THE OXFORD HANDBOOK OF

U.S. HEALTH LAW

THE OXFORD HANDBOOK OF

U.S. HEALTH LAW

Edited by

I. GLENN COHEN, ALLISON K. HOFFMAN

and

WILLIAM M. SAGE

OXFORD
UNIVERSITY PRESS

OXFORD
UNIVERSITY PRESS

Oxford University Press is a department of the University of Oxford. It furthers the University's objective of excellence in research, scholarship, and education by publishing worldwide. Oxford is a registered trade mark of Oxford University Press in the UK and certain other countries.

Published in the United States of America by Oxford University Press
198 Madison Avenue, New York, NY 10016, United States of America.

Library of Congress Cataloging-in-Publication Data
Names: Cohen, I. Glenn, editor. | Hoffman, Allison (Allison K.), editor. | Sage, William M., editor.
Title: The Oxford handbook of U.S. Health Law / edited by I. Glenn Cohen, Allison K. Hoffman, William M. Sage ; foreword by Kathleen G. Sebelius.
Other titles: U.S. healthcare law | United States healthcare law
Description: First edition. | New York : Oxford University Press, 2017. | Includes bibliographical references and index.
Identifiers: LCCN 2016024456 | ISBN 9780199366521 ((hardback) : alk. paper)
Subjects: LCSH: Medical care—Law and legislation—United States.
Classification: LCC KF3821 .O98 2017 | DDC 344.7303/21—dc23 LC record available at https://lccn.loc.gov/2016024456

1 3 5 7 9 8 6 4 2
Printed by Sheridan Books, Inc., United States of America

To Jesse (and Basel) – IGC
To Sam and Elliot Quinn – AKH
For Karen, Abbie, and Harry – WMS

Contents

PART III ORGANIZING AND FINANCING THE HEALTHCARE SYSTEM

A. *Health Professionals and Healthcare Facilities*

B. *Competition and Innovation*

C. *Health Insurance and Finance*

D. *Healthcare Costs*

E. *Public Health Law*

PART IV THE HEALTH LAW FRONTIER

Foreword

U.S. Healthcare Law Enters A New Age

KATHLEEN G. SEBELIUS

This *Handbook* offers a comprehensive analysis of the changing landscape of American healthcare. While the passage of the Affordable Care Act (ACA) in 2010 created a national legal framework for healthcare in America, many other laws have shaped the healthcare system over the last fifty years. The chapter authors capably describe and explain the new legal dynamics of healthcare in both the public and private sectors, and the editors pull together in one volume a range of informed viewpoints on what has changed in health law and what changes to look for in the future. Our understanding of American healthcare, a unique social sector with a huge impact on our population and economy as well as significant global ramifications, is greatly advanced by this *Handbook*.

I think we Americans share several fundamental healthcare values, even if we disagree about the best plan to accomplish the goals. We believe that everyone should have access to healthcare when they need it. We want our doctor's advice to be based on the most current medical information and to be aimed at keeping us healthy and well and, if at all possible, out of the hospital. When faced with a health situation that requires hospitalization, we want to receive the best care possible and the data and information we need to make informed health decisions for our loved ones and ourselves.

For decades, Republican and Democratic presidents talked about healthcare and how the United States could make progress toward universal coverage, joining the rest of the developed world. The battles were contentious, but progress was made for various populations—older Americans, low-income pregnant women and children, disabled individuals, and workers in large companies.

But huge gaps persisted. While the United States had the best healthcare for some people some of the time, as a nation Americans paid more for healthcare than any country on earth. Compared to other developed countries, we had the highest percentage of our population uninsured, and our citizens lived sicker and died younger than most of their peers across the globe. Changing that snapshot was essential for our global competitiveness and for our economy.

Passing Health Reform

When Illinois Senator Barack Obama announced his candidacy for president in February 2007, he committed to passing comprehensive health reform in his first term. His Democratic challenger and even the Republican candidates also had plans for expanded healthcare and proposed various ways to lower medical costs.

So it shouldn't have come as a big surprise to anyone in Congress or the public that health reform was on the new president's must-do agenda. The big surprise, given decades of promises from both Republican and Democratic presidents to reform healthcare, was that President Obama accomplished his goal. Within fourteen months of taking office, on March 23, 2010, he signed into law the Patient Protection and Affordable Care Act (ACA). That same day, the first of many legal challenges was filed, with twenty-seven attorneys general asserting that the law was unconstitutional.

The ACA, often called "Obamacare" by its critics and some of its fans, focused on three primary goals: access to health insurance for those Americans whose jobs, income levels, or health status didn't allow them to qualify for affordable coverage; better health and better care for all Americans; and lower health inflation through improvements to the healthcare delivery system. Most important, Congress created a new national insurance framework, in which individuals would be expected to have coverage but would not be screened or penalized by private insurers for health conditions, premiums would not differ based on gender, and lower-income individuals would be eligible for federal financial subsidies or public coverage. Most of the focus and attention since the passage of the law has been on the new private insurance markets and the expansion of Medicaid, both of which were designed to address access to affordable healthcare for uninsured Americans. The other major elements of the law—with provisions aimed at improving healthcare and underlying health—are just beginning to be well understood.

An even earlier bill signed by President Obama set the stage for this new healthcare system. When President Obama was elected in 2008, most health information was still being exchanged in a paper format. Even though the healthcare industry accounted for approximately a sixth of the nation's GDP, less than 20% of doctors and 10% of hospitals used electronic health records. Tracking payments and outcomes to compare costs of health treatments, provider successes, and drug impacts was often impossible. The 2009 American Recovery and Reinvestment Act (ARRA) included authorization for the Department of Health and Human Services to develop a national strategy for expanding the use of electronic health records and funded financial incentives to hospitals and doctors to adopt new information technology, creating a critical platform for healthcare innovation.

The job of implementing comprehensive health reform was enormous and had to begin immediately after the ACA was passed, even without the recommended congressional funding, with the overhang of a constitutional challenge, and with many states declaring that they would not participate in what was designed as a federal-state partnership. The ACA had a very aggressive timetable, and while the process of putting any detailed statute into effect is complicated, this was particularly difficult.

While legislative language provides the skeleton for any major law, rules and regulations bring it to life, creating the operational roadmap for how the statute will work in the real world. Three major U.S. cabinet-level administrative agencies—the Department of Health and Human Services (which I had the privilege of leading as Secretary), the Department of the Treasury, and the Department of Labor—needed to partner to write all the rules and regulations, because each had key areas of jurisdiction. Meanwhile, Republicans in the House, who had voted against the final passage of the law and then gained a majority in the 2010 elections, opposed funding for implementation and initiated a series of hearings and oversight requests that demanded enormous amounts of time and effort to fulfill.

One can find an historical parallel for the initial opposition to the ACA. There was much furor in the five years after the Social Security law passed in 1935, when taxes were being collected but benefits were not yet in place. The lesson was clear: It is hard to defend against claims about what might happen before a program is fully implemented and benefits are available. Given that the final version of the ACA passed in the House and Senate without any Republican support and was challenged immediately as unconstitutional by state attorneys general, no one should be surprised that the earliest years were very acrimonious. By the time the ACA was fully implemented and benefits became available in January 2014, opponents had spent millions of dollars to discredit the law and discourage people from participating. Unfortunately, attempts to obstruct or reverse the ACA have not yet abated. By contrast, once Americans began collecting retirement benefits in 1940, Social Security was quickly accepted as essential support for older and disabled Americans.

The skill and effort of my department's legal teams to defend against court challenges and respond to a huge volume of adversarial congressional requests, while at the same time collaborating with peers from other federal agencies and states to design a new marketplace for health insurance and to write rules for an historic Medicaid expansion, were extraordinary. The teams also had to work in an uncertain environment for implementation. We were optimistic about a positive outcome from the Supreme Court in the initial constitutional challenges, but no one could (or, as it turned out, did) predict what the Court would decide, and the law's framework had to be designed to work nationally, in spite of major differences in circumstances and politics across the country. I was enormously grateful to work with talented, dedicated lawyers at every step in this process, who made sure that every time a new roadblock was created by the ACA's opponents, we had a plan to advance the ACA's mission within the boundaries of the law. Even so, it remained a great unknown how many of the states opposing the ACA would engage as partners with the federal government in the event that the law was ruled constitutional.

One essential element of the ACA was to create a new virtual marketplace where consumers can compare insurance plans available in their state on price and benefits, and then apply their individualized federal subsidy reflecting on their personal income and family size. Each marketplace was designed to offer products based on state law and premiums based on state competition and oversight, but that also complied with new national insurance rules. And this needed to be in place with or without state cooperation. At the same time, we worked to convince insurers to offer products in marketplaces throughout the country, because we knew that more competition would result in lower prices.

Another complicating factor in implementing the new marketplace framework was that the federal government did not have regulatory authority over the plans sold in the marketplaces because insurance products are regulated at the state level. That was true both before and after the ACA. While the Labor Department had oversight of various "self-insured" plans, no other federal agency was involved in health insurance regulation before the ACA's passage.

This presented two immediate challenges: figuring out what would happen if some states did not fulfill their marketplace oversight role, and quickly adding expertise at the federal level both to partner with states and to administer marketplaces in states that refused to assume or share responsibility. It was unclear how many states would fall into each category, but our job was to ensure that all citizens, regardless of where they lived, had access to the benefits authorized by federal law.

With the help of knowledgeable and creative legal minds, we worked to fashion a flexible approach to marketplace governance: States could choose to be a full partner, could assume some but not all of the oversight functions, or could entirely opt out without jeopardizing their residents' access to the health coverage promised in the ACA.

Coming Online

By the time the Supreme Court issued its favorable decision on the constitutional challenge in June 2012, a presidential election was looming. The future of the Affordable Care Act was one of the major differences between President Obama and his Republican challenger, former Massachusetts governor Mitt Romney. Although Governor Romney only five years earlier had signed into Massachusetts law a bill that provided the template for the ACA, he pledged to repeal federal health reform if elected president. The program therefore continued under a cloud of uncertainty throughout 2012.

Even after President Obama was re-elected, Republicans in the House and Senate continued to attempt to de-fund implementation, to block rule-making, and to pledge to stop the ACA from taking full effect. Because the first open insurance enrollment was scheduled for 2013, it was too late for a nonparticipating state to establish the systems needed to run its own insurance market when the ACA survived the 2012 elections. And on October 1, 2013, the day open enrollment began across the country, the entire federal government was shut down by opponents of the ACA who refused to pass a budget, wreaking billions of dollars of damage on the economy and halting most federal programs from child care to clinical trials. Making things worse, there was also a major technical failure in the online federal marketplace, so millions of people had to wait to select and enroll in health plans.

The federal government was finally reopened fifteen days later, and after eight weeks of round-the-clock efforts to fix the website, the new marketplace was relaunched on December 1 and worked! By the time open enrollment ended in March 2014, 8 million individuals had chosen a new health plan, and millions more had qualified for Medicaid benefits in the states where expansion occurred.

To date, there has been measurable progress on the coverage goals of the ACA, and some positive trends are beginning to develop in areas that will take a longer time to assess definitively. In spite of the Republicans' gaining control of the U.S. Senate in the 2014 election, marketplaces continue to function and more states have decided to expand Medicaid. Over 18 million Americans have new health insurance coverage, representing the largest decrease in the number of uninsured in U.S. history. Insurance rules and selling practices have been thoroughly disrupted, and it seems unlikely that individuals will ever return to an era of being locked out of the market due to preexisting health conditions or being unable to shop online to compare prices and benefits for a variety of insurance products.

While the goals of higher quality care, better population health, and lower costs through improved efficiency will take longer to measure, there are encouraging signs of progress. Annual healthcare inflation has remained well below pre-ACA levels, with some years seeing the smallest increases in half a century. The federal government has committed to using its $1 trillion healthcare buying power to shift as quickly as possible from fee-for-service payments to smarter, value-based purchasing, in which payment is tied to health outcomes rather than the number of services provided. Preliminary results indicate that patient care is improving in hospitals. The occurrence of hospital-acquired conditions—infections and errors—has decreased in the last two years. And preventable readmissions have declined, the result of more attentive follow-up post discharge.

The ACA included a first-ever multiyear investment in prevention strategies, aimed at avoiding many diseases and better managing care for those already struggling with chronic illness. The focus of this investment is on obesity and smoking, the two underlying causes for the vast majority of diseases that cripple and kill people in the United States. Partners in these efforts include many federal government agencies as well as cities, schools, healthcare providers, parents, employers, and health advocates.

With over 80% of healthcare providers now using electronic data measures, aligning payment with desired outcomes, establishing and measuring health goals for patient populations, and rewarding providers who improve health and wellness are finally feasible. In addition, making the government's health data publicly accessible has unlocked private sector investment in new companies and systems aimed at improving care and lowering costs. There have been more health start-ups in the past five years than in the previous twenty. And there is a significant learning collaboration underway between the public and private sectors aimed at improving health and healthcare.

What Comes Next?

Once again, a key issue in the upcoming 2016 presidential election is the survival of the ACA. While critics still demand its repeal if a president is elected who is willing to sign a repeal into law, nobody has proposed a viable alternative approach that could move the United States toward universal healthcare, improve population health, and lower costs in the system. And it seems less and less likely that any elected official could strip millions of American families of the healthcare benefits that they now enjoy.

While there has been significant early progress on the ACA implementation, there are still areas needing legal or legislative attention, where uncertainty or persistent gaps in coverage and cost create real inequities for Americans. The Supreme Court decision in 2012 to make the expansion of Medicaid a voluntary state decision damaged the congressional design of a continuum of coverage for low-income Americans. Politics permitting, new laws could mandate national expansion or give local jurisdictions within a state the authority to partner with the federal government. Another major coverage gap for many Americans derives from the definition of "unaffordable coverage" in a workplace, which triggers a tax subsidy for individuals to purchase coverage in the marketplace. Current regulations consider only the worker's income and individual policy costs, and not the family income and policy costs for a spouse and dependents. This so-called "family glitch" leaves many Americans unable to afford family coverage in the workplace—yet ineligible for the tax subsidy.

Several laws passed by Congress, including the ACA, clearly require parity in care and coverage between those who suffer physical ailments and those patients who experience behavioral health problems. However, this is still not occurring in much of the health system and is not being enforced by insurers. True parity is likely to take sustained effort through regulation and focused litigation to change the status quo.

There is growing concern about the pricing of new drugs and the current ban on Medicare, the largest government purchaser, negotiating lower drug prices for its beneficiaries. In addition to important legal issues regarding incentives for innovation and cost to society, drug pricing raises serious ethical questions about fairness to poorer and sicker Americans that should be debated and hopefully resolved.

As baby boomers age, end-of-life costs and concerns loom large. Who can make decisions for a critically ill patient, when an advance care directive must be followed or can be overridden, and what other legal and ethical issues need to be addressed in a hospital or nursing home setting are being discussed in state legislatures and in the halls of Congress.

With medical science continually offering new ways to extend life and treat disease but at considerable expense, issues of rationing care given finite resources will continue to be debated. And it is almost impossible to predict what opportunities and challenges will result from the next series of advancements.

These difficult issues are made more complicated by our varying religious beliefs and cultural differences. In a nation founded on the separation of church and state, we have already seen faith-based litigation contesting mandatory contraceptive coverage for employees. It is likely that treatment issues such as organ transplantation and various other life-prolonging drugs and procedures will give rise to more religiously motivated lawsuits and legislative battles.

Summing Up

Since 2010, the Affordable Care Act has put this country on a path to expanded access to affordable coverage, better health and better care for our entire population, and reduced costs through improvements to the care delivery system. Hopefully our elected leaders will focus their attention on ways to fully achieve our shared goals and to remedy the health and cost disparities that threaten to make us a less productive and prosperous country. This *Handbook* provides a comprehensive view of the laws that underpin the post-ACA reality of healthcare in America, and offers insights that will help us move forward.

List of Contributors

Keri Arnold Arnold & Porter LLP

Mark Barnes Ropes & Gray LLP

John D. Blum Loyola University Chicago School of Law

Scott Burris Temple Law School

A. M. Capron Gould School of Law, University of Southern California

I. Glenn Cohen Harvard Law School

Nathan Cortez Southern Methodist University Dedman School of Law

Francis J. Crosson The Permanente Federation, Kaiser Permanente

Judith Daar Whittier Law School

Rebecca Dresser Washington University in St. Louis School of Law

Colleen Flood University of Ottawa, Faculty of Law

Michael Frakes Duke University School of Law

Leslie Francis College of Law and Department of Philosophy, University of Utah

Matthew B. Frank Harvard Law School

David M. Frankford Rutgers School of Law, Camden

Barry R. Furrow Drexel University Thomas R. Kline School of Law

Robert Gatter St. Louis University School of Law and St. Louis University College of Public Health and Social Justice

Lawrence O. Gostin Georgetown Law School and Johns Hopkins University

Peter Grossi Arnold & Porter LLP

Lewis A. Grossman American University Washington College of Law

Mark A. Hall Wake Forest University School of Law

B. Jessie Hill Case Western Reserve University School of Law

James G. Hodge, Jr. Sandra Day O'Connor College of Law, Arizona State University

Allison K. Hoffman UCLA School of Law

Sharona Hoffman Case Western Reserve University School of Law and School of Medicine

Jill R. Horwitz UCLA School of Law

Daniel Hougendobler Georgetown Law School

David A. Hyman Georgetown Law School

John V. Jacobi Seton Hall University School of Law

Robert H. Jerry, II University of Missouri School of Law

Sandra H. Johnson St. Louis University School of Law

Marshall B. Kapp Florida State University

Manel Kappagoda ChangeLab Solutions

Eleanor D. Kinney Indiana University Robert H. McKinney School of Law

Joan H. Krause University of North Carolina School of Law

Joseph Lawless Columbia Law School

Zita Lazzarini Community Medicine and Health Care, University of Connecticut

Kristin Madison Northeastern University School of Law and Bouvé College of Health Sciences

Theodore R. Marmor Yale School of Management

Shawn R. Mathis New Mexico Legislative Council Service and Loyola University Chicago School of Law

Dayna Bowen Matthew University of Colorado Law School

Maxwell J. Mehlman Case Western Reserve University School of Law and School of Medicine

Amy B. Monahan University of Minnesota School of Law

Abigail R. Moncrieff Boston University School of Law

Jonathan Oberlander University of North Carolina School of Medicine

Wendy E. Parmet Northeastern University School of Law and School of Public Policy and Urban Affairs

Frank Pasquale University of Maryland Francis King Carey School of Law

Anne Pearson ChangeLab Solutions

David Peloquin Ropes & Gray LLP

Rachel Rebouché Temple Law School

Anna E. Roberts Georgetown Law School

Sara Rosenbaum Milken Institute School of Public Health at the George Washington University, Department of Health Policy and Management

Kyle Rozema Cornell University

William M. Sage School of Law and Dell Medical School, The University of Texas School of Law

Richard S. Saver University of North Carolina School of Law

Nadia N. Sawicki Loyola University Chicago School of Law

Kathleen G. Sebelius 21st U.S. Secretary of Health and Human Services

Elizabeth Sepper Washington University in St. Louis School of Law

Charles Silver The University of Texas School of Law

Anita Silvers Department of Philosophy, San Francisco State University

Michael Ashley Stein Harvard Law School

Timothy Stoltzfus Jost Washington and Lee University

Bryan Thomas University of Ottawa, Faculty of Law

Laura A. Tollen Kaiser Permanente Institute for Health Policy

Paul J. Voss Health Sciences Division of Loyola University Chicago and Office of Research Services, Loyola University Chicago School of Law

Timothy Westmoreland Georgetown Law School

Lindsay F. Wiley American University Washington College of Law

Robin Fretwell Wilson University of Illinois College of Law

INTRODUCTION

I. GLENN COHEN, ALLISON K. HOFFMAN, AND WILLIAM M. SAGE

PERCEPTIONS OF HEALTH LAW AS A FIELD

A decade ago, law professor and legal scholars debated whether health law was a legitimate, coherent field of study.[1] Today, health law is indisputably a prominent, well-accepted field that protects a central aspect of our lives, our health, and sets the ground rules for one-sixth of the U.S. economy.

Health law has become the locus for asking and answering some of the most important legal and social policy questions of our time. For better, and in the mind of some health law scholars certainly for worse, it is a frequent topic of discussion for the Supreme Court. In the year this volume will go to print, the Supreme Court will have considered several health law disputes. The topics of these cases range from state licensure requirements for abortion providers, to the preemptive scope of the Employee Retirement and Income Security Act of 1974 over state healthcare regulations, to religious freedom and insurance benefits. These issues are as technically challenging as they are normatively charged. The voices of health law scholars have been instrumental in helping to guide the Court's deliberations and decisions in these cases and others. The Court's holdings in these cases will have a tremendous impact on access to abortion and contraception services and the feasibility of state efforts to drive down the cost and improve the quality of healthcare. And as health policy becomes an increasingly charged space for partisan conflict, we have every reason to believe the Supreme Court's steady diet of health law cases will continue.

The prominence of health law is also evident from its coverage in law schools across the country. Dozens of top law schools have created centers and programs devoted to health law and policy. Hundreds of law scholars and equal numbers in other disciplines—with dozens of new scholars joining the endeavor annually—focus their research on the many aspects of health regulation and policy. Law school graduates step into roles as regulatory and compliance experts, as healthcare litigators, as business and corporate attorneys, and as advocates

[1] While the exact borders of "health law" are subject to some imprecision, we use it in this volume to cover a series of interconnected topics: health policy, healthcare law, bioethics, public health law, and the law governing drugs, devices, and biotechnology.

for individuals and for the public's health, as employment opportunities in the field of health law proliferate.

The influence and importance of this field of law—intellectually and practically—is incontestable. But it is also a field that is rapidly changing. We compiled this volume precisely because the field is at an inflection point in the United States, as we describe below.

Changing Nature of the Field of Health Law

The fifty chapters in this volume confirm that, as the influence of heath law is growing, so is its breadth and sophistication as a field of legal study and scholarship. Health law has transformed from a niche field of law to an all-encompassing one, in which mastery requires proficiency equally with legal, ethical, and empirical analysis. The scholarship in the field is exploding in quantity and is deepening in quality.

Part of this deepening arises from the fact that health law bears greatly on the development of other fields of law, including administrative law, legislation, antitrust, insurance law, and many others. Experts in health law are equally experts in these other fields and have insight into how ideas developed in other contexts are or are not relevant when applied in the context of health. Teaching health law demands an ability to engage in everything from constitutional law and administrative law to family law to corporate law and antitrust.

Furthermore, health law scholarship is increasingly enriched by theoretical and empirical inquiry. Even the questions that have long been topics of health law, since the days when the field was called "Law and Medicine," such as medical malpractice or informed consent, are now being examined using novel methods and are also benefitting from comparative approaches.

Goal of this Volume

With the 2010 passage of the Patient Protection and Affordable Care Act, the healthcare financing and delivery systems are undergoing substantial change. Not surprisingly, so is the regulation of these systems. While the full ramifications of these changes are yet to be felt, we know enough now to begin chronicling and analyzing the post-ACA picture of health law and also to foreshadow the likely evolution of the field in the decades to come. We think that this critical moment in health law's evolution offers an ideal time to capture the broad contours of the field.

We envision that this volume will give readers a sense of both the breadth and the depth of health law, through the words and insights of some of the best scholars in the field. As the case is with the field itself, many contributions come from law professors, but several come from scholars who are trained in and teach in other disciplines, including political science, economics, and public health. We also include the wisdom of leading practitioners of health law, many of whom wrestle with these issues on a daily basis to help clients comply, shape, and, where necessary, challenge the law. Our hope is that the chapters that follow are equally valuable to readers with no background in the field as to those who write, teach, practice, or make policy in health law.

This volume is divided into several parts. Some of these are conventional (for example, devoting a section to public health law), while others reflect our own way of conceptualizing the field, that groups content more thematically than doctrinally.

The first part of the *Handbook*, "An Overview of the Legal Governance of Healthcare," explains in broad thematic strokes the major features of American healthcare, its recent and past reforms, its relationship to medical ethics and constitutional doctrines related to federalism, and how it compares to the experience of other countries. This part of the book will orient newcomers to American health law and delight experts with the ways in which the authors understand the terrain.

The first chapter in this part, *Relating Health Law to Health Policy: A Frictional Account*, by William M. Sage, examines the ways in which American health *law* does and does not further current goals of American health *policy*. Sage focuses on legal obstacles to meeting renewed expectations of policy to improve both collective fairness and efficiency, such as health law's continued focus on professional self-governance and the physician-patient dyad, and the extent to which health law remains decentralized and adjudicatory rather than being grounded in statute and the administrative state.

I. Glenn Cohen's chapter, *The Relationship between Bioethics and U.S. Health Law: Past, Present, and Future*, explores bioethics as part of U.S. health law and identifies trends in the way the two fields interact. It begins with an overview of the way in which bioethics content has been integrated in health law textbooks over time and then shifts to examine the question of translation. Drawing on recent cases, Cohen describes the mismatch between rich ethical and formalist legal discourse. He also plots a few trends as to where the translation should be going: increased interest in population-level bioethics and the law, including the increased recognition of intellectual property and drug development as topics for both disciplines, and the rise of libertarian bioethics in litigation.

Allison K. Hoffman discusses health reform, with a focus on the Patient Protection and Affordable Care Act, in a chapter called *What Health Reform Reveals about Health Law*. It describes the arc of health reform in the United States over the twentieth century and explores the ACA as a window into the idiosyncrasies of U.S. health law and the values that have shaped health law as a field. In particular, this chapter considers themes such as the influence of market-based ideology, federalism, and professionalism on health law. It illustrates how the ACA policies that most strongly push against these values have resulted in conflict and litigation but may also produce a gradual transformation of legal norms.

In *A View from a Friend and Neighbor: A Canadian Perspective on U.S. Healthcare and the Affordable Care Act*, Colleen Flood and Bryan Thomas compare the path taken in Canada toward universal healthcare and the path taken in the United States with Medicare, Medicaid, and now the ACA. In addition to evaluating the performance of each system, they offer a detailed analysis of the legal and regulatory apparatus governing health systems in both countries, contrasting the five principles of the Canada Health Act with their functional counterparts in the ACA.

Abigail R. Moncrieff and Joseph Lawless's chapter, *Healthcare Federalism*, charts the course of the rise and fall of federalism in U.S. healthcare. From the "Articles of Confederation and

Perpetual Union" to the New Federalism to the Reagan era, the chapter begins with a historical overview of changing legal approaches to federalism in the United States. It then juxtaposes those developments with major health policy initiatives that intersect with federalism: the creation of public health departments and insurance commissions in the mid-1800s, the rise of employer-sponsored insurance during World War II, the introduction of Medicaid and Medicare in the 1960s, and the ACA in the present era. Throughout, the chapter shows how "the federalist structure of the U.S. government has been largely responsible for the piecemeal evolution and perpetual messiness of American healthcare regulation."

The second part of the *Handbook*, "Caring and Receiving Care," explores the legal framework for the patient experience of care from access through treatment to recourse if treatment fails. The chapters in this section focus on individuals with medical needs, whether general or specific, on physicians and other healthcare professionals, on hospitals and health facilities, and on the insurance coverage that makes healthcare possible. Chapters include both core legal material and related ethical considerations. Reflecting the rapid transition in U.S. healthcare to electronic information exchange with its attendant benefits and risks, four chapters are devoted to legal issues involving healthcare information.

The part begins with a section on access to care and financing of care, including hospitals, health professionals, and insurance benefits. The section also addresses discrimination, particularly long-standing racial discrimination, in accessing medical services.

Eleanor D. Kinney's chapter, *Accessing Hospitals and Health Professionals*, opens the discussion. Kinney contrasts the U.S. approach to healthcare access based on private charity and limited legal mandate with the human rights approach taken in much of the world, which confers an affirmative constitutional obligation on government. The chapter goes on to categorize and explain the common law and statutory duties of physicians and hospitals to serve patients not of their choosing, including obligations under the Emergency Medical Treatment and Active Labor Act (EMTALA), federal antidiscrimination laws, and public health insurance programs.

In *Access to Health Insurance and Health Benefits*, Timothy Stoltzfus Jost examines five common forms of payment for healthcare in the United States: out-of-pocket payment, charity, direct public provision, public health insurance, and private health insurance (including employer-sponsored insurance). Jost considers the advantages and disadvantages of each, their current status, and the effect on each of the ACA. The chapter also attempts to explain why the United States retains this patchwork of coverage rather than adopting a single coherent system of healthcare financing.

Dayna Bowen Matthew's chapter, *Legal Battles against Discrimination in Healthcare*, discusses racial and ethnic discrimination in U.S. healthcare, beginning with the adverse health effects of American slavery and the Jim Crow eras. Its central focus, however, is persistent racism in healthcare today, examining the legacy for individual and community health of long-standing discrimination in medicine as well as discussing federal laws currently used to redress and prevent discrimination as interpreted by the Supreme Court. The chapter concludes by outlining concrete steps toward achieving nondiscriminatory healthcare delivery, mainly through civil rights legislation.

Many of the most contentious, unsettled, and important issues in contemporary health law involve information. Asymmetric access to information between expert professionals and uneducated, vulnerable patients—as well as the uncertainty associated with illness and attempted treatment—are fundamental attributes of medical care that undergird both law and ethics in their traditional forms. The second part of this section explores how these assumptions are finally changing as curable informational deficits in healthcare become apparent and new communication and computational technologies are developed. These improvements, however, come at a price that includes risks to data ownership and control, privacy, and reputation.

Frank Pasquale provides a sophisticated overview called *Health Information Law* that examines the complexities of subjecting even basic questions in health data ownership and exchange to the sometimes inconsistent requirements of federal and state statutes, regulatory regimes, constitutional decisions, and international treaties. The chapter explains that information shared between physician and patient, a critical focus of policy concern in the 1960s and 1970s, is now only a small part of information flow in the healthcare system. Although a burgeoning field of information economics has helped resolve the problem of information as simultaneously an input and an output of market activity, there remains a strong tension in health information governance between public commitments to open data and corporate interests in limiting sharing to serve proprietary interests.

Robin Fretwell Wilson's chapter, *The Promise of Informed Consent*, looks at the relationship between ethical goals of individual autonomy with respect to medical care and the legal embodiment of that autonomy through informed consent law. The chapter traces the historical evolution of physicians' obligation to secure a patient's informed consent before focusing on two seminal legal decisions: *Culbertson v. Mernitz* and *Canterbury v. Spence*. These cases present competing standards for determining the scope of disclosure: the professional or "reasonable physician" standard and the patient-centered or "reasonable patient" standard. The chapter also explores the application of duties to secure informed consent to medical research, and describes the efforts of state legislatures to standardize disclosure to patients so as to reduce the burden on and legal risk to physicians without compromising the right of patients to receive needed information.

Communicating Loyalty: Advocacy and Disclosure of Conflicts in Treatment and Research Relationships is Robert Gatter's contribution. The proliferation of agency relationships in healthcare has called many agents' loyalty into question, especially as payment methods change and new profit opportunities arise. Information disclosure has become the mainstay of managing these "conflicts of interest" in both treatment and research relationships. For example, the federal Sunshine Act requires pharmaceutical companies to make public their payments to physicians. Gatter's chapter explores the law and ethics of information designed to protect healthcare consumers and patients from disloyalty.

Medical Privacy and Security, contributed by Sharona Hoffman, addresses privacy and security issues arising from the transition from paper charts to electronic health records (EHRs), as well as "big data" uses of computerized health information. The chapter reviews federal and state privacy laws and their limitations, particularly the Health Insurance Portability and Accountability Act (HIPAA) Privacy Rule. It also considers more general questions about the importance of health privacy in American society.

The next section of this part focuses on the ethics and law of treatments. Chapters in the section relate to specific types of patients or forms of medical care. Experimental treatments for serious conditions, reproductive healthcare, and end-of-life care each merit separate coverage in this part, as do the law and public policy of disability and of healthcare providers with conscientious objections to delivering particular services.

In B. Jessie Hill's chapter, *New, Experimental, and Life-Saving Therapies*, readers explore issues of equity, distributive justice, and patient autonomy connected with government regulation of access to innovative, potentially life-saving medical care. The chapter begins with the politicized, vague terms that are often used to restrict access to life-saving treatments, such as "experimental," "investigational," and "not medically necessary." It then explores the three frames that legal discourse uses to address problems that arise: constitutional law, public health law, and ethics and human rights. Of these, the chapter suggests that the ethics and human rights framework is the most promising approach in substance but is not politically feasible, at least at present.

Mental Health and Other Behavioral Health Services, by John V. Jacobi, examines the clinical and legal history of exclusion for people with mental illness. Over time, mental illness gained conceptual separation from criminality and deviance, and modern psychiatry is premised on a model of mental illness as susceptible of diagnosis and treatment in the same sense as somatic conditions. However, deep suspicions of the mentally ill linger even among behavioral health professionals. The chapter first addresses healthcare delivery challenges. It then turns to the differential treatment of behavioral healthcare by health insurers, differences that are the subject of antidiscrimination and parity efforts in state and federal law. The chapter ends with the difficult issue of personal decision-making autonomy. Throughout, the focus is on understanding where relevant differences *should* alter the law of healthcare for people with behavioral health needs, and where equal treatment should be the order of the day.

Judith Daar, in *Assisted Reproductive Technologies and Abortion*, examines both early and contemporary debates surrounding assisted reproductive technologies (ARTs) and abortion services. After providing historical background on both techniques, describing their integration into modern reproductive life, and comparing the populations who currently access them, the chapter explores the legal and regulatory history of the two procedures and raises the question of whether the law governing the right to avoid procreation also can be applied to the right to access parenthood. The chapter concludes by assessing three areas of overlap between ARTs and abortion: selective reduction of multiple pregnancy, the personhood movement, and perinatal genetic diagnosis.

Elizabeth Sepper's related chapter, *Conscientious Refusals of Care*, examines conflicts of conscience that arise among patients, healthcare providers, and institutions, especially with regard to reproductive health and end-of-life care. Sepper focuses on "conscientious refusal"—a provider's exercise of conscience in refusing to perform or participate in a procedure that is deemed ethically and legally permissible. The chapter begins with the history and development of legislative and court protections for conscientious refusals of care, turns to theoretical justifications for protecting conscience in medicine, discusses recent proposals to strike a balance between patient access and provider conscience (including institutional providers), and concludes with an assessment of future directions for research.

The chapter *Disability and Health Law*, by Leslie Francis, Anita Silvers, and Michael Ashley Stein, examines the disparate histories of health and disability law in the United States and the more recent need to reconcile and integrate them. An appreciation of two different models of disability is central to understanding both the complementary and the conflicting aspects of health and disability law. The "medical model" conceives of disabilities as mental or physical impairments that it is the task of healthcare to address, supplemented by legally mandated support for people with disabilities in conducting activities of daily life.

This welfarist, paternalistic account of disability law contrasts with the "social model" of disability that views disability law as a form of civil rights law according people with disabilities meaningful access to social life on the terms others enjoy rather than special privileges based on need. Disability law therefore has two major strains; one involving provision of benefits such as health insurance and social security, and the other conferring civil rights protections.

Rebecca Dresser writes about *Autonomy and Its Limits in End-of-Life Law*. Her chapter explores the relationship between respect for individual autonomy and the law governing end-of-life treatment decisions involving competent adults, incompetent adults, and children. After touching on legal and ethical difficulties in determining death, Dresser discusses the limitations of an autonomy-based approach in three areas: "futile" treatments, treatment decisions for incompetent patients, and access to physician-assisted death. It concludes that courts and other legal decision-makers will face continuing pressure to incorporate quality of life, cost, medical judgment, and patient vulnerability in end-of-life law.

The final part of this section explains the legal recourse patient may have when medical care that they receive proves unsatisfactory or harmful. Separate chapters are dedicated to private litigation alleging medical negligence (i.e., malpractice), product liability suits for dangerous or defective drugs and medical devices, and complaints filed with state licensing boards and other professional and regulatory entities.

Medical Malpractice Liability: Of Modest Expansions and Tightening Standards by Barry R. Furrow examines the recent evolution of medical malpractice litigation procedures, tort doctrines, and judicial responses to medical injuries. Furrow begins with physician liability, emphasizing new evidentiary practices for proving the standard of care such as increased reliance on practice guidelines, including under the ACA. The chapter also discusses informed consent in promoting patient sovereignty; alternative dispute resolution processes; and liability issues involving hospitals, non-hospital systems, and health professionals other than physicians.

Peter Grossi and Keri Arnold contribute a chapter on *Drug Product Liability at the Crossroads*, which first considers liability for adverse effects of prescription drugs under the established model of regulatory deference before turning to the current debate over liability for the risks of properly prepared drugs and the growing distrust of the FDA's approval and surveillance process. The chapter also reviews court decisions about FDA-approved drug labels preempting state tort claims for failure to warn and more direct "design-defect" claims, and concludes with a discussion of recent tort challenges to the learned intermediary doctrine.

Nadia N. Sawicki's chapter, *Complaints to Professional and Regulatory Bodies*, focuses on patients' ability to express concerns about the quality of care provided by medical practitioners and healthcare institutions. It first considers the procedures employed by state professional licensing boards for patient complaints, as well as the criticisms faced by such boards with respect to both investigation and disciplinary action. The chapter discusses federal regulation of providers and institutions that participate in Medicare and Medicaid, private organizations that receive complaints such as the Joint Commission, and medical professional associations as oversight bodies. Finally, the chapter looks at online consumer reviews and healthcare ratings websites as alternative mechanisms for patient feedback, including complaints.

The third part of this *Handbook*, "Organizing and Financing the Healthcare System," captures the changing nature of healthcare regulation as the healthcare system becomes increasingly complex. It begins with an examination of the providers in the healthcare system—professionals and facilities—and how they are licensed, organized, and monitored. This part of the book also considers research and innovation and the challenges of defining and encouraging high-value healthcare and avoiding wasteful spending. The part also illuminates the multifaceted system for financing healthcare, including how public and private health insurance overlap and blur following the ACA. Finally, it identifies increasing attention to public (population) health as an integral part of the healthcare system and healthcare law, rather than as an afterthought.

The first section of this part focuses on health professionals and healthcare facilities.

In *Structure of Governmental Oversight of Quality in Healthcare*, Sandra H. Johnson considers how states have used gatekeeper laws—licensure, registration, and certification—to attempt to set quality standards. Although licensure is often thought of as a state-level responsibility, Johnson shows how federalism concerns arise in areas with concurrent federal regulatory authority. She also looks at how private controls, such as accreditation of hospitals or staff privileges for physicians in hospitals, complement government regulation. Next, she describes the standards used to measure quality of care, as well as informed consent-based alternatives. Finally, the chapter examines how unlicensed practice of medicine and scope of practice laws draw social and economic boundaries, considering specific examples such as the regulation of assistance at childbirth.

John D. Blum, Shawn R. Mathis, and Paul J. Voss examine *The Hospital-Physician Relationship* and how it has evolved in the context of the Affordable Care Act. This chapter considers the many forces that have shaped this relationship over time, from the rise of health insurance to the changing workforce to the structure of healthcare reimbursement and the introduction of Medicare's prospective payment system and, recently, bundled payments. It traces the healthcare system's evolution from regarding physicians and hospitals as distinct entities, bound together only loosely by mutual interests, to seeing them as inextricably intertwined through organizational structures, contractual and employment relationships, and, increasingly, a shared focus on population health.

Jill R. Horwitz's chapter, *Nonprofit Healthcare Organizations and the Law*, considers and illustrates the exceptional legal treatment of nonprofit healthcare organizations—when compared both with nonprofits outside of the healthcare industry and with functionally similar for-profits in the healthcare industry. She examines reasons for this special treatment, including a misunderstanding of what is demanded from nonprofits and a false expectation that they must relieve poverty to warrant nonprofit status. Interestingly, such expectations sometimes lead to standards favoring these organizations and other times to more demanding expectations under the law.

David A. Hyman and Charles Silver consider medical malpractice reform in *It Was on Fire When I Lay Down on It: Why Medical Malpractice Reform Can't Fix Healthcare*. This chapter reviews an abundance of empirical evidence to make the point that conventional tort reforms (those aimed at reducing litigation involving physicians and hospitals) offer little promise to improve healthcare quality or reduce costs. Instead, the authors advise looking to reform of the healthcare financing and delivery systems to make the market work better, with medical malpractice reform a concordant but not dominant element.

The second section of this part examines competition and innovation.

In *The Biomedical Research Enterprise*, Mark Barnes and David Peloquin examine the wide variety of state and federal regulations governing biomedical research and offer a succinct overview of an especially complex area of healthcare regulation. They survey conflicting regulatory regimes focused on human subjects protections, privacy laws, financial disclosure requirements, and research misconduct, and then offer ways to improve each of these regimes. The chapter ends with considerations that arise specifically when research is federally funded.

William M. Sage, in *Antitrust Enforcement and the Future of Healthcare Competition*, analyzes the interaction of competition policy with the highly regulated U.S. healthcare system. The chapter reviews the essentials of American antitrust law, and applies it to current controversies involving hospital and health insurance mergers, potentially anticompetitive contracting practices, and specific interactions between competition and other laws governing accountable care organizations, medical licensing, and generic drugs. It also discusses deeper issues involving market failure, regulation, and dislodging the status quo without replacing an overly fragmented system with an excessively consolidated one.

Lewis A. Grossman's chapter, *Drugs, Biologics, and Devices: FDA Regulation, Intellectual Property, and Medical Products in the American Healthcare System*, examines the U.S. Food and Drug Administration's approval process for pharmaceuticals and medical devices. It first sets out the basic framework of FDA approval for drugs, biologics, and medical devices. Then, it considers financial interests created by intellectual property and exclusivity rules, including the Hatch-Waxman Act and the Biosimilars Price Competition and Innovation Act. Finally, it looks at the forces that are reshaping regulation in this area, such as the rise of precision medicine and the FDA's increasing role in regulating the actual practice of medicine.

In *Health Law's Uneasy Relationship with Delivery System Innovation*, Richard S. Saver examines how health law constrains and advances welfare-enhancing delivery system reforms. Saver first defines delivery system innovation and then describes several recent efforts at reform, ranging from more modest efforts, such as comparative effectiveness research, to more fundamental or "disruptive" ones, such as accountable care organizations. The chapter describes how the law both promotes and simultaneously restricts these efforts and considers reasons for the law's duality with respect to such innovation.

Kristin Madison explores *Legal and Policy Issues in Measuring and Improving Quality*. The chapter describes tools that policy-makers have relied on to measure and report the quality of healthcare as doing so has become a more prominent regulatory concern. In particular, laws to promote the development of electronic medical records has been foundational to capturing data in ways that can support data aggregation. The chapter reviews ways to refine the accuracy of measurement approaches and explains how patients and providers can remedy faulty quality information. Finally, the chapter suggests an agenda for the next era of policy-making and research on quality reporting.

The third section of this part discusses health insurance and finance.

Mark A. Hall writes the first chapter, *Employment-Based Health Coverage*, which provides an overview of employers' dominant position in the private health insurance market in the United States, and considers resulting legal and policy complexities. He first describes the legal and economic factors that spurred and sustained the dominance of employer-based coverage, including tax law and preemption of state laws for many employer-based plans. The chapter then examines how the ACA is likely to shape the future of employer-based coverage, through a mandate that requires most large employers to offer affordable coverage or pay tax penalties and by galvanizing the use of private insurance exchanges to allow employees to shop for benefits. Finally, Hall considers the complexities that result from the differential regulation of individual health insurance and employment-based coverage, following the ACA, and previews possible areas of conflict that may arise in the coming years.

In *Risk and Regulation in Private Insurance*, Robert H. Jerry II examines the regulation of risk in private health insurance and how health insurance is both similar to and different from other forms of insurance. The chapter begins with a discussion of how and why insurance is used as a risk-management technique for uncertain and adverse future events and contextualizes insurance within a larger picture of risk management strategies. It continues with a description of market categories for insurance and legal definitions of what constitutes insurance in order to frame consideration of how health insurance differs from other forms of insurance—both in terms of how it operates and how it is and should be regulated.

Theodore R. Marmor and Jonathan Oberlander's chapter, *Medicare at Fifty*, illuminates how Medicare has become the program it is today and what its future might hold. After describing the historical origins of the program, the chapter traces how it has changed over the past fifty years, influenced by both politics and economics. The authors detail successes and challenges in the initial implementation of the program; the evolution of cost containment policies and benefit changes in the 1970s and 1980s; the increasing influence of promarket approaches, including on outpatient prescription drug coverage under the Medicare Modernization Act; and how Medicare figured into the Affordable Care Act's universal health insurance agenda. The authors conclude with lessons from the past half-century and reflections on how Medicare might evolve and how it should evolve in the coming decades.

Medicaid at Fifty, by Sara Rosenbaum, reflects on Medicaid as a companion program to Medicare and private insurance—one that provides a safety net and covers people and care that is excluded by these programs, such as long-term services and supports. This chapter begins with a discussion of Medicaid's aims, parameters, and impact, including reflections on Medicaid's many purposes. It explains the critical role Medicaid plays in expanding access under the ACA and current challenges the program faces, including operational hurdles and ambiguities about who has access to courts to enforce Medicaid's rules. The chapter concludes with a reflection on Medicaid's future.

Amy B. Monahan's chapter, *The Interactions between Public and Private Health Insurance*, discusses how private and public health insurance are converging in the United States, as each system incorporates features of the other. The chapter starts with an overview of public and private sources of health insurance and the interactions between the two before the Affordable Act, including ways that private insurance draws on Medicare's administrative and payment systems and cost-shifting from one payer to the other. It examines how the ACA embraces a public model for health insurance, but still relies in part on private insurance to achieve this goal. The chapter closes with two case examples of innovation at the public/private boundary in Arkansas and Vermont.

The next section of this part examines healthcare costs.

Francis J. Crosson and Laura A. Tollen examine innovative approaches to cost control and managing care, drawing on case studies from Kaiser Permanente, in *Managing the Care and Costs of a Defined Insured Population*. This chapter surveys different tools for cost control, including the use of benefit design and increased cost-sharing and the creation of relationships with providers that promote lower reimbursement levels. The authors describe Kaiser Permanente and illustrate through two case examples how the company has successfully managed care and spending: hypertension detection and management, and pharmaceutical cost management. Finally, the chapter considers what it would take to replicate Kaiser Permanente's successes more broadly in the U.S. healthcare system.

In *Paying for Healthcare*, David M. Frankford expounds on the sociopolitical aspects of and mechanisms of payment for healthcare in the United States. He begins with a historical account of how payment structures developed and resulted in a hybrid system with few cost controls. With a focus on Medicare, he describes the creation of and shortcomings of one attempt at cost control: prospective payment for inpatient care and resource-based payment for physician services. Finally, he pulls the lens back out to see why this example is illustrative of the larger ways in which social and political influences have thwarted and misdirected efforts at payment reforms.

In *Integration, Fragmentation, and Human Nature: The Role of Fraud and Abuse Laws in a Changing Healthcare System*, Joan H. Krause explains how changes in models of healthcare delivery are posing new challenges for rooting out healthcare fraud. She offers an overview of healthcare fraud, including the strategy behind and results of federal fraud and abuse detection efforts over the past decade, and outlines the key healthcare fraud laws, such as the Anti-Kickback Statute, the Stark Law, and the Civil False Claims Act. Finally, the chapter describes increased integration in healthcare delivery and explains how integration creates new opportunities for providers to exploit the system and demands smarter and more systemic ways to counteract fraud.

Invisible Forces at Work: Health Legislation and Budget Processes, by Timothy Westmoreland, reveals one of the deepest secrets of federal health policy, which is its frequent dependence on fiscal politics and the peculiarities of budgetary accounting as practiced by the Congressional Budget Office. The chapter begins by describing the basics of federal budgeting, and illustrates these admittedly dry facts with gripping accounts of health policy successes and failures driven by budgetary considerations. In particular, the chapter makes a speculative but plausible argument that, but for the ACA's politically determined budget limits and the arcana of assigning costs to an additional enrollee in a public versus a private insurance program, the Supreme Court would not have declared the law's Medicaid expansion unconstitutionally coercive.

This section closes with a pair of chapters looking at rationing healthcare from two very different vantage points.

A. M. Capron's chapter, *The Ethics of Rationing Healthcare*, examines the policy or practice of consciously limiting access to medical interventions of known benefit, and the legal and ethical analysis thereof. After reviewing the myriad contexts in which healthcare is rationed in the United States, Capron offers a novel topography of forms of rationing and reviews the principles underlying ethical healthcare rationing—focusing on beneficence, nonmaleficence, respect for persons, and justice along with competing concepts of utilitarian distribution versus allocation.

The Economics of Healthcare Rationing, by Michael Frakes, Matthew B. Frank, and Kyle Rozema, begins by drawing some distinctions as to forms of rationing from the economics perspective: the scarcity of healthcare goods or services due to financial versus physical limitations; rationing at the micro versus macro level; and rationing between healthcare and other goods versus rationing within healthcare. They then discuss the use of cost-benefit analysis and cost-effectiveness analysis, challenges with economic methods of rationing, and real-world uses of these techniques by insurers, provider networks, and governments.

The final section of this part focuses on public health law.

American Public Health Law, a chapter by Lawrence O. Gostin, Daniel Hougendobler, and Anna E. Roberts, examines the topic through a wide-angle lens. It focuses on public health law's five essential characteristics: government, populations, relationships, services, and power. It examines the way these characteristics play out in seven models of legal intervention in public health including taxation and spending, alterations to the built environment, and indirect regulation through tort law.

Zita Lazzarini's chapter, *Communicable Disease Law and Emerging Issues: Antibiotic Resistance*, focuses on communicable diseases. Among other things it describes the relevant federal and state power to protect the public from contagion, the relative roles of voluntary and coercive public health programs, and legal limits on the exercise of the police power in this domain. It then shifts to a more in-depth discussion of two cutting-edge issues: the use of public health interventions to reduce antibiotic resistance and public health surveillance data.

In *Public Health: Noncommunicable Disease Prevention*, Lindsay F. Wiley, Manel Kappagoda, and Anne Pearson write about law and policy interventions to prevent noncommunicable diseases. As they note, the primary drivers of premature deaths in the United States are diseases stemming from problems with diet and tobacco use. The chapter discusses a series of interventions that might be used to target these and other noncommunicable diseases: mandated information disclosures and restrictions on marketing, taxation and pricing strategies, product and retailer regulation, licensing and zoning strategies, spending and procurement strategies, and indirect regulation through tort liability. They also focus on the legal obstacles to these interventions, especially First Amendment objections.

The final chapter in this part, James G. Hodge Jr.'s *Public Health Emergency Legal and Ethical Preparedness*, examines the law's response to catastrophic events that threaten the public's health, particularly in the post-9/11 era. After discussing the complex and shifting landscape of federal, state, and local powers in this area, Hodge flags a number of difficult challenges for implementing these practices in real time: triaging legal and medical resources, dueling declarations of state of emergency, and the liability hospitals, providers, nonprofits, and volunteers face when delivering care in emergency contexts.

The last part of the *Handbook*, "The Health Law Frontier," examines issues that we believe will take on an increasing importance not only for healthcare but also for health law—and for which we think new paradigms may be needed.

The first chapter in this part, *Who's In?: Immigrants and Healthcare*, by Wendy E. Parmet, looks at the undertheorized overlap between health law and immigration law. She argues that the United States has never treated immigrants as fully equal and deserving users of the healthcare system, but instead has feared them for bringing diseases and for the costs they supposedly place on taxpayers. The chapter examines the pre- and post-ACA treatment of various types of immigrants by American health law and reflects on the future of this body of law.

Marshall B. Kapp's chapter, *Aging Population*, examines the issues raised for health by aging as it affects the population, the family, and the individual. Kapp thoroughly reviews the demographics and the epidemiology of aging. He focuses in particular on legal problems of decisional capacity relating to aging, the social support system for aging patients, and the standard of care for physicians treating aging patients.

In *Globalization*, Nathan Cortez examines six forms of globalization of U.S. healthcare: hospitals, health insurance, patient care, drugs and medical devices, telemedicine, and medical personnel. The chapter focuses on two central ideas that knit together these disparate areas. The first is the lack of international law and the limitations faced by domestic law in creating meaningful regulation of healthcare globalization. The second is the way the market is pressing the healthcare industry in various jurisdictions to converge into becoming more alike. Cortez examines the ramifications of each for health law.

The Social Determinants of Health, the *Handbook* chapter by Rachel Rebouché and Scott Burris, explores the resources and conditions in our social and physical environments that influence exposure and vulnerability as well as immunity to proximate causes of acute or chronic illness, including toxins or pathogens. It examines the impacts of race, low income, inequality, and education status on health outcomes and critically analyzes how successful the ACA will be in wrestling with these issues. It closes by discussing the role for public health strategies and law in fostering a "culture of health."

Finally, Maxwell J. Mehlman's chapter, *Genomics and the Law*, examines the past, present, and future of the intersection between human genomics and health law. Among the topics he covers are regulation of genomic research on human subjects, so-called "incidental findings," ownership of DNA samples, germ-line gene editing, genomic screening and testing (including liability issues), forensic use of genomic evidence, and genomic discrimination.

Acknowledgments

We thank Amal El Bakhar, Shailin Thomas, Kenneth Kennedy, Mariah Ford, Erynn Embree, Molly Colvard Harding, Kelley McIlhattan, and Preston Moore for their excellent research assistance line editing these chapters. Jennifer Minnich was extremely helpful in coordinating logistics for the project.

PART I

AN OVERVIEW OF THE LEGAL GOVERNANCE OF HEALTHCARE

CHAPTER 1

RELATING HEALTH LAW TO HEALTH POLICY

A Frictional Account

WILLIAM M. SAGE*

I Introduction

Five years into the "Obamacare" era, health law and health policy in the United States would strike a casual observer as one and the same. In 2010, the U.S. Congress legislated a thousand-page statute remaking American healthcare, which President Obama proudly signed. Since then, the executive branch has dedicated massive elements of its administrative apparatus to executing congressional directives and regulating under its delegated authority. At the same time, the federal judiciary has considered and resolved dozens of challenges and disputes, with three cases requiring definitive rulings from the nation's highest legal authority, the U.S. Supreme Court. In sum, public discussions, media reports, and scholarly publications are crowded with constitutional and administrative law because of the Patient Protection and Affordable Care Act (ACA).

In fact, the interaction between health law and health policy is profound but complex, consisting of frictions much more than synergies—frictions that go far beyond the constitutional and administrative infighting that has attracted so much recent attention. Policy and law overlap considerably in their principles, institutions, and processes, but are far from identical along any dimension. This chapter focuses on the principles underlying contemporary health law and health policy, which share a common history but increasingly find themselves in opposition.

Health law and health policy are not incompatible, but neither are they interoperable. Put more bluntly, consensus policy objectives of American healthcare reform involving competition and efficiency will be nearly impossible to achieve without engaging in a structured evaluation and reconciliation of the health law environment. To a lesser extent, the same

* James R. Dougherty Chair for Faculty Excellence, School of Law, and Professor (Department of Surgery and Perioperative Care), Dell Medical School, University of Texas at Austin. The author thanks University of Texas students John Wang and Preston Moore for excellent research assistance.

is true of the ACA's ambitious distributional goals, which in the existing healthcare system have been framed around special programs of indigent coverage, private charitable services, and professional ethical obligations endorsed and supported by health law.

Physician service to patients has been the founding principle of American health law. Applications of this principle encompass the normal operation of the service relationship, its financial and material support, its organizational context, its limits, and its occasional failures. Both welfare and redistribution have found expression in health law, but in ways largely defined by the medical profession and limited to each physician-patient dyad, such as ethical obligations of loyalty, competence, and charity. Because of its "micro" orientation, health law tends to be contextual and inward-looking, drawing on various legal constructs to solve self-contained sectoral problems. This pragmatism and incrementalism has sometimes attracted criticism, as health law often seems less a coherent body of logical or deontological reasoning than an amalgam of doctrines and strategies directed at one object in the real world—like the much maligned "law of the horse."[1]

Health policy also facilitates physician service to patients, but health policy is charged with the whole of health system performance, including improving both productive and allocative efficiency as well as making resources available for those not effectively served by private insurance markets because of sickness, poverty, or both. As the healthcare system has become industrialized and its aggregate cost has risen, legal processes such as legislation, administrative rule-making, and even adjudication have reoriented toward these larger welfarist and redistributive goals. Health policy is also necessarily concerned with spillover effects on other public sectors, and is therefore subject to constraints (both political and legal) with respect to federalism, budgetary discipline, and personal liberty.

As the chapter will discuss, substantial tensions exist between health law and health policy as a result of their divergent premises and objectives. Both health law and health policy espouse a commitment to medical science, for example, but differ in the rigor attached to that commitment, its relationship to professional experience, and its interaction with political preferences. When considering the rights of individuals, health law emphasizes the patient role, while health policy also considers the individual as consumer, taxpayer, and citizen. Health law often subordinates corporate to professional interests, while health policy has become more receptive to the potential performance advantages of corporate engagement and even corporate control. With respect to the role of government, health law tends to honor its common law origins by remaining decentralized and largely adjudicatory, with many regulatory functions still delegated to medical professional bodies. Even policy-relevant healthcare legislation, notably the Medicare program, for many years financed care without significantly regulating it, but recently has adopted a more assertive regulatory posture.

In part because of the unsettled relationship between law and policy, America's healthcare system cannot reasonably claim superiority to those of other developed countries. To the contrary, the cost of our care is outpacing both our wealth and any measure of value that care provides, while basic health indicators in the United States lag much of the developed world.[2] Fortunately, the pursuit of "value-based health care" is now a focus of American

[1] Frank H. Easterbrook, *Cyberspace and the Law of the Horse*, 1996 U. CHI. LEGAL F. 207 (1996).

[2] WORLD HEALTH ORGANIZATION, WORLD HEALTH STATISTICS: 2013, 46 (2013) (detailing global health indicators by country), http://www.who.int/gho/publications/world_health_statistics/EN_

health policy, with the phrase achieving broad usage and surprising policy consensus in the years since the ACA's passage.[3] Other countries also struggle with the value of the healthcare they fund, but they have always attached primacy to assuring universality of access, and therefore, unlike the United States, they have better resisted pressures to expand the supply of low-benefit but costly services.[4]

The "value" movement, however, as yet offers clear answers to only two of three key questions. The first of these is "where do we need to go?," which is now understood and accepted in medical circles as offering well-constructed, fairly priced, safe, reliable and effective care that is oriented to the needs of engaged participant-recipients.[5] The second question is "how can we get there?," which is usually presented in managerial terms as measuring costs and outcomes, expecting payment only for successful care, building "integrated practice units" and "focused factories," and embracing health information technology.[6] For example, a large amount of value-based activity emphasizes packaging disaggregated services into bundles that cover an episode of care at a fixed price for patients with a clear medical need such as hip replacement, cardiovascular surgery, or diabetes management.

The third key question, on which policy-makers seldom linger, is "why aren't we there already?" In an old academic joke, an economist sees a $20 bill lying on the sidewalk, looks at it briefly, then walks past. When asked why, he replies: "If it had been real, someone would have picked it up already." In efficiency terms, the U.S. healthcare system has billions of $20 bills lying in the streets. How this could possibly be true often eludes both clinicians and managers, who tend to hand-wave explanations about lack of information and misaligned incentives.

The concrete—and correct—answer known mainly to health lawyers is that the accumulation of professional privileges, judicial decisions, statutes and regulations, and unconditional public subsidies over the course of more than a century has severely distorted U.S. healthcare markets and crippled competition. Because of long-term regulation, production of health services is fragmented, price competition is minimal, entry barriers are high, geographic markets are small and often bottlenecked, large insurers and large providers are mutually entrenched, and innovation is channeled toward inputs that best suit flawed production

WHS2013_Part3.pdf; Gerard F. Anderson et al., *It's the Prices, Stupid: Why the United States Is So Different from Other Countries*, 22 HEALTH AFF. 89 (2003). *See generally* INST. OF MED., BEST CARE AT LOWER COST: THE PATH TO CONTINUOUSLY LEARNING HEALTH CARE IN AMERICA (2012) (discussing improved efficiency in healthcare and estimating annual waste at $750 billion).

3 Author's note: In 1993 and 1994, a talented young management consultant and I volunteered as healthcare advisers to a prominent Democratic gubernatorial candidate. We suggested "value" as her healthcare platform. Her equally young policy director—now a major television executive—took us aside and gently but firmly reminded us that nobody was interested in the "value" of care, only its accessibility and quality. Times do change.

4 Laurence R. Jacobs, *Politics of America's Supply State: Health Reform and Technology*, 14 HEALTH AFF. 143 (1995).

5 *See* INST. OF MED., CROSSING THE QUALITY CHASM: A NEW HEALTH SYSTEM FOR THE 21ST CENTURY 83 (2001); INST. OF MED., TO ERR IS HUMAN: BUILDING A SAFER HEALTH SYSTEM 37 (1999); INST. OF MED., BEST CARE AT LOWER COST: THE PATH TO CONTINUOUSLY LEARNING HEALTH CARE IN AMERICA (2012).

6 MICHAEL E. PORTER & ELIZABETH O. TEISBERG, REDEFINING HEALTH CARE: CREATING VALUE-BASED COMPETITION ON RESULTS (2006); Michael E. Porter & Thomas H. Lee, *The Strategy That Will Fix Health Care*, 91 HARV. BUS. REV. 50 (2013).

processes. For example, the sale of assembled products with warranties—routine practice in every other complex consumer industry—is vanishingly rare in healthcare.[7] The lesson for health policy is that if competition to deliver value-based care is to improve, regulation must also improve.

How does established health law perpetuate both operational (static) and innovative (dynamic) inefficiency in healthcare delivery? Among the principal causes of inefficiency are piecemeal fee-for-service payment by both public and private insurers; lack of coordinated production models for physicians, other health professionals, and health facilities; and overinvestment in expensive acute care to the detriment of community-based prevention and disease management strategies. These factors in turn are heavily influenced by legal incentives, restrictions, and mechanisms of accountability. As a consequence of law, physicians possess plenary power over clinical decision-making, hospitals are treated as suppliers to physicians rather than as integrated producers in their own right, health insurers function primarily as clearinghouses for eligibility and claims rather than as either buyers or managers of clinical care, and new competitors offering innovative forms of healthcare delivery and financing face significant barriers when attempting to enter the market.

The chapter begins with an overview of the policy-making function, both generally and as applied to healthcare. It then turns to health law, identifying characteristics that result in a stunted version of health policy that is long on physician agency and short on system performance. Most public policy in the United States displays a preference for the efficiency and dynamism of private markets. By contrast, health law has generally enforced a non-market default based on medical professionalism (both expertise and ethics) and patient dependence.

Next, the chapter reviews the post-Medicare history of U.S. health policy, focusing on its inability to generate cost-efficiencies. Medicare, the most significant health policy commitment ever made in the United States, marked its fiftieth anniversary in 2015. Yet substantially more than fifty years of accreted health law has obstructed effective competition in the healthcare system, and therefore has blunted the efficiencies that competition can generate. Finally, the chapter examines the health law–health policy relationship under the ACA. The central message of this section is that the deep history of health law continues to constrain health policy in its pursuit of efficient care delivery. The chapter also comments in passing on the ACA's distributional goals, stressing the importance of efficiency to affordably supporting the needs of the sick and poor in a nation still lacking social solidarity around health and healthcare.

An important disclaimer is that the chapter does not draw a clean line dividing law from policy or articulate a general theory of the relationship between them. Law has many roles in our polity, such as grounding a common moral philosophy (our heritage), serving as an adjunct to citizenship (our Constitution) or politics (our representative government) or bureaucratic expertise (our administrative state), or—in some views—representing the last bastion of individual rights and remedies against governmental or corporate encroachment (our judiciary). The chapter does not attempt to prioritize or harmonize these functions, but concerns itself primarily with identifying seldom recognized constraints on health policy-making that result from accreted health law.

7 William M. Sage, *Assembled Products: The Key to More Effective Competition and Antitrust Oversight in Health Care*, 101 Cornell L. Rev. 609 (2016).

II Public Policy and the Regulatory State

Whereas both law and medicine are ancient callings, public policy is a relative newcomer as a professional and scholarly field—even if government bureaucrats are as ancient a presence in society as physicians or advocates. Policy is an even more recent addition to the American healthcare vocabulary. A casual search of PubMed for articles containing the word "policy" in the biomedical literature reveals a marked upswing in usage since the passage of Medicare in 1965 even if one controls for the overall growth of published research:

- 1966–1973—423 articles (53 per year)
- 1974–1992—24,902 articles (1,310 per year)
- 1993–2008—103,323 articles (6,458 per year)
- 2009–present—78,262 (14,229 per year)

Yet the meaning of "public policy" can be elusive, even among educational institutions offering top programs in the field. The Goldman School at the University of California–Berkeley offers the following, slightly circular, definition:

> Public policy is a newer field, developed in the late 1960s, whose theories and methods draw upon a variety of disciplines, such as economics, political science, statistics, and other social sciences. Its central focus is on the environment, substance, and effects of policies. Within that context, bureaucracies and organizations are examined as major sites for policy formulation, advocacy and implementation.

More concretely, public policy is what the government does.[8] According to Robert Salisbury, "Public policy consists in authoritative or sanctioned decisions by governmental actors. It refers to the 'substance' of what government does and is to be distinguished from the processes by which decisions are made. Policy here means the outcomes or outputs of governmental processes."[9]

Every decision by government is not necessarily a policy, but micro actions can cumulate into a macro activity that expresses a policy.[10] Definitions of policy also may distinguish between "outputs," which are formally announced decisions explaining the intended consequences of government action (including spending commitments) and "outcomes," which are second-order effects of policies in the real world. This distinction can be important because not all policies that are formulated or announced are actually implemented, and some have different outcomes from those originally intended.

Policies adopted in the public interest are aimed at accomplishing a limited number of regulatory objectives.[11] In a democratic society, these policy goals include increasing aggregate

[8] Mark V. Nadel, *The Hidden Dimension of Public Policy: Private Governments and the Policy-Making Process*, 37 J. Pol. 2 (1975).

[9] Robert Salisbury, *The Analysis of Public Policy: A Search for Theories and Roles*, *in* Political Science and Public Policy 151 (Austin Raney ed., 1968).

[10] Theodore J. Lowi, *Decision Making vs. Policy Making: Toward an Antidote for Technocracy*, 30 Pub. Admin. Rev. 313 (1970).

[11] *See* Economic Analysis of Federal Regulations under Executive Order 12866, Jan. 11, 1996, https://www.whitehouse.gov/omb/inforeg_riaguide/.

welfare, fostering distributive justice, furthering individual liberty (which is also often a justification for refraining from regulation), and building an informed citizenry capable of participatory self-governance.

The most detailed taxonomy of public policy objectives attaches to efficiency gains, which can be thought of in general terms without engaging in a formal exposition or critique of particular welfare standards (Pareto, Kaldor-Hicks, utilitarian, etc.).[12] In addition to exercising personal freedom, individuals acting in their own interests under conditions of free exchange should be able to produce goods and services at the lowest possible cost and deploy them to their highest valued uses. However, policy interventions may be warranted for one or more of three possible reasons, which are often labeled "market failures." First, individual decision-making when transaction costs cannot practically be overcome may impose excessive spillover harms on others (negative externalities) or may result in insufficient investment in activities with spillover benefits (positive externalities). Second, individuals may not possess or be able to rationally process the information necessary to make efficient decisions, or insufficient information may exist regarding those decisions (information itself having characteristics of a public good). Third, sellers of goods may have market power, enabling them to reduce production and raise prices for consumers, especially if potential new competitors are excluded or disadvantaged. Improving the efficiency of existing statutes and regulations is also a recognized justification for government intervention, which has particular salience for the health law–health policy tensions described later in this chapter.

Because government's power to tax is central to its history, goals of taxation offer a useful example. These comprise financing public goods such as national defense that otherwise would be subject to free-riding, redistributing resources more fairly among citizens, and discouraging undesired behavior through "sin taxes," either paternalistically or to avoid spillover harms. However, appropriating one citizen's private property for another's purely private advantage—including the "rent seeking" that accompanies the rough-and-tumble of interest group politics—should be considered an abuse rather than a justified use of regulatory authority because it limits personal freedom without offsetting social benefits.

Public policy has evolved a well-defined regulatory toolkit to accomplish its goals. Efficiency-enhancing measures, for example, can be arrayed from least to most coercive. Mandates to produce and disclose information are among the least restrictive, followed by financial incentives of various types (taxes, subsidies, price controls, and administered pricing systems), antitrust remedies (prioritizing structural over conduct-related measures), and "command and control" regulation (screening new products, or imposing substantive performance or design standards on existing products). Redistributive policies can be achieved through taxation and corresponding welfare assistance (either cash or in-kind), through private insurance markets (although efficiencies associated with expanding insurance markets can be undercut by redistributive measures), or by adopting social insurance programs that are not explicitly means-tested but create a universal minimum entitlement. Finally, explicit or implicit limits—rationing—can be placed on scarce resources for reasons of both fairness (distribution) and efficiency (allocation). An important qualification is that

12 *See* Eric Posner & Matthew D. Alder, New Foundations of Cost-Benefit Analysis (2006).

self-regulatory processes with varying degrees of public supervision can complement or substitute for direct government action in most if not all of these domains, delegation of standard-setting and enforcement to professional bodies being a highly relevant example for health law and health policy.

Public policy-making is also vulnerable to risks—"government failures" that not infrequently outweigh the "market failures" invoked to justify regulating in the first place. Special interests may use money and political influence to capture legislators or administrative agencies, thereby subverting public programs for private benefit. Political ideology may trump operational effectiveness; the politics of fiscal accounting (i.e., what constitutes taxation and spending) has particular salience in this regard. Personal ambitions can interfere. Finally, policy-making can simply be irrational because of cognitive biases on the part of government officials or the broader public, or because political activity is subject to many of the same inefficiencies as private markets, such as inadequate information and high transaction costs of collective action.

Regulatory interventions are typically adopted through legal processes—usually legislation and rule-making by administrative agencies but sometimes court or agency-based adjudication or governmental delegation of its regulatory prerogatives to private actors such as professional bodies. In addition, important nonregulatory legal norms routinely shape and constrain policy-making. These include substantive constitutional rights (such as First Amendment limits on coerced or restricted speech), our federal system with its multiple sovereign actors, and various participatory or procedural requirements attached to regulatory action (e.g., hearings, notice and comment, judicial review), all of which are embedded in a system of common law adjudication that serves to enforce private entitlements and obligations and to resolve individual disputes.

III "Health Policy": Distributing Care or Improving Value?

As with "public policy" overall, "health policy" has rapidly increased over the last twenty years in usage as a phrase and in popularity as a field of study. Some definitions of "health policy" are very general, offering little beyond the notion of being a subset of a larger policy whole. According to Jonathan Weiner of the Bloomberg School of Public Health, for example, "Health policy is the planning, development, and implementation of interventions designed to maintain and improve the health of a group of individuals."[13] Similarly, the World Health Organization offers the following definition:

> Health policy refers to decisions, plans, and actions that are undertaken to achieve specific health care goals within a society. An explicit health policy can achieve several things: it

[13] Jonathan P. Weiner, Health Policy and The Delivery of Health Care: Introduction and Private Health Plan Case Study (2008), http://ocw.jhsph.edu/courses/IntroHealthPolicy/PDFs/IHP_lec7_weiner.pdf.

> defines a vision for the future which in turn helps to establish targets and points of reference for the short and medium term; it outlines priorities and the expected roles of different groups; and it builds consensus and informs people.[14]

These two definitions both finesse the relationship between medical care for individuals, which has traditionally been under the control of the medical profession, and the health of groups, which has been overseen by public health officials. Indeed, one of the principal criteria for "health policy" today is that it should bridge the institutional, cultural, and regulatory gap that for many years has separated individual and population health. The emerging literature on "accountable care organizations" (ACOs), for example, incorporates principles of both individual care coordination and "accountable communities," with the result that ACOs (at least in theory) can be seen as both comprehensive healthcare providers and regional health planning organizations.[15]

Considering the newness of the discipline and the rapidity of change within it, the goals of health policy are surprisingly immured. Students in healthcare fields learn to invoke a "Holy Trinity" of health policy t consisting of Access to Care, Cost of Care, and Qality of Care. In my own teaching, I offer my students three additional dimensions of health policy. First, because dynamic change in biomedical science has been a hallmark of the U.S. healthcare system, I point to innovation as a policy criterion. Second, because "care" has often been framed around reaction to illness or injury, I suggest more explicit attention to prevention and population health. Third, because the most substantial drivers of health are nonmedical, I ask students to consider explicitly these social determinants and the health disparities that result from them. But these supplements have not seriously challenged the existing catechism.

University of Pennsylvania physician William Kissick is often credited with popularizing the access-cost-quality trinity. Kissick has been described by his Penn colleague Arnold Rosoff as a "Zelig of health policy"—a reference to an obscure figure in an eponymous film who witnesses most of the world's great events.[16] For example, Kissick was a junior health agency staffer both when Medicare was adopted and when Surgeon General Luther Terry's first report on tobacco appeared.

Kissick's 1994 book, *Medicine's Dilemmas: Infinite Needs Versus Finite Resources*, asserted that "no society in the world has ever been—or will ever be—able to afford providing all the health services its population is capable of utilizing."[17] Accordingly, he conceived of access, cost, and quality as an "Iron Triangle" delimiting the trade-offs that would become necessary if one were to design a national health policy to achieve a desired level of any one or two parameters. The book was written during the Clinton health reform debate, which was the first attempt in more than a generation to universalize health insurance coverage. Following twenty-five years of persistent increases in

[14] *Health Policy*, World Health Organization, http://www.who.int/topics/health_policy/en/ (last visited Sept. 30, 2015).

[15] *See* Stephen M. Shortell & Lawrence P. Casalino, *Health Care Reform Requires Accountable Care Systems*, 300 J. Am. Med. Ass'n 95 (2008); Harold H. Luft, *Becoming Accountable—Opportunities and Obstacles for ACOs*, 363 N. Engl. J. Med. 1389 (2010).

[16] Hoag Levins, *Remembering William Kissick, 1932–2013*, LDI Health Economist (July 2013), http://ldihealtheconomist.com/he000071.shtml.

[17] William Kissick, Medicine's Dilemmas: Infinite Needs Versus Finite Resources (1994).

healthcare costs, it was also the first to consider the effects of expanded coverage both on medical expenditures and—through higher taxation and government crowd-out of private activity—on overall economic growth.

Health policy in the early 1990s therefore can be seen as a tentative step toward rationing, even though the Clintons explicitly rejected government allocation of scarce health resources as the basis for national reform. The paradigmatic example of this thinking was the Oregon Health Plan, which purported to expand access to coverage while controlling expenditures by prioritizing Medicaid coverage based on the cost-effectiveness of specific treatments.[18] Significantly, the Oregon reform suffered from two blind spots that might have helped it better achieve its goals: It accepted contemporary methods of delivering medical care as optimal, and it ignored the social determinants of health. The "cost-benefit" policy language of the Oregon reform therefore sounded efficiency-driven, but the principal effect was redistributive both within the healthcare system and between healthcare and other uses of scarce public dollars.

An implication of Kissick's assumption that everyone wants more medical care than they can afford is that more and more social problems will be medicalized, reducing resources available for other shared needs. Explicitly socialized healthcare systems like Great Britain's appear to avoid this only by instituting strict capital controls and global budgets—Ulysses contracts by which voters as citizens act in advance to constrain their future desires as patients. Although the Oregon reform was initially framed in similar terms, an ironic effect of its early implementation was to channel additional government resources to healthcare because the "line" that was to be drawn between covered and uncovered treatments also divided patients with hope from patients without, and forced legislators to confront more directly the personal consequences of limiting health spending than limiting spending in other areas.[19]

One can argue, however, that Kissick's iconic health policy framework was already outdated when he published it. Kissick's formulation placed existing healthcare expenditures on a Pareto frontier, making "guns or butter" trade-offs necessary. But what if healthcare was just massively inefficient? As government health spending grew rapidly after Medicare was enacted in 1965, politicians often vaguely cited "waste, fraud, and abuse" as culprits. Beyond obvious venality and corruption, however, questioning the necessity of care meant questioning the scientific underpinnings of medicine and challenging the medical profession's authority to advance and interpret that science, something politicians were seldom inclined or equipped to do. A transitional alternative was "managed care," which plausibly offered a way to improve efficiency by delegating to private insurers the otherwise impossible task of saying "no" to physicians and patients. Managed care seemed politically palatable in the early 1990s, particularly in connection with a well-regulated system of universal coverage, but collapsed later in the decade when apparently profit-motivated care denials by insurers

[18] James F. Blumstein, *The Oregon Experiment: The Role of Cost-Benefit Analysis in the Allocation of Medicaid Funds*, 45 Soc. Sci. & Med. 545 (1997). *See also* John Kitzhaber & Mark Gibson, *The Crisis in Health Care—The Oregon Health Plan as a Strategy for Change*, 3 Stan. L. & Pol'y Rev. 64 (1991); Robert J. Moossy, *Health Care Prioritization and the ADA: The Oregon Plan 1991–1993*, 31 Hous. L. Rev. 265 (1994).

[19] Jonathan Oberlander et al., *Rationing Medical Care: Rhetoric and Reality in the Oregon Health Plan*, 164 Canadian Med. Ass'n J. 1583 (2001).

caused a public outcry that resonated with both publicity-averse employers and scandal-seeking legislators.

By the time Obama health reform took shape a generation after the Clinton effort, an irrefutable body of scientific evidence had accumulated that challenged not only the high cost of conventional healthcare but also its quality and safety, as well as raising dire warnings about the long-term economic implications of rapid increases in chronic disease and the inevitable aging of the U.S. population.[20] "Rules of 3" apparently being as indispensable to health policy as car metaphors like "Cadillac tax," the successor to Kissick's Iron Triangle of access, cost, and quality is the "Triple Aim," which was the brainchild of Harvard pediatrician Donald Berwick and the Institute for Healthcare Improvement that he founded. The "Triple Aim" consists of the following:

1. Improving the patient experience of care (including quality and satisfaction)
2. Improving the health of populations
3. Reducing the per capita cost of healthcare

In sharp contrast to Kissick, Berwick asserted that all three parts of the Triple Aim could be achieved simultaneously.

The Triple Aim was the outgrowth of decades of research documenting costly variability in clinical medicine with overinvestment in specialized services and concomitant neglect of primary care and prevention. In addition to integrating individual and population health, the Triple Aim altered policy thinking in two important respects. First, it took the existing healthcare system off the Pareto frontier, making the crux of the debate productive efficiency rather than rationing. Thus was the concept of "value" introduced to health policy as well as healthcare management.[21] Second, and relatedly, it emphasized incremental improvement, not seeking a definitive political settlement regarding trade-offs among access, cost, and quality.[22]

If the Triple Aim has a weakness, it is that it arrogates to the healthcare system the amelioration of social determinants of health that the system may not be capable of addressing, even though its theoretical foundation envisions a more inclusive, community-based set of individuals and institutions than the physicians and hospitals that prior medicalization movements have deployed. Another important limitation is that advancing the Triple Aim might improve the affordability of large-scale redistribution toward the poor and sick but will by no means render it unnecessary.

U.S. health policy therefore has been caught between two formulations, one zero-sum redistributive and one efficiency-driven. Both the Iron Triangle and the Triple Aim are common knowledge among policy-makers, but the differences in their potential regulatory prescriptions are not often appreciated. Recognizing that the relative importance of markets and of nonmarket decision-making in health policy is still subject to debate, and that the

[20] *See* Inst. of Med., Living Well with Chronic Illness: A Call for Public Health Action (2012), http://www.nap.edu/read/13272/chapter/1.

[21] Porter & Teisberg, Redefining Health Care.

[22] Compounding the irony, Berwick was attacked politically for favoring government rationing when in fact his approach is more based on reducing demand for medical care and improving efficiency in providing clinical services.

future healthcare system will almost certainly require both increased productive efficiency and some degree of allocative-distributive rationing, the chapter now turns to the effects of "health law" on health policy-making.

IV Health Law and Deference to Physicians

Modern health law is complex, varied, and changeable. It is also plausibly incoherent, a concatenation of other laws applied to healthcare that is no more a discrete legal domain than our much vaunted "healthcare system" is in fact a system. One can, however, discern an overarching historical pattern: American health law strongly supports the medical profession. It protects the public from individuals and therapies not ordered or administered by physicians, though in so doing it often discourages self-help. It funds physicians' tools and defends their quality, both directly and by assuring insurance coverage for physician-recommended treatment. It insulates physicians from corporate control and the press of market forces in a variety of instances. It mediates disputes between physicians and patients. And it applies medical criteria to many ethical issues. Moreover, in nearly all of these areas, health law delegates substantial rule-making and disciplinary authority to the medical profession.

Rather than using regulation to further the welfarist and redistributive goals that are the usual stuff of public policy decisions, health law leaves both functions primarily to physicians. Health law has justified this approach in terms of physicians' scientific power to heal and their ethical duty not to harm. Deference to the medical profession is a policy choice of sorts, but it differs from the policy choices described above in two important respects. First, it is an accreted policy choice, a norm that has developed over more than a century of often reactive, decentralized legal change. It has, however, undeniably foreclosed other options and brought a strong sense of path dependence to health system governance.

Second, although health law has empowered physicians both to produce and to distribute healthcare, deference to the medical profession assumes a fiduciary construct focused on a single professional serving a single, typically insured patient. It rarely acknowledges scarcity and routinely tempts physicians to elevate (and indeed to rationalize elevating) self-interest over the common good. As such, it cannot easily substitute for an explicit health policy, despite some early economists' efforts to label physicians' superior expertise as the principal source of private market failure in healthcare and the trustworthiness of the medical profession as the nonregulatory cure.[23]

As Ronald Gilson has observed, "a necessary precondition to professionalism may be market power."[24] Shielded from competition but spared direct public control, medical ethics proved inadequate as a basis for either harnessing the industrial power of the healthcare system or effectively serving the poor. Minimal attentiveness to the financial consequences of care, much less bedside rationing, faded as public funds channeled through Medicare lavishly subsidized

[23] Kenneth Arrow, *Uncertainty and the Welfare Economics of Medical Care*, 53 Am. Econ. Rev. 941 (1963). *See also* James C. Robinson, *The End of Asymmetric Information*, 26 J. Health Pol. Pol'y & L. 1045 (2001).

[24] Ronald J. Gilson, *The Devolution of the Legal Profession: A Demand Side Perspective*, 49 Md. L. Rev. 869 (1990).

capital investment, specialized training, and costly treatments. The result, as national wealth grew and medical science improved, was to promote both extravagance and disorganization while neglecting access to services and underlying health at the population level.

Over the decades, health law has shortchanged many aspects of governance because of its need to protect physicians from outside interference. The agency relationship between physician and patient that sits at the center of health law has been policed half-heartedly. The legal duty of competence, enforced through licensing standards and malpractice law, is resented by physicians even though their customs establish the standard of care and their members control state medical boards. The legal duty of loyalty has been an afterthought at most. In bioethics, for example, courts and legislatures announced in theory a right of patient self-determination, especially at the end of life, while ignoring realities of clinical practice that often denied patients that autonomy.

More comprehensive health regulatory regimes that do exist also tend to give physicians a pass. Food and Drug Administration regulation, for example, strictly controls pharmaceutical production and marketing but allows physicians to use approved drugs for other purposes with minimal federal oversight. The Joint Commission promulgates detailed standards for hospitals and other health facilities in which physicians practice, but requires little of physicians themselves. Medicare, which might have defined and pursued general regulatory goals through its coverage and payment policies, was hamstrung from its inception by a politically necessary pledge of noninterference with medical practice. Through powerful advisory bodies such as Medicare's Relative Value Scale Update Committee, moreover, physicians as a group not only determine what they should be paid to deliver but also recommend how much money they should receive.[25] Managed care regulation never succeeded in setting clear rules for the ethical corporate practice of medicine, hoping instead that "good" (i.e., physician-run) health maintenance organizations (HMOs) would somehow emerge.

What is it about medicine that has produced so much law without also articulating substantial public policy? The historical association of healthcare with state law and judicially enforced common-law duties explains some but not all of its patchwork quality. Nor does the mere fact of self-regulation necessarily detach a social or economic activity from conventional policy goals, constraints, or methods. Notwithstanding the risks it creates of underregulation and protectionism, self-regulation has distinct advantages in terms of expertise, flexibility, responsiveness to industry change, ease of enforcement, and reduced budgetary impact. Many industries reasonably regulate themselves through standard-setting bodies that are directly supervised by government, through corporate compliance programs, or through codes of conduct that certify their quality to consumers. Even many professions that enjoy broad legal privileges to self-regulate, such as law and accounting, do so in ways that are more collectively self-aware.

Undoubtedly, the uniquely long history and tradition of the medical profession plays a role. Medical authority seems to predate government authority in the United States, although how much of its asserted foundation is truly historic and how much merely is contrived to appear so remains an interesting question. There have been periods in American history,

[25] *See* Miriam J. Laugesen, Roy Wada, & Eric M. Chen, *In Setting Doctors' Medicare Fees, CMS Almost Always Accepts the Relative Value Update Panel's Advice on Work Values*, 31 Health Aff. 965, 968–970 (2012).

ranging from the Jacksonian era to the feminist revolution of the 1960s and early 1970s, when professional authority has been met with deep skepticism. There are also examples of institutions that have relatively recently adopted ceremonies and symbols in order to convince the public of their purported legacies, such as the British monarchy in the nineteenth century or the former Confederate states under Jim Crow in the twentieth.

Of greater importance is the relational focus of medical professionalism, which (as I have observed in other writing) tends to be "role-governed" more than "rule-governed."[26] There is an underlying reality to the therapeutic bond between a sufferer and a healer that not only provides service but also helps replace fear with trust. There is a lot of myth as well, which not infrequently acts as an enabler for habit, disorganization, self-interest, and paternalism. Yet almost all of health law envisions medical care as a dyadic relationship between one physician and one patient. Health law begins with fiduciary obligation: forming a physician-patient relationship, its premise of personal intimacy, its duty of personal care, and the limited grounds on which it can be terminated. "Patient autonomy"—a relatively late concept in health law—is in some ways an oxymoron. By labeling someone a patient, one is often asserting that they cannot be, and may not wish to be, autonomous.[27] Requirements of regulatory compliance that further most public policy goals are alien to this framework; it more resembles the private sphere of responsibility that binds parents to their children, in which government intervenes only under exceptional circumstances.

Much medical expertise is also nonregulatory. Physicians' work is often portrayed as contextual and individualized, the product of deep experience and skilled craftsmanship that constitutes the "art" rather than the "science" of medicine. The gap between objective science and medical practice is evident in a variety of legal contexts: deference to physician judgment in enforcing standards for "medical necessity" in health insurance contracts, close attention to "severity adjustment" in physician quality ratings lest professional reputations be harmed, acceptance of "off-label" prescribing by physicians for indications not approved by the Food and Drug Administration, the traditional orientation of the malpractice "standard of care" to customary rather than proven treatment, the struggles of courts to reconcile the *Daubert* standard for reliability of scientific testimony with the nondata-based opinions of many medical expert witnesses. In most clinical areas, "evidence-based" medicine remains more aspirational than ingrained; the challenge for policy-makers seeking regulatory benchmarks for both quality and cost is still a daunting one.

Moreover, the conventional understanding of medical expertise is shared wisdom within a self-governing professional community. Medicine sets many of its own standards and polices its members largely through peer review, a loosely defined concept that encompasses a range of practices from "curbside consultation" to guidelines set by medical specialty societies to hospital-based committees that grant or refuse practice privileges to new applicants, opine on ethical dilemmas, or examine recent episodes of patient care that were associated with unexpected morbidity or mortality. Health law often consists primarily of not impeding these practices, notwithstanding their peculiarities and potential for abuse. One of the stronger arguments regarding physician-assisted suicide and euthanasia, for example, is that

[26] William M. Sage, *Physicians as Advocates*, 73 Hous. L. Rev. 1529 (1999).

[27] Carl E. Schneider, The Practice of Autonomy: Patients, Doctors, and Medical Decisions (1998).

criminal prosecution of physician aid in dying deters individual physicians from discussing terminal cases with their colleagues and results in worse care.[28]

Peer review creates substantial barriers to effective oversight by the bureaucrats and judges who administer public policy in accordance with democratic principles of procedure and proof. It is not unusual, for example, for conscientious hearing officers in state medical board proceedings to develop a record from the evidence placed before them, only to have the board itself overrule them based on the physician members' personal experiences and beliefs (when the board in turn is reversed by a court, it makes the health law casebooks, but those instances are rare).[29] Hospitals in particular function as feudal hierarchies with a physician aristocracy that is often fiercely self-protective. In the 1980s, for example, the federal courts concluded that physicians constituting the independent medical staffs of hospitals might violate federal antitrust laws by collectively denying practice privileges to potential competitors.[30] Congress responded by immunizing "bona fide peer review," which required only physician good faith and a modicum of procedure, rather than attempting to subject judgments regarding the competence of newly arrived medical professionals to rigorous standards of proof.[31]

Beyond expertise and professional self-governance, medical care often seems antiregulatory by nature. A person falls gravely ill or is seriously injured, and must be saved. The victim is lying there, afflicted, suffering. Time is of the essence. *Lives are at stake.* The imagery of healthcare is vivid and emotional, the impulse to rescue irresistible. Regulatory policy typically concerns "statistical lives"; by contrast, the lives at stake in healthcare seem identifiable even when they are not. As I have written previously, it is almost impossible to engage in sound policy-making when every proposed change in the current healthcare system is judged by its potential effect on one's sick child or parent.[32] This emphasis on physician heroism (with the occasional fallen hero) may also explain why physicians and the public assign medical malpractice law much greater importance to health policy than it merits based on aggregate data.[33]

V Stunted Policy: Social Solidarity, Consumerism, and the ACA

Central aspects of the structure of American government perpetuate the gap between health law and health policy. American constitutionalism emphasizes so-called negative liberties—individual freedoms from government control or coercion—rather than affirmative entitlements as benefits of citizenship. By favoring freedom over entitlement, constitutional law

[28] *See, e.g.*, Charles H. Baron et al., *Model Statute Act to Authorize and Regulate Physician-Assisted Suicide, A Statute*, 33 Harv. J. on Legis. 1, 8 (1996).

[29] *See, e.g.*, Guanzon v. State Med. Bd. of Ohio, 123 Ohio App. 3d 489 (Ohio Ct. App. 1997), Storrs v. State Med. Bd., 644 P.2d 547 (Alaska 1983).

[30] Patrick v. Burget, 486 U.S. 94 (1988), reversing Patrick v. Burget, 800 F. 2d. 1498 (9th Cir. 1988).

[31] Health Care Quality Improvement Act of 1986, § 412(a), 42 U.S.C. 11112(a) (2015).

[32] William M. Sage, *Legislating Delivery System Reform: A 30,000-Foot View of the 800-Pound Gorilla*, 26 Health Aff. 1553 (2007).

[33] Tom Baker, The Medical Malpractice Myth (2005).

creates an important antiregulatory bias in health system governance.[34] This bias is often operationalized by empowering physicians as proxy guardians of patients' liberty interests.

At the same time, American federalism lodges plenary "police powers" in states rather than the central government, yielding fifty different approaches to regulating health and safety. These two structural features are related; the Supreme Court's rejection of a federal mandate to purchase health insurance was based in part on its view of shared sovereignty as safeguarding individual liberty.[35] In a federalist system, moreover, adjudication tends to be fragmented, with local judges often making state-specific rulings in individual controversies rather than uniform laws being created by federal administrative agencies or specialized central courts (such as the Federal Circuit for patent cases). The recent constitutional and statutory challenges to the ACA are exceptions that prove the rule—unusual forays of the federal judiciary and administrative apparatus into core aspects of the nation's healthcare system.[36]

As a result, the role of the national government in domestic policy has been largely a fiscal one—both because taxation and spending are enumerated powers under the Constitution and because redistribution at the national level is perceived to be fairer. Until the ACA, Medicare policy essentially constituted health policy at the federal level. The U.S. Department of Labor's exclusive supervisory authority over employee benefit plans, for example, long consisted of a "vacuum" that precluded state regulation of employer-sponsored health coverage but failed to generate substantive federal oversight.[37] Even so, forced federal redistribution is disfavored by much of the public, while more popular "developmental" investments of tax revenues in areas such as education and infrastructure are often state or locally controlled. Health, which is both a developmental investment and a redistributive one, has often struggled in this environment. Federal investment in biomedical research through the National Institutes of Health (NIH) is substantial, but tends to support a long-term agenda remote from basic health and healthcare needs.

It is particularly striking how muted social solidarity with respect to healthcare has become in recent decades, a trend that the ACA should but may not reverse. Very little of the American identity involves "health security."[38] For all its importance and controversy, for example, the ACA never assigned a brand name to its embrace of universal coverage, nor did its supporters emphasize the "in-this-togetherness" of health reform.[39] Critical redistributive elements of the ACA, such as expanding Medicaid and subsidizing the purchase

[34] Abigail R. Moncrieff, *The Freedom of Health*, 159 U. Pa. L. Rev. 2147 (2011) (offering a prescient libertarian argument in support of constitutional challenges to the ACA's individual mandate based not on objections to a general federal police power but on unduly burdening the "freedom of health").

[35] Nat'l Fed'n of Indep. Bus. v. Sebelius, 132 S. Ct. 2566 (2012); *see also* Abbe Gluck, *Intrastatutory Federalism and Statutory Interpretation: State Implementation of Federal Law in Health Reform and Beyond*, 121 Yale L.J. 534 (2011).

[36] *Id.*; King v. Burwell, 135 S. Ct. 2480 (2015).

[37] Marry Ann Chirba-Martin & Troyen A. Brennan, *The Critical Role of ERISA in State Health Reform*, 13 Health Aff. 142 (1994).

[38] This formulation was central to the failed reform effort in the early 1990s. *See* Health Security Act, H.R. 3600, 103d Cong. (1994).

[39] William M. Sage, *Why the Affordable Care Act Needs a Better Name: "Americare,"* 29 Health Aff. 1496 (2010); William M. Sage, *Solidarity*, *in* Connecting American Values with American Health Care Reform 10 (Thomas H. Murray & Mary Crowley eds., 2009); William M. Sage, *Brand New Law! The Need to Market Health Care Reform*, 159 U. Pa. L. Rev. 2121 (2011).

of private coverage by low-income Americans, have seldom been trumpeted by the Obama administration. This stands in sharp contrast to other developed nations, who value universality of coverage with equality of access to healthcare as a core attribute of citizenship.[40] Consider the British, whose emotional connection to their National Health Service was energetically demonstrated by dancers portraying nurses and young patients leaping on and off hospital beds circling a giant "NHS" sign in the opening ceremony for the 2012 London Olympic Games.

The closest the United States has gotten to a collectivist health policy is a consumerist one. Recasting medical relationships as consumer transactions paves the way for more policy-oriented health law to improve efficiency, even if it lacks an equally developed mechanism for collective entitlement and shared sacrifice. President Obama's White House remarks on the Supreme Court's decision to uphold the legality of tax subsidies in federally facilitated health insurance exchanges are telling:

> And unlike Social Security or Medicare, a lot of Americans still don't know what Obamacare is beyond all the political noise in Washington. Across the country, there remain people who are directly benefitting from the law but don't even know it. And that's okay. There's no card that says "Obamacare" when you enroll. But that's by design, for this has never been a government takeover of health care, despite cries to the contrary. This reform remains what it's always been: a set of fairer rules and tougher protections that have made health care in America more affordable, more attainable, and more about you—the consumer, the American people.[41]

Based on these comments, "consumers" appear synonymous with "the American people" in the Obama administration's health policy. This is not a new phenomenon or one unique to the ACA. The rhetorical appeal of smaller government, and its association with both deficit reduction and tax relief, have led at least two generations of political leaders to position health reform in terms of competition and consumerism, and have increased the popularity of market-facilitating regulatory tools such as information disclosure (transparency), payment incentives, and antitrust enforcement.[42] For Republicans, the asserted goal has often been privatization.[43] For Democrats, it has been individual empowerment and consumer choice, coupled with a politically acceptable degree of redistribution. Compare President Obama's comments to President Clinton's second inaugural address, delivered in 1997:

> Today we can declare: Government is not the problem, and government is not the solution. We, the American people, we are the solution. . . . As times change, so government must change. We need . . . a government humble enough not to try to solve all our problems for us, but strong enough to give us the tools to solve our problems for ourselves.

40 Laurence R. Jacobs, *Politics of America's Supply State: Health Reform and Technology*, 14 HEALTH AFF. 143 (1995).

41 President Barack Obama, Remarks in the Rose Garden of the White House on the Supreme Court's Decision in King v. Burwell (June 25, 2015).

42 *See* Nathan Cortez, *The Elusive Ideal of Competition in United States Health Care*, *in* HEALTH CARE AND EU LAW (J. W. van de Gronden et al. eds., 2011), http://papers.ssrn.com/sol3/papers.cfm?abstract_id=2225436.

43 *See* Thomas R. Oliver et al., *A Political History of Medicare and Prescription Drug Coverage*, 82 MILBANK Q. 283 (2004).

Consistent with the shift in health policy debate from Kissick's Iron Triangle to Berwick's Triple Aim, the political rhetoric of government-facilitated consumer choice invites increased reliance on markets and competition, rather than centralized controls, to reduce the high and rapidly growing cost of care. However, preconditions for effective healthcare markets include not only a sound regulatory theory, such as "managed competition" has offered since the 1980s,[44] but also a substantial revamping of American health law.

VI Coverage Expansion Without Cost Control

Pending such an overhaul, the cost problem in American healthcare has been substantially worsened by interactions between law and policy over the past half century. Although healthcare prices and aggregate costs had been rising at rates sufficient to alarm observers since the 1930s,[45] the enactment of Medicare and Medicaid in 1965 markedly accelerated those economic trends for hospitals, physicians, and other inputs such as prescription drugs and medical devices. Medicare, which applied only to the elderly was carefully designed not to disrupt existing patterns of physician control. The political negotiations that resulted in an eleventh-hour truce between the American Medical Association and the Johnson administration over Medicare therefore reinforced "path dependency" in U.S. health policy, with the path determined in large part by conventional health law.[46]

In exchange for its support of the Medicare legislation, the medical profession received a formal pledge of noninterference with clinical practice, payment based on its "customary and prevailing" fees, separate payment streams for physicians and hospitals (leading eventually to an antifraud regime that discouraged many potentially efficient hospital-physician transactions), a voluntary coverage rather than social insurance model for physician services (albeit with generous support from general tax revenues), and claims administration by familiar private carriers such as Blue Shield plans rather than by government itself. Within a few years, the federal government realized that it had grossly underestimated the dollar costs of this generosity, as both prices and utilization of services rose rapidly, but the structural damage was already done.

Proposals to expand health insurance coverage beyond Medicare and Medicaid were aired episodically from the 1970s to the 1990s, but with heightened concern over its inflationary potential, especially in connection with direct government outlays. Efforts also were made to modify Medicare practices in order to reduce cost growth while maintaining access

[44] Alain Enthoven & Richard Kronick, *A Consumer-Choice Health Plan for the 1990s*, 320 N. Engl. J. Med. 29 (1989); Paul Starr & Walter A. Zelman, *A Bridge to Compromise: Competition Under a Budget*, 12 Health Aff. 7 (Supp. 1993).

[45] Paul Starr, The Social Transformation of American Medicine 261 (1982) (discussing the Committee on the Costs of Medical Care, which was convened in 1926 by fifteen economists, physicians, and public health specialists).

[46] For an eyewitness account, *see* Joseph A. Califano, America's Health Care Revolution: Who Lives? Who Dies? Who Pays? (1986).

and quality, but frontal assaults on Medicare's inflationary structure were politically unpalatable.[47] Still, hospitals' incentives for efficiency improved in 1983, when Medicare terminated cost-plus reimbursement for most hospitals and instituted prospectively determined case rates based on diagnosis at discharge.[48] Medicare also began to phase out its practice of making supplemental payments to hospitals to support their capital costs, which had been adopted by analogy to public utilities.[49]

Diagnosis-Related Groups (DRGs) forced hospitals to examine their cost structures, and brought them into potential conflict with physicians over excessive length of hospital stay. Financial management of community hospitals became professionalized, clinical coding of patients' diagnoses and treatments assumed greater strategic importance, the home health industry boomed (at least temporarily), and the hospital sector underwent a wave of consolidation aimed at reducing the excess inpatient capacity that had been revealed by the Medicare's new payment approach. Overall healthcare costs failed to stabilize, however, as technologically sophisticated care was shifted to the outpatient sector, where fewer cultural checks on overuse existed, and economic recovery sapped further reforms of motivation and support. Parallel changes to Medicare payment to physicians—the resource-based relative value scale (RBRVS) and the rarely enforced sustainable growth rate (SGR)—had similarly limited effects.

The recessionary period of the early 1980s was also a wake-up call for the Medicaid program, which was expanding in scope as new needs were identified and was straining state budgets whenever the economy dipped. Also in 1983, California repealed its prohibition on selective contracting between non-HMO health plans and hospitals in order to allow its Medi-Cal program to bargain for lower per diem rates in exchange for assurances of volume. Other states followed, ultimately creating through revised regulation the process by which private managed care companies bargain with hospitals over network participation that still prevails today. As discussed below, however, this bargaining process is often more show than substance, largely because legal restrictions channel competition into a limited set of activities, impede productive efficiency, and discourage competitive entry and innovation.

The political fortunes of universal health insurance were revived by the first Clinton administration, only to be dashed once again. Healthcare costs had continued to rise, and an economic recession in the early 1990s provoked fears of layoffs with consequent loss of health insurance. Support built for assuring employer-based coverage, but reform proponents were unable to overcome fears of massive growth in taxation and public spending, an employer mandate causing a double-dip recession, and government intruding excessively on personal healthcare decisions. When legislation stalled, private managed care filled the void, with insurance companies forming contractual networks of healthcare providers with negotiated prices and attempting to control utilization of services through pre-approval of services and primary care "gatekeeping." These profit-motivated behaviors prompted a

[47] Aaron Blake & Chris Cillizaa, *Medicare: The New Third Rail of American Politics?*, WASH. POST (May 26, 2011), http://www.washingtonpost.com/blogs/the-fix/post/medicare-the-new-third-rail-of-american-politics/2011/05/25/AGzWLuBH_blog.html.

[48] U.S. DEP'T OF HEALTH AND HUMAN SERVICES, Medicare Hospital Prospective Payment System, at 5 (2001), https://oig.hhs.gov/oei/reports/oei-09-00-00200.pdf.

[49] U.S. SOCIAL SECURITY ADMINISTRATION, MEDICARE PROGRAM DESCRIPTION AND LEGISLATIVE HISTORY (2012), http://www.ssa.gov/policy/docs/statcomps/supplement/2012/medicare.html.

second political backlash, with most states and the federal government enacting "patient protection" laws intended to constrain the cost-containment efforts of managed care organizations and preserve the traditional prerogatives of physicians and hospitals, with predictable consequences for healthcare spending.[50]

The ACA, enacted in 2010 following a decade of continued cost growth, is unique among national health reform efforts for its explicit pursuit of performance improvement at both the individual and population levels alongside its declared commitment to near-universal insurance coverage. The first two titles of the statute address coverage, rewriting the rules of access to private insurance in Title I, and creating an enlarged, nationally uniform Medicaid program in Title II. These sections articulate and advance a major transfer of healthcare resources from wealthier to poorer and from healthier to sicker Americans by rendering everyone "insurable" in private markets, subsidizing premiums and cost-sharing through federal tax credits, and expanding public coverage for those most financially disadvantaged.

Though still controversial, Titles I and II take a considerably more systematic regulatory approach to redistribution than the existing patchwork of partial public insurance, organized private charity, and professional generosity was able to achieve. Title III goes further, taking aim at the quality and efficiency of healthcare delivery, while Title IV invests in population health. Although these later sections are often overlooked in the continuing controversy over the ACA's landmark coverage expansion, the law's aspiration to go beyond coverage reflects both its health policy roots in "managed competition" theory and its embrace of the "Triple Aim" as state-of-the-art health policy analysis.

VII Competition, Efficiency, and the Need for Legal Change

With respect to productive efficiency in healthcare delivery, the ACA articulates not a regulatory or deregulatory but rather a "re-regulatory" agenda. Among its provisions intended to catalyze a transformation to value-based healthcare are payment reforms, structural changes in care delivery such as ACOs and patient-centered medical homes, innovation centers such as the Center for Medicare and Medicaid Innovation (CMMI, now often called simply the Innovation Center) and the Patient-Centered Outcomes Research Institute (PCORI), transparency initiatives such as HCAHPS Star Ratings on the government's Health Care Compare website, and health information technology improvements such as Stage 3 Meaningful Use requirements. The ACA is also noteworthy for its experimental approach to delivery system reform, emphasizing pilot programs, demonstration projects, and state applications for waivers. This strategy admits of several interpretations: a genuine uncertainty about how best to proceed, a desire to include or appease particular stakeholders, or a fear of having any single, mandatory approach rejected as "government rationing."

[50] Robert J. Blendon et al., *Understanding the Managed Care Backlash*, 17 Health Aff. 80, 94 (1998) (examining the depth and breadth of the public backlash against managed care and the underlying causes).

In conjunction with the ACA, Medicare now requires data regarding provider compliance with clinical best practices and various outcome measures, some patient reported, to be collected and transmitted to the government. Made possible by substantial federal grants for electronic health record (EHR) adoption and use, this information can be standardized and made available online to consumers in connection with quality ratings of hospitals and, increasingly, physicians. Medicare's expansion of the Bundled Payments for Care Improvement (BPCI) program, its implementation of Comprehensive Care for Joint Replacement payment bundles in seventy-five markets, and the repeal of its long-standing SGR formula for paying physicians are additional significant reforms.[51] In early 2015, moreover, the Secretary of Health and Human Services announced an ambitious goal of tying 90% of Medicare payments to quality or value by 2018, with 50% governed by payment arrangements other than fee-for-service.[52]

In three respects, however, these measures are incomplete in their potential to spur value-based competition. First, some of the most pernicious legal and regulatory regimes from a competitive perspective, such as licensing laws that constrain the healthcare workforce and medical staff practices that partition physicians and healthcare facilities, exert their effects under deep cover at the state and community levels rather than being creatures of federal law. Second, payment and delivery reforms pioneered by Medicare will only be transformative if they are integrated into the fabric of private health insurance, which is also mainly a product of state rather than federal regulation notwithstanding the ACA. Third, many value-oriented reforms depend on partnerships or collaborations that blur the lines between conventional payers and conventional providers, a process that risks harming competition by removing a clear "buyer" from the equation. This last phenomenon is not new—the "convergence of coverage and care" was a major theme of managed care from the 1970s until the 1990s—but earlier programs were more tightly organized and more closely associated with fully prepaid practice models such as Kaiser Permanente.[53]

a. Physician Control

Physicians remain the masters of the healthcare universe, with their ordering and referral behavior accounting for roughly two-thirds of national health expenditures. State boards

[51] *See* Suzanna Delbanco, *The Payment Reform Landscape: Bundled Payment*, HEALTH AFF. BLOG (July 2, 2014), http://healthaffairs.org/blog/2014/07/02/the-payment-reform-landscape-bundled-payment; Robert E. Mechanic, *Mandatory Medicare Bundled Payment—Is It Ready for Prime Time?*, 373 N. ENGL. J. MED. 1291 (2015); Steven A. Farmer et al., *Breaking Down Medicare's Bold New Proposal to Transform Hip and Knee Replacements*, BROOKINGS (Aug. 11, 2015), http://www.brookings.edu/blogs/health360/posts/2015/08/joint-replacement-model-care; Billy Wynne, *May the Era of Medicare's Doc Fix (1997–2015) Rest in Peace. Now What?*, HEALTH AFF. BLOG (Apr. 14, 2015), http://healthaffairs.org/blog/2015/04/14/may-the-era-of-medicares-doc-fix-1997-2015-rest-in-peace-now-what.

[52] U.S. DEP'T OF HEALTH AND HUMAN SERVICES, *Better, Smarter, Healthier: In Historic Announcement, HHS Sets Clear Goals and Timeline for Shifting Medicare Reimbursements from Volume to Value* (Jan. 26, 2015), http://www.hhs.gov/news/press/2015pres/01/20150126a.html.

[53] *See* William M. Sage, *"Health Law 2000": The Legal System and the Changing Health Care Market*, 15 HEALTH AFF. 9 (1996).

controlled by physicians set standards for medical licensing, and unlicensed practice is a criminal act. Many other licensed health professions exist, some with extensive training in diagnosis and treatment (e.g., advanced practice nurses), but their permitted scope of practice is constrained compared with physicians, and they are often subject to physician oversight.[54] In many states, authority to prescribe drugs still rests almost exclusively with physicians, as does the right to provide nearly all surgical care.

In addition, laws in several states (including California, Texas, and New York) continue to ban the "corporate practice of medicine" on the formal grounds that a corporation cannot fulfill the requirements for physician licensure. With a few important exceptions, such as professional corporations and in some states licensed hospitals, these laws also prohibit corporations from employing physicians and billing for their services. As a result, although far more physicians are salaried now than twenty years ago, they usually are employed by physician-owned medical groups rather than integrated provider organizations. Even hospitals that employ substantial numbers of physicians typically focus on ancillary medical functions such as radiology and pathology, or purchase general medical practices in order to assure referrals for inpatient care.[55] It is still uncommon for a clinical department in a U.S. hospital to be run as a corporate unit.

Physicians are held accountable, if at all, for quality but not for cost. Because health insurance provides a financial cushion, moreover, even egregious physician billing practices have only begun to provoke public outrage.[56] High-cost, low marginal benefit diagnostic testing is widespread, as are expensive prescriptions and referrals for specialist consultations. Often styled "defensive medicine" by tort reform advocates, these practices are less a matter of rationally defending against the risk of a malpractice suit than capitulating to an overall legal environment that rewards overtreatment.

b. Hospitals and Physician-Hospital Relations

Inpatient care, still the largest component of healthcare spending, has been particularly inattentive to improving its production methods and reducing its costs because of legally mandated physician discretion and control. It is difficult to characterize the relationship between physicians and hospitals in ordinary market terms. It is not a horizontal relationship, in which each party performs similar services and potentially competes with the other. But neither is it vertical, in which one provides inputs to the other's production processes, or in which one distributes or sells what the other has produced. The most one can confidently assert is that hospitals and physicians are fragmented co-producers of complex clinical services.

[54] INST. OF MED., THE FUTURE OF NURSING: LEADING CHANGE, ADVANCING HEALTH (Oct. 5, 2011), http://www.nap.edu/read/12956/chapter/1.

[55] Robert Kocher & Nikhil R. Sahni, *Hospitals' Race to Employ Physicians—The Logic Behind a Money-Losing Proposition*, 364 N. ENGL. J. MED. 1790 (2011).

[56] *See, e.g.*, Elisabeth Rosenthal, *The Odd Math of Medical Tests: One Scan, Two Prices, Both High*, N.Y. TIMES (Dec. 15, 2014), http://www.nytimes.com/2014/12/16/health/the-odd-math-of-medical-tests-one-echocardiogram-two-prices-both-high.html; Erin Fuse-Brown, *Irrational Hospital Pricing*, 14 HOUS. J. HEALTH L. & POL'Y 11 (2014).

For most of the past half century, physicians also have been hospitals' de facto customers. Hospital utilization and revenue generation depend almost entirely on physician decision-making. A physician (not an insurer) has almost always been the patient's buying agent for hospital care. This dynamic has had deleterious effects on the productive efficiency, cost-effectiveness, and aggregate expense of hospital care. It is reasonable for patients to rely on their primary care physicians for guidance when hospitalization is necessary. The problematic aspect derives from the proliferation of community hospitals in the United States in emerging towns and cities across the country as populations migrated and grew. These hospitals adopted "open" medical staff models that allowed not only primary care physicians but also medical specialists in independent office practices to admit patients to the hospital, treat them using the hospital's technology and staff, and bill separately for the services rendered.

Several inflationary consequences flow from American physicians' nearly unique prerogatives to use hospital resources at will. First, ready access to hospitals has resulted in a larger proportion of physicians becoming specialists in the United States than in other countries, with more expensive practice habits and higher earnings expectations. At the same time, medical licensing laws have precluded nurses and other health professionals from delivering less costly primary care. Second, hospitals have been obligated to compete not merely for admissions, but for the allegiance of those physician specialists. This has led to the duplication of expensive technology that must then be overutilized in order to justify its purchase. The often-invoked image of a "medical arms race" resulted from this dynamic, not from competition for patients or insurance contracts, or even from the starry-eyed ambitions of hospital trustees.

Third, because much of their capital costs are funded by hospitals, specialist physicians have been able to remain in undercapitalized solo or small group practices with inadequate information systems and idiosyncratic habits. Fourth, co-production of medical care within hospitals is inefficient because independent physicians are treating patients with insufficient coordination among themselves or with the facility. Fifth, physicians being courted by hospitals for admission have weaker incentives to avoid hospitalizations and to care for patients in less expensive settings.

Health law bears considerable responsibility for perpetuating these inefficiencies. In part because of concerns over the corporate practice of medicine, state law traditionally defined a hospital's "medical staff" as an independent entity with its own charter, bylaws, and committees that oversee clinical care. The Joint Commission, a private accrediting body heavily influenced by physicians to which states and the federal Medicare program delegate substantial authority for hospital oversight, mirrors that independence in its accreditation standards. Several states have reduced medical staff independence as the business practices of hospitals grew in sophistication, reasoning that medical staff authority is derivative of the authority of the hospital's governing board. But many hospital operations are still based on an independent medical staff model.

Most U.S. hospitals are charitable institutions under law. Although proprietary hospitals have been successful in certain locations and lines of business, the nonprofit form facilitated charitable donations that helped hospitals to form and operate before health insurance was widespread. Furthermore, federal tax law allows hospitals to finance their capital costs with tax-exempt bonds that historically cost the hospitals less than borrowing commercially. For many years, moreover, the tax benefits of hospital bond issuance were essentially unrestricted by Congress and only lightly monitored by the Internal Revenue Service (IRS), creating strong incentives for overbuilding and overborrowing at taxpayer expense.

Arguably, however, nonprofit status isolated hospitals from other components of cost-effective healthcare and compromised productive efficiency more than it promoted true charity or reduced managerial incentives to maximize income.[57] For many years, for example, the IRS required nonprofit hospitals to have open medical staffs, and continues to discourage or prohibit contractual collaborations with physicians or other for-profit businesses. Violations of federal fraud law can also put hospitals' tax-exempt status at risk, magnifying its deterrent effect on integrated care.

c. Health Insurance

Health insurance laws have also facilitated physician control and increased healthcare spending. In the early 1930s, less than $4 bought a night in the hospital, and hospitals apologized to patients for surcharges of a few cents necessitated by "new state and federal regulations."[58] Succeeding decades brought a rapid expansion of Blue Cross plans run collectively by hospitals,[59] separation of these hospital service plans from insurance coverage of physicians' services (Blue Shield), pass-through reimbursement of charges by commercial indemnity insurers who became subject to legal restrictions on selective contracting with providers in many states, federal tax subsidies for employment-based health insurance that further attenuated price-consciousness, and the enactment of Medicare and Medicaid with its attendant inflationary characteristics.

Health insurance benefit packages, which are strictly regulated at the state level, are structured by type of provider, facility, or supply (e.g., physician care, hospital care, drug or device) rather than by medical condition. Outside of true HMOs such as Kaiser, the result is to pay claims for disaggregated professional process steps and technical inputs, not assembled services that meet demonstrated patient needs. In particular, separate streams of third-party insurance payment (somewhat oddly termed "reimbursement") flow to facilities and to health professionals, a partition established in the early days of health insurance because of hospitals' greater need to assure payment for serious illnesses and physicians' resistance to corporate control or fee limitations in any form. Medicare replicated this division of payment in order to overcome the American Medical Association's opposition to "socialized medicine."

For nearly two decades, moreover, Medicare paid hospitals on a cost-plus basis, with separate funding streams for operating and capital expenses, before shifting to the DRG system and phasing out additional capital support.[60] Cost-plus reimbursement further blunted

[57] Guy David, *The Convergence Between For-Profit and Nonprofit Hospitals in the United States*, 9 INT'L J. OF HEALTH CARE FIN. & ECON. 403, 409 (2009) (discussing the growing similarity in capacity of for-profit and nonprofit hospitals and their history).

[58] Mercy Hospital (San Diego) Invoice, dated Dec. 5, 1934 (on file with the author).

[59] D. ANDREW AUSTIN & THOMAS L. HUNGERFORD, THE MARKET STRUCTURE OF THE HEALTH INSURANCE INDUSTRY, CRS REPORT R40834 4 (2009), http://fas.org/sgp/crs/misc/R40834.pdf (discussing the expansion of Blue Cross).

[60] U.S. DEP'T OF HEALTH AND HUMAN SERVICES, *Medicare Hospital Prospective Payment System* 1, 18 (2001), https://oig.hhs.gov/oei/reports/oei-09-00-00200.pdf (history of Medicare hospital payment systems).

hospitals' incentives both to reduce care costs directly and to encourage physicians to be more cost-sensitive in their clinical recommendations. Even today, many hospitals focus on their Medicare "cost reports" to the exclusion of modern accounting practices that might enable them to accurately measure and therefore reduce the actual cost of patient care.[61]

Once physicians were empowered to channel virtually unlimited public funds to hospitals and other parties through Medicare, the federal government began to recognize the risks of abuse. However, its response was to characterize many financial relationships between physicians and other providers or suppliers as potential violations of fraud and abuse law, discouraging contractual arrangements that might have reduced fragmentation and improved efficiency.[62] When Medicare of necessity changed its payment methodology for hospitals to DRGs, Congress responded to fears that physicians might be bribed to discharge patients prematurely by enacting the Civil Monetary Penalty law, further chilling physician-hospital collaboration.[63] Fortunately, these laws (along with IRS tax-exemption standards) are now being revisited to allow greater physician-hospital "gainsharing" and the formation of integrated organization such as ACOs.

In sum, a half century of heavily subsidizing health insurance and individual healthcare services under legal restrictions that center health policy narrowly on the physician-patient dyad has harmed the efficiency of care delivery in the following ways:

- Fragmentation of production
- Minimal price competition
- Many barriers to competitive entry (e.g., lack of non-MD primary care)
- Needlessly small geographic markets (e.g., barriers to telemedicine)
- Excessive market concentration from insurance bottlenecks (e.g., "must-have" hospitals in presumptively broad provider networks)
- Large insurers and large hospitals with strong incentives to maintain current practices
- Constrained innovation (e.g., mainly drugs and medical devices that match current production processes)
- Few healthcare services sold as "assembled products" with warranties.

In addition to compromising the performance of acute and complex care, health law and the stunted health policy it fosters has prevented a vast potential domain of "upstream health" from developing. The United States is in the throes of an epidemic obesity of chronic disease: 35% of American adults are obese, and 45% have diabetes, cardiovascular disease, or a similar condition. This broad population is poorly served by healthcare providers as we know them. Instead of focusing on "patients" who have been separated from their lives and communities in order to undergo diagnosis and treatment, population health can be advanced more efficiently and effectively by enabling people to maintain their health and receive basic services in the course of their daily activities.

[61] Robert S. Kaplan & Steven R. Anderson, *Time-Driven Activity-Based Costing*, 82 HARV. BUS. REV. 131 (2004).

[62] James F. Blumstein, *The Fraud and Abuse Statute in an Evolving Health Care Marketplace: Life in the Health Care Speakeasy*, 22 AM. J.L. & MED. 205 (1996).

[63] 42 U.S.C. § 1320a-7a (2015).

In the upstream realm, should it manage to thrive, discrete episodes of dyadic care would be replaced by less well-defined, often asynchronous encounters. Physician control would give way to more widely distributed information and more diffuse authority. Fortress-like hospitals would be largely replaced by community-based providers and fluid enterprises offering mobile and virtual services. Online price brokerages and ordinary consumer financing vehicles would complement traditional health insurance. And medical equipment designed to be used only by or on the authority of physicians in conventional care settings would be supplemented by home, portable, and implantable technologies. This potentially more effective and efficient approach to basic health and healthcare invites the emergence of a new body of "upstream health law."[64]

VIII Conclusion

Despite its wealth and its newfound commitment to near-universal coverage, the United States faces serious and unsolved health policy problems, including most shockingly annual "waste" of approximately $1,000,000,000,000. As this chapter has described, health law remains a significant obstacle to improving health system performance.

Policy and law need not be an inflationary mix in U.S. healthcare. Although it is unlikely that all of the ACA's aspirations will be achieved, the ACA is sufficiently aligned with industry trends that it is fair to say that the healthcare system has come to a crossroads and has embarked on a new path to better value. Structural integration, bundled and episodic payment, and accountability for outcomes through both financial incentives and transparency are now widely discussed and expected among policy-makers and the educated public.

The key question, however, is whether the ACA will change health law or remain its captive. In keeping with health policy trends that began in the 1980s, the ACA emphasizes individual choice through informed consumerism, rather than public entitlement supported by collective restraint, as the source of efficiency. Yet the ACA is not immune to the legal pathologies the chapter has identified, and indeed defers in several respects to conventional legal understandings of the healthcare system.

Accountable care organizations, for example, mix progressive goals of integrated, community-based care with nostalgia for physician- rather than payer-managed care. For fear of government rationing, PCORI is limited by statute to consider only the clinical effectiveness of treatments, not their cost-effectiveness, and cannot restrict coverage based on its findings. The Independent Payment Advisory Board (IPAB) may never become operational because it would challenge established political-professional processes for determining physician fees. And medical liability reform, which might have helped secure physician acceptance of other efficiency-enhancing measures, was omitted entirely from the ACA and remains governed exclusively by state law.[65]

64 William M. Sage & Kelley McIlhattan, *Upstream Health Law*, 42 J.L. Med. & Ethics 535 (2015).

65 William M. Sage & David A. Hyman, *Let's Make a Deal: Trading Malpractice Reform for Health Reform*, 33 Health Aff. 53 (2014).

More optimistically, it is possible that the ACA will become a "superstatute" of quasi-constitutional status, disrupting established patterns of legal interpretation and inculcating new norms over time.[66] Such an understanding, should it occur, might bridge the law-policy divide both doctrinally and politically, creating an administrative law infrastructure on a par with other nationally regulated activities that deploys comprehensive federal regulation to achieve both efficiency-based and redistributive goals.

What would these new norms be? Some norms would involve insurability, including redistribution from healthy to less healthy, acceptance of illness as misfortune rather than misbehavior, and a shared obligation to procure and maintain coverage. Other norms would involve affordability of insurance, including redistribution from wealthy to less wealthy, recognition of healthcare as an investment in human capital rather than a handout, rebalancing of financial responsibility from states to the federal government, and acceptance of increased reliance on the tax system to raise revenue and administer subsidies. Still other norms would promote efficient and effective care, including reducing professional control, embracing greater market competition, protecting individual privacy, overcoming fears of rationing, encouraging "upstream" innovation, and reconciling personal responsibility with communal support for health improvement.

An apt metaphor for the precarious state of U.S. health policy is the ambiguity that inheres in the meaning of "policy" itself. Scholars have noted that the word "policy" derives from two different Greek roots, one meaning "demonstration or proof" and the other meaning "citizenship."[67] Only by integrating these two meanings—achieving both rationality and solidarity—can the American healthcare system become a sustainable part of our national identity.

[66] Historical examples commonly cited include the Sherman Antitrust Act of 1890, the Social Security Act of 1934, and the Civil Rights Act of 1964. William N. Eskridge & John Ferejohn, *SUPER-STATUTES*, 50 Duke L.J. 1215 (2001).

[67] David Falcone, *Health Policy Analysis: Some Reflections on the State of the Art*, 9 Pol'y Stud. J. 188 (1980); Anne Crichton, Health Policy Making: Fundamental Issues in the United States, Canada, Great Britain, Australia (1981).

CHAPTER 2

THE RELATIONSHIP BETWEEN BIOETHICS AND U.S. HEALTH LAW

Past, Present, and Future

I. GLENN COHEN*

I Introduction

"Oh, you are a professor. What is it that you teach?" This is a question that people frequently ask me when they first meet me. My standard answer is, "I am a law professor specializing in the intersection of bioethics and the law."[1] For many that is enough, or more than enough. But the more intrepid sometimes follow up with, "What exactly does that entail?"

This chapter, one of the thematic chapters in this book, is an attempt to better understand how to answer that question. My standard answer historically was to list topics, but in this chapter I seek to give a more satisfying answer. I also use this chapter to telescope the way in which the field has and continues to change.

I set upon this task using different methods of inquiry. As we will see, the results they yield are not always consonant. The first method is inductive. I examine the way several major textbooks in the field that cover bioethics and the law have changed over time, both in terms of their content and the way they organize the field. This genealogy constitutes Part II. Part III examines the issue of "translation." I draw on several recent cases including *Sherley v. Sebelius*[2] (on federal funding for stem cell research) and *Isaacson v. Horne*[3] (on the constitutionality of bans on abortion at the twenty-week stage based on concerns about fetal pain) to discuss a challenge for the field: the ways in which the rich ethical discourse gets translated into a much more formalist legal discourse. Part IV is my own assessment of where the field

* I thank Jose Lamarque and Ethan Stevenson for excellent research assistance.

[1] Throughout this chapter I use the term "bioethics," which is slightly broader than "medical ethics" though I am not sure much turns on it.

[2] 644 F.3d 388 (D.C. Cir. 2011). [3] 716 F.3d 1213 (9th Cir. 2013).

is going. In particular there are two vectors I want to explore: The first is a scholarly one—the rise of population level bioethics as intersecting with law, including the increased recognition of intellectual property and drug development as topics for bioethics and the law. The second is more focused on litigation, the rise (or perhaps more accurately reconfiguration) of libertarian bioethics, which I discuss in the context of two circuit court cases from the last decade: *Abigail Alliance v. Eschenbach*[4] (on terminally ill patient access to experimental drugs) and *Flynn v. Holder*[5] (on selling bone marrow).

II What Is Bioethics and the Law: A Genealogy

I was inspired by "What Is Family Law: A Genealogy," a project of my colleague Janet Halley that tried to map the development of family law by studying changes in textbooks covering the subject (indeed originally "domestic relations") over the years.[6] I want to construct a similar genealogy to understand how the relationship of bioethics and the law changed over time.

a. Materials

In preparation for this task, with the help of a research assistant, I reviewed eight prominent health law or bioethics and the law textbooks aimed for law teaching. The earliest of these casebooks begins in 1960, but most have their first edition in the 1980s or 1990s. In Table 2.1 is a list of the original title and year of publication of each of the books, and the most recent version, though their authorship and in sometimes titles have changed.

To take a look at how things were presented "through the looking glass," I also examined the various editions of one prominent bioethics textbook *not* meant for law schools that nonetheless had a significant amount of legal materials in it, Tom L. Beauchamp and LeRoy Walters et al.'s *Contemporary Issues in Bioethics*, with a first edition from 1978 and a most recent eighth edition published in 2013.

b. Results

For those interested in a full book-by-book analysis of changes edition by edition, I am happy to share that off the page. While I surveyed all of these sources, here I am going to focus my discussion on the main books in the field that are used to teach the "survey" or "basic health

4 495 F.3d 695, 696 (D.C. Cir. 2007) (en banc).

5 684 F.3d 852 (9th Cir. 2011).

6 Janet Halley, *What Is Family Law?: A Genealogy: Part I*, 23 Yale J.L. & Human. 1 (2011); Janet Halley, *What Is Family Law?: A Genealogy, Part II*, 23 Yale J.L. & Human. 189 (2011).

Table 2.1 Health Law and Bioethics Books Reviewed

Original authorship and title	Year of 1st edition	Most recent version
William J. Curran and Donald E. Shapiro, *Law and Medicine*	1960	8th ed. (2013)[a]
Tom L. Beauchamp, LeRoy Walters et al., *Contemporary Issues in Bioethics*	1978	8th ed. (2013)
Michael Shapiro, Roy Spece, Rebecca Dresser, and Ellen Clayton, *Cases, Materials and Problems on Bioethics and Law*	1981	2nd ed. (2003)
Barry Furrow, Thomas Greaney, Sandra Johnson, Timothy Jost, and Robert Schwartz, *Health Law, Cases, Materials and Problems*	1982	8th ed. (2013)
Lawrence Gostin, Judith Areen, Patricia King, and Steven Goldberg, *Law, Science, and Medicine*	1984	3rd ed. (2005)
Clark C. Havighurst, James F. Blumstein, and Troyen A. Brennan, *Health Care Law and Policy: Reading, Notes and Questions*	1988	2nd ed. (1998)
Lars Noah, *Law, Medicine, and Medical Technology, Cases and Materials*	2002	3rd ed. (2012)
Janet Dolgin and Lois L. Shepherd, *Bioethics and the Law*	2005	3rd ed. (2013)
Jonathan Herring, *Medical Law and Ethics*	2006	4th ed. (2012)

[a] Now titled *Health Care Law and Ethics* and authored by Mark A. Hall, Mary Anne Bobinski, & David Orentlicher.

law course"—the books that are now known as *Health Law, Cases, Materials and Problems*, by Furrow, Greaney, Johnson, Jost, and Schwartz, and *Health Care Law and Ethics*, by Hall, Bobinski, and Orentlicher. Why focus on these two books? Numerically they are the best sellers, most commonly used in teaching, and are also, I think, regarded by the field as the most important survey books in the field.

The first trend over time in both books is the increasing amount that is explicitly promoted/discussed as bioethics in these volumes. The evolving title of the oldest casebook in the set is a great example of this. It goes from *Law and Medicine* in 1960 (1st edition) to *Law, Medicine, and Forensic Science* in 1970 (2nd edition), and 1982 (3rd edition), to *Health Care Law, Forensic Science, and Public Policy* in 1990 (4th edition), to beginning to explicitly include "ethics" in its title only starting in 1998 (5th edition) as *Health Care Law and Ethics*, a title it has maintained in all subsequent editions. By contrast, *Health Law, Cases, Materials and Problems* has maintained that title since its inception in 1982 and has not emphasized the bioethics aspects of its coverage in its title.

But this is the proverbial judging of a book by its cover. Let us go inside.

i. Hall et al.

First, let us discuss what is currently in the Hall et al. book. It takes on more and more bioethics in the course of its development over time, and indeed the inclusion of bioethics topics slightly prefigures the titular change.

The first edition (1960) is focused much more on explaining medical education and the medical process to lawyers—major sections purport to provide an "Orientation to Medical Science and the Medical Professions," instruction on "The Process of Medical Diagnosis and Case Management, "An Anatomy of Trauma," as well as significant background on how medical malpractice is tried. What bioethics there is in that edition is subsumed in the book's section on "Psychiatry and the Law"—primarily focused on sex offenders and criminal responsibility (including the insanity defense) and in the last part of the book on "Government Regulation in Medicine and Public Health." This part largely discusses medical societies and credentialing, but there is some discussion of quarantine and compulsory treatment including sterilization.

The next revision of the book does not occur for ten years. The second edition (1970) shifts dramatically—so much so as to be almost a new book—with a central distinction between "medical sciences" and "forensic sciences." In terms of bioethics content, on the one hand the law and psychiatry materials are reduced, but on the other two new chapters are added (out of eleven) with heavy bioethics content. A chapter on "Medical-Moral Problems in a Changing Society now includes birth control (including *Griswold v. Connecticut*[7]), abortion (*Roe* has not yet occurred to *People v. Belous*[8] as the main case), artificial insemination, "The Quality of Life and the Issues of Human Death," and perhaps most intriguingly a section on "Sexual Morals and Mores," with note materials on "sexual deviation," "sexual psychopath legislation," and "transexualism." One thing that struck me as a reader is the way in which the medicalization of certain sexual categories created a space for discussing them in this era, while today they would not typically form a part of most health law courses (or, as we shall see, textbooks). The second new chapter refers to "Innovations in Medicine" and includes sections on human experimentation, organ transplantation, the legal definition of death, and again somewhat amusingly, "Computers in medicine." It also adds the first discussion of "the issue of patient consent," though the classic case in this area (*Canterbury v. Spence*[9]) has not yet been decided.

It takes another twelve years for the next edition, which is a much less drastic revision. Besides updating some cases, the third edition (1982) removes the quality of life materials, but adds in materials in a chapter titled "Patients' Rights and Ethical-Legal Issues in Treatment" coverage of patients' bills of rights, the right to treatment, refusal of treatment, compulsory measures, and care of the terminally ill. It also adds around 6sixtypages of materials on informed consent, although grouped with the malpractice materials not so much as a bioethics topic.

At this point, I would say we have a book that roughly reflects two-thirds of the current shape of the field of bioethics and the law in its coverage—abortion, sterilization, assisted reproductive technology, end of life (including refusal of treatment and definitions of death, though not yet assisted suicide), informed consent, human experimentation, and organ

[7] 381 U.S. 479 (1965). [8] 71 Cal. 2d 954 (1969). [9] 464 F.2d 772 (D.C. Cir. 1972).

transplantation (though not yet much discussion of rationing). What is missing is the law and psychiatry materials that were originally part of the book, discussion of FDA approval, pricing, and Intellectual Property (IP) issues (which have more recently entered the field as bioethics topics rather than purely IP/FDA law topics), as well as some topics in public health and global health ethics (quarantine, medical migration, etc.).

I would venture to say that in most law schools these topics are thought of as more peripheral to the basic health law class, and often taught in specialized courses in public health law or FDA law, such that these omissions do not disrupt my feeling that this edition is where the field ossifies.

The fourth edition (1990) drops some of the prior bioethics content (such as the materials on human experimentation) but adds in materials on AIDS and more on drug "drug and alcohol abuse and dependence."

The fifth edition (1998) restructures the book with most of the bioethics materials (with the exception, arguably of confidentiality) now appearing in their own part entitled "The Patient, the Provider, and the State" with chapters devoted to "The Right and "Duty" to Die," "Organ Transplantation: The Control, Use and Allocation of Body Parts," "Reproductive Rights," and "Public Health Law." This structure persists with the main changes being the addition of a few new cases or subtopics. To give a few prominent examples, *Abigail Alliance v. Eschenbach*[10] is added on access to experimental drugs, as is *Gonzales v. Oregon* in end of life and *Baxter v. State*[11] (wherein Montana decides that assisted suicide is permissible under Montana law), and *Gonzales v. Carhart*[12] on the abortion rights. The most important innovations in the bioethics portion come in the form of materials on the ownership of tissue (*Moore v. Regents of California*[13]) and patenting of the human genome.

The subsequent editions (the 6th, 7th, and 8th editions in 2003, 2007, and 2013, respectively) do not change much in the basic contours of the field.

ii. The Furrow et al. book

In its very first edition (1981), three of the Furrow et al. book's eleven chapters are devoted to what are explicit bioethics topics, with some additional materials sprinkled in other chapters.

The three main chapters come at the book's end. The first title, "Establishing Personhood"[14] begins with the ominous title "Problem: Death During Pregnancy." It begins with some philosophical essays on when life begins and definitions of death, and from there it jumps very quickly into the debate over definitions of death, including writings from religious and secular perspectives and excerpts from the Uniform Brain Death Act and the Uniform Definition of Death Act. I think this organization is quite interesting in that it tracks the philosophical approach to the materials (birth and death both raise questions about when personhood begins and ends) more than the doctrinal categories. The next topic is labeled "Issues Related to Procreation" and contains materials on wrongful life liability, contraception, a relatively short explicit section on abortion (all of six pages, including a short version of *Roe*), "tort

[10] 495 F.3d 695, 696 (D.C. Cir. 2007) (en banc). [11] 224 P.3d 1211 (Mont. 2009).

[12] 550 U.S. 124 (2007). [13] 793 P.2d 479 (Cal. 1990).

[14] This is quite a brave title for the time! But it actually is not a great fit for the material covered in that some of the topics do not require an assumption about personhood of fetuses one way or the others, and at least some of the materials would reject that personhood is ever established in the pre-birth period.

remedies for failed reproductive control," and then a section on "Facilitated Reproduction" with largely noncase materials on artificial insemination by donor and surrogacy.

The next chapter, "Life and Death Decisions" comprises a section on the "right to die" of competent and then incompetent patients, patients with former competence, powers of attorney and living wills, Do not Resuscitate orders, "tort liability for failure to terminate life support systems," and "The right to die—seriously ill newborns." The words "assisted suicide" and "euthanasia" are not visible in the table of contents and do not seem to be discussed in-depth, though this may be a reflection of the terminology of the era.

The third chapter is entitled "Interdisciplinary Decisionmaking and Health Care Institutions" and is a bit of a hodgepodge. One section is on "regulation of medical research—IRBS (Institutional Review Boards)" and includes historical materials, the Nuremberg Code and portions of what we now think of as the "Common Rule." Another section is on "Institutional Ethics Committees." The final portions are on "National and State Commissions" and "Doctor-Lawyer Relations and the Need for Interdisciplinary Training."

Elsewhere in the book other typical bioethics topics are tucked in. In a chapter on "Access to Health Care," mostly on duty to treat, hospitals' duty to provide emergency care, and Medicare and Medicaid eligibility, there is a section on "Access to Advanced, Expensive Technology." In fact, almost all of that last section is focused on organs, with a discussion of "Allocation and rationing" followed by a longer discussion of increasing supply of organs through cadaveric and live donation. In a chapter on "The Relationship of Physician and Patient," informed consent is covered in-depth, and confidentiality and duties to disclose to third parties more briefly, though both are presented in the context of liability concerns (and grouped with issues like exculpatory clauses).

It takes nine years for the introduction of a second edition (1991). The major change for our purposes is that the chapter on "Establishing Personhood" has been split into two and retitled. The first half becomes "Human Reproduction and Birth," with topics of "When Does Human Life Become a 'Person,'" "Medical Intervention in Reproduction," and the two new topics of "Fetal Maternal Conflict" and "Genetic Screening and Engineering." The second half of the original chapter is retitled "Defining Death" with largely the same content as before. The "Life and Death Decisions" section retains its title and its content for the most part, with the removal of "Tort Liability for Failure to Terminate Life Support Systems" and addition of the "The United States Constitution and the 'Right to Die.'" The rest of the bioethics materials remain largely unchanged.

The third edition (1997) adds a new chapter, "Defining, Evaluating and Distributing Health Care: An Introduction" up front and moves the materials on rationing and procuring organs to this section. It is fascinating, especially with the hindsight of the infamous "death panels" kerfuffle in the Affordable Care Act's passage,[15] that both this and the other major textbook treat organs as the main situs for discussing rationing in healthcare, when they are in some ways "exotic" compared to the more everyday rationing possibilities of ordinary care. The remainder of the bioethics chapters retain largely the same structure and content with a few additions—a note on cloning is included with the reproductive technology materials, "anencephalic infants" becomes the new section heading, DNRs are dropped, and the reference to "Competent Patients" is changed to "Patients with Decisional Capacity," and

[15] *E.g.*, Lois Shepherd, *The End of End-of-Life Law*, 92 N.C. L. REV. 1693, 1695 (2014).

"Incompetent Patients" is replaced with "Patients Without Decisional Capacity." The only big change is turning "Legal, Social and Ethical Issues in Human Genetics" into its own chapter. With this change comes a significant shift in focus to "privacy, confidentiality, consent, and discrimination." Legislative materials from California, academic work on genetic discrimination, and several cases about disclosure of genetic results are added. A smaller but I think significant change is that "physician assisted death" finally gets its own subheading in the chapter on end of life decision-making.

The fourth edition (2001) makes very few changes. The only notable one is adding a section on "genetic screening" and a section heading on the "dead donor rule."

The fifth edition (2004) also makes relatively few changes relevant to our discussion. It removes the "genetic screening" section that was recently added and adding "public health and bioterrorism" (including *Jacobson v. Massachusetts*[16] and materials on quarantine and isolation) in the opening chapter and a section on "Regulation of End-of-Life Care: The Case of Medical Marijuana" in the end of life chapter.

The sixth edition (2008) removes the marijuana materials as well as coverage of the Nuremberg code in the research ethics section. It revamps the research ethics materials adding materials on "Protection, Exclusion, and Inclusion" and "Commercialization of the Research Enterprise," and "Tissue and Data Banks: Research Property or Human Subjects?," among making other changes.

Finally, the most recent seventh Edition (2013) somewhat surprisingly removes the public health materials that had been added at the beginning of the book but otherwise leaves things relatively unchanged.

iii. Other Books

In much more brevity let me mention a few other books.

Clark C. Havighurst et al.'s *Health Care Law and Policy: Readings, Notes and Questions* has had two editions—one in 1988 and 1998. The first edition has very little in the way of bioethics, focused much more on the business of medicine, the organization of healthcare institutions, antitrust, and liability. What little bioethics there is appears at the end of the book, in its last sixty-two of thirteen hundred pages in a final chapter called "Cross-Cutting Issues: Ethics, Law, and Economics" that discusses the impacts of AIDS on the healthcare system, very briefly the cost of care at the end of life, and technology assessment, along with fifty pages or so in another part of the book on informed consent. The 1998 version has, if anything, less bioethics, omitting the "Cross-Cutting Issues" materials. This is not to fault the book; it is just not "that kind of book," but I do think it indicates a not uncommon marginalization of the bioethics topics in the traditional survey course.

Shapiro et al.'s *Bioethics and the Law* has two editions, one from 1981 and one from 2003, with the latter being almost double the length. The 1981 edition is divided into five parts: (1) The Field of Bioethics, which includes a section on experimentation and research, the "new biology," and an introduction to ethical theory; (2) "Control of Mind and Behavior," which includes a sections on "synthetic normality" and "rights of access to behavior control techniques," and an "overview of mind and behavior controls"; (3) Genetic

[16] 197 U.S. 11 (1905).

Control, including "Genetic control and procreational autonomy" and "Gathering and Acting on Genetic Information: Screening, Counseling, and Reproductive Decisions"; (4) "Reproductive Control"; (5) "Death Control," including materials on the nature of death and dying, and "Who Does and Who Ought to Decide Whether to Prolong Life, Prolong Dying, Allowing Death, Kill . . .?"; and Finally (6) Organ transplantation, covering procurement and allocation of organs.

In reading its table of contents, one is struck by how strong a "point of view" is being expressed. The image is of the individual besieged on all sides by attempts at state control, whether pushing her to "synthetic normality" or trying to control her death.

The 2003 edition retains largely the same structure as the 1981 edition, though some of the section titles are different (e.g., "Reproductive Control" becomes "Reproductive Choice"), and it adds a new part on human enhancement. The main additions in terms of topics are materials on artificial organs and tissues, performance-enhancing drugs, genetic engineering, in vitro fertilization, embryo and fetal tissue research, cloning, and more on litigation surrounding organ procurement.

Finally, let us go through the looking glass and see how law topics are taught in one of the leading bioethics textbooks—Beauchamp et al.'s *Contemporary Issues in Bioethics*, which has had eight editions between 1978 and 2013. In the 1978 edition, the main legal materials are as follows: *Canterbury v. Spence*[17] and a discussion of the legal requirements of informed consent; *Tarasoff v. Regents of California*[18] of California and a discussion of confidentiality; *Roe v. Wade*[19] and a discussion thereof; a discussion of whole-brain versus other definitions of death; discussions of "Euthanasia and Prolonging Life," including *In Re Quinlan*[20] and distinctions between passive and active euthanasia; the Nuremberg Code on research ethics as well as materials on research with prisons and children; psychosurgery and involuntary mental hospitalization; genetic screening and prenatal genetic diagnosis.

The second edition (1982) adds a few additional cases (including *Superintendent of Belchertown State School v. Saikewicz*[21] on competency to refuse treatment), a chapter on health policy that discusses rationing more in depth, chapters on personhood, health policy, materials on mental illness as a diseases, and materials on the recombinant DNA debate. Curiously, it removes much of the treatment of reproductive technology.

The third edition (1987) updates existing materials (e.g., adding a report from the Netherlands on euthanasia,). It also adds materials on "Frontiers in Biology and Medicine" and on reproductive/genetic/transplantation technologies, "Competition and Profit in Health Care," and, most notably, on state coercion of the gay community regarding HIV and AIDS screening.

This focus on the AIDS epidemic warrants its own chapter in the fourth edition (1994)—it includes topics like the duty to warn and mandatory HIV screening, and adds one reading on a "A Global Perspective" in the AIDS section. This edition also removes the more general chapters on personhood, health and disease, and animal and human research in favor of a variety of other emerging topics of the time (more on end-of-life decisions, gendered and

[17] 464 F.2d 772 (D.C. Cir. 1972). [18] 551 P.2d 334 (Cal. 1976). [19] 410 U.S. 113 (1973).
[20] 355 A.2d 647 (N.J. 1976). [21] 370 N.E.2d 417 (Mass. 1977).

aged patient populations, reproductive technology, and the Oregon Medicaid experiment with rationing.

The fifth edition (1999) and sixth edition (2003) make no major structural changes, but continue to update the text as to emerging issues; the fifth edition updates the clinical research material to discuss issues pertinent to the AIDS epidemic chapter and adds content on cloning and genetic enhancement, while the sixth edition adds content on autonomy rights, bioterrorism, and palliative care options.

The seventh edition (2007) adds chapters on "Organ Transplantation" and "Biotechnology and Bioscience" (e.g., stem cell research, genetic enhancement, GMOs) and revamps selections in the "Public Health" chapter and "Justice and Health Care" chapter "to take account of recent philosophical and public policy debates." Finally, the eighth edition (2013) makes few major content changes, but does retitle many of the chapters.

c. Analysis

Taking a step back, how might we characterize the development of the field as seen by these books over the past forty or so years? I give pride of place in the analysis to the two major health law textbooks because they are what most students in these fields will "learn on" in the basic health law class, and the focus of this chapter is how bioethics is taught to soon-to-be lawyers as part of health law. That said, it is interesting that another major book, the Havinghurst et al. book, has almost no bioethics content at all.

The first observation is that the field becomes relatively stable beginning in the early 1980s and crystallizes around the following topics: reproductive technology and the regulation of reproduction (abortion, contraception, sterilization, maternal-fetal conflicts); end-of-life decision-making, assisted suicide, and the definition of death; organ transplantation (procurement and rationing); and research ethics. In the late 1990s, legal and ethical issues with genetics join these as a standard topic. HIV/AIDS and bioterrorism come in at the moments when they are most in the news. Bioterrorism turns out to be more of a passing fancy, while issues related to HIV/AIDS remain present, although many of these books later reconfigure them as more general public health law and ethics materials.

Perhaps more interesting are what's *not* in these books. "Law and psychiatry" begins as part of bioethics and the law in what is now the Hall et al. book, but quite quickly gets cut from its ambit. Public health topics briefly enter what is now the Furrow et al. book in a short subsection but quickly get dropped, though they remain in the Hall book and some of the other books.

There is overall very little discussion of drug development or the ethical issues raised by it (both trial design, access to experimental drugs for the terminally ill, distributional issues). Global health issues in bioethics get no meaningful treatment in the major health law books, and more generally these books cover very little in global health law or comparative health law relevant to bioethics.

Rationing (a topic covered by two other chapters in this volume) is understood primarily through the context of organ transplantation, rather than the more day-to-day rationing questions of Medicaid coverage decisions or managed care. This is in contrast to the way I think most of bioethics sees it: Rationing decisions are omnipresent, as Alex Capron's chapter in this volume emphasizes, and the special topic of rationing in organs waxes and wanes in significance. Perhaps the reason for this short shrift stems from the fact that rationing is a dirty word politically? One of the editors of this volume, Bill Sage, tells the following anecdote about working on the Clinton Task Force:

> Ethics was absent for about a month until a recent Yale Law grad who had worked with Larry Gostin at ALSME got permission to bring a bunch of ethicists into the White House to work on the reform proposal (Larry, Zeke Emanuel, Art Caplan, etc., with Nancy Dubler and the late Marian Secundy chairing). Many of them arrived expecting to work on resource prioritization/rationing in connection with universal health coverage. After about a month of back-and-forth, Ira Magaziner held a rare meeting of all the working groups, and in passing and as if nobody could reasonably think otherwise, expressed his gratitude to the ethicists for their help, told them and everyone else that Bill Clinton was not going to be the first president to ration health care, and that he wanted the ethicists to do what they did best, which was craft a lofty preamble for the legislation explaining why it mattered and then go back to working on end-of-life issues.

As the infamous (and inaccurate) "death panels" episode of the 2012 election cycle illustrates, this antipathy toward rationing seems to transcend political lines, and perhaps in the end has made it into the health law academy as well.

I will have more to say about potential reasons for these lacunae later in this chapter.

III Lost in Translation?

This analysis of the various casebooks is a useful backdrop to examine the issue, or perhaps better put *the problem* of translation.

When one teaches pure bioethics, deeply normative arguments are always on the table. For example, questions like: What are the relevant criteria/criterion for personhood that help us determine when legal personhood should begin or when individuals are dead? How should we understand philosophical conceptions of coercion or exploitation, to help us understand whether organs or women's eggs should be sellable? What rights claims can we make to health, and what is it we owe one another in terms of solidarity?

Teaching bioethics in a law school, by contrast, always requires a kind of double vision. One tees up these fascinating issues, but when one comes to the relevant "case" in the unit, much feels lost in translation. With a few exceptions (such as wrongful life cases, where the court does do more to directly engage with the bioethical concepts),[22] normative and conceptual arguments must be translated into extremely formalist garb.

Let me illustrate by way of a few recent cases in the circuit courts. *Abigail Alliance v. Eschenbach*,[23] which I will return to in the next part, was an initially successful attack on the U.S. Food and Drug Administration (FDA) and its ability to regulate access to pharmaceuticals but attacking at one of its weakest links: the denial of access to terminally ill patients for drugs that have successfully completed Phase I of clinical testing but not gone further

[22] *E.g.*, Siemieniec v. Lutheran General Hospital, 512 N.E.2d 691 (Ill. 1987); Turpin v. Sortini, 643 P.2d 954 (Cal. 1982).

[23] 495 F.3d 695 (D.C. Cir. 2007) (en banc).

in the drug approval process. With the help of a sympathetic plaintiff class—individuals who were dying and, in the words of one scholar, wanted to a assert a right of "medical self-defense"[24] to try something even if risky—they convinced a panel of the D.C. Circuit to recognize a constitutional right to access such drugs, and would thus have put the onus on the FDA on remand to show that it could survive strict scrutiny. The decision was ultimately overturned at the en banc stage[25] (full disclosure, I was one of the lawyers who represented the Department of Justice in the en banc petition in the case), but has spawned considerable scholarly and litigation interest.[26] When one talks about the case in bioethics circles, *Abigail Alliance* is about the right we have to risk everything on our deathbed and the effect that uncontrolled access would have on clinical trial development.[27] The D.C. Circuit's opinion, by contrast, is relatively formalistic. It is about whether the right sought has an analogy to one available at the time of the framing of the Fourteenth Amendment.[28] I do not want to push the point too far—in considering various analogies the court *does* back into self-defense, but for a bioethicist nonlawyer the treatment would feel oddly desiccated.

The same is true regarding other recent bioethics conflicts that have made their way to court.

Sherley v. Sebelius[29] concerned a challenge to federal funding for research on human embryonic stem cell lines. Bioethics discourse on this question turns on issues such whether embryonic stem cells meet the criteria for personhood and what should those criteria be and when is one morally complicit in an enterprise by funding it through tax dollars?[30] The litigation, though, turned instead on a narrow matter of statutory interpretation: whether the text of the Dickey-Wicker Amendment, which bans the National Institutes of Health (NIH) from funding "research in which a human embryo or embryos are destroyed, discarded, or knowingly subjected to risk of injury or death greater than that allowed for research on fetuses in utero,"[31] applied to research on stem cell lines that had (through private funding) been derived from an embryo. Rather than engage in any bioethical discussion at all, the D.C. Circuit treated this as a matter of administrative law and statutory interpretation and resolved the case using the *Chevron* doctrine.

Similar, but less extreme, is the Ninth Circuit decision in *Isaacson v. Horne*.[32] The case concerned the constitutionality of Arizona's ban on abortions at the pre-viability twenty-week stage on the ground that the legislature found that fetuses at that age experienced pain,

[24] Eugene Volokh, *Medical Self-Defense, Prohibited Experimental Therapies, and Payment for Organs*, 120 HARV. L. REV. 1813 (2007).

[25] 495 F.3d 695, 696 (D.C. Cir. 2007) (en banc).

[26] *E.g.*, Volokh, *supra* note 24; Abigail R. Moncrieff, *The Freedom of Health*, 159 U. PA. L. REV. 2209 (2011).

[27] *E.g.*, Mark S. Stein & Julian Savulescu, *Welfare Versus Autonomy in Human Subjects Research*, 38 FLA. ST. U. L. REV. 303 (2011); Ezekiel J. Emanuel, *Drug Addiction*, NEW REPUBLIC, July 3, 2006, at 9; Volokh, *supra* note 24.

[28] *Abigail Alliance*, 495 F.3d at 695.

[29] 644 F.3d 388, 394 (D.C. Cir. 2011).

[30] *E.g.*, I. Glenn Cohen, "Personhood," *Journal of Law (2 The Post)* 2, no. 1 (2012): 437–444, at 438; CYNTHIA B. COHEN, RENEWING THE STUFF OF LIFE: STEM CELLS, ETHICS, AND PUBLIC POLICY 59–87 (Oxford: Oxford University Press, 2007); John A. Robertson, *Causative vs. Beneficial Complicity in the Embryonic Stem Cell Debate*, 36 CONN. L. REV. 1099 (2004).

[31] Pub. L. No. 111–117, § 509(a)(2), 123 Stat. 3034, 3280–3281 (1996).

[32] 716 F.3d 1213 (9th Cir. 2013).

a so-called "fetal pain" ban. Bioethics discourse on this topic has focused on issues like: What does it mean to feel pain? How do we know when an entity like a fetus feels pain? Is it the experience of pain or merely the neuro precursors that should matter? Is the prevention of pain a justification strong enough to overcome a woman's right to have an abortion or not, and on what account is the basis for the abortion right?[33] The majority opinion by the Ninth Circuit treated the issue as a narrow doctrinal one—it read *Roe*, even as modified by *Casey*, as rendering bans on pre-viability abortions per se unconstitutional and thus found the twenty-week ban violated that rule.[34]

What should we make of this divergence between the cases and the bioethical thinking? It has a somewhat storied history, reaching its apotheosis in the famous "philosopher's brief" in *Vacco* and *Glucksberg*.[35] It is undisputed that "there is no explicit reference to the 'Philosopher's Brief' in either case," though some have argued that the brief influenced the court's decision without making an explicit appearance.[36] In that respect it appears to be, of a piece, with most amici briefs.

This leads me to two hypotheses—though I fear they may be untestable.

The first hypothesis is the Legal Realist take: Judges are influenced by all sorts of things, including bioethical reasoning, but in constructing their opinions they must frame their arguments within the formalities of legal reasoning; their opinions cook the books, but bioethics provides the ingredients, even if those ingredients may not always be taste-able in the final dish. Indeed one might add that this is part of a more general trend toward formalism in opinion writing—the rise of textualist and originalist modes of interpretation has required even their critics so speak at times in that idiom.

The second hypothesis we might call "divergence": Bioethics reasoning does not, in fact, often influence major court decisions on bioethical subjects. These decisions read as formalistic because they *are* formalistic, and the bioethics discourse has not changed that (and perhaps cannot change that?).

As I said, I do not know how one could readily test which hypothesis is at work, nor do I suspect that, even if one could, one would find the answer to be clearly one way or the other.

Let us, though, for a moment, assume that the divergence hypothesis is correct. Should one, as an academic bioethicist in a law school, be depressed by this? I think not, or not yet, for a few reasons.

First, even if academic bioethics has not succeeded in convincing courts, it has very likely inspired the legislatures/agencies that pass the statutes/regulations that are challenged, as well as the groups that bring those challenges. One way of understanding what is going on

33 *E.g.*, I. Glenn Cohen & Sadath Sayeed, *Fetal Pain, Abortion, Viability, and the Constitution*, 39 J. L. Med & Ethics 235, 237 (2011); John A. Robertson, *Abortion and Technology: Sonograms, Fetal Pain, Viability, and Early Prenatal Diagnosis*, 14 U. Pa. J. Const. L. 327, 369 (2011); just Amanda C. Pustilnik, *Pain as Fact and Heuristic: How Pain Neuroimaging Illuminates Moral Dimensions of Law*, 97 Cornell L. Rev. 801, 843 (2012).

34 Isaacson v. Horne, 716 F.3d 1213, 1225 (9th Cir. Ariz. 2013). A concurring opinion by Judge Kleinfeld did engage with the issues identified by the bioethics discourse a little more, but still not very much. *See id.* at 1231 (Kleinfeld, J., concurring).

35 Washington v. Glucksberg, 521 U.S. 702 (1997); Vacco v. Quill, 521 U.S. 793 (1997); Ronald Dworkin et al., *Assisted Suicide: The Philosophers' Brief*, N.Y. Rev. Books, Mar. 27, 1997, at 41.

36 Thom Brooks, *Does Philosophy Deserve a Place at the Supreme Court?*, 27 Rutgers L. Rec. 1, 13 (2003).

here is that bioethics' influence operates on a continuum from regulation to litigation, with more influence on the regulatory side.

Second, it may be that there are positive sides to the divergence: The inclusion of bioethical reasoning in case law would likely have to depart from liberal commitments not to subscribe to any comprehensive moral theory. The somewhat desiccated vernacular of the courts on these topics "takes the political charge out of contentious issues and deflects expressive contention away from" these issues.[37]

This, of course, leads to a much broader discussion of whether courts would be better or worse forums for the deeper normative debates of bioethics. There are many elements to this debate (including very meta-questions about whether the ideals of liberal legality can withstand too much engagement with comprehensive moral views), but let me focus on a brass tacks one: institutional competence. Much bioethics writing, my own included for better or worse, involves detailed reconstructions of abstract arguments or analogies, the generation of variations and hypotheticals, and sometimes subscriptions to overarching normative theories. Although some of this has very strong mirrors in common law reasoning, other elements may be quite unfamiliar and outside of the training of most judges (who, after all, typically come from the bar of practicing lawyers). Asking judges to do what bioethicists do when considering these cases might lead to opinions that are neither satisfying to bioethicists nor to lawyers, the worst of both worlds. It might also make it harder to build a precedential base or to satisfy the primary "consumers" of legal opinions in this area, physicians, hospitals, patients, drug companies, etc., who seek to adjust their own behavior. I say "might" because it is a little hard to imagine how all this would play out in the real world, though perhaps one might learn something from comparative study of other legal systems where bioethics court decision-making is less formalistic.

Whichever thesis is correct, should it change the way we teach bioethics as part of health law? For example, it might move us away from pairing the bioethics materials with cases and instead toward having them on their own or paired with the legislation, regulation, or other decisions that are being challenged rather than the decisions. Certainly the use of some of this case law is useful for pedagogical purposes—for showing the very mismatch I have been writing about in this section. But how much? At the very least, one might think it useful to include some more "meta" materials—discussions about the ways in which scholars and courts diverge in their engagement with bioethical controversies, as well as some comparative institutional assessments of whether we would want more court involvement in these issues or less.

IV Where Is the Field Going?

John Berger once wrote, "Never again will a single story be told as though it's the only one."[38] I invoke that epigraph to signal that this kind of course charting I am about to undertake

[37] I borrow this language from Dan Kahan, *The Secret Ambition of Deterrence*, 113 Harv. L. Rev. 413, 415–416 (1999).

[38] John Berger, G, 133 (1972).

always bears the risk of idiosyncrasy. Fair enough. Through my lens there have been two interesting directional developments, one scholarly—increased focus on population-level bioethics topics—and the other litigation-oriented—a reinvigorated role for libertarian bioethics and a shift in its targets. I will also briefly discuss how these topics might be better "brought into the fold" of the health law textbooks I discussed above.

a. The Rise of Population-Level Bioethics and Its Significance for Law

In its earliest versions, bioethics offered a way of integrating normative philosophical and theological thinking into the clinical encounter. Its chief audience was the healthcare provider. Early bioethics was largely a dyadic affair, the relationship of the patient to the physician or care team, and how to ethically mediate it when disagreements arose. I want to be careful not to caricature the field at this stage of its development. Always there were third parties lurking in the background or even foreground—family members of patients, payers, hospital administration, and so forth. But these stakeholders influenced the dyadic relationship much more than constituting a primary relationship of their own.

In the mid-2000s, though, a different vision for bioethics began to consolidate (it was there before but became a force around then.) It goes under many rubrics, but perhaps the best known is what Daniel Wikler and Dan Brock referred to it as "population-level bioethics." As they put it: "Where clinical bioethics speaks of the rights and responsibilities of patients and doctors, bioethics at the population level assesses the obligations of societies toward their members and each other and the norms governing complex relationships of individuals, groups, and the state."[39] Among the topics they listed as falling into population bioethics analysis are: society's responsibility for health, individual responsibility for health, health and human rights, priority-setting, cost-effectiveness analysis, health measurement, health and economic development, vulnerable populations and emergency humanitarian interventions, risks and the people who bear them, environmental equity, populations and genes, the balance between protecting health and civil liberties, global aging, global health equity, inequalities in health within countries, and social determinants of population health.[40]

In the *Routledge Companion to Bioethics*, the late John Arras and his co-editors trace the development of the increased interest in population-level bioethics to three interlocking phenomena:

> First, the globalization of our economy, culture, and communications has forced bioethicists to examine how research and care are imported, exported, and delivered across national borders and economic and cultural divides. For example, relatively new key issues in bioethics include research designed and funded by individuals and groups from rich countries and performed in poor countries, duties to provide health care and resources to other countries,

[39] Daniel Wikler & Dan W. Brock, *Population-Level Bioethics: Mapping a New Agenda*, *in* Global Bioethics: Issues of Conscience for the Twenty-First Century 15, 16 (Ronald Michael Green, Aine Donovan, & Steven A. Jauss eds. 2008).

[40] *Id.*

> international pharmaceutical patenting policy, medical tourism, and the importation of medical values and practices into other countries and the attendant risks of cultural imperialism.
>
> Second, many of the most important, visible, and ethically charged contemporary threats to health can only be understood at the level of populations rather than individuals. The risks of global climate change and pandemics raise key ethical questions, such as resource allocation during a widespread crisis, duties to future generations, and the relationship between health risks and economic and social vulnerability. Tropical diseases such as malaria and sleeping sickness comprise a huge share of the global disease burden yet command a tiny share of our research dollars, raising questions about the social obligations of those who fund and conduct research. New genetic technologies generate questions about indirect eugenics and the long-term effects of manipulating our gene pool.
>
> Third, bioethicists and health care professionals more broadly have become increasingly aware of the social determinants of health and systematic health disparities. We now understand that individual health and access to health care are shaped in complex ways by race, class, education, geography, and cultural conditions such as eating practices and the car-based culture of suburbia. Thus the choices and health status of individual patients, and their relationships to their health professionals, must be situated within a broader social and economic context before their ethical contours can be clearly discerned.
>
> For all of these reasons, bioethics is moving beyond its traditional set of concerns, including the rights of individuals to health care, and embracing an intensified focus on issues of justice more broadly construed, health equity, public and population health, social systems, and incorporating a new sensitivity to social and cultural context into its methods.[41]

I want to emphasize that this vector is related to but intellectually distinct from a move toward "global" bioethics or "global health ethics." While many of the topics covered by population-level bioethics focus on the relationship between countries, *intra*national issues are also fair game. One example is whether countries must have universal healthcare system, and for those that do, how to determine what should be covered by those systems. A specific example is whether it makes sense for insurers within the United States to cover the cancer drug Avastin or not.[42] An older but more famous example is Oregon's ill-fated experiment with allocating Medicaid dollars based on cost-effectiveness, which would have led it to prioritize tooth capping over appendectomies.[43] Population-level bioethics also concerns itself with issues that arise in domestic healthcare decision-making relating to how much responsibility to impose on individuals for their own health—the West Virginia scheme to tier Medicaid benefits based on whether individuals enrolled in certain health promoting programs is a good example of this kind of controversy.[44]

Legal scholars operating in the bioethics tradition have paid increasing attention to issues of population-level bioethics. The topic that has received the most attention, I would say,

[41] John D. Arras et al., The Routledge Companion to Bioethics xxii–xxiii (2014).

[42] *E.g.*, Christopher Robertson, *The Split Benefit: The Painless Way to Put Skin Back in the Health Care Game*, 98 Cornell L. Rev. 921, 935 (2013).

[43] *E.g.*, Einer Elhauge, *The Limited Regulatory Potential of Medical Technology Assessment*, 82 Va. L. Rev. 1525, 1602 (1996); Arti Kaur Rai, *Rationing Through Choice: A New Approach to Cost-Effectiveness Analysis in Health Care*, 72 Ind. L.J. 1015 (1997); David C. Hadorn, *Setting Health Care Priorities in Oregon: Cost-Effectiveness Meets the Rule of Rescue*, 265 JAMA 2218 (1991).

[44] *E.g.*, Erin E. Patrick, Comment, *Lose Weight or Lose Out: The Legality of State Medicaid Programs That Make Overweight Beneficiaries' Receipt of Funds Contingent Upon Healthy Lifestyle Choices*, 58 Emory L.J. 249, 250 (2008).

has been the pricing of drugs for the developing world and incentives in drug development that mitigate against drug development for the so-called "neglected diseases" that constitute the majority of the global burden of disease.[45] Other topics include antibiotic resistance,[46] conflicts of interest,[47] capacity building in the developing world and medical migration ("the brain drain"),[48] organ shortages and the possibility of markets or other interventions,[49] medical tourism,[50] population-level genetic sequencing for scientific or forensic use,[51] the ownership of genetic information,[52] immigration and healthcare,[53] and many others.

[45] *E.g.*, William W. Fisher & Talha Syed, *Global Justice in Health Care: Developing Drugs for the Developing World*, 40 UC DAVIS L. REV. 581 (2007); Kevin Outterson, Should Access to Medicines and Trips Flexibilities Be Limited to Specific Diseases?, 34 AM. J.L. & MED. 279 (2008); Cynthia Ho, Beyond Patents: *Global Challenges to Affordable Medicine, in* THE GLOBALIZATION OF HEALTH CARE: LEGAL AND ETHICAL ISSUES 302 (I. Glenn Cohen ed. 2013); Amy Kapczynski et al., Addressing Global Health Inequities: An Open Licensing Approach for University Innovations, 20 BERKELEY TECH. L.J. 1031 (2005).

[46] *E.g.*, Kevin Outterson, *The Legal Ecology of Resistance: The Role of Antibiotic Resistance in Pharmaceutical Innovation*, 31 CARDOZO L. REV. 61103 (2010); Kevin Outterson, *The Vanishing Public Domain: Antibiotic Resistance, Pharmaceutical Innovation and Intellectual Property Law*, 67 U. PITT. L. REV. 67, 122–123 (2005).

[47] *E.g.*, MARC A. RODWIN, CONFLICTS OF INTEREST AND THE FUTURE OF MEDICINE: THE UNITED STATES, FRANCE AND JAPAN (2011); Christopher Robertson et al., *Effect of Financial Relationships on the Behavior of Healthcare Professionals*, 40 J. L. MED. & ETHICS 452 (2012); Christopher Robertson et al., *A Randomized Study of How Physicians Interpret Research Funding* Disclosures, 369 N. ENGL. J. MED. & ETHICS 1119 (2012).

[48] *E.g.*, Lawrence O. Gostin, *Redressing the Unconscionable Health Gap: A Global Plan for Justice*, 4 HARV. L. & POL'Y REV. 271 (2010); Vivien Runnels, Corinne Packer, & Ronald Labonté, *Global Policies And Local Practice in the Ethical Recruitment of Internationally Trained Health Human Resources, in* THE GLOBALIZATION OF HEALTH CARE: LEGAL AND ETHICAL ISSUES 233 (I. Glenn Cohen ed. 2013); Margaret Bomba, *Exploring Legal Frameworks to Mitigate the Negative Effects of International Health-Worker Migration*, 89 B.U. L. REV. 1103, 1103 (2009).

[49] *E.g.*, Phillip J. Cook & Kimberley D. Krawiec, *A Primer on Kidney Transplantation: Anatomy of the Shortage*, 77 LAW & CONTEMP. PROBS. 3, 1 (2014); Alexander M. Capron, *Six Decades of Organ Donation and the Challenges That Shifting the United States to a Market System Would Create Around the World*, LAW & CONTEMP. PROBS. 3, 25 (2014); I. Glenn Cohen, *Regulating the Organ Market: Normative Foundations for Market Regulation*, 77 LAW & CONTEMP. PROBS. 3, 71 (2014).

[50] *E.g.*, I. GLENN COHEN, PATIENTS WITH PASSPORTS: MEDICAL TOURISM, LAW, AND ETHICS (2014); Y.Y. Brandon Chen & Colleen M. Flood, *Medical Tourism's Impact on Health Care Equity and Access in Low- and Middle-Income Countries: Making the Case for Regulation*, 41 J.L. MED & ETHICS (2013); Nathan Cortez, *Patients Without Borders: The Emerging Global Market for Patients and the Evolution of Modern Health Care*, 83 IND. L.J. 71 (2008); Frank Pasquale, *Access to Medicine in an Era of Fractal Inequality*, 19 ANNALS HEALTH L. 269, 273 (2010).

[51] *E.g.*, David E. Winickoff, *Partnership in U.K. Biobank: A Third Way for Genomic Property?*, 35 J.L. MED. & ETHICS 440 (2007); Henry T. Greely, *Iceland's Plan for Genomics Research: Facts and Implications*, 40 JURIMETRICS J. 153 (2000); *but see* Erin Murphy, *Relative Doubt: Familial Searches of DNA Databases*, 109 MICH. L. REV. 291 (2010); Dov Fox, *The Second Generation of Racial Profiling*, 38 AM. J. CRIM. L. 49, 50 (2010).

[52] *E.g.*, Russell Korobkin, *"No Compensation" or "Pro Compensation": Moore v. Regents and Default Rules for Human Tissue Donations*, 40 J. HEALTH L. 1, 27 (2007); Gail H. Javitt, *Take Another Little Piece of My Heart: Regulating the Research Use of Human Biospecimens, in* HUMAN SUBJECTS RESEARCH REGULATION: PERSPECTIVES ON THE FUTURE 237 (I. Glenn Cohen & Holly Fernandez Lynch eds. 2015).

[53] *E.g.*, Brietta Clark, *The Immigrant Health Care Narrative and What it Tells Us about the U.S. Health Care System*, 17 ANNALS OF HEALTH L. 229 (2008); Janet L. Dolgin & Katherine R. Dieterich, *When*

Quite a few of these topics are covered in *this* book. However, as the survey discussed above suggests, the health law casebooks have focused less on these topics. One possible reason is the *case* element of the *case*books. As I have noted elsewhere, doctrines of standing and mootness (among others) make it much harder to bring litigation related to health on behalf of statistical rather than identified lives,[54] and most of these topics involve harms and benefits to statistical lives. It may also be that casebook authors find it much easier to include litigation rather than regulatory materials, though I will say that on the healthcare finance and delivery side, these books are replete with the latter.

It is also possible that the global nature of some of these topics has encouraged the health law professoriate to "zone" them outside the traditional health law course (there is so much material already!) However, as I suggested above, for at least some of these topics there are domestic-only versions of the same dilemma, so it would be wrong to think that incorporating population-level bioethics into a health law course requires a teacher to incorporate global health law into his or her syllabus. To the extent some of these topics are global health–oriented, it may also be time that we become more open to the reality of globalization in our field and embrace these topics into our standard curricula.

Thinking very practically about the health law textbooks we use, how might this material be better integrated?

One element of the challenge is the way in which bioethics topics and health law topics are often severed in the major casebooks. This is, I think, a function of the "law of the horse" nature of health law and also the fact that the curriculum tends to divide them. My impression is that many law professors teach a "health law survey course" that allocates only a quarter of the teaching time to "the bioethics stuff," and the casebooks offer a smorgasbord of topics to cover. Others teach a bioethics class focused primarily on those topics—indeed, the two leading casebooks come in versions where you can order a split-off containing *only* the bioethics materials—and not on the non-bioethics elements of health law.

To better integrate population-level bioethics topics, it might be necessary to better reintegrate some of these issues into the non-bioethics portions of the book in order to draw deeper parallels between the issues. For example, in the Medicaid materials one might talk about responsibility for health by discussing states that have experimented with Medicaid benefits adjusted for health-promoting versus health-diminishing activities by patients. One might tie issues of governmental rationing in the organ context to private rationing decisions by insurers in the managed care sections. One might combine issues pertaining to immigration and global justice more generally with discussions of who is left out of healthcare reform more generally, which might spring-board into more theoretical discussion of what a state owes its citizens in terms of providing healthcare, and continuing debates about what is and is not health and its particular moral importance over other goods.[55] And so on.

Others Get Too Close: Immigrants, Class, and the Health Care Debate, 19 CORNELL J. L. & PUB. POL'Y, 283, 286–288 (2010).

[54] I. Glenn Cohen, *Identified versus Statistical Lives in U.S. Civil Litigation: Of Standing, Ripeness, and Class Actions*, *in* IDENTIFIED VERSUS STATISTICAL LIVES AN INTERDISCIPLINARY PERSPECTIVE 161 (I. Glenn Cohen, Norman Daniels, & Nir Eyal eds. 2015).

[55] *See generally* NORMAN DANIELS, JUST HEALTH: MEETING HEALTH NEEDS FAIRLY (2008).

b. The Reinvigoration of Libertarian Bioethics in Litigation

Bioethics has always had a libertarian strain to it. Autonomy has always been a central value in just about every articulation, most notably as one of Beauchamp and Childress's canonical four principles.[56] But *politically* libertarian organizations have, in recent years, taken an increasing interest in litigating bioethics questions. I am not claiming that this has become *all* of bioethics litigation, but instead that it has become an increasingly prominent form.

To be sure this is not a wholly new phenomenon. In law and psychiatry, for example, we had many rounds of litigation aimed at de-institutionalization, which had a distinctly libertarian flavor.[57] Another good example is litigation over assisted suicide. Although these arguments failed at the federal constitutional level in *Glucksberg*, advocacy groups with libertarian arguments nonetheless have achieved success in several states.

What has changed? In the past, the targets of these litigations were in areas of more overlapping consensus between liberals and libertarians. Even if it were necessary to clothe one's arguments in libertarian garb in court filings, the aims were ones that many liberals could like or at least abide with.

In recent years, though, I would argue that the libertarian legal movement in bioethics has taken on much more of a life of its own and has come to threaten institutions that many liberals would much rather retain. I am thinking of three particular examples, though others could easily be added too.

The first is *Abigail Alliance v. Eschenbach*.[58] As discussed above, this was an initially successful attack on the FDA and its ability to regulate access to pharmaceuticals but attacking at one of its weakest links: the denial of access to terminally ill patients for drugs that have successfully completed Phase I of clinical testing but have not gone further in the drug-approval process. The plaintiffs argued for a very libertarian conception of their rights, including, in the words of one scholar, a right of "medical self-defense"[59] to try something even if risky. While they ultimately lost at the en banc stage, the case spawned considerable scholarly and litigation interest. There are also related phenomenon—the increasing attempts to introduce "right to try" laws in various states,[60] and First Amendment challenges to restriction on off-label prescribing, which have been brought by libertarian litigators in the last few years.[61]

The second kind of example I have in mind is *Flynn v. Holder*,[62] which involved a challenge to the National Organ Transplant Act of 1984 (NOTA) that prohibits the buying and selling of some organs. The challenge was brought by a group of plaintiffs with various interests, including parents of children with leukemia and aplastic anemia, which can be fatal

[56] Tom L. Beauchamp & James F. Childress, Principles of Biomedical Ethics (7th ed. 2013).

[57] *See generally, e.g.*, Nancy K. Rhoden, *The Limits of Liberty: Deinstitutionalization, Homelessness, and Libertarian Theory*, 31 Emory L.J. 375 (1982); Samuel R. Bagenstos, *The Past and Future of Deinstitutionalization Litigation*, 34 Cardozo L. Rev. 1 (2012).

[58] 495 F.3d 695 (D.C. Cir. 2007) (en banc).

[59] Volokh, *supra* note 24.

[60] *See, e.g.*, Rebecca Dresser, *The "Right to Try" Investigational Drugs: Science and Stories in the Access Debate*, 93 Tex. L. Rev. 1631 (2015).

[61] *E.g.*, United States v. Caronia, 703 F.3d 149 (2d Cir. 2012); Amarin Pharma, Inc. v. FDA, 2015 WL 4720039 (SDNY Aug. 7, 2015).

[62] 684 F.3d 852 (9th Cir. 2011); I. Glenn Cohen, *Selling Bone Marrow- Flynn v. Holder*, 366 New. Eng. J. Med. 296, 297 (2012).

without bone marrow transplantation; a parent of mixed-race children, for whom sufficiently matched donors are especially scarce; and MoreMarrowDonors.org, a California nonprofit corporation that wanted to offer $3,000 awards in the form of scholarships, housing allowances, or gifts to charities selected by donors, initially to minority and mixed-race donors of bone marrow cells.

Before the district court, the plaintiffs raised two primary arguments. First, they argued that the NOTA prohibition on selling bone marrow violates the substantive due process protections of the Constitution, which protect a person's power to possess or do certain things despite the desire of the government to the contrary. Specifically, the plaintiffs argued that when a patient needs an organ to survive and someone is willing to sell it to the patient, the Constitution prohibits the state from interfering with that exchange. In Flynn, the district court rejected this argument, drawing an analogy between the blood-stem-cell case and the D.C. Circuit Court decision in *Abigail Alliance* to reject this argument, an issue that was not appealed by the plaintiffs.

Second, the plaintiffs argued that as applied to bone marrow, NOTA violated the Equal Protection Clause, because there is no rational basis for allowing compensation for providing blood, sperm, and eggs while disallowing compensation for providing bone marrow. Both the district court and the Ninth Circuit rejected this challenge and found several possible rational bases for the ban on selling bone marrow, including that it is morally wrong to sell bone marrow (just as it is wrong to sell other body parts) because doing so would turn human beings into commodities; that poor people would be coerced by financial pressure into selling their organs; that the rich would be at a substantial advantage in obtaining organs; that donors would have a strong incentive to provide an inaccurate medical history; and so forth.

Before the Ninth Circuit, the plaintiffs also pressed a third argument—that the term "bone marrow" as used in NOTA does not encompass blood stem cells obtained through apheresis as opposed to aspiration. The Ninth Circuit accepted this argument. Because the case was decided on these narrow grounds it represented a relatively minor win for the foes of NOTA and a libertarian agenda in favor of organ sales.

The buying and selling of organs, like the FDA restriction on access to experimental drugs, represents something of a new target for libertarian bioethics and one where, once again, there is more of a cleave between libertarians and liberals than older topics like deinstitutionalization or assisted suicide.

Let me also connect the dots to one more prominent case arguably in the shadowlands between bioethics and more general healthcare law: *NFIB v. Sebelius*, involving the challenge to the individual mandate of the Affordable Care Act.[63] The mandate had many purposes, but one way of viewing it was as an attempt to establish a solidaristic sharing of benefits and risks among all members of society with cross-subsidization through risk pooling, very consonant with bioethics concepts of justice and sharing of benefits. While the challengers were forced to channel their arguments into the federalist garb of Commerce Clause and Taxing Clause arguments, the libertarian impulses behind them were unmistakable and indeed discussed by many of the lower courts who found in their favor.[64]

[63] NFIB v. Sebelius, 132 S. Ct. 2566 (2012).

[64] *See, e.g.*, Abigail R. Moncrieff, *Safeguarding the Safeguards: The ACA Litigation and the Extension of Indirect Protection to Nonfundamental Liberties*, 64 Fla. L. Rev. 639, 643 (2012).

I do not want to speculate too much on the cause for this reinvigoration of libertarian bioethics litigation, though it does seem to me to be part of a zeitgeist that has given birth to the Tea Party movement. Instead I will just observe that it has a counterpart in public health as well, most notably in the backlash and litigation over anti-obesity legislation such as the ill-fated New York City drink ordinance, discussed elsewhere in this book.

V Conclusion

In this chapter I have tried to chart the development of the way in which bioethics is taught as part of health law—showing that it reaches relative stability in the 1980s as to the topics covered, at some point sloughs off law and psychiatry as within its ambit, and largely ignores global health issues, rationing beyond organ distribution, and comparative bioethics topics. I have discussed the way in which many of the recent cases from the circuit courts on bioethics topics have tended to shy away from the rich normative terrain of bioethics and the law in favor of formalistic reasoning borrowed "off the rack" from other areas of law (administrative law, constitutional law). The cause and significance of this phenomenon are open to dispute, but I have made some suggestions as to why those in the field should not find this result depressing, and also how our pedagogy might better engage with this reality.

Finally, and looking forward, I have suggested there have been two significant trends in the last few years—the rise of interest in population-level bioethics and the law at the scholarly level and the reinvigoration of libertarian bioethics litigation in the courts, with new targets leading to more divergence with liberals. The former phenomenon is one that has not yet made its way sufficiently, in my view, into the typical casebooks used to teach bioethics and the law, but I am hopeful it will.

CHAPTER 3

WHAT HEALTH REFORM REVEALS ABOUT HEALTH LAW

ALLISON K. HOFFMAN

If someone unfamiliar with the U.S. healthcare system and laws picked up and read the Patient Protection and Affordable Care Act (ACA),[1] she would be baffled. And rightfully so. The only way this 2010 healthcare reform law makes sense is when understood in the context of the system predating it. In turn, the ACA is a reflection of this system and the values that shaped it.

The ACA offers a unique window into the idiosyncrasies and ideologies of U.S. healthcare law. The law bends when it touches on issues dealing with healthcare—a health law exceptionalism. New doctrines and standards develop in areas like contract and tort. Old rules develop new exceptions in antitrust and tax law. And a whole host of laws has been created in a mostly futile attempt to excise profit motives from medicine, such as prohibitions against the corporate practice of medicine and antifraud laws against kickbacks and self-referral. What results is a very complex and sometimes counterintuitive field of law, explained throughout this volume. It is within this context that the ACA attempts to reshape how healthcare is financed and delivered. Lawmakers had to contend with a preexisting legal structure, as well as the usual political and fiscal barriers. Not surprisingly, the ACA is reform in a path-dependent vein—a renovation on the current foundation, rather than a gut rehab.[2]

This introductory chapter aims to use a few of the most important ACA policies to illuminate key principles that shape the field of health law more broadly. It is not a summary of the

[1] Pub. L. No. 111-148, 124 Stat. 119 (2010), *amended by* Health Care and Reconciliation Act of 2010, Pub. L. No. 111-152, 124 Stat. 1029 (2010). Subsequent references in this chapter to the Patient Protection and Affordable Care Act refer to the Act, as amended.

[2] *See*, e.g., Jonathan Oberlander & Theodore R. Marmor, *The Health Bill Explained at Last*, N.Y. Review of Books, Aug. 19, 2010. "Path-dependence" is a term initially used by social scientists to describe historically rooted evolution. The theory has been applied in a number of other fields, including economics and, by Paul Pierson, in political science with respect to the development of social policy. *See* Paul Pierson, *Increasing Returns, Path Dependence, and the Study of Politics*, 94 Am. Pol. Sci. Rev. 251 (2000).

ACA's policies.[3] Rather, this chapter offers a thematic overview, focusing on the law's most transformative efforts contained in Titles I–III that reform healthcare financing and delivery. It shows how key ACA policies can offer insight into the legal and regulatory structure predating the ACA and the values that shaped it.

I The Path of Health Reform

No one thinks the ACA is the ideal health reform law. The ACA was signed into law on March 23, 2010, by President Barack Obama, after a year of contentious debate and dissent in Congress.[4] As is true of any legislation that makes it to the president's desk for signature, it is the product of political compromise and fiscal realities. Even more challenging for this law, it was not starting on a clean slate. Its goal was to reconfigure an industry that comprises one-sixth of the U.S. economy and is highly regulated.

Not surprisingly, the ACA takes a pragmatic approach. Congress built on preexisting structures and upset vested interests as little as possible, while not losing sight of the potential for fundamental change. The result is a system that looks largely the same as the one in place before, and also different in some meaningful ways.

a. A Brief Note on the Political History and Context of the Affordable Care Act

The ACA was a long time coming. Over the century preceding it, almost every president attempted reform to create a national system for healthcare financing.[5] All failed to achieve this ambitious goal, but a few succeeded in more modest ways. The failures and incremental successes, alike, offered tactical insights and substantive guidance to the architects of the ACA.

President Lyndon Johnson signed Medicare and Medicaid into law in 1965 as part of his Great Society, and the programs have since been considered the greatest success of twentieth-century U.S. health reform.[6] Even so, Medicare and Medicaid were a failed attempt at universal healthcare financing.[7] They pay for healthcare for the elderly, the "deserving poor," and

[3] For a summary, *see* Kaiser Family Found., Summary of the Affordable Care Act (Apr. 25, 2013), http://kff.org/health-reform/fact-sheet/summary-of-the-affordable-care-act/. Many of the policies mentioned in this chapter are described in greater detail in other chapters in this volume (*see* Timothy S. Jost, Amy Monahan, Mark Hall, and Robert Jerry, this volume).

[4] *Remarks on Signing the Patient Protection and Affordable Care Act*, 2010 Daily Comp. Pres. Doc. 196 (Mar. 23, 2010).

[5] *See*, e.g., Stuart Altman & David Schactman, Power, Politics, and Universal Health Care: The Inside Story of a Century-Long Battle (2011), David Blumenthal & James A. Morone, The Heart of Power: Health and Politics in the Oval Office (2009); Paul Starr, Remedy and Reaction: the Peculiar American Struggle Over Health Care Reform (2011).

[6] Social Security Amendments of 1965, Pub. L. No. 89-97, 79 Stat. 286 (1965) (codified as amended at 42 U.S.C. §§ 1395, 1396 (2012)).

[7] Theodore R. Marmor, The Politics of Medicare 95–96 (1970).

people with disabilities, selecting out more vulnerable populations for public insurance and leaving others to fend for themselves. These programs launched a half-century of incremental reform to fill in the gaps.

This incrementalism is at the root of the fragmented system of healthcare financing in the United States.[8] In 2010, the year the ACA became law, public insurance programs covered a combined 90 million Americans,[9] less than one-third of the population. Because Medicare and Medicaid did not fully occupy the healthcare financing space, private financing filled in the gaps. Health insurance developed as an employment benefit throughout the twentieth century and has become deeply entrenched as such.[10] Prior to the ACA, the U.S. private health insurance market was the source of coverage for 195 million Americans.[11] Most of these privately insured Americans have employer-sponsored insurance—coverage through their jobs.[12]

Without access to employer-sponsored insurance, individuals are left to seek out coverage on their own from a private insurance company. Six to seven percent of the nonelderly (about 15 million people) had coverage through this "individual market" prior to the passage of the ACA.[13] Historically, individual-market coverage was relatively more expensive than other forms of coverage with similar benefits, in part because administrative costs were as high as 15% to 20% of total costs. Low-income or unhealthy individuals were excluded from the individual market.[14] As many as three in five people who applied for policies before the ACA could not afford the high premium prices or were denied coverage, and many people remained uninsured or underinsured.[15]

In the half-century since Medicare and Medicaid's passage, many presidents have attempted to move the American hybrid of public and private financing systems toward more universal coverage. Some efforts failed in grand scale, such as President Bill Clinton's

[8] *See* EINER ELHAUGE, ED., THE FRAGMENTATION OF U.S. HEALTH CARE: CAUSES AND SOLUTIONS (2010).

[9] Carmen DeNavas-Walt et al., U.S. CENSUS BUREAU, INCOME, POVERTY, AND HEALTH INSURANCE COVERAGE IN THE UNITED STATES: 2009, at 71 tbl. C-1 (2010). Other public programs in addition to Medicare and Medicaid include the State Children's Health Insurance Program for near-poor children, Indian Health Services for American Indians and Alaskan Natives, and TRICARE and the Veteran Administration's program for active duty military personnel, veterans, and their families.

[10] While employers are not required to offer employees health insurance, many do, in part because expenditures on health benefits are excludable from taxes for both the employer and employee. The beneficial tax treatment means that health benefits have become a less expensive way to compensate employees; health insurance costs employers approximately $.65 per dollar of benefits. Jonathan Gruber, *Covering the Uninsured in the United States*, 46 J. ECON. LITERATURE 571, 574 (2008).

[11] DeNavas-Walt et al., U.S. CENSUS BUREAU, at 71. Over 250 million Americans are insured, some with both private and public coverage.

[12] KAISER COMM. ON MEDICAID & THE UNINSURED, THE UNINSURED: A PRIMER, SUPPLEMENTAL TABLES at 1, tbl. 1 (2015) (58.8% of all adults have private employer-sponsored insurance).

[13] Paul Fronstin, *Sources of Health Insurance and Characteristics of the Uninsured: Analysis of the March 2009 Current Population Survey*, EBRI ISSUE BRIEF, no. 334, Sept. 2009, at 5.

[14] *See, e.g.*, Melinda Beeuwkes Buntin et al., *The Role of the Individual Health Insurance Market and Prospects for Change*, 23 HEALTH AFF. Nov.–Dec. 2004 at 79, 81; SARA R. COLLINS ET AL., THE COMMONWEALTH FUND, SQUEEZED: WHY RISING EXPOSURE TO HEALTH CARE COSTS THREATENS THE HEALTH AND FINANCIAL WELL-BEING OF AMERICAN FAMILIES 3–4 (2006).

[15] Michelle M. Doty et al., *Failure to Protect: Why the Individual Insurance Market Is Not a Viable Option for Most U.S. Families*, COMMONWEALTH FUND PUB. NO. 1300 at 1–3 (2009).

attempt in 1993 to pass a reform called the Health Security Act, an effort led by a task force under the command of First Lady Hillary Rodham Clinton. Explanations for the Clinton failure abound: delay in producing draft legislation halted forward momentum; the policy-making was too covert and under the thumb of the White House, which alienated Congress; public support was lacking; and the administration failed to manage interest groups effectively, including the insurance lobby, among others.[16] As another example of a failed reform attempt, several years before the Clinton reform, President Ronald Reagan signed the Medicare Catastrophic Coverage Act, which expanded Medicare benefits and prescription drug coverage, into law, only to see it repealed a year and a half later by President George H. W. Bush in response to beneficiaries' concerns about costs. These failures played strongly in the minds of the architects of the ACA, who hoped to avoid such missteps.[17]

On the other hand, there were some notable health reform successes in the decades after the passage of Medicare and Medicaid. At the federal level, Congress passed the Health Insurance Portability and Accountability Act (HIPAA) in 1996, incremental reform salvaged from the failed Clinton Health Security Act efforts.[18] HIPAA's insurance reforms aim to enable people to keep insurance coverage when changing jobs. To achieve this portability, HIPAA limits the exclusion of preexisting conditions in employer health plans and requires insurers to issue coverage to any employer groups who apply.[19] HIPAA succeeded in increasing access to healthcare for people whose employers offered health benefits, but it did little for people without access to employer plans in the first place.[20] Another example of a relatively successful reform, the Medicare Prescription Drug, Improvement, and Modernization Act of 2003 (known as "Medicare Part D"), was signed into law by President George W. Bush.[21] Both Republicans and Democrats, as well as many seniors, were early skeptics of the law.[22] Yet, most people consider it a success in practice. Medicare beneficiaries now have outpatient prescription drug benefits for a small monthly premium (the ACA strengthens these benefits further[23]), achieving what both the Medicare Catastrophic Coverage Act and Clinton's Health Security Act hoped to and failed to do. One defining feature of Medicare Part D is that private insurance companies administer the program's benefits. The law expanded Medicare benefits and simultaneously created a windfall for these private insurers, who enjoyed a new, lucrative market. This law served as a model for how private industry could play a central role in significant health reform.

Throughout the 1980s, most health insurance reform activity occurred at the state level. A few states required that insurers issue coverage to everyone who apply ("guaranteed issue")

[16] DAVID BLUMENTHAL & JAMES A. MORONE, THE HEART OF POWER: HEALTH AND POLITICS IN THE OVAL OFFICE 381–384 (2009).

[17] JOHN MCDONOUGH, INSIDE NATIONAL HEALTH REFORM 1–4 (2011).

[18] Health Insurance Portability and Accountability Act of 1996, Pub. L. No. 104–191, 110 Stat. 1936 (1996).

[19] *Id.*

[20] Robert Kuttner, *The Kassebaum-Kennedy Bill—The Limits of Incrementalism*, 337 NEW ENG. J. MED. 64, 64 (1997). *See also* Allison K. Hoffman, *Oil and Water: Mixing Individual Mandates, Fragmented Markets, and Health Reform*, 36 AM. J. L. & MED. 7, 57–59 (2010).

[21] Pub. L. No. 108-173, 117 Stat. 2066 (2003).

[22] PAUL STARR, REMEDY AND REACTION: THE PECULIAR AMERICAN STRUGGLE OVER HEALTH CARE REFORM 148–149, 151 (2011).

[23] Patient Protection and Affordable Care Act § 3301, 42 U.S.C. §1395w (2012).

and some states limited premium variation among enrollees. For example, some states instituted community-rated premium prices, which means that insurers must charge the same or similar prices to all applicants, regardless of an individual's health, or rate bands, which allow only limited variation between the least and most expensive premium for the same plan. All states mandated coverage of certain categories of benefits, ranging from a high of sixty-nine such mandates in Rhode Island to a low of thirteen in Idaho.[24]

The most comprehensive state-based reform was in Massachusetts, which in 2006 passed a health reform law which ironically came to be called "Romneycare," after Governor Mitt Romney, who signed it into law and then opposed the very same policies when running for president in 2008. The ACA is loosely based on the Romneycare policies, including the individual mandate, healthcare exchanges, and sliding scale subsidies—not surprising since key architects of the Massachusetts law, including John McDonough and Jonathan Gruber, also helped to design the ACA.[25]

This past century of reform, failures, and successes, paved a path for the ACA's passage. The Clinton failure offered tactical and substantive guidance. Tactically, President Obama made health reform a priority, and Congress moved more swiftly than in past attempts, with the ACA signed into law a little over a year after President Obama took office. Proponents of reform managed industry interest groups more adeptly, creating opportunities for industry input, or at least the appearance of it, through high-profile meetings with industry representatives at the White House.[26] And the health insurers were neutralized through early public relations efforts that portrayed them as public enemy number one. These efforts set them on the defensive so they were less able to launch attacks like those that maimed the Clinton-era reforms.

President Obama rarely took a public position on the content of the ACA prior to its passage, so much so that his lack of input was remarkable.[27] He could rely, unlike Clinton, on a presumptive vision of what form the policies would take, based on Massachusetts's reform and President Clinton's proposal. The Democratic primaries in 2008 clarified a vision of reform, when Barack Obama and Hillary Clinton debated twenty-one times, often discussing health policy.[28] This vision was then massaged into legislation by Congress and the Democratic leaders, who were in support of reform, including then Senate Finance Committee Chairman Max Baucus, then Senate Committee on Health, Education, Labor, and Pensions Committee Chairman Edward Kennedy, and Speaker of the House Nancy Pelosi, whose heroic effort secured the eventual passage of the law in the House of Representatives.

Substantively, perhaps most important is what Clinton's proposal and the law in Massachusetts were not: a coherent, single system of healthcare financing—a Medicare for all. As in Medicare Part D, private insurance and competition were central to reform. The Clinton plan was based on Alain Enthoven's theory of managed competition, where private

[24] Victoria Craig Bunce & J. P. Wieske, Council for Affordable Health Insurance, Health Insurance Mandates in the States 2010 (2010).

[25] John McDonough, Inside National Health Reform 6 (2011).

[26] *Id.* at 5, 55; Jonathan Cohn, *How They Did It*, New Republic, June 10, 2010, at 19.

[27] *See*, e.g., William M. Sage, *Brand New Law! The Need to Market Health Care Reform*, 159 U. Penn. L. Rev 2121 (2011).

[28] Starr, Remedy and Reaction at 15–16.

health insurers compete for insureds in a carefully structured market and can only profit by providing a better product, not by cherry-picking healthy applicants.[29] Massachusetts's reform and the ACA are both loosely based on this concept, with regulated private markets and health insurance exchanges forming the arena for competition.[30]

Even with the luxury of insight from these past failures and successes, the ACA's passage was a narrow one. The law adhered to the path already carved out and norms of incrementalism and the primacy of private markets, to a large extent. Yet, it promised enough change to the existing system that passage was contentious and supported by a tenuous majority that just barely held together in the end.[31] The narrowness of this win has made the law more vulnerable to repeated attack, both in the legislature and in the courts, as described in Part III, below.

b. An Overview of the Main Goals of the Affordable Care Act

The ACA's primary and most ambitious goal is progress toward universal coverage. In the year before the ACA's passage, 16.3% of Americans were uninsured, including 18.4% of people under age sixty-five, and many more were underinsured.[32] Titles I and II of the ACA are an attempt to solve these problems. These Titles regulate private health insurance markets so that more people can afford good coverage, and they expand public coverage, most importantly extending Medicaid eligibility to cover more low-income Americans.

A secondary core goal of the ACA is to test—and perhaps catalyze—changes in healthcare delivery, contained primarily in Title III. Healthcare in the United States is notoriously more expensive and less effective than in any other developed country.[33] The Institute of Medicine estimates that as much as one-quarter of total spending is wasteful—at best unnecessary and in many cases often harmful.[34] The ACA rolls out a series of experiments to improve this situation. For example, it links Medicare payment more directly to achievement of quality

[29] Alain C. Enthoven, *The History and Principles of Managed Competition*, 12 HEALTH AFF. 24 (1993).

[30] Other aspects, including saving money through Medicare cuts, and an employer mandate (albeit much less demanding than the employer mandate in the Clinton Act) were also similar. *See* Jonathan Oberlander, *Learning from Failure in Health Care Reform*, 357 NEW ENG. J. MED. 1677 (2007).

[31] The history of the legislation in its final machinations is fascinating and detailed nicely in a number of sources including Cohn, *How They Did It*. One of the most interesting developments was Senator Ted Kennedy's death, just months before passage of the ACA. Scott Brown, a Republican, won Kennedy's Massachusetts's Senate seat and left the Senate Democrats without a filibuster-proof majority. At that point, the only way forward for health reform was for the House to pass the Senate bill, as written, and then to use a reconciliation budget bill to amend the Senate bill to incorporate some of the provisions from the House bill (a reconciliation bill requires only a simple majority of votes).

[32] DEP'T OF HEALTH & HUMAN SERVS., OFFICE OF THE ASSISTANT SEC'Y FOR PLANNING AND EVALUATION, OVERVIEW OF THE UNINSURED IN THE UNITED STATES: A SUMMARY OF THE 2011 CURRENT POPULATION SURVEY (2011), http://aspe.hhs.gov/health/reports/2011/cpshealthins2011/ib.shtml.

[33] Karen Davis et al., *Mirror, Mirror on the Wall, 2014 Update: How the Performance of the U.S. Health Care System Compares Internationally*, COMMONWEALTH FUND PUB. NO. 1755 (2014).

[34] INST. OF MED. OF THE NAT'L ACADS., BEST CARE AT LOWER COST: THE PATH TO CONTINUOUSLY LEARNING HEALTH CARE IN AMERICA (2012).

outcomes,[35] tests new models for patient care such as accountable care organizations, and establishes a Center for Medicare and Medicaid Innovation (now just called "The Innovation Center") to evaluate these experiments.[36] This part of the ACA is a small step toward what will be the next big challenge: healthcare delivery reform.

Elsewhere, the law contemplates an increased emphasis on public health efforts (Title IV). It makes significant investments in building a stronger healthcare workforce with an emphasis on recruiting providers into primary care and underserved areas (Title V), requires increased disclosure of providers' financial interests (Title VI), improves access to biological drugs (Title VII), and establishes a social insurance program for long-term care that was later repealed (Title VIII).

The ACA is light on controls on healthcare spending (the notion of "Affordable" in its title is a bit of a misnomer). The law does roll out a series of demonstration projects that, if effective and scaled, could reduce spending growth in the future, but cost control is not its primary goal. In fact, had it been, the law would never have passed.

In sum, the ACA touches in large and small ways on many aspects of healthcare in the United States. At the heart of the ACA is financing reform, and healthcare delivery reform is a close second.[37] Thus, the rest of this chapter focuses on these policies at the heart of the reform and the insight they can offer into health law.

II What the ACA Reveals about Health Law

Several key ACA provisions illuminate the most enduring values and themes that have shaped both health law and healthcare delivery. First, the ACA's centerpiece is an elaborate system to regulate private health insurance. This approach shows an enduring allegiance to markets and competition as a core component of healthcare financing. In turn, ACA regulations must find the balance where market competition and larger social goals can coexist—a challenge that has long shaped health law. Second, the Medicaid expansion and the healthcare exchanges illustrate how health law and policy has adhered to norms of federalism and turned to states to implement federal programs. These policies also show the challenges that federalism produces for the field. Finally, healthcare delivery reform efforts shine a light on the slowly eroding web of laws that served to privilege and protect medicine as a learned profession and is becoming obsolete in the new era of health law.

[35] David Frankford, this volume. Since the ACA's passage, the Department of Health and Human Services has expressed an intention to apply these payment reforms broadly in the Medicare program.

[36] Patient Protection and Affordable Care Act, 42 U.S.C. § 1315a (2012); CMS Innovation Center, http://innovation.cms.gov/index.html (last visited Dec. 14, 2015).

[37] For a somewhat different view of the ACA's key goals, *see* William M. Sage, *Putting Insurance Reform in the ACA's Rear-View Mirror*, 51 Hous. L. Rev. 1081 (2014) (describing the Title I and II insurance reforms, Title III delivery reforms, and Title IV public health reforms as coequal and interdependent goals of the ACA).

a. Private Market Reforms and the Stronghold of Market-Based Ideology

The centrality of the private market in U.S. healthcare has spawned a regulatory morass to curb private market tendencies when in conflict with larger social goals. For example, the ACA's primary goal of more universal access to healthcare is diametrically opposed to the result that will occur in an unregulated private health insurance market. Without careful regulation, insurers profit by excluding the most expensive beneficiaries, and find many creative ways to do so.[38]

Nonetheless, the ACA's quest toward universal coverage relies heavily on private health insurance, for reasons both political and pragmatic. Politically no law would have passed without the support of—or at least without active opposition from—the insurance industry. During the Clinton reform efforts, a coalition of health insurers, under the name Health Insurance Association of America (HIAA), financed negative advertising campaigns that hampered reform.[39] In one now iconic advertisement, a couple named Harry and Louise lament that reform would result in few insurance choices and increased prices.[40] During the ACA debates, the mere mention of a public insurance plan option, which someone could choose instead of private insurance, provoked horror stories of socialized healthcare.[41] Designing a law that built on and privileged private insurance markets avoided such controversy. Notably, Harry and Louise returned in a 2009 advertisement, but this time in favor of the reform.[42]

The central role of private insurance was, however, not all politics. Pragmatically, building on the preexisting structure of private insurance reduced disruption. Since most Americans already had good private coverage, this approach meant easier implementation and less cause for opposition from among the already insured. Accordingly, both during the legislative process and after the law's passage, one of President Obama's favorite public speaking points was to assure voters: "If you like your health-care plan, you'll be able to keep your health-care plan, period."[43]

[38] *See* Regina Austin, *The Insurance Classification Controversy*, 131 U. PENN. L. REV. 517 (1983); Tom Baker, *Health Insurance, Risk, and Responsibility after the Patient Protection and Affordable Care Act*, 159 U. PENN. L. REV. 1577, 1608 (2011) (describing the possibility of "risk classification by design" even after the ACA's insurance regulations); Donald W. Light, *The Practice and Ethics of Risk-Rated Health Insurance*, 267 J. AM. MED. ASS'N 2503 (1992).

[39] JACOB S. HACKER, THE ROAD TO NOWHERE: THE GENESIS OF PRESIDENT CLINTON'S PLAN FOR HEALTH SECURITY 145–146 (1997). (The HIAA is now part of the group called America's Health Insurance Plans). How large of a negative impact these ads had is debated. *See* Paul Starr, *What Happened to Health Care Reform?*, 20 AMERICAN PROSPECT 20 (1994).

[40] *Harry and Louise on Clinton's Health Plan* (political advertisement 1994), https://www.youtube.com/watch?v=Dt31nhleeCg.

[41] Jacob S. Hacker, *The Road to Somewhere: Why Health Reform Happened*, 9 PERSPECTIVES ON POLITICS 861, 864 (2010).

[42] The 2009 advertisement was financed by Families USA and PhRMA. Michael Scherer, *Top 10 Health-Care-Reform Fight Ads*, TIME, Aug. 19, 2009, http://content.time.com/time/specials/packages/article/0,28804,1917490_1917489_1917475,00.html.

[43] Glenn Kessler, *Obama's Pledge that "No One Will Take Away Your Health Plan,"* WASH. POST, Oct. 30, 2013, https://www.washingtonpost.com/news/fact-checker/wp/2013/10/30/obamas-pledge-that-no-one-will-take-away-your-health-plan/ (giving examples of President Obama's many iterations on this

Yet, the fact that the ACA relies so heavily on private insurance created a herculean regulatory task. A main concern of health law for the past half-century has been the regulation of private insurance markets, but regulation has been inconsistent, both among private insurance markets and among states.[44] Prior to the ACA, Congress enacted a few important health insurance laws, including HIPAA, as discussed above in Part I.[45] However, most of the regulation of health insurance, especially in the individual market, was done at the state level.[46] The result was a largely unregulated private market.[47] In most states, if someone was buying insurance on her own, insurers could issue, decline, design, or price insurance based on her health (or perceived health) or any other criterion the insurer chose—a practice known as medical underwriting or "risk rating."[48]

The ACA in effect had to reclaim the regulation of private health insurance from the states in order to bend it to serve policy goals. The tools the ACA employs were familiar, most of them part of the 2006 health reform in Massachusetts. Insurers were required to guarantee issue insurance to any applicant.[49] They were not allowed to consider preexisting conditions in determining eligibility or price.[50] In fact, premiums for a policy were allowed to vary based on only four factors: age, geography, family size, and tobacco use status.[51] The medical underwriting that had long been the source of private insurer profits was prohibited. Even if an insurer devised a way to cherry-pick out healthier applicants, the law intended to disgorge any resulting profits through reinsurance and risk-adjustment arrangements.[52] And the

idea). The particular wording above was from a speech to the American Medical Association on June 15, 2009. *Id.* This promise has since caused the administration considerable grief, as time has proven it impossible to keep. Although nothing in the law explicitly requires most people to change their health plan, it rolled out major changes to insurance markets that inevitably were going to—and have—made substantial changes to what plans employer and insurers are now making available.

44 Hoffman, *Oil and Water*, at 18.

45 Health Insurance Portability and Accountability Act of 1996, Pub. L. No. 104–191, 110 Stat. 1936 (1996). Other examples include the Employee Retirement Income Security Act of 1974, which set minimum standards for employee health plans, and the Genetic Information Nondiscrimination Act of 2008, which restricted the use of genetic information in health underwriting. Employee Retirement Income Security Act of 1974, Pub. L. No. 93-406, 88 Stat. 829 (1974); Genetic Information Nondiscrimination Act of 2008, Pub. L. No. 110-233, 122 Stat. 881 (2008).

46 McCarran-Ferguson Act, ch. 20, 59 Stat. 33 (1945) (codified as amended at 15 U.S.C. §§ 1011–1015 (2012)).

47 Only six states required that insurers guarantee issue policies to all applicants, and only one-third of states regulated the variability in premium prices allowed among insured. *Individual Market Guaranteed Issue (Not Applicable to HIPAA Eligible Individuals)*, Kaiser Family Found., http://kff.org/other/state-indicator/individual-market-guaranteed-issue-not-applicable-to-hipaa-eligible-individuals/ (last visited Dec. 14, 2015).

48 *See* Donald W. Light, *The Practice and Ethics of Risk-Rated Health Insurance*, 267 J. Am. Med. Ass'n 2503 (1992).

49 Patient Protection and Affordable Care Act § 1201, 42 U.S.C. § 300gg (2012).

50 *Id.*

51 *Id.*

52 *Id.* at § 1341–1342, 42 U.S.C. § 18061–18062. These provisions of the ACA are not working as smoothly as envisioned in early years of implementation because the contributions from insurers intended to cover these payments have fallen well short of the amount CMS owes insurers in claims. Timothy Jost, *Risk Corridor Claims by Insurers Far Exceed Contributions*, Health Aff. Blog (Oct. 1, 2015), http://healthaffairs.org/blog/2015/10/01/implementing-health-reform-risk-corridor-claims-by-insurers-far-exceed-contributions/.

ACA reshaped what benefits health insurance policies must include. Requirements included preventative care without cost-sharing and ending lifetime and annual limits on benefits for most plans and coverage of a set of essential health benefits for individual-market and small-group plans.[53]

These regulations can exacerbate the problem of adverse selection, or the tendency of healthier people to wait to buy coverage until they need it, since they know they can get good insurance and will not be charged more, once they get sick.[54] Such opting out creates two problems. First, it results in higher premium prices for people who do buy insurance. Insurance pools need to include both healthy and sick people to moderate premium prices, and if the health opt out, the average price per policy is higher. Second, some people who opt out because they think they do not need health insurance bet wrong. They end up uninsured and in need of expensive care. To prevent these problems, the ACA's individual mandate requires that most Americans carry health insurance that offers "minimum essential coverage," or else pay a penalty.[55] Plus, the ACA provides financial support to help lower-income individuals comply with this mandate. Anyone who earns from 100% to 400% of the federal poverty level ($11,700 to $46,800 for an individual in 2015) and does not have another source of insurance, such as through an employer or Medicaid, is eligible for subsidized premiums, and some are also eligible for cost-sharing subsidies.[56]

Nearly two hundred pages of the ACA are devoted to the endeavor of regulating private insurance. And it takes pages here just to summarize the high points. The law creates a complex scheme of interlocking and interdependent policies, each of which is vulnerable to popular and legal attack and each of which is difficult to implement. Viewed in isolation, this approach makes no sense.

Yet, when understood in light of the preexisting system of law and regulation and the values that shaped this system, this approach can be seen as an incremental way to pursue transformative policy goals. This path-dependent approach was probably a necessary condition of successful reform. But it also meant the law had to fill a void left by years of light federal regulation of insurance and inconsistent state regulation for private insurance to operate in more inclusive and less discriminatory ways. This was no small task. The ACA arguably transformed what private health insurance means. Optically, the ACA preserved preexisting private market structures and values. Practically, however, it bent and reshaped them dramatically—a fact that has not gone unnoticed by ACA opponents, as evinced by the legal challenges to the law discussed in Part III, below.

[53] Patient Protection and Affordable Care Act at § 1302, 42 U.S.C. § 18022; id. at § 1001, 42 U.S.C. § 300gg-11 (2012), 42 U.S.C. § 300gg-13 (2012).

[54] Leigh Wachenheim & Hans Leida, Milliman Consulting, The Impact of Guaranteed Issue and Community Rating Reforms on States' Individual Insurance Markets (2012) (describing adverse selection in state reforms prior to the ACA).

[55] Patient Protection and Affordable Care Act § 1501, 26 U.S.C. § 5000A (2012). Some people are exempted from the penalty for reasons including religious objection or affordability, defined as when premiums cost over 8% of household income. *Id.*

[56] *Id.* at § 1401, 26 U.S.C. § 36B (providing for "premium tax credits"); *Id.* at § 1402, 42 U.S.C § 18071 (providing for "cost-sharing reductions"). The employer plan must be "adequate" and "affordable." Adequate is defined as an actuarial value of at least 60% and affordable is when the employee's share of premium cost is under 9.5% of her income.

b. Exchanges, Medicaid, and Federalism's Influence and Ambiguity

Two of the most important policies of the ACA—the health insurance exchanges and the Medicaid expansion—follow a deeply rooted health law tradition of shared governance among national and state regulators. Cooperative federalism predated the modern welfare state; even in the nineteenth and early twentieth century, local governments and organizations retained responsibility to administer aspects of nationally funded programs.[57] During the New Deal's response to the Great Depression, cooperative federalism became institutionalized as a central policy design feature; for example, in the Works Progress Administration, federal funding supported state efforts to address medical emergencies and chronic illness and old age.[58] Cooperative federalism remains a defining feature of modern healthcare law and policy.

The ACA continues in this tradition by relying on state governments to implement the Medicaid expansion and the creation of healthcare exchanges, marketplaces where people can shop for health insurance policies. The states' key role in each of these efforts reflects the practical benefits of building on an administrative foundation already in place, and, equally, the symbolic importance of engaging state regulators in implementation.[59] Yet, by relying on state implementers in meaningful ways, these policies have also tested the boundaries of modern federalism.

As part of the private insurance expansion, the law established a state-based system of exchanges where individuals and small groups can purchase insurance.[60] The ACA gave states the option to elect to create them and, if a state did not do so by the 2014 deadline, provided that the federal government would establish and operate an exchange for the state.[61] This approach makes sense. It entrusts state insurance regulators, who have historically been in charge of health insurance regulation and who have well-established relationships with insurance companies licensed in the state, with the responsibility of building out new insurance infrastructure. The ACA also gave states the leeway to test different models of exchanges, consistent with the classic "states as laboratories" goal of federalism.[62]

Yet, this approach was not the only one possible or even imagined in Congress. The health reform bill that the House passed provided for a single nationally run exchange for all states. There is also logic to this approach. Building an exchange, including the technical backbone, is intensive, and doing it fifty separate times is inefficient. And since the ACA's insurance regulations will preempt most state insurance regulation, there is less need for an exchange to accommodate different state-based regulatory regimes. In the end, the Senate bill became law and

[57] Eileen Boris & Jennifer Klein, Caring for America 22–39 (2012). [58] *Id.*

[59] Michael S. Sparer, Federalism and the Patient Protection and Affordable Care Act of 2010: the Founding Fathers Would Not Be Surprised, 36 J. Health Pol. Pol'y & L. 461 (2011).

[60] Patient Protection and Affordable Care Act § 1311(b), 42 U.S.C. § 18031(b) (2012).

[61] *Id.* at § 1321, 42 U.S.C. § 18041. This structure, giving the state the right of first refusal, grows out of the "anti-commandeering doctrine" from *Printz v. United States*, where the court established that Congress cannot direct action of state executive authority. Printz v. United States, 521 U.S. 898, 935 (1997).

[62] New State Ice Co. v. Liebmann, 285 U.S. 262 (1932); *see* Abbe Gluck, *Federalism from Federal Statutes: Health Reform, Medicaid, and the Old-Fashioned Federalists' Gamble*, 81 Fordham L. Rev. 1749, 1764 (2013).

imbued the states with a key role in the continued oversight of the private health insurance markets. This model was federalist in structure yet created ambiguity and opportunity for legal challenges in the space of overlap between state and federal authority, as discussed in Part III.

The Medicaid expansion even more closely followed a well-paved tradition of cooperative federalism, growing the existing program to include more beneficiaries. Prior to the ACA, poverty was not enough to qualify for Medicaid. It was a program for low-income pregnant women, children, elderly, and disabled individuals, and, depending on the state, parents of dependent children.[63] Childless adults were not eligible. The ACA eliminated this "categorical eligibility" and expanded Medicaid eligibility to anyone earning below 138% of the federal poverty level.[64]

Congress's decision to build on Medicaid adhered to logic and past precedent.[65] The administrative apparatus was well worn, and the benefits and delivery system are tailored to the particular healthcare needs of lower-income patients. Medicaid had been expanded many times before to include new eligible populations so this expansion looked to most knowledgeable observers like another chapter in Medicaid's evolution.[66] And the federal government promised to pick up nearly all of the costs of healthcare spending for the newly eligible population for at least the first decade of the program.

Both the establishment of the exchanges and the Medicaid expansion rely on state administrators to give content to the ACA's broad strokes by interpreting and implementing the law. Both policies are examples of federalism in an age of statutes, a model one scholar has called "intrastatutory federalism."[67] Unlike a concept of federalism based on constitutional protection of states' autonomy, in this new model, states are not independent agents. Rather, they carry out the will of Congress and, in the process, give meaning to federal laws.[68]

The fact that two of the most important policies of the ACA rely on state-level implementation reflects both a history of shared governance in health regulation and also Congress's opinion (at least in the Senate) that this federalist norm was important to preserve. It would have been simpler to replace the preexisting fragmented financing systems with a universal, national solution, a Medicare for all. But instead Congress opted for existing structures and norms over a more eloquent solution.

Ironically, the very fact that Congress took a path-dependent approach and preserved an important role for states in administering the private insurance expansion and Medicaid fueled legal challenges to these policies. Both challenges reached the Supreme Court, despite the questionable merit of the legal claims, and the Supreme Court held in one—the challenge to the Medicaid expansion—that Congress had exceeded its authority, as discussed in Part III, below.[69]

63 For example, the eligibility level for parents of dependent children was less than 50% of the federal poverty level, or below $6,000 in annual household income, in some states and nearly four times that amount in others. *Federal Poverty Level*, HEALTHCARE.GOV, https://www.healthcare.gov/glossary/federal-poverty-level-FPL/; KAISER FAMILY FOUND., WHERE ARE STATES TODAY? MEDICAID AND CHIP ELIGIBILITY LEVELS FOR ADULTS, CHILDREN, AND PREGNANT WOMEN (2015).

64 Patient Protection and Affordable Care Act § 2001, 42 U.S.C. § 1396a(k).

65 Sara Rosenbaum, this volume. 66 *Id.*

67 Abbe Gluck, *Intrastatutory Federalism and Statutory Interpretation: State Implementation of Federal Law in Health Reform and Beyond*, 121 YALE L. J. 534 (2011); Gluck, *Federalism from Federal Statutes*.

68 Gluck, *Intrastatutory Federalism and Statutory Interpretation*, at 1753.

69 *See also* Sara Rosenbaum, this volume.

c. Delivery System Reform and Legal Impediments to Change

Finally, the ACA offers a window into how healthcare regulation can have paralyzing effects on innovation, especially in healthcare delivery. Health law has entrenched an antiquated notion of medicine—that of a doctor as a revered professional and lone wolf. As a result, attempts to make fundamental changes to how healthcare is provided, such as models that promote increased communication and collaboration among doctors and hospitals, bump up against legal barriers erected in the service of preserving a particular, outdated notion of professionalism. These legal barriers have been justified as necessary to protect individual practitioners' autonomy and to preserve the sanctity of medical decisions. In reality, however, many of these laws were sought out by interest groups, including the American Medical Association, seeking to insulate the profession from competition and from corporate and regulatory control.[70]

The ACA experiments with new modes of healthcare delivery, testing many new models rather than implementing any single one. Such experiments include tying payment explicitly to achieving outcomes in Medicare, the creation of a Patient-Centered Outcomes Research Institute to oversee comparative effectiveness research, and investments in new models of primary care, especially in underserved areas.[71] The experiment getting the most attention is an investment in testing and growing accountable care organizations (ACOs). ACOs are a new riff on an old theme.[72] Like health maintenance organizations, the goal is to use payment reform to create incentives for higher quality, lower cost care. ACOs are more dynamic than HMOs in terms of organizational structure—an ACO can have a hospital, insurer, or physician organization as the hub of the organization[73]—but otherwise they are quite similar.

The ACA developed a new ACO initiative called the Medicare Shared Savings Program.[74] To participate, an ACO must serve at least 5,000 Medicare fee-for-service patients for at least three years. There are two models of risk-sharing. In both, if a participating ACO meets quality standards and saves money for the Medicare program, the ACO earns a share of the savings. A few more experienced ACOs agreed to share also in downside risk of increased spending and in return could get a greater share of any savings.[75]

[70] 198 (1982). Some healthcare laws, such as the Stark Law, were genuine attempts by influential politicians, such as Pete Stark, to root out problems caused by profiteering in medicine, and nonetheless can impede innovation. *See* Joan H. Krause, this volume, for more in-depth consideration of these laws.

[71] Richard S. Saver, this volume.

[72] Theodore R. Marmor & Jonathan Oberlander, *From HMOs to ACOs: The Quest for the Holy Grail in U.S. Health Policy*, 27 J. GEN. INTERNAL MED. 1215, 1215 (2012).

[73] The Centers for Medicare & Medicaid Services describes ACOs as "groups of doctors, hospitals, and other healthcare providers, who come together voluntarily to give coordinated high quality care to their Medicare patients." *Accountable Care Organizations*, CMS.GOV (Jan. 6, 2015), http://www.cms.gov/Medicare/Medicare-Fee-for-Service-Payment/ACO/index.html.

[74] Patient Protection and Affordable Care Act § 3022, 42 U.S.C. 1395jjj (2012).

[75] *Pioneer ACO Model*, CMS.GOV (Dec. 7, 2015), http://innovation.cms.gov/initiatives/Pioneer-ACO-Model/. PAUL SPITALNIC, DEP'T. OF HEALTH & HUMAN SERVS., CERTIFICATION OF PIONEER MODEL SAVINGS (Apr. 10, 2015), https://www.cms.gov/Research-Statistics-Data-and-Systems/Research/ActuarialStudies/Downloads/Pioneer-Certification-2015-04-10.pdf.

As providers began to consider establishing ACOs, they encountered significant legal barriers. For over a century, health law imagined providers as autonomous individuals. In fact, some laws explicitly prohibit the type of collaboration and organizational integration that a successful ACO would need to adopt, ostensibly to protect doctors from the presumptive corrupting influence of profit motives.[76] Laws on gainsharing, kickbacks, and self-referral explicitly prohibit health professionals from being paid a percentage of an organization's profits or earning any benefit in exchange for referring patients to a particular provider, especially when the doctor has a financial interest.[77] Yet, the success of ACOs depends on better coordination among ACO doctors, including referring patients to each other. In turn, the doctors benefit financially if the ACO succeeds. This is exactly the type of activity health law historically tried to root out.

As another example, hospitals must meet the terms of Internal Revenue Code § 501(c)(3) to maintain tax-exempt status.[78] Especially when ACOs are collaborations between nonprofit and for-profit entities, the nonprofit partner could risk losing its tax-exempt status. Likewise, state "corporate practice of medicine" laws prohibit the practice of medicine by unlicensed individuals in order to keep medical decisions in the hands of licensed doctors (and, more cynically, to preserve the profession's monopoly).[79] Although these laws are dormant in many states, they have been interpreted to prohibit corporations from employing doctors and could in theory be triggered by ACO structures where management has too much influence over medical operations or decisions, even if physicians are not employed. For example, the Medical Board of California website describes activities that must be performed by a licensed person, including maintaining "[r]esponsibilty for the ultimate overall care of the patient, including treatment options available to the patient" and "[d]etermining how many patients a physician must see in a given period of time or how many hours a physician must work."[80] This language suggests that organizational policies on how to reduce wasteful treatment, patient safety measures initiated by hospital leadership, or even efforts by administrators to schedule working hours to enable coordination might violate the law in California.

Even the structure of medical liability law is inconsistent with coordinated care or centralized oversight.[81] Patient safety has been the responsibility of individual practitioners, not of organizations. When something goes wrong in medical care, a plaintiff must identify who negligently caused a harm to recover damages. Typically, practitioners hold liability insurance to protect against successful claims. The idea in an ACO is that many people, across the organization, are together responsible for any one person's outcomes. It would

[76] Two examples include two fee referral laws known as the Stark Law, 42 U.S.C. § 1395nn (2012), and the anti-kickback law, 42 U.S.C. § 1320a-7b(b)(2012).

[77] *Id. See* Joan H. Krause, this volume.

[78] I.R.C. § 501(c)(3) (2012).

[79] Jill R. Horwitz, this volume. *See* Mark Hall, *Institutional Control of Physician Behavior: Legal Barriers to Health Care Cost Containment*, 137 U. PA L. REV. 431 (1988). *See*, e.g., CAL. BUS. & PROF. CODE § 2052 (West 2011).

[80] *Corporate Practice of Medicine*, MEDICAL BOARD OF CALIFORNIA, http://www.mbc.ca.gov/Licensees/Corporate_Practice.aspx (last accessed Dec. 14, 2015).

[81] *See* Einer Elhauge, *Obamacare and the Theory of the Firm*, *in* THE FUTURE OF HEALTHCARE REFORM IN THE UNITED STATES 202, 203–206 (Anup Malani & Michael H. Schill eds., 2015).

make sense then to manage risk and liability at the institutional level.[82] Yet, the idea of institutional liability so strongly flouts the norm of physician autonomy that past attempts to enact it have been repeatedly quashed.[83]

Because of all of these ways the law has discouraged new models of care, regulators had to issue reams of new rules and guidance, with exceptions, safe harbors, and winks and nods to allow parties to establish ACOs without taking on excessive legal risk.[84] But these regulations apply narrowly to participants in the Medicare Shared Savings Program. This means that providers might have to abide by two sets of rules: a more forgiving one that applies to ACO patients in this program and a less forgiving one for patients outside of the program. Further, the law and regulations do not remove all barriers to coordination. As one example, even in the Shared Savings Program, Medicare still reimburses doctors and hospitals separately—preserving one of the greatest historical barriers to integration. The ACA and its regulations ameliorate but do not remove barriers.

The takeaway is that the ACA provoked genuine engagement with testing models for better care at lower costs and, in doing so, illuminated a morass of health law in the way. Years of legal developments based on an old model, one designed to elevate the individual, autonomous physician on his pedestal, must give way to enable new models. The ACA has shown that one of the greatest challenges for health law over the next decades will be to continue to honor some of the laudable intentions behind existing laws while not impeding innovation in the way healthcare is delivered.

III Challenges to the Law at the Points of Greatest Divergence from the Path

Even though the ACA is path dependent, it is nonetheless transformative. Its most transformative policies demand flexibility—ideological and practical. Not surprisingly, these aspects of the ACA have been met with the greatest ire and, in many cases, legal challenges. In the first five years of implementation of the ACA, three legal challenges have already been decided by the U.S. Supreme Court, each of which can be understood as resistance to transformation.

[82] Individual liability is not inconsistent with hospitals choosing to engage in risk management practices. *See* Joanna Schwartz, *A Dose of Reality for Medical Malpractice Reform*, 88 N.Y.U. L. Rev. 1224 (2013). But it does not create strong incentives for them to do so.

[83] *See* William M. Sage et al., *Enterprise Liability for Medical Malpractice and Health Care Quality Improvement*, 20 Am. J. L. & Med. 1 (1994).

[84] E.g., Medicare Program; Medicare Shared Savings Program: Accountable Care Organizations, 76 Fed. Reg. 67,802 (Nov. 2, 2011) (to be codified at 42 CFR Part 425); Medicare Program; Final Waivers in Connection with the Shared Savings Program, 76 Fed. Reg. 67,992 (Nov. 2, 2011) (to be codified at 42 CFR chs. IV-V); Statement of Antitrust Enforcement Policy Regarding Accountable Care Organizations Participating in the Medicare Shared Savings Program, 76 Fed. Reg. 67,026 (Oct. 28, 2011); Notice Regarding Participation in the MSSP Through an ACO, I.R.S. Not. 2011-20, 2011-16 I.R.B. 652 (Apr. 18, 2011).

a. Private Markets and NFIB v. Sebelius, King v. Burwell, and Burwell v. Hobby Lobby

Most of the high-profile ACA challenges arose in response to the law's changes to the private insurance market. Even though in structure the ACA preserved the primacy of private insurance, its policies required these markets to bend in significant ways.[85] Perhaps most conspicuously, the individual mandate demands near universal participation in insurance markets, a requirement contrary to private market norms.[86] Had Congress instead opted for a tax-funded system of health insurance for every American, universal participation would be unsurprising. But because the law built on and co-opted the private-market structure, the universal participation requirement stood out as anachronistic, as an assault on the basic principles underlying a free market. It thus became the target of resistance to the ACA, motivating and surviving two separate legal challenges, both of them carefully architected by libertarian legal scholars and think tanks.[87]

The first ACA case to reach the Supreme Court, *National Federation of Independent Business v. Sebelius*, was a direct assault on the individual mandate.[88] This case was framed on the surface as a challenge to Congress's authority to enact the mandate. Yet, not far below the surface was a libertarian aversion to a regulation that demanded Americans carry health insurance.

The government defended the mandate as legitimate based on three different sources of Congress's Article I authority: as part of its ability to regulate interstate commerce under the Commerce Clause (the authority that Congress explicitly asserted it was relying on in the text of the ACA[89]), as a "necessary and proper" means to carry out authorized acts, and as a tax "for the . . . general welfare of the United States."[90] Most of the debate and the federal district and appeals court decisions leading up to the Supreme Court focused on the first two rationales, especially the first.

To the surprise of many,[91] Chief Justice Roberts preserved the individual mandate based on the third rationale, Congress's tax power, joined by the four more liberal justices.[92] The Chief Justice made a point to reject the government's other arguments explicitly. He wrote

[85] Allison K. Hoffman, *A Vision of an Emerging Right to Health Care in the United States: Expanding Health Care Equity through Legislative Reform*, *in* THE RIGHT TO HEALTH AT THE PUBLIC/PRIVATE DIVIDE: A GLOBAL COMPARATIVE STUDY (Aeyal Gross and Colleen Flood eds., 2014).

[86] Hoffman, *Oil and Water*, at 17–19.

[87] David G. Savage, *Obamacare Case Began When Conservative Lawyer Saw Possible Flaw in Law*, L.A. TIMES (Mar. 3, 2015, 5:12PM), http://www.latimes.com/business/la-fi-court-case-origins-20150304-story.html; Eric Lichtblau, *Challenge to Health Overhaul Puts Obscure Think Tank in Spotlight*, N.Y. TIMES (Mar. 4, 2015), http://www.nytimes.com/2015/03/05/us/challenge-to-health-law-puts-obscure-think-tank-in-spotlight.html.

[88] 132 S. Ct. 2566 (2012).

[89] Patient Protection and Affordable Care Act § 1501(a), 42 U.S.C. § 18091 (2012).

[90] U.S. CONST., art. I, § 8.

[91] Jack Balkin was one of the earliest experts defending the mandate as an appropriate use of taxing power. Jack Balkin, *Tax Power: The Little Argument That Could*, CNN (June 30, 2012, 10:21AM), http://www.cnn.com/2012/06/28/opinion/balkin-health-care/.

[92] Nat'l Fed'n of Indep. Bus. v. Sebelius, 132 S. Ct. 2566 (2012).

that compelling individuals to *engage* in commerce is not a legitimate regulation of commerce[93] and that the mandate is improper, even if necessary,[94] giving the "proper" of necessary and proper new independent force.[95]

Justice Roberts's opinion can be read as a reprimand to Congress. He acceded that Congress could tax people for not complying with a regulation but made equally clear that Congress overstepped by attempting to require them to act in a way inconsistent with norms of private commerce. The particular reasoning that he adopted is important symbolically because it casts the individual mandate in way more consistent with these norms. Jack Balkin describes that Roberts "accepts the new social contract but redefines it in a way more palatable to conservatives."[96] In practice, however, Roberts's specific reasoning may have little impact on how the mandate works. His opinion preserved the ACA's policy goals, but did not explicitly legitimate a participation mandate as a means to the end. The individual mandate thus survived a first challenge, but not unscathed.

This vulnerability left a window for a second challenge, different in form but similarly motivated, in a case called *King v. Burwell*.[97] This case was one of a series of lawsuits spearheaded by a think tank called the Competitive Enterprise Institute. Technically, this case concerned the question of when premium-support subsidies are available in healthcare exchanges,[98] but it was for all intents and purposes another jab at the individual mandate.

The four plaintiffs challenged the IRS rule that made tax credits available for purchase of health insurance on the federally facilitated exchange. They argued that when the ACA defines these premium subsidies as for an insurance plan purchased in an exchange "established by the state,"[99] it meant *only* by the state. In other words, the ACA did not allow someone to receive a subsidy to buy a policy on the federally facilitated exchange.[100]

Two-thirds of states failed to set up their own state exchanges, including the plaintiffs' home state of Virginia, and were thus relying on the federally facilitated exchange. An estimated 6 million Americans were receiving premium supports for policies bought through this exchange.[101] Without these premiums subsidies, the plaintiffs claimed they would be statutorily exempted from the individual mandate because their unsubsidized insurance premium rates would exceed 8% of their household income.[102] Not only did the Supreme Court agree to hear this case (one that nearly all experts agreed lacked legal merit), it did

[93] *Id.* at 21.

[94] *Id.* at 30.

[95] *Cf.* Samuel L. Bray, *"Necessary AND Proper" and "Cruel AND Unusual": Hendiadys in the Constitution*, 102 VA. L. REV. 687 (2016) (describing and critiquing the interpretation of "proper" as independent from "necessary").

[96] Jack Balkin, *The Court Affirms the Social Contract*, *in* THE HEALTH CARE CASE: THE SUPREME COURT'S DECISION AND ITS IMPLICATIONS 15 (Nathaniel Persily et al. eds., 2013).

[97] King v. Burwell, 576 U.S. __, 135 S. Ct. 2480 (2015).

[98] 26 C.F.R. § 1.36B-2(a)(1) (2015).

[99] 26 U.S.C. §§ 36B(b)–(c). Patient Protection and Affordable Care Act § 1311, 42 U.S.C. § 18031 (2012).

[100] Brief for Petitioners at 8–9, King v. Burwell, 135 S. Ct. 2480 (U.S. 2014) (No. 14-114).

[101] *State-by-State Effects of a Ruling for the Challengers in King v. Burwell*, KAISER FAMILY FOUND., http://kff.org/interactive/king-v-burwell-effects/ (last visited Dec. 15, 2015).

[102] Brief for Petitioners at 1–5, King v. Burwell, 135 S. Ct. 2480 (U.S. 2014) (No. 14-114).

so proactively, when procedurally it could have chosen not to intervene.[103] Although it is impossible to know what motivated the Supreme Court to step in, the fact that the individual mandate was once again implicated undoubtedly contributed.

The Supreme Court's decision was refreshingly straightforward. In an opinion again written by Chief Justice Roberts, the Court jabbed at the law as sloppily drafted but then held that when the words "established by a state" were read in context, it was clear that Congress intended that subsidies be available through both the state-run and federally facilitated exchanges.[104] It is especially remarkable that Justice Roberts's reasoning was rooted in the role of the subsidies in preventing adverse selection—the very same policy goal that he found unpersuasive with respect to the individual mandate in the *NFIB v. Sebelius* opinion. This time around, Justice Roberts deeply engaged with the complexity and interdependency of the ACA policies in regulating the private insurance markets. Rather than just barely preserving the mandate as the Court did in *NFIB v. Sebelius*, this opinion solidified its legitimacy. Surviving two bouts in the Supreme Court, the mandate stands (at least for now) as an enduring element of U.S. healthcare regulation that nods to while also bending private market norms.[105]

The third Supreme Court decision on the ACA's private insurance reforms, called *Burwell v. Hobby Lobby*, dealt with the requirement that all health insurance, including employer-sponsored plans, must include benefits for preventive care and screening with no cost-sharing.[106] The Department of Health and Human Services defined preventive health services to include all Federal Drug Administration approved contraceptive methods, including some that would cause a fertilized egg not to develop.[107] Hobby Lobby and several other closely held, for-profit companies who were subject to this requirement challenged it as a violation of their rights under the Religious Freedom Restoration Act of 1993 (RFRA).[108] This law says the government may not "substantially burden a person's exercise of religion" unless the burden is the "least-restrictive means" to further a "compelling governmental interest."[109]

In the majority opinion, Justice Alito wrote that requiring closely held, for-profit corporations to provide health-insurance benefits that are inconsistent with owners' sincerely held religious beliefs violates the RFRA.[110] To reach this decision, the Court recognized for the first time that for-profit corporations can exercise religion and thus benefit from RFRA's protections, which could have broad-reaching legal impact.[111] With specific regard to health law, the Court effectively preserved the sanctity of deregulation in the space of employer-health benefits.[112] The *Hobby Lobby* decision gave employers a way out from under one of the

[103] Jonathan Cohn, *Obamacare Returns to the Supreme Court*, New Republic (Nov. 7, 2014), https://newrepublic.com/article/120198/supreme-court-grants-cert-obamacare-challenge-king-v-burwell.

[104] King v. Burwell, 135 S. Ct. 2480, 2492, 2496 (2015).

[105] Congress might still repeal it, depending on its composition following the 2016 elections.

[106] Burwell v. Hobby Lobby Stores, Inc., 134 S. Ct. 2751 (2014); 42 U.S.C. §300gg-13(a)(4)(2012).

[107] Group Health Plans and Health Insurance Issuers Relating to Coverage of Preventive Services Under the Patient Protection and Affordable Care Act, 77 Fed. Reg. 8,725–8,726 (Feb. 15, 2012).

[108] 42 U.S.C. § 2000bb et seq.

[109] 42 U.S.C. § 2000bb-1.

[110] Burwell v. Hobby Lobby Stores, Inc., 134 S. Ct. 2751, 2785 (2014).

[111] *See* Elizabeth Sepper, this volume, for a more detailed discussion of this opinion.

[112] This norm is evinced by the Supreme Court's jurisprudence on the preemptive force of the Employee Retirement Income Security Act of 1974 (ERISA). This result of a series of Court decisions has been broad preemption of state law with respect to employer health benefit plans, despite the fact that

few substantive requirements the ACA placed on employer health plans; its reasoning could extend to any other federal coverage requirements on these plans.

b. NFIB v. Sebelius and Expanded Public Coverage

Perhaps the most unexpected Supreme Court decision on the ACA regards the Medicaid expansion. The Court held that Congress exceeded its authority by expanding Medicaid eligibility to anyone earning up to 138% of the federal poverty level.[113] The Medicaid expansion is one of the most path-dependent and tested aspects of the ACA, as described above and in the Sara Rosenbaum chapter in this volume. It continues a tradition of incremental expansion of the program over fifty years, since its inception.[114] Yet, the Court held that the ACA expansion was unconstitutionally coercive, in a 7–2 ruling. The Court's reasoning was influenced by a belief that the expansion, even though federalist in design, was inconsistent with federalist norms.

It is well established that under its Spending Clause power Congress can condition grants of money to the states, so long as state participation is truly voluntary[115] and the conditions of participation are clear in the federal law.[116] The Court conceded that Congress met the latter condition with a clear statement in the original Medicaid statute that Congress has the "right to alter, amend, or repeal any provision" of the statute.[117] That is in effect what the ACA did by requiring expanded eligibility as a condition of state participation in the program.

However, the Court characterized the expansion as too much of a change to be a modification of the existing program. It called it a "shift in kind, not merely degree."[118] Because states that did not expand eligibility would lose their existing federal Medicaid funds, which account for nearly 14% of total state spending,[119] Roberts described the expansion as "a gun to the head" of the states—unconstitutionally coercive.[120] The Court remedied this defect by severing the penalty from the eligibility expansion; if a state did not expand eligibility, it would not lose existing funds.[121] In effect, the Court gave states the option to expand or not.

The Court's reasoning accuses Congress of stepping too far into the states' decision-making space. Ironically, the Court had the opportunity to find this incursion only because Congress relied on a cooperative-federalism program to expand coverage. Congress clearly would have

ERISA imposes very few substantive federal requirements on these plans. The Supreme Court recently affirmed this principle in Gobeille v. Liberty Mutual Ins., 577 U.S. ___ (2016).

[113] Nat'l Fed'n of Indep. Bus. v. Sebelius, 132 S. Ct. 2566 (2012).

[114] Brief of Amici Curiae Health Law & Policy Scholars and Prescription Policy Choices in Support of Respondents on the Constitutional Validity of the Medicaid Expansion at 4–11, Nat'l Fed'n of Indep. Bus. v. Sebelius, 132 S. Ct. 2566 (U.S. 2012).

[115] *See*, e.g., Steward Machine Co. v. Davis, 301 U.S. 548 (1937); South Dakota v. Dole, 483 U.S. 203 (1987).

[116] Pennhurst State Sch. & Hosp. v. Halderman, 451 U.S. 1, 17 (1981).

[117] 42 U.S.C. § 1304 (2012).

[118] Nat'l Fed'n of Indep. Bus. v. Sebelius, 132 S. Ct. at 2506 (2012).

[119] NAT'L ASS'N STATE BUDGET OFFICERS, STATE EXPENDITURE REPORT: EXAMINING FISCAL 2012–2014 STATE SPENDING 45–47 (2014) (Medicaid spending is 24.5% of state spending, 56.6% of which is from federal funds).

[120] Nat'l Fed'n of Indep. Bus. v. Sebelius, 132 S. Ct. at 2604 (2012).

[121] *Id.* at 2607.

had the authority to provide coverage to the expansion population through a nationally run public insurance program. The very attempt to carve out a role for states is also what gave the Supreme Court the opportunity to say that Congress did too much. And the Court did so based on what some experts critique as an outdated and overly narrow conception of federalism as meaning noninterference with state autonomy.[122] By attempting to build on Medicaid and its model of shared governance, the ACA unearthed strong disagreement about what federalism means.

At least in the short term, this holding has had a significant negative impact on low-income Americans. As of January 2016, nineteen states had not adopted the Medicaid expansion.[123] A state's decision not to expand creates a coverage gap for some of the lowest-income residents in these states, people who do not earn enough to be eligible for subsidies on the exchanges (over 100% of the federal poverty level) and are also not eligible for Medicaid under the old rules. The Congressional Budget Office initially predicted that the ACA's Medicaid expansion would result in 17 million additional enrollees by 2021,[124] but subsequently lowered its estimates by 6 million in light of the Supreme Court's decision.[125]

All of these legal challenges have arisen because the ACA tested the boundaries of pre-existing systems and norms. They demonstrate that when legal battles over values such as the sanctity of private markets and federalism are played out in health law, the decisions can have strong doctrinal *and* social impact.

c. Future Legal Challenges

Challenges to the ACA will inevitably continue, but the magnitude of threats to the law's survival should diminish over time as it becomes slowly engrained and its benefits accrue to newly insured. Some examples of ongoing litigation include lawsuits that test the limits of the *Hobby Lobby* decision and whether courts will uphold the Obama administration's work-around, which requires insurers or third-party administrators to provide contraceptive coverage in cases when an employer objects based on religious beliefs. In another lawsuit, *House v. Burwell*, the House of Representatives challenges the Obama administration's authority to delay the enforcement of the employer mandate and to fund cost-sharing subsidies for exchange plans without an annual appropriation by the House.

Congress will also continue to chip away at parts of the law. As one example, Congress threatened to repeal the Independent Payment Advisory Board (IPAB), a board composed of fifteen

[122] Gluck, *Federalism from Federal Statutes*, at 1765. *See also* at 1767–1769 for a discussion about how this opinion leaves Congress without clear direction on the boundaries of their powers to create federalist regulations and might, in turn, create incentives for a greater national concentration of power.

[123] *Status of State Action of the Medicaid Expansion Decision*, Kaiser Family Found. (Jan. 12, 2015), http://kff.org/health-reform/state-indicator/state-activity-around-expanding-medicaid-under-the-affordable-care-act/.

[124] *CBO's Analysis of the Major Health Care Legislation Enacted in March 2010: Before the Subcommittee on Health, House Committee on Energy and Commerce* at 18 (Mar. 30, 2011) (statement of Douglas W. Elmendorf, Director, Congressional Budget Office), https://www.cbo.gov/sites/default/files/03-30-healthcarelegislation.pdf.

[125] Cong. Budget Office, Estimates for the Insurance Coverage Provisions of the Affordable Care Act Updated for the Recent Supreme Court Decision TBL. 1 (July 2012), https://www.cbo.gov/sites/default/files/cbofiles/attachments/43472-07-24-2012-CoverageEstimates.pdf.

members appointed by the president and confirmed by the Senate whose role is to reduce Medicare spending when projected growth exceeds a target.[126] Because of the unusually slow growth in Medicare spending since the ACA's passage, the IPAB has not yet been formed or required to act.[127] If it is eventually constituted and makes recommendations to reduce spending, these recommendations become law unless Congress acts to supersede them.[128] This design, which pushes at the bounds of executive authority, will unquestionably trigger new litigation.

Industry will continue to assail the fees and taxes levied on them by the ACA and lobby Congress to repeal them, especially in light of successes so far. A coalition that goes by the name "The Alliance to Fight the 40: Stop the 40% Tax on Health Benefits" or "Fight the 40" for short, is targeting the so-called Cadillac Tax, an ACA policy that caps the amount of health benefits excludable from taxes. The medical device lobby has likewise resisted its industry tax. These groups' efforts resulted in a two-year delay of the ACA's medical device tax and the Cadillac Tax as part of the 2016 Appropriations Act.[129]

Most of these efforts could cause the ACA aesthetic, not structural, harm, but wholesale repeal is still a possibility. After more than fifty attempts at repeal, in January 2016, Republicans in the Senate attempted to use the budget reconciliation process, which requires a simple majority of votes, for a more substantial repeal of ACA policies, but the law was predictably vetoed by President Obama.[130] It is impossible to know whether Republicans in Congress were merely grandstanding or whether they would pass such legislation if there were a president who might sign it into law, in light of the highly visible harm it would cause millions of newly insured Americans. The fervor of Congress's repeal-and-replace efforts in the future will depend on the results of the 2016 elections.

IV Conclusion

When it crafted the ACA, Congress did not upend the existing institutional and legal structure, but neither did it shy away from serious renovation. The points where the ACA's renovations are most ambitious have provoked litigation. So far, the ACA has held up reasonably well to these challenges, but its fate is not guaranteed.

Nearly every chapter in this volume includes discussion of the ACA and its impact on health law and health policy. Those of us who teach health law must examine and illuminate the ways that the ACA modified the legal regulation of treatment relationships, of insurance and financing, and of the business of healthcare. The ACA catalyzed changes that have already raised many novel and intriguing legal questions, and it will continue to reshape and redefine health law for years to come.

126 Patient Protection and Affordable Care Act, 42 U.S.C. § 1395kkk (2012).

127 Some have questioned the likely effectiveness of this board, which the ACA provides may not ration care, raise revenues, or beneficiary premiums, and, in early years, reduce reimbursements that were already reduced in the ACA. 42 U.S.C. § 1395kkk (c)(2).

128 42 U.S.C. § 1395kkk (e).

129 Louise Radnofsky, *Spending Deal's Adjustments to Health Law Seen as Step to Permanent Change*, Wall Street J. (Dec. 16, 2016).

130 D. J. Wilson, *Pres. Obama's Veto Message on ACA Repeal*, State of Reform (Jan. 13, 2016), http://stateofreform.com/news/federal/aca/2016/01/pres-obamas-veto-message-on-aca-repeal/.

CHAPTER 4

A VIEW FROM A FRIEND AND NEIGHBOR

A Canadian Perspective on U.S. Healthcare and the Affordable Care Act

COLLEEN FLOOD AND BRYAN THOMAS

I INTRODUCTION

HEALTHCARE reform is a topic of perennial debate in Canada and the United States, with pundits in both countries looking to their neighbor for guidance or cautionary lessons. Thus, most Canadians remain strongly committed to a universal public healthcare, and point to the U.S. system as illustrating the perils of greater privatization; a vocal minority has advocated the liberalization of parallel private financing as an escape valve for wait times in the public system.[1] For their part, U.S. progressives point to Canada as evidencing the improved accessibility and efficiency of single-payer systems, while Canadian wait times are fodder for opponents of "socialized" healthcare. Recent reforms under the Patient Protection and Affordable Care Act (ACA)[2] provide an opportune moment to re-evaluate these familiar talking points.

Our discussion begins (Part II) with a brief historical overview, describing how the United States and Canada set out on divergent paths of healthcare reform in the latter half of the twentieth century. We then situate the present day U.S. and Canadian systems in an international context, in terms of cost, access, depth of coverage, and healthcare outcomes. Here we illustrate how common perceptions about the U.S. system's high level of performance contrast with reality. We explain as well that Canada, while outperforming the United States in some metrics, is itself a poor performer on the international stage, facing its own ongoing

[1] Ipsos, *Majority (53%) of Canadians Prefer Mixed-Model Healthcare, with Services Offered by Both the Public and Private Sectors*, IPSOS NEWS & POLLS, June 28, 2012.

[2] Patient Protection and Affordable Care Act, Pub. L. No. 111-148, 124 Stat. 119 (2010), *amended by* Health Care and Education Reconciliation Act of 2010, Pub. L. No. 111 152, 124 Stat. 1029 (2010). *See* Rule 4.2.

challenges related to access, quality, and expenditure. Next (Part III) we offer a more detailed analysis of the legal and regulatory apparatus governing health systems in both countries, contrasting the five principles of the Canada Health Act[3] with their functional counterparts in the ACA. In the final substantive section of this chapter, we draw out some common challenges facing the two countries, both ideological and administrative. Both countries have faced setbacks in achieving and maintaining universality, owing to desire by some to "opt out." And both countries have faced difficulties with cost containment, owing partly to fee-for-service billing and high rates of pay for physicians.

II What Can Be Learned from North of the Border?

To outsiders, mutual lesson-drawing in health system design between Canada and the United States must seem like a case of the blind leading the blind, as both countries spend an outsized percentage of their gross domestic product (GDP) to achieve health outcomes that are middling by international standards. In various studies over the past decade, the U.S. health system has ranked last among developed nations, with Canada ranked second to last.[4] Despite having these poor overall rankings in common, the two countries are distinguishable in two respects: access and cost. For all its shortcomings, Canada's system does achieve universal coverage, and at a significantly lower cost than the United States. Before delving into the statistics, let us briefly trace the meandering paths of reform that have led these two countries to their current health systems.

a. From Common Origins to Divergent Paths

Throughout the 1950s and into the early 1960s, private employer-based health insurance predominated in both Canada and the United States,[5] with public financing targeted primarily at preventative services and the operation of public hospitals. Physicians enjoyed considerable independence, as, for example, quality control of healthcare practices was delegated to self-regulated professional organizations in both countries; efforts to guard this independence, and protect physicians' incomes, would shape the path of reforms in both countries.[6] The two countries diverged in the 1960s, as Canada headed down the path to universal healthcare.

Canadian reforms originated in the prairie province of Saskatchewan, under an "agrarian socialist" government led by the now-iconic Tommy Douglas. The Saskatchewan

[3] R.S.C. 1985, c. C-6 (Can.).

[4] Karen Davis et al., The Commonwealth Fund, Mirror Mirror on the Wall—How the Performance of the US Health Care System Compares Internationally 13 (2014).

[5] Carolyn H. Tuohy, Accidental Logics: The Dynamics of Change in the Health Care Arena in the United States, Britain, and Canada (1999).

[6] *Id.*

Hospitalization Act, 1946 established that hospital and diagnostic services in the province would be fully subsidized by the provincial government and provided free of charge to all residents. Though the single-payer approach was successful and efficiently administered from the outset, it met vehement opposition from physicians in the province, who sensed a threat to their incomes and professional autonomy. A compromise was reached wherein the government would pay the bills and physicians would be left to decide who, how, and when to treat.[7] These features of the Saskatchewan Hospitalization Act have cast a long shadow over the future of healthcare in Canada.[8]

Support for this model spread and, in 1957, the federal government stepped in with legislation offering financial support (50% of the costs) to any provincial government willing to publicly insure hospital and diagnostic services to all residents on "uniform terms and conditions."[9] By 1961, all provinces had taken up the offer and implemented universal hospital programs.[10] Saskatchewan then expanded universal coverage to include physician services outside of hospitals, again drawing opposition from organized medicine, largely due to entrenched interests in private physician-sponsored medical insurance plans.[11] A doctors' strike was eventually resolved with the assurances that doctors would remain independent professionals, billing government on a fee-for-service basis.[12] The federal government, emboldened by the success of Saskatchewan's expanded scheme, rolled out the Medical Care Act, 1966, again paying 50% of the costs to those provinces that included within their public insurance plans physician services outside of hospitals.[13]

The 1970s saw the emergence of accessibility issues, as physicians in some provinces demanded additional payments from patients, on top of fees paid by provincial insurers ("extra-billing").[14] Responding to this problem, the federal government eventually enacted the Canada Health Act (CHA)[15], requiring that provincial insurance plans prohibit these practices as a condition of federal funding. In response, all ten provinces have implemented a variety of laws that effectively prohibit physicians from charging patients above what is paid by the public plan.[16] The prohibition on extra-billing was met by vociferous opposition from organized medicine, which reverberates even today, as physicians bring constitutional challenges to provincial laws that effectively prevent them from either private practice or topping up their public incomes by billing patients more.[17] This is portrayed as opposition to "socialized medicine," though given the overall independence afforded to physicians it is better characterized as opposition to "socialized insurance."[18]

[7] For a discussion of the accommodations reached, see *Id.*

[8] GREGORY P. MARCHILDON, THE EVOLUTION OF MEDICARE IN CANADA (REPORT ON BEHALF OF THE ATTORNEY GENERAL OF BRITISH COLUMBIA) 4 5 (2013).

[9] Hospital Insurance and Diagnostic Services Act, S.C. 1957, c. 28 (Can.).

[10] MARCHILDON, EVOLUTION OF MEDICARE IN CANADA, at 7 8.

[11] *Id.* at 9 13.

[12] *Id.* at 9.

[13] *Id.* at 25 27.

[14] *Id.* at 27 28.

[15] Canada Health Act, R.S.C. 1985, c. C-6 (Can.).

[16] Colleen M. Flood & Tom Archibald, *The Illegality of Private Health Care in Canada*, 164 CANADIAN MED. ASS'N J. 825 830 (2001). *See also* C. David Naylor, *Health Care in Canada: Incrementalism Under Fiscal Duress*, 18 HEALTH AFF. 9, 12 (1999).

[17] Chaoulli v. Quebec, [2005] 1 S.C.R. 791 (Can.).

[18] Robert G. Evans, *Canada*, 25 J. HEALTH POL. POL'Y L. 889 (2000).

U.S. healthcare reform meanwhile tracked a very different trajectory. This is often traced to the divergent approach taken by U.S. reformers: While Canadian reforms were incubated in the provinces, American reformers focused their energies on the federal level. Following failed attempts to gain support for national universal health insurance, reformers adopted an incrementalist strategy. In 1965, this approach bore fruit with the passage of Medicare, a federal plan insuring Americans 65 and older, and Medicaid, a program for low-income Americans jointly funded by both levels of government and managed at the state level. However, the passage of these reforms saw American policy-makers make significant concessions to providers and private insurers and, by extending coverage to the most vulnerable demographics of the population, slowed momentum toward universal health insurance.[19]

There have been various expansions of the Medicare and Medicaid programs over time,[20] but attempts to introduce national health insurance to the United States (under the Carter regime in the 1970s and again by the Clinton government in the 1990s) have failed. It was not until 2010 when the Obama administration passed the Patient Protection and Affordable Care Act (ACA) that there was any significant progress toward universality.[21] Just as the Canada's national system was modeled on the Saskatchewan Medical Care Insurance Act, Massachusetts's 2006 Act Providing Access to Affordable, Quality, Accountable Health Care served as a template for the ACA.[22] The Massachusetts act was a landmark law that provided near-universal healthcare coverage for the citizens of Massachusetts. Following the Massachusetts model, the ACA introduced, inter alia, the expansion of public programs, the creation of health insurance exchanges, subsidies for low- and moderate- income individuals, and an individual mandate.[23] However, unlike Canadian Medicare, the ACA is not a state-sponsored universal health insurance scheme. While the ACA did expand the scope of Medicaid eligibility to include an additional 16 million Americans, its primary modus operandi is to regulate private health insurance and to offer federal subsidies for low-income workers to purchase private insurance. [24] The ACA also introduced the controversial requirement that most individuals secure and maintain affordable health coverage or face a tax penalty.[25] While the ACA brings the U.S. system closer to that of the Canadian system, it achieves this end via a very different system of regulation of private insurance.

[19] TUOHY, ACCIDENTAL LOGICS, at 60.

[20] *See, e.g.*, the Medicare Prescription Drug, Improvement, and Modernization Act of 2003, Pub. L. No. 108 173, 117 Stat. 2066. The act, among other things, expands Medicare to include out-patient prescription drugs.

[21] TUOHY, ACCIDENTAL LOGICS, at 71.

[22] Kevin Sack, *A Lesson on Health Care from Massachusetts*, N.Y. TIMES, Mar. 29, 2009.

[23] SHARON K. LONG, WHAT IS THE EVIDENCE ON HEALTH REFORM IN MASSACHUSETTS AND HOW MIGHT THE LESSONS FROM MASSACHUSETTS APPLY TO NATIONAL HEALTH REFORM?, TIMELY ANALYSIS OF IMMEDIATE HEALTH POLICY ISSUES (2010).

[24] Section 102 of the Patient Protection and Affordable Care Act prohibits insurers from denying coverage to any American, irrespective of health status; restricts the rates that insurers can charger for coverage; requires insurers to cover a minimum set of services; and limits user fees. *See* Katie Keith & Tanya Baytor, *Outlook for ObamaCare: The Patient Protection and Affordable Care Act of 2010 Was a Landmark Achievement, But the Fight for Reform Is Not Over*, 7 CAIRO L. REV. 84, 90 (2012).

[25] *Id.*

b. Reconciling Universality with Division of Powers

We have just seen that Canada's progress toward universality was incubated at the provincial level. Yet the federalist division of powers that allows for this provincial model has in other respects been a hindrance to reform efforts, both in Canada and the United States. In Canada, attempts to introduce universal healthcare in the post-World War II period were complicated by constitutional division of powers, which assign the provinces jurisdiction over the "establishment, maintenance, and management of hospitals" and "matters of a local and private nature"—interpreted by modern courts as general jurisdiction over healthcare. As explained, the federal government has relied on its broad spending powers to induce provincial compliance with the national scheme and has the power (if not the actual fortitude) to withhold funding to provinces that allow extra-billing, and so on.[26] As healthcare costs have risen as a percentage of provincial budgets, and federal contributions have dwindled as an overall percentage of health spending, this has arguably become a less effective, and less exercised, enforcement mechanism.[27]

Standoffs over the division of powers have likewise been an obstacle to universality under U.S. federalism. First, private health insurance is regulated by both the federal and state governments, depending on where a consumer works and lives, leading to fragmented rules for insurers. Political compromises related to the division of powers have complicated the federal government's efforts to achieve uniform standards for private health insurance: Under the ACA, the federal government relies upon states to adopt and enforce standards. Like private health insurance, public programs—such as Medicare and Medicaid—similarly rely on cooperation from both levels of government.[28] In 2012, disagreements over the division of powers gave rise to a U.S. Supreme Court ruling, mostly upholding the constitutionality of the ACA in a 5 4 decision, and finding that the legislation's individual mandate was a valid use of the federal government's taxation power.

c. The Situation Now: Current Performance in International Perspective

Both Canada and the United States have charted meandering paths toward universality, meeting resistance from physicians groups and private insurers, and amid ongoing jostling between levels of government. In what follows, we compare the two systems' current performance, relative to other mature health systems, along a range of variables: cost, accessibility, wait times, and health outcomes. As explained, the two countries are both middling performers, but with Canada clearly outperforming the United States on cost and accessibility.

[26] Tuohy, Accidental Logics, at 90 91.

[27] William Lahey, Canadian Health Law and Policy 1 (Jocelyn Downie, Timothy Caulfield, & Colleen Flood eds., 4th ed. 2011).

[28] Tuohy, Accidental Logics, at 87 88.

i. Cost

The United States infamously spends more on healthcare than any other country on earth: 17.7% of GDP in 2011, nearly twice the Organization for Economic Cooperation and Development (OECD) average of 9.3%.[29] Though single-payer systems are touted for their efficiency, Canada is itself no role model on cost containment, ranking as the OECD's fifth biggest spender, at 11.2% of GDP.[30] The United States also stands apart from other high-income countries insofar as public financing accounts for less than half of health spending (48%). Again, although Canadians pride themselves on their progressive approach to financing, yet, with its 70/30 mix of public to private financing, Canada is well below the less than 80% levels of public financing found in many European countries.[31] Arguably, this outsized component of privately financed care is linked to the unusually high levels of overall spending in the two countries. For example, levels of public financing for pharmaceuticals are exceptionally low in both countries (35% and 32%, respectively, against an OECD average of 54%),[32] and spending in this area inordinately high: The two countries rank first and second in the OECD for their overall spending in this category.[33] Prices for drugs are high in both jurisdictions relative to other countries, but, as evidenced by the phenomenon of Americans crossing into Canada to purchase cheaper brand name drugs, shelf prices are lower in Canada than in the United States. In part this is likely due to Canada's Patented Medicine Prices and Review Board, which is tasked with establishing maximum prices for brand name drugs. The United States has no counterpart agency.

Another feature common to the U.S. and Canadian systems, which may drive high costs, is a heavy reliance on fee-for-service billing. In any health system, patients are seldom well positioned to question the care prescribed by health professionals (the problem known in economic terms as "information asymmetry"); moreover, when a third-party insurer is paying the bill, patients have no financial incentive to contain costs (the economic problem of "moral hazard"). This problem is exacerbated under fee-for-service billing, wherein physicians have an incentive to provide more of their own services—as compared to salary or capitation models, where more services do not mean greater pay. In the Canadian context, some studies have concluded that "physician-induced demand" accounts for between 30% and 40% of total health spending.[34] In recent years, some Canadian provinces have seen a shift toward alternative payment methods such as capitation, salary, and blended payment methods, which some physicians embrace because it provides them greater stability of income and frees them to spend longer with patients where necessary.

There are also real concerns about the efficiency incentives for hospitals within the Canadian system. Hospitals account for about 36% of health expenditures in Canada and are

[29] OECD, Health at a Glance 2013: OECD Indicators 157 (7th ed. 2013) [hereinafter OECD Indicators].

[30] *Id.*

[31] Canadian Institute for Health Information, National Health Expenditure Trends, 1975 to 2013, at 73 (2013).

[32] OECD Indicators, at 165. [33] *Id.* at 161.

[34] G. L. Stoddart et al., Why Not User Charges? The Real Issues—A Discussion Paper 6 (1993).

funded mostly by global budgets (i.e., a fixed sum every year).[35] Some provinces are looking at alternative payment methods here as well, notably activity-based funding, which would reimburse the volume and type of specific services provided and allow hospitals to retain any savings as an incentive for efficiency.

A further concern is to correct the silos that now exist between physicians and hospitals, which compromise overall efficiency and coordination of care. For the most part, physicians working within hospitals serve as independent contractors, again remunerated on a fee-for-service basis. Thus unlike large health maintenance organizations (HMOs) in the United States, such as Kaiser Permanente, that can create both incentives for and a culture within their subsystems, this is a much more difficult agenda in Canada as a whole. Indeed, many look to some of the large HMOs such as Kaiser and Group Health as a potential role model for reform. One proposal, for example, is to enable group-based profit-sharing, whereby the savings from pursuing cost-effective treatment options would be shared between hospitals and physicians.[36]

These commonalities with respect to cost should not be overstated, as Canada's system is comparatively cost efficient, at $4,522 per capita annually in 2011, compared to $8,508 in the United States (both figures $US Purchasing Power Parity). In explaining these lower costs, experts point to, among other things, the greater bargaining power enjoyed by public insurers under single-payer schemes. Whether Canadian governments are making the most of this bargaining power is an open question, on which the evidence is mixed. For example, in 2012, the province of Ontario announced that the public drug plan would flex its monopsony buying power to cut prices on the top ten generic drugs by 20%.[37] However, it appears that containing fee-for-service rates paid to physicians is less politically palatable. The province of Quebec recently agreed to changes in fee-for-service rates amounting to 67% increase in physician remuneration over five years, despite evidence that prior increases in remuneration have delivered little by way of improved access to care.[38] Canadian physicians earn less than their U.S. counterparts, but both are very well remunerated by OECD standards, according to economist Mark Stabile.[39] To be clear, it does not seem that in the U.S. system more care is delivered. For example, the average number of doctor visits per person in the United States is 4.0 compared to 7.9 in Canada. However, the price of services paid for those same visits is much higher in the United States than in Canada.[40]

[35] A. Constant et al., Research Synthesis on Cost Drivers in the Health Sector and Proposed Policy Options 5 (2011), *available at* http://www.cfhi-fcass.ca/SearchResultsNews/11-02-18/029025cd-350f-4f7f-87cf-b207f8514aa6.aspx.

[36] Canadian Foundation for Healthcare Improvement, Accelerating Healthcare Improvement in Canada: A Review of Policy Options to Sustain, Improve and Transform Healthcare (2013), *available at* http://www.cfhi-fcass.ca/sf-docs/default-source/reports/Review-Policy-Options-Milicic-E.pdf?sfvrsn=0.

[37] Marina Strauss & Karen Howlett, *Pharmacies Take Hit as Ontario Cuts Generic Drug Payments Again*, The Globe and Mail, Apr. 23, 2012. This was the third in a series of cutbacks, first limiting generic prices to 50% of brand name counterparts, then 25%, and finally 20%.

[38] Tommy Chouinard, *Médecins: Couillard Veut Protéger les Hausses de Salaire*, La Presse, Mar. 11, 2014.

[39] Mark Stabile, *The Doctor Will See You Now*, The Globe and Mail, May 28, 2012.

[40] The Commonwealth Fund, International Profiles of Health Care Systems, 2014, at 7 (2014).

In addition to bargaining power, cost savings under Canada's single-payer system are also traced to lower administrative and transaction costs. Under a single-payer scheme, public insurers are not burdened with risk selecting and risk rating, or with scrutinizing individual claims. From the standpoint of providers as well, dealing with a single payer greatly simplifies the associated paperwork, resulting in lower administrative costs.[41]

ii. Access to Coverage

The United States also stands out among developed nations in lacking universal first-dollar healthcare coverage. Thus 64% of the population depends on private insurance, and 34% is covered by publicly funded insurance (including Medicare, Medicaid, and military healthcare programs), leaving 42 million Americans (13 14%) uninsured by one recent estimate.[42] Various features of the ACA are meant to address this problem: The extension of Medicaid to individuals with an income below 133% of the Federal Poverty Level, insurance subsidies for low- and middle-income individuals, and the elimination of copayments for recommended preventative services and immunizations. The creation of state health insurance marketplaces and mandated essential health benefits for individual and small group plans has also helped in narrowing this coverage gap.

By contrast, the Canadian healthcare system provides universal first-dollar coverage for a core set of "medically necessary" physician, diagnostic, and hospital services (including inpatient prescription drugs).[43] Relative to other mature health systems around the world, Canadian Medicare is rightly criticized for its limited basket of coverage.[44] Despite the fact that pharmaceuticals constitute over 15% of its healthcare expenditures,[45] Canada's is the only universal health insurance system not to fully include prescription drug coverage (coverage varies from province to province).[46] Similarly, long-term care is largely excluded from Canada's universal plan, despite costs approximating CAD $3.4 billion per year.[47] This patchy coverage reflects the antiquated origins of the Canadian system, established in the 1960s when hospitals and physician services predominated healthcare spending. As a result of these gaps, most Canadians (69%)[48] hold supplementary private insurance for prescription drugs, psychotherapy, physiotherapy, vision, and dental.[49] Though there is a patchwork of provincial schemes covering these gaps in Medicare for seniors and low-income people,

[41] David U. Himmelstein et al., *A Comparison of Hospital Administrative Costs in Eight Nations: US Costs Exceed All Others by Far*, 33 HEALTH AFF. 1586, 1589 (2014).

[42] THE COMMONWEALTH FUND, INTERNATIONAL PROFILES OF HEALTH CARE SYSTEMS, 2014, at 153 (2014).

[43] *Id.* at 21.

[44] VALÉRIE PARIS ET AL., HEALTH SYSTEMS INSTITUTIONAL CHARACTERISTICS—A SURVEY OF 29 OECD COUNTRIES, 50 OECD Working Papers 1, 20 (2010).

[45] Aslam H. Anis, *Pharmaceutical Policies in Canada: Another Example of Federal Provincial Discord*, 162 CMAJ 523, 523 (2000).

[46] Steven G. Morgan & Jamie R. Daw, *Canadian Pharmacare: Looking Back, Looking Forward*, 8 HEALTHCARE POLICY 14, 16 (2012).

[47] Peter C. Coyte, *Home Care in Canada: Passing the Buck*, 33 CAN. J. NURS. RES. 11 (2001).

[48] OECD INDICATORS, at 165.

[49] PARIS, HEALTH SYSTEMS INSTITUTIONAL CHARACTERISTICS, at 20 21.

there are concerns about these systems being strained to the breaking point as Canada's population ages in the coming decades.

iii. Wait Times

Much has been made of the problem of wait times in the Canadian healthcare system—corroborated by 2014 Commonwealth Fund survey data, finding that wait times for specialists, elective surgery, and emergency room treatment are worse in Canada than in any of the other eleven developed nations under study. The surveys found the United States to be comparatively average.[50] Similarly, a 2010 study ranked Canada last among eleven countries in terms of wait times, finding that 33% of Canadian patients reported waiting six or more days for an appointment with a doctor or nurse, 41% reported waiting two months or more to see a specialist, and 25% reported waiting four months or more for elective surgery.[51]

It is not clear, however, that long wait times are endemic to single-payer financing. Certainly, jurisdictions with single-payer finance such as England have largely eliminated wait times. Within Canada, there has been some success in tackling wait times in priority areas of care: For example, a recent study found that all provinces were able to provide radiation therapy to at least nine out of ten patients within a benchmark timeframe of twenty-eight days.[52] The province of Quebec, facing pressure from the courts, established maximum wait times for certain services, whereupon the province will pay for patients to obtain care in private clinics or abroad if necessary.[53] Wait times in the United States are comparable to those in Canada for patients looking to get same- or next-day appointments, as well as those requiring specialized tests (e.g., CT, MRI).[54] The cost of medical treatment also hinders timeliness of care in the United States, where more people chose not to seek recommended medical care or not to fill prescriptions than in any other country.[55] In short, while Canada could do a better job managing wait lists—most provinces having no system for prioritizing patients outside of emergency and urgent-care settings—the American approach reduces wait times in part through gaps in coverage.[56]

iv. Health Outcomes

By many metrics, the United States has some of the worst health outcomes among developed countries, with Canada faring only slightly better. The recent Commonwealth Fund report, mentioned previously, analyzed healthcare in eleven developed countries and found that the

50 Davis, The Commonwealth Fund, at 21.

51 Canadian Institute for Health Information, Health Care in Canada, 2012: A Focus on Wait Times 13 (2012), *available at* https://secure.cihi.ca/free_products/HCIC2012-FullReport-ENweb.pdf; Cathy Schoen et al., *How Health Insurance Design Affects Access to Care and Costs, by Income, in Eleven Countries*, 29 Health Aff. 2323, 2327 (2010).

52 Canadian Institute for Health Information, Wait Times for Priority Procedures in Canada, 2014 (2014), *available at* https://secure.cihi.ca/free_products/2014_WaitTimesAiB_EN.pdf.

53 Tracey A. LaPierre, *Comparing the Canadian and US Systems of Health Care in an Era of Health Care Reform*, 38 J. Health Care Fin. 1, 77 78 (2012).

54 Davis, The Commonwealth Fund, at 21.

55 *Id.* at 20.

56 Robert Evans & Noralou P. Roos, *What Is Right About the Canadian Health Care System?*, 77 Millbank Q. 393 (1999).

United States had the highest rates of infant mortality and mortality amenable to healthcare and the second shortest healthy life expectancy at age 60.[57] Canada ranked an unenviable seventh, ninth, and fourth in these measures, respectively. In 2011, life expectancy at birth in the United States was 78.7, below the OECD average of 80.1. Though Canada's life expectancy was above average at 81.0, it lagged behind those of many other developed countries such as the United Kingdom, Australia, New Zealand, and the Netherlands.[58] In both Canada and the United States, these aggregate numbers mask major disparities in health outcomes for vulnerable populations. Among Canada's aboriginal population, for example, one finds shorter life expectancies, owing to higher rates of chronic disease, obesity, hypertension, alcoholism, drug addiction, and suicide.[59]

III A Comparison of the Canada Health Act and the Affordable Care Act

As mentioned, the cornerstone of the Canadian healthcare system is the Canada Health Act (CHA), the overarching aim of which is "to protect, promote and restore the physical and mental well-being of residents of Canada and to facilitate reasonable access to health services without financial or other barriers."[60] Each of the ten provinces design and administer their own public insurance schemes, but federal funding is (in theory at least) contingent on compliance with the CHA's criteria. As mentioned earlier, the CHA requires that provincial plans prohibit extra-billing (where physicians can charge over and above the public tariff) and user charges (where the plans themselves impose charges on patients for medically necessary hospital and physician care). In addition, the CHA imposes five broad principles on provincial insurance plans: public administration, universality, comprehensiveness, portability, and accessibility.[61] We discuss each of these in turn below, reflecting on the extent to which a counterpart can be found in the ACA.

We preface this section by noting that our analysis focuses on the express principles and values contained in the foundational legislation of Canadian and U.S. healthcare. A further question hinted at earlier—but not explored here due to limitations of space—concerns whether and how these principles and values are adhered to on the ground. For example, in the Canadian context, the federal government is meant to enforce the CHA by withholding a portion of transfer payments for noncompliance.[62] For example, in the spring of 2010, the province of Quebec floated the idea of a CAD $25 user fee for doctor visits, and the federal government expressed no objection despite this being a clear violation of the CHA.[63]

[57] Davis, The Commonwealth Fund, at 26.

[58] OECD Indicators, at 24.

[59] M. King, *Chronic Diseases and Mortality in Canadian Aboriginal Peoples: Learning from the Knowledge*, 31 Chronic Diseases in Canada 2 (2010).

[60] Canada Health Act, R.S.C. 1985, c. C-6 § 3 (Can.).

[61] *Id.* § 7.

[62] It is generally held that individual *citizens* are not empowered to litigate a provincial government's noncompliance with the five principles. *But see* Sujit Choudhry, *The Enforcement of the Canada Health Act*, 41 McGill L. J. 461 (1996).

[63] *Quoted in* Robert Silver, *The Canada Health Act Is Dead*, The Globe and Mail, Apr. 9, 2010.

Leading pundit Andrew Coyne explained, "[w]ith the cost of health care nearing 50 per cent of provincial budgets, no federal government has any intention of withholding federal transfers in retaliation, from Quebec or any other province. The *Canada Health Act* is a dead letter."[64] A caveat to this is that while the CHA may be unenforced by the federal government it is de facto enforced by the Canadian people, who rapidly punish any strain of government at the polls looking to radically change Medicare.

a. Public Administration

To begin, the CHA mandates that provincial health insurance plans be "administered and operated on a non-profit basis by a public authority appointed or designated by the government of the province."[65] Thus government does not have to directly administer the plan (e.g., through ministries of health) as many assume, but the designated entity must maintain at least arm's-length accountability to government.[66] Beyond ensuring political accountability, the public administration criterion avoids costs associated with having multiple insurers involved (e.g., overhead, profit-taking).

Importantly, the CHA's principle of public administration does not encompass the *delivery* of health services. As we have seen, physicians are not government employees under the CHA, nor are they typically employees of hospitals or other clinical institutions.[67] Instead, they operate as private for-profit contractors, paid on fee-for-service basis. Likewise, hospitals are often private not-for-profit institutions and are not subject to top-down government management.[68] This arrangement protects physician autonomy over clinical decision-making, but at the same time can impede government's ability to drive systems-level initiatives to improve patient safety and clinical practice.[69]

In general, multi-payer systems like that of the United States are subject to higher administrative, marketing, and regulatory costs than are single-payer systems. In Canada in 2009, administrative costs accounted for 3.2% of public spending on healthcare, but made up 15.1% of spending financed through private insurance.[70] A recent study found that, for 2010, U.S. spending on health insurance overhead and government health administration totaled $587 per capita, more than three times Canada's expenditure of $147 per capita (both figures Purchasing Power Parity adjusted US$).[71]

Because provincial insurance plans cover all provincial residents, governments can attempt to engage in monopsony fee negotiations with providers and secure lower rates

64 Andrew Coyne, *It's Like Putting a Puzzle Together*, MACLEAN'S MAGAZINE, Apr. 9, 2010.

65 Canada Health Act, R.S.C. 1985, c. C-6 § 8(1)(a) (Can.).

66 LAHEY, CANADIAN HEALTH LAW AND POLICY, at 36.

67 *Id.* at 17.

68 This distinguishes the Canadian system from many others. In the United Kingdom, for example, the National Health Service (NHS) operates hospitals, and many doctors are directly employed by the NHS.

69 LAHEY, CANADIAN HEALTH LAW AND POLICY, at 17.

70 STEVEN G. MORGAN ET AL., RETHINKING PHARMACARE IN CANADA, 384 C.D. Howe Institute Commentary 1, 15 (2013).

71 Himmelstein et al., *Comparison of Hospital Administrative Costs*, at 1590.

than may be possible in multi-payer systems. Other cost-saving mechanisms include the use of global hospital budgets.[72]

The ACA does not impose public administration of health insurance and thus does not deliver the administrative efficiencies and improved bargaining power available under the CHA.[73] Still, the ACA represents progress on this front. Prior to its enactment, a key failing in the U.S. system related to the purchase of insurance by individuals and small groups, where weak bargaining power resulted in inflated prices for coverage. The ACA brings transparency and affordability to this market, by requiring insurance companies to disclose their expenditures and issue rebates to enrollees if the proportion of premium revenues spent on clinical services and quality improvement is below 80% in small group plans (an 85% rule applies to large group plans, reflecting their stronger bargaining position). A Centers for Medicare and Medicaid Services report finds that "[i]n 2012, the 77.8 million consumers . . . covered by this 80/20 rule saved $3.4 billion upfront on their premiums because of the 80/20 rule and other Affordable Care Act programs. Additionally, consumers will save $500 million in rebates, with 8.5 million enrollees due to receive an average rebate of approximately $100 per family."[74]

The ACA's mandate of state-based health insurance exchanges is another important step in streamlining the administration of health insurance, to facilitate the purchase of adequate coverage in individual and small group markets.[75] The exchanges must be administered by either a government agency or a nonprofit organization, and plans on offer must have "adequate provider networks, contract with essential community providers, contract with navigators to conduct outreach and enrollment assistance, [and] be accredited with respect to performance on quality measures."[76] These requirements are in addition to other ACA

[72] Karla Lant, *An American's Perspective on Health Insurance: Canada versus the United States*, Life Insurance Canada News, Jan. 13, 2014, *available at* http://lsminsurance.ca/life-insurance-canada/2014/01/americans-perspective-insurance. The potential for global hospital budgets to control costs should be regarded with caution, however. A report by the Canadian Health Services Research Foundation suggests that "global budgets can be an effective cost-control instrument and can be combined with other funding mechanisms to accomplish various policy goals," but that global budgets provide little incentive to improve access, quality, or efficiency of care. Canadian Health Services Research Foundation, Evidence-Informed Options for Hospital Funding (2010), *available at* http://www.cfhi-fcass.ca/Libraries/Hospital_Funding_docs/PolicyBrief_Hospital_Funding_ENG_Final.sflb.ashx.

[73] Barry R. Furrow, *Cost Control and the Affordable Care Act*, 13 Nev. L. J. 822, 830 (2013). He writes, "A fragmented reimbursement structure means two things. First, administrative costs are high compared to single-payer or highly regulated systems [. . .] Hundreds of private insurers market their wares to thousands of employers and individuals, while a variety of federal and state programs exist in tandem for their eligible insured. Second, the lack of a single strong payer or coordinated payers means that no single powerful agency confronts providers in the private insurance market in their demands for rising incomes and revenues."

[74] Centers for Medicare and Medicaid Services, 80/20 Rule Delivers More Value to Consumers in 2012 (2013), *available at* http://www.cms.gov/CCIIO/Resources/Forms-Reports-and-Other-Resources/Downloads/2012-medical-loss-ratio-report.pdf.

[75] Timothy S. Jost, *Loopholes in the Affordable Care Act and Border Crossing Techniques and How to Address Them*, 5 St. Louis U. J. Health L. & Pol'y 27 (2011).

[76] The Henry J. Kaiser Foundation, Summary of the Affordable Care Act 5 (2013) [hereinafter Summary of the ACA], *available at* https://kaiserfamilyfoundation.files.wordpress.com/2011/04/8061-021.pdf.

regulations that apply to health insurance plans across the board, such as mandated guaranteed issue and renewability, and regulation of premium rate variations.[77] If a state fails to create an insurance exchange on its own, it defaults to one created by the federal government.

b. Universality

To satisfy the universality criterion, the CHA mandates that the health insurance plan of each province "entitle one hundred per cent of the insured persons of the province to the insured health services provided for by the plan on uniform terms and conditions."[78] Residents of a province cannot be excluded from coverage for any reason, including medical history, pre-existing conditions, age, or lifestyle choices.[79] The system is funded out of general tax revenues, and Canadians bear absolutely no out-of-pocket costs for publicly insured care.[80] As mentioned, provinces have on rare occasions mused about imposing copayments, counting on the federal government's lax enforcement of the CHA. For the most part, there is little appetite in Canada for imposing copayments or deductibles as a means to address problems of moral hazard. It is widely thought that user fees would disproportionately deter low-income people from seeking care and also lead to the postponement of treatment, resulting in greater costs in the long run.[81] These concerns are reinforced by Canada's experiences with privatized pharmaceutical coverage, where out-of-pocket costs cause many patients to avoid seeking treatment or skimp on their prescriptions, leading to dangerous and costly complications.[82]

While the CHA formally mandates universality, there has been long-standing concern over the emergence of "two-tiered care" in Canada, whereby patients pay out-of-pocket to receive faster or better treatment outside of the universal public system. Privately financed care is not illegal in Canada, though the provinces employ a variety of regulations to tamp two-tiered care, such as prohibiting private insurance for medically necessary care, prohibiting physicians who participate in Medicare from engaging in dual practice (i.e., moonlighting in the private sector), and prohibiting physicians who opt out of Medicare from charging private patients higher fees for services available under the provincial plan (leaving

[77] Variations in premium rates can be calculated on the basis of just four factors—age, premium rating area, family composition, and tobacco use—and even then the ACA only allows variation to specific maximum ratios. *See id.*

[78] Canada Health Act, R.S.C. 1985, at c. C-6 § 10 (Can).

[79] Certain residents are covered through other programs, e.g., members of the Canadian Forces, members of the Royal Canadian Mounted Police, and federal prison inmates. LAHEY, CANADIAN HEALTH LAW AND POLICY, at 36.

[80] There have been recent court challenges concerning access to care for refugee applicants in Canada. The Canadian Federal Court recently ruled that withdrawal of basic coverage to refugees constituted cruel and unusual punishment under Canada's Charter of Rights and Freedoms. *See* Canadian Doctors for Refugee Care et al. v. Canada (Attorney General) et al. 2014 FC 651.

[81] Canadian Foundation for Healthcare Improvement, *Myth: User Fees Ensure Better Use of Health Services*, 19 J. HEALTH SERV. RES. POLICY 121 (2014).

[82] Gillian L. Booth et al., *Universal Drug Coverage and Socioeconomic Disparities in Major Diabetes Outcomes*, 35 DIABETES CARE 2257 (2012); R. Tamblyn et al., *Adverse Events Associated with Prescription Drug Cost-Sharing Among Poor and Elderly Persons*, 285 JAMA 421 (2001).

physicians little incentive to opt out to private practice).[83] The result is that most physicians in Canada operate solely in the public sphere, billing only provincial governments for medically necessary services.

Regulating the scope of private practice in physician and hospital services has not entirely shut down private medicine in Canada. There are an increasing number of private clinics offering certain surgical and diagnostic services,[84] raising concerns about the integrity of universality in Canadian healthcare. As some of the services offered by private clinics (e.g., MRIs) overlap with, or expedite, publicly insured services, there is concern that wealthier patients are able to secure preferential treatment by circumventing wait times in the public system.[85]

A vocal and growing minority in Canada have advocated increased privatization as a way of addressing wait times, on the theory that pressure on the public system would be relieved if paying patients opt out in favor of private care. There are good reasons to be skeptical of this suggestion,[86] but that has not prevented challenges to laws restricting private medicine. In its 2005 *Chaoulli* decision, the Supreme Court of Canada ruled that, where there are long wait times for publicly financed care, prohibitions on private health insurance for medically necessary care infringe patients' rights to life and security of the person under Quebec's Charter of Human Rights and Freedoms.[87] The decision has since spurred broader litigation under the Canadian Charter of Right and Freedoms, in British Columbia, Alberta, and Ontario, challenging restrictions on user fees, extra-billing, and dual practice, in addition to prohibitions on private insurance. If these challenges succeed and are affirmed at the Supreme Court level, Canadian provinces will need to find alternative means of limiting two-tiered care and preserving universality.[88]

Turning to the ACA, the law aspires to secure near universality in the sense of ensuring that all Americans have access to health insurance irrespective of age, medical history, or preexisting conditions. It attempts to meet this goal through a combination of mandates and subsidies, requiring all U.S. citizens and legal residents to have health coverage on pain of a tax penalty, with premium and cost-sharing credits available to low- and moderate-income individuals and families who purchase insurance on the state exchanges.[89] In terms of increasing coverage for the uninsured, the ACA has been successful—the Congressional

[83] Colleen M. Flood & T. Archibald, *The Illegality of Private Health Care in Canada*, 164 CMAJ 825 (2001).

[84] Provincial health plans do not cover most cosmetic surgery, and while MRIs undertaken in hospitals are covered by Medicare, private clinics are allowed to operate as well.

[85] ROY J. ROMANOW, BUILDING ON VALUES: THE FUTURE OF HEALTH CARE IN CANADA 7 (2002), *available at* http://publications.gc.ca/site/eng/237274/publication.html.

[86] COLLEEN M. FLOOD ET AL., SEEKING THE GRAIL: FINANCING FOR QUALITY, ACCESSIBILITY, AND SUSTAINABILITY IN THE HEALTH CARE SYSTEM, INTRODUCTION TO EXPLORING SOCIAL INSURANCE: CAN A DOSE OF EUROPE CURE CANADIAN HEALTH CARE FINANCE? 1, 13 16 (Colleen M. Flood et al. eds., 2008).

[87] Chaoulli v. Quebec (Attorney General), [2005] 1 S.C.R. 791 (Can.).

[88] One option is for governments to negotiate restrictive contracts that specify the time physicians must devote to public patients, or that limit the time that physicians can practice privately. *See* Colleen M. Flood et al., *Restricting Private-Sector Practice Using Contracts*, 187 CMAJ 583 (2015).

[89] Those with an income between 133% and 400% of the Federal Poverty Level are eligible for premium credits designed to limit their premium contributions to between 2% and 9.5% of their income. SUMMARY OF THE ACA, at 5.

Budget Office (CBO) estimates that about 12 million more people will have health insurance in 2014 than would have had it without the insurance coverage provisions of the ACA, and that 26 million more people will be insured each year from 2017 through 2024 than would have been the case without the ACA.[90]

Despite these advances, significant gaps in coverage remain and will persist into the future. When the ACA was originally signed into law it featured a requirement that states expand Medicaid coverage to all adults under 65 with incomes of up to 133% of the Federal Poverty Level (FPL), but this was blunted by a U.S. Supreme Court ruling making the expansion voluntary for states.[91] As of April 2015, some twenty-two states had opted not to expand their Medicaid programs, and in these states the median income limit for parents to qualify for Medicaid is 44% of the FPL.[92] The ACA targets subsidies at those earning 100 400% of the FPL, meaning that a large coverage gap has opened in states that have not expanded Medicaid, affecting some 4 million people who earn too much to qualify for Medicaid yet too little to qualify for subsidies.[93]

Altogether, the CBO projects that in 2024, 31 million people in the United States will lack health insurance, a figure that breaks down as follows:

> [A]bout 30 percent of those uninsured people are expected to be unauthorized immigrants and thus ineligible either for exchange subsidies or for most Medicaid benefits; about 5 percent will be ineligible for Medicaid because they live in a state that has chosen not to expand coverage; about 20 percent will be eligible for Medicaid but will choose not to enroll; and the remaining 45 percent will not purchase insurance to which they have access through an employer, an exchange, or directly from an insurer.[94]

Thus despite important gains flowing from the ACA, true universality is still some way off for the United States. Whereas documented residents of Canadian provinces contribute to Medicare automatically through their income taxes and qualify for benefits, Americans can, by choice or by circumstance, find themselves lacking coverage.

The ACA also does not share the CHA's stipulation that insurance be *uniform*. This is by design: The ACA aims to preserve consumer choice with respect to insurance plans and foster competition among insurers. Different plans will feature different premiums, deductibles, and copayments; they will cover different drugs and services (subject to certain minimum standards); and insurers will contract with different provider networks.

Some uniformity among plans is achieved through regulation. For plans offered through exchanges, the ACA creates four different benefit tiers—categorized as bronze, silver, gold, and platinum plans—plus a *catastrophic* plan for individuals.[95] The legislation mandates

90 Congressional Budget Office, Updated Estimates of the Effects of the Insurance Coverage Provisions of the Affordable Care Act 3 (2014), *available at* http://www.cbo.gov/sites/default/files/cbofiles/attachments/45231-ACA_Estimates.pdf.

91 National Federation of Independent Business v. Sebelius, 567 U.S. (2012).

92 The Henry J. Kaiser Foundation, The Coverage Gap: Uninsured Poor Adults in States that Do Not Expand Medicaid—An Update (2014), *available at* http://kff.org/health-reform/issue-brief/the-coverage-gap-uninsured-poor-adults-in-states-that-do-not-expand-medicaid-an-update/.

93 *Id.*

94 Congressional Budget Office, Updated Estimates of the Effects of the Insurance Coverage Provisions of the Affordable Care Act 3 (2014), http://www.cbo.gov/sites/default/files/cbofiles/attachments/45231-ACA_Estimates.pdf. at 4

95 Summary of the ACA, at 5.

the percentage of benefit costs that a plan in a given category must pay, imposes limits on patients' annual out-of-pocket costs, and requires plans to cover certain "essential" health benefits, including (among other things) emergency services, hospitalization, prescription drugs, and preventive services.[96] One of the ACA's laudable features is its emphasis on preventive care: All plans offered through exchanges must cover a long list of preventive services without cost-sharing (i.e., no copayments or deductibles).[97] Other provisions require that variations in premium rates be calculated on the basis of just four factors—age, premium rating area,[98] family composition, and tobacco use—and variation is regulated so as not to exceed specific maximum ratios.[99] Finally, a 40% excise tax on so-called "Cadillac" insurance policies is intended to curb overall spending, by discouraging the moral hazard that occurs when individuals are insulated from deductibles, copays, and caps on coverage.

Overall, as concerns universality, the state of health coverage in the United States under the ACA is somewhat inverted by comparison to Canada. Coverage isn't quite as deep as in Canada in the sense that millions in the United States will remain without health insurance; nor is coverage free at point of access—the scheme of multiple private insurers requires people to pay deductibles and user fees. By the same token, regulations imposed on qualifying private insurance plans under the ACA make the coverage offered broader in the sense of the basket of goods and services that are insured. This brings us to the next CHA principle, comprehensiveness.

c. Comprehensiveness

Earlier we saw that Canadian Medicare progressed first by covering hospital services and soon expanded to physician services. This is formally expressed through the CHA's criterion of comprehensiveness, which states that provincial health plans must cover hospital services that are "medically necessary for the purpose of maintaining health, preventing disease or diagnosing or treating an injury, illness or disability" and all physician services that are "medically required services rendered by medical practitioners."[100] But what do "medically necessary" and "medically required" mean? The CHA does not spell this out.[101] A specific enumeration of ensured services would be unwise in enduring framework legislation such as

[96] Patient Protection and Affordable Care Act, § 1302(b)(1).

[97] U.S. Centers for Medicare & Medicaid Services, Preventive Care Benefits [hereinafter Preventive Care Benefits], *available at* https://www.healthcare.gov/what-are-my-preventive-care-benefits.

[98] States must submit a plan to divide regions of the state into rating areas composed of either counties, metropolitan statistical areas, or three-digit zip codes. When insurers calculate premiums, all households within a given rating area will have the same adjustment factor applied. All households in the same rating area and with similar age and smoking characteristics will pay the same amount in premiums for a particular plan. *See* The Center for Consumer Information & Insurance Oversight, Market Rating Reforms: State Specific Geographic Rating Areas (2014), *available at* http://www.cms.gov/cciio/programs-and-initiatives/health-insurance-market-reforms/state-gra.html.

[99] Summary of the ACA, at 5.

[100] Canada Health Act, R.S.C. 1985, at c. C-6 § 2 (Can.).

[101] It is worth noting that similar difficulties confront the Affordable Care Act. *See* B. Jessie Hill, *What Is the Meaning of Health? Constitutional Implications of Defining "Medical Necessity" and "Essential Health Benefits" Under the Affordable Care Act*, 38 Am. J.L. & Med. 445 (2012).

the CHA, the argument goes, given the ever-evolving nature of healthcare. Returning to our earlier discussion, an attempt to spell out a basket of coverage might also have drawn greater political opposition, as an affront to physician's professional autonomy. Whatever the explanation, the result has been that medical necessity has largely come to mean "what physicians and hospitals do."[102] The result is that, for better or worse, physicians (in concert with their patients) make treatment decisions without constraint.

That said, the range of services that doctors can order is not entirely limitless; fee tariff schedules in different provinces specify which services practitioners can bill to Medicare and are determined by a process of negotiation between governments and the relevant provincial medical associations.[103] In addition, provinces sometimes decline to cover new procedures and treatments, and from time to time, specific services are de-listed due to budget concerns. Moreover, as we have seen, there is a host of important health services that have been excluded from the outset, including prescription drugs consumed outside of hospitals, most dental care, services provided by "other" healthcare professionals such as psychologists and physiotherapists, and long-term care. Finally, of course while treatments are available in theory if the health insurance system is insufficiently resourced and/or inadequately managed, there may be delays for service or unavailability of service in particular areas.

In the United States, for individual and small group plans where bargaining power is assumed to be weak, the ACA directs the Secretary of Health and Human Services (HHS) to define a set of "essential health benefits" that health insurance plans must include, subject to the requirement that every plan cover at least the following ten categories of benefits defined in the ACA itself: ambulatory patient services, emergency services, hospitalization, maternity and newborn care, mental health and substance use disorder services, prescription drugs, rehabilitative and rehabilitative services and devices, laboratory services, preventive and wellness services and chronic disease management, and pediatric services (including oral and vision care).[104] Rather than establishing national standards for the scope of these benefits (specifying which particular services are covered under each category), the HHS has directed each state to designate an existing plan as a "benchmark" for *all* plans in the state.[105] While other plans do not have to exactly replicate the benchmark plan, their benefits and limitations on coverage must be "substantially equal" to those of the benchmark plan.[106] Similarly, substitutions of benefits under the ten categories are

[102] LAHEY, CANADIAN HEALTH LAW AND POLICY, at 38; Cathy Charles et al., *Medical Necessity in Canadian Health Policy: Four Meanings and . . . a Funeral?*, 75 MILLBANK Q. 365, 369 371 (1997).

[103] COLLEEN M. FLOOD ET AL., WHAT IS IN AND OUT OF MEDICARE? WHO DECIDES?, IN JUST MEDICARE: WHAT'S IN, WHAT'S OUT, HOW WE DECIDE 17 30 (Colleen M. Flood ed., 2006).

[104] Patient Protection and Affordable Care Act, § 1302(b)(1).

[105] The plans which states can choose to serve as the benchmark plan include the following: one of the three largest small-group plans in the state by enrollment, one of the three largest state employee health plans by enrollment, one of the three largest federal employee health plans by enrollment, or the largest health maintenance organization plan offered in the state's commercial market by enrollment. Amanda Cassidy, *Health Policy Brief: Essential Health Benefits*, HEALTH AFF., May 2, 2013, at 2, *available at* http://healthaffairs.org/healthpolicybriefs/brief_pdfs/healthpolicybrief_91.pdf.

[106] Patient Protection and Affordable Care Act; Standards Related to Essential Health Benefits, Actuarial Value, and Accreditation, 78 Fed. Reg. 12,834 (Feb. 25, 2013); CENTER FOR CONSUMER INFORMATION AND INSURANCE OVERSIGHT, ESSENTIAL HEALTH BENEFITS BULLETIN 12 (2011), *available at* http://www.cms.gov/CCIIO/Resources/Files/Downloads/essential_health_benefits_bulletin.pdf.

permitted, but must be "actuarially equivalent" to the original benefits in the benchmark plan.[107]

Arguably, the ACA has an edge over Canada's approach in terms of regulating to ensure comprehensiveness and better reflects the realities of modern medicine. To be clear, the major advantage of the ACA over the CHA is that it is not the kind of provider (physician services) or place of provision (hospitals) that attracts insurance coverage but the actual nature of the service—thus allowing for delivery by a range of different healthcare providers and in a range of different settings. But while the ACA has this major advantage over the CHA, the adherence to market-like principles means that U.S. insurance plans may differ in terms of cost-sharing and the specific services covered.[108] Cost-sharing in the form of deductibles and copayments may deter people from filling prescriptions or seeking treatment. Even with respect to the mandatory preventive health services that individual and small group plans must cover without copayments or deductibles,[109] insurers will still have "considerable flexibility in determining the frequency, method, treatment, and setting of these preventative treatments if specific guidelines and recommendations are not provided."[110]

d. Portability

The CHA's portability criterion requires provincial insurance plans "must not impose any minimum period of residence in the province, or waiting period, in excess of three months before residents of the province are eligible for or entitled to insured health services."[111] It also requires that provincial plans cover residents while they are traveling in other provinces and the cost of emergency care received out of country (calculated according to fee schedules of the home province). Payment for *elective* services obtained in another province or abroad generally requires prior approval from the province's health authority.[112] By contrast, U.S. Medicare and Medicaid do not provide coverage out of country, and enrollees are encouraged to purchase supplementary coverage when traveling abroad.

Canadian public coverage is also portable in the sense that patients are covered irrespective of which hospital or physician provides care. This contrasts with the American system under the ACA, which preserves health insurance "networks" whereby healthcare providers contract with insurance plans to provide services at lower cost to its members. Depending on the plan, insured patients who receive out-of-network care are penalized with a larger deductible, and in some cases out-of-network services may not be covered at all.[113] That said, the ACA does offer a few advancements in coverage portability. Health plans could

[107] Cassidy, *Health Policy Brief*, at 2. *See also* Patient Protection and Affordable Care Act; Standards Related to Essential Health Benefits, Actuarial Value, and Accreditation; Final Rule 78 Fed. Reg. 12,834 (Feb. 25, 2013).

[108] LaPierre, *Comparing the Canadian and US Systems of Health Care*, at 5.

[109] PREVENTIVE CARE BENEFITS.

[110] LaPierre, *Comparing the Canadian and US Systems of Health Care*, at 5.

[111] Canada Health Act, at c. C-6 s 11 s (11)(a).

[112] Canada Health Act, at c. C-6 s 11 ss (1)(b)(ii), (2).

[113] FAIR HEALTH, IN-NETWORK VS. OUT-OF-NETWORK CARE (2014), *available at* http://fairhealthconsumer.org/reimbursementseries.php?id=15.

previously limit reimbursement for out-of-network emergency room services or require members to get prior approval for emergency care provided outside its network. Under the ACA, out-of-network emergency care is covered to the same extent as in-network emergency care.[114]

Another improvement, under the ACA, relates to the portability of coverage under employer-based plans. Under the previous rules, members of an employer-based group plan (i.e., the vast majority of insured people) who left their jobs could be denied coverage under an individual plan because of preexisting conditions or face higher premium surcharges under a new plan based on their health status.[115] Because the ACA requires guaranteed issue and eliminates restrictions based on health status or preexisting conditions, these obstacles to portability have been eliminated.

e. Accessibility

Finally, the CHA requires that insured services be available in a manner that does not impede reasonable access by insured persons.[116] To differentiate from other CHA criteria, one can imagine, for example, a system of universal, comprehensive coverage where the criterion of reasonable accessibility is breached by a lack of service provision in rural areas, or user fees that block low-income people from receiving care. Clearly, value judgments are involved in deciding what constitutes an unreasonable access barrier. Lahey speculates, for example, that overlong wait times might constitute a violation of the accessibility criteria "whether the cause of the problem was the inadequacy of public funding, sub-optimal allocation of funding or the failure to manage waiting lists and waiting times in a coordinated and coherent fashion."[117] As discussed previously, some worry that the growth of two-tiered care may siphon practitioners from the public system, and this too might constitute a violation of the accessibility criteria.

In the U.S. context, accessibility is difficult to tease out as a freestanding value. To be sure, the ACA improves access to healthcare by getting people insured, by requiring guaranteed issue by insurers, and by eliminating restrictions based on preexisting conditions and health status. Projections are that eventually about 90% of American residents will have some variety of health insurance under the ACA system, with benefits that extend well beyond physician and hospital services.[118] Yet, within this move toward universal coverage, individuals

114 DEPARTMENT OF HEALTH AND HUMAN SERVICES, ER ACCESS & DOCTOR CHOICE (2013), *available at* http://www.hhs.gov/healthcare/rights/drchoice/index.html.

115 This improves upon prior rules under the 1996 Health Insurance Portability and Accountability Act (HIPAA), which eliminated preexisting condition exclusions for workers whose prior coverage was "creditable and continuous." THE HENRY J. KAISER FOUNDATION, HEALTH INSURANCE MARKET REFORMS: PORTABILITY 1 (2013), *available at* http://kaiserfamilyfoundation.files.wordpress.com/2013/03/8421.pdf.

116 Canada Health Act, R.S.C. 1985, at c. C-6 s 11 s 12(1)(a) (Can.).

117 LAHEY, CANADIAN HEALTH LAW AND POLICY, at 43.

118 CONGRESSIONAL BUDGET OFFICE, UPDATED ESTIMATES OF THE EFFECTS OF THE INSURANCE COVERAGE PROVISIONS OF THE AFFORDABLE CARE ACT 3 (2014), http://www.cbo.gov/sites/default/files/cbofiles/attachments/45231-ACA_Estimates.pdf. at 4.

will continue to face barriers in access to the care they are entitled to, given that the scheme relies upon consumer choice and competition among insurers. Many have anticipated, for example, that the influx of newly insured brought about by the ACA will result in longer wait times, depending on the type of insurance held, and some preliminary surveys have confirmed this fear.[119] In the logic of the ACA, insurers who fail to address wait times problems (e.g., by expanding their provider network or improving coordination) are punished by a loss of enrollees; this market mechanism may be particularly strong in the individual market and less so in employer plans. Similarly, the ACA has no aspirations toward eliminating user fees and deductibles—as we have seen, it regulates these and relies upon them to contain rising spending on health.

The ACA nevertheless contains initiatives and investments intended to improve access to care. It includes a long list of improvements to Medicare and Medicaid, initiatives for increasing service capacity and training more doctors and nurses, and incentives for more practitioners to work in underserved areas.[120] It also increases funding by USD $11 billion for community health centers and $1.5 billion for the National Health Services Corps and establishes new support for school-based health centers and nurse-managed health clinics.[121]

IV Common Challenges Facing the United States and Canada

To this point, we have traced the divergent paths of reform taken by the United States and Canada, reviewed the two countries' recent performance in international context, and compared the federal statutory frameworks undergirding the two countries' health systems. Throughout, we have highlighted how both countries face significant challenges, and in this remaining section we want to draw that theme together a little, exploring two shared challenges: one a kind of ideological challenge related to distributive justice in healthcare, the other a pragmatic challenge related to cost containment.

a. Universality vs. Choice

The Canadian and U.S. health systems both aspire to provide universal coverage, pooling the risks and resources of healthy and sick individuals. Both countries apply diverse regulation, prohibitions, and penalties, and in both countries, these coercive measures have come under constitutional scrutiny from those asserting a right to choose how their healthcare is financed. This plea for freedom of choice in healthcare financing is reinforced from various

119 Merritt Hawkins, An AMN Healthcare Company, Physician Appointment Wait Times and Medicaid and Medicare Acceptance Rates (2014), *available at* http://www.merritthawkins.com/uploadedFiles/MerrittHawkings/Surveys/mha2014waitsurvPDF.pdf.

120 Summary of the ACA, at 11 13.

121 *Id.* at 13. The National Health Service Corps offers scholarships and loan repayment assistance to medical students and current healthcare practitioners who agree to work in underserved communities. *See* National Health Service Corps, http://nhsc.hrsa.gov/ (last visited Mar. 15, 2015).

perspectives, including physicians groups, private insurers, free market think tanks, and so on. As a result, when discussion turns to other key challenges facing these systems—wait times in Canada and high levels of overall spending in both countries—the default solution, it seems, is to dismantle laws and regulations designed to safeguard universality and accessibility. Although this is frequently portrayed as allowing the "market" to operate in a less encumbered way, this is not a an accurate description of what is being sought as proponents for reform largely want to keep universal tax-financed coverage for everyone but allow those with means to buy more timely and higher quality care. In other words, they want their public cake with private toppings, enabling the wealthy to collect a bigger share of healthcare and for physicians and other providers to earn more.

In the Canadian context, this pressure is felt in ongoing court challenges to provincial laws restricting two-tiered care, such as prohibitions on parallel private insurance for medically necessary care, prohibitions on dual practice, and so on. In the highly controversial *Chaoulli* case, discussed above, the co-plaintiffs alleged that, given wait times in the public system, Quebec's ban on private insurance breached patients' rights to life and security of the person, under both s. 1 of Quebec's Charter of Human Rights and Freedoms[122] and s. 7 of the Canadian Charter of Rights and Freedoms. In a 4 3 decision, the Supreme Court sided with the claimants and overturned the prohibition of private insurance. The majority relied upon on a crude international comparison of health systems to conclude that the growth of a parallel private tier would not threaten the quality and accessibility of universal public healthcare.[123]

Chaoulli was the first battle in a larger war to create opportunities for more private financing of medically necessary care, and similar litigation is now occurring across Canada. A new generation of constitutional cases are being litigated across Canada, building on the precedent of *Chaoulli*. The most important of these is in British Columbia where a private-for-profit clinic, Cambie Surgical Corporation (Cambie), is contesting the constitutional validity of provisions under British Columbia's Medicare Protection Act[124] that are protective of public Medicare including a law that bans extra-billing and user charges and a law that requires physician to be in the public system or to opt out to practice privately. Cambie is represented by Dr. Brian Day, a past president of the Canadian Medical Association.[125]

Controversies surrounding freedom of choice in healthcare have taken a different form in the United States. Whereas in Canada, claimants like *Chaoulli* have asserted the right to privatized coverage as a safety valve against wait times in the public system, in the United

[122] Charter of Human Rights and Freedoms, R.S.Q., c. C-12, § 1 (Can.) ("Every human being has a right to life, and to personal security, inviolability and freedom.").

[123] *See* Colleen M. Flood, *Chaoulli: Political Undertows and Judicial Riptides*, HEALTH L.J. 211 (2008) for a thorough discussion on the flaws of the Supreme Court of Canada's international comparative exercise.

[124] Medicare Protection Act, R.S.B.C. 1996, c. 286 (Can. B.C.).

[125] Cambie Surgeries Corp. v. British Columbia (Medical Services Commission), 2010 BCCA 396 (Can.). This case is part of an early round of this constitutional battle concerning the ability of the Medical Service Commission to audit Dr. Day's clinic. The audit sampled 468 services provided by two private clinics (Cambie and Specialist Referral Clinic) and found that almost half were illegally billed. *See* MINISTRY OF HEALTH, AUDIT & INVESTIGATIONS BRANCH, SPECIALIST REFERRAL CLINIC (VANCOUVER) INC. AND CAMBIE SURGERIES CORPORATION AUDIT REPORT (2012), *available at* http://www.health.gov.bc.ca/msp/legislation/pdf/srccsc-audit-report-2012.pdf.

States debate focuses on the right to settle for little or no coverage. Plaintiffs in *National Federation of Independent Business v. Sebelius*,[126] alleged, among other things, that the ACA's mandate fell outside of congressional powers as enumerated in the U.S. Constitution. In oral arguments and media reporting, slippery slope arguments figured prominently: If Congress could mandate the purchase of health insurance, what would stand in the way of a mandate to purchase broccoli? Risk pooling through the mandate is of course essential to achieving the ACA's goals of "guaranteed issue" and "community rating," and so the "big picture" issue here, as in *Chaoulli*, is whether a solidaristic scheme will unravel in deference to individual rights. In its historic ruling, the U.S. Supreme Court narrowly allowed the mandate, deeming it a valid exercise of Congress's taxation powers. The ruling also addressed the constitutionality of the ACA's scheme to expand Medicaid, finding that the conditions set for states—expand Medicaid coverage to everyone earning under 133% of the Federal Poverty Level or forfeit federal funding—were unduly coercive. As of early 2015, only twenty-eight states and the District of Columbia had expanded Medicaid coverage.

To our knowledge, these constitutional challenges to universality are largely unique to Canada and the United States. Across Western Europe, individuals are required to participate in universal tax-funded schemes or social health insurance schemes, and various policy and regulatory provisions discourage two-tier care, yet somehow this has not given rise to great controversy or momentous court challenges.[127] Indeed, in some parts of the world, individual rights are asserted to advance rather than undermine universal health systems.[128]

i. Containing Costs, Achieving Value for Money

This philosophical undercurrent of free-market individualism may partly explain why, as explained, Canada and the United States achieve such poor health outcomes relative to their high levels of spending on healthcare. In the discussion above, we have highlighted how vested private interests have shaped various aspects of both countries' health systems, including the financing of care (maintaining a strong role for private insurance) and the delivery of care (allowing physicians to operate independently and be remunerated largely on a fee-for-service basis). Overall, Canada and the United States have much more in common than is frequently portrayed in the polarized debates over public versus private insurance.

It is of course oversimplifying to expect a linear correlation between increased spending on healthcare and improvements in health outcomes.[129] Ample evidence suggests that health outcomes depend to a significant degree upon a range of social determinants, including access to a decent income, housing, employment, and education.[130] Adverse social and

[126] 567 US ___ (2012).

[127] Colleen M. Flood & Amanda Haugan, *Is Canada Odd? A Comparison of European and Canadian Approaches to Choice and Regulation of the Public/Private Divide in Health Care*, 5 HEALTH ECON. POL'Y L. 319 (2010).

[128] THE RIGHT TO HEALTH AT THE PUBLIC/PRIVATE DIVIDE: A GLOBAL COMPARATIVE STUDY (Colleen M. Flood & Aeyal Gross eds., 2014).

[129] R. G. Evans & G. L. Stoddart, *Producing Health, Consuming Health Care*, 31 SOC. SCI. MED. 1347 (1997).

[130] WORLD HEALTH ORGANIZATION, CLOSING THE GAP IN A GENERATION: HEALTH EQUITY THROUGH ACTION ON THE SOCIAL DETERMINANTS OF HEALTH (2008), *available at* http://whqli bdoc.who.int/publicationsh008/9789241563703-eng.pdf.

material living conditions lead to chronic stress, compromising health psychologically and physiologically. Chronic stress and exhaustion can cause people to follow an unhealthy lifestyle (smoking, poor diet, lack of exercise, and excessive use of alcohol). While the United States' record on addressing social inequality is well known,[131] Canada has enjoyed an undeserved reputation as a "health promotion powerhouse."[132] Yet health policy experts have amply demonstrated that Canadian rhetoric differs starkly from reality in this regard, detailing how the rise of neoliberal thought in the 1970s and onward has led to the gradual erosion of public policies that support health, across variables such as income equality, housing accessibility, and early childhood development.[133]

V Conclusion

Oliver Wendell Holmes, in his 1857 work *The Autocrat of the Breakfast Table*, notes, "Nothing is so common-place as to wish to be remarkable." The same is very true in healthcare—each healthcare system sets itself up as being the world's best (or for detractors seeking reform, the worst) when in fact the truth is somewhere in the middle. Setting up the juxtaposition of the Canadian system as the path to salvation or damnation for the United States is a similar sort of black-and-white story. In truth, there are more similarities than difference between these two countries from an international comparative perspective. As friends and neighbors they have much to learn both from their differences and from their similarities, so as be able to truly claim they each have high-performing healthcare systems. Both countries need to rapidly move forward in insisting that governments, private insurers, physicians, and other providers do a substantially better job than they presently do in delivering high-quality healthcare.

[131] Michael G. Marmot & Ruth Bell, *Action on Health Disparities in the United States: Commission on Social Determinants of Health*, 301 JAMA 1171 (2009).

[132] Dennis Raphael, *Health Equity in Canada*, 29 Soc. Alternatives 41 (2010).

[133] *Id.*

CHAPTER 5

HEALTHCARE FEDERALISM

ABIGAIL R. MONCRIEFF AND JOSEPH LAWLESS

THE last few decades of American constitutional law have experienced a federalism revival. For the nearly half-century between the New Deal revolution of 1937 and the "New Federalism" movement of the 1970s and 1980s, the U.S. Supreme Court had abandoned constitutional notions of state sovereignty and limitations on national power. But with the rise of the New Federalism, the Court once again began constraining Congress in favor of state governments, invalidating national regulations across a wide range of American life—from gun control[1] and radioactive waste disposal[2] to election law[3] and gay marriage.[4]

One of the more controversial targets of the Supreme Court's federalism revival has been the Patient Protection and Affordable Care Act (ACA, or "Obamacare"):[5] Congress's landmark reform of American healthcare law. In *National Federation of Independent Businesses v. Sebelius* (*NFIB*),[6] the Court held that the national government may not require individuals to buy health insurance (but may tax those who refuse to do so), and it prohibited Congress from compelling state governments to expand eligibility for their Medicaid programs.[7] Although *NFIB* was considered an overall victory for the ACA, the Court's doctrinal limitations on national regulation impose real barriers to the coherent management of the American healthcare economy. Congress will never be allowed to require individuals to buy health insurance rather than paying the tax, and for now at least, state resistance to Medicaid

[1] *See* U.S. v. Lopez, 514 U.S. 549 (1995) (invalidating the Gun Free School Zones Act as beyond Congress's power to regulate interstate commerce).

[2] *See* New York v. U.S., 505 U.S. 144 (1992) (invalidating core provisions of the Low-Level Radioactive Waste Policy Amendments Act for impermissibly commandeering state governments).

[3] *See* Shelby County v. Holder, 133 S.Ct. 2612 (2013) (invalidating core provisions of the Voting Rights Act for treating different states differently).

[4] *See* U.S. v. Windsor, 570 U.S. 12 (2013) (invalidating the Defense of Marriage Act for impermissibly interfering with the states' prerogative to regulate marriage).

[5] Patient Protection and Affordable Care Act, Pub. L. No. 111-148, 124 Stat. 119 (2010) (codified in scattered sections of the U.S.C.), *amended by* Health Care and Education Reconciliation Act of 2010, Pub. L. No. 111-152, 124 Stat. 1029.

[6] 132 S.Ct. 2566 (2012).

[7] Medicaid is a public insurance program for the "medically needy" or "deserving" poor, which is administered jointly between the national and state governments.

expansion, facilitated by the Court's holding, continues to undermine the goal of universal access to medical care.

Even before the Supreme Court's federalism revival, though, the presumed primacy of the American states in regulating health and medicine had been an important stumbling block for the growth of a rational healthcare system. The American experience of overspending and under-regulating in the medical sector is partly a story of laissez-faire economic roots, but it is also a story of the United States' federalist structure. Cries for the protection of states' rights and condemnation of nationalistic growth—which are sometimes barriers to national intervention throughout the American political economy—have been particularly strong in health policy.

Indeed, in the earlier eras of constitutional federalism, the now-discredited *Lochner* Era Court had given the states unusually broad latitude to regulate health and medicine, even while prohibiting the states from regulating other aspects of economic life and even while prohibiting the national government from regulating health or medicine at all. As a result, the Court unwittingly empowered an emerging lobby for physicians, the American Medical Association (AMA), to secure its preferred regulatory approach in the states but not in the national government. The AMA—itself a federalist organization made up of state medical societies—gained an oversight role in state-based medical licensure statutes, and it also convinced state governments more generally to adopt a professional self-regulatory approach to health law.

Having won its preferred regulatory approach at the state level during the *Lochner* Era, the AMA fought hard throughout the later postindustrial growth of the national administrative machinery to protect states' presumed primacy in regulating health and medicine. This political federalism—largely led by the AMA and other moneyed interests—has caused American healthcare policy to evolve through a series of disjointed historical accidents and contingencies rather than through a thoughtful decision as to the best regulatory approach for this complex industry. Understanding American federalism is therefore central to understanding the unruly mess that is American health law.

This chapter briefly reviews the rise and fall and rise again of constitutional federalism in the United States. It then traces the respective roles of the state and national governments in managing (and mismanaging) the ever-growing healthcare sector of the American economy. In the process, the chapter demonstrates the ongoing role of both political and constitutional federalism in the piecemeal evolution of American health law. In the conclusion, the chapter offers some predictions for the future of healthcare federalism.

I American Federalism

a. Early History

When the American colonies won their independence from the British Empire, their first attempt at unionized nationhood was a loose confederation of thirteen sovereign states under the "Articles of Confederation and Perpetual Union." Under the Articles, the states printed individual currencies and maintained their own militias. The national government was not allowed to tax or spend for the nation's collective welfare or to keep a standing army. Furthermore, the states retained exclusive power to regulate the citizenry, including the exclusive power to protect the general health and welfare of the populations within their borders. The national government's only affirmative powers under the Articles were those of international diplomacy and declarations of war.

Eight years after adoption of the Articles, it became clear that the central government needed more power. The states were failing to cooperate with one another and, most significantly, refusing to pay the nation's debts from its recent Revolutionary War. Without a central taxing power, payment of national debts depended on each state's willingness to contribute its share, and many states were holding out.

To remedy the failure in interstate cooperation, a handful of American statesmen convened the Constitutional Conventions, proposing dramatic overhaul of the national governmental structure. Despite the states' problems as a collection of sovereigns, though, the thirteen colonies-cum-states insisted on retaining individual sovereignties in any revision they made to the Articles.

In 1789, the states addressed the conflicting priorities of enhancing coordination but retaining sovereignty through the current Constitution of the United States, which expanded the national government's powers while nevertheless reserving significant authority for the states. The Constitution enumerated several regulatory powers that would become the business of the national government, including most importantly the power to tax and spend for "the common defense and general welfare" and the power to regulate "commerce . . . among the several states."[8] But the Constitution also specified that the states retained all powers not specifically delegated to the national government.[9]

Unlike the Articles, which were relatively prolix for a document that delegated such limited powers, the Constitution is parsimonious. It does not clearly delineate the intended scope of national power or the intended balance between national and state power; instead, it enumerates several nationalized powers in broad and ambiguous terms and reserves any and all remaining regulatory authority to the states. As early as 1819, the Chief Justice of the U.S. Supreme Court presciently noted that "the question respecting the extent of the power actually granted" to the national government "is perpetually arising, and will probably continue to arise, as long as our system shall exist."[10]

As the country evolved in its first century, the early Supreme Court—having charged itself with interpreting and clarifying the Constitution's ambiguities[11]—settled on a model of "dual federalism" to define the constitutional balance. The Court held not only that the national government may not encroach on realms reserved to the states but also that the states may not encroach on realms delegated to the national government. For instance, it seemed clear that, because the Constitution gave the national government power to regulate commerce *among* the states, Congress should be forbidden from regulating commerce *within* a state, but the Court held that the converse was also true: The states were forbidden from regulating commerce between or among themselves.[12] The relationship between national and state governments was akin to the relationship between two different states' governments; they had no business trotting on each other's regulatory fields.

[8] U.S. CONST. art. I, § 8. [9] U.S. CONST. amend. X.

[10] McCulloch v. Maryland, 17 U.S. 316, 405 (1819).

[11] *See* Marbury v. Madison, 5 U.S. 137 (1803).

[12] *See generally* Gibbons v. Ogden, 22 U.S. 1 (1824) (denying the power of states to regulate interstate commerce concurrently with the national government).

b. The Civil War

The American Civil War was at once a human rights revolution and a federalism crisis. The conflict between the northern and southern states turned not only on the moral and legal status of black slaves but also on the sovereign status of the American states. The southern states argued that, given the Constitution's limited enumeration of national powers, Congress could not trump states' definitions of human property and citizenship. When Abraham Lincoln was elected president, the southern states, seceding in protest, issued the country's most profound challenge to the concept of state sovereignty in American federalism: They asserted their authority to exercise sovereignty outside of the 1789 constitutional arrangement.

The Union's victory in the Civil War resolved both the human rights issues and the federalism questions. With the Reconstruction Amendments to the Constitution, the Union decided that slavery would not be permitted;[13] that all humans born in the United States, regardless of their race, would be citizens rather than slaves;[14] that the states, notwithstanding their sovereignty, lacked power to abridge any "privileges or immunities" of national citizenship, to deprive American citizens of due process, or to deny to American citizens the equal protection of laws;[15] and that the national government had the authority to protect its citizens from discriminatory treatment by state governments.[16]

The Reconstruction Amendments did not, however, answer the question of secession's permissibility, a question that had to wait for judicial resolution. In *Texas v. White*, the Supreme Court answered that question in the negative, holding that the act of secession was unconstitutional and that the secessionist governments were therefore nullities.[17]

Nevertheless, the *Texas* opinion preserved state sovereignty as a residuum of the constitutional federalism. Despite the tragedies that had arisen from their claims of sovereign power, the states after the Civil War insisted upon retaining sovereignty, just as they had following the crises of the Articles of Confederation, and the Supreme Court acceded by retaining its antebellum doctrine of dual federalism. In the *Texas* opinion, the Court famously described both the antebellum and postbellum federal structure as one of an "indestructible Union, composed of indestructible States."[18] In the end, notwithstanding the states' abuses of their sovereignty leading up to and during the Civil War, the postwar states retained exclusive regulatory power over many arenas of American life, including public health and medicine.

c. The Lochner Era

As the American Civil War ended, the world entered an industrial revolution. The rapid growth of industrial technology dramatically changed the organization of socioeconomic life, altering the regulatory landscape in ways that all the world's governments needed to confront. But in the United States, unlike in many civil law countries, the Supreme Court's common-law path dependence made it impossible for constitutional power to evolve in pace with the changing world. The Supreme Court remained bound by legal precedents that it had

[13] U.S. Const. amend. XIII. [14] U.S. Const. amend. XIV, § 1.
[15] U.S. Const. amend. XIV, § 1. [16] U.S. Const. amend. XIV, § 5.
[17] 74 U.S. 700 (1869). [18] *Id.* at 725.

created for an agrarian economy, even though the agrarian economy was rapidly disappearing. From the end of the nineteenth century until the New Deal revolution of the 1930s, the Court retained a set of so-called laissez-faire constitutional doctrines that had functioned reasonably well for the antebellum nation but that started to fail in the industrializing world.

The twin pillars of the laissez-faire constitutional order were a "freedom of contract," which invalidated most legislative attempts at economic regulation by state and national governments alike, and the "dual federalism" that had reigned since the formation of the Union. But a problem gradually arose with dual federalism in an industrializing world: The crucial doctrinal line between intrastate and interstate commerce became much more difficult to draw as emerging railroads facilitated an enormous increase in interstate transportation of goods.

The postindustrial order needed to create some new distinctions to delineate the scope of national power. The Supreme Court, in an attempt to retain its basic laissez-faire posture despite industrialization, limited national authority to regulation of goods that were, at the time of their regulation, in a "stream" or "current" of commerce. The national government could touch commodities while they traveled from one state to another or while they merely paused in one state to prepare for further shipment,[19] but once a commodity reached a "terminus" of interstate commerce, that commodity became the exclusive jurisdiction of the terminus state. The "stream of commerce" doctrine became a central feature of the so-called *Lochner* Era: the period of Supreme Court jurisprudence from the end of the Civil War through the New Deal.

The other pillar of the *Lochner* Era Court—the freedom of contract—had a significant impact on healthcare federalism. Under the freedom of contract, the Court invalidated economic regulation unless it governed a business "affected with a public interest."[20] The Court also drew fine-grained distinctions between economic and noneconomic regulations, allowing noneconomic regulation even for businesses that were *not* "affected with a public interest." For example, the Court held that maximum hour laws were sometimes permissible as regulations of public health—because maximum hour statutes were noneconomic regulations of the human body—while minimum wage laws were generally unconstitutional—because wage controls were economic price-fixing statutes. Even though wages and hours are flip sides of the same coin in a labor contract, the Court held that regulatory power extended only to hours.

Under this series of cases, the *Lochner* Court upheld many state-created public health and safety regulations either as regulations of "businesses affected with a public interest" or as "noneconomic" regulations. Indeed, the *Lochner* Court allowed state regulation of both the practice of medicine and the business of insurance—both businesses that, according to the Court, were "affected with a public interest" such that even their purely economic aspects could be regulated. The *Lochner* Court thus rejected freedom of contract challenges to a medical licensure statute,[21] to a mandatory vaccination regime,[22] and to a rate-fixing statute for fire insurance.[23]

[19] *See generally* Swift & Co. v. U.S., 196 U.S. 375 (1905).

[20] *See generally* Barry Cushman, *A Stream of Legal Consciousness: The Current of Commerce Doctrine from* Swift *to* Jones & Laughlin, 61 FORDHAM L. REV. 105 (1992).

[21] Dent v. West Virginia, 129 U.S. 114 (1889).

[22] Jacobson v. Massachusetts, 197 U.S. 11 (1905).

[23] German Alliance Ins. Co. v. Lewis, 233 U.S. 389 (1914).

According to *Lochner* Era thinking, however, only the state governments, not the national government, had constitutional power to regulate public health, medicine, or insurance.[24] Because health, medicine, and insurance were highly localized businesses in the early twentieth century, they rarely if ever entered the "current of commerce" and therefore rarely if ever entered the national government's regulatory jurisdiction. And, under dual federalism, what belonged to the states did not belong to the nation.

d. The New Deal Revolution

With the ever-increasing interconnectedness of business and industry in the first part of the twentieth century, many of the *Lochner* Era's precedents—including doctrinal distinctions between "public" and "private" businesses, between "public health" regulations and "price-fixing" statutes, and between goods in the "current of commerce" and those at the "terminuses of commerce"—became increasingly irrational. Indeed, all of the formalistic doctrinal distinctions of the laissez-faire constitutional order had been subject to a prolonged Progressive attack starting before the turn of the century, including several attacks from within as Progressive Justice Oliver Wendell Holmes repeatedly criticized his colleagues' analyses. When the industrial economy collapsed in the Great Depression, the Progressive critique started to look not only right but prophetic. Long before the Great Depression, the intellectual tide had turned against the legal formalism of the *Lochner* Era,[25] and the Great Depression finally brought business and labor interests in line with intellectual thinking. The need for regulatory change became so desperate that *Lochner* Era doctrines simply had to make way.

By the time Franklin D. Roosevelt (FDR) was elected president, having promised to give Americans a "new deal" of social and economic rights, the laissez-faire constitutional order had lost its hold. Immediately upon assuming office, FDR and the New Deal Congress began challenging the Court's limitations on national power. In the first hundred days of FDR's presidency, Congress passed sweeping regulatory reforms in almost every sector of the economy. The national administrative state exploded. And the New Deal agenda openly flouted many *Lochner* Era doctrines.

Unsurprisingly, the path-dependent and slow-moving Court was not immediately ready to give up its long-standing constitutional rules. Throughout FDR's first term, the Court resisted the political branches' regulatory expansions, invalidating several core New Deal programs. Despite the overall picture of Supreme Court resistance to political branch innovations, however, several of the Court's opinions from FDR's first term foreshadowed revolutionary change in constitutional doctrine. In the 1934 decision of *Nebbia v. New York*, for instance, the Court exploded the category of "businesses affected with a public interest"—and thereby rendered irrelevant the distinction between public health regulations and price-fixing statutes—by upholding a regulation of milk

[24] The one exception was that national power extended to quarantine and insurance regulations for workers in interstate commerce, like merchant marines and longshoremen.

[25] *See generally* Morton Horwitz, The Transformation of American Law, 1870–1960: The Crisis of Legal Orthodoxy (1992).

prices.[26] Similarly, in *United States v. Butler*, the Court held that the national government's spending power is a separately enumerated and independent power to promote the general welfare, not limited to spending in pursuit of the Constitution's other enumerated national powers.[27]

But it was not until after FDR's landslide re-election in 1936 that the Court fully jettisoned both of the formalistic doctrines that had been blocking Progressive and New Deal legislation throughout the *Lochner* Era: both the freedom of contract and the concept of dual federalism. The change occurred in a series of 1937 opinions, three of which became famously representative of the "New Deal revolution." In *West Coast Hotel v. Parish*,[28] the Court abandoned its strict scrutiny of regulation under the freedom of contract, holding that economic regulation would be permissible as long as it was rational; in *NLRB v. Jones & Laughlin Steel*,[29] the Court abandoned its distinction between "stream of commerce" and "terminus of commerce" regulations, holding that the national government could regulate anything that had a substantial effect on interstate commerce; and in *Steward Machine Co. v. Davis*,[30] the Court explicitly abandoned the model of dual federalism in favor of a model of "cooperative federalism." After *Steward Machine*, no regulatory question would belong exclusively to the state or national government; the two levels of American government would share jurisdiction over all regulatory domains, with the Constitution's Supremacy Clause clarifying that national regulation would triumph in case of otherwise irreconcilable conflict.

From 1937 until the rise of the "New Federalism" in the 1970s and 1980s, the national and state governments alike enjoyed virtually unconstrained power to regulate the American economy, and they held concurrent power over all regulatory questions. Leveraging the possibility of concurrent regulatory power and attempting to harness the regulatory machineries of the states, Congress frequently chose to regulate concurrently either by exercising overlapping regulatory jurisdiction or by creating so-called "cooperative federalism" programs. In "cooperative federalism" (like Medicaid), the national government sets legal ground-rules and provides funding to the states, but the state governments use their own regulatory machineries to manage the day-to-day implementation of the program. Under such arrangements, *Steward Machine* held, Congress may not simply force the states to participate, but it may offer financial inducements to *encourage* participation as long as the financial inducements do not pass "the point at which pressure turns into compulsion."[31]

After the New Deal revolution, the Supreme Court essentially gave up its role as an enforcer of constitutional limitations on national power. Although the official holdings of the 1937 cases did not eliminate all constitutional boundaries, the New Deal Court created a long-lasting presumption that judges should generally defer to Congress's assessments of what does and does not fall within the national government's constitutional authority.

e. The New Federalism

From 1937 to 1969, the American appetite for national regulation seemed insatiable. Congress entered fields previously thought unsuitable for national attention, including civil

[26] 291 U.S. 502 (1934). [27] 297 U.S. 1 (1936). [28] 300 U.S. 379 (1937).
[29] 301 U.S. 1 (1937). [30] 301 U.S. 548 (1937). [31] 301 U.S. at 590.

rights reform, social welfare support, and—with the passage of the Medicare and Medicaid Acts in 1965—health and medicine. By 1969, however, newly elected President Richard Nixon decided that enough was enough. Although he supported national legislation to promote universal private health insurance (similar in many respects to Obamacare[32]), Nixon also announced a plan for a "new federalism," by which he would devolve national programs back to state control and would provide "revenue sharing" with state governments through unrestricted block grants. Rather than giving the states funding within "cooperative federalism" programs that restricted the states' use of the funds, Nixon argued, the national government should give the states unrestricted funding to manage their own economies however they saw fit.

In the three years between the call for a new federalism in 1969 and the start of the Watergate scandal in 1972, President Nixon made some headway in giving power back to the states. Watergate, however, distracted the president's and the country's attention from Nixon's domestic policy agenda, and the new federalism lost traction. Presidents Ford and Carter were uninterested in the devolution project, so it was not until Ronald Reagan was elected eight years later that new federalism regained traction. Upon his election in 1980, President Reagan promised to pick up where Nixon had left off.

Ultimately, Reagan's most ambitious attempts to devolve power to the states failed;[33] Congress was not sufficiently dedicated to the federalism agenda to pass the necessary legislation. But Reagan's appointees to the Supreme Court—including a Nixon appointee whom Reagan elevated to Chief Justice, William Rehnquist—took charge of new federalism and began to re-establish constitutional limitations on national power that had lain dormant since the New Deal revolution.

In a series of cases from 1991 to today, the Supreme Court has revived constitutional federalism. Three doctrines are of particular importance. First, the Court held in a pair of cases in the 1990s that, although Congress may invite the states to administer national programs and may (as *Steward Machine* had held) use financial inducements to persuade them to do so, Congress may not simply order states to participate in cooperative federalism arrangements.[34] Congress may not require states to use their own regulatory machineries to administer national policies. This is the "anti-commandeering" doctrine. Second, cabining the holding from *Jones & Laughlin*, the Rehnquist Court held in a pair of cases that Congress's power to regulate interstate commerce—and to regulate activities that substantially affect interstate commerce—does not extend to intrastate, noneconomic activity, even if Congress believes that the regulated activity does indeed "substantially affect" the interstate economy.[35] With those holdings, the Court revived the Commerce Clause as a meaningful limitation on national regulatory power. Finally, in 2012, the Roberts Court held for the first time that a financial incentive to induce state participation in a national scheme had, as *Steward*

[32] *See* Farah Stockman, *Recalling the Nixon-Kennedy Health Plan*, BOSTON GLOBE, June 23, 2012.

[33] *See* Robert Pear, *Reagan Modifies "New Federalism" Plan*, N.Y. TIMES, January 26, 1983.

[34] New York v. United States, 505 U.S. 144 (1992); Printz v. United States, 521 U.S. 898 (1997).

[35] United States v. Lopez, 514 U.S. 549 (1995); United States v. Morrison, 529 U.S. 598 (2000); *see also* Nat'l Federation of Independent Businesses v. Sebelius, 132 S.Ct. 2566 (2012) (holding that the individual mandate could not be justified under the Commerce Clause because it regulated economic "inactivity" rather than economic "activity").

Machine put it, "passed the point at which pressure turns into compulsion." The Court invalidated Obamacare's Medicaid expansion as unconstitutionally "coercive."[36]

II Healthcare Federalism

a. Progressive-Era Regulation

Throughout the *Lochner* Era, health, medicine, and insurance had received unusual treatment from the Supreme Court. Even while the Supreme Court blocked most economic regulation, the *Lochner* Court carved exceptions to the freedom of contract for medicine and insurance, holding that both were "businesses affected with a public interest." The Court thus allowed unusually broad state regulation of healthcare and insurance. During that era, however, medical and insurance contracts were regulable *only* by the state governments because such contracts never entered the "stream of commerce."

As a result of these *Lochner* Era doctrines, legislative intervention in medicine arose early in the Progressive erosion of individualist and laissez-faire thinking that had characterized the earlier Jacksonian Era.[37] The vast majority of the Progressive regulation of medical practice, however, was state-based rather than national. Congress's only foray into healthcare during the Progressive Era was the Pure Food and Drug Act of 1906—a precursor to the current regulatory regime for food and pharmaceuticals, overseen by the Food and Drug Administration (FDA)—which could claim constitutionality by limiting its reach to drugs as they actually traveled between or among states (in other words, while they were in the stream of commerce).[38] Other than that, thanks largely to the Court's slowness in catching up to Progressive thinking, national regulation of medical practice remained constitutionally impermissible long after state regulation became possible.

Starting as early as the 1850s and gathering steam in the 1870s and 1880s, states started to take advantage of their authority to regulate healthcare. They re-established medical licensure statutes that they had repealed during the Jacksonian Era, and they created public health departments and insurance commissions.[39] During the same era, despite some early lobbying efforts by labor unions and support from Progressive presidential candidate (and former Republican president) Theodore Roosevelt, the national government made no attempt to regulate.[40]

[36] *NFIB*, 132 S.Ct. 2566.

[37] Laissez-faire philosophy had moved government out of medical contracts in the early nineteenth century, eroding pre-Jacksonian licensure and pricing regulations in the states. Thanks to the Supreme Court's doctrinal distinctions, however, the erosion of the Jacksonian Era's laissez-faire thinking occurred earlier for medicine than it did for other regulatory fields. *See* Paul Starr, The Social Transformation of American Medicine 60–64 (1982).

[38] *See* Pure Food and Drug Act, 34 Stat. 768 (1906).

[39] *See* David A. Johnson & Humayun J. Chaudry, Medical Licensing and Discipline in the United States: A History of the Federation of State Medical Boards 23–25 (2012); Starr, *supra* note 37, at 102–112.

[40] *See* Paul Starr, Remedy and Reaction: The Peculiar American Struggle over Health Care Reform 29–34 (rev. ed. 2013).

The *Lochner* Era thus gave rise to a stark division of labor between state and national governments in the regulation of American healthcare. States had unusually broad authority to regulate while the national government entirely lacked regulatory power. One consequence of this stark division was that a lobby emerged in healthcare, and it won legislative and regulatory victories in the states that could, quite unusually for the time, survive constitutional scrutiny. The American Medical Association (AMA), founded in 1847, became responsible not only for the passage but also for the enforcement of early state regulations, especially including medical licensing statutes and accreditation standards for medical schools.[41] Although the AMA's power and efficacy built gradually in its first half-century, by the early 1900s, the organization had effectively captured state regulatory machineries.[42] Thanks to the Supreme Court's unusual allowance of economic regulation in the medical field, the AMA won significantly more control over the shape of state regulation than its lobbying counterparts of the era, such as labor unions and other trade associations.

b. New Deal Failure

Throughout FDR's three terms as president, the national administrative state exploded, and constitutional barriers to national regulation all but disappeared. Even at this rare sociopolitical moment of nationalistic expansion, however, the AMA levied strong opposition to nationalization of healthcare law, and its opposition proved an insurmountable barrier to the rise of a holistic, national regulatory system for health and medicine—even as other areas like labor law and retirement insurance shifted to the new centralized regulatory system.

By the time the *Lochner* Era ended in 1937, the AMA had not only developed close lobbying relationships with state regulators but had actually entrenched itself in the states' regulatory machineries. State licensing boards—whose members were originally appointed directly by the AMA—retained close relationships with the state medical societies that made up the AMA's national organization.[43] Indeed, in 1901, the AMA had reconstituted itself as a federalist organization in order to bolster and formalize its relationships with state medical societies and licensure boards. Starting in 1901, delegates to AMA national conventions would be apportioned among state medical societies, and dues-paying members of state societies would automatically become AMA members as well.[44] The medical societies that were so powerful in state government were thus subunits of the AMA, giving the national lobby an unusually strong hand in state-level regulation. Furthermore, the states' overall regulatory approach, enacted through AMA leadership, left the day-to-day practice of medicine almost entirely to professional self-regulation, with AMA oversight of licensing and accreditation and only modest public discipline from medical malpractice lawsuits. The AMA and its members—private physicians—thus held enormous power over the practice of medicine throughout the United States, and it did so through state-based law and laissez-faire philosophy.

[41] Johnson & Chaudry, *supra* note 39, at 24.

[42] Starr, *supra* note 37, at 102–112.

[43] Johnson & Chaudry, *supra* note 39, at 24.

[44] Starr, *supra* note 37, at 109–110.

With the Great Depression and the New Deal—and with European countries almost all enacting some form of government funding for medical care—came a rising call for compulsory health insurance. Halfway through his second term, FDR started to explore the possibility of adding healthcare to his landmark Social Security legislation. But from the AMA's perspective, Social Security's regulatory structure was an unknown quantity. The most powerful members of the organization therefore feared (probably rightly) that compulsory public insurance would disrupt the professional self-regulatory approach that they had won from the states. The AMA therefore strongly opposed any New Deal effort to nationalize the regulation of medicine—or even to provide national aid to states for the implementation of compulsory insurance. The organization, thanks in part to a conservative turn in Congress after the 1938 election cycle, successfully blocked any national effort at funding or regulating medical care.[45]

In the end, even as constitutional barriers to nationalization disappeared, political opposition to national healthcare regulation remained strong—and, indeed, stronger in healthcare than in many other fields. Perhaps because the Court had allowed the states an unusually broad license to regulate medicine, the states' early regulatory efforts and the AMA's favored regulatory approach had become so deeply entrenched that it proved impossible to change.

In a similar and parallel public choice story, state insurance commissioners—which were created during the *Lochner* Era's broad grant of state (but not national) power to regulate insurance contracts—strongly opposed national takeover of *their* industry.[46] In the 1944 case *Southeastern Underwriters*, the Supreme Court held for the first time that Congress held constitutional authority to regulate insurance,[47] but state insurance commissioners, just as the AMA had done, strongly opposed national intervention. In reaction to the Court's *Southeastern Underwriters* opinion and at the urging of the National Association of Insurance Commissioners, Congress quickly passed the McCarran-Ferguson Act,[48] which still today instructs courts to assume that national statutes do not apply to insurance unless the statutes explicitly mention the industry.[49]

c. World War II and Employer-Sponsored Insurance

The first national intervention in medicine and health insurance occurred quite accidentally. During the Great Depression, labor unions and hospitals started to establish prepaid medical plans to help patients cover their medical costs, and these prepaid plans ultimately took the form of private health insurance—an innovation of the era. In the 1930s, employers and unions started to offer private health insurance plans as a benefit of employment. Although AMA physicians took a bit longer than hospitals and unions to hop on the bandwagon of private health insurance, they embraced the movement by the start of the 1940s.[50] By the

45 STARR, *supra* note 37, at 270–279; *see also* STARR, *supra* note 40 (describing the many historical defeats of national healthcare regulation).

46 *See, e.g.*, Susan Randall, *Insurance Regulation in the United States: Regulatory Federalism and the National Association of Insurance Commissioners*, 26 FLA. ST. U. L. REV. 625 (1999) (describing the role of the National Association of Insurance Commissioners in opposing national regulation).

47 322 U.S. 533 (1944).

48 *See* Randall, *supra* note 46, at 633–634.

49 *See* 15 U.S.C. § 6701.

50 *See* STARR, *supra* note 37, at 306–310.

time World War II began, hospitals had set up Blue Cross payment plans; physicians had set up Blue Shield plans; labor unions had started providing trust-funded medical care for their members; and a handful of commercial insurers had started offering medical coverage.

With America's entry into World War II, a newly established War Labor Board undertook the Herculean task of restraining wage inflation and promoting war-goods production in the face of a domestic labor shortage—an inevitable consequence of fighting a large-scale foreign war, as the men went overseas. It occurred to the Board and to the Internal Revenue Service (IRS) that the value of an employee's fringe benefits—like vacations, pensions, and these new health insurance policies—was less likely to inflate than the value of cash wages. The Board and IRS therefore decided to exclude from income taxation the value of any in-kind benefits provided in exchange for labor. Benefits thus became cheaper for employers to provide than wages and more valuable for employees to receive than cash wages of an equivalent value.

As a result, employer-sponsored health insurance became an attractive element of employee compensation. Employees grew increasingly accustomed to receiving benefits as part of their compensation packages, and in the 1954 Internal Revenue Code,[51] Congress codified the wartime exemption. Still today, Americans do not pay national income taxes on their employer-sponsored health insurance benefits. Employer-sponsored insurance (ESI) thus became a widespread and long-lasting mechanism for providing Americans with financial access to medical care.[52]

d. Medicare and Medicaid

As a result of the (accidental) tie between health insurance and employment, Americans' access to healthcare had, by the 1960s, become quite unequal. Because health insurance was an incident of employment, anyone lacking well-compensated employment—such as retirees, the unemployed, the working poor, and the self-employed—also lacked easy access to affordable health insurance. Furthermore, even with the passage of some national funding for public healthcare in the late 1950s, different states were investing quite different amounts in public care for the indigent.[53]

With the election of progressive and bullish President Lyndon B. Johnson in 1964, the time was finally right for a strong push for public health insurance, at least for the groups that had been left without access to tax-free private insurance. Congress responded in 1965 with the Medicare Act, providing fully nationalized public health insurance for retirees—and for anyone else over the official retirement age of sixty-five—who had contributed to the program through employment taxes. The Medicare Act, however, was a compromise bill to accommodate the AMA's continuing resistance to national regulation of the medical profession—and the lingering sense that, although the national government had a broad spending power, its regulatory power over localized commerce like medical care ought to be more limited.

[51] Internal Revenue Code of 1954 § 106, Pub. L. 83-591 (1954).

[52] *See generally* Robert B. Helms, Tax Policy and the History of the Health Insurance Industry 6–9 (2008), https://www.aei.org/wp-content/uploads/2011/10/healthconference-helms.pdf.

[53] *See* Laura Katz Olson, The Politics of Medicaid 23–24 (describing the Kerr-Mills federal funding program that preceded Medicare and Medicaid).

Although Medicare created compulsory national insurance for the elderly, the Act officially forbade national regulation of the practice of medicine.[54] This official condemnation of medical regulation through Medicare now looks somewhat silly given the program's deep impact on medical decision-making, but the statute's acknowledgment that it did not intend to regulate medicine is a lasting tribute to the very real limits of Americans' political appetite for national healthcare regulation. Furthermore, the Medicare statute left significant control in the hands of the state decision-makers that the AMA had so effectively captured in the early part of the 1900s. Medicare benefits are, still today, administered by state-based Medicare Administrative Contractors (MACs), which are usually the state's Blue Cross and Blue Shield organizations.

As something of an afterthought to the Medicare Act, Congress also passed the Medicaid Act to cover the "medically needy" poor or the "deserving" poor—the indigent groups that were most in need of medical care, such as the blind and disabled. Medicaid was an attempt to improve state funding of care for the indigent, but like Medicare, the Medicaid Act tried to do so without interfering with the prevailing private models of insurance and care. Unlike the Medicare Act, however, Medicaid did not shift primary regulatory power to a national machinery. In the Medicaid program, each state retains significant flexibility to set its own rules for eligibility and benefits, and each state retains the responsibility to administer the program on a day-to-day basis. State administrators determine which individuals are eligible to join the program and which claims for coverage are worthy of payment. That said, the Medicaid Act also set some baseline national requirements for eligibility and benefits within state programs, and it provided additional national funding to the states in an effort to boost state investment and to reduce state-to-state differentiation in care.[55] Following the guidelines for cooperative federalism established in *Steward Machine*, states were not required to participate in Medicaid, but the offer of national funding—which was contingent on compliance with national guidelines—served as a strong incentive for states to play by Congress's rules in establishing and administering state-run Medicaid programs.

Importantly, both Medicare and Medicaid retained the long-standing model of privately employed doctors (now occasionally reimbursed with public dollars), and both programs retained roles for private insurance companies: features that emerged from the AMA's powerful influence and from the generally individualistic and laissez-faire roots of American regulation. But sympathy for the elderly allowed Medicare to become the country's first national health insurance program while ambivalence toward the indigent (and lobbyist opposition to nationalization) forced Medicaid to split the difference between national and state power.

Medicaid thus joined many cooperative federalism programs in which the national and state governments share financial and regulatory responsibility. Unfortunately, through such a structure, the effort to smooth funding across state lines largely failed; only some states have accepted the national government's various invitations to expand their eligibility and benefits beyond the mandatory national floor. As a result, inequality persists in indigent Americans' access to healthcare; citizens of different states receive widely divergent benefits.

[54] 42 U.S.C. § 1395 ("Nothing in this title shall be construed to authorize any Federal officer or employee to exercise any supervision or control over the practice of medicine or the manner in which medical services are provided, or over the selection, tenure, or compensation of any officer or employee of any institution, agency, or person providing health services; or to exercise any supervision or control over the administration or operation of any such institution, agency, or person.").

[55] *See generally* Olson, *supra* note 53, at 21–26 (describing the passage of the Medicaid Act).

e. The Employee Retirement Income Security Act of 1974 (ERISA)

Twenty years after the accidental creation of employer-sponsored health insurance, another important historical accident fundamentally altered the federalist balance of private health insurance regulation. In 1974, Congress passed the Employee Retirement Income Security Act (ERISA) to nationalize the regulation of pension funds. Although the statute claimed—consistently with the McCarran-Ferguson Act—that Congress did not intend to displace state regulation of the business of insurance[56] and although the statute contained very little substantive regulation that made sense for health insurance benefits, the statute did apply to all self-funded employee benefit plans, including those that might displace private health insurance policies as a benefit.[57] In other words, if an employer bought a commercial health insurance policy for its employees, then the insurance would remain subject to state regulation, according to ERISA's exemption of insurance from its reach. But if an employer instead set aside a trust fund to finance medical care on its employees' behalf—acting as its own health insurer—then the self-funded employer-sponsored insurance would become subject to ERISA regulation rather than state regulation. Relative to state insurance laws, however, ERISA provided a much more relaxed regulatory environment, and the statute prohibited states from supplementing the relatively lax ERISA regulations with any more-stringent regulation of those employee benefit plans that fell within the national statute's jurisdiction.[58]

Because the ERISA framework was so much more relaxed than most states' laws, many employers began to self-fund their health insurance benefits in order to move their health plans from state to national jurisdiction. Rather than purchasing a commercial insurance policy for their employees on the private market, employers started to set aside their own funds to pay for their employees' healthcare costs—thereby becoming self-funded benefit plans that fell under ERISA regulations rather than states' insurance regulations. The creation of a lax regulatory space for self-funded employer-sponsored plans decreased regulatory compliance costs for employer-sponsored insurance, widening the cost gap between employer-sponsored insurance and private-market insurance that had first arisen from the World War II tax exemption.

f. Obamacare

Medicare and Medicaid had filled two coverage gaps that the rise of employer-sponsored insurance had left open—the elderly and the "medically needy" poor—but the programs left

[56] *See* 29 U.S.C. § 1144(b)(2)(A) ("[N]othing in this subchapter shall be construed to exempt or relieve any person from any law of any State which regulates insurance[.]").

[57] *See* 29 U.S.C. § 1144(b)(2)(B) ("Neither an employee benefit plan . . . nor any trust established under such a plan, shall be deemed to be an insurance company or other insurer . . . or to be engaged in the business of insurance . . . for purposes of any law of any State purporting to regulate insurance companies [or] insurance contracts[.]").

[58] *See generally* Russell Korobkin, *The Battle over Self-Insured Health Plans, Or "One Good Loophole Deserves Another,"* 5 Yale J. Health Pol'y L. & Ethics 89 (2005) (describing the preemption and regulation provisions of ERISA).

large coverage gaps for the self-employed and the able-bodied poor as well as for anyone who did not receive insurance as an employment benefit, including many small-business and part-time workers. In most states, Medicaid offered no coverage for able-bodied childless adults under age sixty-five, even if those adults were living in poverty and were unable to pay their medical bills. Furthermore, millions of middle-class American workers lacked employer-sponsored insurance for one reason or another. Many such individuals simply forwent healthcare coverage, but some purchased individual insurance policies on the residual private market that self-funded employers and government programs had left behind.

Unfortunately, before the 2010 passage of the Patient Protection and Affordable Care Act (ACA, or "Obamacare"), the private market for individual health insurance policies was extremely small, not well regulated, and quite dysfunctional. Remember that, largely thanks to the lingering power of insurance commissioners, the regulation of private health insurance remained almost entirely the province of state governments. The national government had, as of 2010, regulated the private insurance market in only two noteworthy ways. First, as noted, ERISA had accidentally carved out a national regulatory space for self-funded employer-sponsored insurance. Second, a modest national statute called the Health Insurance Portability and Accountability Act (HIPAA) had forbidden some discriminatory insurance practices in the small-group and individual markets and had authorized the Department of Health and Human Services to implement privacy regulations.[59]

Overall, however, regulation of the private market for individual health insurance policies had been fragmented across state lines, notwithstanding the nationalization of so many other policy regimes since the New Deal. Before Obamacare, individual policies sold in Massachusetts complied with a completely different set of regulatory requirements than policies sold in Texas, even if the policies were sold by the same company.

One result of state power is that a large company can simply opt out of a regulatory regime it dislikes, without needing to go out of business. If Massachusetts passes a costly set of insurance regulations, Aetna can stop selling policies in Massachusetts while continuing to make a profit from its patients in Texas. Large insurers therefore had tremendous power over the shape of insurance law, and most states' laws (before Obamacare) allowed insurers tremendous leeway in setting the terms of their policies. Insurers were allowed to refuse to cover patients' preexisting medical conditions, to cap the benefits they would pay in a given year or over the course of a patient's lifetime, to cancel a policy if a patient got too sick, and to keep an unlimited percentage of the premiums they collected as profits or other administrative costs (rather than spending the money on patients' medical care). In other words, most state laws treated health insurance policies as ordinary commodities, leaving patients to bargain for favorable terms.

But thanks to the piecemeal—and almost entirely accidental—evolution of healthcare coverage policies in the United States, only a small percentage of Americans were left to purchase individual plans on each state's private market. Because the vast majority of Americans received coverage through their employers or through Medicare and Medicaid, only a small residual population—the self-employed, the childless working poor, the part-time workers, and some small-business employees—was even potentially shopping on the private market. And, thanks to federalism, each state's market was freestanding with no competition

59 *See* Health Insurance Portability and Accountability Act of 1996, Pub. L. 104–191, 110 Stat. 1936.

across state lines. Each market for individual insurance policies was therefore too small to support many providers, and most states' markets were oligopolistic or even monopolistic. Furthermore, the populations that were shopping on the individual market within a state lacked any mechanism for banding together to gain the collective bargaining power that employers, unions, and governments were providing for other covered populations.

In the end, the combination of commissioner-won state jurisdiction over insurance, insurance-company-won laissez-faire state laws that presumed a functioning and competitive market, and largely accidental national exclusion of large swaths of Americans from the private market effectively destroyed the market for individual health insurance policies. Neither effective regulation nor economic competition existed to discipline insurance company behavior. Before Obamacare, individual insurance policies were, for most Americans, prohibitively expensive and undependable. Unsurprisingly, many Americans chose not to buy insurance.

Notice here that both the competitive and regulatory failures in the individual market arose largely from federalism, whether political or constitutional or both. Resistance to national regulation, largely led by the AMA and the insurance commissioners, was responsible for both the incompleteness of prior national healthcare reforms and the preservation of state-by-state fragmentation of insurance markets.

In 2010, Congress passed Obamacare to fill the coverage gaps and to rectify both the market and regulatory failures in the individual health insurance market. Although Obamacare represented the first national attempt at comprehensively reforming American healthcare law, the statute did not enact a comprehensive national healthcare policy. Its purpose and effect was to fill coverage gaps and to rationalize insurance law for the (still residual) private market. To accomplish that limited goal, Obamacare enacted four principal reforms.

First, the "Medicaid expansion": The statute asked states to expand their Medicaid programs to cover anyone living on an income at or below 133% of the Federal Poverty Line, whether "medically needy" or not. For the first time, the national government would require state programs to cover able-bodied and young childless adults who were living in poverty. The national government offered to pay 90% of the cost of care for anyone who would be newly covered under the expanded programs, but the statute also seemed to threaten to withdraw all of the national government's prior Medicaid funding from any state that refused to expand its program. Expansion of the program became a new requirement for the receipt of *any* national Medicaid funding.[60]

Second, the "market reforms": Obamacare enacted a series of regulatory reforms to the private insurance market, prohibiting health insurers from engaging in many of the practices they had been using to protect themselves from large claims or sick patients. The statute banned preexisting condition exclusions, policy rescissions, and lifetime and annual caps on coverage, and it required insurers to spend at least 85% of the premiums they collected on medical claims, allowing the companies to keep only 15% of patients' money for profits and other administrative costs. Obamacare also required insurers to charge all covered patients the same amount in premiums, prohibiting them from charging sicker patients more for insurance except in a few narrow ways.[61]

60 *See NFIB*, 132 S.Ct. at 2601–2608.

61 *See generally* 42 U.S.C. §§ 300gg *et seq.*

Third, the "individual mandate": Obamacare requires all Americans to maintain health insurance coverage at all times unless the cost of insurance exceeds 8% of the individual's household income. Any individual who fails to carry coverage—and who does not fall under the affordability threshold—owes a tax penalty.[62] To help offset the cost of coverage and to ensure that very few Americans are excused from carrying insurance due to cost, Obamacare also offers national subsidies to anyone making between 100% and 400% of the federal poverty line who purchases insurance through the newly reformed individual market.[63]

Finally, the "exchanges": Obamacare created new government-run marketplaces through which individuals could purchase insurance policies, called health insurance exchanges. The exchanges are responsible for ensuring that all policies sold through the individual private market comply with Obamacare's market reform regulations; they provide unified marketplaces that allow buyers to compare easily among competing policies, giving some bargaining power to the buyers' side of the market; and the exchanges distribute subsidies to qualifying purchasers. The exchanges thus simultaneously introduce regulatory and competitive discipline into the individual health insurance market. That said, however, the exchanges retain the state-by-state segregation of the market. Although the initial draft of the Obamacare statute would have created a single national exchange—which would have significantly broadened competition among insurance policies but would have diminished insurance commissioners' power—the final version left exchange establishment in the hands of the states.[64] And although the statute provided that the national government would establish an exchange for any state that failed to do so—which ended up meaning that the national government manages the exchanges in thirty-four states—the nationally established exchanges in nonestablishing states are still state-specific.[65] The national exchange's website has thirty-four different subsites—one for each of the thirty-four nonestablishing states.

In the end, two aspects of Obamacare truly nationalized healthcare policy: the market reforms and the individual mandate. Both the Medicaid expansion and the exchanges perpetuated state-by-state fragmentation and differentiation in healthcare law. Furthermore, starting in 2017, the national government will begin offering "state innovation waivers," which will excuse states from Obamacare requirements if they want to experiment with different approaches to accomplishing Obamacare's goals.[66] Even the market reforms and the mandate, therefore, could return to state control in states that apply for and receive Obamacare waivers in the future.

g. Obamacare in the Supreme Court

Two important aspects of Obamacare fell prey to the Supreme Court's revival of constitutional federalism. In *NFIB v. Sebelius*,[67] the Court held that Congress may not force individuals to carry health insurance but that it may tax individuals for failing to insure, and it held that Congress may not make states' continuing participation in pre-Obamacare Medicaid conditional on their willingness to expand their programs.

[62] *See* 26 U.S.C. § 5000A.
[63] *See* 26 U.S.C. § 36B.
[64] *See* 42 U.S.C. § 18031.
[65] *See* 42 U.S.C. § 18041.
[66] *See* 42 U.S.C. § 18052.
[67] 132 S.Ct. 2566 (2012).

In the Medicaid portion of the opinion, the Court prohibited the national government from discontinuing its financial support of Medicaid in states that refuse to expand their programs. The statute's apparent threat of withdrawing preexisting funding, the Court held, violated the *Steward Machine* prohibition on financial inducements that pass "the point at which pressure turns into compulsion." Because all states are dependent on national Medicaid funds, the threat of withdrawing that funding is unduly coercive of state governments.

Nevertheless, the Court did not invalidate the Medicaid expansion in its entirety. Instead, Chief Justice Roberts's majority opinion held that the expansion must be voluntary. After *NFIB*, therefore, Obamacare continues to offer to pay 90% of the cost of coverage for the expansion population, requiring state governments to cover a mere 10% of the cost of healthcare for the "undeserving" poor, but Obamacare no longer threatens to withdraw preexisting national funding from states that refuse to expand. Because Obamacare has been so politically unpopular among conservative Americans, nineteen states had declined to adopt the Medicaid expansion at the time of this writing despite the generosity of the national funding offered.[68]

In nonexpanding states today, the poorest Americans—if they were ineligible for Medicaid before Obamacare went into effect—are receiving no governmental help in obtaining healthcare coverage. Americans who earn between 100% and 400% of the federal poverty line are receiving subsidies to buy private insurance coverage, but those living below the poverty line receive no help unless they fall into one of the "medically needy" categories that Medicaid covered before Obamacare. This result is, of course, a conscious choice of the state governments in nineteen states, but the oddity of providing coverage for the near-poor and lower middle class without providing coverage for the truly impoverished highlights the nonsensical and arbitrary nature of the overall system. And that oddity is almost entirely thanks to Americans' long history of political and constitutional federalism.

The second holding in *NFIB* was that the national government's power to regulate interstate commerce cannot sustain the individual mandate. The mandate, according to Chief Justice Roberts, does not regulate existing commerce; it compels people to engage in commercial transactions that they might not otherwise enter. Importantly, Roberts did not question the national significance of the individual mandate or the mandate's substantial effect on interstate commerce; he simply asserted that it would be improper for the national rather than state governments to enforce compulsory participation in private insurance markets. This holding was made possible by the new federalism's revival of Commerce Clause limitations in the 1990s, but it created and enforced a new distinction between regulable economic "activity" and nonregulable economic "inactivity"—an economically specious distinction that seems somewhat reminiscent of *Lochner* Era distinctions between public health regulations and price-fixing statutes.

Nevertheless, Roberts did not invalidate the individual mandate. Instead, he argued that the statute could be interpreted as merely taxing individuals who forwent insurance, not truly requiring any individual to engage in the commercial activity of buying insurance.

[68] *See* Kaiser Family Foundation, Current Status of State Medicaid Expansion Decisions, http://kff.org/health-reform/slide/current-status-of-the-medicaid-expansion-decision (accessed March 6, 2016).

And, according to Roberts, the national government's power to tax and spend for the general welfare—unlike its power to regulate interstate commerce—is broad enough to sustain the mandate. On this understanding, the national government may never truly *require* individuals to buy insurance; it must leave them free to choose between purchasing insurance and paying the tax.

Given that Roberts's understanding did not alter the statutory consequences for anyone who failed to buy insurance, his insistence that the provision be understood as a tax to withstand constitutional scrutiny might seem beyond silly. But Roberts's holding forbids future congresses from intensifying the consequences of refusing to insure. Under constitutional limits on the national taxing power, a tax may not be penal.[69] For Obamacare's mandate to remain a constitutionally permissible tax rather than a constitutionally impermissible regulation, therefore, Congress must leave Americans monetarily indifferent between buying insurance and paying the tax. Even if Americans over time become more comfortable with the idea of compulsory health insurance, thanks to Roberts's constitutional federalism, future national governments will never be able to truly compel universal participation in health insurance markets.

III The Future of Healthcare Federalism

Despite some politicians' assertions that Obamacare represents a national "takeover" of healthcare, the future does not seem much more likely than the past to give rise to a rational, holistic system. Obamacare preserved the segmentation of the private market between employer-sponsored and individual insurance policies, and by insisting upon state-specific exchanges, the statute preserved state-by-state fragmentation of the individual insurance market even while imposing some uniform national regulations on the business of health insurance. Furthermore, by providing for "state innovation waivers," Obamacare invites state to make up alternative regulatory systems for their insurance providers. Obamacare is truly a federalist—not nationalist—statute.

There are only two reasons to hope (or fear, depending on one's perspective) that the national government will gradually take a stronger role in American healthcare regulation. First, most states have opted not to establish their own health insurance exchanges, preferring to let the national government run the exchanges within their borders. Also, the states that did establish their own exchanges have had some financial difficulties with exchange management.[70] Perhaps all states will eventually turn their exchanges over to the national government, particularly since the Supreme Court recently held in *King v. Burwell* that Obamacare did not include any punishment for states that refused to run their own marketplaces.[71] If most states end up turning over their markets to nationally run exchanges, then

[69] *See* Bailey v. Drexel Furniture Co., 259 U.S. 20 (1922).

[70] *See* Lena H. Sun & Niraj Choski, *Almost Half of Obamacare Exchanges Face Financial Struggles in the Future*, Wash. Post (May 1, 2015) (noting that half of the seventeen states that established their own exchanges have experienced financial shortfalls and predict further shortfalls in the future).

[71] *See* King v. Burwell, 576 U.S. ___ (2015).

the state governments and insurance commissioners might start to feel less invested in regulating their individual insurance markets. We might then see few applications for waivers from Obamacare's baseline national regulations. Furthermore, if the national government ends up running the exchanges in all states, political resistance to the creation of a single, nationwide exchange might gradually weaken as insurance commissioners give up their holds. In other words, the states' current resistance to national healthcare regulation might, perversely, lead to greater nationalization.

Second, the Supreme Court has recently issued a strange set of holdings relating to Medicaid—and to cooperative federalism more generally—that might eventually push the Medicaid program to nationalize.[72] In *NFIB*, the Court, for the first time in American history, enforced a constitutional limit on the national government's power to threaten withdrawal of Medicaid funds from states. But the threat of withdrawing funds is the only enforcement mechanism the national government has for ensuring that states comply with the Medicaid Act when implementing their programs. *NFIB* therefore creates some uncertainty as to the national government's practical ability to enforce statutory requirements against states in their cooperative federalism programs.

In an unrelated case, *Armstrong v. Exceptional Child Center*, the Supreme Court held that individuals cannot use private litigation to force the states to comply with the Medicaid Act.[73] Instead, the Court said, individuals who are harmed by state violations of the Medicaid Act should try to get the national government to enforce the Act against the states, perhaps through litigation against the national administrative agency charged with such enforcement, the Centers for Medicare and Medicaid Services (CMS). But if CMS's only enforcement tool is sometimes unconstitutional to use, then the Supreme Court's holdings might leave the agency in quite a bind. CMS might end up with court orders to deny funding to noncompliant states but with uncertain constitutional authority to execute those orders.

One way out of this bind would be for Congress to authorize CMS to take over state Medicaid programs from states that refuse to comply with the Medicaid Act—just as Obamacare authorized the national government to take over exchange establishment from states that refused to establish their own exchanges. Given that many states dislike the task of managing Medicaid, it wouldn't be completely surprising if these two Supreme Court holdings—both outgrowths of the New Federalism—eventually led to greater nationalization of Medicaid in the same (slightly perverse) way that states' resistance to exchange establishment might eventually lead to nationalization of the individual health insurance market.

Of course, nationalization of exchanges and Medicaid—even if such nationalization occurred—would not rationalize American healthcare regulation. The segmentation of insurance pools through employer-sponsored insurance and Medicare, which are relics of past federalism, seems quite deeply entrenched. The United States does not seem at all close to accepting a fully national system such as a centrally administered single-payer plan, for instance. Even as the national government takes a greater supervisory role of healthcare regulation through Obamacare, the fragmentation that has arisen from past federalism seems extremely likely to remain.

[72] For fuller analysis of this prediction, *see* Abigail R. Moncrieff & Jonathan Dinerstein, *Will Uncooperative Federalism Survive* NFIB?, 76 MONT. L. REV. 75 (2015).

[73] 575 U.S. ___ (2015).

If my tentative predictions of greater nationalization in exchanges and Medicaid prove wrong, then the future of American healthcare regulation will be more of the same tension between national and state regulation that has prevailed since the New Deal. Perpetual tug-of-war between national and state governments has become the dominant feature of so-called "statutory federalism,"[74] and it is a core feature of both Medicaid and Obamacare.

IV Conclusion

The federalist structure of the U.S. government has been largely responsible for the piecemeal evolution and perpetual messiness of American healthcare regulation. Long ago, the *Lochner* Court created an unusually stark division between state and national power to regulate the component parts of the healthcare industry, and that message of state primacy in healthcare regulation has proven unbelievably sticky. Even as national power has grown across every other regulatory regime and even as the national economy has become increasingly interconnected across state lines, lobbyists, politicians, and justices alike continue to assert the states' prerogative in regulating health and medicine. The result is a fragmented regulatory structure that fails to capture many of the benefits of careful, coherent, centralized attention.

[74] *See, e.g.*, Abbe R. Gluck, *Our [National] Federalism*, 123 YALE L.J. 1626 (2014) (explaining statutory federalism and the idea that state power comes primarily through states' execution of Congress's federal statutes); Jessica Bulman-Pozen & Heather Gerken, *Uncooperative Federalism*, 118 YALE L.J. 1256 (2009) (describing the emerging culture of states' resistance to national directives in their implementations of statutory federalism).

PART II

CARING AND RECEIVING CARE

A. Access to Healthcare

CHAPTER 6

ACCESSING HOSPITALS AND HEALTH PROFESSIONALS

ELEANOR D. KINNEY

I INTRODUCTION

UNLIKE other developed countries, the United States has never assured universal or comprehensive health insurance coverage for its population. Nor has the United States or its states adequately addressed the multiple barriers to access to physicians and hospitals that burden individuals who are unable to pay directly for healthcare services. Only in 2010 did Congress enact the Patient Protection and Affordable Care Act (ACA),[1] as amended by the Health Care and Education Reconciliation Act of 2010,[2] to expand coverage and advance health reform.

First, this chapter examines the five dimensions identified by Roy Penchansky and J. William Thomas in their model of access to healthcare. Second, the chapter reviews the constitutional powers of states and the federal government with respect to health as well as relevant health law. This chapter closes with how the United States fails to realize the human right to health in international treaties. Based on international norms, the United States falls short in significant ways when it comes to access to physicians and hospitals for its population.

As will be discussed in Part III, the law governing access to physicians and hospitals falls into three categories: (1) direct obligations of physicians and hospitals to provide free care to the indigent; (2) federal programs to provide health insurance or healthcare services to vulnerable populations; and (3) laws that affect the delivery of care at the point of access based on the patient's physical characteristics and immigration status.

The first category addresses the obligations of physicians to treat patients under state contract, tort, and regulatory law, as well as the obligations of hospitals under state corporate,

[1] Patient Protection and Affordable Care Act (ACA), Pub. L. No. 111-148, 124 Stat. 119 (2010).

[2] Health Care and Education Reconciliation Act of 2010, Pub. L. No. 111-152, 124 Stat. 1029 (2010).

charity, and tax law, and under federal tax law, to provide charitable care. The second category addresses public health insurance programs for vulnerable populations under the federal Social Security Act, as well as direct services programs for the poor under the federal Public Health Service Act and Chapters 73 and 74 of United States Code Title 38, Veterans Benefits.[3] The third category addresses federal and state antidiscrimination laws and emergency treatment statutes. The third category also includes immigration law pertaining to undocumented immigrants and access.

II Dimensions of Access to Care

Access to physicians and hospitals is more than a problem of lack of funds or health insurance to pay for healthcare services. Access also has to do with the demographics and socioeconomic status of patients and the organization, characteristics, and dispositions of providers to serve these patients.

Other chapters in this book address the general problem of health disparities in the United States.[4] But any analysis of health law must recognize that access to care for many individuals is not simply a result of lack of health insurance or funds to purchase healthcare services.

a. Impact of Social Inequality

People with lower socioeconomic status generally are in poorer health and have diminished access to physicians and hospitals. The annual disparities report of the Agency for Health Services Research and Quality defines disparity:

> The factors that influence the socioeconomic position of individuals and groups within industrial societies also influence their health. Socioeconomic position has continuous and graded effects on health that are cumulative over a lifetime. The socioeconomic conditions of the places where persons live and work have an even more substantial influence on health than personal socioeconomic position.[5]

Inequality is known to result in undesirable social and health problems such as mental illness (including drug and alcohol addiction), obesity, teen pregnancy, lower life expectancy, higher infant mortality, and poor educational performance by children.[6] Social inequity is reflected in higher rates of homicide and imprisonment. Social mobility is compromised along with personal health.

[3] Pub. L. No. 79-293, An Act to Establish a Department of Medicine and Surgery in the Veterans Administration (1946), 59 Stat. 675 (codified as amended at 38 U.S.C., chs. 73 & 74).

[4] *See* Rebouche and Burris' as well as Matthew's articles in this volume.

[5] Center for Disease Control and Prevention, *CDC Health Disparities and Inequalities Report—United States, 2013* (2013).

[6] Richard Wilkinson & Kate Pickett, The Spirit Level: Why Greater Equality Makes Societies Stronger (2010).

Table 6.1 Dimensions of Access under the Penchansky-Thomas Model of Access to Medical Care

Availability is the relationship of the volume and type of existing services (and resources) to the clients' volume and types of needs. It refers to the adequacy of the supply of physicians, dentists, and other providers; of facilities such as clinics and hospitals; and of specialized programs and services such as mental health and emergency care.

Accessibility is the relationship between the location of supply and the location of clients, taking account of client transportation resources and travel time, distance, and cost.

Accommodation is the relationship between the manner in which resources are organized to accept clients (including appointment systems, hours of operation, walk-in facilities, telephone services) and the clients' ability to accommodate to these factors and the clients' perception of their appropriateness.

Affordability is the relationship of prices of services and providers' insurance or deposit requirements to the clients' income, ability to pay, and existing health insurance. Client perception of worth relative to total cost is a concern here, as is clients' knowledge of prices, total cost, and possible credit arrangements.

Acceptability is the relationship of clients' attitudes about personal and practice characteristics of providers to the actual characteristics of existing providers, as well as to provider attitudes about acceptable personal characteristics of clients. In the literature, the term appears to be used most often to refer to specific consumer reaction to such provider attributes as age, sex, ethnicity, type of facility, neighborhood of facility, or religious affiliation of a facility or provider. In tum, providers have attitudes about the preferred attributes of clients or their financing mechanisms. Providers either may be unwilling to serve certain types of clients (e.g., welfare patients) or, through accommodation, make themselves more or less available.

Source: Roy Penchansky & J. William Thomas, *The Concept of Access: Definition and Relationship to Consumer Satisfaction,*, 19 MEDICAL CARE 127–140 (1981).

b. The Penchansky-Thomas Model of Access to Care

One can analyze laws governing access using Roy Penchansky and J. William Thomas's empirically tested model of access to care.[7] Under the Penchansky-Thomas model, there are five dimensions of access: availability, accessibility, accommodation, affordability, and acceptability. These dimensions are presented in Table 6.1. How the various areas of American health law address these five dimensions of access is discussed at the conclusion of the description of each area of law.

i. *Availability*

Availability relates the volume and type of existing services and resources to the clients' volume and types of needs.[8] Realistically, physicians can practice wherever they want, and hospital sponsors can locate hospitals wherever they want consistent with local zoning

[7] Roy Penchansky & J. William Thomas, *The Concept of Access: Definition and Relationship to Consumer Satisfaction*, 19 MED. CARE 127(1981).

[8] Penchansky & Thomas, *The Concept of Access*.

ordinances. Not surprisingly, physicians practice in more affluent urban and suburban settings. Hospitals are located in these areas as well. In the main, the geographic distribution of hospitals and physicians reflects socioeconomic conditions in the country.

State and federal policy-makers have recognized that there are insufficient numbers of physicians and hospitals in medically underserved areas and among underserved populations. Some hospitals, by virtue of their corporate mission, have addressed these deficiencies through their charitable services. These hospitals often purposely locate in underserved areas to provide services to underserved populations. However, as discussed below, federal and state programs have had to step in to meet the needs of all underserved populations.

ii. Accessibility

Accessibility is the relationship between the location of supply and the location of clients, taking account of client transportation resources and travel time, distance, and cost.[9] Health law does little to address specifically the location of healthcare providers and associated transportation issues for patients. Only the programs under the Public Health Service Act, discussed below, have specifically addressed these issues by locating grant-funded community health centers and other assets in specifically defined and designated underserved areas.

iii. Accommodation

According to the Penchansky-Thomas model,[10] accommodation is the relationship between the manner in which the supply resources are organized to accept clients (including appointment systems, hours of operation, walk-in facilities, telephone services) and the clients' perception of their reasonableness and appropriateness.

In general, physicians have considerable flexibility to set the conditions under which they will practice. They set their hours, location, services, and policies. There is no legal requirement that they must be accommodating.

Hospitals have less flexibility regarding accommodation. If they are not-for-profit corporations or municipal corporations, they are subject to additional antidiscrimination laws which prohibit discrimination on the basis of status, including disability. If not-for-profit hospitals want to be tax exempt under federal and/or state law, being accommodating enhances their required community benefit.

iv. Affordability

Affordability is the relationship of prices of services and providers' insurance or deposit requirements to the clients' income, ability to pay, and existing health insurance, as well as client's perception of value and knowledge of prices, cost, and credit arrangements.[11] Most Americans obtain health coverage through private means. According to the U.S. Census Current Population Report, 66% of the U.S. population had private health insurance coverage in 2014.[12] The great majority, 55.4%, obtained coverage through their employer. The

[9] *Id.* [10] *Id.* [11] *Id.*

[12] Jessica C. Smith & Carla Medalia, *Health Insurance Coverage in the United States: 2014*, at 26, Table 8 (U.S. Census Bureau, Current Population Survey, 2015).

remainder purchased health coverage through the private commercial insurance market or through the Medicare and Medicaid programs or other public program. In 2014, 10.4% of the U.S. population was uninsured,[13] down from 16.3% of the population in 2010.[14] This high rate of uninsurance, as well as the prevalence of underinsurance, creates serious problems of affordability.

The primary purpose of the Patient Protection and Affordable Care Act (ACA), enacted in 2010, was to expand health insurance coverage for the uninsured population. Several issues are implicated in assessing whether that insurance expansion will successfully enhance access to the services of physicians and hospitals. First is whether the covered benefits are adequate to assure comprehensive care. The ACA specifies categories of "essential health benefits" and cost-sharing limits for health plans that can be offered through the health insurance exchanges or market places.[15] Second is whether the provider payment levels for covered services are sufficient to ensure participation by physicians, hospitals, and other providers. Third is whether the sponsor of the insurance is able to provide a broad enough network of providers so that beneficiaries have access to high-quality and necessary care. So far, insurance plans under the ACA meet these conditions. The ACA is even having some success in addressing racial and ethnic health disparities.[16]

v. *Acceptability*

Acceptability is a measure of both clients' attitudes toward providers and providers' attitudes toward clients.[17] Providers often have preferences regarding clients' attributes, including sources of financing. As a result, they either may be unwilling to serve certain types of clients or, through accommodation, may make themselves less available.

Physicians do not have a duty to treat particular patients unless they practice in a setting, such as an emergency room, where a patient could reasonably expect the physician to provide care. Hospitals may have such a duty, depending on their corporate form, whether they participate in the Medicare program, and the details of charity or municipal law. These obligations are discussed below.

A major question in the launch of any government health insurance program is whether providers will participate. Historically, physicians have been reluctant to participate in the Medicaid program, in large part because of low payment rates. The authors of the ACA appreciated that the Medicaid expansion would be the major source of coverage expansion for the uninsured.[18] Accordingly, the ACA provides for significant enrichment of the

[13] *Id.*

[14] Carmen DeNavas-Walt, Bernadette D. Proctor and Jessica C. Smith, *Income, Poverty and Health Insurance Coverage in the United States: 2011* (U.S. Census Bureau, Current Population Survey, 2012), at 25, Table 8.

[15] ACA § 1301(a) (codified as amended 42 U.S.C. § 18022).

[16] Lisa Clemans-Cope et al., *The Affordable Care Act's Coverage Expansions Will Reduce Differences in Uninsurance Rates by Race and Ethnicity*, 31 HEALTH AFF. 920 (2012).

[17] Penchansky & Thomas, *The Concept of Access.*

[18] Peter J. Cunningham, Mounting Pressures: Physicians Serving Medicaid Patients and the Uninsured, 1997–2000 (Center for the Study of Health System Change, Dec. 2002); Janet D. Perloff, Phillip Kletke, & James W. Fossett, *Which Physicians Limit Their Medicaid Participation, and Why*, 30 HEALTH SERVICES RESEARCH 8 (1995).

reimbursement formulas for primary care providers. By contrast, there is no indication that physicians and hospital are reluctant to care for people who have obtained coverage expansions through reform of the private health insurance market unless the insurance is clearly inadqeuate.

With respect to original Medicare, the response to payment reforms in the ACA by physicians and hospitals also has been encouraging. Physicians and hospitals have embraced many of the payment reforms, given the leeway in the ACA for provider innovation and leadership. For example, shared savings through accountable care organizations has proven promising for enhancing access to higher quality care at lower costs.[19] However, there is some concern that reductions to funding for Medicare Advantage Plans in the ACA will reduce access to physicians and providers because sponsors of plans will restrict provider networks in order to reduce costs.[20]

III American Law Governing Access to Physicians and Hospitals

Under the federal system of the United States, states as sovereigns have legislatures, executives, and a judiciary to govern their populations and territories. In the federal constitution, the states conferred specific powers on the government of the United States, which are discussed below.

However, states retain a general police power that includes the power to regulate and promote health and healthcare. The state police power is the foundational power of sovereign states irrespective of authorizing constitutional provisions.[21] Of note, the constitutions of a few states expressly recognize the importance of health in the exercise of state power.[22]

The federal government has the power to tax and spend, take other measures to promote the general welfare, and regulate interstate commerce.[23] The power to tax and spend authorizes the federal government to commit financial resources to provide services and also to encourage states and the public to engage in activities that achieve national policy goals.

[19] *See* Eleanor D. Kinney, *The Affordable Care Act and the Medicare Program: The Engines of True Health Reform*, 8 Yale J. Health Pol'y L. & Ethics 253 (2013).

[20] Medicare Advantage and the Affordable Care Act: Hearings before the Health Subcommittee of the House Energy and Commerce Committee (Dec. 4, 2013), http://www.c-span.org/search/?searchtype=Videos&personid[]=9278857&bioid[]=664495.

[21] *See* Markus Dirk Dubber, The Police Power: Patriarchy and the Foundations of American Government (2005); William J. Novak, *The Legal Origins of the Modern American State*, *in* Looking Back at Law's Century 249 (Austin Sarat, Bryant Garth, & Robert A. Kagan eds., 2002). *See also* Glenn H. Reynolds & David B. Kopel, *The Evolving Police Power: Some Observations for a New Century*, 27 Hastings Const. L.Q. 511 (2000).

[22] Eleanor D. Kinney, *The International Human Right to Health: What Does This Mean for Our Nation and World?*, Indiana L. Rev. 1457, at 1465–1466 (2001). *See* Alaska Const. art. VII, § 5; Haw. Const. art. IX, § 1; S.C. Const. art. XII, § 1; Wyo. Const. art. 7, § 20; Mont. Const. art. II, § 3.

[23] U.S. Const. art. I, sec. 8.

It is the power to tax and spend that supports federal health insurance and most federal health promotion and protection programs. In *National Federation of Independent Business v. Sebelius*, the Supreme Court of the United States upheld the ACA as an appropriate exercise of the power to tax and spend.[24]

The Supreme Court has ruled that the government does not have to provide specific benefits in its public health insurance programs as a matter of constitutional law.[25] In *DeShaney v. Winnebago County Department of Social Services*,[26] the Supreme Court stated that "the Due Process Clauses generally confer no affirmative right to governmental aid, even where such aid may be necessary to secure life, liberty, or property interests of which the government itself may not deprive the individual."[27]

Nevertheless, once the government decides to provide a healthcare benefit through a public program, it is bound to the constitutional guarantees of procedural due process. In *Goldberg v. Kelly*,[28] the Supreme Court ruled that government entitlement programs created property interests in benefits eligible for protection under the procedural Due Process Clauses of the Fifth and Fourteenth Amendments. As such, before benefits can be finally terminated, government agencies must provide notice and an opportunity to be heard in a meaningful time and manner. However, the Supreme Court has cut back significantly on the scope of procedural due process protection for beneficiaries of government entitlement programs since this decision.[29]

a. State Law Pertaining to Obligations of Physicians and Hospitals to Provide Care

Important issues in the law of access are the number and geographic distribution of primary care physicians and hospitals. In 2010, there were 208,807 primary care physicians, 55,625 nurse practitioners, and 30,402 physician assistants.[30] Presented in Table 6.2 is the distribution of healthcare professionals in the United States in 2010.

There are 5,723 hospitals in the United States, of which 4,999 are so-called community hospitals. According to the American Hospital Association, community hospitals are non-federal short-term general or other specialty hospitals. Table 6.3 presents data on American hospitals.

[24] 132 U.S. 2566 (2012) (serious injury to a child by his father while under the supervision of social services for child abuse).

[25] Maher v. Roe, 432 U.S. 464 (1977); Harris v. McRae, 448 U.S. 297, 309 (1980).

[26] 489 U.S. 189 (1989). [27] *Id.* at 196. [28] 397 U.S. 254 (1970).

[29] *See* Sidney A. Shapiro & Richard E. Levy, *Government Benefits and the Rule of Law: Toward a Standards-Based Theory of Due Process*, 57 ADMIN. L. REV. 107 (2005); Richard J. Pierce, Jr., *The Due Process Counterrevolution of the 1990s?*, 96 COLUM. L. REV. 1973 (1996). *See also* TIMOTHY STOLTZFUS JOST, DISENTITLEMENT? THE THREATS FACING OUR PUBLIC HEALTH-CARE PROGRAMS AND A RIGHTS-BASED RESPONSE 24–51 (2003).

[30] AHRQ, *Primary Care Workforce Facts and Stats No. 3* (Jan. 2012), http://www.ahrq.gov/research/findings/factsheets/primary/pcwork3/index.html.

Table 6.2 Geographic Distribution of Healthcare Professionals, 2010

Geography	All specialties			Primary care					U.S. population
	NP	PA	MDs	NP	PA	Family MDs/GPs	General internal medicine	General pediatrics	
Urban	84.4%	84.4%	89.0%	72.2%	75.1%	77.5%	89.8%	91.2%	80%
Large rural	8.9%	8.8%	7.1%	11.0%	11.7%	11.1%	6.7%	6.2%	10%
Small rural	3.9%	3.8%	2.6%	7.7%	6.9%	7.2%	2.4%	1.8%	5%
Remote rural/ Frontier	2.8%	3.0%	1.3%	9.1%	6.3%	4.2%	1.1%	0.8%	5%

Source: AHRQ, Primary Care Workforce Facts and Stats No. 3 (Jan. 2012), http://www.ahrq.gov/research/findings/factsheets/primary/pcwork3/index.html.

i. The Relationship between Physician and Patient under State Contract, Tort, and Regulatory Law

Under the state police power, there are many statutes and common law doctrines that address access to physician services. The basis of these obligations is the physician-patient relationship.

(a) The Physician-Patient Contract

The point of access into the healthcare system for any person is a physician. There is a body of law of what constitutes the physician-patient relationship. Under the laws of most states, the physician-patient relationship is based on contract.

Contract principles define whether there is a duty to accept a patient and whether treatment can be terminated. The physician-patient relationship is a contractual relationship to which both parties must agree. The content of the treatment relationship is also determined by state statutes and tort law. Judicial decisions in several states have affirmed this principle of contract law and have further decided that physicians do not have to care for persons with whom they do not have a contract.[31]

Principle VI of the Code of Medical Ethics of the American Medical Association reflects the reasoning in this case and states:

> [A] physician shall, in the provision of appropriate patient care, except in emergencies, be free to choose whom to serve, with whom to associate, and the environment in which to provide medical services.[32]

[31] *See* Ricks v. Budge, 91 Utah 307, 64 P.2d 208 (1937); Hurley v. Eddingfield, 156 Ind. 416, 59 N.E. 1058 (1901); Childs v. Weis, 440 S.W.2d 104 (Ct. Civ. App. Tex. 1969). *See also* Valarie Blake, *When Is a Patient-Physician Relationship Established?*, 14 *Virtual Mentor, Am. Med. Ass'n J. Ethics* 403 (2012).

[32] American Medical Association (AMA), " Principle VI" in AMA, *Code of Medical Ethics* (Chicago: AMA, 2014), http://www.ama-assn.org/ama/pub/physician-resources/medical-ethics/code-medical-ethics/principles-medical-ethics.page?.

Table 6.3 Data on U.S. Hospitals from 2012 AHA Annual Survey of Hospitals

Total Number of All U.S. Registered* Hospitals	**5,723**
Number of U.S. Community Hospitals**	**4,999**
Number of Nongovernment Not-for-Profit Community Hospitals	2,894
Number of Investor-Owned (For-Profit) Community Hospitals	1,068
Number of State and Local Government Community Hospitals	1,037
Number of Rural Community** Hospitals	1,980
Number of Urban Community** Hospitals	3,019
Admissions in Community** Hospitals	34,422,071
Number of Other Types of U.S. Hospitals	
Number of Federal Government Hospitals	211
Number of Nonfederal Psychiatric Hospitals	413
Number of Nonfederal Long-Term Care Hospitals	89
Expenses for U.S. Hospitals	
Total Expenses for All U.S. Registered* Hospitals	$829,665,386,000
Expenses for Community** Hospitals	$756,916,757,000

Definitions:

* Registered: Registered with the AHA (Not necessarily a member).

** Community hospital: The AHA defines a community hospital as a nonfederal short-term general or other specialty hospital, excluding hospital units of institutions.

Source: AHA, Fast Facts on US Hospitals (Jan. 2014), http://www.aha.org/research/rc/stat-studies/fast-facts.shtml.

There are circumstances in which the physician-patient relationship continues despite a physician's desire that it terminate. If a physician does not terminate a relationship properly, the physician may be liable for medical malpractice by exposing the patient to injury. The AMA Code of Medical Ethics has an apt provision on termination:

> Physicians have an obligation to support continuity of care for their patients. While physicians have the option of withdrawing from a case, they cannot do so without giving notice to the patient, the relatives, or responsible friends sufficiently long in advance of withdrawal to permit another medical attendant to be secured.[33]

In sum, physicians make the decisions about where and when they practice medicine. Thus, it is up to physicians to decide if they want to practice medicine in ways that address health disparities in the population. The most effective way in which they do so is by practicing in underserved areas or working for federally funded community health centers or safety net

[33] AMA, "Opinion 8.115, Termination of the Physician-Patient Relationship" in AMA, *Code of Medical Ethics*, http://www.ama-assn.org/ama/pub/physician-resources/medical-ethics/code-medical-ethics/opinion8115.page.

hospitals. In making individual decisions about where to practice, medical students must balance ideological commitments to treating the underserved with monetary considerations when choosing between primary care and specialty residencies.[34]

(b) *Medical Licensure and Discipline*

States authorize physicians and other professionals to practice within the scope of their state conferred licenses. While these provisions set forth the educational and character requirements for medical practice in a state, they do not generally call for physicians to provide healthcare services to people who cannot pay for services.[35]

One important role of state medical licensing boards is delineating the scope of telemedicine, which has served to enhance access to physicians and hospitals for residents of underserved and particularly rural areas.

Fifty-seven state boards require that physicians engaging in telemedicine be licensed in the state in which the patient is located.[36] Over ten state boards issue various types of special licenses or certificates to practice medicine across state lines, and one state requires registration to do so.

(c) *Medical Malpractice*

The tort of medical malpractice imposes obligations on physicians once they undertake the care of a patient. That duty includes not exposing a patient to a reasonably foreseeable risk of injury. There have been malpractice actions against physicians who have tried to terminate relationships with patients who are unable to pay on the theory that once having accepted a patient, the physician must complete care. These obligations arise often in the provision of emergency care, for which physicians by virtue of their employment or other circumstances may be obligated to initiate care for patients.

An exemplary case is *Mead v Adler*,[37] a 2009 decision of the Oregon Supreme Court. In this case, an emergency room physician consulted an on-call neurosurgeon about a patient. The neurosurgeon examined the patient and recommended admission but not surgery. Later, the patient had surgery and had permanent damage. Upon being sued, the neurosurgeon argued that a patient-physician relationship had not been established and thus he had no duty. However, the court held that "in the absence of an express agreement by the physician to treat a patient, a physician's assent to a physician-patient relationship can be inferred when the physician takes an affirmative action with regard to the care of the patient."[38]

A physician-patient relationship and a duty of care will be imputed to on-call physicians treating emergency patients.[39] Similarly, a physician employed by a health maintenance organization (HMO) will have an implied duty of care to a patient who presents to the HMO for treatment.[40]

[34] *See* Mohsen Bazargan et al., *Impact of Desire to Work in Underserved Communities on Selection of Specialty among Fourth-Year Medical Students*, 98 *J. Nat'l Med. Ass'n* 1460–1465 (2006).

[35] *See* Regulation of the Healthcare Professions (Timothy Stoltzfus Jost ed., 1997); FRANK P. GRAD & NOELIA MARTI, PHYSICIANS' LICENSURE AND DISCIPLINE: THE LEGAL AND PROFESSIONAL REGULATION OF MEDICAL PRACTICE (1979).

[36] Federation of State Medical Boards, *Telemedicine Overview: State-by-State Approach* (June 2013), http://www.fsmb.org/Media/Default/PDF/FSMB/Advocacy/GRPOL_Telemedicine_Licensure.pdf.

[37] 231 Ore. App. 451, 220 P.3d 118 (Ore. 2009).

[38] *Id.*

[39] *See* Talavera ex rel. Gonzalez v. Wiley, 725 F.3d 1262 (10th Cir. 2013).

[40] *See* Blake, *When Is a Patient-Physician Relationship Established?*

ii. *The Obligations of Hospitals to Provide Care under State Corporate, Charity, and Tax Law and Federal Tax Law*

The duty to treat is more complicated for hospitals. With the advent of third-party payment from health insurers, hospitals have evolved into large, wealthy institutions. However, hospitals can be established and operate under any corporate form permitted under state corporate law. American hospitals are organized under three corporate forms: (1) public, (2) private, not-for-profit, and (3) for-profit. Public hospitals and private, nonprofit hospitals have obligations to provide free care. For-profit hospitals, except to the extent that they are bound by requirements of public health insurance programs, do not.

(a) State Corporation Law

Hospitals are organized under state corporation laws. As demonstrated in Table 6.3, most hospitals are organized as not-for-profit corporations. The remainder are divided between public hospitals and for-profit hospitals.

Public Hospitals. Historically under the English Poor Law, localities had an obligation to provide aid to the poor, including care of the sick.[41] These arrangements were implemented in the American colonies. In the nineteenth century, municipalities and counties built and operated public hospitals for the poor.[42] Public hospitals are usually organized as municipal corporations and are bound by the duties set forth in statute or ordinance.

Nonprofit Hospitals. In general, not-for-profit corporations have all the powers of for-profit corporations except they cannot divert funds to purposes outside those for which the corporation is organized.[43] State not-for-profit corporation laws impose obligations on hospitals chartered under these laws. The obligations generally are to act in the public good and to perform services for which compensation at profit-making levels is not expected.[44]

State law does not require nonprofit hospitals to provide free care simply by virtue of their organizational form. However, hospitals can impose this obligation upon themselves in their articles of incorporation. Any such obligation can be modified or terminated by the board of directors.

(b) Private Hospitals and the Law of Charities

In the eighteenth and nineteenth centuries, hospitals were the quintessential charitable organizations. Religious or eleemosynary organizations as well as individual philanthropists established private, so-called "voluntary" hospitals that had a mission to care for the poor.[45]

[41] Poor Law Amendment Act of 1834, 4 & 5 Will. 4 c. 76.

[42] America's Essential Hospitals, *History of Public Hospitals in the U.S.* (No Date), http://essentialhospitals.org/about-americas-essential-hospitals/history-of-public-hospitals-in-the-united-states/.

[43] *Corporations, in* Corpus Juris Secundum 19, at § 656 (2014).

[44] Marion R. Fremont-Smith, Governing Nonprofit Organizations: Federal and State Law and Regulation (2004).

[45] Alice A. Noble, Andrew L. Hyams, & Nancy M. Kane, *Charitable Hospital Accountability: A Review and Analysis of Legal and Policy Initiatives*, 26 J. L. Med. & Ethics 116–137 (1998); Robert S. Bromberg,

Thus, a cultural and social expectation developed in the United States that these hospitals would provide care of last resort for people without the ability to pay.

Many nonprofit hospitals were established as charitable trusts or charitable corporations. As such, they are bound by duties imposed in the relevant declaration of trust or corporate charter.[46] The state law of trusts does not automatically require a charitable trust set up to promote healthcare to forgo fees. Unless otherwise specified in the declaration of trust or corporate charter, even a charitable hospital is not obligated to provide all or mostly free care.

The attorney general of each state oversees gifts to charitable organizations to ensure that the recipient honors the donative intent expressed in trust or gift instruments.[47] State attorneys general and co-trustees of the charitable trust enforce free care obligations set forth in charitable trust instruments.[48] Efforts to challenge hospital decisions to reduce services or close facilities because they are charitable trusts, however, have been generally unsuccessful.[49] On the other hand, state attorney generals have acted to protect the public interest when nonprofit hospitals and Blue Cross and Blue Shield plans have converted to for-profit corporations.[50]

(c) State and Federal Tax Law

The law of tax-exempt organizations is another source of nonprofit hospitals' legal duties to provide free care. Such duties apply to both nonprofit corporations and charitable trusts as the law of tax exemption is agnostic on organizational form.

State Tax Law. The law of property tax exemption varies from state to state. Also, some states have programs by which a not-for-profit hospital may make a contribution to the public coffers in lieu of property taxes.[51]

At least two state courts have ruled that nonprofit hospitals did not provide sufficient charity care to justify state property tax exemption. In *Utah County v. Intermountain Health*

The Charitable Hospital, 20 CATH. U. L. REV. 237 (1970–1971). *See also* Evelyn Brody, *The Limits of Charity Fiduciary Law*, 57 MD. L. REV. 1400 (1998).

46 *Charities, in* CORPUS JURIS SECUNDUM 14, at § 84 (2014).

47 *Charities, in* AMERICAN JURISPRUDENCE 15, at § 4 (2014).

48 *See* Craig Kaufman, *Sympathy for the Devil's Advocate: Assisting the Attorney General When Charitable Matters Reach the Courtroom*, 40 REAL PROP. PROB. & TR. J. 705 (2006); Mary Kay Lundwall, *Inconsistency and Uncertainty in the Charitable Purposes Doctrine*, 41 WAYNE L. REV. 1341 (1995).

49 *See, e.g.*, Jackson v. Cleveland Clinic Foundation, 2011 WL 4007732 (N.D. Ohio, Sept. 2011); Lorens v. Catholic Health Care Partners, 356 F.Supp.2d 827 (N.D. Ohio, 2005); Grant v. Trinity Health–Michigan, 390 F.Supp.2d 643 (E.D. Mich. 2005); Burton v. William Beaumont Hospital, 347 F.Supp.2d 486 (E.D. Mich. 2004).

50 *See* Thomas L. Greaney & Kathleen M. Boozang, *Mission, Margin, and Trust in the Nonprofit Health Care Enterprise*, 5 YALE J. HEALTH POL'Y L. & ETHICS 1 (2005); Kenneth E. Thorpe, Curtis S. Florence, & Eric E Seiber, *Hospital Conversions, Margins, and the Provision of Uncompensated Care*, 19 HEALTH AFF. 187 (2000); Jill A. Marsteller et al., *Nonprofit Conversion: Theory, Evidence, and State Policy Options*, 33 HEALTH SERVICES RES. 1495 (1998); Bradford H. Gray, *Conversion of HMOs and Hospitals: What's at Stake?*, 16 HEALTH AFF. 29 (1997).

51 *See* Evelyn Brody, *All Charities Are Property-Tax Exempt, But Some Charities Are More Exempt Than Others*, 44 NEW ENG. L. REV. 621 (2010).

Care, Inc.,[52] the Supreme Court of Utah reversed the tax commissioner's grant of a property tax exemption. In a lengthy opinion tracing the changes in the modern hospital and third-party payment, the chief justice concluded:

> [W]e believe that the defendants in this case confuse the element of gift to the community, which an entity must demonstrate in order to qualify as a charity under our Constitution, with the concept of community benefit, which any of countless private enterprises might provide. We have no quarrel with the assertion that [the hospitals] meet great and important needs of persons within their communities for medical care. Yet this meeting of a public need by a provision of services cannot be the sole distinguishing characteristic that leads to an automatic property tax exemption.[53]

More recently, in *Provena Covenant Med. Center. v. Department of Revenue*,[54] the Supreme Court of Illinois affirmed an appellate court decision that a not-for-profit Catholic hospital was not entitled to a state property tax exemption. The corporate charter of the parent health system stated that its purpose was to coordinate the activities of Provena's health system "as they pursue their religious, charitable, educational and scientific purposes" and "to offer at all times high quality and cost effective healthcare and human services to the consuming public."

The court found that Provena Covenant had not met the requirements for charities under Illinois case law. Specifically, its funds were not derived mainly from private and public charity and held in trust but were generated, overwhelmingly, by providing medical services for a fee. The court also faulted the hospital's provision of charity care.

Federal Tax Law. Not-for-profit hospitals have always been eligible for federal tax exemption under Internal Revenue Code § 501(c)(3).[55] In the 1960s, hospitals moved away from primary reliance on charitable gifts and income to support operations with the growth of third-party payment from private health insurance and the Medicare and Medicaid programs.[56] In 1969, the Internal Revenue Service (IRA) issued a ruling stating that the provision of free care was not required for tax-exempt status under federal tax law and that hospitals could meet their tax obligations with other community benefits.[57] The IRS noted:

> In the general law of charity, the promotion of health is considered to be a charitable purpose. A nonprofit organization whose purpose and activity are providing hospital care is promoting health and may, therefore, qualify as organized and operated in furtherance of a charitable purpose. If it meets the other requirements of section 501(c)(3) of the Code, it will qualify for exemption from Federal income tax under section 501(a).[58]

[52] 709 P.2d 265 (Utah 1985). [53] *Id.* at 276.

[54] 236 Ill.2d 368 925 N.E.2d 1131 (Ill. 2010), *aff'g*, 384 Ill. App.3d 734, 894 N.E.2d 452 (2009).

[55] IRC § 501(c)(3). *See* Internal Revenue Service, *Exemption Requirements—501(c)(3) Organizations* (Mar. 2014), http://www.irs.gov/Charities-&-Non-Profits/Charitable-Organizations/Exemption-Requirements-Section-501(c)(3)-Organizations.

[56] Social Security Amendments of 1965, Pub. L. No. 89-97, §§ 101–111, 121–122, 79 Stat. 291–360 (codified as amended at 42 U.S.C. §§ 1395 & 1396; S. Rep. No. 89-404, (1965), reprinted in 1965 U.S. Code Cong. & Admin. News 1943, 1965.

[57] Rev. Rul. 69-545, 1969-2 C.B. 117. [58] *Id.*

An earlier IRS revenue ruling had required some free care for tax exemption.[59] The 1969 ruling explicitly limited this obligation in the following statement: "Revenue Ruling 56-185 is hereby modified to remove therefrom the requirements relating to caring for patients without charge or at rates below cost."[60]

In recent years, there has been controversy about whether nonprofit hospitals are fulfilling their community benefit obligations in a meaningful way.[61] One major concern has been the rigor of the federal community benefit standard for tax exemption.[62] Most observers see value in tax exemption but suggest different methods for determining eligibility.[63]

In 2008, the U.S. Government Accountability Office (GAO), a congressional watchdog agency, reported considerable variation and substandard performance with respect to this obligation.[64] The IRS published a report on nonprofit hospitals that focused on their benefit to the community, which justifies their tax-exempt status notwithstanding the generous compensation of their top executives.[65]

Uncompensated care was the largest reported community benefit expenditure for nearly all hospitals, irrespective of their geographic or annual revenue grouping. After uncompensated care, the next largest categories of community benefit expenditures were medical education and training, research, and community programs.

The ACA tightened requirements for hospital community benefit programs.[66] Now, in addition to meeting the IRS's community benefit standard, tax-exempt hospitals must conduct a community needs assessment and develop a strategy to address identified needs. They must also clearly and widely communicate their financial assistance policies.[67] The ACA also prohibits hospitals from charging uninsured patients more than insurers paying discounted prices would be charged.[68]

[59] Revenue Ruling 56–185, C.B. 1956-1, 202. [60] Rev. Rul. 69–545, 1969-2 C.B. 117.

[61] *See* Gary J. Young et al., *Provision of Community Benefits by Tax-Exempt U.S. Hospitals*, 368 New Eng. J. Med. 1519 (2013).

[62] *See* John Carreyrou & Barbara Martinez, *Grassley Targets Nonprofit Hospitals on Charity Care*, Wall St. J., Dec. 18, 2008; The Tax Exempt Hospital Sector: Hearing before the House Committee on Ways and Means, U.S. House of Representatives, 109th Cong., 1st sess. (May 26, 2005). *See also* John D. Colombo, *The Failure of Community Benefit*, 15 Health Matrix 29 (2005); James J. Fishman, *Improving Charitable Accountability*, 62 Md. L. Rev. 218 (2003); David A. Hyman, *The Conundrum of Charitability: Reassessing Tax Exemption for Hospitals*, 16 Am. J.L. & Med. 327 (1990).

[63] David A. Hyman & William M. Sage, *Subsidizing Health Care Providers through the Tax Code: Status or Conduct?*, 25 Health Aff. W312 (2006); Jill R. Horwitz, *Nonprofit Ownership, Private Property, and Public Accountability*, 25 Health Aff. W308 (2006); Jill R. Horwitz, *Why We Need the Independent Sector: The Behavior, Law, and Ethics of Not-for-Profit Hospitals*, 50 UCLA L. Rev. 1345 (2003); Lars G. Gustafsson, *The Definition of "Charitable" for Federal Income Tax Purposes: Defrocking the Old and Suggesting Some New Fundamental Assumptions*, 33 Hous. L. Rev. 587(1996); Mark A. Hall & John D. Colombo, *The Charitable Status of Nonprofit Hospitals: Toward a Donative Theory of Tax Exemption*, 66 Wash. L. Rev. 307 (1991).

[64] U.S. Government Accountability Office, *NONPROFIT HOSPITALS: Variation in Standards and Guidance Limits Comparison of How Hospitals Meet Community Benefit Requirements* (Sept. 2008).

[65] Internal Revenue Service, *IRS Exempt Organizations (TE/GE) Hospital Compliance Project: Final Report* (2009).

[66] ACA § 9007(a) (codified as amended at 26 U.S.C. §501(r)). [67] *Id.* [68] *Id.*

(d) *Tort Liability*

In general, private hospitals may treat whom they want so long as they do not discriminate unlawfully. However, common law principles may support duties to treat people without funds. Most involve tort theories, including medical malpractice, and often arise in connection with delays and errors treating patients in emergencies.[69]

(e) *Contributions of Hospitals to Addressing Health Disparities*

There has been much debate about whether corporate form influences corporate behavior in the healthcare sector. The empirical evidence is mixed.[70]

There is no doubt that some nonprofit and public hospitals are serious about their mission to serve the poor. According to America's Essential Hospitals, a trade association for public and nonprofit hospitals with a specific mission to care for the uninsured and Medicaid patients, its members provided 17% of all uncompensated care nationally.[71] These hospitals also specifically address the dimensions of access in the Penchansky-Thomas model, including acceptability. These hospitals go to great lengths to make their institutions and operations more accessible and accommodating to people of lower socioeconomic status.

b. Federal Law Establishing Health Coverage Programs

The federal government has enacted numerous statutes, primarily as amendments to the Public Health Service Act (PHSA) or the Social Security Act (SSA), to address issues of access to physicians and hospitals through the provision of both health insurance and direct services. In 2010, the ACA expanded health coverage and improved healthcare delivery for uninsured and underserved groups.

i. *Public Health Insurance Programs under the Social Security Act*

The federal government and states using federal funding have provided health coverage for some of the most vulnerable in American society—including the aged, poor women and children, and the seriously disabled.

(a) *The Medicare Program*

The federal government funds Medicare, a social insurance program under Title XVIII of the Social Security Act that provides basic coverage to the aged, severely disabled, and people with certain catastrophic conditions such as end-stage renal disease.[72] The

[69] *See* Abdel-Samed v. Dailey, 294 Ga. 758, 755 S.E.2d 805 (2014); Thompson v. Sun City Community Hosp., Inc., 141 Ariz. 597 688 P.2d 605 16634-PR (1984) (en banc); Guerrero v. Copper Queen Hospital, 112 Ariz. 104, 537 P.2d 1329 (1975) (en banc); Wilmington General Hospital v. Manlove, 54 Del. 15, 174 A.2d 135 (1961).

[70] Mark Schlesinger & Bradford H. Gray, *How Nonprofits Matter in American Medicine, and What to Do About It*, 25 Health Aff. W287–W303 (2006).

[71] America's Essential Hospitals, *Essential Hospitals Vital Data—Results of America's Essential Hospitals' Annual Hospital Characteristics Survey, FY 2012* (July 2014).

[72] 42 U.S.C. § 1395.

Medicare program has been an important force in moving the elderly out of poverty and in reducing health disparities among the elderly.[73] Also, the Medicare program was an important force in mitigating segregation of African Americans in healthcare facilities after its enactment—a phenomenon that did much to reduce health disparities for African Americans.[74]

(b) The Medicaid and SCHIP Programs

The Medicaid program, which the federal government and the states jointly finance and administer, is the largest health insurer in the United States, covering an estimated 70 million children and adults—more than one-fifth of the population.[75] Historically, Medicaid covered only categories of poor that seemed deserving of public support, such as children, pregnant mothers, and the aged and disabled. Finally, State Childrens Health Insurance Program (SCHIP) provides supplemental financial assistance to states through a federally funded block grant, enabling them to cover all children up to 200% of the federal poverty level.[76]

The Medicaid and SCHIP programs are important programs for addressing health disparities. By definition, Medicaid and SCHIP recipients have lower socioeconomic status. Of interest, half of all Medicare beneficiaries had annual incomes below $22,500 in 2012.[77] Median income for black and Hispanic Medicare beneficiaries was $15,250 and $13,800, respectively, compared to $24,800 for white beneficiaries.

Title II of the ACA contains provisions to cover many more lower income, uninsured people through the Medicaid program.[78] Under the new law, beginning in 2014, Medicaid will cover nonelderly individuals with incomes up to 138% of the federal poverty line—about $29,000 for a family of four.[79] Had all states agreed to the ACA's Medicaid expansion, there would have been about 8.7 million adults and 5.2 million children newly eligible for Medicaid.[80]

(c) Insurance Market Reform

Title I of the ACA establishes mandates to purchase health insurance for individuals and businesses. Title I also includes measures to expand health coverage through improved regulation of private insurers and the establishment of health insurance marketplaces in which consumers and employers can purchase adequate and affordable health insurance.[81]

[73] *See* June Eichner & Bruce C. Vladeck, *Medicare as a Catalyst for Reducing Health Disparities*, 24 Health Aff. 365–375 (2005).

[74] *See* Theodore R. Marmor, The Politics of Medicare (1970).

[75] Social Security Amendments of 1965, tit. II (codified as amended at 42 U.S.C. § 1396). *See* Johnathan Engel, Poor People's Medicine: Medicaid and American Charity Care 1965 (2006).

[76] 42 U.S.C. § 1397aa.

[77] Gretchen Jacobson et al., *Wide Disparities in the Income and Assets of People on Medicare by Race and Ethnicity: Now and in the Future* (Kaiser Family Foundation, Sept. 20, 2013).

[78] ACA §§ 2001-2006 (codified at scattered sections of 42 U.S.C. § 1396).

[79] Kaiser Family Foundation, *Medicaid Expansion under the Affordable Care Act*, 309 JAMA 1219 (2013).

[80] Kaiser Family Foundation, *Number of Uninsured Eligible for Medicaid under the ACA* (May 2014).

[81] ACA §§ 1001–1563.

Regulatory reforms include the abolition of lifetime and annual limits, mandatory coverage of select preventive services, extension of dependent coverage to age twenty-six, and prohibition of rescissions, among a variety of other provisions to improve health coverage. Also included in Title I are tax subsidies to make health insurance more affordable for individuals and small businesses.

(d) Impact of the ACA on Health Disparities

The ACA coverage expansions should improve health and reduce health disparities.[82] One study suggests that the health insurance benefits in Titles I and II of the ACA have raised the average income of the poorest 5% of the population by more than 6%.[83] The ACA also contains requirements to account for health disparities in establishing quality measures, conducting research, and implementing primary care and public health initiatives and other measures under the ACA.[84]

The bipartisan Congressional Budget Office had estimated that by 2019, 16 million more adults and children would enroll in Medicaid because of the ACA.[85] Should that occur, the Medicaid program expansion would provide greater access to health insurance than the reforms under Title I.

However, the Supreme Court's decision in *National Federation of Independent Business v. Sebelius* gave the states broad latitude to decline the ACA's Medicaid expansion.[86] As a result, many states will not proceed with the expansion, at least not in the near future.[87] Nearly two-thirds of the people who were originally expected to be covered by the Medicaid expansion live in the states that are not planning to expand Medicaid.[88] Texas, Florida, and Georgia contain over half of the uninsured in the states not going forward with the expansion.

Nevertheless, by the end of April 2014, an estimated 8 million people had gained coverage or enrolled in a new healthcare plan under the ACA.[89] Another 5 million people had purchased health insurance directly from insurers. A substantial number of individuals received subsidies to defray some of the cost of health insurance premiums.[90] As of April 2014, 6 million people have obtained coverage through Medicaid or SCHIP.[91]

[82] *See* Benjamin D. Sommers, Katherine B. Baicker, & Arnold M. Epstein, *Mortality and Access to Care among Adults after State Medicaid Expansions*, 367 NEW ENG. J. MED. 1025 (2012).

[83] HENRY J. AARON & GARY BURTLESS, POTENTIAL EFFECTS OF THE AFFORDABLE CARE ACT ON INCOME INEQUALITY (Brookings Institution, Jan. 2014).

[84] *See* ACA § 2010, § 3013, §3201, §3501, §4003, § 4004, § 4201, § 5307, § 5405 & § 6301 & Title 7.

[85] Letter from Douglas W. Elmendorf, Director, Congressional Budget Office, to Nancy Pelosi, Speaker, U.S. House of Representatives (Mar. 20, 2010).

[86] 132 S. Ct. 2566 (2012).

[87] Benjamin D. Sommers & Arnold M. Epstein, *U.S. Governors and the Medicaid Expansion — No Quick Resolution in Sight*, 368 NEW ENG. J. MED. 496 (2013).

[88] JOHN HOLAHAN, MATTHEW BUETTGENS, & STAN DORN, THE COST OF NOT EXPANDING MEDICAID (Kaiser Family Foundation, Commission on Medicaid and the Uninsured, July 2013).

[89] David Blumenthal & Sara R. Collins, *Health Care Coverage under the Affordable Care Act—A Progress Report*, 37 NEW ENG. J. MED. 275 (2014).

[90] AMY BURKE, ARPIT MISRA, & STEVEN SHEINGOLD, *Premium Affordability, Competition, and Choice in the Health Insurance Marketplace*, 2014 (DHHS, ASPE ISSUE BRIEF, June 18, 2014).

[91] Blumenthal & Collins, *Health Care Coverage under the Affordable Care Act—A Progress Report*.

ii. The Public Health Service Act

The PHSA is an important federal law addressing access to hospitals and physicians and social determinants of health.[92] The PHSA authorizes federal grants and other funding to states for public health disease prevention and control activities,[93] as well as direct service programs for medically underserved areas and populations.

The Health Resources and Services Administration (HRSA) oversees the federal government's work with states to enhance access to healthcare services for vulnerable groups. The agency's mission is:

> improving access to health care by strengthening the health care workforce, building healthy communities and achieving health equity. HRSA's programs provide health care to people who are geographically isolated, economically or medically vulnerable.[94]

Through HRSA, the federal government also has several programs that provide direct services to specified groups through block grants to states and other means.[95]

(a) Designations of Health Professional Shortage Areas

To target funding for community health centers and other programs, HRSA designates medical underserved areas and populations under the PHSA.[96] HRSA defines Health Professional Shortage Areas (HPSAs) as areas where the secretary has determined insufficient health professionals are available. The three types of health HPSAs are Primary Care HPSAs, Dental HPSAs and Mental HPSAs. The criteria for designation are set by the secretary but must include the ratio of health professionals to the relevant population group, other indicators of need, and the percentage of physicians serving the area or population.

(b) Community Health Centers and Primary Care

A crucial federal program provides direct services to the poor through community health centers.[97] Community health centers, which are also funded by states and private health systems, are programmatically designed to care for the uninsured and Medicaid and SCHIP recipients.[98]

In 2013, nearly 1,300 community health centers operated over 9,200 service delivery sites that provided care to more than 21.7 million patients in every state and territory.[99] Of these patients, 62% were members of ethnic and minority groups and 35% had no health

[92] Pub. L. No. 78-410, 58 Stat. 682, Ch. 373 (codified as amended at 42 U.S.C. ch. 6A). *See Public Health Service Act, 1944*, 59 PUBLIC HEALTH REPORTS 468 (1944).

[93] 42 U.S.C. Ch. 6A, Subch. II, Pt. G.

[94] HHS, HRSA, *About HRSA* (2014), http://www.hrsa.gov/about/index.html.

[95] 42 U.S.C. §§ 300w to 300y-11.

[96] 42 U.S.C. § 254e. *See* HHS, HRSA, *Medically Underserved Areas/Populations, Guidelines for MUA and MUP Designation* (2014).

[97] 42 U.S.C. § 254b.

[98] *See* BONNIE LEFKOWITZ, COMMUNITY HEALTH CENTERS: A MOVEMENT AND THE PEOPLE WHO MADE IT HAPPEN (2007).

[99] HHS, HRSA, *Affordable Care Act and Health Centers* (No Date), http://bphc.hrsa.gov/about/healthcenterfactsheet.pdf.

insurance. One in every fifteen people living in the United States relies on a HRSA-funded clinic for primary care.

The ACA established the Community Health Center Fund that provides $11 billion to improve community health centers and the primary healthcare services they provide. According to HRSA, health centers are poised to play an essential role in ACA implementation in the following manner:

> In particular, health centers emphasize coordinated primary and preventive services or a "medical home" that promotes reductions in health disparities for low-income individuals, racial and ethnic minorities, rural communities and other underserved populations. Health centers place emphasis on the coordination and comprehensiveness of care, the ability to manage patients with multiple health care needs, and the use of key quality improvement practices, including health information technology. The health center model also overcomes geographic, cultural, linguistic and other barriers through a team-based approach to care that includes physicians, nurse practitioners, physician assistants, nurses, dental providers, midwives, behavioral health care providers, social workers, health educators, and many others.[100]

(c) The National Health Service Corps

Established in 1972, the National Health Service Corps (NHSC) offers financial and other support to primary care providers and sites in underserved communities.[101] Currently, 9,200 NHSC members provide culturally competent care to more than 9.7 million people at 4,900 NHSC-approved healthcare sites in urban, rural, and frontier areas.[102] In addition to Corps providers currently providing care, nearly 1,100 additional members are in school or residency.

The NHSC offers financial and other support to Corps members, including scholarships and loan repayment to primary care providers in NHSC-eligible disciplines. NHSC providers, in turn, commit to serving for at least two years at an NHSC-approved site located in a HPSA. Many choose to continue serving at their sites beyond the initial NHSC service commitment.

(d) Other PHSA Programs to Promote Primary Care

HRSA administers a large number of grant programs that address the needs of underserved areas and specific underserved populations.[103] HRSA funds healthcare providers who provide services to a high percentage of medically underserved populations or other special populations, including nurse-managed health clinics. Addressing deficiencies in rural areas, HRSA supports rural healthcare services outreach, rural health network development, and small healthcare provider quality improvement programs, as well as a rural emergency medical service training and equipment assistance program. HRSA has also invested in the development of telemedicine.

HRSA funds programs to provide healthcare services to specific populations, such as for pregnant women, Pacific Islanders, and Indians and other people with diabetes. Finally,

[100] *Id.* [101] 42 U.S.C. § 254b-2.

[102] HHS, NHSC, *About the NHSC* (No Date), http://nhsc.hrsa.gov/corpsexperience/aboutus/index.html.

[103] 42 U.S.C. §§ 254b & 254c.

HRSA funds centers for strategies on facilitating utilization of preventive health services among various populations.

(e) Impact of PHSA Programs on Health Disparities

PHSA programs are directly targeted to reducing health disparities. Community health centers purposefully address all five dimensions of access to healthcare identified by Penchansky and Thomas as discussed above.[104] There is considerable evidence that community health centers and specific HHS efforts to alleviate disparities have been relatively successful.[105] HHS is also committed to reducing racial and ethnic health disparities in all its programs.[106]

iii. The Veterans Health Administration

Another important source of direct services for particular populations is the Veterans Health Administration.[107] After World War II, the federal government appreciated the need to take care of the veterans who were returning from war and enacted the GI Bill to meet their needs.[108]

In 1946, Congress authorized the establishment of a Department of Medicine and Surgery, now the Veterans Health Administration (VHA), within the Department of Veterans Affairs (VA).[109] Its primary purpose was to ensure an adequate and complete medical service for veterans. The federal government invested heavily in hospitals and other healthcare facilities for the VA. The VA also co-located many of its hospitals in academic medical centers and invested heavily in biomedical and later health services research.[110] Over time, the VA developed a comprehensive, integrated health system for veterans. Today, the Veterans Health Administration is America's largest integrated healthcare system, with over 1,700 sites of care, serving 8.76 million veterans annually.[111]

Because of the way in which the VA prioritizes the veterans it serves, giving preference to lower income veterans with service-connected disabilities, its patient population is generally

[104] National Association of Community Health Center, *Fact Sheet: Health Centers' Role in Reducing Racial and Ethnic Health Disparities* (May 2008), http://www.nachc.com/client//DisparitiesFS.pdf.

[105] David A. Haggstrom, Steven B. Clauser, & Stephen H. Taplin, *The Health Disparities Cancer Collaborative: A Case Study of Practice Registry Measurement in a Quality Improvement Collaborative*, 5 Implementation Science 42 (2010); LeRoy S. Hicks et al., *Impact of Health Disparities Collaboratives on Racial/Ethnic and Insurance Disparities in US Community Health Centers*, 170 Archives of Internal Med. 279 (2010); LeRoi S. Hicks, *The Quality of Chronic Disease Care in U.S. Community Health Centers*, 25 Health Aff. 1712 (2006).

[106] HHS, *HHS Action Plan to Reduce Racial and Ethnic Health Disparities: A Nation Free of Disparities in Health and Health Care* (No Date), http://minorityhealth.hhs.gov/npa/files/Plans/HHS/HHS_Plan_complete.pdf.

[107] Veterans Administration, Veterans Health Administration, Health Care Benefits Overview (2012).

[108] Pub. L. No. 78-346, Servicemen's Readjustment Act of 1944, 58 Stat. 284. *See* Glenn Altschuler & Stuart Blumin, The GI Bill: The New Deal for Veterans (2009).

[109] Pub. L. No. 79-293, § 3, 59 stat. 675 (codified as amended at 38 U.S.C., chs. 73 & 74).

[110] VA, Office of Academic Affiliations, *Still Going Strong—The History of VA Academic Affiliations, Transcript* (2014), *available at* http://www.va.gov/OAA/videos/transcript_affiliation_history.asp.

[111] *Id.*

of lower socioeconomic status with large numbers of racial and ethnic minorities.[112] The VA has given great attention to research and analysis of health disparities.[113] The VA has also taken measures to reduce health disparities throughout the VA system, such as establishing primary care centers for homeless veterans.[114]

c. Federal and State Laws that Directly Affect Access to Physicians and Hospitals

There are state and federal statutes that affect access to physicians and hospitals at the point of delivery of care. These include antidiscrimination statutes that prohibit discrimination on the basis of status or disability. They also include statutes that require providers to treat a patient in an emergent condition. Other federal law addresses access for undocumented immigrants.

i. Federal and State Antidiscrimination Laws and Emergency Treatment Statutes that Address Access to Physicians and Hospitals

The two categories of state and federal statutes directly address access to physicians and hospitals and operate in comparable manners—antidiscrimination statutes and statutes requiring emergency treatment.

(a) State and Federal Antidiscrimination Laws

Federal civil rights laws prohibit discrimination in public accommodations and access to government programs on the basis of race, religion, gender, and national origin.[115] States also have civil rights laws that prohibit discrimination on the basis of disability, race, creed, gender, and national origin.[116]

The Hospital Survey and Construction Act of 1946 (Hill-Burton Act), which provided funding for hospital construction, required funded hospitals to provide services to all persons residing in the area, regardless of ability to pay.[117] Under this community service obligation, Hill-Burton hospitals had to maintain emergency rooms, provide emergency services without regard to patients' ability to pay, and accept Medicare and Medicaid patients. Hill-Burton obligations have almost all expired, but the act established important access norms for the construction and operation of modern hospitals.

[112] *See* David I. Auerbach, William B. Weeks, & Ian Brantley, Health Care Spending and Efficiency in the U.S. Department of Veterans Affairs 4–5 (2013).

[113] Spotlight: Health Equity and Health Disparity Research (Jan. 2013), http://www.hsrd.research.va.gov/news/feature/health_equity.cfm.

[114] VA, Health Services Research & Development, *Racial and Ethnic Disparities in the VA Healthcare System: A Systematic Review* (June 2007).

[115] *See* 42 U.S.C. § 2000a(a) (pertaining to federal civil rights authorities).

[116] *Civil Rights*, American Jurisdiction, 2d, at §§ 223–231 (2014).

[117] Hospital Survey and Construction Act, Pub. L. No. 79-725, 60 Stat. 1040 (1946) (codified as amended at 42 U.S.C. § 291); 42 C.F.R. § 124, subpt. G. *See* HHS, HRSA, *Hill-Burton Free and Reduced-Cost Health Care* (No Date)), http://www.hrsa.gov/gethealthcare/affordable/hillburton/.

Several federal laws specifically address discrimination on the basis of physical disability and, thereby, establish an important source of obligations and rights regarding access to healthcare. Section 504 of the Rehabilitation Act prohibits discrimination in employment against individuals with handicaps by entities that contract with or receive funds from the federal government.[118] The Americans with Disabilities Act even more broadly prohibits discrimination against the disabled in employment, public services, accommodations, and telecommunications.[119]

The enforcement of antidiscrimination laws, especially those prohibiting discrimination against people with disabilities, has been problematic.[120] Hospitals are not all alike, and some lack the capacity to care for patients with certain serious medical conditions. Technically these decisions may be discrimination, but they also reflect an assessment of whether the institution can meet the patient's needs.

Discrimination through physical inaccessibility is another significant concern in healthcare institutions. Hospitals and clinics have not always accommodated the needs of disabled people in the delivery of care.[121] For example, they have not always had physical spaces and medical equipment designed specifically for paralyzed and other disabled people who cannot easily use conventional facilities.

(b) State and Federal Emergency Treatment Laws

Most states have statutes that require hospitals to treat people in emergencies.[122] Many of these laws were enacted to address the problem of patient "dumping" in the mid-1980s when financially strained hospitals appeared to be turning away the uninsured.[123] In 1986, Congress enacted the Emergency Medical Treatment and Labor Act (EMTALA), which imposes a duty on hospitals that receive federal funding to provide certain emergency services to people who are unable to pay.[124]

Under EMTALA, when a patient presents at the emergency room, a hospital must provide a medical screening exam. If a hospital determines that the individual has an emergency medical condition, the hospital must provide further medical examination and treatment to stabilize the medical condition. EMTALA defines stabilizing care as that which ensures that no material deterioration of the condition is likely to result from or occur during the transfer of an individual from a facility. If a hospital lacks the capability to stabilize a patient or if a patient requests, the hospital may transfer a patient to another appropriate facility.

[118] Rehabilitation Act of 1973, Pub. L. No. 93-112, § 504, 87 Stat. 355, 394 (codified at 29 U.S.C. § 794).

[119] Americans with Disabilities Act of 1990, Pub. L. No. 101-336, 104 Stat. 327 (codified at 42 U.S.C. § 12101).

[120] *See* Elizabeth Pendo, *Shifting the Conversation: Disability, Disparities and Health Care Reform*, 6 FLA. INT'L U. L. REV. 400 (2011).

[121] Elizabeth Pendo, *Reducing Disparities through Health Care Reform: Disability and Accessible Medical Equipment*, 4 UTAH L. REV. 1057 (2010); Elizabeth Pendo, *Disability, Doctors and Dollars: Distinguishing the Three Faces of Reasonable Accommodation*, 35 UC DAVIS L. REV. 1175 (2002).

[122] Maria O'Brien Hylton, *The Economics and Politics of Emergency Health Care for the Poor: The Patient Dumping Dilemma*, BYU L. REV. 1023 (1992) (contains a compendium of state laws).

[123] *See* Karen H. Rothenberg, *Who Cares: The Evolution of the Legal Duty to Provide Emergency Care*, 26 HOUS. L. REV. 21 (1989).

[124] Emergency Medical Treatment and Active Labor Act of 1986 (EMTALA), Pub. L. No. 99-272, 100 Stat. 82 (codified as amended at 42 U.S.C. § 1395dd); 42 C.F.R 489.24.

Failure to comply with EMTALA potentially subjects a hospital to loss of its provider agreement with the Medicare program. More commonly, civil monetary penalties may be imposed on hospitals and physicians. HHS also may exclude physicians from the Medicare program for repeated or flagrant violations of EMTALA.

The ACA continues EMTALA's mandate to provide emergency care. The ACA provides: "Nothing in this Act shall be construed to relieve any health care provider from providing emergency services as required by State or Federal law, including section 1867 of the Social Security Act (popularly known as 'EMTALA')."[125]

It is difficult to assess the impact of EMTALA on access to physicians and hospitals because of lack of data on emergency room encounters and imprecise enforcement data.[126] However, the obligation of every Medicare participating hospital with an emergency room to screen patients regardless of ability to pay should detect emergent conditions in need of treatment among thousands of people who otherwise might not be served.

ii. Federal Immigration Law Addressing Access to Physicians and Hospitals

In 2012, 13% of the population of the United States was foreign born, of which less than half being U.S. citizens.[127] Access to physicians and hospitals is a serious problem for immigrants,[128] especially undocumented immigrants.[129] Immigrants tend to work in areas with high uninsurance rates. Linguistic and cultural barriers as well as low income also limit access. Of note, over half of the approximately $5 billion per year in uncompensated emergency healthcare is generated by undocumented immigrants.[130]

Federal law poses a significant barrier for access to health insurance for immigrants. In 1996, Congress enacted the Personal Responsibility and Work Opportunity Reconciliation Act (PRWORA), which clarified the eligibility rules for federal programs for noncitizens.[131] PRWORA defined "qualified aliens" for public programs as legal permanent residents, asylees, and refugees, as well as other narrowly defined groups.[132] Only "qualified aliens," excluding undocumented immigrants, are eligible for "federal public benefits," which include "[a]ny retirement, welfare, health, disability, public or assisted housing, postsecondary education, food assistance, unemployment benefit" and "any other similar benefit for which payments or assistance are provided to an individual, household, or family eligibility unit."[133]

[125] ACA § 1304(d).

[126] GAO, *EMERGENCY CARE, EMTALA: Implementation and Enforcement Issues* (June 2001).

[127] Anna Brown & Eileen Patten, *Statistical Portrait of the Foreign-Born Population in the United States, 2012* (Pew Research Hispanic Trends Project, Apr. 2014), http://www.pewhispanic.org/2014/04/29/statistical-portrait-of-the-foreign-born-population-in-the-united-states-2012/.

[128] *See* Wendy E. Parmet, *Holes in the Safety Net—Legal Immigrants' Access to Health Insurance*, 369 NEW ENG. J. MED. 596 (2013).

[129] Benjamin D. Sommers, *Stuck between Health and Immigration Reform—Care for Undocumented Immigrants*, 369 NEW ENG. J. MED. 593 (2013).

[130] Steven P. Wallace et al., *Undocumented Immigrants and Health Care Reform: Final Report to the Commonwealth Fund* (UCLA Center for Health Policy Research, Aug. 31, 2012).

[131] *See* Pub. L. No. 104-193, 110 Stat. 2105 (codified as amended in scattered sections of 42 U.S.C.).

[132] PRWORA § 431 (codified as amended at 8 U.S.C. §§ 1611–14 (2010)).

[133] PRWORA § 401 (codified as amended at 8 U.S.C. § 1611).

On the other hand, the Medicare Modernization Act of 2003 established an emergency services benefit for undocumented immigrants.[134] The Children's Health Insurance Program Reauthorization Act of 2009 also authorizes states, at their option, to provide health coverage with federal funding to lawfully residing immigrant children and pregnant women through the Medicaid and SCHIP progras.[135]

More recently, there have been reports of hospitals transferring uninsured immigrants, even those legally in the United States, to their country of origin.[136] Neither EMTALA nor state laws seem to address this situation.

The ACA fails to improve access for undocumented immigrants. In addition to the prohibitions in the PRWORA discussed above, the ACA prohibits undocumented immigrants from purchasing health insurance with their own money through the state and federal market places.[137] The ACA also specifically provides that undocumented immigrants are ineligible for nonemergency Medicaid services and other public programs, including EMTALA.[138]

IV Obligations under International Law

Although it is not widely understood or appreciated, the United States is obligated under some international human rights instruments that recognize a right to health. Compared to international norms, the United States falls short in significant ways when it comes to access to physicians and hospitals for its population.

a. United Nations Human Rights Instruments

In 1948, the United States signed two instruments of the United Nations that established an international human right to health. The first was the constitution of the World Health Organization (WHO). The second is the Universal Declaration of Human Rights (UDHR). Because neither of these instruments are treaties requiring ratification by Congress, the United States committed itself to the statements therein by signing.

The WHO Constitution defines "health" broadly as "a state of complete physical, mental and social well-being and not merely the absence of disease or infirmity."[139] The WHO Constitution then states that "[t]he enjoyment of the highest attainable standard of health is one of the fundamental rights of every human being without distinction of race, religion, political belief, economic or social condition."[140]

[134] Medicare Prescription Drug, Modernization and Improvement Act, Pub. L. No. 108-173 § 1011, 17 Stat. 2066 (codified as amended 42 U.S.C. § 1395dd).

[135] Children's Health Insurance Program Reauthorization Act of 2009, Pub. L. No. 111-3 § 214, 123 Stat. 8 (2009) (codified as 42 U.S.C. § 1396b(v)).

[136] *See* Jennifer M. Smith, *Screen, Stabilize, and Ship: EMTALA, U.S. Hospitals, and Undocumented Immigrants (International Patient Dumping)*, 10 Hous. J. Health L. & Pol'y 309 (2010).

[137] ACA § 1312(f)(3). [138] ACA § 2201.

[139] Constitution of the World Health Organization, pmbl., July 22, 1946, 62 Stat. 6349, 14 U.N.T.S. 185, *reprinted in* 15 Department of State Bulletin 211 (Aug. 4, 1946).

[140] *Id.*

The Universal Declaration of Human Rights includes a right to health and healthcare as a recognized international human right.[141] As a declaration rather than a treaty, the United States is committed just by signing the declaration. Article 25 of the UDHR states:

> Everyone has the right to a standard of living adequate for the health and well-being of himself and of his family, including . . . medical care . . . and the right to security in the event of . . . sickness [and/or] disability. . . .[142]

Subsequently, the U.N. adopted two covenants to implement the Universal Declaration—the International Covenant on Civil and Political Rights (ICCPR)[143] and the International Covenant on Economic, Social and Cultural Rights (ICESCR).[144] The ICCPR prohibits state discrimination regarding societal benefits and recognizes that all people have a right to life. Because the United States has signed the Universal Declaration and the WHO Constitution and has ratified the ICCPR, the United States and its states and localities are bound to implement and enforce these instruments under international law.

b. Content of the International Human Right to Health

According to Article 12 of the ICESCR, the right to health includes "the enjoyment of the highest attainable standard of physical and mental health."[145] Article 12 then enumerates several steps to be taken for "full realization" of this right, one of which is highly relevant—"[t]he creation of conditions which would assure to all medical service and medical attention in the event of sickness."[146]

In 2000, the U.N. Committee on Economic, Social and Cultural Rights published General Comment 14 to the ICESCR that outlines the content of the international right to health under this covenant.[147] Because the United States has not ratified the ICESCR, it is not bound to it or to General Comment 14. Nevertheless, General Comment 14 sets forth a global consensus on state obligations to their populations regarding the provision of healthcare services and the promotion of health. General Comment 14 imposes three types or levels of obligations: the obligations to respect, protect, and fulfill the international human right to health.

i. The Obligation to Fulfill

Under General Comment 14, the "obligation to fulfill" requires states to "adopt appropriate legislative, administrative, budgetary, judicial, promotional and other measures

141 *See* Eleanor D. Kinney, *Recognition of the International Human Right to Health and Health Care in the United States*, 60 Rutgers L. Rev. 337 (2008); Kinney, *The International Human Right to Health*.

142 Universal Declaration of Human Rights art. 25, G.A. Res. 217 (III) A, U.N. Doc. A/RES/217 (III) (Dec. 10, 1948).

143 International Covenant on Civil and Political Rights (Mar. 23, 1976), G.A. Res. 2200 (XXI) A, U.N. Doc. A/RES/2200(XXI).

144 International Covenant on Economic, Social, and Cultural Rights art. 2 & art. 12 (Dec. 16, 1966), G.A. Res. 2200 (XXI) A, U.N. Doc. A/RES/2200(XXI).

145 *Id.* at art. 12(d). 146 *Id.*

147 U.N. Econ. & Soc. Council [ESOSOC], Comm. on Econ., Soc. & Cultural Rights, General Comment No. 14 (art. 12), U.N. Doc. E/C.12/2000/4 (Aug. 11, 2000).

towards the full realization of the right to health."[148] With respect to this obligation, the federal government and U.S. states have fallen short. Before the ACA, over 15% of the population of the United States lacked health insurance and many more had inadequate insurance. The ACA made a major contribution to the realization of the obligation to fulfill.[149]

ii. *The Obligation to Protect*

The obligation to protect under General Comment 14 requires states "to take measures that prevent third parties from interfering with article 12 guarantees."[150] This obligation implicates federal and state civil rights law. The record of the federal government and U.S. states on enforcement of antidiscrimination laws has been mixed, especially in view of past discrimination against AIDS victims.[151] Further, U.S. law actually institutionalizes discrimination against undocumented immigrants as discussed above.

iii. *The Obligation to Respect*

The obligation to respect, under General Comment 14, "requires States to refrain from interfering directly or indirectly with the enjoyment of the right to health."[152] In general, the federal government and U.S. states and localities have complied with the obligation to respect in the sense that law and policy have not specifically interfered with individuals accessing physicians and hospitals. The fact that some people have less access to physicians and hospitals largely reflects socioeconomic factors.

However, the PRWORA directly contradicts the obligation to respect. Indeed, it establishes barriers to access for undocumented immigrants. Healthcare providers may even be required to verify immigrant status before conferring benefits. In the Deficit Reduction Act of 2005, Congress required Medicaid providers to ascertain the immigrant status of beneficiaries before service.[153] This law is an affront to the international human right to health.

[148] *Id.*

[149] *See* Gwendolyn Roberts Majette, *Global Health Law Norms and the PPACA Framework to Eliminate Health Disparities*, 55 HOWARD L.J. 55 (2011–2012); Kinney, *Recognition of the International Human Right to Health and Health Care in the United States.*

[150] U.N., Comm. on Econ., Soc. & Cultural Rights, General Comment No. 14.

[151] *See* Mark A. Schuster et al., *Perceived Discrimination in Clinical Care in a Nationally Representative Sample of HIV-Infected Adults Receiving Health Care*, 20 J. GENERAL INTERNAL MED. 807 (2005); Sheryl Thorburn Bird, Laura M. Bogart, & Douglas L. Delahanty, *Health-Related Correlates of Perceived Discrimination in HIV Care*, 18 AIDS PATIENT CARE AND STDs 19 (2004). *See also* Michael L. Closen, *The Decade of Supreme Court Avoidance of Aids: Denial of Certiorari in HIV-AIDS Cases and Its Adverse Effects on Human Rights*, 61 ALB. L. REV. 897 (1998).

[152] U.N., Comm. on Econ., Soc. & Cultural Rights, General Comment No. 14.

[153] Pub. L. No. 109-171 § 6306, 116 Stat. 716 (codified as amended 42 U.S.C. §1396b).

c. Progress of Individual States towards Realization of the International Human Right to Health

In 2008, the Vermont Legislature enacted legislation, Act No. 128, that explicitly adopted human rights principles as the basis for a policy trajectory toward universal coverage.[154] In 2011, the legislature enacted Act No. 48 to establish a comprehensive, publicly financed universal health care system in Vermont by 2017 with the leadership of the newly-elected Democratic Governor.[155] Because of high costs and the need to greatly increase taxes to support the system, the same governor reluctantly ended the push to a single-payer system.[156]

Nevertheless, just recently, Colorado has a ballot initiative to adopt a single payer system in 2016.[157] The ballot initiative seeks to establish a constitutional right to health care in Colorado.[158]

V Conclusion

In sum, the American law addressing access to physicians and hospitals falls into three categories: (1) direct obligations of physicians and hospitals to provide free care to the indigent; (2) federal programs to provide health insurance or health services to vulnerable populations; and (3) laws that affect the delivery of care at the point of access based on the patient's physical characteristics and immigration status.

Historically, laws creating direct obligations of hospitals and physicians have not enabled hospitals and physicians to meet the needs of people who are unable to pay for healthcare or were of lower socioeconomic status. They have not done so even when augmented by state and federal statutes to provide emergency care or not to discriminate on the basis of status. The government has had to step in and provide health insurance programs for vulnerable

[154] An act relating to health care financing and universal access to health care in Vermont, 2010 Vt. Acts & Resolves, Act No. 128. Available at http://www.leg.state.vt.us/DOCS/2010/ACTS/ACT128. PDF. See Anja Rudiger, Reviving Progressive Activism: How a Human Rights Movement Won the Country's First Universal Health Care Law: A Case Study of Vermont's Healthcare Is a Human Right Campaign (National Economic and Social Rights Initiative, Aug. 19, 2011), http://www.nesri.org/sites/default/files/Case_study_8-19.pdf; Mariah McGill, Human Rights from the Grassroots Up: Vermont's Campaign for Universal Health Care, 14(1) Health and Human Rights (2012).

[155] An act relating to a universal and unified health system, 2011, Vt. Acts & Resolves, Act No. 48. Available at http://www.leg.state.vt.us/DOCS/2012/ACTS/ ACT048.PDF. See Abby Goodnough, A Doctor's Push for Single-Payer Health Care for All Finds Traction in Vermont, New York Times (May 21, 2011). See also Adventure in Democracy, Editorial, The Times Argus, May 5, 2011, http://www.nesri.org/sites/default/files/Adventure_in_democracy.pdf.

[156] Reid Wilson, Vermont Ends Push for Single-Payer Health Care, New York Times (Dec. 18, 2014).

[157] The Associated Press, Universal Health Care to Appear on Colorado Ballot in 2016, New York Times (Nov. 9, 2015).

[158] Electa Draper, Colorado Ballot Initiative Calls for $25B Single-Payer Health System, The Denver Post (Jun. 12, 2015).

groups or direct services under the PHSA. In the ACA, however, Congress has taken enormous if incomplete steps to expand coverage for underserved populations, as well as to address health disparities that compromise access.

In the final analysis, health insurance and direct service programs, including programmatic strategies targeted at reducing health disparities, can only do so much to improve healthcare if social determinants remain unaddressed. In the United States, much can be done to improve the economic circumstances of the underserved population. Large proportions of the population work full time but do not make a living wage. Certainly a higher minimum wage, enhanced educational opportunities, and more generous social services program would do much to improve access to physicians and hospitals.

In sum, it is important to realize that the United States is an outlier when it comes to compliance with the international norms for access established in the WHO Constitution and the UDHR. At the very least, these instruments represent an international consensus on normative principles regarding access to healthcare. That the United States falls so short of these norms is distressing.

CHAPTER 7

ACCESS TO HEALTH INSURANCE AND HEALTH BENEFITS

TIMOTHY STOLTZFUS JOST

HEALTHCARE products and services are very valuable.[1] Most obviously, they extend the duration of human life by eliminating or curing diseases and permitting recovery from injuries. Healthcare relieves pain and suffering and contributes to human productivity and well-being. Finally, healthcare meliorates the limiting effects of disabilities, even when it cannot cure them, making it possible for individuals with physical and mental limitations (including limitations due to advanced age) to lead more "normal" lives.

The value of healthcare is attested to by the amounts Americans are willing to spend on it. In 2012, the most recent year for which we have more or less complete data, Americans spent $2.8 billion on healthcare; $8,915 per person and 17.2% of our gross domestic product.[2] We spend more on healthcare than we do on food, housing, or transportation—more than we do on anything else.

Assuming, however, that we place a high value on healthcare, we must find a way to pay for it. Individuals pay for most goods and services in our society out of pocket, or, in the case of large-ticket items, by borrowing to pay for them. Until the second half of the twentieth century, Americans paid for most healthcare items and services out of pocket as well. Out-of-pocket expenditures still make up a substantial share of healthcare expenditures. Healthcare services are also often purchased on credit, either extended by providers of services or through commercial credit cards.

But there are serious limitations to the possibilities of paying for healthcare out of pocket. The distribution of healthcare costs is dramatically skewed. In 2010, 1% of healthcare consumers were responsible for 21.4% of healthcare costs, 5% for 49.9% of costs, and 10% for 65.6% of costs.[3] Healthcare can also be very costly, particularly hospital and nursing-home

[1] DAVID CUTLER, YOUR MONEY OR YOUR LIFE: STRONG MEDICINE FOR AMERICA'S HEALTH CARE SYSTEM (2005).

[2] Anne B. Martin et al., *National Health Spending in 2012: Rate of Spending Growth Remained Low for the Fourth Consecutive Year*, 33 HEALTH AFF. 67, 68 (2014).

[3] Steven B. Cohen & Namrata Uberoi, *Differentials in the Concentration in the Level of Health Expenditures Across Population Subgroups in the U.S., 2010* (2013), *available at* http://meps.ahrq.gov/mepsweb/data_files/publications/st421/stat421.shtml.

care and pharmaceuticals. The costs of treatment for major diseases or traumatic injuries can easily run into six, even seven, figures. Few people can afford these costs out of pocket, and although some individuals may be able to purchase services on credit, individuals with serious health problems are poor credit risks.

Moreover, income distribution in the United States is also dramatically skewed. Americans in the bottom quintile of the American income distribution, who earned less than $20,500 in 2012, can hardly afford healthcare costs that average $8,915 per person.[4] Many Americans simply cannot afford to pay for any but the most basic healthcare services out of pocket. If healthcare is going to be available to those who need it most, some means must be found to move resources both to those who need the highest cost medical items and services and to those who cannot afford healthcare.

There are a number of approaches available to accomplish this. One is charity. The earliest hospitals were run by religious orders or denominations, or were established through gifts from wealthy benefactors. Charity still plays a role in the provision of healthcare, such as provision through free clinics. The charitable origins of healthcare delivery also survive in the presence of nonprofit, tax-exempt, providers of services. But the need for healthcare services long ago outstripped the resources conceivably available through charitable donations.

The institution most capable of moving resources on a large scale from the healthy to the sick, from the wealthy to the poor, is the government. In virtually all wealthy countries—and even in many poor countries—the government is the primary payer for healthcare items and services. In fact, even in the United States, the government bears almost half the cost of healthcare. In some countries, the government provides healthcare directly, through government-owned hospitals and clinics. In many more countries, public insurance programs pay for healthcare provided by private or quasi-public providers.

Healthcare can also be funded, however, by private insurance. Insurance, by definition, shifts costs from individuals who suffer loss to others who could potentially suffer loss, but in fact do not. Absent regulation, however, private insurance is likely to be risk underwritten, making it very expensive for individuals who are already suffering from costly medical problems, or those who are highly likely to incur high medical costs, such as the elderly or disabled. Moreover, individual private insurance is likely to be unaffordable to lower-income individuals absent some kind of subsidy.

One approach to providing private insurance that has proven quite serviceable, however, is employer-sponsored insurance (ESI). ESI has been the primary means of insuring healthcare in the United States since the middle of the twentieth century. Employers, and in particular large employers, can offer coverage that covers unhealthy as well as healthy and low-wage as well as high-income employees. Employees make up diverse risk pools that permit widespread, affordable coverage. Tax subsidies in the United States have made ESI very attractive to both employers and employees.

ESI cannot cover everyone, however. Many of those most likely to incur high medical costs—the elderly and disabled in particular—are unlikely to be employed. Some of these individuals may have retiree coverage, but it has become increasingly uncommon in the

[4] Carmen DeNavas-Walt et al., U.S. Census Bureau, U.S. Department of Commerce, *Income, Poverty, and Health Insurance Coverage in the United States: 2012*, 9 (2013), *available at* https://www.census.gov/prod/2013pubs/p60-245.pdf.

United States. Moreover, many of the poorest Americans do not participate in the workforce, work in low-wage jobs that do not offer health insurance, work part-time or seasonably and are not eligible for ESI, or cannot afford the employee's share of the ESI premium. Some other approach must be found if they are to have coverage.

Each of these five approaches to paying for healthcare—out-of-pocket, charity, direct government provision, public insurance, and private insurance (including ESI)—can be found in the United States. This article discusses each of these forms of payment for healthcare, analyzing their history, advantages, disadvantages, and current status in the United States. It concludes by considering the 2010 Affordable Care Act and how it incorporates each of these approaches to paying for healthcare coverage.

I Out-of-Pocket Payment

As noted earlier, most Americans pay for most of the goods and services they consume out of pocket, or on credit, which is effectively the same if the debt is eventually paid in full. Many uninsured Americans routinely pay for services entirely out of pocket or on credit, although they sometimes purchase healthcare at a discounted rate.[5] Both publicly and privately insured Americans, however, also pay for much of the care they consume out of pocket through cost-sharing.

Cost-sharing takes a number of forms. First, many healthcare consumers must cover a deductible before their insurance begins to pay for services. After individuals satisfy a deductible requirement, they may continue to be obligated to pay a percentage of the additional cost of care through a coinsurance. Alternatively, individuals may owe a flat-dollar payment for a particular service or item—a copayment. If a healthcare provider is not contractually obligated to an insurer to provide services for the amount the insurer is willing to pay, the provider may balance bill the insured in some cases, that is, charge the insured the amount of the provider's bill that exceeds the amount the insurer is willing to pay. Under federal law, however, health insurance coverage is subject to an out-of-pocket limit, beyond which the insurer must absorb all covered costs for services provided in network.[6] Of course, items and services not covered by the insurer, like over-the-counter drugs or alternative medicine, are the responsibility of the insured.

While out-of-pocket costs may in fact be paid out of pocket, many Americans pay for them through special healthcare accounts. Account-based programs allow individuals to claim tax subsidies for some of their out-of-pocket costs and, in some instances, to obtain help from their employers in covering these costs. The federal tax laws have long allowed employees to authorize their employers to direct part of their pay—before it is subject to federal taxes—to flexible spending accounts, which can be used to cover out-of-pocket expenses.[7] More recently Congress and the Internal Revenue Service (IRS) have created approaches—health reimbursement accounts[8] and health savings accounts—that allow employers to provide

[5] I.R.C. § 501(r)(4) requires tax-exempt hospitals to offer free or discounted care to needy patients. I.R.C. § 501(r)(4) (2014).

[6] 42 U.S.C. § 18022(c)(1) (2014).

[7] I.R.C. § 125 (2014).

[8] I.R.S. Notice 2002-45, 2002-02 CB 93; Rev. Rul. 2002-41, 2002-2 C.B. 75.

employees directly with pretax funds with which to cover out-of-pocket expenses if various conditions are met.[9]

Before the middle of the twentieth century, the vast majority of healthcare costs were covered out of pocket.[10] Providers of goods and services would usually bill for services at the time they were received, although some physicians would extend credit. Extending credit was a risky business, as the patients who recovered might believe they would have in any event, and patients who did not might believe that the physician had provided nothing of value (which was often the case). Physicians also widely practiced price discrimination—charging high prices to their wealthy patients and little or nothing to patients who could not afford their services.

As insurance became common in the mid-twentieth century (see below at Section V), out-of-pocket charges remained common. This was particularly true with indemnity coverage, which did not pay providers directly but rather reimbursed covered individuals once they had paid for services, often not paying the full amount charged. Gaps in coverage were also common—insurance originally covered only hospital care, and, although coverage of surgical and medical services was quite common by the 1960s, coverage of pharmaceutical coverage came even later. Deductibles, coinsurance, and balance billing remained common until the late 1980s.[11]

With the coming of managed care in the 1980s and 1990s, deductibles diminished or disappeared, and coinsurance was largely replaced with copayments.[12] Managed care plans primarily relied on care management strategies such as utilization review or capitation rather than cost-sharing to manage demand. Tiered copayment plans for pharmaceuticals also became common, with low copayments for generic drugs, higher copayments for on-formulary patented drugs, and highest copayments for off-formulary and specialty drugs.

But higher cost-sharing returned with the new millennium. In particular, high-deductible plans became common after the Medicare Modernization Act of 2003 made tax-subsidized health savings accounts available when coupled with high-deductible health plans.[13] Individual coverage had always had high deductibles, but as healthcare costs continued to increase, employers also increasingly turned to higher cost-sharing to shift the costs of coverage to employees.

Economists generally believe that high cost-sharing reduces healthcare expenditures. Moral hazard is a persistent problem with insurance. If a product is free to the consumer, the consumer will use more of the product. Without cost-sharing, insurance reduces the cost of a product almost to zero. (The consumer must still spend the time and undergo any discomfort inherent in receiving the service, so it is never entirely free.) Consumers who do not face cost-sharing, therefore, would be expected to use more healthcare items and services than they would if they had to pay out of pocket. Moreover, if consumers must spend a significant amount of their own discretionary funds before insurance begins picking up the tab, they are arguably more likely to shop carefully for healthcare items and services, which could increase price transparency and competition among providers.

[9] I.R.C. § 223 (2014).

[10] Timothy Jost, Health Care at Risk: A Critique of the Consumer-Driven Movement 42–53 (2007).

[11] *Id.* at 65–66.

[12] *Id.* at 66–68.

[13] I.R.C. § 223(c)(1)(A) (2014).

The hypothesis that healthcare costs could be reduced by imposing higher cost-sharing was borne out by the Rand Health Insurance Experiment, one of the few controlled trials ever carried out with respect to healthcare financing.[14] The experiment, conducted between 1974 and 1982, assigned different groups of insured individuals to different cost-sharing levels. As expected, consumers with higher cost-sharing consumed fewer healthcare services.

But the Rand experiment also demonstrated the problems attendant on high cost-sharing. Consumers reduced consumption of healthcare services adjudged by experts to be medically necessary to the same degree that they reduced unnecessary services. Although most participants did not seem to suffer adverse consequences from the reduction in healthcare services, some, and particularly low-income participants, did. Further studies have shown that high cost-sharing does can cause poorer compliance with drug treatment regimens.[15] Individuals with high cost-sharing also tend not to follow up with recommended tests and to avoid seeking medical help, including emergency care, when they need it.[16]

Moreover, the small percentage of users who account for a high percentage of healthcare costs quickly meet their deductible. Cost-sharing primarily influences costs by discouraging consumers from initiating contact with the healthcare system. Once an insured sees a physician or enters a hospital, professionals largely take over control of provision of items and services. There is also some evidence that reduction in expenditures due to high cost-sharing may be temporary—that it may simply lead to postponing the use of services, which may cost more later.[17]

The primary problem with high cost-sharing, however, is the financial insecurity that it causes insureds. Individuals with high cost-sharing health insurance tend to incur medical debt, reduce expenditures on other life necessities, be harassed by collection agencies, and declare bankruptcy more often.[18] Health insurance exists not only to ensure access to healthcare services but also to guarantee that sickness or injury will not result in impoverishment. High cost-sharing impedes the accomplishment of both of these goals.

II Charity

While out-of-pocket cash payment was historically the primary means of financing healthcare prior to the emergence of health insurance, charitable provision of care always supplemented it. The modern hospital grew out of institutions established by religious orders, local governments, and wealthy donors to care for sick paupers.[19] Physicians often provided their

[14] Joseph P. Newhouse & the Insurance Experiment Group, Free for All?: Lessons from the Rand Health Insurance Experiment (1993).

[15] Dana P. Goldman, Geoffrey F. Joyce, & Yuhui Zheng, *Prescription Drug Cost Sharing: Associations with Medication and Medical Utilization and Spending and Health*, 298 JAMA 61 (2007), *available at* http://www.amcp.org/WorkArea/DownloadAsset.aspx?id=12161.

[16] On emergency department care, *see* Katy B. Kozhimannil et al., *The Impact of High-Deductible Health Plans on Men and Women: An Analysis of Emergency Department Care*, 51 Med. Care 639 (2013).

[17] *Id.*

[18] Alison Galbraith et al., *Nearly Half of Families in High-Deductible Health Plans Whose Members Have Chronic Conditions Face Substantial Financial Burden*, 30 Health Aff. 322 (2011).

[19] Paul Starr, The Social Transformation of American Medicine 147–154 (1982).

services in these institutions gratis, subsidizing their service from their paid practice. These institutions were by and large miserable and dangerous places, in which a patient was as likely to die as to be cured. Respectable people who could afford the cost of medical care had surgeries performed in their homes rather than risk entering one of these institutions.

Over time, the modern hospital emerged. Advances in medical science (and in particular of antisepsis), standardization of hospital care, the changing nature of medical practice, and the emergence of public and private insurance coverage created the modern hospital. The notion of the hospital as a charity, however, has continued in law if not in reality. Most private hospitals are organized as nonprofit corporations, and most nonprofit hospitals are exempt from federal and state taxation.

Under federal income tax law, as well as under the laws of many states, hospitals are not tax exempt as hospitals but rather as "charities" (Horwitz, this volume).[20] The meaning of "charitable" under state law varies from state to state, but most states consider it to include service to the community, and more specifically, care for indigents. The definition of "charitable" under federal tax law has changed over time, but under amendments made by the Affordable Care Act (ACA), a hospital claiming tax exemption must regularly assess needs in its community, have and publicize a financial assistance plan, limit its charges to individuals eligible for financial assistance, and limit its billing and collection practices against individuals eligible for financial assistance.[21] Additionally, the Emergency Treatment and Active Labor Act requires all hospitals that participate in Medicare and that have an emergency department to provide emergency services without regard for ability to pay, although hospitals can charge for emergency services after they are received.[22]

Charitable provision of care is not limited to hospitals. Free clinics, through which physicians and other health professionals donate their services to assist lower-income individuals, exist throughout the country. Some pharmaceutical companies also make their drugs available to low-income uninsured individuals at little or no cost.[23]

While charitable provision of care is valuable to the low-income individuals who directly benefit from it, charity is dependent on the goodwill and resources of those who support it (and on tax subsidies that encourage supporters to give). Charity can be demeaning to those who receive it but have no entitlement to it. Charity cannot begin to meet the needs of all Americans who cannot afford the particular care they need either because their income is too low or because their medical needs are too great. It must be supplemented by public provision or public or private insurance.

III Direct Government Provision

Viewed from an international perspective, direct public provision of care is not uncommon. In particular, hospitals in many other countries are often publicly owned. Perhaps surprisingly, public provision of healthcare used to be more common in the United States than it is

20 I.R.C. § 501(c)(3) (2014). 21 I.R.C. § 501(r) (2014). 22 42 U.S.C. § 1395dd (2014).

23 *See* Medicare.gov, *Pharmaceutical Assistance Program*, http://www.medicare.gov/%28X%281%29S%28v2u10kncabpqce45mb010l55%29%29/pharmaceutical-assistance-program/index.aspx?AspxAutoDetectCookieSupport=1 (last visited Apr. 19, 2014).

now. In 1930, 73% of all hospital beds in the United States were found in public hospitals—primarily mental hospitals.[24]

A number of U.S. states still have public hospitals, however, which are often operated by counties. Counties also have public health departments that offer some forms of care, like immunizations or well-baby checkups. The federal government has several large programs that provide care directly to special populations. The U.S. Department of Veterans Affairs, for example, operates with more than 1,700 hospitals, clinics, community living centers, domiciliaries, readjustment counseling centers, and other facilities, making medical care available for certain veterans with certain conditions.[25] Indian Health Service (HIS) provides services in almost 150 hospitals, clinics, health stations, and urban IHS projects.[26] More than 1,100 federally qualified community health centers provide services to lower-income Americans.[27]

Direct government provision can offer a secure entitlement to care to all residents (or citizens) who qualify for the coverage. International evidence suggests that government provision effectively constrains healthcare costs, because payments for healthcare all flow through a single budget.[28] Direct provision also avoids administrative costs of claims presentation and processing that providers and insurers must incur under insurance-based programs and the costs of underwriting and risk bearing that accompany private insurance. Direct government provision of care can improve equity of access to care, as access does not depend on ability to pay. International evidence suggests, however, that health status, and even healthcare, inequities persist in countries that provide healthcare directly.[29] Finally, direct government provision can also balance public and population health with individual healthcare needs, as the government as provider is responsible to the entire populace and not just to individual purchasers of care.

Direct provision of care also has disadvantages. Healthcare financed through general revenues must compete for funding with other public needs and will be limited by the government's capacity to tax. Although all approaches to financing healthcare depend on "rationing," defined as allocating healthcare resources among claimants who need services, direct government provision results in a particularly public and political rationing process. Direct government provision can also result in a greater constraint on the supply of care than occurs in systems where sources of funding are more diverse and less constrained. Where individuals who can afford to pay for care are denied government provision, they may turn to complementary (and competing) private systems for healthcare finance. This may in turn weaken political support for the public system.

In the United States, public provision programs—for Native Americans, veterans, prisoners, the mentally ill, and lower-income populations—have achieved some successes. However, public provision of care as an approach to providing healthcare generally—true

[24] Committee on the Cost of Medical Care, *Medical Care for the American People, 82* (1932).e, 82.

[25] *See* U.S. Department of Veterans Affairs, http://www.va.gov/health/ (last visited Apr. 19, 2014).

[26] *See* Indian Health Service, http://www.ihs.gov/locations/includes/themes/newihstheme/display_objects/documents/ihs_facilities.xlsx (last visited Apr. 19, 2014).

[27] *See* Kaiser Family Foundation, *Number of Federally-Funded Federally Qualified Health Centers*, http://kff.org/other/state-indicator/total-fqhcs/ (last visited Apr. 19, 2014).

[28] Jost, Health Care at Risk, at 182–183.

[29] Michael Marmot et al., The Strategic Review of Health Inequalities in England Post-2010, *Fair Society, Healthy Lives: The Marmot Review* (2010), *available at* http://www.ucl.ac.uk/whitehallII/pdf/FairSocietyHealthyLives.pdf.

socialization of medicine—faces intense political opposition and has marginal support in the United States. Although it might be possible to expand programs to provide care directly to low-income uninsured Americans, socialization of healthcare generally is not conceivable politically in the United States.

IV Public Health Insurance

Public financing of the provision of care by private providers (or by public providers operated by independent government entities) may be the most common form of healthcare financing worldwide, but is less prominent in the United States than elsewhere. Social health insurance originated in Germany in the 1870s and gradually spread throughout the world. Social insurance funds are legally established quasi-public entities that may be self-governing.

Social insurance countries, such as Germany or France, finance coverage through hypothecated taxes—usually payroll taxes assessed against employers and employees.[30] Other countries, for example, Canada and Australia, finance public insurance programs through general revenue funds. Where general revenue funds are used to pay public providers, public insurance can look a great deal like direct government provision.

Attempts to enact public health insurance programs at the state level in the United States began in the Progressive Era, long before private health insurance became common.[31] The idea of including health coverage among the social insurance programs covered by the Social Security Act was mooted by the Roosevelt administration during the Great Depression but faced stiff political opposition and did not go far. Repeated attempts to create a universal public health insurance program during the postwar period also proved unsuccessful. Although President Truman campaigned for a national health insurance program more vigorously than had Roosevelt before him, the United States turned rightward following the war, electing a Republican congressional majority.

There was some expansion of public healthcare coverage for the poor after World War II. The Social Security Act Amendments of 1950 for the first time committed the federal government to match, to a very limited extent, state expenditures for in-kind medical services for the elderly, blind, disabled, and families with dependent children. The anticommunist hysteria of the late 1940s and early 1950s and continued opposition from organized medicine, however, put a hold on any further attempts to create a national health insurance program.

With the election of President Kennedy in 1960, efforts to provide healthcare for the elderly were redoubled. The landslide election of President Johnson and of a liberal Democratic Congress following the assassination of President Kennedy finally made health reform possible. In 1965 Congress created the Medicare program to insure hospital and medical services for the elderly and the Medicaid program to pay for healthcare services for public assistance recipients and the medically needy.[32]

[30] Reinhard Busse, Richard B. Saltman, & Hans F. W. Dubois, *Organization and Financing of Social Health Insurance Systems: Current Status and Recent Policy Developments, in* Social Health Insurance Systems in Western Europe 33, 34 (Richard B. Saltman, Reinhard Busse, & Josep Figueras eds., 2004).

[31] Starr, The Social Transformation, at 243–257.

[32] Theodore R. Marmor, The Politics of Medicare (2d ed. 2000).

Public insurance advocates had hoped that Medicare and Medicaid would be followed up by expansion of public insurance to the entire population. The 1970s, however, brought little progress as Democrats in Congress failed to reach agreement with the Nixon administration on the way forward. Medicare coverage was expanded to the disabled in 1972, however, and to cover outpatient drugs in 2003. Medicaid was expanded through the 1970s, 1980s, and 1990s to cover pregnant women and children up to age eighteen with incomes below the poverty level. A new program, the Children's Health Insurance Program (CHIP) was created in 1997 to cover children of families just above the Medicaid level.

Medicare, Medicaid, and CHIP are today the largest public insurance programs in the United States. Medicare covers almost fifty million elderly and disabled Americans and pays 20% of American healthcare expenditures.[33] Part A of Medicare is a classic social insurance program, funded through dedicated payroll taxes, but Parts B and D are funded through general revenues and individual premiums. Medicaid covers over sixty-six million Americans and accounts for 15% of American healthcare expenditures.[34] It is financed through federal and state general revenue funds.

The great advantage of public insurance is that it enables universal coverage of an entire population. Coverage depends neither on the ability of any individual to pay for coverage nor the willingness of a private insurer to take on the risk of insuring any particular individual. Public insurance programs can create secure rights to healthcare that can be asserted through administrative or judicial proceedings. Public insurers also have considerable market power and thus have far more bargaining power in negotiating with providers and suppliers over price and quality than do individuals, or even private insurers. Of course, the government can through regulation also set the prices that providers charge public insurance programs or standards for the quality of care. International evidence suggests that social insurance programs with dedicated funding sources are less likely to ration visibly as they are not as constrained in expenditures as programs through which governments provide care directly.[35]

Public insurance also has its limitations, however. Public insurance is subject to the political process. On the one hand, this can mean that public insurance funding can be limited, resulting in resources falling short of demand. On the other hand, special interest provider groups can bring political pressure on public insurance programs to ensure coverage or enhanced payment for their services. Public insurance is also subject to the threat of moral hazard as are all insurance programs.

In the United States we have failed to capture the full benefits of public insurance, as our public insurance programs have remained limited to particular populations—the elderly, the disabled, children, some poor parents, veterans, and Native Americans. These populations

[33] Kaiser Family Foundation, *Total Number of Medicare Beneficiaries*, http://kff.org/medicare/state-indicator/total-medicare-beneficiaries/ (last visited Apr. 19, 2014); Martin et al., *National Health Spending*, at 75.

[34] Kaiser Family Foundation, *Total Medicaid Enrollment, FY 2010*, http://kff.org/medicaid/state-indicator/total-medicaid-enrollment/ (last visited Apr. 19, 2014); Martin, et al., *National Health Spending*, at 75.

[35] Timothy Soltzfus Jost, *Funding Health Services: The Optimal Balance*, in COLLEEN M. FLOOD, MARK STABILE, & CAROLYN HUGHES TUOHY, EXPLORING SOCIAL INSURANCE: CAN A DOSE OF EUROPE CURE CANADIAN HEALTH FINANCE? 163, 173 (2008).

have been generally provided secure and affordable healthcare. But the influence of special interests have kept the government from fully using its market power to constrain prices, and public insurance programs have only begun to use their purchasing power to improve quality of care.

V Private Health Insurance

For most Americans, almost 70%, health insurance means private insurance.[36] Most of these people are covered though employer-sponsored health insurance, but some purchase private medical insurance in the individual market, while others purchase private insurance to supplement public insurance, particularly Medicare.

Private health insurance is available almost everywhere in the world.[37] In some countries, like Canada, private health insurance covers items and services not covered by the public program, such as dental or vision care. In other countries, such as France, private insurance covers cost-sharing imposed by the public insurance program. In yet others, like England, private insurance allows enrollees to avoid queues that might exist for particular services, such as elective surgery for knee replacements. In a few countries, such as Germany, lower- and middle-income individuals must enroll in the public insurance program, but wealthy individuals may instead enroll in private insurance. Finally, in a few countries, notably the Netherlands and Switzerland, most individuals are insured for most healthcare items and services through heavily regulated and publicly subsidized private insurance plans.

Private health insurance came into being in the United States in the first half of the twentieth century as advances in medicine made healthcare of real value and as increases in the cost of healthcare rendered it increasingly less affordable to those with serious medical problems. Modern health insurance was born in 1929, when the Baylor Hospital in Dallas, Texas, launched the first "hospital service plan."[38] Baylor entered into a contract under which white public school teachers paid fifty cents a month into a prepaid hospital services plan with the assurance that they would be covered for up to twenty-one days of hospital care, and a one-third discount on the next 344 days. Hospital service plans spread quickly during the 1930s. In 1936, the American Hospital Association established the Commission on Hospital Services, which ultimately became the Blue Cross Association. Blue Cross plans negotiated "service benefit" contracts with the hospitals, under which the plans would cover a fixed number of days of hospitalization for a per diem fee established in the contract. The success of the hospitals prepaid benefit plans was soon noticed by physicians. In 1939 the first of the physician service benefits plan that came to be known as Blue Shield plans appeared.

As it became increasingly clear in the late 1930s that there was a substantial market for hospital benefits, private commercial insurers entered the group insurance market as well, a market they had previously eschewed as too risky. Unlike Blue Cross plans, commercial insurers covered not only hospital care but also offered surgical coverage. Commercial

[36] DeNavas-Walt, U.S. Census Bureau (2013), at 22.

[37] Timothy Stoltzfus Jost, *Private or Public Approaches to Insuring the Uninsured: Lessons from International Experience with Private Insurance*, 76 N.Y.U. L. Rev. 419 (2001).

[38] Starr, The Social Transformation, at 295–306.

plans even began to cover medical costs (nonsurgical physician's services) in the hospital. Commercial health insurance was sold on an indemnity basis. Indemnity policies paid fixed sums per service, which were set beforehand in the insurance contract.

In the booming American economy following World War II, private health insurance coverage expanded dramatically. By 1950, seventy-five million Americans, or half the population, had hospitalization insurance, fifty million had surgical benefits, and twenty-one million had medical benefits.[39] By 1965, the year Congress established Medicare and Medicaid, private hospital insurance covered 156 million Americans, about 80% of the population.[40]

As coverage expanded, it also became more comprehensive.[41] In the early 1950s, commercial insurers began to offer major medical coverage, which provided catastrophic coverage for hospital and medical care. Major medical policies usually supplemented basic hospital and surgical-medical coverage. Comprehensive coverage was the next innovation, bundling basic and major medical coverage into a package to provide the most complete coverage available. Finally, during the 1960s and 1970s, insurance coverage began to expand to cover dental care and pharmaceuticals, while basic coverage expanded to include maternity care, mental health, and some preventive services.

This expansion of private health coverage was driven by several concurrent forces. One important trend following World War II was increased employer responsibility for employee health benefits. Unions were at the peak of their strength in the mid-twentieth century, and improved fringe benefits were a high priority for collective bargaining. The National Labor Relations Board clarified in 1949 that employee benefits were included within the "terms of conditions of employment" subject to collective bargaining under the National Labor Relations Act, giving new impetus to union demands for health benefits.[42]

Nonunion firms also increasingly offered liberal fringe benefits to forestall unionization. Employers saw health insurance as a means to stabilize employment (by making it more difficult for employees to change jobs), to keep workers healthy and productive, and to ward off national social health insurance. By 1988, employers paid for 90% of the cost of individual coverage and 75% of the cost of family coverage.[43]

Tax policy also played a role in expanding coverage. The 1954 Internal Revenue Code explicitly recognized the nontaxability of employment-related benefits to either the employer or employee.[44] Tax subsidies played a particularly important role in increasing the share of premiums covered by employers and the scope of coverage.

A final factor that drove the expansion of employee coverage was the enactment of the Employee Retirement Income Security Act (ERISA) in 1974.[45] By blocking the application of state insurance regulation to self-insured plans, ERISA allowed employers that self-insured to escape state premium taxes, insurance mandates (which became common in the early 1980s), capital and reserve requirements, and risk pool contribution requirements. Whereas

[39] *Id.* at 1–2.

[40] Health Insurance Institute, Source Book on Health Insurance Data, 1966, at 5, 10–13 (1966).

[41] Jost, Health Care at Risk, at 61.

[42] Inland Steel Co. v. N.L.R.B., 170 F.2d 247 (7th Cir. 1948), *cert. denied*, 336 U.S. 960 (1949).

[43] Jon Gabel et al., *Employer-Sponsored Health Insurance in America*, 8 Health Aff. 116, 120 (1989), *available at* http://content.healthaffairs.org/content/8/2/116.full.pdf?origin=publication_detail.

[44] I.R.C. §§ 105, 106 (2014).

[45] 29 U.S.C. §§ 1001, et seq.

only 5% of group health claims were paid by self-insured plans in 1975, an estimated 60% of employees were in self-insured plans by 1987.[46]

One factor that did not play a major role in the expansion of coverage was World War II itself. It is a commonplace misconception that American health insurance began with wage and price controls during World War II. These controls, it is argued, exempted fringe benefits from wage limits and thus stimulated the growth of health insurance. There are a number of reasons, however, to treat with skepticism the assertion that World War II wage and price controls created modern health insurance.[47] First, health insurance as an employee benefit was already well established and growing rapidly before the war began. Second, wartime employment and health insurance coverage grew much faster before than after wage and price controls went into effect in 1943. Employment-related insurance coverage increased again rapidly after wage price stabilization controls expired in 1946. The wage stabilization policy was routinely circumvented, as it allowed wage increases that accompanied promotions, which quickly became common. Finally, throughout the war, Blue Cross coverage, the most common form of health insurance, was generally paid by employees rather than employers. By the end of the war only 7.6% of Blue Cross enrollees were participants in groups to which employers contributed.[48] Wage controls would have only encouraged broader coverage if employers were paying for that coverage.

Whatever the factors that drove private insurance expansion, by the 1980s the United States seemed to have solved for most Americans through private initiative (supplemented by public programs to cover those whom private markets could never protect), the problem of health security that other nations addressed through social insurance or public provision.

As early as the 1970s, however, America's private health security system began to unravel. The driving disruptive force was the increase in healthcare costs. Inflation was a general problem during the 1970s, but healthcare costs grew even more rapidly than other costs. Public initiatives were adopted to restrain healthcare costs—including health planning, professional standards review organizations, and, in some states, state rate review—but none achieved great success.[49]

In response to growing healthcare prices, private health insurers turned from being passive payers for care to becoming care managers. Within a decade, conventional indemnity insurance and service benefit plans gave way to plans—initially called health maintenance organizations (HMOs) and preferred provider organizations (PPOs)—that offered limited provider networks, attempted to review and control utilization, and experimented with incentives structures that would discourage rather than encourage provision of services. For a time, this strategy worked. By the mid 1990s, healthcare cost growth had fallen dramatically; indeed, it briefly fell in line with the growth of the economy generally.[50]

But cost increases also began to have an impact on coverage. Beginning with the 1980s, the percentage of Americans with health insurance began to decline. The first to lose coverage were retirees, who fell victim to the steady increase in healthcare costs, and after 1990, to a

[46] Jon Gabel et al., *The Changing World of Group Health Insurance*, 7 HEALTH AFF. 48, 58 (1988), *available at* http://content.healthaffairs.org/content/7/3/48.full.pdf?origin=publication_detail.

[47] JOST, HEALTH CARE AT RISK, at 59–61.

[48] S. Rep. No. 82-359, at 67 (1951).

[49] Timothy Stoltzfus Jost, *Eight Decades of Discouragement: The History of Health Care Cost Containment in the USA*, 15 F. FOR HEALTH ECON. & POL'Y 53, 55–58, 63 (2012).

[50] *Id.* at 67.

change in accounting standards that required firms to carry the cost of future retiree health obligations on their books as a current liability.[51]

Small businesses had never insured their employees to the same extent as larger businesses, and as the United States shifted from a manufacturing-based economy to a service-based economy, and concomitantly from large unionized employers to small businesses, the percentage of employees who were insured fell further.

Small groups were underwritten based on the expected claims costs of their members, and coverage was very expensive, even difficult to find, for older groups or groups in hazardous occupations. A number of states enacted laws in the 1990s attempting to make health insurance more accessible for small groups, including laws guaranteeing insurance issuance and renewal, limiting variations in rating among groups, and restricting preexisting condition exclusions.[52] A few states even required community rating. The 1996 federal Health Insurance Portability and Accountability Act (HIPAA) established guaranteed issue and renewal requirements throughout the country for small group plans and imposed limits on preexisting condition exclusions in group plans generally.[53] Since health insurers could still vary premiums based on health status, however, insurance remained beyond the reach of many small groups.

Even for larger groups, managed care only temporarily stemmed the growth of healthcare costs. There was a serious backlash against the more extreme forms of managed care. Although Congress failed to adopt a national managed care bill of rights when the issue came before it in 2001, most states adopted legislation restraining managed care in the late 1990s.[54] As the economy improved in the late 1990s and early 2000s, healthcare moved to broader provider networks and away from strict utilization controls.

Healthcare costs began to rise dramatically again around 2000, however.[55] As the economy worsened again in the early 2000s, the cost of employment-related health insurance began to reach levels that employers found intolerable. Employers reacted primarily by increasing employee cost-sharing, although some employers dropped coverage or increased the employee share of health insurance premiums.[56] Many employers shifted to high-deductible policies. As health insurance became more costly and less valuable to employees, more employees passed up employment-related coverage. Whereas by 2005, 98% of large firms offered health insurance (60% of employers overall), only 66% of employees of firms that offered health insurance were insured through their own employer.[57]

The massive layoffs and economic retrenchment that accompanied the economic decline in 2008 and 2009 accelerated the decline in private coverage as well as the expansion of

[51] Paul Fronstin & Nevin Adams, *Employment-Based Retiree Health Benefits: Trends in Access and Coverage, 1997–2010* (2012), *available at* http://www.ebri.org/pdf/briefspdf/EBRI_IB_10-2012_No377_RetHlth.pdf.

[52] Mark A. Hall, Reforming Private Health Insurance (1994).

[53] Pub. L. 104–191, 110 Stat. 1936 (1996).

[54] Barry Furrow et al., Health Law 492–508 (2d ed. 2000).

[55] Jost, *Eight Decades*, at 72, 74.

[56] Gary Claxton et al., Kaiser Family Foundation, *Employer Health Benefits: 2010 Annual Survey*, 38, 72–73, 107, 119 (2010), *available at* http://kff.org/health-costs/report/employer-health-benefits-annual-survey-archives/#2010.

[57] Gary Claxton et al., Kaiser Family Foundation, Employer Health Benefits: 2005 Annual Survey 32, 40 (2005).

public coverage. By 2009, only 55.8% of Americans had employment-based coverage, down from 62.1% in 1989.[58] Retiree coverage declined even more rapidly. Only 28% of large firms that offered health benefits covered retirees in 2010, down from 66% in 1988.[59]

Nevertheless, tax-subsidized employment-based private health insurance has on the whole worked reasonably well for the United States. It has resulted in broad, reasonably generous, coverage of workers and their dependents. Employee groups covered by large employers, which still include most Americans, are usually big enough and cover enough healthy employees to constitute reasonable risk pools. Laws that have since 1996 prohibited discrimination within groups on the basis of health status and other laws that prohibit discrimination in favor of highly compensated employees (subject to many exceptions) provide some protection for lower-income and less healthy employees.[60] Private employment-related insurance is less dependent on political decisions and taxation capacity than public insurance. It is also ideologically acceptable to Americans who oppose government involvement in healthcare.

But employment-sponsored insurance has significant defects as a strategy for covering a nation's population. Most important, it leaves many people uncovered. As long as employers are free to decide whether or not to offer insurance, many employers, particularly those who employ primarily a low-wage workforce, will not offer it. Part-time, seasonal, temporary, and recently hired employees, as well as retirees, are often uncovered. Prior to the adoption of the ACA, insurers could set premiums for small groups based on claims experience or the health status of employees and exclude some preexisting conditions. This rendered coverage unaffordable for some small groups. Private insurance also imposes high administrative costs, which are bigger for small groups than large.

A small fraction of Americans—about eleven million in early 2014—have been insured through the individual market, where they get insurance directly from an insurer, not from an employer.[61] Administrative costs are high in the individual market and premiums have varied sharply from individual to individual based on health status, age, gender, and other underwriting factors. Individual insurance, however, has often been the only alternative available for a number of Americans, including the self-employed, early retirees, the unemployed, part-time and temporary workers, and other individuals who do not have insurance available through their place of employment.

A number of states attempted in the 1990s to reform the individual market, but in most states individual market reforms were less ambitious than small group market reforms.[62] In contrast to its more comprehensive reforms for group coverage, HIPAA required only guaranteed renewal and imposed limits on preexisting conditions' exclusions only for individuals who transferred to the individual market after having group insurance or some equivalent public insurance for a year and a half prior to seeking individual coverage.[63] Many

[58] Carmen DeNavas-Walt, U.S. Census Bureau, U.S. Department of Commerce, *Income, Poverty, and Health Insurance Coverage in the United States: 2009*, at 71 (2010), *available at* http://www.census.gov/prod/2010pubs/p60-238.pdf.

[59] CLAXTON ET AL., KAISER FAMILY FOUNDATION, SURVEY 2010, at 163.

[60] I.R.C. §§ 105(h), 125(b) (2014).

[61] Gary Claxton et al., *Data Note: How Many People Have Nongroup Health Insurance* (2014), *available at* http://kff.org/private-insurance/issue-brief/how-many-people-have-nongroup-health-insurance/.

[62] FURROW ET AL., HEALTH LAW, at 477–478.

[63] 42 U.S.C. §§ 300gg-41, 300gg-42 (2014).

states also established high-risk pools for otherwise uninsurable individuals, but premiums were generally high and participation often limited.[64]

VI The Affordable Care Act

The Affordable Care Act of 2010 (ACA) is a fundamentally conservative law. Like American health reform attempts that preceded it, the ACA does not attempt to revolutionize, unify, or even rationalize healthcare financing in the United States but rather to fill gaps and continue to try to patch up and hold together a diverse nonsystem of healthcare finance.

The ACA makes the greatest changes in the individual market, which was, as just described, the most dysfunctional insurance market prior to the reform. The ACA creates health insurance marketplaces, called exchanges, where individuals can compare and purchase individual coverage.[65] Each state is allowed to create its own exchange, but a national fallback exchange is also created for states that decide not to establish their own, which in the end has been most of them. Individual (and small group) coverage is categorized by "metal levels" of platinum, gold, silver, and bronze, based on actuarial value, defined as the percentage of total healthcare costs borne by the insurer as opposed to the percentage paid for out of pocket. Federal premium tax credits are made available to households with incomes between 100% and 400% of the federal poverty level.[66] Households with incomes below 250% of the poverty level can also qualify for cost-sharing reduction payments if they purchase a silver-level plan.[67]

Health insurers that sell policies in the individual market may no longer discriminate based on health status.[68] Indeed, they may not consider any factors other than age, geographic location, family size, and tobacco use in setting premiums.[69] They must standardize cost-sharing to fit within the four metal tiers.[70] Individual market enrollees are also protected by various insurance reforms included in the legislation, including a ban on lifetime and annual dollar limits and rescissions (except for fraud), and an out-of-pocket maximum cap.

The ACA also attempts to shore up and modestly improve employer-sponsored health insurance. Large employers (those who employ more than fifty full-time or full-time-equivalent employees) must offer "minimum essential coverage" to their full-time employees (those who work thirty hours a week or more) or pay a tax of $2,000 for each full-time employee if any uncovered employees receive premium tax credits through the exchange.[71] Employers who do not offer affordable and adequate coverage (including coverage of hospital and physician services) must pay a $3,000 tax for each employee who actually gets premium tax credits through the exchange.[72] Large employers are not required to cover a particular package of benefits but do face some constraints under the law—for example, if

[64] Deborah Chollet, *Expanding Individual Health Insurance Coverage: Are High Risk Pools the Answer?*, 10 HEALTH AFF. 349 (2002).

[65] 42 U.S.C. §§ 18031 (2014). [66] I.R.C. § 36B (2014). [67] 42 U.S.C. §§ 18071 (2014).

[68] 42 U.S.C. § 300gg-4(a) (2014). [69] 42 U.S.C. § 300gg(a) (2014).

[70] 42 U.S.C. § 18022(d) (2014). [71] I.R.C. § 4980H(a) (2014).

[72] I.R.C. § 4980H(b) (2014).

they offer insurance, they must cover preventive services without cost-sharing, limit out-of-pocket costs on certain core benefits, and limit waiting periods to ninety days.

Small employer group coverage is regulated more extensively. Small employers are under no obligation to provide coverage and face no penalties if they fail to do so. Small employers who offer coverage, however, must cover a package of ten essential health benefits (subject to exceptions).[73] They also cannot offer coverage that has an actuarial value of less than 60%.[74] Small employers can purchase coverage through the Small Business Health Options (SHOP) program. Very small employers with predominantly low-wage employees can qualify for tax credits under the ACA for coverage purchased through the SHOP exchange.[75] Insurers may no longer impose preexisting condition requirements on small groups or discriminate among small groups on the basis of health status.[76]

The ACA, as written, expanded the Medicaid program to cover very low-income Americans who cannot afford commercial health insurance—those with incomes up to 133% of the poverty level (actually 138%, as the law included an automatic 5% income disregard).[77] The Supreme Court, however, held that states could decide whether to expand Medicaid or not.[78] To date, about half of the states have decided to expand Medicaid and half have decided not to, with the breakdown largely along political lines (Rosenbaum, this volume).

The ACA makes minimal changes in the Medicare program (Marmor, this volume). It expands preventive service coverage and eliminates the "doughnut hole" that had previously required beneficiaries whose prescription drug expenses exceeded a certain level to bear the full cost of drug coverage until they reached the catastrophic coverage level. The ACA pays for coverage expansion in part by limiting the growth of future Medicare expenditures.

In order to expand coverage, the ACA contains an individual responsibility mandate, which requires Americans who are not otherwise insured (through private or public insurance), who can afford coverage for 8% or less of their household income (after taking into account premium tax credits and employer contributions to coverage), and who do not fall into a number of other exceptions to purchase health insurance or pay a tax penalty.[79] The individual responsibility requirement is intended to ensure that the individual market, now open to all regardless of health status, will include healthy as well as unhealthy participants, as well as to relieve the burden of uncompensated care that hospitals and other providers have borne. The requirement has proven intensely controversial, however. In a lawsuit brought by twenty-six states and a number of private parties, the Supreme Court upheld the requirement as a valid exercise of the power of Congress to tax and spend, although it also held that Congress did not have the authority to enact the requirement as an exercise of its authority to regulate interstate commerce.[80]

The ACA is still, four years after its enactment, a work in progress. Enforcement of some requirements, such as the employer mandate, has been delayed. Initial deployment of the exchanges was a disaster—it took two months to get the federal exchange fully open for business, and some of the state exchanges failed to become fully operational during the first year of open enrollment. But by the spring of 2014, over eight million Americans had chosen a

[73] 42 U.S.C. § 18022(b) (2014). [74] 42 U.S.C. § 18022(d) (2014).

[75] I.R.C. § 45R (2014). [76] 42 U.S.C. §§ 300gg(a), 300gg-3, 300gg-4(a) (2014).

[77] 42 U.S.C. § 1396a(a)(10)(A)(i)(VIII) (2014).

[78] *N'l Fed'n of Indep. Bus. v. Sebelius*, 132 S.Ct. 2566, 2601–2608 (2012).

[79] I.R.C. § 5000A (2014). [80] *Nat'l Fed'n of Indep. Bus.*, 132 S.Ct. at 2584–2601.

health plan through the exchanges, millions more had enrolled in Medicaid, and the number of the uninsured was dropping dramatically.[81]

Nevertheless, the healthcare financing "system" of the United States, if it can be called a system, remains extraordinarily complex. Healthcare is covered by out-of-pocket expenditures; charity; direct public provision; public insurance; and private insurance, both group and individual. Other developed nations also have a mix of healthcare financing; indeed, most developed nations probably include all of these forms of financing. But most developed nations have a dominant public insurance system, with other forms of financing playing a complementary or supplementary role. In the United States, the dominant form of coverage in terms of numbers covered has been employment-related group private insurance, but the massive public Medicare and Medicaid programs pay for a larger portion of the national healthcare budget than does private insurance because the populations covered by these programs are more in need of services than the privately insured population.

VII Why This Patchwork of Coverage?

Why have we retained this patchwork of coverage in the United States and not developed a consistently private or public system? It is easiest to explain why we have not developed a universal system of private coverage. Given the high cost of healthcare in the United States and the distribution of income, individual private insurance is simply unaffordable for a significant proportion of the population. If health status underwriting is permitted, coverage will also be unaffordable, even unavailable at any price, to individuals with high healthcare needs. Tax-subsidized employer coverage has worked reasonably well in covering a majority of Americans, but it cannot cover the unemployed or unemployable, including the disabled and many of the elderly. As was mentioned at the outset, universal coverage means moving resources from the wealthy to the poor, from the healthy to the sick. Private markets cannot do this; thus some form of public financing is necessary.

Why have we then not moved to universal public coverage, like other nations? There are many answers to this question, no one of them alone wholly explanatory. One reason is the power of interest groups.[82] Public health insurance was for decades effectively opposed by organized medicine, which took the lead in opposing expansion from the 1910s until the 1980s. Universal public insurance would today face vigorous opposition from private insurers, whose revenues would be limited or eliminated by public financing.

Public insurance has, moreover, always faced entrenched political opposition and had no powerful constituency of its own.[83] The United States has never had a significant socialist or

[81] Timothy Jost, *Implementing Health Reform: A Summary Health Insurance Marketplace Enrollment Report*, *available at* http://healthaffairs.org/blog/2014/05/01/implementing-health-reform-a-summary-health-insurance-marketplace-enrollment-report/.

[82] Jill Quadagno, One Nation, Uninsured: Why the U.S. Has No National Health Insurance (2006).

[83] Timothy Stoltzfus Jost, *Why Can't We Do What They Do? National Health Reform Abroad*, 32 J. Law. Med. & Ethics 433, 438 (2004).

labor party. The Republican Party has opposed even the conservative reforms of the ACA. But even Democrats have offered little support for universal public insurance. Indeed, even a public plan alternative to the private insurance covered under the ACA was unable to get Democratic approval in the Senate. An entirely public insurance system never had more than minimal support, particularly in the Senate.

A national public insurance system would require a dramatic increase in public funding. The United States budget regularly runs a deficit, and the national debt of the country is continually rising. A public healthcare system would require new taxes. Of course, the funding of the current Medicare and Medicaid programs, as well as the tax subsidies currently provided for employment-related insurance and for advance premium tax credits could be folded into a public system. It would be difficult to recapture state revenues spent on Medicaid, however, and the sum total of all funds currently being spent would likely fall well short of the cost of a comprehensive program. Imposing a tax sufficient to fund a public insurance system would likely be politically impossible.

A public insurance system would also run contrary to the ideology of many Americans. Americans tend to like public insurance programs once they are in place but are in general skeptical about government.[84] Americans tend to believe that government is inefficient and wasteful and that the private sector does a better job of providing goods and services. Moreover, the current system works reasonably well for most Americans, who will resist the disruption of current arrangements that would be necessary for a move to a universal public system.

American political institutions also make the radical changes that would be necessary to move from a mixed financing system to a largely or exclusively public insurance system very difficult.[85] Legislation creating a national public insurance system would have to pass the House, garner sixty votes in the Senate, and be signed by the president—and most likely be blessed by the Supreme Court. The ACA experience demonstrates how difficult this is to achieve, even when the legislation basically affirms rather than changes the current institutions.

Finally, the absence of universal public insurance in the United States is consistent with a general theory of path dependency.[86] The theory of path dependency emphasizes the power of inertia within political institutions. Once nations get into the habit of doing things in a particular way, they tend to keep on doing them. This is not purely a theory of historical determinism, however. From time to time, "critical moments or junctures" appear when a confluence of factors in the broader political arena makes major institutional changes in healthcare systems possible. This happened in the United States when both Lyndon Johnson and Barack Obama were elected to office with large congressional majorities following dramatic events—the assassination of President Kennedy and the near-collapse of the American economy. Even on these occasions, however, only gap-filling legislation was possible, not radical restructurings of our insurance system.

[84] *Id.* [85] *Id.* at 437–438.

[86] CAROLYN HUGHES TUOHY, ACCIDENTAL LOGICS: THE DYNAMICS OF CHANGE IN THE HEALTH CARE ARENA IN THE UNITED STATES, BRITAIN, AND CANADA (1999).

VIII Conclusion

So where do we go from here? The United States will almost certainly continue along its current path. Large employers are likely to continue to offer health insurance coverage to their full-time employees. Both the ACA's employer and individual mandates will increase the pressure on large employers to do so. But the main reasons they will continue to offer coverage are the tax subsidy and the role that benefits play in recruitment and retention of employees. Although some conservatives and libertarians advocate ending the tax subsidy for employment-based insurance, this would be massively disruptive and is unlikely to happen any time soon. Amendments to the ACA to change the definition of full-time employee or of small employer are quite possible, but not a wholesale change in employer coverage.

Many small employers are also likely to continue to offer coverage. Even though small employers are not subject to the mandate, their employees do need to find coverage somewhere because of the individual mandate, and group coverage is still likely to cost less than individual coverage because administrative costs are lower. Small employers that employ predominantly low-wage employees, however, are more likely to drop coverage, as their employees will be able to get a better deal with premium tax credits and cost-sharing reduction payments through the exchanges.[87]

Employers, large and small, are likely to continue, however, to shift costs to employees. They are likely to require both increased premium contributions from employees and increased cost-sharing in the form of deductibles, coinsurance, and copayments for insured employees. If, as is widely expected, employers begin to move from defined benefit to defined contribution plans, employees may be faced with the choice of either paying more up front for more generous plans or at the time they use services, through higher cost-sharing with less generous plans.

Medicare is likely to continue on course with few major changes. If Republicans take control of Congress and the presidency, and the Senate abolishes the filibuster entirely, it is possible that a premium support proposal could be adopted that would shift more of the costs of the program to beneficiaries. It is likely, however, that cost-saving measures will continue to focus on limiting growth in provider payments and perhaps on assessing more carefully whether covered items and services are cost-effective.

I do not foresee major changes in the Medicaid program either. If Republicans gain control of the Congress and the presidency, they may roll back the ACA Medicaid expansions, and even try to turn Medicaid funding over to the states in block grants without eligibility and benefit requirements. But if the Medicaid expansion remains in place, it is likely that most states will eventually expand. The only arguments for resisting expansion are political, and the moral and economic arguments for expansion will in all likelihood eventually prevail.

87 Amy Monahan & Daniel Schwarcz, *Will Employers Undermine Health Care Reform by Dumping Sick Employees?*, 97 VA. L. REV. 125 (2011).

The biggest unknown is what will happen to Americans who are not covered by employer-sponsored coverage or public health insurance. If the health insurance market reforms, exchanges, premium tax credits and cost-sharing reduction payments, and individual mandate all remain in place, the number of uninsured will continue to drop while coverage through the exchanges increases. If one or more of these reforms are repealed, however, the number of uninsured is likely to grow again. Republican reform proposals, if adopted, might make health insurance more affordable for higher income, healthy individuals, but are unlikely to address the plight of most uninsured Americans.

For the foreseeable future, however, many American residents are likely to remain uninsured. First, nothing in the ACA or in widely supported modifications to the ACA will provide coverage for millions of undocumented aliens. Second, millions of Americans who cannot find health insurance coverage with premiums at 8% or less of their household income will be exempt from the individual mandate, and many of them will remain uninsured. Finally, an undetermined number of Americans are likely to remain uninsured and either pay the individual mandate penalty or find a way to evade it.

In sum, America will continue to muddle along, with its unique public-private mix. This system has, however, provided reasonably good access to healthcare financing for most Americans. The ACA should expand coverage for many who have heretofore been left out—if it remains in place. But the high cost of private coverage and high cost-sharing that coverage in the individual market, including exchange coverage, imposes on most insureds, will continue to hamper access to care. We continue to tinker with the current system but seem incapable of making the changes that are necessary to cover all Americans.

CHAPTER 8

LEGAL BATTLES AGAINST DISCRIMINATION IN HEALTHCARE

DAYNA BOWEN MATTHEW

HEALTHCARE is unique among American industries because historically institutionalized, overt racial and ethnic segregation—primarily enforced by hospitals—ended quietly and seemingly overnight. Without marches, sit-ins, or growling dogs and fire hoses ripping at the backs of civil rights protestors, sometime soon after 1964, hospitals compliantly took down their "whites-only" and "colored-only" signs. Somewhere in the dead of night, orderlies wheeled black and white patient beds onto the sidewalk, shuffled them together, and returned them to ostensibly integrated hospital rooms. The motivation for this "voluntary" desegregation was money. The mechanism that communicated the motivation was a new law—Title VI of the Civil Rights Act of 1964.

The battle for health desegregation was fought in the courts and the halls of Congress, rather than in the streets. Under the newly enacted antidiscrimination law, Congress threatened to withhold federal Medicare and Medicaid reimbursement funds from any person or institution, which, "on the ground of race, or national origin," discriminated or denied benefits "under any program or activity receiving Federal financial assistance."[1] By 1966, nearly 20 million Americans over age 65 were Medicare enrollees; medical providers did the math and quickly determined that overt segregation in healthcare did not pay. But minority patients and their physicians soon learned that achieving facial desegregation of hospitals was only a partial and temporary victory.

Title VI exempted physicians from compliance. Nursing homes largely escaped the antidiscrimination law's coverage, and therefore, in these institutions, discrimination continued to flourish. Even where hospitals were concerned, their apparent acquiescence to integration did not mean an end to race discrimination. In fact, Medicare hospital discharge data reveals that in many areas of the country, racial and ethnic segregation persists to this day.[2]

[1] 42 U.S.C. § 2000d (2012).

[2] David B. Smith, *The Racial Segregation of Hospital Care Revisited: Medicare Discharge Patterns and their Implications*, 88 AM. J. PUB. HEALTH 461 (1988).

Moreover, today, a scant fifty years after the civil rights law's passage, discrimination against patients of color, based solely on their race or ethnicity continues to cause black, Latino, and Native American patients to live sicker and die quicker than white patients in this country. This chapter confronts the evidence that health inequality is medically unjustifiable, entirely avoidable, and arguably illegal.

In doing so, it is important to properly frame the problem. Health inequality refers to differences in access to and the quality of healthcare, not due to clinically appropriate differences or patient preferences. These differences are the result of discrimination at the patient, provider, and institutional levels,[3] and they produce inferior health outcomes in vulnerable populations called "health disparities." By definition, two forms of healthcare discrimination are *not* considered here. This chapter is not about clinically driven differences in medical care. For example, when providers include sickle cell anemia or Crohn's disease in the differential diagnosis for patients of one ethnic group but do not consider these illnesses for patients of another ethnic group for whom the disease prevalence is rare, inequality is not implicated. This discrimination is medically supported and not of concern. Second, the discrimination problems discussed here are not the result of overt bigotry. The malicious discrimination that grows out of a genuine and intentional belief that one people group is inherently inferior to another is no longer the major source of discrimination in American healthcare. Therefore this form of racism is not the focus here. However, the invidious racial hatred that characterized American healthcare at the nation's inception has left a legacy that is at the heart of this chapter. The inequality that plagues our healthcare system today resembles its predecessor because it is historically driven, structurally reinforced, and systemically operationalized. Both the discrimination of the American slavery and Jim Crow eras, and the more subtle form of racism prevalent in healthcare today impose injuries to health and healthcare through individual and institutional conduct. By adversely affecting health outcomes, both forms of discrimination deny people an equal opportunity to participate in education, employment, recreation, and a healthy life, based on their ethnicity or skin color. Both cut short the lives and life chances of those who are not white, merely because they are not white. And yet the forceful legal prohibitions of America's federal antidiscrimination laws forbid only the overt forms of discrimination that seldom find expression in modern America. Federal law apparently ignores the pervasive prejudice that devalues minority lives daily throughout the healthcare system. This chapter outlines concrete steps toward achieving nondiscriminatory healthcare delivery in America.

The chapter begins by contextualizing racism in American healthcare. The legacy of discrimination in medicine is historically rooted and costly in terms of lost productivity, increased healthcare costs, and the number of minority lives that are cut short due to health disparities. Next, the chapter explains the federally enacted legal tools currently available to address discriminatory healthcare, and the ways in which they fall short. The focus in this chapter is on the federal law known as "Title VI." Although this statute was inspired by the need to address explicit, hate-driven racial discrimination, the text of the law has not changed since 1964, and the interpretation of the law has narrowed, while racial and ethnic discrimination in American healthcare have shifted and arguably expanded dramatically.

[3] Brian D. Smedley et al., Unequal Treatment: Confronting Racial and Ethnic Disparities in Health Care (Brian D. Smedley et al. eds., 2003).

The following section describes how the U.S. Supreme Court has responded to contemporary trends in racial discrimination and suggests that the struggle for the soul of antidiscrimination law appears to have moved from the federal legislature to the Supreme Court. Congress appears to have abdicated its responsibility to set the nation's modern civil rights agenda. The third section of the chapter explains why. American lawmakers' efforts to combat health inequity are confounded by a transformation in healthcare from "old-fashioned" discrimination rooted in racism and overt bigotry, to subtle discrimination resulting from implicit racial bias. The shift has allowed unconscious racism to pervade healthcare delivery but escape the law's notice. The chapter concludes with suggested legislative amendments to reform an ineffective civil rights law that currently fails to control discrimination in healthcare and other publicly funded sectors of the economy.

While the focus here is on racial and ethnic discrimination, compelling evidence suggests that health providers also discriminate against patients based on gender, physical disabilities, sexual orientation, and mental health status. However, while these forms of prejudice and the harms they cause are beyond the scope of this chapter, much of the discussion here supports the claim that none of these violations should be beyond the reach of the law in a nation committed to equality. The cost of discrimination is high and climbing. While showing this to be the case for racial and ethnic discrimination, the reader should be mindful that health discrimination against *any* minority population is deadly and dead wrong.

I The Legacy of Discrimination in American Healthcare

Racial and ethnic discrimination in healthcare has been a part of the American historical fabric since the founding of the confederacy. African slaves brought to American shores were thought to warrant and therefore received the quality of medical care afforded to livestock, as colonists protected their financial investments in people they regarded as property. Copious historical records document the filthy shelters where slaves lived, and the limited medical treatment they received. Most owners provided medical treatment for slaves when motivated principally by the need to return the afflicted workers profitability as quickly as possible.[4] As institutional healthcare emerged, so did separate and unequal access to American medicine. Although the nation's first inpatient hospital, built in 1751 to provide charitable care for the poor and insane, initially served patients from all racial backgrounds, records show that by 1825, the Pennsylvania General Hospital, admitted black patients only into segregated wards, giving the facility its designation as "Anglo-America's First Hospital."[5]

From the beginning, Americans of European ancestry received superior healthcare as compared to all others who shaped our country. Native Americans who lacked immunological protections against European-borne illnesses such as smallpox, measles, and influenza,

[4] *See, e.g.*, *Patients' Voices in Early 19th Century Virginia: Letters to Doct. James Carmichael & Son*, Univ. of Va. (2005), http://carmichael.lib.virginia.edu/story/slavecare.html.

[5] William H. Williams, *The Early Days of Anglo-America's First Hospital: The Pennsylvania Hospital, 1751–1775*, 220 JAMA 115 (1972).

suffered egregiously from the new forms of disease the settlers introduced. Their mortality rates increased to "catastrophic" proportions after Columbus and the colonists arrived. Even more devastating, crowded and unsanitary living conditions on the reservation system imposed between the 1830s and 1870s, concentrated and isolated the diseased, and quickly decimated the Indian population. Episodic appropriations bills produced an inadequate Indian healthcare system that shifted the burden on this population from acute, communicable diseases, to chronic infections such as malaria, venereal diseases, tuberculosis, consumption, scrofula, and alcoholism. Thus the seeds of the 500-year-long problem of American Indian health disparities were sown.[6]

Chinese workers who arrived as laborers during the American Industrial Revolution suffered an affirmative brand of racial discrimination in healthcare. For example, in May 1900, the San Francisco Board of Health passed a resolution requiring that *only* the city's 25,000 Chinese residents submit to a "Haffkine Prophylactic" vaccine or be quarantined to prevent the spread of bubonic plague. The plague, it turned out, was conjecture, the vaccine was harmful, and the city's resolution was ultimately held unconstitutional.[7] Still other laws directed toward the Chinese immigrant community forced them to live in prescribed ghettos, where overcrowded and unsanitary conditions provided a vector for communicable diseases.[8]

Mexican laborers working to build American railways during the early 1900s were also early recipients of affirmatively discriminatory American healthcare. In 1916, twenty-six people, twenty-two of whom were Mexican railroad workers, contracted typhus. The five typhus victims who died were all Mexican. As a result, the Mexican community became the target of intrusive hygiene inspections and an aggressive educational and sanitation campaign, because they were declared, as a people group, "pathogenic."[9] State-sponsored efforts at containing the typhus epidemic simply overlooked unsanitary living and unhealthy working conditions the workers endured. This irony of this discriminatory public health effort prompted one group of Mexican workers to write a letter objecting not only to the "offensive and humiliating" treatment they received at the hands of health inspectors but also to wages too low "for the nourishment of one person," the lack of adequate bathroom facilities, the location of overtaxed bathrooms near cooking and sleeping areas in their camps, and "many other details which compromise our good health and personal hygiene."[10]

Unsurprisingly, the historical legacy of discriminatory healthcare has resulted in persistently inferior health outcomes for African, Asian, Latino, and Native American patients when compared to their white counterparts. These health disparities are rooted in structural inequalities beyond the healthcare system. But the structural inequalities that minority Americans face are exacerbated by the discrimination they experience within the healthcare system. The data that confirms health and healthcare disparities is widely reported and

[6] David S. Jones, *The Persistence of American Indian Health Disparities*, 96 AM. J. PUB. HEALTH 2122 (2006).

[7] Jew Ho v. Williamson, 103 F. 10 (1900).

[8] *But see In re* Lee Sing, 43 F. 359 (C.C.N.D. Cal. 1890), where a California court declared one such municipal ordinance unconstitutional.

[9] Natalia Molina, *Borders, Laborers, and Racialized Medicalization*, 101 AM. J. PUB. HEALTH 1024 (2011).

[10] *Id.* at 1026.

affects racial and ethnic minorities across all major disease modalities.[11] The Institute of Medicine's 2003 report titled *Unequal Treatment* remains the most comprehensive review of literature documenting racial and ethnic health disparities.[12] However, the data documenting persistent and pervasive health disparities continue to grow. Recounting a few examples here will help describe the broad scope and impact of the present-day healthcare discrimination problem in America.

II Racial and Ethnic Health Discrimination Today

Heart disease is the leading cause of death in the United States. Although mortality rates due to heart disease and stroke are decreasing, they remain highest among African American and Latino populations. Indeed, the prevalence rate of hypertension in black American adults is the highest in the world,[13] and African Americans are two to three times more likely to die from heart disease than whites. Yet the disturbing fact is that "people of color are far less likely to receive effective treatment and have less frequent access to newer and more costly invasive procedures such as cardiac catheterization, percutaneous coronary intervention, coronary artery bypass graft, implantation of defibrillators," and other treatments that represent the highest quality of care.[14]

Cancer incidence and death rates vary considerably across patients of different racial and ethnic groups. However, for all four major cancer sites (lung, colon, breast, and prostate), and for all cancer sites combined, African American men have a 14% higher incidence rate and a 33% higher death rate than white men. Black women, on the other hand, have a 16% higher death rate for all cancers combined, though they have a 6% lower incidence rate. Generally, other racial groups suffer a lower incidence and death rate from cancer than blacks and whites, but this is not the case for cancers associated within infectious agents such as uterine, cervix, stomach, and liver cancers where the incidence is generally higher in all minority populations than among whites.[15] All minority populations are more likely than non-Hispanic whites to be diagnosed at later stages of the disease than whites for all four major cancer sites. Discriminatory access to cancer care, and the inferior quality of healthcare that minority patients receive, both play a major role in cancer outcome disparities. The impact of discriminatory healthcare is confirmed by the data on cancer survival rates, particularly for black patients. The five-year survival rate for cancer is lower among blacks than for whites for every stage of diagnosis, for nearly every type of cancer; these outcomes are

[11] David B. Smith, *The Racial Segregation of Hospital Care Revisited: Medicare Discharge Patterns and Their Implications*, 88 Am. J. Pub. Health 461(1988).

[12] *See id.*

[13] Alan S. Go et al., *Heart Disease and Stroke Statistics—2013 Update: A Report from the American Heart Association*, 127 Circulation e6 (2013).

[14] Clyde W. Yancy et al., *Coalition to Reduce Racial and Ethnic Disparities in Cardiovascular Disease Outcomes: Why CREDO Matters to Cardiologists*, Elsvier Inc. (2011).

[15] Rebecca Siegel, Deepa Naishadham, & Ahmedin Jemal, *Cancer Statistics, 2013*, 63 CA: Cancer J. Clinicians 11 (2013).

not due to differences in comorbidities but are due to the fact that access disparities mean that black patients are less likely to receive early diagnosis when cancers are localized. Blacks are not only less likely to receive standard cancer treatments than whites, they also generally receive less extensive treatments. Studies show that African Americans who get cancer treatment and medical care similar to the care that white Americans receive experience similar outcomes.[16] In short, discriminatory treatment for minority cancer patients is deadly.

The story is the same across a vast array of medical conditions. Although minorities have a lower incidence of mental illness than whites, black children enjoy less access to high-quality mental healthcare than children of other races.[17] Studies show that 37.6% of whites receive care when diagnosed with a need for mental health or substance abuse treatment, but only 22.4% of Latinos and 25% of African Americans[18] receive treatment.[19] Blacks are less likely than whites to receive or even to be told about the option of a kidney transplant, the treatment for renal failure, though they represent a disproportionately large number of patients with end-stage renal disease.[20] The prevalence of asthma among children in the United States is highest among Puerto Rican children (16.5%), non-Hispanic black children (16%), and American Indian and Alaska Natives (10.7%), and lowest among Asian (6.8%), Hispanic children overall (7.9%), and non-Hispanic white children (8.2%). Minority children miss school more often, exercise less often, and are four times more likely to die due to asthma than white children.[21]

Notably, not all of the costs that discriminatory healthcare imposes upon individual patients are plain to see. Notwithstanding some improvements narrowing disparate life expectancy and infant mortality gaps, the immediate consequences of racial and ethnic health disparities include higher morbidity and mortality rates, decreased access to medical goods and services, and decreased quality of life for the patients who are not afforded equal access to healthcare. However, discrimination visits significant harms upon minority patients even beyond these burdens. Minority patients report that perceived discrimination is a stressor that increases their distrust of the healthcare system.[22] Their mistrust leads these patients to delay seeking further medical care, and decreases the likelihood of adherence to treatment recommendations. These outcomes further decrease minority access to care and ultimately lead to an underutilization of the healthcare system. Several studies demonstrate that perceived discrimination also increases patients' feelings of depression and hopelessness

[16] *Id.*

[17] GENEVIEVE M. KENNEY ET AL., URB. INST., RACIAL AND ETHNIC DIFFERENCES IN ACCESS TO CARE AND SERVICE USE FOR CHILDREN WITH COVERAGE THROUGH MEDICAID AND THE CHILDREN'S HEALTH INSURANCE PROGRAM 12 (2013), *available at* http://www.urban.org/UploadedPDF/412781-Racial-and-Ethnic-Differences-in-Access-to-Care-and-Service-Use-for-Children.pdf.

[18] I use the terms "black" and "African American" interchangeably to denote people descendent from Africa. *See, e.g.*, Lee Sigelman & Steven A. Tuch, *What's in a Name? Preference for "Black" Versus "African-American Among Americans of Descent*, 69 PUB. OPINION Q. 429 (2005).

[19] Thomas G. McGuire & Jeanne Miranda, *Racial and Ethnic Disparities in Mental Health Care: Evidence and Policy Implications*, 27 HEALTH AFF. 393 (2008).

[20] MICHELLE VAN RYN, CTR. CHRONIC DISEASE OUTCOMES RES., RESEARCH ON THE PROVIDER CONTRIBUTION TO RACE/ETHNICITY DISPARITIES IN MEDICAL CARE (2005).

[21] PRESIDENT'S TASK FORCE ON ENVTL. HEALTH RISKS & SAFETY RISKS TO CHILDREN, U.S. ENVTL. PROTECTION AGENCY, COORDINATED FEDERAL ACTION PLAN TO REDUCE RACIAL AND ETHNIC ASTHMA DISPARITIES (2012).

[22] Sarah Stark Casagrande et al., *Perceived Discrimination and Adherence to Medical Care in a Racially Integrated Community*, 22 J. GEN. INTERNAL MED. 389 (2007).

generally,[23] and leads to adverse birth outcomes of African Americans when compared with other racial groups.[24] Emerging evidence also indicates that discrimination is related to physiological changes in minority patients such as increased blood pressure, higher incidence of cardiovascular disease, and immunological compromises.[25] Also, considerable evidence suggests that discrimination perceived by minority patients is associated with increased risk of cigarette smoking, alcohol use, and abuse of prescription and illicit drugs.[26]

Economists have aggregated these individual impacts to quantify the cost to society that discrimination in healthcare imposes.[27] Estimates include the loss of productive human capital calculated in years of potential life lost, the loss of days away from work estimated from occupational health statistics, and the increased costs of medical care, including "excess" hospital admissions and delayed treatment for chronic illness in a sicker population.

It is well understood that lower socioeconomic status is related to poor health and health treatment for patients of *all* races. Thus, the intersectionality between poverty and poor health worsens the risk of discrimination in the healthcare system for racial and ethnic minorities. For example, black and Hispanic Americans suffer the highest poverty levels, lowest net worth, and lowest educational achievement levels of all racial groups in America. Thus, there is a significant correlation between their race and socioeconomic status that influences the discrimination that these groups suffer due to their poverty.[28] However this fact must not confuse or diminish the impact that discrimination solely due to racial or ethnic status has in producing health disparities for at least two reasons.

First, because most racial minorities are overrepresented when compared to whites among the poor, they bear a disproportionate burden of socioeconomic discrimination when compared to whites. As a population group, minorities are also disproportionately represented among those who have lower wealth and education than whites, though Asian Americans are the exception to this rule. Second, the empirical record confirms that race and ethnicity are independelty associated with poor health outcomes, at all socioeconomic leves. Studies continue to show that race and ethnicity independently predict poor health outcomes when disaggregated from confounding socioeconomic factors. Indeed the differences in the quality of healthcare and health outcomes are greater across racial groups than they are among socioeconomic levels within each racial group for minorities, but the reverse is true for whites.[29] In other words, as their income increases, whites enjoy dramatically

[23] Gilbert C. Gee et al., *Self-Reported Discrimination and Mental Health Status Among African Descendants, Mexican Americans, and Other Latinos in the New Hampshire REACH 2010 Initiative: The Added Dimension of Immigration*, 96 AM. J. PUB. HEALTH 1821 (2006).

[24] Cheryl L. Giscombe & Marci Lobel, *Explaining Disproportionately High Rates of Adverse Birth Outcomes Among African Americans: The Impact of Stress, Racism, and Related Factors in Pregnancy*, 131 PSYCHOL. BULL. 662 (2005).

[25] David R. Williams & Selina A. Mohammed, *Discrimination and Racial Disparities in Health: Evidence and Needed Research*, 32 J. BEHAV. MED. 20 (2009).

[26] *Id.*

[27] THOMAS A. LAVEIST, DARRELL J. GASKIN, & PATRICK RICHARD, JOINT CTR. POL. & ECON. STUD., THE ECONOMIC BURDEN OF HEALTH INEQUALITIES IN THE UNITED STATES (2009).

[28] Thomas A. LaVeist, *Disentangling Race and Socioeconomic Status: A Key to Understanding Health Inequalities*, 82 J. URB. HEALTH: BULL. N.Y. ACAD. MED. iii26 (2005).

[29] Melissa M. Farmer & Kenneth F. Ferraro, *Are Racial Disparities in Health Conditional on Socioeconomic Status?* 60 SOC. SCI. & MED. 191 (2005).

better health and healthcare, while improvements in socioeconomic status for minorities offers diminishing returns, primarily because their race continues to be a dominant determinant of the quality and quantity of healthcare they receive. Discrimination in healthcare based on poverty is indeed objectionable and harmful. Certainly, policy solutions addressed at reducing the social gradient that associates low socioeconomic status with poor health outcomes will improve minority health and health outcomes as well as the outcomes that whites experience. Nevertheless, these solutions will have no impact on the problem of racial and ethnic discrimination in healthcare or the disparately poor outcomes associated with this prejudice. Therefore, the remainder of this chapter focuses on the form of discrimination that the American legal system aspires to prohibit: discrimination against patients based on their race, color, or national origin.

III Federal Antidiscrimination Law—Past, Present, and Future

Title VI of the Civil Rights Act of 1964 provides that "[no] person in the United States shall, on the ground of race, color, or national origin, be excluded from participation in, be denied the benefits of, or be subjected to discrimination under any program or activity receiving Federal financial assistance."[30] Title VI was designed to further the U.S. Constitution's prohibition against denying to any person the equal protection of the laws. However, over time, an individual's right to bring suit for equitable and legal relief under this law has been cut off, and intent has been elevated to become an essential part of the constitutional violation. Section 601 of Title VI has been read to prohibit disparate treatment—that is intentional discrimination under any program or activity receiving federal funds. The current Supreme Court reads Section 602 of Title IV to give sole authority for enforcing disparate impact claims that do not require proof of intent, to federal departments and agencies "authorized and directed to effectuate the provisions of [Title VI]" but not to individual litigants.[31] These narrow readings of the Title VI statute are unfortunate, first and foremost because they defy the legislative language and intent of the 88th Congress, which enacted the Civil Rights Act of 1964, and second because they ignore completely that racial discrimination has taken a new but no less invidious form in this country.

According to the legislative history of Title VI statute, addressing healthcare inequity was central to Congress' purpose. The civil rights statute's proponents repeatedly cited a hospital desegregation case in their speeches advocating for the new law. The watershed case was *Simkins v. Moses H. Cone Memorial Hospital*.[32] The *Simkins* plaintiffs were black physicians, dentists, and patients who challenged racial segregation in a hospital that received public funds under the Hill-Burton Act. The Fourth Circuit had held that the separate but equal language in the Hill-Burton Act was unconstitutional and on March 2, 1964, three weeks before the bill proposing Title VI came before the full Senate for debate, the Supreme

[30] 42 U.S.C. § 2000d (2012). [31] Alexander v. Sandoval, 532 U.S. 275 (2001).

[32] Simkins v. Moses H. Cone Memorial Hosp., 323 F.2d 959, 969 (4th Cir. 1963), *cert. denied*, 376 U.S. 938 (1964).

Court denied certiorari to the defendant hospital in *Simkins*. The Court let stand the Fourth Circuit's condemnation of discrimination in the "massive use of public funds and extensive state-funding," and thus its justification for the holding in *Simkins*: "But we emphasize that this is not merely a controversy over a sum of money. Viewed from the plaintiffs' standpoint, it is an effort by a group of citizens to escape the consequences of discrimination in a concern touching health and life itself. . . . Such involvement in discriminatory action it was the design of the Fourteenth Amendment to condemn."[33] Senator John Pastore of Rhode Island cited *Simkins* with approval as he argued passionately for passage of Title VI: "The Supreme Court declined to review [*Simkins*]; so it is the law of our land. . . . That is why we need title VI of the Civil Rights Act, H.R. 7152—to prevent such discrimination where Federal funds are involved. Title VI intends to insure once and for all that the financial resources of the Federal Government—the commonwealth of Negro and white alike—will no longer subsidize racial discrimination."[34] Succinctly, another proponent said, "Title VI rests on the principle that 'taxpayers' money, which is collected without discrimination, shall be spent without discrimination.'"[35]

It is plain that at the time the civil rights law was enacted, Congress intended to grant a right of private enforcement to plaintiffs who claimed to suffer any form of discrimination in order to prohibit the scourge "once and for all." Indeed, until 2001, the U.S. Supreme Court had repeatedly, though not consistently, construed Title VI to prohibit both intentional and unintentional discrimination.[36] However, the Supreme Court has progressively eroded the protections against unintentional discrimination, and circumscribed the private cause of action under Title VI. The Supreme Court's narrow reading of Title VI visits particular harm upon minority patients in the American healthcare system because copious empirical evidence demonstrates that the racial and ethnic discrimination that produces health inequality arises most often from unintentional and unconscious discrimination, rather than from the legally prohibited intentional bigotry.

a. The Nature of Discrimination in American Healthcare

Studies show that most Americans are not overt racists. Physicians, hospital administrators, nurses, respiratory therapists, technicians, and the host of people who provide healthcare today are no exception to the national trend away from explicit racial prejudice. Moreover, health providers are members of a profession trained to deliver care dispassionately and committed to "first, do no harm." Therefore, the persistence of racial discrimination and

33 *Id.*

34 Of course, even once Congress enacted Title VI, federal law continued to sanction separate but unequal health care under the Hill-Burton Act, which controlled outside the reach of the Fourth Circuit's decision in *Simkins*.

35 Guardians Ass'n v. Civil Serv. Comm'n of New York, 463 U.S. 582, 599 (1983) (citing 110 CONG. REC. 6546 (1964) (statement of Sen. Ribicoff)).

36 *See* Lau v. Nichols, 414 U.S. 563 (1974); *Guardians Ass'n*, 463 U.S. 582 ("The Court squarely held in *Lau v. Nichols*, that Title VI forbids the use of federal funds not only in programs that intentionally discriminate on racial grounds but also in those endeavors that have a disparate impact on racial minorities."); Alexander v. Choate, 469 U.S. 287 (1985). *But see* Regents of the Univ. of Cal. v. Bakke, 438 U.S. 265 (1976).

health disparities in medicine requires an explanation. The scientific evidence points to the fact that discrimination has changed from conscious to unconscious forms of racism in medicine, in the same way that discrimination has evolved in other aspects of society. Healthcare providers, like employers, law enforcement officers, judges, and juries, today discriminate against minority patients unintentionally, based on unconsciously and implicitly held biases rather than based on explicit and intentionally malicious bigotry. While the evidence of implicit racial bias in other settings is well developed, the evidence of unconscious racism in healthcare is only recently emerging. Yet social scientists, relying on the science of implicit social cognition, have amassed a sufficient record to compel legal attention to this new form of invidious discrimination in healthcare.

Racism due to implicit bias is especially dangerous because it is ubiquitous and operates surreptitiously in contradiction to a person's sincerely held nonprejudiced beliefs. An implicit bias is a negative attitude that develops over time about a group of people. Implicit biases are developed subconsciously, as individuals gather knowledge about a particular social group from their environment and cumulative life experiences. Everything from the music we hear, to conversations held in our homes, schools, and places of worship, to news, political, or sports programs, to the experiences we have or that our peers report, to motion picture, television, and media representations of minorities—all constitute a lifetime of experiences that contribute to unconsciously stored information about racial and ethnic minorities. Gradually, this stored social group knowledge becomes the information that our brains are unconsciously triggered to retrieve as stereotypes when we encounter and identify a person of a different race. In this way, negative implicit biases are automatically activated to become negative stereotypes, prejudice, and ultimately discrimination without any intentionality on the part of the actor. The key finding that research has consistently shown is that implicit biases can directly contradict explicit personal preferences and more powerfully influence behavior and judgments than firmly but expressly held egalitarian principles. This explains how well-intentioned, fair-minded individuals can be responsible for discriminatory behavior. Implicit racial and ethnic biases operate unconsciously but dominate the choices we make when we interact with members of different racial and ethnic groups.

Social scientists can quantifiably measure implicit racial biases. Although the method is not without controversy and limitations, the Implicit Association Test (IAT) has become the tool of choice for measuring implicit bias. The IAT is a computer-based test that measures the time a person takes to associate words with photographs. The test asks subjects to quickly pair positive words such as "pretty," "nice," or "clean" with photographs of phenotypically African- or European-American faces. The test measures the time a subject takes to make associations between words that are positive, and photographs of white, black, and Hispanic faces to produce a score ranging from −2 to +2. Based on the principle that people more quickly associate photographs with words that are consistent with their implicitly held beliefs about those pictures, a low IAT score is interpreted as a pro-black implicit preference, a high IAT score is interpreted as a pro-white implicit preference, and a person who scores an IAT of zero is interpreted as having no implicit racial preference between the two groups.[37] Using the IAT, researchers have confirmed that the majority of both physicians and patients

[37] Anthony G. Greenwald & Linda Hamilton Krieger, *Implicit Bias: Scientific Foundations*, 94 Cal. L. Rev. 945 (2006).

have measurable implicit preferences for whites over blacks and non-white Hispanics. Researchers have known for some time that physicians discriminate in favor of whites and men as compared to blacks and women in their treatment decisions. A 1999 study of how doctors treat patients with cardiovascular disease famously demonstrated this discrimination.[38] However the evidence that physicians are not generally overt racists seemed to contradict these findings. The ability to measure unconscious racism using the IAT has shed considerable light on these dichotomous findings. Studies such as those summarized in the following section show that physicians and patients' implicit racial and ethnic biases appear to operate before, during, and after the clinical encounter between doctors and patients to profoundly influence the quality of healthcare that minority patients receive, and therefore the quality of health they experience, notwithstanding the good and egalitarian intentions to which most healthcare providers expressly adhere.

i. Physicians and Implicit Bias

Physicians and other healthcare providers are particularly susceptible to unconscious discrimination arising from their implicit biases. Unconscious racism pervades settings in which actors must make important, discretionary judgments under conditions of uncertainty and time pressure, with access to limited information. Medical decision-making occurs in just such a setting. Moreover, sorting clues into categories helps all of us make sense of the complexity we encounter in our daily lives; this adaptive behavior helps us to cross the street safely avoiding fast cars, remember to dress appropriately for the weather, and use caution when we encounter unfamiliar situations, for example. In medicine, this sorting function is especially important to the process of identifying the correct explanation for a person's illness and determining the best treatment to resolve a patient's complaint. However, these seemingly innocuous applications of making implicit judgments turn into odious discrimination when they systematically involve inequitable treatment of minority as compared to white patients.

The most often studied question in this field is whether physicians, because of their implicit biases, prescribe inferior treatments to minority patients than to white patients. The evidence cuts both ways. In one study, physicians watched videos of black and white actors dressed as patients, each relating the same personal history and medical information. They described their coronary artery disease. When the doctors were asked to make a treatment decision, the researchers found that those doctors with high IAT scores—showing stronger pro-white/anti-black implicit biases—more readily discriminated against their black patients by giving them inferior treatment modalities, while more often giving the treatment of choice to their white patients.[39] The findings in this study were remarkable especially because the 287 physicians who participated also overwhelmingly declared they had no explicit preferences for white patients over black ones. The IAT study showed that even when doctors are not overtly prejudice, they might unconsciously discriminate nonetheless. However another study found differently.

[38] Kevin A. Schulman, *The Effect of Race and Sex on Physicians' Recommendations for Cardiac Catheterization*, 340 NEW ENG. J. MED. 618 (1999).

[39] Alexander R. Green, *Implicit Bias Among Physicians and its Prediction of Thrombolysis Decisions for Black and White Patients*, 22 J. INTERNAL MED. 1231 (2007).

In contrast to this first experiment, when 138 physicians were studied to determine whether their treatment of hypertension patients varied with changes in their levels of implicit racial bias, researchers found no association between physician bias and treatment decisions.[40] Moreover, this study showed no association between physician bias and patients' medical adherence or hypertension control outcomes. If the hypertension study is correct, then at least where hypertension is concerned, physicians' implicit racial and ethnic biases do not have any impact on their treatment decisions or on the differences in medical outcomes between black and white patients. Such a conclusion is counterintuitive but can possibly be explained. First, hypertension is a well-understood malady that patients generally know how to control. The study was conducted over a three-year period so that patient visits might have been infrequent and irregular, compromising the accuracy of results. The health facilities where the patients from this study were seen are large, integrated health systems where most patients generally have access to quality preventative care from primary care providers. Finally, the study does not account for patients who stopped going to the doctor, which is a group that evidence shows often includes minority patients who believe they have been the victims of discrimination. In summary, the nature of the disease, the healthcare setting, and patient behavior are important factors that may make this careful study an outlier.

Other researchers have found associations between pediatricians' implicit bias, and differences in their willingness to prescribe pain medication to black and white children with pain, but did not see any differences in these doctors' treatment of children with asthma, attention deficit hyperactivity disorder (ADHD), or urinary tract infections.[41] When medical students were studied, these doctors-in-training were found to share the same pro-white levels of implicit bias that others in the general population held. However, unlike older, experienced physicians, there was almost no association between these younger providers and treatment decisions they made.[42] Taken together, these studies of possible medical treatment discrimination due to implicit bias paints a mixed picture. While the evidence of physician discrimination appears strong when we look at the overwhelming evidence of patient health disparities, the link between biased treatment decisions and healthcare discrimination is not conclusive, that is, until researchers consider the *entire* scope of physician and patient encounters.

ii. Discrimination in Healthcare at the Clinical Level

Physicians and patients are affected by implicit racial and ethnic biases before, after, and during the clinical relationship, not only at the point of treatment decisions. Discrimination permeates every aspect of provider-patient interaction in order to yield the discriminatory results we call health disparities. The social psychology evidence to support this assertion

[40] Irene V. Blair et al., *An Investigation of Associations Between Clinicians' Ethnic or Racial Bias and Hypertension Treatment, Medication Adherence and Blood Pressure Control*, 2014 J. GEN. INTERNAL MED. 987.

[41] Janice A. Sabin & Anthony G. Greenwald, *The Influence of Implicit Bias on Treatment Recommendations for 4 Common Pediatric Conditions: Pain, Urinary Tract Infection, Attention Deficit Hyperactivity Disorder, and Asthma*, 102 AM. J. PUB. HEALTH 988 (2012).

[42] Adil H. Haider et al., *Association of Unconscious Race and Social Class Bias with Vignette-Based Clinical Assessments by Medical Students*, 306 JAMA 942 (2011).

describes six different pathways or "mechanisms" through which unconscious racism operates to cause discrimination in healthcare. Biased perceptions constitute the first mechanism connecting unintentional discrimination to disparities. Physicians hold implicit biased perceptions that cause discriminatory assumptions about patients' likely education and resources available for adherence even before they enter the hospital or examination room.[43] Perceptions made in advance may cause physicians to surmise that a black patient will be unfriendly or uncooperative, while a Hispanic patient will exaggerate their symptoms, and Native American, African American, and Hispanic American patients will lack the educational resources to deal with complicated treatment plans. These perceptions may work to the detriment of the treatment that minority patients receive. Social scientists have shown that biased perceptions also influence a second mechanism before doctors and patients meet. Statistical discrimination provides a second mechanism to link bias to disparate health outcomes.[44] In some cases, doctors may improperly generalize data they know to be true about some patients who are members of a racial minority, and conclude without evidence that the data is true about all patients of that racial group. Therefore, physicians may err by ascribing data about a patient's social group that does not fit that individual patient at all. For example, physicians have been shown to make incorrect generalizations about minority patients' educational attainment or resources available to adhere to complex treatment regimes.[45] Similarly, statistical discrimination occurs when a physician infers the likely cause of a patient's problem and the steps to address it based on assumptions about unobservable variables. In this instance a physician may choose to make a prediction about the medication a patient will best respond to, based on information about a patient's social group characteristics simply by analyzing unrelated racial and ethnic cues she can observe. Thus, a doctor may resort to stereotypes such as presumptions about patients' susceptibility to abusing narcotics or frequency of sexual activity that result in misdiagnosis or disparate treatment decisions. Another form of statistical discrimination arises when physicians allow the "noise" of certain probability data to distract their accurate evaluation of a patient's symptoms. For example, knowing that black patients have a lower probability of depression than whites may influence a physician to incorrectly truncate her search for the source of an African American patient's report of lethargy and missed work over the past two weeks. Thus implicit bias can operate throught the first two mechanisms—biased physician perceptions and statistical discrimination to affect health disparities even before a doctor and patient ever meet.

The third and fourth mechanisms through which unconscious racism can travel to produce discriminatory healthcare occur during the face-to-face communication exchange between patient and provider. Considerable scholarly attention is devoted to examining physician verbal and nonverbal communication with patients generally and minority patients in particular. The third mechanism involves physician communication. Studies have shown that physicians' posture, eye contact, tone of voice, questions, and information content, and the

[43] Michelle van Ryn & Jane Burke, *The Effect of Patient Race and Socio-Economic Status on Physicians' Perceptions of Patients*, 50 Soc. Sci. & Med. 813 (2000).

[44] Ana I. Balsa & Thomas G. McGuire, *Statistical Discrimination in Health Care*, 20 J. Health Econ. 881 (2001).

[45] *Id.*; van Ryn & Burke, *The Effect of Patient Race and Socio-Economic Status on Physicians' Perceptions of Patients*.

length of the clinical visit differs with minority as compared to white patients. Among black patients, one study showed that physicians' implicit racial bias was associated with physicians exercising more verbal dominance in patient conversations, longer visits, slower speech, less patient centeredness, and receiving poorer patient ratings of interpersonal care.[46] Studies even show that physicians, who are in no way prejudiced overtly, display heightened levels of anxiety and even hostility when interacting with minority patients.[47] Medical discrimination that adversely impacts minority health can result from these communication differences.

Moreover, it turns out that patients pick up these discriminatory cues from their physicians and respond in turn with discriminatory feedback of their own contributing to the fourth mechanism. A remarkable study by Dr. Louis Penner showed that black patients react most negatively to physicians who report low explicit racial or ethnic prejudice, but who also display high IAT scores, suggesting greater anti-black implicit bias.[48] Indeed, black patients tested showed more favorable responses to physicians with very high explicit biases than to the doctors who had contradictory implicit and explicit bias measures. Researchers have coined the term "aversive racist" for those who are explicitly race-neutral but implicitly race-biased, and there is evidence that interactions with such doctors adversely impacts minority patient health. Black patients who judge their physicians' communication as less informative, supportive, and partnering ultimately have lower satisfaction ratings after the clinical encounter. These patients also show correspondingly lower adherence rates as well, resulting in the likelihood that their health outcomes will be worse than white patients experience.

To complete the interaction between the third mechanism—communication and conduct, on the physician side, and the fourth mechanism—communication and conduct on the patient side, Dr. Lisa Cooper has called the communication reciprocity between physician and patient, a "feedback loop." When patients ask few questions, seem reluctant rather than forthcoming with medical information, or fail to participate in medical decision-making, physicians may also sense bias and discrimination toward them and respond by limiting the information or time they give to minority patients.[49] Researchers have yet to quantify the extent of discrimination that comes from bias-tainted communication, but the importance has been identified by social scientists and could not be overstated.[50] Some evidence suggests minority patients who are dissatisfied with their providers will simply stop seeking medical care, or change providers often. The result is that discrimination by both parties to the clinical encounter can diminish the quality and continuity of patient care. A provider's negative perceptions may be reinforced through negative communication, discriminatory interpretation of patient data, and unwittingly biased interpretation of patient conduct. The cumulative and complex interaction of these unconscious biases is likely a more significant source of disparities in medical treatment than policy-makers have understood to date and may

[46] Lisa A. Cooper et al., *Associations of Clinicians' Implicit Attitudes About Race with Medical Visit Communication and Patient Ratings of Interpersonal Care*, 102 AM. J. PUB. HEALTH 979 (2012).

[47] Richard L. Street Jr., Howard Gordon, & Paul Haidet, *Physicians' Communication and Perceptions of Patients: Is It How They Look, How They Talk, or Is It Just the Doctor?* 65 SOC, SCI. & MED. 586 (2007).

[48] Louis A. Penner et al., *Aversive Racism and Medical Interactions with Black Patients: A Field Study*, 46 J. EXPERIMENTAL SOC. PSYCHOL. 436 (2010).

[49] Howard S. Gordon et al., *Racial Differences in Doctors' Information-Giving and Patients' Participation*, 107 CANCER 1313 (2006).

[50] Lisa A. Cooper, *Delving Below the Surface: Understanding How Race and Ethnicity Influence Relationships in Health Care*, 21 J. GEN. INTERNAL MED. 521 (2006).

explain the contradictory data researchers have seen in studies that examine the next mechanism through which discrimination impacts minority patients.

Several studies have shown that physicians' implicit racial and ethnic biases are associated with inferior medical treatment decisions for minority patients as compared to white patients, and thus disparate physician treatment decisions constitute the fifth mechanism.[51] However, as discussed earlier, a single study reached contradictory results finding that primary care physicians' medical treatment decisions of hypertension patients were not associated with their implicit bias levels.[52] In addition to the possibility that this aberrational study does not account for patients who discontinue treatment when they perceive physician discrimination, the hypertension study may add the straightforward but limited conclusion that physician biases affect primary care physicians differently than other specialists, with respect to a single disease.

Racial discrimination due to implicit bias continues to operate even after patients leave the hospital, clinic, or physician's office, through the sixth and final mechanism: patients' adherence decisions. Patients who do not trust their physicians do not accept their medical advice, seek medical care less frequently, and are less likely to adhere to treatment recommendations. Thus, these patients are also more likely to have inferior health outcomes when compared to patients whose communication allows them to build a trust relationship with their providers.[53] Taken together, the research supports the conclusion that unconscious racial and ethnic discrimination is a contributing cause to the inferior quality of health and healthcare that minority patients experience in America.[54]

The six mechanisms that describe how individual cognitive biases infiltrate healthcare delivery comprise a conceptual model of implicit bias in healthcare that has been called "The Biased Care Model."[55] The model elucidates the pathways through which individual biases travel to affect minority patient health outcomes. However, physician and patient level biases do not tell the entire story. These interpersonal interactions are replicated throughout the large and complex organizational structures that increasingly characterize the healthcare industry, to produce institutional discrimination at institutional and systemic levels.

iii. Discrimination at Organizational and Systemic Levels

Dr. Joseph Betancourt and others have identified organizational and structural sources that produce discrimination and inequities in American healthcare.[56] Institutionalized

[51] *See, e.g.*, Alexander R. Green et al., *Implicit Bias Among Physicians and Its Prediction of Thrombolysis Decisions for Black and White Patients*, 22 J. INTERNAL MED. 1231, 1231–38 (2007); Sabin & Greenwald, *The Influence of Implicit Bias on Treatment Recommendations.*

[52] Blair et al., *An Investigation of Associations.*

[53] Louis A. Penner et al., *The Experience of Discrimination and Black–White Health Disparities in Medical Care*, 35 J. BLACK PSYCHOL. 180 (2009).

[54] Dara H. Sorkin et al., *Racial/Ethnic Discrimination in Health Care: Impact on Perceived Quality of Care*, 25 J. GEN. INTERNAL MED. 390 (2010).

[55] *See* Dayna Bowen Matthew, *Just Medicine: A Cure for Inequality in Healthcare and Beyond* (New York Univ. Press 2015) (on file with author).

[56] *See, e.g.*, Joseph R. Betancourt et al., *Defining Cultural Competence: A Practical Framework for Addressing Racial/Ethnic Disparities in Health and Health Care*, 118 PUB. HEALTH REPS. 293 (2003) (describing how "organizational, structural, and clinical cultural competence interventions" can improve health disparities).

discrimination occurs in hospital systems, managed care networks, and accountable care organizations that adversely impact minority health broadly.[57] For example, the lack of diversity in the leadership of healthcare organizations makes it more likely that institutions are defined by majoritarian cultural norms. These norms may ignore minority patient needs for translators, signage, or a sufficiently diverse workforce to give minority patients interactions with minority providers who have been shown to produce higher patient satisfaction and improved outcomes for vulnerable patients. Also, organizational biases systemically fail to account for minority patients' unique cultural norms associated with important processes such as informed consent.[58] The lack of diversity in the healthcare delivery workforce has been associated with some poor minority patient outcomes.[59] Minority physicians have been shown more likely than white physicians to offer more effective care to minority patients and more likely to deliver care to minority populations. Yet, minorities are significantly underrepresented within the faculties, administration, student populations, and curricular content of American medical schools and schools of public health. Moreover, formal hierarchies and bureaucratic internal structures that characterize these academic institutions and healthcare deliverer overall tend to perpetuate discrimination through specialization, proliferation of titles, chains of command, and narrow spheres of control. Large institutional providers often segregate women and minorities in subordinate positions, such as nursing staffs, orderlies, janitorial staff, and support workers that lack discretion to significantly impact the quality of patient treatment decisions.

The need to construct solutions that address health inequality at the organizational and systemic levels has been described as "urgent."[60] However the evidence is that providers have been slow to respond to this urgency, and the research that would support evidence-based changes in healthcare delivery is nascent. For example, few institutional studies have assessed changes in health disparities as a primary outcome. Some limited evidence suggests that clinical reorganization, multidisciplinary patient case management, peer support, collaborative socio-medical care models and, health education directed toward reducing disparities may have a positive impact on minority health outcomes, especially when accompanied by community outreach and partnership.[61] However, more research exploring the relationship between organizational discrimination and disparate health outcomes is needed. While discriminatory institutions outside of the healthcare industry such as residential segregation and political governance have been shown to significantly impact disparate outcomes,[62]

[57] Michele J. Gelfand et al., *Discrimination in Organizations: An Organizational-Level Systems Perspective*, CORNELL UNIV. ILR SCHOOL, Mar. 1, 2007, *available at http://digitalcommons.ilr.cornell.edu/cgi/viewcontent.cgi?article=1471&context=cahrswp*.

[58] Dayna Bowen Matthew, *Race, Religion, and Informed Consent: Lessons from Social Science*, 36 J.L., MED. & ETHICS 150 (2008).

[59] *See*, e.g., A. L. Stanton, *Determinants of Adherence to Medical Regimens by Hypertensive Patients*, 10 J. BEHAV. MED. 377 (1987).

[60] Marshall H. Chin et al., *Interventions to Reduce Racial and Ethnic Disparities in Health Care*, 64 MED. CARE RES. & REV. 7S (2007) (literature review of interventions using cultural leverage, pay-for-performance, and public reporting of performance measures to reduce disparities).

[61] *Id.*

[62] *See*, e.g., Gilbert C. Gee, *A Multilevel Analysis of the Relationship Between Institutional and Individual Racial Discrimination and Health Status*, 92 AM. J. PUB. HEALTH 615 (2002).

researchers and policy-makers have paid inadequate attention to addressing the sources of health inequality that foment from within healthcare institutions and systems.

b. Toward Nondiscriminatory Healthcare

Recall that racial and ethnic discrimination by entities that receive federal dollars is against the law. In 2011 the federal government paid 27.6% of the $2.7 trillion spent on healthcare nationally, to reimburse hospitals, nursing homes, and physicians for discriminatory care. Recall also the extent to which African, Latino, Asian, and Native Americans are suffering from disease and death when compared to whites. By one analyst's count, discrimination in healthcare is responsible for over 84,000 "excess" or avoidable minority deaths annually.[63] In spite of the fact that the American Medical Association first issued a report calling for the elimination of disparities in 1994, by most recorded measures the majority of health disparities in quality and access to care continue to persist or grow. Notwithstanding a nationwide effort to impose largely voluntary standards for nondiscriminatory healthcare.[64] Finally, recall the plain language and statements of legislators who enacted the national law prohibiting racial and ethnic discrimination by federal contractors. The urgency of reforming and enforcing antidiscrimination law in healthcare could not be clearer.

In 2003, the Institute of Medicine's landmark report *Unequal Treatment* identified patient-, treatment-, and systems-level variables that may contribute to health disparities. Yet, in the decade that has followed, systemic interventions have been limited while the evidence that discrimination harms and even causes premature deaths in minority patient populations continues to grow. It may be reasonably argued that this disproportionate response provides a compelling basis to require legal accountability for discrimination that produces inequity in healthcare at clinical, institutional, and systemic levels. Currently, however, the antidiscrimination laws are inadequate to address the unconscious discrimination that characterizes clinical, institutional, and systemic discrimination in healthcare. The remainder of this chapter argues for a change in antidiscrimination law that is commensurate with the urgency, severity, and reality of unconscious discrimination in American healthcare.

c. Restoring American Antidiscrimination Law

Title VI of the Civil Rights Act remains the most direct prohibition against racial and ethnic discrimination in American law. Yet, as discussed earlier, this law is powerless to address the unintentional rather than intentional discrimination that has been shown to permeate American healthcare. This has not always been the case. Ironically, as the national expression of racial discrimination has evolved from explicit and overt bigotry, to more advanced

[63] David Satcher, George E. Fryer, & Jessica McCann, *What If We Were Equal? A Comparison of the Black-White Mortality Gap in 1960 and 2000*, 24 HEALTH AFF. 459 (2005).

[64] National Standards for Culturally and Linguistically Appropriate Services in Health Care (CLAS Standards) have governed health providers since 2001 and are largely ineffective. *See* Lisa C. Diamond et al., *Do Hospitals Measure Up to the National Culturally and Linguistically Appropriate Services Standards?* 48 MED. CARE 1080 (2010).

and subtle forms of unconscious racism, the Supreme Court has retreated from the congressional aspiration and promise expressed when enacting Title VI, that the federal government would "no longer subsidize racial discrimination." By returning to its original intent for the federal antidiscrimination law, Congress could effectively and substantially reduce health and healthcare disparities. Unfortunately, to restore the statute to its original purpose, Congress must act to reform the language of Title VI in order to counteract the U.S. Supreme Court's tortured interpretation of the law.

In 1974 and again in 1983, the Supreme Court affirmed that the provisions of Title VI prohibited unintentional discrimination. "The Court squarely held in *Lau v. Nichols*, that Title VI forbids the use of federal funds not only in programs that intentionally discriminate on racial grounds but also in those endeavors that have a disparate impact on racial minorities."[65] In *Guardians Association v. Civil Service Commission of New York*, even though the Court in that case limited recovery for unintentional discrimination to declaratory and injunctive relief, Justice White opened the *Guardians Assn.* opinion by declaring, "[t]he threshold issue before the Court is whether the plaintiffs in this case need to prove discriminatory intent to establish a violation of Title VI. . . . I conclude, as do four other Justices in separate opinions, that the Court of Appeals erred in requiring proof of discriminatory intent."[66] Justice White concluded the *Guardians* opinion writing, "[i]n conclusion, for the reasons expressed above, I am convinced that discriminatory intent is not an element of a Title VI violation. . . ."[67]

Justice White also pointed to congressional inaction as evidence Congress intended to prohibit unintentional discrimination. Justice White explained, "I discern nothing in the legislative history of Title VI, . . . that is at odds with the administrative construction of the statutory terms [reaching disparate impact discrimination]. Congress, furthermore, has consistently administered the Title, in this manner for almost two decades without interference. It must be concluded that Title VI reaches unintentional, disparate-impact discrimination as well as deliberate racial discrimination."[68] Similarly citing congressional inaction, Justice Marshall pointed out in his dissent from the majority's holding that in 1966 a proposal to prohibit only intentional discrimination under Title VI never emerged from committee. In fact, Marshall said, "[s]ince the passage of the 1964 Act, Congress has also enacted 10 additional statutes modeled on §601 of Title VI, none of which define discrimination to require proof of intent."[69] In 1992, even Justice Clarence Thomas wrote separately in *United States v. Fordice* to explain that a Title VI claim does not require "proof of a present intent to discriminate" if an elementary school policy originated during a period of *de jure* segregation.[70] Yet, in 2001 the Supreme Court asserted with conviction, "it is similarly beyond dispute—and no party disagrees—that §601 prohibits only intentional discrimination."[71] This statement, apparently relying upon a view denounced by five Justices in *Guardians*, is simply not supported by the Court's prior opinions.

In a second reversal of Title VI jurisprudence, the *Sandoval* Court swept away the rights of private parties to bring disparate impact claims saying that Congress had created none "and the courts may not create one, no matter how desirable that might be as a policy matter,

[65] Guardians Ass'n v. Civil Serv. Comm'n of New York, 463 U.S. 582, 589 (1983).

[66] *Id.* at 584. [67] *Id.* at 607. [68] *Id.* at 593. [69] *Id.* at 620.

[70] United States v. Fordice, 505 U.S. 717, 746 (1992).

[71] Alexander v. Sandoval, 532 U.S. 275, 280 (2001).

or how compatible with the statute."[72] Admittedly, Title VI does not contain an explicit provision empowering "private attorneys general" to enforce its prohibitions. However the Supreme Court in *Cannon v. University of Chicago* expressed its approbation of lower court rulings that found that Title VI implied a private cause of action.[73] Comparing Titles VI and IX the *Cannon* Court said, "[n]either statute expressly mentions a private remedy for the person excluded from participation in a federally funded program. The drafters of Title IX explicitly assumed that it would be interpreted and applied as Title VI had been during the preceding eight years."[74] That Congress had also approved implied private causes of action under Title VI[75] was of no moment to the *Sandoval* Court.

Justice Scalia went on to further erode Title VI protections in *Alexander v. Sandoval*, saying, "we must assume for purposes of deciding this case that regulations promulgated under §602 of Title VI may validly proscribe activities that have a disparate impact on racial groups even though such activities are permissible under §601."[76] Scalia's opinion in *Sandoval* stands in stark contrast to Justice Thurgood Marshall's statement of the rule of law that had controlled §602 of Title VI for more than thirty years. In *Alexander v. Choate*, Justice Marshall wrote for the majority to hold that a state's reduction in Medicaid covered services did not violate the Rehabilitation Act of 1973.[77] In 1985 Marshall explained, "the Court [has] held that actions having unjustifiable disparate impact on minorities could be redressed through agency regulations designed to implement the purpose of Title VI. In essence, then, we held that Title VI had delegated to the agencies in the first instance the complex determination of what sorts of disparate impacts upon minorities constituted sufficiently significant social problems, and were readily enough remediable to warrant altering the practices of federal grantees that had produced those impacts."[78] The *Sandoval* Court, in contrast, dismissed the decades of Title VI precedent it reversed by referring to "the understanding of private causes of action that held sway 40 years ago when Title VI was enacted" as "the *ancient regime*."[79]

A thorough review of the Court's departure from Congress's view of Title VI is important for at least two reasons. First, it would appear that during the half century that followed passage of the landmark Civil Rights Act of 1964, the U.S. Supreme Court has replaced Congress as the authority to protect the civil rights of minorities against discrimination using its plenary power of judicial review to enact a new and narrower civil rights agenda. The Supreme Court has not only contradicted Title VI's plain language that expressly forbids federally funded providers from discriminating or denying healthcare benefits to minorities, as well as the best evidence of Congress's intent to enact a law that "recognize[s] no prejudice,"[80] but the Court has also ignored the best empirical evidence concerning the unintentional nature of racial and ethnic discrimination in America. This points to the second reason to closely scrutinize the Supreme Court's Title VI jurisprudence. The Court's focus on intentionality[81] comes at a time when empirical evidence that even unintentional discrimination can be intentionally controlled has mounted. For the past twenty years, social scientists have published evidence that implicit biases are malleable. This is an important and underappreciated

[72] *Id.* at 286–87. [73] Cannon v. Univ. of Chi., 441 U.S. 677, 696 (1979). [74] *Id.* at 696.
[75] *See* 42 U.S.C. § 2000d-7. [76] *Sandoval*, 532 U.S. at 281.
[77] Alexander v. Choate, 469 U.S. 287 (1985). [78] *Id.* at 293. [79] *Id.* at 287.
[80] 110 CONG. REC. 7045, 7064 (1964) (statement of Sen. John O. Pastore) (arguing for passage of Title VI).
[81] Washington v. Davis, 426 U.S. 229 (1976).

fact that bears repeating. Substantial scientific evidence shows that unconscious racism is not inevitable, though it operates automatically; is not inaccessible to deliberate human control, though it occurs unintentionally; and implicit biases are not inaccessible even though they form subconsciously. Individuals as well as institutions, it turns out, can substantially mitigate implicit racial biases.

The negative stereotypes previously viewed as inevitable, involuntary attitudes, in fact are merely patterns of thought activation that are simultaneously determined by the context and weight of new information and connected to existing and underlying beliefs. Scientists call this the "connectionist" model of implicit bias, and it long ago replaced the old theories of automaticity. Psychologists now conclude that "stereotypes are quite elastic and thus any individual could hold and even change an infinite number of representations of a social category's members when viewed across time and place."[82] Implicit biases are constructed over time, and therefore can be deconstructed over time as well. In plain language, implicit biases are like a bad driving habit: with practice, the habit can be changed.

Given "the now bountiful evidence that automatic attitudes—like self-reported attitudes—are sensitive to personal, social, and situational pressures,"[83] individuals as well as institutions may reasonably be held accountable for taking action, or failing to take action, to reduce the discrimination that results from unconscious racism. In healthcare, for example, the malleability evidence provides a rational way for providers to align the specific, remedial interventions that effectively disrupt implicit biases, with each of the six mechanisms in clinical healthcare relationships that act as pathways for discrimination to ultimately harm minority health outcomes. With this evidentiary basis, moreover, policy-makers have a compelling basis to incentivize a change in the social norms surrounding the presumed ubiquity and lack of culpability that has sheltered unconscious racism from censure. Finally, based on the malleability evidence, lawmakers can reconsider the assumption that those who are unconscious racists lack discriminatory purpose; antidiscrimination law may prohibit intentional disregard for the scientifically proved interventions that can reduce unintentional as well as intentional discrimination based on race, color, or national origin.

Congress could restore the civil rights law to its original purpose and take back the ground ceded to the current Supreme Court in setting a civil rights agenda for this nation by amending the plain language of Title VI. Amending the Civil Rights Act to expressly prohibit unintentional discrimination will account for the fact that, in the words of Justice Ginsburg, joined by Justice Breyer, "[i]t is well documented that conscious and unconscious race bias, even rank discrimination based on race, remain alive in our land, impeding realization of our highest values and ideals."[84] Next, an amendment restoring a private cause of action for disparate impact claims will empower minority patients and their advocates to use structural reform litigation to combat systemic unconscious discrimination that has gone unchecked in healthcare, as well as in other publicly funded sectors.

[82] Alison P. Lenton, Martin Bruder, & Constantine Sedikides, *A Meta-Analysis on the Malleability of Automatic Gender Stereotypes*, 33 Psychol. Women Q. 183 (2008).

[83] Irene V. Blair, *The Malleability of Automatic Stereotypes and Prejudice*, 6 Personality & Soc. Psychol. Rev. 242 (2002).

[84] Grutter v. Bollinger, 539 U.S. 306, 345 (2003) (Ginsburg, J., concurring). [Typically only the author of the concurrence would be included.]

A further amendment creating an affirmative defense for government grantees who can show they have taken reasonable, evidence-based steps to reduce discrimination due to implicit bias will incentivize all federal contractors to engage in ex ante, self-analysis and undertake the interventions social scientists have proved effective to mitigate discrimination. This amendment would introduce a flexible negligence standard into the statute that would serve two purposes. In the first instance, a negligence standard would incentivize government grantees—say a hospital—to employ all reasonable methods that social scientists have demonstrated will reduce discrimination due to unconscious racism. For example, a hospital may replace ineffective programs such as cultural competency seminars, with the type of multiweek stereotype negation training for medical staff that measurably reduces implicit biases over the long term. Responding to evidence from the malleability literature reviewed in this chapter, the same hospital can aggressively signal a social consensus that implicit as well as explicit discrimination is no longer the accepted norm and can back up these signals with affirmative hiring, promotion, and retention plans that ensure patients and providers regularly interact with minority leaders who provide counterstereotypes throughout their organizations.

The second purpose the negligence standard would serve is to encourage the industry to develop creative, structural solutions to the problem of implicit bias that have hitherto been discussed as merely in the context of an individual burden. In light of healthcare consolidation due to the Affordable Care Act reforms, defeating unconscious discrimination in healthcare will have to be driven by institutions, which will operate as the cheapest cost avoider by virtue of the increased influence they will exercise over the healthcare workforce. Finally, the statute should allow for compensatory damages in cases of intentional discrimination, punitive damages against nongovernmental entities in cases of intentional discrimination, and equitable remedies, including attorneys' fees, in all other Title VI cases. In summary, Title VI should be amended to 1) expressly prohibit unintentional discrimination, 2) restore a private cause of action for disparate impact cases, 3) establish a negligence standard for disparate impact discrimination, and 4) clarify damages. Taken together, these four amendments will operate preventatively to prospectively influence health providers to reduce their discriminatory behavior.[85]

Indeed, the 111th Congress evinced its firm commitment to addressing discrimination in healthcare with the passage of the Affordable Care Act Section 1557.[86] This is a promising new civil rights statute, dedicated specifically to healthcare. The Affordable Care Act reaffirms and leaves Title VI and its regulations in place. However, the new statute significantly enlarges Title VI protections in at least four ways. First, Section 1557 prohibits discrimination based on age, disability, and sex in addition to prohibiting discrimination based on race,

[85] Jerry Kang, *The Missing Quadrants of Antidiscrimination: Going Beyond the "Prejudice Polygraph,"* 68 J. Soc. Issues 314 (2012).

[86] Section 1557 of the Affordable Care Act provides:

> [A]n individual shall not on the ground prohibited under title VI of the Civil Rights Act of 1964, . . . title IX of the Education Amendments of 1972(20 U.S.C. 1681 et seq.), the Age Discrimination Act of 1975 (42 U.S.C. 6101 et seq.), or section 50 of the Rehabilitation Act of 1973 (29 U.S.C. 794), be excluded from participation in, be denied the benefits of, or be subjected to discrimination under, any health program or activity, any part of which is receiving Federal financial assistance, including credits, subsidies, or contracts of insurance, or under any program or activity that is administered by an Executive Agency or any entity established under this title. . . .

color, and national origin. Second, the Affordable Care Act's civil rights provision covers a larger range of participants in the healthcare industry than Title VI.[87] The new civil rights law includes health insurers, hospitals, and the newly created health insurance exchanges. The act gives the Office of Civil Rights authority to investigate complaints under Section 1557.[88] For example, the Office may use the breadth of this new antidiscrimination tool to address institutional bias and discrimination in the way insurers and health plans organize networks, selectively contract with providers, and make coverage decisions. Third, the Affordable Care Act Section 1557 grants individuals the right to file administrative complaints alleging violations of the nondiscrimination provision, and fourth, the new provision could plausibly be read to acknowledge a private right of action to protect civil rights,[89] though admittedly, the restoration of a private right of action is by no means clear. Section 1557's incorporation of "the enforcement mechanisms provided for and available under "the civil rights provisions in Title VI, Title IX, §504, and the Age Discrimination Act,[90] could be read to prohibit both intentional disparate treatment and unintentional disparate impact discrimination. However, until the Department of Health and Human Services promulgates and enforces the regulations to establish the reach of this expanded civil rights law, federal antidiscrimination law will remain vulnerable to the uncertainty of case-by-case judicial construction of the law.

Members of Congress most recently evinced interest in broadening federal civil rights law during the 2012 legislative session. The 112th Congress considered a bill to strengthen Title VI that failed to pass the Senate Committee on Veteran's Affairs. The language of that proposed bill, however, provides guidance for a comprehensive Title VI overhaul that could once again make the law an effective weapon against inequality in health, healthcare, and beyond. Four amendments are needed to fully restore Title to effectively prohibit the use of federal funds to discriminate against or deny benefits to minority patients. First, Section 601 could be amended to expressly define disparate impact to include a prohibition against unintentional discrimination. Second, to operationalize this prohibition, Congress would add language approving an affirmative defense for those who have taken reasonable steps to reduce unconscious discrimination under Section 601 so that it would read as follows:

Section 601 of Title VI:

(a) No person in the United States shall, on the ground of race, color, or national origin, be excluded from participation in, be denied the benefits of, or be subjected to discrimination under any program or activity receiving Federal financial assistance.
(b) Discrimination based on disparate impact with respect to a program or activity is established under this section only if–
    (1) a Federal department or agency, or any person aggrieved, demonstrates that an entity subject to this title has a policy or practice with respect to the program or activity that causes a disparate impact on the basis of race, color, or national origin; and

[87] *See generally*, 42 U.S.C. §18116. [88] 42 U.S.C. §18116(c).

[89] Sidney D. Watson, *Section 1557 of the Affordable Care Act: Civil Rights, Health Reform, Race, and Equity*, 55 How. L.J. 855 (2012).

[90] 42 U.S.C. §18116(b).

(2) the entity fails to demonstrate that it has taken reasonable steps to reduce discriminatory harms due to unconscious or unintentional biases; and
(3) the entity fails to demonstrate that the challenged policy or practice is related to, and necessary to achieve, the substantial and legitimate nondiscriminatory goals of the program or activity; or
(4) a Federal department or agency, or the person aggrieved, demonstrates that a less discriminatory alternative policy or practice exists, and the entity refuses to adopt such alternative policy or practice.

(2) In this subsection, the term "demonstrates" means meets the burdens of production and persuasion.

Third, Congress should amend Section 602 language to restore a private right action to prosecute disparate impact claims, and affirm the authority of agencies and departments to enforce the statute. Fourth, the reformed statute would add the following language to the end of Section 602 to provide for appropriate remedies:

(b) Any person aggrieved by the failure of an entity to comply with section 601 may bring a civil action in any Federal or State court of competent jurisdiction to enforce such person's rights and may recover equitable relief, reasonable attorney's fees (including expert fees), and costs. The aggrieved person may also recover legal relief (including compensatory and, from nongovernmental entities, punitive damages) in the case of noncompliance based on evidence of intentional discrimination. In an action brought by an aggrieved person based on evidence of disparate impact, the aggrieved person may recover equitable relief, reasonable attorney's fees (including expert fees), and costs.

(c) Nothing in subsection (b) limits the authority of a federal department or agency to enforce Section 601.

IV Conclusion

These four proposed changes to Title VI would transform federal antidiscrimination provisions to reaffirm Congress's original intent for the civil rights law and to meet the challenge of today's new forms of racial and ethnic discrimination. Yet, these suggested amendments are not entirely free from the risk of overinclusiveness in light of the ubiquity of unconscious bias. Nor are they free from possible underinclusiveness, given the flexibility of the negligence standard proposed here. Nevertheless, a summary of the information set out in this chapter will help to underscore the severity of the harm and urgency of the need to reduce disparities that justify reform of federal antidiscrimination law. First, the evidence that modern-day racial discrimination is caused by implicit bias belies the notion that discrimination has disappeared from the American landscape just because overt bigotry is no longer the societal norm. Instead, the historical legacy of discrimination is alive and well, operating through unseen implicit biases, but nonetheless visiting severe harm upon the health and well-being of racial and ethnic minorities. Second, discrimination due to unconscious bias is not only alive and well but also operates throughout the context of healthcare delivery to quite literally prevent patients who belong to ethnic and racial minority groups from living well or as long as their white counterparts. Unconscious racism in healthcare precludes minority patients from equal access to healthcare and from an equal opportunity to live healthy lives that whites enjoy. And third, studies show that individuals and institutions can *intentionally* reduce unintentional discrimination that arises from implicit biases. Therefore, the malleability evidence that unconscious racial discrimination may be consciously mitigated provides a sound evidentiary and moral basis to reimagine when and how the law may justly prohibit unconscious discrimination against minorities by the healthcare industry.

Thus, a reconceptualization of Title VI, the cornerstone of federal landmark civil rights law, will reach far beyond merely rectifying inequities in healthcare. Indeed, returning Title VI to its original stature as a potent prohibition against state-funded racial and ethnic discrimination could save and improve the quality of life for tens of thousands of minority patients in America each year.

B. Legal Issues in Information Exchange

CHAPTER 9

HEALTH INFORMATION LAW

FRANK PASQUALE

HEALTH information law is one of the most dynamic and unsettled areas of American jurisprudence. Statutes at the state and federal level, as well as complex regulatory regimes, constitutional decisions, and international treaties, each with diverse and oft-conflicting aims, can render even simple questions (like, "Who owns an electronic health record?") replete with nettlesome complexity and caveats.[1] Health information lawyers are increasingly called on to guide clients through unprecedented patient and regulatory demands.

Several trends in medical practice have framed recent developments in law and policy. Information shared between physician and patient (a critical focus of policy concern in the 1960s and 1970s) is now only a small part of information flow in the healthcare system. Myriad players, ranging from insurers to pharmacy-benefit managers to group-purchasing organizations, have a keen interest in information about patterns of sickness and health, treatment interventions, hospital and physician effectiveness, population health measures, and health disparities. As Latanya Sweeney's Data Map project has shown, even in the period between 1997 and 2012, the number of players in the health information space has rapidly expanded—mirroring larger societal transformations in the amount of data generated, collected, analyzed, and used.

Information presents something of a paradox for economics. Is it a necessary condition for the efficient functioning of a market? Or is it a product like any other, to be created and disseminated according to laws of supply and demand? Akerlofian accounts of information asymmetries, and a burgeoning field of information economics, have helped ameliorate the tension between information as simultaneous *input* and *output* of market activity. Nevertheless, there is a lingering tension between public commitments to open data and corporate proprietary interests in shielding extant rent-seeking and oligopolistic market structures by hiding, shading, or simply failing to record critical data about effectiveness, cost, and accessibility.

There can also be a tension between patients' interest in privacy and larger systemic goals of promoting research and innovation. Most health information privacy laws presume a

[1] And the question may not even matter that much. *See*, e.g., Barbara Evans, *Much Ado About Data Ownership*, 25 HARV. J.L. & TECH. 69, 70 77 (2011) (arguing that the "debate should be about appropriate public uses of private data and how best to facilitate these uses while adequately protecting individuals' interests").

patient prerogative to limit the disclosure of information gathered about the patient's clinical encounters and health needs. However, the more information is available about a patient or population, the better researchers might be able to determine maximally effective interventions. For decades, this tension was alleviated (if not resolved) via relatively clear conceptual boundaries between care and research—with heightened ethical obligations for providers engaged in the latter mission. However, with the rise of big data-driven observational research, the models of a "Learning Health Care System" and "Precision Medicine" are breaking down barriers between clinical and observational research.[2] As promoted by President Barack Obama, the leveraging of data can change the model of care from one that addresses the "average patient" to an approach that takes into consideration individual differences in genes, environments, and lifestyles.[3] Both healthcare systems and researchers are still struggling with legal and ethical implications of this evolution in medical practice.

Conflicts between privacy and research goals have accelerated as the Health Information Technology for Economic and Clinical Health Act of 2009 (HITECH) has provided subsidies to accelerate the adoption of electronic health records (EHRs). Digital records are more subject to replication, transmission, and analysis than paper records. To address privacy concerns, HITECH also implemented a complex update to (and strengthening of) the Health Insurance Portability and Accountability Act of 1996 (HIPAA). The Office of Civil Rights (OCR) in the Department of Health and Human Services (HHS) also stepped up enforcement against violations. Meanwhile, the Office of the National Coordinator of Health Information Technology (ONCHIT) and the Centers for Medicare and Medicaid Services (CMS) tried to balance privacy, research, and accountability imperatives by setting standards for the implementation of EHRs as part of the HITECH subsidy programs.

The convergence of mandatory reporting (to government agencies) and mandatory disclosure (to private sector partners or the general public) is ensuring that information previously accessible only in physical form is now routinely posted by those regulators on the Internet. Both bottom-up consumerism and top-down mandates for reporting have profoundly expanded the amount of information now available about healthcare outcomes. Yet myriad areas of opacity remain. And government efforts to improve the information environment—by, say, requiring certain standards of efficacy before a pharmaceutical firm can market a drug for a certain condition—are under attack as violations of the First Amendment to the U.S. Constitution.

This chapter traces important trends in the development of health information law in the United States over the past decade. Health information exchange is critical, but its advance depends on much higher levels of interoperability than are presently achieved. Policy-makers must navigate intellectual property and privacy rights skillfully. Moreover, private information-gathering services may be both adjuncts to and rivals of the regulatory

[2] Nancy E. Kass, Ruth R. Faden, Steven N. Goodman, Peter Pronovost, Sean Tunis and Tom L. Beauchamp, *The Research-Treatment Distinction: A Problematic Approach for Determining Which Activities Should Have Ethical Oversight*, Hastings Center Report, Jan. 11, 2013 (offering "a critical assessment of five characterizations of research that have been used in policy documents and the scholarly literature to try to make a sharp distinction between research and practice.").

[3] Press Release, White House, *Fact Sheet: President Obama's Precision Medicine Initiative* (Jan. 30, 2015), *available at* https://www.whitehouse.gov/the-press-office/2015/01/30/fact-sheet-president-obama-s-precision-medicine-initiative.

enterprise. Part I discusses the promise and limits of rankings and ratings as aids to patients, payors, and policy-makers in choosing among providers, pharmaceuticals, devices, and other interventions. Part II explores the dissemination of electronic health records. As U.S. regulators subsidize electronic health record systems designed to secure protected health information, they are also demanding more access to key data those systems collect.[4] Part III focuses on medical research: major breakthroughs are tantalizingly close, but the data necessary to drive them forward are still fragmented. Moreover, moving from data to knowledge to action will still require leaders in the healthcare sector to run a gauntlet of entrenched interests and regulatory inertia.

I Patient Privacy in the Digital Age

The privacy concerns of patients have slowed adoption of some digital records, often quite justifiably.[5] Unfair, invasive, and irremediable violations of the privacy of individuals have been documented in many medical settings.[6] An HHS "Wall of Shame" documents, in grim detail, numerous breaches of protected health information. Even when HIPAA-covered records are properly secured, shadow health profiles, generated by entities outside the formal health sector, may expose individuals' sensitive health conditions—or, almost as bad, cause them to be treated as if they had certain health conditions.[7] There are numerous health privacy threat scenarios.

The "rapid-learning health system" poses new threats to privacy.[8] The data collected is no longer limited to specific medical encounters. As the understanding of how individuals live and its effect on healthcare expands, old distinctions between health and other data have

[4] An electronic health record is "an electronic record of health-related information on an individual that is created, gathered, managed, and consulted by authorized health care clinicians and staff." 42 U.S.C. § 17921 (2006).

[5] *See generally*, Roger S. Magnusson, *The Changing Legal and Conceptual Shape of Health Care Privacy*, 32 J.L. Med. & Ethics 680, 685 (2004). Patient concerns are not hypothetical; data breaches have been on the rise. *Reported Health Data Breaches Rose by 97% in 2011*, iHealthBeat (Feb. 1, 2012), http://www.ihealthbeat.org/articles/2012/2/1/health-data-breaches-increased-by-97-in-2011-report-finds.aspx; Scott Gibson, *Stolen Medical Records One of the Most Lucrative Forms of ID Theft*, Health Care Tech Rev. (Dec. 13, 2011), http://healthcaretechreview.com/stolen-medical-records-lucrative/.

[6] Over 21 million patients have suffered data security breaches reported to the federal government over the past three years. *See* Section 13402(e)(4) of the HITECH Act, *in* Health Information Services, Department of Health and Human Services, Breaches Affecting 500 Patients or More, *available at* http://www.hhs.gov/ocr/privacy/hipaa/administrative/breachnotificationrule/breachtool.html (last visited Nov. 11, 2012). Even nonbreached data can lead to serious negative consequences. *See, e.g.*, Chad Terhune, *They Know What's in Your Medicine Cabinet*, Bloomberg BusinessWeek (July 22, 2008), http://www.businessweek.com/magazine/content/08_31/b4094000643943.htm; Sharona Hoffman, *Employing E-Health: The Impact of Electronic Health Records on the Workplace*, 19 Kan. J.L. & Pub. Pol'y 409, 422 (2010) (raising the possibility of a growing use of "complex scoring algorithms based on EHRs to determine which individuals are likely to be high-risk and high-cost workers").

[7] Nicolas Terry, *Big Data Proxies and Health Privacy Exceptionalism*, 24 Health Matrix 65 108 (2014).

[8] Exec. Off. Of the President, *Big Data: Seizing Opportunities, Preserving Values* 23 (2014).

begun to blur.[9] Sensitivity to the "social determinants of health" may well lead informed physicians to gather more information about patients' home circumstances, relationship status, gun ownership, job satisfaction, and varied intimate questions. Increased interoperability of data systems further complicates the picture, as more information is collected and linked in a manner that is not adequately addressed by privacy laws.[10] As data accumulates, certifying its provenance and how it is to be used becomes more difficult.[11]

Criminal breach and use of data raises the stakes of health privacy law. A health data black market has emerged. Consumer health data may be valued by criminal elements at a higher level than other forms of consumer data such as credit card numbers or social security numbers.[12] By some estimates, consumer medical information is worth ten times more than credit card numbers on the black market.[13] Stolen health data can be used in a variety of ways: not only to create fake IDs, but to also purchase medical equipment and drugs that can be resold.[14]

Hacked patient information may also enable criminals to fraudulently bill for medical services.[15] Hackers or purchasers of stolen information can impersonate patients.[16] Victims may only learn of this fraud when they are unable to access services themselves or debt collectors begin to contact them for services they have never utilized.[17] Data controllers should also fear breaches. Hackers can use data to engage in corporate extortion.[18] They can ransom the information, counting on embarrassed firms to pay up.[19]

This criminal activity has seemed to increase over the past several years, though it is hard to tell exactly how common it is because hackers may not leave traces.[20] Many providers still rely on aging computer systems that do not use the latest security features.[21] However diligently HHS prescribes technical and administrative safeguards, the agency is hard pressed to directly monitor thousands of hospitals and hundreds of thousands of physicians. Current auditing levels are a start, but they are not sufficient. Even worse, medical identity theft is often not immediately identified by a patient or healthcare provider.[22] Hackers may continue to sell and use stolen healthcare data years after breaches.[23]

As the recent cyberattack on Anthem showed, even healthcare data at the most well-established firms is not immune to data breaches.[24] While healthcare providers and health business entities must publicly disclose data breaches affecting more than five hundred

[9] *Id.* [10] *Id.*

[11] Sharona Hoffman, *Big, Bad Data: Law, Public Health, and Biomedical Databases*, JLME (2012).

[12] Aarti Shahani, *The Black Market for Stolen Health Care Data*, NPR (Feb. 13, 2015), *available at* http://www.npr.org/sections/alltechconsidered/2015/02/13/385901377/theblackmarketforstolenhealthcaredata.

[13] Caroline Humer & Jim Finkle, *Your Medical Record Is Worth More to the Hackers Than Your Credit Card*, Reuters (Sept. 24, 2014), *available at* http://www.reuters.com/article/2014/09/24/uscybersecurityhospitalsidUSKCN0HJ21I20140924.

[14] *Id.* [15] *Id.* [16] *Id.* [17] *Id.*

[18] Shahani, *The Black Market for Stolen Health Care Data*.

[19] Humer & Finkle, *Your Medical Record Is Worth More to the Hackers*.

[20] Shahani, *The Black Market for Stolen Health Care Data*.

[21] Humer & Finkle, *Your Medical Record Is Worth More to the Hackers*. [22] *Id.*

[23] *Id.*

[24] Reed Abelson & Matthew Goldstein, *Millions of Anthem Customers Targeted in Cyberattack*, N.Y. Times (Feb. 5, 2015), http://www.nytimes.com/2015/02/05/business/hackers-breached-data-of-millions-insurer-says.html?_r=0.

people, the deterrent effect of such disclosures is questionable, especially given how common they have been.[25] Moreover, given the fragmentation of records, there is no single place for individuals to identify and correct problems with their medical information.[26]

Given the arms race among hackers and defensive security professionals to detect (and then defuse) security threats, policy-makers will need to consider creative approaches to reducing the risks posed by data loss. For example, policy-makers should go beyond "notice and consent" models of privacy and prohibit the use of certain types of data in certain situations. In employment or basic banking services, for instance, health data should not even enter the calculus of decision-making without explicit affirmation by either the party affected or a dedicated regulator.

Implementing these solutions will take some time and effort. But they should be worth it, because in a growing variety of contexts, rights to privacy are critical to motivate the creation of knowledge. Why should I honestly enter in all the calories and food I eat in a day in the LoseIt app (or a provider-sponsored EHR) if my employer or potential life insurer can demand it and negatively judge me if I betray a weakness for fatty foods? And what would be the public health consequences if people became too scared to use a Google search to help themselves determine if they might have bird flu, or were afraid to approach a doctor about possibly embarrassing conditions?

Rather than focusing on the efficiency or fairness of single transactions in the knowledge economy, policy-makers need to incentivize the development of information ecologies that embed security-by-design and regularly update such protective mechanisms. As digitization of health data has increased, both the terms "medical" and "privacy" are inadequate to convey the magnitude of the issues raised by the volume, variety, and velocity of big data methods of information collection and analysis. For example, we now more often use the acronym EHR (electronic health record) than EMR (electronic medical record) because we realize that many social determinants and indicators of health lie beyond traditional medical care. For example, health status can increasingly be probabilistically attributed (if not definitively discovered) by reference to nonmedical records.

Thus the concept of a sectoral health privacy law like HIPAA (and its 2009 update, HITECH) fully protecting health privacy by applying a complex set of rules to a narrow range of "covered entities" in the medical sector appears increasingly quaint. Pressure comes from the other side as well: The greater the ability of data aggregation to improve care, and the more sophisticated tools of deidentification that are developed, the less privacy will appear as a prime motivator of health data policy than as one of many social objectives at stake in the management of increasingly comprehensive and interconnected data systems.

Health data solutionism tends to prioritize issues that technology can address: small, algorithmically decomposable bits of wicked problems. It will continue to captivate a small army of lawyers and computer scientists. But it is hard to see how old patterns of notice and consent can address new problems posed by big data. Policy-makers must be willing to delve far deeper into actual business and employment practices with substantive, verifiable, auditable standards of nondiscrimination and fair data practices.

[25] Humer & Finkle, *Your Medical Record Is Worth More to the Hackers.* [26] *Id.*

II The Promise and Limits of Ratings and Rankings

In her 2007 book *Who Killed Health Care*, Harvard Business School Professor Regina Herzlinger posed an interesting thought experiment: What if, instead of the FDA's binary approval or disapproval of drugs, the agency instead offered ratings and rankings of their safety and effectiveness? What if it followed the example of financial regulation, outsourcing assessments of quality to private, for-profit rating agencies like Moody's and Standard & Poor's? Herzlinger has long advocated for "consumer-directed health care." She states: "People can choose from 240 models and makes of cars pretty intelligently . . . Why do we assume they can't do the same when it comes to their health?"[27]

There has been a good deal of interest in using rankings and ratings to guide the decisions of patients, providers, insurers, and government and private third-party payors. Internet-savvy patients aim to find high-quality doctors in a world of uneven care. Insurers also aim to direct resources to reliable providers. As Ellen Nakashima reports, "data-driven surveillance offers the prospect of using incentives to steer patients to care that is both effective and sensibly priced."[28] The data can have important results. According to one survey, "users who picked a top-performing hospital or surgeon from the latest available report had approximately half the chance of dying as did those who picked a hospital or surgeon from the bottom quartile."[29]

Kristin Madison has summarized the government's efforts to make data "bigger," that is, more comprehensive, flowing at faster rates, and more in-depth.[30] New technology has made it much easier and cheaper to collect, store, and analyze ever greater amounts of data. She describes governmental roles as data generator, collector, aggregator, facilitator, and funder. As a data generator, government has contributed to the growth of big data in healthcare by sharing the data generated by Medicare and other programs.[31] As a collector of healthcare information, government researchers rely on a broad range of healthcare and health service surveys and health quality data, an area where the federal government is leading collection efforts.

The pool of information will only expand as the reporting requirements of the ACA are implemented.[32] These reporting requirements are many and varied, including:

> **Sec. 2217 Ensuring the quality of care**: Requires reporting on the prevention of hospital readmission.[33]

[27] Regina Herzlinger, *Who Killed Health Care* (2007).

[28] Ellen Nakashima, *Doctors Rated but Can't Get a Second Opinion*, Wash. Post, July 25, 2007, at A1.

[29] Ashish K. Jha & Arnold M. Epstein, *The Predictive Accuracy of the New York State Coronary Artery Bypass Surgery Report-Card System*, 25 Health Aff. 844, 844 (2006).

[30] Kristin Madison, *The Law and Policy of Health Care Quality Reporting*, 31 Campbell L. Rev. 215 (2009); Madison, *Health Regulators as Data Stewards*, 92 N.C. L. Rev. 1605 (2014).

[31] *See*, e.g., http://www.healthdata.gov/ (generally), and, for example, http://www.cms.gov/Research-Statistics-Data-and-Systems/Statistics-Trends-and-Reports/NationalHealthExpendData/index.html. The numbers have also come under scrutiny. For example, the trustees reports (http://www.cms.gov/Research-Statistics-Data-and-Systems/Statistics-Trends-and-Reports/ReportsTrustFunds/index.html) have systematically overestimated financial problems of Medicare.

[32] *Id.*

[33] Eleanor D. Kinney, *The Affordable Care Act and the Medicare Program: Linking Medicare Payment to Quality Performance*, 68 N.Y.U. Ann. Surv. Am. L. 567 (2012); http://www.foley.com/ppaca-will-drive-quality-health-care-reform-05-21-2010/.

Sec. 3001. Hospital Value-Based Purchasing Program: Allows the Secretary to make performance standards that take into consideration practice experience, historical performance, improvement, and opportunity for improvement.

Sec. 3002. Improvements to the physician quality reporting system: The Secretary has to report on the providers' progress in reporting quality data, as well as create an informal appeal process for those who are determined to not have satisfactorily submitted the required data.

Sec. 3004. Quality reporting for long-term care hospitals, inpatient rehabilitation hospitals, and hospice programs: Extends quality reporting requirement to all the institutions listed in the title. It is the Secretary's duty to develop and institute the quality measure, making the results available to the public by publishing them on a website.

Sec. 3005. Quality reporting for PPS-exempt cancer hospitals: Creates a quality reporting program for cancer hospitals, which were historically exempt. The Secretary is tasked with developing and instituting the measures, making the results available to the public by publishing them on a website.

Sec. 3007. Value-based payment modifier under the physician fee schedule: Obliges the Secretary implement a plan for differential payments to physicians dependent on the quality of care they provide.

Sec. 10322. Quality reporting for psychiatric hospitals: Starting in 2014, psychiatric hospitals must provide quality measures. The Secretary is tasked with developing and instituting the measures, making the results available to the public by publishing them on a website.

Sec. 10327. Improvements to the physician quality reporting system: This section adds an incentive payment for 2011 through 2014 for physicians who provide quality data though Maintenance of Certification Program.

The plethora of new data generated by such requirements itself needs to be presented, analyzed, and displayed carefully, lest information overload overwhelm any positive effects it may have. As an aggregator, government has aided research by making its data available to others, which can then be integrated into larger or more sophisticated databases. Recombination of information helps increase overall information available for comparisons and performance markers. The government can also facilitate interactions among private entities, such as is done with the Mini-Sentinel Initiative.[34]

Another challenge is that the quality of Internet reviews of doctors has been questioned.[35] At the same time, more formal rating systems can have perverse consequences, such as encouraging doctors to shun the sickest patients. For example, a cardiac surgeon may turn away very ill patients in order to keep the mortality rate associated with his practice low.[36] At least one journalist has contended that gaming of ratings was common in New York after

[34] Efthimios Parasidis, *Patients over Politics: Addressing Legislative Failure in the Regulation of Medical Products*, 5 WIS. L. REV. 929, 971 (2011) (discussing Mini-Sentinel); Frank Pasquale, *Grand Bargains for Big Data: The Emerging Law of Health Information*, 72 MD. L. REV. 682, 744 (2013) (discussing its potential expansion).

[35] *See* Ron Lieber, *The Web Is Awash in Reviews, but Not for Doctors. Here's Why*, N.Y. TIMES, Mar. 10, 2012, at B1 (discussing patients' "unquestioning mind-set that may cause such low participation (or disproportionately positive reviews) at many review sites").

[36] *See, e.g.*, Robert Kolker, *Heartless*, N.Y. MAG., Oct. 16, 2005, *available at* http://nymag.com/nymetro/health/features/14788/ ("An anonymous 1999 survey of bypass surgeons revealed that 62% of cardiac surgeons refused to treat at least one patient in the preceding year who was perceived to be high risk."). For related problems, *see* Rachel M. Werner & David A. Asch, *The Unintended Consequences of Publicly Reporting Quality Information*, 293 J. AM. MED. ASS'N 1239, 1239 (2005).

the state "ma[d]e public the mortality rates of its heart surgeons."[37] In the few years after this public reporting standard was adopted, the Cleveland Clinic "received 31% more referrals from New York hospitals than they had previously received," and these referrals were "sicker than those who were referred from other states."[38] Although later work questioned this specific finding, the fact remains that rating systems can be gamed by focusing care on the patients most likely to enjoy positive outcomes.

Risk adjustments can solve simple gaming; for example, mortality figures can be adjusted to reflect the sickness of patients or the complexity of a procedure.[39] But risk adjustments themselves can be gamed.[40] Doctors might even add unnecessary procedures during a routine surgery to avoid reputational damage once the patient takes an unexpected turn for the worse.[41] That is obviously illegal, but there are many subtler, legal ways to manipulate one's score in even sophisticated ranking and rating systems.

Not only state and federal authorities but also private insurers are trying to rate doctors' quality.[42] Insurers and other raters try to make reams of tables and graphs accessible to consumers by boiling them down into grades and scores.[43] Highly rated physicians appreciate the publicity and endorsement, but others "say that the data often contain errors and that doctors often lack the ability to correct them."[44] Conflicts proliferate, including "a lawsuit in Seattle" and a "physician revolt in St. Louis."[45] These acts of resistance reflect both guild protectionism and legitimate concerns about misleading patients or casting aspersions on high-quality physicians.

[37] *Id.*; *see also* Frank Pasquale, *"Best Doctors": Shaming Shirkers or Shunning the Sickest?*, Concurring Opinions (July 28, 2007), http://www.concurringopinions.com/archives/2007/07/doctor_ratings.html (providing specific examples of "gaming" that took place in New York).

[38] *Id.*

[39] *See* Kristin Madison, *The Law and Policy of Health Care Quality Reporting*, 31 Campbell L. Rev. 215, 229 (2009) ("[I]n an ideal world, report card measures would focus on clinical outcomes. Patients care about outcome measures such as lower mortality rates, not whether physicians are board-certified or the frequency of beta blocker prescriptions in hospital settings. These alternative measures are imperfect at best, and are used mainly because it can be costly and difficult to measure outcomes and to risk-adjust them properly, so that they reflect the providers' quality, rather than underlying patient characteristics. In practice, very few report cards measure outcomes, and the outcomes they capture tend to be a limited subset of what patients may care about.").

[40] For more on the problem of manipulation of ratings in healthcare, *see* Nic Terry, *Fear of Facebook: Private Ordering of Social Media Risks Incurred by Health Care Providers*, 90 Neb. L. Rev. 703, 746 747 (2012) (discussing "sockpuppetry" and "astroturfing.").

[41] *See* Kolker, *Heartless* ("If the patient died, it wouldn't affect that surgeon's mortality rate . . . Certainly it was done strictly to manipulate the data.").

[42] *See* Kristin Madison, *Defragmenting Health Care Delivery Through Quality Reporting*, *in* The Fragmentation of U.S. Health Care: Causes and Solutions 87, 97 (Einer Elhauge ed., 2010) (discussing various entities that are developing ways to measure performance quality within the healthcare industry). I have also called for more data development as a goal of healthcare policy in an essay on specialty hospitals. *See* Frank Pasquale, *Ending the Specialty Hospital Wars: A Plea for Pilot Programs as Information—Forcing Regulatory Design*, *in* The Fragmentation of U.S. Health Care: Causes and Solutions 140, 165, 235, 250 251 (Einer Elhauge ed., 2010) (describing research commissioned by the U.S. government in efforts to rate level of care provided by specialty hospitals).

[43] *See* Ann Marie Marciarille, *"How's My Doctoring?" Patient Feedback's Role in Assessing Physician Quality*, 14 DePaul J. Health Care L. 361, 362 (2012) ("User-generated feedback on physicians has found multiple fora on the Internet, including: Angie's List, Yelp, and specialty sites like RateMDs.com.").

[44] Nakashima, *Doctors Rated*.

[45] *Id.*

Fearing an unfair tiering of its members, the Washington State Medical Association filed suit against Regence BlueShield, an insurance company that evaluated doctors using allegedly inaccurate and outdated information.[46] The doctors claimed that Regence used four-year-old data, relied on small sample sizes, and focused on the cost of claims rather than the quality of care.[47] The complaint alleged defamation and violation of the Consumer Protection Act, among other causes of action.[48] After ten months of litigation, Regence agreed to settle with the Washington State Medical Association "in an effort to better understand physician concerns,"[49] voluntarily withdrawing the Select Network program. The settlement agreement, effective for at least two years, promises transparency in evaluations and fair methodology.[50]

To the extent that insurance companies are rating and ranking doctors to guide members to the most effective care, they should be free to use properly anonymized claims data and to publish their results. If such rating systems are primarily driven by commercial concerns such as steering patients away from high-cost doctors, however, that goal needs to be disclosed and perhaps deterred. Quality regulators have already adopted some of these principles, but they need to be more clearly articulated as rating sites proliferate.

In New York, then-Attorney General (and now Governor) Andrew Cuomo launched an investigation of insurers' physician ratings that culminated in settlement agreements in 2007. Cuomo claimed that the evaluation programs were confusing and unfair to both physicians and consumers.[51] After negotiating with his office, insurance companies eventually agreed to follow the ranking guidelines in a national model provided by the Office of the Attorney General (in cooperation and consultation with the American Medical Association and other

[46] *See* Amy Lynn Sorrel, *Washington Doctors Sue Blues Plan over Performance Standards*, AM. MED. NEWS, Oct. 16, 2006, available at http://www.ama-assn.org/amednews/2006/10/16/prsd1016.htm; Judith VandeWater, *Doctors Level Charges at Health Insurer*, ST. LOUIS POST-DISPATCH, May 26, 2005, at A1; *see also Lawsuit: Insurance Commission Physician Tiering Program Flawed*, SURGISTRATEGIES (June 25, 2008), http://www.surgicenteronline.com/hotnews/insurance-commission-physician-tiering.html ("The Washington State Medical Association filed suit in 2006 against the Regence Blue Shield over its physician ranking program.").

[47] *See* Judith VandeWater, *BJC Warns It May Drop United Healthcare*, ST. LOUIS POST-DISPATCH, Mar. 18, 2005, at A1 (describing physician concerns); *Doctors Outraged at Ratings*, *Oregonian*, May 26, 2006, at D4.

[48] *Id.*

[49] Judith VandeWater, *BJC, Health Insurer Resolve Dispute*, ST. LOUIS POST-DISPATCH, June 24, 2005, at A1.

[50] *Id.* Had the suit gone to trial, First Amendment defenses may have been raised. *See* Frank Pasquale, *Beyond Innovation and Competition: The Need for Qualified Transparency in Internet Intermediaries*, 104 NW. U. L. REV. 105, 117 119 (2010) (discussing the successful First Amendment defense of the Avvo lawyer ratings site). There were several possible causes of action. *See* CHRISTINE C. RINN, AM. HEALTH LAWYERS ASS'N, TIERED PHYSICIAN NETWORKS: A NEW TWIST ON AN OLD ISSUE 4 7 (2008), *available at* http://www.crowell.com/documents/Tiered_Physician_Networks_AHLA_Rinnpdf.pdf (discussing potential causes of action in ranking and rating cases, including: "breach of contract"; "defamation"; "consumer protection violations"; "unfair insurance practices"; "tortious interference with contractual relations"; "fraud"; and "conspiracy"); Lawrence P. Casalino et al., *Will Pay-for-Performance and Quality Reporting Affect Health Care Disparities?*, 28 HEALTH AFF. (WEB EXCL.) w405, w405 412 (2007) (suggesting design elements likely to help create fair evaluation methods).

[51] *See* Agreement Between Andrew M. Cuomo, Attorney Gen. of the State of N.Y., and CIGNA Healthcare of N.Y., Inc., Concerning Physician Performance Measurement, Reporting and Tiering Programs 3 (Oct. 29, 2007), *available at* http://www.ag.ny.gov/sites/default/files/press-releases/archived/

provider trade organizations). The model agreements required "insurers to fully disclose to consumers and physicians all aspects of their ranking system." Since there is mandatory disclosure of all data and methodologies, the problem of the "black box" evaluation system is greatly reduced under the model agreements. Other large insurers also capitulated to state or professional demands, starting a trend toward transparent, quality-based rankings with public methodologies. A Patient Charter for Physician Performance Measurement has also emerged as a project of the Consumer-Purchaser Disclosure Project. The specific terms of the charter call for evaluations that are "meaningful to consumers" and bar decontextualized ratings based solely on cost.[52]

These developments are encouraging, but even the regulated rating systems are far from reaching their potential. Patients may seek more granular data. For example, a group that does very well with one subset of patients (say, diabetics) may not be as adept at treating others. Moreover, as Madison has argued, "particularly for process-oriented and outcome-oriented measures, limitations on available data and statistical techniques complicate efforts to develop statistically reliable quality measures that differentiate providers sufficiently to make quality ratings meaningful."[53] The developing national health information infrastructure, as well as state-level health information exchanges and system-level network building, need to address this data drought. One model for further intervention is the Patient Charter. The goal of the Patient Charter is to make sure all Americans have access to publicly reported healthcare information. The Charter calls for healthcare providers to be measured on topics including quality and cost-efficiency information. Measurements should also include patient experience, since that is both independently important to consumers and can affect quality outcomes. The Charter advocates the use of measures based on national standards, and recommends that insurers have independent healthcare quality standard review organizations review their evaluations of providers. In addition, physicians are allowed to request reviews of results they believe are unfair.[54]

As further evaluative mechanisms are developed, healthcare practitioners should receive more formal roles in the evaluative process. Many practitioners have complained about subjective evaluations skewing the results of rankings and ratings. They could help evaluators develop more objective, outcome-focused measures. State certification boards could also help evaluators recognize top providers, and tap those near the bottom for retraining and more extensive monitoring. Independent "reviewers of the reviewers" could also help identify efforts to "game" rating and ranking systems.

CIGNA%20Settlement%20Final.pdf ("The Attorney General finds that any initiatives to measure quality and cost-efficiency of physicians . . . have the potential to cause confusion . . . and could result in a violation of law.").

[52] Press Release, N.Y. Att'y Gen. Office, Attorney General Cuomo Announces Doctor Ranking Agreement with GHI and HIP (Nov. 20, 2007), *available at* http://www.ag.ny.gov/press-release/attorney-general-cuomo-announces-doctor-ranking-agreement-ghi-and-hip.

[53] Kristin Madison, *The Law and Policy of Health Care Quality Reporting*, 31 Campbell L. Rev. 215, 228 (2009). A quick consultation of sites like Hospital Compare and Nursing Home Compare helps validate Madison's contention here. Very disparate entities can appear almost indistinguishable given the crudeness of the categories used to assess quality. Conversely, something like Google's Zagat ratings, now applied to some hospitals, wraps a nontransparent process of evaluation in a patina of objectivity, and in my experience has applied mysterious and unjustified scores to healthcare entities.

[54] *See* Kristin Madison, *The Law and Policy of Health Care Quality Reporting*, 31 Campbell L. Rev. 215, 246 (2009); Marciarille, *"How's My Doctoring?"*, at 389.

Even if these policy tools are implemented, future challenges to ranking and rating systems are apparent. Some analysts already worry they may proliferate unnecessarily. For example, in 2015 a *Health Affairs* article criticized four major hospital ranking systems for rarely agreeing on the identity of "top performers."[55] Indeed, "only 10% of the 844 hospitals rated as a high performer by one rating system were rated as a high performer by any of the other rating systems" examined in the article. Consumers could be forgiven for ignoring rating systems that agree so rarely. And policy-makers will need to balance concerns about finding the one best rating system against justifiable demand for diverse rating methods to reflect a pluralistic society's inevitable disagreements about the nature of quality in care.

For example, consider what might happen if a single rating system were indeed accepted by all patients as optimal and true. The hospitals it ranks as best may start attracting more and higher-paying patients, while those it ranks as worst may fall into a death spiral—lacking even the minimum patient base needed to maintain its operations. No one mourns an ordinary business that fails because of bad outcomes and consequent poor rankings. But if the "worst hospitals" are concentrated in certain regions, their failure imposes real costs on communities—and it is by no means clear that any better providers will soon replace them. Thoughtlessly pursued, the ambition to rank and rate all providers may only end up reinforcing old patterns of health disparities and inadequate care.

III The Law of Electronic Health Record Dissemination

Computational innovation may improve healthcare by creating stores of observational data to complement traditional clinical research.[56] Despite the polarized health policy landscape, a consensus emerged following the "Great Recession" to subsidize electronic health records. The United States took a major step toward building such an infrastructure in the HITECH Act of 2009.[57] The Act established incentive programs for eligible hospitals and professionals

[55] J. Matthew Austin et al., *National Hospital Ratings Systems Share Few Common Scores and May Generate Confusion Instead of Clarity*, 34(3) Health Aff. (2015), at http://content.healthaffairs.org/content/34/3/423.abstract.

[56] Office of the Nat'l Coordinator for Health Info. Tech., Dep't of Health and Human Services, Accelerating the Adoption of Health Information Technology Implementation (2010), *available at* http://www.hhs.gov/recovery/reports/plans/onc_hit.pdf; SAMHSA, Substances Abuse and Mental Health Administration, SAMHSA's Weekly Financing News Pulse: National Edition, July 23, 2010, at 3, *available at* http://www.samhsa.gov/financing/file.axd?file=2010%2f10%2f2010_10_WeeklyFinancingNewsPulseNationalEditionfinal20100723.pdf (reporting that the new program will direct $27 billion for CMS and $2 billion for the ONC). About $30 billion in subsidies were appropriated for this purpose. *CMS Medicare and Medicaid EHR Incentive Program Timeline*, Centers for Medicare and Medicaid Services (Nov. 15, 2010), https://www.cms.gov/EHRIncentivePrograms/Downloads/EHRIncentProgtimeline508V1.pdf.

[57] American Recovery and Reinvestment Act of 2009, Pub. L. 111-5, 123 Stat. 115 (2009); Mark Faccenda & Lara Parkin, *Meaningful Use—What Does It Mean to You?*, 23 Health L. 10, 10 (2011) (citing ARRA, Title IV, Subtitles A and B). *But see generally* Larry Wolf, Jennie Harvell, & Ashish K. Jha, *Hospitals Ineligible for Federal Meaningful-Use Incentives Have Dismally Low Rates of Adoption of*

to adopt and meaningfully use certified electronic health record (EHR) technology.[58] President Obama called HITECH "an investment that will take the long overdue step of computerizing America's medical records to reduce the duplication and waste that costs billions of health care dollars and medical errors that cost thousands of lives each year."[59]

The Act has already catalyzed diffusion of electronic medical records by providing billions of dollars to hospitals and physicians. But the Act does more than subsidize; it conditions funding on the "meaningful use" of electronic medical records.[60] Regulations define how functional an EHR system has to be before its user can receive federal payments.[61] Electronic health records are to include basic information, clinical health information, and medical history.[62] Meaningful use requirements are phased in over a six-year period, in three stages. Stage 1 focused on basic information and patient demographics.[63] Overall, the law creates incentives to improve quality, safety, efficiency, and care coordination; engage patients and families; and promote population health, all while protecting privacy, confidentiality, and security.[64]

The HITECH Act also mandated that the Department of Health and Human Services (HHS) establish procedures for certifying health information technology so that providers can be assured that their technology meets basic standards.[65] The "Standards Rule"

Electronic Health Records, 31 HEALTH AFF. 505 (2012) (discussing providers explicitly excluded from incentive programs).

[58] Bob Brown, *What Is a "Certified EHR?,"* 12 J. HEALTH CARE COMPLIANCE 31, 31 (2010); *see generally* Nicolas P. Terry, *Certification and Meaningful Use: Reframing Adoption of Electronic Records as a Quality Imperative*, 8 IND. HEALTH L. REV. 43 (2011) (examining meaningful use as the condition for receiving EHR subsidy funds).

[59] President Barack Obama, Remarks at Stimulus Bill Signing (Feb. 17, 2009), *available at* http://www.sequelmed.com/Stimulus/; *see also* Federico Girosi, Robin Meili, & Richard Scoville, *Extrapolating Evidence of Health Information Technology Savings and Costs*, RAND CORP. MONOGRAPH (2005), http://www.rand.org/pubs/monographs/2005/RAND_MG410.pdf. *But see* Steve Lohr, *Digital Records May Not Cut Health Costs, Study Cautions*, N.Y. TIMES, Mar. 5, 2012, at B1 (citing more recent data); CONGRESSIONAL BUDGET OFFICE, EVIDENCE ON THE COSTS AND BENEFITS OF HEALTH INFORMATION TECHNOLOGY 4 (2008), *available at* http://www.cbo.gov/sites/default/files/cbofiles/ftpdocs/91xx/doc9168/05-20-healthit.pdf (criticizing the RAND study). Given such conflicting findings, it is reassuring to note that a meta-study concluded that 92% of recent articles on health IT did find positive benefits overall. M. B. Buntin et al., *The Benefits of Health Information Technology: A Review of the Recent Literature Shows Predominantly Positive Results*, 30 HEALTH AFF. 464, 465 (2011).

[60] Camella B. Boateng, *Federal Electronic Health Records Incentive Programs: What They Mean for Compliance Officers*, 12 J. HEALTH CARE COMPLIANCE 17, 18 (2010) ("The meaningful use objectives are divided into two groups: (1) core set and (2) menu set objectives. The core set contains 14 required objectives that eligible hospitals must fulfill to receive bonus payments. The menu set has 10 objectives, and hospitals must select and meet five objectives for payment purposes.").

[61] David Blumenthal & Marilyn Tavenner, *The "Meaningful Use" Regulation for Electronic Health Records*, 363 NEW ENG. J. MED. 501, 501 (2010).

[62] 42 U.S.C. § 300jj(13)(2006).

[63] *See* Medicare and Medicaid Programs, 75 Fed. Reg. 44,314, 44,328 (proposed July 28, 2010) (to be codified at 42 C.F.R. pts. 412, 413, 422) (listing the "core set of meaningful use objectives" for Stage 1).

[64] Nicolas P. Terry & Leslie P. Francis, *Ensuring the Privacy and Confidentiality of Electronic Health Records*, 2007 U. ILL. L. REV. 681, 691 696.

[65] 45 C.F.R. § 170 (2010); Proposed Establishment of Certification Programs for Health Information Technology, 75 Fed. Reg. 11,328 (proposed Mar. 10, 2010) (to be codified at 45 C.F.R. pt. 170); Health Information Technology: Initial Set of Standards, Implementation Specifications, and Certification

focuses on basic benchmarks for data entry and portability.[66] Such certified EHRs must include capacities that "enable providers to achieve meaningful use as it is currently constituted in Phase 1 of HHS's regulations."[67] The Office of the National Coordinator for Health Information Technology (ONC) delegates certification authority to Authorized Testing and Certification Bodies (ATCBs), which will follow standards developed by the International Organization for Standardization (ISO).[68]

The meaningful use and certification standards are a comprehensive, complex effort to create the rules and standards that can support an open twenty-first-century health information technology (IT) infrastructure. Unfortunately, other developments in health information technology threaten to undermine these policies.[69] Phillip Longman worried in 2009 that subsidies could be directed to proprietary systems that prevent widespread study and utilization of health records.[70] That concern proved prescient: Even in 2015, the ONCHIT complained that "current economic and market conditions create business incentives for some persons and entities to exercise control over electronic health information in ways that unreasonably limit its availability and use."[71] In 2011, EHR experts Sharona Hoffman and Andy Podgurski sounded a different alarm about the development of digitized health infrastructure.[72] They argued that early rounds of regulations relating to health information technology failed to address safety concerns: "General system safety is a property that is attainable only through rigorous processes for development and evaluation. The regulations, however, do not address certification of EHR vendors' software development processes or even require vendors to analyze and mitigate potential safety hazards."[73]

A related legal concern is the potential increased risk of liability clinicians may face through the use of predictive analytics. Specifically, as data is collected and integrated into decision support systems, new legal duties may emerge.[74] For example, data systems may raise the public's expectations concerning performance and affect the standard of care to which clinicians are held for medical malpractice purposes.[75] Though it may well be

Criteria for Electronic Health Record Technology, 75 Fed. Reg. 44,590 (proposed July 28, 2010) (to be codified at 45 C.F.R. pt. 170).

[66] Brown, *What Is a "Certified EHR?"*, at 66.

[67] Sharona Hoffman & Andy Podgurski, *Meaningful Use and Certification of Health Information Technology: What About Safety?*, 39 J.L. MED. & ETHICS S77, S78 (Supp. 2011).

[68] *Id.*

[69] Cost of implementation is the first impediment; one study estimated that the first sixty days of implementation in a primary care setting would cost over $30,000 and consume 134 hours of physician time. N. S. Fleming et al., *The Financial and Nonfinancial Costs of Implementing Electronic Health Records in Primary Care Practices*, 30 HEALTH AFF. 481, 482 (2011).

[70] Phillip Longman, *Code Red: How Software Companies Could Screw Up Obama's Health Care Reform*, 41 WASH. MONTHLY 19, 20 22 (2009).

[71] The Office of the National Coordinator for Health Information Technology (ONC), "Report on Health Information Blocking," http://www.healthit.gov/sites/default/files/reports/info_blocking_040915.pdf (Apr. 2015).

[72] Hoffman & Podgurski, *Meaningful Use*. These concerns were anticipated in Sharona Hoffman & Andy Podgurski, *E-Health Hazards: Provider Liability and Electronic Health Record Systems*, 24 BERKELEY TECH. L.J. 1523, 1527 (2009).

[73] Hoffman & Podgurski, *Meaningful Use*, at S78 (footnote omitted).

[74] I. Glenn Cohen et al., *The Legal and Ethical Concerns that Arise from Using Complex Predictive Analytics in Health Care*, 33 HEALTH AFF. 1139, 1141 (2014), at 1144.

[75] Hoffman & Podgurski, *E-Health Hazards*, at 1523, 1528.

appropriate for clinicians to act contrary to decision support recommendations, there also is a risk that evidence of a doctor overriding alerts may prove damaging in litigation.[76]

Further complicating safety is the fact that not only are physicians capable of error but so are data, models, and communication systems that generate clinical decision support. A critical mass of incidents has demonstrated the dangers of malfunctioning and insecure software.[77] It has been suggested that in the case of a data model error, courts are likely to fault a physician for failing to question bad advice given by the system.[78] There have been instances of data systems generating erroneous medication lists or incorrect drug doses, putting patients at risk.[79] Potential liability would not be limited to clinicians but would extend to the healthcare system that implemented the data model.[80] Though the FDA regulates medical device informatics, not all data systems and technology are subject to FDA oversight.[81] As such, it appears that clinicians and health systems bear the burden of data errors, which can heighten skepticism about data initiatives.[82]

The ongoing solicitude of ONC-health IT toward IT vendors may be compromising the effectiveness of the emerging EHR infrastructure.[83] For example, although healthcare settings often encounter urgent, unexpected situations, ATCBs will use testing requirements to certify EHRs that do not even attempt to approximate the "varied operating conditions" that will challenge information systems over the long term.[84] Since a system that is "safe at one facility can experience safety problems when customized by other users," this may prove a serious source of preventable errors and substandard care.[85]

Whereas Hoffman and Podgurski critique the certification process for *technology* for lack of rigor, Nicolas Terry focuses on meaningful use requirements for *providers* that similarly shrink from genuine accountability.[86] Terry worries that even "meaningful use" of EHRs may leave data trapped in silos and inaccessible for many important purposes.[87] Without

[76] *See* Cohen et al., *Legal and Ethical Concerns*, at 1144.

[77] *Bad Health Informatics Can Kill*, INSTITUTE OF HEALTH INFORMATICS (Oct. 19, 2012), *available at* http://iig.umit.at/efmi/badinformatics.htm (providing "summaries of a number of reported incidents in healthcare where [insecure software] was the cause or a significant factor"); Steven Lohr, *Seeing Promise and Peril in Digital Records*, N.Y. TIMES, July 17, 2011, at BU3.

[78] *See* Cohen et al., *Legal and Ethical Concerns*, at 1144.

[79] Associated Press, *Veterans Given Wrong Drug Due to Glitch*, NBCNEWS.COM, Jan. 14, 2009, *available at* http://www.nbcnews.com/id/28655104/ns/health-health_care/t/veterans-given-wrong-drug-doses-due-glitch/#.VVZXZpVFBxQ.

[80] *See* Cohen et al., *Legal and Ethical Concerns*, at 1144.

[81] Food and Drug Administration, *FDASIA Health IT Report: Proposed Strategy and Recommendations for a Risk-Based Framework* 4 (2014).

[82] *See* Cohen et al., *Legal and Ethical Concerns*, at 1144.

[83] For a case study in vendor resistance to more ambitious standards, *see* Anthony Guerra, *Health IT Advisers Blast Data Exchange Policies*, INFORMATIONWEEK (Apr. 1, 2011), http://www.informationweek.com/healthcare/leadership/health-it-advisers-blast-data-exchange-p/229400737 (discussing tensions between the PCAST and the approach to fair information practices being developed by Tiger Team (Workgroup on Privacy and Security)).

[84] Hoffman & Podgurski, *Meaningful Use*, at s78.

[85] *Id.* at s79.

[86] *See* Terry, *Certification and Meaningful Use*, at 48 (citing the "lack of provider enthusiasm for investing in EHR technology").

[87] Nicolas P. Terry, *Anticipating Stage Two: Assessing the Development of Meaningful Use and EMR Deployment*, 21 ANN. HEALTH L. 103, 110 (2012) ("Where PCAST was insightful (and clearly differed

"metadata that provides patient identifying information, privacy protocols, and provenance relating to that data element," EHRs cannot achieve their full potential in monitoring and improving aggregate health outcomes.[88] Though ONC has begun to develop such standards for summary care records,[89] it may be a case of too little, too late.

Nor have patients' perspectives been adequately acknowledged and incorporated into standards.[90] Many patients want to download their health data onto their own computers and applications.[91] Several entities have provided platforms for doing so,[92] promoting "personal health records" (PHRs).[93] At their best, PHRs may help patients better manage their own conditions and join communities of interest online. For example, social networks like PatientsLikeMe.com have proven invaluable sources of support and advice.[94]

The Center for Democracy and Technology has recommended that HHS require PHR vendors "to provide opportunities for consumers to amend, correct or annotate information in a PHR," and "to have policies for handling disputes concerning information in the PHR."[95] If regulators followed the same model as credit reporting, patients should be able

from the CMS/ONC approach) was in viewing data exchange as a major priority (for patient care, health research, and to create network value and so stimulate adoption) and in its skepticism for useful data exchange emerging from the current generation of EMRs, even when supported by Health Information Exchanges ("HIE").").

[88] *Id.* at 111.

[89] *See* 45 C.F.R. § 170 (2010) (creating Metadata Standards to Support Nationwide Electronic Health Information Exchange).

[90] Health Research Inst., Putting Patients into "Meaningful Use" 3 (2011), *available at* http://www.pwc.com/us/en/health-industries/publications/putting-patients-into-meaningful-use.jhtml (finding that "[p]atient awareness of and access to available health IT tools is low").

[91] Dep't of Health & Human Services, Office of the Nat'l Coordinator for Health Info. Tech., Roundtable: Personal Health Records, Understanding the Evolving Landscape (Dec. 3, 2010), *available at* http://www.healthit.hhs.gov/portal/server.pt/community/healthit_hhs_gov_personal_health_records_-_phr_roundtable/3169 (transcript).

[92] *See* Microsoft HealthVault, http://www.microsoft.com/en-us/healthvault/ (last visited Oct. 25, 2012); Aetna CareEngine, http://www.aetna.com/showcase/phr/ (last visited Oct. 25, 2012); My HealtheVet, https://www.myhealth.va.gov/index.html (last visited Nov. 17, 2012); Blue Button, http://www.va.gov/bluebutton/ (last visited Oct. 25, 2012).

[93] A Personal Health Record is "an electronic record . . . that is managed, shared, and controlled by or primarily for the individual." 42 U.S.C. § 17921(11) (2006); *see also* 16 C.F.R. § 318.2(d) (2012); Dep't of Health & Human Services, Office of the Nat'l Coordinator for Health Info. Tech. (describing the range of personal health record systems).

[94] PatientsLikeMe, http://www.patientslikeme.com (last visited Dec. 16, 2012). Of course, these networks raise some difficult legal issues once patients' privacy rights are considered. For example, PatientsLikeMe was subject to a "scraper" which connected health information to some site users' handles. Julia Angwin & Steve Stecklow, *"Scrapers" Dig Deep for Data on Web*, Wall St. J., Oct. 11, 2010, at A1. Sites like Spokeo can in turn reconnect handles back to individuals. Spokeo, http://www.spokeo.com/ (last visited Nov. 17, 2012). For a compelling analysis of how to address these concerns, *see* Nicolas P. Terry, *Physicians and Patients Who "Friend" or "Tweet": Constructing a Legal Framework for Social Networking in a Highly Regulated Domain*, 43 Ind. L. Rev. 285, 286 (2010) (discussing both tort and administrative models of protection).

[95] Ctr. for Democracy & Tech., Comments of the Center for Democracy & Technology to the Office of the National Coordinator's PHR Roundtable 3, 19 (2010), http://www.cdt.org/files/pdfs/CDT_Comment_to_ONC_PHR_Roundtable.pdf (arguing the need to build in a number of consumer safeguards to assure that other stakeholder interests do not trump patients' interests).

to review their reports without charge and make corrections.[96] Still, consumer control will not solve the problem of incorrect or outdated clinical information, suggesting that a personalized health record model has limits. Despite a growing "quantified self"[97] movement that embraces such records, incompatible data entry standards have stymied even the most technologically advanced companies.[98] According to one doctor, "an inaccurate diagnosis of gastrointestinal bleeding on a heart attack patient's personal health record could stop an emergency room doctor from administering a life-saving drug."[99] For the critically or chronically ill, the record is literally a life-or-death matter.

In addition, the more control individuals have over a PHR (and the more accurate it becomes), the more likely it may become that "[e]mployers, health plans, and others" would require "individuals to open PHR accounts as a condition of employment, membership, or for any other reason."[100] To verify participation in a wellness program, an employer may want access to an employee's PHR, particularly if it is much easier for its own computer systems to read and understand than existing "objective" health records. The employer may also want to ensure that the contents of the PHR are validated by third parties, such as doctors' offices, fitness clubs, scales, or blood sugar monitors. What happens if an employer tries to condition participation in a wellness program on an employee's agreement not to try to change whatever is reported by those trusted third parties?[101] Patients must "buy in" to EHR for it to work effectively, and many may avoid data-sharing environments where medical history can lead to the denial of employment opportunities.[102]

Presently, these are largely hypothetical issues in the United States.[103] One has to look to other countries for more advanced adoption of health information technology.[104] A few

[96] For a discussion of the Fair Credit Reporting Act model, *see* Frank Pasquale, *Reputation Regulation, in* THE OFFENSIVE INTERNET 111 (Martha Nussbaum & Saul Levmore eds., 2010).

[97] *See*, e.g., QUANTIFIED SELF, http://quantifiedself.com/ (last visited Dec. 14, 2012) ("A place for people interested in self-tracking to gather, share knowledge and experiences, and discover resources.").

[98] Lisa Wangsness, *Electronic Health Records Raise Doubt*, BOS. GLOBE, Apr. 13, 2009, at C1. Google Health has since ceased operations. *See* David Talbot, *How a Broken Medical System Killed Google Health*, MIT TECH. REV. (June 29, 2011), http://technologyreview.com/news/424535/how-a-broken-medical-system-killed-google-health/.

[99] Wangsness, *Electronic Health Records Raise Doubt.*

[100] CTR. FOR DEMOCRACY & TECH., COMMENTS OF THE CENTER FOR DEMOCRACY & TECHNOLOGY TO THE OFFICE OF THE NATIONAL COORDINATOR'S PHR ROUNDTABLE 3, 19 (2010), http://www.cdt.org/files/pdfs/CDT_Comment_to_ONC_PHR_Roundtable.pdf.

[101] Frank Pasquale, *The End of "Notice and Consent" as Meaningful Privacy Protection, Cyberlaw Jotwell* (Feb. 3, 2012), http://cyber.jotwell.com/the-end-of-notice-and-consent-as-meaningful-privacy-protection/ (offering an overview of the likely responses of data subjects).

[102] *See Id.* (discussing patient distrust over privacy of personal data and examining three possible responses to avoid the harms of full disclosure).

[103] Nicolas P. Terry, *Personal Health Records: Directing More Costs and Risks to Consumers?*, 1 DREXEL L. REV. 216, 226 (2009).

[104] News Release, The Commonwealth Fund, 100% of Primary Care Doctors in Denmark Use Electronic Medical Records (Mar. 11, 2010), *available at* http://www.commonwealthfund.org/~/media/Files/News/News%20Releases/2010/Protti%20Release%20Final%203910.pdf ("All primary care doctors in Demark use electronic medical records"); THE COMMONWEALTH FUND, INTERNATIONAL HEALTH POLICY SURVEY OF PRIMARY CARE PHYSICIANS IN ELEVEN COUNTRIES (2009) (noting that the United States is near the bottom in measures of electronic medical record penetration and use among primary care physicians).

pioneer programs are leading the way, but they tend to be integrated into well-established health systems that have focused on information technology for decades.[105] As rules expanding meaningful use to PHRs are promulgated, it is important that concerned patients' voices are heard. Ideally, technological advances could accurately and completely populate PHRs with inputs from providers, apps, and even radio frequency identification chips.[106]

Effective health information technology depends on sophisticated surveillance: watching, recording, and analyzing patients, populations, and providers.[107] In 2010, the President's Council of Advisors on Science and Technology (PCAST) warned against health information technology adoption that is uninspired by a vision for data use and sharing that would enable healthcare to achieve the quality and efficiency gains characteristic of the modern information economy.[108] Unfortunately, the EHR industry's rejection of the PCAST approach has heavily influenced ONC.[109] Public dialogue on health IT has been limited, and the main commenters are usually industry players.[110] A predictable pattern has developed: HHS announces ambitious goals in proposed rules, commenters raise concerns about technical feasibility, and requirements are scaled back somewhat in final rules.[111] The broader purposes of health information technology often remain in the background. It therefore may be time to revive the PCAST's (and others') ambitious goals for health IT.

IV Medical Research and Data

Digitized health data should enable extraordinary new possibilities for medical research.[112] Observational research based on actual patients' experience with drugs and procedures may turn out to be more useful than clinical trials once a critical mass of outcomes has been

[105] *Id.* at 217 nn.10 11.

[106] Scott Peppet, *Unraveling Privacy: The Personal Prospectus and the Threat of a Full-Disclosure Future*, 105 Nw. U. L. Rev. 1153, 1153 1156 (describing data-gathering apps); Mireille Hildebrandt, Profiling the European Citizen 15 (2009) (describing ubiquitous health data-gathering apps).

[107] *See* Kenneth W. Goodman, *Ethics, Information Technology, and Public Health: New Challenges for the Clinician-Patient Relationship*, 38 J.L. Med. & Ethics 58 (2010) (arguing that surveillance is necessary to ensuring useful health information is not ignored).

[108] President's Council of Advisors on Sci. & Tech., Report to the President Realizing the Full Potential of Health Information Technology to Improve Healthcare for Americans: The Path Forward 14 (2010), *available at* http://www.whitehouse.gov/sites/default/files/microsites/ostp/pcast-health-it-report.pdf.

[109] Terry, *Anticipating*, at 111 112.

[110] *See* Health Research Inst., Putting Patients into "Meaningful Use", at 1 (noting that "[t]he industry" has expressed concerns that the proposed requirements and timelines for Stage 2 of meaningful use may be too aggressive).

[111] Blumenthal & Tavenner, *"Meaningful Use" Regulation*, at 502 (noting that the final regulations for Stage 1 of meaningful use incorporated changes in response to comments that the regulations were too demanding).

[112] President's Council of Advisors on Sci. & Tech., Report to the President Realizing the Full Potential of Health Information Technology to Improve Health Care for Americans: The Path Forward 5 (2010), *available at* http://www.whitehouse.gov/sites/default/files/microsites/ostp/pcast-health-it-report.pdf (describing potential improvements in care).

recorded and researchers can control for environmental and other variations.[113] However, vendors of EHR software currently can exploit a combination of trade secrecy law and licensing agreements to help providers "lock up" data in proprietary formats. If any particular entity retains excessive control over data, many important forms of research may be unduly limited. Scientists also worry about a trend toward obscurity in the computational modeling of medical interventions.[114]

Legal scholars have examined the trade-offs between data portability, standardization, privacy, and innovation in EHRs.[115] One key to policy success in the EHR field will be distinguishing between raw data (which should be both portable and, when properly anonymized, subject to academic research) and its interpretation and organization (which are more justifiably considered intellectual property of a particular person or firm).[116] For example, Hoffman and Podgurski have detailed how advanced programs of research on effectiveness could work.[117] Their proposal for new forms of personalized medicine takes to the individual level what Efthimios Parasidis envisions for population-wide analysis:

> We propose the development of a broadly accessible framework to enable physicians to rapidly perform, through a computerized service, medically sound personalized comparisons of the effectiveness of possible treatments for patients' conditions. A personalized comparison of treatment effectiveness . . . for a given patient (the subject patient) would be based on data from EHRs of a cohort of patients who are similar to the subject patient (clinically, demographically, genetically), who received the treatments previously and whose outcomes were recorded.[118]

As Hoffman and Podgurski explain, such a database query could identify "for a given patient, an appropriate reference group (cohort) of similar, previously treated patients whose EHRs would be analyzed to choose the optimal treatment for the patient at issue."[119] Their proposal is a logical extension of an idea promoted in an Institute of Medicine report known as the "Wilensky Proposal," which called for more targeted comparative effectiveness research.[120] Research has already demonstrated that pharmacogenetic algorithms, for example, can outperform algorithms that consider only clinical factors.[121]

[113] Jennifer Kahn, *Modeling Human Drug Trials—Without the Humans*, WIRED, Dec. 2009, at 156, 157, 194 ("All the calculations happen inside a black box. And that's a problem because there's no way to tell whether the model's underlying assumptions are right.'").

[114] PRESIDENT'S COUNCIL OF ADVISORS ON SCI. & TECH., REPORT TO THE PRESIDENT REALIZING THE FULL POTENTIAL OF HEALTH INFORMATION TECHNOLOGY TO IMPROVE HEALTH CARE FOR AMERICANS: THE PATH FORWARD 5 (2010), *available at* http://www.whitehouse.gov/sites/default/files/microsites/ostp/pcast-health-it-report.pdf (describing potential improvements in care).

[115] *Id.* at 66 67.

[116] *See* Greg R. Vetter, *Slouching Toward Open Innovation: Free and Open Source Software for Electronic Health Information*, 30 WASH. U. J.L & POL'Y 179, 179 186 (2009); Marc Rodwin, *Patient Data: Property, Privacy & the Public Interest*, 36 AM. J.L. & MED. 586, 586 589 (2010).

[117] Hoffman & Podgurski, *Improving Health Care Outcomes Through Personalized Comparisons of Treatment Effectiveness Based on Electronic Health Records*, 39 J.L. MED. & ETHICS 425, 425 (2011).

[118] *Id.*

[119] *Id.* at 426.

[120] *See* INST. OF MED., CHALLENGES FOR THE FDA: THE FUTURE OF DRUG SAFETY 52 (2007) (addressing comparative effectiveness).

[121] J. Woodcock & L. J. Lesko, *Pharmacogenetics—Tailoring Treatment for the Outliers*, 360 NEW ENG. J. MED. 811, 811 (2009).

The PCAST also endorsed aggressive use of health data to improve research.[122] The PCAST authors concluded that many clinical research studies today are "out of date before they are even finished," "burdensome and costly," and too narrowly focused.[123] They endorsed health information technology that is enabled for "syndromic surveillance," "public health monitoring," and "adverse event monitoring" by aggregating observational data.[124]

Of course, there are challenges to this type of research. Systems must move beyond mere transparency to data entry standards that provide the greater intelligibility required for personalized medicine.[125] As Hoffman and Podgurski recognize, the ability "to code all presenting comorbidities" and to identify "patients who have the specific condition to be studied" is crucial to data quality.[126] In developing such systems, there is a tension between encouraging innovation by vendors at any given time and enabling patients, doctors, insurers, and hospitals to compare their records over time and to transport information from one system to another.[127]

For example, one system may be able to understand "C," "cgh," or "koff" as "cough," and may well code it in any way it chooses.[128] But to integrate and to port data, all systems need to be able to translate symptoms, diagnoses, interventions, and outcomes into commonly recognized coding.[129] Patients want their providers to seamlessly integrate records.[130] In addition to personalized medicine and research, competition among vendors also depends on data portability: Healthcare providers can only credibly threaten to move their business away from an unsatisfactory vendor if they can transport those records.[131]

Postmarket surveillance of pharmaceuticals for safety and efficacy exemplifies the feasibility issues involved in transforming healthcare into an information industry that achieves the productivity gains we associate with Silicon Valley.[132] As Parasidis notes of the FDA's deployment of "Mini-Sentinel":

[122] PRESIDENT'S COUNCIL OF ADVISORS ON SCI. & TECH., REPORT TO THE PRESIDENT REALIZING THE FULL POTENTIAL OF HEALTH INFORMATION TECHNOLOGY TO IMPROVE HEALTH CARE FOR AMERICANS, at 64 (recommending use of "large datasets" to address numerous issues in clinical research).

[123] *Id.* at 63. [124] *Id.* at 64.

[125] *See* Hoffman & Podgurski, *Improving Health Care Outcomes*, at 429 (explaining the benefits of personalized comparisons of treatment effectiveness (PCTEs), a form of personalized medicine, that uses information obtained through a large database search to "find a cohort for a patient needing treatment").

[126] Hoffman & Podgurski, *Improving Health Care Outcomes*, at 433.

[127] Sharona Hoffman & Andy Podgurski, *Finding a Cure: The Case for Regulation and Oversight of Electronic Health Record Systems*, 22 HARV. J.L. & TECH. 103, 151 (2008).

[128] *Id.* at 152 (noting that "medical terminology is complex, variable, and evolving").

[129] *Id.* at 153 (promoting a "common exchange representation" (CER), an artificial language that represents information).

[130] David Lagesse, *Deloitte: Patients Want Electronic Health Records*, U.S. NEWS & WORLD REPORT (Mar. 4, 2008), http://money.usnews.com/money/blogs/daves-download/2008/03/04/deloitte-patients-want-electronic-health-records_print.html (noting that a survey by the Deloitte Center for Health Solutions reported that "3 of 4 consumers want their doctors to provide online access to an integrated medical record and that 1 in 4 would pay more for the service").

[131] Niva Elkin-Koren, *User-Generated Platforms*, IN WORKING WITHIN THE BOUNDARIES OF INTELLECTUAL PROPERTY 111, 121 122 (Rochelle C. Dreyfus, Harry First, & Diane L. Zimmerman eds., 2010) (describing the importance of data portability).

[132] *See* Parasidis, *Patients over Politics*, at 984 986 (proposing integration of postmarket drug surveillance into an extant health IT infrastructure); Hoffman & Podgurski, *Improving Health Care*

> Rather than creating a centralized database, Mini-Sentinel uses a distributed data network that is linked by a coordinating center. The Mini-Sentinel data network incorporates EHRs from diverse data sets that are maintained by public and private stakeholders. Each data partner retains control over its own patient-level data and permits others to access its aggregated and de-identified medical data.[133]

Querying of distributed databases from diverse public and private sector partners could vastly accelerate the FDA's ability to advance standards of care. As this example demonstrates, creative partnerships between government, private sector contractors, and providers or suppliers can build institutional capacity to improve healthcare and promote public health.

V Conclusion

To achieve the triple aim of individual quality enhancement, population health improvement, and cost control, new approaches to healthcare have been investigated and developed. One such approach is through data collection and use at each stage of the healthcare delivery process. A "learning health system" draws on electronic health records and other data sources to rapidly advance the evidence base for clinical care.[134] The potential benefits extend not only to improving and coordinating care in the present but also to ensuring a more dynamic approach to the development and dissemination of new medical interventions.

Through precision medicine initiatives and the use of predictive analytical modeling, the goal of a twenty-first-century healthcare system is to provide clinicians and researchers the tools to better understand the complex mechanisms underlying a patient's health, disease, or condition, and to better predict which treatments will be most effective.[135] Though this approach has the ability to greatly improve health outcomes as well as to reduce the costs associated with healthcare, there are legal complexities in the collection, aggregation, and use of data in this context, primarily arising out of informed consent, contract, medical research, intellectual property, and privacy laws. To ensure that data is not only easily accessible for research and clinical purposes but also sufficiently protective of patients' privacy, these legal issues must be identified and addressed with nuance and respect for all stakeholders' interests.

Outcomes, at 425 (proposing the development of a "broadly accessible framework" that enables doctors to quickly perform comparisons of treatments); Hoffman & Podgurski, *Finding a Cure*, at 151 (recommending regulations that require doctors to use IT to improve practices).

133 Parasidis, *Patients over Politics*, at 971.

134 Lynn M. Etheredge, *Rapid Learning: A Breakthrough Agenda*, 33 Health Aff. 1155 (2014).

135 *Id.*

CHAPTER 10

THE PROMISE OF INFORMED CONSENT

ROBIN FRETWELL WILSON*

I Introduction

Some ideas are elegantly simple—deceptively so. In 1914, Justice Cardozo famously observed that "[e]very human being of adult years and sound mind has a right to determine what shall be done with his body."[1] Although it took nearly half a century before patients could sue to enforce that right, patients today are assured that "[a]ll medical care requires the consent of the patient (or someone who is authorized to consent for the patient) before care is given."[2] For that consent to be *informed*, a patient "must understand the risks and drawbacks of the plan to decide if the benefits [she] expect[s] are worth it." Premised on autonomy, self-determination, and patient well-being, the duty to secure a patient's informed consent for medical procedures is a thoroughly American notion.[3]

As this chapter illustrates, the simple notion that patients may direct their care is actually quite complex. The law operationalizes the duty to secure a patient's informed consent with legal tests that sometimes frustrate private enforcement through litigation. Further, in

* Roger and Stephany Joslin Professor of Law and Director, Family Law and Policy Program, University of Illinois College of Law. I am grateful to Anna Gotfryd, Lindsey Lusk, Nick Phillips, and Breanna Taylor for their expert research assistance. I have been retained as an expert in connection with the litigation over the SUPPORT Study discussed *infra*. *See* Dreshan Collins, et al., v. Sheila D. Moore, et al., United States District Court For The Northern District Of Alabama.

[1] Schloendorff v. Soc'y of N.Y. Hosp., 105 N.E. 92, 93 (N.Y. 1914).

[2] American Cancer Society, "Informed Consent," *available at* http://www.cancer.org/acs/groups/cid/documents/webcontent/003014-pdf.pdf.

[3] *See* Jessica W. Berg et al., Informed Consent: Legal Theory and Clinical Practice 14 (2d ed. 2001) (noting that "[t]he values underlying informed consent—autonomy and concern for individual well-being—are deeply embedded in American culture, religious traditions, and Western moral philosophy"); Bernard Lo, Resolving Ethical Dilemmas: A Guide of Clinicians 21 (2d ed. 2000) ("[I]ncreased sense of control, self-efficacy, and adherence to plans for care" are also benefits of patient participation in decision-making).

practice, patients do little more than sign a "paper consent form," never having the "face-to-face" conversation that the form should memorialize. For most patients, there is a gaping gulf between their desire to participate in choices about their care and what actually transpires.[4] Complicating the possibility of reform, not all patients are alike. Some patients want be the decision-maker; others, a passive participant; yet others, a trusted partner in making medical decisions together with their physician. While there is a nascent movement toward shared decision-making, that concept means different things to different people.[5]

Duties to secure informed consent apply to medical research as well. Birthed from the Nuremberg tribunal's prosecution of physicians for experimentation on Jews and others interred in Nazi concentration camps, the right to voluntarily consent to participation in research arose contemporaneously with that in medical treatment. Its contours have been shaped by both case law and regulation. Codified in federal regulations known as the Common Rule, most federally funded research requires voluntary, informed consent where participants weigh the risks and benefits of contributing to human research. But, decades later, some question whether this core duty should be extended to the study of public-domain data like Twitter feeds and other frontier research, while others argue that a subset of research on the standard of care, should require less, not more, disclosure. In both instances, regulators have left existing duties untouched.

A dialogue between professional ethics and formal law has shaped the doctrine's evolution. In recent years, informed consent has also increasingly been the subject of statutory reform. A growing number of states regulate disclosure practices about medical teaching, requiring greater transparency about whether a procedure is being performed for the patient's care or the student's training. One state provides a statutory safe harbor, standardizing disclosure for specific procedures. Other states have sought to dictate what physicians must say to patients about the one healthcare procedure that continues to divide the country: abortion. These laws test the boundary between conduct, which the state has greater leeway to regulate, and speech.[6] Some mandated disclosures have survived challenges that they unconstitutionally infringe providers' free speech rights, others have been struck.

As the economics of healthcare and medical research have changed across time, plaintiffs have sought to expand disclosure duties accordingly. Financial conflicts of interests implicate care, as do the existence or cost of alternative treatment. The nature of medical practice itself has pushed the envelope, as well. Physicians must disclose their relative inexperience in some jurisdictions, and a growing number of states require specific consent to the substitution of another physician to do scheduled surgery or to intimate pelvic exams when done for teaching purposes rather than the patient's benefit. Many of these cases can yield damage

[4] Linda Brom et al., *Congruence between Patients' Preferred and Perceived Participation in Medical Decision-making: A review of the Literature*, 14 BMC MED. INFORM. DECIS. MAK. 25 (2014), *available at* http://www.ncbi.nlm.nih.gov/pubmed/24708833 (reviewing results of forty-four studies that included fifty-two different patient samples).

[5] G. Makoul & M. L. Clayman, *An Integrative Model of Shared Decision Making in Medical Encounters*, 60 PATIENT EDUC. & COUNSELING 301 (2006) (describing the "murkiness" of definitions of shared decision-making).

[6] *See* Robert Post, *Informed Consent to Abortion: A First Amendment Analysis of Compelled Physician Speech*, 3 U. ILL. L. REV. 939 (2007).

awards for fear of undisclosed outcomes that never materialize, challenging whether "materialized risk" really acts as an element of an informed consent claim.

Today, much work remains to be done to realize the promise of informed consent. The common-sense idea that patients—armed with sufficient information to weigh the trade-offs of receiving or foregoing care—may direct their care proves surprisingly challenging to realize on the ground.

II The Genesis of the Duty

Early on, informed consent played little to no role in doctor-patient relationships. Doctors "knew best," and patients routinely looked to physicians to guide their care.[7] "Simple consent"—that is, nearly any indication that the patient consented to being cared for, whether or not armed with sufficient information about risks and benefits—sufficed to authorize the physician to provide whatever treatment the physician deemed best. Absent that simple consent, a patient would have a claim for battery against the physician.[8]

This culture started to change in the years after World War II, both for treatment and research. In medical research, the duty to use only "informed volunteers" arose from a long conversation between law and ethics that later became codified in the Federal Policy for the Protection of Human Subjects, known as the Common Rule.[9] In 1946, the Nuremberg war crimes tribunal prosecuted twenty Nazi doctors for experiments done without consent on those held in prison camps during the war. "The Doctors' Trials" resulted in the death penalty for seven physicians and imprisonment for the others.[10] "Prompted by the Nazis' defense lawyers' surprisingly disconcerting arguments regarding questionable conduct of human research in the United States, particularly research conducted in prisons," the American Medical Association (AMA) commissioned a report by Drs. Andrew Ivy and Leo Alexander of "ethical and legal conventions, or rules, for human experimentation." Adopted by the AMA House of Delegates in 1946 and published in *The Journal of the American Medical Association*, the "rules emphasized voluntary and informed consent, as well as avoidance of inappropriate risk": "Consent of the human subject must be obtained. All subjects must have been volunteers in the absence of coercion in any form. Before volunteering the subjects have been informed of the hazards, if any . . ."[11]

Despite the AMA's role, courts were slow to impose on physicians meaningful disclosure duties for ordinary treatment. As late as the 1950s, trial courts resisted recovery by patients even when patients expressly told the doctor *not* to render certain treatment. Consider *Corn v. French*.[12] There, Ruth Corn consulted Dr. James French about a lump under her right

[7] *See* James F. Childress, Who Should Decide? Paternalism in Health Care (1982).

[8] John Duncan et al., *Using Tort Law to Secure Patient Dignity*, 42 Trial Mag. 42, 44 (Oct. 2004).

[9] *See generally* Presidential Commission for the Study of Bioethical Issues, "Ethically Impossible": STD Research in Guatemala from 1946 to 1948 (Sept. 2011), *available at* http://bioethics.gov/node/654.

[10] *Id.* at 99.

[11] Final Report, Advisory Committee on Human Radiation Experimentation (1995), *available at* http://biotech.law.lsu.edu/research/reports/ACHRE/chap2_2.html.

[12] 71 Nev. 280, 282–285 (1955).

breast. Suspecting breast cancer, Dr. French said the breast might need to be removed. He phoned the hospital to arrange a procedure and request particular tools. Mrs. Corn immediately told Dr. French, "If that's my breast you are talking about, you are not going to remove it." Dr. French responded, "I have no intentions of removing your breast. I wouldn't think of doing so without first making a test," explaining that a biopsy for cancer required the same tools.

At the hospital, Mrs. Corn signed a form "giv[ing] [her] consent to James B. French, M.D., to perform an operation for mastectomy . . . upon [her], and to do whatever may be deemed necessary in his judgment." Mrs. Corn would later testify that she had never heard of a mastectomy and Dr. French never explained the term "mastectomy." Mrs. Corn told Dr. French a second time that she wanted only a test. Dr. French removed her breast anyway.

The trial court granted Dr. French's motion to dismiss Mrs. Corn's suit for "unauthorized and unnecessary amputation of her right breast." In the court's estimation, Mrs. Corn dispositively gave consent by signing the form, "whether or not she understood the meaning of it." Were it otherwise, no "doctor in the country . . . would be safe from suits of this sort." Mrs. Corn appealed to the Nevada Supreme Court, which reversed and remanded for a new trial on the issue of whether Mrs. Corn had withdrawn her consent. At trial, however, Mrs. Corn could not convince the jury to hold Dr. French liable.

In this era, physicians also escaped liability when soft-peddling risks. In 1955, the Supreme Court of North Carolina upheld a trial court's dismissal of a malpractice action brought by a formerly "ablebodied" mechanic, Charles Hunt, against his surgeon, Dr. Howard Bradshaw.[13] Bradshaw removed a "sharpedged piece of steel" from beneath Hunt's collarbone, saying there was "nothing to [the operation], it was very simple."

When Hunt awoke from surgery, he "couldn't use [his] fingers at all"—a problem that never went away. Hunt sued Dr. Bradshaw for advising him that the "operation was simple, whereas it was serious and involved undisclosed risks."

After Hunt's evidence, the trial court granted Dr. Bradshaw's motion for judgment of nonsuit. The Supreme Court of North Carolina affirmed. Bradshaw "understandabl[y] wanted to reassure" Hunt so he would not "go to the operating room unduly apprehensive." While Dr. Bradshaw's "[f]ailure to explain the risk involved . . . may be considered a mistake on the part of the surgeon," it could not "be deemed such want of ordinary care as to import liability."

A scant two years later, the California Supreme Court coined the term "informed consent" in *Salgo v. Leland Stanford Junior University Board of Trustee*.[14] Martin Salgo's estate sued Stanford University Hospital and his surgeon, Dr. Frank Gerbode, for malpractice, claiming that an aortography Stanford performed at Dr. Gerbode's direction paralyzed Salgo from the waist down; he "was not informed that anything in the nature of an aortography was to be performed."

At trial, the judge gave "a rather broad instruction" that physicians must "disclose to the patient 'all the facts which mutually affect his rights and interests and of the surgical risk, hazard and danger, if any.'" Dr. Gerbode and the Stanford physician who performed the procedure both disputed the lack of disclosure but admitted that "details . . . and the possible

[13] Hunt v. Bradshaw, 242 N.C. 517, 518, 522, 523 (1955).

[14] 317 P.2d 170, 181 (Cal. App. 1957).

dangers" were not explained. The jury found for Salgo, awarding damages later reduced to $213,355. The defendants appealed, arguing that the jury instructions prejudiced them.

Finding other errors necessitating a new trial, the California Supreme Court directed that the broad instruction be scaled back to indicate that physicians retain discretion in certain instances to not make disclosures. Although "[a] physician violates his duty to his patient and subjects himself to liability if he withholds any facts which are necessary to form the basis of an intelligent consent by the patient to the proposed treatment," or "minimize[s] the known dangers . . . in order to induce his patient's consent," he or she must "recognize that each patient presents a separate problem, that the patient's mental and emotional condition is important and in certain cases may be crucial, and that in discussing the element of risk a certain amount of discretion must be employed consistent with the full disclosure of facts necessary to an informed consent."

Although providing physicians flexibility to not cause undue alarm, *Salgo* signaled a meaningful shift from the barest consent precluding liability to imposing a duty to secure informed consent. As the next part explains, courts have fleshed out the contours of the duty to disclose in importantly different ways, measuring the content of disclosure by "reasonable physicians" in some places and by "reasonable patients" in others.

III Contours of the Duty

Today, by statute and common law, physicians in every state must obtain informed consent to medical procedures.[15] Generally, to recover on a claim for breach of the duty to secure informed consent, plaintiffs must demonstrate four elements: (1) failure to disclose a specific risk in violation of the governing standard; (2) materialization of that risk; (3) "causation"—that is, if the risk been disclosed, the patient, or a prudent person in the patient's position, would not have proceeded as she did[16]; and (4) that no exception, like emergency, excuses the failure to disclose. As with other claims, plaintiffs must also show an injury suffered as a result of the breach.

As this part shows, in the paradigmatic cases fleshing out the contours of this duty, courts have adopted different benchmarks for deciding what patients must be told to satisfy the duty—and what patients must show to recover for breach. Consequently, patients are far less likely to be able to enforce this duty in some jurisdictions than in others.

a. Dueling Standards for Adequate Disclosure

In the pantheon of famous health law cases, every casebook, treatise, and scholarly treatment of informed consent includes two seminal cases establishing what physicians must disclose

[15] Ryan M. Hrobak & Robin Fretwell Wilson, *Emergency Contraceptives or "Abortion-Inducing" Drugs? Empowering Women to Make Informed Decisions*, 71 Wash. & Lee L. Rev. 1386, 1415 (2014).

[16] *See* Mark Hall et al., Health Care Law and Ethics 215 (7th ed. 2007).

to patients to satisfy the duty of informed consent: *Culbertson v. Mernitz* and *Canterbury v. Spence*.

The law of nearly every U.S. jurisdiction follows one of these two approaches for determining the scope of disclosure. Currently, twenty-five states and the District of Columbia rely on *Canterbury*'s patient-centered material risk test; twenty-three states follow *Culbertson*'s professional or reasonable physician standard.[17] Colorado and Georgia, however, take "hybrid" approaches blending "aspects of the patient[-centered] and professional standards, without expressing a clear preference for either."

Even though courts use different benchmarks for gauging adequate disclosure, both standards yield common disclosure requirements. Patients must be informed of the nature of the intervention, the expected benefits, the risks, and the likely consequences. And physicians have a duty to apprise patients of *alternatives* to treatment,[18] as well as the risk of "doing nothing."[19]

i. The Professional or "Reasonable Physician" Standard

The landmark decision establishing the professional or "reasonable physician" standard for determining the adequacy of disclosure, *Culbertson v. Mernitz*, grew out of facts that would make most wince.[20] Dr. Roland Mernitz believed that Patty Jo Culbertson's problems with incontinence and vaginal discharge stemmed from her bladder bulging into her vagina, multiple uterine fibroid tumors, and cervicitis. A Marshall Marchetti Krantz procedure (MMK), Dr. Mernitz advised, would "suspend the bladder," while "a hysterectomy or cryosurgery [would] freeze the infected tip of the cervix." Although Dr. Mernitz warned Culbertson that infection, severe vaginal discharge, and inability to control her bladder might result, he did not inform her that her cervix could adhere to her vagina. When the latter occurred, Culbertson required a total hysterectomy, removal of both ovaries, and suspension of her bladder a second time.

Culbertson filed a complaint with the Indiana Department of Insurance (Department) and sued in state court. The Department's medical review panel found no breach of the duty to secure informed consent because physicians generally do not consider the cervix's adhesion to the vagina to be a risk of MMK. Relying on that determination, the trial court granted summary judgment for Dr. Mernitz.

Culbertson appealed, arguing that the adequacy of disclosure should be judged by what a reasonable patient would consider material, not what a reasonable physician would disclose. Under the former standard, expert medical testimony would not be necessary to find

[17] David M. Studdert et al., *Geographic Variation in Informed Consent Law: Two Standards for Disclosure of Treatment Risks*, 4 J. EMPIRICAL LEGAL STUD. 103, at 105, 106 (2007).

[18] *See generally* John H. Derrick, Annotation, *Medical Malpractice: Liability for Failure of Physician to Inform Patient of Alternative Modes of Diagnosis or Treatment*, 38 A.L.R. 4th 900 (originally published in 1985).

[19] Wecker v. Amend, 918 P.2d 658, 661 (Kan. Ct. App. 1996) (concluding that the professional standard requires providing patients the option of forgoing treatment when it's a "reasonable medically acceptable option").

[20] 602 N.E.2d 98, 98–103 (Ind. 1992).

Dr. Mernitz liable. Instead, the jury could decide whether disclosure of a given risk would have dissuaded a reasonable patient from having the procedure.

On appeal, the Indiana Supreme Court rejected the reasonable patient standard, measuring disclosure instead by what "reasonable physicians" would disclose. It would require expert testimony to show what a reasonable physician would have disclosed, except when "the situation is clearly within the realm of laymen's comprehension." In Culbertson's case, the risk of adhesion was beyond an "ordinary layman's comprehension."

The *Culbertson* court directly grappled with whether the professional standard represented a return to the older era of paternalism, "destroying the patient's right of self-decision." In its view, the fact that the AMA had developed ethical standards obligating physicians "to present the medical facts accurately to the patient" should "assuage this fear." Further, "the patient possesses enough information to enable an intelligent choice."

Moreover, measuring disclosure by the reasonable physician is only fair. Physicians should not be forced to be "mind reader[s]," guessing what the patient would like to know regarding a proposed treatment. For risks not obvious to the layman, a physician "should only be required to do that which he is trained to do, namely conduct himself as a reasonably prudent physician."

ii. The Patient-centered or "Reasonable Patient" Standard

An equally poignant case established the competing approach to measuring the scope of disclosure, the "reasonable patient" standard. *Canterbury v. Spence* was an "understandable search for reasons" to explain how, nine years after what should have been a routine surgery, a nineteen-year-old FBI clerk, Jerry Canterbury, was left partially paralyzed, incontinent, and wearing "a penile clamp."[21]

Canterbury had consulted neurosurgeon Dr. William Spence about pain between his shoulder blades. After ordering a myelogram, which injects dye into the spine to visualize it, Dr. Spence recommended a laminectomy to alleviate pressure on a ruptured disc. A legal minor at nineteen, Canterbury could not legally consent to the surgery. Canterbury's mother, who signed the consent form when she arrived at the hospital after the surgery was over, was not present when Dr. Spence allegedly told Canterbury the surgery was "no more serious than an ordinary, everyday operation."[22] Canterbury voiced no objection and signed nothing himself. The parties gave contradictory testimony regarding whether Canterbury's mother consented to his surgery over the phone.

Although Dr. Spence performed the laminectomy skillfully and instructed the hospital staff that Canterbury should not leave the hospital bed even to urinate, tragedy struck. Two physicians modified Dr. Spence's orders to allow Canterbury first to sit up in bed and then "to stand at bedside and attempt to void." Needing to urinate, Canterbury rolled out of his elevated bed and fell, injuring his spine. A second operation could not repair the damage.

Canterbury then sued Dr. Spence for failing to obtain informed consent. Canterbury's lawsuit faced significant hurdles. Because the statute of limitations on battery had run, that

[21] 464 F.2d 772, 778 (D.C. Cir. 1972).

[22] Alan Meisel, *Canterbury v. Spence: The Landmark Case*, *in* Health Law & Bioethics: Cases in Context 9, 17, 18, 19 (Sandra H. Johnson, Joan H. Krause, Richard S. Saver, & Robin Fretwell Wilson eds., Aspen Publishers 2009).

straight-forward claim was unavailable, requiring Canterbury to allege negligence and raising the question whether expert testimony about disclosure was required. Unlike today, a "conspiracy of silence" reigned among medical doctors, and obtaining an expert from the same locality as Dr. Spence was nearly impossible. Canterbury's attorney "engage[d] in the risky procedure of calling Dr. Spence as an expert;" Dr. Spence admitted "that even without trauma paralysis can be anticipated 'somewhere in the nature of one percent' of the laminectomies performed . . ."

Finding insufficient evidence for a jury to decide that either the doctor or the hospital had breached the duty of care to Canterbury, the trial court granted the defendants' motions for a directed verdict. Canterbury appealed. The D.C. Circuit's lengthy opinion detailed the requirements for obtaining informed consent. The court held that physicians must behave reasonably under the circumstances, meaning that they must disclose all material risks. The duty to disclose arises from the fiduciary nature of the doctor-patient relationship and extends to those risks a reasonable patient would likely find significant "in deciding whether or not to forego [*sic*] the proposed therapy." This necessarily includes "the incidence of injury and the degree of harm threatened." Because the jury may determine which risks a reasonable patient would consider material to an informed decision about proposed treatment, lawsuits can proceed without expert testimony about physician disclosure practices.

Although *Canterbury* continues to exert a significant influence on American law, for Canterbury, it was "the most Pyhrric of victories." The D.C. Circuit remanded for a new trial "to decide whether [a 1% chance of paralysis] was of sufficient magnitude to bring the disclosure duty into play." Canterbury's claim ultimately failed.[23] Canterbury admitted he voluntarily underwent a second laminectomy to relieve new back pain—a fatal admission seen as impeaching his testimony that he would not have agreed to the original laminectomy had he been adequately informed of its risks. Of course, "it was far more reasonable for Canterbury to accept the risk of paralysis a second time because he already was partially paralyzed."

iii. Core Trade-off

The dueling standards for measuring the scope of disclosure result from a difference in judgment about what one can reasonably expect of physicians. The *Culbertson* court found the reasonable patient standard too "onerous," requiring doctors "to speculate as to what a hypothetical reasonable prudent patient would 'need to know.'"[24] In this view, doctors should not be forced to waste "valuable clinical time" unnecessarily "learning a patient's every idiosyncrasy."[25] Doctors can be tasked, however, with knowing what other reasonable physicians would do in like situations.

The *Canterbury* court also rejected "full" disclosure about each and every risk a given patient may find material as "unrealistic" and overly "prohibitive." Nonetheless, across patients, a set of risks are material to decisions facing prudent patients, which sometimes will not mirror what physicians choose to disclose. The material risk standard avoids placing burdens on patients, who simply do not know enough to ask doctors intelligent questions

[23] *Id.* at 22, 23. [24] *Culbertson*, 602 N.E.2d at 106.

[25] Robert Gatter, *Informed Consent Law and the Forgotten Duty of Physician Inquiry*, 31 Loy. U. Chi. L.J. 557, 559 (2000).

about treatment risks. Without a forced transfer of information, patients cannot vindicate their autonomy interests in deciding what happens with their bodies.

As Parts V and VI illustrate, state legislatures have increasingly sought to standardize disclosure to patients in certain settings in order to reduce the burden on and legal risk to physicians, while assuring that patients receive needed information.

b. Causation: Would Disclosure Have Changed the Outcome?

Plaintiffs in informed consent cases bear the burden of both decision causation and injury causation.[26] To satisfy injury causation, the patient must demonstrate an injury resulting from treatment. To satisfy decision causation, patients must show that, had the risk leading to the injury been disclosed, the patient—or a reasonable patient under similar circumstances—would have forgone the procedure.

The reasonable person standard is the dominant standard for judging decision causation.[27] Objectively, the fact-finder asks what "a prudent person in the patient's position would have decided if suitably informed of all perils bearing significance." If adequate disclosure could reasonably be expected to have caused that person to decline the treatment . . ., causation is shown, but otherwise not."[28] A jury can decide without the patient's testimony what a reasonable patient would have done.[29]

A distinct minority (four states) ask instead only whether *this particular* patient would have foregone the procedure. Since plaintiffs can give self-serving testimony, some see the standard as almost impossible to disprove. Yet "juries are regularly asked to determine the credibility of witnesses."[30]

Objective causation reduces informed consent to a nearly useless claim when a statistical majority of patients would choose to proceed with treatment regardless of the risks. For emergency procedures, causation will prove "almost impossible to satisfy" since reasonable patients would accept treatment even if better informed. Causation will also be difficult to establish when no real alternative treatment exists other than nontreatment.

c. Exceptions to the Duty to Disclose

Five general exceptions exist to the duty to provide informed consent: "threats to public health, medical emergency, therapeutic privilege, waiver of informed consent by the patient, and a patient's lack of competence to make decisions."[31] Physicians are also excused from

[26] Evelyn M. Tenenbaum, *Revitalizing Informed Consent and Protecting Patient Autonomy: An Appeal to Abandon Objective Causation*, 64 OKLA. L. REV. 697, 710 (2012).

[27] Kate Greenwood, *Physician Conflicts of Interest in Court: Beyond the "Independent Physician" Litigation Heuristic*, 30 GA. ST. U. L. REV. 759, 777 (2014).

[28] *Canterbury*, 464 F.2d at 791.

[29] *See, e.g.*, Hartke v. McKelway, 707 F.2d 1544, 1544 (D.C. Cir. 1983).

[30] Tenenbaum, *supra* note 26, at 730.

[31] THOMAS MAY, BIOETHICS IN A LIBERAL SOCIETY: THE POLITICAL FRAMEWORK OF BIOETHICS DECISION MAKING 21 (paperback ed. 2009).

telling patients things that "patients of average sophistication would already be aware" of, such as the commonly known risk of not having an annual pap smear.[32]

The therapeutic privilege, a central reason in *Salgo* for preserving physician discretion, has fallen into disfavor. To modern courts, permitting physicians not to disclose—when in their professional opinion given the patient's fragile emotional state, the harm from learning information outweighs the benefit—is too easily leveraged to "overrid[e] a patient's values."[33]

As *Canterbury* illustrated, a patient's incompetence does not erase the duty to secure consent—instead, consent must be given by the individual legally charged with decision-making. In addition to parents and formal guardians serving in that capacity, patients may appoint "surrogate decision-makers" though a healthcare proxy or durable power of attorney.[34] If the patient does not appoint a surrogate decision-maker, many states specify who can provide informed consent for individuals "incapable of giving informed consent."[35]

IV Informed Consent to Human Research

Duties to secure informed consent apply not only to clinical treatment but to medical research as well. A linchpin of ensuring the safety of human subjects, informed consent permits those placed at risk, or their legally authorized representatives, to weigh the risks and benefits for themselves. Currently, 80% of clinical studies on humans are interventional studies,[36] the most common of which are to test the safety and efficacy of drugs and biologics. At any one time, more than 100,000 drug and biologic studies are ongoing.

For consent to be informed, researchers must explain that participation is voluntary and must describe: (1) the purposes, procedures, and duration of the research; (2) any reasonably foreseeable risks or discomforts; (3) any benefits; (4) advantageous alternative procedures; (5) the confidentiality of records; (6) whether any compensation or any medical treatments are available if injury occurs; and (7) where to seek answers to questions about the research and participants' rights.[37]

In the United States, the regulation of most federally funded research occurs at the institutional level, overseen by local institutional review boards (IRBs). The Common Rule outlines how IRBs are to provide independent ethical review, minimize avoidable risks, and ensure informed consent to participation.[38] Fifteen governmental departments have codified the Common Rule (Common Rule agencies), requiring that the human research they fund adhere to it.

[32] *See* Cathy J. Jones, *Autonomy and Informed Consent in Medical Decisionmaking: Toward a New Self-Fulfilling Prophecy*, 47 Wash. & Lee L. Rev. 379, 393–394 (1990).

[33] May, *supra* note 31, at 26–30.

[34] For a discussion of healthcare proxies, *see* Alan Meisel & Kathy L. Cerminara, The Right to Die: The Law of End-of-Life Decisionmaking, Third Edition (Aspen 2014).

[35] *See, e.g.*, Kan. Stat. Ann. § 65-4974 (2014).

[36] *Trends, Charts, and Maps*, U.S. National Institutes of Health, *available at* https://clinicaltrials.gov/ct2/resources/trends.

[37] General Requirements for Informed Consent, 45 C.F.R. § 46.116.

[38] *The Common Rule*, U.S. Dept. of Health and Human Services, *available at* http://www.hhs.gov/ohrp/humansubjects/commonrule/.

As this part explains, unconscionable studies conducted with government support led to regulatory protections for participants that have changed little across time, despite the changing nature of human research. As with consent to medical treatment, private litigation has also played a crucial role in policing disclosure.

a. History of Unconsented-to Research

As Part II explained, the duty to secure voluntary, informed consent to human research crystallized after the Nazi war tribunals. In the following decades, reports of unconsented-to research in the United States led to greater oversight and safeguards here.

In 1972, explosive details emerged of the now-infamous "Tuskegee Study of Untreated Syphilis in the Male Negro" conducted under the auspices of the U.S. Public Health Service (PHS). Begun in 1932, PHS researchers followed 600 black men, 399 of whom were diagnosed with syphilis, for forty years without notice to the men—decades after treatment for syphilis became available.[39] PHS researchers instructed local doctors that the men were "not to be provided penicillin treatments for syphilis."[40]

More recently, in October 2010, the United States publicly apologized to Guatemala for intentionally exposing thousands of Guatemalans to sexually transmitted infections without their knowledge or consent in the 1940s.[41] Notes on the experiment were found in the papers of Dr. John Cutler, who conducted the Tuskegee study. That discovery prompted the Presidential Commission for the Study of Bioethical Issues (Presidential Commission) in 2011 to review the regulation of federally sponsored research involving human volunteers.[42]

b. Efforts to Expand, and Restrict, Federal Oversight

The Common Rule remains unchanged since its publication in 1991 even as research has expanded to include large multisite studies, Internet research, and DNA studies. In 2011, the federal government proposed a massive overhaul of the Common Rule to reflect this "vastly altered" landscape. For example, the overhaul would have required written consent for research on biospecimens even when stripped of identifiers, and extended federal oversight to all studies conducted by a U.S. institution receiving funding from a Common Rule agency, regardless of the funding source for the particular study. The proposals sparked strong objections that federal oversight would become far too cumbersome, which doomed the reforms. Subsequent studies of the Common Rule have suggested changes to research

39 Centers for Disease Control and Prevention, *The Tuskegee Timeline* (Dec. 10, 2013), *available at* http://www.cdc.gov/tuskegee/timeline.htm.

40 FRED D. GRAY, THE TUSKEGEE SYPHILIS STUDY 74–79 (1998).

41 Rob Stein, *U.S. Apologizes for Newly Revealed Syphilis Experiments Done in Guatemala*, WASH. POST, Oct. 1, 2010, *available at* https://www.washingtonpost.com/wp-dyn/content/article/2010/10/01/AR2010100104457.html?nav=emailpage.

42 PRESIDENTIAL COMMISSION FOR THE STUDY OF BIOETHICAL ISSUES, MORAL SCIENCE: PROTECTING PARTICIPANTS IN HUMAN SUBJECTS RESEARCH (Dec. 2011), *available at* http://bioethics.gov/node/558.

categories to better accommodate new research that does not use actual human subjects, such as social science research of public Twitter feeds. It is not clear what impact, if any, these recommendations will have.

More recently, a raging debate has arisen over the need to disclose risks to participants in studies that compare the effectiveness of competing treatments already in use. A large multicenter study known as the SUPPORT study was designed to identify how much oxygen to give to premature, extremely low birth weight (ELBW) infants to avoid a litany of ills associated with too much oxygen—Retinopathy of Prematurity (ROP), an eye injury which can lead to blindness, chronic lung disease, and other disorders—without neurologically impairing the infants from too little oxygen. The study randomized ELBW infants into two groups that would receive "levels of oxygen saturations on the high and low side of the currently utilized levels."[43] Ultimately, researchers reported in the *New England Journal of Medicine* that "one additional death [resulted] for approximately every two cases of severe [ROP] that [were] prevented."[44]

That result led many to question precisely what the parents of enrolled babies were told about the possible trade-off between death and blindness from receiving oxygen at the high and low ends of conventional care. The consent form explained the study's purpose as:

> pinpoint[ing] the exact range that should be used to help prevent some of the problems that occur with premature babies such as [ROP].... The benefit of higher versus lower levels of oxygenation in infants, especially for premature infants, is *not known*. In going back and looking at how babies in the past were managed, it is being suggested that the use of lower saturation ranges may result in a lower incidence of severe ROP.[45]

As to existing treatment, the form said that "[s]ometimes higher ranges are used and sometimes lower ranges are used. All of them are *acceptable ranges*." The form suggested an upside from participating ("fewer babies with severe [ROP]") but no downside:

> There is *no known risk* to your baby from monitoring with the pulse oximeters used for this study. The possible risk of skin breakdown at the site will be minimized by your baby's nurse moving the oximeter to another arm or leg a couple of times a day.

HHS's Office for Human Research Protections (OHRP) sent a Determination Letter to one of the sites, the University of Alabama at Birmingham.[46] In OHRP's view:

> It would have been appropriate for the consent form to explain (i) that the study involves substantial risks, and that there is significant evidence from past research indicating that the level of oxygen provided to an infant can have an important effect on many outcomes, including whether the infant becomes blind, develops serious brain injury, and even possibly whether the infant dies; (ii) that by participating in this study, the level of oxygen an infant receives

[43] Surfactant Positive Airway Pressure and Pulse Oximetry Trial in Extremely Low Birth Weight Infants (SUPPORT Study) Protocol at 2.

[44] SUPPORT Study Group, Target Ranges of Oxygen Saturation in Extremely Preterm Infants. 362 New Eng. J. Med. 1959 (2010).

[45] "Revised" Consent Form for the SUPPORT study signed by Sharissa Cook on October 7, 2006, as the legally authorized representative of DreShan Collins, at 2, 4, 5 (on file with author) (discussing "Possible Risks" and "Possible Benefits") (emphasis added).

[46] OHRP Mar. 7, 2013 Letter at 9, 10 (citing 45 CFR § 46.116(a)) (emphasis added).

> would in many instances be changed from what they would have otherwise received, though it is not possible to predict what that change will be; (iii) that some infants would receive more oxygen than they otherwise would have, in which case, if the researchers are correct in how they suppose oxygen affects eye development, those infants have a greater risk of going blind; and (iv) that the level of oxygen being provided to some infants, compared to the level they would have received had they not participated, could increase the risk of brain injury or death.

Citing this letter, within weeks the *New York Times* would call the study an "Ethical Breakdown."[47]

OHRP then held a rare public meeting to explore whether existing disclosure duties should be modified for "standard of care" research. After the public commentary, OHRP issued draft guidance reaffirming existing duties to disclose foreseeable risks. In OHRP's view, "[p]atients randomized to different standards of care in a comparative effectiveness trial should accordingly be made aware of the risks of the standards of care that are being compared."[48] Video consent and other forms of technology can assist to explain study risks "in an efficient and cost-effective way, thus respecting [the] ability [of participants] to choose which risks they are willing to be exposed to." OHRP accepted written comments on the draft guidance through December 23, 2014, but has yet to finalize it.

c. The Role of Private Litigation in Regulating Consent Practices

Private litigation challenging the adequacy of consent to human research has occurred alongside federal regulation. Consider, for example, *Berman v. Hutchinson Cancer Center*.[49] Allen Berman sued Fred Hutchinson Cancer Research Center after his wife, Katherine Hamilton, died while undergoing treatment for recurring Stage IV breast cancer. Katherine enrolled in a cancer research study but, Berman contended, was not informed that less risky, alternative treatments with higher success rates existed, that the chemotherapy drug cocktail she would receive might damage her organs, or that seven prior participants had died, one from organ failure. Neither was Katherine told that she would not receive the planned dosage if she was unable to take it orally. Berman also brought additional claims, including common law fraud and breach of assurance.

Noting that the Cancer Center's "failure to disclose the unavailability of intravenous [drugs] invalidated Katherine Hamilton's consent to participate" in the study, the court granted Berman partial summary judgment on that claim, reserving the others for the jury. The suit settled before trial for an undisclosed amount.[50]

47 *An Ethical Breakdown*, N.Y. Times, Apr. 15, 2013, *available at* http://www.nytimes.com/2013/04/16/opinion/an-ethical-breakdown-in-medical-research.html?_r=0.

48 OHRP, HHS, Draft Guidance on Disclosing Reasonably Foreseeable Risks in Research Evaluating Standards of Care, 79(206) Fed. Reg. 63629, 63632 (Oct. 24, 2014).

49 Berman v. Hutchinson Cancer Center, *available at* http://biotech.law.lsu.edu/research/wa/Berman_v_Hutchinson.pdf.

50 David Heath, *Hutch Settles Consent Case Out of Court*, Seattle Times, Jan. 15, 2003, *available at* http://community.seattletimes.nwsource.com/archive/?date=20030115&slug=hutch15.

Berman illustrates the special challenges in explaining the risks of participating in a research study. As some have pointed out, medical treatment and human research have fundamentally different goals:

> Research is not treatment. Experiments require measurements and conditions that may not be therapeutically significant. The disappointment of patient-participants [in receiving a placebo rather than the drug under study or the "best treatment" for them] is not the result of a wrong inflicted on them; they are frustrated in not receiving a potential cure, but they were permitted to have the drug for the purpose of research—the [researchers'] purpose not theirs. They were the incidental, gratuitous beneficiaries of the research. . . . Research is not standard; it is speculation, approximation, and inquiry.[51]

Compounding the need to clearly explain the difference between treatment and research is the "therapeutic misconception"—a participant's unspoken hope that she will receive a positive outcome despite explicit disclaimers of benefit and clear warnings of potential risks.[52] One study found that 51% of participants had "unrealistic beliefs about the nature or likelihood of benefit to themselves of participating in the study."[53]

The therapeutic misconception makes informed consent challenging in the best of circumstances. However, consent forms often muddy the line between research and treatment. For example, 50% of gene transfer studies described the intervention as "gene therapy"[54]—a label that suggests a proven therapy. After Jesse Gelsinger became the first person to die in such a study in 1999, bioethicist Ruth Macklin bluntly observed, "Gene therapy is not yet therapy."[55]

Litigation alleging defective consent has pushed researchers to be more careful when describing risks as well as benefits. The consent form Jesse Gelsinger signed was rife with partial truths about the risks Jesse faced.[56] "[T]he maximum dose of virus" Jesse would receive "is still below that which has caused any severe problems in mice or monkeys," it read. This statement stands in striking contrast to the candid disclosure of the death of monkeys and mice in prior studies, contained in the consent form circulated to the approving IRB and federal oversight authorities four years before: "In mice and monkeys high doses of the virus have been associated with evidence of liver inflammation (hepatitis), hepatic necrosis and *death*."

[51] E. Haavi Morreim, *Litigation in Clinical Research: Malpractice Doctrines Versus Research Realities*, J. L., MED. & ETHICS 474, 476 (2004).

[52] *See* Paul S. Appelbaum et al., *False Hopes and Best Date: Consent to Research and the Therapeutic Misconception*, 17 HASTINGS CENTER REP. 20 (1987).

[53] Mildred K. Cho & David Magnus, *Therapeutic Misconception and Stem Cell Research*, NATURE.COM, Sept. 27, 2007, *available at* http://www.nature.com/stemcells/2007/0709/070927/full/stemcells.2007.88.html (citing P. Appelbaum, C. Lidz, & T. Grisso, *Therapeutic Misconception in Clinical Research: Frequency and Risk Factors* IRB: ETHICS HUM. RES. 26, 1–8 (2004)).

[54] Cho & Magnus, *supra* note 53.

[55] Robin Fretwell Wilson, *Estate of Gelsinger v. Trustees of University of Pennsylvania: Money, Prestige, and Conflicts of Interest In Human Subjects Research, in* HEALTH LAW & BIOETHICS 229, 234.

[56] Robin Fretwell Wilson, *The Death of Jesse Gelsinger: New Evidence of the Influence of Money and Prestige in Human Research*, 36 AM. J.L. MED. 295, 303, 304, Fig. 6 (2010) (reproducing Gelsinger Consent Form at 7).

After Jesse's death, his family sued the researchers and sponsoring institutions, alleging breach of the duty to secure informed consent and fraud, among other claims.[57] Within weeks, the family settled for an undisclosed amount. The federal government also sued, alleging violations of the federal False Claims Act. Researchers and sponsors failed to disclose not only animal deaths but "significant adverse events" experienced by earlier participants in the same trial—"important evidence," the FDA said, "of increased risk."[58] Further, "the study had produced toxicities in humans that should have resulted in termination," clinical findings "misrepresented" in reports filed with federal authorities.

Like the family, the government settled with the researchers. The sponsoring institutions together paid more than a million dollars in fines in 2005, while admitting no wrongdoing. The settlement placed restrictions on the researchers' clinical research activities, with the toughest controls placed on Wilson, who held a sizable financial stake in the research's outcome—a stake the consent form downplayed.

Informed consent claims have been leveraged to force researchers to also be more forthright about alternatives to participating in a research trial. In *Stewart v. Cleveland Clinic Foundation*, Cleveland Clinic physicians enrolled Daniel Klais in a Phase III clinical trial after an oropharyngeal tumor at the base of his tongue metastasized.[59] The trial was designed to evaluate whether adding experimental chemotherapy before radiation and surgery improved the chances of remission. Researchers randomized participants into one of two arms: treatment with the standard radiation-therapy-followed-by-surgery-only or radiation and surgery combined with preoperative chemotherapy.

Klais executed a five-page informed consent document. Randomized into the standard treatment arm, Klais never received chemotherapy. He remained cancer free for nearly five years until an x-ray indicated that the cancer had metastasized to his lungs. He succumbed to cancer the next year.

In the intervening months, he and his wife filed suit against the Cleveland Clinic and his treating doctors, alleging medical negligence in diagnosing and treating him. Later they added a defective consent claim. Deposed before his death, Klais stated that no one informed him that he had a right to be treated with radiation *and* chemotherapy, or that other cancer centers treated similar patients with chemotherapy and radiation—a combination that he believed offered the "most . . . opportunity for a cure."[60] His physicians never suggested that he opt out of the study to ensure chemotherapy treatment.

Concluding that genuine issues of material fact existed as to whether Klais gave informed consent to treatment and participation in the clinical trial, the Court of Appeals of Ohio reversed and remanded. The case later settled quietly.[61]

57 Estate of Gelsinger, *supra* note 55, at 230, n.18.

58 Press Release, U.S. Settles Case of Gene Therapy Study that Ended with Teen's Death (Feb. 9, 2005) (on file with author); Letter from Steven A. Masiellos Dir., Office of Compliance & Biologics Quality, F.D.A. Ctr. for Biologics Evaluation & Research to Mark L. Batshaw, Children's Nat'l Med. Ctr. 7 (Nov. 30, 2000) (Warning Letter), *available at* http://www.fda.gov/foi/nidpoe/n14l.pdf.

59 736 N.E.2d 491, 493 (1999). 60 *Id.* at 494.

61 Jerry Menikoff & Edward P. Richards, What the Doctor Didn't Say: The Hidden Truth about Medical Research 131 (2006).

V Pushback Against Informed Consent

Critics charge that duty to secure informed consent goes too far in a number of directions: It unfairly provides recovery when medical malpractice cannot be shown; physicians rely on paper consent rather than engaging their patients in meaningful dialogue; disclosure taxes scarce physician time, leading one state to provide off-the-rack disclosures to reduce the burden; and the doctrine is premised on notions of autonomy that do not map well to patients with diminished capacity.

a. Second Bite at the Malpractice Apple

Most civil suits for breach of the duty to secure informed consent also claim malpractice, leading some to contend that defective claims are an unfair second bite at the malpractice apple.[62] Conceptually, the two claims differ. Malpractice concerns whether the doctor performed the procedure with due care. Defective consent concerns whether the physician disclosed sufficient information for the patient to arrive at an informed decision. Claims based purely on "failure to instruct patient," and not on medical errors, constitute only 1% of malpractice claims against doctors and 2% of claims against hospitals[63]—lessening concerns that informed consent claims are tacked onto every malpractice claim.

Outside of trespass or battery claims involving the total absence of consent, moreover, it is difficult to identify a patient who recovered *in negligence* for defective consent to a procedure that was medically indicated and properly performed. Nonetheless, attorneys say that informed consent claims form an important part of the litigation strategy. Challenging the sufficiency of consent can undermine perceptions of the quality of care provided and undercut a jury's confidence in the physician—making juries feel more sympathetic at the margin. This dynamic raises the case's settlement value even if it is not ultimately heard by a jury. Moreover, in material risk jurisdictions, claims of defective consent may proceed without expert testimony, making them less costly for plaintiffs to pursue. Of course, today, tort reform and other trends have made all malpractice claims harder to maintain.

b. "Not Worth the Paper It Is Written On"

Ideally, the duty to secure informed consent precipitates an individualized dialogue with the patient. Yet, doctors face enormous time constraints. In 2014, doctors spent an average of between 8 and 15 minutes with each patient[64]—a modest improvement over 7-minute visits

[62] William J. McNichols, *Informed Consent Liability in a "Material Information" Jurisdiction: What Does the Future Portend?*, 48 Okla. L. Rev. 711, 715 (1995).

[63] Peter H. Schuck, *Rethinking Informed Consent*, 103 Yale L.J. 899, 923 n.105 (1994).

[64] Roni Caryn Rabin, *15-minute Visits Take Toll on Doctor-Patient Relationship*, Kaiser Health News & USA Today, Apr. 23, 2014, *available at* http://www.medscape.com/viewarticle/823992; Pauline W. Chen, M.D., *For New Doctors, 8 Minutes Per Patient*, N.Y. Times, May 30, 2013, *available at* http://well.blogs.nytimes.com/2013/05/30/for-new-doctors-8-minutes-per-patient/.

the decade before.[65] Further, time spent educating patients is time that cannot be billed to insurers.

Although doctors have an obligation to disclose risks and obtain the patient's informed consent, physicians sometimes rely on consent forms prepared by the admitting facility, rather than spending scarce time on oral explanations. Ironically, despite the central role facilities play in facilitating consent, "[m]ost courts today still follow the traditional common law rule that hospitals do not have the responsibility to obtain the informed consent of patients before treatment, viewing it as a duty solely of the treating physician."[66] Consent forms do memorialize the patient's agreement in a record that can later be produced in court.

Paper consent raises additional concerns. Some worry about "consent fatigue."[67] Like warning labels generally, "overdisclosure" makes it difficult for patients to distinguish meaningful risks from trivial ones. Patients who receive shorter consent forms gain a better understanding of the procedures they are undertaking, while longer forms produce less comprehension.[68]

Others charge that disclosure duties operate too narrowly, requiring disclosure only of a procedure's risks—without accounting for the patient's own goals for medical treatment, which are critical to effective treatment. Rather than a "one-size-fits-all" approach, Professor Robert Gatter sees the duty to secure informed consent as expansive enough to require doctors to learn about their patients and recommend a treatment that fits them.[69]

In a study called "Not worth the paper it's written on?," researchers analyzed the process for obtaining informed consent in Norway's research biobank.[70] Trust, they contend, grows from "a complex mixture of experiences, knowledge, ignorance, feelings, intuitions, relationships, values, political governance, economical infrastructure and various other factors," which may be "undermined by the demands of a formalistic ethics." They urge that "[t]he concreteness of a signature . . . [as] an expression of an improved research ethics" should be resisted because researchers can gain "trust through the process of obtaining informed consent." The Presidential Commission expressed the same intuition in its 2011 report on human research. "The government, in collaboration with institutions and investigators, should refocus on the importance of the process of informed consent lest the procedures, ostensibly derived from ethical principles, serve to obscure the values they were intended to implement."[71]

65 Peter Salgo, *The Doctor Will See You for Exactly Seven Minutes*, N.Y. TIMES, Mar. 22, 2006, *available at* http://www.nytimes.com/2006/03/22/opinion/22salgo.html?_r=1&.

66 Richard S. Saver, *Darling v. Charleston Community Memorial Hospital: A Broken Leg and Institutional Liability Unbound*, *in* HEALTH LAW & BIOETHICS, *supra* note 22, at 27, 44–45.

67 HEALTHCARE INFO. & MGMT. SYSTEMS SOC'Y, INFORMATION PRIVACY IN THE EVOLVING HEALTHCARE ENVIRONMENT 124 (Linda Koontz ed. 2013).

68 *See* Lynn Chaikin Epstein & Louis Lasagna, *Obtaining Informed Consent*, 123 ARCH. INTERN. MED. 682 (1969).

69 Robert Gatter, *Informed Consent Law and the Forgotten Duty of Physician Inquiry*, 31 LOY. U. CHI. L.J. 557, 558–559 (2000).

70 John-Arne Skolbekken, Lars øystein Ursin, Berge Solberg, Erik Christensen, & Borgunn Yttherhus, *Not Worth the Paper It's Written On? Informed Consent and Biobank Research in a Norwegian Context*, 15(4) CRITICAL PUBLIC HEALTH 335, 335, 345 (Dec. 2005).

71 Moral Science, *supra* note 42.

c. A Burden on Physicians

From the beginning, the duty to secure informed consent has raised questions of fairness to physicians, who must guess at what patients want to be told or discern what other physicians disclose. One state, Texas, reduces the burden on physicians, facilitating disclosure with an unconventional approach: providing a "safe harbor" to physicians who use standardized disclosures. If the patient signs the prescribed disclosure prior to treatment, a presumption arises in litigation that the physician satisfied the duty of informed consent. A panel of experts specifies the information patients must be given about common procedures after reviewing evidence of the inherent risks and benefits. Prescribed disclosures are not intended to replace a dialogue between the physician and the patient about a given procedure, but to supplement it.

The marketplace is also developing tools to reduce the time commitment associated with securing informed consent. With the advent of computerized, multimedia software, patient education and informed consent have entered the digital age. Millions of patients at hundreds of hospitals now watch video consent programs. Doctors can e-mail informed consent videos for particular procedures to patients to view on their own. Researchers who want to design their own informed consent videos have the benefit of guidance from the National Institute of Mental Health.[72]

"[W]hen patients watch, stopping and starting [videos] to review information, they create an electronic trail. Hospitals have used that data in court to argue that patients were informed about specific risks because they watched portions of the program where risks were detailed."[73] Video consent may be practical for routine procedures, such as blood transfusions, or in research studies that present a limited universe of risks. Outside these areas they are unlikely to work well, however.

d. Patients with Diminished Capacity

Some question the value of disclosure in cases of diminished capacity. Concerned that a narrow focus on autonomy will lead to "poor" choices, bioethicists Allen Buchanan and Dan Brock have proposed an alternative "risk-relativity" test for deciding whether informed consent is required of patients who lack capacity.[74] Under this sliding scale, the doctor or the patient's designated surrogate decision-maker may overrule a less-than-fully-competent patient's expressed wishes when she chooses a risky course of action, like refusing antibiotics.

"Risk-relativity" establishes gradations of competence that would be minimally necessary for rejecting different procedures. The riskier the action a patient endorses, the greater the need to be sure she understands the consequences of her decisions. Thus, risk relativity

[72] Nat'l Inst. of Mental Health, Elements of a Successful Informed Consent Video (Feb. 16, 2015), *available at* http://www.nimh.nih.gov/funding/grant-writing-and-application-process/elements-of-a-successful-informed-consent-video.shtml.

[73] Lindsey Tanner, *Hospitals Try High-Tech to Better Inform Patients*, YAHOO News (Nov. 10, 2010, 9:37 PM), *available at* http://news.yahoo.com/hospitals-try-high-tech-better-inform-patients.html.

[74] Allen E. Buchanan & Dan W. Brock, Deciding for Others: The Ethics of Surrogate Decision-Making 17–50 (1989).

analysis permits patients who *agree* with accepting a common and valuable treatment to have less capacity than those who *disagree*. Proponents justify this sliding scale as assisting hospital staff, faced with an intransigent patient who wants to be left alone to die, to override the patient's irrational choices.

Some see "risk-relativity" as nothing more than the old wine of paternalism in a new bottle.[75] Decisional capacity, critics say, is not "a genuine property of persons"; moreover, "judgments regarding decisional capacity" are not made on a "relatively consistent and defensible basis." A healthcare provider's decision that a conscious patient lacks capacity may be "purely a projection of [that provider's] values" about whether the patient should accept treatment.

VI Questions at the Frontier of Informed Consent

Changes in healthcare delivery resulting in a greater emphasis on managed care and costs generally have pushed the limits of the duty to disclose particular facts. An emerging body of cases now address whether physicians must disclose financial incentives or the existence or costs of alternative treatment. Other cases test the need to disclose physician-specific risks, like whether the physician is performing a risky procedure for the first time or herself poses a risk to the patient, say of transmitting a communicable disease. New state legislation has politicized the disclosure duty in one specific context, abortion, implicating physicians' countervailing free speech rights.

a. Disclosing the Economics of Treatment and Research

Changes in the economics of medical care and research have tested whether the duty to secure informed consent is narrowly focused on disclosing risks of the specific procedure or whether it instead encompasses a more holistic evaluation of the wisdom of accepting treatment. This part examines emerging case law and regulation on disclosure of treatment alternatives, costs, and physician financial incentives that have taken on greater significance in an era of managed care and commercially focused research. Among other things, these cases often challenge the concept of "materialized risk" as an element of an informed consent claim.

i. Economics of Treatment and Research

As Part III.a noted, under both the professional standard and the material risk standard, physicians must disclose alternatives to recommended treatment. In an era of economic restraint, however, the disclosure of available alternatives will sometimes be pointless because no realistic possibility exists of paying for it. Moreover, as Professor Joan H. Krause points out, "patient knowledge can be expensive" and both physicians and insurers

[75] David Checkland, *On Risk and Decisional Capacity*, 26 J. Med. & Phil. 36, 36 (2001).

have "incentives to withhold information about treatments that are not covered under the patient's insurance policy."[76] Courts have yet to squarely address the tension between obligating doctors to fully inform patients of uncovered, costly treatment alternatives and healthcare cost containment strategies. In fact, the legal duty to review alternatives appears not to have seeped into the consciousness of providers or the public. When asked "what the term *informed consent* meant to them, less than 1% of the public, and only 14% of physicians, mentioned the disclosure of treatment alternatives."[77]

Just as costs of competing treatment options may influence one's decision, so, too, may a provider's or researcher's financial stake. In *Moore v. Regents of the University of California*, the California Supreme Court ruled that doctors have a legal duty to disclose personal interests to patients prior to procedures.[78] There, John Moore underwent a successful splenectomy at UCLA Medical Center after being diagnosed with hairy cell leukemia. Thinking that Moore's cells were unique and would be of great research value, Dr. David Golde instructed Moore to return to UCLA to have bodily fluids drawn. This continued for seven years under the guise of treatment. Golde and UCLA subsequently developed a commercial cell line and derivative products. Moore sued Golde, UCLA, and the pharmaceutical companies to recover the profits of his cell line.

The California Supreme Court allowed Moore's claims against Golde for breach of fiduciary duty and informed consent to go forward. The court noted that "[t]he possibility that an interest extraneous to the patient's health has affected the physician's judgment [. . .] is material to the patient's decision and, thus, a prerequisite to informed consent." The case later settled for an undisclosed amount.[79] Requiring disclosure of financial conflicts of interests challenges the concept of "materialized risk" as an element of an informed consent claim. Unlike failing to disclose that a particular procedure carries a particular risk, which risk must then materialize in order to warrant recovery, an undisclosed financial stake applies to every procedure, whatever is disclosed.

Bland disclosures of significant financial stakes have received exacting scrutiny in recent years. After the high-profile death of Jesse Gelsinger in a gene transfer study described above, the *Wall Street Journal* reported that one researcher, Dr. James Wilson, held shares in a sponsoring biotech company, Genovo, valued at $13.5 million. Years earlier, Wilson's employer, the University of Pennsylvania (Penn), evaluated Wilson's interests in Genovo as a part of its duty under federal regulations to eliminate or manage any "significant financial interests" (SFIs) over $10,000 by the time grant funds are distributed.[80] At that time, internal Penn documents implicitly valued Wilson's interest in Genovo at between $28.5 and $33 million.

Most people see equity ownership as more problematic than receiving per capita payments or other financial conflicts.[81] However large Wilson's stake, the consent form Jesse signed blandly noted:

[76] Joan H. Krause, *Reconceptualizing Informed Consent in an Era of Health Care Cost Containment*, 85 IOWA L. REV. 261, 264, 265, 281–282, 293, 307 (1999).

[77] *Id.* [78] 793 P.2d 479, 481–482, 484, 485 (Cal. 1990).

[79] Dennis McLlellan, *John Moore, 56; Sued to Share Profits from His Cells*, L.A. TIMES, Oct. 13, 2002, *available at* http://articles.latimes.com/2001/oct/13/local/me-56770.

[80] 42 C.F.R. § 50.603 (2008).

[81] *See* Kevin P. Weinfurt et al., *Effects of Disclosing Financial Interests on Attitudes Toward Clinical Research*, 23 J. GEN. INTERNAL MED. 861, 863 (2008); Lindsay A. Hampson et al., *Patients' Views on Financial Conflicts of Interest in Cancer Research Trials*, 355 NEW ENG. J. MED. 2330, 2336 (2006).

SPONSOR INFORMATION

Please be aware that the University of Pennsylvania, Dr. James M. Wilson (the Director of the Institute for Human Gene Therapy), and Genovo, Inc., (a gene therapy company in which Dr. Wilson holds an interest) have a financial interest in a successful outcome from the research involved in this study.[82]

Following Jesse's death, Wilson's interests in Genovo naturally elicited the question: Would different decisions have been made in the absence of financial conflicts? Not all individuals respond to financial conflicts the same way. When faced with identical conflicts, some trust researchers less, others trust them more. In 2009, Wilson published his *Lessons Learned* from Jesse's trial, a condition precedent to being readmitted to human research without restriction. Wilson rejected the idea that financial ties influenced his choices, saying instead that he was motivated by "leadership and notoriety and accomplishment."

Today, the regulation of financial conflicts of interest remains largely the same as it was when Jesse died, although the duty to disclose and manage SFIs is now triggered by SFIs over $5,000.[83] In 2011, HHS finalized a framework for "identifying, managing, and ultimately avoiding investigators' financial conflicts of interest" that eliminates researchers' historical discretion to report only SFIs related to PHS-supported research. Instead, researchers must disclose all SFIs related to their institutional responsibilities. Further, the SFIs of senior personnel must be publicly accessible online or provided upon request within five business days.

b. Disclosure of Physician-specific Risks

Also testing the limits of the duty to secure informed consent are physician-specific risks. Must a physician disclose the fact that she is performing a risky procedure for the first time on the patient, or that she herself poses a risk to the patient of contracting AIDS? Must she disclose that another, possibly less-qualified physician will actually perform a needed procedure? Are patients entitled to know that students are performing procedures for the student's training?

i. *Physician Inexperience*

In *Johnson v. Kokemoor*, a physician's failure to disclose the fact that he was performing a specific aneurysm surgery for the first time, had never been board certified in neurosurgery, and was not an aneurysm subspecialist formed the backbone of the patient's claim of defective consent.[84] Dr. Richard Kokemoor performed surgery on Donna Johnson to clip an aneurysm, leaving her an incomplete quadriplegic, unable to walk or control her bowel or bladder. Johnson sued Kokemoor for failing to obtain her informed consent. At trial, the judge allowed Johnson to present evidence that a physician in good standing would have

[82] *Death of Jesse Gelsinger, supra* note 56, at Fig. 8 (reproducing Gelsinger *Consent Form*at 11).

[83] Press Release, U.S. Dep't of Health and Human Services National Institute of Health, HHS Tightens Financial Conflict of Interest Rules for Researchers (Aug. 23, 2011), *available at* http://www.nih.gov/news/health/aug2011/od-23.htm; 42 C.F.R. pt. 50.

[84] Johnson by Adler v. Kokemoor, 545 N.W.2d 495, 497, 499, 499 n.11, 509 (Wis. 1996).

notified Johnson that she could have sought an alternative lower risk surgery with a more experienced surgeon in a better facility. The jury found that Kokemoor failed to adequately inform Johnson of the surgery's risks and advantages and a reasonable person in her shoes would have not consented if fully informed. Relying on the prudent patient standard for what physicians are required to disclose, on appeal the Wisconsin Supreme Court concluded that the lower court did not err in admitting evidence of possible treatment by more experienced physicians since the surgery's difficulty was central to the case.

ii. Ghost Surgery

Modern medicine often means a team of professionals treats a given patient. While perfectly appropriate, patients may believe they are consenting to treatment by a specific physician even though another professional will actually perform the procedure. The AMA's Code of Medical Ethics condemns substitutions "without the patient's knowledge and consent"—known as "ghost surgery"—as "deceitful."[85]

Recovery for this bait-and-switch has traditionally sounded in battery. As a battery claim, the plaintiff does not have to show negligent performance or elicit expert testimony. But as an intentional tort, battery is excluded under most malpractice liability policies, presenting an additional challenge to recovery.

An emerging trend is to treat "ghost surgery" as breach of the duty to secure informed consent. *Perna v. Pirozzi*, a New Jersey medical malpractice case, provides the seminal example.[86] Following the advice of his family physician, Thomas Perna sought urological consultation and tests at St. Joseph's Hospital in May 1977. The urologist who examined Perna, Dr. Pirozzi, recommended he undergo surgery to remove kidney stones. The medical group Dr. Pirozzi belonged to shared patients, meaning no doctor had their own patients; the "team" decided which surgeon would operate just before surgery, though patients could request specific physicians.

Unaware of this practice, Perna alleged he specifically requested that Dr. Pirozzi perform his procedure, an allegation uncontradicted by the defendants. Perna did meet with another physician prior to surgery, Dr. Ciccone, who explained that two group members would be present during the procedure, but did not say who would operate. Perna signed a consent form naming Dr. Pirozzi as the operating surgeon and authorizing him, and unnamed "assistants," to perform the procedure. On the day of Perna's procedure, however, Dr. Pirozzi was not even on duty; instead, Dr. Ciccone and group member Dr. Del Gaizo conducted the operation.

Perna was readmitted to the hospital several weeks later for postsurgical complications, and then learned that Pirozzi did not operate on him. He sued all three doctors, alleging malpractice in the diagnosis, treatment, and surgery. He also alleged they failed to obtain his informed consent to Dr. Del Gaizo's operation, saying he only consented to Dr. Pirozzi performing the surgery.

[85] American Medical Association, *Opinion 8.16—Substitution of Surgeon Without Patient's Knowledge or Consent*, AMA Code of Medical Ethics,(June 1994), *available at* http://www.ama-assn.org/ama/pub/physician-resources/medical-ethics/code-medical-ethics/opinion816.page?.

[86] 457 A.2d 431, 433–434, 438–441 (1983).

The trial court entered a verdict of no cause of action, and Perna appealed. The Supreme Court of New Jersey reversed and remanded for a trial. On the "ghost surgery" claim, the court distinguished the failure to obtain *informed* consent, an act of malpractice, from the failure to obtain *any* consent, a battery. Perna could succeed on a battery claim against Drs. Del Gaizo and Ciccone if he proved his factual claim that those surgeons operated on him without consent. On the informed consent claim, the court noted how crucial it is for patients who place their lives in a doctor's hands to have trust and confidence in that doctor. Thus, it is medical malpractice whether "the right surgeon operates on the wrong part or the wrong surgeon operates on the right part of the patient."

Like *Canterbury*, the outcome in *Perna v. Pirozzi* resulted from a dialogue between formal law and professional ethics. As the court emphasized, the American College of Surgeons and the AMA both condemn ghost surgery as misrepresenting the identity of an operating surgeon, a "deceit" that breaches the surgeon's fiduciary duty to the patient.

iii. Safety Risks Posed by the Physician

Medical treatment often involves invasive procedures, where the only barrier to contagion between provider and patient are surgical dressing and gloves. More often than not, the patient poses a risk to the provider; but in some instances, the provider poses the risk—raising questions about disclosure duties. *Faya v. Almaraz* imposed just such a duty on surgeons to disclose their health status before operating on patients.[87] Former patients Sonja Faya and Perry Mahoney Rossi brought negligence actions against the estate of surgeon Rudolph Almaraz, who died from AIDS, and John Hopkins Hospital, claiming that Almaraz acted as the hospital's agent or employee.

Almaraz knew he was HIV positive when he operated on Faya and Mahoney Rossi but did not inform them prior to surgery. Both learned of Almaraz's status after reading of his death in the newspaper more than a year after their operations. They sued despite testing negative for HIV. Initially dismissed by the trial court, the Maryland Court of Appeals reversed and remanded. The court acknowledged that although the risk of transmission was low, the consequences were severe, requiring disclosure under the material risk standard. The court held that Faya and Mahoney Rossi could recover for fear and its physical manifestations in the "window of anxiety" before testing negative for HIV, but could not recover after that point. Thus, as with *Moore* above, this novel informed consent claim may succeed even if the undisclosed risk of acquiring AIDS never materializes.

Courts are split on whether physicians must disclose other personal issues to patients, such as alcoholism or drug addiction. Some conclude it would change a patient's decision, while others note that it would be impossible to develop standards of what in a doctor's personal life must be disclosed.[88]

[87] 620 A.2d 327, 337–339; 339, n.6 (Md. 1993).

[88] *See* Albany Urology Clinic PC. v. Cleveland: 272 Ga. 296, 528 S.E.2d 777 (Ga. 2000) (failing to disclose a cocaine habit did not void informed consent); *but see* Hidding v. Williams, 578 So. 2d 1192 (La. Ct. App. 5th Cir. 1991) (failing to disclose struggles with alcoholism voided consent to spinal surgery).

iv. *Care in the Context of Medical Training*

In the last decade, reports of medical students performing pelvic exams for training purposes on anesthetized women without their consent have produced outrage and calls for greater regulation.[89] News of unauthorized exams continues to emerge after oversight bodies like Association of American Medical Colleges in 2003 condemned allowing students to perform such examinations as "unethical and unacceptable."[90] Some medical educators defend the choice to perform educational exams without specific consent on a number of grounds: "it's pretty much all covered in the overall consent form"[91]; "accepting care at a teaching hospital gives implicit consent"; "it has always been considered a part of ordinary medical practice in the specialty."[92]

However, a close reading of admission forms for major medical centers reveals that patients generally authorize care for their own benefit, not for the student's education—refuting actual consent. Implied consent is also difficult to defend. Factually, many patients have no idea that they are being seen at a teaching hospital; indeed, with the rise of community teaching hospitals, neither the name nor location of the hospital would alert patients to the hospital's status. More fundamentally, many patients see intimate exams as different in kind from other teaching procedures and want to be asked for permission—even though they consent in overwhelming numbers when asked.

In 2012, Hawaii joined California, Illinois, Oregon, and Virginia in prohibiting intimate pelvic examinations on female patients for medical teaching purposes without the patient's consent.[93] California and Virginia fold the disclosure duty into existing accreditation standards for graduate medical education, leveraging medical regulators, rather than litigation, to ensure compliance.

c. When Disclosure Collides with Physician Free Speech Rights

Informed consent law has recently acquired a constitutional gloss, with some courts holding that a legally mandated disclosure obligation may be in tension with a physician's right to free speech. A series of state laws and private lawsuits for breach of the duty to provide informed consent test where the boundary between conduct and speech falls as to abortion, a procedure that remains controversial more than forty years after *Roe v. Wade*.

A handful of states have enacted much-debated "speech and display provisions," specifying elaborate procedures that physicians must follow in order to secure "informed consent"

[89] *See* Robin Fretwell Wilson, *Autonomy Suspended: Using Female Patients to Teach Intimate Exams Without Their Knowledge or Consent*, 8:2 J. of Health Care L. & Pol'y 240, 240 (2005); Shawn S. Barnes, *Practicing Pelvic Examinations by Medical Students on Women under Anesthesia*, 120 Obstetrics & Gynecology 941, 943 (2012).

[90] Press Release, Ass'n of Am. Med. Colls., AAMC Statement on Patient Rights and Medical Training (June 12, 2003), *available at* http://www.aamc.org/newsroom/pressrel/2003/030612.htm.

[91] Autonomy Suspended, *supra* note 89, at 242.

[92] *Id.* at 242, 251–255, 258, 262, n.131.

[93] Va. Code Ann. § 54.1-2959 (2010); 410 ILCS 50/7 (2010); Cal. Bus. & Prof. Code § 2281 (2010); OR Rev. Stat. § 676.360 (2013); Haw. Rev. Stat. § 453-18 (2013).

for abortions. For example, in Texas, before terminating a "known pregnancy," a physician must perform a sonogram, show and describe the image to the woman—which includes giving "a medical description of the dimensions of the embryo or fetus, the presence of cardiac activity, and the presence of external members and internal organs"—and make audible any heartbeat and explain it.[94] North Carolina, Oklahoma, and Wisconsin have enacted similar laws. Not surprisingly, providers have challenged the provisions as tantamount to an endorsement of state speech, as well as an undue burden on a woman's right to obtain an abortion.

Courts have split on the merits of these challenges. While courts have enjoined North Carolina's and Oklahoma's laws,[95] mandated disclosures in Texas and Wisconsin have survived challenge.[96] In 2014, a federal district court struck North Carolina's speech and display provisions as infringing on free speech, a decision affirmed by the United States Court of Appeals for the Fourth Circuit.[97] In that case, the district court reasoned that the requirements constitute "an effort by the state to require health care providers to deliver information in support of the state's philosophic and social position discouraging abortion and encouraging childbirth."[98] As "content-based" regulations of speech, the provisions must satisfy heightened scrutiny.

By contrast, an undivided panel of the United States Court of Appeals for the Fifth Circuit upheld nearly identical provisions in *Texas Medical Providers Performing Abortion Services v. Lakey*.[99] It "conclude[d] that the . . . disclosures and written consent . . . are within the State's power to regulate the practice of medicine, and therefore do not violate the First Amendment."[100]

The speech and display laws represent only one variety of a new crop of abortion "informed consent" laws. Other states require explicit disclosures by doctors before performing an abortion. In Kansas, physicians must inform the woman that the procedure "will terminate the life of a whole, separate, unique, living human being."[101] In South Dakota, physicians must disclose the risk of suicide after an abortion, a law that has been sustained against challenge.[102]

[94] *See, e.g.*, TEX. HEALTH & SAFETY CODE ANN. § 171.011. Texas also requires elaborate disclosures for a chemical abortion, which spill over to prescriptions for some forms on emergency contraceptives, like *ella*. *See* Cameron Flynn & Robin Fretwell Wilson, *Speaking Candidly About EC and Abortion: What Should Guide Disclosure*, 43(1) J.L. MED. & ETHICS 72 (Spring 2015).

[95] *See Stuart v. Camnitz*, __F.3d__, 2014 WL 7237744 (affirming injunction against the North Carolina Women's Right to Know Act); Nova Health Sys. v. Pruitt, 2012 OK 103, 292 P.3d 28, as corrected (Dec. 5, 2012) (enjoining as unconstitutional under *Casey* 63 OKL. STAT. ANN. § 1-738.3d, which required display of ultrasound/sonogram to women prior to abortion).

[96] For a review of pending challenges, *see generally* Sonia Suter, *The First Amendment and Physician Speech in Reproductive Decision Making*, 43(1) J.L. MED. & ETHICS (2015).

[97] Stuart v. Camnitz, __F.3d__ 2014 WL 7237744.

[98] Loomis, at *3.

[99] 667 F.3d 570 (5th Cir. Jan. 10, 2012).

[100] *Lakey*, 667 F.3d at 580.

[101] KAN. STAT. ANN. § 65-6709.

[102] Planned Parenthood Minnesota, North Dakota, South Dakota v. Rounds, 686 F.3d 889, 899, 912 (8th Cir. 2012).

d. Decision-making Beyond Informed Consent

Across dozens of patient samples, four in ten patients report a mismatch between the participation in decision-making they hoped for and what actually happened.[103] Not every medical decision is equally difficult to make.[104] Moreover, patients differ in their appetite for participating. In one study, a fourth of patients wanted physicians to make the decision for them, while a significant majority, roughly one-half in one study and 68% in another, wanted to select the treatment option together with their physician.[105] Certain kinds of patients tend to opt for a more passive role: cancer patients, patients over forty-five, and men.[106] Premised on the decisional authority of the patient, the doctrine of informed consent does not account well for the many patients who place great trust in their physicians' expertise and medical training.[107]

Over the last decade, healthcare professionals have embraced a "process of interacting with patients who wish to be involved in arriving at an informed, values-based choice among two or more medically reasonable alternatives" known as shared decision-making (SDM).[108] In *Critical Decisions: How You and Your Doctor Can Make the Right Medical Choices Together*, Peter Ubel casts SDM as "foster[ing] a sense of partnership in decision making among doctors and patients so that each can coach the other to share—information, preferences, a range of choices, and the power and burden of decision."[109]

Few deny that the impulse to "return decision-making power to patients is a noble one." Yet the partnership envisioned by SDM may be one that neither physicians nor patients are ready for. Many patients prefer to rely on their doctors' expertise entirely.[110] Even patients who desire a bigger role may not be willing to endure the extra time and confusion necessary for genuinely informed consent. Complicating reform, SDM is a concept that means different things to different people. Some question the whole enterprise, arguing that "the skimpiest reflection reveals that [SDM] is ambiguous unto incoherence."[111]

[103] Brom et al., *supra* note 4.

[104] *See* Simon N. Whitney et al., *Beyond Shared Decision Making: An Expanded Typology of Medical Decisions*, 28 MED. DECISION MAKING 699, 701–702 (2008) (contrasting situations where one viable treatment option exists with situations where there is disagreement among competing options).

[105] *See* R. B. Deber, N. Kraetschmer, & J. Irvine, *What Role Do Patients Wish to Play in Treatment Decision-Making?*, 154 ARCHIVES INTERNAL MED. 1414, 1414–1420 (1996); Dennis J. Mazur & David H. Hickam, *Patients' Preferences for Risk Disclosure and Role in Decision Making for Invasive Medical Procedures*, 12 J. GEN. INTERNAL MED. 114, 115 (1997).

[106] Brom et al., *supra* note 4.

[107] Schuck, *supra* note 63, at 904.

[108] Annette O'Connor, Hilary A. Llewellyn-Thomas, & Ann Barry Flood, *Modifying Unwarranted Variations in Health Care: Shared Decision Making Using Patient Decision Aids*, HEALTH AFF. 63, 64 (2004), *available at* http://geiselmed.dartmouth.edu/ cfm/education/PDF/shared_decision_making.pdf.

[109] Zackary Berger, Review of Peter Ubel, *Critical Decisions: How You and Your Doctor Can Make the Right Medical Choices Together*,, 13 AM. J. BIOETHICS 53–54 (2013) (reviewing Peter Ubel, *Critical Decisions: How You and Your Doctor Can Make the Right Medical Choices Together* (2012)).

[110] CARL SCHNEIDER, THE PRACTICE OF AUTONOMY: PATIENTS, DOCTORS, AND MEDICAL DECISIONS (1998).

[111] Carl E. Schneider, *Void for Vagueness*, 37 HASTINGS CTR. REP. 10, 10–11 (2007).

VII Conclusion

"At times exalted, at times maligned,"[112] the duty to secure fully informed consent to treatment took decades to develop as a doctrine. While following parallel paths in U.S. jurisdictions, the notion that patients should be the ones to evaluate the risks they are taking when deciding to be treated, or participating in human research, remains surprisingly hard to realize in practice.

The dueling approaches to disclosure means that patients in some jurisdictions can vindicate their interests in deciding what happens with their bodies, but others cannot. Moreover, the doctrine yields disclosures about the risks of a medical procedure, largely divorced from any discussion of the patient's own goals for treatment. Understandably, physicians default to paper consent, risking both overdisclosure of minute risks and underdisclosure of risks that may be important to only a handful of patients.

Over time, regulators and legislatures have become more prominent than courts in policing what physicians and researchers must tell patients. This development has operated to shut down unethical practices that individual lawsuits were unlikely to police, such as the use of women under anesthesia to teach intimate exams without their consent. Of course, courts can, and have, bent the rules to permit recovery for defective consent in egregious cases, such as when physicians induce patients to agree to tests for the physician's private gain, dispensing with the need to show that an undisclosed risk actually materialized.

While legislation and regulation can make concrete physicians' disclosure duties, they complicate the nature of disclosure and threaten to politicize informed consent.[113] In the abortion realm, laws compelling the disclosure of certain information by physicians encroach, in the words of one court, on physicians' prerogatives not to act as "mouthpieces" for the state.

Like the larger pursuit of transparency in healthcare today—from honesty regarding medical errors to providing comprehensive price and quality information as discussed in several other chapters in this volume—regulators have sought to empower patients' decision-making. This pursuit of empowerment is evidenced not just by forcing detailed disclosures under the rubric of informed consent, as the Common Rule does with human research and state legislators have done with medical teaching of pelvic exams. Regulators have also made publicly available, on a wholesale basis, the kinds of information that the duty of informed consent ideally would disclose on a piecemeal, retail basis—such as the outcomes of prior studies so that later participants can meaningfully decide to participate, or not. Disclosure of prior results may have been mandated in a material risk jurisdiction, but it is less clear that it would be required under the professional standard—highlighting how statutes and regulations can have a unifying impact in this area that the common law may not.

[112] Krause, supra note 76, at 264.

[113] Caitlin Borgmann, *Fourth and Fifth Circuits Confront Abortion Exceptionalism*, Jurist (Jan. 15, 2015), *available at* http://jurist.org/forum/2015/01/caitlin-borgmann-abortion-exceptionalism.php.

CHAPTER 11

COMMUNICATING LOYALTY

Advocacy and Disclosure of Conflicts in Treatment and Research Relationships

ROBERT GATTER[1]

THIS chapter examines financial incentives that give rise to potential conflicts of interest (COIs) in treatment and research relationships and the law's regulation of those potential COIs.[2] In particular, it evaluates both financial incentives for healthcare providers to reduce spending on clinical care and financial incentives for researchers and their institutions to pursue commercially viable biomedical discoveries. These incentives, which are endorsed by the law, may generate economic efficiencies. Yet, they also increase risks for patients and human subjects. In the treatment setting, they tempt physicians, hospitals, provider networks, and delivery systems—either consciously or unconsciously—to place their financial interests ahead of the medical interests of their patients. Similarly, these incentives increase the risk that researchers and research institutions will not adequately safeguard individuals on which they experiment because they are pursuing discoveries that could be commercially successful.

At core, this chapter addresses a clash of societal expectations that arise from the law's use of the market economy to discipline historically trust-based relationships. The fiduciary's duty of loyalty—and, in particular, its demand that fiduciaries avoid COIs—might seem to be the right starting place for critiquing this policy and calling for its prohibition; however, an outright prohibition of these COIs is unrealistic. For decades, the United States has committed itself to using financial incentives to generate efficiencies in healthcare delivery and in biomedical research. Given such stability of political will, this chapter presumes that

[1] Robert Gatter is Co-director and Professor of Law, Center for Health Law Studies, Saint Louis University School of Law and Professor of Health Policy and Management, Saint Louis University College of Public Health and Social Justice. Special thanks to Srishti Miglani for her research assistance. This chapter is dedicated to David R. Garfield in gratitude for his caring advice at just the right time in my early career; it has made all the difference.

[2] "Conflict of interest" is used throughout this chapter to refer to circumstances in which a healthcare professional, researcher, or institution has a financial self-interest that conflicts with a responsibility the professional, researcher, or institution has to serve the interests of one or more other persons.

disclosure requirements and advocacy protections are the primary tools available under the law to regulate COIs, and that prohibitions will play an important but secondary role.

Part I identifies key financial incentives in both the treatment and research settings, and it explains how these incentives have the potential to create COIs. Part I also demonstrates that financial incentives and COIs are not merely a feature of individual relationships between doctors and patients or researchers and human subjects. Instead, they are inherent in institutional relationships with patients and insurance beneficiaries as well as between human subjects and research institutions.

These observations highlight the importance of disclosure requirements and advocacy protections to account for the increased risks associated with our use of financial incentives to generate greater efficiency in clinical treatment and biomedical research. By not prohibiting the use of financial incentives, the law increases the risks of harm to individual patients, pools of insurance beneficiaries, individual human subjects in medical experiments, and the public at large. Accordingly, the law must—through robust disclosure requirements—better equip patients, research subjects, insurance beneficiaries, and the public generally to protect themselves from this increased risk. Moreover, healthcare professionals and researchers are dependent on institutions and networks that increasingly have financial interests that can conflict with the best interests of patients and human subjects. To encourage professionals to advocate within those institutions for the best interests of patients and human subjects, the law must also protect those professionals from the risk that their advocacy will result in institutional retaliation.

Part II identifies the goals the law should attempt to achieve through the regulation of these potential COIs given our sustained political will to use financial incentives to control healthcare costs and to generate commercially viable products from biomedical research. Fundamentally, the primary goal cannot be pursuing and maintaining trust relationships in a pure and traditional sense. Permitting potential COIs among clinical providers and medical researchers is plainly inconsistent with a purely fiduciary relationship. Instead, the law should be designed to promote self-protection among those at risk of harm, to generate data for regulators, watchdog organizations, and the public at large about those potential conflicts and their link to increased harm, and to preserve public confidence (differentiated from trust) in healthcare delivery and biomedical research.

Part III critiques current law with respect to COI disclosure and advocacy protections. It reveals that, while disclosure requirements have expanded, they remain insufficient to achieve these goal because they are focused almost exclusively on COIs of individual physicians and researchers without accounting for the potential COIs of institutions through which those professionals work. Part III also finds that the law does not require adequate disclosure of potential COIs to patients, insurance beneficiaries, or human subjects. Instead, it requires that providers and manufacturers disclose financial information only to institutions and to regulators. While this helps promote public accountability with respect to these financial interests, it does little to enable patients, insurance beneficiaries, and human subjects to protect themselves. Finally, Part III shows that the law provides only a patchwork of incomplete protections for healthcare and research professionals who advocate within their institutions for the interests of patients or human subjects.

Last, Part IV proposes changes to the law. Each proposal is designed to more closely align disclosure law with the goals described above.

I Potential COIs in Treatment and Research Relationships

Financial incentives of one form or another have always existed in healthcare delivery and biomedical research, and they have always affected the way physicians and hospitals care for their patients and the way researchers and their institutions have experimented on human subjects. More recently, however, policy-makers have attempted to use financial incentives through the law to improve economic efficiency in these fields. This part identifies COIs that can result from such deliberate use of financial incentives in both the treatment and research settings. In particular, this part focuses on Medicare's Shared Savings Program, which reintroduces capitation to healthcare delivery but in a new form that redirects its incentives toward large provider organizations. The law endorses the use of capitation incentives as a way of reducing utilization and thereby slowing the rate of escalating healthcare costs. Additionally, this part examines now decades-old policy that gives intellectual property rights to researchers and research institutions for biomedical discoveries they make. Here the goal of lawmakers is to encourage researchers and their institutions to pursue discoveries that have immediate commercial value.

While the financial incentives at play in healthcare delivery and biomedical research are quite different, as are the economic purposes they are designed to serve, they share certain features. First, the law is using both deliberately to generate economic efficiencies, which, in turn, create potential COIs that increase the risk of harm to patients and human subjects. Second, these incentives—and the potential COIs and risks they create—affect healthcare and research institutions, and not just medical and research professionals. Given the role institutions play in safeguarding patients and human subjects, this expands the potential effect of COIs and their risks. All of this is explored in greater detail below.

a. Financial Incentives and Potential COIs in Healthcare Delivery

The ways we pay healthcare providers for their services to patients have always created conflicts between the medical interests of patients and the financial interests of providers.[3] For example, physicians paid on a fee-for-service basis generate more personal income when they provide more care. Consequently, they tend to have significantly higher utilization rates than do physicians on salary.[4]

In the late 1980s and early 1990s, however, public concern peaked over potential COIs caused by the widespread use of capitated provider payments. This method of reimbursement gives physicians a financial incentive to reduce utilization. While capitation is intended

[3] Robert H. Brook, *Physician Compensation, Cost, and Quality*, 304 JAMA 795 (2010).

[4] Toby Gosden et al., Capitation, Salary, Fee-for-Service and Mixed Systems of Payment: Effects on the Behaviour of Primary Care Physicians (2000), http://onlinelibrary.wiley.com/doi/10.1002/14651858.CD002215/abstract.

to reduce wasteful clinical spending, it can incentivize physicians to withhold potentially necessary care, and it triggered an outcry over providers' divided loyalties. For a variety of reasons the use of capitation declined dramatically in the late 1990s.[5] Yet, the need remained to control healthcare costs while still assuring access to quality healthcare.

More recently, the Patient Protection and Affordable Care Act (ACA) introduced a new form of capitation through the Medicare Shared Savings Program (MSSP), which is the latest effort to use provider financial incentives to reduce utilization and encourage lower-cost treatment.[6] While MSSP is not merely a reinstatement of capitation, it nevertheless makes substantial use of provider risk-sharing and thereby creates similar potential COIs between providers and patients.

Unlike capitation arrangements with individual physicians in the 1980s and 1990s, Medicare, under MSSP, enters into agreements with organizations that integrate professional and institutional providers, known as accountable care organizations (ACOs). To qualify as an ACO, an organization must employ shared governance that assures significant control by affiliated healthcare professionals over the organization's decision-making. Under MSSP, ACOs take responsibility for the overall care of a population of Medicare beneficiaries numbering at least 5,000, and they also agree to bear financial responsibility for the treatment decisions their providers and beneficiaries make.[7] Based on the beneficiaries assigned to an ACO, Medicare sets a spending benchmark. When actual costs are less than the benchmark, Medicare shares the savings with the ACO so long as the ACO also meets certain quality standards for its population of beneficiaries. ACOs that exceed benchmark costs, however, are responsible to Medicare for its excess spending. Thus, MSSP creates a financial incentive for networks of providers through ACOs to meet financial benchmarks and trigger shared-savings while also avoiding reimbursement obligations.

Like capitation, shared-savings programs create potential conflicts between the interests of patients to receive all care that could provide a medical benefit and the financial interests of providers to provide care that costs less than the benchmark set by Medicare. These are "potential" conflicts because lower utilization under a shared-savings program as compared to utilization under other payment mechanisms could result from eliminating unnecessary care and providing necessary care more efficiently. In those instances, the interests of providers and patients are well aligned. The incentive to trigger shared-savings payments remains, however, even after all clinical efficiencies have been achieved, and this could lead providers to skimp on necessary care. Of course, the interests of providers to meet population quality markers required under MSSP as well as in avoiding bad clinical outcomes and malpractice liability could offset any financial incentive to withhold medically necessary care. Yet, each of these interests is relatively blunt and cannot be so finely tuned to assure that providers only cut fat and never bone.

An important feature of MSSP is that it employs shared-savings plans only in the context of integrated organizations, such as ACOs. The potential COI created by federal law thereby exists primarily at the organizational level rather than the individual provider level. Thus, an ACO, as an organization, has a financial interest to trigger shared-savings payments by incurring costs lower than the spending benchmark set by Medicare, and this can conflict

[5] James C. Robinson, *The End of Managed Care*, 285 JAMA 2622 (2001).

[6] Medicare Shared Savings Program, 42 C.F.R. pt. 425 (2015).

[7] *Id.*

with the interests of the Medicare beneficiaries served by that ACO to receive all potentially beneficial medical care. Meanwhile, the individual professionals who, in the 1990s, might have felt directly the full weight of incentives created by capitation, are less directly affected by a shared-savings payment from Medicare when working as part of an ACO.

Instead, providers delivering healthcare services to Medicare beneficiaries through ACOs are incentivized by their obligations to the ACOs with which they affiliate. Those obligations include promises to abide by ACO policies and procedures for clinical practice and other forms of organizational oversight, which, in turn, are affected by the ACO's financial interest in triggering shared-savings payments. Incentivizing providers to reduce utilization in this way therefore create potential "conflicts of obligation"[8] as well as potential COIs for individual providers delivering patient care through modern integrated organizations.

This does not delegitimize ACOs or MSSP or the financial incentives inherent in similar shared-savings programs. Incentives that correct the tendency of providers to overtreat or that otherwise eliminate waste or find efficiencies have real value. Yet, they are not without their risks, and a national policy to harness financial incentives to increase clinical efficiency must acknowledge and account for those risks.

b. Financial Incentives and Potential COIs in Human Subjects Research

Just as COIs can exist in healthcare delivery, they also exist in research involving human participants. For example, researchers and their institutions may have ownership interests in the intellectual property produced by or tested as part of an experiment, which can result in opportunities for both to profit by selling or licensing that intellectual property to commercial developers. Additionally, a researcher might own equity or options in the company that is developing the drug or device being tested in a human clinical trial, giving the researcher an incentive to generate research results that will support the licensing and marketing of the product. A researcher or research institution also might enter into sponsorship agreements with a company developing a drug or device pursuant to which the company underwrites all of the costs associated with research on that company's drug or device. This is valuable to research institutions because it relieves them from the obligation to cover those costs.

These are not the only kinds of financial relationships that exist between private industry and researchers and their institutions. They are, however, emblematic of relationships featuring financial incentives that can conflict with the obligation of research institutions and researchers to safeguard the well-being of human subjects participating in clinical experiments conducted within those institutions.

These conflicts grow out of a tension inherent in federal policies that, on the one hand, encourage close cooperation between medical researchers and commercial developers and

[8] "Conflict of obligation" is distinguishable from a conflict of interest. The term is used here to refer to circumstances in which a healthcare professional, researcher, or institution simultaneously has responsibilities to serve the interests of two or more other persons where these responsibilities conflict with each other such that the provider, researcher, or institution must sacrifice the interests of one of these persons in order to serve the interests of the other.

that, on the other hand, make researchers and research institutions responsible for the safety of human subjects participating in medical experiments. Since the passage of the Bayh-Dole Act in 1980, federal law has incentivized researchers, research institutions, and drug and device developers to invest cooperatively in experiments that can lead to new commercial products. In particular, it allows scientists and their institutions to own, license, or sell the results of publicly funded research they conduct, and it permits federal laboratories to work cooperatively with private industry.[9] Thus, each medical discovery has the potential to enrich the researcher who made the discovery as well as her institution. Moreover, commercial developers have an incentive to channel research and development funding into academic medical centers now that academic researchers have a greater interest in the commercial viability of their discoveries. As public funding has diminished, academic research institutions and their researchers have become more reliant on funding from private industry.[10]

In this way, federal policy has resulted in close financial ties between drug and device manufacturers, on the one hand, and medical researchers and their institutions, on the other. A survey of university technology transfer managers states that universities received nearly $5 billion in research grants from private industry in 2013, which represented an increase of 11% over the prior year.[11] Additionally, researchers and their universities in 2013 executed more than 6,500 agreements under which private industry paid to license or obtain options on the results of research, and these new agreements contributed to a total of more than 43,000 active licenses and options that year. While these data encompass more than just human subjects research partnerships between academia and private industry, they demonstrate the scope of commercial influence on all academic research.

Meanwhile, federal regulations also obligate research institutions to safeguard human subjects who participate in clinical experiments those institutions house.[12] Each research institution must have an institutional review board (IRB), typically composed of individuals affiliated with the institution, which is charged with the responsibility of assuring the safety of human research subjects.[13] The IRB cannot approve a research protocol unless the risks to human subjects, when minimized, are reasonable in light of expected benefits to those subjects.[14]

In addition to the duties imposed on research institutions, federal regulations also separately obligate researchers to safeguard human subjects on which they conduct experiments. The researcher must obtain the informed consent of each subject to participate in a clinical protocol.[15] Additionally, if an unanticipated problem arises during the research, including an

[9] Bayh-Dole Act, Pub. L. No 96-517 (1980); Stevenson-Wydler Technology Transfer Act of 1980, Pub. L. No. 96-480; Federal Technology Transfer Act of 1986, Pub. L. No. 99-502; Omnibus Trade and Competitiveness Act of 1988, Pub. L. No. 100-418; National Competitiveness Technology Transfer Act of 1989, Pub. L. No. 101-189.

[10] Edgar Walters, *Biomedical Turning More to Private Funds*, Tex. Tribune (June 10, 2015), http://www.texastribune.org/2015/07/10/ut-system-partners-pharma-company/.

[11] Ass'n of Univ. Tech. Managers, Highlights of AUTM U.S. Licensing Activity Survey: FY2013 (2013), http://autmvisitors.net/sites/default/files/images/Highlights%20FNL.pdf [http://perma.cc/DRE9-ALBN].

[12] 45 C.F.R. pt. 46 (2015) (promulgated by the Department of Health and Human Services); 21 C.F.R. pt. 50 (2015) (promulgated by the Food and Drug Administration).

[13] 45 C.F.R. § 46.109 (2015); 21 C.F.R. § 56.109 (2015).

[14] 45 C.F.R. § 46.111 (2015); 21 C.F.R. § 56.111 (2015).

[15] 45 C.F.R. § 46.116 (2015).

adverse event indicating a higher risk of harm to research subjects than previously known, the researcher must report the adverse event to the IRB for further action.[16]

When a researcher or research institution has a financial tie to the sponsor of a clinical protocol or to the object being researched, the potential COIs and conflicts of obligation are obvious. The very investigator and institution that must act to comply with regulations designed to protect the welfare of human subjects simultaneously may have incentives, endorsed by federal law, to serve their own financial interests and those of private developers to which they have obligated themselves by contract. This, in turn, creates incentives for researchers to take—and for research institutions to permit—risks that could unduly threaten human subject safety.[17]

Consider, for example, the now infamous case of Jesse Gelsinger's death in a clinical trial.[18] Jesse suffered from a genetic liver illness that did not have a cure and was often fatal to newborns and young children. He participated in a clinical trial at the University of Pennsylvania designed to test the safety of using a modified cold virus to transport a genetic fix—that might be developed in the future—to the human genome. Jesse was nineteen years old, and he understood that he would not receive any medical benefit from participating in this trial. At the time of the study, Jesse was permitted to participate despite having some risk indicators that should have disqualified him, and he was given a dose of the test vector that was much larger than permitted under the protocol. The dose proved highly toxic, and Jesse died of multi-organ system failure a few days later.[19]

One of the three investigators on the study, Dr. James Wilson, had a large equity interest in the biotech company, Genovo, that sponsored the study and owned the intellectual property rights to any discoveries that resulted. Dr. Wilson had created Genovo and held an equity interest in it worth tens of millions of dollars.[20] Additionally, the University of Pennsylvania, which housed the study in which Jesse participated, signed an agreement with Genovo under which Genovo promised to pay $21 million over five years to sponsor Dr. Wilson's research at the university's Institute for Human Gene Therapy and to give Penn a 5% equity interest in Genovo.[21] Thus, both Dr. Wilson as an investigator and Penn as the research institution stood to benefit financially if this research showed that the vector could be used safely in humans.

Several missteps occurred with respect to this clinical study and Jesse's participation in it. First, the portion of the written protocol that set clinical criteria for the participation of human subjects was amended to allow participation of subjects with higher levels of baseline ammonia.[22] Second, Jesse was permitted to participate in the study despite having ammonia levels slightly higher than those permitted by even the amended protocol.[23] Third, the informed consent documents replaced a disclosure that animals had died in prior studies of the vector with a different disclosure saying that animals had not shown toxic effects at the doses of the vector that would be used in Jesse's study.[24] Fourth, Jesse was given a dose

[16] 45 C.F.R. § 46.103 (2015); DEP'T OF HEALTH & HUMAN SERVS., GUIDANCE ON REVIEWING AND REPORTING UNANTICIPATED PROBLEMS INVOLVING RISKS TO SUBJECTS OR OTHERS AND ADVERSE EVENTS (2007), http://www.hhs.gov/ohrp/policy/advevntguid.html#Q1.

[17] Robert Gatter, *Walking the Talk of Trust in Human Subjects Research*, 52 EMORY L.J. 327 (2003).

[18] Robin Fretwell Wilson, *The Death of Jesse Gelsinger: New Evidence of the Influence of Money and Prestige in Human Research*, 36 AM. J.L., MED. & ETHICS 295 (2010).

[19] *Id.* [20] *Id.* [21] *Id.* [22] *Id.* [23] *Id.* [24] *Id.*

of the vector much higher than allowed for under the protocol as approved.[25] Each of these missteps either increased the risk that Jesse would be harmed by participating in the study or partially hid from Jesse the complete picture of those risks.

It is hard to know whether each of these problems would have occurred in the absence of any financial interest of Dr. Wilson and Penn in the study, or if those interests had been disclosed to Jesse. Yet, we do know that Dr. Wilson was involved in decisions about the study, including some decisions related to the risks that were important in Jesse's case.[26] We also know that Penn was concerned that Dr. Wilson's financial interest in both Genovo and the research could bias the study, and so it prohibited him from analyzing the research data. Nonetheless, the institution permitted Dr. Wilson to be involved in the design of the study, and—except for the data analysis prohibition—Penn merely requested that he avoid participating in the protocol otherwise.[27] Thus, the financial interests of one of the investigators and of the overseeing institution provide at least one plausible explanation for the missteps that led to Jesse's death, suggesting that the exercise of discretion both by a researcher and a research institution can be influenced by financial interests.

Overall, financial incentives operating in modern medical treatment and biomedical research settings evince a political commitment in the United States to harnessing the power of incentives to generate efficiencies in each setting. Given the obligation of physicians and healthcare institutions to serve the medical interests of patients and of researchers and their institutions to protect the safety of human research subjects, the potential COIs—both of professionals and institutions—become clear, as do the risks those potential conflicts create. Thus, the question is how the United States can balance its use of financial incentives to harness economic efficiencies with the need to protect the public from the risks associated with COIs those financial incentives potentially create, and what role the law should play in achieving such a balance. That is addressed next in Part II.

II Protecting Against the Risks of Potential COIs Through Disclosure and Advocacy

As stated at the outset, it is tempting to argue that financial interests giving rise to potential COIs in treatment and research relationships should be prohibited because they violate the fiduciary duty of loyalty and its prohibition against self-dealing. This approach, however, is of little help given the now long-term political will in the United States—as reflected in federal law—to leverage the financial interests of professionals and institutions in clinical medicine and in biomedical research in pursuit of both better control over healthcare spending and evermore commercially viable biomedical discoveries. It is settled, as a practical matter, that financial incentives will continue to operate in treatment and research settings with the law's blessing, and so the application of loyalty concepts must account for this fact.

One might conclude that contemporary providers, researchers, and research institutions are not fiduciaries subject to a duty of loyalty precisely because they are expected to serve societal interests as well as those of individual patients and human subjects. Given

[25] *Id.* [26] *Id.* [27] *Id.*

the requirement to serve potentially conflicting interests simultaneously—so goes this line of thinking—a fiduciary construct simply does not fit. Indeed, some have argued that researcher-human subject relationships never have been fiduciary in nature precisely because a researcher's first obligation is to serve the interests of science.[28] Likewise, courts have limited the application of the fiduciary duty against self-dealing in the face of contemporary health law that endorses the use of financial incentives to reduce utilization.

Consider, for example, a state court ruling in *Bush v. Dake*.[29] A patient sued her physician for breach of fiduciary duty when he treated her while under contract with her insurance plan to be paid on a capitated basis, which gave him a financial incentive to reduce utilization and thereby to withhold potentially necessary care. She claimed that she was injured when the defendant-physician refused to refer her for ongoing specialty care, and she alleged that the physician's decision resulted from the incentives inherent in the capitation system under which the physician was paid. The court dismissed her fiduciary claim because capitation had been endorsed by state statute as a method of controlling healthcare costs.

Similarly, the Supreme Court of the United States in *Pegram v. Herdrich* held that physicians treating patients through a prepaid clinic model did not breach the fiduciary obligation under the Employee Retirement Income Security Act (ERISA) to serve only the interests of plan beneficiaries simply because they had made allegedly harmful clinical judgments while under the influence of shared-savings incentives.[30] In that case the plaintiff claimed that a physician at a clinic under contract with the plaintiff's health maintenance organization (HMO) failed to refer the plaintiff for immediate imaging outside the clinic when the plaintiff presented with symptoms of appendicitis. The plaintiff claimed that the physician's financial incentives created a COI that violated fiduciary obligations imposed by ERISA. The Court disagreed in part because Congress had endorsed, through separate legislation, both the imposition of fiduciary obligations on employee benefit plans through ERISA and the development HMOs that employed physician-level financial incentives.

Because law has endorsed the use of financial incentives in these arenas as a way of promoting economic efficiency, mandatory disclosure rather than prohibition is the primary mechanism to account for the risks associated with potential COIs. Population health depends on both public and personal confidence in providers and insurers not to skimp on needed medical care despite shared-savings programs designed to reduce unnecessary spending. Similarly, biomedical research depends on a supply of willing human subjects to advance knowledge, and, in turn, this requires that would-be subjects and the public at large feel they can rely on researchers and research institutions to protect human safety despite incentives to pursue commercially viable discoveries. Thus, even if it is unrealistic for the law to prohibit providers, researchers, and research institutions from serving any interests other than those of patients and human subjects, a rigorous regime of COI disclosure can bolster public confidence that, despite potential COIs, the medical needs of patients and the safety of human subjects will be served.

[28] William M. Sage, *Some Principles Require Principals: Why Banning "Conflicts of Interest" Won't Solve Incentive Problems in Biomedical Research*, 85 Tex. L. Rev. 1413 (2007).

[29] No. 86-25767 NM-2 (Mich. Cir. Ct. Apr. 27, 1989). An edited version of this opinion appears in Barry R. Furrow et al., Health Law: Cases, Materials and Problems 292 (American Casebook Series, 3d ed. 1997).

[30] Pegram v. Herdrich, 530 U.S. 211 (2000).

Moreover, mandatory disclosure of financial incentives is not inconsistent with the fiduciary duty of loyalty. The Restatement (Third) of Agency provides that an agent must neither "acquire a material benefit from a third party . . . through the agent's use of the agent's position" nor "deal with the principal as or on behalf of an adverse party," and the agent must "refrain from competing with the principal and from taking action on behalf of or otherwise assisting the principal's competitors."[31] Yet, an agent may conduct herself in ways that would violate each of these prohibitions so long as the agent has disclosed all material information to the principal concerning her conduct and the principal consents to such conduct.[32] Disclosure and consent is, in essence, a waiver by a principal of at least some of the protections afforded by the fiduciary duty of loyalty. Thus, even assuming that professionals and institutions in both clinical medicine and biomedical research are fiduciaries with respect to patients and human subjects, and further assuming that working under financial incentives that give rise to potential COIs in each of those settings violates the duty of loyalty, disclosure of those incentives to would-be patients and research subjects would be at least partially consistent with common-law agency principles.

The justification for shifting COI risks through a disclose-and-consent regime is that the principal has knowingly and voluntarily assumed the disclosed risks. This justification, in turn, rests on at least three important assumptions. First, it assumes that complete information about the risks to the principal of relying on an agent with a COI is available and can be communicated to the principal in a way that she can understand. Second, it assumes that the principal can rely on the agent to fairly inform the principal about the COI and its risks. Third, it assumes that the principal is in a position either to renegotiate or to walk away from the relationship if she believes that the risks of relying on an agent with the disclosed COI are too high.

Each of these assumptions is challenged in the context of the financial incentives at work in clinical medicine and biomedical research. First, the financial incentives themselves are not always easy to understand, whether it is the inner workings of a shared-savings program or holding equity in a start-up that owns the intellectual property rights to matter being tested in human subjects research. Moreover, a patient or human subject might not understand how even a well-described financial incentive might bias the judgment of a provider, researcher, or institution in such a way as to create or increase a risk of harm to that patient or human subject. Second, the very financial incentives that must be disclosed are likely to bias disclosures by providers, researchers, and research institutions operating under those incentives. Providers will be reluctant to disclose their financial incentives under shared-savings programs as will researchers and research institutions to explain their financial incentives to profit from discoveries made as part of human subjects research for fear, in both cases, that it will drive away potential patients or human subjects or undermine their confidence. Third, patients and human subjects are relatively powerless to dictate the terms of their relationships with providers, researchers, and research institutions. For one, they lack expertise. Additionally, as a result of their symptoms, diagnoses, prognoses, and insurance plans, patients and human subjects might have few, if any, options other than to consent to a disclosed COI.

[31] Restatement (Third) of Agency, Chapter 8. [32] *Id.*

More fundamentally, requiring the disclosure of potential COIs rather than prohibiting them sends a very different "loyalty" message to individuals and to the public at large. It signals that those who must entrust their interests to another can count on being warned about a potential COI but that, apart from such a warning, they will need to protect themselves from any associated risks. While a disclosure regime is more likely to engender public confidence than one allowing potential COIs without any disclosure, it is less likely to promote public trust in the way a regime might that prohibits altogether the financial incentives that can result in COIs.

None of this means that mandatory disclosure of financial incentives in clinical medicine and biomedical research is not feasible, but executing the strategy effectively remains challenging. For example, a disclosure regime must require disclosure of financial incentives to those who will experience most directly the risks of those incentives and at times when those individuals are most likely to have alternatives to consenting to those risks. Additionally, the law should pursue standardization of disclosures to assure they are complete and understandable.

Moreover, while disclosure to individuals is necessary, it is not sufficient. Public disclosure is also necessary so as to permit private watchdogging and public regulation that can backstop whatever power individual patients and human subjects possess to decrease the risks of potential COIs. Finally, an effective disclosure regime should be supplemented with legal protections for individual professionals who advocate for the interests of a particular patient or human subject. This is particularly important in the medical and research settings where institutions have financial incentives that create risks for patients and human subjects.

Overall, then, the purposes of laws mandating disclosure of the financial incentives discussed in this chapter are to (1) safeguard patients and human subjects against risks arising as a result of those incentives, (2) communicate respect for patients and human subjects as they decide what, if any, risks they will assume, (3) equip individuals and the public generally to protect their interests despite financial incentives at work in clinical medicine and biomedical research, and (4) gather data about those financial incentives. These goals provide a basis for critically examining existing law. Part III takes on that task.

III Assessing Current Law

Legal mandates to disclose financial interests exist in clinical medicine and in biomedical research, but their use is insufficient to achieve the goals outlined above. Specifically, while the law increasingly requires such disclosure by professionals to institutions and by institutions to the public, it is less likely to require that financial incentives be disclosed to individuals. Consequently, patients and human subjects must do their own legwork to learn about these incentives and assess their associated risks; they must read public disclosures or ask questions of the providers or researchers. Additionally, the financial interests of research institutions undermine the effectiveness of regulations requiring researchers to disclose their own financial interests to those institutions so that any COIs can be identified and managed institutionally. Further, publicly disclosed information about financial incentives remains difficult to interpret so as to assess the nature and extent of any resulting risk.

Finally, while some protections exist for professionals who advocate on behalf of patients or research subjects, they are incomplete and uneven state to state.

Part III first examines requirements applicable to financial interests in clinical medicine, starting with public disclosure obligations, moving to disclosures that must be made directly to individual insurance beneficiaries or patients, and finishing with legal protections for providers who advocate for the well-being of particular patients despite institutional pressures arising from shared-savings programs. Part III then turns to disclosure requirements and advocacy protections in biomedical research, addressing first regulations requiring professionals to disclose financial interests to their institutions as well as the option for institutions to disclose those financial interests to human subjects, examining next obligations of research institutions and drug and device manufacturers to disclose their financial relationships publicly, and then considering advocacy obligations and protections.

a. Disclosure Mandates in Clinical Medicine

Not all mandates to disclose financial incentives in clinical medicine are equal. An important variable is the target of a required disclosure. Often mandatory disclosures are made to the public generally, and, occasionally, they are made directly to individuals. Additionally, laws vary based on whether disclosure is made routinely or only by request and whether they apply only to health plans or also to providers. Each of these variables affects how well individuals can protect themselves from the risks associated with potential COIs and how completely regulators and the public understand the use and risks of these incentives.

With respect to *public* disclosure requirements, a patchwork of federal and state laws exists. While it is unlikely that individual insurance beneficiaries or patients even know about such disclosures, these mandates are useful to regulators, researchers, and private watchdog organizations.

Each ACO participating in MSSP, for example, is obligated under federal law to report annually the amount of their shared-savings or losses as well as how shared-savings are distributed among its providers.[33] While this disclosure mandate has substantial reach, there remain many health plans and delivery systems that use financial incentives but are not subject to the mandate because they are not ACOs or they do not participate in MSSP. Another limitation of this mandate is that it does not require centralized reporting. Instead, the disclosed information is available to the public through each ACO's website, imposing a substantial burden on those seeking to survey the use of financial incentives nationally.

Federal law requires that health plans contracting with Medicare or Medicaid to serve beneficiaries of those programs disclose to the Centers for Medicare and Medicaid Services financial incentives they incorporate into the ways they pay their affiliated physicians, including capitation payments or returned withholdings.[34] Plans that fail to do so can be subject to civil monetary penalties.[35] Again, this mandate encompasses a substantial portion of health plans; nonetheless, it is limited to plans contracting with Medicare or Medicaid.

[33] Ctrs. for Medicare & Medicaid Servs., Medicare Shared Savings Program Public Reporting Guidance (version 2, 2014).

[34] 42 C.F.R. § 417.479 (2015).

[35] 42 C.F.R. § 1003.100 (2015).

State law may also impose similar disclosure mandates, requiring health plans to disclose to insurance regulators financial incentives they incorporate into their contracts with providers. Yet, such disclosure mandates may be limited to prepaid plans, and they may expressly exclude capitation as a financial incentive that must be disclosed.[36] Moreover, such state law mandates are preempted by ERISA with respect to employers offering self-funded group coverage to their employees.[37]

To a lesser extent, the law may require insurers to disclose their use of financial incentives directly to *individual enrollees*, but those requirements often are not triggered until an enrollee requests such a disclosure. For example, while ACOs and health plans contracting with Medicare and Medicaid must publicly report financial incentives and in this way make them available to beneficiaries who are searching for such information, federal law requires health plans to make such disclosures directly to beneficiaries only when a beneficiary specifically asks for such information.

A Minnesota statute is an exception because it mandates that health plans disclose to plan enrollees the general methods by which providers are paid, including any financial incentives to reduce utilization. Moreover, this mandate applies whether or not an enrollee asks for it.[38] Under the statute, plans in Minnesota must make a general disclosure in writing at the time of enrollment and annually thereafter during open enrollment. However, the statute does not require plans to inform enrollees about financial incentives that are at work in the care they receive from their particular physicians unless an enrollee affirmatively asks for the additional information.

In the late 1990s it appeared that federal courts might interpret ERISA to require that employer-sponsored health plans disclose directly to beneficiaries any financial incentives incorporated into their physician payment methodologies that encouraged physicians to withhold or delay potentially necessary medical care. For example, the Eighth Circuit in *Shea v. Esensten*[39] ruled that the spouse of a deceased HMO beneficiary adequately stated a claim against the plan for breach of fiduciary duty under ERISA, holding that the plan had a duty to disclose to the beneficiary financial incentives it gave its affiliated physicians not to refer patients for specialty care.

Circuit courts since *Shea*, however, have narrowed the scope of that holding. Three years after *Shea*, the Fifth Circuit interpreted ERISA's fiduciary obligations to not require that employer-sponsored health plans disclose to beneficiaries financial incentives in physician contracts designed to reduce utilization unless a beneficiary asks for such information or unless other special circumstance exists.[40] The Fifth Circuit distinguished *Shea* as involving special circumstances because the patient had requested specialty care and had offered to pay for it out of pocket. In 2003, the Third Circuit followed the lead of the Fifth Circuit, holding that ERISA does not impose a fiduciary duty on plans to disclose financial incentives to beneficiaries, and it too distinguished *Shea* on the grounds that it had involved special circumstances.[41]

In addition to laws concerning financial incentive disclosures by health plans and ACOs, we must also account for any requirements imposed on individual physicians to disclose

36 *E.g.*, Mo. Ann. Stat. § 354.443 (West 2015).

37 29 U.S.C § 1144.

38 Minn. Stat. Ann. §.62J.72 (West 2015).

39 Shea v. Esensten, 107 F.3d 625 (8th Cir. 1997).

40 Ehlman v. Kaiser Found. Health Plan of Tex., 198 F.3d 552 (5th Cir. 2000).

41 Horvath v. Keystone Health Plan E., Inc., 333 F.3d 450 (3d Cir. 2003).

such information to individual patients. State common law—through the informed consent doctrine—controls whether and, if so, what physicians must disclose to their patients.

The law of every state imposes a duty on physicians to disclose material treatment information to their patients when their patients are considering whether or not to consent to a proposed treatment plan. While financial incentives inherent in physician payment methods may seem "material" because of the risks they can create for patients, state courts generally have rejected this notion as a matter of law. Consider, for example, *Neade v. Portes* in which a patient's estate claimed that the patient's physician had a fiduciary duty under Illinois common law to disclose to the patient the financial incentive the physician had under his contract with the patient's health plan to deny specialist referrals and tests outside the office.[42] The estate alleged that the patient's primary care physician twice refused to authorize a test that could have identified whether the patient's persistent chest pains resulted from arterial blockage in his heart and that the physician's refusal resulted in the patient's death. The Illinois Supreme Court dismissed the disclosure claim, holding that it duplicated the estate's medical malpractice cause of action, which, according to the court, was sufficient to provide compensation where a financial incentive resulted in a physician's having provided injurious, substandard care.

A notable exception is the ruling in *Moore v. Regents of the University of California.*[43] Moore, a patient with leukemia, sued the employer of his treating physician for, among other things, breach of fiduciary duty for the physician's failure to disclose as part of seeking consent to various treatments that the physician had a financial interest in Moore's cells. The physician collected cells from Moore's spleen, blood, skin, bone marrow, and sperm over several years. The physician conducted research on these cells, and, from them, he developed a cell line that produced valuable protein mediators. The physician and the university patented the cell line and licensed its use to a company for commercial development. The issue on appeal to the California Supreme Court was whether Moore had stated a legally cognizable claim. The court held that Moore's allegations were sufficient to state a claim for failure to obtain informed consent. The court reasoned that a physician's financial interest in obtaining cells as part of a medical procedure is material to the decision of a reasonable person in Moore's position about whether or not to consent to such a procedure.

Although *Moore* broke new legal ground, few courts have followed its lead. Instead, the case is often distinguished on the grounds that it involved a research relationship.[44] In the end, plaintiffs have not succeeded in establishing a duty for physicians to routinely disclose to their patients financial incentives designed to reduce utilization, which could create COIs in clinical decision-making.[45]

Of course, a patient can make almost any information "material" by asking for it. Informed consent common law requires physicians to provide any information asked for by their patients.[46] Thus, common-law informed consent, like most state statutes and ERISA, enforces a policy that individuals do not have a right to know about payment methods that

[42] Neade v. Portes, 739 N.E.2d 496 (Ill. 2000).

[43] Moore v. Regents of Univ. of Cal., 271 Cal. Rptr. 146 (1990).

[44] *E.g.*, Hecht v. Kaplan, 645 N.Y.S.2d 51, 53 (1996).

[45] Kate Greenwood, *Physician Conflicts of Interest in Court: Beyond the "Independent Physician" Litigation Heuristic*, 30 GA. STATE UNIV. L. REV. 778 (2014).

[46] Hooks v. Humphries, 692 S.E.2d 845 (Ga. App. 2010).

give providers an incentive to withhold or delay potentially necessary medical care unless the individual affirmatively asks for it.

While Congress or state legislatures could override common law with legislation mandating the disclosure of these financial incentives, they have not done so. As discussed above, federal statutes require public disclosure in some instances, but they do not require routine disclosure to individual insurance beneficiaries or patients. The same is true of state legislation.

In sum, the law provides an uneven patchwork of disclosure mandates applicable to financial incentives that result in potential COIs in clinical medicine; a patchwork that favors public over individual disclosure. The broadest use of disclosure mandates is found in federal and state statutes requiring some health plans and ACOs to disclose their use of provider financial incentives publically. The law is far less likely, however, to require that health plans or providers routinely disclose such financial incentives to plan enrollees or patients, opting instead to mandate disclosure only when enrollees or patients affirmatively ask for such information.

By favoring public over individual disclosure, the law empowers regulators, researchers, and watchdog organizations while leaving individual insurance beneficiaries and patients to fend for themselves. Regulators, researchers, and watchdog organizations with the time, obligation, and resources to locate and interpret public disclosures are very likely to pursue the information available from those disclosures. Individual consumers of health insurance and individual patients, however, are much less likely to do so. This seems particularly true for patients. As a result of an illness or injury, they may be less able to research public disclosures than healthy individuals. Moreover, patients are traditionally deferential to their treating physicians and, therefore, unlikely to ask their physician for information about the ways they are paid.

Under such a legal regime, the law is unlikely to achieve the goal of protecting insurance beneficiaries and patients from the risks associated with financial incentives that can create COIs in the clinical setting. Certainly, public disclosures enable regulators to create regulatory protections, they help researchers to explain more completely the relationships between financial incentives, costs, and patient risks, and they empower watchdog organizations to advocate for public protections. The law's current policy of disclose-only-if-asked with respect to individuals, however, leaves beneficiaries and patients largely unequipped to protect themselves through the exercise of individual choice of a plan, a provider, and a treatment option.

For the same reason, the current legal regime fails to achieve another goal, which is for the law to sufficiently communicate respect to individual insurance beneficiaries and patients. Burdened with the responsibility to discover for themselves that financial incentives to limit utilization are at work in their clinical relationships, individuals may perceive that the law, health insurers, and providers have abandoned them in a marketplace that is difficult for consumers to navigate.

b. Advocacy and Clinical Medicine

If ACOs operating under shared-savings incentives become the dominant vehicle for health-care delivery in the United States, key policy questions will include: (1) who will advocate for the interests of individual patients within those organizations, and (2) how will advocates be protected against retaliation. In general, common-law corporate negligence duties help align the interests of institutional providers, health plans, and patients. Hospitals have a duty to safeguard the well-being of the patients treated in their facilities.[47] The same duty has been extended to managed care organizations,[48] and it is likely applicable to ACOs as well.[49] Additionally, as noted above, ACOs participating in MSSP are obligated to meet population-based quality standards as a condition of receiving any shared-savings payments. Nonetheless, the obligation to safeguard patients will be in tension with the incentives of an institutional shared-savings program. As always, physicians will play an important role as advocates for their patients within this clinical setting, and the law should assure that they are protected within that role.

The law does not impose an affirmative duty of patient advocacy on providers. Instead, the common-law duty for physicians to treat patients in ways that meet the standard of care creates an incentive for physicians to advocate on behalf of their patients for care that is at least sufficient to satisfy this duty. In fact, there is case law suggesting that, when a physician fails to provide care adequate to meet the standard of care, she cannot justify her failure on the ground that the patient's health plan initially denied coverage for that care.

In *Wickline v. State of California*, a Medicaid beneficiary in California sued the public program—called Medi-Cal—for injuries allegedly caused by Medi-Cal's refusal to cover an extension to her hospital stay.[50] The patient had been admitted for arterial surgery on one of her legs, and, following complications, she underwent two additional surgeries over five days. Her surgeon sought coverage approval from Medi-Cal for the patient to remain in the hospital an additional eight days as a result of these complications. Medi-Cal approved only an additional four days. Without pursuing an appeal, the physician discharged the patient at the end of the four-day extension. Following her discharge, the patient suffered still more complications, which eventually resulted in the amputation of her leg. She did not sue the physician; instead, she sued only Medi-Cal for negligently causing her to be prematurely discharged from the hospital.

The trial court entered judgment for the plaintiff based on a jury verdict, and the state appealed. The intermediate court of appeals reversed, holding that the Medi-Cal had met its statutory obligation to provide the patient with coverage for services consistent with the medical standard of care because medical experts at trial testified that the timing of the patient's discharge did not fall below the standard of care.

In dicta, the *Wickline* court also announced that a treating physician could be held responsible under the law for failing to provide treatment as required by the standard of care even if an insurer refused to cover the cost of such treatment.

> [T]he physician who complies without protest with the limitations imposed by a third party payor, when his medical judgment dictates otherwise, cannot avoid his ultimate responsibility

47 Thompson v. Nason Hospital, 591 A.2d 703 (Pa. 1991).

48 Shannon v. McNulty, 718 A.2d 828 (Pa. 1998).

49 H. Benjamin Harvey & I. Glenn Cohen, *The Looming Threat of Liability for Accountable Care Organizations and What to Do About It*, 310 JAMA 141 (2013).

50 Wickline v. State of Cal., 239 Cal. Rptr. 810 (Cal. App. 1986).

> for his patient's care. He cannot point to the health care payor as the liability scapegoat when the consequences of his own determinative medical decisions go sour.[51]

While this dictum indicates that the law might require a physician to make a reasonable attempt to persuade a health plan to reverse its initial denial of coverage, this principle has never been tested in a lawsuit against a physician.

A 1988 complaint in Maryland, *Wilson v. Chesapeake Health Plan, Inc.*,[52] suggests that, in the face of a health plan's denial of coverage, a physician may have a legal duty to recommend to a patient that she find some means to pay for care that the physician believes is necessary to meet the standard of care. Additionally, when a physician is aware of social workers or other professionals who can assist a patient to find a means to pay for such care, the physician may also have a legal duty to direct the patient to receive such assistance.

In that case, a physician diagnosed a patient with cirrhosis of the liver and recommended a liver transplant. Unfortunately, the patient's health plan denied coverage. At that point, the patient's wife belatedly began her efforts to find alternative financing, but the patient died before she could do so. The patient's estate sued both the health plan and the treating physician, claiming that each had a duty either to direct the patient to others who could help the patient accurately determine whether or not his plan would cover the transplant or to advise the patient to identify immediately alternative means of payment as a backup. The defendant-physician settled before trial, but not before a trial court refused to dismiss this claim against him, indicating that the duty is cognizable under Maryland law. Yet, the nature of the duty is somewhat clouded by the allegation that the physician had stated affirmatively and erroneously that the patient's plan would cover the recommended transplant.

In any case, any obligation under the law for a provider to advocate that her patient receive particular care likely ends at the point a physician has satisfied the medical standard of care. In short, the law would not hold a provider liable for failing to treat above and beyond the medical standard of care. Accordingly, the law would not obligate a physician to advocate for such treatment either. Both the dicta in *Wickline* and the alleged duty from *Wilson* are consistent with this likely limitation. The *Wickline* court was careful to note that all experts had agreed that the patient had been treated in a manner consistent with the standard of care. Likewise, the alleged duty in *Wilson* arose out of a case in which a liver transplant was required by the standard of care given the patient's diagnosis.

Nonetheless, the law must adequately protect physicians who choose to advocate for their patients when those physicians practice within ACOs, as employees of healthcare institutions, or as part of any delivery network that seeks to generate cost savings through greater clinical efficiency. One way for ACOs to generate savings is to create and enforce clinical policies and procedures that steer affiliated physicians and institutions to the most cost-efficient care. A physician who regularly deviates from such clinical policies and procedures undermines the ACO's effort to lower its costs below its Medicare target. Therefore, an ACO has an incentive to terminate or bring into line with the ACO's cost goals any of its affiliated providers with higher than average utilization rates.

[51] *Id.*

[52] No. 88019032/CL76201 (Baltimore Circuit Court, 1988).

Some state statutes provide partial protection to physicians. Many states in the 1990s enacted statutes prohibiting managed care organizations and other payors from terminating provider contracts as a result of a physician's having advocated in good faith for medical care on behalf of a beneficiary.[53] For example, a Missouri statute declares that "[n]o health carrier shall terminate a contract or employment solely or in part because a health care provider in good faith . . . [a]dvocates on behalf of an enrollee."[54] The limited protection provided by the Missouri statute, however, is unlikely to create the protected space necessary for physicians to advocate on behalf of their patients inside of ACOs. First, the statutory prohibition only applies to "health carriers," which likely does not include ACOs or other independent provider networks. Second, it applies only to the "termination" of contractual or employment relationships. Consequently, a health carrier would be free under the statute not to offer a new contract to a provider whose contract expires of its own terms.[55] Last, even if nonrenewal of an expired contract were treated as a contract termination under the statute, there are methods other than termination or nonrenewal that ACOs and networks might use to punish physicians who advocate for expensive medical care, including, for example, lowering or eliminating any distribution such physicians receive of shared-savings payable to the organization.

A California statute provides a better model. First, it declares that "[i]t is the public policy of the State of California that a physician and surgeon be encouraged to advocate for medically appropriate health care for his or her patients."[56] It then creates a broad prohibition: "No person shall terminate, retaliate against, or otherwise penalize a physician and surgeon for that advocacy, nor shall any person prohibit, restrict, or in any way discourage a physician and surgeon from communicating to a patient information in furtherance of medically appropriate health care." Moreover, it assigns broad meaning to the phrase "to advocate for medically appropriate health care" so that it includes:

> to appeal a payor's decision to deny payment for a service pursuant to the reasonable grievance or appeal procedure established by a medical group, independent practice association, preferred provider organization, foundation, hospital medical staff and governing body, or payer, or to protest a decision, policy, or practice that the physician, consistent with that degree of learning and skill ordinarily possessed by reputable physicians practicing according to the applicable legal standard of care, reasonably believes impairs the physician's ability to provide medically appropriate health care to his or her patients.[57]

Unlike Missouri's statute, this provision applies to more than just health carriers, and it protects against any form of retaliation or penalty. Without the additional legal protection found in California's statute, we should expect physician advocacy to be "chilled," especially within ever-larger and more highly integrated delivery systems incentivized by law and payors to generate cost savings.

[53] Linda Fentiman, *Patient Advocacy and Termination from Managed Care Organizations: Do State Laws Protecting Health Care Professional Advocacy Make Any Difference?*, 82 NEB. L. REV. 508 (2003).

[54] MO. ANN. STAT. § 354.609 (West 2015).

[55] Mark A. Hall, *Managed Care Patient Protection or Provider Protection? A Qualitative Assessment*, 117 AM. J. MED. 932 (2004).

[56] CAL. BUS. & PROF. CODE § 2056 (West).

[57] *Id.*

c. Disclosure and Human Subjects Research

Financial incentives that can result in COIs related to human subjects research, unlike potential COIs in treatment relationships, are directly regulated by the federal government through (1) the conditions it sets on the eligibility of investigators and institutions to receive public research funds from the Public Health Service at the Department of Health and Human Services (HHS), which includes the National Institutes of Health (NIH), (2) the requirements imposed on medical drug and device manufacturers applying to the Food and Drug Administration (FDA) for approval to market a new product, and (3) standards for the eligibility of drugs and devices to be covered as part of Medicare and Medicaid. In each instance, federal law requires the disclosure of financial relationships that can bias research. Yet, these regulations do not require disclosure of potential COIs directly to human subjects, and they rely heavily on research institutions—biased by their own financial incentives—to review, manage, and publicly report these financial arrangements.

i. HHS Disclosure Regulations

As a condition of applying for and receiving federal research funding from NIH or any other part of the Public Health Service at HHS, research institutions must enforce a financial COI policy with respect to any of their investigators who will participate in HHS-funded experiments. Each institution is required to solicit information from its affiliated investigators about "significant financial interests" they have that "reasonably appear[] related to [their] institutional responsibilities."[58] A financial interest is "significant" and thus reportable by an investigator to her research institution when the total value of all forms of remuneration by a private company to the investigator exceeds $5,000 during the prior twelve months or when the interest is in the form of income-generating intellectual property rights regardless of the dollar value.[59]

Each research institution is also required to determine whether any significant financial interest reported to the institution by an investigator is "related to" the proposed protocol and, if so, whether it constitutes a "financial conflict of interest," meaning that it "could directly and significantly affect the design, conduct or reporting of PHS-funded research."[60] An institution must then enforce a plan to "manage" any financial COIs it reasonably determines to exist, which could include requiring that the investigator divest or take no part in the protocol, arranging for an independent party to oversee the protocol, disclosing the COI publicly, or any other step necessary to account for the bias introduced by the financial interest.[61]

The research institution must report all of this information to the funding source at HHS.[62] It also must provide information to anyone who requests it about any financial COIs the institution determines an investigator to have with respect to funded research and about the steps the institution is taking to manage the conflict.[63] By making institutions the locus

58 42 C.F.R § 50.603 (2015); 45 C.F.R. § 94.3 (2015). 59 *Id.*

60 42 C.F.R. § 50.604(f) (2015); 45 C.F.R. § 94.4(f) (2015).

61 42 C.F.R. § 50.604(g) (2015); 50.605; 45 C.F.R. § 94.4(g) and 94.5 (2015).

62 42 C.F.R. § 50.605(b) (2015); 45 C.F.R. § 94.5(b) (2015).

63 42 C.F.R. § 50.605(a)(5) (2015); 45 C.F.R. § 94.5(a)(5) (2015).

both for investigator disclosure and government reporting, these regulations harness the expertise of those institutions, their close proximity to and authority over the work of their researchers, and their interest in qualifying for public funding. Yet, the regulations are limited in their ability to promote fidelity of researchers to the well-being of research subjects.

First and most fundamentally, they do not mention research subjects or require any disclosure of financial COIs directly to them. Second, the regulations do a poor job of accounting for each institution's own financial interest in receiving research grants and generating marketable research results. For example, they do not require institutions to report or even keep records concerning their own financial ties to funded research that could affect institutional judgments about whether an affiliated investigator has a financial COI and, if so, how best to manage that conflict. HHS acknowledged the need for safeguards against institutional conflicts of interest, but it did not promulgate any relevant regulations.[64] Third, the regulations do not require institutions to disclose information about the significant financial interests of their affiliated investigators that those institutions determine *not* to be financial conflicts of interest. Consequently, regulators and the public have no way to know if an institution is downgrading some of its investigators' financial interests so as to avoid the obligation of reporting and managing them.

ii. FDA Disclosure Regulations

Drug or device manufacturers submitting data from clinical investigations involving human research subjects to FDA in support of applications to market a new drug or device must also disclose to FDA whether each investigator involved in the collection of such data had any of several defined financial interests in the outcome of the investigation.[65] Ideally, FDA then uses that information to determine whether to rely on or disregard the data resulting from studies that failed to account adequately for the bias that such financial interests can create.[66]

The reporting obligation is vested in drug and device manufacturers,[67] and not the academic institutions that might employ an investigator conducting human subjects research sponsored by the manufacturer. Thus, the manufacturer relies upon the veracity of reports submitted by the investigator to the manufacturer.

Reportable financial interests include: (1) any compensation tied directly to the outcome of a clinical study, (2) any equity interest in the sponsor of the clinical study in excess of $50,000, (3) a patent, trademark, copyright, or licensing agreement with respect to the tested product, and (4) any payment to an investigator or her supporting research institution by a research sponsor greater than $25,000 excluding the costs of conducting the sponsored research.[68]

While these regulations promote some degree of accountability among manufacturers and investigators for financial COIs that could threaten the well-being of human research subjects, they are not aimed primarily at assuring the safety of subjects. As discussed above, IRBs are the primary mechanism for assuring research safety. Instead, these regulations are designed to help FDA account for potential bias in the design or execution of an experiment that could undercut the reliability of the data from that research.[69]

[64] 76 Fed. Reg. 53256-01.4 (Aug. 25, 2011). [65] 21 C.F.R. § 54.4 (2015).
[66] 21 C.F.R. § 54.6 (2015). [67] 21 C.F.R. § 54.3 (2015). [68] 21 C.F.R. § 54.2 (2015).
[69] 21 C.F.R. § 54.5 (2015).

Nonetheless, the ability of these regulations to promote safety even indirectly suffers from several limitations. As in the case of HHS regulations, FDA regulations do not require disclosure to human subjects. Unlike HHS regulations, however, FDA does not impose an obligation on investigators or manufacturers to make any of this information available to anyone who requests it. Additionally, the $50,000 and $25,000 thresholds for reporting certain financial interest are relatively high, which allows for financial interests below these thresholds to avoid scrutiny. Thus, federal law does not require FDA to prohibit the use of data generated from a protocol that, as a result of reportable financial interests of a researcher and a research institution, took undue risks with the safety of human subjects so long as the data appears unbiased.

iii. Physician Payments Sunshine Provision of ACA

As of March 2013, the Physician Payments Sunshine provision of the ACA requires manufacturers of drugs and devices covered under Medicare or Medicaid to report to HHS any payments they make to physicians or academic hospitals valued at more than $10.[70] Additionally, manufacturers must inform HHS of any ownership or investment interests they have granted to physicians or their family members. The reports must identify the hospital or physician and include the kind of payment made (e.g., cash, in-kind services, stock, or stock options) as well as the purpose for which each payment is made (e.g., consulting fee, honoraria, research support). A manufacturer failing to comply is subject to civil monetary penalties for each violation capped at $150,000 annually. The penalties for a knowing violation are ten times higher and capped at $1 million each year.

The Sunshine provision not only requires HHS to compile these reports but also to make them publicly available. HHS has complied with this requirement by posting the data on a searchable website called "Open Payment."[71] Given that HHS and FDA disclosure regulations discussed above do not require public disclosure, this federal statute requiring the publication of manufacturer payments to physicians and hospitals is an important step forward. Nonetheless, this reporting system contains a major gap that severely undermines its ability to inform the public generally, and human research subjects in particular, about potential financial COIs in medical research.

First, the Physician Payments Sunshine provision permits "delayed publication for payments made pursuant to product research or development agreements and clinical investigations."[72] A manufacturer making an otherwise reportable payment to a physician or hospital for the purpose of research on a new medical technology or a new application of an existing medical technology need not be reported until the earlier of either (1) approval of the new technology or new application by FDA, or (2) four years from the date of the payment. This, of course, would shield from public view all potential financial COIs associated with virtually all human research until well after the research is completed and research subjects have been exposed to all of the risks associated with such research.

[70] *See* 42 U.S.C. § 1320a-7h.

[71] *See* Ctrs. for Medicare and Medicaid Servs., Open Payments, http://www.cms.gov/openpayments (last visited July 31, 2015).

[72] 42 U.S.C. § 1320a-7h(c)(1)(E).

Second, all information posted on the "Open Payment" website is at least six months and perhaps as much as eighteen months out of date. Manufacturers file one annual report at the end of March, which discloses all payments made in the prior calendar year.[73] HHS then has until the end of June in the year a report is made to post the information on its website.[74] So, for example, any payment by a manufacturer to a physician on January 1, 2015, which is reportable and not eligible for "delayed publication," will not be reported to HHS until March 30, 2016, and will not be posted to the "Open Payment" website until June 30, 2016. Thus, the system does not allow for the kind of real-time disclosure necessary for individuals to make choices about whether or not to participate in research.

Third, the "Open Payment" reporting system is a public reporting system only. Thus, it puts the burden to seek this information on individuals who might place themselves in harm's way by participating in clinical research. The Sunshine provision does not require a manufacturer, hospital, or physician to disclose to a would-be research subject that the "Open Payment" website exists or what information it contains. Thus, an individual considering whether to participate in a protocol at a particular hospital or conducted by a particular physician must not only search for the information herself, but she must also think to inquire about financial COIs in the first place. This has led some to wonder whether this reporting system can be effective.[75]

In the end, this reporting system is a useful tool for journalists and watchdog organizations to hold researchers, research institutions, and manufacturers accountable for their financial relationships. Yet, it enables such accountability only in the medium and long terms after research has finished, clinical risks have been taken, and money has been lost or made.

iv. Common Law

The common-law informed consent doctrine does not impose a duty on manufacturers or research institutions to disclose to research subjects their financial ties with each other or with a researcher. While the California Supreme Court held in *Moore* that a claim was stated for breach of fiduciary duty when a patient alleged that the physician treating him for leukemia failed to disclose that the physician was conducting research on the patient's cells and had a pecuniary interest in that research, no court has applied that duty to either a research institution or a drug or device manufacturer.[76]

Furthermore, courts have limited *Moore*'s reach where a patient seeks to apply a duty to disclose to a physician-researcher. For example, in *Greenberg v. Miami Children's Hospital Research Institute*, a federal court declined to extend *Moore*'s duty of disclosure to encompass the intent of a researcher to patent and license a gene sequence discovered as part of experimentation on bodily tissue samples donated for the research effort.[77] The court reasoned that

[73] Ctrs. for Medicare & Medicaid Servs., User Guide for Industry: Open Payments—Creating Public Transparency into Industry-Physician Financial Relationships (2013), https://www.cms.gov/Regulations-and-Guidance/Legislation/National-Physician-Payment-Transparency-Program/Downloads/Open-Payments-User-Guide-%5BAugust-2013%5D.pdf.

[74] *See* 42 U.S.C. § 1320a-7h(c)(1)(C).

[75] Merideth B. Rosental & Michelle M. Mello, *Sunlight as Disinfectant: New Rules on Disclosure of Industry Payments to Physicians*, 368 N. Eng. J. Med. 2052 (2013).

[76] *See, e.g.*, Suthers v. Amgen, Inc., 372 F. Supp. 2d 416 (S.D.N.Y 2005).

[77] Greenberg v. Miami Children's Hospital Research Inst., 264 F. Supp. 2d 1064 (S.D. Fla. 2003).

requiring disclosure of researchers' economic interests would, among other things, "chill medical research."

In the end, the common law does not provide a reliable duty to disclose information about a researcher's potential COIs. Moreover, it does not impose any duty on research institutions or drug or device manufacturers to disclose payments that could create COIs.

d. Advocacy and Human Subjects Research

Federal statutes and regulations pertaining to clinical research impose affirmative obligations on researchers and research institutions to protect human subjects even after they have consented to participate in a protocol. For example, federal regulations require researchers to report promptly adverse events or other unanticipated problems to their IRBs or other appropriate institutional heads when those events or problems suggest that the research places subjects at greater risk for harm than previously known.[78] They also obligate IRBs to conduct continuing review of approved research with more frequent ongoing review where risks to subjects are highest.[79]

So, if the financial interests of a researcher or a research institution related to a protocol result in either unanticipated harms to subjects or a deviation from an approved protocol, this would trigger obligations for both the researcher and the institution to take action to protect subjects from harm. Where an investigator or institution fails to take sufficiently protective action, a human subject harmed as a result would likely have grounds for a private cause of action sounding in tort.

Consider, for example, *Grimes v. Kennedy Krieger Institute, Inc.*[80] In that case, parents of children who participated in nontherapeutic research on the effects of lead paint abatement sued the research institution for negligence, claiming that the institution had breached a duty to prevent research that placed children at unnecessary risk for harm and a duty to warn parents of those children about all of the risks associated with participation in research. In reversing the trial court's grant of summary judgment, the Court of Appeals of Maryland held that the claimed duties exist because federal law imposes obligations on researchers and research institutions to protect human subjects, which creates a special relationship justifying state law recognition of similar duties remediable through negligence actions.

By recognizing a private right of action for human subjects to enforce these duties created by public research regulations, the law enforces a limited duty for researchers and research institutions to advocate for the interests of human subjects. This, in turn, creates an incentive for researchers and their institutions to account for their own financial bias toward permitting potentially undue research risks for human subjects.

Moreover, injured human subjects are aided by the fact that federal law imposes obligations: (1) on researchers to report their financial interests to their institutions, (2) on research institutions to identify and manage any conflicts of interest, and (3) on manufacturers to

[78] 45 C.F.R. § 46.103(b)(5) (2015); DEP'T OF HEALTH & HUMAN SERVS., GUIDANCE ON REVIEWING AND REPORTING UNANTICIPATED PROBLEMS INVOLVING RISKS TO SUBJECTS OR OTHERS AND ADVERSE EVENTS, http://www.hhs.gov/ohrp/policy/advevntguid.html#Q1.

[79] 45 C.F.R. § 46.109(e) (2015); 21 C.F.R. § 56.109(f) (2015).

[80] Grimes v. Kennedy Krieger Inst., 782 A.2d 807 (Md. App. 2001).

report to the federal government their payments to researchers and research institutions. Those who pursue negligence claims against researchers or research institutions will be able to discover fairly easily financial information that created economic incentives for the defendants to have taken the risks that were allegedly injurious. That kind of information, if admissible, could help undercut arguments from such defendants that they were merely researchers pursuing scientific discoveries. Although motive is not relevant to a claim of research negligence, a court addressing the admissibility in an informed consent claim of evidence related to a physician's potential financial COI held that such evidence could be introduced because it was relevant to the physician's meeting or breaching his disclosure obligations.[81]

IV Proposals for Reform

There are several ways to improve current law with respect to both disclosure and advocacy concerning financial interests that can cause COIs in both the clinical and research settings. These improvements should (1) prepare consumers to protect themselves from any risks associated with incentivizing greater efficiency among providers, researchers, and research institutions, (2) promote accountability among these players for financial interests that can lead to COIs, and (3) do both of these things in the context of ever-increasing institutionalization of both clinical medicine and biomedical research. Several proposals are offered here that pursue these goals. Additionally, they address gaps in the law identified above, particularly with respect to requiring that individuals be provided with information about financial interests.

a. Proposals for Mandating Disclosure and Protecting Advocacy in Clinical Medicine

The law should require health plans to disclose the methods by which they pay providers and the incentives these methods create. Disclosure should be required both at the time a consumer is shopping for a plan and at the time she is enrolling in a plan. By requiring disclosure at the time consumers are shopping, the law signals to consumers that they should account for provider incentives when choosing a health plan, and, of course, it better equips them to do so. By requiring disclosure at the time of enrollment, the law reminds consumers that, as beneficiaries, they should consider provider incentives as they choose a primary care provider from the plan's network, as they choose whether to pay for a second opinion outside of the plan's network, or as they consider treatment options. Where plan information is provided by a third party, such as brokers advising consumers in the individual market or benefits administrators advising employees in large employer groups, those third parties should share information about each plan's provider incentives.

[81] Shapira v. Christiana Care Health Servs., Inc., 99 A.2d 217 (Del. 2014).

Current state laws fall well short, relying almost exclusively on public reporting, which requires consumers to request information before an obligation to disclose is triggered.[82] By placing the burden on consumers to ask about the financial incentives of providers, state law fails to account for an assumption among consumers that healthcare providers do not have COIs that pose any risks to patients. After generations of patients' having been treated by providers under a traditional or discounted fee-for-service payment system, and with managed-care-style capitation largely abandoned after a relatively short period of use, consumers remain unaccustomed to conceiving of their physicians and hospitals as having financial interests to conserve medical resources during treatment. Moreover, consumers are accustomed and even encouraged to think of the treatment relationship as one based in trust.[83] By mandating disclosure of these interests routinely, the law can help re-educate consumers to discourage an attitude of blind faith toward their healthcare professionals and to account for how the incentives inherent in shared-savings programs may affect treatment.

Similarly, federal law does not require health plans to disclose to consumers or enrollees the methods by which they pay their affiliated providers. Instead, through its silence, federal law permits plans to treat provider payment methods as proprietary and confidential. This is true despite the many requirements in the ACA that group and individual plans disclose important plan information to consumers in a standardized format so as to encourage consumers to shop on the basis of that information.[84] Instead, the law should require health plans and providers to report publicly on an annual basis the various methods by which they are paid and the percentage of their incomes that come from each form of payment.

State and federal law should also require professional and institutional providers to disclose the methods by which they are paid by a patient's health plan. This mandate would not require that providers reveal payment incentives each and every time they seek the consent of a patient to a treatment plan. Instead, this disclosure requirement—like the Health Insurance Portability and Accountability Act's requirement that providers covered by its privacy rule notify patients of their privacy policies—would be satisfied when providers disclose their payment incentives as part of other information-sharing between a patient and a provider at the outset of their treatment relationship and periodically (e.g., annually) for as long as the treatment relationship exists. Such a requirement could reinforce with each patient that a potential COI exists in her treatment relationship, encourage conversation with the provider about how such COIs are managed, and potentially cause the patient to reflect on how she might protect herself against any risks created by such a COI.

Meanwhile, the law must better protect professionals who advocate for the interests of particular patients especially when doing so will undercut organizational interests under a shared-savings program. Given the inconsistencies among state law, a federal statute is needed. It should be modeled on the California statute, described earlier, which protects from any form of retaliation a physician who advocates in good faith on behalf of a particular patient. At the same time, federal law should not prohibit ACOs and other networks from terminating physicians whose aggregate records over a significant time period reveal substantially higher utilization than warranted by their particular patient mixes. In other words,

[82] Fred J. Hellinger, *Regulating Financial Incentives Facing Physicians in Managed Care Plans*, 4 Am. J. Managed Care 663 (1998).

[83] Mark A. Hall, *Law, Medicine and Trust*, 55 Stan. L. Rev. 463 (2002).

[84] 42 U.S.C. § 300gg-15; 42 U.S.C. § 18022.

the law should protect physicians who advocate for greater than average spending in outlier cases, but it should not protect physicians who advocate for most patients to be treated as outliers.

b. Proposals for Mandating Disclosure and Protecting Advocacy in Biomedical Research

Current federal law inadequately protects the safety of human subjects from the risks arising from the financial interests of researchers, research institutions, and drug and device manufacturers. Again, the law relies almost exclusively on reporting by the research enterprise to governmental agencies. Better protecting human subject safety requires changing what, when, and to whom information is disclosed.

The existence and scope of each financial interest of a researcher and a research institution in a protocol should be disclosed to any person solicited to participate in the protocol together with: (1) the determination by the institution about whether each of these financial interests constitutes a COI and why or why not; and (2) the plan to manage any financial tie determined by the institution to be a COI (including a plan to take no managerial action with respect to a financial tie) along with a description of the managerial options considered and the rationale for selecting the managerial plan chosen. Additionally, such disclosure must occur at the time a would-be human subject is first approached about participating in a research protocol, which may or may not coincide with the informed consent process. This timing respects individual decision-making to the greatest degree possible by maximizing the period during which one can consider, ask questions about, and otherwise engage with this information. This is the greatest failure of current law. While disclosure requirements related to financial COIs have increased, those requirements have not included any disclosures to human subjects. Instead, they impose obligations to disclose to government agencies and to the public generally.

The method of disclosure must also help individuals to engage with the information disclosed. Thus, regulators should consider ways to standardize the disclosure of financial interests in clinical research to individuals.[85] Federal standards under the ACA for disclosing health insurance coverage information to consumers as well as for categorizing the financial risk associated with each insurance plan (platinum, gold, silver, and bronze) could serve as an example.[86] Ideally, a would-be human subject would receive a disclosure statement that would not only provide the relevant information about a researcher's and a research institution's financial interests in a clinical protocol but would also categorize the riskiness of such financial interests to one who participates in the protocol.

Finally, the law must better account for institutional bias by holding research institutions accountable for their management of potential COIs. Federal law should require research institutions to account publicly for their review of all financial interests that, under HHS regulations, researchers must disclose to their affiliated institutions, and not just the review

[85] William M. Sage, *Regulating Through Information: Disclosure Law and American Health Care*, 99 Colum. L. Rev. 1701 (1999).

[86] 42 U.S.C. §§ 300gg-15 and 18022.

of the few financial interests that an institution determines to be COIs related to a clinical protocol. Such a law would mandate that research institutions publicly disclose the financial interests they review, the decisions they reach with respect to each, and the rationale for their decisions. Only then can regulators and the general public understand if and how institutional bias affects an institution's determination that a financial interest be exempt from any management plan.

V Conclusion

Giving financial incentives to providers for the purpose of lowering utilization in clinical medicine and to researchers and research institutions for the purpose of increasing the commercial viability of biomedical research is risky business because it attempts to leverage economic efficiencies by using a profit motive in traditionally trust-based relationships that affect vulnerable individuals. Disclosure and other reporting requirements are generally palatable, if not universally appealing, to those concerned with economic efficiency and those concerned with promoting trustful medical relationships.[87] Nonetheless, deploying such requirements is challenging. Sage described it best as "building a system of public accountability on a foundation of relational accountability."[88]

This chapter has assumed that financial incentives in clinical medicine and biomedical research are here to stay. The chapter offers proposals designed to help consumers protect themselves from any risks associated with the use of financial incentives and to hold institutions in both settings more accountable for how they manage the use of those incentives.

[87] Sage, *Regulating Through Information.*

[88] William M. Sage, *Some Principles Require Principals: Why Banning "Conflicts of Interest" Won't Solve Incentive Problems in Biomedical Research*, 85 Tex. L. Rev. 1413 (2007).

CHAPTER 12

MEDICAL PRIVACY AND SECURITY

SHARONA HOFFMAN

MEDICAL privacy has long been among Americans' most cherished values. The advent of new technology in general and electronic health records (EHRs) in particular raises new questions about the meaning of privacy in the contemporary world and the extent to which it can be safeguarded. Consequently, health privacy is a far more complex topic today than ever before. This article will discuss the transition from paper records to EHRs and the many uses to which computerized health information, popularly referred to as "big data," can be put. It will analyze federal and state privacy laws and their significant coverage limitations. It will also raise several questions about the importance of privacy in American society. The chapter will end with several recommendations for maintaining and improving medical privacy protection.

I Background

A formalized concept of privacy emerged in the legal literature in 1890 in a *Harvard Law Review* article authored by Samuel Warren and Louis Brandeis. The two scholars posited that privacy is "the right to be let alone."[1] Although the term "privacy" does not appear explicitly in the constitution, the U.S. Supreme Court, in numerous decisions, has found that the U.S. Constitution embodies this right. For example, in the 1965 case, *Griswold v. Connecticut*, the Court declared that "the First Amendment has a penumbra where privacy is protected from governmental intrusion" and deemed a Connecticut statute forbidding use of contraceptives to be unconstitutional because it violated the right of marital privacy.[2] Similarly, in the 1973 case, *Roe v. Wade*, the Court famously determined that the right to privacy encompasses a woman's decision to terminate her pregnancy, subject to appropriate state regulation.[3]

[1] Samuel D. Warren & Louis D. Brandeis, *The Right to Privacy*, 4 HARV. L. REV. 193, 195 (1890).
[2] Griswold v. Connecticut, 381 U.S. 479, 483, 485–486 (1965).
[3] Roe v. Wade, 410 U.S. 113, 153 (1973).

Privacy is of particular importance in the realm of healthcare, and the remainder of this section will set the stage for a detailed discussion of its legal, ethical, and policy implications.

a. Medical Privacy

Three separate terms relate to protecting patients' interests: privacy, confidentiality, and security. "Privacy" refers to the gathering, storage, and use of personal health information and focuses on the questions of whether information can be obtained and used, by whom, and under what circumstances. "Confidentiality" is the principle that health professionals must maintain secrecy concerning patient information unless patients authorize disclosure. The "security" of medical records is the degree to which they are protected, through technical measures and procedures, from being accessed by unauthorized personnel or improperly disclosed.[4] For the sake of brevity, however, the term "privacy" will at times be used in this article to encompass all three concepts.

Why has medical privacy generated so much discussion and concern? The answer is that medical records often contain individuals' most intimate details, including reproductive and sexual health, psychiatric conditions, disabilities, chronic illnesses, genetic information, and other details that are predictive of individuals' ongoing health status and even life expectancy. This data might be of interest to anyone with a stake in an individual's future. Employers wish to hire workers who are healthy, with a low risk of absenteeism or productivity problems, and who are unlikely to require frequent insurance reimbursement for expensive medical care. Various types of insurers (e.g., life, disability, long-term care) seek clients who will never need benefits or need them only in the very distant future, and thus their premium payments will far exceed claims. Lenders are interested in borrowers who are physically and mentally able to work and to pay off their loans. Advertisers and marketers hope to sway doctors' prescribing choices and to persuade patients to purchase or ask their doctors for particular products. Political operatives may hope to use health data to disqualify or embarrass opponents, and those with criminal intent, such as perpetrators of blackmail, fraud, or identity theft, may seek such information for their own financial gain.[5]

b. Electronic Health Records

The digitization of medical records in recent years has exacerbated privacy concerns. The healthcare industry is being transformed by implementation of electronic health record (EHR) systems. In the near future, the familiar paper medical records that are placed in manila folders and stored in large file rooms will be a thing of the past.

Unfortunately, EHRs are potentially vulnerable to improper disclosure through a variety of breaches. Occasionally, computers in hospitals and clinics have been hacked. Laptops or

[4] Comm. on Health Research & the Privacy of Health Info.: The HIPAA Privacy Rule, IOM, Beyond the HIPAA Privacy Rule: Enhancing Privacy, Improving Health Through Research 76 (Sharyl J. Nass et al. eds., 2009).

[5] Sharona Hoffman & Andy Podgurski, In Sickness, Health, and Cyberspace: Protecting the Security of Electronic Private Health Information, 48 B.C. L. Rev. 331, 334–335 (2007).

other portable electronic devices with unencrypted personal health information have been stolen or misplaced. E-mails are all too often sent to the wrong address. At times, healthcare professional have themselves knowingly disclosed patient data to third parties. For example, medical students reportedly have posted on Facebook videos of patient encounters in which the patients were recognizable. Even worse, healthcare professionals involved in bitter custody disputes have allegedly attempted to obtain information about their spouses from EHRs in order to use it in litigation. Sadly, privacy breaches are reported all too frequently. A Department of Health and Human Services (HHS) website listed 736 large breaches that affected 500 or more individuals and occurred between September of 2009 and the end of 2013.[6] In what is likely the largest data theft case to date, hackers breached the security of Anthem Blue Cross and Blue Shield in early 2015. They accessed records of up to 80 million Anthem customers and employees, including names, Social Security numbers, birthdays, mailing addresses, email addresses, and employment information.[7]

c. Big Data

An additional source of privacy concerns is the nonclinical (also known as secondary) use of digitized health information. "Big data" is now a common term and will be used in this article to mean large collections of biomedical data, including EHRs and genomic information from perhaps millions of patients. Big data has generated much enthusiasm among academics, scientists, and even the press because of its potential to facilitate medical discoveries, to improve healthcare outcomes, and to promote public health. At the same time, however, the big data trend has caused consternation among some privacy and autonomy advocates.

i. The Promise of Big Data in Medicine

A large number of private and public sector entities are creating data resources that will be used for nonclinical purposes. These initiatives are too numerous to list, but a handful are discussed below by way of illustration.

Governmental agencies at the national, regional, and local levels have launched a variety of big data initiatives. For example, a federal-state-industry partnership sponsored by the Agency for Healthcare Research and Quality has developed the Healthcare Cost and Utilization Project, which offers the State Inpatient Databases (SID). The SID contain a wealth of de-identified data that are included in hospital discharge abstracts, and the SID files are available for purchase in some states.[8] The Centers for Medicare and Medicaid Services maintains the Chronic Condition Data Warehouse. This database houses information about

[6] U.S. Department of Health and Human Services, *Health Information Privacy: Breaches Affecting 500 or More Individuals*, at http://www.hhs.gov/ocr/privacy/hipaa/administrative/breachnotificationrule/breachtool.html.

[7] Tara Siegel Bernard, *What Anthem Customers Should Do Next After Data Breach*, N. Y. TIMES, Feb. 6, 2015, at http://www.nytimes.com/2015/02/07/your-money/what-anthem-customers-should-do-next-after-data-breach.html.

[8] Healthcare Cost and Utilization Project, *Overview of the State Inpatient Databases (SID)*, at http://www.hcup-us.ahrq.gov/sidoverview.jsp.

Medicare and Medicaid beneficiaries, claims for services, and assessment data. The Food and Drug Administration (FDA)'s Sentinel system will enable the agency to access health information from one hundred million patients in order to track the safety of drugs and devices after they are approved and marketed.

Numerous private enterprises have entered the business of big data as well. Geisinger Health Systems, based in Pennsylvania, operates MedMining, which extracts EHR data and offers it to researchers after it is de-identified. Similarly, a private company called Explorys has collected information derived from electronic health records belonging to major healthcare organizations that have partnered with it. Using a cloud-computing platform, Explorys provides purchasers with aggregated and standardized health information from millions of patients. A third example is the Electronic Medical Records and Genomics Network (e-MERGE), a consortium of five institutions with DNA repositories that are linked to EHRs so that genetic information is supplemented by clinical data about patients. This combination of resources is particularly valuable for large-scale research projects.[9]

The federal government and the Institute of Medicine have enthusiastically promoted comparative effectiveness research (CER), defined as "research evaluating and comparing health outcomes and the clinical effectiveness, risks, and benefits of 2 or more medical treatments, services, and items. . . ."[10] It is hoped that CER will fill many of the considerable knowledge gaps that still exist in twenty-first-century medical practice. Such research is sorely needed because according to experts, even today "more than half of medical treatments are used without sufficient proof of their effectiveness."[11]

Big data is expected to be employed in many other arenas as well. Healthcare institutions can use their patient records to engage in assessment of their quality of care and implement measures to achieve quality improvement. Public health agencies such as state health departments and the Centers for Disease Control and Prevention derive critical information from EHRs concerning numerous health risks such as chronic illnesses and infectious disease outbreaks. It is even likely that big data will increasingly be used in litigation. Plaintiffs may attempt to mine databases in order to prove that exposure to a particular manufacturer's product caused a specific illness. Defendants, in turn, may rely on EHR databases in order to attempt to establish that the culprit was a different company's product or a genetic abnormality.

ii. Big Data Privacy Concerns

Big data collections often consist of de-identified EHRs. Under the Health Insurance Portability and Accountability Act (HIPAA) Privacy Rule, disclosure of fully de-identified EHRs to third parties is not prohibited and does not require patient authorization. Thus, many patients will never discover that their records have been incorporated into a database and will have no say in the matter.

[9] Sharona Hoffman & Andy Podgurski, *The Use & Misuse of Biomedical Data: Is Bigger Really Better?*, 39 AM. J. L. & MED. 497, 503–506 (2013).

[10] 42 U.S.C. §1320e(a)(2)(A) (2010).

[11] Eric B. Larson, *Building Trust in the Power of "Big Data" Research to Serve the Public Good*, 309 JAMA 2443, 2444 (2013).

The HIPAA Privacy Rule states that health information can be considered de-identified if (1) a qualified expert determines that there is only a "very small" risk that the data could be re-identified, and (2) the expert documents his or her analysis.[12] In the alternative, the Privacy Rule lists eighteen items that should be removed in order to achieve full de-identification. They are:

> (A) Names;
> (B) All geographic subdivisions smaller than a State, including street address, city, county, precinct, zip code, and their equivalent geocodes, except for the initial three digits of a zip code if, according to the current publicly available data from the Bureau of the Census:
> (1) The geographic unit formed by combining all zip codes with the same three initial digits contains more than 20,000 people; and
> (2) The initial three digits of a zip code for all such geographic units containing 20,000 or fewer people is changed to 000.
> (C) All elements of dates (except year) for dates directly related to an individual, including birth date, admission date, discharge date, date of death; and all ages over 89 and all elements of dates (including year) indicative of such age, except that such ages and elements may be aggregated into a single category of age 90 or older;
> (D) Telephone numbers;
> (E) Fax numbers;
> (F) Electronic mail addresses;
> (G) Social security numbers;
> (H) Medical record numbers;
> (I) Health plan beneficiary numbers;
> (J) Account numbers;
> (K) Certificate/license numbers;
> (L) Vehicle identifiers and serial numbers, including license plate numbers;
> (M) Device identifiers and serial numbers;
> (N) Web Universal Resource Locators (URLs);
> (O) Internet Protocol (IP) address numbers;
> (P) Biometric identifiers, including finger and voice prints;
> (Q) Full face photographic images and any comparable images; and
> (R) Any other unique identifying number, characteristic, or code. . . .[13]

De-identification in accordance with the Privacy Rule's guidelines in theory makes it impossible to determine who the data subject is. Nevertheless, there is a very small chance (estimated by some to be 0.01%–0.25%) that highly skilled and motivated attackers, in some circumstances, will be able to re-identify records that have undergone HIPAA-compliant de-identification.[14]

[12] 45 C.F.R. § 164.514(b)(1) (2013).

[13] 45 C.F.R. § 164.514(b)(2)(i) (2013). In addition, information will not be considered de-identified if an entity has "actual knowledge that the information could be used alone or in combination with other information to identify an individual who is a subject of the information." *Id.* at §164.514(b)(2)(ii).

[14] NAT'L COMM. ON VITAL & HEALTH STATISTICS, REPORT TO THE SECRETARY OF HEALTH AND HUMAN SERVICES ON ENHANCED PROTECTIONS FOR USES OF HEALTH DATA: A STEWARDSHIP

The risk of re-identification is not the only privacy-related concern of patient advocates. Individuals who have no opportunity to decide whether their records will be included in a database could potentially suffer dignitary harms and thus prefer that their records remain inaccessible to researchers. They may worry that research that focuses on patients of a particular gender, sexual orientation, or ethnicity will stigmatize a group to which they belong. Data subjects may also oppose use of their data for research relating to certain controversial treatments, such as abortion. Finally, some may object to the fact that a pharmaceutical company or device manufacturer could ultimately profit from use of their data without sharing those profits with them.[15] Individuals with these concerns may be disinclined to have their records included in research regardless of whether their information is effectively de-identified.

d. Rights and Ownership Questions

Although Americans often speak of a "right to privacy," it is not at all clear that patients have a right to keep their health information to themselves. The Supreme Court has provided little guidance. To the contrary, in a 2011 case, *National Aeronautics & Space Administration v. Nelson*, which involved employment background checks, the Supreme Court explicitly declined to determine whether the Constitution establishes a right to informational privacy.[16]

The question of data ownership further muddies the water. While individuals in theory own their health information, once information is documented in medical records, the records themselves are generally viewed as the property of the physicians and institutions that create them rather than the property of patients.[17] This principle has been confirmed in both state statutes and judicial decisions.[18]

This, however, does not mean that healthcare providers are free to divulge patient information without restriction. Instead, they must comply with a myriad of state and federal regulations.

Framework for "Secondary Uses" of Electronically Collected and Transmitted Health Data 36 n.16 (2007), *available at* www.ncvhs.hhs.gov/071221lt.pdf; Sharona Hoffman & Andy Podgurski, *Balancing Privacy, Autonomy, and Scientific Needs in Electronic Health Records Research*, 65 SMU L. Rev. 85, 105–107 (2012), at 105–107.

[15] Mark A. Rothstein, *Is Deidentification Sufficient to Protect Health Privacy in Research?*, 10 Am. J. Bioeth. 3, 5 (2010).

[16] National Aeronautics and Space Administration v. Nelson, 131 S.Ct. 746, 756–757 (2011).

[17] Marc A. Rodwin, *The Case for Public Ownership of Patient Data*, 302 JAMA 86, 87 (2009); Mark A. Hall, *Property, Privacy, and the Pursuit of Interconnected Electronic Medical Records*, 95 Iowa L. Rev. 631, 642 (2010).

[18] *see* Estate of Finkle, 90 Misc.2d 550, 552 (N.Y.Sur. 1977); Holtkamp Trucking Co. v. Fletcher, 932 N.E.2d 34, 43–44 (Ill. App. Ct. 2010); Young v. Murphy, 90 F.3d 1225, 1236 (7th Cir. 1996); FLA. Stat. Ann. §456.057(1) (West); Miss. Code. Ann. § 41-9-65; S.C. Code Ann. § 44-115-20 (Law. Co-op); Tenn. Code Ann. § 68-11-304(a)(1); Va. Code Ann. § 32.1–127.1:03A (Michie). *But see* Person v. Farmers Insurance Group of Companies, 52 Cal.App.4th 813, 815 (1997) (finding that health records belong to the patient).

II Federal and State Privacy Laws

The federal and state legislatures have not ignored public anxiety about medical privacy. All states have enacted statutes intended to protect privacy in healthcare.[19] Likewise, a number of federal laws and regulations address the subject. For example, the Americans with Disabilities Act requires that employers protect the privacy of any medical information they obtain about employees through work-related examinations.[20] Likewise, the Family Educational Rights and Privacy Act (FERPA) governs records held by educational institutions, including those containing health information.[21] In the area of medical research, the federal research regulations, also known as the "Common Rule," mandate that research participants generally be asked to consent to research involving identifiable private health information so that they can autonomously decide whether they wish to have such data disclosed to researchers.[22]

The most ambitious regulatory initiative to protect patient privacy came in the form of the HIPAA Privacy Rule, which became effective in 2003,[23] and the HIPAA Security Rule, which took effect in 2005.[24] These regulations were promulgated pursuant to the Health Insurance Portability and Accountability Act of 1996 and were amended in accordance with the Health Information Technology for Economic and Clinical Health (HITECH) Act of 2009.[25] Because the regulations have been both much heralded and controversial, they merit detailed discussion in this article.

a. The HIPAA Privacy and Security Rules

The HIPAA Privacy Rule governs the disclosure of electronic and hard-copy medical information and provides patients with a degree of control over their medical records. Key provisions establish that, with some exceptions, covered entities must obtain patients' permission before disclosing their medical information to third parties,[26] must furnish patients with notices of their privacy practices concerning protected health information,[27] and must allow patients to inspect their health records and request that they be modified or used restrictively.[28] In addition, covered entities must notify affected individuals and the Department of Health and Human Services of any breaches of unsecured protected health information, and in the case of large breaches, must notify the media as well.[29]

19 American Health Lawyers Association, State Healthcare Privacy Law Survey (2013).

20 42 U.S.C. § 12112(d)(4)(B) (2010).

21 20 U.S.C. § 1232g (2010).

22 45 C.F.R. §§ 46.102(f) & 46.116 (2013). These issues are dealt with more comprehensively in Mark Barnes and David Peloquin's article in this volume.

23 45 C.F.R. §§ 160.101–534 (2013).

24 45 C.F.R. §§ 164.302–.318 (2013).

25 42 U.S.C. §§ 1320d-1320d-9 (2010); Health Information Technology for Economic and Clinical Health (HITECH) Act, Title XIII of Division A and Title IV of Division B of the American Recovery and Reinvestment Act of 2009 (ARRA), Pub. L. No. 111-5 (Feb. 17, 2009).

26 45 C.F.R. §§ 164.508–510 (2013).

27 45 C.F.R. § 164.520(a) (2013).

28 45 C.F.R. §§ 164.520, 164.522 (2013).

29 45 C.F.R. §§ 164.400–408 (2013). The media must be notified if a breach involves "more than 500 residents of a State or jurisdiction." *Id.* at § 164.408.

The HIPAA Security Rule has garnered less attention than the Privacy Rule but is equally important. It delineates administrative, physical, and technical safeguards to protect the confidentiality, integrity, and availability of electronic health information (EHI).[30] The administrative safeguard standards focus on security management processes, workforce security, information access management, security awareness and training, security incident procedures, and contingency plans.[31] Physical safeguards include facility access controls, workstation security, and device and media controls.[32] Technical safeguards are procedures to control access to EHI (e.g., encryption), to audit activity related to processing EHI, to protect EHI from improper modification or elimination, and to obtain authentication from those seeking access to EHI.[33]

The HIPAA Privacy and Security Rules preempt weaker state laws that conflict with the federal requirements. However, they do not preempt more stringent state statutes.[34] Consequently, one must consider both federal and state law when assessing privacy protections.

b. State Law

All states have recognized a common law or statutory right to privacy.[35] In addition, all of the states and the District of Columbia have statutes that address privacy concerns. To varying degrees, the state law provisions accomplish the following: (1) grant patients access to their medical records; (2) restrict data use and disclosure by a range of entities including providers, employers, government agencies, and others; (3) establish privileges, for example, the psychotherapist-patient privilege; (4) institute requirements relating to specific conditions, such as alcohol or substance abuse, cancer, genetic testing, sexually transmitted disease, HIV/AIDS, and mental health; and (5) require breach notification in particular circumstances.[36]

At the same time, all states have established reporting requirements. Generally, healthcare providers must report to state government agencies the occurrence of particular conditions, such as infectious disease, HIV/AIDS, cancer, and congenital defects, and their reports must include details that constitute personally identifiable information.[37] The states, therefore, have large collections of patient information.

The states have also adopted "duty to warn" statutes that either permit or require healthcare providers to disclose patient information in particular circumstances. Generally, disclosure can or must be made to law enforcement authorities and potential victims if a patient

[30] 45 C.F.R. §§ 164.302–318 (2013). [31] 45 C.F.R. § 164.308 (2013).

[32] 45 C.F.R. § 164.310 (2013). [33] 45 C.F.R. § 164.312 (2013).

[34] 45 C.F.R. § 160.203 (2013).

[35] Corrine Parver, *Patient-Tailored Medicine, Part Two: Personalized Medicine and the Legal Landscape*, 2 J. Health & Life Sci. L. 1, 32 (2009).

[36] American Health Lawyers Association; LawAtlas, *Public Health Departments and State Patient Confidentiality Laws Map*, at http://lawatlas.org/preview?dataset=public-health-departments-and-state-patient-confidentiality-laws.

[37] Joy L. Pritts, *Altered States: State Health Privacy Laws and the Impact of the Federal Health Privacy Rule*, 2 Yale J. Health Pol'y, L. & Ethics 325, 335 (2002).

appears intent on harming himself or others, such as in instances in which the patient has discussed with a clinician a well-formed plan to engage in violence.[38]

Under state common law or statutory provisions, patients may seek remedies for privacy breaches. The tort theories that apply are invasion of privacy and breach of confidentiality, and some state laws provide statutory causes of action as well.[39]

c. The Limitations of Legal Protection

It may seem that the state and federal governments have done everything possible to protect patient privacy and confidentiality. In truth, however, many gaps remain in the regulatory scheme, and patients' records may be disclosed to numerous parties even without the data subjects' knowledge. To the disappointment of many strong privacy advocates, the HIPAA Privacy Rule and state laws do not establish a blanket consent requirement for medical data disclosure. In fact, they protect only a fraction of existing patient information.

i. The HIPAA Rules' Coverage Gaps

The federal regulations' limitations are rooted primarily in four factors: (1) the definition of "covered entity"; (2) the numerous Privacy Rule exceptions; (3) the definition of "protected health information"; and (4) the lack of a private cause of action.

(a) The Limited Range of "Covered Entities"

The HIPAA Privacy and Security Rules cover only a subset of those who handle private health information. The regulations define "covered entities" as including health plans, healthcare clearinghouses, healthcare providers who transmit health information electronically for purposes of HIPAA-relevant transactions, and their business associates.[40] However, the HIPAA regulations do not cover numerous other parties that might obtain and process private health information, such as employers, marketers, website operators, insurers issuing life, disability, or long-term care policies, and others.[41] Noncovered entities and individuals are not bound by any of the obligations imposed by the HIPAA regulations, including implementation of strong security measures to prevent breaches.

Those outside the healthcare industry come in contact with health information surprisingly often. Employers, for example, can obtain medical data in a variety of ways. They frequently require potential employees to provide authorizations for release of medical records prior to the commencement of employment. They also can obtain records for purposes of workers' compensation claims, wellness programs, reasonable accommodation requests by

[38] National Conference of State Legislatures, *Mental Health Professionals' Duty to Protect/Warn* (2013), at http://www.ncsl.org/research/health/mental-health-professionals-duty-to-warn.aspx (including a chart of all relevant state laws).

[39] *Id.*; Sharona Hoffman & Andy Podgurski, *E-Health Hazards: Provider Liability and Electronic Health Record Systems*, 24 Berkeley Tech. L. J. 1523, 1558–1560 (2009).

[40] 45 C.F.R. §§ 160.102–160.103 (2010); 42 U.S.C. §17934 (2010).

[41] Hoffman & Podgurski, *In Sickness*, at 337.

individuals with disabilities, or Family Medical Leave Act (FMLA) requests.[42] Under the Americans with Disabilities Act, employers are obligated to treat all medical information in their possession as confidential and store it in separate files, but they are not subject to the much more detailed requirements of the HIPAA Privacy and Security Rules.[43]

Moreover, patients themselves may unwittingly submit health information to noncovered entities, such as websites or apps, and create records that could potentially be traced back to them. For example, WebMD's Symptom Checker asks the user to indicate whether she is the patient and to provide details about her age, sex, zip code, e-mail, and symptoms.[44] HIPAA does not govern how WebMD stores and secures this information or what it does with it.

Finally, a growing number of providers outsource work such as medical transcription, billing, and reading radiological tests (X-rays, CT scans, MRIs) to developing countries in order to save labor costs.[45] Nathan Cortez's article in this volume further addresses this globalization of healthcare. While those engaged in this work offshore are technically covered by HIPAA as "business associates," the reality is that it is extremely unlikely that any enforcement action will be initiated against foreign individuals or entities in cases of noncompliance. Thus, the practice of outsourcing to offshore professionals creates another gap in the HIPAA Rules' reach and generates further privacy vulnerabilities for patients.

(b) Regulatory Exceptions

The HIPAA regulations' scope is limited not only by the narrow definition of "covered entity" but also by the Privacy Rule's many exceptions to the use and disclosure prohibition. First, covered entities may divulge patients' medical information without their consent for purposes of treatment, payment, and healthcare operations.[46] In fact, experts estimate that during the course of a typical hospitalization, approximately one hundred fifty individuals see the patients' records, including doctors, nurses, medical technicians, and billing clerks.[47]

In addition, healthcare providers need not obtain patient authorization for disclosures that are: (1) required by law; (2) necessary for public health activities; (3) related to victims of abuse, neglect, or domestic violence; (4) required for purposes of health oversight activities; (5) necessary for judicial and administrative proceedings; (6) required for law enforcement purposes; (7) about deceased individuals; (8) made in order to facilitate cadaveric organ, eye, or tissue donation; (9) provided for medical research purposes, with particular types of oversight to safeguard privacy; (10) necessary to avert a serious threat to health or safety; (11) needed for specialized government functions, such as national security and intelligence activities; and (12) authorized by law in order to provide workers' compensation.[48]

[42] Sharona Hoffman, *Employing E-Health: The Impact of Electronic Health Records on the Workplace*, 19 SPG KAN. J.L. & PUB. POL'Y 409, 409–410 (2010).

[43] 42 U.S.C. §12112(d) (3)(B)((2010).

[44] WebMD, *WebMDsymptomchecker*, at http://symptoms.webmd.com/#introView.

[45] Nir Kshetri & Dholakia Nikhilesh, *Offshoring of Healthcare Services: The Case of the Indian Medical Transcription Offshoring Industry*, 25 J. HEALTH ORG. & MANAGEMENT 94, 94 (2011).

[46] 45 C.F.R. §164.506 (2013).

[47] Judy Foreman, *At Risk of Exposure: In the Push for Electronic Medical Records, Concern is Growing about How Well Privacy Can Be Safeguarded*, L.A. TIMES, June, 26, 2006, *available at* http://articles.latimes.com/2006/jun/26/health/he-privacy26.

[48] 45 C.F.R.§§ 164.502, .512 (2013).

(c) *The Definition of "Protected Health Information"*

Yet another important limitation arises from the type of information protected by the privacy regulations. Protected health information (PHI) is defined as "individually identifiable health information" that is electronically or otherwise transmitted or maintained.[49] Increasingly, however, information is stored in de-identified form in databases used for nonclinical purposes such as research, quality assessment, and public health surveillance.[50] These databases are often entirely exempt from HIPAA coverage.

The HIPAA Privacy Rule allows for de-identification by a variety of means. For example, it lists eighteen identifiers, as noted above, whose removal should theoretically make it impossible for readers to connect a record with a patient's name.[51] Data that meets de-identification standards is not covered by HIPAA and thus can be disclosed to third parties without the patient's consent and stored without the safeguards required by the HIPAA Security Rule.[52] This exclusion has troubled commentators because it is not absolutely impossible for a highly motivated and skilled attacker to re-identify data, and furthermore, some patients may object as a matter of principle to having their health data disclosed to third parties even in de-identified form.[53]

Databases of de-identified medical data are not the only source of personal health information that is not considered HIPAA-protected PHI. In addition, there is a proliferation of what one scholar calls "medically inflected data."[54] Data collectors interested in garnering health information about individuals for a variety of reasons, including a desire to sell it to marketers, may mine the information from a large number of sources.[55] These include: supermarket cards, credit card transactions, web browsing histories, social media interactions, phone call records, and more. For example, several experts analyzed the Facebook "likes" of approximately sixty thousand volunteers and were able to predict "sexual orientation, ethnicity, religious and political views, personality traits, intelligence, happiness, use of addictive substances, parental separation, age, and gender."[56] In the words of law professor and journalist Jeffrey Rosen, "Google and AT&T can track us more closely than any N.S.A. agent."[57]

The sale of health-related information for marketing purposes is a growing phenomenon that has generated much controversy, including a case that reached the Supreme Court. In *Sorrell v. IMS*,[58] data miners and pharmaceutical companies challenged the constitutional validity of a Vermont statute that prohibited the sale, without doctors' consent, of pharmacy

[49] 45 C.F.R. § 160.103 (2013). [50] Hoffman & Podgurski, *The Use & Misuse*, at 506–515.

[51] *See* note 13 and accompanying text for full list of eighteen identifiers.

[52] 45 C.F.R. § 164.514(b)(2)(i) (2013).

[53] Mark A. Rothstein, *Is Deidentification Sufficient to Protect Health Privacy in Research?*, 10 Am. J. Bioethics 3, 6–7 (2010).

[54] Nicolas P. Terry, *Big Data Proxies and Health Privacy Exceptionalism*, 24 Health Matrix 65, 67 (2014).

[55] Hoffman & Podgurski, *In Sickness*, at 349.

[56] Michal Kosinskia,1, David Stillwella, & Thore Graepel, *Private Traits and Attributes Are Predictable from Digital Records of Human Behavior*, 110 PNAS 5733, 5733 (2013), *available at* http://www-psych.stanford.edu/~knutson/bad/kosinski13.pdf.

[57] Jeffrey Rosen, *Madison's Privacy Blind Spot*, N.Y. Times, Jan. 19, 2014, at http://www.nytimes.com/2014/01/19/opinion/sunday/madisons-privacy-blind-spot.html?ref=opinion&_r=0.

[58] Sorrell v. IMS Health Inc., 131 S.Ct. 2653 (2011).

records that revealed physicians' prescribing practices. The Supreme Court held that the law violated the First Amendment. While this case involved information about physicians rather than about patients, it confirmed the prevalence and legitimacy of big data trafficking by industry.

(d) *The Absence of a Private Cause of Action*

The HIPAA Privacy Rule does not establish a private cause of action for aggrieved individuals. Instead, enforcement is left up to the Department of Health and Human Services (HHS) and state attorneys general offices.[59] The HHS provides enforcement information on its website but does not indicate how often it imposes civil penalties.[60] While HIPAA authorizes the government to punish violators with harsh fines and imprisonment,[61] the regulations' efficacy may be compromised by limited government enforcement resources and the absence of a threat of private litigation.

ii. *The Patchwork of State Laws*

As noted above, state laws that are not contrary to the HIPAA Privacy Rule or that exceed its requirements are not preempted by the federal regulations and thus must be considered in the privacy calculus. Determining whether a state law is contrary to or more stringent than HIPAA, however, may itself be a very challenging task.[62]

A careful analysis of the myriad state privacy laws is beyond the scope of this article. Each state generally has multiple statutes and even more regulations that relate to medical privacy.[63] Suffice it to note that the laws vary widely and are often described as a "patchwork." For example, unlike the HIPAA Privacy Rule, Texas law defines "covered entity" broadly to include "any person who . . . engages . . . in the practice of assembling, collecting, analyzing, using, evaluating, storing, or transmitting protected health information."[64] Other states require consent to disclosures for which HIPAA does not mandate patient authorization. Thus, Michigan law does not feature an exception for disclosures made in the context of legal proceedings, and California has narrower exceptions than HIPAA for the disclosure of psychotherapy notes, drug and alcohol treatment records, and HIV test results.[65] California's Confidentiality of Medical Information Act, which is considered one of the most

59 45 C.F.R. §160.306; 42 U.S.C.A. § 1320d–5(d).

60 U.S. Department of Health & Human Services, *Health Information Privacy Enforcement Data*, at http://www.hhs.gov/ocr/privacy/hipaa/enforcement/data/index.html.

61 42 U.S.C.A. §§ 1320d-5–1320d-6.

62 *See, e.g.*, Jill D. Moore, *Legal Requirements for Consent to Disclose Patient Information for Treatment Purposes: Alignment of North Carolina and Federal Laws*, Report to North Carolina Health & Wellness Trust Fund Commission (2010), at http://www.ncdhhs.gov/healthit/exchange/NCLaws_alignment.pdf (struggling to interpret North Carolina law and concluding that it is characterized by many ambiguities that make it difficult determine the status of state law vis-à-vis HIPAA).

63 *See* LawAtlas, *Public Health Departments*.

64 Tex. Health & Safety Code Ann. § 181.001(b)(2) (West). *See also* CA Civil Code § 56.06 (West) (adopting a significantly broader coverage scope than HIPAA).

65 Steiner v. Bonanni, 807 N.W.2d 902, 906 (Mich. App. 2011); CA Health & Safety Code Ann. §§ 11845.5 & 120975; CA Civil Code § 56.104 (West).

comprehensive privacy protection laws in the United States, also offers a private cause of action for those aggrieved by violations of the statute.[66]

The inconsistencies between federal and state laws may cause confusion and frustration for patients who have medical records in multiple states. They may also constitute obstacles for policy-makers and health information technology experts who seek to build large, regional and national databases for research, public health, or other purposes or to establish interoperable[67] EHR systems that will link records from geographically diverse facilities.[68]

III Is Privacy Still a Priority Value?

The collage of federal and state laws and the significant coverage gaps that they leave are not the only sources of complexity in the realm of medical privacy. Several other important questions are raised by contemporary technology, trends, and priorities.

a. Do Contemporary Americans Care Deeply about Privacy?

Public opinion surveys repeatedly show that Americans assert that they care deeply about privacy. A 2010 Markle survey found that 80% of patients and doctors "express[ed] the importance of privacy protections as a requirement to ensure that public investment in health IT will be well spent."[69] In a different study that focused on biobank research, 90% of the 4,659 adults surveyed stated that they would be concerned about privacy if they were research participants.[70]

Yet the actions of many contemporary Americans may belie the notion that they treasure their privacy. It is now common practice to publicize intimate details of one's life and thoughts through Facebook, Tweets, and other social media. This phenomenon has not been ignored by scholars and has been the subject of several research projects.

The studies conclude that social media users retain a desire for privacy, though they may have very naive beliefs about the degree to which their privacy is safeguarded online. While survey respondents, especially those who are under twenty-five, generally indicate that the benefits of Facebook outweigh the privacy risks, over 60% attempt to manage access to their data through privacy settings. Observers have also noted an emerging trend of "Facebook

[66] Cal. Civ. Code § 56.36(b) (West).

[67] Interoperable systems can communicate with each other, exchange data, and operate seamlessly and in a coordinated fashion across organizations. Biomedical Informatics: Computer Applications in Health Care and Biomedicine 952 (Edward H. Shortliffe & James J. Cimino eds., 2006).

[68] Michael D. Greenberg & M. Susan Ridgely, *Patient Identifiers and the National Health Information Network: Debunking a False Front in the Privacy Wars*, 4 J. Health & Biomedical L. 31, 46 (2008).

[69] Markle, *The Public and Doctors Overwhelmingly Agree on Health IT Priorities to Improve Patient Care*, Jan. 31, 2011, at http://www.markle.org/publications/1461-public-and-doctors-overwhelmingly-agree-health-it-priorities-improve-patient-care.

[70] David J. Kaufman et al., *Public Opinion about the Importance of Privacy in Biobank Research*, 85 Am. J. Hum. Genet. 643, 645 (2009).

quitters," approximately half of whom cite privacy concerns as their reason for closing their Facebook accounts.[71]

b. Should Privacy Be Prioritized over Competing Values?

Regardless of the degree to which Americans prize and protect their privacy, one must ask whether privacy should in fact prevail over other values. Indeed, a strong argument can be made that promoting the common good through EHR-based studies is equally if not more important than ensuring individual privacy and informational control.

As noted earlier in this article, both the private and public sectors are launching initiatives to establish large databases of de-identified electronic health records (EHRs) and genomic data that will be used for research, quality assessment and improvement, public health surveillance, postmarketing surveillance of drugs and devices, and other purposes. These enterprises may yield significant medical advances and promote public health. For example, an analysis of Medicaid and pharmacy data showed that a common antibiotic, Zithromax, can cause a small increased chance of sudden death. However, researchers also discovered that this adverse event is most common in patients at risk of heart disease, and these combined findings are important tools for physicians making prescribing decisions. Similarly, a study of chicken pox vaccinations revealed that children whose parents declined to have them vaccinated were nine times more likely to contract the disease, thus confirming the efficacy of the injection.[72]

In light of such significant benefits, it is arguable that the common good should supersede concerns about privacy. Along these lines, Larry Gostin and James Hodge argued in a 2002 article:

> Individuals should not be permitted to veto the sharing of personal information irrespective of the potential benefit to the public. Privacy rules should not be so arduous and inflexible that they significantly impede, for example, health services research or surveillance necessary to promote the public's health. Provided that the data are used only for the public good (e.g., research or public health), and the potential for harmful disclosures are negligible, there are good reasons for permitting data sharing.[73]

Broad rules that never permit disclosure without consent, even for de-identified information, might generate a "free rider" problem. Everyone in society benefits from medical advances and public health surveillance, and it is perhaps unfair to allow some to enjoy the fruits of these endeavors without contributing their data.

[71] Bernard Debatin et al., *Facebook and Online Privacy: Attitudes, Behaviors, and Unintended Consequences*, 15 J. COMPUTER-MEDIATED COMMUNICATION 83, 86 & 100 (2009); Maja van der Velden & Khaled El Emam, *"Not All My Friends Need to Know": A Qualitative Study of Teenage Patients, Privacy, and Social Media*, 20 J. AM. MED. INFORM. ASSOC. 6, 20 (2013); Stefan Stieger et al., *Who Commits Virtual Identity Suicide? Differences in Privacy Concerns, Internet Addiction, and Personality Between Facebook Users and Quitters*, 16 CYBERPSYCHOLOGY, BEHAVIOR, & SOCIAL NETWORKING 629, 632 (2013).

[72] Sally Okun et al., *Making the Case for Continuous Learning from Routinely Collected Data*, Discussion Paper, Institute of Medicine 5 (2013), at http://www.iom.edu/makingthecase.

[73] Lawrence O. Gostin & James G. Hodge, *Personal Privacy and Common Goods: A Framework for Balancing under the National Health Information Privacy Rule*, 86 MINN. L. REV. 1439, 1441–1442 (2002).

Some individuals may object as a matter of principle to having their information shared in any format with third parties without their authorization. Regrettably, tracking down millions of individuals whose records will be included in a database and obtaining meaningful consent from them may be extremely costly, burdensome, and, in some cases, impossible. It would be especially unrealistic to consent all data subjects repeatedly for each research project.[74] On the other hand, many patients are genuinely concerned about the privacy of their personal health data. Surveys show that up to 89% of respondents are willing to allow their data to be used for beneficial nonclinical purposes if their identity will be protected.[75] Fortunately, for such patients, the values of privacy and the common good most often are not in tension, and both can be promoted simultaneously. The remainder of this article outlines recommendations for enhancing privacy protection in a world of big data and multiple data uses.

IV Recommendations

A number of interventions can be implemented to improve informational privacy protections. By necessity, only a few can be discussed in this article, so the following is a nonexhaustive list. First, any entity that stores or processes private health information should be constantly vigilant about data security and adopt all appropriate technologies to maintain it. In addition, those preparing EHR data for secondary purposes, such as research or public health initiatives, must ensure that the identity of data subjects cannot be discerned. Data use agreements between database operators and users are also advisable. Finally, the HIPAA Privacy and Security Rules should be modified to enhance their scope of coverage.

a. Data Security

Data security is essential in the electronic age and must be a priority for anyone concerned about protecting patient privacy. Securing EHR systems is quite challenging for many healthcare providers because they are in the business of medicine rather than information technology (IT) and often do not have robust IT departments. Nevertheless one's privacy policies are only as good as one's security safeguards, because once security is breached, there is no way to ensure that information will remain private.

The HIPAA Security Rule details administrative, physical, and technical standards and implementation specifications to secure personally identifiable health information that is stored electronically. Examples are risk analysis, workforce training, access control and validation procedures, encryption, and automatic logoff.[76] Any entity that houses or processes health data, including entities that are not governed by HIPAA, should follow the practices required by the Security Rule. Moreover, security practices should be maintained even for databases that contain only de-identified information that is exempted from HIPAA

[74] Hoffman & Podgurski, *Balancing*, at 114–123.

[75] Okun et al., *Making the Case*, at 8.

[76] 45 C.F.R. §§ 164.302–318 (2013).

coverage because of the possibility of re-identification. Although one hopes that database operators would be responsible enough to implement state-of-the-art security technologies, regulators would be prudent to consider amending the Security Rule so that it formally extends to de-identified information.

Many resources are available on the Internet to assist with HIPAA Security Rule compliance. For example, the Department of Health and Human Services offers a page featuring relevant educational papers, guidance, and special publications by the National Institute of Standards and Technology.[77] Moreover, those without strong IT departments may wish to hire security consultants in order to ensure that they adopt the most up-to-date and effective security technology.

b. Identity Concealment Techniques

When researchers and others use EHRs for secondary purposes, they may employ several methods to protect the identity of data subjects. Two of the most well-known are (1) de-identification of records that are collected in EHR databases, and (2) secure statistical analysis of distributed databases.

i. Record De-identification

When large databases are created in order to enable big data analysis, database operators can protect patient privacy through de-identification. Experts may use a variety of techniques to de-identify data.[78] Several options endorsed in guidance issued by the Department of Health and Human Services are:

1. *suppression*, which involves removal or elimination of particular data features prior to dissemination (e.g., zip codes, birthdates, income);
2. *generalization*, which involves transforming particular information into more abstract representations (e.g., indicating a ten-year age range instead of exact age); and
3. *perturbation*, which involves replacing certain data values with equally specific but different values (e.g., changing patients' ages).[79]

The HIPAA Privacy Rule provides detailed guidance concerning suppression, listing eighteen identifiers that should be removed in order to render data fully de-identified.[80] However, experts have determined that even with redaction of the eighteen identifiers,

[77] U.S. Department of Health and Human Services, *Security Rule Guidance Material*, at http://www.hhs.gov/ocr/privacy/hipaa/administrative/securityrule/securityruleguidance.html.

[78] *See* note 12 and accompanying text.

[79] U.S. Department of Health and Human Services, *Guidance Regarding Methods for De-identification of Protected Health Information in Accordance with the Health Insurance Portability and Accountability Act (HIPAA) Privacy Rule* (2012), at http://www.hhs.gov/ocr/privacy/hipaa/understanding/coveredentities/De-identification/guidance.html#guidancedetermination (noting that techniques such as suppression and generalization are often used in combination).

[80] 45 C.F.R. § 164.514(b)(2)(i) (2013); *see* note 13 and accompanying text.

there is a very small chance, estimated by some to be 0.01%–0.25%, that records could be re-identified by skilled attackers who have access to certain publicly available information, such as voter registration records.[81] Though the very fact that records could ever be re-identified raises serious concerns, the possibility is extremely small, and de-identification remains a very important tool for protecting patient privacy.

Whenever possible, database operators, whether or not they are covered by HIPAA, should fully de-identify data that is released to third parties. Because some who manage data resources are not covered entities, thorough de-identification is not always accomplished. For example, a 2013 survey found that thirty-three states release patient hospital discharge data to the public, and quite a number do not meet HIPAA de-identification standards because they include information such as five-digit zip codes.[82] Since states are not covered entities, this lapse is not a violation of law, but it could compromise patient privacy. In fact, Latanya Sweeney, one of the survey authors and now a Harvard faculty member, is famous for having identified Massachusetts' Governor William Weld's records based on anonymized hospital discharge data and voter registration information when she was a graduate student in 1996.

A possible objection to de-identification, other than that it is burdensome, is that HIPAA-compliant de-identification may strip away too much data that is useful or necessary for certain scientific research or other analysis. The absence of details such as dates or localities may indeed impact research quality in some instances. Consequently, the HIPAA Privacy Rule allows for disclosure and use of "limited data sets" without patient consent if data recipients sign data use agreements containing specified restrictions and privacy protections. Limited data sets are largely de-identified, but they do contain dates and geographic locales, though not patients' exact addresses.[83] While these details may be valuable for analysts, they may also make it considerably easier for skilled attackers to link records to particular patients.[84]

ii. Secure Statistical Analysis of Distributed Databases

An alternative research technique that should be considered by investigators is secure statistical analysis of distributed databases, which allows analysts to query the records of entities that participate in a federated system. Parties in a federated system agree to collaborate so that all EHRs remain housed in their facilities of origin and no separate research database is created, but queries can be sent to member establishments through a standard web service. Researchers submit statistical queries via the Internet, and these are processed by a query service. What researchers receive back is summary statistics with no individually identifying information. To illustrate, a researcher might submit a query asking for the prevalence of disease X among the federated systems' patient population. After statistical analysis, the

[81] *See* note 14 and accompanying text.

[82] Sean Hooley & Latanya Sweeney, *Survey of Publicly Available State Health Databases* (2013), at http://dataprivacylab.org/projects/50states/1075-1.pdf.

[83] 45 C.F.R. §§164.514(e)(1)–(4).

[84] Kathleen Benitez & Bradley Malin, *Evaluating Re-identification Risks with Respect to the HIPAA Privacy Rule*, 17 J. Am Med. Inform. Assoc. 169, 128 (2010) (estimating that the risk of re-identification is between 10% and 60%, depending on the state).

investigator would obtain an estimate of the percentage of the population that is afflicted with that disease.

Several federated systems already exist. The FDA's Sentinel System is being implemented in stages and used for postmarketing surveillance of drugs and devices. It allows the FDA to query data sources such as EHRs and insurance claims databases in order to identify potential product safety problems.[85] Likewise, the Distributed Network for Ambulatory Research in Therapeutics (DARTNet) was created in 2008 and is funded by the Agency for Research Healthcare and Quality.[86] DARTNet links separate member organizations' databases, containing information such as vital signs, family histories, and physical examination findings, so that a single query can draw information from all of the databases. The project's goal is to promote quality improvement in primary healthcare.

In terms of privacy, an advantage of a federated system is that records are queried at their facilities of origin, and no central database is created. Thus, there is no risk of leaks during the process of constructing the database and transmitting information to it. In addition, researchers receive only summary statistics or aggregated data, and thus they have no access to anonymized patient records that they could try to re-identify or that may not have been thoroughly de-identified in the first place. However, just as fully de-identified data sets cannot be used for some studies that require more detail, statistical queries will not be appropriate for all research projects.[87]

iii. Data Use Agreements and Privacy Training

A third privacy safeguard for secondary use of private health information is data use agreements. Such agreements are required by the HIPAA regulations for limited data sets, but they should be adopted for fully de-identified information as well. Anyone seeking access to a database that contains patient information should be required to sign data use agreements that specify conditions for utilizing the resource. Data use agreements generally require users to provide assurances of the following:

1. they will not attempt to re-identify data;
2. they will store data in secure environments;
3. they will not publish information in forms that could enable others to identify individuals or establishments;
4. they will use the data only for one or more projects described in the document;
5. they will destroy or return the dataset after the projects' completion;
6. they will not release the data to anyone other than individuals who are listed or described in an attachment to the agreement.[88]

[85] U.S. Food and Drug Administration, *FDA's Sentinel Initiative* (2014), at http://www.fda.gov/Safety/FDAsSentinelinitiative/ucm2007250.htm.

[86] Agency for Healthcare Research and Quality, *Distributed Network for Ambulatory Research in Therapeutics, Topic Abstract*, at http://effectivehealthcare.ahrq.gov/index.cfm/search-for-guides-reviews-and-reports/?productid=317&pageaction=displayproduct.

[87] Hoffman & Podgurski, *Balancing*, at 131–133.

[88] *See, e.g.*, Healthcare Cost and Utilization Project.

Prior to signing a data use agreement, applicants should be required to undergo web-based privacy training. This approach has been adopted by the Healthcare Cost and Utilization Project for those seeking access to the State Inpatient Databases. Although training and data use agreements will not guarantee that users will avoid misconduct, they could prevent many privacy breaches that would arise from carelessness or ignorance.

c. HIPAA Revisions

The HIPAA statute and regulations could be modified in several ways to enhance their reach and efficacy. These changes include expanding the definition of "covered entity," explicitly prohibiting attempts to re-identify data, and adding a private cause of action.

i. Expanding the Definition of "Covered Entity"

The HIPAA Privacy and Security Rules currently cover only healthcare providers, health plans, healthcare clearinghouses, and their business associates. This definition leaves out numerous parties that handle health information. In order to improve privacy protection, the definition should be revised both in the Privacy Rule and the enabling HIPAA statute[89] to be far more inclusive. A strong precedent is set by Texas law, which provides:

> "Covered entity" means any person who:
>
> (A) for commercial, financial, or professional gain, monetary fees, or dues, or on a cooperative, nonprofit, or pro bono basis, engages, in whole or in part, and with real or constructive knowledge, in the practice of assembling, collecting, analyzing, using, evaluating, storing, or transmitting protected health information. The term includes a business associate, health care payer, governmental unit, information or computer management entity, school, health researcher, health care facility, clinic, health care provider, or person who maintains an Internet site;
> (B) comes into possession of protected health information;
> (C) obtains or stores protected health information under this chapter; or
> (D) is an employee, agent, or contractor of a person described by Paragraph (A), (B), or (C) insofar as the employee, agent, or contractor creates, receives, obtains, maintains, uses, or transmits protected health information.[90]

A broad definition such as the Texas statute's would extend HIPAA's privacy and security mandates essentially to any party in possession of individually identifiable health information.[91] It would thus offer much more comprehensive privacy protection to the American public.

[89] 45 C.F.R. §160.103 (2013) and 42 U.S.C. §1320d-1(a) (2010).

[90] Tex. Health & Safety Code Ann. 181.001(b)(2) (West).

[91] Note that the definition of "protected health information" would also need to be revised to eliminate exceptions for individually identifiable health information held by educational institutions and employers. 45 C.F.R. § 160.103 (2013). Likewise, the definition of "health information" would need

ii. Prohibit Re-identification

In general, the HIPAA Rules apply only to individually identifiable information. However, the regulations should include one mandate that governs use of de-identified information as well: an explicit prohibition of any effort to re-identify anonymized health information. This restriction is listed as an element of data use agreements that are to be signed by limited data set recipients. Recipients must promise not to "identify the information or contact the individuals."[92] A similar regulatory proscription should extend to anyone utilizing fully de-identified information, and violators should be subject to HIPAA's enforcement provisions and penalties.

iii. Add Private Cause of Action

Government oversight should be supplemented by private enforcement through a private cause of action. The threat of private litigation could go far in deterring covered entities from violating HIPAA standards. In its absence and in light of severely limited federal and state enforcement resources, some covered entities may calculate that the risk of being penalized by the government is extremely small. Therefore, they may be tempted to cut corners with respect to HIPAA compliance, which can be costly and burdensome.

Under HIPAA's breach notification provisions, covered entities must report any breaches that they identify both to affected individuals and to the HHS.[93] Consequently, patients will know about all breaches, and this reporting requirement may raise the specter of a deluge of litigation. However, plaintiffs would need to have suffered damages in order to sue. Thus, plaintiffs will have standing if perpetrators obtain credit card numbers from medical records and use them for purchases or publicize sensitive medical details about patients and cause embarrassment or reputational harm. Specific injury will not be provable in many cases, such as those in which computer equipment was lost or stolen, and no private health information was used by third parties for malicious purposes.

Numerous state privacy laws feature private causes of action for aggrieved individuals.[94] The recommended revision therefore would follow well-established precedent. A private cause of action may serve as an important enforcement tool that both deters regulatory violations and provides a means to compensate victims of unlawful conduct.

V Conclusion

The extent to which the privacy of patients' medical records is and should be protected is an immensely complicated question. The transition to electronic health records and the

to be revised because it is currently limited to information that is "created or received by a health care provider, health plan, public health authority, employer, life insurer, school or university, or health care clearinghouse." *Id.* It thus fails to include data handled by financial institutions, marketers, website operators, and others.

[92] 45 C.F.R. §164.514(e)(4)(ii)(C)(5) (2013).

[93] 45 C.F.R. §§ 164.404–410 (2013).

[94] Hoffman & Podgurski, *E-Health Hazards*, at 1559, note 225.

phenomenon of big data collections have made privacy both increasingly important and more difficult to safeguard. The federal and state legislatures have enacted a myriad of privacy statutes and regulations, but public authorities cannot rest on their laurels. Health information technology experts and policy-makers must be ever vigilant about privacy and data security and continue to develop mechanisms for improvement. To that end, this article has formulated a number of technical and legal recommendations. At the same time, society should not be so overzealous about privacy that it abandons big data initiatives and relinquishes their enormous potential benefits. The healthcare community has many challenges ahead of it in the twenty-first century. Not least among them is grappling with how best to protect privacy in the digital age while simultaneously facilitating scientific advancement through widespread data use.

C. *Ethics and Law of Treatments*

CHAPTER 13

NEW, EXPERIMENTAL, AND LIFE-SAVING THERAPIES

B. JESSIE HILL

THE breakneck pace of pharmaceutical and technological innovation has increasingly led to the development of experimental or life-saving therapies to which individuals may not always have access at will, whether because of their expense, government regulation, or manufacturers' decisions to withhold them from the market. For example, some newer cancer drugs may increase life span by only a few months on average, but at an enormous cost. Payers, whether public or private, must make decisions about coverage of such drugs that will, in most cases, translate into a decision about whether the individual patient has access to the therapy at all. On the other hand, patients sometimes seek access to drugs that, although inexpensive, are off-limits because they have not been approved as safe and effective by the U.S. Food and Drug Administration (FDA). Occasional outbreaks of lethal diseases such as Ebola, with their concomitant threat of a global epidemic, place pressure on national governments and the medical community to act quickly by bringing even relatively untested therapies to suffering populations, while sharpening concerns about access and research ethics.[1] Finally, some treatments—such as stem-cell derived therapies or sex reassignment surgery for minors—may raise ethical concerns in their own right, even bracketing the problem of who should have access and under what conditions.

The existence of such cutting-edge therapies provoke numerous questions—in particular, how to engineer fair distribution; how best to ensure individual decision-making autonomy in light of imperfect knowledge and information asymmetries; and how to evaluate the institutional competency and proper role of the government vis-à-vis the market in regulating access to these new therapies. There are three principal frameworks deployed within legal discourse in attempting to address these challenges: the constitutional framework, the public health framework, and the ethics and human rights framework. Each framework grapples with all of the problems described in Part III, though each emphasizes some over others, with greater or lesser degrees of success in resolving them. No one approach dominates U.S. health policy; consequently, fundamental conflicts persist over the existence and meaning of a right

[1] *See, e.g.*, Steven Joffe, *Evaluating Novel Therapies During the Ebola Epidemic*, 312 JAMA 1299, 1299 (2014).

to healthcare, as well as over the proper allocation of scarce healthcare resources, in both judicial and political fora. Moreover, although the ethics and human rights frameworks hold the most promise for solving the three types of challenges raised by new, innovative, and life-saving therapies, it is also the least likely to predominate in U.S. law and policy.

I Some Definitions

An initial challenge for conceiving a regulatory framework for experimental therapies is defining the term "experimental," as well as specifying when experimental therapies can be considered medically necessary. "Experimental," "medically necessary," and similar terms do not correspond to fixed legal categories. Rather, they are often left vague and undefined, and they are mobilized in different ways, for different purposes, in a variety of contexts. These definitional challenges reflect, to some extent, the decentralized nature of medical decision-making in the United States as a whole: decisions regarding the necessity and propriety of various treatments have historically been made primarily by individual payers or physicians, rather than by governmental entities.[2]

Of course, the charge of vagueness could likely be made about numerous legally important terms, but that does not necessarily obviate their usefulness. Nonetheless, the definitional vagueness of key terms pertaining to experimental and life-saving therapies, together with their often politicized nature, aggravates some of the difficulties in meeting the challenges posed by new medical technologies. In particular, the lack of a clear understanding of what constitutes medical necessity, on either an individual scale or a broader population level, inhibits decision-making regarding insurance coverage and fair distribution of healthcare resources.

a. "Experimental"

To begin with, the term "experimental" often carries meanings in legal and popular discourse that do not correspond to most medical understandings of the term. In medical usage, "experimental" usually means not only that the particular therapy's safety or efficacy has not been thoroughly tested or that its acceptance in the medical community is not widespread but also that it is being used with an intent to develop knowledge about the therapy's safety or efficacy—in other words, that it is being administered as part of a more or less controlled experiment.[3] Thus, courts and even insurers sometimes use the term "experimental" when they actually mean something more like "innovative," because they are referring primarily to the therapy's new and untested nature.[4] Moreover, the Medicaid program, which is

[2] *See, e.g.*, B. Jessie Hill, *What Is the Meaning of Health? Constitutional Implications of Defining "Medical Necessity" and "Essential Health Benefits" Under the Affordable Care Act*, 38 Am. J. L. & Med. 445 (2012) (noting the traditionally decentralized nature of medical decision-making and discussing the implications of the move toward a more centralized system with the Affordable Care Act).

[3] Dale Cowan, *Innovative Therapy Versus Experimentation*, 21 Tort & Ins. L.J., 619, 622–623 (1986)).

[4] Richard S. Saver, *Reimbursing New Technologies: Why Are The Courts Judging Experimental Medicine?*, 44 Stan. L. Rev. 1095, 1096 & n.6 (1992).

the largest insurer in the country, does not define "experimental," although it permits states to exclude experimental treatments from their programs; Medicaid also does not define "medical necessity," although the term is central to determining which procedures may be reimbursed under the program's rules.[5]

Nonetheless, regulators, insurers, and courts are often called upon in borderline cases to determine whether a treatment qualifies as "experimental," usually in order to determine whether it falls under an insurance exclusion for such treatments. In reviewing determinations that a treatment is experimental and therefore excluded from coverage, courts often consider factors such as the newness of the therapy, the degree of acceptance in the medical community, and FDA approval or other authoritative evidence of safety and efficacy.[6]

b. "Medical Necessity"

"Medical necessity" likewise has no authoritative clinical or legal definition.[7] Although "medically necessary" is sometimes contrasted with "experimental"—insofar as a particular therapy may be categorized as either experimental (and therefore excluded from coverage) or medically necessary (and therefore covered)—the terms are not exactly opposites. In the coverage context, medical necessity generally refers to a determination that a particular treatment will have therapeutic effect by alleviating pain or illness or restoring normal functioning.[8] This determination, by definition, precludes treatments that are experimental—in the sense of new and untested—from its scope, but it does not necessary include all established therapies. Though the concept of medical necessity comprises an element of therapeutic effect, it would not be accurate to assert that every treatment that is likely to bring any therapeutic benefit to a patient, no matter how small, is medically necessary. Such an understanding of medical necessity is far too broad in that it would sweep in expensive treatments that are only minimally therapeutic. The concept of medical necessity thus appears to include some degree of cost-benefit balancing as well.[9]

5 *See* The Kaiser Commission on Medicaid and the Uninsured, *Medicaid: A Primer* v-16 (2013), *available at* http://kff.org/medicaid/issue-brief/medicaid-a-primer/.

6 *See, e.g.*, Rush v. Parham, 625 F.2d 1150, 1156 (5th Cir. 1980); Oklahoma Chapter of the American Academy of Pediatrics v. Fogarty, 366 F. Supp. 2d 1050, 1117 (N.D. Okla. 2005); McLaughlin v. Williams, 801 F. Supp. 633 (S.D. Fla. 1992).

7 The American Medical Association defines medical necessity as: "Health care services or products that a prudent physician would provide to a patient for the purpose of preventing, diagnosing or treating an illness, injury, disease, or its symptoms in a manner that is: (a) in accordance with generally accepted standards of medical practice; (b) clinically appropriate in terms of type, frequency, extent, site, and duration; and (c) not primarily for the economic benefit of the health plan and purchasers or for the convenience of the patient, treating physician, or other health care provider." American Medical Association, *Statement of the American Medical Association to the Institute of Medicine's Committee on Determination of Essential Health Benefits* 3 (Jan. 14, 2011), *available at* http://www.iom.edu/~/media/Files/Activity%20Files/HealthServices/EssentialHealthBenefits/2011-JAN-13%20and%2014/Gerald%20Harmon%20Statement.pdf. For private insurers, too, the term "medically necessary" is generally used to describe medical treatment that is appropriate and rendered in accordance with widely accepted standards of medical practice. Gillian I. Russell, *Terminology*, *in* FUNDAMENTALS OF HEALTH LAW 1, 25 (5th ed. 2011).

8 Einer Elhauge, *Allocating Health Care Morally*, 82 CAL. L. REV. 1449, 1467 (1994).

9 M. GREGG BLOCHE, THE HIPPOCRATIC MYTH: THE HIPPOCRATIC MYTH: WHY DOCTORS ARE UNDER PRESSURE TO RATION CARE, PRACTICE POLITICS, AND COMPROMISE THEIR PROMISE TO HEAL 11 (2011).

The necessity of determining therapeutic impact and of weighing it against the procedure's cost raises the question of who, precisely, will conduct this balancing. In many cases, the individual treating physician will receive substantial deference, both from courts and insurers, although obviously disagreements may and do arise. In some contexts, government agencies have created lists of covered health services, which has the advantage of eliminating the need to define medical necessity on a case-by-case basis in many instances. For example, Medicaid publishes a list of services that must be covered by state Medicaid programs. Similarly, the Affordable Care Act requires most plans to cover certain categories of "Essential Health Benefits," such as "emergency services," "maternity and newborn care," "mental health and substance use disorder services," "rehabilitative and habilitative services and devices," and "preventive and wellness services and chronic disease management."[10] The precise services that fall into those categories are left to the individual states to determine, however. Finally, in the 1990s, the state of Oregon established a relatively comprehensive prioritized list of hundreds of diagnoses and treatments and ranked them in order of importance. It then drew a line above which the Oregon Medicaid program would cover services and below which it would not; the line would—in theory at least—move up or down based on the financial resources available to the program.[11]

Whether defined on an ad hoc basis or with reference to a predetermined list, medical necessity is a concept that is intensely fraught with profound political and moral implications. One set of problems arises from the implicit or explicit element of cost-benefit balancing that occurs when a particular therapy is determined to be, or not to be, medically necessary. This determination raises profound ethical questions about the value of individual lives, quality of life, and the just allocation of scarce but vital resources. Those difficulties may be magnified by concerns about the reliability and legitimacy of the decision-makers and decision-making methods.

A second set of problems centers around the value judgments that are required in order to determine that a treatment is medically necessary because it is essential for "normal" human functioning, or even normal appearance. For example, when the Obama administration decided to designate contraceptives as preventive care, to be included within the essential health benefits covered by all employers, a political firestorm ensued. Indeed, the place of reproductive healthcare within healthcare more generally has long been contested. Similar problems lurk in deciding when a procedure to restore or even initiate "normal" functioning is medically necessary. For example, some controversy attends the use of cochlear implants, which enable congenitally deaf children to hear, but which are viewed as a threat by the deaf community. The designation of obesity as a treatable medical condition rather as than as the result of poor lifestyle choices similarly raises baseline questions about what the range of "normal" is and about the role of free will in human behavior. The dividing line between the

[10] 42 U.S.C.A. §18022(b)(1).

[11] *See, e.g.*, Thomas Bodenheimer, *The Oregon Health Plan—Lessons for the Nation*, 337 JAMA 651, 651 (1997). The list was actually created by the Oregon Health Services Commission, which reported to the governor, acting under a mandate from the state legislature. *See* OR. REV. STAT. § 414.720. The plan's medical directors were also empowered to authorize payment for below-the-line treatments on a case-by-case basis. Bodenheimer, *The Oregon Health Plan*, at 654.

cosmetic and the therapeutic is also often blurred; for example, short stature may be treated by payors either as a medical condition or as a normal variation in physical appearance. Finally, open questions remain about whether emotional and even social considerations should come into play in defining a normal state of "health."[12]

c. Individual and Collective Terms

A final tension lurks in the definition of both "experimental" and "medically necessary": namely, that these terms can be understood at either the individual or the collective level. The quality of a decision-maker's ultimate determination whether a treatment is experimental or medically necessary is naturally limited by the state of medical knowledge and the existence of research at the time of decision, as well as by the often ad hoc balancing that must occur in individual cases. Thus, for example, while medical necessity often pertains to individual patients and their unique medical circumstances, the term is also used on the programmatic level to designate services that are reimbursable. Alternately, therapies may be experimental in all cases, because new and untested, or they may be well-tested but used for new types of indications or patients, and therefore not reimbursable.

Because of the individualized nature of judicial decision-making, the tension between the individual and the collective becomes particularly acute when courts are tasked with making medical necessity determinations. Courts tend to focus on the individual patient before them in discerning whether a particular therapy is experimental, weighing the costs of the therapy against the benefits to that one person.[13] Indeed, in countries that recognize a constitutional right to health, this problem can have significant economic implications. In countries such as Brazil and Colombia, for example, courts have been flooded with individual claims for access to particular therapies, resulting in serious financial impacts for those healthcare systems.[14] Multiple individual courts were tasked with deciding individuals' particular needs, without national-level coordination or the ability to conduct a cost-benefit analysis on a systemic scale. In South Africa, by contrast, the courts have recognized a right to health but have created a wide realm of discretion for government regulators in determining which therapies are required, so as to avoid the problem of the judicial branch allocating scarce medical resources in a way that undermines broader policy objectives adopted by the political branches.

[12] For example, "health" is sometimes defined in the United States to include mental and emotional health, as well as social factors. Doe v. Bolton, 410 U.S. 179, 192 (1973); United States v. Vuitch, 402 U.S. 62, 71–72 (1971). In international human rights scholarship, much attention is given to the role played by social determinants in achieving a state of health. *See, e.g.*, Thana Cristina de Campos, *Health as a Basic Human Need: Would This Be Enough?*, 40 J.L. MED. & ETHICS 251, 252 (2012).

[13] Saver, *Reimbursing New Technologies*, at 1113–1114 (discussing *Rollo v. Blue Cross-Blue Shield of New Jersey*, 1990 WL 312647 (D.N.J. Mar. 22, 1990)).

[14] Leonardo Cubillos et al., *Universal Coverage and Litigation in Latin America*, 26 J. HEALTH ORG. & MGMT. 390, 395, 401–402 (2012) (noting that, in 2009, one municipality in Brazil spent 16% of its entire health budget to treat eighty-six new patients as a result of litigation, and that Colombia used 5% of its national health budget to pay for individual right-to-healthcare suits).

II History

Protection of public health and safety has long been considered the core function of the state; indeed, it is arguably the raison d'être of the state itself.[15] But because the professionalization of medicine is a relatively recent phenomenon, and because the line between dangerous quackery and legitimate, proven treatment was, for a long time, relatively blurry, governments in the United States did not take an active role in regulating medical therapies until the early twentieth century.[16] The Pure Food and Drug Act, predecessor to the federal Food, Drug, and Cosmetic Act (FDCA), was passed in 1906. The act provided the Bureau of Chemistry in the Department of Agriculture—later named the Food and Drug Administration (FDA)—with enforcement powers over adulterated and misbranded drugs that moved in interstate commerce. While fairly limited in scope at the outset, the FDA's powers increased with the passage of the FD&C Act in 1938, which was at least partly a response to the widespread problem of false therapeutic claims, which were not regulated by the earlier statute, resulting in serious harm to individuals who ingested unregulated medications. The focus of the new statute was on requiring premarket approval of drugs, along with proper labeling.

Though the FD&C Act has largely retained the same form since 1938, the history of regulation of new and experimental therapies had, in some respects, only begun in that year. After World War II, the world learned of the horrific involuntary experiments conducted on prisoners by Nazi doctors, which led to the promulgation of the Nuremberg Code. The code is a set of ten principles for the ethical conduct of medical research that was initially formulated as part of the American judges' verdict in trial of the Nazi doctors for war crimes. Though never acknowledged as binding law, the Nuremberg Code's influence—particularly its emphasis on informed consent as the centerpiece of ethical research—has extended into U.S. law and research regulations, as well as other international documents. For example, it is the basis for the Helsinki Declaration, which also grew out of World War II but was not officially adopted by the World Medical Association until 1964. Drawing in part on the Helsinki Declaration, but also in response to pressing need and ethical concerns raised by the HIV/AIDS crisis of the 1980s and 1990s, the Council for International Organizations of Medical Sciences (CIOMS), an affiliate of the World Health Organization (WHO), issued the International Ethical Guidelines for Biomedical Research Involving Human Subjects.

The history of the regulation of new and experimental therapies is thus, to a great extent, a history of responding to medical, political, and moral crises. These crises have called on physicians to consider the responsibilities created by their twin roles as healers, who must focus on the individual patient, and researchers, who must focus on improving the health of the population at large. Indeed, government regulators and nongovernmental entities promulgating rules of scientific research ethics share these same goals: protecting individuals, on the one hand, and improving overall health and medical knowledge on the other. The resulting principles have therefore tried to mediate the tension between individuals and the

[15] *See, e.g.*, Wendy E. Parmet, *From* Slaughter-House *to* Lochner: *The Rise and Fall of the Constitutionalization of Public Health*, 40 AM. J. LEGAL HIST. 476, 478–479 (1996).

[16] *See, e.g.*, Maxwell J. Mehlman, *Quackery*, 31 AM. J.L. & MED. 349, 350 (2005).

population by affirming that individuals cannot be treated as mere instruments to serve the greater good, stressing instead the protection of individual autonomy through voluntary participation in research. Later, the research ethics principles, like U.S. law, came to include a requirement of peer review and approval of research protocols (for example, through institutional review boards) as an additional procedural safeguard.

III Challenges

Because life-saving therapies are often both expensive and lacking in assurances of safety and efficacy, they raise numerous challenges for regulators and policy-makers. One of the most widely discussed challenges is distributive justice: by what means should we decide who gets access to these expensive drugs, given limited societal healthcare resources? In addition, the newness of the therapies and the often desperate situations in which patients find themselves may raise questions about the ability of patients to give fully informed consent to new and experimental treatments. The opportunity to undergo experimental treatments may thus pose a threat to patient autonomy. At the same time, regulatory and financial barriers that put innovative therapies off limits may pose a threat to patient autonomy from the opposite direction: they may leave patients unable to exercise true autonomy in healthcare decision-making. Finally, new and experimental therapies raise questions concerning the institutional competency of government regulators and other governmental decision-makers, who are often, but not always, the gatekeepers that control access to new therapies.

a. Equity and Distributive Justice

Innovative therapies sharply raise a problem that afflicts healthcare more generally as well: determining the proper allocation of scarce healthcare resources. Some treatments are so expensive that only the wealthiest individuals could afford to pay for them out-of-pocket; for all others, private or public insurers will inevitably be forced to make rationing decisions. Such a system sets up the specter of distributing life-saving healthcare on the basis of wealth—an unappealing notion, to say the least.[17] Health disparities due to economic inequality are particularly stark in the developing world, for example, in part due to the economic incentives that drive the pricing structure of pharmaceuticals.[18] Thus, some degree of rationing seems to be both a useful and an inevitable way of dealing with limited healthcare resources.

[17] Indeed, the Canadian province of Québec attempted to avoid this problem and ensure that healthcare resources would be distributed primarily on the basis of need rather than wealth, by adopting prohibitions on private insurance for healthcare services. Those prohibitions were held unconstitutional by the Canadian Supreme Court in *Chaoulli v. Québec*, [2005] 1 S.C.R. 791 (Can.).

[18] Anand Grover, Brian Citro, Mihir Mankad, & Fiona Lander, *Pharmaceutical Companies and Global Lack of Access to Medicines: Strengthening Accountability under the Right to Health*, 40 J.L. Med. & Ethics 234, 235 (2012).

Yet, rationing is itself controversial. Indeed, Oregon's prioritized list for Medicaid coverage provoked controversy when it was first established, because it was viewed as an instance of healthcare rationing, particularly for the poor. Full-fledged embrace of a rationing regime would seem to fly in the face of an implicit but widely embraced moral imperative to preserve human life at any cost, without making distinctions respecting quality of life.[19] Even setting this fundamental moral impulse aside, or assuming a just and egalitarian method of rationing could be identified, skepticism about the competence and motives of the rationers—whether government agencies or private insurers—further complicates the possibility of rationing in a transparent fashion. Finally, it must be noted that rationing itself entails significant political, social, and administrative costs.[20]

b. Autonomy

New and innovative therapies also create challenges for patient autonomy. Truly informed consent can be elusive even under optimal conditions, but patients in desperate circumstances, faced with incomplete information about new or experimental treatment options, are particularly ill-situated to make fully informed choices.[21] Indeed, the flip side of patient autonomy to choose medical treatment is the need to protect patients from untested and possibly unregulated drugs and procedures.

In the United States, a complex regulatory regime attempts to ensure that informed consent is achieved as fully as possible in certain contexts, such as federally funded clinical research involving human subjects.[22] But not all experimental treatment occurs within those confines. For example, in 2005, private physicians developed a nonsurgical therapy using stem cells, which they used to treat orthopedic pain and degeneration. Until the federal Food and Drug Administration successfully sought to exercise jurisdiction over the stem cell procedure, it was practiced without any regulatory oversight.[23]

Autonomy concerns may arise in the context of clinical trials, as well. Patients have begun militating for continued access to experimental and unapproved drugs even after the end of the trial, for example—a problem that is largely unaddressed by research regulations in the United States.[24] Patients often reasonably expect that, at least when they receive a benefit from the drug, they will be allowed to continue it indefinitely after the trial is complete. Indeed, in some cases, informed consent documents and research protocols explicitly

[19] *See, e.g.*, Elhauge, *Allocating Health Care Morally*, at 1457.

[20] Maxwell J. Mehlman, *Rationing Expensive Lifesaving Medical Treatments*, 1985 WIS. L. REV. 239.

[21] *See, e.g.*, George J. Annas, *Faith (Healing), Hope and Charity at the FDA: The Politics of AIDS Drug Trials*, 34 VILL. L. REV. 771, 775–778 (1989).

[22] *See, e.g., Protection of Human Subjects*, 45 C.F.R. § 46 (2005), *available at* http://www.hhs.gov/ohrp/humansubjects/guidance/45cfr46.html. *See also Informed Consent of Human Subjects*, 21 C.F.R. § 50.20 (2011), *available at* http://www.gpo.gov/fdsys/pkg/CFR-2000-title21-vol1/content-detail.html.

[23] United States v. Regenerative Sciences, LLC, 741 F.3d 1314, 1317–1318 (D.C. Cir. 2014).

[24] Richard S. Saver, *At the End of the Clinical Trial: Does Access to Investigational Technology End as Well?*, 31 W. NEW ENG. L. REV. 411, 426 (2009). However, FDA regulations do contain provisions for "compassionate use," allowing access to unapproved drugs by individuals with severe or life-threatening conditions and no other suitable treatment options. *See Expanded Access to Investigational Drugs for Treatment Use*, 21 C.F.R. § 312.300 (2009).

promise continuing access to the therapies that prove beneficial.[25] Relatedly, in the case of *Abigail Alliance for Better Access to Developmental Drugs v. Von Eschenbach*, terminally ill patients who were not themselves participants in clinical trials unsuccessfully sought access to experimental drugs that had not yet completed the FDA testing and approval process, based in part on their constitutional autonomy rights.[26] Thus, the need to respect autonomy gives rise to potentially conflicting demands in this context—requiring protection of patients who may not be well positioned to provide fully informed consent but eschewing paternalism toward terminally ill patients who have little left to lose and wish to take their chances on a possibly beneficial therapy.

c. Institutional Competency and the Role of Government

Determining the proper role of government actors in regulating access to experimental and innovative therapies also presents challenges. Even bracketing the problems raised by rationing, there are other ways in which the various government institutions responsible for setting the conditions and limits of access to experimental drugs and therapies may lack the competency to do so. To begin with, courts are regularly called upon to decide on insurance coverage of experimental treatments. They may also have to decide whether patients have a right to access experimental drugs outside of the clinical trial context, whether on contract, estoppel, or constitutional theories. Yet, as noted above, judicial decision-making is unavoidably ad hoc and particularized; judges can only decide the case before them, and the broader public health and public policy consequences of permitting access to an unapproved therapy in a particular instance may fall into the background, as the suffering of an individual plaintiff is foregrounded. Moreover, judges are famously generalists and therefore possibly ill-equipped to analyze highly technical medical or epidemiological information. Finally, the quality of the decision-making is dependent on the quality of the evidence before the court, which in turn depends upon the abilities and motivation of the attorneys in any given case.

A logical solution may be to devolve decision-making to specialized agencies; however, this solution is also imperfect. Though they possess relevant technical expertise, agencies are susceptible to charges of capture and even political bias. For example, political controversy attended FDA decision-making about the over-the-counter availability of emergency contraception, as evidence-based decisions about the drug's availability made by scientists within the agency were twice overruled by political appointees.[27] Similar

[25] *See, e.g.*, Abney v. Amgen, Inc., 443 F.3d 540, 544 (6th Cir. 2006); *see also* Saver, *At the End of the Clinical Trial*, at 429.

[26] 495 F.3d 695, 717 (D.C. Cir. 2007) (Rogers, J., dissenting).

[27] In 2005, the FDA commissioner delayed making emergency contraception available over the counter despite a positive recommendation by the FDA's Center for Drug Evaluation and Research. Susan F. Wood, *The Role of Science in Health Policy Decision-Making: The Case of Emergency Contraception*, 17 HEALTH MATRIX 273, 284 (2007). Then, in 2011, the director of the Department of Health and Human Services overruled the FDA's decision that the drug could be made available over the counter to minors. Gardiner Harris, *Plan to Widen Availability of Morning-After Pill Is Rejected*, N.Y. TIMES, Dec. 11, 2011, *available at* http://www.nytimes.com/2011/12/08/health/policy/sebelius-overrules-fda-on-freer-sale-of-emergency-contraceptives.html?_r=0.

charges of political decision-making have surrounded the repeated rejection of petitions to reschedule cannabis as a less-restricted drug under federal law. Growing discontent has led to the adoption of ballot initiatives in several states making marijuana legal for medical uses, and in some cases for nonmedical uses, despite the continuing federal prohibition.

To allay concerns about the competence and incentives of the various institutions involved, an alternate model would be to loosen regulation and leave availability of new therapies to the market to decide, at least to a significant degree. However, market incentives are particularly skewed in this context, such that they are highly unlikely to result in a fair or efficient allocation of healthcare resources. For example, patients receiving an experimental drug in the context of a clinical trial may have an incentive to continue the therapy after the end of an inconclusive trial if they believe the drug has been beneficial; the drug's manufacturer, however, may lack an incentive to make the drug available if its therapeutic applications turn out to be too limited to make it profitable. Patients, particularly those in dire circumstances, tend to be relatively inattentive to cost, as are their physicians, whereas manufacturers are arguably overly attentive to economic concerns. Moreover, pharmaceutical companies stand to gain much more from selling costly, highly profitable drugs to wealthy and insured patients in the developed world than from dealing with the most pressing public health concerns. Thus, the vast majority of private research and development dollars are currently directed toward illnesses that account for only a very small percentage of the global disease burden.[28]

IV Frameworks

Within American law, there are the multiple approaches to the problems posed by new, experimental, and life-saving therapies. Each approach grapples with the problems described above, though each emphasizes some over others, with greater or lesser degrees of success in resolving them. First, the constitutional framework focuses on a "negative right to health" or a right to "medical self-defense"; it is primarily concerned with circumscribing the role of the government in mediating access to potentially beneficial therapies. The public health framework, by contrast, emphasizes the role of the state in protecting the health and safety of the populace over individual rights claims; this approach to regulation may best be described as "biopolitical," to borrow a term from Michel Foucault, meaning that it views one of the primary functions of the state to be the management of individuals' health, physical capacity, and reproduction[29]. Finally, the ethics and human rights frameworks attempt to combine distributive justice and positive rights of access with respect for individual autonomy. Since no one approach dominates, conflicts over healthcare allocation continue to play out simultaneously on the national political stage, as well as in individual judicial fora.

[28] Grover et al., *Pharmaceutical Companies and Global Lack of Access to Medicines*, at 235.

[29] Michel Foucault, 1 The History of Sexuality 135–159 (Robert Hurley trans., 1978).

a. The Constitutional Framework

American constitutional law has long resisted recognizing positive rights or entitlements to government services flowing from the existence of constitutional rights. It has, however, implicitly recognized a right to make medical treatment decisions—or at least some of them—free from governmental interference.[30] Alternately, the right can be conceived as a right to "medical self-defense," with affiliations to the common-law and now constitutional self-defense right, when one's life or health is seriously threatened.[31]

The existence of this right has long been assumed, even if its contours are unclear. Indeed, some of the earliest individual rights claims to be asserted in the twentieth century involved a claimed right to resist compulsory vaccination, often because of fears about vaccination's health effects, and to make medical care decisions free from governmental interference.[32] In *Cruzan v. Director, Missouri Department of Health*, the U.S. Supreme Court obliquely acknowledged the existence of a constitutional right to refuse medical treatment, finding its origins in the common-law recognition of unwanted treatment as a battery or as a violation of informed consent.[33]

The right to access experimental or life-saving treatments may be inferred from this constitutional right, together with the more general substantive due process right to privacy. Indeed, the early cases identifying a right to privacy and autonomy—that is, a right to freedom from governmental interference in important personal decisions involving procreation—arose, after all, in the context of medical decision-making. In particular, *Roe v. Wade*'s emphasis on the medical aspects of abortion has been widely noted; *Roe* can thus be understood as a case about, among other things, the constitutional right to access medical treatment and make health-related decisions autonomously. Even more to the point, an unbroken line of abortion cases from *Roe* onward has recognized that women have a right to choose abortion, even after the fetus is viable, when the procedure is necessary to preserve her life or health.[34] Given that the state's interest in a viable fetus is considered to be compelling, the fact that the woman's right to protect her own health is sufficient to overcome that state interest indicates that the right is an extraordinarily robust one.

The question remains, however, how far this right extends. Courts have generally proven unsympathetic to other sorts of claims by plaintiffs seeking to assert a right to access a particular therapy in the face of legal prohibitions. As discussed in section IV.b., the persistence of the public health approach may be one reason for this. Thus, claims for access to

[30] *See, e.g.*, B. Jessie Hill, *The Constitutional Right to Make Medical Treatment Decision: A Tale of Two Doctrines*, 86 TEX. L. REV 277 (2007); John A. Robertson, *Embryo Culture and the "Culture of Life": Constitutional Issues in the Embryonic Stem Cell Debate*, 2006 U. CHI. LEGAL F. 1 (2006).

[31] District of Columbia v. Heller, 554 U.S. 570, 635 (2008) (recognizing a constitutional right to possess a handgun for self-defense); Eugene Volokh, *Medical Self-Defense, Prohibited Experimental Therapies, and Payment for Organs*, 120 HARV. L. REV. 1813 (2007).

[32] MICHAEL WILLRICH, POX: AN AMERICAN HISTORY 14 (2011).

[33] Cruzan v. Director, Mo. Dep't of Health, 497 U.S. 261, 277–279 (1990).

[34] Although the Supreme Court declined to strike down a federal law banning a particular abortion procedure for lack of a health exception in *Gonzales v. Carhart*, 550 U.S. 124 (2007), it upheld the law only because it found that facial invalidation would be inappropriate in light of medical disagreement over whether the procedure was ever medically indicated, *id.* at 163. It nonetheless assumed that any abortion regulation creating significant health risks for women would be unconstitutional. *Id.* at 161.

experimental and unapproved therapies such as medical marijuana and laetrile (or amygdalin, a substance found in apricot pits believed by some to be a treatment for cancer) were consistently turned away without any serious credence being given to the constitutional claims at issue. Nonetheless, advocates continue to present claims of a constitutional right to access medical treatment without government interference. In the closely watched *Abigail Alliance* case, the plaintiffs claimed a substantive due process right to access new drugs that had completed only the first stage of clinical trials. Although the D.C. Circuit court of appeals initially recognized "a right of terminally ill patients to make an informed decision that may prolong life," it later reversed itself.[35] Rather than weighing the patients' interests in health and bodily integrity against the asserted state interests in ensuring the drugs' safety and efficacy, the court simply held that there was no constitutional right to access unapproved drugs.[36] Thus, this constitutional right remains one of uncertain standing.

Of the various challenges for dealing with access to experimental treatments, the constitutional framework is most clearly focused on autonomy. It generally balances individuals' interest in protecting their health and making important healthcare choices without government interference against the state's interests, such as the state interest in ensuring the safety and efficacy of drugs that are made available to the public. In *Cruzan*, a case dealing with whether care should be continued for a patient in a persistent vegetative state when some evidence indicated that she would have wanted care to be terminated, the Supreme Court explicitly balanced the individual's right to refuse health care against the state's interests in protecting vulnerable individuals[37]. Similarly, the original panel in *Abigail Alliance* clearly contemplated such balancing—a balancing that could ultimately weigh against access to unapproved drugs that had completed only the first phase of clinical trials.[38] Given the relatively sparse jurisprudence on this issue and the fact that every claim of access to unapproved medicines has ultimately been rejected by the courts, it is difficult to say exactly how the constitutional balance would be struck, if courts were to recognize a right to protect one's health outside the reproductive health context. Beyond concerns about the safety and efficacy of particular drugs—concerns that are arguably minimal with respect to terminally ill patients for whom all other therapies have failed—the balancing would have to take account of the broader risks posed by access to experimental therapies outside the clinical trial context. In particular, it might be argued that patients would have little incentive to participate in clinical trials, in which they may be assigned to the control group that receives only a placebo rather than the potentially efficacious drug, if they can gain access to the drug through constitutional litigation. If patients no longer sign up for clinical trials, the entire system for testing and approval of new drugs could unravel. Such concerns may be sufficient to outweigh any individual interest in accessing unapproved drugs, except in the most extreme circumstances.

[35] Abigail Alliance for Better Access to Developmental Drugs & Washington Legal Found. v. von Eschenbach, 445 F.3d 470, 477 (D.C. Cir. 2006), *vacated on reh'g en banc sub nom.* Abigail Alliance for Better Access to Developmental Drugs v. von Eschenbach, 495 F.3d 695 (D.C. Cir. 2007).

[36] Abigail Alliance for Better Access to Developmental Drugs v. von Eschenbach, 495 F.3d 695, 707 (D.C. Cir. 2007).

[37] *Cruzan v. Dir., Missouri Dep't of Health*, 497 U.S. 261, 279 (1990).

[38] *Id.* at 715 (Rogers, J., dissenting) (citing *Abigail Alliance*, 445 F.3d 470, 486 (D.C. Cir. 2006), vacated upon grant of rehearing en banc by *Abigail Alliance*, 495 F.3d 695).

Because the U.S. constitutional framework is a negative one, equality concerns are not directly addressed: there is no affirmative right to government assistance or subsidy for healthcare in the negative model, which comprises only a right to avoid government interference with healthcare decisions. Although equal protection norms would generally forbid discriminatory distribution of healthcare resources along racial, ethnic, religious, or gender lines, ability to pay is largely irrelevant to the constitutional framework. Thus, if patients are unable to access needed healthcare due to a lack of financial resources, the constitutional framework will not provide a basis for relief: it is the individual's own indigence, not government action, that creates the obstacle to access.[39]

Finally, the constitutional framework implicitly assumes that the institution most suited to decide individual access claims is the judiciary. Constitutional rights claims by nature call on the courts as ultimate arbiters, since successful constitutional claims trump law enacted by the legislature. Thus, the question whether a constitutional right to make medical treatment decisions should be recognized impliedly raises the question whether the judiciary is the right institution to make decisions about access to experimental or life-saving therapies. Institutional-competence questions such as these tend to be underemphasized in constitutional argument, however, in favor of argument about the normative desirability of the substantive right itself.[40]

b. The Public Health Framework

Coexisting with the constitutional framework is the public health framework, which emphasizes the police power of the state and the government's traditional role in safeguarding the public's health and safety. Included within that traditional role, virtually since the beginning of modern medicine, is the power to regulate medical practice and practitioners. Thus, U.S. law has long placed claims of access to medical therapies in the context of the broad power and discretion granted to the state to decide best how to protect the public. This tradition coexists uncomfortably alongside the more recent recognition of a constitutional right to make certain medical treatment decisions.

The early twentieth-century case of *Jacobson v. Massachusetts* exemplifies the public health framework. In that case, Henning Jacobson had refused to be vaccinated against smallpox, despite a city ordinance requiring virtually universal vaccination and imposing criminal penalties for refusal. He claimed that the Constitution gave him the right "to care for his own body and health in such way as to him seems best."[41] The U.S. Supreme Court flatly rejected this individual rights claim, focusing instead on the state's power to protect the public. Taking a population view rather than an individual rights view, the Court insisted that "the rights of the individual in respect of his liberty may at times, under the pressure of great dangers, be subjected to such restraint, to be enforced by reasonable regulations, as the safety of the general public may demand."[42] The claim of the individual simply gave way in the face of a claim of public necessity; no meaningful balancing or scrutiny was required.

[39] *See* Maher v. Roe, 432 U.S. 464, 474 (1977).

[40] *See generally* Andrew B. Coan, *Is There a Constitutional Right to Select the Genes of One's Offspring?*, 63 HASTINGS L.J. 233 (2011).

[41] Jacobson v. Commonwealth of Massachusetts, 197 U.S. 11, 26 (1905).

[42] *Id.* at 29.

This line of thinking persists in American law, though little effort has been made to reconcile it with the constitutional framework. For example, in *Eisenstadt v. Baird*, the case in which the Supreme Court recognized the right of unmarried persons to access contraceptives and the "right of the *individual*, married or single, to be free from unwarranted governmental intrusion into matters so fundamentally affecting a person as the decision whether to bear or beget a child," the dissent embraced the public health view.[43] Chief Justice Burger emphasized the state's traditional role and prerogative in regulating medicine and protecting health.[44] Similarly, the lower court in *Griswold v. Connecticut* had dismissed the claim of a constitutional right to access contraception, stating, "[C]ourts may not interfere with the exercise by a state of the police power to conserve the public safety and welfare . . . if the law has a real and substantial relation to the accomplishment of those objects. The legislature is primarily the judge of the regulations required. . . . "[45]

Claims of access to experimental and unapproved therapies are mostly treated under this public health framework, as demonstrated by the Supreme Court's cursory dismissal of patients' claimed right to access to laetrile in *United States v. Rutherford*.[46] Suits for access to cannabis for medical use and to drugs that have passed only Phase I clinical trials have been treated similarly by lower courts.[47]

Several features characterize the public health approach. The public health approach is *biopolitical* in nature; it views the primary purpose of the state as both protecting and managing human health and physical well-being.[48] The public health approach operates primarily at the population level: biopolitics, like public health but in contrast to the constitutional framework, focuses primarily on statistics and large groups, not individuals and their particular health needs.[49] Moreover, the biopolitical public health framework is not merely a negative one, intent on preventing harm and disease. It is also a *positive* approach to governing, explicitly concerned with improving health and lengthening the average lifespan and quality of life.[50] Thus, for example, the public health approach to access to experimental therapies emphasizes the role of the FDA in protecting the public from unsafe and ineffective drugs, but it is also attentive to the FDA's role in facilitating the approval of new drugs to improve health, which must be protected by avoiding any approach that would permit widespread access to unapproved drugs outside the carefully controlled clinical trial process or its limited exceptions, such as compassionate use.

[43] Eisenstadt v. Baird, 405 U.S. 438, 453 (1972). [44] *Id.* at 465–472 (Burger, C.J., dissenting).

[45] State v. Griswold, 200 A.2d 479, 480 (1964), *rev'd*, 381 U.S. 479 (1965).

[46] 442 U.S. 544 (1979).

[47] *See, e.g.*, Abigail Alliance for Better Access to Developmental Drugs v. von Eschenbach, 495 F.3d 695 (D.C. Cir. 2007); Raich v. Gonzales, 500 F.3d 850, 864–866 (9th Cir. 2007).

[48] Michel Foucault, 1 The History of Sexuality 135–159 (Robert Hurley trans., 1978).

[49] *See, e.g.*, Lawrence O. Gostin, Public Health Law: Power, Duty, Restraint 11–14 (2000). Indeed, Foucault suggests that the birth of the rights to privacy and bodily integrity are themselves a response to the rise of the biopolitical state. Those claimed rights are a reaction—but stated in the government's own language, the language of rights—against the state's seizure of control over the body and human life through its new comprehensive biopolitics. *Supra* note 48, at 145.

[50] Gostin, Public Health Law, at 327 ("The field of public health is purposive and interventionist. It does not settle for existing conditions of health, but actively seeks effective techniques for identifying and reducing health threats.").

Thus, in contrast to the constitutional framework, the public health framework minimizes the importance of individual autonomy in favor of protecting the public.[51] The principal autonomy concern for the public health framework is that of ensuring that meaningful informed consent to experimental treatment can be obtained in the face of patients' desperation, their possibly unrealistic expectations of miracle cures and, occasionally, political rhetoric that overstates the benefits and understates the potential harm of experimental drugs.[52]

However, the public health approach is more likely than the constitutional framework to be attentive to concerns of equity and distributive justice, albeit not always explicitly. Because the public health framework is concerned with the distribution of healthcare resources across a population, the primary goal is to determine how resources may be allocated most effectively—that is, to identify the allocation of resources that will provide the largest public health benefit per governmental dollar spent. Unsurprisingly, such an approach would tend to disfavor expensive and untested new therapies and favor alleviating the most common and most treatable diseases in the developing world.[53] Given that decisions must be made on a population level rather than on an individual case-by-case basis, questions about the fairest allocation of resources are easily built into the public health calculus.

The public health approach, too, includes certain implicit assumptions about which institutions are best suited to make decisions regarding access to experimental and life-saving medical treatment. The biopolitical state is heavily reliant on more or less independent agencies to gather, study, and analyze vast amounts of data, embracing the disciplines of epidemiology and demography, among others. Thus, the public health framework gives priority to the FDA and other specialized agencies in the functions of coordinating and implementing access to new and innovative therapies. Additionally, the legislative arm of the state retains the power and duty to protect the public health. However, the judiciary and the various players in the marketplace—pharmaceuticals manufacturers, physicians, and patients—are seen as too limited and individualized in their focus to make decisions that will best serve the collective good; as such, their decision-making must be subject to oversight. For this reason, too, individual rights are often given less weight than the state's interests in health and safety.

Finally, the public health framework has traditionally assumed a second kind of institutional division of labor. It assumes a federalist approach to protecting health: the state is charged with the regulation of the medical profession and medical practice, whereas the federal government regulates the sale and marketing of innovative drugs and devices that move in interstate commerce. This has long been the classic structure of American health regulation. Yet, there is reason to doubt the durability of this traditional model. The adoption of the Affordable Care Act, including the expansion of Medicaid, appears to have enlarged the federal government's role in the regulation and delivery of healthcare. At the same time, recent cases recognize a wide scope for federal preemption of state laws by means of federal

[51] *See, e.g.*, Wendy E. Parmet, *Public Health and Constitutional Law: Recognizing the Relationship*, 10 J. Health Care L. & Pol'y 13, 23 (2007) ("One quick, but I think ultimately unsatisfactory, answer is that the interdependency of risk demonstrated by epidemiology argues for the need for constitutional law to give less weight to 'individual rights' and more leeway for government actions taken in the name of public health.").

[52] Annas, *Faith (Healing), Hope and Charity at the FDA*, at 782–788.

[53] *Cf.* Christopher T. Robertson, *The Presumption Against Expensive Health Care Consumption*, 49 Tulsa L. Rev. 101 (2014).

labeling and safety standards.[54] Thus, it may be that the future of federalism in healthcare is uncertain.

c. The Ethics and Human Rights Frameworks

The ethics and human rights framework in fact comprises two related approaches, both of which are fundamentally concerned with fairness and with the dignity of the individual. The ethics framework, which dominates the field of bioethics in the United States, is built around four fundamental principles: autonomy, beneficence, nonmaleficence, and justice.[55] These principles, too, arguably originated with the Nuremberg Code. The first of the ten Nuremberg Code principles is that the patient must voluntarily consent to the experiment; this aligns with the bioethics principle of respect for patient autonomy. Similarly, the Nuremberg Code embodies the principle of beneficence by requiring that experiments must benefit society and cannot be random or unnecessary. Finally, several of the Nuremberg Code requirements forbid causing harm to the subject; this aligns with the nonmaleficence principle. Thus, the origins of bioethics appear to lie in human rights concerns about protecting patients in the context of experimental therapies.

While compatible with the ethics framework, the human rights approach tends to take a more international perspective, considering the global impact of particular health policy decisions with respect to experimental therapies. The human rights approach to healthcare is characterized by the recognition of a universal right to health, understood as a positive entitlement to at least some of the elements necessary to achieving a state of health, along with the fundamental principles of equality and nondiscrimination. Thus, numerous treaties and many national constitutions drafted in the modern era specify a right to health, which is generally understood to mean a right "of everyone to the highest attainable standard of physical and mental health."[56] This may imply a right of access to some life-saving treatments and some experimental treatments outside the context of clinical trials. In addition, the emphasis on the right "of everyone" to health denotes a requirement of moral fairness in the allocation of healthcare resources. However, one of the difficulties in fulfilling the promise of the human right to health is precisely the indeterminacy and potential breadth of the term "health."

With respect to innovative, experimental, and life-saving therapies, the human rights framework is represented by numerous documents including the Nuremberg Code, the Helsinki Declaration, the U.N. Universal Declaration on Bioethics and Human Rights, and the U.N. Human Rights Guidelines for Pharmaceutical Companies, in Relation to Access

[54] *See, e.g.*, Mut. Pharm. Co. v. Bartlett, 133 S. Ct. 2466 (2013) (holding that a patient's state tort law claim based on inadequate warning of a generic drug's dangers was preempted by federal labeling regulations, which prohibited unilateral alternation of a drug label); PLIVA, Inc. v. Mensing, 131 S. Ct. 2567 (2011) (finding preemption of state-law claims for brand-name drugs based on federally approved drug label); Riegel v. Medtronic, 128 S. Ct. 999 (2008) (holding that common-law claims against a medical device manufacturer were preempted by FDA requirements); *But see* Wyeth v. Levine, 183 Vt. 76, 944 A.2d 179 (2006), *cert. granted*, 129 S. Ct. 1887 (2008) (holding that state law failure-to-warn claims were not preempted by federal law).

[55] Beauchamp & Childress, Principles of Biomedical Ethics 12–13 (6th ed. 2009).

[56] *See, e.g.*, Campos, *Health as a Basic Human Need*, at 252.

to Medicines. As the last document in particular indicates, the human rights obligation to safeguard the right to health is not limited to states; private parties such as pharmaceutical manufacturers share in this duty. In addition, those documents share, in common with the ethics framework, a focus on protecting patient autonomy and well-being.

Because of its global focus, the human rights framework is particularly relevant to controversies involving experimental therapies abroad. For example, the rise of medical tourism, in which patients travel abroad for medical treatment, may result in profound healthcare inequities. Patients may engage in medical tourism to access procedures they would be prohibited from accessing in their home country (for example, in vitro fertilization, stem cell therapies, or experimental drugs), or in order to access healthcare services that may be legal in their home country but so expensive as to be out of reach. Because patients from developed countries who travel to developing countries are usually willing and able to pay a much higher price for medical services than the destination country's residents, healthcare providers have an incentive to serve as many tourists as possible, while limiting the care provided at a lower cost to their fellow citizens. In addition, the lucrative practice of medical tourism may even result in poorer nations investing public dollars in expensive, cutting-edge healthcare technologies that will inevitably be beyond the financial reach of their citizens.[57]

Another pressing controversy to which the ethics and human rights framework is often applied is the conduct of clinical trials abroad—particularly clinical trials of new drugs by U.S. or European pharmaceutical researchers in the developing world. In some cases, researchers have been accused of taking advantage of another country's less patient-protective legal standards and needier patient population in order to conduct trials that would not be permissible at home. The temptation to go abroad to recruit clinical trial participants is particularly great in light of Americans' increasing reluctance to participate in clinical trials and the need for large numbers of subjects in order to pass the three phases of clinical trials required for FDA approval.[58] The practice of conducting clinical trials in developing countries raises questions about whether subjects are truly giving voluntary consent, when in many cases no other healthcare may be available for them. It also raises questions about the researchers' and manufacturers' duty to extend post-trial access to subjects who otherwise have little or no access to effective treatment. Finally, standards for the ethical design of clinical trials in developing countries must be considered. For example, federally sponsored researchers controversially conducted placebo-controlled trials of a drug to reduce mother-to-child transmission of HIV in developing countries in Africa, Asia, and the Caribbean. The use of placebos was ethically questionable, because another effective (but expensive) treatment was known.[59]

Because the human rights and ethics frameworks foreground equality and distributive justice, controversies concerning medical tourism and clinical trials in the developing world must be resolved with a goal of recognizing human dignity and the equal entitlement of all

[57] I. Glenn Cohen, *Medical Tourism, Access to Health Care, and Global Justice*, 52 VA. J. INT'L L. 1, 3–5 (2011).

[58] *See generally* Adam H. Laughton, *Somewhere to Run, Somewhere to Hide?: International Regulation of Human Subjects Experimentation*, 18 DUKE J. COMP. & INT'L L. 181 (2007).

[59] *See* Peter Lurie & Sidney M. Wolfe, *Unethical Trials of Interventions to Reduce Perinatal Transmission of the Human Immunodeficiency Virus in Developing Countries*, 337 NEW ENG. J. MED. 853 (1997).

persons to a standard of health, however defined. For example, denying post-trial access to drugs arguably constitutes exploitation of trial subjects—treating them "as mere means to the end of testing a drug."[60] This is especially true in cases where the therapy being tested, if proven effective, is likely to be unaffordable for the vast majority citizens of the country in which it was tested. In Brazil, which recognizes a fundamental constitutional right to health, courts have thus enforced a right to post-trial access and have required pharmaceutical companies to foot the bill.[61] Furthermore, the Helsinki Declaration requires—at least presumptively—that trials be conducted in compliance with the ethical standards of both the sponsoring country and the country that is the site of the trials, as well as that placebos not be used for testing new therapies when another effective treatment exists.[62]

But at the same time, the requirements of equality and justice may not always be straightforward. Controversies over access to treatment often involve conflicting interests and incentives. For example, while post-trial access to drugs may serve the interests of justice for individual subjects, recognizing a broad right to post-trial access may undermine the entire system of randomized, controlled clinical trials. Moreover, if pharmaceutical companies are forced to bear the costs of post-trial access, they may decline to conduct trials in that country altogether; at the same time, in cases where the experimental therapy is proven to be effective but financially out of reach for most citizens, it seems unfair to award access only to certain individuals because they had the good luck to be chosen to receive it in the context of a clinical trial. Similarly, though the potentially negative consequences of medical tourism may militate in favor of heavily regulating or even outlawing it, global justice also requires recognition that host countries may benefit economically from it, and in some cases the benefits may outweigh the costs. Nonetheless, the ethics and human rights framework engages productively with these difficult questions. Moreover, some innovative solutions have been proposed or adopted, such as compulsory drug licensing, which is already in use in numerous countries, and the Health Impact Fund, which would provide financial rewards for drug companies whose products have a meaningfully positive global health impact.

Autonomy is an equally important value in the ethics and human rights frameworks. Because of the ethics and human rights frameworks' attentiveness to global disparities in wealth and bargaining power, they also recognize that autonomy is inextricably intertwined with the values of equality and justice. This concern is particularly visible in the overriding focus of the Nuremberg Code, the Helsinki Declaration, and other such documents on informed consent and preventing exploitation of vulnerable populations. In general, the human rights approach combines robust protection for individual autonomy in the form of a right to access necessary healthcare—essentially, both a negative and a positive right to health—with the recognition that individual decision-making may be influenced by economic circumstances in ways that may place a particularly heavy responsibility on researchers and drug manufacturers for ensuring true and voluntary informed consent. Moreover,

[60] Daniel Wei L. Wang & Octavio Luiz Motta Ferraz, *Pharmaceutical Companies vs. the State: Who Is Responsible for Post-Trial Provision of Drugs in Brazil?*, 40 J.L. MED. & ETHICS 188, 189 (2012).

[61] *Id.*

[62] World Medical Association, *Declaration of Helsinki: Ethical Principles for Medical Research Involving Human Subjects*, paras. 10, 33, 310 JAMA 2191 (2013). The Helsinki Declaration does permit the use of a placebo in trials, even where another effective treatment exists, if there are compelling scientific reasons for doing so and there is no significant risk to patients. *Id.* para. 33.

it is at least due to the principles embraced by the ethics and human rights frameworks that the use of independent ethics committees, such as institutional review boards, is required in connection with research on human subjects. The use of such committees, which is required by the Helsinki Declaration and by federal regulations, is intended to ensure that research on human subjects is conducted ethically, with respect for the autonomy and well-being of those subjects.

Institutional competency concerns are the least comprehensively addressed challenge within the ethics and human rights frameworks. Rather, the human rights and ethics frameworks draw on a mix of courts, legislatures, international bodies, and even private actors to determine, operationalize, and regulate access to experimental and life-saving treatments. The overriding mandate is to serve the substantive ends of justice, rather than to respect preexisting institutional constraints or to maximize efficiency.

V Conclusion

In combination, the ethics and human rights frameworks are the most promising. They address all three challenges of access to new, experimental, and life-saving therapies in a comprehensive and nuanced manner, with attention to the implications of decisions about access to healthcare not just in the United States but also globally. This global focus is appealing, because it fills an apparent normative gap in the constitutional and public health frameworks. Given the increasing globalization of both the economy in general and the healthcare sector in particular, it is of pressing importance to consider how health conditions abroad impact healthcare and economics at home. In addition, an important strength of the ethics and human rights frameworks is that they combine a focus on equality with a deep concern for autonomy. The ethics and human rights frameworks insist on distributive justice, while making room for cost-benefit analysis and for creative solutions to the severe and growing problem of health disparities.

To some degree, the ethics and human rights frameworks have been embraced in American healthcare law and policy. The Affordable Care Act may be viewed as an initial step, however tentative, toward elaborating a positive statutory right to healthcare in the United States. Furthermore, widespread recognition of human rights abuses flowing from unethical, federally sponsored research—such as the syphilis experiments in Guatemala in the post-World War II era and those at home in Tuskegee, Alabama from 1932 to 1972—has led to the adoption of mandatory ethics standards for the conduct of clinical trials, including the requirement of institutional review board approval. For the most part, however, the ethics and human rights frameworks, while somewhat influential, do not command the force of law in the United States. The Nuremberg Code and Helsinki Declarations are nonbinding, and no positive constitutional right to health has been recognized.

Thus, although the ethics and human rights frameworks are the most promising solution to the pressing challenges surrounding access to experimental and life-saving therapies, they are the least likely to be adopted in the United States. Indeed, the FDA has moved away from requiring international research accepted by the agency to adhere to the relatively restrictive ethical prescriptions of the Helsinki Declaration, issuing a rule in 2009 that sanctioned the alternative, less restrictive good clinical practice (GCP) regulations created by the International Conference on Harmonisation. The GCP regulations do not address some of the issues that are particularly germane to the ethics and human rights frameworks, such as the use of placebos and post-trial access. In addition, the ethics and human rights frameworks are generally less attentive to institutional issues, such as separation of powers and institutional competency, that are often central to American legal discourse. Finally, the documents that outline the ethics and human rights approaches lack enforcement mechanisms, and positive-rights jurisprudence and rhetoric have yet to gain a foothold in the United States. Once again, politics is shown to be inseparable from healthcare.

CHAPTER 14

MENTAL HEALTH AND OTHER BEHAVIORAL HEALTH SERVICES

JOHN V. JACOBI

THE clinical and legal history of people with mental illness is one of exclusion. Mental illness was long treated as deviant, and the mad were lumped together with criminals as outcasts, housed in prisons or prison-like asylums. This exclusion was both caused by and reinforced a deep fear and distrust of people exhibiting symptoms of mental illness. Over time, mental illness gained conceptual separation from criminality and deviance. The emerging discipline of psychiatry established madness as an illness, subject to courses of clinical intervention and potential cure.

Mental illness, notwithstanding therapeutic advances, continues to be thought of as fundamentally different from somatic illness. Psychiatry is premised on a model of mental illness as susceptible of diagnosis and treatment in the same sense as are somatic conditions. Researchers have found, however, that deep suspicions of the mentally ill linger even among behavioral health professionals:

> The clinicians in our study [psychiatrists and psychologists] associated the psychological causation of mental illness with intentionality, controllability, responsibility, and blameworthiness on the part of the patient, and they tended to view behaviors with a biological etiology as unintentional, uncontrollable, not within the patient's sphere of personal responsibility, and less blameworthy.[1]

These misattributions signal that clinicians have incompletely transitioned from a relationship of blame to one of therapeutic engagement with the mentally ill. The picture is complicated by the fact that for some purposes and in some circumstances, mental illness *is* different. Just and equitable treatment of those with behavioral conditions depends on understanding where differences simply don't matter—but also where differences matter a great deal.

[1] M. Miresco & L. Kirmayer, *The Persistence of Mind-Brain Dualism in Psychiatric Reasoning About Clinical Scenarios*, 163:5 AM. J. PSYCHIATRY 913, 916–917 (2006).

Rights to personal autonomy in healthcare decision-making are nearly inviolable for most Americans, but take on a different aspect when that healthcare implicates the very impairments of cognitive processes necessary to exercise meaningful choice. Healthcare treatment itself tends to poorly serve people with behavioral health conditions, in part due to continuing separation of behavioral and physical clinical services. Treatment disparities also, however, reflect continuing fear and discomfort in this context, and the uncomfortable fact that those with behavioral health symptoms can be difficult patients. In insurance coverage, determinations of the medical necessity of treatments for behavioral health conditions can be more uncertain than such determinations for medical or surgical treatments; health insurance procedures reflect that uncertainty, but differential insurance rules seem to exceed those necessary to reflect clinical uncertainty. Legal and ethical analysis of behavioral healthcare must struggle with the imperative to assure equitable treatment for all while carefully and respectfully facing situations where difference matters.

This chapter first addresses the difficult issue of personal decision-making autonomy in the behavioral health context, where the line can blur between bias and unwarranted paternalism, on one hand, and appropriate, genuine concern for patients, on the other. It then turns to healthcare delivery challenges. American healthcare is unquestionably fragmented, and for people with mental illness, this fragmentation can be devastatingly harmful. Efforts to ensure that access to behavioral and somatic care is appropriately available and integrated is the subject of substantial effort and frustrating legal confusion. Finally, the chapter turns to the differential treatment of behavioral healthcare by health insurers, differences that are the subject of antidiscrimination and parity efforts in state and federal law. Throughout, the focus is on understanding where there are relevant differences that should drive the law of healthcare for people with behavioral health needs, and where equal treatment should simply be the order of the day.

I Personal Autonomy and the Right to Choose/Refuse Treatment

The right to direct one's own medical care is well established in American law. Even in situations where treatment is necessary to sustain life, common law and constitutional principles accord a competent adult the right to refuse that treatment. Difficult cases arise where a court has determined that a patient has lost the capacity to consent. In such cases, courts struggle with questions of discerning what the patient would choose if competent, or what course of action is in the incompetent patient's best interest. Some older cases limited the right to protect minor children who would suffer from the death of the patient. More recent cases have removed that exception, and patient autonomy to accept or reject treatment is now broadly recognized.[2] As a result, the law generally upholds patients' right to refuse treatment if they have not been declared incompetent.

[2] Application of the President and Directors of Georgetown College, 331 F.2d 1000 (D.C. Cir. 1964) is an example of a case limiting a patient's range of choices to prevent harm to her children. Fosmire v. Nicoleau, 551 N.E.2d 77 (N.Y. 1990) is an example of a more recent case rejecting that exception to the general autonomy rule. For cases on the general right to refuse treatment, *see* Bouvia v. Superior Court,

Our society and our courts have not resolved the question of whether and under what circumstances people with mental illness retain or lose that right. Confusion over the extent to which competent people with mental illness may be deprived of the right to choose their own healthcare arises in two contexts. First, the law is unsettled on whether and to what extent patients who have been involuntarily committed to a psychiatric hospital, but who have not been determined by a court to have lost decisional capacity, may be deprived of their right to direct their own medical care. Second, in many jurisdictions, autonomy rights are further curtailed through "involuntary outpatient commitment," a process by which people neither in need of institutionalization nor adjudged incompetent are deprived of decisional autonomy due to their mental illness. In both settings, the treatment is unequal; we allow people with physical illness to refuse care even if most would disagree, but we do not accord those with mental illness the same right to make apparently bad choices. It is, therefore, important to assess the validity of the differential treatment.

a. Decisional Autonomy in Psychiatric Institutions

It was long the practice of mental health practitioners to conflate the determination to subject a person to involuntary commitment (usually after a court finding that he is an imminent danger to himself or others) with the decision that the person is incompetent to make treatment decisions. That conflation was understandable on the surface, as the decision to commit is a weighty one involving a dramatic loss of liberty, and it was widely assumed that the arguably greater deprivation (involuntary hospitalization) implied the arguably lesser (loss of decisional power). The conflation seems inconsistent, however, with the general rule that a person retains decisional autonomy unless and until he is adjudged incompetent to control his own treatment. The standard for institutional commitment does not entail a judgment of decisional incompetence, but in practice often (although not in all jurisdictions) is treated as though it does.

Central to the concept of decisional autonomy is the notion that people are free to make decisions with which we disagree. The modern doctrine of informed consent generally empowers patients to make their own treatment decisions even where those decisions run counter to the medical advice they receive. Physicians are generally obliged to inform patients of their choices, and of the risks and benefits of different options. The information is sometimes technical, and the ability to assess all of the implications of medical conditions and treatments necessitates medical judgment. The information about the choices, then, is medical, but the American notion of decisional autonomy means that patients may act on this information according to their risk tolerance, life goals, and personal circumstances. The advice is expert; the weighing of options (e.g., tolerance for side effects; particular

225 Cal. Rptr. 297 (1986) (competent patient may refuse life-sustaining treatment); Lane v. Candura, 376 N.E. 2d 1232 (Mass. App. 1978) (same); Cruzan by Cruzan v. Director, Missouri Department of Health, 497 U.S. 261, 279 (1990) (assuming without deciding that Cruzan had a Fourteenth Amendment liberty interest in refusing treatment, finding lack of "clear and convincing evidence" that currently incompetent patient would have chosen to withdraw treatment if competent); In re Conroy, 98 N.J. 321, 346–348 (1985) (recognizing common law right to refuse life-sustaining treatment, finding sufficient evidence that currently incompetent patient would have chosen to refuse life-sustaining treatment).

aversion to possible negative outcomes; and unwillingness to become dependent on others) is not, and foolish choices are generally as protected as wise ones. The right to decisional autonomy can be negated by a court's finding that a person is incompetent—cognitively unable to understand and act upon important decisions. Commitment standards ordinarily do not include a judgment of incompetence, but turn on a prediction of dangerousness, and it therefore does not follow that a committed person should be deprived of decisional autonomy. Competency laws require a court to find a lack of capacity that is entirely distinct from a presence of dangerousness. The puzzle of why courts might conflate the two is an important one, and courts have come to different conclusions.

Federal courts often treat institutionalized persons as having lost much of their right to choose, relying on *Washington v. Harper*. In *Harper*, a state prisoner was housed in a prison's mental health unit, where he initially consented to the administration of antipsychotic drugs. When he later revoked his consent to treatment, a committee of prison employees, including a psychiatrist, a psychologist, and a prison administrator found that he "suffer[ed] from a mental disorder and [was] gravely disabled or dangerous." The prisoner sued, claiming that his rights under the Due Process Clause of the Fourteenth Amendment protected his right to judicial process before he could be forcibly medicated. The Washington State Supreme Court agreed, holding that the prisoner's liberty interest in controlling his medical treatment entitled him to judicial process through which the state was required to prove by "clear, cogent, and convincing evidence" that the administration of medication to a competent, nonconsenting prisoner was "both necessary and effective for furthering a compelling state interest."[3]

On appeal, the U.S. Supreme Court reversed, finding that the non-judicial prison process adequately protected the prisoner's rights. While the prisoner's liberty interest in medical autonomy was acknowledged to be substantial, the Court found the prison's process constitutionally sufficient, thereby permitting the involuntary medication of competent prisoners without providing access to any judicial or quasi-judicial process.[4] The Court's majority assumed that a treating psychiatrist would only prescribe appropriate medications, and that the panel of prison employees was an appropriate body to review the treating psychiatrist's judgment. The panel's decision, the Court found, was a mixed medical and penal one, presenting issues in which courts should seldom interfere.

Harper might have been regarded as an anomalous case, limited in its application to prisoners. But the rationale of *Harper* has been applied broadly by courts faced with federal due process challenges to the involuntary administration of drugs. In *DRNJ v. Velez*, for example, the U.S. Court of Appeals for the Third Circuit in 2015 applied the *Harper* rule to a claim by patients involuntarily committed to a psychiatric hospital. The court found that permitting the hospital's medical and administrative personnel, and not courts, to review involuntary treatment decisions was appropriate because, as the *Harper* Court had found, "[t]he risks associated with antipsychotic drugs are for the most part medical ones, best assessed by medical professionals."[5]

[3] Washington v. Harper, 494 U.S. 210 (1990). [4] See id.

[5] Disability Rights New Jersey, Inc. v. Commissioner, 796 F.3d 293, 308 (3d Cir. 2015) *quoting* Washington v. Harper, 494 U.S. at 233.

The modern informed consent doctrine, however, explicitly removes medical decision-making from the medical realm and, by according individuals a right to make the choice, places it in the legal realm. The informed consent doctrine is rooted in the "concept, fundamental in American jurisprudence, that '[e]very human being of adult years and sound mind has a right to determine what shall be done with his own body. . . .'"[6] The reservations for children and those not of "sound mind" help to explain the differential treatment of people with mental illness. Like children, people with mental illness have conditions that implicate the nature and quality of their cognitive abilities. Those courts that deny autonomy rights to people with mental illness likely believe that these cognitive differences render paternalism more appropriate than autonomy.

But there is a well-established legal process in each state for evaluating the decisional competence of adults, and that process involves the right to judicial review. In explaining why those committed because of their mental health lack a right to judicial process, the *DRNJ* court elided the distinction between the dangerousness standard that must be met for *commitment* purposes, and the capacity standard that must be met for *competency* purposes:

> It would be passing strange if due process were to permit the State to forcibly medicate a criminal whose conviction bears no suggestion of physical dangerousness without a judicial hearing, while mandating judicial hearings for mentally ill people who have already been adjudicated to be so dangerous as to require civil commitment.[7]

But why would such a result be "passing strange"? Individuals who have been civilly committed are deprived of their freedom of movement, but not of all legal rights. What justifies losing the right to refuse psychotropic medication? The need to protect prison guards, hospital personnel, and other patients from possible harm is significant, but does not explain why competency determinations are "medical" for people with a psychiatric diagnosis, and legal for everyone else. The decision to act over the patient's objection is paternalistic—reflecting a desire to help the mentally infirm—in a way that does not arise, for example, when a person refuses a life-saving operation for personal or religious reasons.

Not all courts acquiesce in *Harper*'s brand of medical paternalism. Several state courts interpreting state law have held that the fact of involuntary commitment does not permit a competent person to be involuntarily medicated as a matter of medical judgment. Instead, these courts require judicial process—as is required for any non–mentally ill person whose treatment judgments are challenged. The court, and not a doctor, determines whether the patient's right to decisional autonomy should be abrogated for his own good or the good of those with whom he resides.[8]

Although society often limits the autonomy of people in categories that bespeak diminished decision-making ability, *Harper* and *DRNJ* involved neither children nor people

[6] Canterbury v. Spence, 464 F.2d 772, 780 (1972) *quoting* Schoendorff v. Society of New York Hospital, 105 N.E. 92, 93 (N.Y. 1914) (Cardozo, J.). Not all jurisdictions accept the patient-centered doctrine of informed consent. About half of the states continue to treat the choice of treatment as largely a medical one. *See* Jaime Staples King & Benjamin Moulton, *Rethinking Informed Consent: The Case for Shared Decisionmaking*, 32 AM. J. L. & MED. 429 (2006).

[7] DISABILITY RIGHTS NEW JERSEY, INC., 796 F.3d at 308.

[8] *See, e.g.*, Rivers v. Katz, 495 N.E. 2d 337 (N.Y. 1986); Rogers v. Commissioner, 448 N.E. 2d 308 (Mass. 1983).

determined by a court to be incompetent but people with mental illness who had been physically committed to a psychiatric institution. As the law presumes competence absent a judicial finding to the contrary, the new category of paternalistic intervention requires some justification. Those generally relied on by courts—relative accuracy of medical treatment choices and the inconvenience of invoking judicial process—would swallow the general presumption of competence rule entirely if taken at face value, and no one would be entitled to a judicial determination of incompetence. The justification is likely otherwise and simple: a seldom-articulated belief that people with mental illness serious enough to justify involuntarily commitment also substantially lack decision-making capacity. However, it is one thing to say that committed patients likely do not have decisional capacity. It is another to deprive someone who has been committed of a generally applicable right to judicial process when he challenges that assumption.

b. Paternalism in the Service of Patient Safety: Involuntary Outpatient Commitment

Paternalistic treatment of people with mental illness finds expression in the community as well as in psychiatric hospitals. The involuntary commitment process for people with serious mental illness has undergone a number of changes over the last fifty years. Prior to the 1960s, hospital commitment often followed a somewhat circular finding that the patient was "in need" of inpatient psychiatric care. With the advent of effective medications and the emergence of the due process revolution after mid-century, the standard generally shifted to one of dangerousness, and permitted the state to exercise its police power when the patient was dangerous to others or its *parens patriae* power when he was dangerous to himself. Coupled with fiscal pressures for deinstitutionalization, these new standards may have been too restrictive, leading to the emergence of a class of homeless people unable to care for themselves but not presenting an imminent danger. The legal pendulum therefore swung back, relaxing to some degree the standard for dangerousness and allowing commitment on the grounds of self-neglect presenting a threat of grave harm.[9]

More recently, controversies have arisen in the context of amendments to commitment laws permitting a court to order not hospitalization, but "involuntary outpatient commitment" (IOC) or "assisted outpatient treatment" (AOT). Under these amendments, courts apply some variant of a dangerousness or self-neglect test to a person with mental illness not alleged to need inpatient care. If the patient meets this outpatient standard, he is ordered to undergo a specific course of outpatient care. These amendments are often justified by the argument that, although the individual is less likely to be dangerous than the inpatient standard would require, the IOC infringements on liberty are also less severe, so that the balance struck between the deprivation of liberty and the danger to self or others is therefore appropriate.

[9] See Donald H. Stone, *Confine Is Fine: Have the Non-Dangerous Mentally Ill Lost Their Right to Liberty: An Empirical Study to Unravel the Psychiatrist's Crystal Ball*, 20 VA. J. SOC. POL'Y & L. 323 (2012–2013).

Under IOC, a court orders the person to participate in treatment without any finding that the person is incompetent to make treatment decisions. Mechanisms for enforcing the order vary, but include the overt or implicit threat of inpatient commitment. IOC, then, is paternalistic to an extent that goes beyond traditional commitment law. The application of IOC in this setting raises a question very similar to that raised in connection with *Harper* and *DRNJ*: Why override the treatment choices of competent people with mental illness but not competent people with physical illness? Isn't a person who refuses a blood transfusion or cancer care similarly at grave risk of harm?

American legislation and regulation has pockets of "hard paternalism" in which government prohibits behavior on the grounds that an actor is harming (almost always) himself by acting incorrectly; criminalization of heroin, motorcycle helmet mandates, and limitations on the size of sugary drinks offered for sale come to mind. IOC, however, seems a version of "soft paternalism" through which government attempts to protect a person's "true" choice when that person may be acting under duress, ignorance, incapacity, or any other circumstance that threatens autonomy.[10]

Is IOC an acceptable form of government paternalism? The answer to this question requires grappling with a paradox of difference: Are people with mental illness improperly being treated differently by IOC or do their differences render IOC acceptable? It may be that depriving people with mental disabilities of autonomy is best explained by residual fear and distrust of the mentally ill, with the result that society continues to treat them as second-class citizens. If so, then federal antidiscrimination law may have something to say about the differential treatment.

A series of federal antidiscrimination statutes were enacted in the last quarter of the twentieth century to benefit either people with mental illness or people with disabilities more generally.[11] The Americans with Disabilities Act (ADA), enacted in 1990, is the most important of these, and was intended by Congress to combat the historical stigma experienced by people with disabilities.[12] It generally prohibits disparate treatment of people with mental disabilities in access to care, including in an unequal, separate, or segregated setting.[13] From this perspective, IOC seems to be an unequal application of governmental control, separately treating people with mental illness. Moreover, the availability of IOC may lower the threshold of commitment for a judge considering the fate of a person with mental illness—tempting her to impose coercive treatment on a marginal patient whom she might have released given only institutionalization as an alternative.

In most cases, however, the ADA is triggered only if treatment is stigmatizing in comparison to another, similarly situated group. People with mental illness may not to be similarly situated to people with physical illness when facing possible commitment. Other than very rare cases involving people with communicable diseases, it is only people with mental illness

[10] *See* JOHN KLEINIG, PATERNALISM 8–14 (1984). The distinction between weak and strong paternalism is not universally accepted, and definitional concerns among philosophers abound.

[11] *See* The Rehabilitation Act of 1973, 29 U.S.C. §§ 791–794; Civil Rights for Persons in Institutions Act, 42 U.S.C. §§ 1997 *et seq.*; The Americans with Disabilities Act, 42 U.S.C. §§ 12101–12213.

[12] *See* 42 U.S.C. §§ 12101(a)(2), (3), and (5). *See also* MARTHA NUSSBAUM, HIDING FROM HUMANITY: DISGUST, SHAME, AND THE LAW 309–311 (2004) (discussing the stigma felt by people with disabilities).

[13] 42 U.S.C. §§ 12182(b)(1)(A)(ii), (iii), and (iv).

who are subject to involuntary confinement. In addition, one of the central purposes of the ADA was to protect people with disabilities from social isolation, as is described in the next section's discussion of the Supreme Court's *Olmstead* decision.[14] From that perspective, IOC can be seen as a positive step, as it may shift care for people with severe mental illness from institutional settings to the community, in essence creating a middle ground that benefits people with mental illness. Instead of substituting for release, IOM may lead judges to commit to outpatient care a marginal patient who would otherwise have been institutionalized.

II Healthcare Delivery—Fragmentation and Community Care

a. Deinstitutionalization

Mental healthcare experienced a leap forward in the mid-twentieth century when the norm for the care of people with significant mental illness shifted from institutional to community care. Deinstitutionalization was a social movement to allow people with mental illness to escape isolation and rejoin society by providing them with community-based health services. In mid-century, approximately 550,000 people were long-term patients in psychiatric hospitals. The daily census of psychiatric hospitals has dropped tenfold to approximately 50,000. The shift in the default from inpatient to outpatient care was accelerated by *Olmstead*, a 1999 U.S. Supreme Court case that recognized a limited right conferred by the ADA on institutionalized persons to receive optimal care in the community.[15]

People leaving hospitals were not, however, cured of their illnesses, and their freedom was dependent on access to clinical treatment and social services. Institutional closure was meant to coincide with an increase in access to community services facilitated by new laws such as the Community Mental Health Centers Act of 1963 and the Medicaid Act in 1965, which promised injections of new federal funds for community care that only partly materialized.[16] Although the daily census of psychiatric institutions has dropped dramatically, moreover, admissions to inpatient mental healthcare remain very common, running approximately 660,000 per year. "Deinstitutionalization," then, is best thought of as a sharp reduction in long-term institutionalization, with a complicated successor: community care augmented for those with serious mental illness with periodic returns to a hospital environment.

b. Therapeutic Advances Allowing Community Care

Community care succeeds when it permits people to maximize their independence and quality of life, reduce the severity of their symptoms, and avoid the need for more intensive

[14] Olmstead v. L.C. ex rel. Zimring, 527 U.S. 581 (1999). [15] *Olmstead*, 527 U.S. 581.

[16] Community Mental Health Centers Act of 1963, P.L. 88–164, codified as amended in scattered provisions of 42 U.S.C. ch. 33. The statute creating the Medicaid program amended the Social Security Act, P.L. 89–97, codified at 42 U.S.C. §§ 1396 *et seq.*

care. This care must include in the first instance the therapeutic advances that permitted the depopulation of the psychiatric hospitals. The first wave of effective antipsychotic medications such as chlorpromazine came into use beginning in the 1950s, allowing relief for many patients from severe symptoms such as hallucinations and delusional thinking. These sometimes caused side effects including weight gain, lethargy, restlessness, and—more rarely—tardive dyskinesia, an irreversible neurological disorder associated with involuntary muscular tics and movements. A second generation of "atypical" antipsychotics such as olanzapine was introduced in the last two decades and may allow relief with fewer side effects. Several drugs now treat major depression, including monoamine oxidase inhibitors, tricyclic antidepressants and selective serotonin reuptake inhibitors (SSRIs) such as paroxetine. Bipolar disorder symptoms may be addressed by a range of drugs including mood stabilizers, lithium, and antipsychotics. Of course, the side effects of many of the drugs prescribed for mental illness require close medical management.

Substance use disorders often coexist with mental disorders. Addiction to and misuse of drugs such as opioids, cocaine, and methamphetamine can cause disengagement from social responsibilities, loss of control, and physical health problems. Treatments for substance use disorders include psychotherapeutic counseling, group counseling, and peer support. For opioid addiction, these treatments are sometimes supplemented with pharmacological agents such as methadone, buprenorphine, or extended-release injectable naltrexone. These drugs reduce cravings for opioids, and improve retention in psychotherapeutic treatment programs. As is true with antipsychotic drugs, medical management of these treatments is important.

There are several types of psychotherapeutic treatment, including psychodynamic therapies, by which patients address how past experiences affect current mental states, with an emphasis on uncovering unconscious reasons for psychiatric symptoms; behavioral therapies, which focus not on past experiences but on present mind states in order to address mental abnormalities; and humanistic therapy, which focuses on the patients' subjective feelings and self-awareness to improve patients' mental states.[17]

Acceptance of psychotherapy's efficacy in treating mental illness has waxed and waned over time, but in recent years some forms have gained broad acceptance as evidence-based treatments. It is well established, for example, that cognitive behavioral therapy (a short-term, goal-oriented approach to psychotherapy) can be effective in the treatment of anxiety disorders, depression, and schizophrenia. Many patients are attracted to these forms of therapy instead of or in addition to drug therapy because drugs are ineffective or only partially effective in the treatment of some symptoms, can cause significant physical side effects, and leave unaddressed many of the social deficits many people with mental illness experience. Perhaps for these reasons, a recent metastudy found that patients are three times more likely to prefer psychological counseling than drug therapy.[18]

[17] *See* U.S. Department of Health and Human Services, Mental Health: A Report of the Surgeon General 65–67 (1999), http://profiles.nlm.nih.gov/ps/access/NNBBHS.pdf.

[18] See R. McHugh et al., *Patient Preference for Psychological vs. Pharmacological Treatment of Psychiatric Disorders: A Meta-Analytic Review*, 74 J. Clinical Psychiatry 595 (2013) (meta-analysis of patient preferences). See also T. Wykes et al., *A Meta-analysis of Cognitive Remediation for Schizophrenia: Methodology and Effect Sizes*, 158 Am. J. Psychiatry 472 (2011) (meta-analysis finding support for cognitive remediation therapy for schizophrenia); T. Wykes et al., *Cognitive Behavior Therapy for Schizophrenia: Effect Sizes, Clinical Models, and Methodological Rigor*, 34 Schizophrenia

c. The Uncoordinated Nature of Community Care

As has been observed by many, the development of community services failed to keep pace with the shift of care from institutions to the community. These failures often left individuals with mental illness at a loss when they left hospitals, with many continuing to be isolated in ramshackle facilities with little or no follow-up care. Without a suitable safety net, these individuals often became homeless or incarcerated. The frequency of incarceration, typically after conviction for minor "quality of life" offenses, spawned the term "transinstitutionalization"—capturing the reality that people with mental illness often left psychiatric hospitals not to lead an independent life in the community but only to move to another institution.[19]

One feature of the healthcare system dominates the clinical and legal analysis of the harms experienced by people with behavioral conditions: its fragmentation. The subject of voluminous scholarship,[20] fragmentation is a byproduct of success. The twentieth century saw dramatic advances in medicine. New modalities of care were developed for cardiovascular, oncological, and other conditions that had been largely untreatable. These new treatments were often delivered in acute (frequently surgical) settings, with one or a few episodes of intense service. Partly as a result of those advances, the number of Americans living with chronic conditions is large and growing. Curing previously fatal conditions also has increased longevity, and the incidence of chronic illness rises inexorably with age.

Coordination is necessary to provide appropriate health treatment for people with behavioral health conditions. The side effects of many psychoactive drugs can be significant, and close attention to the appearance of those side effects is critical. Similarly, the effects of the drugs employed in medication-assisted substance abuse treatment must be carefully monitored. In addition, the interplay of drug therapy and talk therapy for people with conditions such as schizophrenia, anxiety disorders, and depression calls for coordination among the

Bull. 523 (2008) (meta-analysis finding support for cognitive behavioral therapy for schizophrenia); D. Turkington et al., *Cognitive Behavior Therapy for Schizophrenia*, 163 Am. J. Psychiatry 365 (2006) (same).

[19] *See* H. Lamb & L. Bachrach, *Some Perspectives on Deinstitutionalization*, 52 Pscyhol. Servs. (2001); J. Talbot, *Deinstitutionalization: Avoiding the Disasters of the Past*, 1979 Hosp. & Community Psychiatry 621. For a somewhat more positive analysis of the history of deinstitutionalization, *see* S. Bagenstos, *The Past and Future of Deinstitutionalization Litigation*, 34 Cardozo L. Rev. 1 (2012).

The extent to which transinstitutionalization has occurred and, if so, what might be its causes and cures is a subject of much discussion in the literature and is beyond the scope of this chapter. *See, e.g.*, A. Primeau, *Deinstitutionalization of the Mentally ill: Evidence for Transinstitutionalization from Psychiatric Hospitals to Penal Institutions*, 2 Comp. Psychol. 1 (2013); Steven Raphael & Michael A. Stoll, *Assessing the Contribution of the Deinstitutionalization of the Mentally Ill to Growth in the U.S. Incarceration Rate*, 42 J. Legal Stud. 187 (2013); Seth J. Prins, *Does Transinstitutionalization Explain the Overrepresentation of People with Serious Mental Illnesses in the Criminal Justice System?*, 47 Community Mental Health J. 716 (2011); Chris Koyanagi, Kaiser Commission on Medicaid and the Uninsured & Judge David L. Bazelon Center for Mental Health Law, Learning From History: Deinstitutionalization of People with Mental Illness as Precursor to Long-Term Care Reform (2007), https://kaiserfamilyfoundation.files.wordpress.com/2013/01/7684.pdf.

[20] *See, e.g.*, The Fragmentation of U.S. Health Care: Causes and Solutions (Einer Elhauge ed. 2010); Robert L. Kane et al., Meeting the Challenge of Chronic Illness (2005); Comm. on Quality of Health Care in Am., Inst. of Med., Crossing the Quality Chasm: A New Health System for the 21st Century (2001).

various professions providing the different treatments. Many people with major mental illness also have a co-occurring substance use disorder, which amplifies this need.

Looming over these coordination challenges within mental healthcare is the fact that people with behavioral health conditions as a group also suffer relatively poor access to *physical* healthcare. As a result, people with serious mental illness experience highly elevated mortality and morbidity rates. Research has demonstrated that patients treated in state public mental health systems (presumably those with very serious illnesses) died, on average, twenty-five years younger than the general population. Some of this excess mortality is due to suicide or accidents related to the mental illness. Most, however, is not: "the majority of excess deaths [are] due to medical illness rather than 'unnatural' causes such as suicide."[21] The years of potential life lost are often attributable to treatable chronic conditions such as vascular, respiratory, and cardiac disease.

Notwithstanding laws such as the ADA, denials of care still occur. A large study of people with schizophrenia conducted by Joseph McEvoy and colleagues found high rates of hypertension, obesity, elevated cholesterol, and diabetes; it also found that those individuals very often were not receiving treatment. Thirty percent of subjects with diabetes were not receiving treatment, nor were 62% of those with hypertension, and 88% of those with elevated cholesterol.[22] Significantly, the study's subjects were all patients of mental health programs at major universities with sophisticated capacity to provide needed physical health services. Many things contribute to these shortfalls in treatment. Because of the at-times-difficult behaviors that characterize the lives of those with substance use disorders and mental illness, people with behavioral conditions may not be the favorite patients in physicians' offices. In addition, the life challenges faced by those with behavioral conditions, including difficulty finding and maintaining employment, housing, family connections, and broader social networks, can interfere with their ability to make and keep medical appointments.

d. Integrated Care and Its Barriers

In behavioral healthcare, lack of coordination is exacerbated by the gulf that often exists between physical and behavioral care. The problem manifests in two ways. First, people with serious mental illness often have access to care through dedicated university clinics and community mental health centers. The focus of these clinics and centers is the amelioration of serious behavioral conditions such as bipolar disorder, schizophrenia, and major depression. The task of keeping patients under care, fostering engagement in receiving treatment, and working with patients to achieve recovery can be daunting. The press of these tasks diverts attention from physical health needs, which often are regarded as someone else's

[21] Benjamin G. Druss & Thomas H. Bornemann, *Improving Health and Health Care for Persons with Serious Mental Illness*, 303 J. Am. Med. Ass'n 1972 (2010). *See also* Craig W. Colton & Ronald W. Manderscheid, *Congruencies in the Increased Mortality Rates, Years of Potential Life Lost, and Causes of Death Among Public Mental Health Clients in Eight States*, 3 Preventing Chronic Diseases A42 (2006).

[22] Joseph P. McEvoy et al., Prevalence of the Metabolic Syndrome of Patients with Schizophrenia, Schizophrenia Research 19–32 (2005).

concern. Specialization in professional training tends to accentuate that separation, which reimbursement and licensing rules for healthcare facilities further reinforce.

Second, primary care physicians and nurses, hospital-based primary care clinics, and community health providers such as Federally Qualified Health Centers (FQHCs) serve patients' basic medical needs, but often not their behavioral health needs. A very high percentage of patients with mental health or substance abuse conditions present initially in primary care settings. Others remain with primary care practitioners for treatment, often because of difficulty locating appropriate sources of referral for behavioral healthcare, or because the primary care practitioner elects to provide it.[23]

The problems in these two settings mirror each other. Behavioral health specialists often fail to identify chronic physical health problems, or find themselves ill-equipped to manage them or refer the patient elsewhere for primary care. Primary care providers and community health clinics often fail to recognize behavioral health issues, or find themselves unable to manage or refer the patient elsewhere for care of mental health or substance use disorders.

Many caregivers work hard to patch together a system of care for patients with complex needs. In addition, much good work has been done to initiate novel clinical models that integrate care. Some models bring primary care practitioners together with those serving patients with serious mental illness. For example, the Cherokee Health System in Tennessee was a provider of behavioral health services that moved to an integrated practice mode, embedding a primary care team in its behavioral health practices. The Cherokee model has reduced the incidence of emergency department use by coordinating care for complex patients.[24] Others bring mental health and substance use disorder services into primary care settings such as FQHCs and other community health clinics. Community Health Center in Connecticut, for example, is an FQHC that has incorporated behavioral health services into its range of services. All patients receive behavioral health screening in the primary care

[23] *See* Jürgen Unützer et al., *Transforming Mental Health Care at the Interface with General Medicine: Report for the President's Commission*, 57 Psychiatric Serv. 37 (2006); U.S. Dept. Health & Human Servs., Report of a Surgeon General's Working Meeting on the Integration of Mental Health Services and Primary Health Care (2001), http://www.surgeongeneral.gov/library/mentalhealthservices/mentalhealthservices.PDF4; Sarah Klein & Martha Hostetter, *In Focus: Integrating Behavioral Health and Primary Care*, Commonwealth Fund (August/September 2014), http://www.commonwealthfund.org/publications/newsletters/quality-matters/2014/august-september/in-focus.

[24] *See, e.g.*, Deborah J. Cohen et al., Agency for Healthcare Research and Quality. A Guidebook of Professional Practices for Behavioral Health and Primary Care Integration: Observations from Exemplary Sites (2015), http://integrationacademy.ahrq.gov/sites/default/files/AHRQ_AcademyGuidebook.pdf (identifying CHS as one of eight high-performing primary care organizations with integrated behavioral health and primary care); Chris Collins et al., Milbank Memorial Fund, Evolving Models of Behavioral Health Integration in Primary Care 36 (2010), http://www.milbank.org/uploads/documents/10430EvolvingCare/EvolvingCare.pdf (highlighting CHS as an example of a unified primary and behavioral health program); Nat'l Ass'n of Community Health Ctrs., Educational Health Centers: Teaching and Learning in the Community, at 1, 8 (Nov. 2015) (identifying CHS as a "Best Practice" Educational Health Center Site: "CHS is known across the country as being one of the nation's leading 'best-practice' programs in the integration of behavioral health and primary care, and they have also become known for their ability to train health professionals in this 21st-century, integrated, collaborative-care model"), http://www.nachc.com/client/Educational%20Health%20Centers%20Teaching%20and%20Learning%20in%20the%20Community%20Case%20Studies%20Final%20Report%20November%202015.pdf.

setting, and receive a "warm handoff" to a behavioral health professional in the same examination room.[25]

Nonetheless, practical barriers can impede the integration of behavioral health and physical health services among previously unconnected providers or of creating integrated systems within a single healthcare center. First, primary care professionals may be unused to working with behavioral health caregivers, and cultural accommodations in the workplace may be necessary.[26] Second, record-keeping concerns may arise, as the privacy requirements differ for different types of health records.[27] Third, reimbursement programs based on fee-for-service payment have long been wary of care methods that involve multiple professionals billing separately on the same day.[28] On the other hand, changes in payment and delivery in connection with the implementation of the Affordable Care Act, such as bundled payments, behavioral health homes, and gainsharing programs, offer bridges to more comprehensive care.[29]

Another barrier is the licensure of facilities seeking to provide integrated care. Progress here has been slower, perhaps because state law tends to evolve in an unpredictable, piecemeal fashion. Most healthcare facilities larger than a single professional's office—including FQHCs, mental health centers, and community health clinics—require licensure. Licensure of each type of facility is often controlled by a dedicated state agency, and is commonly governed by distinct standards. This separateness has its roots in both concern over protecting people with mental illness and fear (however unwarranted) that behavioral health patients might pose a danger to physical health patients. Efforts to bring modern licensure rules into

[25] *See* Chris Collins et al., *supra* note 24. *See generally* David Mechanic, *Seizing Opportunities Under the Affordable Care Act for Transforming the Mental and Behavioral Health System*, 31 Health Aff. 376 (2012); Emily Woltmann et al., *Comparative Effectiveness of Collaborative Chronic Care Models for Mental Health Conditions Across Primary, Specialty, and Behavioral Health Care Settings: Systematic Review and Meta-Analysis*, 169 Am. J. Psychiatry 790 (2012); Thomas W. Crogan & Jonathan D. Brown, *Integrating Mental Health Treatment into the Patient Centered Medical Home* (Mathematica Policy Research for U.S.D.H.H.S., Agency for Healthcare Research and Quality, June 2010), *available at* https://pcmh.ahrq.gov/sites/default/files/attachments/Integrating%20Mental%20Health%20and%20 Substance%20Use%20Treatment%20in%20the%20PCMH.pdf; Deborah M. Scharf et al., Rand Corp. for N. Y. State Health Found., An Examination of New York State's Integrated Primary and Mental Health Care Services for Adults with Serious Mental Illness (2014), http:// nyshealthfoundation.org/uploads/resources/integrated-primary-care-mental-health-services-rand-sept-2014.pdf.

[26] *See* Chris Collins et al., *supra* note 24, at 15.

[27] Federal law, for example, protects the confidentiality of alcohol and drug treatment and prevention records. Federal laws recognize the stigma and potential discrimination surrounding addiction, and therefore carry enhanced confidentiality and patient consent requirements. *See* 42 U.S.C. §§ 290dd-2 *et seq.*; 42 C.F.R. §§ 2.1 *et seq.*

[28] *See* John V. Jacobi et al., Integration of Behavioral and Physical Care: Licensing and Reimbursement Barriers and Opportunities in New Jersey 41–52 (2016), https://issuu.com/seton-hall-law-school/docs/integration-of-behavioral-and-physi?e=19054437/34560793.

[29] *See* Deborah Bachrach et al., *State Strategies for Integrating Physical and Behavioral Health Services in a Changing Medicaid Environment* (Commonwealth Fund, August 2014), *available at* http://www. commonwealthfund.org/~/media/files/publications/fund-report/2014/aug/1767_bachrach_state_ strategies_integrating_phys_behavioral_hlt_827.pdf; Benjamin G. Druss et al., *Budget Impact and Sustainability of Medical Care Management for Persons with Serious Mental Illness*, 168 Am. J. Psychiatry 1171 (2011); Chris Collins et al., *supra* note 24.

harmony with clinical preferences for integration run into bureaucratic inertia and agency infighting. Without that cooperation, the financial burden of filing for separate licenses from separate agencies can be significant. Even more troubling is the requirement of physical separation between the two groups of patients, extending in some cases to separate waiting rooms, hallways, and even entrances.[30]

One spur to progress in this area is the threat of scrutiny under disability discrimination law. The ADA, enacted in 1990, is the most important of several federal antidiscrimination statutes were enacted in the last quarter of the twentieth century.[31] An important role of the ADA is to combat the historic tendency to "isolate and segregate individuals with disabilities."[32] In addition to its prohibition of unwarranted institutional isolation, as embodied in the *Olmstead* opinion discussed above, the ADA protects access to private doctors' offices and hospitals. Under Title III of the ADA, however, access to such places of "public accommodation" still may be restricted for a person with a disability if equality could be achieved only by fundamentally altering the facility.[33]

Title II of the ADA applies to government, including state regulators responsible for licensing programs. State agencies must administer their programs consistent with the ADA's "integration mandate," must "make reasonable modifications in policies, practices, or procedures" to avoid discrimination, and "must administer services, programs, and activities in the most integrated setting appropriate to the needs of qualified individuals with disabilities."[34] A requirement that a facility offering both physical and behavioral health services maintain separate entrances, clearly and visibly treats people differently on the basis of their need for behavioral health services. In the event a facility were to comply with a policy mandating separate structures and amenities, it might appear that the facility itself and not the public agency is the entity performing the discriminatory act. However, state agencies that enforce "keep separate" rules violate Title II, unless the agency is able to offer an affirmative defense.[35] Title II of the ADA states:

> [A] public entity may not establish requirements for the programs or activities of licensees that would result in discrimination against qualified individuals with disabilities. For example, a

[30] *See* Jacobi et al., *supra* note 28, at 15–30.

[31] *See* The Rehabilitation Act of 1973, 29 U.S.C. §§ 791–794; Civil Rights for Persons in Institutions Act, 42 U.S.C. §§ 1997 *et seq.*; The Americans with Disabilities Act, 42 U.S.C. §§ 12101–12213.

[32] 42 U.S.C. § 12101(2). *See* 42 U.S.C. § 12101(5) ("individuals with disabilities continually encounter various forms of discrimination, including . . . overprotective rules and policies, failures to make modifications to existing policies and practices, . . . [and] segregation.").

[33] 42 U.S.C. § 12182(b)(2)(A)(i) and (ii).

[34] 28 CFR § 135.130(b)(6), (7) and (8)(d). *See* Jacobi et al., *supra* note 28, at 39–40.

[35] It may be that public health and safety motivates the policy. Such concerns, however, only form a defense to differential treatment on the basis of actual or perceived disability if the differential policies "are based on actual risks, not on mere speculation, stereotypes, or generalizations about individuals with disabilities." 28 CFR § 135.130(h). In the alternative, it may be that the policy is motivated by a concern that people with behavioral conditions present a threat of harm to others using the facility. A defense based on such a threat is only valid, however, if the public entity makes "an individualized assessment, based on reasonable judgment that relies on current medical knowledge or on the best available objective evidence, to ascertain: the nature, duration, and severity of the risk; the probability that the potential injury will actually occur; and whether reasonable modifications of policies, practices, or procedures or the provision of auxiliary aids or services will mitigate the risk." 28 CFR § 135.139(b).

public entity's safety standards may not require the licensee to discriminate against qualified individuals with disabilities in its employment practices.[36]

The provision of separate facilities and services on the basis of behavioral diagnosis without a particularized, evidence-based justification therefore runs afoul of the ADA's integration mandate and antidiscrimination provisions. These barriers should fall away over time, as state agencies grow to understand both the clinical need to break down the treatment walls and the mandates of disability discrimination law.

III Coverage or Care: Mental Health Parity

Health insurance companies historically thrived by understanding differences in healthcare need among individuals, and applying that understanding to decisions regarding underwriting (i.e., deciding who to insure) and rating (i.e., deciding how much to charge). When insurers had broad discretion to use actuarial analysis to differentiate among classes of risk on the basis of both the expected cost of providing coverage and the level of uncertainty in the computation of the expected costs, discriminatory practices followed. Young men were charged less than young women because the latter group, but not the former, could be expected to incur pregnancy costs. People with mental illness often found themselves excluded from coverage. These differences have always been muted in group policies, and were nearly nonexistent in large group coverage because the number of covered lives assured ample distribution of risk, laws prohibited favoring one set of employees over another, and most large employers self-funded their coverage. Culminating in the passage of the Affordable Care Act (ACA), however, federal and state laws have changed in recent years to substantially restrict the ability of health insurers to select among applicants on the basis of risk in small group and even individual coverage.[37]

a. The Americans with Disabilities Act

Shortly after the ADA was signed into law, advocates began to argue that insurers' refusal to cover, or differently cover, care for particular disabling conditions such as AIDS constituted unlawful discrimination. As *Olmstead* and other cases established, the ADA was a dramatic endorsement of the notion that people with disabilities belong in society and should not be shunted off to the side. *Olmstead* recognized this integrationist intent when it mandated, at least in some circumstances, community-based care for people who did not medically require institutionalization.

[36] TAM § II-3.7200. *See* Reeves v. Queen City Transportation, Inc., 10 F. Supp. 2d 1181, 1185–1187 (D. Colo. 1998) (distinguishing for Title II purposes between discriminatory acts of a regulated business that are, and are not, mandated by a public entity).

[37] *See* Deborah A. Stone, *The Struggle for the Soul of Health Insurance*, 18 J. Health Pol., Pol'y & L. 287 (1993); Leah Wortham, *Insurance Classification: Too Important to Be Left to the Actuaries*, 19 J. L. Reform 349 (1986).

When the ADA was employed to attack insurance plans that differentially treated people with disabilities, however, advocacy efforts failed. The ADA was ineffective in combating differential insurance treatment due to the ADA's "insurance safe harbor" provision. That provision allowed insurers to use the traditional tools of the insurance trade to assess and classify risks, choosing to cover some and not others, so long as those methods were consistent with preexisting insurance law and were not employed as a "subterfuge" to avoid the antidiscrimination goals of the ADA. Under that stringent test, a challenge to a plan design that omits or restricts coverage of treatments for people with disabilities (including those with mental illness) must show more than actuarial difference. The challenge must show a conscious plan to discriminate. Such a showing is, in practice, nearly impossible to make, as the insurer can justify almost any difference as a cost-saving measure. As a result, the ADA was unable to force mental healthcare into the mainstream of insurance coverage.

b. State Parity Laws

State legislatures attempted to address insurance inequity by enacting a variety of mental health parity laws beginning in the 1970s. These laws shared the goal of improving coverage of treatment for mental health conditions, but their methods differed. Some of the early statutes prescribed minimal coverage for substance use disorder or mental health treatment. Later statutes required that behavioral health benefits be offered to purchasers of medical insurance. Others required the coverage of treatment for all people with "serious" mental illness; for all conditions listed in the DSM including substance use disorder; for all conditions in the DSM except for substance use disorder; or for "biologically based" mental illness.

In addition, the requirements of these laws sometimes differed among the individual, small group, and large group markets. More importantly, a growing number of people with nongovernmental coverage—now about 50%—became enrolled in self-funded plans that were exempt from state regulation altogether because of the federal Employee Retirement Income Security Act (ERISA) statute.[38] Consequently, state mental health coverage laws conferred at best a patchwork of access for persons with mental illness.

c. Federal Parity Laws

Federal parity protection resulted from the uneven nature of states' responses to inequity in coverage and the limits on state power imposed by ERISA. Federal intervention came in three steps: the passage of the Mental Health Parity Act (MHPA) in 1996, the passage of the Paul Wellstone and Pete Domenici Mental Health Parity and Addiction Equity Act (MHPAEA) in 2008, and the passage of the ACA in 2010. The MHPA's passage was widely regarded as more symbolic than functional. It did not mandate mental health coverage, but imposed some requirements should it be included. It stated only that—for large group health

[38] See John V. Jacobi, *Parity and Difference: The Value of Parity Legislation for the Seriously Mentally Ill*, 29 AM. J. L., MED. & ETHICS 185 (2003).

plans voluntarily including mental health benefits—annual and lifetime limits could not be more restrictive for mental than for physical health coverage. There were no requirements for types of treatment covered, and plans were still free to impose different scope, duration, and cost-sharing provisions. Moreover, the MHPA did not apply to individual and small group coverage.

Like the MHPA, the MHPAEA does not mandate that health plans provide mental health coverage, but sets conditions on such coverage should a plan include it. It applies by its terms primarily to large employer groups, although the Affordable Care Act extended its application to include individual and small group plans. The most important contributions of the MHPAEA were that it extended the reach of federal parity law to substance use disorder and that it directly regulated the *content* of coverage. If mental health services are provided, it requires "general equivalence" in coverage decisions for both mental health and substance use disorder services, and any treatment limits or cost-sharing provisions must be no more restrictive than limits applied to substantially all medical/surgical benefits.

The final MHPAEA regulations, adopted for plan years beginning in 2014, add detail to the statutory definition of parity. Determining whether a plan is "no more restrictive" for behavioral health services requires scrutiny of several categories of coverage, including inpatient in-network, inpatient out-of-network, outpatient in-network, outpatient out-of-network, emergency, and prescription drug. Cost-sharing and treatment or day limits for each of those six types of service must be comparable between physical and behavioral health services. For example, a plan cannot impose a coinsurance charge for an out-of-network inpatient mental health stay that exceeds that for a comparable stay for cardiac care, and limits on in-network outpatient visits must be at least as generous for substance use disorder as for hypertension care.

These numerical or "quantitative" limits on coverage are important and are also relatively easy to compare. As drafters of the final regulations discerned, however, some instances of plan management are more difficult to describe and assess. In addition to quantitative limits on coverage, plans may use nonquantitative treatment limitations (NQTLs). The regulations require that NQTLs in behavioral healthcare are "comparable to, and are applied no more stringently than" those limits in physical healthcare. The regulations also provide a non-exhaustive list of NQTLs, including medical management standards limiting or excluding benefits based on medical necessity, formulary design, network tier design, standards for in-network status for providers, reimbursement rates for different providers, use of fail-first or step therapy, exclusions based on failure to complete a course of treatment, and restrictions based on facility type or provider specialty.

MHPAEA notwithstanding, the use of these tools for plan management can be free of discriminatory intent and consistent with sound and lawful insurance practices. It is, for example, proper for an insurer to refuse payment for treatment in a context for which there is no medical or scientific justification, and it can be appropriate to exclude from a network a professional with a history of providing substandard care. On the other hand, it is clear that the use of NQTLs presents an opportunity for discriminatory treatment, and regulators will strive to fashion tests evaluating the propriety of their use. Objective measurement of medical necessity, for example, is elusive at best and it is challenging to disentangle the many factors that go into formulary management to discern disparate intent or effect. Evaluation of NQTLs therefore is likely to be a flash point for behavioral health parity for the foreseeable future.

d. The Affordable Care Act: Behavioral Healthcare Becomes Essential

The ACA firmly moved the health insurance underwriting system away from competing on how well insurers attract healthy people and avoid those in genuine need of coverage. It largely ended preexisting condition exclusions and denials of coverage based on medical history. For these reasons, people with a history of mental illness or substance use disorder are less likely to be shut out of the insurance market today. The importance of this shift in law and policy toward insurance as a vehicle to connect people equally to care is difficult to overstate.

The ACA built on the protections of the MHPAEA by placing mental health and substance use disorder treatment front and center. The ACA describes ten "essential health benefits" that must be included in any individual or small group plan. Listed among those requirements are mental health and substance use disorder treatments: Individual and small group plans are required to offer those treatments and to do so in compliance with the terms of the MHPAEA. Together, the MHPAEA and the ACA extend parity protections to most large group plans—whether self-funded or insured—that choose to offer behavioral health coverage (most do), as well as to all individual and small group plans.

Because of these parity laws, coverage for behavioral health services has come a long way. Over time, the practice of denying enrollment to people with a history of mental illness or substance use disorder has found disfavor, and the passage of the ACA seems to have irrevocably ended that form of exclusion from coverage. As federal and state parity laws evolved, moreover, advocates for the rights of people with behavioral health conditions acquired more legal tools to challenge disparate plan design. Notably, the parity regulations call out for sanction many improper uses of quantitative treatment limits. The disparate use of NQTLs may be a last frontier for improper treatment of people with behavioral health concerns by health insurers.

The stakes are high. As is true for all people with significant chronic illness, people with mental illness or substance use disorder can be quite expensive to insure. The higher cost of covering those with behavioral health conditions creates an incentive—whether or not it is acted upon—for insurers and sponsors of health plans to cut corners on behavioral healthcare. Such stinting would serve two (now unlawful) purposes: It would immediately cut the plan's costs, and it would drive expensive insureds to competitors' plans. Risk adjustment and reinsurance mechanisms notwithstanding, health plans still have much to gain by shortchanging behavioral healthcare. For that reason, principled enforcement of the ban on improper use of NQTLs will be needed to permit effective utilization management by plans while guarding against discrimination against people with behavioral health conditions in a new guise.[39]

[39] The final regulations were published at 78 FR 68240 (Nov. 13, 2013). For discussion of the issues raised by the final regulations *see, e.g.*, John V. Jacobi, Tara Adams Ragone, & Kate Greenwood, *Health Insurer Market Behavior after the Affordable Care Act: Assessing the Need for Monitoring, Targeted Enforcement, and Regulatory Reform*, 120 PENN ST. L. REV. 109 (2015); Ellen Weber, *Equality Standards for Health Insurance Coverage: Will the Mental Health Parity and Addiction Equity Act End the Discrimination?*, 43 GOLDEN GATE L. REV. 1079 (2013).

IV Conclusion

The history of society's treatment of people with behavioral health conditions is replete with instances of differential treatment. Some treatment differences remain the result of mistrust and fear; others spring from more benign if paternalistic motives. The task of the law is to encourage the impulse to assist, but prohibit invidious, unjustifiably isolation or exclusion of those with mental illness or substance abuse disorders. People with mental illness are far from monolithic, and most are as competent to choose their care and reject unwanted treatment as any other patient.

Healthcare delivery has long treated behavioral modalities of care separately from those for physical illness. The continuation of this practice is now understood to be harmful to people with behavioral illness in most cases, as it deprives their caregivers of the ability to coordinate care. Enforcing separation of patients on the basis of their primary diagnosis therefore should be rejected unless the separation can be empirically justified on clinical or public health grounds

Health insurance is a key predicate for the receipt of integrated behavioral healthcare. After years of sanctioned exclusion of behavioral health services from many insurance products, the combination of mental health parity laws and the recognition in the ACA of behavioral healthcare as an essential health benefit have generated great progress in equalizing coverage.

Across these three critical domains—medical self-direction, organization of clinical services, and insurance coverage—people with behavioral health conditions should not be subjected categorically to differential treatment, whether as an act of invidious discrimination or as a reflection of the impulse to misguided paternalism. Rather, they should be treated as individuals, with their needs, capacities, and rights assessed accordingly.

CHAPTER 15

ASSISTED REPRODUCTIVE TECHNOLOGIES AND ABORTION

JUDITH DAAR

SAVE biblical celebrations, human reproduction has never been a solitary activity. In the modern era, procreation is increasingly yielding to multiparty involvement both as a means to produce and to avoid the birth of offspring. The use of assisted reproductive technologies (ART) and abortion, while seemingly occupying opposite ends of the procreative spectrum, share the commonality of invoking strong opinions, deep analysis, and impactful regulation surrounding the various medical procedures that comprise the reproductive realm. At first blush, it may appear that ART and abortion rest in entirely separate silos; the former committed to aiding those who wish to attain biologic parenthood, the latter available for averting the birth of a developing child. At their heart, each technique falls under the reproductive healthcare rubric which, ideally, should be calibrated to facilitate fair and equitable access to both procreative arenas.

This article introduces readers to the historic and contemporary debates surrounding ART and abortion, ideally setting the foundation for understanding future challenges. Part I reveals that both techniques are of ancient origin, helping explain their durable integration into modern reproductive life. This part further details the current usage of ART and abortion in American life. Comparing the populations who access these techniques is mostly a study in contrast, but a few shared interests do emerge. Part II discusses the regulatory landscape surrounding both areas, including legislative attempts to control the exercise of reproductive autonomy as well as judicial responses to that activity. A discussion of reproduction as a fundamental right follows, with emphasis on the constitutional basis for regulating a person's efforts to engage in or avoid procreation. At the heart of this constitutional discussion, set out in Part II, is the debate over whether the existing jurisprudence surrounding the right to avoid procreation applies equally to the right to access parenthood through assisted conception. As is essential to any analysis involving constitutional rights, differing interpretations are presented and assessed.

Finally, Part III considers three areas in which ART and abortion have recently and uncharacteristically overlapped—selective reduction of multiple pregnancy, the personhood movement, and perinatal genetic diagnosis. Each of these areas attracts a variety of stakeholders who take up occupancy on previously vacant common ground. Classical distinctions between pregnancy-inducing and pregnancy-avoiding behavior are called into question, particularly in light of emerging technologies that impact reproductive decision making. The rapid growth of genetic detection technologies for embryonic selection and fetal diagnosis has blurred the historically bright line between the pre- and postpregnancy states, giving contemporary verdure to Justice O'Connor's long ago observation that a static reproductive analytic framework was "on a collision course with itself."[1] Today's collision course brims with activity beyond the contemplation of its original framers, making it ripe for current inspection.

I Beyond Intimacy: Reproduction and Collaboration

In the legal realm, reproduction is regarded as a semipublic activity. While the physical act that introduces male sperm into the female reproductive tract is, in the main, a private expression of intimacy between two parties, efforts to change the course of one's reproductive destiny requires the aid of trained professionals who are strangers to the intimate act. These strangers take shape as medical professionals, most often trained in obstetrics and gynecology with specialized knowledge to assist in the promotion[2] or termination of pregnancy.[3] Physicians who toil in the reproductive arena must be equipped to deftly navigate between two worlds, one demanding strict adherence to sacrosanct principles of patient privacy and confidentiality, the other exposed to relentless public scrutiny, judgment, and agitation at every turn.

Correspondingly, any individual who seeks reproductive medical assistance necessarily abandons the intimacy of natural processes and enters a semipublic relationship where personal choices are subject to external inputs in the form of practice standards, societal norms, and legal regimes. What is striking about this transition from private individual to semipublic patient in the reproductive arena is its historic longevity. Nearly as far back as recorded history permits, one can trace the medical curiosity surrounding human reproduction and its impact on private lives. A brief look back at reproductive medicine's humble beginnings beckons, if only to remind us of the progress we have made to arrive in this modern medical era.

[1] City of Akron v. Akron Center for Reproductive Health, Inc., 462 U.S. 416, 458 (1983) (O'Connor, J., dissenting).

[2] According to the American Society for Reproductive Medicine, ART physicians are typically obstetricians and gynecologists with advanced training in reproductive endocrinology and infertility (REI). ASRM website, About Us, http://www.asrm.org/detail.aspx?id=150.

[3] ACOG Committee Opinion, Committee on Health Care for Underserved Women, *Abortion Access and Training*, Number 424, Jan. 2009, http://www.acog.org/Resources_And_Publications/Committee_Opinions/Committee_on_Health_Care_for_Underserved_Women/Abortion_Access_and_Training.

a. A Brief History of the Medicalization of Reproduction

The provision of abortion and infertility services as medical treatments track the development of modern medicine in general, from a field dominated by homeopaths, midwives and other "irregulars" until the emergence of university-trained physicians as a dominant group in early nineteenth century. Debate continues over whether near exclusive control of the provision of these health services should be captured by the medical profession. Relatedly, scholars and advocates ponder whether the response to women's reproductive health been overmedicalized.[4] For better or worse, today's reproductive patient can look to a panoply of medical techniques and technicians capable of producing outcomes unthinkable only a generation ago. A look back reveals the trajectory of reproductive medicine from ancient formulas to modern technologies.

i. Assisted Reproduction: From Hippocrates to the Modern Era

The awareness of infertility as a treatable condition can be traced back to the fifth-century BC writings of Greek physician patriarch Hippocrates (460 to 377 BC), who concocted a number of Egyptian-inspired recipes to open a woman's cervix that was thought to be "closed too tightly." Eight hundred years later, third-century AD Talmudic records show that Jewish thinkers discussed the possibility of human insemination by artificial means. During the Middle Ages, infertile men were prescribed a steady diet of testicles and livers from young stags, while women were diagnosed as infertile if their breath failed to display a garlicky odor after cloves of garlic were placed in their vagina. While quaint or perhaps bizarre to the modern mind, these recipes reflect how little was known about the inner workings of human reproduction for much of our early history.[5]

It would take nearly a millennium and a half and the invention of the microscope before medical science became vested in the problem of infertility. The ability to visualize male sperm and contemplate its role in human reproduction encouraged scientists to consider alternate methods of delivering this essential ingredient into the female reproductive tract. By the turn of the nineteenth century, physicians understood that separating sex from reproduction was essential to treating certain forms of male infertility, ushering in the technique we know modernly as artificial insemination. By the mid-1950s, the ability to freeze and thaw viable sperm assured the continued success of insemination by donor, a technique that today accounts for approximately sixty thousand U.S. births annually.[6]

Around this same time, interest in treating female infertility grew as increasing scientific attention was paid to women's health. In the 1960s, doctors began to investigate and prescribe ovulation inducing drugs to stimulate egg production as a treatment for female infertility. The concept of removing those eggs from the body began to percolate, helped along by veterinary protocols. Heartened by successful French experiments in which rabbit eggs were removed and fertilized in vitro (literally, in glass), two British physicians considered

[4] *See, e.g.*, Elizabeth Britt, Conceiving Normalcy (2001).

[5] Judith Daar, Reproductive Technologies and the Law 26–38 (2d ed. 2013).

[6] Inst. for Sci., Law & Tech. Working Group, *ART into Science: Regulation of Fertility Techniques*, 281 Science 651 (1998) (reporting 60,000 births by artificial insemination by donor (AID) annually).

the viability of such a procedure in humans. As the ART world now well knows, Louise Brown—the first human being conceived using in vitro fertilization (IVF)—was born due to the efforts of Drs. Patrick Steptoe and Robert Edwards on July 25, 1978. In the nearly four decades since, five million IVF-conceived children have populated the world, making family formation through IVF a viable option for many who experience involuntary childlessness.

While IVF remains a staple in treating infertility, it has given rise to even more sophisticated techniques for assuring the birth of a healthy child. In the early 1990s, scientists introduced a method for surveying the genetic health of early embryos, known as preimplantation genetic diagnosis (PGD). Today, prospective parents undergoing IVF and PGD can access intricate details about the genetic makeup of their children-to-be, even discovering the child may someday experience a disabling disorder that will only manifest well into adulthood.[7] This ability to access—and act upon—information about one's future child has emerged as a straddling tie between ART and abortion. While the techniques may present as functionally opposite ends of the reproductive spectrum, their shared parental choice feature brings them much closer as cogs in a larger procreative wheel. The role of genetics in modern healthcare is also further discussed in another article, "Genomics and the Law."

ii. Abortion throughout the Ages

The history of abortion, while replete with periodic medical advances similar in scope to those accompanying ART, is far more steeped in social and political upheaval than its baby-producing counterpart. In fact, abortion is often described historically via its reigning position at law rather than its development as a medical technique.[8] Setting aside for now its intense relationship with law and policy, abortion's development from a crude and dangerous invasive procedure to a relatively safe and effective means for pregnancy termination mirrors similar arcs in modern medicine.

According to scholars, abortion was ubiquitous in premodern societies, with references to the technique as far back at as 2700 BC. Two and a half millennia later Hippocrates wrote about the methods for procuring an abortion, favoring insertion of gradually larger dilators over suppositories. Abortion at the time of the Roman Empire was performed by "skilled abortionists," which until the eighteenth century referred to midwives rather than trained physicians.[9] Advances in gynecology beginning around the nineteenth century brought more physician providers into the practice, but the procedure remained dangerous due in part to the large percentage of untrained doctors who were willing to provide this type of care. In fact, it was the move by university-trained physicians to rid the profession of incompetent abortion practitioners that ushered in the most deadly era of women's reproductive health in our nation's history.[10]

Beginning with the founding of the American Medical Association (AMA) in 1847, physician members agitated to criminalize abortion—primarily to suppress the activities of untrained practitioners who had operated freely during the first part of the nineteenth

[7] DAAR, REPRODUCTIVE, at 290–291; 334–341.

[8] *See, e.g.*, Mark A. Graber, RETHINKING ABORTION 41–44 (1996).

[9] Carole Joffe, *Abortion and Medicine: A Sociopolitical History*, *in* MANAGEMENT OF UNINTENDED AND ABNORMAL PREGNANCY 1–9 (M. Paul et al. eds., 2009).

[10] Laurence H. Tribe, ABORTION: THE CLASH OF ABSOLUTES 30–34 (1990).

century. What followed was a "century of criminalization" in which illegal abortions, and their deadly consequences, were widespread. Thousands of women died or sustained serious injury from "back alley butchers" who lacked the technical skill and infection control acumen to safely deliver a woman of her unwanted fetus. Advances in abortion techniques stagnated during this period, a logical consequence of the procedure's disfavored legal status.

The devastating impact of illegal abortion on women and their families began to gain public attention by the middle of the twentieth century. Fortunately, public agitation for legalization began in earnest in the 1950s and saw much progress by 1970 when the AMA reversed its position on abortion criminalization. At this same time, advances in the science of abortion began to emerge. Specifically, development of the vacuum aspirator, cervical anesthesia methods, and the Karman cannula all improved the safety of abortion and permitted its provision in nonhospital settings.[11] An even greater advance in terms of health outcomes came with the introduction of medical (rather than surgical) abortion in the late 1980s. Physicians in the United States gained access to Mifepristone (RU 486) in 2000, a drug that acts as an abortifacient in early pregnancy. Today, about 20% of all U.S. abortions performed at eight weeks or earlier are medically induced, dramatically improving the safety of pregnancy termination.

ART and abortion share the commonality of a rich history dating back to ancient times, with both experiencing significant technical advancement at the turn of the twenty-first century. In a limited but important way, advances in ART have obviated the need for abortion when prospective parents make preferential choices among embryos prior to transfer. Choosing to discard an embryo rather than later abort a fetus of undesired characteristics strikes some as an immoral act of equal significance to abortion; others view preimplantation selection as an ethical salvation from the more maternally traumatic abortion procedure. While pregnancy remains a vital demarcation between embryo manipulation via ART and fetal demise via abortion, advances in both fields suggest the two fields are beginning to intersect. As the ability to maintain an embryo outside the body extends postfertilization and the opportunity to investigate the health of an in utero embryo presents earlier in the pregnancy, the time between ART and abortion grows ever shorter. The history of ART and abortion as distinct and oppositional medical techniques is clearly set to add a new chapter detailing the pair's shared interests and concerns.

b. Reproduction in the Modern Era: The View from Usage and Demographics

Abortion and ART may one day intersect on a technical level, but they are likely to remain distinct enterprises based on the demographics of their patient populations. ART users tend to be older, whiter, and wealthier than women who undergo abortions, making the techniques vulnerable to disparate treatment by law and public opinion. Data collection in both fields is ongoing, enabling an informed analysis of who becomes a patient and why.

[11] Joffe, *Abortion*, at 3. Strides in safety were reflected in the reduction of abortion-related deaths between 1955 and 1972, falling from 100 to 3 in every 100,000 legal abortions performed. *See* TRIBE, ABORTION, at 36.

i. ART Usage in the United States

Since 1997, the Centers for Disease Control (CDC) has annually published a compendium of IVF usage and outcomes in the United States. As set out in the Fertility Clinic Success Rate and Certification Act of 1992, ART clinics are required to report standardized pregnancy success rates (including data about IVF indications and usage) to the CDC, which is charged with publishing the annual report.[12] Over time, the CDC has increased the amount and type of data reported, including summary profiles that track ART trends based on clinical outcomes. The most recent report, released in February 2014, tallied over 65,000 infants born of more than 176,000 cycles of IVF performed during 2012.[13]

While the CDC data is highly instructive on the incidence and treatment of medical infertility (typically defined as the failure to achieve pregnancy after one year of unprotected intercourse), the national database does not report on certain treatments used by those who experience social infertility—the inability to achieve pregnancy due to a person's sexual orientation or social status. Because the CDC limits reporting to IVF, little is known about usage and outcomes with artificial insemination by donor (AID), a treatment option for single women and lesbian couples. As noted earlier, rough estimates peg annual AID offspring at around sixty thousand, rivaling the number of IVF-conceived births during the same period. Together, children conceived by these two techniques currently account for three of every hundred children born in the United States annually,[14] far exceeding the number of families formed through neonatal adoption.[15]

The incidence of medical infertility among women in the United States is fairly well tracked by periodic surveys conducted by the National Survey of Family Growth. It is estimated that approximately 12% of U.S. women of reproductive age (15–44) have sought fertility care at some point in their lives, with around 1.2 million women seeking treatment each year. The survey also concludes that 7% of married couples in which the woman is of reproductive age experience infertility.[16] Even though the survey queries unmarried women, only those who are cohabitating and intimate with a male partner are included. Excluding single women and lesbian couples from national survey efforts means that even medical infertility among these cohorts (for example, failure to become pregnant after twelve months of AID)

[12] *See* Fertility Clinic Success Rate and Certification Act of 1992, 42 U.S.C. §263a-1 et seq. One criticism of the act's reporting requirement is the lack of any real penalty surrounding nonreporting. If a clinic fails to report, the law simply requires that the name of the nonreporting clinic be included in the annual report. Typically, about 10% of ART clinics fail to report their data. For a critique of this "shaming" technique as ineffective, *see* Theresa Glennon, *Choosing One: Resolving the Epidemic of Multiples in Assisted Reproduction*, 55 VILL. L. REV. 147 (2010).

[13] Preliminary 2012 Data, CDC ART Fertility Clinic Success Rates Report, http://www.cdc.gov/art/artreports.htm.

[14] CTRS. FOR DISEASE CONTROL & PREVENTION, U.S. DEP'T. OF HEALTH AND HUM. SERVS. 2011 ASSISTED REPRODUCTIVE TECHNOLOGY: NATIONAL SUMMARY REPORT (forthcoming 2014) (reporting birth of 61,610 IVF-conceived infants in 2011). There were 3.95 million babies born in the United States in 2011, meaning IVF and AID offspring accounted for over 3% of all births. *See* Joyce A. Martin et al., 62(1) NATIONAL VITAL STATISTICS REPORT 1 (2013).

[15] *See Domestic Adoptions: Perception and Reality*, Adoptive Families, http://www.adoptivefamilies.com/articles.php?aid=1618 (estimating 18,000 domestic newborn nonrelative adoptions in the United States annually).

[16] *See* CTRS. FOR DISEASE CONTROL & PREVENTION, U.S. DEP'T. OF HEALTH AND HUM. SERVS. 2011 ASSISTED REPRODUCTIVE TECHNOLOGY: FERTILITY CLINIC SUCCESS RATES REPORT 3 (2013).

will go unreported. Thus, we know very little about incidence of all forms of infertility—medical and social—among all those interested in becoming biological parents.

In addition to deficits in data measuring infertility in single individuals and same-sex couples, there is much to be learned about the racial and ethnic divisions among those who are unable to reproduce without medical assistance. Epidemiologic studies do reveal that women of color experience infertility at higher rates than white women and that they tend to seek treatment at lesser rates. We also know that treatment is generally less effective in minority women, a result attributed to a variety of factors including environmental, socio-cultural, economic, and genetic correlates that influence reproductive health and health-care.[17] Among racial groups, data reveal that whites fare best in terms of ART outcomes (measured by live birth), followed by Asians, Hispanics, and then African Americans.[18] In one study, African American women had live birth rates of 29.6% compared to 35.8% for white women.[19] These disparities are even more troubling against a backdrop of ART success in the general population, where pregnancy rates among women younger than thirty-five improved from 37% to over 41% per cycle between 2005 and 2009.[20]

ART by the numbers displays its increasing utilization and success, though disparities between and among subgroups are a dominant factor in assessing this contemporary practice. Since infertility among women is often attributable to advanced age (i.e., over thirty-five), and a single cycle of IVF costs roughly $12,000, age and wealth-status serve as palpable divides among those who can and do access ART compared to those who can't and don't. The stratification of ART use among older, whiter, and wealthier women can be compared to the demographics of those who utilize abortion, a cohort dominated by patients who are younger, poorer, and more racially diverse.

ii. Abortion Usage in the United States

The number of women who access abortion annually is nearly ten times the number who access ART. According to the Guttmacher Institute, a private research group supporting abortion rights, approximately 1.1 million abortions were performed in 2011; during that same year ART clinics reported performing 163,069 IVF cycles.[21] While the incidence of ART usage has increased over the past two decades, the number of abortions reported each year has declined over this same period, with both fields reporting record numbers in 2014.[22]

[17] Samantha F. Butts & David B. Seifer, *Racial and Ethnic Difference in Reproductive Potential Across the Life Cycle*, 93 FERTILITY & STERILITY 681 (2010).

[18] Melissa F. Wellons et al., *Race Matters: A Systematic Review of Racial/Ethnic Disparity in Society for Assisted Reproductive Technology Reported Outcomes*, 98 FERTILITY & STERILITY 406 (2012).

[19] Eve C. Feinberg et al., *Comparisons of Assisted Reproductive Technology Utilization and Outcomes Among Caucasian and African American Patients in an Equal-Access-to-Care Setting*, 85 FERTILITY & STERILITY 888 (2006).

[20] *Id.*

[21] Guttmacher Institute, *U.S. Abortion Rate Hits Lowest Level Since 1973*, http://www.guttmacher.org/media/nr/2014/02/03/index.html; 2011 ART Report, at 3, 24.

[22] In February 2104, the Guttmacher Institute reported 2011 marked the lowest U.S. abortion rate since 1973. *Id.* At the same time, ASRM reported a record number of IVF-conceived infants born in the United States. http://www.asrm.org/SART_Technology_Releases_New_Annual_Report_on_In_Vitro_Fertilization_Procedures/.

The demographic features of abortion- and ART-seeking patient are also quite distinct. In terms of age, 75% of all women who undergo abortion are under the age of thirty. In comparison, roughly 61% of all patients who access ART are thirty-five or older.[23] In terms of wealth status, 69% of all women who access abortion have annual incomes below 200% of the annual federal poverty level ($10,830 for a single woman with no children). While the income levels of ART patients are not collected or reported, the cost of treatment ($12,000 for a single IVF cycle) and the general lack of insurance coverage for infertility care suggest these patients enjoy a far higher family income than women seeking medical assistance to end their pregnancies.

Data on the racial and ethnic makeup of patients who undergo abortion show this group to include more women of color than those seeking ART. As reported by the Guttmacher Institute, non-Hispanic white women account for 36% of abortions, non-Hispanic black women for 30%, Hispanic women for 25%, and women of other races for 9%. Similarly robust data showing the race and ethnicity of ART patients is not easily accessed, as many clinics fail to include this information in their annual reporting to the CDC.[24] We do know that infertility rates are higher among women of color compared to white women and that treatment seeking is lower among minority women, especially among certain subpopulations of women.[25]

While ART and abortion appear to share little in common in terms of their usage and patient populations, questions have arisen over whether the two share a clinical link—that is, does having an abortion increase a woman's chance of becoming infertile and thus needing to access ART?[26] Unsurprisingly, stakeholders and advocates on all sides of the abortion debate have a keen interest in the answer to this query, thus ample research has been conducted to identify the relationship, if any, between induced abortion and subsequent infertility. The weight of reported research concludes that first-term abortion poses no long-term risk of infertility. However, certain side effects from abortion can pose problems for later pregnancies, including low birth weight offspring and preterm delivery.[27] Notably, both of these complications are associated with IVF usage, making assessment of causative factors in the cohort of postabortion ART patients more complex.

In sum, patients who avail themselves of abortion or ART, or both, are part of a millennia-old pairing of healthcare providers and women seeking to control their reproductive lives. Today's ART and abortion patients differ tremendously in their demographic characteristics, but they share in their desire to enlist medical professionals who can freely assist with their treatment needs. The liberty of physicians to provide and patients to access

[23] Guttmacher Institute, *Facts on Induced Abortions in the U.S.*, http://www.guttmacher.org/pubs/fb_induced_abortion.html; 2010 CDC ART Report, National Summary, at 3, http://www.cdc.gov/art/ART2010/PDFs/Section_508_PDF_2010_SLIDES.pdf.

[24] Wellons et al., *Race Matters* (noting 35% of reported ART cycles do not include information on the patient's race or ethnicity, despite this category being a mandatory reporting field for SART clinics).

[25] Desireé M. McCarthy-Keith, *Will Decreasing Assisted Reproductive Technology Costs Improve Utilization and Outcomes Among Minority Women?*, 94 Fertility & Sterility 2587 (2010) (reporting infertility rates among black women (11.5%), Hispanic women (7.7%) and white women (7%). This study revealed lower utilization among Hispanic women despite low-cost access to care.

[26] Another link may be the stigma experienced by women who deviate from reproductive norms. *See generally* Kimberly Mutcherson, *Transformative Reproduction*, 16 J. Gender, Race & Justice 187 (2013).

[27] *See* Does Abortion Cause Infertility, http://healthdailyonline.com/2012/11/does-an-abortion-cause-infertility/.

pregnancy-inducing and pregnancy-reducing reproductive care, like the clinical relationship between ART and abortion, is marked by points of divergence and intersection. The story of reproductive liberty continues to evolve, yet much is discovered in its retelling.

II Regulating Intimacy: Reproduction and Law

The history of abortion as a clinical practice is replete with interactions with the legal system, mostly in the form of legislation limiting or outlawing the procedure in the nineteenth and early twentieth centuries. While ART did not provoke similar legal scrutiny during its ascension as a medical treatment, questions about the limits of governmental authority to regulate assisted conception were considered from the outset.[28] Well-traveled by scholars, students, advocates, and lawmakers, the reproductive liberty road has become a shared path for discerning the constitutionality of state action that impacts both ART and abortion.

a. Distinguishing Affirmative and Negative Rights to Reproduce

At the height of World War II, the U.S. Supreme Court issued a ruling that has become central to the development of reproductive liberty as an enduring jurisprudential concept. In *Skinner v. Oklahoma*, the Court struck down a eugenics-era law authorizing state officials to sexually sterilize those convicted two or more times for felony crimes involving "moral turpitude."[29] Writing for a unanimous court, Justice William O. Douglas described the case as "touch[ing] a sensitive and important area of human rights . . . the right to have offspring."[30] In repudiating the law and protecting Mr. Skinner and countless others from forced sterilization, Justice Douglas declared: "Procreation involves one of the basic civil rights of man . . . fundamental to the very existence and survival of the race."[31] These broad-minded pronouncements about the import of reproduction in everyday life have launched countless debates about the propriety of freeing procreative choice—both the choice to have and to not have children—from governmental interference.

i. The Right to Engage in Reproduction

The decision in *Skinner* is seminal in American law for many reasons (marking the demise of laws authorizing eugenical sterilization and abortion, planting the seed for judicial recognition of fundamental rights, opening the Court to matters involving intimate association), but in the ART world the case stands out as a solitary beacon in an otherwise empty sea. To

[28] *See, e.g.*, Kara W. Swanson, *Adultery by Doctor: Artificial Insemination, 1890–1945*, 87 Chi.-Kent L. Rev. 591 (2012).

[29] Skinner v. Oklahoma, 316 U.S. 535, 541 (1942). [30] *Id.* at 536. [31] *Id.* at 541.

date, *Skinner* remains the only high court decision to discuss the affirmative right to engage in procreation as a matter of constitutional right. True enough, as discussed below in Section II(a)(ii), the Court has handed down numerous reproduction-related decisions since 1942, but all focusing on the right to avoid procreation—either through birth control or abortion. To discern the limits of governmental regulation of the right *to* procreate, one must rely on the wisdom of a court whose worldview of reproduction was far simpler than the configurations available to today's prospective parents. Would *Skinner* support the right of an individual to access all forms of ART, and if not what limitations would likely pass constitutional muster?

As a preliminary matter, we might consider the rights surrounding reproduction holistically, as encouraged by Professor John Robertson in his influential book, *Children of Choice*. "Procreative liberty," he avers, "is a negative right against state interference with choices to procreate or to avoid procreation."[32] It is not "a positive right to have the state or particular persons provide the means or resources necessary to have or avoid having children."[33] Thus, under Robertson's configuration, procreative liberty is essentially the right to be left alone (by the state) in one's quest to achieve or avoid parenthood. While *Skinner* supports the right of individuals to be free from state interference (at least in the form of involuntary sterilization) in decisions and activity surrounding natural conception, Robertson tackles the question of whether this right extends to procreation via ART. After considering the parallel values and interests that fertile and infertile persons have in reproducing, he concludes, "[n]oncoital reproduction should thus be constitutionally protected to the same extent as is coital reproduction, with the state having the burden of showing severe harm if the practice is unrestricted."[34] Robertson's broad thesis has garnered praise and critique in the two decades since its publication.

One line of critique challenges the assertion that natural and assisted conception are constitutional equals because, by definition, the latter invokes the participation and rights of third parties. While coital reproduction may deserve fundamental right status to protect the intimacy of this closed two-party activity, assisted conception is a collaborative process devoid of sexual intimacy. ART requires third-party participants—in the form of physicians, gamete donors, and gestational surrogates—who do not necessarily benefit from the level of scrutiny applied to regulations impacting the exercise of fundamental rights. The potential conflict of interest between and among parties to an ART arrangement arguably cautions against its treatment as a fundamental right, principally because such an approach would preference the rights of the intended parents over those of the third-party collaborators.[35] A related critique of Robertson's thesis is its failure to account for the unique harms visited upon ART children. Higher rates of multiple pregnancy, lower birth weights, higher incidence of preterm delivery, and genetic bewilderment owing to not knowing one's genetic parent can befall ART offspring in far greater numbers than naturally conceived children. Thus, a constitutional primacy of procreative liberty accords insufficient weight to the well-being of ART children when balancing the interest of would-be parents against protective regulations that impact access to reproductive technologies.[36]

[32] John A. Robertson, CHILDREN OF CHOICE 23 (1994). [33] *Id.* [34] *Id.* at 39.

[35] *See generally* Radhika Rao, *Constitutional Misconceptions*, 93 MICH. L. REV. 1473 (1995) (Children of Choice book review) (arguing *Skinner* "is too weak a reed to carry so much constitutional weight" and cautioning such a broad right to access ART "threatens to swallow up other constitutional privacy right").

[36] *See generally* Ann MacLean Massie, *Regulating Choice: A Constitutional Law Response to Professor John A. Robertson's Children of Choice*, 52 WASH. & LEE L. REV. 135 (1995) (arguing Robertson underplays

Academic debate about the limits of procreative liberty as applied to ART might abound, but judicial illumination is scarce. As noted, *Skinner* remains the only time the Court has directly addressed the affirmative right to reproduce, though the right to procreate as a general matter has been reaffirmed many times since, typically as a starting point for discussing other conduct of a personal nature.[37] The Court had an opportunity to break its silence in 2012 when it considered the rights of posthumously conceived children to receive Social Security benefits as dependents of their deceased genetic parent. In *Astrue c. Capato*,[38] the plaintiff underwent IVF to conceive twins using sperm deposited by her husband prior to his death from cancer. At issue was whether the Social Security Act (SSA)'s eligibility language embraced children conceived after their parent's death. In a unanimous decision, the Court held that the SSA's definition of "child" incorporates state intestacy law, which, in the case at hand, excluded postmortem conception children as intestate takers. Though no law impacting access to ART was involved, the case did present an opportunity for the Court to comment on the current use of reproductive technologies. While disappointing to some ART watchers, the Court declined to offer any dicta.

The lack of Supreme Court commentary on the bundle of rights surrounding ART is logically linked to the paucity of legislation directly regulating assisted conception. Only one federal law specifically addresses ART, and to date no cases have arisen under that law.[39] At the state level, a handful of jurisdictions have enacted laws addressing different aspects of ART, but none have become the subject of a full-blown constitutional attack.[40] One federal case that does provide guidance as to possible future interpretation of ART law involved a physician's challenge to state restrictions on abortion. In *Lifchez v. Hartigan*,[41] an ART physician challenged as vague and an infringement on reproductive liberty a provision in an Illinois abortion law that prohibited experimentation on a fetus. The plaintiff argued such a restriction could be interpreted to prohibit certain ART procedures, such as embryo transfer. The court agreed, noting that particular procedure is designed to enable an infertile woman to bear her own child. Importantly, the court then stated:

> It takes no great leap of logic to see that within the cluster of constitutionally protected choices that includes the right to have access to contraception, there must be included within that

interests of ART children, which should be focus of responsible social policy governing assisted reproduction). *But see* I. Glenn Cohen, *Regulating Reproduction: The Problem with Best Interests*, 96 Minn. L. Rev 423 (2011) and *Beyond Best Interests*, 96 Minn. L. Rev.1187 (2012) (arguing assertions of child welfare as rationale for regulating reproduction cannot be justified in most cases).

[37] *See, e.g.*, Washington v. Glucksberg, 521 U.S. 702 (1997) (upholding state assisted suicide laws which deprive terminally ill patients the right to physician aid in dying); Cruzan v. Director, MO Dep't of Health, 497 U.S. 261 (1990) (upholding right of competent adults to refuse life-sustaining medical treatment); Michael H. v. Gerald D., 491 U.S. 110 (1989) (discussing right of biological father to establish paternity and right to visitation of child born to married woman living with her husband); Bowers v. Hardwick, 478 U.S. 186 (1986), overruled by Lawrence v. Texas, 539 U.S. 558 (2003) (upholding constitutionality of Georgia sodomy statute as applied to homosexual conduct).

[38] Astrue v. Capato, 132 S. Ct. 2021 (2012).

[39] *See* note 12.

[40] *See* Daar, Reproductive, at 662–665 (discussing direct and indirect regulation of ART by state governments).

[41] Lifchez v. Hartigan, 735 F. Supp. 1361 (N.D. Ill. 1990).

cluster the right to submit to a medical procedure that may bring about, rather than prevent, pregnancy.[42]

The decision in *Lifchez* sets out the view later embraced by Professor Robertson and others that procreative choice includes a bundle of rights touching upon disparate reproductive activities. And while the activities range in scope from avoiding reproduction through abortion to seeking biological parenthood through a surrogate parenting arrangement, the legal standards governing state interference with any of these activities are the same. As noted above, these standards have developed exclusively in the realm of negative reproduction, that is, in cases assessing the constitutionality of regulation impacting the right to avoid procreation through medical assistance. Thus, understanding whether a law impacting ART would pass constitutional muster requires great familiarity with the evolved jurisprudence surrounding contraception and abortion regulation.

ii. The Right to Avoid Reproduction

The jurisprudential history of the right not to procreate has been exhaustively documented and analyzed by countless scholars, historians, commentators, and others. For purposes of discussing the relationship between ART and abortion on a constitutional level, a brief and highly selective review of this rich body of law will suffice. We begin by tracing the emanations from *Skinner* to the next major precedent to consider restrictions on reproductive conduct. In 1965, Justice Douglas once again authored an opinion striking down a state law prohibiting the use of contraception. In *Griswold v. Connecticut*, the Court declared such state action infringed upon the married couple's right of privacy under the Due Process Clause.[43] The Court made plain that this protected "zone of privacy" includes the "intimate relation of husband and wife and their physician's role in one aspect of that relation."[44] Seven years later, the Court expanded the reach of reproductive privacy, striking down a Massachusetts law that banned the sale of contraceptives to unmarried individuals. In *Eisenstadt v. Baird*, Justice Brennan penned the oft-quoted pronouncement, "If the right of privacy means anything, it is the right of the individual, married or single, to be free from unwarranted governmental intrusion into matters so fundamentally affecting a person as the decision whether to bear or beget a child."[45]

Taken together, *Griswold* and *Eisenstadt* provide solid ground for requiring strict scrutiny of any regulation that infringes upon an individual's reproductive choices, including barriers to access the means to operationalize those choices. The seminal 1973 decision in *Roe v. Wade* extended the fundamental right to avoid procreation to the abortion arena, setting out the doomed trimester framework that allocated decision making and regulatory rights according to stages in the pregnancy.[46] *Roe* and its companion case, *Doe v. Bolton*,[47] invalidated forty-six states' abortion laws, including the nineteenth-century prohibitory statutes enacted as part of the physician movement to "professionalize" the technique, as well as mid-twentieth-century laws that legalized but heavily regulated access to abortion.[48] The

[42] *Id.* at 1376. [43] 381 U.S. 479 (1965). [44] *Id.* at 482.
[45] 405 U.S. 438, 454–44 (1972). [46] 410 U.S. 113 (1973). [47] 410 U.S. 179 (1973).
[48] *See* Caitlin E. Borgmann, *Roe v. Wade's 40th Anniversary: A Moment of Truth for the Anti-Abortion-Rights Movement?*, 24 STAN. L. & POL'Y REV. 245 (2013).

cornerstone of *Roe*—that a woman is protected against government interference in her right to seek an abortion prior to the end of her first trimester—withstood attack for nearly two decades.

In 1992, the Court reaffirmed *Roe*'s essential holding but reconfigured the legal standard under which future abortion regulation would be judged. Instead of viewing abortion rights as largely unfettered during the early stages of pregnancy, the Court in *Planned Parenthood of Southeastern Pennsylvania v. Casey* reformulated the test for evaluating state regulation of elective abortion, weighing the woman's liberty interest against the government's interest in potential life.[49] State abortion regulation, the Court declared, will be invalid if it poses an "undue burden" on the right to decide whether to terminate a pregnancy. An undue burden exists "if its purpose or effect is to place a substantial obstacle in the path of a woman seeking an abortion before the fetus attains viability."[50]

The undue burden test remains the centerpiece of the Court's abortion jurisprudence, though the high court has taken precious little opportunity to elucidate exactly when state action constitutes an undue burden on a reproductive liberty. In the years since *Casey*, the Supreme Court has cited the 1992 case over two dozen times, but only two of these decisions involved the direct regulation of abortion.[51] With no express limitation, the concept of undue burdens and procreative liberty need not be limited to the abortion context.[52] The same procreative liberty supporting the right to choose to end one's pregnancy arguably applies equally to actions intended to initiate conception and childbirth. If this logical inference is sound, then state action that interferes with the decision *to* procreate should also be evaluated under the undue burden analysis. Imagine, for example, that the undue burden test was the reigning analysis in 1942 when the *Skinner* court evaluated the Oklahoma law authorizing state officials to sexually sterilize certain convicted felons. We can be quite confident that Justice Douglas would have found that law to pose an undue burden on the right to procreate. Query whether contemporary laws that indirectly regulate reproductive choice can likewise withstand constitutional challenge.

b. Regulating around the Core of Reproduction

In the post-*Casey* era, regulatory activity surrounding reproductive choice has focused largely on discrete aspects of the medical procedures used to achieve and avert pregnancy, rather than on comprehensive schemes designed to fundamentally alter access to ART and abortion. Overall, legislative attention on abortion has been far more robust than lawmaking surrounding assisted conception, though occasionally proposed regulations impact both fields equally. For example, personhood measures that declare human life—and thus legal personhood—begin at fertilization would, under a plain meaning analysis, ban all

[49] 505 U.S. 833 (1992). [50] *Id.* at 878.

[51] *See* Stenberg v. Carhart, 530 U.S. 914 (2000) (declaring unconstitutional Nebraska statute banning "partial birth abortion" as unduly burdening right to choose abortion); *Gonzales v. Carhart*, 127 S. Ct. 1610 (2007) (upholding federal Partial-Birth Abortion Ban Act of 2003 as not imposing a substantial obstacle to late-term abortion because alternative methods, not banned by the act, are available).

[52] *But see* Borgmann, *Roe v. Wade's*, at 257 (calling the undue burden standard an "abortion-specific test").

abortion (for killing a human being) and significantly restrict current IVF practice (for discarding and freezing unwanted and excess embryos).[53] The personhood movement and its ambitious agenda aside for now,[54] legislative activity impacting reproductive choice has focused around rather than at the core of ART and abortion.

i. Abortion Regulation: On Incremental and Radical Approaches

In the abortion arena, state and federal lawmakers have considered myriad bills in recent years.[55] Offering a bird's-eye perspective, Professor Caitlin Borgmann observes a "strategy [among anti-abortion advocates] of incrementally whittling away at the right to abortion . . . to change 'hearts and minds' about abortion by giving it disfavored treatment in the law through as many channels as possible, without actually banning the procedure."[56] This incrementalism, she explains, takes shape as a steady stream of restrictions offered up to state legislatures and Congress that test the limits of the undue burden standard by pushing back on virtually every aspect of the abortion experience. The success of this incremental approach from a clinical perspective remains to be seen, with supporters citing the recent decline in abortion as a sign of victory while pro-choice advocates point out that data collection occurred before the bulk of the regulations were put in place.[57] Success from a legislative perspective, however, is clear.

Proffered and enacted bills range in scope from parental consent requirements, waiting periods, scripted counseling mandates, facility regulations, practitioner credentialing, mandatory ultrasounds, outright bans on medically preferred late-term abortion techniques, and fetal homicide laws. Of late, these incremental restrictions have grown more aggressive, gnawing at *Roe*'s essential holding by prohibiting previability abortions on several grounds. A handful of state laws now prohibit abortion based on sex selection or fetal anomaly, while others impose outright bans on abortion elected after a fetal heart rate is audible, generally occurring well before the end of the first trimester. In the main, advocates for this cornucopia of controls have made inroads at the legislative level. Judicial review, however, has yielded a more mixed result.

Ongoing abortion litigation is too immense and volatile to properly document herein, but mention of a few recent cases will serve to sketch the landscape. Recent cases navigate the constitutionality of several increasingly restrictive state laws touching upon preprocedure requirements, physician qualifications, and the pregnancy point at which abortion can be banned. The dispute at issue in each case provokes fundamental—or perhaps ideological—disagreement over whether the particular regulatory impact constitutes an undue burden

[53] *See* Jonathan F. Will, *Beyond Abortion: Why the Personhood Movement Implicates Reproductive Choice*, 39 AM. J. L & MED. 573 (2013).

[54] *See* text accompanying notes 82–90 for a discussion of the personhood movement.

[55] *See, e.g.*, Guttmacher Institute, *Laws Affecting Reproductive Health and Rights: 2013 State Policy Review* (reporting passage of seventy bills in twenty-two states restricting abortion rights), https://www.guttmacher.org/statecenter/updates/2013/statetrends42013.html.

[56] *Id.* at 245. This strategy is contrasted with the radical approach taken by others in the anti-abortion movement who seek nothing short of the overturning of *Roe* and a ban on all abortions.

[57] *See* Erik Eckholm, *Abortions Declining in U.S., Study Finds*, N.Y. TIMES, Feb. 3, 2014, at A10.

on a woman's right to choose or survives as a legitimate exercise of the state's interest in potential life.

One group of laws seeks to make abortion more unattractive to woman by requiring they visualize their fetus before deciding to abort. In November 2013, the Supreme Court denied certiorari in *Pruitt v. Nova Health Systems*,[58] in which the Oklahoma Supreme Court struck down a state law that would have required the performance, display, and explanation of a pre-abortion ultrasound. State lawmakers defended the bill as allowing women to make an informed decision before undergoing abortion, but the state high court found the measure facially unconstitutional under *Casey*. In contrast, a similar "informed consent" law enacted in Texas withstood challenge and became effective in January 2012.[59]

Other laws are design to suppress access to abortion by beefing up the credentialing requirements providers and facilities must meet. One such Texas law survived to implementation in November 2013 when the Supreme Court refused to temporarily block a new law requiring physicians performing abortions to have professional privileges at a hospital within thirty miles of the clinic site.[60] Providers challenging the law estimated that a third of the state's clinics would be forced to close, depriving twenty thousand women a year access to abortion, while imposing delays and increased risk of complications on countless other patients.

A final example includes laws from 20% of U.S. states that prohibit abortion after twenty weeks postfertilization, based on the medically contested assertion that the fetus senses pain at this point in development. In January 2014, the Supreme Court declined to hear a case testing the constitutionality of an Arizona fetal pain law banning most abortions, save those involving a medical emergency, after twenty weeks gestation.[61] The decision means that a Ninth Circuit decision striking down the ban as unconstitutional will stand.[62] Given the Court's unwillingness to weigh in on the legality of a law that moves the *Roe* viability standard forward by at least several weeks, the status of similar laws in other states is unclear, particularly in jurisdictions where the laws have not been challenged.

Perhaps more critically, laws like the Arizona twenty-week ban seem to mark a transition from incrementalism to radicalism on the part of abortion-rights foes. Laws banning previability abortion with almost no exception move the needle from chipping away at abortion rights to blowing them up altogether. It takes little leap of logic to conclude that if abortion can be banned at twenty weeks based on the state's purported concern for fetal pain, a law prohibiting the procedure once fetal movement can be detected (typically within the first weeks postfertilization) could likewise withstand legal challenge under a "state's interest in potential life."[63] The future of abortion access and restriction

[58] 134 S. Ct. 617 (2013).

[59] Texas Medical Providers Performing Abortion Servs. V. Lakey, 667 F.3d 570 (5th Cir. 2012) (also requiring physician to broadcast fetal heartbeat to patient).

[60] Planned Parenthood of Greater Texas Surgical Health Servs. v. Abbott, 734 F.3d 406 (5th Cir. 2013). While the law has been implemented, it remains under review by the 5th Circuit.

[61] Horne v. Isaacson, __ S.Ct. __, 2014 WL 102430 (U.S.), 82 USLW 3193.

[62] Isaacson v. Horne, 716 F.3d 1213 (9th Cir. 2013) (law violates the U.S. Constitution by depriving women the ultimate decision to terminate their pregnancy prior to fetal viability).

[63] In July 2013, a federal district court struck down a North Dakota law that would have banned most abortions once a fetal heartbeat is detected, typically at six weeks gestation. In signing the bill, Gov. Jack Dalrymple, a Republican, called it "a legitimate attempt by a state legislature to discover the boundaries

remains in play, guided only by a set of aging and ill-defined legal standards that permit oppositional interpretation.

ii. ART Regulation: A Quieter and Gentler World

An unfortunate moniker stalks reproductive medicine from a regulatory perspective, with many labeling the field, "the wild west of medicine."[64] Such an accusation conjures up an image of lawless and greedy physicians preying upon desperate wannabe parents with no regard for the well-being of either patient or prospective offspring. While the ART world has endured its share of scandal, malfeasance, and downright criminality, such occurrences are not the exclusive—or even causative—product of an absent regulatory scheme. Nevertheless, the perception persists.

Briefly stated, ART is regulated by a bevy of federal and state laws that touch on various aspect of assisted conception. On the federal side, ART providers are subject to usage and outcome reporting requirements,[65] as well as health and safety parameters affecting donated gametes and embryos.[66] States, in their traditional role as protectors of the public's health, welfare, and safety, regulate a range of ART activity, including informed consent for IVF, surrogate parenting arrangements, gamete and embryo donation, parental assignment in third-party reproduction, posthumous use of reproductive material, and disposition of gametes and embryos maintained in frozen storage.[67]

The critique of U.S. ART as a largely unregulated field does have merit from a comparative global perspective. Many countries have enacted comprehensive regulatory schemes that govern the delivery and monitoring of ART services, typically vesting authority in a national agency. Robust regulation in different corners of the world, including Canada, Australia, Brazil, Israel, and England and other European nations, highlight the lack of a federal approach in the United States. Even at the state level, the nature of ART regulation does not rise to the level of clinical management exercised by non-U.S. overseers. For example, several countries limit the number of embryos that can be transferred in any single IVF cycle (in order to reduce the incidence of multiple pregnancy), while no such restrictions exist within the United States. Instead, best practices are disseminated through a self-regulatory system in which industry experts publish voluntary guidelines for adoption by practicing clinicians.[68]

of Roe v. Wade." Erik Eckholm, *Judge Blocks North Dakota Abortion Restrictions*, N.Y. Times, July 22, 2013, at A10. For an analysis of the state's interest in potential life and in preventing fetal pain as distinct interests, *see* I. Glenn Cohen & Sadath Sayeed, *Fetal Pain, Abortion, Viability and the Constitution*, 39 J. L. Med. & Ethics 235 (2011).

64 For citations to this reference, *see* Judith Daar, *Federalizing Embryo Transfers: Taming the Wild West of Reproductive Medicine?*, 23 Col. J. Gender & L. 257, 258 (2012).

65 *See* note 12.

66 *See* Human Cells, Tissues, and Cellular and Tissue-Based Products, 21 C.F.R. §1271, at http://www.accessdata.fda.gov/scripts/cdrh/cfdocs/cfcfr/CFRSearch.cfm?CFRPart=1271.

67 *See generally* Daar, Reproductive, at 662–665 (discussing state regulation of ART).

68 For example, the American Society for Reproductive Medicine publishes practice guidelines on its website at http://www.asrm.org.

In contrast to the flurry of legislative interest that besieges abortion, congressional and state house activity surrounding ART is relatively low, though not nonexistent. While Congress has not meaningfully considered a bill touching on ART practice in recent years, many state legislatures have contemplated various measures. Over the past five or so years, bills have been introduced that would have limited embryo transfers per cycle, criminalized commercial surrogacy, restricted IVF to married patients, banned payments to egg donors, and outlawed the freezing of embryos for future use—though none of these measures emerged enacted. A few new laws have been added to the rolls, including requirements surrounding egg donor solicitation and formalization of parental rights in surrogacy arrangements.[69] Thus, ART regulation takes shape as an incremental process marked by tweaks, rather than dramatic shifts, in the legislative arena.

The relatively low level of legislative activity compared with abortion is attributable to many factors, including the lack of a national movement to ban the technique in its entirety. Abortion-rights advocates frequently spar with well-organized groups such as the National Right to Life Committee and Americans United for Life. While the Catholic Church continues to oppose all forms of fertilization that substitute for the conjugal act, no other organized group of national prominence advocates for complete suppression of medically assisted conception. In addition, the widespread use of ART for family formation probably plays a role in its "under the radar" position relative to abortion. Since we know that three in one hundred Americans are born via assisted conception, we can surmise that most lawmakers have themselves or know someone who has benefited from the practice. Working to ban family formation technologies in the face of one's own children or children within one's family circle could present an insurmountable conflict for many legislators, prompting restraint rather than activism.

III Emerging Issues at the Intersection of ART and Abortion

The broad range of reproductive choices a person can make in a lifetime are central to that individual's identity, touching upon such vital decisions as whether, when, how, and with whom to become a parent. In most instances, decision making about reproductive activity is binary—one pathway leads to the birth of a child and the other avoids or averts this outcome. Earlier we considered, in similar binary fashion, whether the right to be left alone in the pursuit of medically assisted parenthood enjoys the same jurisprudential treatment as the right to avoid procreation via access to abortion. Now we move to consider the conflation of these two reproductive activities, so disparate in their ultimate goals. At least three areas challenge us to consider the intersection of ART and abortion: selective reduction of multiple pregnancy, the personhood movement, and emerging technologies that challenge heretofore sacred notions about the events that mark the beginning of pregnancy.

[69] Cal. Health & Safety Code §125325; Cal. Fam. Code §7962.

a. Selective Reduction: Abortion in the Name of Parenthood?

Selective reduction, also called multifetal pregnancy reduction,[70] is a surgical procedure performed between late first and early second trimester of pregnancy to "reduce" the number of fetuses in a multiple pregnancy, typically in order to enhance the survival and well-being of the remaining fetuses.[71] The use of selective reduction has increased dramatically with the rise in ART usage, owing to the still imprecise nature of fertility treatment. Predicting with certainty the number of live-born offspring to emerge from any IVF or ovulation induction cycle remains an elusive goal.[72] We do know that the rate of twin and higher-order multiple births has risen between 1980 and 2009, with over 27% of all IVF pregnancies currently yielding two or more fetuses.[73] The morbidity and mortality associated with multiple birth for both mother and babies has been well documented, prompting some patients to consider the emotionally painful, medically risky, and ethically wrenching reduction procedure.[74]

Commonalities and distinctions between selective reduction and abortion are, at first blush, fairly easily teased out. The procedures share the ultimate outcome—the death of a fetus upon completion of a medical intervention. Both are performed, generally speaking, well before the end of the second trimester at the request of a (ideally, fully informed) pregnant woman. Both can be justified under current constitutional jurisprudence as an expression of a woman's reproductive autonomy. On the other hand, selective reduction and abortion are distinguishable in two primary ways—technique and intent. The abortion technique, whether medical or surgical, involves the expulsion of the fetus from the woman's body. Done correctly, an abortion should leave the uterus empty of fetal material. Selective reduction is accomplished by injected a needle containing potassium chloride directly into the fetal heart to produce death of the fetus in the uterus. The dead fetus is not removed or

[70] Many clinicians and scholars distinguish between the terms "multifetal pregnancy reduction" in which a (typically healthy) fetus is reduced to improve the outcome in high-order multiple pregnancy based on technical considerations, primarily the location of the fetus in the uterus, from "selective reduction" in which a patient elects fetal reduction based on the sex or health status of a fetus in a multiple pregnancy. This article adopts the term "selective reduction" to describe the technique of fetal reduction, regardless of impetus.

[71] American College of Obstetrics and Gynecology, Committee on Ethics, *Multifetal Pregnancy Reduction*, Committee Opinion No. 553 (Feb. 2013).

[72] Even predicting that a singleton birth will result from a single embryo transfer is uncertain given the increased risk of monozygotic twinning in IVF cycles. *See* Jaime Knopman et al., *Monozygotic Twinning: An Eight-Year Experience at a Large IVF Center*, 94 Fertility & Sterility 502 (2010). Another oft-quoted factor impacting the high rate of ART multiple pregnancies in the U.S. is the lack of insurance coverage for most patients. Several studies show a correlation between multiple birth rates and mandated IVF coverage. *See, e.g.*, J. Ryan Martin, Jason C. Bromer, Denny Sakkas, Pasquale Patrizio, *Insurance Coverage and* In Vitro *Fertilization Outcomes: A U.S. Perspective*, 95 Fertility & Sterility 964 (2011) (data show clinics in states without insurance mandates have higher multiple pregnancy rates because they transfer more embryos than clinics in states with coverage).

[73] *Id.* The twin rate increased 76% between 1980 and 2009, while the triplet or greater rate shot up more than 400% between 1980 and 1998. Since then, the rate of higher-order multiple deliveries has decreased by 29% as a result of a reduction in the number of embryos transferred per cycle and the increased use of selective reduction.

[74] Risks of multiple birth to offspring include prematurity, cerebral palsy, learning disabilities, chronic lung disease, and developmental delays. Maternal risks include hypertension, preeclampsia, gestational diabetes, and postpartum hemorrhage. *Id.*

expelled from the body but rather is gradually resorbed as the pregnancy progresses. Done correctly, selective reduction leaves a woman pregnant with a more medically manageable number of fetuses.

On deeper analysis, selective reduction and abortion raise complex legal and moral questions about the path of a woman's reproductive journey in contemporary society. In particular, two questions are worthy of discussion. First, to what extent do state and federal abortion laws apply to selective reduction? Given the panoply of post-*Casey* abortion obstacles lawmakers have contemplated, approved, and implemented, would a woman seeking to continue her pregnancy through selective reduction be subject to these regulatory measures? Second, to the extent selective reduction is justified as a risk-reduction technique in a "balance of harms" analysis, does it remain justified when a woman elects to reduce twins to a singleton for social rather than medical reasons? Both of these questions delve into the nature and durability of a pregnant woman's reproductive autonomy.

Do abortion laws apply to selective reduction? It depends. Mostly the answer is tied to the definition of abortion set forth in any given statute. In Texas, for example, a state with relatively robust abortion restrictions including mandated ultrasound, required counseling, and provider credentialing, abortion is defined as "the use of any means to terminate the pregnancy of a female known by the attending physician to be pregnant with the intention that the termination of the pregnancy by those means will, with reasonable likelihood, cause the death of the fetus."[75] On the question of whether this language applies to selective reduction, University of Texas law professor John Robertson opines:

> Since protection of fetuses is a main purpose of such statutes, a natural reading of the statute would be to view the termination of the pregnancy of a particular fetus, as occurs with selective reduction, to be covered. On the other hand, precision in language is also necessary. Since the intention of the physician is not to terminate the entire pregnancy, one could argue (perhaps with less support) that selective reduction where at least one fetus remains and the pregnancy continues is not covered.[76]

Other state laws are more explicit about the "fetal protection" aim of their abortion laws, including a Virginia statute that provides, "if any person administer to, or cause to be taken by a woman, any drug or other thing, or use means, with intent to destroy her unborn child, or to produce abortion or miscarriage, and thereby destroy such child, or produce such abortion or miscarriage, he shall be guilty of a Class 4 felony."[77] Since selective reduction "administer[s] to . . . a woman . . . with intent to destroy her unborn child," the law's plain language would appear to apply. In states like Virginia, where abortion is defined primarily by the intentional killing of a fetus, relief from liability would have to be found in maternal health exceptions, if any, or in any safety zone carved out for previability terminations.

Even if selective reduction can be distinguished from abortion under laws enacted to apply to the former, should all forms of fetal reduction be entitled to equal protection? We

[75] V.T.C.A. Health & Safety Code §171.002.

[76] John Robertson, Is Selective Reduction Covered by State Abortion Law? Harvard Bill of Health Blog (Apr. 10, 2013), http://blogs.law.harvard.edu/billofhealth/2013/04/10/john-robertson-on-is-selective-reduction-covered-by-state-abortion-law-online-abortion-and-reproductive-technology-symposium/.

[77] Va. Code Ann. §18.2-71.

can imagine a legislative debate in which lawmakers agree to exclude selective reduction of higher-order multiple pregnancy (triplets or greater) from the general abortion laws under the principle of proportionality. Since selective reduction produces a net benefit for both the pregnant woman and her remaining fetuses as measured against the loss of one or more fetal lives, the procedure can be justified as offering greater protection to fetal well-being than nonintervention. Decades of medical data support this analysis.[78] But the medical benefits of reducing a healthy twin pregnancy are less certain.[79] Can lawmakers effectively ban selective reduction in some cases but not others? Here, arguments likely turn to assertions of reproductive autonomy since the proportionality of benefits to harms is, at best, in equipoise.

Applied broadly, reproductive autonomy would not distinguish between higher-order and twin pregnancy reduction, just as it is unconcerned with a woman's reasons for seeking a previability abortion under any circumstances. But if a woman's liberty to elect reduction is measured against competing state interests in fetal life, twin reduction could be in jeopardy. Reducing one healthy twin for nonmedical reasons would invoke the same bare "respect for life" objections that motivate current anti-abortion laws.

Moreover, the stigma associated with abortion could be even greater in the case of a woman who intentionally seeks out ART knowing the high risk of multiple pregnancy.[80] For this woman to initially intend the consequences of her choice—to become pregnant through assisted conception—and then take measures to reverse one of its well-known sequelae, may strike some as a breach of her duty to maintain a healthy twin pregnancy. Clinically speaking, multiple pregnancy following ART is more foreseeable than pregnancy following consensual intercourse, arguably giving rise to a heightened duty to the resulting fetuses. But linking the exercise of reproductive rights to the nature or impetus of a woman's pregnancy has dangerous implications for the survivability of procreative liberty and should be eschewed. At its core, a woman's right to control her reproductive destiny should be clinically neutral, thus treating abortion and reduction as equally viable choices.[81]

b. The Personhood Movement: ART and Abortion Rights Find Common Ground

The personhood movement was launched in 2008 with a Colorado ballot initiative that would have amended the state constitution to provide, "the term 'person' or 'persons' shall include any human being from the moment of fertilization."[82] Though rejected by 73% of the electorate, the measure energized its backers to found Personhood USA, a nonprofit

[78] *See* Mark I. Evans & David W. Britt, *Multifetal Pregnancy Reduction: Evolution of the Ethical Arguments*, 28 Seminars in Reprod. Med. 295 (2010).

[79] *But see id.* (reduction to singleton pose less risk than twin pregnancy).

[80] *See generally* Paula Abrams, *The Scarlet Letter: The Supreme Court and the Language of Abortion Stigma*, 19 Mich. J. Gender & L. 293 (2013).

[81] *See generally* Laura Purdy, *Women's Reproductive Autonomy: Medicalisation and Beyond*, 32 J. Med. Ethics 287 (2006).

[82] *See* Colo. Initiative 36 (2008) (proposed Colo. Const. art. II, §23), http://www.sos.state.co.us/pubs/elections/Initiatives/ballot/contacts/2008ballotinitiativecontactlist.pdf.

Christian ministry committed to "moving churches and the culture to make the dehumanization and murdering of preborn children unthinkable."[83] In the ensuing years, the group has sponsored several ballot measures and state bills, to date only one of which has been tentatively approved.[84] The movement, renouncing an incremental approach to suppressing access to abortion, gives its full-throated support for "filling the Blackmun Hole," a reference to the language in *Roe* that "[i]f this suggestion of personhood is established, the appellant's case, of course, collapses, for the fetus' right to life would then be guaranteed specifically by the Amendment."[85] While academic and policy debate continues over whether a personhood law would in fact be interpreted to render all abortion illegal, the movement is committed to this outcome. One very interesting aspect of the personhood movement is the ART stumbling block it has repeatedly encountered.

Pre- and postelection polling revealed that many a ballot was cast not on the voter's position on abortion or the definition of human life, but rather on worries that a personhood law would impact the availability and use of IVF. Even in states where the percentage of abortion rights supporters in the electorate hovers in the single digits, personhood initiatives fell handily, largely out of fear such a change in the law would hinder access to medically assisted conception.[86] These results obtained in the face of significant efforts on the part of personhood supporters to assure voters through messaging and tweaks in the proposals' language that IVF would proceed unaffected by the laws' passage. ART access was likewise a concern in state houses in which similar bills were considered. A 2012 personhood effort was defeated in the Virginia legislature, with opponents persuasively arguing that the bill could prohibit IVF.[87]

Whether a personhood law would impact ART remains to be seen, but such concerns are hardly unfounded.[88] Imbuing a zygote with full legal rights could call into question the legality of common aspects of IVF, including preimplantation genetic screening, embryo transfer, cryopreservation, and embryo discard. Each of these techniques poses some risk of embryo loss and thus could be banned in the name of protecting human life. Even restricting only certain aspects of IVF could dramatically impact clinical outcomes. For example if cryopreservation were banned (on the grounds that 20%–40% of embryos fail to survive the freezing process), patients would have to accept transfer of all embryos that are formed. Given the still imprecise science surrounding in vitro embryo formation, physicians could be compelled to transfer a high-order number of embryos, posing significant risk to both

[83] *See About Us, What is Personhood?*, PERSONHOOD USA, http://www.personhoodusa.com/about-us/.

[84] In 2013, the North Dakota legislature approved a measure amending the state constitution to guarantee the protection of human life at any stage of development. Before it becomes operational, the measure will be placed before voters for approval in 2014. *See North Dakota Measure 1* at *id.*

[85] Roe v. Wade, 410 U.S. at 156–157.

[86] *See* Will, *Beyond Abortion*, at 585 (reporting in 2011, Mississippi voters rejected personhood Measure 26 with 31% of voters saying their vote was based on concerns about availability of IVF; only 8% voted based on pro-choice concerns).

[87] *See* Anita Kumar, *"Personhood" Bill Killed for This Year by Virginia Senate*, WASH. POST (Feb. 23, 2012), http://www.washingtonpost.com/blogs/virginia-politics/post/personhood-bill-killed-for-this-year-by-virginia-senate/2012/02/23/gIQAyXvBWR_blog.html.

[88] *But see* I. Glenn Cohen & Jonathan F. Will, *Mississippi's Ambiguous 'Personhood' Amendment*, N.Y. TIMES, Oct. 31, 2011 (arguing personhood law would apply to common ART procedures, including embryo discard).

mother and offspring. Additionally, taking cryopreservation off the table means patients would have to undergo repeat cycles of ovarian stimulation after a failed cycle or to initiate another pregnancy, something avoided when frozen embryos are available for transfer.

Politically, the personhood movement brought ART and abortion closer than they had ever been. Prior to the movement, interaction between groups such as the National Abortion Rights Action League (NARAL) and the American Society for Reproductive Medicine (ASRM) was rare. Perhaps both saw their missions as nonintersecting. NARAL describes itself as a pro-choice organization working to protect women's access to safe, legal abortion while reducing the need for abortion through improved access to birth control. The group also pledges support for women who choose to carry their pregnancies to term.[89] ASRM states its mission as "a multidisciplinary organization dedicated to the advancement of the art, science, and practice of reproductive medicine."[90] Reproductive medicine is a branch of medicine dedicated to enabling people to have children at a time of their choosing. With pregnancy as a dividing line, ASRM focused on the events before, while NARAL looked only at choices available after this defining event.

The seeming disconnect between the groups' core missions may have kept the organizations at arm's length for fear of contaminating or confusing their respective messages. It is not unsurprising that ART advocates would be wary of tangling in abortion politics—forcing them to acknowledge the degree of embryo loss associated with IVF. Such confessions have largely been avoided by focusing on the child-bearing goals of treatment. At the same time, abortion rights advocates may have seen ART as a thriving enterprise serving a very different patient population, hardly in need of its limited resources. But the two sides found much common ground when faced with the same enemy. Both are strong and vocal opponents of the personhood movement, both acknowledge the threat to the other's domain.[91] As historic allegiances tied to pre- and postpregnancy choice coalesce around the definition of human life, can the role of pregnancy as a true biologic marker distinguishing ART and abortion be sustained? The emergence of new genetic technologies raises this very question.

c. On Choosing: Reproductive Decision Making in the Genomic Era

Current configurations of ART and abortion support a person's right to avoid becoming a parent to a child afflicted by a life- or health-threatening genetic anomaly. Since the early 1990s, patients undergoing IVF could elect to investigate the genetic makeup of their embryos through preimplantation genetic diagnosis (PGD). PGD involves the extraction and genetic analysis of one of the totipotent cells of the early embryo, traditionally performed

[89] *See What Is Choice?*, NARAL Pro-Choice America, http://www.prochoiceamerica.org/what-is-choice/.

[90] *See* Mission Statement, American Society for Reproductive Medicine, http://www.asrm.org/mission/.

[91] *See* ASRM Position Statement on Personhood Measures, http://www.asrm.org/ASRM_Position_Statement_on_Personhood_Measures/ (discussing impact on abortion); "Personhood Measure: Extreme and Dangerous Attempts to Ban Abortion, http://www.prochoiceamerica.org/media/fact-sheets/abortion-personhood.pdf (discussing impact on IVF).

on the third day of embryonic development. With results in hand, prospective parents can choose to transfer or discard embryos on the basis of their genetic health.[92] Postpregnancy options for fetal diagnosis have progressed from ultrasound to amniocentesis to chorionic villus sampling (CVS) to maternal serum screening, with each technique yielding actionable information well into the second trimester of pregnancy.[93] Moreover, both amnio and CVS are invasive procedures and pose risk of fetal loss, making them unattractive to many women who might otherwise want access to information about their child's health.

Recent advances in both pre- and postpregnancy genetic testing are bringing the previously distinct processes closer together, as measured by the time each is performed and the degree of invasiveness each poses. In the PGD arena, the standard of care is moving to removing cells from the placental portion of an embryo (the trophectoderm) at day five, rather than extraction of a single cell from the embryo itself at day three. This move to trophectoderm biopsy provides more cell material to analyze, thus improving accuracy while reducing embryo loss following the procedure.[94] The procedure also avoids invasion of the embryo by taking cells from the area destined to become the placenta.

Postpregnancy prenatal genetic testing is undergoing rapid change with the advent of cell-free fetal DNA analysis, a technique in which fetal genetic material is culled from maternal blood and subject to in depth analysis. While still experimental, scientists report it is possible to noninvasively sequence the entire fetal genome, thus facilitating prenatal diagnosis of virtually any genetic anomaly.[95] This breadth of data may soon be available as early as the fifth week of gestation, with at least one study reporting the presence of cell-free fetal DNA at eighteen days post–embryo transfer in an IVF pregnancy.[96] With less than three weeks separating the search for an embryo's genetic makeup for purposes of initiating a pregnancy from that same search for purposes of possibly terminating a pregnancy, the distinction between ART and abortion is, at the very least, diminished. While ART stakeholders have resisted and rejected claims that embryo selection after PGD is akin to prepregnancy abortion, the compression of time between embryo discard and early first-trimester abortion does provoke thought about the durability of pregnancy as a unique and irreplaceable biologic marker.

Comparing cell-free fetal DNA analysis with trophectoderm biopsy raises one final point. Both advances are designed to be less invasive than prior techniques; maternal blood draw avoids disturbing the intact uterine cavity while day five PGD leaves the developing embryo untouched. The question is whether this retreat from physical interaction with the

[92] PGD also detects the embryo's sex. While nearly all ART clinics facilitate embryonic selection on the basis of health, some do not offer PGD for nonmedical sex selection. *See* Susannah Baruch, David Kaufman, & Kathy L. Hudson, *Genetic Testing of Embryos: Practices and Perspectives of US* In Vitro *Fertilization Clinics*, 89 Fertility & Sterility 1053 (2008) (reporting 93% of clinics offer PGD for chromosomal abnormalities but only 42% offer nonmedical sex selection).

[93] *See* Ruth M. Farrell, *Women and Prenatal Genetic Testing in the 21st Century*, 23 Health Matrix 1 (2013).

[94] *See* Ruthi B. Lathi et al., *Outcomes of Trophectoderm Biopsies on Cryopreserved Blastocysts: A Case Series*, 25 Reprod. Biomed. Online 504 (2012), http://www.rbmojournal.com/article/S1472-6483(12)00414-2/abstract.

[95] *See* H.C. Fan et al., *Noninvasive Prenatal Measurement of the Fetal Genome*, 487 Nature 320 (2012).

[96] *See* J. Guibert et al., *Kinetics of SRY Gene Appearance in Maternal Serum: Detection by Real Time PCR in Early Pregnancy after Assisted Reproductive Technique*, 18 Human Reprod. 1733 (2003).

developing child has any impact on reproductive decision making? Is initiating or terminating a pregnancy a less meaningful life-defining event when it reaches only the periphery of the somatic self? True enough, IVF still requires embryo transfer into the uterus, and abortion involves the departure of the fetus the same place, both techniques invading the woman's bodily integrity. But technological advances have paved the way for a more hands-off approach to the early stages of reproduction. When Justice O'Connor warned that the *Roe* abortion framework was on a collision course with itself, she likely did not contemplate how closely the acts of engaging in and avoiding reproduction would one day align.

IV Conclusion

ART and abortion have traditionally occupied distinct realms, invoking participation from demographically diverse communities, engendering different legal analysis, spurring disparate legislative activity, and conjuring distinctive public images tied to the intended consequences of each technique. But these pregnancy-inducing and pregnancy-avoiding processes are becoming increasingly intertwined, legally, politically, and technically. In all likelihood, overlaps will continue to emerge as our knowledge about embryonic development progresses. It will be interesting to observe how each camp regards the other, given their shared reliance on reproductive medical professionals who facilitate all aspects of procreative choice. Today, the decision to abort a pregnancy invokes obstacles and reactions that are quite distinct from those accompanying a decision to access parenthood via ART. But at their heart, both decisions are about the propriety of utilizing medical assistance to define one's reproductive future. Building on this shared truth can surely strengthen both foundations.

CHAPTER 16

CONSCIENTIOUS REFUSALS OF CARE

ELIZABETH SEPPER

THE mention of conscience in medicine likely calls to mind the doctor who will not perform abortions due to his deep-seated religious belief that to do so would be to take a human life. Willing to sacrifice his career rather than violate his very sense of self, he would leave the profession if compelled to provide an abortion.

Conscience in medicine, however, proves more diverse than this archetype allows. Patients exercise conscience in choosing abortion, contraception, assisted suicide, and other contested care. Providers disagree with one another, based on opposing but equally fundamental moral judgments. Healthcare facilities also set religious restrictions on care, often in tension with the religious, moral, and ethical commitments of individuals who practice within them.

Conflicts of conscience between patients, providers, and institutions arise across medicine but are most salient with regard to reproductive and end-of-life care. In these areas in particular, patients' rights to control treatment decisions in accordance with their values may collide with the judgments of medical providers. Futility determinations are a classic example, relying on decisions about the nature of life and death. Providing condoms as part of HIV counseling, sterilization, contraception, removal or refusal of respirators, artificial hydration or nutrition, vaccination, blood transfusions, circumcision, fertility treatments, euthanasia, psychotropic drugs, pain management, stem-cell-derived therapies, and, of course, abortion also figure prominently.

In the course of these disagreements, doctors and nurses, as well as their patients, may invoke conscience. Although there is no single definition, "conscience" generally refers to consciousness of and decision-making about right and wrong. Individuals will disagree over fundamental questions of right and wrong, but each experiences conscience in determining the morality of his or her own actions. To exercise conscience, a person identifies moral principles, assesses context, and decides whether to do or omit a particular act. Across many moral traditions, these judgments of conscience must be obeyed, or the individual will have acted immorally.[1] Conscience is significantly broader than religion and is informed by education, experience, and introspection.

[1] VATICAN II, DIGNITATIS HUMANAE (1965) ("He is bound to follow this conscience faithfully in all his activity so that he may come to God, who is his last end. Therefore he must not be forced to act

In medicine, "conscientious refusals" take place when a provider consults her conscience and determines that she cannot participate in a procedure that the profession has determined to be ethically and legally permissible. The exercise of conscience arises in the specific circumstance where a patient, an institution, or the state requests or requires that she perform the procedure.

Legislators have acted to protect conscientious refusals. Across the United States, legislation protecting refusal to provide contested medical care—commonly known as "conscience clauses"—shield objectors from adverse employment decisions, defunding, professional discipline, and criminal and tort liability based on their refusal. They extend both to individual healthcare providers and to facilities, typically hospitals. Originally confined to abortion and sometimes sterilization, their scope is broadening. Once thought to protect religious organizations involved in healthcare and individual adherents who object to an act they view as killing, conscience legislation has extended to individuals and entities remote from the contested act and devoid of religious identity.

Refusal to deliver healthcare (or insure particular procedures) has moved from the legislatures to the courts. In response to new requirements in the Affordable Care Act, for-profit corporations demanded the right to refuse to cover contraception in employee health plans, using abortion conscience legislation as evidence that for-profits occupy the same religious ground as religious organizations. In 2014, in *Burwell v. Hobby Lobby*, the U.S. Supreme Court sided with the challengers and held—for the first time ever—that for-profit corporations can exercise religion.[2] It concluded that, at minimum, for-profit corporations must be exempted from compliance with the contraceptive rule on the same terms as nonprofit religious organizations.[3]

Legislatures and courts—as well as much of the scholarly literature—oversimplify the dilemmas created by conscientious refusal. Virtually all legislation neglects the access problems that arise when no alternate provider exists to deliver care or when patients need emergency treatment. Statutes often treat refusal as synonymous with conscience. As a result, they both include non-normative refusals and exclude claims of conscience by patients seeking controversial care and providers committed to delivering it. Courts and legislatures alike extend conscience protections to refusing institutions with weak theoretical support. They ignore the significant practical impact of institutional protections on individual conscience.

Part I of this article sets out the expansionist history of legislative protections for refusals of healthcare and the recent recourse to the courts for exemptions from requirements to provide insurance for contested care. Part II explores the theoretical justifications for protecting conscience in medicine and reviews proposals to balance patient access and provider conscience. Part III contends that current legislation works to prioritize refusal over true exercise of conscience by failing to examine the basis of a provider's refusal and by excluding countervailing claims to conscience from providers and patients. Part IV argues that

contrary to his conscience."); Hannah Arendt, The Life of the Mind 186 (Harcourt 1978) (arguing for the importance of being consistent with oneself, which Socrates epitomizes); Thomas E. Hill, *Four Conceptions of Conscience, in* Ian Shapiro & Robert Merrihew Adams, Integrity and Conscience 17 (1998) ("Kant's moral theory holds that each of us must, in the end, treat our own (final) moral judgments as authoritative, even though they are fallible.").

[2] Burwell v. Hobby Lobby Stores, Inc., 134 S. Ct. 2759 (2014).

[3] *Id.*

institutional conscience rests on shaky theoretical foundations and poses practical and theoretical impediments to the protection of conscience. Part V identifies paths for future research.

I History and Development of Protection for Conscientious Refusals of Care

This section traces legislation protecting refusal of controversial healthcare from their origins forty years ago to their manifestations in contemporary healthcare. It begins with a brief overview of the common law, statutory, and ethical duties of healthcare providers. It explains the ways in which conscience legislation works to exempt providers from these duties and to modify the relationship between healthcare institutions, personnel, patients, and the state—initially with regard to abortion and now with regard to an expanding universe of healthcare. It concludes by describing recent litigation that brings conscientious refusal into the courts.

As a general rule, medical personnel and institutions have no legal or ethical duty to accept any specific person as a patient or to deliver any particular service. Federal and state statutes, however, set some limits. Most significantly, in hospital emergency rooms, all patients suffering from emergency conditions or in active labor must be stabilized.[4] In many states, providers must offer emergency contraception to sexual assault survivors.[5] In others, they must counsel terminally ill patients about palliative care.[6] Providers generally must comply with laws and ethical norms that prohibit discrimination—as is most relevant here—on the basis of sex, sexual orientation, religion, and gender identity.[7]

Moreover, having accepted a person as a patient, providers have a legal and ethical duty to treat her in accordance with the standard of care, inform her of treatments and of their risks and benefits, and refer her for services that they are not able to provide.[8] As a matter of common law and constitutional doctrines, patients—not providers—control medical treatments and may refuse even life-saving care.[9] A doctor may not abandon a patient and may be held

[4] *See, e.g.*, Emergency Medical Treatment and Labor Act, 42 U.S.C. § 1395dd (2006).

[5] *See, e.g.*, 410 Ill. Comp. Stat. 70/2.2 (2011); N.M. Stat. Ann. § 24-10D-3(A) (West 2011); Ohio Rev. Code Ann. § 2907.29 (LexisNexis 2010); S.C. Code Ann. § 16-3-1350(B) (2003).

[6] N.Y. Pub. Health Law § 2997-c(2) (McKinney 2012).

[7] American College of Obstetricians and Gynecologists (ACOG), Committee on Ethics Opinion, The Limits of Conscientious Refusal in Reproductive Medicine 2 (Nov. 2007); American Medical Association (AMA) Council on Ethical and Judicial Affairs, Report 6-a-07, Physician Objection to Treatment and Individual Patient Discrimination (2007), *available at* http://www.ama-assn.org/resources/doc/ethics/ceja_6a07.pdf.

[8] 61 Am. Jur. 2d Physicians, Surgeons, Etc. § 121 nn.5-7 (2002).

[9] Cruzan v. Director, Mo. Dep't of Health, 497 U.S. 261, 278 (1990) ("The principle that a competent person has a constitutionally protected liberty interest in refusing unwanted medical treatment may be inferred from our prior decisions."); Pub. Health Trust of Dade Cnty. v. Wons, 541 So. 2d 96, 98 (Fla. 1989) (stating, with regard to a Jehovah's Witness's refusal of a blood transfusion, that "the courts, quite properly, have given great deference to the individual's right to make decisions vitally affecting his private life according to his own conscience[]").

liable if she unilaterally ends the relationship without reasonable notice while a patient still needs medical attention.[10]

Conscience legislation at the national level and in almost every state operates to exempt providers—to varying degrees—from these common law, statutory, and ethical obligations. The first conscience clauses responded to court decisions around sterilization and abortion. In 1973, a district court in Montana enjoined a Catholic hospital from refusing to permit tubal ligations,[11] prompting outcry from Catholic healthcare institutions. That same year, the Supreme Court established abortion as a constitutional right in *Roe v. Wade*. The U.S. Congress quickly passed the Church Amendment, which made clear that receipt of federal funds did not require an individual or institution to perform sterilizations or abortions if it "would be contrary to religious beliefs or moral convictions."[12] State legislatures followed suit.

In most states, laws now safeguard refusals to provide abortion (and sometimes sterilization and contraception) and to comply with a patient's request to withdraw or withhold life-sustaining treatment. The stated purpose of this legislative activity is protection of the consciences of medical providers who otherwise might face demands to deliver such care. Although many statutes protect "refusal" without stating its basis, more specific statutes require "ethical, moral, or religious grounds" for refusal.

Under most statutes, entire healthcare facilities may deny specified procedures to patients. The Church Amendment, for instance, states that federal funding will not require an entity to "make its facilities available for the performance of any sterilization procedure or abortion if the performance of such procedure or abortion in such facilities is prohibited by the entity on the basis of religious beliefs or moral convictions." [13] At the state level, typical statutory language reads "a hospital is not required to admit any patient for the purpose of performing an abortion."[14] Another common version immunizes healthcare institutions that decline to follow an advance directive because it "is contrary to . . . the written policies of the institution."[15]

This legislation modifies statutory and common law relationships in three significant ways. First, it imposes a duty on healthcare institutions to accommodate individual providers who refuse to participate in delivering contested procedures. Institutions cannot discriminate against them in hiring, promotion, or staff privileges. Conscience legislation thus functions as employment law, ensuring that employees do not face demands from employers that they cannot fulfill.[16] Second, the state may not discriminate against or penalize refusing providers in government programs. Finally, the legislation shifts the burden of any

[10] *See, e.g.*, Ricks v. Budge, 64 P.2d 208, 211–212 (Utah 1937).

[11] Taylor v. St. Vincent's Hosp., 369 F. Supp. 948 (D. Mont. 1973).

[12] 42 U.S.C. § 300a-7(b) (2000).

[13] *Id.* at § 300a-7(b)(2).

[14] Ariz. Rev. Stat. Ann. § 36-2154(A) (2009).

[15] Wyo. Stat. Ann. § 35-22-410 (2009).

[16] *See* Shelton v. Univ. of Med. & Dentistry of New Jersey, 223 F.3d 220 (3d Cir. 2000) (involving labor and delivery nurse who objected to participation in abortions and was offered a transfer); Grant v. Fairview Hosp. & Healthcare Serv., No. Civ. 02-4232JNEJGL, 2004 WL 326694 (D. Minn. Feb. 18, 2004) (involving ultrasound technician who preached to women contemplating abortion); Kenny v. Ambulatory Ctr. of Miami, 400 So. 2d 1262, 1267 (Fla. Dist. Ct. App. 1981) (discussing claims of nurse who objected to gynecological procedures and was employed in an operating room where 16% of procedures were gynecological); Swanson v. St. John's Lutheran Hosp., 597 P.2d 702 (Mont. 1979) (finding for a nurse-anesthetist although employer could only procure a part-time substitute fifty-five miles away).

harm caused by refusal onto specific patients and the general public by immunizing refusing institutions and individuals from civil and criminal liability or professional discipline. Patients harmed by refusal have no recourse to courts or state medical boards. Under all but a few conscience clauses, patients may be refused care even in emergencies.[17] For example, whereas a pregnant woman normally would have an informed consent claim if deprived of information about prenatal testing, some conscience laws strip her of this right. Similarly, delaying an abortion procedure for a woman who is miscarrying—as Catholic hospitals often require—may contravene the standard of care; yet, under conscience legislation, the patient's injuries—from, for example, going septic—go unremedied.[18]

In recent years, legislatures across the United States have expanded the reach of conscience laws substantially. More procedures have been specified as appropriate subjects of conscientious objection. Several states have moved from abortion to sterilization to contraception. The broadest legislation—in Mississippi, Illinois, and Washington—permits conscientious objections to any medical treatment at all.[19] In these states, Jehovah's Witnesses could refuse to transfuse patients. A vegan could withhold vaccines that contain egg proteins on the ground that the use of animal products is morally wrong.

Under some statutes, healthcare providers may withhold information, refuse to refer for treatment, and deny patients care distant from the contested procedure. In Oklahoma, for example, a nurse could refuse to take the blood pressure of a woman after she has had an abortion.[20] In Illinois, doctors may decline to "counsel, suggest, recommend, refer or participate" in "any phase of patient care."[21] With the country's broadest conscience legislation, Mississippi permits refusal to participate in "patient referral, counseling, therapy, testing, diagnosis or prognosis" for any medical procedure.[22] A clinic could withhold information

[17] Only a few state conscience clauses contain an emergency exception. *See* Cal. Health & Safety Code § 123420(d) (West 2006) (containing an exception for emergency for abortion); Fla. Stat. § 765.1105(1)(a) (2010) (containing an exception for emergency); 745 Ill. Comp. Stat. 70/6, 70/9 (2010) (containing exception for any procedure); Iowa Code § 146.1 (2005) (containing an exception for "medical care which has as its primary purpose the treatment of a serious physical condition requiring emergency medical treatment necessary to save the life of a mother"); La. Rev. Stat. Ann. § 40:1299.34, 34.5, 35.9 (2008) (containing exception for abortion); Nev. Rev. Stat. § 632.475(3) (2008) (containing exception for abortion); S.C. Code Ann. § 44-41-40 (2002) ("[N]o hospital or clinic shall refuse an emergency admittance" with regard to abortion); Tex. Occ. Code Ann. § 103.004 (West 2012) ("A private hospital or private health care facility is not required to make its facilities available for the performance of an abortion unless a physician determines that the life of the mother is immediately endangered."). *See also* California v. United States, No. C 05-00328 JSW, 2008 WL 744840 (N.D. Cal. Mar. 18, 2008) (reviewing state's challenge to federal conscience clause as potentially conflicting with state law requiring hospital to provide or refer for abortions in emergencies but dismissing claims on standing and ripeness grounds).

[18] Nat'l Health Law Program, Health Care Refusals: Undermining Quality Care for Women 15, 40, 57 (2010), *available at* http://www.healthlaw.org/images/stories/Health_Care_Refusals_Undermining_Quality_Care_for_Women.pdf; Angel M. Foster et al., *Do Religious Restrictions Influence Ectopic Pregnancy Management? A National Qualitative Study*, 21 WOMEN'S HEALTH ISSUES 104, 106 (2011).

[19] MISS. CODE ANN. § 41-107-5 (2009); 745 ILL. COMP. STAT. 70/4-5 (2010); WASH. REV. CODE § 48.43.065(2)(a) (2008).

[20] 63 OKL. ST. ANN. 1-741 (West 2004) ("No person may be required to perform, induce or participate in medical procedures which result in an abortion, which are in preparation for an abortion or which involve aftercare of an abortion patient. . . .").

[21] 745 ILL. COMP. STAT. §§ 70/3(a), 70/5, & 70/6 (2002).

[22] MISS. CODE ANN. §§ 41-107-3 & § 41-107-5 (West 2009).

about HIV testing. A doctor could fail to tell a patient about the terminal nature of his cancer in order to ensure aggressive treatment, instead of hospice care. Under such broad conscience laws, these actions could generate no tort liability, professional discipline, or adverse employment action.

Finally, a growing number of individuals and entities can claim rights to accommodation. In addition to direct providers like doctors and nurses, the new generation of conscience legislation covers pharmacists, medical secretaries, orderlies, billing clerks, and the like. The category of entities covered has also widened from hospitals to other healthcare facilities and even to insurance companies. With the inclusion of additional actors, conflicts of conscience potentially become more frequent and complex. Consider, for example, a physician, patient, and clinic that agree that emergency contraception is the medically appropriate and morally correct course of treatment but are impeded by a pharmacy that will not dispense the drug or a medical translator who will not explain the dosage to the patient.

Insurance coverage has become a flashpoint, moving demands for accommodation from the legislatures to the courts. In several jurisdictions, individuals have insisted that they cannot pay premiums toward an insurance plan that covers abortion or contraception for others. In California, students at public universities brought suits objecting to paying into the university health system because it covered abortion.[23] Employers across the country filed suit under the Religious Freedom Restoration Act (RFRA) against requirements in the Affordable Care Act that employees' insurance plans cover contraception. Under the RFRA, the federal government may only substantially burden a person's exercise of religion when the burden "(1) is in furtherance of a compelling governmental interest; and (2) is the least restrictive means of furthering that compelling governmental interest."[24]

In 2014, in *Burwell v. Hobby Lobby*, the Supreme Court sided with employers objecting to the contraceptive mandate. It held that closely held, for-profit corporations can claim religious exemptions under the RFRA and that their exercise of religion was substantially burdened by the requirement that insurance plans cover contraceptives.[25] The Court concluded that the government had less restrictive means to further its interests in public health and gender equality. The government could either directly provide access, or extend to for-profit corporations the accommodation that it granted to nonprofit religious organizations. Under the nonprofit accommodation, employers may exclude contraceptives from employment-based plans, but must file a form with their insurance company or third-party administrator that ensures employees still have access to contraceptive coverage through a separate, freestanding plan.[26] While the Court insisted its decision was "very specific" with "precisely zero" effect,[27] only days later it enjoined enforcement of the accommodation in a case involving a nonprofit that objects to filing this form.[28] In so doing, the Court suggested that only direct government provision of contraceptive coverage may be permissible under the RFRA. Although the *Hobby Lobby* decision concerns contraceptive coverage, its effects may be

[23] Goehring v. Brophy, 94 F.3d 1294 (9th Cir. 1996); Erzinger v. Regents of Univ. of Cal., 137 Cal. App. 3d 389 (1983).

[24] 42 U.S.C. § 2000bb–1(a) & (b).

[25] Burwell v. Hobby Lobby Stores, Inc., 134 S. Ct. 2759 (2014).

[26] Group Health Plans and Health Insurance Issuers Relating to Coverage of Preventive Services under Patient Protection and Affordable Care Act, 78 Fed. Reg. 8456, 8462 (Feb. 6, 2013).

[27] *Hobby Lobby*, 134 S.Ct. at 2760.

[28] Wheaton Coll. v. Burwell, 134 S. Ct. 2806 (2014).

far-reaching. In particular, the opinion expressed skepticism about the compelling nature of interests in public health and gender equality, which could result in religious exemptions to other public health efforts and create a judicially enforceable right to refuse medical services.

II Scholarly Debates over Conscientious Refusal

Conscientious refusals have generated lively debate among bioethicists and, to a lesser degree, legal academics. Scholars initially divide into pro- and anti-accommodation camps and further differ on the appropriate balance between conscience and care. This section examines the rationales for protecting conscience in medicine and the balance of access and conscience through the conventional compromise of information and referral.

a. The Foundations of Conscience in Medicine

The majority of legal scholars and bioethicists take the position that acting according to conscience—including through refusal of healthcare—has significance because it is central to each person's moral integrity or sense of self.[29] Accommodation is thus most compellingly justified not by the objective truth of the objector's moral commitments but by the harm to the whole person.[30] Prohibiting a person from acting in accordance with conscience might inflict "a psychological schism that violates the integrity of the person as a unity of body, soul, and psyche."[31] In a pluralist society, individuals recognize the value of maintaining their own moral integrity, and "this gives them in turn a reason to value and respect the moral integrity of others."[32]

This reason—diverse scholarly accounts argue—is heightened in medicine due to its life-or-death nature. Scholars frequently analogize doctors engaging in refusal to conscientious objectors to military service who are willing to be imprisoned rather than engage in killing.[33]

29 Daniel P. Sulmasy, *What Is Conscience and Why Is Respect for It So Important?*, 29 Theor. Med. Bioeth. 135, 138 (2008); Martin Benjamin, *Conscience*, *in* The Encyclopedia of Bioethics 510, 514 (Stephen G. Post ed., 3d ed. 2004); Mark R. Wicclair, *Conscientious Objection in Medicine*, 14 Bioethics 205, 214 (2000).

30 James F. Childress, *Conscience and Conscientious Actions in the Context of MCOs*, Kennedy Inst. of Ethics J. 7.4 403, 403 (1997); Steven D. Smith, *What Does Religion Have to Do with Freedom of Conscience?*, 76 U. Colo. L. Rev. 911, 935 (2005) (asserting that the most plausible rationale for respecting conscience is that it is central to personhood).

31 Edmund D. Pellegrino, *The Physician's Conscience, Conscience Clauses, and Religious Belief: A Catholic Perspective*, 30 Fordham Urb. L.J. 221, 240 (2002).

32 Dan W. Brock, *Conscientious Refusal by Physicians and Pharmacists: Who Is Obligated to Do What, and Why?*, 29 Theor. Med. & Bioethics 187, 189 (2008).

33 *See, e.g.*, James Childress, *Civil Disobedience, Conscientious Objection, and Evasive Noncompliance: A Framework for the Analysis and Assessment of Illegal Actions in Health Care*, 10 J. Med. Phil. 63 (1985); Huseina Sulaimanee, *Protecting the Right to Choose: Regulating Conscience Clauses in the Face of Moral Obligation*, 17 Cardozo J.L. & Gender 417, 435 (2011).

With regard to traditional objections to abortion and removal of life support, the objecting healthcare provider, like the draftee, has clear causal and proximate responsibility for an act with serious consequences.[34] In its origins, conscience legislation, thus, targeted direct responsibility for an alleged killing. It shielded providers only to the extent they might be called upon to directly perform or to participate in the performance of an act that, in their view, wrongly results in death or ends the potential for life.

In addition to its life-or-death nature, medicine has other characteristics that may render conscience essential to its practice. The intimacy of relationships and providers' shared role in decision-making differentiate healthcare from many other pursuits.[35] Relationships in healthcare cannot be arm's-length; they require the provider to share in the patient's decision.[36] Medicine also raises unique and ethically complex questions. For example, "quality of life" requires judgments that vary according to how each person defines a good, or sufficient, life. To navigate these issues, physicians need ethical virtues as well as clinical skills.[37]

For some, the very nature of the healthcare profession warrants accommodation of refusals. Edmund Pellegrino, for example, argues that allowing patients to demand a procedure "is to challenge a conscientious physician's integrity as a physician. It depreciates his expertise, reduces his discretionary latitude in decisionmaking, and makes him a technical instrument of another person's wishes."[38] Other scholars see providers' refusals of care for religious or moral reasons as potentially compatible with professional obligations, but only permissible when rooted in shared professional norms—such as the relief of pain and suffering or the avoidance of death.[39] Professional ethical codes also tend to take this

[34] Diverse philosophical traditions invoke these factors to determine whether one is complicit in another's wrongdoing. *See, e.g.*, Edmund D. Pellegrino, *Societal Duty and Moral Complicity: The Physician's Dilemma of Divided Loyalty*, 16 INT'L J. L. PSYCH. 371 (1993); Noam J. Zohar, *Cooperation Despite Disagreement: From Politics to Healthcare*, 17 BIOETHICS 121 (2003); Sulmasy, *What Is Conscience*.

[35] David C. Thomasma *Beyond Medical Paternalism and Patient Autonomy: A Model of Physician Conscience for the Physician–Patient Relationship*, 98 ANN. INTERN. MED. 243, 246 (1983) (arguing in favor of professional conscience rooted in beneficence and the condition of the patient); William P. Cheshire, *When Conscience Meddles with Ethics*, 27 ETHICS & MED. 139, 139 (2011) ("Conscience is at the heart of the medical profession's commitment to honesty, compassion, and taking responsibility to prevent harm.").

[36] Jacob M. Appel, *May Doctors Refuse Infertility Treatments to Gay Patients?*, HASTINGS CTR. REP., Jul./Aug. 2006, at 20, 21 ("The nature of the doctor-patient relationship is fundamentally more intimate than the sorts of interactions that occur between landlords and tenants or innkeepers and guests."); Mark A. Hall, *Law, Medicine, and Trust*, 55 STAN. L. REV. 463, 471 (2002) (arguing the doctor-patient relationship has a "deeply personal type of trust paralleled only in fraternal, family, or love relationships").

[37] Piers Benn, *Conscience and Health Care Ethics*, *in* PRINCIPLES OF HEALTH CARE ETHICS 345, 345 (R.E. Ashcroft et al. eds., 2007); *see also* Laurence B. McCullough, *The Nature and Limits of the Physician's Professional Responsibilities*, 29 J. MED. & PHIL. 3, 4 (2004) (arguing for importance of intellectual and moral integrity in medicine).

[38] Edmund D. Pellegrino, *Patient and Physician Autonomy: Conflicting Rights and Obligations in the Physician-Patient Relationship*, 10 J. CONTEMP. HEALTH L. & POL'Y 47, 59 (1993).

[39] *See, e.g.*, HOLLY FERNANDEZ LYNCH, CONFLICTS OF CONSCIENCE IN HEALTH CARE 34 (2008) (limiting objection to "refusals grounded in values that are widely held within the profession and have even been accepted as clinical standards"); Jeffrey Blustein, *Doing What the Patient Orders: Maintaining*

position.[40] With this limiting principle, conflicts manifest themselves between the values of a patient and the values of the profession, not a single provider.

A minority of scholars rejects the accommodation of conscientious refusal altogether. Even accepting the value of conscience generally, they suggest that legal and ethical interventions to allow conscientious refusal are particularly inappropriate to medicine and, ultimately, incompatible with professionalism.[41] Alta Charo, for example, argues that conscientious refusal expresses moral approbation of the patient.[42] On this account, unlike draftees, healthcare providers have chosen their profession, specialty, and place of employment.[43] They have consented to role-based obligations that they cannot abandon at will. Immunizing providers from liability when they deny care, by contrast, destabilizes the medical profession's duties to do no harm and respect patient autonomy. Refusal pits the provider against a vulnerable patient. It endangers the very trust upon which the profession relies.

b. Balancing Patient Access to Care

While conscience legislation may have the benefit of protecting conscience (a questionable assumption as we shall see in the next section), it comes at the cost of patients' access to care. Due to licensing requirements, healthcare providers act as gatekeepers to treatment.[44] Their refusals consequently can deprive patients of access altogether. Emergency situations and institutional refusals up the ante. Harms to bodily integrity may be severe. The question of access, therefore, becomes central to the accommodation of refusal.

The preponderance of scholarly literature recommends ensuring access through some combination of informed consent and referral from the provider in return for the right to

Integrity in the Doctor-Patient Relationship, 7 BIOETHICS 289, 312 (1993) (arguing whether refusal is permissible depends on "ethical consensus within the profession"); Carolyn McLeod, *Referral in the Wake of Conscientious Objection to Abortion*, 23 HYPATIA, 30, 38 (2008) ("[P]hysicians cannot make conscientious objections in their practices that violate established norms of the profession that are morally justified"); Wicclair, *Conscientious Objection*, at 217 ("[A]n appeal to conscience has significant moral weight only if the core ethical values on which it is based correspond to one or more core values in medicine.").

[40] ACOG, *Limits of Conscientious Refusal*, at 2; American College of Emergency Physicians, Management of the Patient with the Complaint of Sexual Assault (reaffirmed 2008); American Academy of Pediatrics Committee on Bioethics, *Physician Refusal to Provide Information or Treatment on the Basis of Claims of Conscience*, 124 PEDIATRICS 1689, 1691 (2009).

[41] Rosamond Rhodes, *The Ethical Standard of Care*, AM. J. OF BIOETHICS, Mar./Apr. 2006, at 76; Joel Frader & Charles L. Bosk, *The Personal Is Political, the Professional Is Not*, 151C AM. J. OF MED. GENETICS 62 (2009); Julian Savulescu, *Conscientious Objection in Medicine*, 332 BRIT. MED. J. 294, 294 (2006).

[42] R. Alta Charo, *Health Care Provider Refusals to Treat, Prescribe, Refer or Inform: Professionalism and Conscience*, 1 J. ACS 120, 128 (2007).

[43] LYNCH, CONFLICTS OF CONSCIENCE, at 48–56 (critiquing the consent paradigm based on dynamic nature of profession, existence of conscience protections, and lack of substantive standards to assess existing norms).

[44] Charo, *Health Care Provider*, at 129.

refuse services.[45] Professional societies concur.[46] Under this compromise, medical professionals should inform patients of diagnoses and treatment options and refer patients for medically appropriate treatments that they cannot in good conscience provide. Significantly, the vast majority of medical providers agree referring for and counseling patients about procedures they find morally objectionable.[47] In theory at least, this ethical compromise would avoid patient harm by ensuring care through an alternate provider.

Whether referral and information suffice to avoid harm, however, depends on how "harm" is defined. The predominant view is that patients experience no harm in being denied medical care—based either on a libertarian rationale according to which providers may reject a patient's offer to contract or on a professional independence rationale tied to the common law no-duty-to-treat rule. On this account, provided a patient ultimately can access an alternate provider, she has not been harmed. Refusal may inconvenience, but does not harm.[48]

However, even with referral and access to another provider, refusal generates two distinct harms. First, the delay of care is a foreseeable consequence of refusal, even when a patient is referred to another provider. Delay itself can constitute injury. A woman who seeks an abortion, for example, carries the pregnancy further, suffers additional days of anxiety, and likely pays an increased price for the procedure. The effects fall disproportionately on poor and working-class women, who may lack transportation and leisure time to seek out alternatives easily.[49] Delay may irreparably harm patients with regard to end-of-life care as well. For example, if providers prove unwilling to honor his advance directive indicating minimal comfort care, a terminally ill

[45] *See, e.g.*, Thomas May & Mark P. Aulisio, *Personal Morality and Professional Obligations: Rights of Conscience and Informed Consent*, PERSPECTIVES IN BIO. & MED., Winter 2009, 30, 35; LYNCH, CONFLICTS OF CONSCIENCE, at 229 (proposing, instead, self-referral by providing patients who have been denied services by one doctor a list of willing providers); Blustein, *Doing* (arguing that physicians have a duty to refer for ethically acceptable services out of respect for moral sincerity of others).

Some scholars, however, would permit providers to refuse to refer patients for treatment. They argue that, like performance or participation in a procedure, referral makes a provider complicit in the patient's wrongdoing. A. A. Howsepian, *On Referring*, 25 ETHICS & MED. 31, 40–41 (2009). Others would go so far as to allow providers to withhold information. Robert John Araujo, *Conscience, Totalitarianism, and the Positivist Mind*, 77 MISS. L.J. 571 (2007). Some state legislatures share these views and have adopted new broad conscience legislation allowing withholding of information or referrals from patients.

[46] ACOG, *Limits of Conscientious Refusal*, at 2; American College of Emergency Physicians, Management of the Patient with the Complaint of Sexual Assault (reaffirmed 2008); American Academy of Pediatrics Committee on Bioethics, *Physician Refusal to Provide Information or Treatment on the Basis of Claims of Conscience*, 124 PEDIATRICS 1689, 1691 (2009); American Medical Association (AMA) Council on Ethical and Judicial Affairs, Report 6-a-07, Physician Objection to Treatment and Individual Patient Discrimination (2007), *available at* http://www.ama-assn.org/resources/doc/ethics/ceja_6a07.pdf.

[47] Ryan E. Lawrence & Farr A. Curlin, *Physicians' Beliefs About Conscience in Medicine: A National Survey*, 84 ACAD. MED. 1276, 1278 (2009); John D. Yoon et al., *Moral Controversy, Directive Counsel, and the Doctor's Role: Findings from a National Survey of Obstetrician-Gynecologists*, 85 ACAD. MED. 1475, 1477 (2010) (reporting that 97% of ob-gyns agreed that a physician should provide all relevant facts without influencing the patient's decision one way or another regarding morally controversial decisions).

[48] *See, e.g.*, Elizabeth Fenton & Loren Lomasky, *Dispensing with Liberty: Conscientious Refusal and the "Morning-After Pill,"* 30 J. MED. & PHIL. 579 (2005).

[49] Eileen P. Kelly et al., *Crisis of Conscience: Pharmacist Refusal to Provide Health Care Services on Moral Grounds*, 23 EMPLOYER RESPONSIBILITIES & RTS. J. 37, 41 (2011) (suggesting that a referral an hour's drive or forty-five miles away is inconvenient, but not harmful).

patient may suffer intubation until another provider can be found. That said, it may be possible to avoid all delay through institutional mechanisms. For example, hospitals could be required to ensure a willing provider is always available to step in when another refuses.

Second and fundamentally, the experience of being denied care for moral reasons can inflict substantial psychological and dignitary harm. Take a pharmacist's refusal to dispense emergency contraception. Refusal to provide a woman with legal, ethically acceptable care sends the message that society does not value her ability to make decisions about her life and her body.[50] It suggests to her that she has transgressed by engaging in sex, whether voluntary or coerced. This harm can only be mitigated in some instances. For example, in an institution of adequate size, a refusing pharmacist could hand off a prescription to a willing colleague without making the patient aware of his judgments. In other contexts, seamless transfers will be impossible. A physician's refusal will be apparent to a patient who has asked him to perform an abortion or prescribe contraception. Moreover, the existence of institutional conscience protections undermines any potential mitigation of harm.

The compromise position (referral and refusal) also depends on the existence of an accessible willing provider. Legislative protection for entire healthcare facilities, however, renders access illusory. In many parts of the country, only one hospital is accessible.[51] Even in communities with more than one hospital, hospital mergers may mean all nearby hospitals operate under religious restrictions. Willing institutions—whether pharmacies or hospitals—also may prove unable to deliver controversial care if their employees refuse. In the most difficult cases, a service can become unavailable in a community because the sole specialist (or a number of specialists) refuses to provide it—as is the case in the nine out of ten U.S. counties that lack an abortion provider.[52]

Institutional refusal also complicates access in emergencies where patient's interests are at their apex. The American Medical Association states that "from an ethical standpoint, physicians are not free to refuse to provide services to patients in need of emergency care."[53] The definition of emergency, however, remains contested. Does an emergency require "risk of death";[54] "an avoidable, serious, irreversible consequence on a patient at this moment or in the very near future";[55] or need for care "measured in minutes"?[56] Is the focus on future risk or current status? Carolyn McLeod, for example, argues that these definitions are overly narrow; the need for emergency contraception constitutes an emergency even though the woman may not become pregnant or could abort if she does become so, just as a small house fire is an emergency even though the house might not burn down or could be rebuilt if it does.[57]

50 Carolyn McLeod, *Harm or Mere Inconvenience? Denying Women Emergency Contraception*, HYPATIA, Oct.–Dec. 2008, at 19.

51 Lawrence E. Singer, *Does Mission Matter?*, 6 HOUS. J. HEALTH L. & POL'Y 347, 376–377 (2006).

52 Richard Florida, *The Geography of Abortion*, ATLANTIC CITIES (Jun. 11, 2012), http://www.theatlanticcities.com/politics/2012/06/geography-abortion/1711/.

53 AMA; *but see* Edmund D. Pellegrino, *The Physician's Conscience, Conscience Clauses, and Religious Belief: A Catholic Perspective*, 30 FORDHAM URB. L.J. 221, 232 (2002) (concluding that doctors have no obligation to treat in emergencies or remote areas).

54 Marcus P. Adams, *Conscience and Conflict*, 7 AM. J. OF BIOETHICS 28, 29 (2007).

55 LYNCH, CONFLICTS OF CONSCIENCE, at 227.

56 Fenton & Lomasky, *Dispensing with Liberty*, at 582.

57 Carolyn McLeod, *Harm or Mere Inconvenience? Denying Women Emergency Contraception*, HYPATIA, Oct.–Dec. 2008, at 24.

Several scholars have engaged in creative solutions to the problems caused by the absence of alternate providers or occurrence of emergencies. Some propose requiring an objector to render necessary care if no substitute provider can be found, creating incentives for the individual refuser to work in proximity to willing providers and for the state to remove obstacles to access.[58] Holly Fernandez Lynch advocates that licensing boards bear the responsibility of ensuring sufficient access by assessing patient demand and fostering a supply of physicians willing to meet it, such that refusing physicians (or institutions) are never "the last doctor in town."[59] Others suggest developing joint ventures and partnerships that link religious institutions, in particular, to willing providers.[60]

Despite this thoughtful scholarly engagement, the statutory framework does not reflect an attempt to balance access and conscience. To the extent that statutes require referral and information, they do so only by implication; they exempt providers from performing or participating in the performance of contested care, but are silent as to referral. Several conscience clauses reject the ethical compromise explicitly, allowing providers to withhold from patients referrals and information about their diagnosis and options. In practice, a significant minority of physicians does not believe that physicians must give referrals or deliver information about procedures to which they object.[61]

Conscience legislation also ignores the difficulties created by the lack of willing providers and fails to offer clear guidelines for emergencies. Even where there is no alternate provider, virtually all conscience clauses allow institutions and providers to refuse care without qualification. The status of emergencies is less clear. In some states, conscience laws may supersede state emergency medical treatment acts and authorize the denial of care in emergencies. Irrespective of state law, however, essentially all hospitals retain obligations under the federal Emergency Medical Treatment and Labor Act (EMTALA), but its narrow definition of emergency—where "the absence of immediate medical attention could reasonably be expected to result in placing the health of the individual . . . in serious jeopardy, serious impairment to bodily functions, or serious dysfunction of any bodily organ or part"[62]—excludes many situations in which refusal would nonetheless result in harm. The U.S. Congress also has repeatedly proposed to amend EMTALA to permit any person or entity to refuse patients treatment in emergencies for moral—rather than medical—reasons.[63]

The issue of access ultimately remains overlooked in the statutory protections and unresolved by the scholarly literature. As the next two parts argue, the dichotomy between patient access and provider conscience is oversimplistic. Conscience is more varied than refusal. Thus, even as it neglects patient access to care, legislation does not adequately or comprehensively protect conscience.

58 Robert Baker, *Conscience and the Unconscionable*, 23 BIOETHICS ii, iii (2009).

59 LYNCH, CONFLICTS OF CONSCIENCE, at 111.

60 Kathleen M. Boozang, *Deciding the Fate of Religious Hospitals in the Emerging Health Care Market*, 31 HOUS. L. REV. 1429, 1493 (1995).

61 C. Ben Mitchell, *Conflicts of Conscience Matter Because Medicine Matters*, 27 ETHICS & MED. 133, 133 (2011) (extrapolating from survey data to conclude that nationwide forty million Americans may be cared for by doctors who don't believe obligated to inform and nearly one hundred million by doctors who don't believe have to refer).

62 42 U.S.C. §1395dd(e)(1) (1985).

63 Respect for Rights of Conscience Act, S. 1467, 112th Congress, 2011–2012.

III Rectifying the Priority of Refusal over Conscience

The goal of conscience legislation—as the name indicates—is to protect conscience. Yet it falls woefully short. This section argues that current law is both overinclusive, drawing in unprincipled refusals, and underinclusive, excluding people of conscience who seek to access or to deliver care.

a. Testing the Sincerity of Refusals

Medical conscience legislation tends to assume all refusals are motivated by conscience. Many statutes protect "refusal" without limiting it to religious, moral, or ethical beliefs. None requires providers to show the sincerity or depth of their convictions. Current legislation simply favors refusal writ large.

Christopher Meyers and Robert Woods provide an example.[64] Faced with requests to perform a second trimester abortion, all four ob-gyns at a public hospital signed a form, as required by state law, claiming "a moral, ethical, or religious objection" and were excused as conscientious refusers. But further inquiry showed that none clearly exhibited moral reasoning. One expressed concern over losing patients at his fertility clinic. Another wanted to limit his practice to gynecology. A third said providing abortions was inadequately lucrative. The final physician stated that second trimester abortions are "complex and frankly ugly."

The tendency to accept refusal no matter the reason has broad effect. For example, the vast majority of ob-gyns never provide abortions.[65] But only 7% are morally opposed to all abortions.[66] The remainder has reasons far removed from conscience, including physical danger, inconvenience, fear of controversy, lack of support by professional community, and gaps in medical education.

To remedy the permissiveness of the status quo, statutory text should at a bare minimum: (1) include a clear definition of conscience, requiring religious, moral, or ethical reasoning; and (2) require notice of refusal. Legislation that simply provides "no medical provider will be required to provide abortion" should be disfavored. Meyers and Woods' example, however, suggests that these reforms will be insufficient to discourage refusals based on less weighty concerns than conscience.

As many scholars propose, the solution might lie in bringing medical refusal into line with the military model.[67] To secure an exemption from military service, a draftee must show

[64] Christopher Meyers & Robert D. Woods, *An Obligation to Provide Abortion Services: What Happens When Physicians Refuse?*, 22 J. of Med. Ethics 115 (1996).

[65] Debra B. Stulberg et al., *Abortion Provision Among Practicing Obstetrician-Gynecologists*, 118 Obstetrics & Gynecology 609, 609 (2011) (86%).

[66] Lisa H. Harris et al., *Obstetrician-Gynecologists' Objections to and Willingness to Help Patients Obtain an Abortion*, 118 Obstetrics & Gynecology 905, 905 (2011).

[67] Robert F. Card, *Conscientious Objection, Emergency Contraception, and Public Policy*, 36 J. Med. & Phil. 53, 55–56 (2011); Lori Kantymir & Carolyn McLeod, *Justification for Conscience Exemptions*

his sincerity before a draft board and assume noncombat duty or civilian service in return for exemption. To claim the right to deny legal, necessary services, healthcare professionals could similarly offer an explanation of their refusal before a decision-maker—whether a hospital, licensing board, or professional society.[68] This process would acknowledge that the exercise of conscience itself requires a process of examination and judgment, informed by specific circumstances.[69] A provider acting conscientiously should be willing to articulate her judgments, setting forth those beliefs central to her sense of self and how they apply in context.

An additional—or substitute—reform would have providers shoulder alternate burdens when they refuse services widely accepted within their field.[70] With the purpose of ensuring that refusers provide service to society, burdens have the added benefit of testing sincerity. For example, requiring twenty hours of charitable care likely would deter refusals from doctors who consider abortion provision inadequately lucrative.

Sincerity testing and alternate burdens would elevate conscience above non-normative motivations for refusal with positive impact on patient access to care. The problem of overinclusion thus could be resolved. The problem of underinclusion, discussed in the next section, proves stickier.

b. Restoring Balance to Conscience Protection

While legal and ethical frameworks include refusals with no basis in conscience, they simultaneously exclude the consciences of patients who require care and providers who seek to deliver it. Indeed, the term "conscience" is often employed interchangeably with refusal. Conscience, however, exists and should be equally protected on both sides of the moral divide.

First and significantly, the consciences of patients go unacknowledged within existing legislation. Yet, patients make conscientious judgments to seek contraception, abortion, or fertility treatments, and to ensure compliance with their wishes about death. They have an interest in preserving their moral integrity in medical decision-making at least equal to, if not stronger than, medical providers' interests.

Second, providers' religious and moral beliefs do not always pit them against their patients. While the archetypal doctor whose conscience prohibits performance of an abortion or withdrawal of life support looms large in the discourse, providers also have fundamental moral, religious, and ethical commitments in favor of delivering contested treatments to patients. These medical providers have equal claims of conscience.

for Health Care, 28 BIOETHICS 16 (2014); Sylvia A. Law, *Silent No More: Physicians' Legal and Ethical Obligations to Patients Seeking Abortions*, 21 N.Y.U. REV. L. & SOC. CHANGE 279, 303 (1995).

[68] LYNCH, CONFLICTS OF CONSCIENCE, at 158 (proposing professional discipline boards take over this function).

[69] Brock, *Conscientious Refusal*, at 189 (contending "[a] claim of justification requires some process in which reasons have been offered and considered").

[70] Adam J. Kolber, *Alternative Burdens on Freedom of Conscience*, 47 SAN DIEGO L. REV. 919, 930 (2010); Ronald A. Lindsay, *When to Grant Conscientious Objector Status*, AM. J. BIOETHICS, June 2007, at 25, 25–26.

Like their refusing colleagues, willing nurses and doctors primarily experience conflicts of conscience, not with the law but with the policies of entities with which they are associated. A physician in an orthodox Jewish nursing home might avoid providing futile care to dying patients who do not want it. A nurse practitioner in a refusing group practice might prescribe contraception to a patient whose insurance limits her to one ob-gyn exam annually, finding it morally wrong to impede patient decisions about reproduction. A Catholic physician might give condoms to people at risk of HIV infection in contravention of institutional policy. More widely, 37% of ob-gyns in religiously affiliated institutions (and over half of those in Catholic institutions) report having experienced conflict with the religious institution where they work regarding its religion-based policies for patient care.[71]

These willing providers, nonetheless, are largely absent from the legislative radar. Legislation commonly authorizes entire institutions to restrict reproductive and end-of-life care for religious or moral reasons—without regard to the consciences of willing providers. Baptist and Seventh Day Adventist hospitals, for example, may prohibit nontherapeutic abortions. Catholic facilities restrict a wide array of care, including reproductive and end-of-life care, and limit information to "morally legitimate alternatives."[72] Employees and medical staff of all faiths, beliefs, and backgrounds must then abide by the institutional policy of refusal, even when their consciences counsel otherwise.

While lawmakers have resolved conflicts in favor of refusing providers by requiring willing institutions to accommodate them, only in the exceptional case does legislation acknowledge the *willing* individual provider. Most notably, the Church Amendment prohibits discrimination against "any physician or other health care personnel, because he performed or assisted in the performance of a lawful sterilization procedure or abortion . . . or because of his religious beliefs or moral convictions respecting sterilization procedures or abortions."[73] Alabama's conscience statute also is unusual in providing that "[n]o person may be discriminated against in employment or professional privileges because of the person's *participation* or refusal to participate in the withholding or withdrawal of life-sustaining treatment."[74]

By and large, legislative and ethical frameworks are underinclusive. People of conscience are excluded. The patient's interest in living in accordance with her conscience is rarely considered. Willing individual providers must cede to institutional policies of refusal, even as refusing doctors and nurses secure accommodation from institutional demands. Equivalent conscientious beliefs of providers are treated asymmetrically.

Respect for conscience—that is, for the moral integrity of each individual—requires treating like claims alike. It requires recognizing that conscience hangs in the balance for patients as well as providers. It demands remedying asymmetry, consistently favoring either individual conscience or institutional interest irrespective of its content.[75]

[71] Debra B. Stulberg et al., *Obstetrician-Gynecologists, Religious Institutions, and Conflicts Regarding Patient Care Policies*, 207 AM. J. OF OBSTETRICS & GYNECOLOGY 73 (2012).

[72] United States Conference of Catholic Bishops. Ethical and Religious Directives for Catholic Health Care Services para. 27 (5th ed. 2009), *available at* http://www.nccbuscc.org/meetings/2009Fall/docs/ERDs_5th_ed_091118_FINAL.pdf.

[73] 42 U.S.C. § 300a-7(c) (2000).

[74] ALA. CODE § 22-8A-8(b) (2010) (italics added).

[75] For a more thorough critique of the asymmetrical treatment of conscience, *see* Elizabeth Sepper, *Taking Conscience Seriously*, 98 VA L. REV. 1501 (2012).

IV The Question of Corporate Conscience

Legislation has long authorized refusal of care by healthcare institutions without examining the deeper questions of whether a corporate entity can exercise conscience and, if so, under what circumstances. The Supreme Court's endorsement of religious exercise by for-profit corporations in the *Hobby Lobby* case portends the expansion of this model throughout commercial life. This section critiques the two theories of institutional conscience and draws out the difficult legal and philosophical questions they leave unanswered.

Two mutually exclusive theories undergird discussions of institutional conscience. The first—the mission-operation theory—locates conscience in the mission statement and operational structure of the corporation. In this view, the corporation has moral agency and an identity larger than its constituents. Beth Israel Hospital, for example, remains Beth Israel Hospital, even when a shift changes or its administrators are replaced.[76] As a moral agent, the institution expresses its identity through its corporate documents and then, like a human being, maintains its integrity by conforming decisions to the mission.[77] Several conscience clauses adopt this approach, requiring healthcare entities to reference reasons for refusal in its "existing or proposed religious, moral or ethical guidelines, mission statement, constitution, bylaws, articles of incorporation, regulations or other relevant documents."[78]

The second—the moral-collective theory—indicates that, though an institution itself does not have a conscience, individuals collectively further their moral convictions through the formation of partnerships, limited liability companies, and corporate structures.[79] As challenges to the Affordable Care Act's contraceptive mandate proceeded to the Supreme Court, a number of courts and commentators reflected this view. Discomfited by the idea that a for-profit business has a moral core, they concluded that the owners or shareholders of a business nevertheless exercise conscience through its operation. Taken to an extreme, this theory envisions a "moral marketplace" in which there are a wide variety of medical institutions with clear moral positions and employees and customers who embrace or reject a business's moral norms.[80]

Neither the mission-operation nor the moral-collective theory, however, convincingly establishes conscience for institutions. The mission-operation theory's focus on formal rules without reference to context proves too rigid and formalistic to establish corporate

[76] Peter A. French, *Collective Responsibility and the Practice of Medicine*, 7 J. of Med. & Phil. 65, 74–75 (1982).

[77] Pellegrino, *The Physician's Conscience*, at 235 ("The ethical 'code' or commitment of a specific institution is now customarily expressed in its mission statement. This is in a way the 'conscience' of the institution."); Kevin W. Wildes, *Institutional Integrity: Approval, Toleration and Holy War or "Always True to You in My Fashion,"* 16 J. of Med. & Phil. 211, 214–215 (1991).

[78] Miss. Code Ann. § 41-107-3(h) (West 2009).

[79] Suzanne Davis & Paul Lansing, *When Two Fundamental Rights Collide at the Pharmacy: The Struggle to Balance the Consumer's Right to Access Contraception and the Pharmacist's Right of Conscience*, 12 DePaul J. Health Care L. 67, 100 (2009); Robert K. Vischer, Conscience and the Common Good: Reclaiming the Space Between Person and State 179 (2009).

[80] *See generally* Vischer, Conscience and the Common Good; Robert K. Vischer, *Conscience in Context: Pharmacist Rights and the Eroding Moral Marketplace*, 17 Stan. Law & Pol'y Rev. 83, 86, 95 (2006).

conscience as analogous to individual conscience. It suggests institutional norms can be determinative in every situation. But mission statements typically include only broad principles, upon which people may agree but will apply differently in context. At the same time, under this theory, the institution's exercise of conscience depends on individual human beings. Because the institution lacks consciousness and agency, individuals must necessarily interpret and apply principles to specific situations (potentially exercising individual conscience).

Like the mission-operation theory, the moral-collective theory does not describe conscience as such. Conscience is not simply shared moral values or religious affiliation but each individual's sense of self. The moral-collective theory assumes that individuals who agree on general principles can predict their moral judgments in specific situations. But even affiliation with the same religion, for example, does not significantly reduce conflicts between physicians and healthcare facilities over patient treatment.[81] This theory also falls short in that it fails to ascribe conscience to an institution at all. The "conscience" at issue belongs to individuals.

Even assuming the existence of institutional conscience, one must consider whether—and why—to protect it. Recall that protection of individual conscience is most persuasively rooted in concern for the moral core of the human person. Do concerns about moral integrity extend to a corporation? Could a business experience a psychological schism or abandonment of self? Is there a basis for preserving institutional identity irrespective of content?

The mission-operation theory does not answer these questions in a coherent way. It suggests that the delivery of a contested service would degrade norms that the institution has developed and fostered, even to the point of destroying its identity. Given the diversity of missions, however, it is difficult to conclude that society has an interest in preserving the text of a mission statement (or its interpretation by some collection of individuals). Nor is it clear that society should be agnostic as to the pursuits of businesses, allowing them to further the mission regardless of its content. More fundamentally, while a person can experience a psychological schism or abandonment of self, a business entity—even if it has an interest in mission coherence—cannot experience a similar harm. The institutional "self" is an artificial construct of law and contract.

Perhaps for this reason, proponents of the mission-operation theory often default to suggesting that religious organizations are special.[82] The religious character of an organization may act as a proxy for sincerity of belief. The alternative—and the logical conclusion of the mission-operation theory—is to allow any business to find conscience through amendment of corporate documents. But religiously affiliated hospitals are not necessarily more mission-driven than their nonsectarian competitors. Their primary mission—providing medical care to patients—cannot be distinguished from that of other hospitals. They typically only have formalistic connections to a religious group or church. Religious orders no longer deliver care directly, boards of directors are diverse, and churches rarely have a financial stake.

[81] Debra B. Stulberg et al., *Religious Hospitals and Primary Care Physicians: Conflicts over Policies for Patient Care*, 25 J. OF GEN. INTERNAL MED. 725, 728 (2010).

[82] Kent Greenawalt, *Objections in Conscience to Medical Procedures: Does Religion Make a Difference?*, 2006 U. ILL. L. REV. 799, 824 (2006); Ana Smith Iltis, *Institutional Integrity in Roman Catholic Health Care Institutions*, 7 CHRISTIAN BIOETHICS 95, 98–102 (2001).

The moral-collective theory provides a more compelling reason for recognizing institutional conscience: It ensures individuals can live out their conception of the good life in community with others, disassociate themselves from acts or individuals of whom they disapprove, and agree on institutional norms that reinforce their own convictions. Failure of the state to accommodate institutions interferes with associative interests at least in some subset of healthcare facilities that this theory may accurately describe (small family practices, for example).

Nonetheless, the moral-collective theory does not support the current scope of conscience legislation. First, hospitals, the most common subjects of institutional conscience, are large and pluralistic. Their employees and affiliates are drawn by working conditions, pay, and convenience, among other things. Recognizing institutional conscience for these large institutions departs radically from a theory that values individuals associating with one another based on shared moral convictions. It results, not in a true moral association, but in the imposition of certain individuals' moral beliefs on others (whether patients or providers). Second, current protections of public and for-profit facilities are out of step with the institution as moral collective. With regard to public facilities, one might expect commitment to provide all legal, medically necessary treatment to be the public conscience. But, in most states, public hospitals may deny reproductive or end-of-life care to patients. Within for-profit businesses, even though moral convictions might come into play, the profit motive (in some cases, an obligation to maximize shareholder wealth) must drive decision-making.

Ultimately, protection of institutional refusal across facilities of all kinds rests on shaky theoretical foundations. Nonetheless, in the latest iteration of battles over conscience with regard toinsurance coverage for contraception, the Supreme Court identified healthcare conscience legislation as precedent for the religious accommodation of large, for-profit businesses.[83] The *Hobby Lobby* opinion employed the mission-operation and moral-collective theories interchangeably, despite their tension with one another. It ascribed religious exercise to the corporation as a separate legal entity and pointed to the existence of corporate documents using religious language as evidence of the corporate religion.[84] At the same time, it invoked associational interests—despite the fact that large, for-profit corporations employ people of all beliefs and send no discernable moral message.[85] It described the corporation as a vehicle for shared aims, dismissing the potential for religious conflicts among shareholders and concrete burdens on employees.[86] Even as it moved the medical model into commercial life, the Supreme Court failed to provide a coherent concept of institutional conscience. It ignored the inherent tension between protection of corporate and individual conscience.

[83] Burwell v. Hobby Lobby Stores, Inc., 134 S. Ct. 2759, 2773 (2014).

[84] *Id.* at 2764, 2766 (noting plaintiff Conestoga Wood's "Vision and Values Statements" and "Statement on the Sanctity of Human Life" and Hobby Lobby's statement of purpose but also linking those statements to the shareholder's beliefs).

[85] *Id.* at 2768 ("A corporation is simply a form of organization used by human beings to achieve desired ends. An established body of law specifies the rights and obligations of the people (including shareholders, officers, and employees) who are associated with a corporation in one way or another. When rights, whether constitutional or statutory, are extended to corporations, the purpose is to protect the rights of these people.").

[86] *Id.* at 2784, n.43.

V Emerging Questions

The expansionist character of conscience protection calls for greater empirical and theoretical inquiry. With this in mind, this section suggests potential avenues for future research.

a. Reviewing the Scientific Evidence

Traditional refusals invoked disagreements over the meaning of life and death. Despite rifts over the morality of the procedure—whether withdrawal of life support or abortion—opposing sides did not necessarily contest its scientific definition or mechanism. Under such circumstances, objectors raised claims that could not be tested. Legislators reasonably could conclude that the law was ill-equipped to evaluate the correctness of answers to these metaphysical questions and, accordingly, could safeguard conscience without regard to its truth.

Some objections, however, depend on misinformation, rather than metaphysics. In the early days of AIDS research, for example, Catholic bishops prohibited dispensing condoms to patients, suggesting that they could result in the spread of AIDS. Today, many Americans express moral concerns about the human papilloma virus (HPV) vaccine based on the belief that it causes promiscuity. Some claim that abortion leads women to commit suicide. Others insist that vaccines cause autism.

Unlike claims that life begins at conception, these objections are susceptible to empirical testing. Courts, nonetheless, have hesitated to examine the reasonableness or factual basis of belief in evaluating claims for religious exemption.

Inquiries into the scientific facts, nonetheless, may be particularly appropriate in medicine, as ACOG and Mark Wicclair argue.[87] In the context of healthcare, the objector simultaneously is a member of a religious tradition and a professional community. Being a healthcare professional carries a duty to possess and exercise scientific knowledge, which the public depends on and the law should reinforce.

Consider a pharmacist who asserts that he cannot dispense Plan B because he believes that: (1) life begins with the fertilization of an egg; (2) providing medications that interfere with the implantation of a fertilized egg is killing; and (3) Plan B is a medication with this mechanism of action. One could accept the first two contentions, but reject the third because the scientific evidence—of which he should be aware—establishes that Plan B does not affect a fertilized egg. The pharmacist's refusal would not be accommodated, because the drug does not work as she believes and thus does not create the moral dilemma she assumes. By contrast, a pharmacist who is morally opposed to Plan B because it prevents fertilization is not incorrect on the scientific evidence and could be accommodated.

Making accommodation of refusals depend on the strength of the scientific evidence is not without difficulties. How would one inquire into such beliefs? Can the empirical be cleanly disentangled from the metaphysical? What is the evidentiary burden? As with

[87] ACOG, *Limits of Conscientious Refusal*, at 3–4; Mark R. Wicclair, *Reasons and Healthcare Professionals' Claims of Conscience*, Am. J. Bioethics, June 2007, at 21, 22.

sincerity testing, the jurisdictional question—what institution could evaluate the scientific bases of refusal?—arises.

b. Reviving the Anti-discrimination Framework

Religious and moral refusals are often discussed as though they were inherently nondiscriminatory. Yet women and sexual minorities disproportionately bear their brunt. Consider typical conscientious refusals. Fertility clinics refuse to perform intrauterine insemination for lesbian patients.[88] Physicians deny fertility treatments to HIV-positive women. Others do not prescribe contraception to unmarried women. Hospitals prohibit abortions unless the woman is miscarrying. Others do not dispense emergency contraception unless the woman has experienced sexual assault.

Now re-imagine each of these refusals. A physician denies fertility treatments to interfaith couples. Another withholds contraception from people of his own race, because of a religion-based conviction about promulgating the race. A hospital prohibits abortions unless the woman agrees to sterilization. Another refuses to deliver emergency contraception to a woman who has been raped by her husband based on religious teaching that rape cannot occur within marriage. Although these horribles seem obvious examples of discrimination, no principle clearly distinguishes them from run-of-the-mill refusals.

Indeed, virtually all conscience clauses authorize selective refusals, when a provider withholds a treatment only from a select category of patients as in the examples above. Recent research suggests that, at least with regard to assisted reproductive technology, physicians routinely refuse services selectively for moral reasons.[89] Further empirical research is needed to understand the ways in which selective refusals operate to discriminate based on race, sexual orientation, religion, and disability.

Scholars should also consider the appropriate role of consistency in conscience protection. Traditional religious and moral refusals often are defended as expressing concern for life, whether of a fetus or a terminally ill adult, rather than denoting discrimination. Understanding objection as a refusal to engage in killing, however, seems to imply consistency vis-à-vis a particular procedure. The claim that emergency contraception ends a life is hard to square, for instance, with a willingness to provide the drug to sexual assault and incest survivors.

Finally, further thought should be given to conscience legislation as sex discrimination. Although legal arguments that the denial of abortion violates equal protection historically have failed, conscientious refusals across reproductive healthcare—from abortion and sterilization to contraception and assisted reproductive technologies—disfavor women in impact and, perhaps, in purpose. Only women require abortions or contraception. They receive the preponderance of fertility treatments. They bear the costs of reproduction. If

[88] North Coast Women's Care Med. Group, Inc. v. San Diego County Superior Court, 189 P.3d 959 (Cal. 2008).

[89] Ryan E. Lawrence et al., *Obstetrician-Gynecologists' Beliefs About Assisted Reproductive Technologies*, 116 OBSTETRICS & GYNECOLOGY 127 (2010) (surveying ob-gyns and finding, for example, 73% would discourage a patient with HIV from assisted reproduction and 47% would refuse to help; 14% if partner female (12.7% would not help)).

denials clustered around treatment only needed by one ethnic or racial group, would they be considered discriminatory? Evaluating the effect and discerning animus behind ever expanding conscience protections calls for critical and sustained examination.

VI Conclusion

For years, the legal status of conscientious refusals seemed settled. But, in the last decade, skirmishes over conscience began to stir with the legalization or proliferation of new practices, such as assisted suicide, advance directives, and emergency contraceptives. Long-standing conscience legislation for abortion and end-of-life care failed to stem demands for additional accommodation of refusals. Rather, having secured exemptions for pharmacists and pharmacies by arguing by analogy to medicine, advocates of refusal laws today argue by analogy to pharmacists to extend conscience protections beyond healthcare to businesses that refuse to serve same-sex couples for religious or moral reasons.

The expansion of conscience protections reveals fissures in the theory behind the medical model. For too long, refusal and conscience have been used interchangeably. The inclusion of non-normative refusals and the exclusion of patients and providers of conscience in the legal framework have denigrated the true exercise of conscience. Attempts at balancing have been warped, as provider conscience has been placed on one side of the balance and patient access on the other. The status of the institution as a conscientious entity has been accepted without adequate scrutiny, despite the serious impediment that institutional refusal poses to patient care.

A society committed to tolerance of religious belief, moral pluralism, and individual conscience, by contrast, should accommodate equal claims of conscience equally. Its laws should negotiate between public health and professional conscience. They should take into account competing claims of conscience of health providers and of the facilities in which they work—whether they refuse or are willing to deliver care. As for-profit businesses assert their corporate consciences and the medical refusal model extends more broadly into commercial life, it is urgent that we draw principled lines to protect conscience or, at minimum, lay bare unprincipled attempts to restrict access to care.

CHAPTER 17

DISABILITY AND HEALTH LAW

LESLIE FRANCIS, ANITA SILVERS, AND MICHAEL ASHLEY STEIN

HEALTH law in the United States developed largely independently from disability law and theory. Yet today the two intersect in both complementary and conflicting ways. Core to understanding these intersections are contrasting conceptualizations of disability and disability law.

On the so-called "medical model" of disability, differences associated with disability are seen as mental or physical impairments that it is the task of healthcare to address. Concomitantly, disability law is understood as addressing the needs of people with disabilities for support in executing the activities of daily life; on this view, disability law is largely welfarist and paternalistic in character. To the extent that U.S. health law has been concerned with needs of people with disabilities for care, it would appear aligned primarily with welfarist perspectives.

Pursuant to the contrasting "social model" of disability, arrangements in the built and social worlds are critical to how well people with disabilities are able to function, and disability law is a form of civil rights law according people with disabilities meaningful access to social life on the terms others enjoy. What Martha Minow called "dilemmas of difference"[1]—how equality requires different treatment in some cases of relevant differences between groups of people—are at play here as well: If differences legitimate different treatment, differences in support can be seen as a civil right rather than as a special privilege for someone in need.

Health law, as traditionally taught in American law schools, was a combination of the constitutional law, tort, contract, and regulatory issues affecting healthcare providers and the institutions in which they work. Disability law was primarily welfare or disability rights law, affecting healthcare at best tangentially. Disability advocates, moreover, resisted the medicalization of disability and the incorporation of approaches from healthcare into disability rights as perpetuating welfarist paradigms. More recently, commentators have advocated

[1] MARTHA MINOW, MAKING ALL THE DIFFERENCE: INCLUSION, EXCLUSION, AND AMERICAN LAW (1990).

moving disability rights perspectives into health law, pressing the incorporation of social justice concerns, especially for access to care.[2]

Disability law itself has two major strains. The welfarist strain involves provision of benefits such as health insurance, social security, and related programs. This strain of disability law originated in civil war pensions for disabled veterans and continues today in such public programs as workers' compensation, disability insurance, Medicaid, Medicare for qualifying persons who are permanently disabled, and Social Security Disability Insurance (SSDI). A more recent strain in disability-related law is civil rights protection for people with disabilities, including prohibitions on employment discrimination, discrimination in public services such as Medicaid, and discrimination in public accommodations such as physicians' offices or hospitals. Each of these strains of disability law impacts a wide range of issues in health law.

Take medical malpractice as just one example. In his famous article on the disabled in the law of tort, Jacobus tenBroek argued that tort law should entitle people with disabilities to full participation in the life of the community and not submit them to double standards.[3] On this view, standards of care that would countenance different treatment of people because of their disabilities, or damages remedies that would discount harms on account of disabilities, are discriminatory and a matter for civil rights to address.

The field of health law is protean, and we have perforce been selective. We emphasize areas of health law where disability law has had important impacts, areas of health law with serious implications for people with disabilities, and areas of health law undergoing rapid change. The impact of the Patient Protection and Affordable Care Act (ACA) on access to care is an especially significant development in the intersection between these fields.

I Disability and Classic Issues in the Provider-Patient Relationship

In the second half of the twentieth century, while bioethics was developing as an independent field, health law confronted an important range of cases about patients' rights and the provider-patient relationship. Many of these cases have become classics of bioethics as well as health law. This section considers some of these enduring issues in the provider-patient relationship as they interconnect with disability rights: informed consent, decision-making at the beginning of life, and decision-making at the end of life.

Much of this litigation arose during the time of concern for civil rights generally but before the full extension of this law to disability discrimination.[4] In *Cleburne*, the central

[2] Lindsay F. Wiley, *Health Law as Social Justice*, 24 Cornell J. L. & Pub. Pol'y 47 (2014); Jessica L. Roberts, *Health Law as Disability Rights Law*, 97 Minn. L. Rev. 1963 (2013); Ani B. Satz, *Overcoming Fragmentation in Disability and Health Law*, 60 Emory L.J. 277 (2010).

[3] Jacobus tenBroek, *The Right to Live in the World: the Disabled in the Law of Torts*, 54 Calif. L. Rev. 841 (1966).

[4] The initial statute protecting the civil rights of people with disabilities in the United States was the Rehabilitation Act of 1973, which applied to the federal government and federally funded activities. Rehabilitation Act of 1973, Pub. L. No. 93-112, 87 Stat. 355.

constitutional law case for disability decided in 1985, persons with intellectual disabilities were characterized as being exceptionally dependent and needing benevolent public support. This construction led to the conclusions that disability does not delineate a suspect classification and that laws treating persons with disabilities differently do not warrant strict scrutiny.[5] *Cleburne* involved the application of local zoning regulations to bar locating a group home for people with intellectual disabilities. In refusing to characterize disability as a suspect class, the U.S. Supreme Court opined that state legislatures had generally acted benignly toward people with disabilities and that these efforts were to be applauded: "Such legislation thus singling out the retarded for special treatment reflects the real and undeniable differences between the retarded and others. That a civilized and decent society expects and approves such legislation indicates that governmental consideration of those differences in the vast majority of situations is not only legitimate but also desirable."[6]

These contentions by the Court were met with a stinging dissent from Justice Marshall, who observed that "the mentally retarded have been subject to a 'lengthy and tragic history'"[7] and that "[f]or the retarded, just as for Negroes and women, much has changed in recent years, but much remains the same; out-dated statutes are still on the books, and irrational fears or ignorance, traceable to the prolonged social and cultural isolation of the retarded, continue to stymie recognition of the dignity and individuality of retarded people."[8] To be sure, the Court struck down the zoning ordinance in question as not even passing a rational basis test. But the welfarist views asserted by the Court about the exceptional needs of people with disabilities continue to this day and were apparent in much of the development of health law as it applied to providers and their patients.

a. Disability, Informed Consent, and Healthcare Decision-making

Informed consent to healthcare treatment is a core value in bioethics and a long-standing legal requirement.[9] Treatment without consent is a battery, even if the patient receives benefit (the damages are nominal in such cases). Consent processes that do not meet the standard of care can be challenged as negligent. In some jurisdictions, this means that disclosures should be what the average reasonable provider discloses, and in others, this means what the average reasonable person would want to know. Average reasonable provider standards may incorporate judgments that are discriminatory but not recognized as such because of their prevalence in the profession. Average reasonable person standards have come under fire in other areas of law, such as sexual harassment, where they are charged with perpetuating perspectives of dominance. For example, standards of reasonableness about whether sexual advances are welcome may differ from male and female perspectives.[10] The extent

[5] City of Cleburne v. Cleburne Living Center, Inc., 473 U.S. 432 (1985).

[6] *Id.* at 444.

[7] *Id.* at 461 (Marshall, J., concurring in part and dissenting in part).

[8] *Id.* at 467 (Marshall, J., concurring in part and dissenting in part).

[9] Schloendorff v. Society of New York Hospital, 105 N.E. 92 (N.Y. 1914), *abrogated by* Bing v. Thunig, 2 N.Y.2d. 656 (N.Y. 1965).

[10] *E.g.*, Ellison v. Brady, 924 F.2d 872 (9th Cir. 1991).

to which ideas of reasonableness in tort law reflect different perspectives[11] might lead disability advocates to question whether the reasonable patient standard affords a standard of relevance to them.

Informed consent has been of uncertain value for people with disabilities, moreover, especially for people with intellectual disabilities. Decision-making capacity is a standard precondition for individuals to consent to their own healthcare, yet if people are too readily perceived to lack capacity, unwarranted paternalism may result. Guardianship, especially in its plenary form, extinguishes the legal power of individuals to enforce their own decisions and replaces them as decision-makers. Characterizing people with disabilities as a "vulnerable" population, however well meaning, may both reflect and foster such protectionist attitudes.[12] The legal case of Mary Northern, anthologized in many bioethics texts, illustrates. Ms. Northern was a seventy-two-year-old woman with gangrene in both feet. When she refused amputation, the Tennessee Department of Human Services went to court to compel treatment. Despite her lucidity otherwise, the Tennessee Court of Appeals found her incompetent based on her physician's testimony that she was "functioning on a psychotic level" with respect to her feet.[13]

Historical approaches to decision-making capacity treated it as an "either/or" determination, largely aimed at protecting people who could not protect themselves. More recent approaches emphasizing the rights of people with disabilities rather than their special needs prefer either limited guardianship or supported decision-making. In the United States, constitutional liberty protections support limited guardianship determinations, although this is frequently not realized in practice.[14] The U.N. Convention on the Rights of Persons with Disabilities (CRPD)[15] advances supported decision-making with persons with disabilities. The goal is to foster the individual's ability to exercise legal capacity to the greatest possible extent, rather than to resort to judgments substituting choice by a proxy for choice by or with the person with disabilities.[16] Some jurisdictions in Canada give legal recognition to supported decision–making, and this idea is beginning to garner support in the United States as well.[17]

Informed consent has also played an important role in the legal standards applied to participation of human subjects in research. Reflecting the World Medical Association

[11] Gregory C. Keating, *Reasonableness and Rationality in Negligence Theory*, 48 STAN. L. REV. 311 (1996).

[12] Michael Ashley Stein et al., *Health Care and the UN Disability Rights Convention*, 374 THE LANCET 1796 (2009).

[13] Department of Human Services v. Northern, 563 S.W.2d 197 (Tenn. Ct. App. 1978); *see also* Elyn R. Saks, *Competency to Refuse Treatment*, 69 N.C. L. REV. 945 (1991).

[14] *E.g.*, Susan G. Haines & John J. Campbell, *Defects, Due Process, and Protective Proceedings: Are our Probate Courts Unconstitutional?*, 33 REAL PROP. PROB. & TR. J. 215 (1998).

[15] United Nations Convention on the Rights of Persons with Disabilities, Art. 12, http://www.un.org/disabilities/convention/conventionfull.shtml (last visited Mar. 16, 2015); Nandini Devi, *Supported Decision-making and Personal Autonomy for Persons with Intellectual Disabilities: Article 12 of the UN Convention on the Rights of Persons with Disabilities*, 41 J.L. MED. & ETHICS 792 (2013).

[16] Michael Ashley Stein, Janet E. Lord, & Dorothy Weiss Tolchin, *Equal Access to Health Care under the UN Disability Rights Convention*, *in* MED. & SOC. JUST. 245 (Rosamond Rhodes, Margaret Battin, & Anita Silvers eds., 2012).

[17] National Resource Center for Supported Decision-Making, *Everyone Has the Right to Make Choices*, http://www.supporteddecisionmaking.org/Education (last visited Mar. 17, 2015).

Declaration of Helsinki[18] and the Belmont Report,[19] U.S. federal regulations for the protection of human subjects in research require protection of the autonomy of research subjects through informed consent.[20] For persons not considered capable of informed consent, the regulations require special protection; the regulations do not single out disability in this way, although many institutions reviewing research do require such protections for people with cognitive impairments and people with mental disabilities. If these policies present unjustifiable barriers to people entering research studies or discourage valuable research about conditions affecting people with such impairments, however, people in these categories may lose benefits from research that could be valuable to them.[21]

b. Disability and the Beginning of Life: Prenatal Testing and Reproductive Liberty

Trisomy 21 (Down syndrome) and neural tube malformations are the conditions for which prenatal testing is most widely performed. Abortion is frequently the option chosen by parents when test results are positive. Yet the practice of letting newborns with these conditions die—also at one point accepted in the medical profession—met with outcry following a critical report in 1973 in the *New England Journal of Medicine*.[22] Adrienne Asch—although a supporter of reproductive liberty and the right to abortion generally—powerfully argued that selective abortion for disability likewise treats disability unjustly.[23] Opponents of selective abortion for disability are also concerned that parents choosing abortion may have been unduly influenced by biased and disparaging reports—framed as neutral and informative by health professionals—about the difficulties of parenting children with disabilities and about the children's capabilities, prognoses, or quality of life. This approach is a critique of disability discrimination in reproductive liberty rather than a commitment to the right-to-life position found in much of the opposition to abortion.

The right to choose abortion remains a constitutionally protected liberty right, despite the many restrictions imposed on it by state legislatures.[24] Nonetheless, some states have not repealed statutes prohibiting abortion that are enjoined from enforcement. These statutes may contain exceptions for the life of the mother or for fetal anomalies that are inconsistent with prolonged life but may not permit abortion on the basis of other disabilities.[25]

[18] World Medical Association, Declaration of Helsinki (1964), *available at* http://www.wma.net/en/30publications/10policies/b3/.

[19] Office of the Secretary, Dep't of Health, Education, and Welfare, Belmont Report (1979), *available at* http://www.hhs.gov/ohrp/humansubjects/guidance/belmont.html.

[20] 42 C.F.R. § 46.116 (2014).

[21] Ana Iltis et al., *Addressing Risks to Advance Mental Health Research*, 70 JAMA Psychiatry 1363 (2013).

[22] Raymond S. Duff & A. G. Campbell, *Moral and Ethical Dilemmas in the Special-Care Nursery*, 289 New Eng. J. Med. 890 (1973).

[23] Adrienne Asch, *Prenatal Diagnosis and Selective Abortion: A Challenge to Practice and Policy*, 89 Am. J. Pub. Health 1649 (1999).

[24] Planned Parenthood v. Casey, 505 U.S. 833 (1992).

[25] Guttmacher Institute, Policies in Brief: An Overview of Abortion Laws (2015), *available at* http://www.guttmacher.org/statecenter/spibs/spib_OAL.pdf.

States also vary in their willingness to countenance lawsuits claiming that negligent failure to offer or negligent performance of prenatal testing is a wrong to either parents or child. In wrongful birth actions, a form of tort litigation, parents seek compensation for being damaged by physician or hospital negligence that resulted in giving birth to a disabled child. As damages, these parents claim the extra costs of raising a child with a disability over the costs of raising a nondisabled child. They may also claim their emotional distress at the child's condition. Plaintiffs are most likely to be successful in these cases if they allege malpractice in correctly informing prospective parents of the results of prenatal tests or in failing to recommend genetic testing.[26] Much less likely to be successful are cases in which the child sues for wrongful life, claiming that it was a wrong to her to have been born. Courts are reluctant to conclude that wrongful life plaintiffs would have been better off never having been brought into existence. In 1982 the California Supreme Court permitted a child to sue but limited the remedy to objective economic costs of the disability and also precluded damages for such subjective outcomes as general suffering or reduced quality of life due to disability.[27] Several states have statutes barring parents' claims that a child would not have been born alive but would have been aborted; these states thus will not permit parents to sue for negligent prenatal testing if they allege that but for the negligence they would have chosen abortion.[28]

c. Disability and the Beginning of Life: The "Baby Doe" Regulations

In the early 1980s, the federal government responded to public opinion prompted by cases in which infants were denied life-saving surgery due to their disabilities.[29] The Reagan administration's strategy to protect newborn infants against denial of medical treatment in hospitals on the basis of disability initially relied on regulatory action by the Department of Health and Human Services (HHS) under the Rehabilitation Act. The Secretary of HHS invoked Section 504 of the Rehabilitation Act, requiring nondiscriminatory access to federally funded programs and services, to prohibit recipients of federal funds from withholding nourishment or medically indicated treatment from a handicapped child solely because of the handicap.

The medical establishment fought adding such protection to extant statutory prohibitions of disability discrimination by successfully filing suit against HHS's effort to create applicable regulations under Section 504. The HHS regulations prohibited federally funded hospitals from withholding nourishment or other medically beneficial treatment from newborns solely on the basis of their disabilities.[30] The Court concluded that this regulation was arbitrary and capricious because hospitals had no power to impose medical treatment in the absence of parental consent and because HHS had no evidence hospitals ever withheld

[26] *E.g.*, Schirmer v. Mt. Auburn Obstetrics & Gynecologic Associates, Inc., 844 N.E.2d 1160 (Ohio 2006); Quinn v. Blau, 21 Conn. L. Rptr. 126 (Conn. Super. Ct. 1997).

[27] Turpin v. Sortini, 643 P.2d 954 (Cal. 1982).

[28] *E.g.*, Sejpal v. Corson, Mitchell, Tomhave & McKinley, M.D.'s, Inc., 665 A.2d 1198 (Pa. Super. Ct. 1995).

[29] Christopher H. Hoving, *The "Baby Doe" Cases*, 72 A.B.A.J. 50 (Apr. 1986).

[30] Bowen v. American Hospital Association, 476 U.S. 610, 614 (1986).

treatment from infants when parents consented.[31] In so reasoning, the Court did not consider the possibility that the parents' decisions had been influenced by discriminatory portrayals of their infants' prospects by those involved in their treatment. Thus reasoning that there had been no violations of the Rehabilitation Act, the Court also rejected the federal government's claim that it had the power to examine medical records to determine whether the Rehabilitation Act had been violated.[32]

Nor, the Court declared, did Congress intend Section 504 to confer any categorical entitlement to particular medical services or to influence states' priorities in allocating medical resources.[33]

Congress proved ready to embed protective language directly into a statute that left no vagueness about legislative intent to provide for categorical intervention into the medical treatment of children with disabilities. Subsequently, in 1988 Congress amended the Child Abuse Prevention and Treatment Act (CAPTA) to require that, to be eligible for federal funding under this legislation, states must establish procedures to address reported medical neglect, "including instances of withholding of medically indicated treatment from disabled infants with life-threatening conditions."[34] Thus, the infants are protected from abuse, not from discrimination. These so-called "Baby Doe" rules define medical neglect as failure to respond to the infant's life-threatening conditions by providing treatment, which, in reasonable medical judgment most likely will be effective in remedying such conditions, unless the infant is irreversibly comatose, or treatment would be futile in achieving the infant's survival and thus would only prolong dying, or the treatment would be virtually futile and also would be inhumane.

Although the CAPTA language appears inflexible, in practice parents are invited to make decisions about continued treatment based on the child's best interest judged against quality-of-life standards. Physicians are expected to advise parents of the options, expected benefits, risks, and limits of any proposed care; how the potential for human relationship is affected by the infant's condition; and relevant information and answers to their questions.[35] And families are supposed to apply these considerations to decide whether treatment, or withdrawal of treatment, is in the person's best interest.

Very little enforcement activity has attended this version of the Baby Doe regulation. To date, only one court decision[36] has invoked the regulation as legal precedent.[37] Suing unsuccessfully under a theory of failure of informed consent, a family alleged that they should

[31] *Id.* at 630–631. In the (in)famous cases at issue, it was the parents who decided not to treat. United States v. University Hosp., State University of New York at Stony Brook, 729 F.2d 144 (2d Cir. 1984) (Baby Jane Doe); Hoving, *supra* note 29. The Court did not apply its reasoning solely to disabilities: "If, pursuant to its normal practice, a hospital refused to operate on a black child whose parents had withheld their consent to treatment, the hospital's refusal would not be based on the race of the child even if it were assumed that the parents based *their decision* entirely on a mistaken assumption that the race of the child made the operation inappropriate." *Bowen*, 476 U.S. at 631.

[32] *Id.* at 616. [33] *Id.* at 624. [34] 42 U.S.C. § 5106a (2014); 45 C.F.R. § 1340.15 (2014).

[35] American Med. Ass'n, Current opinions of the Judicial Council of the American Medical Association 10.016, http://www.ama-assn.org/ama/pub/physician-resources/medical-ethics/code-medical-ethics.page (last visited May 11, 2015).

[36] Montalvo v. Borkovec, 647 N.W.2d 413 (Wis. Ct. App. 2002).

[37] Michael White, *The End at the Beginning*, 11 Ochsner J. 309 (2011); Irene Hurst, *Letter to the Editor: Baby Doe Rules*, 116 Pediatrics 1600 (2005).

have been given data regarding their pre-term neonate's risks of being disabled and that they therefore lacked fully informed opportunity to refuse consent for life-saving measures immediately after his birth. Further, no state has lost federal funds for violating CAPTA. Explanations include widespread professional support for applying the best interests standard to decision-making involving newborns and children, the possibility that there are few if any inappropriate nontreatment decisions, and continuing reluctance to intervene in parental decisions.[38] There is also one case rejecting a family's battery and negligence claims against a hospital, based on their refusal of consent for resuscitation prior to the child's being born and their contention that the hospital's life support interventions caused the child's disabilities.[39] In this case, the Texas Supreme Court stated that neither parents nor physicians could properly evaluate the child's condition before she was born, and consequently a pre-birth decision by the parents could not prevail over a physician's evaluation in an emergent situation post-birth. The Texas court also concluded that state law rather than federal funding authorities have jurisdiction over which situations require parental consent.

d. Disability and Decision-making at the End of Life

Decision-making with respect to life-sustaining treatment is an area of significant intersection and tension between health law and disability. Some disability advocates, such as Not Dead Yet, charge that themes in healthcare and bioethics such as quality-of-life judgments, cost-effectiveness measures, the need to control healthcare costs, and even autonomy, evidence outright discrimination against people with disabilities. Alicia Ouellette argues that bioethics has ignored these concerns to its peril.[40] Other disability rights proponents argue that it is similarly discriminatory to prevent people with disabilities from exercising the full range of choices with respect to end-of-life decision-making.[41] These issues are highly politicized, and, not surprisingly, health law has been caught in the middle.

That a patient is a person with a disability complicates end-of-life legal issues in two primary ways. One has to do with presumptions about the impact of disability on capacity for decision-making. The other has to do with presumptions about the impact of disability on quality of life. While these effects of disability are independent of each other, they often become entangled or at least entwined.

Being disabled can influence how a person dies. Individuals with cognitive disabilities – whether congenitally or from trauma, dementia, psychiatric, or other illnesses or injuries—may be judged deficient both in understanding and executive function and thereby be considered insufficiently autonomous to exercise the right to refuse aggressive end-of-life treatment by themselves. People with severe to profound cognitive disabilities beginning very early in life typically are judged incapable of formulating conceptions of their good and exercising executive judgment to pursue their goals. In such cases, guardians or other personal representatives are authorized to substitute their judgment as to the disabled person's

38 *Id.* at 316 n.17. 39 Miller *ex rel.* Miller v. HCA, Inc., 118 S.W. 3d 758 (Tex. 2003).

40 Alicia Oeullette, Bioethics and Disability: Toward a Disability-Conscious Bioethics (2011).

41 Anita Silvers & Leslie Francis, *Death, Dying and Disability*, *in* Oxford Handbook of Ethics and the End of Life (Stuart Youngner & Robert Arnold eds., forthcoming 2016).

best interests or to construct conceptions of their good from what is known about the individual or about humans generally.

In cases of incapacitating traumatic neurological injury or neurological illness that onset later in life, a person's former conceptualization of the good may be cited as decisive, as stated by the person in an advance directive or as reconstructed by a surrogate or guardian *ad litem*, under a theory of precedent autonomy. That is, the person's decisions when capacitated are taken as decisive or at least a strong indication of the relevant judgments about the ongoing individual's good. That precedent autonomy should prevail becomes problematic, however, where the now-disabled individual retains ability to express preferences clearly, but these differ from the choices the person formerly would have made.[42]

An important goal of the CRPD is to implement a human rights approach with inclusive social frameworks within which people with disabilities can—with any necessary reasonable and effective supports—work out how to live lives that are good for them.[43] As discussed above, supported decision-making is a method for giving enhanced legal authority for collaboratively made decisions such as those an individual with moderate dementia might make interactively with family members' assistance. It is voluntary, can be revoked at any time, and does not remove legal capacity. More formal models for supported decision-making, including for decisions about the end of life, have been developed in a number of jurisdictions outside of the United States.[44]

Disabilities that are not cognitive also have been advanced as reasons to deny the usual freedom to make decisions for one's self about one's end of life.[45] One contention is that disabilities and illnesses warp reasoning about dying, despite the disabled individual's well-balanced thinking in other respects. Another is that reasonable assessments of their own situations notwithstanding, individuals with disabilities have special obligations to act courageously that restrict how they may approach their own lives' ends. Both versions suppose that disabled people's troubled relationships with nondisabled society may too readily induce them to give up on living.

In 1983, Elizabeth Bouvia—a young woman with extensive dysfunction from cerebral palsy, dependent on others to execute essential activities of daily living, and suffering severe pain from arthritis as well—became a client of the American Civil Liberties Union (ACLU) for a lawsuit against the hospital where she resided to free her from being tube-fed, an intervention for which she had refused consent. After a loss at trial, in which the court decided that the state had an interest in saving her from suicide, the appellate court reversed, ruling that Bouvia, as a competent patient, had a fundamental right to refuse any treatment even at the cost of her life.

[42] *E.g.*, Rebecca Dresser, *Precommitment: A Misguided Strategy for Securing Death with Dignity*, 81 TEX. L. REV. 1823 (2003).

[43] Michael Ashley Stein, *Disability Human Rights*, 95 CALIF. L. REV. 75 (2007).

[44] Janet E. Lord & Michael Ashley Stein, *Contingent Participation and Coercive Care: Feminist and Communitarian Theories of Disability and Legal Capacity*, *in* COERCIVE CARE: RIGHTS, LAW AND POLICY 31 (Bernadette McSherry & Ian Freckelton eds., 2013).

[45] *See* Katharina Heyer, *Rejecting Rights: The Disability Critique of Physician Assisted Suicide*, *in* 54 STUDIES IN LAW, POLITICS, AND SOCIETY: SPECIAL ISSUE SOCIAL MOVEMENTS/LEGAL POSSIBILITIES 77 (Austin Sarat ed., 2011) (for an analysis of the effects of denying a freedom right on the rhetoric of a civil rights movement).

The appellate court noted that, despite the appearance that Bouvia had an overriding interest in living for the two decades projected as feasible with artificial feeding, the prospect of suffering a painful and isolated life suggested that in her case the seeming interest in staying alive was illusory.[46] Bouvia's life was characterized in the following terms: "She herself is imprisoned and must lie physically helpless subject to the ignominy, embarrassment, humiliation, and dehumanizing aspects created by her helplessness."[47]

Disability activists characterized both Bouvia's, and the court's, motivations very differently.[48] Bouvia's self-reports about her own situation seemed suspiciously stereotypical to them. They believed Bouvia was being misrepresented as desiring to die by starvation. They diagnosed her instead as having internalized the rejection and repression that society rains on disabled people. Bouvia thus was accused of having internalized nondisabled society's biased view of the quality of life disabled people can attain. The court was accused of echoing nondisabled society's biased presumptions that she could not live independently, could not have a marriage or a career, could not cope with the multiple hardships of disabled life, and therefore that she—as a person who had to live with such an absence of high-quality life—was worthless.[49]

Bouvia's critics also contended that Bouvia's dependence on nondisabled society for services and to mitigate her loneliness exposed her to being exploited by nondisabled people for their own purposes. They viewed her as voicing ideas inspired by ACLU attorneys who had made her a tool to show that disability made life expendable under a pretext of defending liberty. Finally, they feared her legal pursuit to be free of life-saving medical intervention could negatively impact others like herself, especially those who depended on medical support to survive. To discredit Bouvia's decision that dying was in her interest, disability activists derogated her capacity for self-governance, thereby echoing the prevailing societal picture of disabled individuals who retain executive functioning as nevertheless being coercible because their sense of self is pervaded by anger and shame.[50] Tensions between respect for autonomy, judgments about what autonomy is possible in constrained circumstances, and the apparently well-meaning but not always well-directed desire to protect the lives of people with disabilities are striking in these cases.

In 1997, in denying that a state law prohibiting assisted suicide violates constitutional liberty guarantees, the U.S. Supreme Court reiterated this fear, similarly characterizing disabled people as vulnerable. The Court stated,

> the State has an interest in protecting vulnerable groups including the poor, the elderly, and disabled persons from abuse, neglect, and mistakes. . . . We have recognized . . . the real risk of subtle coercion and undue influence in end of life situations. . . . The risk of harm is greatest for the many individuals in our society whose autonomy and wellbeing are already compromised by poverty, lack of access to good medical care, advanced age, or membership in a stigmatized

46 Bouvia v Superior Court, 225 Cal. Rptr. 297, 299-00 (Cal. Ct. App. 1986).

47 Associated Press, *Woman Won Right to Die But Stays Alive*, Deseret News, Dec. 16, 1993, http://www.deseretnews.com/article/326259/WOMAN-WON-RIGHT-TO-DIE-BUT-STAYS-ALIVE.html?pg=all.

48 Mary Johnson, *Right to Life, Fight to Die: The Elizabeth Bouvia Saga*, http://www.broadreachtraining.com/advocacy/artbouvia.htm (last visited Mar. 17, 2015).

49 *Id.*

50 Paul K. Longmore, *Screening Stereotypes: Images of Disabled People in Television and Motion Pictures*, *in* Images of the Disabled, Disabling Images 65 (A. Gartner and T. Joe eds., 1987).

> social group . . . The State's interest here goes beyond protecting the vulnerable from coercion; it extends to protecting disabled and terminally ill people from prejudice, negative and inaccurate stereotypes, and "societal indifference." . . . The State may fear that permitting assisted suicide will start it down the path to voluntary and perhaps even involuntary euthanasia . . . [I]t turns out that what is couched as a limited right to "physician-assisted suicide" is likely, in effect, a much broader license, which could prove extremely difficult to police and contain. Washington's ban on assisting suicide prevents such erosion.[51]

The high-profile national debate that swirled around the case of Teresa Marie (Terri) Schiavo[52] illustrates how issues of capacity and quality-of-life judgments may become so intertwined in end-of-life situations that the impact of disability and the concerns of people with disabilities are obscured. Schiavo suffered brain damage due to anoxia after collapsing at her home, and after ten weeks in a coma her diagnosis was changed to persistent vegetative state (PVS). After eight years her husband and legal guardian Michael Schiavo petitioned the Sixth Circuit Court of Florida to remove her feeding tube. Her parents, the Schindlers, opposed the action. Over the next seven years, the case spawned fourteen appeals, state and federal legislation, and action by then Florida Governor Jeb Bush and then President George W. Bush. Eventually, Florida courts decided that Schiavo met the state criteria for withdrawal of life support, the feeding tube was removed, and she died of dehydration.

Throughout, the Schindlers argued that their daughter did not meet the criteria for a diagnosis of PVS because she was at least minimally responsive to some stimuli and was capable of swallowing if fed by mouth. Physician testimony introduced by the contesting sides conflicted in regard to these points, but the Florida courts concluded that the evidence supported the determination of PVS. Contending that this judgment subjected Schiavo to disability discrimination, manifested by underestimations of her potential for improved functioning and of her quality of life, some commentators called for applying for protection under the Americans with Disabilities Act (ADA).

Schiavo thus became a national symbol of the vulnerability disability can bring. Yet the ADA neither presses nor prohibits specific scientific or medical treatment decisions; it is a prohibition of discrimination, not a right-to-life statute. Two of the authors of this chapter have argued elsewhere that it is important not to interpret disability perspectives about the Schiavo situation to support permitting bad science to influence decision-making with respect to people with severe intellectual disabilities.[53]

Schiavo is a case in which the usual approaches to address the impact of disability on capacity for decision-making provided a legal resolution but became entangled with ongoing disagreement about the impact of disability on quality of life. In *amicus* briefs in the *Schiavo* case,[54] disability organizations contended without success that prevailing prejudice regarding the poor quality and burdensomeness on others of severely disabled people's lives may taint third-party decisions about withdrawing or withholding life support from them.

51 Washington v. Glucksberg, 521 U.S. 702, 731–732 (1997).

52 Schiavo *ex rel.* Schindler v. Schiavo, 358 F. Supp. 2d 1161, 1164–1165 (M.D. Fla. 2005), *aff'd*, 403 F.3d 1289 (11th Cir. 2005).

53 Leslie Francis & Anita Silvers, *(Mis)Framing Schiavo as Discrimination Against Persons with Disabilities*, 61 U. MIAMI L. REV. 789 (2007).

54 *See, e.g., Brief of Amici Curiae Not Dead Yet* et al. *in Support of Appellants and Requesting Reversal*, Bush v. Schiavo, 885 So.2d 321 (Fla. 2004) (No. SC04-925).

This view about the dangers of underestimating disabled people's quality of life was advanced by the National Council on Disability in a 1997 position paper and remains influential in the disability community today.[55]

II Health Law and the Statutory Framework of U.S. Disability Law

Understanding statutory definitions of disability is critical to understanding the relationship between disability law and health law. United States disability law statutes define disability in different ways and in so doing align with different purposes for disability law. Some statutory approaches to disability employ what can best be characterized as a functional approach to defining disability. These characterize disability in terms of extraordinary limitations on a person's activities that result from combinations of biological anomalies with restrictive social attitudes and structures. Other statutes are primarily impairment-based—that is, they specify a list of conditions that qualify individuals as disabled. These approaches reflect tensions between universalist and "minority group" approaches to disability rights, as described below.[56] They also reflect differences between the medical model of disability on which disability is identified with a diagnosable condition of the individual and the social model of disability on which adverse social arrangements or disparately truncated opportunity are at least partially responsible for the individual's functional limitations.

a. Statutes Employing Functional Definitions of Disability

In the United States, the Rehabilitation Act of 1973 (Rehabilitation Act), the Fair Housing Act (FHA), and the Americans with Disabilities Act (ADA) are the primary statutes of relevance to healthcare laws and policies that employ a functional approach to defining disability. A functional approach to defining disability considers what an individual is—or is not—able to do. To be disabled for one of these statutes, an individual must have a physical or mental impairment that substantially limits a major life activity, have a record of such an impairment, or be regarded as having such an impairment.[57] Because the U.S. Supreme Court issued a series of decisions narrowly interpreting and severely constraining this definition of disability, Congress responded with the ADA Amendments Act of 2008 (ADAAA), stipulating that the definition of disability is to be construed in favor of broad coverage.[58]

[55] Robert L. Burgdorf, Jr., National Council on Disability, Assisted Suicide: A Disability Perspective Position Paper (1997), *available at* http://www.ncd.gov/publications/1997/03241997.

[56] Samuel Bagenstos, Law and the Contradictions of the Disability Rights Movement (2009); Kevin Barry, *Toward Universalism: What the ADA Amendments Act of 2008 Can and Can't Do for Disability Rights*, 31 Berkeley J. Emp. & Lab. L. 203 (2010).

[57] Americans with Disabilities Act of 1990, 42 U.S.C. § 12102(1) (2014); Rehabilitation Act of 1973, 29 U.S.C. § 705(9)(B) (2014); Fair Housing Act, 42 U.S.C. § 3602(h) (2014).

[58] 42 U.S.C. § 12102(4)(A) (2014). Exceptions to this statutory definition of disability that reflect a complex set of congressional moral judgment should be noted. For all three of these statutes, current

Section 504 of the Rehabilitation Act of 1973,[59] which prohibits discrimination in any program or activity receiving federal funding, was the initial U.S. statute prohibiting disability discrimination. Any healthcare facilities receiving federal funding, including Medicare or Medicaid reimbursements, construction funds, or research funds, are subject to the Rehabilitation Act. The FHA, amended to include disability in 1988, prohibits discrimination in the sale or rental of housing; it excludes single-family dwellings and dwellings of three or fewer units (four, if owner-occupied). Of relevance to healthcare, the FHA applies to assisted-living facilities and continuing-care retirement communities, among other senior living communities.[60]

The ADA, the most comprehensive of the American antidiscrimination statutes, prohibits defined forms of disability discrimination in employment, public services, public transit, and public accommodations. Title I of the ADA, the employment discrimination title, applies to all employers engaged in commerce with fifteen or more employees except the U.S. government or Indian tribes; all state and private sector healthcare facilities meeting the minimum size requirement are covered by this Title.[61] This Title I requirement includes the failure of healthcare employers to provide reasonable accommodations for their employees such as light-duty assignments, altered work responsibilities, or adjusted work shifts for otherwise qualified individuals—so long as these do not impose an undue hardship.[62]

Employees of healthcare institutions have brought many claims of employment discrimination under Title I of the ADA. In a well-known case, the University of Maryland Medical Center permanently suspended a neurosurgery resident who had become HIV-positive after a needle stick and he refused the nonsurgical residencies offered to him as alternatives. The court held that the resident was not otherwise qualified for the surgery position if he posed safety risks to others.[63] In reaching this conclusion, the court relied on the medical system's determination that a significant percentage of the procedures Dr. Doe would be expected to perform presented the possibility of exposure to patients despite use of precautions. Although judgments about risk must be based in current best evidence, it remains good law that employees who pose safety risks that cannot reasonably be accommodated are not qualified for positions they seek; their employers may use the "direct threat" defense to the charge of discrimination.

Many employment discrimination cases involve hospital employees seeking accommodations such as lifting restrictions or altered shifts; before 2009, these cases most frequently failed on motions for summary judgment applying the Supreme Court's straitened standards for disability as well as on claims that the employee could not perform the essential functions of the job and thus was not qualified. Despite the ADAAA, indications are that some courts may still be concluding that plaintiffs are not sufficiently limited in their major life activities

illegal use of or addiction to a controlled substance is not a disability; this exclusion does not include adult alcohol addiction, as alcohol use by adults is legal and alcohol is not a controlled substance. Under the ADA and the Rehabilitation Act, being a transvestite, homosexual, or bisexual also is not the basis for a claim to be disabled, nor are certain other conditions such as pyromania, gender identity disorders, or pedophilia. 42 U.S.C. §§ 12208, 12214 (2014).

[59] 29 U.S.C. § 701(a) (2014).

[60] These come under the definition of dwelling, 24 C.F.R. § 100.10 (2014).

[61] 42 U.S.C. § 12111(5) (2014). [62] 42 U.S.C. § 12112(b) (2014).

[63] Doe v. University of Maryland Medical System Corp., 50 F.3d 1261 (4th Cir. 1995).

to qualify as disabled, and other courts are granting summary judgment in favor of employers on the question of the employee's abilities to perform essential job functions.[64] Moreover, the Supreme Court has held that policies with differential impact on persons with disabilities are not discriminatory treatment under Title I of the ADA, absent some further evidence of actual discriminatory motivation on the part of the employer. Consequently, nurses in successful rehabilitation from substance abuse and with exemplary recent records, but who were not hired because a hospital had a policy of not hiring anyone who had had a prior licensing restriction, lost their suit for employment discrimination under the ADA.[65]

Title II of the ADA governs public services provided by any state or local government and so includes public hospitals, clinics, public health departments, and the like, as well as public educational institutions.[66] Title II prohibits exclusion from services or denial of benefits to any individual meeting essential eligibility requirements with or without reasonable modifications.[67] A pre-ADA Supreme Court decision (under the Rehabilitation Act) considering an application to nursing school by a deaf student concluded that she must be able to meet eligibility requirements in spite of her disability and could not do so because her need for lip reading or interpretation might preclude her full participation in clinical settings as when masks are worn.[68] Although much criticized as stereotyping the capabilities of students with disabilities,[69] *Davis* continues to be relied on by courts adjudicating ADA claims in concluding that applicants to educational programs in medicine or other health sciences cannot meet essential eligibility requirements.[70]

Another important early interpretation of the Rehabilitation Act, continuing to set the standard under the ADA, was *Alexander v. Choate*'s determination that Tennessee had provided "meaningful access" to its Medicaid program for persons with disabilities despite cutting back hospital stays to fourteen days per year.[71] The "meaningful access" standard continues to be employed by courts scrutinizing whether plaintiffs with disabilities have received social services in a nondiscriminatory manner. Some courts interpret *Alexander* to require only that people with disabilities have meaningful access to whatever benefit is provided, even if the benefits are limited in ways that make them useless to the individuals due to their disabilities.[72] On this interpretation, all that matters is access. Other courts examine the structure of a benefits program for whether it is difficult for people with disabilities to enjoy due to their disabilities and hence discriminates.[73] On this approach, the nature of the benefit provided also matters: Is the benefit formulated in such a way that people with

[64] Michael Ashley Stein et al., *Accommodating Every Body*, 81 U. CHI. L. REV. 689 (2014). Dismissal of a case on summary judgment is a critical blow to plaintiffs, as it precludes any further exploration of the facts in court or incentives on the part of the defendant to settle the case.

[65] Lopreato v. Select Specialty Hospital-Northern Kentucky, LLC, No. 12-217-DLB-JGW, 2014 WL 6804221 (E.D. Ky. Dec. 3, 2014).

[66] 42. U.S.C. §12131(1) (2014).

[67] 42 U.S.C. § 12132 (2014).

[68] Southeastern Community College v. Davis, 442 U.S. 397 (1979).

[69] Michael Schwartz, *Technical Standards for Admission to Medical School: Deaf Candidates Don't Get No Respect*, 28 BUFF. PUB. INT. L.J. 31 (2009–2010).

[70] *E.g.*, Halpern v. Wake Forest University Health Sciences, 669 F.3d 454 (4th Cir. 2012); Zukle v. Regents of the University of California, 166 F.3d 1041 (9th Cir. 1999).

[71] Alexander v. Choate, 469 U.S. 287 (1985).

[72] *E.g.*, Cohon *ex rel.* Bass v. New Mexico Dep't of Health, 646 F.3d 717 (10th Cir. 2011).

[73] *E.g.*, Henrietta D. v. Bloomberg, 331 F.3d 261 (2d Cir. 2003).

disabilities can enjoy it on terms equivalent to others? Scholars[74] characterize this as the access/benefits distinction; if the issue is framed in terms of nondiscrimination with respect to benefits rather than mere access, civil rights protections will reach far more broadly than they otherwise would. As discussed more fully below, it remains to be seen how the meaningful access standard of *Alexander v. Choate* will be applied by courts to states' reforms of their Medicaid programs in the wake of the ACA.

A third decision interpreting the ADA Title II of critical relevance to healthcare is *Olmstead v. L.C.*'s holding[75] that services must be provided in the most integrated setting appropriate in order to avoid undue segregation of people with disabilities. In *Olmstead*, two patients in state hospitals for persons with intellectual or psychiatric disabilities sought community placements as recommended by their treating physicians. The state objected that requiring community placements for all patients like these would be a fundamental alteration in the state's design of mental health services, imposing excess costs on the state's system. Although adopting the most integrated setting requirement, the Court also held that in determining whether a community placement requirement would be a fundamental alteration in the state's program, and thus allow the state a defense to the discrimination claim, the lower court should take into account the range of services provided by the state to others with mental disabilities, the state's obligation to mete out these services equitably, and the system's overall costs. State programs that require or as a practical matter expect patients to receive benefits in institutional settings rather than home care continue to be challenged by plaintiffs; recent litigation in Florida by medically fragile children claiming that the state program placed them at risk of institutionalization is an example.[76] Litigation following *Olmstead* has often been successful for plaintiffs, with states either losing or settling cases.

Title III of the ADA applies to public accommodations, defined to include physicians' professional offices, pharmacies, hospitals, other service centers, social service centers, and health spas.[77] Like ADA Title II, ADA Title III can be expected to be a rich source of litigation as the ACA continues to unfold. ADA Title III requires public accommodations to afford persons with disabilities the full and equal enjoyment of goods, services, facilities, privileges, advantages, or accommodations.[78] Offices of insurance companies are clearly public accommodations that must be physically accessible, but it is unsettled legally whether the insurance products sold are also subject to the nondiscrimination requirement and what that requirement might entail if they are.

ADA Title III also covers examinations such as the MCAT, professional licensing examinations, and medical board examinations. The statute requires tests to be administered in a place or manner accessible to persons with disabilities,[79] and the regulations construe this to require that examination results "accurately reflect the aptitude or achievement level of individuals with disabilities rather than reflecting the individuals' impaired sensory, manual, or speaking skills."[80] Courts have concluded that examining boards are not required to construct alternative format examinations for persons with cognitive processing disabilities, however.[81]

74 *E.g.*, BAGENSTOS, *supra* note 56.
75 Olmstead v. L.C., 527 U.S. 581 (1999).
76 A.R. *ex rel.* Root v. Dudek, 31 F. Supp. 3d (S.D. Fla. 2014).
77 42 U.S.C. § 12181(7)(F), (K-L) (2014).
78 42 U.S.C. § 12182(a) (2014).
79 42 U.S.C. §12189 (2014).
80 28 C.F.R. § 36.309(b)(i) (2014).
81 *E.g.*, Rawdin v. American Board of Pediatrics, 582 Fed. Appx. 114 (3d Cir 2014).

b. Statutes Employing Condition-based Definitions of Disability

In contrast to a functional definition of disability, other statutes employ condition-based diagnoses to set coverage eligibility limitations. Often resulting from lobbying or advocacy by groups with interests in the condition in question, this approach limits coverage to the enumerated conditions, thus relying on medicalized diagnoses. The Individuals with Disabilities Education Act (IDEA) requires that all children with disabilities be provided with a free and appropriate public education. This includes medical services if they are related to the children's receipt of educational services; examples include administration of ventilator support or medication required for a student to be safely in a school setting.[82] To qualify for IDEA services, children must be diagnosed with one of a listed set of conditions (including mental retardation, hearing or visual impairments, serious emotional disturbance, other health impairment, or specific learning disabilities) by reason of which they need special education services.[83] Children not fitting one of these diagnostic categories will be ineligible for IDEA services.

SSDI is another federal program employing a diagnosis-based understanding of disability. To qualify for Social Security disability income, an individual must have received the age-appropriate number of work credits, be unable to work in any job in the relevant labor market, and have a diagnosed disability that has lasted for more than one year or is expected to result in death. Social Security lists conditions that presumptively qualify for the disability designation.[84] Other conditions may qualify if claimants can demonstrate that they are of equal severity to conditions on the list. Individuals receiving SSDI also qualify for Medicare. Individuals qualifying for SSDI may also receive Supplemental Security Income (SSI) if their assets and income place them below income and resource thresholds and may be eligible for state Medicaid as well.

Several federal statutes protect types of information about individuals' health, sometimes limited to the type of information or treatment. The Genetic Information Nondiscrimination Act (GINA) prohibits genetic discrimination by employers and health insurers. GINA defines genetic information to include genetic tests and family history information, but not information about disease that has become manifest in the individual.[85] GINA's nondiscrimination provisions include prohibiting requirements that individuals undergo genetic tests or submit genetic information to be used by employers or insurers. The federal Substance Abuse and Mental Health Services Act (SAMHSA) and accompanying regulations require specific consent for the disclosure of records of treatment by federally funded alcohol or drug abuse programs.[86] The Health Insurance Portability and Accountability Act (HIPAA) protects the security and privacy of identifiable health information for all patients, whether

[82] Cedar Rapids Community School District v. Garrett F., 526 US 66 (1999).

[83] 20 U.S.C. § 1401(3) (2014).

[84] US Social Security Administration, Disability Evaluation Under Social Security: Listing of Impairments—Adult Listings Part A, *available at* http://www.ssa.gov/disability/professionals/bluebook/AdultListings.htm (last visited Mar. 17, 2015).

[85] Genetic Information Nondiscrimination Act of 2008, Pub. L. 110-223, §201(4), 122 Stat. 881.

[86] 42 C.F.R., Part 2 (2014).

or not they are persons with disabilities. Many state statutes also protect the privacy of various types of health information beyond these federal protections.

Workers' compensation is a state-level insurance program that pays benefits to individuals who have been injured on the job. Typical state programs require employers to carry the insurance, but individual states have a variety of exceptions for smaller employers and employers in certain job sectors such as agriculture. Workers' compensation benefits cover a percentage of income (up to a ceiling) and, depending on the state, may be subject to time limitations in coverage. Workers' compensation also covers necessary medical care, although coverage limits vary by state. In addition, many employers provide disability insurance and life insurance programs for their workers; these are subject to the ADA prohibition on employment discrimination but may incorporate reasonable actuarial calculations to determine premiums. These insurance programs may be offered in the private market and, as mentioned above, may receive ADA Title III protections. Only health insurance is subject to the GINA prohibitions on genetic discrimination and to ACA requirements, however.

III Health Law, Disability, and Access to Care

Nondiscrimination statutes, particularly the Rehabilitation Act and the ADA, address discrimination in the provision of healthcare. Many other aspects of health law also impact access to care, especially structures of public and private healthcare financing. Recent passage of the ACA contains the promise of erasing much disability discrimination from healthcare financing, as insurers will no longer be able to charge premiums based on the individual's health history or exclude preexisting conditions from coverage. How much this promise will be realized remains an evolving conundrum, however, and much remains to ensure meaningful access to healthcare for all people with disabilities in the United States.

a. Access to Healthcare—Providers' and Programs' Obligations Under the ADA

As explained above, the ADA Title III establishes that healthcare providers must not discriminate against people with disabilities by refusing to treat them or by limiting the treatment they provide in a way they would not limit treatment to the nondisabled. In *Bragdon v. Abbott*,[87] the Supreme Court held that it was disability discrimination for a dentist to refuse to treat a person with HIV/AIDS. The dentist had invoked the ADA's "direct threat" defense, claiming that he had a good faith belief that treating patients with HIV would risk transmission of infection. In response, the Court said that the defense would only be available based on objective evidence of risks such as that available from the Centers for Disease Control. Some providers still may be unjustifiably refusing to treat people with disabilities

[87] Bragdon v. Abbott, 524 U.S. 624 (1998).

such as HIV/AIDS, however.[88] *Bragdon v. Abbott* also held that Abbott's HIV was a disability because it substantially limited her fundamental life activity of reproduction. Although the impact of HIV may be far less on reproduction today because of the availability of retroviral medications, HIV likely still qualifies as a disability under the ADAAA because if an HIV positive patient is assessed in her uncorrected state, her immune system function is substantially limited.

Full and equal enjoyment also means that healthcare facilities must be accessible to people with disabilities. Critics have documented limited accessibility in many healthcare facilities, however.[89] Examination tables or scales that cannot be easily used by people with mobility impairments, mammography machines that require standing, or improperly sized equipment are illustrations. Another example is that elders who due to disability use powered mobility devices may find themselves denied access to assisted-living facilities despite qualifying for them. These inadequacies violate the ADA and the Fair Housing Act.[90]

Communication is another important aspect of accessibility. Patients or their personal representatives who due to deafness communicate with sign language rather than speech need effective ways to exchange information with medical professionals. A poignant example is a California case in which a deaf woman was not provided any interpreter services and was unable to communicate about difficult care decisions for her husband who had suffered massive cardiac arrest.[91] The ADA and implementing regulations require that healthcare providers ensure effective communication with patients or patients' companions with sensory impairments. This may require a variety of auxiliary aids. Providers must consult with patients about what types of auxiliary aids are needed, but under the regulations the ultimate responsibility for the decision rests with providers, subject to the requirement that the communication be effective.[92] In addition, under the implementing regulations, providers may not require patients to provide their own auxiliary aids.

b. Medicare

Medicare is the federal health insurance program for qualifying persons over the age of sixty-five, qualifying persons with long-term disabilities rendering them incapable of working, or people with end-stage renal disease. Medicare eligibility tracks Social Security eligibility: People over age sixty-five must have forty credits (work quarters) of paying into the Social Security system, and people under age sixty-five must have achieved the number of credits specified for their age (unless they have been unable to work since childhood or come within certain other limited exceptions). Thus Medicare covers many but by no means all adults with long-term disabilities in the United States.

[88] Brad Sears et al., *HIV Discrimination in Dental Care: Results of a Testing Study in Los Angeles County*, 45 Loy. L.A. L. Rev. 909 (2012).

[89] Elizabeth Pendo, *Disability, Equipment Barriers and Women's Health: Using the ADA to Provide Meaningful Access*, 2 St. Louis U. J. Health L. & Pol'y 15 (2008).

[90] Assisted-living facilities are public accommodations under Title III of the ADA, ADA § 12181(7), and dwellings under the FHA, 24 C.F.R. § 100.10 (2014).

[91] Aikens v. St. Helena Hospital, 843 F. Supp. 1329 (N.D. Cal. 1994).

[92] 28 C.F.R. §36.303(c) (2014).

Medicare primarily covers hospital, outpatient, and pharmaceutical expenses, but with limits of significant importance to people with disabilities. Except for a maximum of one hundred days post-hospitalization (with a $140/day copayment after the first twenty days), Medicare does not pay for any nursing home care, even when skilled care is required. Additional nursing home care or long-term care in the United States must be paid for out of private funds, long-term care insurance policies, or Medicaid for those who have spent down to meet income and asset eligibility ceilings. Mental healthcare is also quite limited under Medicare: Inpatient mental health benefits are limited to 190 days lifetime, and the outpatient benefit requires a 40% copayment.

c. The Implications of the ACA

The ACA aims to improve access to healthcare and overall health status, while at the same time reducing healthcare costs and improving healthcare quality. For persons with expensive healthcare needs, the ACA presents the clear advantage of prohibiting insurers from underwriting decisions based on individual risk profiles or preexisting conditions. While some of these goals might seem uncontroversially beneficial for people with disabilities and indeed for the population as a whole, tensions among the goals as well as between strategies for implementing them remain problematic. This section highlights specific areas of concern: the continuing role of employer-provided insurance, the definition of minimum essential benefits, the use of premium differentials to encourage supposed health-promoting behaviors, the emphasis on wellness programs, and the reliance on Medicaid to expand coverage.

i. Employer Coverage and Minimum Essential Benefits

Cornerstones of the ACA are the requirements for employers to provide or maintain coverage, for individuals to meet the coverage mandate, and for coverage providing minimum essential benefits to be available through exchanges in a manner that does not discriminate against individuals with expensive healthcare needs.[93]

ACA requirements leave large employer plans for the most part unchanged.[94] These plans may not include forms of coverage that matter to employees (or their dependents) with certain kinds of disabilities. Examples are home healthcare, out-of-network care with desired specialists, or coverage for prostheses or other novel assistive devices. Employer plans also may contract separately with pharmacy benefit managers to reduce drug costs to the plan; these arrangements may involve high copayments or a limited formulary of available drugs, posing problems for people with disabilities such as multiple sclerosis who require particularly expensive pharmaceuticals.

Individuals without employer-provided insurance may purchase coverage through exchanges offered in the various states and operated by federal or state governments. All

[93] For a full discussion of ACA requirements, *see* Hall, Hoffman, in this volume.

[94] Amy Monahan, *The ACA, the Large Group Market, and Content Regulation: What's a State to Do?*, 5 St. Louis U. J. Health L. & Pol'y 83 (2011).

plans sold through exchanges must cover minimum essential benefits in a list of ten categories set out in the statute.[95] (Plans offered in the small group market must also meet this requirement.) By regulation, HHS has tied minimum essential benefits to state benchmark plans, defined in terms of plans currently sold in the state; the default is the largest plan by enrollment in the largest product in the state's small group market. Benchmark plans vary by state and like current employer plans may or may not include coverage particularly important to people with disabilities. If benchmark plans omit an essential benefit category, states must require that coverage in this category be included. Disability advocates are concerned that these additions may be inadequate or that states may fail to scrutinize benchmark plans for adequacy in categories they do cover. A particularly important essential benefits category for people with disabilities is rehabilitative and habilitative services. In this category, advocates caution that it is important to cover habilitation (learning a skill) as well as rehabilitation (regaining a skill) and to include a wide range of devices and services.[96]

Coverage for mental healthcare has been a persistent gap in American healthcare. The ACA aims to address the problem of mental health parity by requiring essential mental health and substance use disorder services as part of the essential health benefits package.[97] A primary concern about the use of existing plans as benchmarks is that this strategy will replicate existing inequities in coverage for mental healthcare, despite the requirement to include mental health and substance use disorder services in the essential benefits package.[98] Commentators are especially worried about plan designs that restrict types of therapy or choice of provider in the mental health arena.[99]

ii. *Encouraging Healthy Behavior: Premium Differentials and Wellness Programs*

The ACA permits employer-provided health insurance plans to offer premium discounts or rebates based on behavior and participation in wellness plans.[100] These programs must be made available to all similarly situated individuals and may not be based on health status per se, such as whether an individual has diabetes.

The ACA also permits demonstration projects for the incorporation of wellness programs into plans sold through exchanges. State Medicaid programs, particularly in more

[95] 42 U.S.C. § 18022 (2014).

[96] Consortium for Citizens with Disabilities, Open Letter to the States on Defining Essential Health Benefits Package, https://www.aapmr.org/advocacy/federal-reform/Documents/EHB%20Technical%20Assistance%20For%20Distribution.pdf (last visited Mar. 17, 2015).

[97] Patient Protection and Affordable Care Act, 42 U.S.C. § 18022(b)(1)(E) (2014).

[98] Office of the Assistant Secretary for Planning and Evaluation, U.S. Dep't of Health, Consistency of Large Employer and Group Health Plan Benefits with Requirements of the Paul Wellstone and Pete Domenici Mental Health Parity and Addiction Equity Act of 2008 (2013), *available at* http://www.dol.gov/ebsa/pdf/hhswellstonedomenicimhpaealargeemployerandghpbconsistency.pdf; Stacey A. Tovino, *A Proposal for Comprehensive and Specific Essential Mental Health and Substance Use Disorder Benefits*, 38 Am. J.L. & Med. 471 (2012).

[99] Miriam Ruttenberg, *Choice and Continuity of Care as Significant Issues for Equality in Mental Health Care*, 10 J. Health & Biomedical L. 201 (2014).

[100] 42 U.S.C. § 300gg-4(j) (2014).

conservative states, also have experimented with a variety of "personal responsibility for health" programs.[101] If any conditions for obtaining a wellness plan benefit under the ACA require an individual to satisfy a standard related to a health status factor—an example would be maintaining specified HA1C levels for a diabetic—the reward may not exceed 30% of the employee-only coverage costs. Health target-based programs also must provide reasonable alternative standards for individuals when it is unreasonably difficult or inadvisable for them to meet the prescribed standard because of a medical condition. Plans may seek reasonable verification from the individual's physician of the impact of the health status factor.

While the requirement that these wellness programs be available to all similarly situated individuals may provide some protection for people with health status differences arising from disability, others may find these programs inappropriate interventions at best and coercive impositions at worst. The permissible differential in the employee's premium share—30%—may be highly significant for many lower-income employees and thus may affect the affordability of coverage. Although participation-based programs are theoretically open to everyone, they may be as a practical matter more difficult to access for some (e.g., persons with disabilities who cannot drive and must use public transit or paratransit), and they may not provide the adaptive equipment people with certain disabilities need. Thus the unlimited rewards attached to them may be unfairly distributed.

Normative assumptions built into the programs about what behaviors are healthy—smoking cessation is a primary example, but so are weight reduction and exercise—may be inapposite or ill-advised for people with disabilities such as forms of mental disability.[102] Employees with disabilities may find it very difficult to reach stated targets—for example, weight-loss goals—even if it is medically possible for them to do so. At the very least, efforts to reach these goals impose burdens on some that are not imposed on others who already meet them; as a practical matter, some will experience liberty intrusions that others will not. Moreover, permitting employers to request verification from treating physicians that meeting wellness standards would be unreasonably difficult or medically ill-advised may be seen as violating employees' privacy and subjecting them to paternalistic medical judgments on the part of their physicians.[103] An overarching disability critique of these programs is that, relying on the medical model of disability, they may see bodily differences as an individual "problem," to be addressed by personal responsibility and the acceptance of medical intervention.

iii. Expanding Medicaid (or Not)

Medicaid is the federal-state partnership designed to provide healthcare coverage to certain low-income persons. Medicaid has been particularly important for people with disabilities, as it covers services such as long-term care that are not available under other insurance programs. In 2010, nearly 10 million of the 66 million Medicaid recipients qualified on the basis

[101] Karen J. Blumenthal, *Medicaid Incentive Programs to Encourage Healthy Behavior Show Mixed Results to Date and Should be Studied and Improved*, 32 HEALTH AFF. 497 (2013).

[102] Sherry Leonard, Sharon Mexal, & Robert Freedman, *Smoking, Genetics and Schizophrenia: Evidence for Self Medication*, 3 J. DUAL DIAGNOSIS 43 (2007).

[103] Lindsay F. Wiley, *Access to Health Care as an Incentive for Healthy Behavior? An Assessment of the Affordable Care Act's Personal Responsibility for Wellness Reforms*, 11 IND. HEALTH L. REV. 635 (2014).

of disability. The ACA Medicaid expansion may provide coverage to people with disabilities who are able to earn too much income to qualify for traditional Medicaid. It may also allow people with disabilities to qualify for Medicaid based on their income alone rather than needing also to demonstrate their disability status.[104] The U.S. Supreme Court's decision[105] that the ACA could not require states to expand Medicaid has left a patchwork of imperfect coverage for persons who could otherwise have benefited from the expanded coverage.

Like private insurance plans, Medicaid may also limit benefits in ways that disproportionately affect people with disabilities. Limited provider networks, required managed care plans, and restrictions on available pharmaceuticals are all examples. Restrictions on home healthcare benefits and coverage for durable medical equipment may be especially challenging for people with disabilities. Mental health benefits are a particular problem under Medicaid, especially in states that have not chosen to expand their programs under the ACA. Inpatient psychiatric care for individuals under age twenty-one and inpatient mental disease coverage for those over sixty-five are optional Medicaid benefits and may not be included in state plans.[106] Although Medicaid is the primary payer for nursing home care in the United States, it does not cover mental healthcare provided in small residential facilities such as halfway houses or adult residential foster care homes.[107]

Medicaid expansion itself may also have indirect consequences for people with disabilities. Medicaid is one of the largest items in many state budgets, and constraining program costs is understandably a very high priority for state legislatures. One way states have tried to control their Medicaid budgets is to require recipients to receive care from managed care provider agencies. This may impose serious practical limits on clients' ability to access care by reducing the pool of potential caregivers to those who comply with agencies' business interests and by making caregivers the agency's rather than the client's employees, thus undercutting the guiding premise of the Independent Living Movement.[108]

[104] MaryBeth Musumeci, *The Affordable Care Act's Impact on Medicaid Eligibility, Enrollment, and Benefits for People with Disabilities* (Apr. 8, 2014), http://kff.org/health-reform/issue-brief/the-affordable-care-acts-impact-on-medicaid-eligibility-enrollment-and-benefits-for-people-with-disabilities/.

[105] National Federation of Independent Business v. Sebelius, 132 S. Ct. 2566 (2012).

[106] Substance Abuse and Mental Health Services Administration, Medicaid Handbook: Interface with Behavioral Health Services (2013), p. 3–3, *available at* http://store.samhsa.gov/shin/content//SMA13-4773/SMA13-4773.pdf.

[107] Tovino, *supra* note 98.

[108] A 2014 HHS report, Office of Inspector General. Dep't of Health and Human Services, State Standards for Access to Care in Medicaid Managed Care (2014), *available at* http://oig.hhs.gov/oei/reports/oei-02-11-00320.pdf, raises alarms about whether states have adequate standards for access to Medicaid managed care providers and sufficiently monitor compliance with the standards they do impose. For example, access standards vary from states requiring one primary care provider per 100 enrollees to states requiring one per 2,500 enrollees. Standards for the maximum distance patients might be expected to travel to see primary care providers vary from 5 to 60 miles; these standards also vary widely for rural and urban areas. Many states do not have travel standards that apply to specialists. Standards for wait times to see a primary care provider for routine care vary from 10 to 45 days and some states lack standards for wait times to see specialists. Provider shortages, especially in primary care fields, may also prove challenging as more people receive healthcare coverage. Some studies of patient experience indicate that at least so far most patients with both Medicaid and private coverage are able to obtain needed services, however. Austin Frakt, *Shortage of Medicaid Doctors? Not if You Ask Patients*, N.Y. Times, Nov. 10, 2014, http://www.nytimes.com/2014/11/11/upshot/shortage-of-medicaid-doctors-not-if-you-ask-patients.html?abt=0002&abg=0.

Medicaid reimbursement levels are also a persistent challenge to access to care. Providers contend that Medicaid pays far too little for it to be economically viable for them to treat Medicaid patients and many refuse to take patients on Medicaid. The Medicaid statute[109] requires Medicaid rates to be "consistent with efficiency, economy, and quality of care and . . . sufficient to enlist enough providers so that care and services are available under the plan at least to the extent that such care and services are available to the general population in the geographic area . . ." but states may not be meeting this standard.[110] Home healthcare has proven a particularly thorny area for reimbursement issues. Medicaid has a program (§ 1915) under which requirements of the Medicaid statute can be waived for states wishing to try out different program approaches. One very popular waiver program is for home- and community-based services for people who would otherwise be institutionalized. States may apply to HHS for approval for such programs and must demonstrate that they are cost-neutral to Medicaid and that they will "continuously and effectively assur[e] the health and welfare of waiver participants."[111] Waivers may allow for individuals to direct the services they receive, including hiring their own community workers. In a case argued before the Supreme Court in January 2015, Idaho providers of supported-care facilities for persons with intellectual disabilities under the state's § 1915(c) waiver program sued to enforce § 30(A) reimbursement requirements. Idaho had not raised reimbursement rates since 2006 because the legislature had not appropriated the needed funding, despite its Medicaid agency's cost-based analysis recommending an increase in the rates.

IV Conclusion

Healthcare represents nearly 20% of GDP in the United States. Health law is correspondingly protean in its reach. It is thus not at all surprising that health law intersects in myriad ways with disability law and the lives of people with disabilities.

The impact of disability law on health law for achieving meaningful access to care for persons with disabilities remains a work in progress, however. Much of the law concerning the provider-patient relationship developed before civil rights paradigms had become firmly extended to persons with disabilities. The ADA prohibits discrimination in employment, public services, or public accommodations, but evidence of discrimination persists. Despite the ACA, access to healthcare or reimbursement for it remains uneven. There is no incentive for employers who furnish healthcare insurance to be concerned about expanding coverage to support employees or family members with disabilities, and employer-based coverage that has served people with disabilities could be altered to limit or exclude benefits of importance to them. Coverage in the individual or small group markets may mirror these

[109] 42 U.S.C. §1396a(30)(A) (2014).

[110] *See, e.g.*, Armstrong v. Exceptional Child Center, Inc., No. 14-15, 2015 WL 260361 (argued Jan. 15, 2015).

[111] Centers for Medicare and Medicaid Services, Application for a §1915(c) Home and Community-Based Waiver: Instructions, Technical Guide and Review Criteria (2008), p. 8, *available at* https://www.medicaid.gov/medicaid-chip-program-information/by-topics/waivers/downloads/technical-guidance.pdf.

inadequacies. Many people with disabilities do not have employer-provided insurance and remain dependent on Medicare or Medicaid programs with coverage restrictions or reimbursement constraints that make it difficult for them to receive care in the form they need. If meaningful access to healthcare means access on the terms others enjoy, there is much still to be achieved in health law for people with disabilities.

CHAPTER 18

AUTONOMY AND ITS LIMITS IN END-OF-LIFE LAW

REBECCA DRESSER

END-OF-LIFE law in the United States relies primarily on individual autonomy to resolve treatment questions. The autonomy-based approach underlies defensible rules governing many end-of-life situations, such as the rules allowing competent patients to refuse life-sustaining treatment. But the autonomy-based approach is inadequate to address several other end-of-life situations. Although additional moral and policy considerations merit attention in those situations, courts and lawmakers are often reluctant to depart from their reliance on autonomy. There is controversy over whether factors like patients' quality of life and treatment costs should influence end-of-life law. There is also a lack of agreement on when individual autonomy should be limited to protect broader societal concerns.

This article describes the law's general approach to end-of-life issues. After reviewing the law governing treatment decision-making for competent adults, incompetent adults, and children, as well as the determination of death, the article turns to three topics presenting hard questions for U.S. courts, legislators, and policy-makers. Authorities have yet to formulate clear and defensible rules governing "futile" treatment disputes, treatment decisions for incompetent patients, and access to medically assisted death.[1]

I Decisions on Life-Sustaining Treatment

a. Competent Adults

When courts began to consider permissible limits on the use of life-sustaining medical interventions, they turned first to the matter of the competent patient. They examined the individual patient's interests and balanced them against potential competing interests, such the state's interest in preserving life. Individual self-determination and control over bodily

[1] For a detailed and comprehensive description of U.S. judicial decisions and statutes governing end-of-life treatment, *see* ALAN MEISEL & KATHY CERMINARA, THE RIGHT TO DIE (3d ed. 2004).

integrity were central values in the United States, long recognized and protected by the common law. Courts thought these values were important to protect in the medical context, as well. Courts saw the U.S. Constitution's protection of individual liberty and privacy as relevant to end-of-life choices, too.

It seemed a logical step to give competent patients the legal power to decide about life-prolonging interventions. It was the patients who would be most affected by the treatment decision; thus, they should be permitted to choose for themselves. State officials, hospital administrators, clinicians, and family members did not have the right to force patients to accept treatment, including interventions that could extend life.

The 1976 New Jersey Supreme Court's *Quinlan* decision was the first major U.S. court opinion addressing end-of-life treatment.[2] Although the patient in that case was in a persistent vegetative state, unconscious and unable to make her own treatment choices, the *Quinlan* decision had as its foundation the competent patient's right to decide. Noting the patient's poor prognosis and the invasiveness of the respirator that doctors believed was necessary to sustain her life, the court said it had "no doubt" that the law would (and should) allow her to refuse continued treatment if she were awake and aware of her medical situation. The judges said that the freedom to make such a choice was part of the individual right to privacy protected by the U.S. and New Jersey constitutions.

Other state courts considering whether competent patients could refuse life-sustaining treatment followed *Quinlan*'s lead, citing both common law and constitutional support for protecting the patient's right to refuse. Although a few early court cases authorized compelled blood transfusions for Jehovah's Witnesses, who oppose transfusions on religious grounds, later cases upheld patients' right to refuse even this minimally invasive, highly effective intervention. Eventually the U.S. Supreme Court recognized that the U.S. Constitution protects the competent patient's liberty interest in deciding whether or not to accept life-sustaining treatment.[3]

Courts also rejected the position that individuals had stronger interests in refusing "extraordinary" life-sustaining measures, such as respirators, than in refusing "ordinary" measures, such as medically supplied nutrition and hydration. They failed to distinguish between withholding and withdrawing life-sustaining interventions, too, finding that patients were authorized to make both kinds of choices. And the decisional rights of individuals with terminal and nonterminal conditions were no different, according to the courts. In all of these situations, courts ruled, it was the patient who should decide whether a medical intervention's burdens outweighed the benefits that it could confer.

At the same time, courts observed that the competent patient's interest in refusing treatment was not absolute. Instead, the patient's interest must be balanced against certain competing state interests. According to the courts, states have interests in: (1) preserving life; (2) preventing suicide; (3) protecting innocent third parties, such as a patient's dependent children; and (4) protecting the integrity of the medical profession. Yet the clear consensus among courts has been that none of these state interests outweighs the competent patient's right to refuse life-sustaining treatment.[4]

[2] *In re* Quinlan, 355 A.2d 647 (N.J.), *cert. denied*, 429 U.S. 922 (1976).

[3] Cruzan v. Director, Missouri Dep't of Health, 497 U.S. 261 (1990).

[4] *See* Meisel & Cerminara, The Right to Die, at §§ 2.02, 2.04 and 5.04(F) for case law taking this position.

In rare cases, courts have cited additional state interests relevant to treatment refusal cases. Some courts have ruled that the state's interest in maintaining prison order and discipline is sufficient to override the rights of prison hunger-strikers refusing tube-feeding as part of their protests. And in a case involving a quadriplegic patient who wanted his respirator removed, the Nevada Supreme Court recognized a state interest in "encouraging the charitable and humane care of those whose lives may be artificially extended under conditions which have the prospect of providing at least a modicum of quality living."[5] Although this state interest would not justify depriving the patient of his right to refuse treatment, the court said it would justify a requirement to make him aware of opportunities to receive care in the community.[6]

In the years since *Quinlan* was decided, it has become increasingly clear that U.S. law protects the competent individual's right to decide whether to accept life-sustaining treatment.[7] The rules governing treatment for patients unable to make their own choices are more complicated, however. Judges and legislators have established a legal framework governing treatment decisions for incompetent patients, but as I discuss later, existing law fails to address important ethical questions that can arise in such cases.

b. Capacity to Make Medical Decisions

Although U.S. law seeks to promote individual autonomy in medical decision-making, patients whose mental capacities are impaired by conditions like dementia or brain injury lack the ability to apply their personal beliefs and values to the treatment questions they face. Rather than giving them the freedom to decide for themselves, the law permits guardians, designated proxies, and surrogate decision-makers to choose on their behalf.[8]

United States law presumes that adults are competent to make their own medical choices. A judicial determination of incompetency defeats this presumption. Strictly speaking, the

[5] McKay v. Bergstedt, 891 P.2d 617, 621 (Nev. 1990).

[6] The Nevada court's remarks point to an overlooked problem in end-of-life law. The law gives individuals freedom to decide about treatment, but says little about the disclosure process in end-of-life care. In two states, legislators concerned about patients' access to information enacted laws intended to assure that patients diagnosed with a terminal condition are given information about all of their medical options. *See* California Right to Know End of Life Options Act, Cal. Health & Safety Code §§ 442–442.7 (West Supp. 2013); New York Palliative Care Information Act. N.Y. Pub. Health Law § 2997-c (McKinney 2012).

[7] The law governing competent patients' rights, as well as end-of-life law governing other treatment situations, both resembles and influences medical ethics guidelines on life-sustaining treatment. *See, e.g.*, American Medical Association, AMA Policy on End-of-Life Care, http://www.ama-assn.org/ama/pub/physician-resources/medical-ethics/about-ethics-group/ethics-resource-center/end-of-life-care/ama-policy-end-of-life-care.page; Nancy Berlinger, Bruce Jennings, & Susan Wolf, The Hastings Center Guidelines for Decisions on Life-Sustaining Treatment and Care Near the End of Life (2d ed. 2013).

[8] Guardians are appointed by courts for individuals found legally incompetent. Proxies are decision-makers named in incompetent patients' advance treatment directives. Surrogates are relatives, friends, or others authorized by statute or medical custom to decide for incompetent patients. In the remainder of this article, I use the term surrogate to refer to any individual authorized to decide for an incompetent patient.

term "incompetent" applies only to individuals legally adjudicated as incompetent. In the vast majority of cases, however, clinicians determine when patients are unable to decide for themselves. End-of-life law permits informal evaluations of patients' decisional capacity, because it would be unrealistic and unwarranted to require judicial evaluations in every case. Judicial determinations are sought only in problematic cases involving disputes over patient capacity, an absence of family members to assist with decision-making, or other out-of-the-ordinary circumstances.

Courts, legislators, and clinicians adopt a variety of standards for evaluating medical decision-making capacity. These range from relatively undemanding standards, such as the ability to express a choice, to demanding ones, such as the ability to engage in logical thinking about a treatment decision.[9] In recent years, cases, statutes, and scholarly opinion have favored a standard that builds on the legal and ethical concept of informed consent.[10] According to this standard, patients are competent if they have the capacity to understand and appreciate basic information relevant to the treatment decision they are facing. This means that patients should demonstrate the ability to comprehend facts about different treatment alternatives, including the risks and expected benefits of each alternative. When conversations with patients reveal that they cannot comprehend those facts, someone else should assume the role of medical decision-maker.

This is not to suggest that all capacity determinations are simple and straightforward. A patient's communication difficulties, fear, ambivalence, or hostility to medical professionals can lead evaluators to mistakenly label the patient incompetent. Some clinicians assume that patients who refuse treatment must be depressed and thus incompetent to make decisions about life-sustaining treatment. Rather than assuming that uncooperative or depressed patients are incompetent, clinicians should try to remedy conditions that may be affecting such patients' willingness or ability to decide.[11]

c. Incompetent Adults

End-of-life cases often involve patients who are unable to make their own medical decisions. Illness or injury has impaired their ability to apply their personal values and preferences to decisions about life-sustaining treatment. Some are unconscious; others are conscious and able to experience treatment burdens and benefits, but unable to understand the facts relevant to the choice at hand.

Courts and legislators have adopted three major approaches to decisions about life-sustaining interventions for patients unable to make autonomous treatment choices. Two approaches seek to respect the values and preferences patients held when they were capable of exercising autonomy. The other approach focuses on the welfare of patients in their incapacitated state. Consistent with the law's emphasis on autonomy, the first two approaches are

[9] *See* Jessica Berg, Paul Appelbaum, Charles Lidz, & Lisa Parker, Informed Consent: Legal Theory and Clinical Practice 98–106 (2d ed. 2001).

[10] *See, e.g.*, Lane v. Candura, 376 N.E.2d 1232 (Mass. 1978); Berlinger, Jennings, & Wolf, Hastings Center Guidelines, at 47 (2d ed. 2013).

[11] *See* Paul Appelbaum & Thomas Grisso, *Assessing Patients' Capacity to Consent*, 319 New Eng. J. Med. 1635 (1988).

the preferred legal mechanisms for resolving end-of-life dilemmas involving incompetent patients.

The first approach is the subjective standard (sometimes referred to as the advance directive standard). This approach emerged in the 1970s, when court opinions and living will legislation declared that an incompetent patient's treatment should be governed by the individual's previously expressed wishes.[12] Living wills were an early form of what is now known as the instruction advance directive, which is a written or oral description of the kinds of life-sustaining treatment a competent individual would accept or refuse as an incompetent patient. Another type of advance directive is the proxy directive, which allows competent persons to designate a trusted relative or other individual as their preferred treatment decision-maker if they become incapable of independent choice.

Advance directives allow clinicians and surrogate decision-makers to apply the subjective standard to decisions about life-sustaining treatment. But the subjective standard can also be applied whenever there is evidence that an incompetent patient would make a particular treatment decision if the individual were competent to choose. Some courts applying the subjective standard have accepted a patient's previous general remarks about life-sustaining treatment as sufficient evidence of that patient's wish to refuse treatment.[13] Other courts have refused to authorize nontreatment on the basis of general remarks, however, finding such remarks inadequate to indicate patients' autonomous wishes. In *Cruzan v. Director, Missouri Department of Health*, the U.S. Supreme Court held that it was constitutional for states to require clear and convincing evidence that a patient would refuse a specific intervention before allowing that intervention to be withheld or withdrawn.[14]

Legal authorities may differ on the sort of evidence required by the subjective standard, but their support for this standard is strong. Courts and legislatures consider the subjective standard the best way to determine treatment decisions for incompetent patients. When it is impossible to obtain contemporaneous choices from patients, the next best strategy is to ascertain the choices they expressed when they were competent. Officials see the subjective approach as a way to promote respect for individual autonomy and evade the concerns that arise when healthy people make judgments about the quality and value of an impaired person's life.[15] But because relatively few people express clear and specific treatment preferences in advance directives or other statements,[16] the subjective approach cannot be applied in many cases.[17]

[12] *See, e.g.*, Natural Death Act, Cal. Health & Safety Code §§ 7185–7195 (West Supp. 1978).

[13] *See, e.g.*, McConnell v. Beverly Enterprises-Connecticut, Inc., 553 A.2d 596 (Conn. 1989).

[14] 497 U.S. 261 (1990). But the Court did not rule that states were constitutionally required to adopt Missouri's relatively stringent standard.

[15] *See* Rebecca Dresser & John Robertson, *Quality of Life and Non-Treatment Decisions for Incompetent Patients: A Critique of the Orthodox Approach*, 17 LAW MED. & HEALTH CARE 234, 235 (1989).

[16] In a 2013 survey by the Pew Research Center, 35% of respondents said that they had recorded their preferences in an advance directive or informal document. Pew Research Religion & Public Life Project, *Views on End-of-Life Medical Treatments* (Nov. 21, 2013), http://www.pewforum.org/2013/11/21/views-on-end-of-life-medicaltreatments/. Such documents do not necessarily include specific instructions about treatment preferences, however; instead, they may contain general statements of values or attitudes relevant to end-of-life treatment.

[17] In an effort to promote treatment that is consistent with the patient's or surrogate's preferences, an instrument called the Physician Orders for Life-Sustaining Treatment (POLST) has been adopted, sometimes by law, in many states. The POLST enables physicians to document patient or surrogate

When the available evidence of a patient's former preferences is insufficient to satisfy the subjective standard, courts and legislatures usually turn to some version of the substituted judgment standard (also known as the limited-objective standard).[18] As described in *In re Conroy*, another important decision by the New Jersey Supreme Court, this standard permits forgoing life-sustaining treatment "when there is some trustworthy evidence that the patient would have refused the treatment" and "it is clear that the burdens of the patient's continued life with the treatment outweigh the benefits of that life for him."[19] Like the subjective standard, the substituted judgment standard seeks to ascertain what the patient would choose if competent. But because the evidence of patient preferences is less clear than it is in cases applying the subjective standard, decision-makers must also take into account objective factors like the pain, distress, pleasure, or enjoyment a patient would experience if treatment were administered or forgone. This inquiry into the incompetent patient's welfare is designed to prevent speculative judgments about patients' preferences from legitimizing treatment decisions that would be harmful to patients in their current state.

A third standard, known as the best interest or objective standard, is designed to promote the incompetent patient's welfare, rather than the beliefs and values the patient had as a competent person. The objective standard is applied when there is no clear indication of how a patient's former personal views would influence the treatment question.[20] This standard is also applied in end-of-life cases involving mentally disabled adults who have never been competent and in cases involving minors (see section d., below). Courts developed the objective standard in the course of exercising the state's parens patriae responsibility to protect the welfare of vulnerable persons. This standard is the least favored by legal authorities, however, for it requires them to directly confront questions about the value of life in a compromised condition.

As one advisory group put it, objective treatment standards "reflect a societal consensus, or the perspective of a 'reasonable person,' choosing as most people would choose for themselves."[21] The assumption is that reasonable people making treatment decisions would base their decisions on both survival odds and quality-of-life considerations, such as the pain, distress, loss of dignity, pleasure, or satisfaction that would result from a decision for or against treatment.

But the objective standard is also patient-centered. It requires decision-makers to assess and then balance different features of the individual incompetent patient's medical situation, such as prognosis and quality of life with and without treatment. Judges and other decision-makers consider the burdens and benefits the individual patient would experience

preferences in a medical order, which increases the chance that those preferences will be followed in the treatment setting. *See* Patricia Bomba & Charles Sabatino, *POLST: An Emerging Model for End-of-Life Planning*, ELDER LAW REP., Feb. 2009, at 1.

[18] The substituted judgment standard seeks to determine the choice the incompetent patient would make if competent. Decision-makers applying it infer a patient's preferred choice by examining the person's former values, statements, and behavior (such as their previous attitudes toward medical care). Sometimes the standard is applied in cases in which there is no evidence of a patient's preferences as a competent individual. In those cases, the substituted judgment standard is a version of the objective, best interest standard.

[19] *In re* Conroy, 486 A.2d 1209, 1232 (1985).

[20] *See, e.g., In re* Storar, 420 N.E.2d 64 (N.Y. 1981).

[21] NEW YORK STATE TASK FORCE ON LIFE AND THE LAW, WHEN OTHERS MUST CHOOSE 55 (1992).

if life-sustaining interventions were provided, or conversely, forgone. Then they determine whether the burdens of continued life with treatment would outweigh the benefits the patient would gain if treatment were provided.

Some courts applying the objective standard have authorized nontreatment only in extreme situations. The New Jersey Supreme Court took this position in *In re Conroy*.[22] In that case, which involved a conscious but minimally aware dementia patient, the court ruled that treatment may be withheld or withdrawn if "the recurring, unavoidable and severe pain of the patient's life with the treatment [are] such that the effect of administering life-sustaining treatment would be inhumane."[23] Other courts applying the objective standard have permitted nontreatment in less dire circumstances, however, including in cases involving permanently unconscious patients.[24]

Although the objective standard is the least favored approach to treatment decision-making for incompetent patients, it is often necessary to apply it. Clinicians and surrogates must often act in the absence of an advance directive or other clear evidence of a patient's former treatment preferences. In most cases, they have only general information about patients' former beliefs and values. That information may or may not point to a specific treatment choice. When it does not, decision-makers must determine how best to protect the patients' current welfare. As I discuss later in this article, existing law provides insufficient guidance to those deciding on the incompetent patient's behalf.

d. Children

United States law presumes that minors are incompetent and gives parents the power to make medical decisions for their children. Court decisions and statutes protect parents' autonomy to decide about life-sustaining treatment for their children, but the law also sets limits on parental choice.

When parents refuse medically recommended treatment for their children, whether for religious or other reasons, the parens patriae doctrine authorizes the state to override refusals that endanger the health and welfare of dependent children. Courts applying this doctrine rely on the best interest standard to delineate permissible end-of-life choices for children.[25]

In some cases, the dual goals of respecting parental autonomy and child welfare cannot both be achieved. In such cases, courts evaluate a proposed treatment's benefits and burdens to determine whether to override the parents' treatment refusal. As in cases applying the best interest standard to incompetent adults, courts consider the likely treatment outcome, the pain and distress the patient would experience if treatment were provided or forgone, and other information relevant to the patient's welfare. Courts commonly mandate the use of highly effective and low-burden interventions like blood transfusions; they are less willing to mandate interventions that impose significant burdens and have low success rates, such as some cancer chemotherapy drugs.[26]

[22] *In re* Conroy, 486 A.2d 1209 (1985). [23] *Id.* at 1232.

[24] E.g., *In re* L.W., 482 N.W.2d 60 (Wis. 1992). *See generally* Rebecca Dresser & Peter Whitehouse, *The Incompetent Patient on the Slippery Slope*, HASTINGS CENTER REP., July–Aug., 1994, at 6.

[25] *See, e.g.*, Newmark v. Williams, 588 A.2d 1108 (Del. 1991).

[26] *See, e.g.*, Jehovah's Witnesses v. King County Hosp., 278 F.Supp. 488 (W.D.Wash. 1967); Newmark v. Williams, 588 A.2d 1108 (Del. 1991).

Federal authorities have adopted additional rules that apply solely to treatment decisions for newborn infants. In the early 1980s, federal officials challenged a medical tradition that permitted and even encouraged parents to refuse relatively simple life-sustaining interventions for infants born with conditions like Down syndrome and spina bifida. The federal government initially proposed mandatory treatment regulations in response to two widely publicized cases involving nontreatment of infants with these conditions; the two cases became known as the "Baby Doe" cases.[27] After courts rejected the government's initial efforts to intervene in such cases, Congress enacted the Child Abuse Amendments of 1984 (CAA),[28] which remain in effect.

Some CAA provisions can be interpreted to mandate treatment that would not be required by the best interest standard.[29] For example, the federal law permits clinicians to forgo extremely burdensome interventions only when they are almost certain to be ineffective in sustaining life, while courts applying the best interest standard have allowed nontreatment in less extreme circumstances. The federal law assigns state social service agencies CAA enforcement responsibilities, however, and those agencies have generally been reluctant to interfere in medical decision-making. At the same time, attitudes toward treating infants with disabilities like Down syndrome have changed significantly and much of the past support for withholding life-sustaining treatment from those infants has dissipated.[30]

Although the law governing treatment decision-making for children focuses on parental autonomy, two legal doctrines recognize adolescents' own developing autonomy, allowing minors to make life-sustaining treatment decisions in certain circumstances. The mature minor doctrine allows underage individuals to make decisions if they demonstrate the ability to understand the important facts relevant to a treatment choice. Another doctrine confers decision-making rights on emancipated minors, defined as those who have married, joined the military, established their own residences, or taken other steps to achieve independent status.

e. Determination of Death

Because there is no legal duty to treat a deceased person, the law governing determination of death is an important element of end-of-life law. In contrast to the rules governing decisions about life-sustaining treatment, the rules governing declaration of death rest on considerations other than respect for individual autonomy. In this legal realm, freedom of choice is for the most part subordinated to the societal need for uniformity and ease of application in determining when someone has died. At the same time, there is some support for injecting autonomy into the law governing declaration of death.

Before the advent of modern medical care, the law regarded cessation of heart and lung function as the criterion for death. By the 1960s, however, the emergence of respirators and

[27] *See* Nancy Rhoden, *Treatment Decisions for Imperiled Newborns: Why Quality of Life Counts*, 58 S. Cal. L. Rev.1283 (1985).

[28] 42 U.S.C. § 5106g (2006).

[29] *See* Loretta Kopelman, *Are the 21-Year-Old Baby Doe Rules Misunderstood or Mistaken?*, 115 Pediatrics 797 (2005).

[30] *See* Norman Fost, *Decisions Regarding Treatment of Seriously Ill Newborns*, 281 JAMA 2041 (1999).

other intensive care measures made it possible to maintain heartbeat and respiration in people whose brains were no longer functioning. Legal authorities were asked to decide whether those people were alive or dead. The question had important implications, for the answer would influence decisions not only about continued life support but also about criminal liability, transplant organ retrieval, and other legal and policy matters.

Advisory groups proposed that people should be considered legally dead when they have experienced an irreversible loss of all brain function. This judgment should apply even when circulation and respiration can be maintained by medical technology. According to the President's Commission for the Study of Ethical Problems in Medicine, an influential advisory group, individuals in this state should be defined as dead because "the integrated functioning of the organism as a whole" is no longer possible.[31] The commission said that because integrated functioning is essential to life, individuals whose brains are unable to support such functioning are dead. Legal officials were receptive to this view, and it didn't take long for all states to adopt cessation of whole-brain function as the legal standard for death.

This wide legal acceptance has not eliminated all controversy over the determination of death, however. Sometimes the families of deceased individuals challenge the decision to remove respirators and cease other intensive care measures, claiming that their loved ones are not really dead.[32] Courts have rejected these challenges, although sometimes hospitals will temporarily continue intensive care to give families time to accept a death. At a broader level, certain religious groups continue to see cessation of circulation and respiration as the event that signals death. A law in New Jersey requires physicians to apply the traditional heart-lung criterion when determining death in someone who belongs to one of those religious groups.[33]

Additional challenges come from commentators arguing that the current legal criteria for death are too liberal, or conversely, too restrictive. Some clinicians contend that the whole-brain standard lacks a solid biological foundation, because a number of integrated functions can apparently be sustained in the bodies of at least some individuals meeting the criteria for whole-brain death. This undermines the rationale for considering such individuals dead, they say. Other critics believe the current law is too narrow. Consciousness is the essential feature of human life, they insist, and individuals in the persistent vegetative state, infants with anencephaly, and others lacking the "higher-brain" functions that underlie consciousness should also be considered legally dead.[34] A few commentators seek to insert individual autonomy into the legal framework, arguing that individuals should have the freedom to choose their preferred definition of death.[35] None of these positions has received support from legal authorities, however. Indeed, one court asked to declare an infant with anencephaly dead refused to do so, finding "no basis to expand the common law to equate anencephaly with death."[36]

[31] President's Commission for the Study of Ethical Problems in Medicine and Biomedical and Behavioral Research, Defining Death 15–16 (1981).

[32] E.g., Alvarado v. New York City Health & Hospital Corp., 547 N.Y.S.2d 190 (1989).

[33] New Jersey Declaration of Death Act, N.J. Stat. Ann. § 26.6A–5 (2007).

[34] For review of the debate, *see* Franklin Miller & Robert Truog, Death, Dying, and Organ Transplantation: Reconstructing Medical Ethics at the End of Life (2012); President's Council on Bioethics, Controversies in the Determination of Death (2008).

[35] Robert Veatch, Death, Dying, and the Biological Revolution 25–29 (rev. ed. 1989).

[36] *In re* T.A.C.P., 609 So.2d 588, 595 (Fla. 1992). The drive to secure more organs for transplantation has produced debate over the length of time that must elapse before organs are removed from individuals

II WHERE AUTONOMY FALLS SHORT

Although respect for individual autonomy is the dominant factor in many areas of end-of-life law, there are times when the autonomy-based approach falls short. As noted in section e., above, existing law governing the determination of death relies largely on considerations other than respect for autonomy. Ongoing controversies reveal problems with relying on autonomy to resolve additional end-of-life dilemmas. Debates over the law governing "futile" treatment, treatment for conscious incompetent patients, and physician-assisted death highlight these problems.

a. Futile Treatment

The futile treatment debate addresses potential limitations on a patient's or surrogate decision-maker's autonomy in choices about life-sustaining treatment. According to the general rule, the patient or patient's surrogate, rather than the physician, is authorized to decide when the potential benefits of a life-sustaining intervention are sufficient to justify treatment. Thus, physicians' own judgments about treatment burdens and benefits are not the determining factor in decisions about treatment. But this rule is contested when it comes to cases involving treatment that physicians believe would be futile.

Futile treatment can be defined in different ways. One definition covers treatment that has no reasonable chance of accomplishing its goal. For example, cardiopulmonary resuscitation would be futile for a patient if medical evidence indicates that no one in the patient's condition has ever been successfully resuscitated. In many cases, however, the medical situation is less clear. Perhaps resuscitation sometimes restores heart and lung function to people in the patient's condition, but only for a day or two. Perhaps in rare cases resuscitation has produced longer survival. Physicians may question the value of resuscitation in these circumstances, but patients and surrogates might consider a few days of additional life or a very small chance of survival a sufficient benefit to justify the invasiveness and pain involved in resuscitation.[37]

A broader definition of futile treatment covers interventions that offer a good possibility of extending a patient's life, but in a severely compromised state. This futility definition explicitly incorporates an evaluation of patients' quality of life. People adopting this definition often say that life-sustaining treatment for permanently unconscious patients is futile. Mere biological life is not valuable enough to justify life-sustaining treatment, they say.[38]

declared dead according to the traditional heart-lung criterion. A related debate concerns the so-called dead donor rule, which holds that transplant organs may not be retrieved until an individual is legally dead. Thus far, however, these debates have not influenced the law. *See* Robert Truog, Franklin Miller, & Scott Halpern, *The Dead-Donor Rule and the Future of Organ Transplantation*, 369 NEW ENG. J. MED. 1287 (2013); James Bernat, *Life or Death for the Dead-Donor Rule?*, 369 NEW ENG. J. MED. 1289 (2013).

[37] *See* Robert Truog, Allan Brett, & Joel Frader, *The Problem with Futility*, 326 NEW ENG. J. MED. 1560 (1992); Stuart Youngner, *Who Defines Futility?*, 260 J. AM. MED. ASS'N 2094 (1988).

[38] *See* Lawrence Schneiderman, Nancy Jecker, & Albert Jonsen, *Medical Futility: Its Meaning and Ethical Implications*, 112 ANN. INTERNAL MED. 949 (1990).

A third futility definition encompasses resource allocation considerations as well. Someone applying this definition might claim that intensive care for a patient with advanced dementia is futile not only because of the patient's low quality of life but also because continued care is a "waste" of limited healthcare dollars.[39]

The position that physicians have no duty to provide inappropriate treatment is uncontroversial; the controversy concerns how much discretion physicians should have to determine what treatment is appropriate. The medical profession does not have complete freedom to define its particular role and mission; instead, the profession is subject to socially determined restrictions and obligations. Physicians have no clear authority to deny life-sustaining treatment based on a personal judgment that the treatment would not provide an acceptable quality of life or would be too expensive. Thus, much of the debate over futile treatment concerns whether the law should step in to restrict patients' and surrogates' freedom to choose interventions that physicians consider futile.

Not many courts have considered cases involving disputes over futile treatment. The few rulings that exist fail to directly address the futility question, instead resolving the cases on other grounds. An early example is *In re Wanglie*. In *Wanglie*, the physicians and hospital caring for an irreversibly unconscious eighty-six-year-old woman petitioned for appointment of an independent guardian to make medical decisions on her behalf. The patient's family wanted her to receive continued intensive care, even though physicians said she would not recover. The family claimed that aggressive treatment was consistent with the patient's former pro-life values. Physicians and hospital officials believed such care was medically inappropriate and nonbeneficial to the patient. They tried to transfer the patient, but no other facility would agree to provide her with continued intensive care. The judge deciding the case took no position on the substantive disagreement. Instead, he denied the petition and appointed the patient's husband as guardian, noting that he "was the most suitable and best qualified person among those nominees who are now available." [40]

Other courts handling cases involving requests for allegedly futile treatment have been equally unwilling to confront the substantive questions. The most well-known futile treatment case, *In re Baby K*, involved an infant with anencephaly, a congenital condition in which a large part of the brain is absent. Infants with anencephaly typically die within a few days after birth. But Baby K's mother wanted her child to receive intensive care for the breathing problems and other complications that normally cause death in these infants. A federal court of appeals ruling in the case relied on a law enacted to prevent hospitals from denying emergency care to uninsured people. According to the court's majority opinion, the Emergency Medical Treatment and Active Labor Act (EMTALA) requires uniform emergency medical treatment for all consenting patients, including those for whom care is generally deemed medically or ethically inappropriate. A dissenting judge contested this interpretation of EMTALA, arguing that Congress did not intend "to impose federal control in this sensitive, private area."[41]

[39] *See* Haavi Morreim, *Profoundly Diminished Life: The Casualties of Coercion*, HASTINGS CENTER REP., Jan.–Feb. 1994, at 33.

[40] *In re* Wanglie, No. PX-91-283 (4th Dist. Ct., Hennepin Co., Minn. July 1, 1991), *reprinted in* 2 BioLaw, at U:2161 (Aug.–Sept. 1991).

[41] *In re* Baby "K," 16 F.3d 590, 598 (4th Cir. 1994). In a later decision, however, the same court upheld a do-not-resuscitate order doctors had entered on futility grounds. The court said that the federal emergency treatment statute did not apply in that case because the patient had died twelve days after

Many analysts have called on lawmakers and other officials to enact rules governing futile treatment disputes, but few officials have responded to the calls. Texas is the only state with a law establishing a clear process for resolving futility cases. When physicians object to a patient's or surrogate's life-sustaining treatment request in Texas, a hospital ethics or medical committee must review the request at a meeting in which the patient or surrogate may participate. If the review committee supports the position that treatment would be inappropriate, physicians and other staff must make a reasonable effort to transfer the patient to an alternative care setting where staff would be willing to provide the requested treatment. If a transfer cannot be arranged within ten days (a period that may be extended by court order), the law permits life-sustaining treatment to be withheld or withdrawn.[42]

Although the Texas law has been praised by clinicians, scholars, and other commentators, it also has critics. Critics contend that the law's review process is biased in favor of physicians, because review committees are composed largely of the objecting physicians' professional colleagues. Indeed, a study of forty-seven cases in one health system found that reviewers agreed with physicians' positions in forty-three of forty-seven cases.[43] Moreover, some patients' families have gone to court to challenge review committee decisions.[44]

Clinicians' continued reluctance to accede to requests for what they regard as unjustified treatment, together with ongoing policy efforts to reduce healthcare costs, will fuel future litigation about futile treatment.[45] In the coming years, legal authorities will face pressure to devise acceptable limits on patient and surrogate autonomy in this end-of-life context.

b. Decisions for Incompetent Patients

Each of the three legal standards governing decision-making for incompetent patients raises hard questions that courts and lawmakers have so far avoided. But as the number of people with dementia increases, officials are likely to encounter more cases revealing inadequacies in existing law. Officials will be pressed to fill gaps in the current rules governing treatment decisions for this growing patient population.

The subjective standard for treatment decision-making has several shortcomings. Basing decisions on patients' past preferences has proven more difficult than was initially expected. Few competent people issue advance instructions about the life-sustaining interventions they do and do not want as incompetent patients. And many of the advance instructions that are issued are too general to supply clear guidance to decision-makers at the bedside.[46]

hospitalization. The law requires hospitals to provide only emergency stabilizing treatment, the court said, not "to provide treatment indefinitely—perhaps for years—according to a novel, federal standard of care." Bryan v. University of Virginia, 95 F.3d 349, 351 (4th Cir. 1996). Any remaining liability issues should be resolved according to state tort law, the court noted.

42 Tex. Health & Safety Code Ann. §§ 166.001–166.166 (West 2010).

43 Robert Fine & Thomas Mayo, *Resolution of Futility by Due Process: Early Experience with the Texas Advance Directives Act*, 138 ANN. INTERNAL MED. 743 (2003).

44 E.g., Hudson v. Texas Children's Hospital, 177 S.W.3d 232 (Tex. Ct. App. 2005). *See also* Robert Truog, *Tackling Medical Futility in Texas*, 357 NEW ENG. J. MED. 1 (2007).

45 For an argument that court intervention can be beneficial in futility cases, *see* Douglas White & Thaddeus Pope, *The Courts, Futility, and the Ends of Medicine*, 307 J. AM. MED. ASS'N 151 (2012).

46 *See* Angela Fagerlin & Carl Schneider, *Enough: The Failure of the Living Will*, HASTINGS CENTER REP., Mar.–Apr. 2004, at 30–42.

There are also concerns about the quality of the choices people make in advance. According to the informed consent doctrine, patients making medical decisions should understand basic facts about the risks and benefits of different treatment options. With the possible exception of seriously ill individuals facing a limited number of future treatment situations, competent people cannot make informed choices about the medical treatment they receive as incompetent patients. Most competent people face an unknown medical future presenting a multitude of potential treatment questions. By necessity, the preferences they express in advance are based on limited information.[47]

Besides lacking information about future treatment options, people making advance choices cannot know how those choices will affect them as incompetent patients. Many of the things that matter to them as competent persons might no longer matter after they become incompetent. For example, what they now see as an undignified existence featuring simple interactions and activities might become valuable to them once dementia alters their mental capacities. Or the religious beliefs driving them to want every possible life-sustaining measure might slip away as dementia progresses.[48] In short, the future-oriented autonomy the subjective standard seeks to honor is not as robust as the present-oriented autonomy that underlies rules allowing competent persons to make contemporaneous decisions about life-sustaining treatment.

Similar problems apply to the substituted judgment standard for decision-making. When this standard is applied, surrogates derive patients' treatment preferences from evidence about the patients' former religious beliefs, general conduct, and informal remarks. But like explicit advance treatment choices, competent persons' general beliefs, remarks, and behavior may reflect a lack of knowledge about their later conditions and treatment options. Moreover, a person's general remarks and behavior are a less solid basis for inferring treatment choices than are advance directives. People issuing advance directives or other explicit instructions are making deliberate choices about the care they would prefer as incompetent patients. This deliberate exercise of autonomy is missing when the substituted judgment standard is applied.[49]

In sum, the subjective and substituted judgment standards rely on a weaker version of autonomy than the autonomy supporting the competent patient's right to decide. This is not necessarily a problem, for in many cases, choices based on a patient's former statements, beliefs, and behavior pose no serious threat to the currently incompetent patient's welfare. In those cases, the welfare-based objective standard for decision-making supports the same choices the other two standards support. But sometimes the decision-making standards fail to support the same treatment choices. This can occur in two situations. In one, an advance directive or other evidence of a patient's former preferences calls for forgoing a low-burden

[47] For a review of these findings, *see* Rebecca Dresser, *Precommitment: A Misguided Strategy for Securing Death with Dignity*, 81 TEX. L. REV. 1823, 1830–1834 (2003).

[48] *Id.* at 1835–1837. Studies of human psychology suggest that certain cognitive biases distort individual predictions of how good or bad life would be in various hypothetical medical situations. For discussion of this problem, *see* Dan Brock, *Reflections on the Patient Preference Predictor Proposal*, 39 J. MED. PHIL.153 (2014); Rebecca Dresser, *Law, Ethics, and the Patient Preference Predictor*, 39 J. MED. PHIL. 178 (2014).

[49] *See* Allen Buchanan & Dan Brock, DECIDING FOR OTHERS 115–117 (1989); Daniel Brudney, *Choosing for Another: Beyond Autonomy and Best Interests*, HASTINGS CENTER REP., Mar.–Apr. 2009, at 31.

intervention that could extend a life that now appears to have value to the patient.[50] In the other, a choice in accord with the patient's past preferences would require administering an extremely burdensome intervention to extend a life that now appears to lack value to the patient. Is it more important to honor the patients' past preferences, or to protect their current welfare? This is a question the law has yet to confront.[51]

Protecting patients' current welfare is the focus of the objective standard. But the existing law on this standard has shortcomings, too. Courts have applied the standard in a variety of ways, producing inconsistent outcomes for patients in similar situations.[52] As it stands today, the standard is too indeterminate to furnish adequate guidance to decision-makers at the bedside.

The objective standard applies community norms to determine appropriate treatment for incompetent patients. But to apply the standard, there must be agreement on what counts as the benefits and burdens of life-sustaining treatment. In a diverse country like the United States, such agreement can be elusive. For example, although few people would argue against counting severe pain as a burden, or enjoyment of music as a benefit, the population differs on whether life in an unconscious or "barely conscious" state is a benefit. There is even less consensus about the balance of benefits and burdens that justifies a decision to forgo life-sustaining treatment.[53] Some courts have demanded high treatment burdens to justify a choice to forgo treatment. As noted earlier, in *Conroy*, the New Jersey Supreme Court permitted nontreatment under the objective standard only when "recurring, unavoidable and severe pain" would make continued treatment "inhumane."[54] But other courts have adopted a less demanding version of the objective standard.[55]

A basic question is whether the objective standard should count only benefits and burdens that incompetent patients actually experience. The actual-experience approach considers benefits and burdens from the incompetent patient's perspective, allowing nontreatment solely when a patient's "quality of life with the life-sustaining treatment will be so poor as to be not worth living or worse than no life at all."[56] Under this approach, burdens such as loss

[50] For an example of such a case, *see* Rebecca Dresser, *Dworkin on Dementia: Elegant Theory, Questionable Policy*, HASTINGS CENTER REP., Nov.–Dec. 1995, at 32.

[51] In two state supreme court cases, judges came close to facing this question. The cases involved brain-damaged patients dependent on medical nutrition and hydration. The patients were conscious but had severe cognitive deficiencies. Neither patient appeared to be in pain or distress. In both cases, some relatives offered evidence suggesting that the patients would refuse tube feeding in their current states. But other relatives contested that view. The courts found that evidence of the patients' past preferences was too weak to support a nontreatment decision. They also ruled that the patients' best interests would not be served by a nontreatment decision. Nothing was said about how the cases would have been resolved if there had been clear evidence that the patients would have refused treatment. *See* Rebecca Dresser, *The Conscious Incompetent Patient*, HASTINGS CENT. REP., May–June 2002, at 9; Rebecca Dresser, *Still Troubled: In re Martin*, HASTINGS CENT. REP., July–Aug. 1996, at 21.

[52] For a review and critique of the cases, *see* Rebecca Dresser, *Missing Persons: Legal Perceptions of Incompetent Patients* 46 RUTGERS L. REV. 609, 636–666 (1994).

[53] In the 2013 Pew survey, 31% percent of respondents said that clinicians should "always do everything possible to save a patient." Other respondents said nontreatment would be acceptable in a variety of situations. *See* Pew Research Religion and Public Life Project, *Views on End-of-Life Medical Treatments*, at 1.

[54] *In re* Conroy, 486 A.2d 1209, 1232 (N.J. 1985).

[55] E.g., *In re* L.W., 167 N.W.2d 60 (Wis. 1992).

[56] BUCHANAN & BROCK, DECIDING FOR OTHERS, at 124.

of dignity may count only when there is behavioral or other evidence that patients themselves experience those burdens.

Although the actual-experience approach to the objective standard is highly protective of vulnerable impaired patients, critics say it is too restrictive. Critics contend that the approach rules out nontreatment when many reasonable people would choose this for themselves and their families.[57] For example, a reasonable-person approach to the objective standard could permit nontreatment of patients who have lost the capacity for consciousness and interaction with others, even though such patients are not themselves experiencing the burdens of their loss. But those favoring the actual-experience approach say the reasonable-person approach is too expansive. The reasonable-person approach could, for example, permit nontreatment of patients with mild or moderate dementia who appear comfortable and content, but lead lives that many people see as humiliating and undignified.

This discussion highlights the need for further development of the law governing decisions on life-sustaining treatment for incompetent patients. Courts and legislatures should clarify the scope of permissible treatment decisions when the patient's former treatment preferences are unknown or unclear. They should also acknowledge the potential for conflict between an incompetent patient's former beliefs and current welfare, and should provide guidance on how to resolve such situations. Although officials would like to avoid evaluating the quality and value of life in various compromised states, such evaluations are essential to devising adequate rules governing treatment for incompetent patients.

c. Physician-Assisted Death

In most parts of the United States, physician-assisted suicide and active euthanasia are legally prohibited. A few states have legalized physician-assisted suicide for terminally ill patients, however. The ongoing legalization debate centers on whether the law should assign priority to the individual's freedom to choose assisted dying, or to other considerations that are relevant to physician-assisted death. End-of-life law's emphasis on autonomy fails to provide an easy answer to whether physician-assisted death should be legally permissible.

Calls for legalizing physician-assisted death in the United States became common during the 1990s. A growing number of clinicians and members of the general public argued that the law allowing patients to refuse life-sustaining treatment was insufficient to protect patient autonomy and dignity.[58] Legalization supporters said that terminally and seriously ill persons not dependent on medical interventions to sustain their lives were denied adequate control over the dying process. The law condemned such persons to a protracted and often inhumane death for no good reason, legalization supporters argued.

Legalization opponents contested these views. It is one thing to give people the right to refuse medical interventions that could prolong life, they said. It is a very different thing to give people the right to lethal medical assistance. Legalization opponents saw clear

[57] *See In re* Visbeck, 510 A.2d 125, 133 (N.J. Super. Ct. Ch. Div. 1986) (under restrictive version of objective standard, "large numbers of people will be thoughtlessly and automatically compelled to continue lives of intolerable bleakness").

[58] E.g., Timothy Quill, *Death and Dignity: A Case of Individualized Decision Making*, 324 New Eng. J. Med. 691 (1990).

conceptual and moral distinctions between forgoing life-sustaining treatment and active measures that caused death. They also feared that legalization would reduce public trust in physicians, put pressure on patients to choose death, and lead to inappropriate applications of assisted dying.

In 1997, the U.S. Supreme Court addressed the constitutionality of legal prohibitions on physician-assisted suicide. In *Washington v. Glucksberg*[59] and *Vacco v. Quill*,[60] the Court held that neither the terminally ill patient's constitutionally protected liberty interest nor the patient's claim to equal protection of the laws required states to protect patients' access to lethal medication. The Court's analysis focused on the justifications for drawing legal lines between decisions about life-sustaining treatment and decisions about physician-assisted death.

In *Glucksberg*, the Court majority described a long and persisting refusal to recognize a fundamental individual right to physician-assisted suicide. In the absence of a fundamental right, states need only a rational basis (rather than a compelling state interest) to support their laws prohibiting physician-assisted suicide. According to the Court, states have many legitimate interests in maintaining their prohibitions. These include state interests in preserving life, preventing suicide, protecting the medical profession's integrity and ethics, protecting vulnerable groups from mistaken or inappropriate applications of assisted suicide, and avoiding the slippery slope to voluntary and possibly even involuntary active euthanasia.[61]

Quill was an equal protection case. The patients and physicians who brought the case contended that New York's law prohibiting physician-assisted suicide failed to give all terminally ill patients the same right to hasten death. They claimed it was a violation of the Constitution to give only patients dependent on life-sustaining treatment that choice. But the Court disagreed. The law neither limited a fundamental right nor involved a suspect classification like race; thus, New York had only to offer a rational basis for distinguishing forgoing life-sustaining treatment and assisted suicide.

According to the majority opinion, causation was one rational basis for distinguishing the two practices: "when a patient refuses life-sustaining medical treatment, he dies from an underlying fatal disease or pathology; but if a patient ingests lethal medication prescribed by a physician, he is killed by that medication."[62] According to this analysis, suicide involves an independent cause of death, but when life-sustaining treatment is forgone, the patient's underlying condition is the significant causal factor.

Quill also pointed to differences in the actors' mental states. The primary objective of individuals committing suicide is to end their lives. In contrast, those refusing life-sustaining treatment might have preservation of bodily integrity or other objectives primarily in mind. The opinion also found differences in physicians' mental states: "a physician who withdraws, or honors a patient's refusal to begin, life-sustaining medical treatment purposefully intends, or may so intend, only to respect his patient's wishes and 'to cease doing useless and futile or degrading things to the patient when [the patient] no longer stands to benefit from them.'" In

[59] 521 U.S. 702 (1997). [60] 521 U.S. 793 (1997).

[61] In active euthanasia, physicians, rather than patients, administer the death-producing agent.

[62] *Quill*, 521 U.S. at 801.

contrast, the opinion asserts, a "doctor who assists a suicide . . . 'must, necessarily and indubitably, intend primarily that the patient be made dead.'"[63]

Quill acknowledged that permissible palliative care medications sometimes cause patients to die sooner than they otherwise would. But according to *Quill*, the goal of risky palliative care is to keep patients comfortable, not end their lives. Although the Court acknowledged that the lines between permissible end-of life measures and physician-assisted suicide are not always clear, it said the lines were clear enough to justify the assisted suicide bans.

Glucksberg and *Quill* left states free to prohibit or allow physician-assisted suicide. As of 2014, four states had moved to allow the practice in limited circumstances. Statutes in Oregon, Washington, and Vermont permit physicians to give competent patients with a prognosis of six months or less to live a prescription for lethal medication. Two physicians must agree on the patient's prognosis. There is a mandatory waiting period between the patient's initial request for the prescription and the time the prescription is provided. Physicians must disclose facts designed to promote informed decisions about using lethal medication, such as information about alternatives like hospice and palliative care.[64] The Montana Supreme Court ruled in 2009 that physicians in that state were legally permitted to provide lethal prescriptions to competent terminally ill patients. Thus far, neither the state legislature nor the courts have established procedural rules governing the practice.[65]

In deciding whether to legalize physician-assisted death, states face hard questions about the proper reach of individual autonomy. States maintaining their prohibitions confront difficulties in drawing clear lines between permissible and impermissible conduct. For example, the law allows a competent patient capable of eating normally to refuse ordinary food as well as tube-feeding. In that case, as in assisted suicide, death is produced by a cause unrelated to the patient's underlying illness. States maintaining their prohibitions must also explain why the state interests *Glucksberg* cited justify restrictions on physician-assisted death but not on risky palliative care or forgoing life-sustaining treatment. Pressure on vulnerable patients, erroneous applications, and other concerns *Glucksberg* raised could be present in cases involving the two legally permissible practices.[66]

[63] *Id.* (quoting congressional testimony of Dr. Leon R. Kass). In *McKay v. Bergstedt*, the Nevada Supreme Court also cited mental state differences to distinguish between treatment refusals and suicide. The court observed that patients refusing treatment "have not sought to contract the disease or condition that threatens both the quality and duration of their lives. Rather, they have evaluated their circumstances and determined that a future sustained by radical medical treatment or artificial means. . . is not a valued alternative. . . ." McKay v. Bergstedt, 801 P.2d 617, at 625 (Nev. 1990). According to this analysis, patients refusing treatment are involuntarily assigned to their precarious positions, while individuals attempting suicide make voluntary choices to endanger their lives.

[64] Vermont's law eliminates some of its procedural requirements in 2016, but preserves the substantive eligibility limits.

[65] *See* Baxter v. Montana, 224 P.3d 1211 (Mont. 2009). As of this writing, a New Mexico trial court ruling authorizing physician-assisted suicide for competent terminally ill patients is under consideration by a state appellate court. *See* Erik Eckholm, *"Aid in Dying" Movement Takes Hold in Some States*, N.Y. TIMES, Feb. 7, 2014, http://www.nyti.ms/LXfC4F.

[66] *See* Rebecca Dresser, *The Supreme Court and End-of-Life Care: Principled Distinctions or Slippery Slope?*, *in* LAW AT THE END OF LIFE: THE SUPREME COURT AND ASSISTED SUICIDE 83 (Carl Schneider ed., 2000).

States moving to legalize physician-assisted death face hard questions about the proper reach of individual autonomy, too. The Netherlands and Belgium permit both physician-assisted suicide and euthanasia in a wide variety of situations. In those countries, assisted death has been provided to people suffering from conditions like anorexia nervosa, depression, and fear of disability. Advance directives have authorized assisted death for patients with dementia. Assisted death is permitted for children as well.[67]

States that have legalized assisted suicide could encounter pressure to expand their laws in similar ways. Assisted-dying advocates could challenge the terminal illness requirement, contending that patients with serious but nonterminal conditions should also have access to lethal medications. Advocates could also push for laws allowing individuals to make advance directives requesting assisted dying if they are diagnosed with dementia or a similarly disabling condition. There could be support for allowing assisted dying under the substituted judgment and best interest standards, too. Advocates will argue that if forgoing life-sustaining treatment is permitted in these situations, active assistance should be permitted, as well.[68]

Like the other topics discussed in this section, assisted dying raises questions about the proper reach of individual autonomy. Addressing these questions will require courts and legislatures to decide when to give individuals full control over death and when there are good reasons to limit that control. That won't be easy; decisions for and against legalization will inevitably be criticized. Like abortion law, the law governing assisted dying could remain controversial and unsettled for many years.

III Conclusion

Respect for individual autonomy has proven a reasonable and widely accepted basis for many of the rules governing end-of-life treatment in the United States.[69] With the passage of time, however, it has become clear that autonomy cannot supply a straightforward answer to certain end-of-life dilemmas. In the coming years, courts and legislatures will face growing

[67] *See* Barney Sneiderman & Marja Verhoef, *Patient Autonomy and the Defence of Medical Necessity: Five Dutch Euthanasia Cases*, 34 Alberta L. Rev. 374 (1996); Tony Sheldon, *Dementia Patient's Euthanasia Was Lawful, Say Dutch Authorities*, 343 BMJ d7510 (2011); Cecelia Rodriguez, *Legal Euthanasia for Children in Belgium: Will It Trigger Death Tourism?*, Forbes (Mar. 6, 2014), http://www.forbes.com/sites/ceciliarodriguez/2014/03/06//2378; Naftali Bendavid, *For Belgium's Tormented Souls, Euthanasia-Made-Easy Beckons*, Wall St. J. (June 14, 2013), http://online.wsj.com/news/articles/SB10001424127887323463704578495102975991248.

[68] *See* Yale Kamisar, *Are the Distinctions Drawn in the Debate About End-of-Life Decision Making "Principled"? If Not, How Much Does It Matter?*, 40 J.L. Med. & Ethics 66 (2012); David Orentlicher, *The Alleged Distinction Between Euthanasia and the Withdrawal of Life-Sustaining Treatment: Conceptually Incoherent and Impossible to Maintain?*, U. Ill. L. Rev. 837 (1998).

[69] This article focuses on end-of-life law in the United States. For material on end-of-life law in other nations, *see* Timothy Stoltzfus Jost, Readings in Comparative Health Law & Bioethics 278–340 (2d ed. 2007).

pressure to address unresolved issues involving futile treatment claims, appropriate care for incompetent patients, and physician-assisted death. Resolving these issues will require officials to confront hard questions about the proper role of cost, quality of life, clinical judgment, and vulnerability in determining end-of-life law. Individual autonomy will be one consideration, but not the sole consideration, shaping emerging law in these areas.

D. Recourse for Injury

CHAPTER 19

MEDICAL MALPRACTICE LIABILITY

Of Modest Expansions and Tightening Standards

BARRY R. FURROW

I Introduction

Lawsuits are powerful patient safety tools. Medical liability litigation can serve five important social policies. Tort liability (1) compensates injured patients, reducing the need for an external compensation system; (2) reinforces good medical practice by incentivizing providers to improve their practices; (3) articulates new duties of care; (4) gives voice to mistreated patients and offers them an explanation for their harms; and (5) exposes healthcare organizations that are often resistant to change.[1]

Medical litigation against physicians increased dramatically until the 1970s. Several explanations have been proposed for the increase in litigation. First, medical practice changed: it became more dependent on technologies—surgery, drugs, and diagnostic tools—as medicine treated more illnesses with a wider range of intrusive treatments; the availability of third-party financing for healthcare made such treatments available to more people; and the end result of more invasive treatments was inevitably an increase in the incidence of adverse events that result in patient injury. Second, malpractice litigation became easier for a time: modern rules of pleading and practice made suing easier; modern urban juries were less sympathetic to physicians; and new tort doctrines expanded liability.

In the 1970s tort reforms began to constrain medical malpractice litigation: limits on damage recovery reduced incentives for plaintiff lawyers to bring such suits; new immunity laws

[1] For a full account, *see* Barry R. Furrow, *Adverse Events and Patient Injury: Coupling Detection, Disclosure, and Compensation*, 46 N. Eng. L. Rev. 437 (2012).

made evidence harder to obtain; new procedural hurdles to filing suit were created in every state; specialty societies began to sanction physician experts for plaintiffs; and juries' sympathies often turned against plaintiffs.[2]

This chapter is not the place to sort through the virtues and flaws of litigation as a primary compensation system, nor to trace the special interest lobbying that has displaced compensation through layers of tort reform barriers and disincentives.[3] Strong reform headwinds have reduced the ability of plaintiffs to recover, particularly for smaller claims, by reducing the economic potential of malpractice judgments. These headwinds are discussed elsewhere in this book.

My goal is to look at the processes of malpractice litigation, changes in tort doctrine, and judicial responses to medical injuries to give a snapshot of how malpractice law evolved over the decades. Even in a common law system with fifty state approaches to patient injury, consistency can be seen across state lines. Evidentiary requirements for proving the medical standard of care have led to increased power of the trial judge as gatekeeper. Expert testimony as to the standard of care has grown in reliance on practice guidelines that articulate the parameters of the standards of care. Damage doctrines have allowed plaintiffs to expand their claims where, for example, a doctor missed a diagnosis, reducing a patient's chances of survival. Hospitals have increasingly been targets of suit as agency doctrine and corporate negligence theories have been expanded. Informed consent doctrine has evolved and is expanding into accountable care organizations and other integrated systems. Rapid changes in the U.S. healthcare system driven by reimbursement policies and the Affordable Care Act have spawned new delivery forms that represent the next wave of litigation.

Tort doctrines have a complicated relationship with legal processes. Many malpractice claims have become uneconomical to bring, given the evidentiary and other costs of preparing these complex cases and state reforms that cap damage awards and otherwise reduce plaintiff incentives to sue. On the other hand, insurers' settlement decisions may lead them to pay for smaller claims that would be unsuccessful at trial, to reduce their exposure to actuarial risk. The shadow of doctrine alters insurer behavior, while reforms alter lawyers' incentives. What we see is modest expansion of liability risk for physicians in some areas, accompanied by increasing solidification of the standard of care through practice guidelines, in a larger context of limits on the ability of plaintiffs to sue. Hospitals and other institutional providers also face theoretical expansions in liability exposure as corporate negligence doctrine blooms, impeded by caps on damages enhanced by discovery limitations of peer immunity statutes, and limited by mandatory mediation and arbitration approaches to adverse event claiming.

[2] For a full inventory of malpractice reform strategies, *see generally* MICHELLE M. MELLO & ALLEN KACHALIA, EVALUATION OF OPTIONS FOR MEDICAL MALPRACTICE, MEDICARE PAYMENT ADVISORY COMMISSION (Apr. 2010); for a review of current evidence on tort reform, *see* BARRY R. FURROW ET AL., HEALTH LAW (3rd ed. 2014).

[3] David A. Hyman & Charles Silver, *Double, Double, Toil and Trouble: Justice-Talk and the Future of Medical Malpractice Litigation*, 63 DEPAUL L. REV. 547 (2014).

II Physician Liability

a. Adverse Events and the Physician's Standard of Care: Eroding Professional Custom

The liability of healthcare providers is governed by special negligence principles. Malpractice is usually defined as unskillful practice resulting in injury to the patient, a failure to exercise the "required degree of care, skill and diligence" under the circumstances.[4] The medical profession itself has traditionally set its standards of practice, and the courts have enforced these standards in tort suits. Defendants trying to prove a standard of care normally present expert testimony describing the actual pattern of medical practice, without any reference to the effectiveness of that practice. Professional medical standards are given conclusive weight by most state courts,[5] whereas in tort litigation not involving doctors, courts are willing to reject customary practice if they find the practice dangerous or out of date.[6]

Some courts, however, now allow a *reasonable practice standard* that allows the jury to consider evidence that a custom is no longer reasonable or acceptable. The court in *Nowatske v. Osterloh*[7] expressed it well: "An emphasis on reasonable rather than customary practices, however, insures that custom will not shelter physicians who fail to adopt advances in their respective fields and who consequently fail to conform to the standard of care which both the profession and its patients have a right to expect."[8]

One medical response to a less protective standard of care has been to turn to practice guidelines to bolster a defense of compliance with the standard of care.

b. Expert Testimony: Demanding Grounded Qualifications

The standard or customary practice by those in the defendant doctor's specialty or area of practice is normally established through the testimony of medical experts. Plaintiffs must qualify their medical witnesses as experts; satisfy the court that the expert's testimony will assist the trier of fact; and have the witnesses testify based upon facts that support their expert opinions.[9] Courts have applied very flexible standards in qualifying medical experts, noting that "fields of medicine overlap and more than one type of practitioner may perform the diagnosis or treatment."[10]

4 Bardessono v. Michels, 91 CAL. RPTR. 760, 764, 478 P.2d 480, 484 (Cal. 1970).

5 *See, e.g.*, Holt v. Godsil, 447 So.2d 191 (Ala. 1984).

6 *See* Joseph H. King Jr., *In Search of a Standard of Care for the Medical Profession—The "Accepted Practice" Formula*, 28 VAND. L. REV. 1213, 1236 (1975).

7 198 Wis. 2d 419, 543 N.W.2d 265 (1996).

8 *See generally* Philip G. Peters Jr., *The Role of the Jury in Modern Malpractice Law*, 87 IOWA L. REV. 909 (2002) (contending that many state courts are reconsidering deference to medical custom in malpractice cases).

9 *See* Fed. R. Evid. 702. Testimony by Expert Witnesses.

10 *Id.* at 974.

Expert testimony is needed to establish both the standard of proper professional skill or care and a failure by the defendant to conform. The testimony must be based "upon a reasonable degree of medical and scientific certainty" to satisfy most state courts.[11] The expert must be familiar with the standard of care in the area where the defendant practices[12] and must base testimony on his or her knowledge, education, and experience.[13] An expert has always been able to rely on outside studies in the research literature, and in some cases even admit such outside materials.[14]

The basis of an expert's testimony is now subject to a new level of scrutiny based on Supreme Court decisions as to scientific evidence. Beginning with *Daubert v. Merrell Dow Pharmaceuticals, Inc.*,[15] the Court held that the Federal Rules of Evidence, particularly Rule 702, make the trial judge the gatekeeper of such evidence, with the responsibility to assess the reliability of an expert's testimony, its relevance, and the underlying reasoning or methodology. Expert testimony must have a valid scientific connection to the issues in the case, and be based on "scientifically valid principles."[16]

Daubert set forth a nonexclusive checklist for trial courts to use in assessing the reliability of scientific expert testimony: (1) whether the expert's technique or theory can be or has been tested—that is, whether the expert's theory can be challenged in some objective sense, or whether it is instead simply a subjective, conclusory approach that cannot reasonably be assessed for reliability; (2) whether the technique or theory has been subject to peer review and publication; (3) the known or potential rate of error of the technique or theory when applied; (4) the existence and maintenance of standards and controls; and (5) whether the technique or theory has been generally accepted in the scientific community.

The Court extended the *Daubert* factors to all expert testimony, not just scientific testimony, in *Kumho v. Carmichael*.[17] The trial judge is a gatekeeper to decide whether experts are allowed to testify, and the judge is to apply factors such as the presence of peer review and the rate of error in determining if an expert is reliable.[18] Experts have to be careful to base opinions on a theory that has independent indicia of reliability or has been peer reviewed. Literature support is more likely to be required as a basis of expert opinion. Expert testimony will be subjected to a motion *in limine* to test whether the *Daubert* and *Kumho* factors are satisfied, and in theory this applies to medical malpractice litigation generally.

Courts in medical malpractice cases, however, are flexible about the use of the *Daubert* factors in deciding whether expert testimony is admissible.[19] Recent cases hold that a qualified expert, particularly in medical malpractice cases, is reliable—without going into the underlying scientific qualities of the opinion[20]—so long as the expert refers to widespread, recognized standards of medical care.[21] State courts usually conclude that an expert's

[11] Carter v. Johnson, 187 Ill. Dec. 52, 617 N.E.2d 260, 264 (Ill. App. 1 Dist. 1993).

[12] Kobialko v. Lopez, M.D., 160 Ill. Dec. 90, 576 N.E.2d 1044 (Ill. App. 1991).

[13] *See* Fed. R. Evid. 703, 704.

[14] Young v. Horton, 855 P.2d 502 (Mont. 1993).

[15] 509 U.S. 579 (1993).

[16] *See* Committee Notes on Rules—2000 Amendment, for a full discussion of judicial responses to *Daubert*.

[17] 526 U.S. 137, 119 S.Ct. 1167 (1999).

[18] *The Daubert Challenge to the Admissibility of Scientific Evidence*, 60 AMJUR TRIALS 1 (updated 2013).

[19] Sandretto v. Payson Healthcare Management, Inc., 322 P.3d 168 (Ariz. 2014) Application of the *Daubert* factors, however, particularly to medical testimony like that of Ferrante, requires flexibility.

[20] *See, e.g.*, Potter ex rel. Potter v. Bowman, 2006 WL 3760267 (D. Colo. 2006).

[21] Delta Regional Medical Center v. Taylor, 112 So.3d 11, 28 (Court of Appeals Miss. 2012).

practice experience and acquired knowledge is sufficient without further proof of statistical efficacy.[22] They apply the *Daubert* factors only in special circumstances, for example, when the defense experts introduce studies that attack the standard of care claimed by the plaintiff experts.

c. Practice Guidelines: Solidifying the Standards of Care

Practice guidelines are becoming critical in establishing breach of a medical standard of care. The Institute of Medicine defines clinical guidelines as "statements that include recommendations intended to optimize patient care that is informed by a systematic review of evidence and an assessment of the benefit and harms of alternative care options."[23] The revised definition distinguishes a clinical practice guideline from clinical guidance such as consensus statements and other forms of guidance that lack proper evidence. Guidelines are standardized specifications for using a procedure or managing a particular clinical problem.[24]

The development and proliferation of clinical practice guidelines is one of the transforming forces in current medical practice.[25] Such guidelines provide decision rules based on current medical consensus on how to treat a certain illness or condition.[26] The best guidelines have affected medical practice and settlement patterns, according to surveys of malpractice lawyers.[27] Plaintiffs have used such guidelines to their advantage in malpractice cases, with the guidelines of the American College of Obstetricians and Gynecologists a particularly strong example.[28] And specialty societies are developing substantial efforts toward producing rigorous and useful guidelines.[29]

A widely accepted clinical standard may be evidence of due care, but expert testimony will still be required to introduce the standard and establish its sources and its relevancy, and the sources will determine the weight given the study.[30] Guidelines can also be used to

[22] Reese v. Stroh, 907 P.2d 282 (Wash. 1995).

[23] INSTITUTE OF MEDICINE. CLINICAL PRACTICE GUIDELINES WE CAN TRUST 2 (R. Graham, M. Mancher, D. M. Wolman, S. Greenfield, & E. Steinberg, eds.) (2011), http://www.iom.edu/Reports/2011/Clinical-Practice-Guidelines-We-Can-Trust/Standards.aspx.

[24] The choice of "guideline" with its meaning of a general guidance, not a mandate, suggests a political choice of language, since guidelines are intended to narrow practice variation by standardizing medical responses to specific medical conditions.

[25] *See* Ronen Avraham, *Overlooked and Underused: Clinical Practice Guidelines and Malpractice Liability for Independent Physicians*, 20 CONN. INS. L.J. 273 (2013–2014); Chris Taylor, *The Use of Clinical Practice Guidelines in Determining Standard of Care*, 35 J. LEGAL MED. 273 (2014) The classic article is Arnold J. Rosoff, *The Role of Clinical Practice Guidelines in Health Care Reform*, 5 HEALTH MATRIX 369 (1995).

[26] AHRQ, the Agency for Healthcare Research and Quality created the National Guideline Clearinghouse™ (NGC), a publicly available database of evidence-based clinical practice guidelines and related documents, http://www.guideline.gov/.

[27] *Id.*

[28] *See, e.g.*, Green v. Goldberg, 630 So.2d 606 (Fla. Dist. Ct. App. 1993) (ACOG bulletin on breast cancer treatment used to support expert testimony).

[29] Laxmaiah Manchikanti et al., *An Update of Comprehensive Evidence-Based Guidelines for Interventional Techniques in Chronic Spinal Pain. Part I: Introduction and General Considerations*, 16 PAIN PHYSICIAN S1 (2013).

[30] *See, e.g.*, Bond v. U.S., 2008 WL 655609 (D.C. Oregon 2008).

impeach the opinion of a medical expert.[31] Courts have long been cautious about the use of clinical practice guidelines as evidence of the standard of care,[32] but experts increasingly rely on them as establishing the baseline of a "minimally competent physician,"[33] and more and more courts allow experts to rely on such guidelines.[34] A review of recent case law supports judicial comfort with allowing practice guidelines to be introduced as relevant to the standard of care, even if not mandating its application by the trier of fact.[35]

d. The Affordable Care Act: Discovering and Promoting Best Practices

Current practice guideline development has been soundly criticized:[36] (1) guidelines may suffer from lack of sufficient scientific evidence; (2) authors may be biased due to financial conflicts of interest; and (3) disagreements in the drafting of a guideline may be downplayed or concealed.[37] One of the goals of the Affordable Care Act (ACA) is to create and fund several research entities to develop "best practices" and "practice guidelines."[38] The expectation is that trustworthy guidelines will be created.[39]

The ACA creates four streams of pressure toward measurable specific standards of care.[40] First, outcomes measures will be researched, developed, and disseminated. Section 10303 of the ACA instructs the Secretary of the U.S. Department of Health and Human Services to develop provider-level outcome measures for both hospitals and physicians, as well as other providers. Second, best practices will be researched and disseminated. Third, clinical practice guidelines

[31] *See* Roper v. Blumenfeld, 706 A.2d 1151, 1156 (N.J. Super. A.D. 1998).

[32] Frakes v. Cardiology Consultants, P.C., 1997 WL 536949 (Tenn. Ct. App. 1997) (allowing a consensus statement of the American College of Cardiology and the American Heart Association).

[33] Conn v. United States, 880 F. Supp. 2d 741 (U.S. Dist. Ct., S.D., Miss. 2012).

[34] *See, e.g.*, Delta Regional Medical Center v. Taylor, 112 So.3d 11 (Court of Appeals of Mississippi 2012) (expert relied on American Stroke Association's *Guidelines for the Early Management of Patients with Ischemic Stroke: A Scientific Statement from the Stroke Council of the American Stroke Association*, as an authority).

[35] Delta Reg'l Med. Ctr. v. Taylor, 112 So.3d 11, 18 (Miss. Ct. App. 2012) (regardless of "whether testimony is based on professional studies or personal experience, the 'gatekeeper' must be certain that the expert exercises the same level of 'intellectual rigor that characterizes the practice of an expert in the relevant field.'").

[36] *See generally* Allen Kachalia, Alison Little, Melissa Isavoran, Lynn-Marie Crider, & Jeanene Smith, *Greatest Impact of Safe Harbor Rule May Be to Improve Patient Safety, Not Reduce Liability Claims Paid by Physicians*, 33 HEALTH AFF. 15 (2014).

[37] Justin Kung et al., *Failure of Clinical Practice Guidelines to Meet Institute of Medicine Standards*, 172 ARCHIVES OF INTERNAL MED. 1628, 1628 (2012) (describing a "dizzying array" of clinical practice guidelines that expands year after year).

[38] *See* Conn v. United States, F. Supp. 2d 741 (U.S. Dist. Ct., S.D., Miss. 2012).

[39] *See generally* Barry R. Furrow, *Regulating Patient Safety: The Patient Protection and Affordable Care Act*, 159 U. PENN. L. REV. 101 (2011).

[40] Research findings are now being published under various ACA-funded initiatives. *See, e.g.*, Roger Chou, Carlos Cuevas, Rongwei Fu, Beth Devine, Ngoc Wasson, Alexander Ginsburg, Bernadette Zakher, Miranda Pappas, Elaine Graham, & Sean Sullivan, *Imaging Techniques for the Diagnosis and Staging of Hepatocellular Carcinoma*, COMPARATIVE EFFECTIVENESS REVIEW NUMBER 143 (AHRQ).

will be developed in light of the research on outcome measures and best practice.[41] Fourth, outcomes, best practices, and guidelines will be rapidly disseminated to practice settings. The Center for Quality Improvement and Patient Safety will support research on system improvements and the development of tools "to facilitate adoption of best practices that improve the quality, safety, and efficiency of health care delivery services." The Patient-Centered Outcomes Research Institute will further this effort of developing evidence-based medicine.

Evidence-based guidelines will slowly squeeze out medical practice variation in clinical practice.[42] The tort effect of such narrowing of practice is clear: defenses under liability rules (e.g., respectable minority defenses, variations in practice, proximate causation) will narrow as practice choices narrow. The physician who doesn't keep up with new research will suffer a higher risk of liability for failing to conform to what becomes the new standard of care.

e. Defenses to a Malpractice Suit: Excusing Physician Deviation from Standards of Care

Common law defenses have evolved over the past decades, in the direction of specific immunity statutes and more general tort reform legislation.[43]

i. Standard of Care Exceptions

Defenses to a malpractice suit range from standard of care exceptionalism to hard-edged affirmative defenses like statutes of limitation or Good Samaritan laws. The standard of care defenses typically are incorporated into jury instructions, giving the trier of fact flexibility to accept or reject them. Many state courts acknowledge a "two schools of thought" or "respectable minority" defense, which holds that a provider meets the standard of care so long as a "reasonable and prudent member of the medical profession would undertake under the same or similar circumstances."[44]

ii. Clinical Innovation

Courts may allow a physician to deviate from standard treatment to suit the needs of a particular patient with a particular problem or a desperate situation.[45] Such clinical innovation

[41] Section 1181 (8)(A)(iv) for the ACA specifies that such research findings shall "not be construed as mandates for practice guidelines, coverage recommendations, payment, or policy recommendations . . ." In spite of this prohibitory language, plaintiff lawyers can certainly use the findings as evidence of a standard of care, although of course not as mandates qualifying as a negligence per se finding by the court.

[42] *See generally* BARRY R. FURROW ET AL., HEALTH LAW (3rd ed. 2014).

[43] Passarello v. Grumbine, 87 A.3d (Pa. 2014).

[44] Brook v. St. John's Hickey Memorial Hosp., 380 N.E.2d 72 (Ind. 1978) (the plaintiffs alleged that Dr. Fischer was negligent in choosing an injection site which had not been specifically recommended by the medical community and that this choice of an unusual injection site was a medical experiment).

[45] *See* Anna C. Mastroianni, *Liability, Regulation and Policy in Surgical Innovation: The Cutting Edge of Research and Therapy*, 16 HEALTH MATRIX 351 (2006). The mini-IRB model is outlined by the Partners Human Research Committee, Innovative Therapy and Diagnosis.

does not fit within the requirements for institutional research board (IRB) approval for research, and may harm patients because of this lack of oversight. Some hospitals have therefore implemented a limited peer review process for clinical practices that are more experimental than traditional clinical practice but do not reach the level of research. These "mini IRBs" allow peer physicians to review and critique innovative therapy without hampering innovation by requiring the rigorous and time-consuming approval of an IRB. These peer review procedures help ensure patient safety, particularly when the consequences of using a new and unproven therapy are unknown.[46]

f. Damage Innovations: Refining the "Loss of a Chance" Doctrine

The normal approach to proof of causation and damages is to require the plaintiff to show by a preponderance of the evidence that absent the defendant's negligence, the plaintiff would have lived a normal life. The normal elements of damages, including lost wages, medical expenses past and future, impaired earning capacity, and pain and suffering, are allowed where the negligence of the provider is proved by a preponderance of the evidence.[47]

The adoption by most state courts of the "loss of a chance" doctrine is perhaps the most significant development in damage rules relating to malpractice cases. When a physician is negligent in diagnosing a disease, and the resulting delay reduces the plaintiff's chances of survival (even though the chance of survival was below 50% before the missed diagnosis), a strong argument can be made that the physician should be responsible for the value of the chance that the plaintiff lost,[48] so long as the initial act of the physician was itself negligent.

Courts have cited compelling justifications for the loss of a chance doctrine. First, the loss of an improved chance of survival or improvement in condition, even if the original odds are less than 50%, is an opportunity loss due to negligence. Many treatments aim at extending life for brief periods and improving its quality rather then curing the underlying disease, with a high percentage of the healthcare dollar spent on such treatments. Second, immunizing whole areas of medical practice from liability by requiring proof by more than 50% that the negligence caused the injury fails to deter negligent conduct.[49]

Courts have adopted various measures to calculate the loss of a chance doctrine over the past twenty years. The proportional "loss of a chance" approach has been adopted by many courts that have considered the issue.[50]

46 *See generally* Dan B. Dobbs, The Law of Remedies: Damages—Equity—Restitution (2d ed. 1993).

47 The leading law review article, often relied upon by courts adopting the doctrine, is Joseph H. King Jr., *Causation, Valuation and Chance in Personal Injury Torts Involving Preexisting Conditions and Future Consequences*, 90 Yale L.J. 1353 (1981).

48 721 F.2d 203, 208 (7th Cir. 1983) (Posner, J. dissenting).

49 *See* Matsuyama v. Birnbaum, 452 Mass. 1, 890 N.E.2d 819 (Sup. Jud. Ct., Mass. 2008) (including a full discussion of state courts that have adopted the loss of a chance doctrine).

50 Harbeson v. Parke Davis, 746 F.2d 517 (9th Cir. 1984).

g. Informed Consent: Fostering Patient Sovereignty in Medical Decision-Making

The risks of a medical treatment, and alternatives to it, are perhaps the most important pieces of information for a patient to consider. Risks must be material to a patient's decision-making in order to be disclosed.[51] Courts often state that remote risks can be omitted,[52] as can those commonly known by patients.[53] Risks of drug side effects, however, are singled out for disclosure by some courts, even if the risk of side effect is small.[54]

The threshold of disclosure varies with the product of the probability and the severity of the risk.[55] Probabilities of various risks must be disclosed by physicians in a fashion that accurately informs the patient. Thus, one court has held that if a physician tells a patient that the risks of a particular surgical procedure are increased by 50% by smoking, the physician must also discuss with the patient the base probability of the average risk to an average patient.[56] Some courts have moved beyond a rote compliance with informed consent procedures, often holding physicians responsible to provide more sophisticated and accurate information.[57] This may include disclosure of reliable tests to rule out a patient's condition, even if unrelated to the final diagnosis.[58]

The duty to disclose the risks of treatment may be expanded if the patient inquires more specifically as to particular risks, under both the reasonable patient and the reasonable physician standards. A patient's request puts the physician on notice as to a patient's particular worries, and a standard disclosure is no longer a defense in such cases.[59]

i. *Disclosure of Skill or Status Risks*

Comparative data as to outcomes and success rates in hospitals and of particular medical specialties is proliferating. Hospitals and managed care organizations have been actively engaged in programs to promote high-quality and effective practice. The rapid acceleration of information gathering by healthcare institutions is likely to lead to disclosure of such comparative success rates and outcome data where available.[60]

Informed consent doctrine can be interpreted to require a physician to disclose differential success rates, forcing the physician into the awkward position of presenting his or her

[51] *See, e.g.*, Koapke v. Herfendal, 660 N.W.2d 206, 212 (N.D. 2003).

[52] *See generally* Kissinger v. Lofgren, 836 F.2d 678, 681 (1st Cir. 1988) (risks of infection from operations should be known to every patient).

[53] Cunningham v. Charles Pfizer & Co., 532 P.2d 1377, 1381 (Okla. 1974) (duty to disclose "even though the chances of the adverse reaction occurring are statistically small.").

[54] Canterbury v. Spence, 464 F.2d 772, 789 n. 85 (D.C. Cir. 1972).

[55] Korman v. Mallin, 858 P.2d 1145 (Alaska 1993).

[56] *See, e.g.*, Distefano v. Bell, 544 So.2d 567 (La. App. 1989), *writ denied*, 550 So.2d 650 (La. 1989).

[57] Jandre v. Wisconsin Injured Patients and Families Compensation Fund, 340 Wis. 2d 31 (Wisc. 2012).

[58] Korman v. Mallin, 858 P.2d 1145 (Alaska 1993).

[59] *See* Aaron D. Twerksi & Neil B. Cohen, *Comparing Medical Providers: A First Look at the New Era of Medical Statistics*, 58 BROOK. L. REV. 5, 12–13 (1992) (as statistical validity of data is established, it will become part of litigation).

[60] 545 N.W.2d 495 (Wis. 1996).

"batting average." Production of comparative outcome data on both hospitals and physicians for certain procedures, as mandated by the federal government and some states, raises the possibility that disclosure of such success rates may be required. A duty of a physician, typically a surgeon, to disclose performance data has been adopted in a limited way by some American courts. The best example of such a duty is found in *Johnson v. Kokemoor*,[61] where the surgeon overstated his experience with a difficult aneurysm procedure. The Wisconsin Supreme Court held that the surgeon should have disclosed his own experience with the particular procedure and compared the morbidity and mortality rates among experienced surgeons with those lacking experience, such as himself.

ii. Alternatives

Doctors have also been required to disclose alternative methods of diagnosis or treatment that are generally acknowledged within the medical community as feasible[62]; their risks and consequences; and their probability of success. Some courts have held that alternatives should be disclosed, even if the alternative is more hazardous,[63] or the physician is not capable of performing the procedure or evaluating its risk.[64] Such alternatives might include availability to diagnostic tools such as CT scanners and better equipped facilities.[65] Such disclosure is mandated by statute in some states.[66] Alternatives must be discussed unless an alternative is not considered to be within the standard of care.[67] The definition of treatment has been construed broadly to include diagnostic options and choices of hospitals for performing a procedure. Physicians must disclose diagnostic procedures that might assist patients in making an informed decision about treatment.

iii. Decision Aids and Informed Consent

Decision aids are decision support tools that provide patients with detailed and specific information on options and outcomes, help them clarify their values, and guide them through the decision-making process.[68] The process by which such decision aids are used by the provider and the patient has come to be called "shared medical decision-making," a

[61] *See* Newmark-Shortino v. Buna, 48 A.3d 401, 412 (N.J. Super. Ct. App. Div. 2012).

[62] Gemme v. Goldberg, 626 A.2d 318, 326 (Conn. App. 1993).

[63] *See* Holt v. Nelson, 523 P.2d 211 (Wash. App. 1974).

[64] Martin v. Richards, 531 N.W.2d 70 (Wis. 1995) (failure to inform parents of patient that a CT scanner was available to diagnose head injuries, and that facility lacked neurosurgeon to treat intracranial bleeding).

[65] *See, e.g.*, WISC. ST. ANN. 448.30 (mandating disclosure of the "availability of reasonable alternate medical modes of treatment").

[66] *See* Morris v. Ferriss, 669 So.2d 1316 (La. App. 4 Cir. 1996) (physician did not have to advise patient that psychiatric treatment was an alternative treatment for epileptic partial complex seizures, since it was not accepted as feasible); Lienhard v. State, 431 N.W.2d 861 (Minn. 1988) (managing pregnancy at home rather than in hospital not a choice between alternative methods of treatment; disclosure therefore not required).

[67] *See, e.g.*, Elie A. Akl et al., *A Decision Aid for COPD Patients Considering Inhaled Steroid Therapy: Development and Before and After Pilot Testing*, 15 BMC MED. INFORM. DEC. MAK. 7 (2007).

[68] Jaime Staples King & Benjamin Moulton, *Rethinking Informed Consent: The Case for Shared Medical Decisionmaking*, 32 AM. J. LAW & MED. 429, 431 (2006).

process by which the physician discusses with the patient all treatment options and their risk and benefits, and the patient shares her personal information that may make one treatment more desirable than another. It strives for a mutual medical decision rather than a one-way mechanical disclosure of risk information by the physician.[69]

The Affordable Care Act proposes the use of decision aids for preference-sensitive care to better incorporate patient preferences into the medical treatment plan, but does not mandate their use. Decision aids are, however, beginning to be adopted by some health plans as an improvement over traditional informed consent requirements.[70]

h. Alternative Dispute Resolution: Moving Toward Trial Risk Reduction

The most powerful tool to reduce the risks of malpractice litigation and jury trials is contractual or compelled alternative dispute resolution (ADR). Historically, arbitration agreements in the healthcare setting have been uncommon: insurers calculate that the odds of a physician winning a medical malpractice suit are higher than in arbitration; providers think that it sets the wrong tone for the treatment relationship; and state courts continue to frown on such agreements as too often on the borderline of "unconscionable" contracts that smack of adhesion.[71]

Recent Supreme Court cases strongly favoring arbitration may be tipping the scales toward the use of arbitration agreements in healthcare.[72] The Court has adopted a strong presumption, almost a rule of law, supporting the enforceability of arbitration agreements. In *AT&T Mobility LLC v. Concepcion*,[73] the Court refused to allow state courts to nullify arbitration agreements based on arguments that only the courts can provide proper redress. Fraud, duress, and unconscionability are still possible grounds for setting aside such agreements.[74]

Hospitals are experimenting with nonbinding mediation, but binding arbitration has yet to emerge as a powerful tool in the tort reform arsenal. However, nursing homes, assisted-living facilities, and long-term-care providers have been pioneers of incorporating binding, predispute arbitration clauses into their contracts with patients. State courts continue to resist the forces of arbitration, at least outside the nursing-home settings where arbitration is typically mandatory.[75] However, various forms of arbitration agreements seem likely in the future, given the Supreme Court's heavy-handed support for all forms of arbitration.

[69] *See* Washington State's adoption of such decision aids in Rev. Code Wash § 7.70.060. *See generally* David Arterburn et al., *Introducing Decision Aids at Group Health Was Linked to Sharply Lower Hip and Knee Surgery Rates and Cost*, 31 HEALTH AFF. 2094 (2012).

[70] RAND CORPORATION, RESEARCH BRIEF, BINDING ARBITRATION IS NOT FREQUENTLY USED TO RESOLVE HEALTH CARE DISPUTES (1999).

[71] *See* Richard Frankel, *The Arbitration Clause as Super Contract*, 91 WASH. U. L. REV. 531 (2014).

[72] *See* Myriam Gilles, *Operation Arbitration: Privatizing Medical Malpractice Claims*, 15 THEORETICAL INQUIRIES IN LAW 671 (2014) (predicting that more medical contracts will contain arbitration provisions.)

[73] 131 S.Ct. 1740 (2011).

[74] *See* Franks v. Bowers, 116 So.3d 1240 (Fla. 2013).

[75] Michael I. Krauss, *A Medical Liability Toolkit, Including ADR*, 2 J.L.: Periodical Laboratory of Leg. Scholarship 349 (2012) (good appendix of tort reforms); Franks v. Bowers, 116 So.3d 1240 (Fla.).

Some proposed tort reforms, such as health courts and communication-and-resolution programs (CRPs), assume the benefits of ADR models as the foundation for their approach. Health courts are unlikely to be legislated, but CRPs are already in place. In CRPs, health systems and liability insurers encourage the disclosure of unanticipated care outcomes to affected patients and their families and seek resolutions, which may include an apology; an explanation; and, where appropriate, an offer of reimbursement, compensation, or both.[76]

Such programs have become more common in hospitals, as risk managers search for ways to control their liability costs.[77] Under this approach providers would voluntarily agree to identify and promptly compensate patients for avoidable injuries.[78] When the adverse outcome first occurred, the patient or provider would file the claim with the insurer, who would decide whether the injury was covered. If so, it would make prompt payment. Disputes would be resolved through mediation or arbitration.[79]

III Institutional Liability

Healthcare delivery includes a range of institutional forms of delivery. Hospitals are the classic provider institution, but we have seen the growth of managed care organizations that finance healthcare and contract with physicians and hospitals to provide care, as well as ambulatory care facilities such as surgicenters and ever-larger physician practice groups, along with urgicenters run by large pharmacy chains like Rite Aid and CVS. The ACA has also spawned new forms, such as accountable care organizations and medical homes, to better coordinate care. As more medical care is moved out of the hospital into alternative settings, the liability of these institutional arrangements emerges as a new concern.

[76] Michelle M. Mello, Richard C. Boothman, Timothy McDonald, Jeffrey Driver, Alan Lembitz, Darren Bouwmeester, Benjamin Dunlap, & Thomas Gallagher, *Communication-and-Resolution Programs: The Challenges and Lessons Learned from Six Early Adopters*, 33 Health Aff. 20 (2014).

[77] *See* ECRI Institute, Disclosure of Unanticipated Outcomes (Jan. 2008) (outlining the disclosure steps developed by the American Society for Healthcare Risk Management (ASHRM)).

[78] This approach was first proposed in 1973 by Clark Havighurst and Lawrence Tancredi, and has been recommended in Institute of Medicine, Fostering Rapid Advances in Health Care: Learning from System Demonstrations 82 (2002). *See* Clark Havighurst & Laurence Tancredi, *"Medical Adversity Insurance"—A No-Fault Approach to Medical Malpractice and Quality Assurance*, 51 Milbank Memorial Fund Quarterly 125 (1973).

[79] The University of Michigan Health System, a self-insured system, has developed such a system. It will tender compensation to an injured patient suffering inappropriate care. The offer may include compensation for all elements of loss that are compensable in tort cases, including medical expenses, lost income, other economic losses, and "pain and suffering." A patient must agree that his acceptance is a final settlement. *See generally* Richard C. Boothman et al., *A Better Approach to Medical Malpractice Claims? The University of Michigan Experience*, 2 J. Health & Life Sci. L. 125, 135 (2009) (summarizing the approach); Michelle M. Mello & Thomas H. Gallagher, *Malpractice Reform—Opportunities for Leadership by Health Care Institutions and Liability Insurers* (Mar. 31, 2010 at NEJM.org).

a. Hospitals: Moving from Community Centers to Industrial Networks

The United States has over 5,700 hospitals—almost 3,000 are nonprofit, 1,000 are for profit, and 1,200 are owned by the local, state, or federal government, with the rest psychiatric and long-term care hospitals.[80] Hospitals are major providers of emergency care and highly complicated surgical and other procedures. They are therefore the largest sources of patient harms in the U.S. system. Hospitals provide acute care in severe health crises and, given the possibility of errors and serious adverse events, we also think of institutional liability for those injuries.

The traditional relationship of doctor to hospital has been that of independent contractor or noncontracted member of the medical staff, rather than employee. The hospital is not regularly targeted as a defendant in a malpractice suit. Only if the doctor whose negligence injured a patient was an employee could the hospital be reached through the doctrine of vicarious liability. As medicine has grown more commercial and hospitals have become complex corporate entities, the courts have been less willing to grant a special subsidy in the form of immunities to nonprofit institutions.

i. Agency Doctrine: Stretching to Reach Hospitals

Hospitals are responsible for the torts of their employees, including employee-doctors, under the principle of vicarious liability. The hospital came to be viewed as an enterprise liable for the acts of its employees, and physicians became liable for the acts of their employees, a partner, or another physician working jointly. A master-servant relationship, a partnership, or a joint venture could lead to liability.[81]

Hospitals currently employ more than 200,000 physicians. Many physicians are moving from practicing in small groups to some form of employee status in a changing delivery system. Their terms and conditions of employment are controlled by the hospital, which sets their hours, wages, and working conditions. The test of employee status is based on "control."[82] Physicians need considerable autonomy in practice, given the complexity of their decisions and their relationship to particular patients. Determining the degree of control necessary to create an employment relationship in a medical malpractice claim poses a unique set of difficulties.[83] When employees are negligent, the hospital is vicariously liable for their acts as a result of the master-servant relationship of agency law.[84]

[80] *See* American Hospital Association, Fast Facts on U.S. Hospitals (2013).

[81] 41 C.J.S. Hospitals § 43–Theories of Liability.

[82] The general definition of the term "servant" in the Restatement (Second) of Agency § 2(2) (1957) refers to a person whose work is "controlled or is subject to the right to control by the master." The relevant factor for analyzing the hospital-physician relationship by agency tests is § 220(2)(a), which looks to "the extent of control which, by the agreement, the master may exercise over the details of the work." This becomes a fact-intensive analysis for the trier of fact.

[83] Lilly v. Fieldstone, 876 F.2d 857 (C.A. 10 Kan. 1989).

[84] *See generally* John D. Hodson, *Liability of Hospital or Sanitarium for Negligence of Physician or Surgeon*, 51 A.L.R. 4th 235 (2014).

The hospital-physician relationship, however, is an unusual one by corporate standards and raises more difficult agency questions. Most hospital physicians have been treated as independent contractors, relieving the hospital of any agency-based liability for their negligent acts. The mere grant of staff privileges is not sufficient control to impose vicarious liability on the hospital.[85] The test under agency law is whether the acts are within the "scope of employment," and are derived from events or conditions of employment.[86]

Courts have limited the reach of the independent contractor defense in many malpractice cases.[87] Many jurisdictions have allowed cases to proceed on agency-based theories of ostensible agency or apparent authority.[88] Courts are impatient with the law's role in shielding modern hospitals from liability, noting that modern marketing promotional campaigns deliberately foster patient reliance on the hospital's doctors.[89] The development of hospital-based accountable care organizations or other emerging corporate forms that compete for new patients are likely to directly impact agency relationships, leading to hospital vicarious liability.

ii. Corporate Negligence: Moving Toward Enterprise Liability

A healthcare institution is liable to its patients for negligence in maintaining its facilities; providing and maintaining medical equipment; hiring, supervising, and retaining nurses and other employees; and failing to have in place procedures to protect patients.[90] Hospitals are generally held to a national standard of care for hospitals of their size and treatment category.

Courts have expanded the doctrine of corporate negligence since the 1960s, recognizing the role of the modern hospital in providing care, support, and service, not just a shell for the physicians to use.[91] A hospital is thus directly liable for the failure of administrators and staff to properly monitor and supervise the delivery of healthcare within the hospital. A hospital has a nondelegable duty directly to its patients and is liable for its action or inaction regarding its policies rather than specific negligent acts of one of its employees.[92] Courts have held that Joint Commission standards can establish the standard of care for a hospital, along with state hospital licensure laws and the hospital's own bylaws.[93]

The corporate negligence doctrine was well stated by the Pennsylvania Supreme Court in *Thompson v. Nason Hospital*.[94] Corporate negligence, as the *Nason* court outlines it, involves

[85] Albain v. Flower Hosp., 553 N.E.2d 1038 (Ohio 1990).

[86] Lisa M. v. Henry Mayo Newhall Memorial Hospital, 907 P.2d 358 (1995) (sexual assault by ultrasound technician lacked causal nexus to employee's work); *but see* Roberts v. Blount Memorial Hospital, 963 S.W.2d 744 (Tenn. App. 1997) (no vicarious liability for sexual assault in hospital).

[87] *See* Mduba v. Benedictine Hosp., 384 N.Y.S.2d 527 (N.Y. App. Div. 1976).

[88] Sword v. NKC Hospitals, Inc., 714 N.E.2d 142 (Ind. 1999) (and cases cited).

[89] Clark v. Southview Hospital & Family Health Center, 628 N.E.2d 46 (Ohio 1994) (promotional and marketing campaign stressed the emergency departments); Gragg v. Calandra, 696 N.E.2d 1282 (Ill. App. 1998) (unless patient is put on notice of the independent status of the professionals in a hospital, he or she will reasonably assume they are employees).

[90] Lamb v. Candler General Hospital, Inc., 413 S.E.2d 720 (Ga. 1992) (hospital negligent in failing to use proper replacement parts in a medical instrument).

[91] Alex Stein, *Toward a Theory of Medical Malpractice*, 97 Iowa L. Rev. 1201, 1229 (2012).

[92] Moser v. Heistand, 681 A.2d 1322 (Pa. 1996).

four distinct duties for institutional providers: (1) a duty to use reasonable care in the maintenance of safe and adequate facilities and equipment; (2) a duty to select and retain only competent physicians; (3) a duty to oversee all persons who practice medicine within its walls as to patient care; and (4) a duty to formulate, adopt, and enforce adequate rules and policies to ensure quality care for patients. This recognizes the complexity of the modern healthcare institution and the need to impose a duty that is patient-centered.[95] More than half of American jurisdictions have now adopted the corporate negligence doctrine in some form.[96]

The hospital has an obligation to provide surveillance of the quality of patient care within the hospital. Courts have imposed upon hospitals a duty to follow their own internal procedures,[97] and to monitor risks to patients created by poor treatment by staff physicians.[98] The courts have found that the power of hospitals to improve patient care dictates a corporate negligence analysis. They note that the public perceives a hospital as a complex entity responsible for care provided, and relies on the hospital for this care; that the hospital is in the best position to "monitor and control physician performance," given its opportunities to observe professional practices on a daily basis, to adopt procedures to detect problems; and that such tort liability creates incentives for hospitals to "insure the competency of their medical staffs."[99]

Credentialing and retention of hospital medical staff is the central task of hospitals.[100] Under the Health Care Quality Improvement Act of 1986 (HCQIA), hospitals must check a national database maintained under contract with the Department of Health and Human Services before a new staff appointment is made. This National Practitioner Data Bank contains information on individual physicians who have been disciplined, had malpractice claims filed against them, or had privileges revoked or limited. Even if the hospital fails to check the registry, it is held constructively to have knowledge of any information it might have gotten from the inquiry.

93 Decker v. St. Mary's Hospital, 619 N.E.2d 537 (Ill. App. 1993); Pedroza v. Bryant, 766 P.2d 166, 171 (1984). *But see* Kadlec Med. Ctr. v. Lakeview Anesthesia Assocs., 2006 WL 1328872 (E.D. La.) (holding that the Joint Commission guidelines don't create a cause of action).

94 591 A.2d 703 (Pa.1991).

95 Casillas-Sanchez v. Ryder Memorial Hosp., Inc., 960 F. Supp. 2d. 262 (U.S.D.C. Puerto Rico 2013) (recognizing a hospital's independent duty to patients to: "(1) carefully select the physicians to whom it grants privileges; (2) require that such physicians stay abreast of the most recent developments in their respective fields; and (3) monitor the work of such physicians, intervening, when possible, in the face of an obvious act of medical malpractice by one of them.").

96 *See* Larson v. Wasemiller, 738 N.W.2d 300 (Minn. 2007) (adopting corporate negligence for Minnesota, the court noted that more than half of the state courts have adopted the tort, and it has support in Restatement (Second) Tort sections such as sections 320 and 411).

97 *See, e.g.*, Williams v. St. Claire Medical Center, 657 S.W.2d 590 (Ky. App. 1983).

98 *See, e.g.*, Strubhart v. Perry Memorial Hospital Trust Authority, 903 P.2d 263 (Okla. 1995) (adopts doctrine of independent corporate responsibility, requiring hospitals to ensure that only competent physicians are privileged, and must take reasonable steps to ensure patient safety when it knows or should know that physicians has displayed incompetence); NKC Hospitals, Inc. v. Anthony, 849 S.W.2d 564 (Ky. App. 1993).

99 Schoening v. Grays Harbor Community Hosp., 698 P.2d 593 (Wash. App. 1985).

100 Columbia/JFK Medical Center Ltd. v. Sangounchitte, 977 So.2d 639 (Fla. App. 4 Dist. 2008).

Most jurisdictions have held hospitals to a duty to take reasonable steps to ensure the competence of members of their medical staff.[101] While the medical staff is self-governing, the hospital establishes and implements procedures for staff selection and reappointment.[102] A hospital therefore is held to have an obligation to its patients to investigate the qualifications of medical staff applicants.[103] This duty to investigate is based on a national standard of credentialing practice,[104] although some courts note the problems with a credentialing duty due to peer review immunity statutes.[105]

An obligation to detect physician problems is growing, as hospitals use modern software tools such as data mining to spot eruptions of patient-adverse events.[106] A hospital must properly restrict the clinical privileges of staff physicians who are incompetent to handle certain procedures, and detect concealment by a staff doctor of medical errors.[107] While some courts have limited this duty to only those situations where a hospital has learned of physician insufficiencies,[108] others have talked of "negligent supervision" in terms of an affirmative duty to detect problems.[109]

The Joint Commission issued new standards on medical staff governance in 2010 that prescribe the relationship between the medical staff, the medical staff's executive committee, and the hospital's board. Joint Commission standards have intensified the institutional focus on prospective monitoring of physician quality. One of the standards, for example, specifically provides that the hospital must establish a system for collecting, recording, and addressing individual reports of concerns about individual physicians.[110]

iii. Informed Consent: Developing Institutional Responsibility

Consent forms are universally used in healthcare institutions, where most healthcare is provided. Hospitals use them at several points in a patient's progress through the institution—upon admission, when a generic form is signed; and before surgery or anesthesia, when more detailed forms may be offered. A consent form is treated in many states as presumptively valid consent to the treatment at issue, with the burden on the patient to rebut the presumption.[111]

[101] Welsh v. Bulger, 698 A.2d 581 (Pa. 1997).

[102] *See generally* CNA HEALTHPRO, MEDICAL STAFF CREDENTIALING: EIGHT STRATEGIES FOR SAFER PHYSICIAN AND PROVIDER PRIVILEGING (VP 09-3), https://www.cna.com/vcm_content/CNA/internet/Static%20File%20for%20Download/Risk%20Control/Medical%20Services/MedStaffCredentialing.pdf.

[103] Bell v. Sharp Cabrillo Hosp., 260 CAL. RPTR. 886 (Cal. App. 1989).

[104] Lopez v. Central Plains Regional Hosp., 859 S.W.2d 600, 603 (Tex. App.–Amarillo 1993).

[105] Paulino v. QHG of Springdale, Inc., 386 S.W.3d 462 (Ark. 2012). *See also* J. Taylor White, *Paulino v. QHG of Springdale, Inc., and Negligent Credentialing: A Look into Peer-Review Statutes and the Health Care Quality Improvement Act*, 66 ARK. L. REV. 879, 879 (2013).

[106] Barry R. Furrow, *Data Mining and Substandard Medical Practice: The Difference between Privacy, Secrets and Hidden Defects*, 51 VILL. L. REV. 803 (2006).

[107] Cronic v. Doud, 119 Ill. Dec. 708, 523 N.E.2d 176 (Ill. App. 1988), *appeal denied*, 125 Ill. Dec. 214, 530 N.E.2d 242 (Ill. 1988); Corleto v. Shore Memorial Hospital, 350 A.2d 534 (N.J. Super. Law Div. 1975).

[108] Albain v. Flower Hospital, 553 N.E.2d 1038 (Ohio 1990).

[109] LeBlanc v. Research Belton Hosp., 278 S.W.3d 201 (Mo. App. W.D. 2008); Oehler v. Humana Inc., 775 P.2d 1271 (Nev. 1989).

[110] *See* Joint Commission, Focused Professional Practice Evaluation, Oct. 13, 2008.

The majority view is that the hospital has no duty to obtain a patient's consent to surgery, nor to conduct any kind of inquiry into the quality of the plaintiff's consent.[112] Even the adoption of a hospital regulation that physicians must obtain informed consent is not sufficient to shift the burden of obtaining such consent from the physician to the institution.[113]

The emergence of accountable care organizations (ACOs) as new organizational forms for purposes of Medicare shared savings may expand the duties of hospitals and other institutions that are part of ACOs.[114] The pressures created by the ACA and its new centers, coupled with the mandates imposed on ACOs to promote patient engagement as a central component of their delivery model, will push institutions develop an effective informed consent system as part of shared decision-making.[115]

b. Nonhospital System Liability: Accountable Care Organizations

Managed care plans disappeared from the liability landscape in the 1990s as plans learned that being a "qualified health plan" gave them immunity, through ERISA preemption. The Employee Retirement Income Security Act of 1974 (ERISA) applies either explicitly, or by U.S. Supreme Court interpretation, to the vast majority of managed care plans that are employment-based and ERISA-qualified. ERISA preemption shields most managed care organizations (MCOs) from liability stemming from their physicians' errors and omissions as they pursued cost-cutting strategies.[116] It does not shield the rapidly evolving new payment models such as medical homes and accountable care organizations.

Managed care programs in the 1990s had three relevant features from a liability perspective.[117] While plans have migrated to a less-intense management model since the managed care backlash of the 1990s, the liability issues that the courts faced in the early cases may predict litigation over new forms of delivery like accountable care organizations and medical homes. Potential sources of liability include: (1) program selection of a restricted group of

[111] *See* WEST'S FLA. STAT. ANN. § 766.103(4); GA. CODE § 88-2906.1(b)(2); IDAHO CODE § 39-4305.

[112] *See, e.g.*, Winters v. Podzamsky, 621 N.E.2d 72, 76 (Ill. App. 1993) ("[t]he hospital fulfills its obligations to the patient by requiring the signed consent form before allowing surgery to be performed . . . Any inadequacy of the physician's explanation cannot be imputed to the hospital."); see also Petriello v. Kalman, 576 A.2d 474 (Conn. 1990).

[113] Kelly v. Methodist Hospital, 664 A.2d 148 (Pa. Super. 1995).

[114] *See* FURROW ET AL., HEALTH LAW, at § 8-17.

[115] *See* THE NATIONAL PATIENT SAFETY FOUNDATION'S LUCIAN LEAPE INSTITUTE REPORT OF THE ROUNDTABLE ON CONSUMER ENGAGEMENT, SAFETY IS PERSONAL: PARTNERING WITH PATIENTS AND FAMILIES FOR THE SAFEST CARE (2014), http://www.npsf.org/wp-content/uploads/2014/03/Safety_Is_Personal.pdf?utm_campaign=wihi&utm_source=hs_email&utm_medium=email&utm_content=12660928&_hsenc=p2ANqtz-_PpF8uBYJMQWDn-ZFWtVzBjA5D7OhiUNZ13hCZep72PHMEg1nOQQMI7EMmVUCLGukuaAH4-pWBFoOx9p51j1FYvovC8g&_hsmi=12660928.

[116] Suits are still brought against nonqualified plans with success, however. *See, e.g.*, Bradford v. Jai Med. Sys. Managed Care Organizations, Inc., 439 Md. 2, 93 A.3d 697 (2014).

[117] *See generally* Barry R. Furrow, *Managed Care Organizations and Patient Injury: Rethinking Liability*, 31 UNIV. GA. L. REV. 419 (1997) (reviewing managed care structures and theories of liability).

healthcare professionals who provide services to the program's participants; (2) capitation in some form, accepting a fixed payment per subscriber, in exchange for provision of necessary care; (3) utilization tools to control referrals and hospitalizations.

Physician incentives were central to both quality of care and cost management in managed care plans, and the same is true today with ACOs and other new delivery models. MCOs used utilization review techniques, incentives systems, and gatekeepers to control costs. Medicare pay-for-performance, and the regulatory requirement of ACOs, reintroduce a forceful use of utilization management but within a more highly specified regulatory framework that reduces the discretion of ACOs and other new models.

The ACA has no provisions that directly address agency relationships or corporate negligence, nor does it explicitly alter the existing common law rules relating to vicarious liability and independent contractors. What the ACA does do, however, is create strong pressures—through centers, demonstration projects, and Medicare reimbursement incentives—for providers to integrate and coordinate their delivery of healthcare for Medicare recipients. The goal is to develop better coordinated systems of care.[118]

The Affordable Care Act has accelerated the development of ACOs.[119] In an accountable care organization, a group of primary care physicians, specialists, and other health professionals (or hospitals) agree to accept joint responsibility for the quality and cost of care provided to their patients.[120] If the ACO meets certain targets, its members receive a financial bonus.[121] ACOs strive to improve quality by streamlining and coordinating services from all providers into one, patient-focused plan, and reducing unnecessary and redundant treatment.[122] The goal of an ACO is to keep patients from entering a hospital and cost-effectively treating those that are admitted.[123] ACOs can specifically achieve this goal "by preventing medical errors and eliminating duplication of medical services, including tests, examinations, and other procedures."[124]

ACOs look like mini–health plans and they share some of the design features of the older managed care models. An ACO requires a range of tools to manage patient utilization and to hit quality targets: (1) financial and actuarial tools to establish targets, cost trends, and provider-payment and incentive-distribution models;[125] (2) tools for chronic-disease and

[118] System reforms have been slow in coming to the U.S. healthcare system, with its fragmentation and fee-for-service payment system. For a critical perspective, *see* REPORT TO THE PRESIDENT, BETTER HEALTH CARE AND LOWER COSTS: ACCELERATING IMPROVEMENT THROUGH SYSTEMS ENGINEERING v (May 2014).

[119] For a fuller description of accountable care organizations, *see generally* BARRY R. FURROW ET AL., HEALTH LAW s. 8–17 (West Academic Press 2014).

[120] *See* Timothy L. Greaney, *Accountable Care Organizations—The Fork in the Road*, 364 N. ENG. J. MED. e1(1), e1(1)–(2) (2011), http://www.nejm.org/doi/pdf/10.1056/NEJMp1013404 (discussing the benefits and concerns surrounding the implementation of ACO reform measures).

[121] *See* Mark McClellan et al., *A National Strategy to Put Accountable Care into Practice*, 29 HEALTH AFF. 982, 983 (2010) (discussing different ACO payment models).

[122] Katie Siegel, *Risks: Accountability in the ACO Structure, Risk and Insurance* (Apr. 7, 2014), http://www.riskandinsurance.com.

[123] Centers for Medicare & Medicaid Services, Accountable Care Organizations (ACO), CMS.gov, http://www.cms.gov/Medicare/Medicare-Fee-for-Service-Payment/ACO/index.html?redirect=/ACO.

[124] Section 3022 of the Affordable Care Act is codified at 42 U.S.C. § 1395jjj (2011).

complex-ease management and wellness-prevention to control demand and improve quality of care; and (3) utilization tools for reporting preauthorization, hospital utilization review, high-tech radiology management, specialty referral management, and pharmacy management to limit medically unnecessary services.

The ACO indeed resembles a more sophisticated version of the managed care model of the 1990s, with major structural and incentive differences.[126] The ACO form is likely to confront the same concerns from patients that the MCO model generated in the 1990s: cost-cutting that harms quality, denial of necessary tests and services, and other fears of rationed care.[127] Here is the nub of the liability problem: reducing hospital admissions and reducing tests will in rare cases result in patient harm, and the plaintiffs will argue that the omissions caused their injuries.

MCOs and ACOs, however, have important differences.[128] ACO providers can receive bonuses for keeping patients healthy so that hospitalization is not needed. ACOs will have a governing body to represent ACO providers, suppliers, and Medicare beneficiaries; ACOs will create processes to promote evidence-based medicine, promote patient engagement, internally report on quality and cost, and coordinate care. The federal requirements for ACO operation are much more developed than those that regulate MCOs, which were driven by cost-containment goals in the 1990s. The incentives are different, the tools more advanced, and the coordination mandates much more extensive for ACOs. It is not likely that ACOs and other coordinated-care models will generate the adverse events and patient anger that managed care did at its peak in the 1990s.

ACOs, unlike MCOs, are not protected by preemption under ERISA, unless the ACOs contract with an ERISA-qualified plan sponsored by a private employer. Patients enrolled in ACOs are not barred from suit, and so a flurry of litigation can be predicted early in the life cycle of ACOs, as they perfect the institutional tools required by their enabling legislation.

ACOs present a range of liability risks, but these are mostly transitional risks as new systems and technologies are chosen and mastered. However, other liability risks are inherent in ACO structure as established by federal law and regulations. Some possible risks include the following.

[125] *See* MEDICARE PAYMENT ADVISORY COMM'N, REPORT TO CONGRESS: IMPROVING INCENTIVES IN THE MEDICARE PROGRAM 39–56 (2009), *available at http://www.medpac.gov/documents/reports/Jun09_EntireReport.pdf?sfvrsn=0* (developing an ACO model as a recommendation for reforming Medicare's healthcare delivery system).

[126] *See* Clayton Christensen, Jeffrey Flier, & Vineeta Vijayaraghavan, *The Coming Failure of "Accountable Care": The Affordable Care Act's Updated Versions of HMOs Are Based on Flawed Assumptions About Doctor and Patient Behavior*, WALL ST. J., Feb. 18, 2013, http://online.wsj.com/news/articles/SB10001424127887324880504578296902005944398.

[127] *See* Stephen H. Siegel, *The Law of Unintended Consequences: Will ACOs and Clinical Integration Increase Malpractice Liability?*, *available at* http://www.broadandcassel.com/articles/SHS_Liability.pdf.

[128] Ezekiel J. Emanuel, *Why Accountable Care Organizations Are Not 1990s Managed Care Redux*, 307 JAMA 2261 (2012).

i. *Solidification of the Standard of Care*

As ACOs and their providers adapt to the new demands mandated by federal law and deliver quality care at a lower cost, patients may be able to claim substandard care. ACOs are premised on evidence-based medicine. In establishing best practices, ACOs must create clinical guidelines, presumably using evidence-based guidelines that are being developed by various federal initiatives. Any guideline selection process risks a claim that the guideline chosen is inappropriate when applied to a particular patient. The use of evidence-based medicine criteria, reporting on quality and cost metrics, and documentation to show the coordination of care will likely create new duties for physicians and therefore for the ACO itself.

ii. *Patient Engagement*

The ACO model is built on a concept of patient engagement and "patient-centeredness."[129] ACOs must promote beneficiary engagement, since the ACA ties patient satisfaction to reimbursement, and must meet "patient-centeredness criteria."[130] This patient focus will facilitate patient buy-in and presumably reduce their inclination to sue for adverse events; it also sets high expectations for patient engagement that may be disappointed. It turns the traditional informed consent duty into a more elaborate engagement process.

iii. *Cost Control*

Cost-containment goals and incentive-based payments present a theoretical liability exposure. An ACA provision calling for value-based compensation that pays doctors based on positive outcomes rather than patient volume for Medicare and Medicaid patients is set to go into full effect in 2015.[131] Value-based compensation seeks to balance high-value care and lower cost. Meaningful quality measures must be developed to ensure the use of evidence-based quality measures. Reducing or eliminating some diagnostic tests, for example, will risk a missed diagnosis on occasion. Such a missed diagnosis of a disease, which delays treatment, is the foundation of a "loss of a chance" claim for patient harms suffered. The defense of cost reduction may be a hard sell to juries.[132] Incentive-based compensation may risk resurrecting the old HMO liability arguments of undertreatment leading to patient injury.[133] Incentive-based arguments were, however, rarely if ever successful in suits brought against MCOs, as the courts understand the balance that providers had to strike between cost-containment and quality of care.[134]

[129] Michael L. Millenson, Building Patient-Centeredness in the Real World: The Engaged Patient and the Accountable Care Organization, http://www.nationalpartnership.org/research-library/health-care/building-patient-centeredness-in-the-real-world.pdf.

[130] Patient Protection and Affordable Care Act § 3022, 2 U.S.C. § 1899(b)(2)(H).

[131] Christine Burke Worthen, *Legal Considerations in Negotiating ACO Contracts: The New World of Risk Assumption, Enterprise Data Analytics, and Population Health Management*, http://www.broadandcassel.com/articles/Worthen_AHLAJune2014.pdf.

[132] Benjamin Harvey & Glenn Cohen, *The Looming Threat of Liability for Accountable Care Organizations and What to Do About It*, 310 JAMA 141 (2013).

[133] *Id.*

[134] *See* Furrow et al., Health Law, at § 4–22c.

iv. *Electronic Health Records*

Electronic health records (EHRs) provide a clear record of ACO plan performance, both its failures and successes. They also provide a record of whether care was evidence-based and of document compliance. From a lawyer's perspective, standard of care evidence is critical to any malpractice case, and the EHRs may be a gold mine of information. They also offer a lawyer the possibility of Health Insurance Portability and Accountability Act (HIPAA) privacy or security violations.

v. *Nonphysician Health Professional Liability*

The expanded role of nurses and physician assistants as part of ACO teams will lead to increased liability risks for those providers and for the ACO as the "employer" of these teams. Coordination of care in an ACO requires that all providers master new skills in moving patients around the network and sharing information across providers.[135] Vicarious liability principles apply for provider errors so long as they are within the scope of employment. An ACO, particularly a hospital-based one, will be liable for the acts of its nurses and physician assistants, since they are likely to be treated as employees and not independent contractors.

vi. *Corporate Structure*

An ACO may be found negligent for "failure to uphold the proper standard of care owed its patient."[136] Corporate negligence principles logically apply to integrated organizations that manage care, whether a patient medical home, an ACO, or some other delivery form that the ACA creates. The courts are willing to look beyond the hospital form in deciding whether a healthcare entity might be liable for corporate negligence,[137] looking at the entity's scope of responsibility for "for arranging and coordinating the total health care of its patients" and whether it takes an "an active role in patients' care."

Institutional liability extends beyond hospitals. A group practice has been held to corporate negligence standards for their lack of a formal on-call backup system in the case of a patient who developed erectile dysfunction after receiving heparin for his postsurgery deep vein thrombosis and had to wait at least twelve hours for treatment for heparin-induced priapism on a holiday weekend.[138] Nursing homes likewise have been included as institutions subject to corporate negligence.[139]

[135] *See generally* Marsh & McLennan Companies, *A New Risk Management Frontier: Accountable Care Organizations* (Oct. 2012).

[136] Thompson v. Nason Hospital, 527 Pa. 330, 591 A.2d 703, 708 (Pa. 1991).

[137] Gianquitti v. Atwood Medical Associates, Ltd., 973 A.2d 580 (R.I. 2009).

[138] Gianquitti v. Atwood Medical Associates, Ltd., 973 A.2d 580 (R.I. 2009).

[139] Scampone v. Highland Park Care Center, LLC, 618 Pa. 363, 57 A.3d 582 (2012).

IV Conclusion

Common law tort liability has been improved by several evidentiary and doctrinal changes. Experts are increasingly relying on better quality practice guidelines, which narrows uncertainly for both plaintiffs and defendants in predicting litigation outcomes. Consent doctrine is slowly evolving toward a model of patient engagement and full disclosures. Hospitals are facing expanded liability as they become large multisystem entities run like any corporate enterprise or move into accountable care organizations or other new pay-for-performance models pushed by the ACA. And new healthcare entities are proliferating in response to funding initiatives and market pressures, creating new organizations subject to corporate negligence analysis.

Physicians will rely increasingly on practice guidelines in their treatments; as evidence-based guidelines displace flawed specialty guidelines, settlements can be quicker as uncertainty is reduced. It may be that improved evidence-based standards of care will be as powerful as tort reform in reducing the need for jury trials, leaving it to insurers and plaintiff lawyers to settle cases in the bright light of sharper definitions of good medical practices.

Assume that within a few years ACOs and medical homes are successfully formed and performance-based payment systems proliferate. These reforms do several things at once: they move physicians from solo or small group practice into a partnership position in a group model or a salaried employee position in a hospital; and they shift power, and therefore liability risk, toward enterprises that can buy and coordinate the technologies—from EHRs to case management strategies—to meet the demands of the federal government.

The liability result is clear. First, institutional providers will become liable for patient injury, as well as the physicians causing patient injury directly, because agency law will carry liability upstream from agent to principal. Physicians will be much more integrated into the system, whether or not they are salaried, and any argument of independent contractor status will evaporate.

Second, even if ACOs and other entities operate without a hospital as part of the organization, they have become institutional healthcare providers, subject to liability just as a hospital or managed care organization is, on both vicarious liability and direct negligence principles.[140]

The future of medical malpractice litigation is not bright, in spite of modest expansions of doctrine. Tort reform has done its damage to medical liability litigation.[141] Limits on damages will continue to make litigation unattractive for plaintiff lawyers. However, an enterprise liability model, driven by corporate negligence doctrine, may make a new category of

[140] Laura D. Hermer, *Aligning Incentives in Accountable Care Organizations: The Role of Medical Malpractice Reform*, 17 J. Health Care L. & Pol'y 271 (2014) (arguing for a move to pure enterprise liability for ACOs to produce a consistent liability environment for their operation).

[141] David A. Hyman & Charles Silver, *Double, Double, Toil and Trouble: Justice-Talk and the Future of Medical Malpractice Litigation*, 63 DePaul L. Rev. 547 (2014).

litigation profitable. Provider-adopted settlement models will at least offer patients and their lawyers some prospect of recovery in cases that otherwise might not have been discovered. The burgeoning of practice guidelines will bring two changes: they will reduce unnecessary medical practices, and they will make a malpractice case easier to prove if trustworthy guidelines are not followed by physicians. Patient safety is likely to be improved in response to both changes.

CHAPTER 20

DRUG PRODUCT LIABILITY AT THE CROSSROADS

PETER GROSSI AND KERI ARNOLD

Over the past twenty years, prescription drugs have joined asbestos and tobacco as the prime targets of American tort plaintiffs. Indeed, it has been said more product liability lawsuits are filed against pharmaceutical manufacturers than against all other industries combined.

It was not always so. For many years, the law of drug product liability was limited to a few quaint cases where a druggist reached for the wrong bottle or a manufacturer adulterated its product with some unintended substance. But, until the 1960s, the law of product liability had not much focused on the *inevitable* harm that even *properly prepared* pharmaceuticals visit on a few patients through unavoidable "side effects," even as they benefit many others.

That changed in 1965 when the authors of the Restatement (Second) of Torts were forced to consider how, if at all, their new regime of "strict liability" for consumer products should be applied to drugs. Reflecting on a few prior cases, and then extending them, the Second Restatement set forth two doctrines which have since provided some protection to pharmaceutical manufacturers from liability typically found with more pedestrian products.

First, the Restatement authors decided that the strict liability regime they espoused for virtually all other products, for the most part, should not apply to pharmaceuticals in recognition of the balance federal regulators must strike between their unavoidable risks and life-saving benefits.

Second, the Restatement authors endorsed the evolving rule that, since prescription drugs are available only from physicians, the further balance made by such "learned intermediaries" of the benefits and risks of a drug to each individual patient breaks the chain of causation necessary for tort liability so long as appropriate information is given to the physician.

For forty years after the Second Restatement was issued, those two doctrines, founded on judicial deference to experts at the Food and Drug Administration (FDA) and the medical profession generally remained strong. Over the last fifteen or so years, however, dissatisfaction with the rigor of FDA review, as well as concerns about how prescription decisions are now made, have led commentators and courts alike to reconsider both rules. As discussed below, a number of courts, often expressly reflecting that growing distrust of the FDA, have either rejected outright, or carved significant exceptions to, the earlier deferential theories preempting claims against FDA-approved labels; accepting uncritically prescriber decisions on behalf of individual patients; and excusing "off-label" uses the FDA tacitly permits. The law of drug product liability is thus at a crossroads, with serious doubt as to how those balances between the inherent risks and presumed benefits of drugs will be struck in the future.

I Liability for Prescription Drugs under the Regulatory Deference Model

Until the 1960s, the few cases that had dealt with product liability for prescription drugs had treated them like any other product under a traditional "negligence" standard. That made sense when those products were rudimentary chemicals that had long been used without any rigorous review by regulators. The relatively few cases held that a druggist or manufacturer could be liable if they "unreasonably" sold a drug that was adulterated in some fashion, or if they failed to provide adequate warnings about some clearly improper use. But the *unavoidable* risks of *properly prepared* drugs were generally ignored, since the sale of such products was not "unreasonable" and hence not "negligent."

In the early 1960s, however, two events prompted a more nuanced balance of the inherent risks and benefits of properly prepared drugs. First, in reaction to the tragedy of birth defects caused by the sedative thalidomide, the U.S. Congress substantially broadened the federal Food, Drug, and Cosmetic Act (FD&C Act) to give the FDA much greater authority over the preapproval testing and risk-benefit evaluation of pharmaceuticals. For the first time the FDA was squarely charged with determining—prior to the sale of any drug and on a continuing basis thereafter—whether its benefits exceeded its risks for the general population.[1]

Second, the drafters of the Second Restatement made a dramatic shift in the general law of product liability, applying it "strictly" to consumer products without any demonstration of "negligence." As set forth in Section 402A, such liability is imposed on anyone who sells a product that harms a consumer even though "the seller has exercised all possible care in the preparation and sale of his product."[2]

As part of that change in centuries-old tort law, the Restatement drafters, most notably Dean Prosser, debated the application of such a strict liability regime to "unavoidably unsafe" products, which "in the present state of human knowledge are quite incapable of being made safe for their intended and ordinary use." The Restatement authors recognized that "[t]hese are especially common in the field of drugs."[3]

In their now-famous Comment k, the Restatement drafters gave one example of such an "unavoidably unsafe" drug,

> [t]he Pasteur treatment of rabies, which not uncommonly leads to very serious and damaging consequences when it is injected. Since the disease itself invariably leads to a dreadful death, both the marketing and use of the vaccine are fully justified, notwithstanding the unavoidable high degree of risk which they involve.[4]

[1] For a detailed description of the factors balanced by the FDA and the extent of its New Drug Approval process, *see* Lewis Grossman's article in this volume.

[2] Restatement (Second) of Torts § 402A(2).

[3] Section 402A, Comment k.

[4] *Id.*

This example suggested to some that the Restatement authors did not intend to immunize *every* prescription pharmaceutical, most notably those that are far less beneficial than a life-saving vaccine. Over time a split developed, with some courts requiring a case-by-case assessment of the benefits of a given drug before according it Comment k protection, while others, in states with major pharmaceutical firms, and hence the bulk of drug product cases (California, Florida, New York, North Carolina, Pennsylvania), adopted a more universal approach. The latter group of courts deferred to the expertise of the FDA in approving drugs, with the requisite finding that the product's benefits (be they vaccinations against "dreadful diseases" or treatments for erectile dysfunction) sufficiently outweigh its risks (be they trivial or deadly).[5] In its seminal *Brown* decision, the California Supreme Court argued such deference to FDA regulation was essential:

> Perhaps a drug might be made safer if it was withheld from the market until scientific skill and knowledge advanced to the point at which additional dangerous side effects would be revealed. But in most cases such a delay in marketing new drugs—added to the delay required to obtain approval for release of the product from the Food and Drug Administration—would not serve the public welfare. Public policy favors the development and marketing of beneficial new drugs, even though some risks, perhaps serious ones, might accompany their introduction because drugs save lives and reduce pain and suffering.[6]

A few years later, another court made that deference even more emphatic. In *Grundberg v. Upjohn*, the Utah Supreme Court described the FDA approval process in detail, stressing that it "can require years of testing and review" and consist of "thousands of pages of material describing studies of the drug in several hundred to several thousand patients," which are then reviewed by a wide range of medical professionals, before the drug can be approved.[7] The court added that although such "elaborate pre-approval screening" did not guarantee adverse reactions might not arise after a drug was introduced to the market, the FDA also conducts "extensive post-market surveillance" in which manufacturers are required to submit reports of all adverse reactions whether or not anyone believes they were drug related.[8] The court then drew the conclusion that pharmaceutical manufacturers urge in virtually every case:

> [T]his extensive regulatory scheme [is] capable of and appropriate for making the preliminary determination regarding whether a prescription drug benefits outweigh its risks. The structured follow-up program imposed by law ensures that drugs are not placed on the market without continued monitoring for adverse consequences that would render the FDA's initial risk/benefit analysis invalid. Allowing individual courts and/or juries to continually reevaluate a drug's risks and benefits ignores the processes of this regulatory body. . . .[9]

Other courts similarly extolled the virtues of the FDA regulatory process in concluding that Comment k protection from strict liability should be universal. To be sure, Comment

[5] *See, e.g.*, Buckner v. Allergan Pharm., 400 So. 2d 820 (Fla. App.), *review denied*, 407 So. 2d 1102 (Fla. 1981); Wolfgruber v. Upjohn, 423 N.Y.S.2d 95 (App. Div. 1979), *aff'd*, 52 N.Y.2d 768 (1980); Basiste v. Am. Home Prods., 231 S.E. 2d 269 (N.C. App.), *review denied*, 292 N.C. 466 (1977); Hahn v. Richter, 673 A.2d 888 (Pa. 1996).

[6] Brown v. Superior Court, 751 P.2d 470, 479 (1988). [7] 813 P.2d 89 (Utah 1991).

[8] *Id.* at 96. [9] *Id.* at 97.

k still required that a drug must be "properly labeled and properly marketed." And that, in turn, allowed some plaintiffs to succeed on "failure-to-warn" claims. But legislatures in some of the states with significant pharmaceutical industries (Michigan, New Jersey, Texas) then declared that drug products, and specifically their warning labels approved by the FDA, are at least presumed to be "reasonably safe" and "adequate."[10]

By 2005, some defendant manufacturers decided they should take the next "logical" step and argue that, since their products and their warning labels are subject to *continual* FDA review, *all* state "failure-to-warn" tort claims should be preempted by that federal regulatory process. As discussed below, however, by the time that proposition reached the U.S. Supreme Court, changes in the political environment made that ultimate extension of deference to the FDA one bridge too far.

II The Growing Distrust of the FDA Approval and Surveillance Process

In the three decades following the thalidomide tragedy, and the resulting expansion of the FDA approval process, drug withdrawals were few and far between. And those that did occur from the 1960s to the mid-1990s affected only relatively small numbers of patients.

Commencing in the late 1990s, however, the pattern of withdrawals and, with them, confidence in the FDA, changed dramatically. From 1997 to 2004, there were no fewer than sixteen major drug withdrawals, with at least seven affecting hundreds of thousands, in some cases millions, of patients. All told, the seven larger withdrawals impacted more than 30 million Americans who had taken drugs that, for the most part, were not nearly as "life-saving" as Dean Prosser's rabies vaccine. (1997—Redux and Pondimin (diet medications); 1998—Posicor (antihypertensive); 1998—Duract (pain reliever); 2000—Rezulin (diabetes treatment); 2000—Propulsid ("heartburn" treatment); 2001—Baycol (diabetes treatment); 2004—Vioxx (pain reliever)).

These highly publicized withdrawals of drugs, which in some cases had been approved by the FDA only a year or two before, did not go unnoticed. The Vioxx withdrawal became especially political. In 2004, David Graham, an FDA epidemiologist, testified before Congress that when he and his colleagues concluded that the pain reliever increased the risk of heart attacks and sudden death and should no longer be prescribed to anyone, he was muzzled by his superiors at the agency. According to Dr. Graham, the risk was the equivalent of "2–4 jumbo jet liners . . . dropping from the sky each day, and no one else at FDA was concerned."[11]

The following year another Senate committee similarly heard critics allege that the FDA approval process depended on too few tests, involving too few patients, for too short a period to detect significant side effects; the FDA was the "captive" of the industry, in part because the Prescription Drug User Fee Act enacted in the mid-1990s allowed the manufacturers to

[10] *See, e.g.*, Fla. Stat. § 768.1256; Mich. C.L. § 600.2946(5); N.J. Stat. Ann. 2A:58C-4; Tex. Code, Civil Practice & Remedies § 82.007(a).

[11] Testimony of David Graham Before the Senate Committee on Finance (Nov. 18, 2004), at 3.

fund the process by which the FDA *approves* drugs for market, but not the subsequent effort to *monitor* their side effects; the FDA's reliance on "Phase IV" testing, conducted only after a drug was already on the market, was insufficient in many respects; and the FDA had no power to compel manufacturers to change labels to warn of new, often more serious, side effects after the drugs were initially approved.[12]

A few months later, Congress's Government Accountability Office (GAO) issued an equally scathing report, concluding that the FDA "lack[ed] a clear and effective process for making decisions about, and providing management oversight of, postmarket drug safety issues."[13] The GAO found that, when the agency relied on the drug sponsors themselves to conduct postmarketing studies, less than a quarter were ever completed.[14]

In 2006, the Institute of Medicine (IOM) joined the chorus. In a lengthy report, the IOM again criticized the FDA for having too few tools to address safety issues; for relying too heavily on drug industry funding skewed toward approval rather than safety; and for promising Phase IV studies which the industry too often failed to complete.[15] The IOM then went a step further and criticized the regulatory framework of the FDA itself. According to the IOM, the approval process created in 1962 was "aging and inadequate" to meet 21st-century needs.[16]

Last, but not least, in 2007 a committee of FDA staff members agreed that the agency's authority was too limited and its task too great. The FDA committee again declared that the agency was underfunded, poorly organized, and lacked sufficient regulatory authority—adding that, even when recommendations for changes were made, they were seldom implemented.[17]

In short, in the ten years between 1997 and 2007 there was a growing perception among Congress, industry critics, medical authorities, and, in some quarters, the FDA itself that the agency was no longer protecting American patients. That perception set the stage for a very different, decidedly nondeferential approach to drug product liability, with a number of courts, as Mr. Dooley observed, following the political returns.

III The Preemption Decisions

Even as the perception was growing among industry critics, Congress, and some FDA staff that the agency was not sufficiently controlling the approval and labeling of prescription drugs, the industry's defenders in product liability lawsuits began to argue that FDA

[12] S. Hrg. 109-67, Before the Senate Committee on Health, Education, Labor and Pensions, *FDA's Drug Approval Process* (Mar. 1, 2005).

[13] GAO Report 06-402, *Drug Safety: Improvement Needed in FDA's Postmarket Decision-Making and Oversight Process* (Mar. 2006), at 5.

[14] *Id.* at 28.

[15] Institute of Medicine, The Future of Drug Safety 153–157 (Sept. 2006).

[16] *Id.* at 153.

[17] Report of the Subcommittee on Science and Technology, FDA Science and Mission at Risk (Nov. 2007).

regulation was sufficiently "comprehensive" to preempt state tort actions *entirely* as a matter of federal law. And initially it appeared that *totally* deferential theory might succeed.

In 2001, the Supreme Court rejected a state tort claim that allegedly misleading statements made directly to the FDA, in seeking its approval of a medical device, could constitute a "fraud on the FDA" entitling the device's users to civil damages. In *Buckman Co. v. Plaintiffs' Legal Committee*, the Court deferred to the FDA's plenary authority to police its own proceedings and held that only the agency itself could redress such false statements.[18] Private "attorneys generals" seeking civil tort damages need not apply. Although *Buckman* concerned the somewhat different context of medical devices, and did not directly address more traditional failure-to-warn claims, some commentators and defense counsel began to speculate that those types of claims would be the next to fall to federal preemption.

Five years later, in 2006, the regulatory officials at the FDA—a group somewhat apart from the staff scientists who were simultaneously complaining about a lack of resources—added fuel to the fire by announcing, in a preamble to new labeling regulations, that, at some point, FDA review of drug labels should preempt any second-guessing by state tort juries. According to the FDA attorneys, federal preemption should at least bar state tort "claims that [a drug manufacturer] breached an obligation to warn by failing to include a statement in labeling or in advertising, the substance of which had been proposed to FDA for inclusion in labeling, if the statement was not required by FDA at the time plaintiffs claim [the manufacturer] had an obligation to warn."[19] The FDA lawyers went so far as to argue that state failure-to-warn claims "threaten FDA's statutorily prescribed role as the expert Federal agency responsible for evaluating and regulating drugs."[20]

Emboldened by such pronouncements, some drug companies began to challenge failure-to-warn claims on preemption grounds. And, initially, they succeeded.

In *Colacicco v. Apotex*, manufacturers of similarly labeled antidepressants convinced a divided panel of the Third Circuit—a court especially important in drug product liability as it has jurisdiction over the many pharmaceutical firms headquartered in New Jersey and Pennsylvania—that tort claims alleging the manufacturers had failed to warn sufficiently of the risk of suicide associated with the drugs were preempted because the FDA had decided such a warning was not warranted.[21] In reaching that conclusion, the Third Circuit showed extreme deference to the FDA, both in terms of its labeling process (which the court stressed was designed to balance the benefits and risks of a drug) and the statements the agency lawyers had made about the preemptive effect of such agency review.[22]

In one sense, *Colacicco* was a relatively "easy case" because there the FDA had only recently rejected precisely the warning the state tort plaintiffs contended was warranted. But the foundation of the decision—judicial deference to the expertise of the FDA—was thought by many to be far broader.

That view, however, was short-lived. Only a year later, the Supreme Court held that the preemption doctrine was nowhere near as protective as industry lawyers had argued. In *Wyeth v. Levine*, the Court held that even a fairly extensive history of FDA review of a label would not immunize a drug from state tort claims.[23]

[18] 531 U.S. 341 (2001). [19] 71 Fed. Reg. 3922, 3936 (Jan. 24, 2006). [20] *Id.* at 3935.
[21] 521 F.3d 253 (3d Cir. 2008). [22] *Id.* at 268–269, 274. [23] 555 U.S. 555 (2009).

In *Levine*, a physician's assistant had administered a migraine drug through what she intended to be an intravenous line. Tragically, the drug instead infiltrated the patient's artery, with the result that her arm became gangrenous and had to be amputated. Even more tragically, that was not an unprecedented accident—the label already in effect for the drug expressly warned, six times, of the grave risk of such unintended arterial administration. Indeed, the label, which had been repeatedly reviewed and approved by the FDA, recommended a simple procedure that would have guaranteed the drug could not infiltrate an artery. The only problem, according to the state tort plaintiff, was that those warnings and recommendation were not included, for a seventh time, in the "contraindications" section of the label—a section which is limited by FDA regulation to such clear misuses of a product that they would *never* be appropriate under *any* circumstance. Yet, as the dissenting justices noted, there was medical literature suggesting that such a "contraindication" was not appropriate as there might be circumstances where the drug might be administrated, by a skilled physician, without that simple (but slower) safeguard.[24]

That history of FDA review and approval, however, did not save the manufacturer from the state failure-to-warn claim. The trial court rejected the same preemption theory that had been accepted in *Colacicco* and allowed the state tort plaintiff to urge the lay jury to ignore the FDA's approval of the label's warnings. As plaintiff's counsel summed up that decidedly nondeferential approach in his closing to the jury, "Thank God we don't rely on the FDA . . . to make the safety decision. You will make the decision."[25] The jury accepted that task, found the label inadequate, and awarded substantial damages.

When the case arrived at the Supreme Court, the majority agreed that even fairly detailed FDA review and approval is not sufficient to establish federal preemption unless it is clear that the FDA would have *prohibited* a manufacturer from making the type of label change the state tort plaintiff contends was necessary. According to the *Levine* majority, only "clear evidence" that it was "impossible" for a manufacturer to make such a change could justify preemption.[26]

Having set forth such a "demanding" standard, the majority then hinged its anti-preemption decision on its view that a pharmaceutical manufacturer could always use another FDA regulation to issue a "Change Being Effected" modification of its label without *prior* FDA approval. The majority ignored the fact that the FDA regulation also provides that, after such change is submitted to the agency, it may then "order the manufacturer to cease distribution" of the drug if it disagrees with the change.[27] According to the *Levine* majority, the mere *possibility* of such a unilateral "Change Being Effective" was sufficient to demonstrate that it was not "impossible" for a manufacturer to have made the type of change a state tort plaintiff might subsequently claim was appropriate.[28] And the "adequacy" of warnings and other label provisions, expressly approved by the FDA, thus remained a matter for lay jurors to second-guess in tort cases.

The *Levine* majority likewise gave short shrift to the pro-preemption views of the FDA lawyers in their labeling preamble. Citing various older regulatory pronouncements, the majority held that the agency's "new" views on the force of its label decisions were entitled to no deference at all.[29]

[24] 555 U.S. at 614–618. [25] *Id.* at 606 (Alito, J., dissenting). [26] *Id.* at 571.
[27] 21 C.F.R. § 314.70(c)(7). [28] 555 U.S. at 568–573. [29] *Id.* at 575–79.

As part of their justification for this nondeferential approach, the majority endorsed the view that the FDA was simply not up to the task of protecting the public. Like the earlier congressional critics, the majority lamented that "FDA has limited resources to monitor the 11,000 drugs on the market," adding that FDA advisers had "conclusively" found that "the budget and staff of the Food and Drug Administration are inadequate to permit the discharge of its existing responsibilities for the protection of the American public."[30] The majority then quoted the similar conclusions from the IOM and FDA staff reports discussed in Section II above.[31]

It was left to the three dissenting Justices to reprise the deferential approach so popular only a few years before. Justice Alito reviewed the FDA's consideration of the label at issue, including the various express warnings and recommendations concerning the proper administration of the drug. In his view, the imposition of state tort liability in such circumstances was a clear threat to the agency's ability to balance the risks and benefits of drugs in warning labels:

> To be sure, state tort suits can peacefully co-exist with the FDA's labeling regime, and they have done so for decades. But this case is far from peaceful coexistence. The FDA told [the manufacturer] that [the drug] label renders its use "safe". But the state of Vermont, through its tort law, said: "Not so."[32]

But, despite the dissent's passion, *Levine* was now the law of the land; and a few weeks later, the Supreme Court vacated the Third Circuit's preemption ruling in *Colacicco*. Thus, even where the FDA has recently rejected precisely the label change proposed by a state tort plaintiff, that review will not preclude a state tort jury from rendering a contrary verdict.

Levine has also resulted in a serious disparity between the labeling obligations, and hence potential tort liability, of the "pioneer" ("brand name") company which first develops a drug and the "generic" firms which subsequently market the same drug with no clinical research or monitoring of its effects. As noted, the *Levine* majority rested its decision on the "possibility" that the pioneer company can unilaterally change a label, without prior FDA approval, through a "Change Being Effective." But what of the generic companies who, by federal statute and current FDA regulations, are required to copy the original drug label without deviation?

Two years after *Levine*, a divided Supreme Court considered that issue in *PLIVA v. Mensing* and this time upheld the preemption defense of a generic manufacturer on the grounds that it was required by federal law to copy the pioneer label in every respect.[33] The four dissenting justices (who had all been in the majority in *Levine*) continued to argue that the FDA was no better able to monitor generic than pioneer versions of the same drug. They further asserted that any distinction between the liability for such two identical products with identical labels "makes little sense," especially given that 75% of all prescriptions are today filled with generic versions.[34] Indeed, even the *Mensing* majority seemed troubled by the distinction they were drawing between the generic and pioneer labels on products which, by legal definition, are chemically equivalent and thus undeniably provide the same benefits and risks. According the majority, however, that was a problem for Congress, not the Court, to resolve.[35]

30 *Id.* at 579 n.11. 31 *Id.* 32 *Id.* at 628. 33 131 S.Ct. 2567 (2011).
34 *Id.* at 2583 (Sotomayer J., dissenting). 35 *Id.* at 2581–2582.

The FDA, however, has not waited for such congressional action. In November 2013, the agency proposed a change to its regulations that would put generic manufacturers under the same threat of state tort law as pioneer firms, by making it clear that they too are entitled, indeed obligated, to change their labels *independently* of the pioneer label as soon as they become aware of any new risk.[36] In advancing that novel proposal, the FDA conceded "that there may be concerns about temporary differences in safety-related labeling for drugs that FDA has determined to be therapeutically equivalent, especially if multiple [generic manufacturers] submit . . . labeling changes that differ from each other and from the [brand name version]."[37] But the FDA never addressed those concerns. Rather, the agency justified its proposed rule solely on the current dichotomy between the state tort liability of pioneer and generic companies created by *Levine* and *Mensing*, acknowledging that it was proposing the change "to create parity" between the two types of manufacturers.[38]

The proposed rule is currently working its way through the FDA administrative process; it has been the subject of significant criticism; and its future is uncertain. But, however the matter is ultimately resolved, there will be anomalies: On the one hand, if the proposed rule is rejected, and the current Supreme Court case law is maintained, identical drug products will be labeled the same yet impose radically different degrees of liability on their brand name and generic manufacturers. On the other hand, if the FDA's "parity" proposal is issued as a final regulation, generic firms—which generally do not have safety departments capable of monitoring drugs (the assumption being that the pioneer company will maintain such vigilance)—could be forced to make precipitous changes in their labels solely to avoid the wrath of state tort juries, in a manner that will confuse medical practitioners.[39]

This much is clear: The prior presumption that courts will defer to the expertise of the FDA in formulating and ultimately endorsing drug warning labels, even on the basis of substantial medical evidence, has been eroded to the point where little of that deference is left. Henceforth, such "balances" will generally be made by state tort juries.[40]

[36] 78 Fed. Reg. 67985, 67988-89 (Nov. 13, 2013).

[37] *Id.* at 67989.

[38] *Id.* at 67988–67989.

[39] A few courts have tried to fill the current gap in liability for generic drugs by ruling that where, as is often the case, a prescriber relies on either the original pioneer label (or the generic verbatim copy), the *pioneer* company may be liable to a patient treated with the *generic* version for any deficiencies in the common label, *even though the pioneer company did not make the sale. See* Wyeth v. Weeks, 2014 WL 4055813 (Ala. Sup. Ct. Aug. 15, 2014); Conte v. Wyeth, 85 Cal. Rptr. 3d 299 (Cal. Ct. App. 2008); Kellogg v. Wyeth, 762 F. Supp. 2d 694 (D.Vt. 2010).

The majority of courts, however, have rejected such indirect liability, holding that the pioneer company owes no "duty" to patients who purchased (or were forced by their insurance companies to purchase) the cheaper generic. *See* Foster v. Am. Home Prods., 29 F.3d 165 (4th Cir. 1994) (pre-*Mensing*, applying Virginia law); Smith v. Wyeth, 657 F.3d 420 (6th Cir. 2011) (Kentucky law); Demahy v. Schwarz Pharma, 702 F.3d 177 (5th Cir. 2012), *cert denied*, 134 S. Ct. 57 (2013) (Louisiana Law); Schrock v. Wyeth, 727 F.3d 1273 (10th Cir. 2013) (Oklahoma law); Guarino v. Wyeth, 719 F.3d 1245 (11th Cir. 2013) (Florida law).

Since these conflicting decisions turn on differences in *state* product liability law—and California itself constitutes a large "exception" in any national market policy—this split will likely continue, immune to any Supreme Court reconciliation.

[40] Preemption doctrine concerning medical devices is likewise muddled. In 1976 Congress added a provision to the Medical Device Amendments which ostensibly preempts state safety requirements "different from, or in addition to" any requirement under federal law. 21 U.S.C. § 360k(a). But in 1996, the Supreme Court ruled that provision did not preempt a state tort action alleging defects in the electrical

IV The Direct Challenge to FDA Approval Presented by Design-Defect Claims

The same changing perception about the FDA's competence has also recently prompted one important state supreme court to take another step long debated, but rarely endorsed, and permit state tort plaintiffs to second-guess the FDA's very decision to approve a new drug. Such "design-defect" claims effectively relegate drugs approved by the FDA to the level of consumer products not approved by anyone; and they are clearly contrary to the deference shown to FDA approval in the Second Restatement. That is quite a change. Although, as noted above, some courts have allowed claims of negligent *labeling* to go forward, that is a far cry from a claim that the drug product is "defective" *per se*—like a lawn mower without protective toeguards or an automobile without passenger restraints—and hence subject to strict liability.

The novelty of such a cause of action can be appreciated in the rude reception given to earlier proposals to allow tort juries to second-guess FDA drug approvals under somewhat similar theories. In 1996, shortly before the wave of anti-FDA critiques began, the authors of the Third Restatement tried to deal with that issue, formulating a curious test that ultimately satisfied no one. In their Section 6(c), the Restatement authors appeared to create a chink in Comment k protection by suggesting that an FDA-approved drug might not be "reasonably safe," and hence could be subjected to strict liability, as a result of a "defective design," *if* a plaintiff could establish that the "foreseeable risks of harm posed by the drug are sufficiently great in relation to its foreseeable therapeutic benefits that reasonable health-care providers, knowing of such foreseeable risks and therapeutic benefits, would not prescribe the drug for *any* class of patients."[41] The Restatement authors cautioned that this language was intended to create a "very demanding objective standard . . . to be imposed only in unusual circumstances," noting further that the test still recognized "the unique characteristics of prescription drugs."[42]

This attempt in the Third Restatement to force the square peg of FDA-approved drugs into the round hole of design-defect law only promoted more disputes. As general criticism of the FDA grew, some commentators argued for an even broader basis to subject drugs to classic

leads to a pacemaker, which, like most more common devices, was not reviewed and approved by the FDA through its more rigorous Section 360 process, but rather was merely permitted by Section 501(k), which allows devices "substantially equivalent" to those already on the market. In *Medtronic v. Lohr*, 518 U.S. 470, 492–502 (1996), the Court reasoned that, in such "substantially equivalent" cases, there was no "federal requirement" arising from specific FDA approval to conflict with a state negligence standard.

Twelve years later, the Supreme Court focused on the less common (but arguably more important) situation where a device had been reviewed and approved under the more demanding Section 360 process. In *Riegel v. Medtronic*, 552 U.S. 312, 321–323 (2008), the Court enforced the congressional provision, ruling that the action there, based on one particular state negligence standard, was preempted. But the Court expressly left the door open to state tort actions predicated on artful pleading of negligence standards that "parallel" some federal requirement. *Id.* at 330. Ever since, the lower courts have been grappling with what that means. *See, e.g.*, Pudhel v. Endologix, 2009 WL 2045559 (E.D.Cal. July 9, 2009).

[41] Restatement (Third) of Torts, Section 6(c) (emphasis added).

[42] *Id.* Comment f (emphasis added).

design-defect lawsuits.[43] That, in turn, led the Restatement reporters (acting in a "retired" capacity) to remind everyone that "drug designs are different" from more pedestrian products. A bit apologetically, they explained they never intended Section 6(c) to authorize a traditional design-defect claim where a jury would have free rein to assess the "benefits" and "risks" of a drug. According to the reporters, Section 6(c) would permit such a claim only where a jury reached the rather remarkable conclusion that the FDA had made a "mistake" by "approving worthless drugs that no competent [physician] would prescribe for any class of patients."[44]

Initially, this academic debate had little effect on design-defect claims as to FDA-approved drugs. Indeed, Section 6(c) was almost universally ignored or rejected. Most courts continued to follow the deferential policy in Comment k and hold that a drug approved by the FDA simply could not be viewed as "defective" *per se*.

But that did not discourage tort plaintiffs from including design-defect claims in their complaints. And by 2013 one of them worked its way to the U.S. Supreme Court. In *Mutual Pharmaceutical v. Bartlett*, a patient who had been "horrifically" disfigured by a rare but recognized reaction to a prescription painkiller sued under the product liability law of New Hampshire, alleging both failure-to-warn and design-defect claims. When the prescribing doctor testified he had not relied on the allegedly deficient label, the plaintiff abandoned her failure-to-warn theory and focused instead on her design-defect claim. The trial court permitted that claim to go to the jury under the state's general design-defect law, which required the jurors to consider three factors: "the usefulness and desirability of the product to the public as a whole, whether the risk or danger could have been reduced without significantly affecting either the product's effectiveness or manufacturing cost, and the presence and efficacy of a warning to avoid an unreasonable risk of harm from hidden dangers or from foreseeable risks."[45] The jury rendered a large verdict, and the court of appeals, while recognizing the novelty of the design-defect claim, punted the issue to the U.S. Supreme Court.[46]

The Supreme Court ruled that the design-defect claim was preempted by federal law, but only because the particular product at issue was a generic copy of a brand name drug. Given their decision two years before in *Mensing*, the Supreme Court held that the defendant generic manufacturer could not have changed the "design" of the drug—either chemically (and hence its pharmacological benefits and risks) or its warning label—without prior FDA approval.[47]

But even then the *Bartlett* majority dropped a footnote that suggests it was not entirely shutting the door on design-defect drug claims. According to the majority, the Court was not addressing "state design-defect claims that parallel the federal misbranding statute" which "requires a manufacturer to pull even an FDA-approved drug from the market when it is 'dangerous to health,' even if 'used in the dosage or manner, or with the frequency or duration prescribed, recommended, or suggested in the labeling.'"[48] The *Bartlett* majority added that the FDA appears to agree a drug is so misbranded "when liability is based on new and scientifically significant information that was not before the FDA."[49]

[43] *See, e.g.*, G. Conk, *Is There a Design Defect in the Restatement (Third) of Torts?*, 109 YALE L. J. 1087 (2000).

[44] J. Henderson & A. Twerski, *Drug Designs Are Different*, 111 YALE L.J. 151, 162–163 (2001).

[45] Mutual Pharm. v. Bartlett, 133 S.Ct. 2466, 2475 (2013).

[46] 678 F.3d 30 (1st Cir. 2012).

[47] 133 S.Ct. at 2476–2480.

[48] *Id.* at 2477 n.4 (*quoting* 21 U.S.C. § 352(j)).

[49] *Id.*

Bartlett thus arguably creates a narrow theory under which an enterprising plaintiff can argue that scientific developments, after FDA approval, produced a new imbalance of risks over benefits which mandates withdrawal. Such an exception, of course, presumes the FDA has not already learned of that "new and scientifically significant information" and yet decided to leave the drug on the market. And it thus remains to be seen whether that theory will gain any real traction in typical drug liability cases.

More recently, however, one important state supreme court, relying on criticisms of the FDA and its approval process, has endorsed an even more extreme approach. In *Lance v. Wyeth*, the Supreme Court of Pennsylvania (a state home to more pharmaceutical manufacturers and drug product liability cases than any other) aggressively embraced design-defect theory in the prescription drug context.[50]

Lance concerned two diet drugs that had been withdrawn from the market in 1997 following the discovery of a previously unreported side effect. As in *Bartlett*, the prescriber testified he would not have changed his decision to prescribe the drugs had he known of that side effect, and the plaintiff therefore shifted to a design-defect claim, arguing that the drugs never should have been approved *at all*. The defendant manufacturer responded with a motion to dismiss, which thus presented the unvarnished legal question of whether it is *ever* appropriate to allow a lay jury to second-guess the FDA on its approval of a drug (or its daily "decision" to allow the drug to remain on the market).

Initially, both the state trial and intermediate appellate courts agreed with the manufacturer, rejecting the design-defect claim.[51] But when the question arrived at the state supreme court, it held that such a claim was at least legally permissible.

In reaching that result, the state supreme court, again citing the more recent criticisms of the FDA, shifted the burden to the manufacturer to establish (in some manner never specified by the court) that the FDA's approval of the drug at issue had been justified:

> We have respect for the FDA and its on-going efforts to protect the health of the citizenry. As with other regulatory bodies, however, this is reflected in the practice of Pennsylvania courts permitting defendants to adduce evidence of compliance with governmental regulation in their efforts to demonstrate due care. [The defendant manufacturer in *Lance*] offers little to address the limitations of the federal regulatory process observed by the United States Supreme Court [in *Levine*] or the wealth of commentary discussing the downsides of according absolute deference to a regulatory body. . . . [A]s the proponent of a contraction of existing tort law [the manufacturer] has failed to persuade us that federal regulatory involvement warrants a departure from Pennsylvania's system of civil redress. . . .[52]

The state supreme court then relied heavily on the criticisms of the FDA compiled in *Levine*, noting that there the U.S. Supreme Court had reminded everyone that *federal* law also imposes postmarketing duties on pharmaceutical manufacturers, including the obligation to "[e]nsure that [their] warning remain adequate as long as the drug is on the market."[53] From this the *Lance* court concluded that "a company with actual or constructive knowledge that its product is too dangerous to be used by anyone violates such duty during any period of time which it thereafter continues to market the commodity."[54]

[50] 85 A.3d 434 (Pa. 2014). [51] Lance v. Wyeth, 4 A.3d 160 (Pa. Super. Ct. 2010).
[52] 85 A.3d at 456–457. [53] *Id.* at 453 n.24. [54] *Id.*

The *Lance* court never explained how such a claim should be proved or rebutted. And more litigation is a certainty. But in Pennsylvania, at least, the law may thus have come full circle: Notwithstanding FDA approval, which requires an express finding by the agency that the benefits of a drug exceed its risks for *most* patients, once some new side effect is discovered, a state tort plaintiff may argue that, at some point, the manufacturer knew (or should have known) its product should be withdrawn from the market.

To be sure, the *Lance* court added that the specific case before it was perhaps somewhat easier than most because the drugs had been withdrawn following review by both the FDA and the manufacturer of the new side effect. But its ruling and rationale were applied to an individual who had taken the drugs *before* those reviews had been made. Indeed, the state supreme court seemed to ignore the fact that one of the drugs in question had been approved by the FDA only a year before the plaintiff had taken it. Aggressive plaintiffs thus may argue that *Lance* applies even where the FDA is cognizant of some particular problem and yet still believes the drug is appropriate for the market.

It remains to be seen whether *Lance* will influence other courts, including others equally important to the pharmaceutical industry, to entertain such design-defect claims. But, at very least, the law now seems fractured: Many courts will undoubtedly continue to defer to FDA approval, at least on the direct assaults presented by such claims. Others may take the approach in Section 6(c) of the Third Restatement and permit such claims only where it is clear the drug was so unquestionably defective as to be unsuitable for *any* group of patients. And then there is *Lance*, which arguably permits a lay jury to assess *de novo* whether the overall risks and benefits of the drug were appropriate at any one of a number of points in time (at approval; when the drug was prescribed to the patient in question; or perhaps even on verdict day, with its clarity of 20–20 hindsight)—and thereby second-guess the FDA on its most fundamental regulatory decision. Only time, and more litigation, will tell.

V The Evolving Law Based on Deference to Prescriber Decisions

Much as the courts once deferred to the presumed expertise of the FDA in its balance of the benefits and risks of a drug to the population *as a whole*, they also presumed each individual doctor would carefully balance those benefits and risks for each of his or her patients, based on an intimate knowledge of each patient's specific medical history. The case law conversely assumed that patients themselves played little or no role in the decision to take prescription drugs which are, by FDA definition, too complex to be left to mere patient choice. Quite literally, "Doctor knows best" and "Doctor's orders" were the bywords of a supposedly benign medical paternalism.

In the last fifteen years, however, that perception too has changed as courts have recognized that doctors no longer have the time to make house calls or, indeed, to learn much more about a patient than they can glean from a volunteered history on a clipboard or computer screen. And, even as a doctor's knowledge about a patient may now be far less than complete, the courts are also recognizing that patients themselves are becoming more and more "informed" by the media (social and otherwise) about drug products marketed as the cure for what ails them.

Those changes are affecting the traditional assumption that doctors, acting as gatekeepers, can effectively keep prescription drugs from patients who do not need, or could be harmed by, them. The principal doctrine now under some scrutiny is the "learned intermediary" rule, an exception to the general rule that manufacturers must *directly* warn end users about the risks of their products. Instead, the rule shields prescription drug manufacturers from tort liability so long as they have provided an adequate warning *to the prescribing physician.*

The rule is premised on the "natural" assumption that each doctor is in the best position to assess the risks and benefits of a drug for a particular patient. As the Fifth Circuit put it some forty years ago,

> [a]s a medical expert, the prescribing physician can take into account the propensities of the drug, as well as the susceptibilities of his patient. His is the task of weighing the benefits of any medication against its potential dangers. The choice he makes is an informed one, an individual medical judgment bottomed on a knowledge of both patient and palliative.[55]

The rule itself dates back to the 1940s when a New York court held that the manufacturer of a prescription suppository could not be held liable for allegedly failing to warn the patient's parents of its risks.[56] The court relied on the fact that the manufacturer did not make any representations directly to the patient-plaintiff and that the physician used his own judgment in prescribing the drug. Conversely, the court noted that the allegations would have been sufficient to state a claim "if the product were sold to the public generally as a drug for which no physician's prescription was necessary."[57]

The term "learned intermediary" was first used by the Eighth Circuit in 1967 in *Sterling Drug v. Cornish.*[58] The issue there was whether a drug manufacturer had a duty to warn of a side effect that only occurred in a highly susceptible group of patients (a rather common scenario in drug product liability cases). The Eighth Circuit concluded that the manufacturer *did* have such a duty to warn, but that the duty extended only as far as the doctor. The court optimistically assumed, "If the doctor is properly warned of the possibility of a side effect in some patients, and is advised of the symptoms normally accompanying the side effect, there is an excellent chance that injury to the patient can be avoided."[59]

Since that decision in 1967, the learned intermediary rule has been expressly endorsed by the highest courts in twenty-two states and adopted by statute in North Carolina as well.[60] And, with the exception of the West Virginia Supreme Court discussed below, no state supreme court has expressly rejected the principle that a prescription drug manufacturer satisfies its duty to warn by providing an appropriate warning to the physician.

To be sure, a few courts have found a few exceptions to the rule, primarily for situations where a traditional doctor-patient relationship does not exist. For example, some courts

[55] Reyes v. Wyeth Labs., 498 F.2d 1264, 1276 (5th Cir.), *cert. denied*, 419 U.S. 1096 (1974).

[56] Marcus v. Specific Pharms., 77 N.Y.S.2d 508 (Sup. Ct. 1948).

[57] *Id.* at 509.

[58] 370 F.2d 82 (8th Cir. 1966).

[59] *Id.* at 85.

[60] *See* State ex. rel. Johnson & Johnson v. Karl, 647 S.E.2d 899, 903–904 & n.6 (W.Va. 2007). The Supreme Court of Texas subsequently adopted the rule in 2012. Centocor v. Hamilton, 372 S.W.3d 140 (Texas 2012).

have held that manufacturers of vaccines distributed through mass immunization programs must directly warn recipients of potential adverse consequences.[61]

A few others have held that manufacturers of contraceptives are not shielded from liability if they fail to provide adequate warnings directly to consumers. Those courts have argued that contraceptives are typically used by consumers who are more actively involved in the choice to use them, with prescribing physicians "relegated to a relatively passive role."[62]

A few other courts have recognized an "overpromotion" exception to the learned intermediary rule, for situations where a manufacturer's promotion of a drug allegedly impacted a doctor's decision to prescribe a medication.[63] As the Supreme Court of California argued,

> [A]n adequate warning to the profession may be eroded or even nullified by overpromotion of the drug through a vigorous sales program which may have the effect of persuading the prescribing doctor to disregard the warnings given.[64]

But most courts have limited such an exception to "unusual cases" where a plaintiff can produce "individualized proof" and "well-supported" facts that the manufacturer's excessive promotion "caused the [plaintiff's] physician to initiate or maintain the prescription at issue."[65]

Over the last fifteen years, however, some courts have exhibited broader doubt as to the learned intermediary doctrine. Those courts have argued that our healthcare system, including the manner in which medications are now prescribed and advertised, has changed so dramatically that the presumptions on which the rule were once founded are no longer valid.

In no small measure, this was the doing of the manufacturers themselves. At the same time critics in Congress and some courts began to question the FDA's competence in approving and monitoring the safety of prescription drugs, the manner in which they were marketed changed as well. Most important, since the late 1990s there has been a frenetic increase in the use of direct-to-consumer (DTC) advertisements to promote prescription drugs in a manner many contend circumvents the "gatekeeper" function of the physician. According to the Congressional Budget Office (CBO), annual industry expenditures on DTC ads for prescription drugs went from virtually nothing in 1995 to nearly $5 billion by 2006.[66]

Such ads are criticized on a number of fronts. First, although FDA regulations ostensibly require that each ad contain a "[t]rue statement of information in brief summary relating to the side effects, contraindications, and effectiveness" of the drug product, which must also strike a "fair balance" between those competing factors,[67] many believe that it is a futile

[61] Davis v. Wyeth, 399 F.2d 121 (9th Cir. 1968). *See also* Mazur v. Merck, 964 F.2d 1348 (3d Cir.), *cert. denied*, 506 U.S. 974 (1992).

[62] MacDonald v. Ortho Pharm., 475 N.E.2d 65, 69 (Mass. 1985). *See also* Hill v. Searle Labs., 884 F.2d 1064, 1070 (8th Cir. 1989) (learned intermediary rule does not apply to intrauterine devices (IUDs) because "the treating physician generally does not make an intervening, individualized medical judgment in the birth control decision"); Stephens v. G.D. Searle & Co., 602 F. Supp. 379 (E.D. Mich. 1985) (manufacturer of oral contraceptives has duty to warn consumers directly of side effects).

[63] *See, e.g.*, Salmon v. Parke, Davis, 520 F.2d 1359 (4th Cir. 1975); Hamilton v. Hardy, 549 P.2d 1099 (Colo. Ct. App. 1976); Stevens v. Parke, Davis, 507 P.2d 653 (Ca. 1973).

[64] *Stevens*, 507 P.2d at 661.

[65] *See, e.g.*, Boehm v. Eli Lilly, 747 F.3d 501, 508 (8th Cir. 2014) (*quoting In re Zyprexa Prods. Liab. Litig.*, 649 F. Supp. 2d 18, 33 (E.D.N.Y. 2009)). *See also* Motus v. Pfizer, 196 F. Supp. 2d 984 (C.D. Cal. 2001).

[66] *See* CBO, *Promotional Spending for Prescription Drugs* (Dec. 2009).

[67] 21 C.F.R § 202 (e)(1).

endeavor in a 30 or 60 second spot (which, of course, must also leave room for visuals of mountain lakes, racing cars, or his-and-her bathtubs). The more glossy ads then become fodder for ridicule by plaintiff attorneys in product liability cases.

Second, many critics note that such DTC advertisements typically promote more popular, "lifestyle" drugs, which a consumer might be persuaded to request, rather than the true lifesavers such as antibiotics or chemotherapy, which are important to doctors but not the stuff of consumer desire. The CBO found that the largest DTC expenditures were made for drugs to treat erectile dysfunction, followed, in the top ten, by products that treat common, but hardly life-threatening, problems such as sleeping aids, statin drugs to control high cholesterol (which many contend are overused by a nation that could just as well modify its diet), and stimulants (often used to control appetite). Depending on their particular mindset, other critics suggest the ubiquitous advertisements for contraceptives, diet aids, and hair-growth drugs convince "consumers" (rather than true "patients") to insist that their doctors write them prescriptions to treat "conditions" not really worthy of the title, or to treat "real conditions" (e.g., obesity) that arguably can be remedied without any drugs at all.

Last, but not least, many critics, including the FDA itself, argue that such advertisements interfere with the doctor-patient relationship, one of the principal foundations of the learned intermediary rule, in that they convince a patient that he or she needs some specific drug without regard to that individual's medical condition, the utility of the drug for the patient's specific problem, or the patient's susceptibility to the drug's side effects—the very factors a doctor is supposed to balance in making an individual prescription decision. The critics assert that, even when one doctor refuses to prescribe the desired drug, those overly motivated by DTC advertising promising thicker hair or thinner waists will "doctor shop" until they find another willing to oblige.

Such concerns were apparent in 1999 when the Supreme Court of New Jersey became the first to articulate a broad criticism of the learned intermediary rule in *Perez v. Wyeth*.[68] The court there reversed the ruling of both the trial and intermediate appellate courts that the doctrine precluded a group of plaintiffs from pursuing claims for injuries they allegedly sustained from a contraceptive device on the grounds the manufacturer had failed to warn those patients directly in various advertisements.

The state supreme court recognized it was creating a new exception to the rule for manufacturers who market their products directly to consumers. The court began by harkening back to a rather nostalgic view of healthcare, lamenting that the "Norman Rockwell image of the family doctor no longer exists."[69]

> At an earlier time, medical advice was received in the doctor's office from a physician who most likely made house calls if needed. Neighborhood pharmacists compounded prescribed medicines. . . . For good or ill, that has all changed. Medical services are in large measure provided by managed care organizations. Medicines are purchased in the pharmacy department of supermarkets and often paid for by third-party providers. Drug manufacturers now directly advertise products to consumers on the radio, television, the Internet, billboards on public transportation, and in magazines.[70]

[68] 734 A.2d 1245 (N.J. 1999). [69] *Id.* at 1255. [70] *Id.* at 1246–1247.

According to the court, in our modern healthcare system, "[i]nformed consent requires a patient-based decision rather than the paternalistic approach of the 1970s."[71] Yet, at the same time, managed care allows physicians far less time to talk to their patients about the individualized risks of medications. The court then detailed the growth of DTC advertising, which, it believed, skews the views of those patients.[72]

Thus, while the *Perez* court could have merely invoked the previously recognized exception to the learned intermediary rule for contraceptive devices, it chose to adopt a new and broader exception for all manufacturers who engage in DTC advertising, based on its view that such marketing "belies each of the premises on which the learned intermediary doctrine exists."[73]

In 2007, the Supreme Court of West Virginia went even further and formally rejected the rule entirely where DTC advertisements are at play. In *State ex rel. Johnson & Johnson v. Karl*, the court held that the manufacturer of the gastrointestinal drug Propulsid had the same duty to warn the ultimate users of their product as manufacturers of any other "consumer" product.[74] The court in *Karl* drew on the *Perez* court's analysis of the changes in the healthcare system and, in particular, the alleged adverse effect of DTC advertising on the physician-patient relationship. It then added that the Internet had also become an important method of obtaining prescription drugs, which, in turn, has resulted in a further degradation of the traditional doctor-patient relationship.[75] Given all that, the *Karl* court concluded that the "justifications for the learned intermediary doctrine [are] largely outdated and unpersuasive."[76]

In 2008, a federal district court in New Mexico, relying on both *Perez* and *Karl*, predicted that the state courts there, which had yet to address the issue, would likewise reject the learned intermediary doctrine.[77] The court assumed the New Mexico courts would agree that the justifications for the doctrine have become "outdated" as a result of both the dramatic increase in DTC marketing and patients' use of the Internet to conduct their own "medical research."[78] The court commented on the emergence of "Do-It-Yourself-Doctors," who research their own symptoms, diagnose their own problems, and identify "appropriate" medications, as the "biggest trend in American health care."[79]

Each of these decisions has prompted considerable debate and serious concerns by the industry. Since DTC advertising is as national as a Super Bowl ad, the prospect of differing outcomes in differing states is especially worrisome. And that may well be the situation for some time to come. To date, the trio of decisions has not yet been followed by other courts, some of which, even after *Karl*, have reaffirmed the view that a prescription drug manufacturer fulfills its duty to warn by informing the prescribing physician, not the patient.[80] Others have expressly declined to adopt the DTC exception recognized in *Perez*.[81]

71 *Id.* at 1255. 72 *Id.* at 1255–1256. 73 *Id.* at 1256.

74 647 S.E.2d 899 (W.Va. 2007). 75 *Id.* at 907. 76 *Id.* at 906.

77 Rimbert v. Eli Lilly, 577 F. Supp. 2d 1174 (D.N.M. 2008). 78 *Id.* at 1218. 79 *Id.*

80 *See, e.g.*, Centocor v. Hamilton, 372 S.W.3d 140 (Tex. 2012); Springhill Hosps. v. Larrimore, 5 So. 3d 513 (Ala. 2008); Hyman & Armstrong v. Gunderson, 279 S.W.3d 93 (Ky. 2008), *cert. dismissed*, 557 U.S. 951 (2009); Stevens v. Novartis, 247 P.3d 244 (Mont. 2010).

81 *See, e.g.*, DiBartolo v. Abbott Labs., 914 F. Supp. 2d 601 (S.D.N.Y. 2012); Allgood v. GlaxoSmithKline, 2008 WL 483574 (E.D.La. Feb. 20, 2008); Porter v. Eli Lilly, 2008 WL 544739 (N.D.Ga. Feb. 25, 2008); Beale v. Biomet, 492 F. Supp. 2d 1360 (S.D.Fla. 2007); Cowley v. Abbott Labs., 476 F. Supp. 2d 1053 (W.D.Wis. 2007); *In re* Meridia Prods. Liab. Litig., 328 F. Supp. 2d 791 (N.D.Ohio 2004).

For example, when an intermediate appellate court in Texas followed *Perez* and created its own DTC exception, that decision was reversed by the Texas Supreme Court, which expressly adopted the doctrine and refused to carve out any DTC advertising exception.[82] The state supreme court held that, despite the changes in the healthcare system described in *Perez* and *Karl*, the principles underlying the learned intermediary rule still apply: (1) patients still cannot obtain prescription drugs from anyone but a physician, and (2) each physician is still "best suited to weigh the patient's individual needs in conjunction with the risks and benefits of the prescription drug."[83]

In rejecting any DTC exception, the state supreme court focused on the FDA oversight of such advertising and in part on the unusual facts of that case. Specifically, the court noted that there were no allegations of intentionally misleading statements made by the manufacturer and that the DTC advertising at issue was an informational video provided to patients for individual viewing, "not the type of misleading DTC advertising that concerned the *Perez* court."[84]

Thus, while the Texas court left the door open for some limited exception to the learned intermediary doctrine if presented with more compelling facts, the rule seems safe there at least for the moment. Whether other courts and legislatures will follow *Perez* and *Karl* and reject further protections for prescription drug manufacturers against a duty to warn consumers directly of the inherent risks of their drugs, or will hold fast to the principles underlying the more traditional rule, thus remains to be seen.

VI Off-Label Uses—Liability for Manufacturers between a Rock and Hard Place

Over the last fifteen years, pharmaceutical manufacturers have also confronted a new source of potential product liability, as well as huge civil penalties, from the use of their products "off label." Simply defined, "off-label" is any use of a drug for medical conditions ("indications") or for periods of time beyond those that were clinically tested and thus were the basis for the label approved by the FDA.[85]

Such off-label use is older than the FDA regime itself. And it is widespread. One study concluded that in 2006 as many as 150 million prescriptions in the United States were written off-label.[86] In some specialties, the prevalence is especially high. It has been estimated between 50% and 75% of cancer treatment drugs are prescribed off-label. Oncologists

[82] *Centocor*, 372 S.W.3d 140. [83] *Id.* at 159. [84] *Id.* at 163.

[85] For example, the "fen-phen" diet drug combination, which spawned so much product liability litigation, was an off-label use both because the two different drugs (fenfluramine and phentermine) were never approved by the FDA for use together *and* because the label (and clinical data reviewed by the FDA) for fenfluramine was for only "short-term use." Physicians, however, routinely prescribed the combination for years, consistent with a study funded by the National Institutes of Health.

[86] D. Radley, *Off-Label Prescribing Among Office-Based Physicians*, 166 Arch. Internal Med. 1021 (2006).

assume a drug tested in FDA-controlled studies on some more common form of cancer is also likely to be useful in other, lesser-studied forms.[87] Off-label uses are likewise common in pediatric care—some suggest more than 90% of all pediatric prescriptions—where the difficulties of conducting studies on children often mean a drug is approved without clinical data on its effect on children. Again, pediatricians simply extrapolate lower doses based on their own judgment or perhaps some study the FDA has never reviewed.

The FDA recognizes that off-label uses are a necessary corollary of its mission to regulate drugs without directly interfering with the practice of medicine.[88] The FD&C Act itself acknowledges that it is not intended to "limit or interfere with the authority of a healthcare practitioner to prescribe or administer any legally marketed device to a patient for any condition or disease. . . ."[89]

Yet, at the same time, the FDA prohibits manufacturers from promoting their drugs for such uses which go beyond the clinical data, and therefore FDA approval, set forth in the label. Indeed, the FDA will prosecute a company which "promotes" a drug for an off-label use, and that, of course, includes any discussion of such uses in either professional or DTC advertisements.[90]

This tension between the desires of doctors for information, from whatever source, on off-label uses and the FDA's insistence that an FDA-approved label be based on study data it has reviewed during the New Drug Approval process led to a 1997 amendment to the FD&C Act that allowed manufacturers to provide some information concerning off-label uses, in response to *unsolicited* requests from doctors, under limits set by the FDA.[91] That enactment, which by its terms expired in 2006, prompted a "guidance" from the FDA, which vaguely describes how far manufacturers may go in providing such information, primarily through reprints of medical literature and presentations at medical conferences—far short of the way they normally promote labeled uses.[92] But that FDA "guidance" warns that it does not "establish legality."[93] And its provisions are so vague that a wholesale revision is now in the works.[94]

Beyond this amorphous FDA regulation, another force has developed over the last decade to complicate the off-label landscape still more. The federal government, with state attorneys general often hard on its heels, has filed civil penalty cases against leading manufacturers for allegedly promoting off-label uses and hence massive purchases by the federal and state governments through their Medicare and Medicaid programs of drugs for such "unapproved" uses. Proceeding on the theory that the "knowing promotion" of such off-label uses will

[87] D. Pfister, *Off-Label Use of Oncology Drugs*, 30 J. Clinical Oncology 584 (2012).

[88] *See* Buckman Co. v. Pls.' Legal Comm., 531 U.S. 341 (2001).

[89] 21 U.S.C. § 396.

[90] For a more detailed account of the FDA's approach to off-label uses, *see* Lewis Grossman's article in this volume.

[91] 21 U.S.C. § 360aaa-6(a).

[92] FDA Guidance for Industry, *Good Reprint Practices for Distribution of Medical Journal Articles . . . on Unapproved Uses* (Jan. 2009).

[93] *Id.* at 1.

[94] *Revised Draft Guidance on Distributing Scientific and Medical Publications on Unapproved New Uses* (Feb. 2014).

necessarily lead doctors to issue such prescriptions—which then constitute "false claims" for payment for drugs for purposes other than those for which they are strictly labeled—the federal government has exacted huge penalties under the False Claims Act, a statute enacted during the Civil War to penalize those who sold defective supplies to Union troops.[95]

In one recent case, those federal enforcement theories collided with the First Amendment, when a representative of a drug manufacturer argued he was entitled to make *truthful* statements about the potential off-label uses of a drug. A divided panel of the Second Circuit agreed with the representative, casting some doubt on the government's ability to criminalize *pure speech by an individual* about an off-label use, as opposed to an overall *corporate campaign to promote* such uses—a distinction only a constitutional lawyer could love.[96] Nevertheless, the massive civil penalty cases against the manufacturers continue, not only directly impacting the companies but also providing fodder for product liability plaintiffs who then argue to tort juries that such penalties stigmatize the off-label use itself.

Finally, these continuing disputes over the proper role of drug companies in even acknowledging the possible off-label use of their products have led some courts to question the former view that a manufacturer is not liable if doctors choose, in the exercise of their medical expertise, to use a drug in some manner, or for a longer period of time, than had been approved by the FDA.[97] Some courts have more recently ruled that where the facts suggest a manufacturer could have reasonably foreseen its drug would be used in some off-label manner—especially where it may have provided some information about that use—the manufacturer can be held liable in a product liability action, even where the use went far beyond the ones approved in the label.[98]

In sum, the evolving law concerning off-label uses—ambiguous FDA regulation, sniping by federal and state prosecutors through False Claims Act actions, and the impact of such claims on product liability cases—presents yet another challenge to manufacturers who are caught between the conflicting expertise of the FDA, which still requires clinical proof from FDA-monitored studies before any use may be included in a label, and physicians, who will not wait for such FDA-blessed data before using drugs in an "off-label," but perhaps life-saving, manner.[99]

In each of the doctrinal disputes discussed above, a long-standing policy of deference to the presumed expertise of the FDA, the medical profession, or both is under new scrutiny, if not

[95] The larger settlements for off-label promotion include those by Lilly (*Zyprexa*)—$1.4 billion (2009); Pfizer (*Bextra*)—$2.3 billion (2009); GlaxoSmithKline (*Paxil, Wellbutrin*)—$1.0 billion (2012); Johnson & Johnson (*Risperdal*)—$1.4 billion (2013).

[96] *See* United States v. Caronia, 703 F.3d 149 (2d Cir. 2012).

[97] For the more traditional view, *see, e.g.*, Robak v. Abbott Labs., 797 F. Supp. 475 (D.Md. 1992).

[98] *See, e.g.*, McNeil v. Wyeth, 462 F.3d 364, 369–371 (5th Cir. 2006) (under Texas law, manufacturer liable for extended use beyond label where manufacturer had survey data showing such use was common); Knipe v. SmithKline Beecham, 583 F. Supp. 2d 602, 623–625 (E.D.Pa. 2008) (under New Jersey law manufacturer could owe duty to warn as to dangers of off-label use where manufacturer knew or should have known of dangers).

[99] Over the last decade medical devices have likewise been subject to False Claims Act charges arising from alleged over-promotion of "off-label" uses. *See*, e.g., United States ex rel. Colquitt v. Abbott Labs., 864 F. Supp. 2d 499 (N.D.Tex. 2012); James v. Stryker Corp., 2011 WL 292240 (M.D.Pa. Jan. 27, 2011).

outright attack. To some extent, that may be the legitimate result of significant changes over the last fifteen years in the way drugs are reviewed, monitored, marketed, and prescribed. In other respects, it may be the result of unfair criticisms by politicians seeking votes or tort lawyers seeking verdicts. But whatever the root cause, these continuing debates, among judges and justices, are transforming drug product liability law with consequences for all who depend on those products that are unique in their ability to save, or to destroy, lives.

CHAPTER 21

COMPLAINTS TO PROFESSIONAL AND REGULATORY BODIES

NADIA N. SAWICKI

Civil litigation may be the most commonly recognized mechanism by which patients can seek recourse for injuries associated with medical treatment. However, other mechanisms play an equally important role, both in addressing individual patients' complaints and in responding to broader concerns over the quality of care provided by medical practitioners and healthcare institutions.

Both private and public actors govern quality control in the sphere of American healthcare. Healthcare institutions and providers are regulated most comprehensively by federal and state agencies. The federal government's authority to regulate healthcare quality is exercised primarily though the U.S. Department of Health and Human Services and its operating divisions—among them, the Centers for Medicare and Medicaid Services (CMS), which imposes standards for participation in the federal Medicare program. Provider compliance with federal standards is monitored by state-level Quality Improvement Organizations (QIOs) and survey agencies that contract with the federal government. States also enforce their own quality standards by way of state health departments that are responsible for surveying and licensing healthcare institutions, as well professional licensing boards responsible for setting the standards for professional practice among healthcare practitioners like physicians, nurses, pharmacists, and physician assistants. Some states have also created specific regulatory agencies devoted to issues relating to patient safety and consumer protection in the healthcare sphere—for example, California's Department of Managed Health Care (which provides independent review of plan coverage determinations), and Pennsylvania's Patient Safety Authority (an independent agency aimed at reducing medical error and promoting patient safety).

Private actors with significant influence on healthcare quality include private accreditation organizations like the Joint Commission and the National Committee for Quality Assurance, which set standards and conduct regular surveys of healthcare institutions. Likewise, individual healthcare providers may be certified by private professional associations; the most notable example of this is the certification of physicians practicing in specialty areas by independent certification boards affiliated with the American Board of Medical Specialties. Board certification is a voluntary process, however, and does not affect a physician's legal authority to practice medicine (though some states require independent board certification for physicians who wish to advertise their expertise in a specialty area). Finally, healthcare providers are also subject to significant oversight, including limitations on practice, by the medical staff and peer review organizations of the institutions in which they practice.

At almost every level in this process of regulatory and private control, patients with quality or safety concerns have opportunities to voice these concerns with the knowledge that they will be investigated. State and federal agencies have the authority to investigate and respond to patient complaints, and discipline or sanction offending providers and institutions.[1]

Private organizations such as the Joint Commission and specialty medical associations sometimes offer patients the opportunity to provide feedback on their experiences with healthcare providers and institutions. Hospitals and other healthcare institutions have internal mechanisms for accepting and responding to patient complaints.

Nevertheless, healthcare consumers often feel that these organizations are not sufficiently responsive to their needs. Patients are often unaware of their right to file quality-related grievances with governmental agencies, and resource limitations make this process far less effective than it could be. As a result of the current American political climate, health-related agencies are granted only limited funding and personnel. Therefore, were these agencies better funded, many patient complaints, which can be costly to investigate, might be addressed more carefully. Private organizations, while sometimes available to accept patient complaints, have priorities quite different from those of governmental entities dedicated to the enforcement of regulatory standards. For example, the Joint Commission, a private accreditation authority recognized by state agencies as a key player in ensuring institutional compliance with federal reimbursement requirements, is known for its regular surveys of healthcare institutions far more than its willingness to accept patient complaints. Private medical societies and specialty boards frequently direct concerned patients to state licensing boards rather than accepting and responding to patient complaints themselves. And while healthcare institutions invest significant resources in risk management and complaint resolution, injured patients dissatisfied with this system sometimes have no recourse but to resort to civil litigation.

Perhaps these perceived inadequacies in responsiveness to patient complaints are what led patients to take advantage of the rise of consumer-directed reporting resources on the Internet, like Yelp, Angie's List, and RateMDs. These sites offer consumers the opportunity to input personalized feedback about their experiences with healthcare institutions and providers. While the complaints aired in these forums do not offer the possibility of individual redress, they may nevertheless impact the market for medical services by causing prospective patients to avoid providers and institutions who have received negative reviews.

The importance of having resources by which patients can air their complaints, whether through public agencies, private organizations, or consumer ratings websites, is obvious. While patients are certainly well served by having access to the courts to seek compensation from defendants for their injuries, compensation is clearly not the only thing that is important to them. In addition to financial recourse, injured patients also seek public recognition

[1] While a few agencies have the authority to provide compensation for patient injury in extremely limited contexts (most notably, the National Vaccine Injury Compensation Program), the primary focus of these regulatory bodies is in establishing systems for ensuring quality of care on a larger scale.

of the wrongs that they have suffered and assurance that future patients will not suffer the same wrongs. According to a study of one state medical board's complaint-resolution process, "the majority of complaints were not obviously instrumental in the sense that they requested something specific."[2] Many complainants expressed a desire to "protect others from the same fate in the future."[3] As one patient wrote, "This is not just for my mother but for some little old lady that has no family or no one in the medical field that can recognize gross professional behavior that may fall victim [to this doctor.]"[4] Having the opportunity to bring their concerns to regulatory authorities or air them in the public sphere is an essential mechanism for patients and their advocates—one that has the potential for a far greater impact than regulatory standard-setting and civil litigation alone.

I State Regulation: Professional Licensing Boards

The primary administrative resource for patients with concerns about the quality of care received from medical providers is the state-level system of professional licensing boards. Modern medical practice acts and state agencies for the regulation of the medical profession first arose in the 1800s, driven in large part by pressure from within the organized medical profession, which at the time was resisting an influx of alternative or "irregular" practitioners such as naturopaths, hydropaths, chiropractors, and midwives.[5] Many physicians believed that by establishing a state licensing authority for the exercise of medical practice they could maintain their dominance and limit competition in the domain of patient care.[6]

While modern medical licensing boards focus on patient protection and no longer operate under explicitly anticompetitive principles, their history of self-protective professional regulation necessarily impacts contemporary discussions of their authority and efficacy. Most notably, this can be seen in contemporary disputes about scope of practice among various healthcare professions—for example, medical boards' resistance to expanding the scope of practice and prescribing authority of advanced practice nurses,[7] and dental boards' bans on the "unlicensed practice of dentistry" by nondentists offering teeth-whitening services.[8]

[2] Timothy S. Jost, Linda Mulcahy, Stephen Strasser, & Larry A. Sachs, *Consumers, Complaints, and Professional Discipline: A Look at Medical Licensure Boards*, 3 Health Matrix 309, at 322 (1993).

[3] *Id.* at 321. [4] *Id.*

[5] *See generally* Richard Harrison Shryock, Medical Licensing in America, 1650–1965, at 25 (1967); Carl F. Ameringer, State Medical Boards and the Politics of Public Protection 15–16 (1999); James C. Mohr, Licensed to Practice: The Supreme Court Defines the American Medical Profession 15–16 (2013).

[6] Ameringer, State Medical Boards, at 1, 14–16("Ostensibly created to protect the public, state boards were gatekeepers guarding entry into the medical profession rather than internal police over substandard care."). *But see* Paul Starr, The Social Transformation of American Medicine 107–108 (1984) (noting that the myth of suppression of homeopaths by allopaths is not entirely accurate).

[7] *See* Robert L. Philips, Jr. et al., *Can Nurse Practitioners and Physicians Beat Parochialism into Plowshares?*, 21(5) Health Aff. 133 (2002).

[8] *See* North Carolina State Board of Dental Examiners v. FTC, 717 F.3d 359 (4th Cir. 2013) (currently on appeal to the U.S. Supreme Court, Docket #13–534).

State administrative agencies, thus, must strike a sensitive balance when licensing and regulating healthcare professionals. Over time, states have developed professional licensing standards for a broad range of healthcare professionals—including registered nurses, pharmacists, physical and occupational therapists, social workers, chiropractors, radiologic technologists, physician assistants, dentists, acupuncturists, and a host of other ancillary healthcare providers. Regulatory control may be under the auspices of a single state licensing board for all healthcare professions, or may be broken up into individual boards for major groups of practitioners (most often, separate boards for physicians and osteopaths, nurses, pharmacists, chiropractors, and then other healthcare professionals). Whether structured as a single entity or divided into separate boards for each discipline, these agencies maintain statutory authority for the licensure, regulation, and discipline of a wide variety of medical professionals, and operate in substantially similar ways when it comes to patient complaints.[9] State departments of health, which license and maintain responsibility for quality of care in hospitals, nursing homes, and other healthcare institutions, have similar standards for disciplinary enforcement of regulatory requirements. Because the approaches taken by various state agencies responsible for healthcare quality are somewhat similar, this section will focus exclusively on the patient complaint process for physicians as implemented by medical licensing boards.

a. Authority for Licensure and Discipline

A state medical board will award a physician's license upon proof that an individual has graduated from an approved medical school, completed postgraduate training, passed the U.S. Medical Licensing Exam, and satisfied other state-specific licensing requirements. Boards also have the authority to impose re-registration and continuing medical education requirements, although these requirements are neither stringent nor particularly well-enforced. Finally, and perhaps most important from the perspective of patient advocates, boards have the authority to take disciplinary action against physicians who have fallen short of the standards set out in state medical licensing laws. Indeed, as one author has noted, "[p]rotecting the public from incompetent practitioners has long been recognized as the primary justification for professional licensure."[10]

The substantive grounds for professional discipline vary among the states. However, most state medical practice acts authorize disciplinary action on the basis of aiding the unlicensed practice of medicine,[11] fraudulent misrepresentation, discipline by another state board, substance abuse, controlled substances violations, criminal conviction, professional

[9] This statutory authority is granted pursuant to the state's police powers to regulate the health, safety, and welfare of its citizens. Dent v. West Virginia, 129 U.S. 114 (1889) (noting that it is "[t]he power of the State to provide for the general welfare of its people [that] authorizes it to prescribe all such regulations as, in its judgment, will secure or tend to secure them against the consequences of ignorance and incapacity as well as of deception and fraud.").

[10] Timothy S. Jost, *Oversight of the Competence of Healthcare Professionals*, *in* Regulation of the Healthcare Professions 20 (Timothy S. Jost ed., 1997).

[11] Medical boards may also seek injunctive relief against individuals practicing without a medical license, or refer such individuals for criminal prosecution by the state.

incompetence, physical or mental impairment, and unprofessional conduct. This last category is quite broad and can encompass violations as varied as insurance fraud, breach of patient confidentiality, violations of the American Medical Association's Code of Ethics, as well as other conduct that brings the medical profession into disrepute.[12] Indeed, there are very few constitutional limitations on the substantive criteria state boards use for physician discipline. The U.S. Supreme Court has held only that the criteria for professional licensure and discipline may not be vague, arbitrary, or unattainable, and "must have a rational connection with the applicant's fitness or capacity to practice" his profession.[13] Courts grant a significant degree of deference to board decisions, and it is relatively rare for a medical board's substantive authority to be successfully challenged on judicial review.[14]

b. Procedures for Patient Complaints, Investigation, and Discipline

Patient complaints play a very important role in initiating agency investigation and enforcement of regulatory standards. Indeed, the primary means by which medical boards learn about physician misconduct that might trigger disciplinary action is through direct complaints by patients or families.[15] However, boards also collect relevant information from healthcare institutions, malpractice insurers, government agencies, and other entities required by law to report such information.

Each state board establishes its own procedures by which patients and families can file complaints about medical providers. If a complaint is deemed to be within the board's jurisdiction, an investigator will collect additional information by interviewing the patient and requesting copies of medical records and other relevant documentation. The investigator may also contact the provider for additional information. Based on the information collected by the investigator, a medical expert will review the case and, if appropriate, refer it to the full board for formal disciplinary action. However, most cases are closed before this

[12] *See* Nadia N. Sawicki, *Character, Competence, and the Principles of Professional Discipline*, 13 J. Health Care L. & Pol'y 285, at 293 (2010).

[13] Schware v. Board of Bar Examiners of the State of New Mexico, 353 U.S. 232, 239 (1967). *See also* Dent v. West Virginia, 129 U.S. 114 (1889) ("The nature and extent of the qualifications required must depend primarily upon the judgment of the State as to their necessity. If they are appropriate to the calling or profession, and attainable by reasonable study or application, no objection to their validity can be raised because of their stringency or difficulty. It is only when they have no relation to such calling or profession, or are unattainable by such reasonable study and application, that they can operate to deprive one of his right to pursue a lawful vocation.").

[14] *See* Eleanor Kinney, *Administrative Law Issues in Professional Regulation*, *in* Jost, Regulation of the Healthcare Professions, at 114; Barsky v. Board of Regents, 347 U.S. 442, 469–470 (1954) (noting that states must have "the widest leeway" in the realm of healthcare regulation, and that judicial review of agency discretionary decisions may permissibly be limited); Bettencourt v. Board of Registration in Medicine, 904 F.2d 772, 774 (1st Cir. 1990) (identifying the limited conditions under which the Massachusetts court may set aside a medical board's determination).

[15] Jost, Regulation of the Healthcare Professions, at 23; Richard Kusserow, U.S. Dept. of Health and Human Svcs. Office of the Inspector General, Pub. No. OEI-01-89-00560, *State Medical Boards and Medical Discipline* (1990), at 3 (hereafter, 1990 OIG Report).

point without formal discipline, either because the complaint lacks merit, because the complaint is settled through a consent decree, or because the physician is given only an informal reprimand.[16] According to one study, only 2.5% of patient complaints ultimately result in a formal disciplinary citation.[17]

Where formal disciplinary proceedings are warranted, they are constrained by principles of substantive due process. These entitle physicians to procedural protections, including notice and hearing, clear evidentiary standards, and judicial review. If a claim against a physician is ultimately meritorious, the board can choose from among a wide variety of disciplinary actions—including revocation or suspension of licensure, conditional probation, supervision, fines, mandated professional education, and orders to pursue continuing education or substance abuse treatment.

Notably, medical boards have no authority to provide compensation for individual patients or assist patients in filing malpractice suits. However, there can be significant overlap between the types of patient concerns that are directed to state licensing boards and those that might be grounds for civil liability. A patient who suffers injury as a result of provider negligence, for example, may file an administrative complaint with the state medical board as well as a parallel civil complaint against the provider for litigation before a judge or a jury.[18] While a successful malpractice claim requires the patient to satisfy more stringent legal standards of proof—including demonstrating a causal link between the provider's negligence and the patient's injury—the increased difficulty of litigation is correspondingly tied to the possibility of substantial remuneration not available through the administrative complaint process.

Many commentators have noted parallels between administrative agency complaints and civil litigation. For example, some have suggested that a robust system of licensure and discipline may increase public confidence in the profession's ability to self-regulate and could ultimately reduce demand for remedies arising from civil litigation.[19] Even some state legislatures seem to recognize a connection between the two systems that patients can use to vindicate their concerns. The comprehensive tort reforms passed in Texas in 2003, which included a $250,000 cap on noneconomic damages per claimant,[20] also significantly expanded the scope of the state medical board's authority.[21] Since the passage of these limitations on tort recovery, one study found a significant increase in the number of complaints to and disciplinary actions by the Texas Medical Board—the number of disciplinary actions

[16] 1990 OIG Report, at 14, 17–18; Jost, REGULATION OF THE HEALTHCARE PROFESSIONS, at 25.

[17] Jost et al., *Consumers*, at 310–331.

[18] That said, a 1990 study of complaints to the Ohio State Medical Board found only limited overlap between complainants to the medical board and plaintiffs in malpractice litigations. Jost et al., *Consumers*, at 324–326.

[19] Gary M. Fournier & Melayne Morgan McInnes, *Medical Board Regulation of Physician Licensure: Is Excessive Malpractice Sanctioned?*, 12 JOURNAL OF REGULATORY ECONOMICS 113, at 115–117 (1997).

[20] H.B. 4, Texas Legislature (2003), *adopted as* Tex. Civ. Prac. & Rem. Code Ann. §74.301-303; S.B. 104, Texas Legislature (2003).

[21] Among other things, the new law required that the board adopt a new schedule of disciplinary actions keyed to the severity of violations, required the board to automatically revoke the license of any physician who has been convicted of a crime or whose license to practice medicine has been revoked in another state, and increased board investigation of temporarily suspended physicians for compliance with the conditions of suspension.

taken, for example, increased by 96%, and the number of financial penalties imposed on physicians increased by 367%.[22] This study, again, suggests a correlation between the functions of the civil and administrative complaint systems.

c. Challenges and Criticisms

State medical boards face significant criticism regarding their approach to complaint investigation and disciplinary enforcement. Like many administrative agencies, medical boards are faulted for being subject to professional capture—a phenomenon whereby an industry protects itself rather than the consumer community at large. Critics argue that while state medical boards are tasked with regulating the medical profession, they are often in fact beholden to it and reluctant to take action against one of their own.[23]

Evidence demonstrates that state medical boards discipline physicians only infrequently in response to patient complaints and that most disciplinary actions taken are quite mild. According to one study, only approximately 2.5% of patient complaints result in formal discipline; most complaints are closed without any formal or informal disciplinary action.[24] Estimates suggest that just under half of all disciplinary actions taken against physicians are considered "serious"—that is, involving surrender, suspension, revocation, probation, or restrictions on licensure.[25] Fewer than a quarter of disciplined physician overall lose their ability to practice medicine, even temporarily.[26] For example, in cases where physicians were found to have provided substandard care, fewer than 30% were required to stop practicing.[27] More than half of physicians whose clinical privileges were restricted by the hospitals at which they worked faced no state board discipline whatsoever, despite the fact that these hospital actions were reported to the National Practitioner Data Bank.[28]

[22] Ronald M. Stewart et al., *Tort Reform Is Associated with More Medical Board Complaints and Disciplinary Actions*, 214(4) JOURNAL OF THE AMERICAN COLLEGE OF SURGEONS 567 (2012).

[23] Stanley J. Gross, *The Myth of Professional Licensing*, 33 AMERICAN PSYCHOLOGIST 1109, at 1012 (1978). This concern has been eased somewhat by the inclusion of nonphysician members on state medical boards; however, physicians still make up the majority of board members. *See generally* Andrew K. Dolan & Nicole D. Urban, *The Determinants of the Effectiveness of Medical Disciplinary Boards: 1960–1977*, 7 LAW & HUM. BEHAV. 203 (1983) (finding that the principal determinant of medical board effectiveness was the degree to which the board's composition included non-physician representatives).

[24] Jost et al., *Consumers*, at 330.

[25] Consumer advocacy group Public Citizen regularly collects information about the rates of board discipline based on data made available by the Federation of State Medical Boards. Sidney M. Wolfe, *20,125 Questionable Doctors*, 16(9) PUBLIC CITIZEN HEALTH RESEARCH GROUP HEALTH LETTER 1 (Sept. 2000) (90.6% of disciplinary actions taken were on the basis of "serious offenses," but only 48% of the disciplinary actions themselves were considered "serious"). Public Citizen has also reported that fewer than one half of 1% of licensed physicians face serious action on an annual basis. Sidney M. Wolfe, Cynthia Williams, & Alex Zaslow, *Public Citizens' Health Research Group Ranking of the Rate of State Medical Boards' Serious Disciplinary Actions, 2009–2011* (2012), *available at* http://www.citizen.org/documents/2034.pdf (finding that between 2000 and 2011, state boards took an average of between three and four serious disciplinary actions per one thousand physicians).

[26] Wolfe et al., *20,125 Questionable Doctors*, at 2. [27] *Id.* at 4.

[28] Alan Levine, Robert Oshel, & Sidney Wolfe, *State Medical Boards Fail to Discipline Doctors with Hospital Actions Against Them* (Mar. 2011), *available at* http://www.congresswatchdog.org/documents/1937.pdf (noting that between 1990 and 2009, state medical boards took no action at all against two

Most often, boards tend to opt for informal disciplinary measures, like letters of caution, warnings, or informal agreements to alter practice.[29] News media are replete with examples of "bad doctors" who receive mere slaps on the wrist. A 2000 report by Public Citizen, for example, provided a number of egregious examples of physician misconduct that was punished only weakly—a fine and reprimand for placing an amputated human foot in a crab trap; a reprimand for artificially inseminating a woman with semen from a known HIV-positive donor; a reprimand for administering high doses of drugs leading to a woman's death during a simple breast biopsy.[30]

Many critics also claim that regardless of the number of disciplinary actions taken or the severity of the penalties imposed, state boards are doing a poor job prioritizing their investigations to address physician incompetence.[31] Studies by the Office of the Inspector General in the 1980s and 1990s, for example, consistently concluded that issues of medical quality ranked very low among medical boards' disciplinary priorities.[32] "[W]e've never had a disciplinary action based on malpractice," reported one board director, and "when there is a malpractice case, we tend to look for another basis for disciplinary action."[33] More recent evidence suggests that less than a third of disciplinary actions are taken on the basis of quality-of-care concerns, with the majority of actions being taken for reasons related to conduct outside the sphere of direct clinical practice—such as substance abuse, criminal activity, and behavioral problems.[34] A study of the Ohio state medical board, for example, found that of the sixty-five disciplinary actions taken in 1990, only six were "directly based on allegations of improper clinical practice"; most were based on physical or mental impairment, violation of continuing medical education requirements, unlicensed practice, and criminal convictions.[35] Given that the same study found that 60% of patient complaints related to "subminimal or incompetent" care, the rate of actual discipline on the basis of improper clinical practice seems low. Another study found that the most common substantive reason for discipline was the vague category of "unprofessional conduct" (33.4%); quality concerns were raised in only 10% of cases.[36] As Timothy Jost and others concluded, these data ought to

hundred twenty physicians whose hospital privileges were restricted on the basis of their being an "immediate threat to health or safety.")

29 Jost et al., *Consumers*, at 331 (1993) (finding that in 1990, the Ohio State Medical Board took thirty-two informal actions and only seven formal disciplinary actions as a result of patient complaints); David A. Swankin & Shawn Willette, Citizen Advocacy Center, *Should the Public Have a Right to Comment on Proposed Licensing Board Consent Orders* (1993) (on file with author) (finding that in some states, up to 95% of disciplinary cases are resolved by way of negotiation or consent order prior to a formal hearing).

30 Wolfe et al., *20,125 Questionable Doctors*.

31 Sawicki, Character; David A. Swankin & Marci Rose, Citizen Advocacy Center, *Licensing Board Policies for Prioritizing Complaints* (1993) (on file with author) (noting that the majority of state boards responding to a survey about complaint prioritization had no policies on this matter).

32 1990 OIG Report, at 15; Office of Analysis and Inspections, U.S. Department of Health & Human Services, *Medical Licensure and Discipline: An Overview* (1986), at 13–14, *available at* http://oig.hhs.gov/oei/reports/oai-01-86-00064.pdf [hereafter, 1986 OIG Report].

33 1986 OIG Report, at 14.

34 *See generally* Sawicki, *Character*, at 303–304; Jost et al., *Consumers*; Darren Grant & Kelly C. Alfred, *Sanctions and Recidivism: An Evaluation of Physician Discipline by State Medical Boards*, 32 J. Health Pol. Pol'y & L. 867 (2007).

35 Jost et al., *Consumers*, at 332.

36 Grant & Alfred, *Sanctions*, at 875–876.

"give pause to those who believe that medical licensure boards can play a major role in assuring clinical competence."[37]

Part of the reason why medical boards take disciplinary action for reasons other than clinical incompetence is because investigating substantive complaints about the quality of care is resource-intensive. Given the significant resource limitations many state boards face, it is often simpler to discipline a physician on the basis of an objective standard—criminal conviction, for example—than to investigate a quality-related clinical matter.[38] Thus, while physicians who provide incompetent care are ultimately disciplined, this often occurs because boards are able to bootstrap competence issues onto less subjective complaints.

This reactive (rather than proactive) approach to physician discipline has also been criticized because it fails to address long-term quality-of-care concerns through prevention and management, especially of repeat offenders.[39] Lucian Leape and John Fromson, for example, note that state medical boards "typically do not define prevention of injury as part of their responsibility," contrasting this with the more systemic approach taken by the commercial airline industry to ensure continued competence among pilots.[40] There have, however, been some proposals for making medical boards more proactive in addressing issues of physician quality—these include implementing confidential questionnaires, annual physical examinations, random drug testing, cognitive evaluations of older physician, competency-based maintenance of certification, and development of effective remediation programs. If such measures were implemented, then perhaps there would be less need to respond to patient complaints because the underlying system would be better at ensuring quality of care.

Finally, and perhaps most important from the perspective of patient complainants, medical boards are frequently criticized for not being responsive enough to consumers. Although state statutes and regulations typically require boards to notify complainants of the resolution of their cases,[41] agencies' actual responsiveness (and the level of detail they provide) varies greatly. A study of the Ohio licensing board, for example, found that only seven of two hundred complainants got individual letters from the board responding to their allegations, 70% received a form letter, and 26% were not contacted at all.[42] Given that the length of time a complaint case remains open ranges from approximately 180 days (for cases resolved before or during investigation) to 675 days (for cases that reach a hearing), this lack of responsiveness is troubling.[43] By failing to follow up with complainants, medical boards call into question who they are serving—the community or the profession. This is particularly problematic given the fact that the reason most complainants bring their concerns to state medical board is not only to protect others by giving the board the opportunity to take action

[37] Jost et al., *Consumers*, at 332.

[38] *Id.* ("Disciplinary actions based on allegations of clinical incompetence generally require identifying and then proving up several malpractice cases simultaneously.").

[39] Randall R. Bovbjerg, Pablo Aliaga, & Josephine Gittler, *State Discipline of Physicians: Assessing State Medical Boards through Case Studies*, Final Report to the U.S. Department of Health and Human Services Assistant Secretary for Planning and Evaluation; Office of Disability, Aging, and Long-Term Care Policy (Feb. 2006), at 44–45.

[40] Lucian L. Leape & John A. Fromson, *Problem Doctors: Is There a System-Level Solution?*, 144(2) Annals of Internal Medicine 107, at 109 (Jan. 17 2006).

[41] *See, e.g.*, N.Y. Comp. Codes R. & Regs. tit. 12, § 302-1.10(h); 25 Tex. Admin. Code § 140.214(e).

[42] Jost et al., *Consumers*, at 333.

[43] Bovbjerg, Aliaga, & Gittler, *State Discipline*, at 33.

but also to feel like they have a voice. As noted by Timothy Jost, "[m]any complaints can be seen as ends in themselves, the main purpose being to express dissatisfaction."[44]

State agencies are typically more forthcoming in providing information about the outcome of disciplinary actions to the general public, typically on the basis of a statutory mandate or agency regulations.[45] A 2006 survey of state boards of medicine and nursing by the Citizen Advocacy Center revealed that all of them publicly disclose a substantial amount of information about disciplinary actions taken against individual providers; typically including formal charges, final disciplinary orders, and findings of fact, as well as information about dismissal of charges and negotiated settlements.[46] This information is reported and searchable on most agencies' websites and is often published in newsletters and press releases as well.

Given that state medical boards' stated purpose in responding to patient complaints is to protect the public from dangerous providers and ensure clinical competence, it is far from obvious that the current disciplinary system—which disciplines providers only infrequently, with limited levels of severity, for reasons that may not be related to clinical competence, and fails to communicate with complainants—actually achieves this goal. Medical boards' lack of responsiveness to patient quality complaints calls into question their commitment to public interests and their ability to impose appropriate penalties that keep dangerous physicians out of practice.

II Federal Regulation: CMS, QIOs, and Survey Agencies

A second important resource for patients with quality-related complaints is the federal system for regulating providers and institutions that participate in Medicare and Medicaid. In order to participate in these federal programs, healthcare providers must satisfy a comprehensive set of conditions of participation, which regulate an enormous scope of activity—including quality assurance programs, medical records, patient grievance programs, utilization review, and facility quality and safety. A provider or institution's failure to comply with these conditions can result in a variety of sanctions, including exclusion from federal programs.

Compliance with these regulations is generally overseen by the Centers for Medicare and Medicaid Services (CMS). However, primary responsibility for on-site monitoring and review of healthcare quality at the institutional and provider levels is vested in state-level entities (including private Quality Improvement Organizations [QIOs] and state survey

[44] Jost et al., *Consumers*, at 321.

[45] *See, e.g.*, N.Y. Pub. Health Law § 2995-a (Physician profiles); Cal. Bus. & Prof. Code § 803.1 (medical, osteopathic, podiatry, and physician assistant boards; disclosure of information to public).

[46] Citizen Advocacy Center, Center for Medical Consumers, and New York Public Interest Research Group, *Release of Disciplinary Information to the Public by State Boards of Medicine and Nursing* (2006) (on file with author). *See also* Meredith Larson et al., *Survey of State Medical and Osteopathy Board Disciplinary Web Sites in 2006*, 19 Health Matrix 1 (2009), which found that only five state boards of medicine or osteopathy provided no information at all about board disciplinary action, and that many provided disciplinary information from other authorities (such as hospital discipline, criminal convictions, federal discipline, and malpractice information).

agencies), as well as private accreditation organizations whose standards are recognized by the federal government.[47] This balance of authority is struck for reasons of administrative efficiency; where healthcare institutions are already being reviewed by state agencies or reputable accreditation authorities, federal agencies can rely upon those findings rather than engage in their own independent review. Indeed, the federal government has long recognized the value of nonfederal entities in collecting information about healthcare quality that can be put to use at the national level—the National Practitioner Data Bank, for example, is a clearinghouse maintained by the Department of Health and Human Services to compile information about practitioner competence reported by state licensing boards, healthcare institutions, medical malpractice payers, and professional societies.[48]

a. Authority

The entities primarily responsible for ensuring compliance with federal healthcare quality regulations are Quality Improvement Organizations (QIOs), private (typically nonprofit) organizations that hold three-year contracts with Department of Health and Human Services.[49] They operate as part of the Medicare Quality Improvement Organization program, which is aimed at "promoting the effective, efficient, and economical delivery of health care services, and [] promoting the quality of services" paid for by the Medicare program.[50] These are goals that the federal government has long strived for, and QIOs are but the most recent iteration in a long line of organizations aimed at achieving these goals.

In 1972, Congress authorized the establishment of voluntary peer review organizations to help reduce utilization of unnecessary services within the Medicare program.[51] These Professional Standards Review Organizations (PSROs) (previously called Experimental Medical Care Review Organizations, later called Utilization and Quality Control Peer Review Organizations, and officially renamed Quality Improvement Organizations in 2001) focused primarily on cost containment via retrospective utilization review and were considered by many physicians to be adversarial entities.[52] With the development of healthcare payment reformed aimed at encouraging efficiency of care in the 1980s and 90s, however, QIOs' emphasis on cost containment shifted to a focus on quality improvement writ large.[53] Partly in response to a 1990 Institute of Medicine (IOM) report,[54] which

[47] Healthcare institutions that are voluntarily accredited by private organizations whose standards are as stringent as federal standards (like the Joint Commission, for example) are deemed compliant with federal conditions of participation. 42 C.F.R. § 488.4 488.6.

[48] *See generally* 45 C.F.R. § 60.1 *et seq.*

[49] *See generally* 42 U.S.C.A. § 1320-c *et seq.* For information on the challenges associated with private administration of federal regulations, *see* Timothy Stoltzfus Jost, *Administrative Law Issues Involving the Medicare Utilization and Quality Control Peer Review Organization (PRO) Program: Analysis and Recommendations*, 50 Ohio St. L.J. 1 (1989).

[50] 42 U.S.C.A. § 1395y(g).

[51] Jost, *Administrative Law*, at 4–5.

[52] Institute of Medicine of the National Academies, Medicare's Quality Improvement Organization Program: Maximizing Potential (National Academies Press, 2006), at 40 [hereafter, 2006 IOM Report].

[53] Jost, *Administrative Law*, at 5–6.

[54] Institute of Medicine, Medicare: A Strategy for Quality Assurance (National Academies Press, 1990) [hereafter, 1990 IOM Report].

recommended that Medicare quality assurance efforts shift away from individual case reviews and toward evaluating patterns of practice, QIOs began to position themselves as partners and collaborators, rather than adversaries, with respect to healthcare providers.

The complaint investigation function has been part of QIOs' role since 1986.[55] Even as the 1990 IOM report recommended a newfound emphasis on quality at a systems level, CMS "emphasized the importance of the beneficiary complaint process in carrying out the work of the QIO program."[56] However, after much public criticism, culminating in a 2001 OIG report highlighting the inadequacies of the complaint process,[57] the review organizations' complaint function was reevaluated, redesigned, and supported with additional funding.[58] Reevaluations and changes are ongoing.

Today, QIOs are required by statute to review, investigate, and respond to quality complaints by Medicare beneficiaries.[59] However, the investigation of beneficiary complaints constitutes a relatively small part of their work.[60] The primary part of modern QIOs' responsibilities is still to engage in peer review of treatment provided under the federal programs and establish plans for corrective action, thereby improving overall quality and controlling utilization.

b. Procedures for Patient Complaints, Investigation, and Discipline

When a patient files a quality-related complaint, the QIO investigates the complaint to "assess whether the health care delivered... met professionally recognized standards, was provided economically, was medically necessary, and was supported by adequate documentation."[61] The goal of the complaint investigation process is not to punish physicians with performance problems—rather, it is to help reform systems and improve care.

[55] Diane E. Hoffmann & Virginia Rowthorn, *Achieving Quality and Responding to Consumers—The Medicare Beneficiary Complaint Process: Who Should Respond?*, 5(9) IND. HEALTH L. REV. 9, 13 (2008).

[56] *Id.* at 14.

[57] Department of Health and Human Services Office of the Inspector General, *The Medicare Beneficiary Complaint Process: A Rusty Safety Valve*, OEI-01-00-0060 (Aug. 2001), at 24 [hereafter, 2001 OIG Report].

[58] Hoffmann & Rowthorn, *Achieving Quality*, at 14–15.

[59] 42 U.S.C.A. 1320c-3(a)(14) ("The organization shall conduct an appropriate review of all written complaints about the quality of services... not meeting professionally recognized standards of health care[.]).

[60] Department of Health and Human Services Office of the Inspector General, *Quality Concerns Identified Through Quality Improvement Organization Medical Record Reviews*, OEI-01-06-00170 (May 2007), at 10 [hereafter, 2007 OIG Report] (finding that cases identified via beneficiary complaints comprised only 6% of QIO case reviews); Sally Hart & Toby Edelman, "A Brief Overview of the Current Medicare Beneficiary Complaint Process," Center for Medicare Advocacy, *Beyond QIO: Modeling a Medicare Beneficiary Complaint Process for Quality of Care* (2007), *available at* http://www.medicareadvocacy.org/Projects/QIOConference/Background/BackgroundPaper.Overview.pdf (noting that the investigation of quality-related complaints from Medicare beneficiaries is "a relatively small part of the current Scope of Work for QIOs" and "has never been a central part of the role of QIOs.").

[61] 2006 IOM Report, at 302. *See generally* 42 U.S.C.A. § 1320c-3.

CMS sets out comprehensive procedures for investigating patient complaints in the Quality Improvement Organization Manual.[62] Initial complaints are screened and evaluated by review analysts, and cases requiring further attention are referred to physician peer reviewers. Where a peer reviewer determines that the medical care provided failed to satisfy professionally recognized standards of practice, the QIO will recommend corrective action, often working with the provider to establish a quality improvement plan. Typically, no further action will be taken by the QIO unless the reviewer finds an instance of "grossly and flagrantly unacceptable" conduct,[63] evidence of a pattern of nonstandard care in a substantial number of cases, or if the provider fails to complete the corrective action plan.[64] In such cases, the QIO may recommend sanctions to the Office of the Inspector General of the Department of Health and Human Services (OIG), which has the authority to impose monetary penalties or to permanently or temporarily exclude the provider from federal participation.[65]

Once a complaint has been resolved, federal law requires that the QIO inform the beneficiary of its final resolution as to whether the quality of care provided met professional standards.[66] As of 2014, beneficiaries and providers alike have the right to request formal reconsideration of a QIO determination.[67]

c. Challenges and Criticisms

The modern QIO process, and in particular its responsiveness to beneficiary quality complaints, has been subject to critical review in recent years, most notably in *Medicare's Quality Improvement Organization Program: Maximizing Potential*, a 2006 report by the Institute of Medicine (IOM) that was issued as a requirement of the Medicare Prescription Drug, Improvement, and Modernization Act of 2003.[68] It is worth noting, however, that many of these modern criticisms echo criticisms of prior iterations of QIOs dating back to the 1980s, including concerns about the balance of QIO activity as between large-scale quality improvement and individual case review (either via utilization review or as prompted by beneficiary complaints).

The overarching concern raised in the 2006 IOM report, as well as in other studies by the Office of the Inspector General and by a variety of academic researchers, is that QIOs tend to treat providers, rather than beneficiaries, as their primary clients. CMS's contracts with QIOs prioritize large-scale quality improvement projects and prevention of payment errors

[62] *Available at* http://www.cms.gov/Regulations-and-Guidance/Guidance/Manuals/Internet-Only-Manuals-IOMs-Items/CMS019035.html.

[63] *See* 42 U.S.C.A. § 1320c-5(b)(1).

[64] 2006 IOM Report, at 305–307; 2007 OIG Report, at 14.

[65] Of course, physicians have due process rights before revocation or other significant sanctions and are entitled to appeal and judicial review of the secretary's decision. *See generally* 42 C.F.R. §1101.2001 *et seq*; Fayad v. Sebelius, 803 F. Supp. 2d 699, 706 (E.D. Mich. 2011) (citing Mathews v. Eldridge, 424 U.S. 319, 334–35 (1976)).

[66] 42 U.S.C.A. § 1320c-3(a)(14).

[67] 42 CFR § 476.140(a). Previously, this right was not available to beneficiaries. *See* 77 F.R. 68210, 68514–68515 (Nov. 15, 2012).

[68] 2006 IOM Report.

over complaint investigation and response. Thus, QIOs are in the difficult position of having to collaborate with providers to implement technical quality improvement programs, while at the same time maintaining the regulatory function of overseeing and responding to patient care complaints. Given this inherent tension, it appears that QIOs tend to view their regulatory enforcement function as a lower priority. For example, a 2007 OIG study found that beneficiary complaints comprised only 6% of cases reviewed by QIOs, with the vast majority of QIOs' work dedicated to payment-related and other reviews.[69] This criticism is not new—the OIG raised similar concerns in a 2001 report, finding that CMS's contracts with QIOs "treat complaints as a distinctly minor activity."[70]

Both the OIG and the IOM have found that many Medicare beneficiaries are simply unaware that they have a right to file complaints and have them reviewed by QIOs.[71] As a result, very few beneficiaries actually file complaints—in 2004, for example, only one complaint was filed per every fourteen thousand beneficiaries.[72] Those beneficiaries who are aware of the QIO complaint process, moreover, often have difficulties using the reporting system. A 2007 study found that almost half of all callers to CMS's beneficiary call centers experienced problems accessing information, with approximately 21% of callers hanging up before receiving responses to their questions.[73] An earlier study noted that only four of ten calls to state-level peer review organizations yielded accurate information about how to file a quality-of-care complaint.[74]

A second concern is that QIOs are not responsive enough to those patients who do file complaints. Generally, beneficiaries are contacted once when the complaint is filed, and again at the end of the review process, with minimal, if any, written communication in between.[75] While QIOs have a statutory mandate to inform beneficiaries about the disposition of their complaints,[76] it was not until a 2003 decision by the U.S. Court of Appeals for the District of Columbia that long-standing agency restrictions on information disclosure to beneficiaries were lifted. Historically, CMS barred QIOs from disclosing substantive information about the resolution of complaints to a beneficiary if the treating physician did not consent to such disclosure, and QIO notices to beneficiaries were frequently criticized as lacking. However, in *Public Citizen v. HHS*, a federal appeals court held that the statutory requirement that QIOs disclose the "final disposition of the complaint" requires disclosure of the substantive resolution of the complaint, including the QIO's determination of whether the care provided met "professionally recognized standards of care," regardless of

69 2007 OIG Report, at 10–11.

70 2001 OIG Report, at 14–15.

71 2006 IOM Report, at 113; Department of Health and Human Services, *The Beneficiary Complaint Process of the Medicare Peer Review Organizations*, OEI-01-93-00250 (Nov. 1995), at 5 (finding that 77% of Medicare beneficiaries were not aware of Medicare Peer Review Organizations (the predecessors to QIOs); 2001 OIG Report, at 7 (noting that even those beneficiaries who are aware of PROs lacked adequate understanding of the complaint process).

72 2006 IOM Report, at 113.

73 Office of the Inspector General, *1-800-Medicare: Caller Satisfaction and Experiences*, OEI-07-06-00530 (Sept. 2007) at 8–9.

74 2001 OIG Report, at 7. *See also* Government Accountability Office, *Call Centers Need to Improve Responses to Policy-Oriented Questions from Providers*, GAO-04-669 (July 2004) (finding that that only 4% of providers who called 1-800-MEDICARE obtained "correct and complete" answers to their policy-related questions).

75 2001 OIG Report, at 11.

76 42 U.S.C.A. § 1320c-3(a)(14).

the consent of the practitioner.[77] In addition, CMS requires that QIOs make two additional disclosures if the consent of the provider is granted: It must summarize the medical record and its findings, and provide a description of the corrective action taken.[78] More recently, in 2012, federal regulations were changed to require disclosure of additional information to beneficiaries even without the consent of providers—first, about the standard of care used by the QIO in making its determination, and second, a summary of specific facts pertinent to its findings.[79] It remains to be seen how these new regulations will play out in practice.

The length of the complaint review process has been another long-standing point of criticism. Even with no delays, the QIO complaint resolution process can take over one hundred fifty days.[80] In response to these concerns, CMS recently adopted regulations allowing beneficiaries filing oral complaints to receive quicker resolution by way of a process called "immediate advocacy."[81] Written complaints, however, still have to be processed through the traditional lengthy peer review process. It is unclear how many beneficiaries will be able to take advantage of the expedited system.

From a more substantive perspective, QIOs have been criticized for failing to take meaningful action in response to patient complaints. When investigating complaints, QIOs appear to invest minimal effort, often limiting their investigations to medical record reviews. [82] When quality concerns are found, QIOs tend to categorize them as low level—according to a 2007 review of cases with "confirmed quality concerns," QIOs classified 50% with the lowest level of concern, "care could reasonably have been expected to be better."[83] Thirty-one percent of cases were classified as involving care that "failed to follow generally accepted guidelines or usual practices," and only 2% of cases were found to have involved a "gross and flagrant violation."[84] And with the exception of the last category, corrective actions taken tend to be minimal. QIOs imposed no corrective action at all in 28% of all cases involving confirmed quality concerns; of the remaining cases, most actions taken were limited to providing advice about alternative approaches to future care.[85] Formal quality improvement or corrective action plans were recommended in 25% of cases,[86] and only in fewer than 2%

[77] Public Citizen v. Department of Health and Human Services, 332 F.3d 654 (D.C. Cir. 2003). Notably, a post–Public Citizen study of QIO responses to patient complaints during 2008 and 2009 concluded that almost all responses satisfied the new disclosure requirements. Stuart Wright, *Memorandum Report: Quality Improvement Organizations' Final Responses to Beneficiary Complaints*, OEI-01-09-00620 (Oct. 12, 2010) [hereafter, 2010 OIG Report], *available at* http://oig.hhs.gov/oei/reports/oei-01-09-00620.pdf.

[78] 2010 OIG Report, at 4.

[79] 77 F.R. 68210, 68515 (Nov. 15, 2012); 42 C.F.R. § 476.130(b).

[80] 77 F.R. 68210, 68510 (Nov. 15, 2012). *See also* 2001 OIG Report, at 13 (noting that despite CMS's shortening of the target timeframe for complaint resolution from 220 to 150 days, 43 of 55 complaint reviews examined by the OIG exceeded this limit).

[81] *See* 77 F.R. 68210, 68510-68512 (Nov. 15, 2012); 42 C.F.R. § 476.110.

[82] 2001 OIG Report, at 8–9. Moreover, many QIOs incorrectly view service-related complaints (as opposed to quality complaints) as outside their scope, often referring beneficiaries instead to other entities. *Id.*

[83] 2007 OIG Report, at 13.

[84] *Id.*

[85] *Id.* at 14–16. *See also* 2001 OIG Report, at 9 (noting that the most common intervention is by way of letter to providers, which the PROs consider to be "educational" rather than disciplinary interventions).

[86] 2007 OIG Report, at 14–16. *See also* 2001 OIG Report, at 9 (finding that in only six of sixty-six complaints with confirmed quality concerns did PROs call for a corrective action plan).

of cases did the QIOs initiate formal sanction activity[87] or referral to licensing bodies.[88] Opportunities for large-scale quality improvements, moreover, are minimal; according to the 2001 OIG Report, "PROs tend to treat complaints as individual incidents, rather than as potential signs of systemic problems." [89]

Thus, one of the IOM's primary recommendations for improving the beneficiary complaint process was to separate QIOs' two functions, delegating complaint investigation and enforcement to an independent entity that "recognizes the beneficiary as the primary client."[90] This way, QIOs could focus on peer review, technical assistance, and large-scale quality improvement, with a separate independent entity dedicated to prioritizing patient complaints. The IOM noted that there are many other organizations at the state, regional, and national level that are already charged with investigating patient complaints; if provided with the funds typically allocated to QIOs for complaint investigation, they might be more suitable entities for complaint resolution.[91] Moreover, many of these organizations, like state survey agencies, have greater visibility among consumers than QIOs currently do, which would make the transition a natural one. The proposal to shift complaint resolution to alternate entities was also supported in a 2007 report by the Center for Medicare Advocacy, which suggested that state survey agencies and state medical boards would be best situated to take over this function, because they are visible among consumers, more accessible and responsive, and better able to take corrective action.[92]

State survey agencies contract with CMS to survey hospitals, nursing homes, and other healthcare facilities on a regular basis for compliance with state and federal regulations. In addition to conducting regular surveys, survey agencies also respond to patient complaints about improper care or unsafe conditions in healthcare facilities. CMS defines the survey agency complaint review process as having three primary objectives: responding to incidents with significant potential for beneficiary harm, investigating less serious incidents with an eye toward preventing escalation of problems, and promoting quality and efficiency within the Federal healthcare system.[93] Like QIOs, survey agencies have a number of options for dealing with noncompliant institutions, from developing corrective action pans, taking action under state licensing authority, or reporting to CMS. And because survey agencies'

[87] 2007 OIG Report, at 14–16. *See also* 2006 IOM Report, at 113 ("[T]he number of QIO recommendations for sanctions against physicians and hospitals stemming from beneficiary complaints has dropped from an annual average of 31 to an annual average of 1 over the last 20 years."). Between 1995 and 2003, for example, QIOs nationwide recommended sanctions in only twelve cases. *Id.*

[88] 2007 OIG Report, at 14–16. *See also* 2001 OIG Report, at 10 (noting that only nine of fifty QIOs contacted as part of the survey reported referring providers to state medical boards based on a beneficiary complaint on over a three-year period, and only six6 reported referrals to state certification agencies).

[89] 2001 OIG Report, at 8–11 (also finding that only one out of fifty QIOs reported implementing a quality improvement project based on beneficiary complaints).

[90] 2006 IOM Report, at 114–115. [91] *Id.* at 113.

[92] Diane E. Hoffmann & Virginian Rowthorn, "Medicare Beneficiary Complaint Process: QIOs and Possible Alternatives," Center for Medicare Advocacy, *Beyond QIO: Modeling a Medicare Beneficiary Complaint Process for Quality of Care*, 36–37 (2007), *available at* http://www.medicareadvocacy.org/Projects/QIOConference/Background/BackgroundPaper.LegalPerspective.pdf.

[93] Medicare State Operations Manual, §5000.1, *available at* http://www.cms.gov/Regulations-and-Guidance/Guidance/Manuals/Downloads/som107c05.pdf.

primary focus is surveying institutions for compliance with federal regulations rather than implementing systemic quality improvement measures, concerns about conflicts of interest are limited.

However, shifting the complaint function to state survey agencies may not be a perfect solution. Although the effectiveness of survey agencies in handling patient complaints has not been studied as widely as that of QIOs (evaluations of survey agencies focus primarily on their reviews of nursing homes), many of the other criticisms of QIOs cited above also apply to these entities—including inadequate investigation of complaints, limited corrective actions, and inadequate follow-up on corrective actions.[94] Historically, complaint review has been a greater portion of survey agencies' budgets than QIOs' budgets, but complaint investigation still comprises a minority of survey activities as a whole.[95] Furthermore, there is a great deal of variation in procedures among state survey agencies, with only limited federal oversight.

CMS, in its response to the 2006 IOM report, rejected the recommendation to spin off the beneficiary complaint function to state survey agencies or other organizations. By virtue of its statutory mandate, CMS views the complaint function as essential to QIOs' role, and maintains that QIOs should retain responsibility for the complaint review function. Instead, it proposed that the QIO programs be restructured and improved, though it did not provide specific recommendations beyond greater outreach to beneficiaries.[96]

It is clear that QIOs face a conflict of interest because their responsibilities include both technical assistance to physicians and enforcement of patient complaints. As a result, beneficiary complaints are not handled as effectively as they could be. Whether the solution is to spin off the complaint investigation process entirely, or rather clarify the QIOs' priorities and strengthen their authority, is unclear. While patients are fortunate to have the opportunity to share their concerns about federal quality standards with QIOs, it is not clear that QIOs are responding to these concerns as effectively as they could.

III Private Organizations and Professional Associations

Patients with quality-related complaints about their healthcare providers may also bring their concerns to some private organizations, like the Joint Commission and various

[94] Hoffman & Rowthorn, Medicare.

[95] General Accounting Office, *Nursing Homes: Complaint Investigation Processes Often Inadequate to Protect Patients*, GAO/HEHS-99-80 (Mar. 1999), at 5 (noting that only 20% of the federal funds paid to states for nursing home certification and surveys in 1998 was allocated to complaint investigation).

[96] Michael Leavitt, HHS Secretary, *Report to Congress: Improving the Medicare Quality Improvement Organization Program: Response to the Institute of Medicine Study* 14, 22–23 (2006). The American Health Quality Association, likewise, suggested that QIOs maintain responsibility, but that Congress modernize the programs by replacing the beneficiary complaint process with a Medicare Quality Accountability Program that would provide more concrete directives to QIOs. American Health Quality Association, *Recommendations to Congress for a Medicare Quality Accountability Program* (Mar. 2006) (on file with author).

specialty medical associations. Medical associations, however, focus primarily on furthering the interests of the profession and so are not focused on patient complaints; many do not accept complaints all.

The Joint Commission (formerly the Joint Commission for the Accreditation of Healthcare Organizations) accredits and certifies the vast majority of hospitals and large healthcare organizations in the United States. Its website offers consumers the opportunity to submit complaints about a healthcare organization,[97] but there is limited public information available about how many complaints the Joint Commission receives and how it approaches the complaint investigation process. Its website assures consumers that they will be informed about whether the institution in question was contacted, whether the institution was asked to make improvements, and whether its accreditation standards were impacted,[98] but there is no data evaluating whether the commission is successful in documenting and disclosing its responsiveness.

While most private medical societies do not accept patient complaints, a few do—most notably, the American Hospital Association, the American College of Physicians, and the Accreditation Counsel for Continuing Medical Education. However, detailed information about their procedures for investigation, reporting, and sanctions is generally unavailable to the public; and informal communications with some of these organizations suggest that patient complaints are relatively rare. This is not surprising, given that these organizations are designed primarily to further the goals of the profession rather than address matters of public concern—were they to adopt a more formal investigatory role in response to patient complaints, they would likely face even more accusations of conflicts of interest than state medical boards and QIOs. However, the fact that private medical associations are funded by membership fees suggests that they may have the resources that some of these public agencies lack.

IV Public Consumer Reviews

Some patients are aware of the opportunities to voice quality-related complaints to governmental or private entities; however, many are not. Moreover, even those patients who know about formal systems for complaint resolution may be reluctant to pursue these options, either because of their perceived ineffectiveness or simply because of the time and energy involved in filing a formal complaint. The rise of online consumer ratings systems like HealthGrades, Vitals, and RateMDs demonstrates that patients are seeking new outlets for voicing concerns about healthcare quality outside formal complaint processes.

While consumer reviews of restaurants, hotels, and retail establishments have long been viewed as useful tools for providing public information about the perceived quality of businesses, online reviews of healthcare providers have developed somewhat more recently. Numerous commentators have noted that online ratings sites and social media may be valuable mechanisms for obtaining "insight into quality of care from a patient's perspective."[99]

[97] Https://jcwebnoc.jcaho.org/QMSInternet/IncidentEntry.aspx.

[98] Http://www.jointcommission.org/report_a_complaint.aspx.

[99] Lise M. Verhoef et al., *Social Media and Rating Sites as Tools to Understanding Quality of Care: A Scoping Review*, 16(2) J. Med. Internet Res. e56 (2014).

However, although there are many online resources for reviewing healthcare providers and institutions, few providers are represented on these sites and few patients use them.[100] That said, there is some evidence demonstrating an association between positive online reviews and objective quality-of-care measures (such as mortality and readmission rates),[101] as well as more traditional assessments of patient satisfaction (like the Hospital Consumer Assessment of Healthcare Providers and Systems).[102] It is perhaps because of this connection between self-reported patient experiences and quality measures that healthcare agencies in some non-U.S. countries have established nationally sponsored healthcare ratings websites. The National Health Service Choices website in the United Kingdom, for example, allows patients to rate and provide commentary on their experiences with healthcare providers, physician groups, and hospitals.[103]

Unlike formal mechanisms for patient reporting and complaints, however, healthcare ratings websites offer no direct opportunity for quality improvement. Whereas physicians disciplined by their state medical boards or healthcare facilities sanctioned by federal or state agencies are targeted for improvement, a handful of negative ratings on Yelp is unlikely to impact the average healthcare provider's practice patterns. Thus, while they may be valuable tools for consumers choosing between healthcare providers, such websites are not necessarily effective tools for healthcare quality improvement at large.

V Conclusion

Patients have numerous opportunities to bring concerns about quality of care to the attention of state and federal agencies, as well as some private organizations. But few patients are aware of these opportunities, and widespread criticism suggests that the organizations responsible for complaint investigation and resolution are not as effective as they could be. Many of them have conflicting obligations, often prioritizing protection of the profession over protection of the patient population. Most operate under significant budgetary constraints, with the majority of their budgets dedicated to purposes other than complaint investigation. Finally, many critics argue that these organizations have failed to prioritize and effectively respond to complaints about quality of care.

There is no single solution to this problem. One recommendation is for agencies responsible for resolving patient complaints to instead focus on systemic ex ante approaches to improving care quality, which, if effective, would minimize the number of quality-related

[100] Martin Emmert et al., *Eight Questions About Physician-Rating Websites: A Systematic Review*, 15(2) J. Med. Internet Res. e24 (2013) (citing studies finding that less than 30% of sampled physicians had been rated on online sites); Susannah Fox, Pew Research Center, *The Social Life of Health Information, 2011*, *available at* http://www.pewinternet.org/2011/05/12/the-social-life-of-health-information-2011/ (finding that approximately 15% of Internet users have consulted online rankings or reviews of healthcare providers or facilities, and that fewer than 5% of Internet users have posted such online reviews).

[101] Verhoef et al., *Social Media*.

[102] Naomi S. Bardach et al., *The Relationship between Commercial Website Ratings and Traditional Hospital Performance Measures in the USA*, 22(3) BMJ Quality and Safety 194 (2013).

[103] Http://www.nhs.uk/Services/.

problems that patients experience. Indeed, some federal and state agencies are increasingly choosing to focus their energies on establishing ex ante quality improvement systems with the potential to affect whole populations, rather than responding to ex post patient complaints about individual providers. This trend toward ex ante prevention has been prompted in part by the 2010 Patient Protection and Affordable Care Act, which for the most part set aside issues of recourse for individual injuries in favor of developing systemic approaches for improving quality of care.[104] And indeed, for a healthcare system whose goal is to ensure care quality and protect patients from harm, this seems to be a move in the right direction.

It is difficult to predict the extent to which agencies, in light of these changes, will continue to use their resources to investigate issues brought to their attention by injured patients. Although it may indeed be more cost-effective to focus on preventing injury through regulation rather than responding to complaints after problems arise, it would be unwise for agencies to abandon this role altogether. Even the best ex ante regulatory system will not eliminate errors entirely, and it would be troubling if injured patients were only able to seek recourse through the malpractice system—an inefficient and arguably ineffective system for addressing patients' quality-related concerns. State licensing boards, QIOs, and survey agencies bring significant value to patients whose primary goal is not seeking compensation, but rather seeking acknowledgment that a quality error occurred and a promise to protect other patients from similar harms. While the current regulatory system for investigating and responding to patient complaints about quality of care is far from perfect, it serves a valuable and commendable goal.

[104] *See* William M. Sage & David A. Hyman, *Let's Make A Deal: Trading Malpractice Reform for Health Reform*, 33 HEALTH AFF. 53, at 53–54 (2014) (noting the political opposition to inclusion of malpractice reform measures within the Affordable Care Act).

PART III

ORGANIZING AND FINANCING THE HEALTHCARE SYSTEM

A. Health Professionals and Healthcare Facilities

CHAPTER 22

STRUCTURE OF GOVERNMENTAL OVERSIGHT OF QUALITY IN HEALTHCARE

SANDRA H. JOHNSON

I Structure of Governmental Oversight of Quality in Healthcare

For most consumer goods and services, the market works to set an acceptable level of quality. However, significant intractable barriers impede the influence of the market in creating effective demand for quality in healthcare services. Specific impediments include a lack of relevant, timely, accurate, and understandable information on quality measures and outcomes for professionals and facilities; the limited ability on the part of consumers to evaluate available data; and decision-making processes that place the choice of facility or caregiver in the hands of someone other than the patient. State and federal governments are making efforts to address these barriers, and many of these efforts have focused on collecting and posting quality data. For example, a number of state medical licensure boards are beginning to establish consumer-accessible websites with information on physicians practicing within the state.[1] The federal government also has established several consumer-oriented websites, including the federal *PhysicianCompare* and *Nursing Home Compare* websites.[2] Experience with *Nursing Home Compare*, however, illustrates the challenges of remedying information-related barriers as the site has been heavily criticized for posting information that is dated, inaccurate, and misleading.[3]

[1] *See, e.g.*, Mass. Bd. of Reg. in Med., Online Physician Profiles Website, http://profiles.ehs.state.ma.us/Profiles/Pages/FindAPhysician.aspx (Dec. 28, 2014, 3:22 AM).

[2] Physician Compare, http://www.medicare.gov/PhysicianCompare; Official Nursing Home Compare Data, https://data.medicare.gov/data/nursing-home-compare.

[3] Editorial, *When Five-Star Care Is Substandard: Medicare's Flawed Ratings for Nursing Homes*, N.Y. Times, Aug. 26, 2014.

State and federal governments ultimately respond to this endemic market failure by using a "command-and-control" system of regulation through which the government sets quality standards, monitors for compliance, and imposes sanctions for violations. State governments regulate the quality of healthcare professionals and facilities primarily through licensure. The federal government enforces quality standards for healthcare services chiefly through Medicare and Medicaid contracting.

a. Defining Terms: Licensure, Registration, and Certification

Licensure is the most restrictive of government controls on the provision of healthcare services. If state law requires that individuals or organizations providing certain healthcare services be licensed, any person or facility offering those services without a state-issued license is violating the law and typically can be charged with a crime.[4] State statutes set licensure requirements for the health professions.[5] These laws govern entry into the licensed professions; regulate the healthcare services that licensed professionals may provide; and prohibit the delivery of regulated healthcare services by unlicensed persons. Through individual disciplinary actions, the state licensure agencies, often called "boards," oversee the quality of care provided by licensees and penalize or remove incompetent and unethical practitioners from practice. The composition of state licensure boards varies considerably, although most are still dominated by members of the licensed professions subject to the board's jurisdiction even though the boards typically include at least one consumer member.[6]

Even though only licensed healthcare professionals may treat patients within a healthcare facility, a quality-control regulatory system that stopped with the individual professional would be incomplete. The quality of the institution itself has a significant impact on the quality of care received by patients. The scope of institutional factors that can pose a danger to patients is extensive, ranging from the adequacy of buildings, equipment, maintenance, and sanitation through health information technology; from fiscal and managerial effectiveness through the selection, training, and monitoring of individuals directly providing care; and from staffing levels through food service. The patient safety movement, in fact, focuses on

[4] *See* section III.

[5] A very wide range of healthcare professionals commonly require a license under state law. For example, the state of California requires a license for acupuncturists (Cal. Bus. & Prof. Code § 4935); chiropractors (Cal. Bus. & Prof. Code § 1000-5); clinical laboratory technologists (Cal. Bus. & Prof. Code § 1261.5); clinical laboratory bioanalysts (Cal. Bus. & Prof. Code § 1260); cytotechnologists (Cal. Bus. & Prof. Code § 1270); dentists (Cal. Bus. & Prof. Code § 1634); physicians and surgeons (allopathic) (Cal. Bus. & Prof. Code § 2050); podiatrists (Cal. Bus. & Prof. Code § 2472); speech pathologists (Cal. Bus. & Prof. Code § 2532); physical therapists (Cal. Bus. & Prof. Code § 2630); vocational nurses (Cal. Bus. & Prof. Code § 2859); registered nurses (Cal. Bus. & Prof. Code § 2732), midwives (Cal. Bus. & Prof. Code § 2507); psychologists (Cal. Bus. & Prof. Code § 2903); hearing aid dispensers (Cal. Bus. & Prof. Code § 2538.20); physician assistants (Cal. Bus. & Prof. Code § 3519); osteopathic physicians (Cal. Bus. & Prof. Code § 3600-5); respiratory therapists (Cal. Bus. & Prof. Code § 3701); polysomnographic technologists (Cal. Bus. & Prof. Code § 3575); psychiatric technicians (Cal. Bus. & Prof. Code § 4510); and clinical social workers (Cal. Bus. & Prof. Code § 4996), among others.

[6] *See* section III.a and b.

the quality of systems within healthcare organizations rather than on the behaviors of individual caregivers standing alone. States, therefore, also require that many types of healthcare facilities be licensed as a condition of providing certain services.[7]

While states typically require licensure for a great range of healthcare professionals and organizations, states utilize mechanisms that are less restrictive than licensure for some healthcare providers. For example, states may require only that a particular service provider be registered with the state in order to use a specific title or to provide certain services. When a state requires registration only, and not licensure, the regulated provider ordinarily is not required to pass an examination in order to provide services. Registration-only requirements are quite uncommon, however,[8] and confusion can arise when the term "registered" is used in a professional title. The term may indicate that the professional is registered with the state but not licensed, but it may also be used when the professional is both registered and licensed. The most common example is the common title of "registered nurse" or "RN" RNs typically are both registered with and licensed by the state.[9]

A similar ambiguity arises in the use of the term "certification." As a general matter, certification is a process conducted by a private organization that sets educational standards, conducts examinations, and requires compliance with particular professional standards of behavior and practice. Many states, however, require that an individual seeking licensure for the practice of certain healthcare professions be certified by a particular private organization as a condition of licensure. So, for example, states licensing particular nurse specialists may require that the individual be certified by the appropriate professional organization.[10] States do not require that physicians be certified as a condition of licensure, however. Adding to this definitional confusion the process for assuring that healthcare facilities are in compliance with Medicare and Medicaid requirements is called "certification," although in the case of Medicare and Medicaid, certification is a governmental process.[11]

b. Private Quality-Control Mechanisms as Compared to State and Federal Quality-Control Regulation

In addition to governmental quality-control mechanisms, healthcare professionals and organizations are subject to private nongovernmental efforts related to quality of care. Important private quality-oriented tools include private accreditation of healthcare facilities; board certification of physicians; intra-institutional tools such as staff privileges in hospitals; and private malpractice and negligence litigation, each of which is described in the paragraphs

[7] *See, e.g.*, ALA. CODE § 22-21-20 and 22-21-22, requiring licensure for a dozen types of healthcare facilities including hospitals, ambulatory surgical centers, freestanding dialysis units, skilled nursing facilities, and assisted living facilities. *See also* CONN. GEN. STAT. § 19A-490, for a similar range of facilities requiring licensure.

[8] *See, e.g.*, CAL. BUS. & PROF. CODE § 2529 (research psychoanalysts) and CAL. BUS. & PROF. CODE § 2559.1 (spectacle lens dispensers).

[9] *See, e.g.*, CAL. BUS. & PROF. CODE § 2732.

[10] *See, e.g.*, CAL. BUS. & PROF. CODE § 2746 (nurse midwives) and CAL. BUS. & PROF. CODE § 2829 (nurse anesthetists).

[11] *See* section I.b and c.

that follow. Governmental quality-control regulation, including licensure and governmental approval for Medicaid and Medicare contracting, intersects in meaningful ways with each of these nongovernmental quality-control efforts and those intersections are highlighted in the discussion that follows.

For healthcare facilities, private nonprofit organizations offer voluntary accreditation processes through which facilities can measure their compliance with standards established by their own industry. Consumers can look to this voluntary accreditation as an indicator of quality, viewing accreditation as a de facto seal of approval.[12] The Joint Commission (formerly known as the Joint Commission on Accreditation of Healthcare Organizations and before that as the Joint Commission on Accreditation of Hospitals) has been the most influential and powerful among the several organizations that offer voluntary accreditation to particular segments of the healthcare industry.

Although entirely voluntary, private accreditation is now closely aligned with government regulation of healthcare facilities. For example, most states incorporate Joint Commission standards in licensing hospitals, and many states accept Joint Commission accreditation in lieu of licensure inspection.[13] In addition, the Medicare statute permits the U.S. Department of Health and Human Services (HHS) to accept private accreditation of a healthcare facility in lieu of federal certification under certain circumstances.[14] This process is called "deemed status" because the facility that has been accredited by the private organization is deemed to have met the Medicare conditions of participation by virtue of that accreditation. The Centers for Medicare and Medicaid Services (CMS) within HHS retains the authority to perform validation surveys on accredited facilities, however, as a tool for verifying compliance with Medicare standards and for auditing the performance of the accreditation agency.[15]

Private accreditation organizations that want their accredited facilities to enjoy deemed status must be approved by the CMS. To gain approval, the accreditation organization must provide reasonable assurances that its accreditation program for that type of facility meets federal requirements. Accreditation organizations are required to reapply periodically for CMS approval. This application and review process provides a vehicle for the federal government to require and monitor consistency between the accreditation organization's standards and processes and Medicare standards and processes. For example, accreditation organizations desiring deemed status for accredited facilities generally are required to abandon the custom in accreditation of announcing site visits in advance and instead must conduct unannounced on-site inspections.[16] On the other hand, the reapplication and review process engages the CMS and the private accreditation organizations in a dialogue about appropriate standards of care, allowing industry a route for influencing government standards. Deemed status is a great advantage to healthcare facilities, reducing their compliance costs by requiring a single inspection process for both accreditation and Medicare/Medicaid certification. Currently, deemed status is not available to accredited nursing homes.

[12] *See, e.g.*, Clark C. Havighurst, *Foreword: The Place of Private Accrediting Among the Instruments of Government*, 57 LAW & CONTEMP. PROBS. 1 (1994).

[13] *See, e.g.*, ALA. CODE § 22-21-24; HAW. REV. STAT. § 321-14.5; WASH. REV. CODE § 70.41.122.

[14] 42 U.S.C. § 1395bb(2). [15] 42 U.S.C. § 1395bb(c) (2008).

[16] *See, e.g.*, Approval of the Application by the Joint Commission for Continued Deeming Authority for Hospitals, 74 Fed. Reg. 62333 (Nov. 27, 2009).

In theory, private accreditation more effectively encourages voluntary compliance, avoids some of the prosecutorial environment of government-conducted inspection programs, and strengthens quality standards by adding another incentive for compliance with accepted standards.[17] Still, there are concerns that the private accreditation organizations are too readily influenced by the industry; that the CMS does not adequately assure that accreditation standards and Medicare standards are equivalent; and that delegation of public regulation to private organizations is improper, although legal challenges based on improper delegation typically have failed.[18]

Similar to private accreditation of healthcare facilities, specialty certification of physicians by private professional organizations operates as a quality-control mechanism by identifying practice standards and testing the clinician's skills and knowledge. This "board certification" is entirely voluntary for physicians, unlike the required state license, although many states require certification for some nonphysician healthcare professionals (as a nurse anesthetist or a midwife, for example) as a condition of licensure.[19] Although board certification is not required for licensure of physicians, some payers and healthcare organizations require that physicians be board-certified to receive payment or have access to facilities. In fact, public and private payers exert a strong influence on the quality of care by setting rates of reimbursement[20] and linking payment and performance.[21] However, payers cannot legally prohibit or mandate a particular practice as does licensure; they merely decline to pay for it.

Healthcare facilities themselves also engage in substantial internal quality assurance and improvement efforts. For example, to provide medical care to hospital patients, physicians must have been awarded "clinical staff privileges" by the hospital. Hospitals control the awarding and continuation of staff privileges through a peer-review process called credentialing, a process required by state hospital licensure and by Medicare. The credentialing system for clinical staff privileges within hospitals performs a significant quality-control function as the hospital uses the process to establish and enforce standards for practice within the hospital; actively monitor physician behaviors and outcomes; and exclude practitioners who fail to conform to the hospital's requirements.[22] Unlike the state health professions licensure boards, however, hospitals cannot remove a negligent or incompetent healthcare professional completely from practice but can only exclude the professional from treating patients in the hospital or from contracting or employment with the hospital.

[17] *See, e.g.*, Louise G. Trubek, *New Governance and Soft Law in Health Care Reform*, 3 IND. HEALTH L. REV. 139 (2006).

[18] *See generally* Harold J. Krent, *The Private Performing the Public: Delimiting Delegations to Private Parties*, 65 U. MIAMI L. REV. 507 (2011). *See also* Am. Nurses Ass'n v. Leavitt, 593 F.Supp.2d 126 (D.D.C. 2009), unsuccessful challenge to CMS reliance on Joint Commission staffing standard rather than Medicare staffing standard.

[19] *See, e.g.*, CONN. GEN. STAT. § 20-94A. *See also* section I.a.

[20] *See, e.g.*, Brietta R. Clark, *Medicaid Access, Rate Setting and Payment Suits: How the Obama Administration Is Undermining Its Own Health Reform Goals*, 55 HOW. L.J. 771 (2012); David C. Grabowski et al., *Medicaid Payment and Risk-Adjusted Nursing Home Quality Measures*, 23 HEALTH AFF. 243 (2004).

[21] *See generally* BARRY R. FURROW ET AL., IMPROVING TRADITIONAL MEDICARE: PAYMENT REFORMS UNDER THE AFFORDABLE CARE ACT IN HEALTH LAW, at § 8-16 (Hornbook Series 3d ed. 2014).

[22] *See generally* Furrow et al., *Professional Relationships in the Health Care Enterprise*, §§ 10-2 to 10-12.

Finally, the risk of private malpractice and negligence litigation creates a significant disincentive for substandard care and, unlike licensure, provides financial compensation to injured patients.[23] Malpractice and negligence settlements and judgments raise the cost of negligent practice and only very indirectly may drive some incompetent practitioners and substandard facilities from business. Private litigation, like other private quality-control tools, intersects with governmental quality-control regulatory mechanisms. For example, some states require that judgments and settlements be reported to the state licensure boards,[24] and others require the boards to investigate the substance of malpractice claims to identify professionals who should be removed from practice.[25] At least one state requires that the state medical licensure board revoke the license of a physician with multiple malpractice judgments under certain narrow circumstances.[26] In addition, medical malpractice judgments and settlements must be reported to the federal National Practitioner Data Bank. Although not open for public review, the information in the Data Bank is accessible to state licensure boards for licensure and discipline and to hospitals for credentialing.[27]

c. Federalism in Licensure and Medicare/Medicaid Certification

As a matter of constitutional law, the source of the individual state's power to license healthcare professionals and healthcare institutions is the police power, which is retained by the states in our federal system.[28] Under the police power, the state's regulation must further health, safety, and the general welfare. In reviewing legislation challenged as lying beyond the scope of the state's police power, courts will uphold the legislation if its contribution to health, safety, and general welfare is at least fairly debatable. Challenges to licensure requirements arguing that they are not legitimate exercises of the state police power typically have not succeeded.[29]

While the states have authority to regulate healthcare facilities under their police power, the federal government's primary authority with regard to healthcare providers, with few exceptions, arises from its spending authority exercised as purchaser of healthcare. Thus, the federal government relies on Medicare and Medicaid contracting, rather than licensure, as the primary vehicle for federal quality-control regulation of healthcare services. In general, requirements established under the federal government's spending authority must bear a relationship to the relevant federal payment program.

As administrative agencies, both the state licensure agencies and the federal HHS are limited to the authority granted to them within their enabling statutes. State professional licensure agencies are constrained by the state statutes that establish the particular licensing

[23] *See generally* Furrow et al., Chapters 3 (*The Liability of Health Care Professionals*) and 4 (*Liability and Quality Improvement of Health Care Institutions*).

[24] *See, e.g.*, 225 ILL. COMP. STAT. 60/22(A)(36).

[25] *See, e.g.*, MICH. COMP. LAWS ANN. § 333.16231.

[26] *See, e.g.*, FLA. STAT. § 456.50.

[27] 42 U.S.C. § 11131 *et seq.*

[28] Dent v. West Virginia, 129 U.S. 114 (1889).

[29] *See, e.g.*, Brightonian Nursing Home v. Daines, 999 N.E.2d 510 (N.Y. 2013); Ferrier-Harris, Ltd. v. Sanders, 905 S.W.2d 123 (Mo. Ct. App. 1995); People v. Casa Blanca Convalescent Homes, Inc., 159 Cal. App. 3d 509 (1984).

program, for example, in the medical practice act, the nurse practice act, or the nursing home licensure act. Similarly, the authority of the HHS in setting and enforcing standards for certification for federal payment is defined in the Medicare and Medicaid statutes. Thus, federal and state agencies must conform to statutory boundaries in setting quality standards; in following procedures for adopting standards or investigating and penalizing noncompliance; and in the penalties that they levy against noncomplying healthcare providers. In addition, these regulatory functions on both the state and federal level are subject to constitutional norms, including due process and equal protection.[30] Further, the state health professions boards may be subject to constraints on anticompetitive conduct under the federal antitrust laws.[31]

State and federal regulation of healthcare professionals and facilities intersect at many points. At times this intersection increases regulatory effectiveness and at other times, serious inefficiencies or conflicts in policy occur. Policy issues arise, for example, in regard to state boundaries for professional licensure; the dual federal and state regulation of specific medical practices; and the federal-state partnership that executes the enforcement process for Medicare and Medicaid certification, as discussed in the following paragraphs.

The states confront substantial cross-border limitations in professional licensure as state authority terminates at the state's borders. All states authorize the medical licensure board to penalize doctors practicing within the state when those doctors have been disciplined, for example by revocation or suspension of license, in other states. For decades, however, the states lacked a comprehensive and workable tool for discovering actions taken in other states. In response to this problem, Congress established the federal National Practitioner Data Bank to collect information on disciplinary actions, malpractice judgments and settlements, and adverse credentialing actions against individual physicians. State medical and dental licensing boards are required to report certain disciplinary actions and have access to reports on individual physicians and dentists.[32]

A second substantial cross-border issue in medical licensure by the states is the increasing utilization of telemedicine in which a doctor physically located in one state may use technology to diagnose or treat a patient located in another.[33] The states are taking disparate approaches to regulating doctors engaged in treating patients remotely across state lines, for example, by requiring the physician to register, pay licensing fees, or meet other requirements in each state where his or her patients are located, increasing the cost of this innovation.[34] State medical licensure boards justify such requirements based on their core obligation to protect the citizens of their state from incompetent practitioners even though

[30] *See, e.g.*, Watson v. Superior Court, 176 Cal. App. 4th 1407 (2009) (substantive due process challenge on grounds for discipline); Dandamudi v. Tisch, 686 F.3d 66 (2d Cir. 2012) (equal protection challenge to exclusion from licensure); Beverly Health & Rehabilitation Services, Inc. v. Thompson, 223 F. Supp. 2d 73 (D.D.C. 2002) (vagueness challenge).

[31] *See* sections III.b.i, ii, and iii.

[32] 42 U.S.C. § 11131 *et seq. See also* Furrow et al., §§ 1-6 (*Licensure and Discipline of Health Care Professionals*) and 10-6 (*Professional Relationships in the Health Care Enterprise*).

[33] *See generally* Diane E. Hoffman & Virginia Rowthorn, *Legal Impediments to the Diffusion of Telemedicine* (Symposium Issue on Telemedicine), 14 J. HEALTH CARE & POL'Y 1 (2011).

[34] *See, e.g.*, IND. CODE § 25-22.5-1-1.1(a)(4); ALA. CODE § 34-24-502; OHIO REV. CODE ANN. § 4731.296. *See also* Smith v. Lab. Corp. of Am., No. C09-1662-JCC, 2010 WL 5464770 (W.D. Wash. Dec. 30, 2010).

these requirements raise the cost of care and other less costly methods could be used to assure quality of care. In contrast to medical licensure, a good number of nursing licensure boards have established an interstate compact that affords licensure reciprocity among participating states so that nurses can move from state to state to practice without engaging in costly regulatory processes in each state.[35] The Federation of State Medical Boards, a private association, has recently completed a model interstate compact that state legislatures may eventually enact.[36]

A second illustration of federalism issues in healthcare regulation arises in those activities, such as prescribing, that are subject to both federal and state control. The federal Food and Drug Administration (FDA) controls approval and surveillance of medications; and the federal Drug Enforcement Administration (DEA) enforces standards for the prescription of controlled substances by requiring that healthcare professionals with prescribing authority hold a DEA-issued permit for the prescription of these medications. Finally, the state licensure boards set and enforce standards for and actively monitor prescribing by licensees within the state. This dual federal and state regulation can lead to conflicts. One current example of conflict between federal and state health policy is the legalization of marijuana for medical uses by a number of states while federal law continues to make the use or prescribing of marijuana illegal.[37]

Federalism issues are also prominent in the enforcement of Medicare and Medicaid standards for healthcare facilities. To receive payments under Medicare or Medicaid, an institutional provider must be licensed by the state, if the state licenses that type of facility, and must be approved by the CMS as meeting the Medicare and Medicaid Conditions of Participation (COP), which include standards for quality care.[38] Once certified as having met the program's COP, the facility executes a provider agreement with the CMS. The federal government, however, relies on state agencies to perform most of the inspection and sanction processes under a federally approved state plan.[39] Under the Medicaid statute, the states apply federal standards and use federally approved survey instruments in inspecting Medicaid facilities.[40] The federal government retains the authority to perform validation surveys (inspections), often called "look behind" surveys, to monitor the state inspections.[41] The state agency recommends sanctions to HHS for noncompliance. Both the state and HHS, however, hold the formal authority to sanction providers in the Medicaid program.[42] The state retains authority to levy licensure sanctions apart from HHS; and, if HHS concludes in its own inspection of a facility that the facility does not meet federal standards, the department may levy sanctions independent of the state agency's recommendation.[43] The state-federal partnership can be criticized as producing duplicative efforts and other inefficiencies; however, the federal government has a nondelegable duty to assure that it pays

[35] Nurse Licensure Compact, NAT'L COUNCIL OF ST. BOARDS OF NURSING, https://www.ncsbn.org/nlc.htm (last visited Jan. 4, 2015).

[36] FED'N OF STATE MED. BDS., INTERSTATE MEDICAL LICENSURE COMPACT (2014).

[37] *See generally* Melanie Reid, *The Quagmire That Nobody in the Federal Government Wants to Talk About: Marijuana*, 44 N. M. L. REV. 169 (2014). *See also* Gonzales v. Raich, 545 U.S. 1 (2005); Conant v. Walters, 309 F.3d 629 (9th Cir. 2002), *cert. denied*, 540 U.S. 946 (2003).

[38] 42 U.S.C. § 1396r(a)(3); 42 U.S.C. § 1395i-3(a)(3).

[39] 42 U.S.C. § 1396a(a).

[40] 42 U.S.C. § 1396r(g)(2)(C).

[41] 42 U.S.C. §§ 1396r(g)(3)(A), (g)(3)(D).

[42] 42 U.S.C. §§ 1396r(g)(1)(A), (h).

[43] 42 U.S.C. §§ 1396r(g)(3)(A), (g)(3)(D).

only for adequate quality and state and federal efforts can provide a knowledgeable check on the performance of each. In addition, the states can be a laboratory for quality standards and enforcement innovations.

II Setting Regulatory Standards

a. Defining Standards

Quality-control regulation of healthcare professionals and facilities begins with identifying standards that measure the quality of care. A classic taxonomy of healthcare quality standards divides these standards into structural standards, process standards, and outcome standards.[44]

Structural standards measure the resources available for caring for patients and thus measure the facility's or individual's capacity for rendering quality care. Structural standards for facilities include, for example, the facility's patient–staff ratio and the presence or absence of specific equipment. For healthcare professionals, educational qualifications, including degrees and continuing education credits, are examples of structural standards. Quantifiable structural standards eliminate the variable of individual judgment in the inspection/investigation stage and make it easy to prove noncompliance. Unfortunately, structural standards don't necessarily measure whether the care is actually any good, only that the tools required for good care are present. Individual providers, however, generally might prefer being measured on inputs, such as their education and training, and organizations, by the presence of written policies or required equipment, as such measures shut off inquiry into individualized performance and results and restrict individual discretion in the inspection and penalty process. In fact, landmark litigation regarding nursing home regulation successfully contested the federal government's nearly exclusive reliance on structural standards, arguing that structural standards measured only the facility's capacity to render care and failed to investigate whether the residents actually received quality care. The court held that this narrow approach to quality violated the federal agency's duty to assure that the care that the federal government paid for and residents actually received was adequate.[45]

Process standards relate more directly to the activities that take place in the delivery of care. For example, process standards relating to facility performance regarding medications would examine whether orders are written properly and whether the medications are delivered as prescribed while a structural standard would require that a licensed pharmacist manage the facility's pharmacy. For physicians, a process standard relating to prescribing might require that the physician perform a medical examination of the patient at particular intervals while a structural standard might require that the physician complete continuing education in prescribing medication with particular risks.

[44] Avedis Donabedian, The Definition of Quality and Approaches to Its Assessment (Vol. 1) (1980).

[45] *In re* Estate of Smith v. Heckler, 747 F.2d 583 (10th Cir. 1984).

Process standards depart from structural standards in that they examine the actual process of care, but these standards can perpetuate interventions and procedures that are strongly rooted in custom but lack evidence of positive effect. In the context of medical licensure, for example, licensure boards have used the practice patterns and custom of the profession as the gold standard for identifying substandard care processes. In effect, the custom of the profession, for example as to what diagnostic testing should be done and which medication should be prescribed and for how long, establishes the standards for quality medical care. Using the custom of the profession to define poor-quality care defers to the expertise of medicine and is one of the reasons that the medical licensure and disciplinary system is considered self-regulation. Deference to the medical profession is attractive as a tool for reining in regulatory power and as a reflection of how physicians learn and adapt their treatment decisions to those of their colleagues. Creating such a strong incentive for compliance with customary practice, however, can dampen medical innovation and the diffusion of new clinical knowledge by threatening or penalizing early adopters of useful but not yet widely accepted therapies. Driving physicians to the safety of the herd can also deprive individual patients of the best care in their particular circumstance.[46]

Although structure and process standards continue to play a significant role in governmental quality-control regulation, the current wave of government regulation for healthcare facilities is shifting emphasis toward more reliance on outcome standards. Outcome standards measure the actual effect of care on patients. For facilities, for example, outcome standards include rates of hospital-acquired infections, bed sores, urinary tract infections, and hospital readmissions. Outcome standards for doctors are much less common at this point, perhaps in part due to persistent perceptions that outcomes in individual patients are uncertain. Examples of outcome standards for physicans may include rates of postsurgical complications and "never events" such as wrong-site surgeries.

Outcome standards offset critical weaknesses in structure and process standards by requiring actual examination of the impact of care on patients, by setting norms for expected effects of care, and by holding providers accountable for the results of their work. Outcome measures also have their problems, of course. For example, at times convenience outweighs significance, and outcome measures can focus on items that are easily measured but less important than others. In addition, the identification and measurement of specific outcomes must be sensitive to variations other than quality of care that might determine positive or negative outcomes or they run the risk of making some patient populations less desirable. Furthermore, attaching consequences, such as reduction in payments or public disclosure or penalty, to specific outcomes drives organizational effort toward outcomes that will be measured whether or not this has a negative impact on other processes.

Regulation of the use of restraints in nursing homes provides an example of the weakness of outcome standards in the context of healthcare facility regulation. The rate of falls is a long-standing outcome measure of quality in nursing home care. A high rate of falls indicates a failure in care. Prior to the 1980s, physically restraining a nursing home resident, using lap belts, restraining vests, bed rails and such, was viewed as protective of the patient by preventing falls that could cause significant injury. Regulatory standards of the time actually contributed to the excessive use of restraints by requiring reporting and citations for

[46] *See also* section II.b.

falls but not the use of restraints. Empirical research in the field radically changed views of the appropriateness of using physical restraints. Legal research proved that nursing homes indeed faced liability risks for falls, but that the cases did not support the use of restraints as a preventive measure. Instead, where mobility was encouraged in the resident's care plan, nursing homes were not held liable for falls.[47] Nursing and medical research proved that physical restraints counterintuitively caused injuries rather than protecting patients.[48] This evidence crumbled the foundations of the strong customary practice of the use of physical restraints as protective of patients. In fact, reduction in the use of restraints did not produce an increase in falls.[49] Regulatory standards, first for nursing homes and then for hospitals, changed to reflect both the unintended consequence of the regulatory emphasis on falls alone and the new knowledge concerning the harmful effects of restraints. Although regulatory standards still account for a facility's rate of falls, they also now include detailed restrictions on the use of restraints, allowing their use only in well-defined rare circumstances.[50] Standard-setting is thus a continuous process, constantly reflecting the emergence of new knowledge and response to provider behaviors.

b. Challenges in Setting Standards for Nonconforming Practices

Medical licensure statutes vary among the states, but they typically provide for disciplinary action against doctors who fail to conform to "acceptable," "customary," or "prevailing" medical practice.[51] As discussed in section II.a., standards of care that rely on customary practice can dampen innovation and penalize early adopters of emerging treatments. Departing from professional custom as the source of standards of care, however, raises its own concerns as the efforts of several states to adjust disciplinary standards to accommodate CAM or other nonconforming interventions illustrate.

Physicians who adopt complementary and alternative medicine (CAM), or other nonconforming interventions, in treating their patients can easily run afoul of these statutory standards and risk disciplinary action. In a well-known example, the North Carolina medical board successfully pursued disciplinary action against a popular MD who provided his patients with homeopathic treatment. The board found, and the appeals court affirmed, that the doctor violated the standard of care under the North Carolina medical practice

47 Sandra H. Johnson, *The Fear of Liability and the Use of Restraints in Nursing Homes*, 18 J.L., MED. & HEALTH CARE 263 (1991).

48 Julie A. Braun & Elizabeth A. Capezuti, *The Legal and Medical Aspects of Physical Restraints and Bed Siderails and Their Relationship to Falls and Fall-Related Injuries in Nursing Homes*, 4 DEPAUL J. OF HEALTH CARE L. 1 (2000).

49 Nicholas G. Castle, *Physical Restraints in Nursing Homes: A Review of the Literature Since the Nursing Home Reform Act of 1987*, 55 MED. CARE RES. REV. 139 (1998).

50 42 U.S.C. § 1395i-3(c)(1)(A)(ii)(II); 42 U.S.C. § 1396r(c)(1)(A)(ii)(II); 42 C.F.R. § 483.13(a); APPENDIX PP—GUIDANCE TO SURVEYORS FOR LONG TERM CARE FACILITIES, CMS STATE OPERATIONS MANUAL § 483.13(a), at 69 (2011).

51 *See, e.g.*, GA. CODE ANN. § 43-34-8(7); MO. REV. STAT. § 334.100(5).

act, which called for discipline when a physician failed to conform to "prevailing medical practice."[52]

In response to this litigation the North Carolina legislature amended the state's medical practice act to add a provision that prohibited the board from disciplining a physician who provided "a therapy that is experimental, nontraditional, or that departs from acceptable and prevailing medical practice" unless the board can produce "competent evidence" that the specific treatment has a greater "safety risk" than the prevailing practice or that the treatment is "generally ineffective."[53] This standard certainly expresses the central concerns of risk and benefit that arise in medical treatment and which should be the focus of restrictive regulation; however, data on effectiveness is nonexistent for a significant portion of conventional medicine and much of CAM. Furthermore, it is unlikely that even the most muscular efforts to produce data on effectiveness for conventional treatments and CAM would be able to provide a flow of clinically relevant and conclusive data that would respond to the burden set for the board by this statute.

Other states have adopted modified versions of the North Carolina approach.[54] Alaska, for example, bars the board from finding a licensee guilty of professional incompetence solely on the basis of the use of unconventional or experimental therapies "in the absence of demonstrable physical harm to a patient."[55] This requirement that the board refrain from acting until a patient has been physically harmed radically narrows the traditional authority and core duty of professional licensure and discipline as the boards are expected to act to prevent such harm from occurring.[56]

Even developing a working definition of what practices should be protected from standards relying on customary practice is challenging. Identifying the universe of interventions that physicians may pursue despite their violation of professionally accepted standards must account for constant change in medical knowledge and must maintain boundaries that actually protect patients from risky, fraudulent, or ineffective interventions. For example, both the North Carolina and Alaska approaches to restraining interference with treatment choices protect the use of "experimental" therapies. The term "experimental," however, encompasses a range of quite distinct interventions including those being studied in formal research protocols; clinical innovation reasonably designed to treat a particular patient's condition; and interventions that simply have not been tried before. In fact, many states,[57] including some with these provisions, specifically prohibit physicians from providing patients with experimental therapies outside of established protocols designed to gather data and analyze results or otherwise greatly restrict their use.[58] For example, Alaska prohibits experimental interventions in mental health facilities where there is a "significant *risk*" of harm.[59] A more refined effort at defining the permissible scope of departure from accepted medical practice divides therapies into those that are "invalidated (either implausible or has

[52] *In re* Guess, 393 S.E.2d 833 (N.C. 1990).

[53] N.C. Gen. Stat. § 90-14(a)(6).

[54] *See, e.g.*, Okla. Stat. Ann. tit. 59, § 509.1(2).

[55] Alaska Rev. Stat. § 08.64.326(8)(A).

[56] *See, e.g.*, Bd. of Reg. for the Healing Arts v. McDonagh, 123 S.W.3d 146 (Mo. 2003).

[57] The federal government also strictly regulates experimentation in medicine when the intervention meets the definition of research adopted in federal regulations. *See generally* Furrow et al., *Regulation of Research Upon Human Subjects*, §§ 17-1 to 17-23.

[58] *See, e.g.*, Ariz. Rev. Stat. Ann. § 32-1401(y); Kan. Stat. Ann. § 65-2837(b)(27).

[59] Alaska Rev. Stat. § 47.30.830. *See also* Okla. Stat. Ann. tit. 59, § 637.

failed in controlled studies)," "non-validated (plausible but not yet proven)," and "validated" (proven efficacious) therapies, prohibiting the provision of invalidated therapies and allowing nonvalidated therapies under certain circumstances.[60] While this is not an entirely satisfactory definitional structure, it is more analytical than intuitive and takes a step forward. An alternative and less satisfactory approach would be to look to CAM for a generalizable definition of the landscape of interventions that would be permissible in that realm, but CAM is not amenable to definition either, as has been noted by the Institute of Medicine in its study.[61]

In the face of these definitional challenges, many states, by statute or by board rule or regulation, have adopted quite specific prohibitions or restrictions on particular treatments. The medical practice act in California, for example, lists as unprofessional conduct the use of liquid silicone for breast implants and the prescription or use of laetrile outside of specific restrictions.[62] Once a specific prohibition like these has been adopted, the board must prove only that the prohibition has been violated and not that the medical standard of care has been violated.[63] Precise statutes and rules such as these have the benefit of clearly informing licensees of impermissible practices and of allowing the board to police practices thought to be quackery without bearing the considerable burdens of proof created by more generally stated standards of care or professional conduct. In most situations, however, medical knowledge and practice changes too quickly to be policed through one-off statutory or regulatory prohibitions.

c. Consent-Based Alternatives to Restrictive Standards

The legal requirement and ethical norm of informed consent has elevated the status of patient choice and the more recent movement toward patient-centered care strengthens that claim. Especially in the context of professional licensure, antiregulatory arguments that individuals should have the freedom to choose have gained considerable influence. A core justification for restrictive professional licensure in healthcare, however, is that patients are unable to protect themselves from incompetent, negligent, or fraudulent practices because they lack accurate information, are incapable of competently evaluating information that is available, or are vulnerable to the persuasive power of trusted but untrustworthy physicians. Striking the right balance between freedom of choice and protection in the context of nonconforming practices is challenging. Many states, however, have turned to informed consent to mediate their concerns about the risk of harm when licensees provide nonvalidated, complementary or alternative, and innovative interventions even though a patient's consent is not otherwise a defense to violations of licensure standards.[64]

60 *See, e.g.*, Kentucky Bd. of Med. Licensure, Board Pol'y Statement—Complementary and Alternative Therapies (1999), *available at* http://kbml.ky.gov/board/Pages/Opinion-and-Policy-Statements.aspx.

61 Inst. of Med. of the Nat'l Acads., Complementary and Alternative Medicine in the United States (2005).

62 Cal. Bus. & Prof. Code §§ 2251, 2258. *See also In re* Williams, 573 N.E.2d 638 (Ohio 1991).

63 *See, e.g., In re* Williams, 573 N.E.2d 638. *See also* Mo. Rev. Stat. § 334.100.2(4)(f).

64 *See, e.g.*, Kentucky Bd. of Med. Licensure, Board Pol'y Statement—Complementary and Alternative Therapies (1999), *available at* http://kbml.ky.gov/board/Pages/Opinion-and-Policy-Statements.aspx.

A board regulation from the Missouri state medical board illustrates a rather extreme example of reliance on informed consent.[65] The rule was issued during the course of disciplinary action against a medical doctor for providing chelation therapy for atherosclerosis and other vascular conditions on the grounds that the intervention violated the standard of care in medicine.[66] The Missouri regulation expressly declares that chelation therapy has "no medical value," except for uses approved by the FDA (which do not include use for atherosclerosis), but it states that the board will not take disciplinary action against a physician if the patient signs the required consent form. The prescribed consent form includes the following statements of fact: the FDA has not approved chelation therapy for cardiovascular conditions, and two controlled studies in 1992 and 1994 demonstrated that it was ineffective. The required form also states the board's conclusions that chelation therapy, except for FDA-approved uses, is ineffective and may be harmful and that the board "strongly recommends that Missouri citizens not undergo" this treatment. Still, once the patient has signed the consent form and met the required waiting period, the doctor may provide chelation therapy without interference from the licensure board.

This rule is an example of the trend toward personal liberty and questioning of the knowledge base of conventional or customary medicine. While the consent form provides patients the stark facts as the board sees them, it does not respond to concerns over the capacity and vulnerability of patients. Ironically, the largest National Institutes of Health study of chelation therapy for treatment of patients with heart disease produced surprising results, finding that the therapy reduced the risk of subsequent cardiovascular event when compared to placebo—not a ringing endorsement for the intervention, but a reminder of the limitations of using medical custom as a standard of care.[67]

III Patrolling the Borders of the Licensed Healthcare Professions

a. The Unauthorized Practice of Medicine

Under each state's medical licensure statute, only persons who hold a state-issued medical license are permitted to practice medicine. Unlicensed persons who engage in activities that are considered the practice of medicine are guilty of the unauthorized, or illegal, practice of medicine. The essential inquiry in litigation over violations of the prohibition against unauthorized practice is the interpretation of the statutory definition of the practice of medicine and its application to a particular set of activities. Statutory definitions of the practice of medicine vary among the states. Generally, however, the definitions tend to be quite broad. A typical statute provides that the practice of medicine includes

> the diagnosis, treatment, correction, or prevention of any disease, ailment, defect, injury, infirmity, deformity, pain, or other condition of human beings; the suggestion, recommendation,

[65] Mo. Code Regs. Ann. tit. 20, § 2150-2.165.

[66] Bd. of Reg. for the Healing Arts v. McDonagh, 123 S.W.3d 146 (Mo. 2003).

[67] Gervasio A. Lamas et al., *Effect of Disodium EDTA Chelation Regimen on Cardiovascular Events in Patients with Previous Myocardial Infarction*, 309 J. Am. Med. Ass'n 1241 (2013).

> or prescription or administration of any form of treatment, without limitation; the performing of any kind of surgical operation upon a human being . . . or the penetration of the skin or body orifice by any means, for the intended palliation, relief, or cure; or the prevention of any physical, mental, or functional ailment or defect of any person.[68]

The breadth, generality, and specificity of this definition all conspire to bring a practically limitless range of activity within the exclusive purview of medicine. So, for example, this definition would subject persons providing personal athletic training at the Y or ear piercing at the department store and bloggers galore to the risk of prosecution for the unlicensed practice of medicine. With this broad reach, the medical licensure board has quite broad discretion in deciding whether or not to pursue any specific individual, creating a broad threat or risk of prosecution. Cases interpreting such statutes tend to focus on whether the challenged activities involve diagnosing a condition or prescribing a remedy[69] or specifically proscribed actions such as penetration of the skin.[70] Particularly with respect to assistance in childbirth, the issue may be whether the statute defines the practice of medicine in relation to illness or disease, which categories may not include pregnancy and childbirth, rather than a broader notion of human conditions.[71]

The prohibition against the unauthorized practice of the licensed healthcare profession is intended to protect the public from risks of harm, and healthcare services provided by unlicensed persons can present a danger to patients. In some cases, however, the boards have used the prohibition as a tool for restricting competition. For example, in *North Carolina State Board of Dental Examiners*, the board appealed an order from the Federal Trade Commission (FTC) that the board's actions against nondentists who provided teeth-whitening services amounted to unfair competition in violation of the federal FTC Act. The board claimed that its actions amounted to "state action" and so would be immune from application of federal antitrust laws. The Court of Appeals rejected the board's defense, noting that the members of the board were practicing dentists and dental hygienists elected by their peers (with one consumer member appointed by the governor); the board was not closely supervised by the state; and in this particular case had acted beyond the scope of its authority. The Supreme Court has accepted the case for review.[72] Depending on the ultimate result, the case could heighten scrutiny of the anticompetitive impact of the activities of the health profession boards and trigger more public control of the boards.[73]

Unlicensed CAM providers are among those at risk for prosecution for the unauthorized practice of medicine.[74] A few states desiring to make room for CAM providers who are not otherwise licensed as healthcare professionals have enacted legislation to limit the

68 IND. CODE § 25-22.5-1-1.1(a)(1).

69 *See, e.g.*, Washington State Dept. of Health Unlicensed Practice Program v. Yow, No. 61021-0-I, 2008 WL 4561437 (Wash. Ct. App. Oct. 13, 2008); State v. Pac. Health Ctr, Inc., 143 P.3d 618 (Wash. Ct. App. 2006).

70 *See, e.g.*, State Bd. of Healing Arts v. Beyrle, 7 P.3d 1194 (Kan. 2000).

71 *See, e.g.*, Albini v. Conn. Med. Examining Bd. 72 A.3d 1208 (Conn. App. Ct. 2013). *See also* section III.c.

72 *See, e.g.*, N.C. Bd. of Dental Exam'rs v. FTC, 717 F.3d 359 (4th Cir. 2013), *cert. granted*, 134 S. Ct. 1491 (2014).

73 *See also* section III.b.

74 *See, e.g.*, State v. Pac. Health Ctr., Inc., 143 P.3d 618.

state's statutory prohibition against the unauthorized practice of medicine.[75] Typically, these statutes, often called "Health Freedom Acts," provide that an individual will not be prosecuted for the unauthorized practice of medicine if the patient consents to their treatment and so long as they do not engage in one of the listed prohibited activities. Specifically prohibited activities include, for example, surgery or invasive procedures, administration of prescription drugs or radiation, dental procedures, and setting of fractures, among other items. Some of these statutes include a very long list of prohibited activities, while others include a narrower scope.[76] The statutes usually specifically prohibit the unlicensed person from recommending against compliance with a licensed healthcare professional's treatment. Statutes like these also rely heavily on regulated informed consent.[77] The California statute, for example, requires written consent that includes a statement that the provider is not licensed; a description of the intervention; and a description of the provider's education and other qualifications, among other items.[78] The Colorado statute requires consent from parents and additional information for children between the ages of two and eight years old.[79] In addition, one statute prohibits treating children under the age of two and requires that the unlicensed provider recommend that older children maintain a relationship with a pediatrician.[80] Some states, however, license or otherwise recognize specific CAM practitioners, including, for example, practitioners of homeopathy,[81] naturopathy,[82] and acupuncture.[83] Licensed CAM providers are subject to prosecution for unauthorized practice only if their activities exceed the boundaries of their own licensure.[84] The analysis in such cases falls within questions of scope of practice addressed in the next subsection.

b. Scope-of-Practice Regulation

i. Context for Scope-of-Practice Regulation

A stronger emphasis on preventive care, on primary care, and on chronic disease management all point to a critical and greatly expanded role for advanced nurse practitioners (ANPs) and physician assistants (PAs), among others. The great concern over the shortage of primary care physicians to meet these goals is also fostering a push to expand practice opportunities for these practitioners.[85] Physician-controlled medical care is giving way to a team approach as a core characteristic of healthcare delivery. New vehicles for healthcare

[75] *See, e.g.*, COLO. REV. STAT. § 6-1-724.

[76] *Compare* COLO. REV. STAT. § 6-1-724 *with* CAL. BUS. & PROF. CODE § 2053.5.

[77] *See* section II.c.

[78] CAL. BUS. & PROF. Code § 2053.6.

[79] COLO. REV. STAT. § 6-1-724(6)(n).

[80] COLO. REV. STAT. § 6-1-724(6)(m).

[81] *See, e.g.*, ARIZ. REV. STAT. ANN. § 32-2912; NEV. REV. STAT. § 630A.155.

[82] *See, e.g.*, ARIZ. REV. STAT. ANN. § 32-1521; ALASKA REV. STAT. § 08.45.030; FLA. STAT. § 462.01; WASH. REV. CODE § 18.36A.030. *But see* TENN. CODE ANN. § 63-6-205(making the practice of naturopathy illegal).

[83] *See, e.g.*, CAL. BUS. & PROF. CODE § 4935.

[84] *See, e.g.*, State Bd. of Healing Arts v. Beyrle, 7 P.3d 1194 (Kan. 2000); State v. Pac. Health Ctr., Inc., 143 P.3d 618 (Wash. Ct. App. 2006).

[85] *See, e.g.*, INST. OF MED. OF THE NAT'L ACADS., THE FUTURE OF NURSING: LEADING CHANGE, ADVANCING HEALTH (2011).

delivery, such as retail clinics,[86] are also contributing to pressure for expanding the work of nonphysician healthcare professionals. The Affordable Care Act (ACA) provided significant support for healthcare workforce development[87] and improved payment[88] directed toward advanced practice nursing and other nonphysician health professionals. The ACA, however, defers to state law on the permissible functions of these practitioners,[89] as do Medicaid and Medicare payment policies.[90]

The states regulate the permissible scope of practice of each of the health professions. State medical licensure statutes prohibit any but licensed physicians from practicing medicine. Certain professional practice acts, such as the nursing practice acts, have parallel provisions prohibiting the unauthorized practice of those professions. Medical practice acts generally provide that a violation of the statutory prohibition against the unauthorized practice of medicine is a crime.[91] In addition, a licensed physician who aids and abets an individual, including a licensed nonphysician healthcare professional, in the unauthorized practice of medicine may be subject to disciplinary measures, including license revocation.[92]

Licensed healthcare professionals have a defense against a charge of the unauthorized practice of medicine so long as their activities fall within the statutory bounds of their own licensed profession. Licensed nonphysician healthcare professionals cannot legally practice medicine, but practices that fall within the boundaries of their own licensure are not considered the practice of medicine. A nurse, for example, who is providing services authorized under the state's nurse practice act would not be practicing medicine, while an unlicensed practitioner providing the same services would be guilty of the unauthorized practice of medicine. If a nurse engages in practices that exceed those authorized in the nurse practice act, however, that nurse would be subject to discipline by the nursing board for exceeding the authorized scope of practice of nursing and would also be subject to prosecution through the medical board for violating the statutory prohibition against the unauthorized practice of medicine.

While state regulation of the scope of practice of the nonphysician health professions is justified as protective of the public, scope-of-practice regulation has often been the handmaiden of anticompetitive *animus* among the licensed health professions. Licensing boards, acting within the broad reach of the police power, are not required to prove that limitations on the scope of practice of licensed professionals are grounded in empirical research assessing the risk presented by the provision of services by one particular practitioner as compared to another. At the same time, the conflict between the stated licensure goal of protection

[86] Lauren E. Battaglia, *Supervision and Collaboration Requirements: The Vulnerability of Nurse Practitioners and Its Implications for Retail Health*, 87 WASH. U. L. REV. 1127 (2010).

[87] *See, e.g.*, 42 U.S.C. § 296j-1 (training grants for advanced nurse practitioners); 42 U.S.C.A. § 294q(d)(4)(a)(v)(I), (II) (establishing Health Care Workforce Commission to study and coordinate efforts related to primary care, nursing, and allied health practitioners, among others).

[88] *See, e.g.*, 42 U.S.C. § 1395cc-5. *See also* 42 U.S.C. § 1395l(a)(1)(K) (raising Medicare payment rate for nurse midwives from 65% to 100% of physician level).

[89] *See, e.g.*, 42 U.S.C. §§ 1395cc-5(b)(2)(B).

[90] 42 U.S.C. § 1396d(a)(xvii)(17, (l)(3)(C). *See also* Cal. Soc'y of Anesthesiologists v. Superior Court, 204 Cal. App. 4th 390 (2012); Col. Med. Soc'y v. Hickenlooper, No. 11CA1005, 2012 WL 2928528 (Colo. App. Oct. 7, 2013); Mont. Soc'y of Anesthesiologists v. Mont. Bd. of Nursing, 171 P.3d 704 (Mont. 2007).

[91] *See, e.g.*, State v. Annable, 956 N.E.2d 341 (Ohio Ct. App. 2011).

[92] MINN. STAT. ANN. § 147.091(1)(i).

of the public health and the externality of anticompetitive market control is close to the surface in the turf battles among licensed health professionals. In fact, the Federal Trade Commission has pursued an active policy opposing restrictions on the scope of practice of licensed nonphysician health providers. For example, the agency regularly sends letters of support or concern to state government agencies and legislatures acting to expand or limit the scope of practice of nonphysician licensed healthcare professionals, arguing that such restrictions do not promote quality but rather increase costs and decrease access to care.[93] More recently, the FTC issued a policy paper advising state legislators of the agency's concerns over the anticompetitive effects of restrictive scope-of-practice regulation.[94]

ii. Overview of the Structure of Scope-of-Practice Regulation

Two structural issues tend to breed rather than reduce conflicts in the regulation of the scope of practice of the nonphysician licensed healthcare professions. First, the state regulatory board for each of the licensed healthcare professions has some degree of authority to define the legitimate boundaries of that profession and to exclude others, leading to unproductive battles among boards in the same state. Second, the regulation of scope of practice relies on statutory definitions that are both broad and ambiguous, allowing the boards to threaten action against a broad range of healthcare services.

The disciplinary board charged with supervising the licensure of physicians generally has the primary responsibility for enforcing the prohibition against the unauthorized practice of medicine by healthcare providers licensed in the other healthcare professions. Similarly, boards governing nonphysician licensed professionals, such as nurses, pharmacists, chiropractors, and others, will enforce any statutory prohibitions that exist concerning the unlicensed practice of that particular profession. Unproductive conflicts arise frequently between licensure boards governing different licensed healthcare professions in setting boundaries on authorized scope of practice, producing litigation by one state board contesting the authority of another. Until recently, the medical boards in the states have dominated this border-patrolling function and still retain significant power in scope-of-practice regulation in many of the states. Many states, however, have created a joint board or super board consisting of members of each of the licensed professions to avoid having the frequent turf battles fought out in court. The joint board or super board may be granted authority for delineating and monitoring the scope of practice of the regulated professions or the individual professional boards may be required to consult with the joint board.[95] Generally as a matter of administrative law, courts defer to the medical board's decisions in administering the medical practice act, but the question of deference is more complicated in scope-of-practice litigation because of the involvement of a joint board or multiple boards with overlapping authority.[96]

[93] *See, e.g.*, Letter from FTC to Texas State Senators (May 11, 2011).

[94] DANIEL J. GILMAN ET AL., POLICY PERSPECTIVES: COMPETITION AND THE REGULATION OF ADVANCED PRACTICE NURSES, FTC (2014).

[95] *See, e.g.*, IDAHO CODE ANN. § 54-1402(d); MD. CODE ANN., HEALTH OCC. § 14-306(d)(1).

[96] *See* Mo. Assoc. of Nurse Anesthetists v. State Bd. of Registration for the Healing Arts, 343 S.W.3d 348 (Mo. 2011) (holding that medical board lacked authority to enforce prohibition against aiding and abetting the unauthorized practice of medicine against doctors working with nurse anesthetists; that the board of nursing held the authority to define the practice of nursing; but that state statute required

The second structural issue that fosters conflict in scope-of-practice regulation is more difficult to overcome. Statutory definitions of the practice of medicine tend to be broad and general,[97] and may reasonably be viewed as encompassing activities that are performed both by licensed doctors and by other licensed health professions. While the licensed health professions have a defense to charges that they are practicing medicine without a license, that defense requires that the nonphysician professional be practicing within the boundaries of their own license. Unfortunately, statutory definitions of the legitimate scope of practice of nonphysician licensed healthcare professionals often pose a similar problem of breadth and ambiguity as does the statutory definition of the practice of medicine. The resulting blurred boundaries can stimulate turf wars. Because some degree of overlapping competencies is unavoidable in describing the legitimate work of the full range of health care professionals, however, many states have addressed the problem through procedural mechanisms like the joint boards described in the previous paragraph.

iii. Illustrations: Scope of Practice for Nursing and Physician Assistants

Nurse practice acts parallel the medical practice acts in establishing entry requirements, disciplinary grounds and procedures, and prohibiting the unauthorized practice of the profession. Although nurse licensure statutes originally presented nursing as a practice that required the supervision or direction of a licensed medical doctor, the nursing practice acts enacted in the 1970s adopted a broader definition of the practice of nursing and legally established the practice of nursing as an independent practice requiring that a nurse exercise judgment independent of that of a physician. With the expansion of the practice of nursing, the jurisdictional claims of medicine and nursing began to overlap as the two can encompass the same functions. In *Sermchief v. Gonzales*,[98] for example, the Supreme Court of Missouri issued a landmark opinion interpreting a medical practice act that defined "diagnosis" as the practice of medicine and a general nurse practice statute enacted in 1978 which allowed nurses to make a "nursing diagnosis." The court concluded that "a nurse undertakes only a nursing diagnosis, as opposed to a medical diagnosis, when she or he finds or fails to find symptoms described by physicians' standing orders and protocols for the purpose of administering courses of treatment prescribed by the physician in such orders and protocols." Beyond that foray, however, the court refused to "draw that thin and elusive line that separates the practice of medicine and the practice of professional nursing in modern day delivery of health services." Rather, the court referred to legislative intent to expand the reach of authorized nursing practices in the Missouri nurse practice act and held that the activities of the nurses at issue, which included primary care and family planning, clearly fell within the legislative intent of the statute.

A second wave of legislative reform of the nurse practice acts produced statutes in most states that address advanced practice nursing as distinct from general professional nursing.

that scope-of-practice rules issued by a joint board). *See also*, Int'l Chiropractors Ass'n v. N.M. Bd. of Chiropractic Exam'rs, 323 P.3d 914 (N.M. Ct. App. 2013); Tex. Bd. of Chiropractic Exam'rs v. Tex. Med. Ass'n, 375 S.W.3d 464 (Tex. App. 2012).

[97] *See* section III.a.

[98] Sermcheif v. Gonzles, 660 S.W.2d 683 (Mo. 1983). *See also* Iowa Med. Bd. v. Iowa Bd. of Nursing, 831 N.W.2d 826 (Iowa 2013).

Most of these statutes provide generally for advanced nurse practitioners (ANPs),[99] and some specifically provide for nurse specialties such as nurse midwives[100] and nurse anesthetists.[101] Specific legislative recognition of nursing specialties provides a shield against prosecution of ANPs for the unauthorized practice of medicine. The mere threat of such prosecution, especially against doctors for aiding and abetting the unauthorized practice of medicine, has diminished opportunities for advanced practice nursing as both the ANPs and physicians who would work with them feared the burden of litigating such action.[102]

Nurse practitioner statutes require that the ANP have completed more advanced education and training beyond what is required for licensure as a registered nurse.[103] They also specify a broader scope of practice than for general nursing and describe the required relationship with a licensed physician and the extent of an ANP's prescribing authority. Although some advanced nurse practice statutes are silent on the question of physician participation in the nurse practitioner's practice,[104] most require that nurse practitioners have collaborative practice arrangements with physicians. Specific statutory requirements for collaboration agreements vary considerably among the states, however. Statutes that specify criteria for collaboration typically provide that the collaboration must be within the skills and education of both the nurse and the physician; must provide for coverage of services when the nurse is unavailable; and must describe the nurse's prescribing authority, if any.[105] Some states require that there be a formal written agreement, written protocols and standing orders, geographic proximity between the nurse and the physician, and that a physician review the work of the nurse on a regular basis, requirements that are more akin to supervision rather than collaboration.[106] In fact, some states specifically use language requiring that the nurse practitioner be "supervised" by a physician.[107] While all states authorize prescribing for advanced nurse practitioners, many require physician supervision of that function.[108]

The distinction between collaboration and supervision may be a matter of language only, however. Some statutes requiring "collaboration" may require extensive physician oversight, in terms of record review and presence, while some requiring "supervision" do not demand the doctor's physical presence. Requirements of detailed oversight or reference to physician-delegated functions are inconsistent with the independent practice of nursing envisioned in the legislation of the 1970s and certainly raise the costs of care, as has been noted by the FTC.[109]

99 *See, e.g.*, MO. REV. STAT. § 334.104; FLA. STAT. § 464.012(3).

100 *See, e.g.*, CAL. BUS. & PROF. CODE § 2746.5(b); FLA. STAT. § 464.012(4)(b).

101 *See, e.g.*, FLA. STAT. ANN. § 464.012(4)(a).

102 *See, e.g.*, Sermchief v. Gonzales, 660 S.W.2d 683 (Mo. 1983) (noting impact of threat of disciplinary action).

103 *See generally* Tine Hansen-Turton et al., *Nurse Practitioners in Primary Care*, 82 TEMPLE L. REV. 1235 (2010).

104 *See, e.g.*, N.M. STAT. ANN. § 61-3-23.2(B)(2); MD. CODE ANN. HEALTH OCC. § 8-601.

105 *See, e.g.*, MINN. STAT. ANN. § 148.171.

106 *See, e.g.*, MO. REV. STAT. § 334.104; OHIO REV. CODE ANN. § 4723.431.

107 *See, e.g.*, CAL. BUS. & PROF. CODE § 2746.5 (nurse midwives). *See also* N.J. Ass'n of Nurse Anesthetists v. N.J. Dept. of Health and Senior Servs., 2012 WL 6163180 (N.J. Super. Ct. App. Div. Dec. 12, 2012).

108 *See, e.g.*, CAL. BUS. & PROF. CODE § 2836.1(d); N.J. STAT. ANN. § 45:11-49.

109 *See* section III.b.1. *See also* Daniel J. Gilman & Julie Fairman, *Antitrust and the Future of Nursing: Federal Competition Policy and the Scope of Practice*, 24 HEALTH MATRIX 143 (2014).

In the legislative process, however, the acceptance of a dependent, supervisory relationship may be a practical trade-off in exchange for legislative recognition of a more extensive scope of practice and protection from the threat of prosecution for the unauthorized practice of medicine.

Most medical practice acts allow physicians to delegate appropriate functions to individuals capable of performing the work including physician assistants (PAs) as well as other licensed and unlicensed practitioners.[110] The permissible range of delegation under a general statutory delegation provision will be unclear, however, and will depend on the prevailing custom of the medical profession as to the degree of supervision and control to be exercised by the delegating physician.[111] Where the state provides for licensure (or certification or registration) of PAs, these statutes often will prohibit physicians from delegating a similar range of activities to persons other than those licensed by the state.[112] As dependent practitioners, PAs are required to work under physician supervision.

Typically, the PA statutes specify that any delegation must be appropriate for the training and experience of the specific physician assistant,[113] and many statutes also specify that the physician may delegate only those functions that fall within his or her own expertise and experience.[114] Some PA statutes or medical practice acts provide for the required supervision in detail, addressing geographic proximity and timely review of charts and prescriptions on a regular basis, for example.[115] Some states require that the PA and the physician work in the same facility for a specified proportion of the time worked,[116] while others specify that supervision does not necessarily require the physician to be personally present where the PA is working as long as the physician is accessible by phone.[117] Some set specific limits on the number of PAs that any one physician may employ or supervise[118] or require prospective approval of the board for the specific practice arrangements for the individual PA.[119] Most states grant PAs prescribing authority but set specific requirements for the PA and the supervising physician.[120] Some states require advanced filing with the board of documentation as to the medications (and sometimes the dosages) that the individual PA will be allowed to prescribe[121] or that a supervising physician execute a written protocol that specifies all criteria for the use of the particular drug.[122] Prescribing of medications that are controlled substances typically are subject to further restrictions.[123]

110 *See, e.g.*, MINN. STAT. ANN. § 147.091(1)(i); ALASKA STAT. § 32-1401(16) (providing for medical assistants). *See also* State Bd. of Nursing v. Ruebke, 913 P.2d 142 (Kan. 1996) (midwifery as a delegated function).

111 *See, e.g.*, Jacobs v. U.S., 436 A.2d 1286 (D.C. 1981); Marion OB/GYN, Inc. v. State Med. Bd., 739 N.E.2d 15 (Ohio Ct. App. 2000). *See also* Am. Nurses Ass'n v. Torlakson, 304 P.3d 1038 (Cal. 2013).

112 *See, e.g.*, Mesbahi v. Md. State Bd. of Physicians, 29 A.3d 679 (Md. Ct. Spec. App. 2011).

113 *See, e.g.*, WASH. REV. CODE § 18.71A.020(2)(b)(i).

114 *See, e.g.*, OHIO REV. CODE ANN. § 4730.21(C).

115 *See, e.g.*, CONN. GEN. STAT. § 20-12a(a)(7).

116 *See, e.g.*, MO. REV. STAT. § 334.735(8), (10).

117 *See, e.g.*, WASH. REV. CODE § 18.71A.020(2)(b)(ii).

118 *See, e.g.*, OHIO REV. CODE ANN. § 4730.21(B); N.Y. EDUC. LAW § 6542(3) (McKinney 2013).

119 *See, e.g.*, MD. CODE ANN., HEALTH OCC. § 15-302.

120 *See, e.g.*, MO. REV. STAT. § 334.735(4).

121 *See, e.g.*, W. VA. CODE § 30-3E-3.

122 *See, e.g.*, CAL. BUS. & PROF. CODE § 3502.1(a)(2).

123 *See, e.g.*, CAL. BUS. & PROF. CODE § 3502.1(e); W. VA. CODE § 30-3E-3.

c. Assistance in Childbirth

At least three distinct categories of healthcare providers provide assistance at childbirth: doctors, nurses (typically now as nurse midwives), and direct entry midwives (also called or lay or traditional or professional midwives). State legislation concerning provision of assistance in childbirth varies widely. Most states specifically authorize the practice of nurse midwifery.[124] The majority of states also have statutes that specifically authorize assistance at childbirth by professional midwives who are not nurses.[125] Some of these statutes prescribe particular training or certification requirements,[126] while others do not.[127] Statutes specifically authorizing assistance at childbirth by nurse midwives or direct entry midwives delineate a particular scope of practice and often prohibit specific activities, such as the use of specified obstetrical devices.[128] Violation of those boundaries can result in disciplinary action by the relevant board on the basis that the practitioner exceeded the statutory boundaries of practice or prosecution for the unauthorized practice of medicine or nursing.[129]

In the absence of legislation or regulation authorizing assistance at childbirth by nurses, nurse midwives, or direct entry midwives, individuals providing childbirth assistance are subject to charges of the unauthorized practice of medicine. In such cases, courts will have to interpret the definition of the practice of medicine in the state's medical licensure statute to decide whether the individual has violated the prohibition.[130] Courts have adopted many approaches to analyzing whether services provided in the assistance of childbirth are the unauthorized practice of medicine in the absence of specific legislative authorization of the practice. Results in these cases are decidedly mixed. Some have examined individual actions that may be performed during childbirth, distinguishing, for example, "ordinary assistance in normal cases of childbirth" from the use of obstetrical instruments and prescriptions, which are prohibited as the unauthorized practice of medicine.[131] Others have focused on the character of childbirth, distinguishing it from disease or deformity referenced as the target of medical treatment in the medical or nursing practice act.[132] Others have concluded that lay midwifery is the unauthorized practice of nursing, especially in cases where nurse midwifery is specifically recognized by statute, and there is no provision authorizing lay

[124] *See, e.g.*, ALA. CODE § 34-19-3; ARIZ. REV. STAT. ANN. § 36-752; CONN. GEN. STAT. § 20-86a.

[125] Sarah Anne Stover, *Born by the Woman, Caught by the Midwife: The Case for Legalizing Direct-Entry Midwifery in All Fifty States*, 21 HEALTH MATRIX 307 (2011) (reporting that forty-one states have such statutes).

[126] *See, e.g.*, MINN. STAT. ANN § 147D.01.

[127] *See, e.g.*, ARIZ. REV. STAT. ANN. § 36-755; GA. CODE ANN. § 31-26-2(c).

[128] *See, e.g.*, MINN. STAT. ANN § 147D.03 (excluding assistance at childbirth by direct entry midwife "by artificial or mechanical means"); GA. CODE ANN. §31-26-5 (allowing only attendance at "normal childbirth" and not allowing "internal examinations or manipulations of any kind").

[129] *See, e.g.*, People v. McCall, 154 CAL. RPTR. 3d 471 (2013) (holding that midwife violated both the midwifery act and the medical practice act). *See also* Devers-Scott v. Office of Prof'l. Reg., 918 A.2d 230 (Vt. 2007).

[130] *See also* section III.a.

[131] *See, e.g.*, Leigh v. Bd. of Registration in Nursing, 481 N.E.2d 1347 (Mass. 1985). *See also* People v. Jihan, 537 N.E.2d 751 (Ill. 1989).

[132] State Bd. of Nursing v. Ruebke, 913 P.2d 142 (Kan. 1996). *See also* Albini v. Conn. Med. Examining Bd., No. CV084018329S, 2011 WL 1566994 (Conn. Super. Ct. Apr. 5, 2011).

midwifery.[133] At least one judicial opinion has held that attendance at childbirth by a lay midwife is authorized under the general delegation authority of the physician.[134]

IV Conclusion

Governmental quality-control regulation is undergoing significant change, stimulated at least in part by cultural shifts surrounding healthcare generally. So, for example, increased capacity in information technology is supporting the collection and dissemination of quality data to the general public. These efforts aim at strengthening consumer choice in healthcare and perhaps will narrow the traditional justifications for restrictive quality regulation in favor of market forces. Access to aggregated data on health outcomes is also allowing the regulatory system to adopt more outcomes-oriented quality standards. Even more fundamentally, the commitment to evidence-based medicine has produced skepticism toward customary standards of care. This skepticism is evident in the rather radical efforts that state licensure boards and legislatures are making to reduce reliance on customary or prevailing practice as measure of quality care. At the same time, the effect of this skepticism is magnified by increased claims for consumer choice and patient autonomy which have produced an increasing reliance on regulated informed consent, again putting pressure on the foundations of restrictive licensure in the healthcare professions. Finally, recognition of the need for lower cost quality care, especially in the contexts of primary care, preventive care, and chronic disease management, is strengthening the relative position of nonphysician healthcare professionals and is likely to expand their scope of practice. The coming decade promises to be a time of significant realignment in governmental quality-control regulation.

[133] *See, e.g.*, Sherman v. Cryns, 786 N.E.2d 139 (Ill. 2003) and Hunter v. State, 676 A.2d 968 (Md. Ct. Spec. App. 1996). *See also* Goslin v. State Bd. of Med., 949 A.2d 372 (Pa. Commw. Ct. 2008).

[134] State Bd. of Nursing v. Ruebke, 913 P.2d 142.

CHAPTER 23

THE HOSPITAL-PHYSICIAN RELATIONSHIP

JOHN D. BLUM, SHAWN R. MATHIS, AND PAUL J. VOSS

I Introduction

THE key players in the provision of acute, critical, and emergent care are hospitals and physicians. The hospital provides the resources that allow physicians to practice medicine at the highest levels of their profession, while physicians individually and collectively direct patient care. This relationship has been fraught with tension owing to economic and professional agendas that have not always been aligned or compatible. A certain balance in roles has been achieved over time, which, while not necessarily ensuring cooperation and trust, provides parameters within which to structure and maintain working hospital-physician relationships. However, changes in science, technology, regulation, and reimbursement make the partnership of hospital and physician no longer a foregone conclusion. Today, broader systemic changes under the Patient Protection and Affordable Care Act (PPACA) are driving a radical transformation in the relationship between these partners in healthcare.

This chapter thematically addresses core legal and policy issues pertinent to the hospital-physician relationship, both traditionally and in the wake of the PPACA. Part II explores the historical relationship between hospitals and physicians, focusing on major issues and policies that have shaped this relationship: the changing workforce, health insurance, competition, and health reform. Part III highlights two key regulatory initiatives in healthcare reimbursement—prospective payment and bundled payment—that have particular significance for the hospital-physician relationship. Part IV reviews the legal relationship that physicians have had with hospitals through the organized medical staff in the context of the traditional tripartite structure of hospitals, covering current regulatory mandates in hospital operations. Part V considers alignment strategies that competitive pressures and federal policy promoting integration have forced hospitals to pursue, including contractual arrangements ranging from joint ventures to co-management to employment arrangements. Part VI concludes the chapter, focusing on PPACA provisions that evidence the federal government's intention to make greater use, now and in the future, of hospitals and physicians to promote population health.

II The Origin and Evolution of the Physician-Hospital Relationship

a. History

The earliest focus of the nation's hospitals was one of concern on the part of community leaders for the community's poor, in which hospitals "pursued the value of community service over investor return" and physicians "served in hospitals without remuneration.[1] Driven by a convergence of factors—medical science, technology, financing, and regulation—hospitals emerged as the dominant actors of the twentieth-century American healthcare system. The growth of the hospital industry resulted in a "major change in the hospital's mission: from being primarily an institution of care to an institution of cure."[2] Today, the short-stay acute care hospital (whether public, private, for-profit, or investor-owned) remains a constant, albeit changing, focal point in patient care. It is, as yet, hard to envision a medical care system in which hospitals don't play a pivotal role.

The hospital-physician relationship has evolved over three principal periods in healthcare, beginning with the origin of the medical staff, followed by managed care, and ending with the PPACA. For most of the twentieth century, fee-for-service was the dominant model. Medical autonomy and professional imperatives were protected through a tripartite hospital model consisting of the hospital's governing board, administration, and an independent self-governing medical staff.

Two early-twentieth-century events are seminal to the development of the modern hospital: the publication of the Flexner Report in 1910 and the release of the American College of Surgeons (ACS) Minimum Hospital Standards Statement in 1919.[3] The Flexner Report dealt with an assessment of early-twentieth-century medical education. Its harsh critiques, and related recommendations, were a primary catalyst for the adoption of the German scientific model of medical education and the resultant need for university teaching hospitals to support that model.[4] The ACS hospital standards provided the foundation for acute care institutional structures, which, in turn, evolved into the accreditation, licensing, and certification processes that resulted in a basic clinical and bureaucratic core across the hospital sector. The scientific and operational underpinnings of acute care hospitals all but guaranteed that their relationship with physicians would be central to the institution's capability to deliver patient care and to its ultimate financial viability.

[1] Lawton R. Burns, *The Transformation of the American Hospital: From Community Institution Toward Business Enterprise*, 12 Comp. Soc. Res. 77, 78 (1990).

[2] *Id.* at 84.

[3] Am. Coll. of Surgeons, The 1919 "Minimum Standard" Document (May 25, 2006), http://www.facs.org/archives/minimumhighlight.html.

[4] *See generally* Thomas P. Duffy, *The Flexner Report—100 Years Later*, 84 Yale J. Biological Med. 269 (2011).

While bound together by mutual interests, physicians and hospitals are organizationally and professionally distinct. As they are individually licensed to provide medical services, physicians value autonomy and control over the patient care they provide, chafing at interference from nonmedical administrators.[5] On the other hand, as a result of market and regulatory pressures to meet demands for greater operational efficiency, hospitals are now highly structured healthcare corporations that seek to control physician inputs.[6] While a physician's desire for professional autonomy and a hospital's need for organizational control are ever present sources of tension between them, the dynamics of the relationship are far more nuanced.[7] Physicians in many specialties are dependent on hospital technology; hospitals increasingly depend on revenue streams from physicians performing high-dollar or high-volume procedures. To the extent that hospitals and physicians have effectively collaborated, it can be attributed to the need for a unified front when dealing with third-party payers, regulators—and patients.

Starting in the mid 1980s, the rise of managed care heralded a new era in healthcare. While the medical staff model continued under managed care, hospitals increasingly hired specialists to join insurance networks and to comply with legal requirements for staffing under the Emergency Medical Treatment and Labor Act (EMTALA), usually in hospital-based services such as radiology and anesthesiology. In addition to individual hospital-physician contracts, a variety of organizational structures emerged such as the physician-hospital organization (PHO) and the independent practice association (IPA) that created new interfaces between hospitals, physicians, and third-party payers.[8] Over time, tensions arose as hospitals and physicians both collaborated and competed with each another under strict regulatory oversight.

The current period of system redesign in the wake of the PPACA touches on virtually all aspects of the healthcare delivery system and, as such, has significant implications for hospital-physician relationships. The PPACA dramatically expands both private and public insurance, putting pressure on the delivery system to expand access—a goal that cannot be achieved without innovations in hospital-physician collaboration. In addition, there is considerable emphasis in the PPACA on altering reimbursement, through cost and quality goals that bind hospitals and physicians together and through incentives for a more coordinated and team-based approach.[9] The goals of health reform are, to a large extent, embodied

[5] Ariz. Health and Hosp. Ass'n, *Can This Marriage Be Saved? Physician –Hospital Relationships*, Ariz. Health Futures (Dec. 2005), http://slhi.org/wp-content/uploads/2014/02/pp-2005-12.pdf.

[6] Am. Hosp. Ass'n, *Tax Exempt Status*, http://www.aha.org/advocacy-issues/taxexempt/index.shtml. 80% of America's hospitals are non-profit institutions, which have an obligation under the tax code to provide charity care.

[7] Jonathan Burroughs, *Physician Engagement: What Not to Do*, Hosp. Impact (June 24, 2013), http://www.hospitalimpact.org/index.php/2013/06/24/doc_engagement_what_not_to_do.

[8] Kevin Grumbach et al., *Independent Practice Association Physician Groups in California*, 17 Health Aff. 227 (May/June 1998) (An IPA is "a network of physicians who agree to participate in an association to contract with health maintenance organizations . . . and other managed care plans."); Lawton R. Burns, *Models of Physician-Hospital Organization: Possibilities and Pitfalls*, 2 LDI Issue Brief (Nov. 1995), http://www.upenn.edu/ldi/issuebrief2_7.html. (A PHO "is a joint venture between one or more hospitals and a group of physicians" that "acts as a single agent for managed care contracting, presenting a united front to payers.").

[9] Lawton R. Burns et al., History of Physician-Hospital Collaboration: Obstacles and Opportunities 18–45 (Francis Crosson & Laurel Tolle eds., 2011).

in the PPACA Medicare Shared Savings program, which promotes the development of the accountable care organization (ACO), a type of hybrid managed care organization that joins physician groups with hospitals in a patient-centric model.[10]

b. The Changing Healthcare Workforce

With the aging of the American population, the expansion of insurance coverage and the graying of the physician workforce, shortages in the supply of medical practitioners are of grave concern.[11] It is widely acknowledged that shortages are extreme in some areas critical to hospital services such as general surgery, cardiology, critical care, diagnostic radiology, oncology, and orthopedic surgery.[12] The physician undersupply places considerable pressure on current practitioners, generating lively competition among hospitals and community practices to attract new physicians through high salaries, signing bonuses, and favorable practice arrangements that accommodate lifestyle considerations.[13]

While increasing residency training slots and opening new medical schools may ease physician shortages, changes in the role of the physician, in the makeup and scope of practice of the nonphysician healthcare workforce, and telemedicine may do more to address this problem. In particular, hospitals on both the inpatient and outpatient side have seen a growth in the roles of physician assistants, nurse practitioners, pharmacists, and other allied health professionals who have taken on an increasing number of functions previously performed by physicians, with the role of physicians in hospital settings shifting into a multidisciplinary team-based leadership model.[14]

c. Markets and Competition

Significant portions of healthcare have migrated to outpatient settings, and hospitals and doctors, either jointly or independently, continue to position themselves to compete in the provision of outpatient care.[15] Expansion of the healthcare industry has attracted

[10] Jenny Gold, *FAQ on ACOs, Accountable Care Organizations Explained*, KAISER HEALTH NEWS (Apr. 16, 2014), http://khn.org/news/aco-accountable-care-organization-faq/.

[11] Federation of State Medical Boards, *U.S. Medical Regulatory Trends and Actions Report*, 27 (May 2014), http://www.fsmb.org/state-medical-boards/publications-media/publications/regulatory-trends. In 2012, approximately 75% of licensed physicians were forty or older. An almost equal number of physicians were between forty and forty-nine years old as those between fifty and fifty-nine years old. *Id.*

[12] *Physician Shortages in the Specialties Taking Toll*, NEJM CAREER RESOURCES CENTER (Oct. 31, 2011), http://www.nejmcareercenter.org/article/physician-shortages-in-the-specialties-taking-a-toll/; Eric M. Siegel, *Hospitalists and the Intensivist Shortage*, PHYSICIAN'S WKLY. (Mar. 13, 2013), http://www.physiciansweekly.com/intensivist-shortage-hospitals/.

[13] NEJM Career Resources Center. *See also* Daniel G. Kirch, *A Word from the President: Facing the Facts about the Physician Shortage*, AAMC REP. (Dec. 2013), https://www.aamc.org/newsroom/reporter/december2013/363844/word.html.

[14] Cari Synderman et al., *The Physician as Team Leader: New Job Skills Are Required*, 16 ACAD. MED. 1348, 1348 (2011).

[15] For a discussion on the rise of the ambulatory surgical center, *see generally* Shawn Mathis, *Closing in on Health Care-Associated Infections in the Ambulatory Surgical Center*, 33 *J. Legal Med.* 493 (2012).

entrepreneurs who bring new expertise and capital into both inpatient and outpatient settings.

Many physicians are now able to establish in-office practices that provide complex technologies, and to collectively establish freestanding sites of care, including ambulatory surgery and urgent care. Until recently, most individual physicians and medical groups lacked the necessary capital and support systems required to break their dependency on hospital resources. But changes in the costs and capabilities of technology, reimbursement policies, and the availability of capital have dramatically altered the medical practice landscape. Physician groups can independently acquire complex diagnostic technologies such as PET scanners, and in the future, robotics may be widely used in outpatient care to expand services.

While hospitals as acute care institutions will retain their relevance in resource-intensive services, particularly critical care, and medical research, the future in which hospitals and physicians interact will be marked by much greater fragmentation and diversification, particularly as physician specialists with new technologies and access to capital can practice outside acute care settings.

Meanwhile, a convergence of factors has resulted in the development and growth of competition in healthcare markets. A key tenet of government policy-makers is to regulate in ways that encourage competition, resulting in positive changes in cost and quality. Competition has forced hospitals to adopt strategies to attract patients and insurance contracts, including extensive marketing to promote their areas of distinction and philosophies of patient care, and—in some cases—affiliating with other institutions, branding particular service areas. Perhaps the most striking example of competitive forces at work in hospital markets can be seen in ongoing cycles of mergers and acquisitions that have rendered independent freestanding hospitals a rarity in many parts of the country.[16] In extreme cases, institutions overwhelmed by the pressures of the marketplace have been forced to close their doors.[17]

Integral to hospital competitive strategies is the ability to attract and retain physicians, both in high-margin practice areas and in medical specialties in which there are shortages. While price competition in hospital services rarely occurs, hospitals compete on the complement of services they offer, and—more recently—on quality measurements.[18] Physician involvement is critical for both of these, requiring effective collaboration between hospital and physician. Interestingly, the same competitive factors that drive collaboration foster direct competition between institutions and physicians, as capital and technology have freed doctors from institutional ties, allowing them to pursue niche practices that were formerly hospital-based. Competition is a wild card in hospital-physician relationships as healthcare markets react to regulatory and reimbursement pressures, impacted by geography and

[16] Beth Kutscher, *Ascension Health Plan Joins Joint Venture with Dignity Tenet to Run Arizona Hospitals*, Modern Healthcare (July 21, 2014), *available at* http://www.modernhealthcare.com/article/20140722/NEWS/307239925.

[17] Bob Herman, *18 Hospitals That Closed in 2013*, Becker's Hosp. Rev. (Jan. 2, 2014), http://www.beckershospitalreview.com/hospital-management-administration/hospitals-that-closed-in-2013.html.

[18] Diane Archer, *No Competition: The Price of a Highly Concentrated Health Care Market*, Health Aff. Blog (Mar. 6, 2013), http://healthaffairs.org/blog/2013/03/06/no-competition-the-price-of-a-highly-concentrated-health-care-market/.

tradition. As such, market forces coalesce in different ways. In some locales, large health systems have emerged as dominant players, whereas in other areas, market competition among many actors is more vigorous, with differences between urban and rural health markets.[19]

d. Health Reform

While the PPACA sets out a complex structure of insurance and health system reforms, its primary emphasis lies in the so-called triple aim: reducing the per capita costs of care, improving the patient experience, and addressing challenges of population health.[20] The triple aim clearly has great potential to alter the dynamics of hospital-physician relationships through provisions that require intensive collaboration between the parties, driven by new cost and quality emphases. For example, the law promotes a number of key reimbursement changes that can be broadly classified under the concept of pay-for-performance in which meeting quality and efficiency measures underline payment, as opposed to a volume-based, fee-for-service orientation.[21]

Shifts in reimbursement promoted by PPACA initiatives will require a carefully coordinated approach to treatment that rests on a team-based, highly collaborative model, moving patient care away from the control of a single clinician. In addition, quality metrics will factor into reimbursement, and performance will be tracked and rewarded resting on use of evidence-based measures. Integral to cost containment, quality control, and medical safety enhancement are electronic medical record systems, which were promoted legislatively prior to the PPACA and play a central role in hospital-physician reform efforts.[22] Particularly noteworthy is the PPACA's continuing focus on reducing hospital readmissions, an area that demands a concerted effort between hospital and medical staff to coordinate care and manage care transitions to avoid reductions in reimbursement.[23] In turn, insurers and high-cost providers (primarily hospitals) will need to manage newly insured high-risk patients in ways that avoid or sharply decrease the need for hospitalization.[24]

[19] David A. Balto & James Kovacs, *Consolidation in Health Care Markets: A Review of the Literature* (Jan. 2013), *available at* http://www.dcantitrustlaw.com/assets/content/documents/2013/balto-kovacs_healthcareconsolidation_jan13.pdf. *See also* Robin Respaut, *Rural Hospitals Pressured to Close as Healthcare Systems Change*, REUTERS (Sept. 3, 2014), http://www.reuters.com/article/2014/09/03/us-healthcare-rural-insight-idUSKBN0GY14620140903.

[20] *See generally* Donald M. Berwick et al., *The Triple Aim: Care, Health & Costs*, 27 HEALTH AFF. 759 (2008).

[21] *See generally* Andrew Ryan & Jan Blustein, *Making the Best of Hospital Pay for Performance*, 366 NEW ENG. J. MED. 1557 (2012).

[22] *See generally* David U. Himmelstein & Steffie Woolhandler, *Hope and Hype: The Impact of Electronic Medical Records*, 24 HEALTH AFF. 1121 (2005).

[23] Under the Hospital Readmissions Reduction Program, institutions that exceed a baseline rate of readmissions within thirty days face a penalty. It becomes essential for hospital-based physicians to adopt treatment procedures which minimize readmissions, particularly development of greater sensitivity to discharge planning. *See* 42 C.F.R. §412. *See generally* Shreya Kangovi & David Grande, *Hospital Readmissions—Not Just a Measure of Quality*, 306 JAMA 1796 (2011).

[24] Karen E. Joynt & Ashish Jha, *A Path Forward on Medicare Readmissions*, 368 NEW ENG. J. MED. 1175–1177 (2013).

Two models that emerge from the PPACA—the accountable care organization (ACO) and the patient-centered medical home (PCMH)—both require high degrees of integration in which both clinical and management services need to be coordinated across a wide continuum of medical conditions and services. An ACO requires intensive collaboration among providers; the model does not have to be hospital-centric, as physician networks are just as likely to be at the helm of an entity that is globally budgeted to manage the cost and quality of a given patient population.[25] PCMHs are multidisciplinary primary care practices that provide a comprehensive set of services ideally suited to the chronically ill. If successful, they have the potential to reduce hospitalizations and manage most medical conditions in the outpatient setting.[26]

III The Impact of Reimbursement on the Hospital-Physician Relationship

Few environmental forces have had as great an impact on the hospital-medical staff relationship as the adoption of Medicare in 1965 and the regulations and policies that have emanated from this program. As the single largest payer for healthcare in the United States, Medicare has a profound impact on all aspects of acute care delivery. Indeed, Medicare's influence is so great that physicians lament that Medicare's payment systems "prescribe" the care they furnish, rather than leaving the prescribing to the physician. Medicare underpins the hospital-physician relationship, serving as a catalyst to both unite and divide physician and hospital, against the backdrop of continual development and refinement of payment policies. Within the universe of Medicare reimbursement initiatives, two payment schemes stand out as key illustrations of how this program has impacted the relationship: the long-standing use of prospective payment and the more recent movement to bundled payment.

a. Prospective Payment System

Introduced in 1983, Medicare's prospective payment system (PPS) is a reimbursement system that provides remuneration based on prospectively set rates that are determined by a complex array of categories based on patient care classifications, known as the Diagnosis-Related Groups (DRGs).[27] It provides an output payment triggered by diagnosis in question, combined with a number of variables specific to a given patient and the situs of care.

[25] California Healthcare Foundation, *Arranged Marriages: The Evolution of ACO Partnerships in California* (2013), http://www.chcf.org/publications/2013/09/arranged-marriages-acos.

[26] Am. Acad. of Family Physicians et al., *Joint Principles of the Patient Centered Medical Home*, Patient Centered Primary Care Collaborative (Feb. 2007), http://www.aafp.org/dam/AAFP/documents/practice_management/pcmh/initiatives/PCMHJoint.pdf; Centers for Medicare & Medicaid Services, *Accountable Care Organizations*, CMS.gov. (Jan. 6, 2015, 2:58 PM), http://www.cms.gov/Medicare/Medicare-Fee-for-Service-Payment/ACO/index.html.

[27] *See generally* Judy Sturgeon, *DRGs: Still Frustrating After All These Years*, 21 For the Record 14 (May 25, 2009), *available at* http://www.fortherecordmag.com/archives/052509p14.shtml.

DRGs were first adopted as mandated hospital fiscal management tools, but over the past thirty years have evolved into important measures of patient utilization and quality used by Medicare, Medicaid, and private payers.

The PPS program was changed in 2003, with the adoption of the All-Patient Refined DRG (APR-DRG), shifting away from facility to patient-centric measures.[28] In 2008, Medicare further refined the DRG with the adoption of the Medicare Severity DRG (MS DRG), which included severity of patient disease in the payment algorithm. Broadly speaking, the DRG system shifted control of institutional reimbursement away from providers to regulators and was a primary catalyst in driving a significant amount of patient care from inpatient to ambulatory settings.[29]

Of note, the adoption of prospective payment via the DRG did not alter the fact that physicians continued to be separately reimbursed from hospitals for their services. Whether astute or ill-conceived, PPS used the hospital to achieve cost savings by requiring it to accept a single payment for an entire course of an inpatient's hospital treatment, without mandating or incentivizing physicians to limit their utilization.[30] Since the attending physician makes the decisions regarding patient admission to and treatment in the hospital, a hospital's success in responding to prospective payment incentives depends on buy-in from the attending physician staff.[31]

PPS expanded the power and influence of medical staffs as hospitals gave them a role in administrative decision-making and hospital management. Predictably, this also led to greater hospital intervention in medical staff affairs, particularly in areas such as medical staff credentialing. In fact, the seeds of economic credentialing—the granting or denial of hospital privileges based on criteria other than quality of care or competence (for example, overutilization of costly procedures)—were sown through the adoption of PPS.

PPS has had other long-lasting effects on the hospital-physician relationship. The need for collaboration increased hospital use of "medico-administrative officers" who are hospital employees from within the staff, viewed by many of their medical staff colleagues as "collaborators" in the most pejorative sense of the word.[32] Joint hospital-medical staff committees became more common as a result of PPS and, while fostering cooperation, have been controversial for the degree of authority they exercise.

PPS also triggered legislation to address the anticipated impact of smaller hospital budget surpluses and greater cost-consciousness on access to care for Medicare and indigent patients, impacting hospital-medical staff relations, as well. EMTALA passed in 1986 and required Medicare participating hospitals with an emergency department to screen all patients who present in the emergency department for emergency conditions and to

28 Brandon D. Bushnell, *The Evolution of DRGs*, AM. ACAD. OF ORTHO. SURGEONS (Dec. 2013), http://www.aaos.org/news/aaosnow/dec13/advocacy2.asp.

29 *Id.*

30 Bushnell, *Evolution of DRGs*. It is often noted that physicians account for as much as 75% of the total costs of services provided in hospitals. For an interesting contrast in how physicians see their role in costs, *see generally* Jon C. Tilburt et al., *Views of U.S. Physicians About Controlling Health Care Costs*, 310 JAMA 380 (2013).

31 *See generally* R. J. Schuch & J. A. Levy, *DRGs and Physician Autonomy*, 2 J. MED. PRACTICE MGMT. 13 (1986).

32 *See generally* Bruce Spivey, *The Relationship Between Hospital Management & Medical Staff Under a Prospective Payment System*, 310 NEW ENG. J. MED. 984 (1984).

stabilize emergent patients without regard to ability to pay.[33] Hospitals were required to offer the same complement of ancillary services to such patients (no matter when they presented) as the hospital offered during the workday, requiring hospitals to arrange for after-hours on-call availability of physicians. Again, the Centers for Medicare and Medicaid Services (CMS) chose to make only hospitals subject to this unfunded mandate, without creating reciprocal or complementary obligations of Medicare physicians to be on call.

The issue of who controls and determines "call obligations" to meet EMTALA's requirements has been yet another area of conflict between hospitals and their medical staffs. While the burden to develop on-call policies rests with the hospital, historically institutions have required physicians to provide uncompensated emergency room coverage as a condition of medical staff membership.[34] In recent years, hospitals have reported difficulties in obtaining adequate on-call coverage and have been forced to pay physicians for such services.[35]

b. Bundled Payment

The prospective payment system was organized around hospitalization and directed to institutional reimbursement based on diagnosis. A newer initiative in reimbursement—bundled payment—attempts to provide a single payment to a group of providers involved in care during a specific episode of illness, as opposed to separately reimbursing individual actors. Bundled payments arose from CMS's recognition that the episodic payment approach that has characterized Medicare leads to a largely fragmented system of delivery, with minimal coordination, rewarding quantity of services, rather than quality of care.[36] The bundled payment approach is one of several initiatives in Medicare designed to shift healthcare from volume to value measured by cost reductions and adherence to quality and outcome measures.

Research has shown that bundled payments can align incentives for providers—hospitals, post-acute care providers, physicians, and other practitioners—allowing them to work closely together across all specialties and settings.[37] While the American Medical Association acknowledges that physicians have experience with payments for a grouping of services, it cautions that, with more services included in current bundled payment, physician exposure increases exponentially, impacting both parties and shifting control of payment to the hospital as it parses payment among providers.

[33] Emergency Medical Treatment and Active Labor Act of 1986, 42 USC §1395dd (2012).

[34] Lisa W. Clark, *The Physician On-Call Dilemma: Emerging Solution?*, Duane Morris LLP (2007), http://www.duanemorris.com/articles/static/modern_healthcare_mayo7.pdf.

[35] Wilson Hayman, *OIG Approves Multiple Compensation Methods for Paying Physicians to Take Hospital Calls*, Poyner Spruill Publications (2009), http://www.poynerspruill.com/publications/Pages/OIGAppr.aspx; *see also* Becker's Healthcare, *10 Physician On-Call Compensation Trends*, Becker's Hospital Rev. (June 1, 2010), *available at* http://www.beckershospitalreview.com/compensation-issues/10-physician-on-call-compensation-trends.html.

[36] Centers for Medicare & Medicaid Services, *Bundled Payment for Care Improvement Initiative: General Information*, CMS.gov, http://innovation.cms.gov/initiatives/bundled-payments/ (last visited on June 11, 2015).

[37] *See generally* Robert Mechanic & Christopher Tompkins, *Lessons Learned Preparing for Medicare Bundled Payment*, 367 New Eng. J. Med. 1873 (2012); Bundled Payments for Care Initiative Fact Sheet (BPCI) Fact Sheet – Updated August 2015, https://www.cms.gov/Newsroom/MediaReleaseDatabase/Fact-sheets/2015-Fact-sheets-items/2015-08-13-2.html.

Splitting the bundled payment is of particular concern to physicians and medical societies. For the first time both the medical staff and the hospital have financial "skin in the game." Bundled payment is a long way from being an established reimbursement practice, but it has the potential to promote collaboration among physicians and hospitals, well beyond PPS. For example, the models being tested under the PPACA bundled payment initiative are relevant in addressing complex issues such as readmissions as they promote higher levels of coordination among key actors.[38]

IV The Medical Staff

While the healthcare world in which hospitals and physicians function has changed over time, the foundational legal structure on which their relationship rests has remained relatively constant. The basic operational structures and requisite functions of hospitals are specified in state licensing laws and regulations.[39] Hospital operations are also affected by Medicare Conditions of Participation that require institutions to meet a series of mandates in order to receive federal reimbursement.[40] Hospitals that have been accredited by certain private organizations, such as The Joint Commission (TJC), receive "deemed status" as an alternative to certification by Medicare.[41] While these sets of regulatory mandates are not totally harmonized, they all support a tripartite hospital structure composed of a governing board, administration, and a self-governing medical staff.[42] The distinction between the governing board, the administration, and the medical staff is complicated as acute care institutions are required to have two separate sets of bylaws—one corporate and another for the medical staff. Generally, supplemented by extensive policies and operating manuals, the two types of bylaws provide a framework for hospital structure and operations, and underpin the self-governing authority of the medical staff and the role of its medical executive committee.[43]

a. Combining the Practice of Medicine with Hospital Administration

When licensing and accreditation developed in the mid-twentieth century, there was a sharp distinction between the practice of medicine, and the administration and governance of the hospital. Under this ongoing scheme, physicians are bound to the hospital by membership

[38] Bob Herman, *The Advantages and Disadvantages of CMS' Bundled Payment Initiative: 8 Responses*, Becker's Hosp. Rev. (Oct. 7, 2011), http://www.beckershospitalreview.com/hospital-physician-relationships/the-advantages-and-disadvantages-of-cms-bundled-payment-initiative-8-responses.html.

[39] *For example, see* 210 Ill. Comp. Stat. 85 (2014).

[40] 42 C.F.R. §482.22.

[41] *See generally* Joint Comm'n, 2015 Hospital Accreditation Standards (2014).

[42] Joint Comm'n, *Revision to Hospital Medical Staff Standard MS.01.01.01*, PowerPoint Presentation (Apr. 2010), http://www.jointcommission.org/assets/1/18/MS.01.01.01_FINAL_4-08-10.pdf. It is possible for hospitals in systems to have unified governing boards, but each hospital, in a system, must have its own medical staff.

[43] James Hall & Teresa A. Williams, *Medical Staff Bylaws and Related Documents: Advanced Issues*, Westlaw, AHLA-Papers P11109429.

in the institution's medical staff but are relatively free from professional control and exercise autonomy granted by their medical license to direct patient care within the entity's four walls.[44] While hospital operations and the environments in which such institutions function are markedly changed, the organizational trinity remains intact, with little chance it will be abandoned anytime soon.[45] Rather, efforts to update and even expand the roles of the three actors have accompanied ongoing systemic change, with recent attention focused on institutional governance and the requisite duties of boards.[46]

For physicians, the medical staff has served as the organizational focal point in their relationship with hospitals. The medical staff organization (MSO) is independent and self-governing, while comprising multiple committees, deriving its authority from the hospital board. Under law, this unincorporated association must have its own bylaws, rules, and regulations that delineate structures and functions, including specification of the nature of its accountability to the hospital governing board.

The MSO bylaws must be viewed in tandem with, and are subordinate to, institutional bylaws.[47] The primary functions of the MSO include credentialing (the appointment, reappointment, and delineation of clinical privileges), physician performance improvement, peer review, conduct of disciplinary processes, and providing input on planning and budgeting.[48] Membership in a medical staff is required for individual clinicians to provide patient care in a given institution. Through medical staff credentialing, individuals join the MSO and, in return for this permission to practice in a facility or health system, have certain obligations such as on-call and committee service.

While MSOs traditionally have been composed of only licensed physicians, in recent years the composition of the medical staff has been expanded in most states to include other health professionals, such as advanced practice nurses, physician assistants, and clinical pharmacists, requiring scope-of-practice assessments for these providers.[49] For example, CMS has granted hospitals authority to place podiatrists into MSO leadership roles.[50]

Originally intended as a vehicle to uphold safety and clinical quality, the medical staff is frequently criticized as a vestige of an outdated and highly politicized model. After all, much

[44] *See generally* Robert A. Berenson et al., *Cooperation, Competition, or Separation?*, 26 HEALTH AFF. 31 (Jan. 2007).

[45] Francis J. Crosson & John Combes, *We'll Need a Bigger Boat: Reimagining the Hospital-Physician Partnership*, HEALTH AFF. BLOG (Apr. 17, 2014), http://healthaffairs.org/blog/2014/04/17/well-need-a-bigger-boat-reimagining-the-hospital-physician-partnership/.

[46] *Id. See also* AM. HOSP. ASS'N, GOVERNANCE PRACTICES IN AN ERA OF HEALTHCARE TRANSFORMATION (Dec. 2012), *available at* http://www.americangovernance.com/resources/reports/brp/2012/.

[47] John P. Marren, G. Landon Feazell, Michael W. Paddock, *The Hospital Board at Risk and the Need to Restructure the Relationship with the Medical Staff*, 12 ANN. HEALTH LAW 179, 220 (Summer 2003).

[48] MSOs are complex organizations that have undergone significant organizational changes and as a result are underpinned by a professional core of managers; *see* JODI SCHIRLING, INTRODUCTION TO MEDICAL STAFF SERVICES 1–38 (2011), *found at* http://samples.jbpub.com/9780763784416/84416_CH01_Gassiot.pdf. *See also* 77 ILL. ADM. CODE §250.310. For a description of a large medical staff, *see The Medical Staff at California Pacific*, CPMC MED. STAFF (last visited June 11, 2015), http://www.cpmc.org/about/medstaff.html.

[49] 77 Fed. Reg. 29033 (May 12, 2012); 42 C.F.R. §482.22.

[50] *Id. See also* Karen Cheung Larivee, *Medical Staff Definitions to Include APRNs, PAs*, FIERCE HEALTHCARE (May 11, 2012), http://www.fiercehealthcare.com/story/cms-expands-medical-staff-definition-include-nps-pas/2012-05-11.

of the relationship between the physician and the hospital lies outside the dictates of bylaws and is governed by financial and contractual concerns.[51] The centrality of the medical staff to clinicians is no longer a given, and significant change in the MSO structure and operations seem likely.[52] From a regulatory standpoint, both The Joint Commission and CMS, in particular, have updated mandates in the medical staff area to be responsive to institutional realities.[53] For example, accommodations have been made in medical staff standards to allow for health systems to have a unified medical staff, to expand the human resource component of the staff, and to require medical consultation on hospital policy, but not mandatory physician membership on governing boards.[54]

b. Business Disputes

The medical staff has been the subject of extensive litigation. While many issues involving MSOs, including liability and antitrust, have been litigated, two areas predominate: credentialing disputes and controversies about the legal boundaries between the medical staff and the hospital board. Credentialing, in particular, has been characterized by a long history of disputes in which individual physicians have challenged the legality of hospital decisions that negatively impact their practices, including actions concerning denial of appointment, and termination or restriction of privileges.[55]

While the medical staff, under its delegated authority, carries out the credentialing process, the ultimate responsibility for credentialing decisions rests with the hospital board. The legal battles surrounding physician disputes to practice in a given facility are interlaced with concepts of fairness and due process, as well as federal and state statutory requirements.[56] Integral to credentialing is the peer review privilege, which involves the protection of medical staff quality review functions from disclosure, shielding credentialing records from discovery in litigation. As attorneys representing medical malpractice plaintiffs, among others, would be interested in records of such proceedings, an extensive body of case law concerning the nature and scope of the privilege has developed.[57]

[51] Advisory Bd. Co., *Future of the Medical Staff Organization* (2010), *found at* http://www.capellahealth.com/wp-content/uploads/2013/06/2-Future-of-the-Medical-Staff-Organization-Reengineering-Governance.pdf.

[52] *Id. See also* Cal. Med. Ass'n, *CMA Releases 2014 Annotated Bylaws* (June 5, 2014), http://www.cmanet.org/news/detail/?article=cma-releases-2014-annotated-model-medical; *see also* Alice Gosfeld, *The Organized Medical Staff: Should Anyone Care Anymore?*, 20 J. MED. PRACTICE MGMT. 210 (2005).

[53] Lisa Sprague, *Hospital Oversight in Medicare: Accreditation and Deeming Authority*, NHPF ISSUE BRIEFS, No.802 (May 6, 2015), http://www.nhpf.org/library/issue-briefs/IB802_Accreditation_05-06-05.pdf.

[54] 42 C.F.R. §482.12. An ongoing issue involving MSOs concerns whether medical staffs must remain open or be closed to qualified members; such a policy will vary around the country and may be a matter of state law.

[55] John D. Blum, *Hospital-Medical Staff Relations in the Face of Shifting Institutional Business Strategies: A Legal Analysis*, 14 U. PUGET SOUND 561 (1991).

[56] The Health Care Quality Improvement Act of 1986, 42 U.S.C. §11101-§11152.

[57] *See* El-Attar v. Hollywood Presbyterian Med. Ctr., 301 P.3d 1146 (Cal. 2013). The case provides an excellent example of credentialing disputes between physicians and hospitals, detailing issues of procedure and relevant statutory law in the area.

Individual disputes between a single physician and a hospital, over matters such as credentialing, peer review, and quality assurance, have spilled over into larger disputes between medical staffs and hospital boards/administrations regarding the appropriate bounds of authority separating these entities. Regulatory changes, and the expansion of corporate liability doctrines, have led to increased governance mandates (in finance, quality, safety, community benefits), pushing trustees to become involved in matters once within the exclusive purview of the medical staff. Controversies have arisen when boards, often spurred on by the administration, exert decision-making authority that impinges on physician autonomy and patient care issues. Some hospitals have gone so far as to create rules and policies that exist separate and apart from traditional governance documents, giving boards authority to implement changes in operations outside the strictures of institutional and MSO bylaws.

The expansive nature of board activities has not occurred without pushback as a number of highly publicized disputes have arisen in which attempts of hospital trustees to unilaterally amend medical staff bylaws have been challenged as a violation of the MSO's self-governing authority. Several state courts have held that MSO bylaws constitute a contract between members and the hospital, upon which staff grievances can be adjudicated.[58]

In one well-publicized case, suit was brought by the medical staff against Community Memorial Hospital San Buenaventura alleging, in part, that the hospital improperly interfered with medical staff governance by unilaterally amending MSO bylaws, denying staff self-governance, and imposing a code of conduct, including a conflict of interest policy, without securing the necessary input of staff doctors.[59] Codes of conduct, while mandated by The Joint Commission, have been viewed negatively in some sectors of organized medicine as a mechanism to discipline physicians for actions unrelated to patient care, often dealing with economic matters.[60]

The settlement of the Memorial Community Hospital case required the hospital to: comply with medical staff bylaws (elections, peer review, credentialing, privileging); agree to neither unilaterally amend MSO bylaws nor unreasonably withhold approval of bylaw changes; and to recognize the right of the MSO to hire legal counsel and pursue independent actions against the institution. Following the settlement, the state of California enacted legislation reaffirming the independent self-governing medical staff model and recognizing the right of the MSO to employ independent counsel.[61]

Not all courts view medical staffs as independent and distinct from the hospital, and as a result, disagree with the proposition that bylaws are binding contracts that can serve as the basis for independent MSO legal actions against a hospital. In *Medical Staff v. Avera Marshall Regional Medical Center*, the medical staff challenged the hospital board's unilateral

[58] Anesthesia Bus. Consultants, *Your Other Hospital Contracts the Medical Staff Bylaws*, ANESTHESIA INDUS. EALERTS (May 11, 2009), http://www.anesthesiallc.com/publications/anesthesia-industry-ealerts/382-your-other-hospital-contracts-the-medical-staff-bylaws.

[59] Tanya Albert, *California Deal Reaffirms Medical Staff Autonomy*, AMED NEWS (Sept. 6, 2004), http://www.amednews.com/article/20040906/profession/309069968/2/.

[60] Joint Comm'n, *2015 Hospital Accreditation Standards*, LD.03.01.01. *See also* El-Attar v. Hollywood Presbyterian Med. Ctr., 301 P.3d. 1146 (Cal. 2013).

[61] CAL. BUS. & PROF. CODE §2282.5(a)(5) (West 2004).

amendment of MSO bylaws.[62] The appellate court ruled that the hospital medical staff, an unincorporated association, lacked standing and had neither a statutory nor common law bases on which to sue or be sued. The court did not recognize hospital bylaws as contractual, taking the position that a hospital's inappropriate unilateral action could only be challenged by individual medical staff members in equity to enjoin or compel institutional action.[63]

Medical staff disputes not only involve hospital boards and management but also entail disagreements between the MSO itself and its leadership represented by the medical executive committee and chief medical officer. Lack of cohesion within a medical staff, combined with external friction with the two other core hospital components, poses significant operational challenges that affect a hospital's ability to respond to competitive and regulatory pressures. To address potential dysfunction in the medical staff model, The Joint Commission revised its accreditation policies to address some of the more problematic aspects of this model.[64] The new standards prevent either the governing board or the medical staff from unilaterally amending the medical staff bylaws, and require that rules, procedures, and parameters be developed to allow for collaboration on matters involving patient care, quality, and safety. The Joint Commission standards leave the details of hospital—medical staff collaboration up to each accredited entity, but whatever dispute resolution mechanism is adopted, medical staff bylaws and their amendments must ultimately be approved by the hospital governing board.

c. Economic Credentialing

Typically, credentialing determinations have been delegated to the medical staff. While ultimate decision-making authority concerning appointments, reappointments, and delineation of clinical privileges rests with the hospital board, such governing bodies have historically taken a hands-off approach in this area. With changes in hospital competition, boards acting as fiscal fiduciaries have been forced to consider the implications of physician staffing decisions, not only from a quality perspective but also from the vantage point of operational considerations.[65]

The use of financial analyses by a hospital board to make staffing decisions (known as "economic credentialing") became controversial in the late 1980s. Economic credentialing is a generic term that refers to a variety of independent board decisions impacting MSO membership and privileges that rest on business considerations outside the normal realm of clinical quality evaluation.[66] Typical economic credentialing decisions might entail board

[62] Med. Staff of Avera RMC Regional Med. Ctr. v. Avera Marshall, 836 N.W.2d 549 (Minn. Ct. App. 2013); *see also* Exeter Hosp. Med. Staff v. Bd. of Trustees of Exeter Health Res., Inc., 810 A.2d 53 (N.H. 2012).

[63] *Id.*, *see* both *Avera* and *Exeter Hospital.*

[64] Joint Comm'n, *2015 Hospital Accreditation Standards.*

[65] *See generally* John D. Blum, *Beyond the Bylaws: Hospital-Physician Relationships, Economics and Conflicting Agendas*, 53 Buff. L. Rev. 458 (2005). Hospital boards have broad power to make credentialing determinations based on standards of patient care, patient welfare, character or competency of applicant or staff member, and objectives of the institution.

[66] *See generally* Elizabeth Weeks, *The New Economic Credentialing: Protecting Hospitals from Competition by Staff Members*, 36 J. Health L. 247 (2003).

actions to: (1) close medical staff membership in certain specialties; (2) deny a clinician's reappointment to the staff based on a conflict of interest; and (3) enter into exclusive contracts with medical specialty groups to provide core services such as emergency medicine, anesthesiology, radiology, and—more recently—hospitalist care.[67]

There has been strong resistance to economic credentialing on the part of organized medicine, and a number of laws and organization policies have been developed to limit such practices.[68] Economic credentialing has resulted in a number of highly publicized legal challenges with courts deferring to a hospital board's exercise of authority in the best interests of institutional operations and business considerations.[69] As capitation and changes in both payment and clinical measurement (bundled payment, readmission penalties, value-based purchasing, and quality reporting) have complicated the relationship between cost and quality, casting a credentialing decision as strictly financial has become increasingly difficult.

V Hospital-Physician Alignment Strategies

Traditionally, hospital medical staffs have been dominated by physician members who are independent contractors, and only a small number of clinicians, usually hospital-based specialists, have been directly employed, or worked with a given hospital under explicit contractual arrangements. Recently, relationships between hospitals and physicians have been caught up in a larger shift from volume- to value-based care, with success based on achievement of quality and cost indicators. Hospitals have had to compete with each other to attract physicians committed to a coordinated care model, adopting a variety of alignment strategies achieved through contract, joint venture, or shared equity arrangements, and employment/practice acquisition models.[70] While physicians are required to belong to a medical staff, their business relationship with an institution or health system is based on contracts external to the MSO bylaws.

These contractual and employment arrangements have added a financial dimension to the relationship that was far less explicit in the heyday of the all-voluntary medical staff.

a. Independent Contractors and Service Agreements

It has become common for physicians and medical groups to enter into contractual agreements with hospitals for services considered either essential to institutional operations, or

[67] Kristen Schorsch, *Doctors, Hospitals Feud over the Future of Healthcare*, Crain's Chi. Bus. (May 19, 2014), http://www.chicagobusiness.com/article/20140517/ISSUE01/305179981/doctors-hospital-feud-over-the-future-of-health-care.

[68] 77 Ill. Admin. Code §250.310 (2014).

[69] Cal. Bus. & Prof. Code §2282.5(a)(5) (West 2004). *See also* Joint Comm'n, *2015 Hospital Accreditation Standards*.

[70] Health Research & Educ. Trust and Kaufman, Hall & Assoc., Inc., *A Guide to Physician Integration Models for Sustainable Success* (Sept. 2012), *available at* http://www.hpoe.org/resources/hpoehretaha-guides/883.

in specialty practice areas in which the acute care entity has invested considerable resources. More modest alignment efforts may include on-call services, or particular arrangements for specific functions such as medical director, or physician champion of quality initiatives.[71] In addition, hospitals often enter into agreements for services with hospital-based physician (HBP) groups to provide specialty care, providing the groups with institutional services and equipment. The doctors in the contracted groups are generally employees of the practice in question, and specialty practice agreements are usually exclusive contracts that drive significant patient volume to the group.[72]

Whether the contract at issue is an agreement with an individual or a group, the physicians involved in these arrangements must be credentialed through MSO processes. The contractual relationship is a separate arrangement that undoubtedly adds a commercial dimension to the hospital-physician relationship and may create fissures in the medical staff organization, as physicians under contract may be perceived by their medical staff colleagues as institutional agents instead of independent practitioners.[73]

More ambitious physician alignment arrangements are found in various joint ventures between hospitals and doctors, with parties sharing in the equity and management of a particular entity. In the 1990s, it became common for hospitals and their medical staffs to form physician-hospital organizations (PHOs) to be able to offer various provider products to managed care organizations and employers.[74] PHOs typically involved the creation of a separate legal entity co-owned by a hospital and a group of primary care physicians who would, in turn, contract for specialty services.[75] The closed-panel PHO, restricted to the members of a given medical staff, was a popular vehicle to align hospital and physician interests structurally, but this type of organization proved to be difficult to sell and manage.[76] While the PHO was, in most cases, a joint venture model between a hospital and its medical staff with limited administrative services, some PHOs evolved into integrated health networks that act as conduits for a number of collective functions such as insurance contracting, physician billing and collections, quality improvement, and electronic medical record implementation and management.[77]

[71] Irene Blake, *What Is the Role of a Physician Champion?*, HOUSTON CHRON., *available at* http://work.chron.com/role-physician-champion-2960.html (last visited June 11, 2015).

[72] While each HBP contract may be unique, such contracts typically cover billing, insurance, compensation, benefits, noncompete provisions, legal and regulatory compliance, and termination provisions. *See* Audio Recording: Ann M. Bittinger & Michael F. Schiff, *What's Wrong with This Picture? Negotiating Hospital-Based Physician Group Contracts with Hospitals: The Physician Group Perspective* (2010) (held by American Health Lawyers Association and Physicians and Physician Organizations Institute), http://www.medpagetoday.com/Washington-Watch/Washington-Watch/52086?xid=nl_mpt_DHE_2015-06-12&eun=g153179d0r.

[73] Am. Coll. of Emergency Physicians, *Medical Staff Structure* (June 1998), *available at* http://www.acep.org/workarea/DownloadAsset.aspx?id=8942.

[74] Robert A. Berenson & Paul Ginsburg, *Hospital Cooperation, Competition or Separation?*, 26 HEALTH AFF. 31 (Jan. 2007).

[75] Am. Health Lawyers Assoc., *Physician-Hospital Organization*, http://www.healthlawyers.org/hlresources/Health%20Law%20Wiki/Physician-Hospital%20Organization%20%28PHO%29.aspx (last visited June 11, 2015).

[76] Grumback et al., *Independent Practice Association Physician Groups in California.*

[77] Somewhat akin to PHOs are organized healthcare arrangements (OHAs); these are loosely structured hospital/medical staff practice networks used as vehicles to enter into managed care contracts,

Large-scale joint ventures were replaced by more targeted alignment strategies as institutions wanted to build stronger relationships with physician specialists in high-profit areas.[78] The convergence of available capital and technology gave certain medical specialists the ability to open freestanding treatment facilities that compete with hospitals for healthier and privately insured patients. Joint ventures with physicians in outpatient settings such as ambulatory surgical centers and imaging centers became a way for hospitals to generate revenue and forestall competition posed by independent physician groups.

On the inpatient side, there has been growth in contractual arrangements between hospitals and physician groups in specific clinical departments to co-manage medical services in cardiac catheterization, orthopedics, and digestive disease. Co-management agreements typically include bonus arrangements for participating doctors that are awarded if the entity that oversees the co-management services meets targeted goals in areas such as quality and patient satisfaction. Through such agreements, the hospital is able to harness the expertise of clinical specialists in key operational areas, in a nonemployment model, and enter into a type of partnership that is subject to hospital fiscal oversight.[79] Co-management agreements must be carefully structured to comply with Medicare fraud and abuse laws.[80]

b. Physician Employment and Practice Acquisition

Beyond joint ventures, there is a growing trend for hospitals to employ doctors. Between 2000 and 2011, the number of physicians employed by hospitals grew by 34%, and according to the American Medical Association, 60% of family doctors and pediatricians, 50% of surgeons, and 25% of surgical subspecialists are employees rather than independent contractors.[81] Employment arrangements vary, but in broad terms the institution may either directly employ doctors or may make arrangements with medical groups to hire their physicians. In a quest to realize cost efficiency and care coordination, the concept of physician employment

participate in medical record systems, and perform certain quality improvement functions. *For example, see* Univ. of Pittsburgh Med. Center, *Organized Health Care Arrangements that UPMC Participates in*, http://www.upmc.com/patients-visitors/privacy-info/Pages/arrangements.aspx (last visited June 11, 2015).

[78] Berenson et al., *Cooperation, Competition, or Separation*. For a good overview of joint venture arrangements, *see* Ariz. Health and Hosp. Ass'n, *Can This Marriage Be Saved?*, at 17. The report identifies common hospital-physician joint ventures as including leasing, purchased service agreements, clinical co-management, and gainsharing. It is important to recognize that these arrangements raise a variety of legal issues such as fraud and abuse laws, and tax implications.

[79] John C. Erickson III, *What in the World Is Medical Co-Management?*, Physician's Prac. (Nov. 2011), *available at* http://www.physicianspractice.com/blog/what-world-medical-%E2%80%98co-management%E2%80%99.

[80] *Id. See also* Charles Oppenheim & Sandi Krul, *Clinical Co-Management Arrangements: The OIG Speaks*, Compliance Today, 63–67 (May 2013). The authors provide a detailed analysis of the January 7, 2013, OIG (Office of the Inspector General) Advisory opinion 12-22, which offers guidance on a cardiac catheterization co-management agreement and its implications under the federal anti-kickback and CMP (Civil Monetary Penalties) statues.

[81] Elizabeth Rosenthal, *Apprehensive, Many Doctors Shift to Jobs with Salaries*, N.Y. Times (Feb. 14, 2014).

often entails outright purchases of medical practices. This strategy—popular in the 1990s—has once again become attractive to hospitals.

Institutions and health systems see practice acquisition as a vehicle both to secure physician engagement, as well as to generate new revenue from physician fees for inpatient diagnostic services.[82] For physicians, hospital employment frees them from the burdens of practice management and the pressures of coping with decreasing reimbursement. Younger physicians, in particular, are attracted to employment arrangements that provide a predictable salary, benefits (including malpractice coverage), and standardized work hours. Overall, employment is perceived as resulting in a much more favorable life-work balance than has been the case with private medical practice.[83] While compensation varies depending on the hospital market and specialty, employment arrangements are based on either a straight salary or net income guarantee with a bonus/incentive arrangement, with the latter approach more likely to be the dominant model in the future.[84]

Employment models may present the most direct approach to hospital-physician affiliations, but they are not without considerable complications. It has been well documented that hospitals lose between $150,000 and $300,000 per year during the first three years of physician employment, with losses higher for primary care physicians (PCP) than specialists, as PCP productivity tends to drop during the period these clinicians are adjusting to practice in large system settings.[85] Employing doctors entails salaries and benefits, providing medical liability coverage, as well as office space and staffing, and upgrading information technology.[86] For hospitals to break even on physician employment arrangements, PCPs must generate 30% more visits and new specialists must have a 25% increase in referrals annually to meet institutional productivity goals.[87] For employment arrangements to succeed, hospitals must closely manage physicians through quality-of-care initiatives that minimize unnecessary practice variations and inappropriate use of supplies, thus lowering costs.[88]

[82] *Id. See also* Richard Gunderman, *Should Doctors Work for Hospitals*, ATLANTIC.COM (May 27, 2014), http://www.theatlantic.com/health/archive/2014/05/should-doctors-work-for-hospitals/371638/. The author details several reasons for hospitals to employ physicians beyond those noted in the text: avoidance of the ban on self-referrals (Stark), capturing physician referrals (preventing what is referred to as leakage), and increasing clout with payers (with antitrust concerns factored in).

[83] Victoria Stagg Elliott, *Doctors Describe Pressures Driving Them from Independent Practice*, AMED NEWS (Nov. 19, 2012), http://www.amednews.com/article/20121119/business/311199971/2/. *See also* Beth Kutscher, *Making Physicians Pay Off*, MODERN HEALTHCARE (Feb. 22, 2014).

[84] Bonnie Darves, *Physician Compensation Models: The Basics, the Pros and the Cons*, NEJMCAREERCENTER.ORG (Sept. 2004), http://www.nejmcareercenter.org/article/physician-compensation-models-the-basics-the-pros-and-the-cons.

[85] *Id.*

[86] Joint Comm'n, *2015 Hospital Accreditation Standards; see also* Beth Kutscher, *Some Hospitals Employing Doctors See Great Losses*, MODERN HEALTHCARE (Dec. 30, 2014), *found at* http://www.modernhealthcare.com/article/20141230/NEWS/312309942.

[87] Robert Kocher & Nikhil R. Sahni, *Hospitals' Race to Employ Physicians—The Logic Behind a Money Losing Proposition*, 364 NEW ENG. J. MED. 1790–1793 (May 12, 2011).

[88] *Id.* The *New England Journal* points out that reduction in physician costs "will be achieved through such actions as standardizing surgical supplies, using evidence to choose cost-effective medical devices, requiring use of health information technology, requiring adherence to clinical guidelines, scheduling elective procedures in ways that maximize asset utilization and discharging patients consistently early in the day." A number of factors have been identified that can explain losses hospitals experience during the initial periods of physician employment beyond a drop in productivity, including hospitals

From the physician standpoint, employment represents a loss of autonomy, a major change in the culture of practice, and a shifting of administrative functions such as billing and charge coding to the institution. Doctors employed by hospitals must use institutional services and equipment, particularly electronic medical records. Hiring and office staffing issues are not controlled by individual clinicians but by their employers. While employed physicians still retain authority over clinical decision-making, such control will be affected by care coordination and service integration efforts, promoted by medical group and hospital employers [89] Doctors must follow increasingly detailed clinical guidelines to meet benchmarks that trigger incentive and bonus payments.

Not all employment involves a hospital's acquisition of a physician practice; there has also been a trend to hire full-time hospital-based physicians known as "hospitalists." Hospitalists provide general and specialized inpatient care and play an important role in care coordination, working closely with hospital provider teams.[90] It is estimated that 60% of hospitals employ hospitalists, and with the growth in this area, complex inpatient acute care has been ceded to these institutionally based clinicians, resulting in less inpatient work for community physicians.[91] Like other hospital-based specialists, not all hospitalists are employees of an acute care facility but may be employed by groups of physicians that have contractual arrangements with the institution. In addition to hospitalists, acute care entities also employ or contract with intensivists, who are typically pulmonary care specialists who provide treatment in intensive care units.[92]

c. Teaching and Research

The academic medical center's (AMC) institutional expectations include not only patient care but also teaching and research. Doctors are credentialed through traditional MSO bylaw processes, given a medical school appointment, and required to belong to a faculty practice plan (FPP). Academic medical centers are typically composed of a tertiary hospital or hospitals, a medical school (as well as other health science schools), and an FPP. Physician evaluations are subject to performance and quality measures that consider not only clinician competencies but also include medical school departmental assessments of teaching and research.[93] The FPP acts as a unifying entity to join clinical departments and the AMC

making excessive financial commitments to employed physicians and institutional failures to carefully assess staffing needs, caught up in a type of 'buying frenzy.'" *See* Sabrina Burnett, *Strategic Physician Onboarding: 7 Tactics for Minimizing Losses on Employed Medical Practices*, Becker's Hosp. Rev. (Jan. 7, 2013), http://www.beckershospitalreview.com/hospital-physician-relationships/strategic-physician-onboarding-7-tactics-for-minimizing-losses-on-employed-medical-practices.html.

89 Joint Comm'n, *2015 Hospital Accreditation Standards*.

90 Joe Cantlupe, *A Bigger Role for Hospitalists*, healthleadersmedia.com (Apr. 2013), *found at* http://www.healthleadersmedia.com/content/MAG-290925/A-Bigger-Role-for-Hospitalists.html.

91 *Id.*

92 *Intensivist or Hospitalist, What Is the Difference*, The Happy Hospitalist Blog, http://thehappyhospitalist.blogspot.com/2010/01/intensivist-vs-hospitalist-what-is.html (last visited June 11, 2015).

93 *For example, see* Am. Ass'n of Univ. Professors, *Tenure in the Medical School* (1999), http://www.aaup.org/report/tenure-medical-school.

medical group for purposes of contracting, compensation, marketing, and creating alliances with other health provider entities.[94]

As with other hospitals, AMCs are now faced with profound regulatory and reimbursement challenges, but tend to be slower to implement structural changes.[95] The need to cope with high service volumes, restraints on resident service hours, and Medicare medical education payment cutbacks have forced AMCs to focus on increasing patient revenues to supplement teaching and research activities. As such, teaching hospitals have come to depend on the services of nonteaching physicians to provide increased billings to offset educational program losses. A bifurcated structure has emerged in academic hospitals, split between teaching and nonteaching services, in which the latter area is often staffed by nonacademic hospitalists. Recently, considerable effort has been made to unify the AMC clinical staff, integrating physicians in ways that minimize the academic versus nonacademic divide, pushing the two groups to assume more collaborative functions in a time when Medicaid patient volume is increasing proportionately.[96]

Finally, in the face of increasing reductions in reimbursement from both public and private payers, some health systems such as Johns Hopkins and the Cleveland Clinic are looking outside the United States for ways to increase revenues.[97] Without the constraints of Medicare's Conditions of Participation and other increasingly burdensome healthcare regulations, health systems expanding abroad have more leeway to innovate in forming relationships between healthcare institutions and physicians.[98]

d. The Impact of Healthcare Delivery System Integration

Reforms, including the many discussed above, are clearly moving the healthcare delivery system toward care coordination strategies that require ever increasing collaboration between hospitals and physicians. The American Hospital Association charts provider integration along a continuum, moving from inpatient care management during an episode of illness, to coordination of care among hospital providers, to inter-institutional care coordination, and ultimately to the development of disease management that reaches out to the community, involving patient care before and after a period of acute illness.[99]

[94] UCSF Med. Grp., *Bylaws of the UCSF Clinical Practice Organization* (amended Jan. 1, 2010), http://medgroup.ucsf.edu/sites/medgroup.ucsf.edu/files/med_group_bylaws2010.pdf; *see also* Duane Morris, *Faculty Practice Plans*, http://www.duanemorris.com/practices/healthcare_faculty_practice_plans.html (last visited June 11, 2015).

[95] Typically academic medical centers are composed of a medical college, several hospitals, a physician practice plan, and a research center. These related entities have not followed a shared governance model but have operated independent of one another, driven by interests in subspecialties and research, historically lacking a focus on budget-minded strategies. Health Research Inst., *The Future of the Academic Medical Center: Strategies to Avoid a Margin Meltdown* (Feb. 2012), *available at* http://healthsciences.utah.edu/hcr/2012/resources/the-future-of-academic-medical-centers.pdf.

[96] Bonnie Darves, *Teaching and Nonteaching Services Separate No More*, TODAY'S HOSPITALIST (Nov. 2011), http://www.todayshospitalist.com/index.php?b=articles_read&cnt=1381; *see generally* B. M. Reilly, *Don't Learn on Me—Are Teaching Hospitals Patient Centered?*, 371 NEW ENG. J. MED. 293 (2014).

[97] Allison Van Dusen, *America's Top Hospitals Go Global*, FORBES.COM (Aug. 25, 2008).

[98] *Id. See also* I. GLENN COHEN, PATIENTS WITH PASSPORTS 29 (2015).

[99] Am. Hosp. Ass'n, *The Value of Provider Integration*, TRENDWATCH (Mar. 2014).

No model of integration, regardless of how innovative its design, will be effective unless hospitals and health system sponsors are able to engage their medical staffs in the transformation.[100] Engagement, lying outside the boundaries of bylaws and contracts, must be present to foster physician collaboration.[101] Elements essential to enlist physician buy-in include shared vision, consensus development, workable compensation incentive models, performance recognition, adherence to an institutional culture, and, most significantly, making the delivery system patient-centered. However, the elements of collaboration may be easier to identify than implement, given laws and regulations that more often impede than promote change, particularly in areas such as fraud and abuse, and antitrust.

VI FINDING BROADER VALUE

As state and national leaders continue to grapple with healthcare costs, shifting the focus of the hospital-physician relationship to population health seems inevitable. The relationship will no longer focus only on patient episodic illness, but will be driven by public needs, especially chronic illness and persistent shortfalls in the budgets of public health agencies. In the context of hospital-physician relationships, a focus on population health would expand the relationship beyond traditional patient medical care to goals and objectives focused on community health. While population health is a rather broad and loosely defined concept, it includes not only traditional public health but also activities traditionally rooted in the delivery system.[102]

Improvement of population health is a major pillar of the PPACA, whose measures in access and quality support a delivery system oriented to addressing population health needs. This emphasis serves as a springboard for engaging hospitals and doctors in matters beyond traditional inpatient and ambulatory care. More specifically, the PPACA mandates a number of Medicaid and Medicare preventive services without cost-sharing, and promotes the development of ACOs that are tasked with responsibility for optimizing population healthcare outcomes for thousands of enrollees.[103] Particular reforms such as bundled payment

[100] Thomas H. Lee & Toby Cosgrove, *Engaging Doctors in the Health Care Revolution*, 92 HARV. BUS. REV. 104 (June 2014).

[101] *Id.* Lee and Cosgrove suggest that healthcare organizations engage in collaboration efforts with physicians that parallel the work of sociologist/economist Max Weber. Drawn from Weber's four motivations that drive social action, Drs. Lee and Cosgrove suggest that shared purpose, self-interest, respect, and tradition form the bases of strategies to engage physicians into the types of efforts necessary to promote integrative care.

[102] Michael A. Stoto, *Population Health in the Affordable Care Act*, ACAD. HEALTH (Feb. 21, 2013), http://www.academyhealth.org/files/AH2013pophealth.pdf. Dr. Stoto points out that population health differs from public health perceptually "as it is less tied to government health departments and explicitly includes the health care delivery system which is sometimes seen as separate from or even in opposition to governmental public health."

[103] *Id.* In addition, Stoto points out that the ACA promotes a number of community and population-based activities such as the creation of the National Prevention, Health Promotion and Public Health Council, a Prevention and Public Health Fund, community transformation grants, and a number of workplace wellness initiatives.

and required reductions in readmissions drive coordinated care processes that could be easily expanded into a population health focus akin to the ACO model.

Further, a focus on population health is evident in the PPACA mandate for nonprofit hospitals to conduct a community health needs assessment (CHNA) every three years, together with a mandate requiring annual reporting on how the institution is responding to the identified needs.[104] The planning and implementation of the CHNA is inherently population focused and developed with input from interested parties in the hospital's catchment area; it presents an ideal opportunity for hospitals to engage their medical staffs as partners in this new enterprise. There is no one model that needs to be pursued; target areas, ranging from health education to specialty clinic services in areas such as behavioral health, dentistry, and obesity are selected and directed by community need.[105] The CHNA holds a great potential for improving the overall health status of targeted populations.

The harsh reality of physician and patient demographics will continue to require better utilization of physician resources, with an ever increasing focus on chronic illness that is responsible for so much of the nation's healthcare costs. Models that serve as "physician multipliers," which leverage physicians' time to address population health, are already being used and expanding. One such example is Project Echo, an evidence-based telehealth model that has succeeded in disseminating expertise in the management of chronic conditions of the underserved—such as hepatitis C and diabetes—to primary care physicians, allied health professionals, and community health workers in rural and frontier areas.[106] Using specialists associated with academic medical centers and tertiary hospitals, this model "demonopolizes medical knowledge," creating a platform for specialists to share their medical expertise across distances, increasing the geographic area served by an institution.[107]

Adding further responsibilities to the hospital-physician portfolio is problematic unless there are ways to reimburse the additional work. One approach is a bonus payment to hospitals and physicians for meeting measureable public health targets, similar to other payment incentive programs. In essence, meeting defined population health goals that include both process and outcome measures could trigger a payment for performance that would support this activity.

In addition to reimbursement, hospital regulations could require institutions and their medical staffs to engage in population health activities. On the federal level, the Medicare Conditions of Participation (COP) that delineate hospital operational requirements for

[104] Affordable Care Act, Pub. L. No. 111-148, §9007, 124 Stat. 119 (2010). Institutions that fail to meet the CHNA mandate can be required to pay an excise tax, Section 4959. The CHNA is an organic process developed by a hospital with input from an array of local stakeholders. There is no specific model that must be followed, but plans must be transparent and responsive to local needs. The CHNA plan and implementation process has a close nexus to the community benefit demonstration required by the Internal Revenue Service, Ass'n of State & Territorial Health Officials, *Community Health Needs Assessments*, *available at* http://www.astho.org/Programs/Access/Community-Health-Needs-Assessments/.t

[105] CDC, *CDC Community Health Improvements Navigator*, *available at* http://www.cdc.gov/chinav/index.html.

[106] Sanjeev Arora, M.D. et al., *Demonopolizing Medical Knowledge*, 89 Acad. Med. 30 (Jan. 2014).

[107] *Id.* at 31.

Medicare and Medicaid could be expanded to include population health collaborations between the two parties.[108] State hospital licensing laws could also be changed to require hospitals and their staffs to collaborate to identify and address discrete population health problems. Such requirements could also be incorporated into The Joint Commission's private accreditation of hospitals.

VII Conclusion

The relationship between hospitals and physicians has been, and continues to be, central to the American healthcare landscape. While the medical staff structure has endured over time, regulation, economics, and technology have shaped the hospital-physician relationship. Federal policy-makers appear to envision ever greater collaboration between these two key healthcare players in the coming years to address population health. Adopting a population focus takes today's acute care institution and its staff full circle, back to the American hospital's roots in public service; moving the hospital-physician collaboration into population health is a step toward recapturing the hospital's former institutional mission of responding to community needs.

[108] 42 C.F.R. §482.21. Within the COP itself are possibilities to expand existing regulatory mandates to focus on population health, incorporating population health improvement efforts in the hospital quality assessment and performance improvement program.

CHAPTER 24

NONPROFIT HEALTHCARE ORGANIZATIONS AND THE LAW

JILL R. HORWITZ

I Introduction

The U.S. healthcare industry is different from other American industries in many respects. It has extreme cost growth, great significance to the economy, an outsized role in federal and state budgets (despite the somewhat limited role of government insurance provisions compared to other countries), and a host of market failures. The mix of nonprofit, for-profit, and government firms also makes healthcare markets unique. Although other industries include these three types of firms, they tend to specialize. For example, government schools educate the vast majority of primary and secondary students, while for-profits in higher education largely operate in a different market than public and nonprofit colleges and universities. Uniquely, healthcare organizations of different forms have long competed directly against each other in the same markets.

Scholars and policy-makers—who are far more aware of this facet of the healthcare industry than are patients—have largely focused on two sets of questions about the significance of ownership in healthcare markets. First, there is a considerable body of empirical research identifying differences and similarities among nonprofit, for-profit, and (less commonly) government healthcare organizations. These economic, econometric, and policy studies deal with differences in the quality of medical services offered, pricing and other competitive behaviors, and mix of services offered by different forms of hospitals, insurers, and nursing homes. They have generated mixed findings regarding the value of nonprofit ownership.

A second set of research questions—whether and how nonprofits merit federal and state tax exemptions—has produced far more heat. Legal scholars have engaged in extensive debate regarding exemptions for healthcare organizations; numerous hearings, lawsuits, and legislation have examined hospital and insurer tax exemptions. Because several helpful reference sources, literature reviews, and meta-studies have already canvassed scholarship regarding these two sets of questions, this chapter only briefly addresses them in section II.

This scholarship, even broadly construed, does not exhaust the important questions that should be asked about nonprofits, ownership, healthcare, and related areas of law. Therefore, this review chapter addresses something different. It recognizes that even within the odd terrain of law as applied to the health industry—a terrain in which ordinarily well-behaved laws behave erratically—there are further special rules when nonprofit healthcare entities are involved.

This chapter reviews several major legal and policy areas in which nonprofit healthcare organizations are treated differently from analogous for-profits, and in which nonprofit health providers are treated differently from other types of nonprofits. These differences can be found in such disparate legal areas as tax, antitrust, medical practice, and tort law. They can also be found in statute, common law, and regulation at the federal, state, and local levels of government. Most recently, the phenomenon appears in the Patient Protection and Affordable Care Act (PPACA or the Act).

Although the main ambition of this chapter is to identify salient examples of health law's special treatment of nonprofit organizations and nonprofit law's special treatment of health entities, it also reveals the law's reasoning, reporting explicit justifications for differential treatment where the law makes that possible, and inferring implicit reasons where the law does not. The chapter suggests that in many instances where the law treats analogous nonprofits and for-profits differently, it treats the former as particularly valuable and trustworthy, in part because it misunderstands nonprofits as being primarily dedicated to the relief of poverty and, therefore, imposes more lenient standards. But not always. In other instances, the law treats nonprofits as suspect and imposes additional oversight or regulation.

The chapter demonstrates that there is no consistent justification, and often no justification at all, for the variable treatment of nonprofit health providers, either by health law or nonprofit law. Indeed, their treatment often seems to operate at cross-purposes, with the law sometimes favoring and at other times disfavoring the same entities for the same expected behavior. Seeking a coherent justification across bodies of law as applied to nonprofit healthcare would likely be unfruitful, but identifying the inconsistency gives an accurate sense of the law and guidance for its development.

Finally, the chapter identifies some law and policy questions raised by major changes to the organization of healthcare. Some of these questions have come in the wake of the PPACA and are concerned primarily with its implementation. Others concern ongoing questions about legal ownership and healthcare organizations that have yet to be addressed.

Before proceeding, a note about terminology is in order. This chapter follows the popular convention of using the term "nonprofit" to refer to charities and other nonprofits, rathering than differentiating among nonprofit types. Charities, which are largely the subject of this chapter, are a subset of nonprofits that are organized and operated in a particular manner; they must have one of a list of purposes the law deems as charitable, be established for the benefit of indefinite beneficiaries, and are prohibited from providing impermissible private benefit.[1] There are many noncharitable, nonprofit organizations (e.g., labor unions, trade and professional organizations). Charities and the large majority of other nonprofit entities are exempt from federal and state taxes, and may receive related benefits. Charities, unlike

[1] *See generally* MARION R. FREMONT-SMITH, GOVERNING NONPROFIT ORGANIZATIONS: FEDERAL AND STATE LAW AND REGULATION (2004).

many other nonprofits, are eligible to receive tax-deductible donations and are more likely to be eligible for state and local property tax exemptions.

II Nonprofits vs. For-Profits: Are They different? Do They Merit Special Treatment?

The creation of a nonprofit, including a nonprofit healthcare organization, is generally a matter of state statutory and common law. Until the mid-nineteenth century, founders typically organized nonprofits in the form of trusts, and some older healthcare nonprofits remain legal trusts. Today nonprofits mainly incorporate, although some are formed as trusts, unincorporated associations, or limited-liability companies. As discussed in the next section, whether a nonprofit is eligible for tax exemption is a separate legal question from its legal form.

Several existing literature reviews summarize research comparing nonprofit and for-profit healthcare entities. Although most studies focus on hospitals, others examine insurers, nursing homes,[2] dialysis centers,[3] and hospice providers.[4] Research on quality of care has generated conflicting results,[5] but most articles demonstrate that nonprofits often provide higher quality services than for-profits.[6] Research on the financial behavior of nonprofit health providers, such as the exercise of market power, pricing behavior,[7] or hospital costs, has shown few differences in such behavior. In addition, for-profit hospitals are more likely than nonprofits to "upcode," bill for more profitable diagnoses than necessary.[8] They are also more likely to locate where there is relatively low demand for free and subsidized healthcare.[9]

A few articles examine the effects of nonprofit market share on medical care. Nonprofits with more for-profits in their markets behave like for-profits by offering more profitable services and fewer unprofitable services, and changing their service mix in response to changes

[2] *E.g.*, Anna A. Amirkhanyan et al., *Does the Public Sector Outperform the Nonprofit and For-Profit Sectors? Evidence from a National Panel Study on Nursing Home Quality and Access*, 27 J. Pol'y Analysis & Mgmt. 326 (2008).

[3] *E.g.*, Donald K. K. Lee et al., *Re-Exploring Differences Among For-Profit and Nonprofit Dialysis Providers*, 45 Health Services Res. 633 (2010).

[4] *E.g.*, Frank A. Sloan, *Not-for-Profit Ownership and Hospital Behavior*, *in* Handbook of Health Economics 1141 (Anthony J. Culyer & Joseph P. Newhouse eds., 2000); Mark Schlesinger & Bradford H. Gray, *How Nonprofits Matter in American Medicine and What to Do About It*, 25 Health Aff. W287 (2006).

[5] Karen Eggleston et al., *Hospital Ownership and Quality of Care: What Explains the Different Results in the Literature?*, 17 Health Econ. 1345 (2008).

[6] *E.g.*, Thomas C. Tsai et al., *Variation in Surgical-Readmission Rates and Quality of Hospital Care*, 369 N. Eng. J. Med. 1134 (2013).

[7] *E.g.*, Martin Gaynor & William B. Vogt, *Competition Among Hospitals*, 34 RAND J. Econ. 764 (2003).

[8] *E.g.*, Leemore Dafny & David Dranove, *Regulatory Exploitation and Management Changes: Upcoding in the Hospital Industry*, 52 J.L. & Econ. 223, 224, 246 (2009).

[9] Edward C. Norton & Douglas O. Staiger, *How Hospital Ownership Affects Access to Care for the Uninsured*, 25 RAND J. Econ. 171, 184 (1994).

in financial incentives.[10] Nonprofits in markets with relatively high for-profit market share avoid unprofitable patients,[11] spend less on some patients,[12] and are more responsive to profit-making opportunities.[13]

A second area of research concerns tax exemption, which is discussed at length in section III.a below. Legal scholars have examined the requirements for nonprofit hospitals and insurers to obtain federal income tax exemption, argued over whether those exemptions are justified, and proposed alternative requirements for exemption.[14] Some specifically address community benefit requirements,[15] with some arguing for stricter standards and more enforcement.[16] Others highlight the negative, unintended consequences of reform.[17]

III The Special Case of Nonprofit Health Providers in the Law

The law sometimes treats nonprofit health providers more leniently and at other times more strictly than comparable organizations. This differential treatment occurs in broad (e.g., the

[10] Jill R. Horwitz & Austin Nichols, *Hospital Ownership and Medical Services: Market Mix, Spillover Effects, and Nonprofit Objectives*, 28 J. Health Econ. 924 (2009).

[11] *E.g.*, Mark Schlesinger et al., *The Privatization of Health Care and Physicians' Perceptions of Access to Hospital Services*, 65 Milbank Q. 25 (1987).

[12] *E.g.*, Susan L. Ettner & Richard C. Hermann, *The Role of Profit Status Under Imperfect Information: Evidence from the Treatment Patterns of Elderly Medicare Beneficiaries Hospitalized for Psychiatric Diagnoses*, 20 J. Health Econ. 23 (1987); Daniel Kessler & Mark McClellan, *The Effects of Hospital Ownership on Medical Productivity*, 33 RAND J. Econ. 488 (2002).

[13] *E.g.*, David Cutler & Jill R. Horwitz, *Converting Hospitals from Not-for-Profit to For-Profit Status: Why and What Effects?*, *in* The Changing Hospital Industry: Comparing Not-for-Profit and For-Profit Institutions 45 (David Cutler ed., 2000); Mark G. Duggan, *Hospital Ownership and Public Medical Spending*, 115 Q. J. Econ. 1343 (2000); Elaine Silverman & Jonathan Skinner, *Medicare Upcoding and Hospital Ownership*, 23 J. Health Econ. 369, 371 (2004).

[14] *E.g.*, M. Gregg Bloche, *Health Policy Below the Waterline: Medical Care and the Charitable Exemption*, 80 Minn. L. Rev. 299 (1995); Mark A. Hall & John D. Colombo, *The Charitable Status of Nonprofit Hospitals: Toward a Donative Theory of Tax Exemption*, 66 Wash. L. Rev. 307 (1991); Jill R. Horwitz, *Does Nonprofit Ownership Matter?*, 24 Yale J. on Reg. 139 (2007); Lloyd Hitoshi Mayer, *The "Independent" Sector: Fee-for-Service Charity and the Limits of Autonomy*, 65 Vand. L. Rev. 51 (2012); Usha Rodrigues, *Entity and Identity*, 60 Emory L.J. 1257 (2011); Schlesinger & Gray, *How Nonprofits Matter in American Medicine, and What to Do About It*, W287.

[15] *E.g.*, Gloria J. Bazzoli et al., *Community Benefit Activities of Private, Nonprofit Hospitals*, 35 J. Health Pol. Pol'y & L. 999 (2010); Cecilia M. Jardon McGregor, *The Community Benefit Standard for Non-Profit Hospitals: Which Community, and for Whose Benefit?*, 23 J. Contemp. Health L. & Pol'y 302, 304 (2007).

[16] *E.g.*, John Colombo, *The Failure of Community Benefit*, 15 Health Matrix 29 (2005); Laura L. Folkerts, Note, *Do Nonprofit Hospitals Provide Community Benefit? A Critique of the Standards for Proving Deservedness of Federal Tax Exemptions*, 34 J. Corp. L. 611, 640 (2009).

[17] *E.g.*, Lawrence E. Singer, *Leveraging Tax-Exempt Status of Hospitals*, 29 J. Legal Med. 41, 61–64 (2008); James E. Tyrrell, III, Note, *Non-Profits Under Fire: The Effects of Minimal Charity Care*

required legal form of health exchanges) as well as specific (e.g., the delayed application of rules limiting physician referrals, known as "Stark rules," to nonprofit systems[18]) areas of law.

Cases of relatively lenient treatment are grounded on the assumption that nonprofits are particularly trustworthy: more likely to act in the interest of their patients or other beneficiaries, less likely to interfere in the medical judgments of physicians, and less likely to behave competitively in markets than comparable for-profits. Some of the justifications offered by the law for favoring nonprofits are implausible, such as the claim that they are not market competitors. Others are credible. It is reasonable to assume that nonprofits, because they cannot seek to maximize profits or pay profits to owners, will reinvest profits in advancing their goals, such as providing health services. On the contrary, relatively onerous treatment stems from a suspicion that nonprofit healthcare organizations are merely for-profits in disguise. This treatment is often justified by the erroneous belief that nonprofits are required to relieve poverty, discussed in detail in section III.a.iii, and that they do not adequately do so.

Even within the PPACA, nonprofits receive inconsistent treatment. Many provisions seem to have an incidental effect on nonprofits qua nonprofits. The delay in implementation of the Small Business Health Options Program, for example, disproportionately affects nonprofits, because nonprofits are disproportionately small employers. Other rules explicitly disfavor nonprofits. This is most obvious in new rules regarding the tax treatment of nonprofit hospitals. Other PPACA provisions, such as the tax credit for small employers, less overtly, but no less effectively, disfavor nonprofits.

In several other sections of the PPACA, the Act entrusts nonprofits to advance the public interest, which is sometimes assumed to be the patient's interest, sometimes the government's interest. For example, states that establish exchanges may do so only through a state-established nonprofit entity or government agency.[19] In other states, the federal government may operate exchanges either directly or through an agreement with a nonprofit entity.[20] In addition, eventually all states must have at least two multistate insurance plans, one of which must be nonprofit.[21]

The remainder of this chapter reviews five areas in which nonprofit status, health policy, and various areas of law interact: (1) tax exemption, including new requirements imposed by the PPACA; (2) antitrust law; (3) the corporate practice of medicine doctrine; (4) tort law; and (5) fundamental transactions in corporate organization.

a. Tax Exemption

Federal and state laws impose greater obligations on tax-exempt nonprofits that provide health services than they have on tax-exempt nonprofits in other industries.[22] PPACA provisions

Requirements Legislation on Not-for-Profit Hospitals, 26 J. CONTEMP. HEALTH L. & POL'Y 373, 375–376 (2010).

[18] Delay of the Date of Applicability for Certain Provisions of Physicians' Referrals to Health Care Entities With Which They Have Financial Relationships (Phase III), 72 Fed. Reg. 64161-01 (Ctrs. for Medicaid & Medicare Servs. [CMS], Nov. 15, 2007); *see also* CMS Advisory Op. 2005-08-01 (2005).

[19] 42 U.S.C. § 18031(d)(1) (2012); 45 C.F.R. § 155.100(c) (2015).

[20] 42 U.S.C. § 18041(c) (2012); 45 C.F.R. § 155.105(f) (2015).

[21] 42 U.S.C. § 18054(a)(3) (2012). In addition, navigator grants must go to at least one nonprofit group. 45 C.F.R. § 155.210(c)(2) (2015). And the Consumer Operated and Oriented Plan (CO-OP) encourages nonprofits. 42 U.S.C. §§ 18042(a)(2) (2012); 45 C.F.R. §§ 156.510,156.520 (2015).

amending the Internal Revenue Code impose even more requirements on tax-exempt hospitals. In this respect, nonprofits in healthcare are treated as more suspect than other nonprofits, in need of special regulation and heightened scrutiny to ensure they merit their exemptions.

These heightened requirements are at odds with the centuries-old law of charities from which contemporary tax law descends.[23] Historically, both the common law and statute have treated the provision of healthcare itself, regardless of the socioeconomic status of the patients, as a valid charitable purpose.[24] As far back as 1601, for example, the Statute of Elizabeth permitted gifts for "relief of aged, impotent and poor people, [and] for maintenance of sick and maimed soldiers and mariners."[25] In determining which purposes counted as charitable, including medicine, American courts cited this statute. Moreover, under charitable trust law the traditional list of permissible purposes has always included the promotion of health; indeed, the Restatement of the Law Third, Trusts includes it as one of only five enumerated charitable purposes.[26] Today, hospitals and other healthcare entities may take the nonprofit form in every state.

Although whether an entity is a nonprofit under state law and qualification for tax exemption can be related, they are distinct legal questions. The latter question—whether providing healthcare is sufficient for various tax exemptions and related benefits—has raised controversy over the past few decades. Before the mid-twentieth century, charitable healthcare entities seeking tax exemptions and related benefits available to other nonprofits—including income tax exemption, the receipt of tax-deductible donations, and other benefits—needed to follow the same rules as other charities, such as museums or schools. Yet state and federal policy has increasingly required charitable hospitals to relieve poverty through the provision of free care for indigent patients and similar activities in exchange for various exemptions. No other type of charity is required to relieve poverty to qualify for exemption. Few scholars and policy-makers have focused on these differences.

i. Federal Tax Exemption

The Internal Revenue Code grants federal tax exemption, inter alia, to the subset of nonprofits that have charitable purposes and adhere to other requirements. These purposes include "religious, charitable, scientific, testing for public safety, literary, or educational purposes, or to foster national or international amateur sports competition (but only if no part of its activities involve the provision of athletic facilities or equipment), or for the prevention of cruelty to children or animals . . ."[27]

A series of revenue rulings has imposed particular requirements on hospitals and nonprofit insurers. From 1956 to 1969, an Internal Revenue Service (IRS) revenue ruling required nonprofit hospitals to be "operated to the extent of [their] financial ability for those not able to pay for the services rendered."[28] Since 1969 the IRS has had no explicit charity care

[22] *See* Daniel M. Fox & Daniel C. Schaffer, *Tax Administration as Health Policy: Hospitals, the Internal Revenue Service and the Courts*, 16 J. HEALTH POL. POL'Y & L. 251 (1991); Douglas M. Mancino, *Income Tax Exemption of the Contemporary Nonprofit Hospital*, 32 ST. LOUIS U. L.J. 1015 (1988).

[23] *See generally* Jill R. Horwitz, *Nonprofits and Narrative: Piers Plowman, Anthony Trollope, and Charities Law*, 2009 MICH. ST. L. REV. 989, 1000–1006 (2009).

[24] *See* Jill R. Horwitz, *Nonprofit Ownership, Private Property, and Public Accountability*, 25 HEALTH AFF. W308, W309 (2006).

[25] 43 Elizabeth I c. 4. 26 RESTATEMENT (THIRD) OF TRUSTS § 28(d) (2003).

[27] I.R.C. § 501(c)(3) (2015).

[28] Rev Rul. 56-185, 1956-1 C.B. 202, 203, *available at* http://www.irs.gov/pub/irs-tege/rr56-185.pdf.

requirement for tax-exempt status. Instead a nonprofit hospital could secure exemption by either (1) providing free or subsidized care "to the extent of its financial ability" or (2) meeting an alternative, "community benefit" test, involving treating all patients who were able to pay or were insured and operating an emergency room where needed.[29] Federal regulators have interpreted the term "community benefit" broadly.

During the late 1990s and early 2000s, legislators, litigators, and scholars expressed growing concern that nonprofit hospitals are really "for-profits in disguise." In particular, there was outcry over hospitals billing uninsured patients at higher rates than other patients and using aggressive debt collection techniques. A wave of class action lawsuits were filed in federal courts (alleging hospitals had violated federal tax law) and state courts (alleging violations of consumer-protection statutes). Although these cases largely foundered on procedural grounds such as lack of standing, reports of aggressive billing and debt collection garnered the attention of Congress and state legislatures. Indeed, some plaintiffs went so far as to claim nonprofit hospitals were generally unscrupulous, not only because they provided an insufficient amount of free care but also because their activities were unfair, opaque, and resulted in too much financial benefit for the hospitals, their board members, and private medical groups.[30]

At the federal level, the response to these allegations included a series of hearings and studies.[31] The IRS created a new schedule (Schedule H) for hospitals to file as part of their IRS form 990, the federal information return. The schedule does not explicitly require the relief of poverty; hospitals, in theory, can provide medical care to patients regardless of their wealth or insurance status and still qualify for exemption. However, the relief of poverty figures so prominently throughout different sections of Schedule H that hospitals understand they must provide free care to obtain exemption.

Some scholars had long argued for restrictions on nonprofit providers such as legislation limiting hospitals' abilities to collect debts,[32] imposing a provider tax to provide care for the poor,[33] and other measures that implicitly equate charity with poverty relief.[34] And observers anticipated that free care for indigent patients would increase in response to the new forms,[35] and argued that the changes could help stop nonprofit hospitals from receiving tax exemptions of more value than the community benefit provided.[36] In fact, a recent analysis finds

[29] Rev. Rul. 69-545, 1969-2 C.B. 117, *available at* http://www.irs.gov/pub/irs-tege/rr69-545.pdf.

[30] *See* Nancy M. Kane, *Tax-Exempt Hospitals: What Is Their Charitable Responsibility and How Should It Be Defined and Reported?*, 51 ST. LOUIS U. L.J. 459, 459–461 (2007).

[31] *E.g.*, *The Tax-Exempt Hospital Sector: Hearing Before the H. Comm. on Ways & Means*, 109th Cong. (2005); *Taking the Pulse of Charitable Care and Community Benefits at Nonprofit Hospitals: Hearing Before the S. Fin. Comm.*, 109th Cong. (2006); INTERNAL REVENUE SERV., IRS EXEMPT ORGANIZATIONS (TE/GE) HOSPITAL COMPLIANCE PROJECT—FINAL REPORT (2014), *available at* http://www.irs.gov/pub/irs-tege/frepthospproj.pdf.

[32] *E.g.*, Terri L. Brooks, *Billions Saved in Taxes While Millions Underserved—What Has Happened to Charitable Hospitals?*, 8 HOUS. BUS. & TAX L.J. 391, 424 (2008).

[33] *E.g.*, John D. Colombo, *Federal and State Tax Exemption Policy, Medical Debt and Healthcare for the Poor*, 51 ST. LOUIS U. L.J. 433, 434–435 (2007).

[34] *E.g.*, McGregor, *The Community Benefit Standard for Non-Profit Hospitals*, 302, 304; Jeremy J. Schirra, *A Veil of Tax Exemption?: A Proposal for the Continuation of Federal Tax-Exempt Status for "Nonprofit" Hospitals*, 21 HEALTH MATRIX 231, 236 (2011).

[35] *E.g.*, Lisa Kinney Helvin, Note, *Caring for the Uninsured: Are Not-for-Profit Hospitals Doing Their Share?*, 8 YALE J. HEALTH POL'Y, L. & ETHICS 421 (2008).

[36] *E.g.*, Folkerts, Note, *Do Nonprofit Hospitals Provide Community Benefit?*, 611, 640.

that hospitals largely spend their community benefit dollars on activities related to poverty relief.[37]

The PPACA's most dramatic provision addressing nonprofits adds new conditions for federal tax exemption and related benefits available to organizations eligible for exemption under § 501(c)(3).[38] In addition to meeting existing requirements for exemption, hospitals that are charities must (1) establish financial assistance and emergency medical care policies, (2) limit charges to patients eligible for assistance under those policies, and (3) make reasonable efforts to identify eligible patients before engaging in extraordinary collection actions against them. They must also conduct community health needs assessments and adopt implementation strategies to meet those needs at least once every three years. Hospitals that do not report on and comply with the requirements face a $50,000 tax and risk losing their tax exemptions altogether.

The tax treatment of health insurance companies varies. For-profit insurers have always been taxable. Until the Tax Reform Act of 1986 many nonprofit health insurers were fully exempt from federal taxation under Internal Revenue Code § 501(c)(3) or § 501 (c)(4). That act introduced § 501(m), which makes insurers that provide "commercial-type" insurance as a substantial part of their activities ineligible for exemption.[39] Even after these rules were implemented, certain insurers, such as Blue Cross or Blue Shield organizations, were still able to qualify for preferential tax treatment in the form of special deductions as long as they met certain requirements, such as maintaining high-risk and small-group coverage plans.[40] A large body of tax law addresses health maintenance organizations (HMOs), many of which are organized such that they are not providers of "commercial-type" insurance.

ii. *State Exemptions and Payments in Lieu of Taxes*

States typically grant income tax exemption to entities that are eligible for federal income tax exemption. Other states have statutes or constitutional provisions that include different, usually more stringent, requirements for exemption.[41] Because many nonprofit healthcare entities do not earn significant profits but do own real property, property tax exemptions can be more valuable to them than income tax exemptions. (Indeed, the greatest tax benefit accruing to nonprofit hospitals is the ability to issue tax-exempt debt under IRC § 103).

Local governments, however, feel the loss of property taxes, which are the largest source of local government revenue. On average they constitute 30% of total revenues of localities.[42] Therefore, states and localities, particularly those under financial pressure and those with large numbers of nonprofits, increasingly turn to them for donated services[43] and money. One

[37] Susannah Camic Tahk, *Tax-Exempt Hospitals and Their Communities*, 6 COLUM. J. TAX L. 33 (2015).

[38] I.R.C. § 501(r) (2015); Additional Requirements for Charitable Hospitals, 79 Fed. Reg. 78954-01 (Dec. 31, 2014).

[39] *See* FRANCES R. HILL & DOUGLAS M. MANCINO, TAXATION OF EXEMPT ORGANIZATIONS § 22.06 (2002 & Supp. 2014-2).

[40] I.R.C. § 833 (2015).

[41] *See, e.g.*, Utah Cnty. v. Intermountain Health Care, Inc., 709 P.2d 265, 267–268 (Utah 1985).

[42] Percentage calculated by author from U.S. CENSUS BUREAU, 2012 CENSUS OF GOVERNMENTS: FINANCE (2012).

[43] Evelyn Brody, *The States' Growing Use of a Quid Pro Quo Rationale for the Charity Property Tax Exemption*, 56 EXEMPT ORG. TAX REV. 269 (2007).

form of relief for these governments is Payments in Lieu of Taxes (PILOTs).[44] One form of PILOT is a payment from one level of government to another as compensation for forgone taxes from public and charitable land. For example, Connecticut reimburses municipalities for certain categories of forgone taxes.[45] Another form is a negotiated payment from the charity to the government. These payments are typically restricted to large nonprofits like universities and hospitals, although some states ask more nonprofits to make voluntary payments.[46]

In addition, many states encourage or require hospitals to provide adequate community benefits to justify exemptions.[47] These benefits include requirements that hospitals meet quantitative expenditure targets. For example, Pennsylvania hospitals can meet the requirement by providing uncompensated care in an amount equivalent to at least 5% of net patient revenue.[48] Applicants for a hospital license (or any subsequent successor or acquirer) in Massachusetts must agree to maintain or increase the percentage of patient revenue allocated to uncompensated care.[49] Determining whether a hospital provides adequate community benefits can be difficult given the challenge of distinguishing uncompensated care meant to relieve poverty from ordinary bad debt.

Other states have pushed to eliminate property tax exemption for nonprofit hospitals altogether. In a prominent Illinois case, *Provena v. Department of Revenue*, a plurality of the Illinois Supreme Court held that a medical center and five affiliated hospitals provided insufficient free care to qualify for exemption.[50] After difficult negotiations among stakeholders, Illinois legislated a compromise under which hospitals must provide uncompensated care at least equal to the value of their estimated property tax liability.[51]

iii. Healthcare Providers vs. Other Charities

Unless it provides healthcare, a charity that does nothing to relieve poverty may nonetheless benefit from tax exemption. It can educate rich students in universities, improve the spiritual health of rich congregants in church, or operate a museum that appeals to the tastes of the upper classes. Few scholars have noted either that these rules imply one definition of charity for healthcare and another definition of charity for other types of entities, or that this distinction may impose unintended costs on the provision of healthcare.[52]

The heightened requirements for nonprofit health entities may increase the provision of free care for indigent patients and help hospitals accomplish one method of fulfilling charitable obligations (relieving poverty) at the expense of other patients and other

[44] Fan Fei et al., *Are Pilots Property Taxes for Nonprofits?* (Nat'l Bureau Econ. Res. Working Paper No. 21088, 2015).

[45] Conn. Gen. Stat. §§ 12-19a, 12-20a (2015).

[46] *E.g.*, Town Manager's Office, Town of Andover, Mass., PILOTs: Payments in Lieu of Taxes (2014), *available at* http://andoverma.gov/publish/PilotReport.pdf.

[47] Fred Joseph Hellinger, *Tax-Exempt Hospitals and Community Benefits: A Review of State Reporting Requirements*, 34 J. Health Pol. Pol'y & L. 37, 47 (2009).

[48] 10 Pa. Cons. Stat. Ann. § 375(d)(1)(iii) (2015).

[49] Mass. Gen. Laws ch. 111, § 51G(3) (2015).

[50] Provena Covenant Med. Ctr. v. Dep't of Revenue, 236 Ill. 2d 368 (2010).

[51] 35 Ill. Comp. Stat. 200/15-86(c) (2015).

[52] *E.g.*, Tyrrell, Note, *Non-Profits Under Fire*, 373, 375–376.

obligations.[53] On the one hand, health law (particularly the PPACA) attempts to improve access to care, and conscripting charities in that effort is one way to do so. But if the goal of this provision is to improve access to healthcare, it is unclear why the requirements are levied only on nonprofit hospitals. Those requirements could be imposed on all hospitals including for-profits, not as requirements for exemption (for which for-profits are ineligible) but, for example, as a condition of Medicare participation.

b. Antitrust Law and Nonprofit Hospitals

In theory, U.S. antitrust law treats nonprofits and for-profits alike.[54] Particularly during the 1990s, however, the practice told a different story. Courts deferred to nonprofit hospitals in assessing the anticompetitive outcomes of hospital mergers, finding that nonprofit status "militates in favor of finding their combination reasonable."[55] Federal courts found against the Federal Trade Commission (FTC) or the Department of Justice (DOJ) in every nonprofit hospital merger case from 1994 to 2004.[56] Since then, there has been a shift away from favoring nonprofits.

Judges favored nonprofits for several reasons. In authorizing mergers, they assumed, for example, that nonprofit hospitals: (1) do not compete on price and, therefore, would not raise prices postmerger; (2) would use increased revenues that would result from mergers for "high quality healthcare to economically disadvantaged and elderly members of the community,"[57] and (3) would be constrained by their boards to protect consumers from anticompetitive behavior.[58]

F.T.C. v. Butterworth Health Corp. represents the high-water mark for preferential treatment of nonprofit hospitals seeking to merge. The court held that although the merger in question would result in reduced competition, "a substantial increase in market concentration among nonprofit hospitals is not likely to result in price increases."[59] The defendants argued that unlike for-profits, nonprofits "do not operate in the same manner as profit maximizing businesses."[60] In approving the merger as in the best interest of the public, the court assumed that the hospital board, composed of community members, would protect that

[53] Jill R. Horwitz & David Cutler, *The ACA's Hospital Tax-Exemption Rules and the Practice of Medicine*, Mar. 3, 2015, HEALTH AFFAIRS BLOG (Mar. 3, 2015), http://healthaffairs.org/blog/2015/03/03/the-acas-hospital-tax-exemption-rules-and-the-practice-of-medicine/.

[54] Peter J. Hammer & William M. Sage, *Critical Issues in Hospital Antitrust Law*, 22 HEALTH AFF. 88 (2003).

[55] United States v. Carilion Health Sys., 707 F. Supp. 840, 849 (W.D. Va.), *aff'd*, 892 F.2d 1042 (4th Cir. 1989).

[56] DEP'T OF JUSTICE & FED. TRADE COMM'N, IMPROVING HEALTH CARE: A DOSE OF COMPETITION 14 (2004), *available at* http://www.ftc.gov/reports/improving-health-care-dose-competition-report-federal-trade-commission-department-justice.

[57] United States v. Long Island Jewish Med. Ctr., 983 F. Supp. 121, 149 (E.D.N.Y. 1997).

[58] United States v. Carilion Health Sys., 707 F. Supp. 840, 849 (W.D. Va.), *aff'd*, 892 F.2d 1042 (4th Cir. 1989).

[59] F.T.C. v. Butterworth Health Corp., 946 F. Supp. 1285, 1297 (W.D. Mich. 1996), *aff'd*, 121 F.3d 708 (6th Cir. 1997).

[60] F.T.C. v. Butterworth Health Corp., 946 F. Supp. 1285, 1296 (W.D. Mich. 1996), *aff'd*, 121 F.3d 708 (6th Cir. 1997).

community. Another court predicted that the merger of two nonprofit hospitals would result in greater competitiveness and yield price reductions, in this case because the combination of a small hospital with high fixed costs and limited services with a larger hospital in need of space could more effectively compete in the market.[61]

Scholars have roundly criticized these justifications. Many scholars have argued that nonprofits face the same incentives to restrain trade as for-profits.[62] They have also found that nonprofit hospital mergers result in price increases no lower than those found in markets where for-profits have merged,[63] although recent scholarship suggests that nonprofits do not fully exercise their market power to maximize profits.[64]

Regardless, scholars argue that relying on community benefits "impermissibly allows non-competitive values to be weighed against the virtues derived from competition, which is the core value of the antitrust laws."[65] They further object to favoring nonprofits and allowing them to accrue monopoly profits, even if they use those profits for the provision of public goods (e.g., free care for indigent patients, technological innovation). Allowing nonprofits to spend these profits according to organizational preference, it is argued, shortcuts public debate regarding the type and quantity of public goods that are appropriately available.[66]

Scholars have also been skeptical that community-based boards of directors will prevent nonprofit hospitals from seeking monopoly profits. Blumstein, for example, criticized the *Butterworth* court for its "considerable emphasis on noblesse oblige considerations associated with the leadership of the nonprofit institutions."[67] According to Greaney, relying on private regulation in the form of "supposedly benign nonprofit boards and governmental regulation in the form of the judicially approved controls over prices and profits are dubious substitutes for interfirm rivalry," particularly with no evidence that board members exert such control.[68] Scholars have also offered various explanations for the judiciary's misplaced faith in nonprofit hospitals. These include judges' social affinity with hospital board members[69] and their desire to protect nonprofit hospitals against newly powerful managed care organizations, which they believed were in the business of saving dollars rather than lives.[70]

61 United States v. Carilion Health Sys., 707 F. Supp. 840, 849 (W.D. Va.), *aff'd*, 892 F.2d 1042 (4th Cir. 1989). *See also Blodgett Memorial Medical Center*, 946 F. Supp. 1285 (W.D. Mich. 1996), *aff'd*, 121 F.3d 708 (6th Cir.).

62 *E.g.*, Tomas Philipson & Richard A. Posner, *Antitrust in the Not-For Profit Sector*, 52 J.L. & Econ. 1 (2009).

63 *E.g.*, Gary Young et al., *Community Control and Pricing Patterns of Nonprofit Hospitals: An Antitrust Analysis*, 25 J. Health Pol. Pol'y & L. 1051 (2000); Thomas L. Greaney, *Antitrust and Hospital Mergers: Does the Nonprofit Form Affect Competitive Substance?*, 31 J. Health Pol. Pol'y & L. 511, 520 (2006).

64 David Dranove et al., *How Do Hospitals Respond to Negative Financial Shocks?* (Nat'l Bureau Econ. Res., Working Paper No. 18853, 2013).

65 James F. Blumstein, *The Application of Antitrust Doctrine to the Healthcare Industry: The Interweaving of Empirical and Normative Issues*, 31 Ind. L. Rev. 91, 110 (1998).

66 *E.g.*, Barak D. Richman, *Antitrust and Nonprofit Hospital Mergers: A Return to Basics*, 156 U. Pa. L. Rev. 121 (2007).

67 Blumstein, *The Application of Antitrust Doctrine to the Healthcare Industry*, 91, 111.

68 Thomas L. Greaney, *Wither Antitrust? The Uncertain Future of Competition Law in Health Care*, 21 Health Aff. 185, 188 (2002).

69 Peter J. Hammer & William M. Sage, *Antitrust, Health Care Quality, and the Courts*, 102 Colum. L. Rev. 545, 617 (2002).

70 Greaney, *Antitrust and Hospital Mergers*, 511, 513.

Policy-makers have similarly criticized deference to nonprofits. In 2004, an FTC and DOJ report on competition in the healthcare industry included analysis of federal court decisions regarding nonprofit mergers and postmerger anticompetitive activity.[71] The report disagreed with the courts' lenient approach, noting that nonprofit market concentration is associated with higher prices. It recommended that the "nonprofit status of a hospital should not be considered in determining whether a proposed hospital merger violates the antitrust laws."[72]

Perhaps in response to these criticisms, *Butterworth* was cast in doubt.[73] In 2007, the FTC affirmed a 2005 administrative ruling that Evanston Northwestern Healthcare Corporation's acquisition of another hospital was anticompetitive.[74] The administrative law judge rejected the claim that the hospital's nonprofit status meant it was unlikely to raise prices. In fact, the nonprofit had raised prices after the merger.[75] There remains some disagreement about whether community benefits will still be considered in courts' analysis of nonprofit mergers or if these changes signal a new approach.[76]

Nonetheless, other recent cases suggest a further retreat from favoring nonprofits in antitrust analyses.[77] In 2013, the Supreme Court touched on the question of nonprofit behavior, albeit indirectly. In forbidding a local hospital authority from acquiring a hospital and leasing it to the authority's subsidiary nonprofit health system, the Court rejected the authority's argument that the state's requirement that the system and subsidiary hospitals be nonprofits provided sufficient evidence that the state had considered the anticompetitive effects of the acquisition and judged them to be acceptable.[78] The Court did not explicitly address whether nonprofit hospitals compete, but indicated that the state could rely on the mere fact that the parties were nonprofits as protection against anticompetitive effects.

At least for a time, antitrust law, like other laws discussed in this chapter thus far, applied special rules to nonprofit healthcare entities. Treating nonprofit hospitals as inherently trustworthy—in light of their missions, governance structures, inability to distribute profits, value of the public goods they provide, or for no stated reason at all—courts regarded nonprofit hospitals as if they were not market competitors. Recently, however, courts seem to be rejecting these views in favor of treating nonprofit hospitals as they do for-profits, in need of the regulatory supervision regarding anticompetitive behavior.

[71] DEP'T OF JUSTICE & FED. TRADE COMM'N, IMPROVING HEALTH CARE: A DOSE OF COMPETITION 27 (2004), *available at* http://www.ftc.gov/reports/improving-health-care-dose-competition-report-federal-trade-commission-department-justice.

[72] Id., at 27.

[73] *See, e.g.*, Greaney, *Whither Antitrust?*, 185, 187–188; Toby G. Singer, *Antitrust Implications of the Affordable Care Act*, 6 J. HEALTH & LIFE SCI. L. 57, 77–78 (2013).

[74] *See Commission Rules that Evanston Northwestern Healthcare Corp.'s Acquisition of Highland Park Hospital Was Anticompetitive*, FED. TRADE COMM'N (Aug. 6, 2007), http://www.ftc.gov/news-events/press-releases/2007/08/commission-rules-evanston-northwestern-healthcare-corps.

[75] *See* Erica L. Rice, Note, *Evanston's Legacy: A Prescription for Addressing Two-Stage Competition in Hospital Merger Antitrust Analysis*, 90 B.U. L. REV. 431, 451 (2010).

[76] *E.g.*, Richman, *Antitrust and Nonprofit Hospital Mergers*, 121, 149–150; Barry C. Harris & David A. Argue, FTC v. Evanston Northwestern: *A Change from Traditional Hospital Merger Analysis?*, ANTITRUST (Spring 2006), at 34.

[77] F.T.C. v. OSF Healthcare Sys., 852 F. Supp. 2d 1069, 1085 (N.D. Ill. 2012); F.T.C. v. ProMedica Health Sys., Inc., No. 3:11 CV 47, 2011 WL 1219281 (N.D. Ohio Mar. 29, 2011).

[78] F.T.C. v. Phoebe Putney Health Sys. Inc., 133 S. Ct. 1003 (2013).

c. Corporate Practice of Medicine

Most states prohibit the corporate practice of medicine.[79] In some states the laws are dormant, but in others—including California and Texas—they have an outsized influence on practice. Although restrictions vary, they typically forbid business corporations from employing physicians to provide medical services but permit similar contractual relationships. The restrictions are found in statutes, common law, and, by implication, state medical licensing rules (i.e., only human professionals and not legal persons can practice medicine).[80]

Two common justifications for the rules are: (1) the commercial pressures inherent in corporate or lay employment undermine physicians' independent judgment and their fiduciary duties to patients; and (2) such employment might lead to the exploitation of the medical community, harming the status and income of physicians.[81] The law presumes that contractual relationships do not raise these same risks.

Many states exempt certain entities, frequently nonprofits, from these rules.[82] A typical justification for exempting nonprofits is that because they are not motivated by profit, they will not undermine physicians' independence by entraining them into profit-making behavior.[83] For example, one court distinguished the for-profit defendant from nonprofit caregivers, stating:

> [Nonprofit] activities are not comparable to those of private corporations operated for profit and, since the principal evils attendant upon corporate practice of medicine spring from the conflict between the professional standards and obligations of the doctors and the profit motive of the corporation employer, it may well be concluded that the objections of policy do not apply to nonprofit institutions. This view seems almost implicit in the decisions of the courts and it certainly has been the assumption of the public authorities. . . .[84]

More recently, another court concluded that "concerns about for-profit corporations have nothing to do with non-profit teaching hospitals."[85]

Recently, states that had favored nonprofits have limited or eliminated the nonprofit exemption. California used to exempt all nonprofits but now only exempts licensed charities if they do not charge their patients.[86] According to the California Court of Appeals, "[w]hile

[79] Isles Wellness, Inc. v. Progressive N. Ins. Co., 703 N.W.2d 513, 517 (Minn. 2005).

[80] *See* Jessica A. Axelrod, *Future of the Corporate Practice of Medicine Doctrine Following* Berlin v. Sarah Bush Lincoln Health Center, 2 DePaul J. Health Care L. 103, 106 (1997).

[81] Andrew Fichter, *Owning a Piece of the Doc: State Law Restraints on Lay Ownership of Healthcare Enterprises*, 39 J. Health L. 1, 4 (2006). Occasionally, the corporate practice doctrine has been grounded in the *quo warranto* doctrine. *See, e.g.*, People, by Kerner, v. United Med. Serv., 200 N.E. 157 (Ill. 1936).

[82] Sara Mars, Note, *The Corporate Practice of Medicine: A Call for Action*, 7 Health Matrix 241, 281 (1997); *see also* Berlin v. Sara Bush Lincoln Health Ctr., 688 N.E.2d 106, 111–112 (Ill. 1997); Grp. Health Ass'n v. Moor, 24 F. Supp. 445, 446–447 (D.D.C 1938).

[83] *E.g.*, Nonprofit Corporation Act, Op. Minn. Att'y Gen. 6770 (Sept. 17, 1993), *available at* http://www.ag.state.mi.us/opinion/datafiles/1990s/op06770.htm; *see also* Henry B. Hansmann, *Reforming Nonprofit Corporation Law*, 129 U. Pa. L. Rev. 497, 539–540 (1981).

[84] People ex rel. State Bd. of Med. Examiners v. Pac. Health Corp., 82 P.2d 429, 431 (Cal. 1938).

[85] California Med. Ass'n, Inc. v. Regents of Univ. of California, 94 Cal. Rptr. 2d 194, 199–200 (Cal. Ct. App. 2000).

[86] Cal. Bus. & Prof. Code § 2400.

the principal evils of the corporate practice of medicine may arise from the stress the profit motive places on physicians, [] courts have also noted the danger of lay control—a danger that attends all types of corporations."[87] The court nonetheless concluded that particular nonprofits such as community clinics were exempted. Other states have not always followed this logic.[88] In 2002, for example, the Supreme Court of Illinois maintained that nonprofits, like for-profits, can disrupt the "safeguarding [of] the physician's professional judgment from lay interference or protecting the public's general health and welfare."[89]

The history of exemption for nonprofits from the corporate practice doctrine highlights the presumption that nonprofit status insulates organizations from a degree of profit-seeking that would interfere with the practice of medicine and, therefore, protects patient welfare. As in antitrust law, corporate practice doctrine has grown less likely to assume that nonprofit status offers this protection.

d. Nonprofit Hospitals and Tort Law: The Case of Charitable Immunity

Charitable immunity offers a complete defense against tort liability for nonprofit defendants. Adopted in almost every state around the 1870s, it was dominant law until the 1960s, when many states repealed it.[90] Although a general rule of tort law and not specific to health law, the doctrine largely developed through suits against hospitals, and its lasting importance lies largely in the healthcare sector.

In those few states where charitable immunity still exists, analogous nonprofits and for-profits, equally at fault for negligently caused harm, will be held responsible to different degrees. For example, Arkansas' common law rule prohibits executing an order against financial assets of nonprofits, and a statute restricts liability for negligence to a charity's insurance limits.[91] Massachusetts no longer follows the doctrine in its purest form, but limits recovery in tort for acts committed in furtherance of a charity's purpose to $20,000 or $100,000 for malpractice claims against nonprofit healthcare defendants (both limits exclude interest and costs).[92] New Hampshire has a similar law with higher caps.[93] (Even in states without charitable immunity, nonprofits can structure to create their own immunity, separating their risky activities and their assets into separate organizations.)

Because they are general rules regarding nonprofits that happen to be applied largely to health entities, some of the justifications for immunizing charities are only incidentally relevant for understanding the interaction between ownership and the healthcare industry. For example, some explanations derive from nonprofit law's roots in trust law. Under one

[87] California Physicians' Serv. v. Aoki Diabetes Research Inst., 163 Cal. App. 4th 1506, 1516 (2008).

[88] *See* Mark Hall, *Institutional Control of Physician Behavior: Legal Barriers to Health Care Cost Containment*, 137 U. Pa. L. Rev. 431 (1988).

[89] Carter-Shields, M.D. v. Alton Health Inst., 201 Ill. 2d 441, 460 (2002).

[90] Jill R. Horwitz, *The Multiple Common Law Roots of Charitable Immunity: An Essay in Honor of Richard Epstein's Contributions to Tort Law Scholarship*, 3 J. Tort L. 1, 14 (2010).

[91] Ark. Code Ann. § 23-79-210 (2015); Kathryn A. Sampson, *Nonprofit Risk; Nonprofit Insurance*, 2008 Ark. L. Notes 83, 83 (2008).

[92] Mass. Gen. Laws ch. 231, § 85K (2015).

[93] N.H. Rev. Stat. Ann. § 508:17 (2015).

understanding of trusts, it is impermissible to use charitable trust assets to satisfy a tort liability because the proper defendant is the trustee and not the trust (in these cases, the hospital). The idea is that the alleged tortfeasor, in causing harm, was not acting on behalf of the charity and, therefore, the restricted charitable funds could not be used to satisfy a judgment. (The early immunity cases that rely on these ideas do not account for the fact that often the trustee can be indemnified by the trust when the trustee's tortious act was done in his role of trustee and not in violation of the trust.) Alternatively, the cases presume that charitable hospitals rely on restricted donations, in these cases meant for the provision of healthcare, not for satisfying a tort judgment. Other cases further assume that charitable assets must be protected in this way either so that donors will continue to give or the enterprise can continue to serve, presumably because they provide useful services that other organizations do not.

The most frequent justification for immunity in the early cases focuses specifically on the interaction of medicine and charity. The patient-beneficiary, by accepting free or subsidized medical care, impliedly waives the right to legal recourse for negligently inflicted harm.[94] This waiver theory appears even today as "[i]t is well settled in Virginia that charitable organizations are immune from liability arising from tort claims asserted by persons who accept the organizations' charitable benefits."[95] In other words, those who need free care should not "look a gift horse in the mouth."[96] Some of these cases analogize to the Good Samaritan immunity:

> [I]t would be intolerable that a good Samaritan, who takes to his home a wounded stranger for surgical care, should be held personally liable for the negligence of his servant in caring for that stranger. Were the heart and means of that Samaritan so large that he was able, not only to provide for one wounded man, but to establish a hospital for the care of a thousand, it would be no less intolerable that he should be held personally liable for the negligence of his servant in caring for any one of those thousand wounded men.[97]

For-profit hospitals, which also have free-care programs, may not raise the defense.

The immunity cases envision nonprofit hospitals as trustworthy but fragile institutions in need of protection to carry out good works. Unlike the PPACA, which seeks to protect poor patients from the hospital's inhumane pursuit of payment, the immunity laws are worried about the opposite—that is, protecting good hospitals from greedy patients.

e. Nonprofit Healthcare Entities: Fundamental Transactions

Nonprofit health organizations sometimes make major changes to their legal structures. These include mergers (discussed above in section III.b), consolidations, conversions,[98] and other transactions that involve substantially all of a charity's assets. Conversions from

[94] Powers v. Mass. Homoeopathic Hosp., 101 F. 896, 897–898 (C.C.D. Mass. 1899), *aff'd*, 109 F. 294 (1st Cir. 1901).

[95] Barbara Ann Williams, *Charitable Immunity: What Price Hath Charity?*, 28 U. RICH. L. REV. 953, 953 (1994).

[96] Powers v. Mass. Homoeopathic Hosp., 101 F. 896, 898 (C.C.D. Mass. 1899), *aff'd*, 109 F. 294 (1st Cir. 1901); *see also* Comment, *Tort Responsibility of Charitable Corporations*, 34 YALE L. J. 316, 318 & n.6 (1925).

[97] Basabo v. Salvation Army, 85 A. 120, 122 (R.I. 1912).

[98] "Conversion" is a legal term of art that refers to the transformation of the entity and not, as is commonly used, the transfer of the entity's assets.

nonprofit to for-profit form have played a particularly prominent role in public and scholarly attention to nonprofit healthcare. However, conversions have gone in all directions—hospitals frequently convert from nonprofit to government and vice versa, for-profit to government and vice versa, as well as for-profit to nonprofit. For this reason and because conversions to for-profit have tended to occur among relatively small hospitals, the share of hospitals owned by the three forms has remained remarkably constant over time (among urban hospitals, 74% are nonprofit, 11% for-profit, and 15% government).[99]

Regulatory changes, market developments, and other factors have influenced trends in hospital conversions.[100] The first waves of hospital conversions occurred during the Depression and after World War II, when the government made loans and grants to public and nonprofit hospitals under programs such as the Hill-Burton Act, promoting conversions from for-profit to nonprofit. (In fact, although the program ended in 1997, as of October 2015, 148 facilities still provide care under Hill-Burton.[101]) With new access to reimbursement that came with Medicare and Medicaid in 1965, the tide turned, and for-profits began repurchasing nonprofit hospitals. In the 1980s and 1990s, over 300 hospitals changed from nonprofit to for-profit in another wave of conversions.[102] One scholar called these conversions "the largest redeployment of charitable assets in the United States."[103]

An extensive scholarly debate regarding the welfare consequences of nonprofit to for-profit conversions followed this activity.[104] Some research raised concerns about conversions. For example, converting hospitals provide lower levels of uncompensated care compared to nonprofits that did not convert, and similar levels of unprofitable services as for-profit hospitals (although converting nonprofits tend to be more similar to for-profits than nonconverting nonprofits even before they convert).[105] Another study suggests that one to two years after conversion to for-profit ownership, patient mortality increases and the form is "harmful to elderly patients," possibly because of reductions in staffing; there was no similar decrease or increase in mortality after for-profit to nonprofit conversions and, indeed, several years after such a conversion, mortality rates were lower than those long before the conversion.[106]

[99] Jill R. Horwitz & Austin Nichols, *Rural Hospital Ownership: Medical Service Provision, Market Mix, and Spillover Effects*, 64 HEALTH SERVS. RES. 1452 (2011).

[100] Jack Needleman, *Nonprofit to For-Profit Conversions by Hospitals, Health Insurers, and Health Plans*, 114 PUB. HEALTH REP. 108, 113–114 (1999).

[101] *See Hill-Burton Facilities Obligated to Provide Free or Reduced-Cost Health Care*, U.S. DEP'T OF HEALTH & HUMAN SERVS. (Oct. 7, 2015), http://www.hrsa.gov/gethealthcare/affordable/hillburton/facilities.html.

[102] Phil Kline et al., *Protecting Charitable Assets in Hospital Conversions: An Important Role for the Attorney General*, 13 KAN. J.L. & PUB. POL'Y 351, 351 (2004); *see also* Kevin F. Donohue, *Crossroads in Hospital Conversions—A Survey of Nonprofit Hospital Conversion Legislation*, 8 ANNALS HEALTH L. 39, 40 (1999).

[103] Lawrence E. Singer, *The Conversion Conundrum: The State and Federal Response to Hospitals' Changes in Charitable Status*, 23 AM. J.L. & MED. 221, 224 (1997).

[104] *E.g.*, Donohue, *Crossroads in Hospital Conversions*, 39, 42–43; Frank A. Sloan et al., *Antecedents of Hospital Ownership Conversions, Mergers, and Closures*, 40 INQUIRY 39 (2003); Gary Young et al., *Does the Sale of Nonprofit Hospitals Threaten Health Care for the Poor?*, 16 HEALTH AFF. 137 (1997).

[105] Needleman, *Nonprofit to For-Profit Conversions by Hospitals, Health Insurers, and Health Plans*, 108, 114–115.

[106] Gabriel Picone et al., *Are For-Profit Hospital Conversions Harmful to Patients and to Medicare?*, 33 RAND J. ECON. 507, 508–509, 512–513, 520 (2002).

In addition, research has found that profits increased after conversion among both nonprofit and for-profits,[107] leaving open the question of how these hospitals improved their finances. Studies suggest that bottom lines were improved after conversions through aggressive billing techniques.[108] In fact, hospitals with more ability to pursue these techniques were more likely to affiliate with a for-profit hospital system, suggesting that such hospitals are particularly attractive to for-profit hospitals seeking to manage reimbursement rules aggressively.[109]

Yet, some observers have argued that opposition to conversions is based on outmoded ideas about nonprofit behavior that is unsupported by evidence.[110] For example, a study of some early hospital conversions found that for-profit hospital corporations paid more than a fair price to acquire a given nonprofit and the resulting for-profit hospitals did not reduce community benefits, suggesting that communities received more in terms of financial value in the form of the resulting conversion foundation than the financial value they gave up.[111] However, assessing the effects of conversion by studying the behavior of hospitals that convert is difficult because the hospitals that choose to convert are likely different from those that do not—e.g., financially weak hospitals often convert as a method to obtain needed capital to avoid closure—making it hard to distinguish selection effects from conversion effects.

This mixed evidence and the scale of the charitable assets involved has led to extensive oversight of conversions.[112] States have attempted to ameliorate these risks through the enforcement of common law rules as well as through legislation. As to the former, the state attorney general oversees enforcement of common law rules governing charitable status by exercising the office's responsibility to act on behalf of the public in enforcing the use of charitable assets, including ensuring that fiduciaries act in accordance with the charity's governing documents. These powers, at least in the states that require charities to notify the attorney general of a fundamental transaction, are generally exercised through the attorney general's power to bring suit against a charity in court.

In states that allow conversions—some states forbid nonprofit to for-profit conversions—almost half of the states enacted conversion statutes.[113] Most of these are based on model legislation adopted by the National Association of Attorneys General and, typically, require that charitable assets must be applied to advance the nonprofit's purpose and cannot be used for the purpose of making profits.[114] Accordingly, nonprofits must receive fair market value for

[107] Tami L. Mark, *Analysis of the Rational for, and Consequences of, Nonprofit and For-Profit Ownership Conversions*, 34 HEALTH SERVS. RES. 83, 85, 89, 92 (1999).

[108] Cutler & Horwitz, *Converting Hospitals from Not-for-Profit to For-Profit Status*, 45.

[109] Dafny & Dranove, *Regulatory Exploitation and Management Changes*, 223, 224–225.

[110] *E.g.*, David A. Hyman, *Hospital Conversions: Fact, Fantasy, and Regulatory Follies*, 23 J. CORP. LAW 741 (1998).

[111] Frank A. Sloan et al., *Hospital Conversions: Is the Purchase Price Too Low?*, *in* THE CHANGING HOSPITAL INDUSTRY: COMPARING NOT-FOR-PROFIT AND FOR-PROFIT INSTITUTIONS 29, 41 (David Cutler ed., 2000).

[112] *See* Daniel W. Coyne & Kathleen Russell Kas, *The Not-for-Profit Hospital as a Charitable Trust: To Whom Does Its Value Belong?*, 24 J. HEALTH & HOSP. L. 48, 52, 56–57 (1991); Donohue, *Crossroads in Hospital Conversions*, 39; James J. Fishman, *Checkpoints on the Conversion Highway: Some Trouble Spots in the Conversion of Nonprofit Health Care Organizations to For-Profit Status*, 23 J. CORP. L. 701 (1998).

[113] Jill R. Horwitz, *State Oversight of Hospital Conversions: Preserving Trust or Protecting Health?* (Kennedy School of Government, Wiener Center, Working Paper H-98-03, 1998).

[114] Mary Beckman & Eric Carriker, *State Charities Regulation in a Dynamic Health Care Market* 5 (2013), http://academiccommons.columbia.edu/item/ac:168583.

all charitable assets sold in a conversion. In addition, most state statutes governing conversions require the conversion proceeds and remaining assets to be used for a purpose similar to the original nonprofit. Which purposes count as similar varies, with some states allowing new foundations to have broad healthcare uses and others imposing more stringent rules. Several statutes impose an additional requirement, instructing the state attorney general or other authority to evaluate the effect of the conversion on public health or the community. Conversions and the statutes that govern them raise tensions among the converting nonprofit's healthcare purposes, the appropriate regulation of a charity's assets, nonprofit law, health law, and various conceptions of the public good. Some scholars have argued that stringent regulation may deter assets from moving to the most efficient use, and too much control and discretion undermines the role of charitable boards as stewards of the nonprofit's mission.[115] Additionally, too-strict enforcement of charitable trust law and cy pres may prevent nonprofit charities from remaining flexible in addressing community needs.[116] Others have argued that lax or absent oversight by the state attorney general has allowed states to inappropriately claim private assets as their own.[117]

Many insurers have also converted from nonprofit to for-profit. Although these conversions have involved large amounts of charitable assets and may well have had more significance for healthcare access and quality than hospital conversions,[118] they have received comparatively little scholarly and regulatory attention. The major wave of such conversions occurred in the 1990s when Blue Cross Blue Shield began permitting franchises to convert from nonprofit to for-profit ownership.[119] Many states allowed conversions, in part because the resulting charitable foundations freed billions of dollars for other forms of charitable healthcare. For example, in 1993, California's Commissioner of the Department of Corporations authorized Blue Cross of California's transfer of a majority of its assets to a for-profit subsidiary only after it agreed to distribute over $3.2 billion to two grant-making foundations: the California Endowment, a 501(c)(3) private foundation, and the California HealthCare Foundation, a 501(c)(4) entity.[120] In 2002, New York legislation authorized the conversion of Empire Blue Cross Blue Shield, directing 95% of the proceeds to a fund (held as a public asset) to be used for certain public initiatives and by hospitals, nursing homes,

[115] *E.g.*, Evelyn Brody, *Whose Public? Parochialism and Paternalism in State Charity Law Enforcement*, 79 IND. L.J. 937, 939–940 (2004); Thomas L. Greaney & Kathleen M. Boozang, *Mission, Margin, and Trust in the Nonprofit Health Care Enterprise*, 5 YALE J. HEALTH POL'Y L. & ETHICS 1 (2005).

[116] John D. Colombo, *A Proposal for an Exit Tax on Nonprofit Conversion Transactions*, 23 J. CORP. L. 779, 782–794 (1998).

[117] *See* Jill R. Horwitz & Marion R. Fremont-Smith, *The Common Law Power of the Legislature: Insurer Conversion and Charitable Funds*, 83 MILBANK Q. 225 (2005).

[118] *See* Mark A. Hall & Christopher J. Conover, *For-Profit Conversion of Blue Cross Plans: Public Benefit or Public Harm?*, 27 ANN. REV. PUB. HEALTH 443, 443 (2006); *see also* Christopher J. Conover et al., *The Impact of Blue Cross Conversions on Health Spending and the Uninsured*, 24 HEALTH AFF. 473, 473 (2005); Mark A. Hall & Christopher J. Conover, *The Impact of Blue Cross Conversion on Accessibility, Affordability, and the Public Interest*, 81 MILLBANK Q. 509, 509–510 (2003).

[119] *See generally Blue Cross and Blue Shield: A Historical Compilation*, CONSUMERS UNION (Mar. 2013), https://consumersunion.org/wp-content/uploads/2013/03/yourhealthdollar.org_blue-cross-history-compilation.pdf.

[120] *Blue Cross and Blue Shield: A Historical Compilation*, CONSUMERS UNION 17 (Mar. 2013), https://consumersunion.org/wp-content/uploads/2013/03/yourhealthdollar.org_blue-cross-history-compilation.pdf.

and other agencies for wage increases for healthcare employees; by 2004, the state received a total of $363 million from the sale and, by 2005, the for-profit company had a value of $4.4 billion.[121] Of particular concern in that case is the role the state played in commandeering charitable, but private, assets for public ends. In the other states, state insurance commissioners blocked conversion plans because of anticipated negative consequences.[122]

These issues will only grow more important with the most recent trend of conversions, in which new buyers are not publicly traded for-profits but rather private entities purchasing with private equity.[123] Without the transparency afforded by the nonprofit form or annual reports produced by publicly traded for-profits, it will be more difficult for regulators to understand how converted hospitals are providing care, and more difficult to police conversion agreements.

IV Conclusion

Although there is a rich tradition of scholarship regarding ownership and healthcare, more work is needed to understand the role of nonprofits in health and, therefore, how to govern them more effectively. In addition to surveying the law, this chapter suggests that health law and policy often treats nonprofit entities as more trustworthy than analogous for-profits. Much of the law regards them as particularly appropriate settings for the provision of health services because they will protect patients from the extremes of the market. This faith in the nonprofit form has gone so far as to lead judges to declare that the merger of nonprofit oligopolists would not harm competition. Yet this faith does not extend to their treatment under nonprofit law, where healthcare entities are more suspect than their peers.

In addition to investigating this inconsistent regulation of nonprofits, several other topics offer fruitful areas for exploration. First, whether and to what extent nonprofit health providers should benefit from tax exemption will likely remain controversial topics. Most commentary in this area has focused on federal tax exemption, but state and local tax exemption, access to tax-exempt bonds, and state charitable status likely matter more to many nonprofit healthcare providers.

Second, and more generally, future research should consider the conflicts between the popular understanding of nonprofit charities as primarily dedicated to poverty relief, and the legal requirements, which do not necessarily reflect this understanding. Poverty relief may be an unrealistic goal for healthcare providers, given the operation of healthcare markets and the scale of the funds needed to relieve poverty. It may also be an undesirable one. Indeed poverty relief, which may be most effectively addressed by government programs, may be in tension with other goals of healthcare provision such as quality care for all. More

[121] Horwitz & Fremont-Smith, *The Common Law Power of the Legislature: Insurer Conversion and Charitable Funds*, 225, 229.

[122] James C. Robinson, *For-Profit Non-Conversion and Regulatory Firestorm at CareFirst BlueCross BlueShield*, 23 Health Aff. 68, 69 (2004).

[123] *See, e.g.*, Catherine J. Robbins et al., *Private Equity Investment in Health Care Services*, 27 Health Aff. 1389 (2008); David G. Stevenson & David C. Grabowski, *Private Equity Investment and Nursing Home Care: Is It a Big Deal?*, 27 Health Aff. 1399 (2008).

targeted inquiries could also answer whether requiring more and more specific behavior of nonprofits would risk the benefits of flexibility that they have traditionally produced.

Third, who provides, and who accesses, services from the various forms? Healthcare scholars often jokingly note that individual practitioners and administrators—nurses, doctors, and CEOs—are not nonprofits. But there is something to the joke. Practitioners sort among the types of forms, and it is unlikely that the sorting is random. Although there has been a small amount of scholarship on pay across types, understanding whether those types attract workers with systematically different characteristics would help us explain why ownership matters. In addition, do tax exemptions or other aspects of nonprofit status allow administrators to implement different policies from those at taxable entities? Does the nonprofit form itself, absent regulation, attract certain types of providers, administrators, or patients?

Fourth, several questions related to the PPACA merit exploration. For example, which types of ownership forms are best suited for new entities like healthcare exchanges and accountable care organizations? Should nonprofit organizations change their goals in response to new tax requirements in the Affordable Care Act? If so, how? Of what significance to patients, providers, and markets is the new trend in hospital conversions from nonprofit to privately owned for-profit hospital systems?

Fifth, what type of ownership models can and should play a role in healthcare? New hybrid forms that combine nonprofit and for-profit features exist in virtually every state. These forms—such as social or flexible purpose corporations—may bring needed capital to old nonprofit healthcare providers and allow those providers to remain committed to public purposes. On the other hand, there seems to be a recent trend in hospital conversions from nonprofit to for-profit form, but unlike the conversions from nonprofit to publicly held for-profit companies that were popular in the first waves of conversions, these buyers are private. Little investigation has been done into the role of private equity in healthcare markets.

Sixth, nonprofits need to be understood in context. Law, policy, and scholarship tend, mistakenly, to treat nonprofits as if they exist in a vacuum. However, whether nonprofit health providers will put patients first, as some law presumes they will, depends in part on the competitive environment in which nonprofits operate. There is some evidence that nonprofits behave differently depending on the amount of competition they face and, given a level of competition, the ownership of their competitors. The research in this area is sparse, however, and the law does not take these interactions into account.

In the late 1960s, observers predicted the end of the need for nonprofit medicine. In 1965, the advent of Medicare and Medicaid brought with it the hope of universal access to health insurance. It was widely believed that with these programs, coupled with employment-based insurance and a patchwork of other government programs, there would no longer be any indigent patients. Therefore, as tax reform in 1969 made clear, nonprofit hospitals needn't worry about providing for the poor. These views were based on two fundamental mistakes about healthcare and nonprofits—first, that there would be no more indigent patients; second, that the value of nonprofits lies primarily in treatment of the poor.

Given contemporary tastes for market-based policy solutions, it would be even more tempting for observers to make the same mistakes today. Like Medicare and Medicaid before it, the PPACA brings with it the hope of near universal insurance. One might assume that armed with this insurance, individuals can fend for themselves in for-profit healthcare markets.

But even if the PPACA succeeds, not all insurance will be equally attractive to providers, and nonprofit and government providers are more likely than for-profits to offer services needed by the poor. Moreover, as has always been the case, all patients, regardless of their wealth, are poorly situated to evaluate the care they receive. They need not only to access care, but to trust their providers not to provide too little, too much, or the wrong kind of care.

A fundamental legal requirement of a nonprofit entity is that, although it may strive for profits in some of its activities, it is forbidden from organizing with the purpose of profit-seeking. To the extent it earns profits, those profits must be used to advance the nonprofit's purposes, whether they be related to poverty relief or some other charitable endeavor. These restrictions apply to all nonprofit healthcare providers, and may well explain why they are less responsive to profit-making incentives than are similarly situated for-profits. The restrictions also make nonprofit law a valuable legal tool for health policy.

Acknowledgements

The author thanks Harvey Dale, Marion Fremont-Smith, Allison K. Hoffman, and Ted Parson for helpful comments; Alan Azar, Jesse Martin, and Lynn McClelland for excellent research support and comments; Kathryn Gilbert for editorial assistance, and Jennifer Davis for extensive research and discussion of earlier versions of the chapter.

CHAPTER 25

IT WAS ON FIRE WHEN I LAY DOWN ON IT

Why Medical Malpractice Reform Can't Fix Healthcare

DAVID A. HYMAN AND CHARLES SILVER

I INTRODUCTION: MALPRACTICE CRISES AS KABUKI THEATER

THE United States has experienced three medical malpractice ("med mal") crises during the last forty years. In each instance, premiums spiked and healthcare providers argued that the liability system was driving up costs and limiting access to medical services. In response, plaintiffs' lawyers argued that the liability system was merely doing its job, by requiring careless providers to compensate the patients they harmed. The real problem, they claimed, was that providers were delivering shoddy care.

Editorial writers, policy analysts, and legislators also weighed in. Those on the political right tended to side with physicians, hospitals, and liability insurers, all of which wanted to make it harder and less profitable for patients to sue. Advocates on the political left tended to oppose these proposals, but had limited success overall. Many states restrained lawsuits by imposing one or more of the tort reforms listed in Table 25.1. Damages caps were the favored strategy for reducing the frequency of lawsuits and settlement values, but many states also imposed other constraints.

Although the reforms were touted as policy improvements, little peer-reviewed academic research showed that any of them were likely to have good effects. This should have given legislators pause. There is an abundance of academic research on the medical liability system and the tort system more generally. By and large, these studies neither documented the existence of sizable fluctuations in tort outcomes nor supported the imposition of any of the lawsuit restrictions that were on the table. Instead, they showed that the liability system produced outcomes that varied slowly and predictably in response to changes in the surrounding environment. As the volume of medical services increased, claims become more frequent. Payments reflected patients' losses, and rose with their lost wages, their future medical needs,

Table 25.1 1st, 2nd, and 3rd Generation Tort Reforms

1st Generation

Aimed at size of recovery

Caps on punitive and noneconomic damages; mandatory periodic payment of damages; abrogation of collateral source rule; modification to joint and several liability

Aimed at frequency of claiming

Pretrial screening panels; arbitration; shortened statutes of limitation; attorney fee caps; pre-filing certificate of merit

Insurance reforms

Patient Compensation Funds; Joint Underwriting Associations; Reporting of Closed Claims and Financial Performance

Other

Limitations on Expert Witnesses and Res Ipsa Loquitar

2nd Generation

Specification of standard of care in medical practice guidelines; scheduled damages; mandatory ADR; No-Fault Liability; Enterprise Liability; Private Contracts

3rd Generation

Health Courts; Protections for Apology; Communication and Resolution Programs

The 1st and 2nd generation reforms listed in the table are derived from Eleanor Kinney, *Malpractice Reform in the 1990s: Past Disappointments, Future Success?*, 20 J. HEALTH POL., POL'Y L. 99 (1995).

and the severity of their injuries. Plaintiffs' attorneys screened cases carefully, both because med mal lawsuits are expensive and because strong claims generate payments and fees more often than weak ones. Frivolous med mal cases were uncommon, as were cases involving minor injuries and cases with punitive damages awards. Payments rarely exceeded the limits of providers' insurance coverage, even when the legal value of claims, as measured by jury awards, indicated that plaintiffs deserved more. This is not to suggest that the tort system was perfect. It was slow, costly, and failed to compensate many patients with meritorious claims.

All of this information about the actual performance of the med mal liability and insurance mechanisms was readily available, but it was not a portrait that showed a pressing need to rein in lawsuits. Complementing the lack of evidence of a crisis on the liability side was a large and growing body of research on the medical side, documenting the tendency of the healthcare system to harm patients. Historically, doctors and hospitals had derided malpractice lawsuits as frivolous complaints that were ginned up by greedy contingent fee lawyers. Over time, this public relations strategy became less and less tenable, and it had to be abandoned entirely when the Institute of Medicine validated the charge that medical errors killed 44,000–98,000 hospitalized patients a year.[1] Nor did the bad news end there. A few

[1] INST. OF MED., TO ERR IS HUMAN: BUILDING A SAFER HEALTH SYSTEM (Linda T. Kohn ed., 1st ed. 2000).

years later, Healthgrades doubled the count, putting the annual death toll at 195,000.[2] Then, in 2013, the *Journal of Patient Safety* published a meta-analysis of prior studies which concluded that "preventable harm to patients" caused more than 400,000 premature deaths per year.[3] This estimate tagged medical errors as the third-leading cause of death in the United States, with only heart disease and cancer killing more often.

Providers still wanted to free themselves from legal responsibility for mistakes, of course, but they needed a new line of argument to get there. Several alternatives were available, all of which shared a common theme: The healthcare system had serious problems, and the liability system was responsible for all of them. Costs were high because malpractice lawsuits forced doctors to practice defensive medicine. Access was impaired because lawsuits drove doctors out of risky practice areas and away from plaintiff-friendly states. Quality was deficient because the fear of being sued drove errors underground. The problems of healthcare were real. The new twist was that the legal system was to blame.

The ease with which providers switched tactics should have caused legislators to wonder whether the new arguments were any better than the old ones they replaced. But the politics of tort reform did not encourage dispassionate reflection. C. Northcote Parkinson, the author of Parkinson's Law, once observed that the design of the English Parliament made it easy for members to tell whether or not they agreed with a speaker. If the speaker rose from one's own side of the aisle, one heartily agreed; if from the other side, one strongly dissented. The politics of tort reform were similar. If one was a Republican, one supported restrictions on lawsuits. If one was a Democrat, one opposed tort reforms. Doctors and insurers made campaign contributions and common cause with Republicans. Plaintiffs' lawyers made campaign contributions and common cause with Democrats.

Academic researchers were less polarized, but there were still divisions. Some public health researchers and economists argued that lawsuits impeded quality improvement and drove up costs by causing doctors to practice defensive medicine. Other researchers (most of whom were located in law schools) disputed these assertions. For many years, the extent to which the problems of the healthcare system could be fixed by tinkering with the civil justice system remained an open question.

In this chapter, we argue that the time has come to end this debate. Empirical studies have shed a good deal of light on the connections between the liability system and the healthcare system, and it is clear tort reform has little or no power to cure the problems of cost, quality, and access that plague the American healthcare system. These problems have their roots in our systems for financing and delivering healthcare. Only by reforming those systems can they be solved. When it comes to improving healthcare in the United States, tort reform is a small idea, not a big one.

This chapter proceeds as follows. Part II examines the evidence bearing on the connection between litigation and quality improvement. Part III analyzes the impact of the liability system on healthcare spending (including defensive medicine). Part IV focuses on the effect of tort reform on physician supply. Part V offers four strategies for improving the performance

[2] Patient Safety in American Hospitals, HealthGrades (2004), http://www.providersedge.com/ehdocs/ehr_articles/Patient_Safety_in_American_Hospitals-2004.pdf [http://perma.cc/2UNL-ML9J].

[3] John T. James, *A New, Evidence-Based Estimate of Patient Harms Associated with Hospital Care*, 9 J. Patient Safety 122 (2013).

of the med mal system. Part VI considers the implications of our findings through the lens of the title of Robert Fulghum's best-selling book, *It Was on Fire When I Lay Down on It.*

II Litigation and Healthcare Quality

a. Theory

Standard tort theory contends that malpractice liability will improve the quality of healthcare by forcing providers to internalize the costs of errors that can be prevented by the exercise of reasonable care. The conventional wisdom among patient safety advocates has long been the opposite. They contend that malpractice lawsuits impede efforts to improve healthcare quality by encouraging providers to hide mistakes. The two most influential statements of this position appeared in consecutive publications by the Institute of Medicine (IOM). In *To Err Is Human*, which appeared in 1999, the IOM contended that "[p]atient safety is ... hindered through the liability system and the threat of malpractice, which discourages the disclosure of errors. The discoverability of data under legal proceedings encourages silence about errors committed or observed."[4] In *Crossing the Quality Chasm*, which appeared in 2001, the IOM stated that "[a]lternative approaches to liability, such as enterprise liability or no-fault compensation, could produce a legal environment more conducive to uncovering and resolving quality problems" than the tort system.[5]

Among public health researchers, doctors, organized medicine, tort reform advocates, and even pharmacists, the claim that tort liability impedes quality improvement became an article of faith.[6] Provider groups like the American Medical Association (AMA) contend that they oppose medical malpractice liability because they want to "creat[e] a climate where reporting of errors will occur so that the information can be used to improve the [healthcare] system and avoid repeating [errors] in the future."[7] They advocate the creation of protected spaces in which physicians and other medical professionals can apologize for and discuss mistakes secure in the knowledge that their statements will not be used against them in court. The AMA's official position is that liability has no proper role in the regulation of healthcare professionals.

Many academic commentators agree that incident reporting and quality of care will increase only when malpractice liability is curtailed. For example, a team of researchers at the Harvard School of Public Health asserted that malpractice liability "may well stifle efforts to reduce error" because practitioners are wary "of reporting events that may leave them open to accusations of negligence."[8] That is, "the specter of litigation" currently stands as "the principal barrier to the free flow of information about medical errors," and "removing it would "align[] the foci of the compensation and quality improvement systems and center[] attention

[4] Inst. of Med., To Err Is Human.

[5] Inst. of Med., Crossing the Quality Chasm: A New Health System for the 21st Century 219 (2001).

[6] David A. Hyman & Charles Silver, *The Poor State of Health Care Quality in the U.S.: Is Malpractice Liability Part of the Problem or Part of the Solution?*, 90 Cornell L. Rev. 893 (2005).

[7] *Id.*

[8] David M. Studdert & Troyen A. Brennan, *Toward a Workable Model of No-Fault Compensation for Medical Injury in the United States*, 27 Am. J.L. & Med. 223, 227–228 (2001).

on precisely those injuries that are eradicable." The same team argued that "[m]oving to a system that does not penalize clinicians for reporting adverse events would result in increased reporting and thus increased institutional learning about how to avoid errors in the future."

Why might liability impede quality improvement? The argument is that healthcare providers are strongly motivated to help patients. Therefore, if left to their own devices, they would identify errors, study them in hope of finding their root causes, and implement desirable reforms. The result would be reliable delivery systems that protect patients from avoidable mistakes. But providers are not left alone. The liability system punishes them for slip-ups that harm patients. Wanting to avoid being punished, providers react by refusing to admit errors, failing to study them, and leaving faulty delivery systems in place. As a result, these commentators assert, patients continue to be harmed.

As we have explained at length elsewhere, the theory that liability impedes quality improvement raises a host of questions—the most basic of which is whether the account it offers of providers' motivations is accurate.[9] Is their desire to protect patients from avoidable perils really as strong as the theory's proponents contend? If so, one would expect to see robust discussions of errors and safe delivery systems in contexts where providers are immune from malpractice liability. Do the facts confirm this prediction? The culture of medicine, which is famously perfectionist and punitive, must also be considered. Might medical culture encourage providers to hide mistakes even if the threat of liability were removed? And what impacts do state medical boards, hospital accreditors, and other regulatory bodies have? If the threat of malpractice liability were removed, might not providers still hide errors for fear of being punished by them? Again, studies of contexts in which the risk of being sued is low could shed light on the answer.

Because secrecy about errors may have multiple causes, the possibility that lawsuits are valuable sources of information about mistakes must also be considered. In the course of litigation, medical mistakes are often studied in great detail. Hospital records are examined by independent experts for patients and providers. Witnesses are deposed. Procedures are highlighted, as is the standard of care. Providers are forced to confront this information, as decisions regarding the defense and settlement of claims are made. Plus, after litigation concludes, insurers' claim files become treasure troves that can be mined for data about past mistakes and used to prevent problems from recurring in the future. When it comes to information, litigation may be both productive and stifling. The question is then whether the gain or the loss predominates.

b. Empirical Evidence

In an earlier article, we pointed out that no empirical study had ever documented an inverse correlation between malpractice exposure and the frequency of error reporting.[10] In support, we cited a 2002 statement by Dr. Lucien Leape, a strong proponent of error reporting and a leading advocate for patient safety: "[F]ear of litigation may . . . be overblown. No link between [error] reporting and litigation has ever been demonstrated."[11]

[9] Hyman & Silver, The Poor State of Health Care Quality in the U.S.

[10] Id.

[11] Lucian L. Leape, *Reporting of Adverse Events*, 347 N. ENG. J. MED. 1633, 1635 (2002).

The absence of evidence did not keep the IOM from arguing, in both *To Err Is Human* and *Crossing the Quality Chasm*, that there was such a link. But, neither study included even a single citation to a peer-reviewed statistical study supporting these claims—even though both studies cited a raft of such studies in support of other empirical propositions. (In an ironic twist, Dr. Leape was part of the IOM Committee that prepared both of these reports.) Although the vast majority of commentators on public health issues believe that litigation impedes quality improvement by driving errors underground, the charge rests entirely on anecdotes and the theory's surface plausibility.

The lack of rigorous empirical support was especially damaging because there was a competing line of thought according to which litigation encouraged providers to be more open about mistakes than they would otherwise have been. In the same article where the lines quoted above appeared, Dr. Leape also noted that "several reports indicate that full disclosure reduces the risk of litigation."[12] In other words, given the prospect of litigation, providers might gain by revealing mistakes instead of hiding them. Why? Because patients don't expect providers to be perfect, but they do want to know what happened to them and to be treated with respect.[13] When providers are open and honest about mishaps, patients are less inclined to sue and more inclined to accept modest compensation.

Since we published our earlier article on this subject in 2005, the literature on the connection between liability and error disclosure has grown, but its nature has not changed. It still consists mainly of anecdotal reports. Thus, the authors of a comprehensive literature review published in 2010 reported that "quantitative analysis" of the studies they found was "not appropriate" because most of the studies "were largely descriptive."[14] There still appear to be no studies showing that "full disclosure increases the risk of negative consequences for physicians," and many doctors believe that malpractice suits are less likely when providers discuss errors with patients.[15]

The studies that support the tendency of malpractice liability to impede error reporting typically draw upon interviews in which providers offer the fear of being sued as a reason for keeping quiet. These studies are far from conclusive, however, for two reasons. First, providers often offer many reasons for failing to report adverse incidents, malpractice fears being only one. Other causes are said to be the "shame and blame" culture of medicine, medical training that inculcates students in the tradition of keeping quiet about mistakes, professional embarrassment and career-related concerns, the feeling that errors are inevitable, the belief that reporting is pointless because conditions won't improve, and the fear of provoking closer oversight by corporate managers. With so many causes at work, it is impossible to know whether the frequency of reports would increase to any significant extent if the threat of litigation were reduced or removed.

[12] *Id.*; *see also* Steve S. Kraman & Ginny Hamm, *Risk Management: Extreme Honesty May Be the Best Policy*, 131 ANNALS INTERNAL MED. 963 (1999).

[13] Charles Vincent et al., *Why Do People Sue Doctors? A Study of Patients and Relatives Taking Legal Action*, 343 LANCET 1609 (1994).

[14] Elaine O'Connor et al., *Disclosure of Patient Safety Incidents: A Comprehensive Review*, 22 INT'L J. FOR QUALITY HEALTH CARE 371 (2010).

[15] Catherine Cravens & Jo Anne L. Earp, *Disclosure and Apology: Patient-Centered Approaches to the Public Health Problem of Medical Error*, 70 N.C. MED. J. 140, 142 (2009); Thomas H. Gallagher et al., *US and Canadian Physicians' Attitudes and Experiences Regarding Disclosing Errors to Patients*, 166 ARCHIVES INTERNAL MED. 1605 (2006).

Second, the reasons people offer for failing to report errors may bear little relation to the actual causes of neglect. Implicit in the idea that providers would report adverse events if only they did not fear malpractice suits, embarrassment, or other negative consequences is the hidden assumption that it is natural to identify errors and discuss them. In fact, these are things that most people are reluctant to do, whether they face adverse consequences or not. This is why businesses that want to improve train their employees to report mistakes. They know that, otherwise, error reporting is unlikely to occur. The slogan "Safety Doesn't Happen by Accident" is more than a silly play on words. It communicates the message that safety is not the default condition; it takes planning, training, a supportive culture, and a continuous commitment to error eradication.

The falsity of the belief that providers would naturally improve their delivery systems if the threat of liability were removed becomes apparent when one considers how providers that operate in zero-liability environments perform. For example, quality problems abounded at hospitals run by the Veterans Health Administration (usually called the VA), even though the doctors and nurses who ran these facilities bore no personal liability for medical mistakes. Error reporting occurred no more often at VA hospitals than it did at other facilities. VA hospitals continue to experience quality problems today, and appear to be getting worse. From 2010 to 2014, the number of investigations of adverse events declined by 18% even though the number of medical errors rose by 7% in response to an increase in the number of veterans who were treated.[16] The decline appeared to be due to a degradation of the culture of safety that had been created in prior years.

Historically, most providers also failed to make the best use of closed medical malpractice claims, even though by definition they faced no prospect of future liability on these claims. As mentioned, closed malpractice files contain a wealth of information that could be used to identify deficiencies in delivery systems and reduce the likelihood and dangerousness of mistakes. The American Society of Anesthesiologists (ASA) demonstrated the value of closed claim files by using them to revolutionize the practice of anesthesiology, with demonstrated benefits for patients (who experienced fewer injuries) and practitioners (whose malpractice premiums fell). But for decades, other associations of medical professionals failed to follow the ASA's lead. Instead of mining closed claims in hope of identifying the root causes of mistakes, they lobbied for tort reforms that would make mistakes harmless to their members while leaving patients even more vulnerable than they already were.

Recently, healthcare providers have expressed greater appreciation for the benefits to be derived by communicating openly about mistakes and by studying closed claim files. In survey responses and in-depth interviews, hospital managers who were responsible for risk management, claims management, and quality improvement reported

> [t]hree notable shifts [that] contradict [the] conventional wisdom about the negative effects of malpractice litigation on patient safety: 1) Risk managers increasingly see themselves as responsible for improving patient safety; 2) hospitals are becoming more transparent with patients when errors occur; and 3) hospitals increasingly encourage discussion of errors by hospital staff as a means of improving performance.[17]

[16] Gov't Accountability Office, VA Health Care: Actions Needed to Assess Decrease in Root Cause Analyses of Adverse Event, GAO-15-643 (2015), http://www.gao.gov/assets/680/671748.pdf.

[17] Joanna C. Schwartz, *A Dose of Reality for Medical Malpractice Reform*, 88 N.Y.U. L. Rev. 1224, 1252 (2013).

Seventy-six percent of the respondents said that they "often" or "sometimes" reviewed closed malpractice claims files. The usage rate was even higher for hospital risk managers, almost all of whom reported using closed litigation files "for patient safety lessons." In an especially impressive development, managers who work in multi-hospital systems report that they aggregate closed claims information in a central office, which reports the results of data analyses back to the individual facilities.

Other medical associations are finally stepping up to the plate too, using closed claims to identify the causes of error in emergency room diagnoses, obstetric errors, and surgical errors.[18] Medical associations are being joined and assisted by liability insurers, which have enormous databases of closed malpractice claims on which to draw. We are on the verge of a revolution in "Learning from Litigation," where providers can use closed claim files to identify the root causes of errors and to quantify error rates and trends.[19]

The obvious question: Why didn't the "Learning from Litigation" revolution occur sooner? There are many possibilities, but one worth considering is that the financial consequences for providers of medical mistakes were too low. Injured patients rarely sue, and the tort system is stingy.[20] The most common problems documented by empirical studies of the litigation process are that patients receive less than they are due and that providers bear no personal financial liability for medical mistakes. Conceivably, providers' widespread failure to report adverse incidents could have provided a basis for awarding punitive damages in cases where reports were omitted but should have been made. In fact, punitive awards against doctors and other healthcare providers are incredibly rare and are the first item sacrificed in settlement negotiations. Tort reforms have only made matters worse. Given the secular decline in malpractice cases, the remarkable thing is that the "Learning from Litigation" revolution is finally taking place.[21]

III Litigation and Healthcare Spending

There is universal agreement that Americans spend far too much on healthcare and that an enormous portion of this money, perhaps as much as a third, is wasted on services that have little or no medical value for patients. The question addressed in this section is whether the liability system substantially contributes to these problems.

[18] *Id. See also* M. Ennis & C. A. Vincent, *Obstetric Accidents: A Review of 64 Cases*, 300 Brit. Med. J. 1365 (1990) (study of closed obstetric claims); Atul A. Gawande et al., *Risk Factors for Retained Instruments and Sponges After Surgery*, 348 New Eng. J. Med. 229 (2003) (studying, through closed claims, incidence of retained sponges after surgery); Graham Neale, *Risk Management in the Care of Medical Emergencies After Referral to Hospital*, 32 J. Royal C. Physicians London 125 (1998) (study of claims of medical emergencies in general medicine and gastroenterology).

[19] Chih-Ming Liang, *Rethinking the Tort Liability System and Patient Safety: From the Conventional Wisdom to Learning from Litigation*, 12 Ind. Health L. Rev. 327 (2015).

[20] Hyman & Silver, *The Poor State of Health Care Quality in the U.S.*; Michelle M. Mello et al., *Who Pays for Medical Error: An Analysis of Adverse Event Costs, the Medical Liability System, and Incentives for Patient Safety Improvement*, 4 J. Empirical Legal Stud. 835 (2007).

[21] Myungho Paik, Bernard Black, & David Hyman, *The Receding Tide of Medical Malpractice Litigation: Part 1—National Trends*, 10 J. Empirical Legal Stud. 612 (2013).

a. The Direct Costs of Medical Liability

It is certainly true that the liability system generates some healthcare spending directly by saddling providers with the cost of responding to liability claims. These direct costs include the cost of paying lawyers, satisfying jury verdicts in cases that are lost at trial, funding settlements in cases that are resolved out of court, and so forth. Many of these costs, though not all, are reflected in providers' liability insurance premiums. For this reason, premiums are often used in studies of the direct costs of malpractice liability.

Several studies find that some tort reforms reduce the direct costs of medical liability claims by reducing claim frequencies and payouts.[22] This makes sense. If insurance markets are competitive, all changes that reduce the cost of responding to claims should have this effect. Because tort reforms make lawsuits less profitable for plaintiffs or otherwise harder to bring, providers' direct costs should fall. Of course, the costs of injury do not go away, merely because they are not borne by providers. Instead, they are borne by the negligently injured patients, who now find themselves without recompense.

The direct costs of liability account for a small fraction (less than 1%) of healthcare spending. Mello et al. put the direct costs at $10 billion, or 0.4% of healthcare spending.[23] During med mal crises, physicians complain bitterly about the cost of their malpractice premiums, but those costs are (in the grand scheme of things) insignificant. Moreover, because the rate of med mal claiming has fallen substantially over the past few decades, direct costs have held steady or fallen when adjusted for the quantity of medical services delivered.[24] In sum, direct costs contribute little to overall healthcare spending.

b. The Indirect Costs of Medical Liability

i. Assurance Behavior

As noted above, providers and tort reform advocates contend that fear of litigation adds hundreds of billions of dollars in waste to the healthcare system. The services that generate these costs are known as "defensive medicine" because doctors purportedly order them to defend against the risk of being sued. In this chapter, we refer to the decision to order additional tests and procedures solely to provide a layer of protection against malpractice risk as "assurance behavior," because it gives providers greater assurance against being sued in connection with caring for a given patient.

Assurance behavior consists of "doing more"—that is, more tests and imaging studies, more referrals, and more office visits, to ensure that nothing is missed. Of course, treating patients appropriately also often involves providing services. Consequently, an analytical problem that must be recognized early on is the difficulty of distinguishing positive service levels that are medically appropriate from positive service levels that are not.

[22] Stephen Zuckerman et al., *Effects of Tort Reforms and Other Factors on Medical Malpractice Insurance Premiums*, 27 INQUIRY 167 (1990); Patricia Danzon, *The Frequency and Severity of Medical Malpractice Claims*, 27 J.L. ECON. 115 (1984).

[23] Michelle Mello et al., *National Costs of the Medical Liability System*, 29 HEALTH AFF. 1569 (2009).

[24] Paik et al., *The Receding Tide of Medical Malpractice Litigation*.

Making this difficulty explicit also reveals two related problems. First, some level of assurance behavior is desirable. When physicians or hospitals provide services that are reasonably thought to help patients, they may be engaging in assurance behavior because of the fear of being sued, but they are not contributing to waste. Desirable assurance behavior must therefore be excluded when tallying the cost of defensive medicine, which involves the delivery of services that are not likely to help patients.

Second, providers may have other reasons for delivering services that are medically unnecessary. For example, in a fee-for-service environment, providers are paid for delivering services, including services that patients do not need. Providers have also been said to order unnecessary tests and scans when they own the equipment that is used to perform them or gain financially by sending patients to others. These economic incentives could generate high levels of waste. Local customs could do so as well. A sizable literature contends that doctors follow other physicians in their geographic areas who are practice leaders. If practice leaders deliver unnecessary services, physicians who follow them will do so too.

Still, in theory, defensive medicine involving assurance behavior could contribute tens of billions of dollars to the cost of healthcare. It costs providers little or nothing to deliver services whose sole or primary function is to protect them from liability risks. Consequently, they may find it rational to provide defensive assurance services until the perceived marginal reduction in liability exposure from an additional service is zero. Because many services may be needed to reach the zero point in a given patient/physician interaction and there are billions of interactions each year, the cost of assurance behavior could be enormous.

ii. Avoidance Behaviors

Providers' fear of liability is also said to generate a second form of indirect cost. Known as "avoidance behavior," this effect consists in the refusal to deliver medical services that expose providers to liability risks. The risk may stem from the procedure itself, from the patient to be treated, or from the two in combination. In the limiting case, physicians may leave a practice area or a plaintiff-friendly location entirely. Because avoidance behavior takes the form of "doing less," it tends to reduce healthcare costs, rather than inflate them.

Avoidance behaviors entail analytical complications similar to those we identified when discussing assurance behaviors above. One must subdivide medically appropriate and medically inappropriate denials of care into those that are attributable to liability fears and those that have other causes. Physicians may have many reasons for withholding treatments that are likely to help patients. For example, they may not recognize the value of the treatments or they may not be paid sufficiently for the time that is required. When quantifying the impact of liability fears on patients' welfare, one must also recognize that withholding medically unnecessary treatments is a plus. When a doctor who fears being sued withholds an inappropriate treatment that he or she would otherwise have delivered, the patient is protected from unnecessary risk.

iii. Indeterminacy of the Effects of Tort Reform on Spending

It should now be clear that the impact of tort reforms on spending cannot be stated from an armchair. When providers worry less about liability, they may (1) provide fewer services that are medically appropriate because the risk of being sued for malpractice is reduced; (2) provide more services that are medically unnecessary because they can harm patients with impunity; (3) withhold more services that are medically appropriate because errors of omission are less costly; and (4) withhold fewer services that are medically inappropriate because errors of commission pose less financial risk. Given the options, the overall impact on healthcare spending is indeterminate. Effects (1) and (3) will reduce spending, while effects (2) and (4) will increase it. Liability is simultaneously an accelerator and a brake on the vehicle that is the American health system—and the overall rate of speed is a function of whether the accelerator or the brake predominates.

Consider a concrete example: back surgery. Assurance behavior involves running more tests and multiple imaging studies on those slated to receive back surgery. The same amount of back surgery may be performed, but the cost per surgery will be higher. Avoidance behavior, on the other hand, discourages physicians from performing back surgery on some or all of the patients to whom they would otherwise recommend it. In the limiting case, there is no one available to perform back surgery, as physicians flee jurisdictions that are friendly to plaintiffs. For example, when Illinois considered tort reform in the early 2000s, a constant refrain was "there are no neurosurgeons south of Springfield." To a first approximation, less back surgery means lower healthcare spending.

What happens once liability risk is reduced? In theory, both avoidance and assurance behavior should diminish, or disappear entirely. Physicians will no longer feel the need to run quite so many tests and imaging studies before they perform back surgery. This change will reduce healthcare spending. But, as physicians become willing to provide back surgery to more patients, and do so in locations that previously lacked a back surgeon, the number of back surgeries (and healthcare spending) will go up.

It is ultimately an empirical question whether the net effect of reducing assurance and avoidance behavior will cause healthcare spending to increase, stay the same, or decrease. The direction and magnitude of the net effect may also vary, depending on the specific reforms that are enacted, and the specialty and procedure in question.

iv. Physician Rationality: A Crucial but Unexamined Assumption

The claim that restrictions on lawsuits will reduce wasteful medical spending rests on a number of strong assumptions about providers' behavior and rationality. It assumes that (1) providers believe that assurance behaviors reduce the risk of being sued (and particularly of being sued successfully), and are correct in that belief; (2) providers can accurately perceive the level of liability risk; and (3) providers have no reasons other than fear of liability for engaging in assurance behaviors and will therefore quickly adapt to lowered liability risk by reducing assurance behaviors, and only assurance behaviors. There are good reasons to doubt all three assumptions.

1. Do Assurance Behaviors Work?

The first assumption requires providers to act rationally, in the sense of selecting efficient means to desired ends. Wanting to reduce the likelihood of being sued and believing that defensive practices will accomplish this, practitioners regularly order needless tests, scans, and procedures. Once tort reforms are enacted, they will stop practicing defensively, because doing so will no longer confer any benefit.

This theory certainly sounds plausible, but there isn't much evidence that defensive medicine "works." In other words, no one has shown that doctors who practice defensively are less likely than others to be sued—or less likely to lose, conditional on being sued. One recent study finds that doctors who delivered more expensive services in a given year were less likely face malpractice suits in later years, and that an individual doctor's risk of being sued declined when that doctor's intensity of treatment increased.[25] But, as the authors explain, the lack of outcome measures makes it impossible to know whether the services ordered by doctors with more intensive practice styles were medically unnecessary. If patients who received more expensive medical services enjoyed better outcomes, then the additional services had value, and the lower rate of malpractice claims is easily explained.

There are also good reasons to doubt the defensive medicine theory. One is that every medical service entails a positive risk of harming a patient. The likelihood of being sued should therefore be a positive function of the quantity of services delivered. This being so, doctors who wish to avoid malpractice suits might rationally choose to deliver fewer services, not more. The rationality of doing less may be especially clear in service areas known to have volume/quality relationships. When "practice makes perfect," if the med mal system is doing its job, it may well be rational for low-volume providers to refuse to deliver risky services at all.

A second problem with the defensive medicine theory is that, by delivering a needless service, a provider who injures a patient may make a malpractice suit more meritorious. The physician may provide a basis on which a plaintiffs' expert can persuasively testify that a service should not have been delivered because it had little or no potential to benefit a patient.

For the defensive medicine theory to work, then, the propensity of particular unnecessary services to reduce the frequency of malpractice claims must be proved. Past research has glided over this point. For example, Carrier et al. set out a series of hypotheses concerning the likely behaviors of physicians with especially strong concerns about malpractice liability.[26]

- When treating patients with chest pain, malpractice-sensitive doctors would "use more conventional and more advanced imaging and [] be more likely to have their patients visit the ED [emergency department] or be admitted to the hospital."
- When seeing patients with headaches, "malpractice-sensitive physicians [would] use more advanced imaging and ED referrals."
- When dealing with lower back pain, malpractice-sensitive doctors would "use more conventional imaging and more advanced imaging, and possibly more ED referrals."

The authors offered no evidence that any of the identified procedures actually reduces the likelihood of being sued by a patient with the relevant condition—and seem not to have thought that evidence was required. They simply guessed that certain procedures are liability-reducing,

[25] Anupam B Jena et al., *Physician Spending and Subsequent Risk of Malpractice Claims: Observational Study*, 351 British Med. J. (2015).

[26] Emily R. Carrier et al., *High Physician Concern About Malpractice Risk Predicts More Aggressive Diagnostic Testing in Office-Based Practice*, 32 Health Aff. 1383 (2013).

assumed that doctors would agree, and hypothesized that malpractice-concerned doctors would deliver more of them. This is a bit like trying to figure out where an escaped horse went by standing outside the barn and imagining where one would go if one were a horse.

Without evidence that any of the identified procedures reduces liability, there is little reason to credit the authors' hypotheses that rational doctors wanting to avoid malpractice suits would select the procedures they studied. Such doctors might act as predicted, or they might spend more time with their patients, prescribe more drugs, or deliver other services instead. The assumption that doctors pick efficient means to their desired ends only supports predictions about defensive medicine when the identified practices and procedures actually protect doctors from malpractice suits.

Carrier et al. did not choose procedures at random, of course. They focused on tests, services, and referrals with diagnostic value, believing that malpractice-sensitive doctors would use them especially often to establish or rule out "the most worrisome potential diagnoses." Malpractice-sensitive physicians were thought to have no reason to use other services that "play little role in the diagnosis of potentially worrisome conditions," so their use of other services was expected to mirror that of other physicians. Carrier et al. may have focused on services with diagnostic value because an appreciable number of malpractice suits are based on the negligent failure to diagnose.

But, it is possible that the study was not measuring defensive medicine at all. To explain why, we must briefly describe the study's methodology. Carrier et al. used surveys to gauge the intensity of physicians' concerns about being sued for malpractice. They rated as malpractice-sensitive physicians who voiced the strongest fears. Then they used Medicare records to correlate physicians' responses with the treatments doctors actually delivered. The object was to determine whether treatment patterns reflected the intensity of physicians' malpractice concerns.

Using doctors' expressed fears is problematic, however, for reasons the authors did not appreciate. Doctors vary in quality, and the strength of their concerns about being sued for malpractice may reflect their perceptions of their own abilities or their understandings of other factors that correlate with the risk of being sued, such as how well they interact with patients. Inferior physicians may—and, with any luck, should—worry more about being sued than superior ones. Inferior physicians may also use diagnostic services more heavily than superior ones, not because they worry more about being sued, but because they know their diagnostic skills are weak and rationally have less trust in them. But doctors who prescribe more procedures to offset their own deficiencies are not practicing defensive medicine. They are adapting to their abilities and, plausibly, treating patients better than they otherwise would.

Another possibility is that more intensive evaluation and treatment is just a hallmark of inferior physicians. This behavior could be evidence of their inferiority rather than a rational response to it. Even then, however, intensive treatment would not qualify as defensive medicine. Inferior physicians would use diagnostic tools more intensively than others because they are inferior, not because they hope to ameliorate their malpractice concerns.

Having discussed Carrier et al. in some detail, we finally note that the study's results are all over the map. Doctors who expressed great concern about malpractice claims sometimes treated patients more intensively than others and sometimes did not. The relationship between strength of malpractice concerns and treatment intensity was not always linear either. Doctors who expressed mid-level concerns sometimes treated patients more intensively than those whose expressed fears were stronger.

2. *Do Providers Perceive Malpractice Risks Accurately?*

To this point, we have focused on the assumption that defensive medicine is a rational response to the fear of being sued for malpractice. Although the anti-liability coalition's contention that tort reforms will save money rests on this assumption, it is entirely conjectural. For all anyone knows, doctors may increase the risk of being sued by delivering unnecessary tests and treatments. The prudent course for malpractice-sensitive physicians may be to avoid harming patients by practicing conservatively.

Proponents of tort reform often respond to criticisms like these by contending that physicians' beliefs are all that matter. Physicians think they protect themselves from lawsuits by ordering needless tests and procedures, so they practice defensive medicine. Whether or not the practices actually have the desired effect is said to be irrelevant.

This response has one thing going for it: Doctors often hold faulty beliefs about the operation of the medical malpractice liability system and its likely impact on the risk of a lawsuit. For example, when asked, physicians overestimate the risk of being sued by a factor of three.[27] Because their "extreme dread of malpractice litigation" rests on faulty understandings of the likelihood and consequences of being sued, Carrier et al. raise the possibility that doctors' fears

> might be ameliorated simply by better informing physicians about the actual dynamics of the malpractice claims process. For example, prior studies show that physicians greatly overestimate their risk of being sued; the actual risk of facing a malpractice claim in specialties such as emergency medicine may not be any greater than the average risk for all physicians; only about one in fifty injuries caused by negligence result in a claim; lawsuits are virtually never settled for amounts in excess of a physician's insurance policy limits (and thus involve little personal financial risk for physicians); claims are resolved in ways concordant with their merit three-quarters of the time; and malpractice plaintiffs lose four out of five trials.[28]

If doctors practice defensive medicine because they are misinformed, the obvious corrective is education, not tort reform. Unfortunately, the anti-liability coalition isn't interested in convincing doctors (or anyone else) that the liability system is anything other than an untamed beast. Its members would neither accept the description offered in Carrier et al. nor say anything resembling it to providers.

The reply that only doctors' beliefs matter, regardless of their basis in fact, also has a deeper problem. This assertion abandons any commitment to doctors' rationality. When rational people learn that flawed beliefs led them to select means that were ineffective ways of achieving their desired ends, they update their beliefs and alter their behaviors. The assertion that doctors ignore facts implies that they act irrationally. This undermines the assertion that defensive medical practices will taper when the threat of liability is reduced. If doctors ignore facts, tort reforms may not affect their behaviors. They may continue to exaggerate the threat

[27] Ann Lawthers et al., *Physician Perceptions of the Risk of Being Sued*, 17 J. HEALTH, POL., POL'Y & L. 463 (1992).

[28] Emily R. Carrier et al., *Physicians' Fears of Malpractice Lawsuits Are Not Assuaged by Tort Reforms*, 29 HEALTH AFF. 1585 (2010).

of being sued and practice defensively. In fact, as Carrier et al. point out, "physicians' levels of malpractice fear are not substantially different in states with and without tort reforms." If providers are not means-ends rational, the case for tort reform as a means of curtailing defensive medicine evaporates.

3. *Do Providers Have Other Reasons for Practicing Defensively?*

Doctors may also practice defensively for reasons other than the fear of being sued. The culture of medicine that prevails in the United States is notoriously punitive. Regulators investigate doctors against whom patients file complaints and occasionally revoke, suspend, or qualify their licenses. Hospitals also conduct their own peer review, which can result in revocation of privileges.

In prior work, we noted that although doctors attributed their failure to discuss mistakes to their fear of being held liable for malpractice, doctors who were immune from personal liability, such as those who practice in hospitals run by the Veterans Health Administration, also maintained a code of silence, until they were trained to talk to patients.[29] This suggests that factors other than litigation are responsible for communication failures. Other factors may also explain why doctors practice medicine defensively, assuming they do. If so, tort reforms won't save hundreds of billions of dollars. They might not save any money at all. This possibility seems especially likely when one learns that defensive medicine is also said to be common in the United Kingdom, even though by comparison to the United States its liability system is tame.[30]

In sum, even if one assumes that a positive level of defensive medicine exists, the impact of tort reform on spending cannot be determined on the basis of theory alone. Tort reform could cause total spending to fall, as the level of defensive medicine declines. It could also cause spending to rise, as doctors provide services, including risky ones, at higher levels once the restraint provided by the legal system is removed. Tort reform could also leave spending unchanged, if doctors fail to revise their beliefs and continue practicing as they have in the past. Only empirical studies can tell us whether tort reforms actually save real money. We now turn to those studies.

c. Empirical Studies of Defensive Medicine

i. *Opinion Surveys*

Most studies of defensive medicine are opinion surveys. Doctors are asked whether they prescribe tests, scans, or treatments to alleviate concerns about liability, knowing that the procedures have no medical benefit for patients. The vast majority of physicians respond affirmatively. Some authors use the responses to quantify the cost of defensive medicine.

[29] Hyman & Silver, *The Poor State of Health Care Quality in the U.S.*

[30] Osman Ortashi et al., *The Practice of Defensive Medicine Among Hospital Doctors in the United Kingdom*, 14 BRIT. MED. ETHICS 1 (2013), http://www.biomedcentral.com/content/pdf/1472-6939-14-42.pdf.

Consider one typical study of 1,214 orthopedic surgeons.[31] Over 96% reported having practiced defensive medicine by ordering imaging, laboratory tests, specialist referrals, or hospital admissions mainly to avoid possible malpractice liability. The responses indicated that, on average, 24% of all tests were ordered for defensive reasons, at a cost of approximately $100,000 per orthopedic surgeon per year. The authors then estimated the annual cost of defense medicine for all 20,400 practicing orthopedic surgeons at $2 billion. They gave no weight in their financial calculations to "negative defensive medicine," by which they meant avoidance behavior, even though "84% [of the responding doctors] reported reducing the number of high-risk procedures they performed, and 70% reported reducing the number of high-risk patients they saw."

If one were to credit these results, one would have to infer that enormous numbers of doctors commit fraud routinely—almost 25% of the time, in the case of orthopedic surgeons. By submitting a bill to Medicare, Medicaid, or some other payer, a physician represents that the service delivered was medically necessary. By definition, defensive medical services are unnecessary, at least from the patients' perspective. If these findings are correct, most orthopedic surgeons have committed crimes for which they could be criminally prosecuted. These physicians have also violated the civil False Claims Act, subjecting themselves to massive financial penalties—to the tune of three times the overpayment, plus $5,500 to $11,000 per false claim. Finally, these physicians have violated their ethical duties to their patients by prescribing unnecessary imaging studies, laboratory tests, referrals to specialists, and hospital admissions to protect themselves from liability.

Reframing defensive medicine in this way certainly casts physicians in an unfavorable light. But is this view warranted? Only if physicians' responses to opinion polls are trustworthy. In all likelihood, they are not. Doctors may behave strategically when responding to surveys, hoping to provide support for tort reform. More important, no doctor studies the amount of defensive medicine he or she delivers. Few doctors even know how to conduct such a study, which would have to control for factors other than fear of liability that might influence their judgments. Consequently, there is no reason to think that doctors know the answers to the questions contained in most surveys. They may think they are practicing defensively when, in fact, they are delivering services to make money, to satisfy patients' demands, to adhere to local norms, to maintain good relations with specialists, to create reputations for being thorough, to obtain valuable information, or to compete with other doctors in their local areas. As mentioned, doctors hold many mistaken beliefs about the operation of the malpractice system. Their beliefs about the influence the fear of liability exerts on their behavior may be inaccurate too.

There is also another reason to doubt the validity of opinion surveys about defensive medicine. To avoid or soften the implication that doctors routinely commit fraud, these surveys typically ask physicians about services that are provided "primarily" or "mainly" to avoid malpractice suits. Primarily or mainly is not exclusively. This qualification renders the results of opinion surveys impossible to interpret. If respondents thought the services would also help their patients, then it is far from obvious that they would change their behavior if the risk of liability were to diminish.

[31] Manish K. Sethi et al., *Incidence and Costs of Defensive Medicine Among Orthopedic Surgeons in the United States: A National Survey Study*, 41 Am. J. Orthopedics 69 (2012).

For similar reasons, one should also not credit another opinion doctors often express about defensive medicine. According to the study of orthopedic surgeons referenced above, "[s]eventy-seven percent of [their] respondents reported they would reduce or discontinue practicing defensive medicine if significant medical liability reform were enacted."[32] This finding led the authors to predict that tort reforms would save enormous amounts of money. But as we detail below, post-reform studies of treatment patterns have not borne out this expectation.

ii. Practice-based Studies

Kessler and McClellan performed the first rigorous study of the impact of tort reforms on healthcare spending.[33] Using longitudinal data on Medicare beneficiaries who received cardiac treatments in hospitals for acute myocardial infarction (heart attack) or ischemic heart disease in three nonconsecutive years (1984, 1987, and 1990), they found that damages caps and other reforms that directly limited liability reduced post-treatment medical spending by 5–9%, without adverse health effects. Other tort reforms did not produce statistically significant spending reductions. In response to the criticism that they failed to control for managed care penetration, Kessler and McClellan reanalyzed their data, and found a 4–5% decline.[34]

Kessler and McClellan observed that "if our results are generalizable to other medical expenditures outside the hospital, to other illnesses, and to younger patients, then direct [tort] reforms could lead to expenditure reductions of well over $50 billion per year without serious adverse consequences for health outcomes." Without testing generalizability, tort reform advocates took these figures and ran with them.[35] In various reports, government agencies followed suit.[36] What followed was an inflationary tendency that rivaled the Weimar Republic; estimates in the $100 billion to $400 billion range were common.

Subsequent research found much more modest effects.[37] A Congressional Budget Office (CBO) study in 2006 found that healthcare spending in states that implemented tort reforms in the 1980s was disproportionately affected by the adoption of the Medicare Prospective Payment System in 1983, which Kessler and McClellan did not control for.[38] When CBO controlled for this change, it found that a cap on noneconomic damages had a statistically insignificant effect on Medicare spending—in the range of 1.6%.

[32] *Id.*

[33] Daniel P. Kessler & Mark B. McClellan, *Do Doctors Practice Defensive Medicine?*, 111 Q. J. ECON. 353 (1996).

[34] Daniel P. Kessler & Mark B. McClellan, *How Liability Law Affects Medical Productivity*, 21 J. HEALTH ECON. 931 (2002).

[35] Peter Huber, *Rx: Radical Lawyerectomy*, FORBES, Jan. 27, 1997, at 112.

[36] Hyman & Silver, *The Poor State of Health Care Quality in the U.S.*

[37] *See* CONG. BUDGET OFFICE, LIMITING TORT LIABILITY FOR MEDICAL MALPRACTICE (2004); Frank Sloan & John H. Shadle, *Is There Empirical Evidence for "Defensive Medicine"? A Reassessment*, 28 J. HEALTH ECON. 481 (2009); DARIUS LAKDAWALLA & SETH A. SEABURY, NAT'L BUREAU OF ECON. RES., THE WELFARE EFFECTS OF MEDICAL MALPRACTICE LIABILITY (Working Paper No.: 15383) (2009); CONG. BUDGET OFFICE, LIMITING TORT LIABILITY FOR MEDICAL MALPRACTICE (2004).

[38] CONG. BUDGET OFFICE, MEDICAL MALPRACTICE TORT LIMITS AND HEALTH CARE SPENDING (2006), https://www.cbo.gov/sites/default/files/109th-congress-2005-2006/reports/04-28-medicalmalpractice.pdf.

Premiums for health insurance can proxy for medical spending, because the two vary together. Avraham, Dafny, and Schanzenbach measured the impact of tort reforms on premiums collected by employer-funded health insurance plans that covered over 10 million Americans annually from 1998 and 2006.[39] They found caps on noneconomic damages, abrogation of the collateral source rule, and reform of joint and several liability each reduced premiums for self-funded health plans by 1–2%. They found no effect on premiums charged by fully insured plans.

In two studies, Baicker et al. found no overall association between insurance premiums and Medicare spending, but did find an association for the Medicare Part B spending subcategory "diagnostic, laboratory, and x-ray services."[40] They hypothesized that diagnostic testing is more likely to reflect defensive medicine than medical practice more generally, and thus is more sensitive to liability risk.

In our own work, we found that Texas' adoption of a damages caps resulted in a dramatic decline in claim frequency and payout per claim, reducing overall payouts by approximately 75%.[41] However, this dramatic change in the malpractice environment did not result in significant changes in healthcare spending levels or trends, whether assessed statewide or at the county level. Indeed, we found some evidence of *increased* physician spending post-reform in counties where med mal risk was higher.

Turning from studies of costs to the impact of tort reforms on particular treatments and outcomes, both early and recent studies of childbirth have produced mixed results.[42] Dhankhar et al. find that higher claim rates are associated with improved post-heart-attack outcomes and predict lower treatment costs for less severely ill patients.[43] Frakes examined the impact of noneconomic caps on cesarean rates, episiotomies, and postdelivery hospital lengths of stay, and found that caps predicted roughly 5% fewer episiotomies (depending on specification) and perhaps also a 3% or so decline in hospital length of stay, but did not affect cesarean rates.[44] In contrast, Yang et al. found that noneconomic caps predicted lower primary and total cesarean rates, and higher VBAC (vaginal birth after cesarean) rates.[45]

39 Ronen Avraham et al., *The Impact of Tort Reform on Employer-Sponsored Health Insurance Premiums*, 28 J. L. Econ. Org. 657 (2012).

40 Katherine Baicker et al., *Malpractice Liability Costs and the Practice of Medicine in the Medicare Program*, 26 Health Aff. 841 (2007); Katherine Baicker & Amitabh Chandra, *The Effect of Malpractice Liability on the Delivery of Healthcare*, 8 Frontiers Health Pol'y Res. (2005).

41 Myungho Paik et al., *Will Tort Reform Bend the Cost Curve? Evidence from Texas*, 9 J. Empirical Legal Stud. 173 (2012).

42 *See* Janet Curie & W. Bentley MacLeod, *First Do No Harm? Tort Reform and Birth Outcomes*, 123 Q. J. Econ. 795 (2008); Lisa Dubay et al., *The Impact of Malpractice Fears on Cesarean Section Rates*, 18 J. Health Econ. 491 (1999); A. Russell Localio et al., *Relationship between Malpractice Claims and Cesarean Delivery*, 269 JAMA 366 (1993); Laura-Mae Baldwin et al., *Defensive Medicine and Obstetrics*, 274 JAMA 1606 (1995); David Dranove & Yasutoru Watanabe, *Influence and Deterrence: How Obstetricians Respond to Litigation against Themselves and Their Colleagues*, 12 Am. L. & Econ. Rev. 69 (2010); Gilbert Gimm, *The Impact of Malpractice Liability Claims on Obstetrical Practice Patterns*, 45 Health Services Res. 195 (2010).

43 Praveen Dhankhar et al., *Effect of Medical Malpractice on Resource Use and Mortality of AMI Patients*, 4 J. Empirical Leg. Stud. 163 (2007).

44 Michael Frakes, *Defensive Medicine and Obstetric Practice*, 9 J. Empirical Legal Stud. 457 (2012).

45 Tony Y. Yang, *A Longitudinal Analysis of the Impact of Liability Pressure on the Supply of Obstetrician-Gynecologists*, 5 J. of Empirical Legal Stud. 21 (2008).

iii. Synthesis

In an earlier article, we concluded that the likely effect of tort reform on healthcare spending was far lower than usually suggested in public debate:

> Our results, combined with those from other studies, lets us place some bounds on the likely impact of tort reform on spending. We believe a "credible interval" for the most likely effect of major tort reform on health-care-spending runs from 0 percent to about a 2 percent decline for states that currently lack caps on non-econ or total damages. *Higher* spending cannot be ruled out; indeed, our study finds some evidence suggesting higher spending after reform.[46]

Compare our conclusions with Mello et al., who used Kessler and McClellan's studies to estimate the national cost of defensive medicine at 5.4% of hospital spending, which in their opinion is "a conservative assumption that represents the lower of Kessler and McClellan's original estimates and the midpoint between their latest estimates."[47] This led them to conclude that "$38.8 billion of [hospital] spending could be reduced through direct tort reforms." This figure is 70% of the total estimated cost of the medical liability system, which Mello et al. pegged at $55.6 billion dollars.

The approach taken by Mello et al. raises several issues. Post Kessler & McClellan, other researchers studying a wider variety of medical treatments and using data sets that cover more years found much less impressive results. Mello et al. recognized this by giving a "low" rating to the quality of the evidence supporting their estimate of defensive medicine in hospitals. Given that 70% of their estimated total cost is based on evidence of poor quality, it might have been the better course to offer no number at all, or suggest a range of values.

Mello et al. also took no account in their calculations of the braking effect the liability system may exert on medical spending. Although the authors adopted the definition promulgated by the U.S. Congress Office of Technology Assessment, which posits that defensive medicine occurs "when doctors order tests, procedures, or visits, or *avoid certain high-risk patients or procedures*, primarily (but not solely) because of concern about malpractice liability," they neither quantified the savings from avoidance behavior nor noted the omission when offering their total estimate. In theory, the savings generated by avoidance behavior could equal or exceed the costs attributable to excessive treatments. In fact, not enough is known about the numbers on either side of the balance.

In sum, we believe that Mello et al. took too aggressive a position, but in the public debate over malpractice liability, numbers stick and qualifications are ignored. The $55.6 billion number has been repeated endlessly, often by politicians and interest groups who disregard the caveat regarding the quality of the evidence.

Where does that leave us? First, we believe that our credible interval from 2012 (i.e., 0–2% of total healthcare spending) represents a defensible outer boundary on the likely impact of tort reform on healthcare spending in those states that don't already have damage caps. We hasten to add that a majority of states have already adopted caps on noneconomic or total damages—reducing the potential impact of a national cap well below the figures that currently dominate the public discourse. Second, were we asked to set a new credible interval, the upper boundary would likely be 1% or less—and the lower boundary might be less than

[46] Paik et al, *Will Tort Reform Bend the Cost Curve?*

[47] Mello et al., *National Costs of the Medical Liability System*.

zero (i.e., reducing liability risk might well increase healthcare spending). To summarize, we think it quite likely that tort reform has either no net effect or a very small effect on healthcare spending.

d. Defensive Medicine and the Base Rate of Overutilization

Even if we assume that defensive medicine has a cost that is close to Mello et al.'s estimate, that figure should be understood against a backdrop of waste, fraud, abuse, and unnecessary care that totals hundreds of billions of dollars per year. Medicare's chief actuary estimated that fully 15–30% of healthcare spending is unnecessary—which would total $425 billion to $850 billion per year—dwarfing the amount attributable to defensive medicine.[48] The base rate of overuse and inappropriate utilization is so pervasive that dozens of medical specialty societies have developed lists of "things to question," to aid patients and providers in making better decisions.[49] In a study of more than a million Medicare beneficiaries, 25–42% received at least one of twenty-six useless tests and treatments.[50] Gawande neatly described the basic dynamics of the current healthcare system:

> The medical system had done what it so often does: performed tests, unnecessarily, to reveal problems that aren't quite problems to then be fixed, unnecessarily, at great expense and no little risk. Meanwhile, we avoid taking adequate care of the biggest problems that people face—problems like diabetes, high blood pressure, or any number of less technologically intensive conditions. An entire health-care system has been devoted to this game.[51]

These problems are simply not attributable to the liability system—so tort reform will do little or nothing to fix them. If we wish to address these problems, we will need to do so directly.

IV Litigation and Physician Supply

Even if tort reform doesn't dramatically reduce healthcare spending, it might still affect physician supply. If physicians take liability risks into account in deciding where to practice, damages caps and other lawsuit restrictions are obvious options for attracting more physicians, particularly those who practice in lawsuit-prone specialties. Reform advocates have argued that damages caps have exactly this effect. In Texas, they insisted that physicians were fleeing the state in droves and that a cap on noneconomic damages was needed to halt the exodus. After Texas enacted a comprehensive package of lawsuit

48 Rita F. Redberg, *Squandering Medicare's Money*, N.Y. Times (May 26, 2011), http://www.nytimes.com/2011/05/26/opinion/26redberg.html?_r=0.

49 ChoosingWisely, http://www.choosingwisely.org/resources/ (last visited Oct. 26, 2015).

50 Aaron L. Schwartz et al., *Measuring Low-value Care in Medicare*, 174 J. Am. Med. Ass'n Internal Med. 1067 (2014).

51 Atul Gawande, *Overkill*, New Yorker, May 11, 2015, http://www.newyorker.com/magazine/2015/05/11/overkill-atul-gawande.

restrictions in 2003, proponents insisted that the trend reversed and that physicians were flooding in.[52]

There is, of course, a seeming incoherence in the assertion that tort reforms will reduce healthcare spending while also improving patients' access to medical services. An increase in the number of doctors practicing in a state would predict a rise in the volume of services delivered and a corresponding increase in costs. For supply to increase and costs to fall, the reduction in the cost of defensive medicine would have to be especially large. Because empirical studies have shown that tort reforms have small effects on spending, the conjoint assertion cannot be true.

To their credit, when the politicians in Texas who supported tort reform learned that medical spending had not fallen, they did not dispute the facts. Instead, they argued that their goal all along was to improve Texans' access to healthcare, not to reduce costs.

a. Theory

A simple theory supports the assertion that tort reforms improve physician supply. Doctors consider costs when deciding where to practice and which specialties to enter. Liability costs are sufficiently great to affect some doctors' decisions, driving them away from states and practice areas where these costs are especially great and into those where they are lower. By reducing liability costs, tort reforms should alter doctors' location decisions and make high-risk states and practice areas more attractive.

One obvious limitation on this theory is that it only works when liability risks vary significantly across geographical areas. This is so because states that enact reforms are trying to steal doctors from other states or to discourage doctors they already have from leaving for other states or retiring. But if all states were to adopt tort reforms that kept liability risks uniformly low, there would be no winners. Likewise, if all states were to eliminate their restrictions and reinstate their common law systems, the incentive to relocate would also disappear. Finally, retirement aside, the recruitment game (and gain) is effectively zero-sum. For every locality or specialty that gains a doctor, another locality or specialty loses one. Supply can increase in the longer run, but no one contends that liability laws discourage students from applying to medical schools or otherwise restricts the supply of physicians nationwide.

Another question is whether tort reforms attract the "right kind" of physicians. Tort reform could draw in high-quality physicians who provide services that are beneficial and in short supply. Or they could attract low-quality physicians that provide services that are dangerous. Presumably, a state would prefer to attract more of the former than the latter, but simply counting newly arrived physicians does not tell us whether they are any good.

The matter of physician quality is of great moment. Only in Garrison Keillor's fictional town of Lake Wobegon, where all the children are above average, are all doctors likely to be first-rate practitioners too. In the real world, physicians vary greatly in quality. A study of complication rates following elective surgeries found that "[a] small share of doctors, 11%, accounted for about 25% of the complications" and that "[h]undreds of surgeons across

[52] David A. Hyman et al., *Does Tort Reform Affect Physician Supply? Evidence from Texas*, 42 INT'L REV. L. & ECON. 203 (2015).

the country had rates double and triple the national average." A surgeon who performed prostate removals at Johns Hopkins Hospital "had more complications than all 10 of his colleagues combined—though they performed nine times as many of the same procedures."[53]

Because physicians vary greatly in quality, some are much more likely to incur malpractice claims than others, and those who are malpractice magnets will benefit disproportionately from tort reforms. Consequently, lawsuit restrictions should have the greatest impact on the location and practice decisions of the worst physicians.

A similar dynamic forces one to wonder whether tort reforms attract physicians whose services are in short supply. Presumably, lawsuit restrictions make states more attractive to physicians who practice in specialties that are likely to generate malpractice claims. But the services of these specialists may be easy to obtain because, for example, the doctors are highly compensated. Shortages may exist in areas like pediatric care, family medicine, and geriatrics where salaries are low and malpractice claims are rare. There may also be significant access problem in rural areas and for poor populations that lawsuit restrictions will do little or nothing to address. Finally, even within a particular specialty, it matters what the physicians do once they start practicing. Having more neurosurgeons is a good thing if they are dealing with brain trauma—but much less likely to be beneficial if they are primarily doing back surgery.

A final weakness in the simple theory connecting tort reforms to physician supply is its static nature. In the short run, restrictions on lawsuits should reduce the cost of practicing in a state. But over time, labor markets should respond to this change in employment conditions by adjusting providers' compensation. If Texas were to become more attractive to doctors because of tort reforms or for any other reason, salaries elsewhere would rise as other states tried to hold onto their physicians. Likewise, as the number of doctors migrating to Texas increased, one would expect salaries there to fall, it being easier to lure doctors into the state than it was before. Because labor markets are dynamic and more things matter than just liability costs, tort reforms might have little or no impact on doctors' location or practice decisions.

b. Empirical Evidence

The impact of tort reforms on physician supply has been studied extensively, with mixed results. Damage caps appear to have a small positive impact on physician supply in rural areas and a few specialties, but there is much less evidence of post-reform across-the-board statewide increases.

In one study, states that adopted damage caps had 3.2% more physicians per capita in rural counties.[54] Klick and Stratmann found a 6–7% rise in per capita counts for the five highest-lawsuit-risk specialties, and a 3–4% effect for the ten highest risk specialties, relative to the five

[53] Marshall Allen & Olga Pierce, *Surgery Risks: Why Choosing the Right Surgeon Matters*, PROPUBLICA (July 13, 2015), https://www.propublica.org/article/surgery-risks-patient-safety-surgeon-matters. In fairness, ProPublica's findings have been harshly criticized (and defended) by patient safety researchers.

[54] William Encinosa & Fred Hellinger, *Have State Caps on Malpractice Awards Increased the Supply of Physicians?*, 24 HEALTH AFF. 250 (2005). *See also* David Matsa, *Does Malpractice Liability Keep the Doctor Away? Evidence from Tort Reform Damage Caps*, 36 J. LEGAL STUD. 143 (2007).

(or ten) lowest risk specialties, with risk based on payout per paid claim.[55] Helland and Seabury found a 3–5% drop in physician supply in all but the five to ten highest risk specialties, and 1.5–7% relative increase in physician supply in the high-risk specialties, relative to the drop for other specialties (thus, no increase, relative to non-cap-adopting states, just a nondecrease).[56]

We examined Texas' experience before and after it adopted damages caps in 2003.[57] As noted previously, before Texas adopted tort reform, proponents claimed that physicians were deserting Texas. After tort reform was enacted, proponents claimed there had been a dramatic increase in physicians moving to Texas. We found no evidence to support either claim. Physician supply was not measurably stunted prior to reform, and it did not measurably improve after reform, whether one focused on all patient care physicians in Texas, on high-malpractice-risk specialties, or on rural physicians.

Finally, in a working paper, we examined the impact of noneconomic caps on physician supply in the nine states that adopted tort reform during the third med mal reform wave (2002–2005).[58] Using a variety of analytical methods, we found no evidence that cap adoption predicted an increase in total patient care physicians or in rural physicians. When we examined high-risk specialties, we also found no evidence of an increase in physician supply, with the exception of plastic surgeons.

To summarize, damages caps may play a small role in attracting physicians to rural areas or high-risk specialties. But the evidence is mixed, and some studies find no effect. The best conclusion is therefore that liability reform has limited potential to improve the performance of the healthcare system by improving patients' access to care.

V Where Should We Go from Here?

The liability system is far from perfect. It is costly, slow, and prone to error. Injured patients don't find the system to be humane—and neither do physicians. Even worse, the legal system does far too little to motivate healthcare providers to improve the quality of services they deliver. The conventional list of tort reforms addresses none of these problems. So, if damages caps and other restrictions on lawsuits aren't the right solution, what is?

We propose four concrete steps.

a. Make the Healthcare Market Work Better

When markets work well, civil justice systems can safely play a subordinate role in quality improvement. Their main purpose is to ensure a degree of civility and respect in economic

[55] Jonathan Klick & Thomas Stratmann, *Medical Malpractice Reform and Physicians in High-Risk Specialties*, 36 J. of Legal Stud, 121 (2007).

[56] Eric P. Helland & Seth A. Seabury, *Tort Reform and Physician Labor Supply: A Review of the Evidence*, 42 Int'l Rev. L. & Econ. 192 (2015).

[57] Hyman et al., *Does Tort Reform Affect Physician Supply?*

[58] Paik et al., *Does Medical Malpractice Reform Increase Physician Supply? Evidence from the Third Reform Wave* (Nw. Univ. L. Sch., Law and Economics Research Paper No. 14-11), http://ssrn.com/abstract=2470370.

relationships by taking the roughest edges off disagreements that buyers and sellers cannot work out on their own. In the healthcare sector, law has historically had to shoulder too great a burden because market forces have been too weak.

The main problem with market forces, and the chief cause of mediocrity in the healthcare sector, is the absence of a business case for quality. Time and again, researchers have found that healthcare providers make more money when they deliver error-laden care than when they improve. One recent study examined the billing records for over 34,000 hospital inpatients, each of whom had one of nine common surgical procedures in 2010.[59] Over 1,800 patients (5.3%) experienced at least one potentially preventable complication, such as an infection at the surgery site or a pulmonary embolism. The patients with surgical complications generated $8,084 more in profit on average after the hospitals' variable costs were netted out. Privately insured patients with complications were especially profitable, generating an average of $39,017 more in profit. Another study of a Michigan hospital found that every 1% decline in surgical complications would cost the hospital $1.2 million.[60]

As long as the business case for quality is missing, quality problems will abound. The reason for this is straightforward. The problem of error-laden care is not attributable to a lack of medical knowledge. Providers generally know what works; they just do what works inconsistently. Consistency requires things like checklists, teamwork, root cause analysis, benchmarking, logistics, and culture reform. In other words, consistent delivery of high-quality care requires the application of sound business techniques. By and large, however, managers apply business techniques successfully only when there is a financial case for doing so. Otherwise, they fail to recognize problems and allow them to persist.

In healthcare, the business case for quality is missing for many reasons. Compensation arrangements reward providers for delivering services, regardless of quality or the impact on patients' well-being. Competition is spotty, so providers feel little pressure to do better than their peers. They also have no reason to gather and disseminate information that patients could use to shop intelligently. Third-party payment arrangements reduce the pressure for quality even further. Payers care about costs, not quality. It is widely known that quality metrics play little role in negotiations between insurers and providers. Finally, third-party payment makes patients insensitive to prices, and price competition is one of the forces that motivate providers to compete on the basis of quality and value.

As long as quality improvement continues to be unprofitable, mediocre care will continue to be a problem, and all the tinkering in the world with the legal system won't fix it. Courts cannot exert the large amount of pressure encouraging the delivery of high-quality care that this situation requires. By comparison to the number of errors, the number of malpractice lawsuits is small. Meritorious cases often end without recoveries, because costs discourage plaintiffs' attorneys from handling them and because the liability system tends to err in favor

[59] Sunil Eappen et al., *Relationship between Occurrence of Surgical Complications and Hospital Finances*, 309 JAMA 1599 (2013). The surgeries included in the study were craniotomy, colorectal resection, total or partial hip replacement, knee arthroplasty, coronary artery bypass graft, spinal surgery (laminectomy, excision of intervertebral disk, or spinal fusion), hysterectomy (abdominal or vaginal), appendectomy, and cholecystectomy or common bile duct exploration.

[60] Dan C. Krupka, Warren S. Sandberg, & William B. Weeks, *The Impact on Hospitals of Reducing Surgical Complications Suggests Many Will Need Shared Savings Programs with Payers*, 31 HEALTH AFF. 2571 (2012).

of providers. When injured patients do recover, their compensation tends to be inadequate, with the most severely injured patients incurring the largest shortfalls. Liability insurance dulls the deterrent signal too, by spreading the costs of errors across the entire pool of providers and by insulating negligent providers from personal exposure. Finally, courts decide malpractice cases on the basis of old knowledge (that may or may not be reliable) that has been incorporated into a standard of care (that may or may not be efficient). Litigation can supplement a strong market-based signal for quality improvements, but it cannot replace it.

Instead of trying to correct the problems of healthcare by reforming the legal system, providers should look at their own delivery systems and correct the glaring deficiencies that plague them. When Peter Pronovost first studied the practices for inserting central line catheters that were in use at Johns Hopkins, he discovered that doctors there followed all the recommended steps only about one-third of the time. He also learned that Johns Hopkins had one of the highest rates of central line associated infections of any hospital in the country, and that the hospital's doctors and administrators had no idea how bad the problem was. The idea that one could have fixed these problems by tinkering with the legal system didn't occur to Dr. Pronovost. Nor should it have occurred to anyone else. The problems of healthcare have their roots in the healthcare system. The idea that they can be fixed by imposing restrictions on lawsuits is ridiculous.

If and when healthcare providers injure patients less often or less seriously, the number of lawsuits and the damages recovered will automatically fall.[61] Providers have it in their own power to free themselves from the lawsuits they dread. They need only take a lesson from anesthesiologists and other providers who have put real effort into quality improvement.

b. Roll Back Existing Tort Reforms

The civil justice system operates on the bases of simple principles. It seeks to *compensate* those who are negligently injured. It seeks to *deter* negligence, by denouncing bad behavior and making negligence expensive. Finally, it seeks to ensure *corrective justice*, by restoring the victims of negligence to the positions they would have been in absent the negligent injury.

Tort reforms are deeply at odds with all of these objectives. There has never been any evidence that the liability system systematically overcompensates victims of medical malpractice for their losses. To the contrary, studies have shown time and again that undercompensation is the norm and that the patients whose injuries are the worst suffer the biggest shortfalls. Damages caps and other restrictions on lawsuits simply make these problems worse, by making it harder for victims to obtain full compensation.

For the same reason, tort reforms undermine the justice system's deterrent function. By insulating providers from the costs their defective actions impose on patients, damages caps and other reforms make medical malpractice cheaper than it otherwise would be. In Texas, the package of lawsuit restrictions adopted in 2003 reduced the number of lawsuits by more

[61] Kenneth D. Illingworth, Steven H. Shaha, Tony H. Tzeng, Michael S. Sinha, & Khaled J. Saleh, *The Impact of Tort Reform and Quality Improvements on Medical Liability Claims: A Tale of 2 States*, 30 Am. J. Med. Quality 263 (2015).

than half and cut the flow of dollars through the liability system by more than two-third. On the assumption that potential tortfeasors respond to incentives, tort reforms should cause providers to injure patients *more often*. There is some evidence showing exactly that.[62] The effects are small, in keeping with the liability system's limited potential to force quality to improve.

If we are going to have a tort system, we may as well use it to help address the problem of low-quality care. Reconsideration of past tort reforms is an obvious place to start. Rolling back excessively strict limits on suits and recoveries may also have the side effect of causing providers to treat injured patients with greater respect. More and more risk managers have come to realize that honesty is the best policy when it comes to mistakes.

c. Use Caps Strategically

To date, more than thirty states have enacted caps on damages. These caps apply whether providers have made great effort or no effort to improve the quality of services they provide. How dumb is that? A better strategy, if caps are politically inevitable, is to use them to encourage providers to improve the quality of care they provide. One obvious approach is to reward providers for error reporting and punish them for hiding mistakes. For example, when a provider reports an error within a specified time of its occurrence, she would receive the protection of a limit on noneconomic damages. When a provider fails to report an error in a timely manner, we propose that noneconomic damages be enhanced. One could use a similar strategy to reward providers who improve their performance on certain defined quality benchmarks, by allowing them to take advantage of a second (and lower) cap on noneconomic damages.

d. Experiment!

No one loves the existing liability system, but with few exceptions, the fault-based med mal system is mandatory throughout the United States. This one-size-fits-all approach has its advantages—but it has real costs as well. For example, the fixed costs (and risks) of litigating med mal cases, coupled with the use of contingency fee arrangements, means that over the past two decades, small cases have been systematically squeezed out of the system.[63] Many plaintiffs' lawyers reportedly won't take a med mal case unless there is at least $100,000 in damages.

Rather than effectively require plaintiffs with modest damages to lump it, states and payers should experiment with alternative compensation strategies. Small claims present a good test-bed for a no-fault system, modeled on the workers' compensation system. Or contract. Or health courts. Or whatever. Because not much money is at stake, there is the opportunity to learn what works (and what doesn't), without triggering a duel to the death among those affected.

[62] Frakes, *Defensive Medicine and Obstetric Practice*.

[63] Paik et al., *The Receding Tide of Medical Malpractice Litigation*.

More broadly, we should be experimenting with alternative strategies to simultaneously deter negligent treatment and compensate those who are negligently injured. After all, isn't that what the tort system is supposed to be doing? And, when it falls short, shouldn't we be looking for a better way?

VI Conclusion

In 1989, Robert Fulghum's first book, *All I Really Needed to Know I Learned in Kindergarten*, was published. The book dominated bestseller lists for several years. In 1991, Fulghum followed up with his second book, *It Was on Fire When I Lay Down on It*. Fulghum achieved the unprecedented feat of having two books ranked #1 and #2 on the bestseller list.

Fulghum's title for his second bestseller comes from one of the stories in the book:

> A tabloid newspaper carried the story, stating simply that a small town emergency fire squad was called to a house where smoke was pouring from an upstairs window. The crew broke in and found a man in a smoldering bed. After the man was rescued and the mattress doused, the obvious question was asked: "How did this happen?"
>
> "I don't know. It was on fire when I lay down on it."

What lessons should we draw from Fulghum's tale? It is not surprising that healthcare providers blame the liability system and not themselves for wasteful spending and for problems with quality and access.[64] But, like the man who lay down on a burning mattress, it is the deliberate choices and non-choices made by those who operate the American healthcare system (including but not limited to healthcare providers) that are responsible for the wasteful spending we describe in this chapter. Indeed, those with an unkind bent of mind might suggest that healthcare providers poured gasoline on the mattress and then lit the match—before "laying down on it." If we want to improve the performance of the healthcare system, we will need to focus not on the liability system but on the healthcare system itself—preferably on the massively inefficient ways we have chosen to deliver and pay for healthcare services.

Yogi Berra died while we were completing revisions to this chapter. To baseball fans, Berra is the best catcher in the history of the sport. But to many more Americans, Berra is better known for his Yogi-isms—profound statements about the human condition that appear to be simple-minded banter. Berra was also the inspiration for the cartoon character Yogi Bear—but we leave that important topic (and his contemplated lawsuit) for another day.

Berra offers a simple Yogi-ism about the use of tort reform to achieve health system change: "If you don't know where you're going, you might end up somewhere else." Although tort reformers claim they know where they want us to go (i.e., to better health system performance), they keep picking a route that leads somewhere else. Simply stated, healthcare problems require healthcare solutions. Physician, heal thyself.

[64] David A. Hyman & Charles Silver, *Health Care Quality, Patient Safety and the Culture of Medicine: "Denial Ain't Just a River in Egypt,"* 46 New Eng. L. Rev. 101 (2012).

B. Competition and Innovation

CHAPTER 26

THE BIOMEDICAL RESEARCH ENTERPRISE

MARK BARNES AND DAVID PELOQUIN

I Introduction

Biomedical research in the United States is subject to a wide variety of laws at both the federal and state level. These laws cover a vast range of legal principles, ranging from obtaining informed consent from human subjects to ensuring that federal grant funds are expended appropriately. We offer here a survey of some of these key areas, including human subjects protections, privacy laws, financial disclosure requirements, clinical trials registration and data transparency, processes for handling research misconduct, substantive limitations placed on certain categories of research, protections for research involving animals, and the law of technology transfer. We offer insights throughout regarding the tension that exists between parallel sets of regulations and indicate instances in which conflicting regulatory regimes could potentially be better harmonized.

II Human Subjects Protections

a. The Common Rule

Because much biomedical research involves human subjects, the law of human subject protections is at the core of ethical and compliance concerns in this area. There are two distinct but largely similar regulatory regimes that govern protections for human subjects: (1) the regulations located at 45 C.F.R. part 46, which are administered by the U.S. Department of Health and Human Services (HHS) Office for Human Research Protections (OHRP) (formerly known as the Office for Protection from Research Risks), and (2) the regulations located at 21 C.F.R. parts 50 and 56, which are administered by the Food and Drug Administration (FDA).

The human subjects research regulations administered by OHRP were adopted in the late 1970s and early 1980s to codify in regulation the principles of the *Belmont Report*, which set forth basic ethical principals designed to guide the conduct of research with human subjects.[1] The regulations administered by OHRP consist of four subparts: Subpart A, which sets forth basic rules governing research with human subjects; Subpart B, which provides additional protections for pregnant women, human fetuses, and neonates; Subpart C, which provides additional protections for prisoners; and Subpart D, which provides additional protections for children. Subpart A is often referred to as the "Common Rule," as it has been adopted in common by fifteen federal departments and agencies that have codified its protections in their own regulations, and three additional federal departments and agencies that have agreed to follow its requirements in their own research, though they have not officially codified its provisions in regulation.[2]

Institutions that conduct research funded by an agency that has adopted the Common Rule must provide OHRP with a "Federalwide Assurance" (FWA) in which such institutions agree to abide by the requirements of the Common Rule for all human subjects research they conduct that is supported by a Common Rule agency.[3] Because a large percentage of biomedical research conducted in the United States is funded by grants provided by federal departments and agencies that have adopted the Common Rule, the Common Rule's requirements apply to a large percentage of research conducted in the United States, even when such research is conducted at private universities or in cooperation between public and private entities. The Common Rule also applies to research conducted outside of the United States that is supported by the federal government.[4] Furthermore, many institutions voluntarily elect in their FWA to extend the requirements of the Common Rule to all research conducted at their institution, regardless of the source of funding, thereby voluntarily extending the Common Rule's reach within those institutions.

The Common Rule defines research as "a systematic investigation, including research development, testing and evaluation, designed to develop or contribute to generalizable

[1] *See* The National Commission for the Protection of Human Subjects of Biomedical and Behavioral Research, Ethical Principles and Guidelines for the Protection of Human Subjects of Research (Apr. 18, 1979) [hereinafter the *Belmont Report*]. The *Belmont Report* was drafted in large part in response to unethical practices that occurred in research involving human subjects during the nineteenth and twentieth centuries, such as research conducted without first obtaining informed consent of the subjects and research conducted solely on members of vulnerable or disadvantaged populations.

[2] A listing of the relevant federal departments and agencies may be found at the following link: http://www.hhs.gov/ohrp/humansubjects/commonrule/. It is important to keep in mind that individual departments and agencies that have adopted the Common Rule may issue guidance with agency-specific interpretations of the rule or imposing additional requirements applicable to research funded by the agency in question.

[3] *See* 45 C.F.R. § 46.103.

[4] *See* 45 C.F.R. § 46.101(h) (providing that foreign laws governing human subjects research may be followed in lieu of the Common Law if the applicable department or agency head determines that the foreign law affords protections that are at least equivalent to those provided by the Common Rule); 71 Fed. Reg. 38,645, 38,645 (July 7, 2006) (indicating that the HHS has yet to determine that any foreign regimes governing human subjects research impose requirements comparable to those imposed by the Common Rule).

knowledge."[5] A "human subject" is defined as a living individual about whom the investigator conducting the research obtains (1) "[d]ata through intervention or interaction with the individual" or (2) "[i]dentifiable private information."[6] The Common Rule exempts several types of research from its purview, including research involving the use of educational tests (cognitive, diagnostic, aptitude, or achievement) if certain conditions are met; research involving the review of existing records if the researcher records information in such a manner that the subjects cannot be identified; and research and demonstration projects that are designed to examine public benefit or service programs.[7]

When human subjects research does not fall within an exempt category, the Common Rule imposes several requirements on the research. The first of these is that the institution at which the research takes place must designate an institutional review board (IRB), often referred to outside of the United States as a research ethics committee (REC) or institutional ethics committee (IEC), to review all human subjects research proposals. The IRB must include at least five individuals of diverse backgrounds selected with consideration given to race, gender, and cultural backgrounds, as well as community attitudes.[8] While the Common Rule does not require that IRB members come from certain professional backgrounds, it does indicate that the IRB must include "persons knowledgeable" regarding institutional commitments and regulations, applicable law, and standards of professional conduct and practice, and at least one member whose primary concerns are in scientific areas and one member whose primary concerns are in nonscientific areas.[9] The Common Rule provides that the IRB shall review research for adherence to the following requirements: (1) risks to subjects are minimized; (2) risks to subjects are reasonable in relation to anticipated benefits; (3) selection of subjects is equitable, taking into account the purposes of the research, the setting in which the research is conducted, and the special problems of research involving vulnerable populations, such as children, prisoners, or pregnant women; (4) informed consent will be sought from each prospective subject or the subject's legally authorized representative; (5) informed consent will be appropriately documented; (6) the research plan makes adequate provision for monitoring the data collected to ensure the safety of subjects; and (7) when appropriate, there are adequate provisions to protect the privacy of subjects and to maintain the confidentiality of the data.[10]

While generally the full IRB must review proposed research according to the above criteria, the Common Rule allows in limited instances for "expedited review," that is, review solely by the IRB chair or an experienced reviewer designated by the chair from among the IRB members.[11] Expedited review is available only for certain categories of research, as determined by the Secretary of HHS. Examples of categories for which the secretary has determined expedited review to be available include clinical studies of drugs and medical devices for which an investigational new drug (IND) or an investigational device exemption (IDE) application is not required, collection of blood samples from certain healthy populations, and prospective collection of biological specimens for research purposes by noninvasive means.[12] Even when research falls into a category that the Secretary of HHS has determined allows for expedited review, expedited review is available only if the designated IRB reviewer determines that the research involves no more than minimal risk.

[5] *See* 45 C.F.R. § 46.102(d). [6] *See id.* (f). [7] *See* 45 C.F.R. § 46.101.

[8] *See* 45 C.F.R. § 46.107(a). [9] *See* 45 C.F.R. § 46.107(a), (c).

[10] *See* 45 C.F.R. § 46.111(a). [11] *See* 45 C.F.R. § 46.110.

[12] The complete list of the categories of research eligible for expedited review may be found at the following link: http://www.hhs.gov/ohrp/policy/expedited98.html.

One of the most important roles of the IRB is to review the process by which informed consent will be obtained from human subjects. As a threshold manner, the Common Rule requires that prospective subjects be provided sufficient opportunity to consider whether or not to participate in the research such that the possibility of coercion or undue influence is minimized, and that an informed consent form include no exculpatory language that could waive or appear to waive the subject's legal rights.[13] The Common Rule further requires that several pieces of information be conveyed to prospective subjects, including: (1) an explanation of the purposes of the research; (2) a description of any reasonably foreseeable risks or discomforts to the subject; (3) a description of any benefits to the subject or others that may reasonably be expected from the research; (4) a disclosure of appropriate alternative procedures or courses of treatment, if any, that might be advantageous to the subject; (5) a statement describing the extent, if any, to which confidentiality of records identifying the subject will be maintained; (6) for research involving more than minimal risk, an explanation as to whether any compensation and/or any medical treatments are available if injury occurs; (7) an explanation of whom to contact for answers to pertinent questions about the research and research subjects' rights and whom to contact in the event of a research-related injury to the subject; and (8) a statement that participation is voluntary and that refusal to participate will involve no penalty or loss of benefits to which the subject is otherwise entitled.[14]

The Common Rule permits some or all of the requirements of informed consent to be waived in instances in which an IRB determines all of the following to be true: (1) the research involves no more than minimal risk to the subjects; (2) the waiver or alteration will not adversely affect the rights and welfare of the subjects; (3) the research could not practicably be carried out without the waiver or alteration; and (4) whenever appropriate, the subjects will be provided with additional pertinent information after participation.[15] Informed consent generally must be documented in a written form approved by the IRB and signed by the subject, though the IRB may waive the requirement of obtaining a signed informed consent form when (1) the written informed consent form would be the only record linking the subject to the research, or (2) the research presents no more than minimal risk of harm to the subjects and involves no procedures for which written consent is normally required outside of the research context.[16]

b. Proposed Changes to the Common Rule

After undergoing very few changes since its original adoption, the Common Rule was the subject of an Advanced Notice of Proposed Rulemaking (ANPRM) in the summer of 2011 proposing changes to the rule that were designed primarily to (1) enhance the protection of research

[13] In the past the prohibition on exculpatory language generated confusion as it had been interpreted to prohibit the common practice of using informed consent forms in which individuals acknowledge that they will not receive any rights to revenue from commercial products that are developed through use of their biospecimens and/or data. This interpretation has since been rejected by OHRP and FDA in a draft joint guidance document, which indicates that prohibited exculpatory language includes only language that frees or appears to free an individual or entity from malpractice, negligence, blame, fault, or guilt. *See* OHRP & FDA, *Guidance on Exculpatory Language in Informed Consent*, http://www.hhs.gov/ohrp/newsroom/rfc/exculpatorydraft2011.html (Aug. 19, 2011).

[14] *See* 45 C.F.R. § 46.116.

[15] *See* 45 C.F.R. § 46.116(d).

[16] *See* 45 C.F.R. § 46.117.

subjects, and (2) improve the efficiency of the IRB review process.[17] One of the key issues identified by the ANPRM is that the number of research studies subject to the Common Rule's requirements has steadily increased since the adoption of the rule, which has made it difficult for overworked IRBs to assess appropriately the risk of all studies. The ANPRM thus proposes a move toward a risk-based framework, for example by introducing a default presumption that all protocols that consist of research categories that have been identified by the Secretary of HHS as eligible for expedited review also be considered minimal risk and thus automatically subject to expedited review.[18] The ANPRM further proposes modifying the expedited review procedure such that not all of the criteria required for IRB approval of research, as discussed in section II.a above, need be considered for studies undergoing expedited review.[19] Another of the ANPRM's proposals to streamline the IRB approval process involves mandating that one, central IRB become the IRB of record in instances in which a study is carried out at multiple sites, which is an increasingly frequent phenomenon in clinical trials.

A second goal of the ANPRM is to increase the Common Rule's protections related to privacy risks, that is, risks resulting from inappropriate access to identifiable information collected in research studies, in contrast to the physical and psychological risks on which the Common Rule has traditionally focused. In so doing, the ANPRM proposes to adopt the standards of the Health Insurance Portability and Accountability Act of 1996 (HIPAA) regarding when data pertaining to human subjects are considered "de-identified," in place of its current standard that information is identifiable if the identity of the subject may "readily be ascertained" by the investigator.[20] Such a change is important because research that does not involve interaction with human subjects is only subject to the Common Rule if the researcher obtains "[i]dentifiable private information" regarding the subject.[21] Moving to the HIPAA standard of de-identification, which is a stricter standard than the "readily ascertainable" standard of the Common Rule, could thus effectively result in an expansion of the definition of human subjects research. In the realm of biospecimens, the ANPRM proposes to move beyond the HIPAA definition of "de-identification" by considering all research on biospecimens to be research involving identifiable information, due to new technologies that allow for re-identification of individuals through the use of genetic information contained in their biospecimens.[22] Accordingly, the protections of the Common Rule would be extended to all research on biospecimens, regardless of whether the biospecimens are labeled with identifiers that would traditionally have been considered to render them "identifiable" to researchers.

The ANPRM also proposes a major change to researchers' ability to use data and biospecimens for future research studies. Researchers often wish to perform future research on biospecimens and data collected during a research study despite the fact that at the time of obtaining informed consent for collection of the biospecimens and data the researcher may not know the form the future research will take. Currently, researchers can conduct such future research by (1) removing a sufficient number of identifiers from the data and biospecimens such that the identity of the subject may not "readily be ascertained," or (2) by obtaining a waiver of informed consent from the cognizant IRB. The ANPRM would eliminate these possibilities by requiring that a subject always provide consent in writing for future research uses of his or her biospecimens and data, regardless of whether such biospecimens and data have been stripped of identifiers.[23] The ANPRM

17 *See* 76 Fed. Reg. 44,512 (July 26, 2011). 18 *See id.* at 44,516–517. 19 *See id.* at 44,517.

20 *See id.* at 44,525; for a further discussion of HIPAA's requirements for "de-identification," *see* Sharona Hoffman's article in this volume.

21 *See* 45 C.F.R. § 46.102(f). 22 *See* 76 Fed. Reg. at 44,525. 23 *See id.* at 44,515, 44,519.

attempts to accommodate future research uses of biospecimens and data by indicating that the written consent "need not be study-specific, and could cover open-ended future research"; however, the ANPRM also notes that subjects must be permitted to opt out of all future research uses of their biospecimens and data, and that participation in a research study cannot be conditioned on agreeing to allow future, open-ended research uses of biospecimens.[24] Many researchers have thus been alarmed by the possibility that subjects could "opt out" of all future research uses of their biospecimens and data, thus preventing the use of such materials, in contrast to the present situation, in which IRBs can grant waivers of informed consent for future uses.[25] If, indeed, any significant number of subjects were allowed to "opt out" of future research uses, this could endanger the reliability and representativeness of subject populations in "future use" studies.

It has now been over three years since the issuance of the ANPRM, and there has been no indication of when, if ever, a proposed let alone final rule will be issued. This is likely due to the fact that changes to the Common Rule require agreement among the disparate federal departments and agencies that have adopted it. Nevertheless, representatives from OHRP continue to indicate that the ANPRM is under consideration by HHS.

c. Distinctions between the FDA's Human Subjects Research Regulations and the Common Rule

As noted in section II.a, the second regime of regulations governing human subjects research is that administered by the FDA.[26] These regulations apply when research is a clinical investigation involving a drug for which the FDA has granted an investigational new drug (IND) application, a device for which the FDA has granted an investigational device exemption (IDE) application, or where the research will otherwise be used in support of applications for research or marketing permits for products regulated by the FDA.[27] It is quite common for research to be subject to both the requirements of the Common Rule and those of the FDA, for example, when an IND or IDE trial is supported by funding from the National Institutes of Health (NIH), or when an IND or IDE trial is conducted in an institution that has voluntarily committed to OHRP jurisdiction over all research it conducts.

FDA regulations governing human subjects research are very similar to those of the Common Rule in that they both require IRB review of most research, they contain identical requirements for IRB membership, and their requirements for the content of IRB review are nearly identical. One important area where the two regimes do differ relates to waiver of informed consent requirements. As discussed above, under the Common Rule an IRB may grant a general waiver from informed consent requirements for cases in which the research is determined to involve minimal risk to subjects and certain other conditions are met. The

[24] *See id.* at 44,515, 44,519–520.

[25] *See* Secretary's Advisory Committee on Human Research Protections, Recommendation Relative to the ANPRM, at 27–37 (Oct. 13, 2011); Association of American Medical Colleges, Comments on Docket No. HHS-OPHS-2011-0005, at 16 (Oct. 25, 2011).

[26] Lewis Grossman's article in this volume discusses in greater depth the FDA's regulation of drugs and devices, including its clinical trial regime.

[27] *See* 21 C.F.R. § 50.1.

FDA's regulation do not permit such a general waiver but rather allow for an exception from the informed consent requirement only in instances in which (1) the research subject is faced with a life-threatening condition that renders him or her unable to give informed consent, and (2) there is no time to obtain consent from the subject's legally authorized representative.[28] Thus if research will later be used in support of an application before the FDA, the investigator must take care that the research is not performed under a waiver of informed consent in the absence of a life-threatening condition. The Common Rule and FDA regulations also require a different party to certify compliance with the regulations: The institution receiving federal funding must certify compliance with the Common Rule, whereas the sponsor of a clinical investigation, for example, a pharmaceutical manufacturer, is the certifying party under FDA regulations.

d. State Laws on Informed Consent

In addition to the informed consent requirements imposed by the Common Rule and the FDA, state legislatures have imposed additional informed consent requirements on biomedical research, oftentimes specific to research involving certain types of testing such as genetic testing. Roughly half the states have enacted legislation that requires informed consent prior to the performance of a genetic test and/or the disclosure of genetic information obtained from such a test.[29] Accordingly, researchers performing genetic testing in states with such laws must disclose as part of the informed consent process that genetic testing will take place as part of the research, and they must specify which parties will receive the results of the genetic test.

While state laws regarding genetic testing were often enacted to help individuals understand the meaning of tests they undergo and to prevent discriminatory use of such test results by life or health insurance companies,[30] the wording of some state genetic testing laws has proved problematic for researchers. For instance, New York state law requires that written informed consent for genetic tests provide a general description of each disease or condition tested for and the level of certainty that a positive test result for a disease condition serves as a predictor of a disease.[31] Fulfilling such conditions in the research context is often not feasible because no level of certainty of the meaning of test results has been established, and moreover, research results are oftentimes not returned to subjects. The statute permits modification of the informed consent form by an IRB in instances in which the research protocol would not allow for return of genetic test results, thus requiring researchers conducting genetic testing in New York to seek consideration by the IRB of this point.[32] New York law also requires that if previously collected biospecimens are to be used in research involving genetic tests, an IRB must approve the research, even if the specimens are not identifiable and thus the research would generally not be considered human subjects research under

[28] *See* 21 C.F.R. § 50.24.

[29] *See, e.g.*, Ill. Cons. Stat. tit. 410, § 513/30.

[30] California is an example of a state in which a statutory requirement for consent to genetic testing applies only where the results of the test are requested by an insurance company. *See* Cal. Ins. Code § 10149.1.

[31] *See* N.Y. Civ. Rights Law § 79-*l*(2).

[32] *See* N.Y. Civ. Rights Law § 79-*l*(2)(f).

the Common Rule.[33] These provisions present potential pitfalls to researchers performing genetic tests on specimens derived from New York, as well as researchers who perform this research testing in New York.

Massachusetts provides an example of a state that has taken a more researcher-friendly approach to genetic testing. Like New York, Massachusetts generally requires that prior to undergoing a genetic test, an individual execute a written informed consent that includes a general description of each specific disease or condition tested for, as well as the reliability of test results in detecting such disease or condition.[34] However, in the case of clinical research approved by an IRB, Massachusetts does not require this type of written informed consent. Furthermore, Massachusetts' law allows for disclosure of genetic test results by researchers to third parties without the consent of the subject so long as the results are encrypted or encoded such that the identify of the subject of the test is unknown to the researcher receiving the test results.

III Privacy Laws

a. Health Insurance Portability and Accountability Act of 1996 Research Requirements

In addition to the Common Rule and FDA regulations governing informed consent, biomedical research is also subject to a separate body of law governing the privacy of health information. The primary federal law in this area is the Health Insurance Portability and Accountability Act of 1996 (HIPAA). HIPAA is discussed in great detail in Sharona Hoffman's article of this *Handbook*; here we focus solely on the provisions of HIPAA that are applicable to biomedical research.

Regulations promulgated under HIPAA, referred to collectively as the Privacy Rule, govern the use and disclosure of protected health information (PHI). PHI is defined as individually identifiable health information that is created or received by a "covered entity," such as a healthcare provider or health insurance company.[35] Accordingly, biomedical researchers who conduct research at a covered entity are generally subject to the constraints of HIPAA.

Recognizing that HIPAA could potentially frustrate biomedical research occurring at covered entities, the law has certain provisions intended to ease the process of using and disclosing PHI for "research" purposes, with the term "research" defined consistently with the Common Rule.[36] Where a new research study is being undertaken, permission to use and disclose a research subject's PHI during the course of the research is generally obtained through a "HIPAA Authorization," which is a written form containing several required elements, such as a description of the PHI to be used or disclosed, a description of each purpose of the requested use or disclosure, the name of the persons or class of persons who may receive the information, and an expiration date, which in the case of a research study may

[33] *See* N.Y. Civ. Rights Law § 79-*l*(9).
[34] *See* Mass. Gen. Laws ch. 111, § 70G.
[35] *See* 45 C.F.R. §§ 160.102–103.
[36] *See* 45 C.F.R. § 164.501.

simply state "the end of the research" or "none."[37] While the authorization may be a stand-alone form, the Privacy Rule permits the authorization to be combined with an informed consent form for participation in research. Accordingly, in practice, the HIPAA authorization is often integrated into the informed consent form used for the research, meaning that it is subject to review by an IRB and the research subject supplies one signature for both the HIPAA authorization and the informed consent form.

HIPAA's requirements related to authorizations for research uses and disclosures of PHI became more "researcher-friendly" with the issuance of the HIPAA Omnibus Rule of 2013 (the Omnibus Rule).[38] Prior to the issuance of the Omnibus Rule, the HHS's Office for Civil Rights (OCR), which enforces HIPAA, interpreted the law as requiring that an authorization for the use or disclosure of PHI be research study specific in order to meet the Privacy Rule's requirement that an authorization include a description of each purpose of the requested use or disclosure.[39] Accordingly, a researcher was unable to obtain a "broad authorization" that allows for PHI collected in a given study to be used for future research. In the Omnibus Rule, OCR revised its interpretation to permit a subject to provide authorization for future research so long as the research is "adequately described" such that it is "reasonable" for the data subject to expect that his or her PHI will be used for the given research.[40] Because OCR declined to prescribe specific statements that would "adequately describe" future research, this interpretation provides researchers a degree of flexibility in interpreting the requirement.

In addition to permitting research subjects to provide authorization for future research uses of their PHI, the Omnibus Rule also made it easier for researchers to request such authorization by permitting for the first time the combination of an authorization for use of PHI in the present study with an authorization to use PHI in *another study*, such as for the creation of a research database or repository.[41] In so doing, the HIPAA Omnibus Rule's acceptance of authorizations that allow for collection of PHI for a research database or repository is consistent with the ANPRM's proposal to allow broad consent for future research on biospecimens.

Recognizing that there may be situations in which a covered entity wishes to use or disclose PHI for research purposes in circumstances in which it is not practicable to obtain a signed authorization from the subject of the PHI, HIPAA permits the use and disclosure of PHI for research purposes in the absence of written authorization of the research subject in the following situations:

1. Reviews of PHI "preparatory to research," such as where the PHI is sought solely to prepare a research protocol and the PHI is not removed from the covered entity;
2. Research that takes place solely on the PHI of decedents; and
3. Research involving only a "limited data set," that is, PHI that has been stripped of all identifiers with the exception of dates, such as date of birth or treatment date, and certain geographic information. When a limited data set is used, the party receiving the limited data set must enter into a data use agreement (DUA) with the party supplying the PHI pursuant to which the receiving party agrees to several limitations on its use

[37] *See* 45 C.F.R. § 164.508(c). [38] *See* 78 Fed. Reg. 5566 (Jan. 25, 2013).
[39] *See* 67 Fed. Reg. 53,182, 53,226 (Aug. 14, 2002).
[40] *See* 78 Fed. Reg. at 6513. [41] *See* 45 C.F.R. § 164.508(b)(1)(i).

of the data, including that the receiving party will not use or further disclose the PHI other than as permitted by the DUA and will not attempt to identify the PHI or contact the individuals who are the subject of the PHI.[42]

In addition to the above-cited research exceptions, similar to the Common Rule's provisions allowing for a waiver of informed consent, the HIPAA regulations allow for an IRB or privacy board to grant a waiver of HIPAA authorization in situations in which the use or disclosure of PHI involves no more than a minimal risk to the privacy of individuals, the research could not practicably be conducted without the waiver or alteration, and the research could not practicably be conducted without access to the individually identifiable health information in question.[43]

It is important to keep in mind that the requirements of HIPAA do not apply to health information that has been "de-identified" either through the removal of the eighteen identifiers specified in the Privacy Rule or through certification by a statistical expert that the data are no longer identifiable.[44] Accordingly, in instances in which a researcher does not require information containing any of the eighteen HIPAA identifiers, the researcher may be able to take the research out of the realm of HIPAA by working solely with de-identified data. It remains to be seen whether OCR will curtail the availability of de-identification in biospecimen research by adopting the position proposed by OHRP in the ANPRM and declaring all biospecimens to be identifiable due to advances in technology.

b. State Privacy Law Requirements

In addition to HIPAA, many state privacy laws impact biomedical research. These laws oftentimes apply to health information concerning a specific disease or area of illness deemed to be particularly sensitive, such as mental health, substance abuse, HIV/AIDS, sexually transmitted diseases, mental retardation, and developmental disabilities.[45] Such laws may require that extra precautions be taken to protect the privacy of individuals participating in research that could reveal their status with respect to these diseases or disorders, such as through using "check-the-box" permission in informed consent forms.

IV Clinical Trials Registration and Data Transparency

An additional topic that has recently come to the forefront of biomedical research is the advent of requirements that clinical trials be publicly registered and that summary results

[42] *See* 45 C.F.R. §§ 164.512, 164.514.

[43] A "privacy board," which is a creation of the HIPAA Privacy Rule, is a board with membership and functions similar to that of an IRB. *See* 45 C.F.R. § 164.512(i).

[44] *See* 45 C.F.R. § 164.514(b).

[45] *See, e.g.*, Neb. Rev. Stat. § 38-2136 (providing that mental health practitioners shall only release information pursuant to the written consent of the subject); Cal. Health & Safety Code, § 11845.5 (requiring that all records regarding alcohol and other substance abuse treatment be released only with the prior written consent of the subject).

of trials be made publicly available. The movement to register clinical trials began with the Food and Drug Administration Modernization Act of 1997 (FDAMA), which mandated the establishment of a database of clinical trials of drugs treating "serious or life-threatening conditions," a list of investigational new drug applications for expanded access protocols, and experimental treatments available as Group C cancer drugs.[46] The purpose of the database was to provide a resource for patients suffering from serious diseases to find a clinical trial of an experimental treatment for their disease in which they might seek enrollment. Accordingly, the information to be provided to the database was limited to eligibility criteria for participation in the trial, a description of the location of trial sites, and the point of contact for the trial.[47] FDAMA's statutory mandate regarding a database of clinical trials was fulfilled through the creation of ClinicalTrials.gov in 2000.

The requirement of clinical trial registration expanded greatly in 2007 with the passage of the Food and Drug Administration Amendments Act (FDAAA). FDAAA expanded the clinical trial registration requirement to nearly all drug clinical trials, with the exception of Phase I trials, and to nearly all medical device clinical trials.[48] In addition to expanding the types of trials for which registration is required, FDAAA also introduced for the first time a requirement that summary results of registered trials that form the primary basis of an efficacy claim or are conducted after the drug or device tested has received FDA clearance or approval be submitted for posting on ClinicalTrials.gov. Due to the posting of summary results, regulations promulgated under FDAAA mandate that informed consent forms used in clinical trials subject to FDAAA's reporting requirements include the following language:

> A description of this clinical trial will be available on http://www.ClinicalTrials.gov, as required by U.S. law. This Web site will not include information that can identify you. At most, the Web site will include a summary of the results. You can search this Web site at any time.[49]

The shift to requiring results reporting in addition to registration of ongoing trials significantly changed the rationale for ClinicalTrials.gov. Instead of operating primarily as a tool to help patients suffering from a serious disease to identify enrollment opportunities in ongoing clinical trials, it began to function as a way to provide information that could allow patients, healthcare providers, and researchers to compare the efficacy of different treatments and to verify whether the results of a given clinical trial have been replicable.

Since the expansion of ClinicalTrials.gov to include summary results, there have been many additional efforts to expand the public availability of clinical trial results, as well as the underlying data from certain trials. For example, the medical journal, *BMJ*, began requiring in January 2013 that authors publish or disclose anonymized, subject-level data gathered in clinical trials upon reasonable request. Around that same time, the European Medicines Agency (EMA) announced that it would develop a policy requiring that participant-level clinical trials data used to support a medication marketing authorization

[46] *See* Food & Drug Modernization Act of 1997, Pub. L. No. 105-115, § 113. Group C cancer drugs are investigational study drugs that have "shown evidence of relative and reproducible efficacy in a specific tumor type" and are distributed by the National Institutes of Health under National Cancer Institute protocols for treatment purposes. *See* FDA, Treatment Use of Investigational Drugs, Guidance for Institution Review Boards and Clinical Investigators, *available at* http://www.fda.gov/RegulatoryInformation/Guidances/ucm126495.htm.

[47] *See* Pub. L. No. 105-115, § 113.

[48] *See* FDAAA, Pub. L. No. 110-85, § 801 (2007), 42 U.S.C. § 282(j).

[49] 21 C.F.R. § 50.25(c).

with the EMA be made publicly available. The first phase of this policy was finalized on October 2, 2014; it provides that the EMA will make available at the time a decision is made regarding a drug's marketing authorization "clinical reports," that is, clinical study reports, clinical overviews, and clinical summaries, which correspond to modules 5, 2.5, and 2.7, respectively, of the International Conference on Harmonisation of Technical Requirements for Registration of Pharmaceuticals for Human Use ("ICH") common documents.[50] While the "clinical reports" to be made available under the first phase of the policy generally do not contain participant-level data, the EMA has stated that a second phase of the policy will make participant-level data available. The EMA's draft policy is important to U.S. researchers because clinical data gathered in the United States that are used to support marketing authorizations with the EMA will be subject to the policy. It is also important to note that any future requirement that participant-level clinical trial data be made publicly available will be inconsistent with the language required to be added to informed consent forms under FDAAA, which indicates that "at most" a summary of the results will be made publicly available. This introduces the possibility that informed consent forms will have to be changed in the United States to account for the possibility that participant-level clinical trial data will be made available under a future phase of the EMA's policy.

The FDA has also some shown interest in developing mechanisms for making participant-level clinical trial data available to researchers on request. In June 2013, the FDA issued a request for comments on a proposal to make available for future research participant-level data from medical product applications.[51] The FDA's proposal indicated that data released would be both "masked," meaning that they would be stripped of information that could link them to a specific product or application, and "de-identified," defined to mean that the data would not provide a reasonable basis to believe that the subject of the data could be identified. The FDA received comments evidencing a wide variety of concerns in response to this proposal, including that data could be "unmasked" and/or "re-identified," that masking of data could render them useless to subsequent analysis, and that sponsors of trials for which data were released could suffer competitive harms.[52] There has yet to be any subsequent activity by the FDA on this request for comments.[53]

[50] *See* European Medicines Agency Policy on Publication of Clinical Data for Medicinal Products for Human Use Policy/0070. The clinical study reports to be released under the policy will include the main body of the report, along with the following three appendices: 16.1.1 (protocol and protocol amendments), 16.1.2 (sample case report forms), and 16.1.9 (documentation of statistical methods).

[51] Availability of Anonymized Non-Summary Safety and Efficacy Data; Request for Comments, 78 Fed. Reg. 33,421 (June 4, 2013).

[52] *See* Availability of Anonymized Non-Summary Safety and Efficacy Data; Request for Comments, FDA Docket No. 2013-N-0271, http://www.regulations.gov/#!docketDetail;D=FDA-2013-N-0271.

[53] In addition to the governmental efforts discussed in the text, several pharmaceutical companies have announced voluntary initiatives to make available their clinical trials data to secondary researchers. GlaxoSmithKline (GSK) in particular has created a web portal through which researchers may request access to data from GSK and nine competitor pharmaceutical companies. *See* http://www.ClinicalStudyDataRequest.com. For more information on clinical trial transparency, see the website of the Multi-Regional Clinical Trials Center (MRCT) at Harvard University, which focuses on trial transparency. *See* http://mrct.globalhealth.harvard.edu/.

V Financial Disclosure Requirements

Investigator conflicts of interest are another focus of laws governing biomedical research. Like the regulations governing human subjects research protections, two parallel regulatory regimes exist: one for research funded by Public Health Services Act (PHS) agencies and offices (e.g., the National Institutes of Health) and a second for research involving products regulated by the FDA.[54]

The PHS regulations apply to institutions that receive PHS research funding and are designed to promote objectivity in research by establishing standards that provide a reasonable expectation that research funded under PHS grants will be free from bias resulting from *financial* conflicts of interest.[55] Toward that end, rather than prohibit researchers from having financial interests that could be viewed as creating a conflict of interest, the regulations require disclosure of several types of financial interests held by investigators, as well as their spouses and dependent children. Reportable interests include remuneration received from entities in excess of $5,000, equity interests in excess of $5,000 in publicly traded entities, any equity interest held in a nonpublicly traded entity, and intellectual property rights and interests from which income is received.[56]

Modifications made in 2011 to the PHS financial disclosure rules significantly expanded reporting requirements by mandating the disclosure of all interests meeting the given financial thresholds, whereas previously, investigators were required to disclose only those interests that they deemed "related" to the PHS-funded research in question.[57] Disclosure under the PHS regulations is to be made to an official designated by the institution at which the research occurs, who is to determine whether a financial interest constitutes a financial conflict of interest, that is, whether it could directly and significantly affect the design, conduct, or reporting of the PHS-funded research.[58] Each institution is required to develop its own guidelines for helping the designated official determine whether a financial conflict of interest exists and for managing such conflicts of interest once identified. If the designated official determines that a financial conflict of interest exists, such conflict must be reported to the PHS agency awarding funding for the research.[59]

The FDA's regulations regarding financial conflicts of interest differ from the PHS regulations on this topic in that while requiring disclosure of a narrower category of financial interests, they require disclosure directly to the FDA rather than to the research institution. Such disclosures are generally made by the sponsor of research rather than the investigator or the institution at which the research takes place. An applicant submitting clinical studies in support of FDA approval of a product must disclose the following types of interests to the FDA: (1) financial arrangements between the sponsor of the study and the investigator that

[54] A complete listing of the PHS agencies and offices may be found at the following link: http://www.usphs.gov/aboutus/agencies/hhs.aspx.

[55] *See* 45 C.F.R. § 50.601.

[56] *See* 45 C.F.R. § 50.603. The regulations provide for certain carve-outs from the disclosure requirement for activities that are unlikely to create a conflict of interest, such as income from seminars, lectures, or teaching sponsored by a governmental agency or an institution of higher education. *See id.*

[57] *See* 76 Fed. Reg. 53,256, 53,263 (Aug. 25, 2011).

[58] *See* 42 C.F.R. § 50.604.

[59] *See id.* § 50.605.

could result in the value of the compensation received by the investigator for conducting the study being influenced by the outcome of the study; (2) payment in any form from the sponsor of the study to the investigator having a monetary value in excess of $25,000; (3) any proprietary interest in the tested product held by the investigator, such as a patent, trademark, copyright, or licensing agreement; and (4) any steps taken to minimize the potential for bias resulting from any of the disclosed arrangements.[60] The FDA reviews the disclosed financial interests to determine whether they may impact the reliability of a study submitted to the agency in support of a marketing application for a drug or device. If the FDA determines that the financial interests of a clinical investigator draw into question the integrity of the submitted data, it may take actions such as initiating audits of data, requiring submission of further data analyses, or refusing to consider data from the study.[61] In practice, when an investigator has reported a financial interest to a research sponsor at the outset of a study, the sponsor typically meets with the FDA to determine the best methods of controlling for potential bias in the trial.

It is important to note that neither PHS nor FDA regulations require that research subjects be informed of financial conflicts of interest, nor do they require that the IRB be informed of such potential conflicts of interest. Consequently, research subjects are often not aware that a conflict of interest may exist at the time they decide to participate in research.

VI Research Misconduct

One of the legal issues governing biomedical research that is most often discussed in the popular press is that of research fraud, which is referred to in relevant regulations as "research misconduct." There have been several prominent examples of research misconduct in recent years, such as ex-Harvard researcher Marc Hauser's study of nonhuman primates, in which Hauser was found to have fabricated research data, resulting in the redaction of one published article and the correction of two additional articles.[62] Like many of the other topics discussed in this article, research misconduct is subject to multiple, sometimes overlapping, regulatory regimes.

When funding for research is provided by a PHS agency or department, the HHS Office of Research Integrity (ORI) has jurisdiction over any misconduct that occurs during the research.[63] ORI's regulations indicate that research misconduct includes "fabrication, falsification, or plagiarism in proposing, performing, or reviewing research, or in reporting research results."[64] These activities are defined as follows:

> **Fabrication**: making up data or results and recording or reporting them.
>
> **Falsification**: manipulating research materials, equipment, or processes, or changing or omitting data or results such that the research is not accurately represented in the research record.

[60] *See* 21 C.F.R. pt. 54. [61] *See* 21 C.F.R. § 54.5.

[62] *See* Carolyn Y. Johnson, *Ex-Harvard Scientist Fabricated, Manipulated Data, Report Says*, Boston Globe, Sept. 5, 2012, http://www.bostonglobe.com/news/science/2012/09/05/harvard-professor-who-resigned-fabricated-manipulated-data-says/6gDVkzPNxv1ZDkh4wVnKhO/story.html.

[63] *See* 42 C.F.R. § 93.102. [64] *See* 42 C.F.R § 93.103.

Plagiarism: appropriation of another person's ideas, processes, results, or words without giving appropriate credit.

A finding of research misconduct requires that the misconduct be committed intentionally, knowingly, or recklessly, and that the allegation be proven by a preponderance of the evidence.[65]

Procedurally, an investigation of misconduct generally begins when an institution receives credible allegation of conduct meeting the above definition of research misconduct.[66] The institution must then begin an "institutional inquiry," which involves obtaining custody of all research records and evidence needed to conduct the inquiry. These efforts are generally led by a research integrity officer (RIO). The purpose of the institutional inquiry is to determine whether a reasonable basis exists to conclude that the allegation falls within the federal definition of "research misconduct" and the allegation has any substance.[67] At the conclusion of the "institutional inquiry," the institution must complete a written "inquiry report" laying out its decision regarding whether to pursue an investigation into the alleged misconduct.[68]

If the institution determines through its inquiry that an investigation is warranted, the institution must report the finding and provide a copy of the inquiry report to ORI within thirty days.[69] Once the institution decides to pursue an investigation, it must provide notice to the respondent, obtain custody of all necessary records, interview the respondent and the complainant, and pursue diligently all significant issues and leads discovered that are determined to be relevant to the investigation.[70] The investigation must be completed within one hundred twenty days of its start date, including preparation of a report of findings and providing the report to ORI.[71] The report submitted to ORI must indicate whether research misconduct was uncovered, whether the institution accepts the findings of the investigation, and describe any pending or completed administrative actions taken by the institution against the respondent.[72]

After receiving a research misconduct report from an institution, ORI may review the research misconduct proceedings to determine whether HHS jurisdiction exists, whether the research misconduct proceedings were conducted properly, and whether misconduct actually occurred.[73] Based on these findings, ORI may propose that the HHS take administrative actions, such as clarification, correction, or retraction of the research record, issuance of letters of reprimand, special review of all of the investigator's requests for PHS funding, imposition of supervision requirements on PHS grants, contracts or cooperative agreements, or suspending or debarring an individual from receiving federal funds.[74] Notice of findings of research misconduct may also be published in the *Federal Register*.[75]

Separate and apart from the research misconduct regime that is applicable to PHS-funded research and enforced by ORI, a separate regime of enforcement, administered by OHRP, exists to ensure the integrity of research subject to the Common Rule. Unlike ORI's processes with regard to research misconduct, which focus on fabrication, falsification, or

[65] *See* 42 C.F.R. § 93.104. [66] *See* 42 C.F.R. § 93.307(a).
[67] *See id.* (c)–(d). [68] *See id.* (e).
[69] *See* 42 C.F.R. § 93.309. [70] *See* 42 C.F.R. § 93.310. [71] *See* 42 C.F.R. § 93.311.
[72] *See* 42 C.F.R. §§ 93.312-13. [73] *See* 42 C.F.R. § 93.403. [74] *See* 42 C.F.R. § 93.407.
[75] *See* 42 C.F.R. § 93.411.

plagiarism by an *individual investigator*, OHRP's jurisdiction derives from an *institution*'s failure to abide by the promise contained in its FWA that its human subjects research adhere to the standards of the Common Rule.[76]

Violations of the Common Rule giving rise to an OHRP investigation may include deviation from the research protocol approved by the IRB, failure to obtain or falsification of informed consent forms, enrollment of subjects who do not meet eligibility criteria, and failure to report unanticipated problems involving study subjects. OHRP's investigations occur both in response to specific allegations of Common Rule violations and through not-for-cause evaluations of an institution's compliance with the Common Rule. If OHRP's investigation reveals noncompliance, it will impose a corrective action plan; it may also impose conditions on FWA research conducted while the corrective action plan is completed, or even suspend an institution's FWA entirely, thereby requiring suspension of all federally supported research activities until reinstatement of the FWA.[77]

Products regulated by the FDA are subject to a third research misconduct regime. If an investigator provides false information to the sponsor and the FDA, the FDA may terminate the investigator's ability to receive and use INDs or IDEs, and it may also "debar" such investigator, that is, prohibit him or her from working for anyone with an approved or pending drug product application before the FDA.[78] Recognizing a need for additional guidance in this area, the FDA issued a proposed rule in 2010 entitled "Reporting Information Regarding Falsification of Data" that is designed to ensure the validity of data submitted to the FDA in support of product approvals.[79] This rule puts the onus on sponsors to report falsification of data to the FDA, noting that "sponsors of studies are responsible for ensuring the integrity of study data and are in a better position to discover possible falsification of data through their monitoring, auditing, and reviewing of data."[80] The proposed rule notes that it is needed because the regulations at 42 C.F.R. part 93 apply only to PHS-funded research, which is a narrower category than research on products regulated by the FDA.[81]

In addition to federal regulations governing research misconduct, the policies of scientific journals regarding research misconduct play a significant role in the investigation of and response to research misconduct. The International Committee of Medical Journal Editors (ICMJE) indicates that if substantial doubt arises regarding the honesty or integrity of work that has been submitted or published, it is the responsibility of the editor to ensure that the question is appropriately pursued.[82] Ordinarily, this involves the editor following up with the institution or funding agency to determine the results of any investigation undertaken

[76] *See* OHRP, Compliance Oversight Procedures for Evaluating Institutions, http://www.hhs.gov/ohrp/compliance/evaluation/ohrpcomp.pdf.

[77] For a detailed discussion of the intersection between the research misconduct regime enforced by ORI and that enforced by OHRP, *see* Barbara E. Bierer & Mark Barnes, *Research Misconduct Involving Noncompliance in Human Subjects Research Supported by the Public Health Services: Reconciling Separate Regulatory Systems*, *in* HASTINGS CENTER REPORT: THE INTERSECTION OF RESEARCH FRAUD AND HUMAN SUBJECTS RESEARCH: A REGULATORY REVIEW S2 (Barbara E. Bierer & Mark Barnes eds., 2014).

[78] *See* 21 C.F.R. §§ 312.70, 812.119; 21 U.S.C. § 335a.

[79] *See* 75 Fed. Reg. 7412, 7421–7424 (Feb. 19, 2010) (to be codified at 21 C.F.R. pts. 58, 312, and 812).

[80] *Id.* at 7414. [81] *See id.* at 7417.

[82] *See* ICMJE, *Scientific Misconduct, Expressions of Concern, and Retraction*, http://www.icmje.org/recommendations/browse/publishing-and-editorial-issues/scientific-misconduct-expressions-of-concern-and-retraction.html.

regarding the misconduct. If an investigation has taken place, the editor must notify readers of the outcome of the investigation and, depending on the outcome of the investigation, publish a retraction of the article. Even if no misconduct is proven, ICJME counsels that "an exchange of letters to the editor could be published to highlight matters of debate to readers."[83]

VII Substantive Research Limitations

While the bodies of law discussed above are largely "procedural" in the sense that they regulate the manner in which research is carried out, certain areas of research are subject to substantive limitations imposed by statute or regulation. The substantive area that has received the most attention concerns research involving human embryos and fetuses, particularly embryonic stem cell research. Since 1996, Congress has regularly included a rider to appropriation bills, known as the Dickey-Wicker Amendment, which prohibits the NIH from funding (1) the creation of a human embryo or embryos for research purposes, or (2) research in which a human embryo or embryos are destroyed, discarded, or knowingly subjected to a greater than minimal risk of injury or death.[84] Because harvesting embryonic stem cells for research involves the destruction of human embryos, this amendment effectively prohibits federal funding of the creation of new stem cell lines.

In 2001, President George W. Bush, issued an executive order further limiting federal funding of embryonic stem cell research by indicating that federal funds could only be used if the cells under study were drawn from one of the approximately sixty stem cell lines already in existence at the time of President Bush's declaration.[85] President Barack Obama repealed the Bush Executive Order in 2009 through the issuance of an executive order providing that the NIH may "support and conduct responsible, scientifically worthy stem cell research, including human embryonic stem cell research, to the extent permitted by law."[86] Following the issuance of President Obama's executive order, the NIH issued guidelines permitting NIH funds to be used for embryonic stem cell research projects using cells from lines (1) created by in vitro fertilization for reproductive purposes, (2) no longer needed for that purpose, and (3) voluntarily donated by the individuals who owned them.[87] These guidelines have survived a highly publicized federal court challenge contending that no federal funding of *any* stem cell research is permitted by Dickey-Wicker because all research conducted on embryonic stem cells is necessarily part of the same "research" that involved destruction of the embryos, and thus all such research is prohibited by the Dickey-Wicker Amendment.[88]

[83] *See id.* In addition to ICMJE guidance in the medical field, the Committee on Publication Ethics (COPE), which comprises academic journal editors from a wide range of academic fields, provides further guidelines regarding retraction and expression of concern related to published research. *See* COPE, Retraction Guidelines, http://publicationethics.org/files/retraction%20guidelines.pdf.

[84] *See, e.g.*, Consolidated Appropriations Act, 2012, Pub. L. No. 112-74, § 508 (example of an appropriations bill containing the amendment).

[85] *See* 37 Weekly Comp. Pres. Doc. 1149, 1151 (Aug. 9, 2001).

[86] *See* Exec. Order No. 13,505, 74 Fed. Reg. 10,667 (Mar. 11, 2009).

[87] *See* 74 Fed. Reg. 32,170, 32,173 (July 7, 2009).

[88] *See* Sherley v. Sebelius, 689 F.3d 776, 781 (D.C. Cir. 2012).

Independent of concerns regarding federal funding of embryonic stem cell research, several states have adopted laws that impact research on fetuses and embryos. Because these laws vary widely and are often worded ambiguously, researchers who wish to perform research involving human embryos must be careful to evaluate applicable state laws. For example, Arizona law makes it a felony to destroy human embryos to produce pluripotent stem cells or stem cell lines, whereas Louisiana goes further and prohibits all use of human embryos for research purposes and treats a human embryo as a "juridical person" entitled to sue or be sued.[89] Accordingly, researchers in these two states may not create new human embryonic stem cell lines, even if no federal funding is involved. Other states have laws that could be interpreted broadly to prohibit all research involving human embryos. Pennsylvania, for instance, bans "fetal experimentation" upon any "unborn child," defining "unborn child" as "an individual organism of the species homo sapiens from fertilization until live birth."[90] Because this prohibition begins at *fertilization*, read literally it would appear to prohibit all experimentation involving human embryos, although sources suggest that in practice it has not been interpreted or enforced in such a manner.[91]

VIII Animal Research Requirements

While our focus thus far has been on regulations applicable to research on human subjects, a parallel regulatory regime has developed governing research on animals. The Animal Welfare Act of 1966 was the first law in this area and is administered by the U.S. Department of Agriculture, Animal and Plant Health Inspection Service (APHIS).[92] APHIS regulations apply to any "research facility," such as a university, that uses live animals in research and either transports animals in commerce or receives funds under a grant, award, loan, or contract from the United States for the purpose of carrying out research, tests, or experiments.[93] Importantly, the term "animal" under the regulations is defined to include any warm-blooded animal used for research, but explicitly excludes birds, rats, and mice, bred for use in research.[94] The APHIS regulations impose several requirements, including that subject institutions form an Institutional Animal Care and Use Committee (IACUC) to assess their program for the humane care and use of animals, inspect facilities used in animal research, and review studies involving animals, somewhat akin to an IRB.[95]

When research involving animals is funded by one of the PHS agencies, the research is also subject to the policies of the NIH Office of Laboratory Animal Welfare (OLAW), which was developed to fulfill the Health Research Extension Act of 1985's mandate that the director of the NIH establish guidelines for the "proper care of animals to be used in biomedical and behavioral research."[96] OLAW's policies apply to *all* vertebrate animals and are intended

[89] *See* Ariz. Rev. Stat. §§ 36-2311(1); 36-2313; La. Rev. Stat. §§ 9:124, 9:129.

[90] *See* 18 Pa. Cons. Stat. §§ 3216, 3203.

[91] *See* Commonwealth v. Bullock, 590 Pa. 480, 500 (2006) (Baer, J. concurring); Fotini Antonia Skouvakis, *Defining the Undefined: Using a Best Interests Approach to Decide the Fate of Cryopreserved Preembryos in Pennsylvania*, 109 Penn. State L. Rev. 885, 902 (2005).

[92] *See* Pub. L. No. 89-544 (1966), *codified at* 7 U.S.C. § 2131 *et seq.*

[93] *See* 9 C.F.R. § 1.1.

[94] *See id.*

[95] *See* 9 C.F.R. §§ 2.31, 2.33.

[96] *See* Pub. L. No. 99-158 § 495 (1985).

to complement rather than replace those of APHIS.[97] Like the Common Rule, which many institutions choose to apply to all of their human subjects research regardless of source of funding, many institutions choose to apply the OLAW policy to all research involving animals.

In addition to the APHIS regulations and OLAW policies, many institutions performing research on animals seek accreditation by the Association for Assessment and Accreditation of Laboratory Animal Care International (AAALAC) a private, nonprofit organization that develops standards to promote the humane treatment of animals in science. The NIH and the U.S. Department of Agriculture have indicated that certain programs offered by AAALAC may meet the regulatory and policy requirements that an institution's IACUC regularly assess the institution's program for humane care and use of animals.[98]

IX Additional Considerations Related to Federal Funding of Research

a. Federal Grant Principles

We have mentioned several times in this article the existence of certain regulatory regimes that apply to research conducted with federal funding. The federal government funds research through both grants and contracts. Grants provide funding to support the grant recipient's research, whereas contracts involve the purchase of research services that are of direct benefit to the federal government. Recipients of both federal grants and contracts are subject to a complex set of rules that place restraints on how the federally funded research may be carried out. For federal grants, this includes cost principles that establish standards for which expenses may be charged against a federal grant, administrative requirements that establish standards for institutional administration of federal grants, and audit standards for monitoring the ways in which federal grant funds are spent.

Principles governing all federal grants were previously set forth in various "circulars" maintained by the Office of Management and Budget (OMB), which are codified in separate regulations promulgated by each funding agency. In late 2013, the OMB published final guidance in the *Federal Register* superseding the "circulars" and consolidating in one place the federal government's grant principles.[99] The stated intent of the new guidance is to streamline the federal grant-making and monitoring process, to ease the administrative burden for grant applicants and recipients, and to reduce the risk of waste, fraud, and abuse. These rules are extremely detailed and complex, and thus require a great deal of attention by recipients of federal funding. Importantly, failure of a recipient institution to use funds for intended

[97] *See* Office of Laboratory Animal Welfare, *Public Health Service Policy on Human Care and Use of Laboratory Animals*, http://grants.nih.gov/grants/olaw/references/phspol.htm#Introduction.

[98] *See* Office of Extramural Research Guidance Regarding Reduction of Regulatory Burden in Laboratory Animal Welfare, Notice OD-00-007 (Dec. 21, 1999), http://grants.nih.gov/grants/guide/notice-files/NOT-OD-00-007.html.

[99] 78 Fed. Reg. 78,590 (Dec. 26, 2013). Each federal funding agency is required to promulgate its own regulations implementing these requirements by December 26, 2014.

purposes, or failure to fulfill scopes of work with funds received, or even the production of research of inferior quality and reliability, can subject the recipient institution to civil and even criminal liability under the Federal False Claims Act.[100]

b. Technology Transfer Considerations

Because so much of the biomedical research conducted in the United States is carried out at research universities and their affiliated academic medical centers, a major component of the biomedical research enterprise concerns so-called "technology transfer," that is, the transfer of research results developed in universities or academic medical centers to outside entities for commercialization. Much of the research conducted at universities and academic medical centers is funded by federal government grants or carried out pursuant to federal contracts, and thus a key question that arises is the extent to which discoveries made during the course of such research may be patented by the university or academic medical center at which they were made.

The Bayh-Dole Act of 1980 revolutionized this area of intellectual property law by permitting universities, nonprofit organizations, and small businesses to retain title to innovations developed with federal funding.[101] To carry out this goal, the Bayh-Dole Act empowered the U.S. Department of Commerce to create standard contractual clauses for insertion into contracts providing federal funding for research. These clauses provide that in exchange for being permitted to retain title to an invention made with federal funding, the federal funding recipient must disclose the "subject invention" to the agency that provided the funding in question, elect in writing whether or not to retain title to the invention, file its initial patent application within one year after electing to retain title to the invention, grant the government a nonexclusive, nontransferable license to the invention, require that any entities receiving an exclusive license to sell subject inventions in the United States agree to manufacture substantially in the United States any products using the subject invention, and permit the government to "march in" and require licenses to be granted if the organization holding title has not taken sufficient steps to achieve practical application of the subject invention.[102] If the organization in question is a nonprofit, the standard contractual clauses require that royalties collected on the license be shared with the inventor and that the balance of any royalties collected after payment of patent expenses be used to support scientific

[100] *See, e.g.*, United States *ex rel.* Feldman v. van Gorp, 697 F.3d 78 (2d Cir. 2012) (affirming a False Claims Act judgment of $855,714 against Cornell University Medical College; the acts giving rise to liability included (1) use of NIH grant funds by research staff who had not been listed on the grant application, and (2) research on topics that differed from those set forth in the application). *See also* NIH Grants Policy Statement, The National Institutes of Health as a Grant-Making Organization, General Information, § 2.3.10 (2013), http://grants.nih.gov/grants/policy/nihgps_2013/nihgps_ch2.htm.

[101] Patent and Trademark Law Amendments Act, Pub. L. No. 96-517 (1980). Prior to passage of the Bayh-Dole Act, the federal government retained ownership of all inventions made using federal government money, and it licensed such inventions to the private sector on a nonexclusive basis. This regime resulted in no company having an incentive to develop fully an invention because a competitor could also receive a license from the government for the same technology.

[102] *See* 37 C.F.R. §§ 401.3, 401.14(a). The government's "march-in" rights have attracted public attention in the biomedical realm in instances in which patients harmed by the shortage of a critical drug have

research and education. These standard clauses further require that preference in licensing the subject invention be given to small business firms.

The ability of universities to license subject inventions has given rise to large technology transfer offices that are tasked with developing mechanisms for licensing inventions made at the university to private industry. Applied to the biomedical realm these rights are especially important because a university may retain ownership of a biomedical invention and license the invention to a pharmaceutical or medical device company for further development. Oftentimes the licensee is a start-up biotech company that has been spun off from the university for the purpose of commercializing a particular invention.

X Conclusion

The above discussion has reviewed some of the legal and regulatory regimes that must be taken into account by those conducting biomedical research in the United States. These laws continue to evolve, as the scientific capabilities of research expand and the expectations placed on researchers by society change. For example, the proposed changes to the Common Rule regarding research with biospecimens recognize the reality that biological information is becoming increasingly identifiable. The push for the release of results from clinical trials to permit verification of results and secondary analyses of clinical trials data indicates an increased emphasis on transparency in biomedical research, a desire to harness "big data" for research purposes, and a belief that patients should be able to take a more active role in their medical care. The drive for transparency is also one of the rationales for the move toward an increased interest in investigation and disclosure of instances of research misconduct. These areas of the law will continue to evolve as technology develops and the demands of consumers of biomedical research change.

petitioned the United States to "march in" and require licenses to be granted to permit additional manufacturers to make the drug. To date, however, the United States has never exercised its march in rights. *See, e.g.*, Nat'l Inst. of Health, Office of the Director, *Determination in the Case of Fabrazyme Manufactured by Genzyme Corporation*, (Dec. 1, 2010).

CHAPTER 27

ANTITRUST ENFORCEMENT AND THE FUTURE OF HEALTHCARE COMPETITION

WILLIAM M. SAGE

As in other democratic nations, the U.S. economy generally operates as a competitive market. In this endeavor, it is aided by social norms, sound monetary policy, general laws protecting private property and facilitating commercial transactions, and specific "antitrust" laws prohibiting private anticompetitive organization and conduct. Health systems in these same democracies deviate from market principles to varying degrees and in different respects. Although its largely private health insurers and its almost entirely private healthcare providers have enabled the United States to claim (or be accused of) outlier status in this respect, the ongoing implementation of the Patient Protection and Affordable Care Act of 2010 (ACA) both confirms and challenges the conventional account of U.S. healthcare as uniquely reliant on free enterprise.

In its expansion of health insurance coverage, the ACA honors a long-standing conception of healthcare access, cost, and quality as an iron triangle of national trade-offs requiring mandatory redistribution of resources. As a result, it reduces many competitive pressures on the private insurance industry by prohibiting traditional underwriting practices, subsidizing premiums for low-income individuals, and promoting risk-sharing among competitors. At the same time, however, the ACA rejects explicit rationing, emphasizing instead the "Triple Aim" of reducing inefficiencies at both the individual and population levels that impair quality and waste money. To succeed, this process relies on heightened competition among providers of care (perhaps working collaboratively with insurers) and a greater focus on measurable benefits for consumers.[1]

The ACA therefore contemplates an important role for competition oversight through antitrust law, as well as a reorientation of preexisting healthcare regulation to unleash the dynamism and choice associated with market competition without compromising the law's commitment to near-universal health insurance coverage. Much as the Triple Aim is less an achievement than an iterative process of incremental improvement, optimal governance of

[1] *See* William Sage's chapter on health law and health policy, in this volume.

healthcare competition will necessarily be an adaptive process that continually reconsiders major questions and redirects its enforcement focus. Which types of competition are more desirable, and which less so? How can competitive change be reconciled with the need for universally accessible, financially stable health insurance coverage? What balance of competition and collaboration best advances population health within communities? Can healthcare competition generate substantial savings without chilling biomedical innovation? How compatible is heightened competition with medical ethics, medical professionalism, and other forms of consumer protection?

Although each country has different priorities and constraints, improving the efficiency of healthcare while assuring access to coverage and promoting public health is a global priority for the twenty-first century. In the United States, market competition is most needed to pare down annual waste of approximately $1 trillion tied to outdated production processes, poor information, and blunted incentives. At the same time, however, a powerful set of private actors entrenched by regulation is often able to resist change despite significant market, professional, consumer, and technologic pressures for innovation. Any "competition policy" that guides the U.S. healthcare system must recognize and attempt to address both of these realities.

This chapter begins by summarizing U.S. antitrust law, which constitutes the general framework for the legal defense of competition. It then describes recent and ongoing controversies involving antitrust law and healthcare. Finally, it identifies and discusses questions central to formulating a sound competition policy as the U.S. healthcare system adapts and develops in the post-ACA era. Not unexpectedly, answering these questions turns out to be less about policing purely private anticompetitive activity and more about redesigning healthcare regulation to facilitate competition and competition oversight where and how it is most needed.

I The Basics

There are no special antitrust laws that govern the healthcare sector. Antitrust enforcers and the courts apply the same statutes and procedures when considering healthcare matters as they do with antitrust issues that arise in any other economic sector. Nonetheless, challenging questions may arise when antitrust principles encounter the special needs and traditions of healthcare markets.

a. The Key Antitrust Statutes

Almost all federal antitrust enforcement in healthcare is based on a handful of statutes enacted over a century ago, each of which contains relatively few lines of rather general language. Although the early history of "trust-busting" included multiple goals such as preventing the accumulation of political power by industry and preserving independent small businesses, modern interpretations focus exclusively on "consumer welfare," meaning the economic benefits to buyers of maintaining competitive market conditions. When sellers exercise market power by raising prices, they unfairly appropriate economic surplus from buyers. More importantly, the output restriction necessary to increase price results in goods and services that could be sold for more than the cost of production not being produced at all, which is a "dead-weight" efficiency loss to society.

The Sherman Antitrust Act provides for both civil and criminal liability. Civil remedies may be sought by both private parties and the government, while only the U.S. Department of Justice may prosecute criminal violations. Section 1 of the Sherman Act makes unlawful "[e]very contract, combination . . . or conspiracy in restraint of trade . . ."[2] A violation requires proof of an *agreement* between two independent entities—a party cannot violate Sherman Act Section 1 unilaterally—and that the conduct in question *unreasonably* restrains trade.

Unilateral conduct is the subject of the Section 2 of the Sherman Act, which is aimed at entities that seek to obtain or maintain a monopoly by predatory or exclusionary conduct. To violate Sherman Act Section 2, an entity must have a high market share (generally 60%–70% or more), and have engaged in some form of anticompetitive conduct. Simply possessing monopoly power or achieving it through "growth or development as a consequence of a superior product, business acumen, or historic accident" is not illegal.[3] Courts have wrestled with defining the scope of anticompetitive conduct that can be the basis of a monopolization claim. The challenge is to distinguish between conduct that discourages rivals from competing and conduct, even if aggressive, that enhances productive efficiency. In the United States, charging a monopoly price is not itself an antitrust violation, in part because it makes the market more attractive to new competitors.

Mergers and acquisitions are the subject of Section 7 of the Clayton Act, which prohibits such transactions "where in any line of commerce . . . the effect . . . may be substantially to lessen competition, or to tend to create a monopoly."[4] Under the Hart-Scott-Rodino (HSR) Act,[5] prior notification must be given to the federal antitrust enforcement agencies of transactions that exceed a certain size and which are not otherwise exempt under the statute. This requirement gives the agencies the opportunity to investigate a transaction prior to closing; the Act's provisions do not affect the substantive standards for review. Insurance, hospital, and pharmaceutical mergers and acquisitions generally trigger HSR reporting, but transactions involving physicians often do not (because they typically do not exceed the size of transaction threshold).

There are other antitrust statutes that occasionally are implicated by healthcare matters, but they warrant less attention. The Federal Trade Commission (FTC) is authorized to enforce Section 5 of the FTC Act, which makes illegal "unfair methods of competition." While the potential reach of Section 5 is not entirely clear,[6] the overwhelming majority of cases brought by the FTC also could be initiated under the Sherman or Clayton Acts. Occasionally, questions may arise under the Robinson-Patman Act, which makes it illegal "to discriminate in price between different purchasers of commodities of like grade and quality . . . where the effect of such discrimination may be substantially to lessen competition . . ."[7]

[2] Sherman Act of 1890, 15 U.S.C. § 1 (2012).

[3] United States v. Grinnell Corp., 384 U.S. 563, 570–571 (1966).

[4] Clayton Antirust Act of 1915, 15 U.S.C. § 18 (2012).

[5] 15 U.S.C. § 18a (2012).

[6] *See* Fed. Trade Comm'n, Statement of Enforcement Principles Regarding "Unfair Methods of Competition" Under Section 5 of the FTC Act, 80 Fed. Reg. 57055–59 (Aug. 13, 2015).

[7] 15 U.S.C. § 13 (2012).

Since the 1980s, however, the government has brought almost no cases under the Robinson-Patman Act, and private plaintiffs who have brought such challenges in the healthcare sector (typically involving pharmaceuticals) have succeeded only rarely. Finally, most states have their own state antitrust laws, but for the most part these parallel the federal antitrust statutes and have been interpreted in the same way.

b. Analytical Framework

i. Introduction

The three principal areas of antitrust enforcement—joint conduct under Sherman Act Section 1, unilateral conduct under Sherman Act Section 2, and mergers and acquisitions under Clayton Act Section 7—have several things in common. First, the touchstone under all of these statutes is the effect of the conduct or transaction at issue on the competitive process rather than the fortunes of particular firms. Thus, it is commonly stated that the antitrust laws are aimed at "the protection of competition, not competitors."[8] Second, courts will reject arguments that the antitrust analysis should take into account issues other than competition.[9] There is no exemption under the antitrust laws for healthcare professionals or nonprofit institutions.[10] Third, in undertaking antitrust review, both the agencies and the courts rely on economic evidence, often based on econometric models and historical data. Fourth, in recognition of the complexities of antitrust analysis and the absence of recent Supreme Court precedent on some issues, the federal antitrust agencies have issued statements and guidelines that describe their enforcement policies and priorities. These include statements aimed specifically at antitrust enforcement in healthcare,[11] as well as more general statements dealing with such matters as horizontal mergers,[12] competitor collaborations,[13] and intellectual property.[14] In addition, agency officials often explain their enforcement agenda in speeches, advisory opinions, testimony, reports and other documents. While such pronouncements do not have the force of law, they offer very useful guidance to practitioners and market participants, and often may be persuasive to courts.

[8] Brown Shoe Co. v. United States, 370 U.S. 284, 320 (1962).

[9] *See, e.g.*, United States v. Topco Assocs., 405 U.S. 596 (1972).

[10] *See* Am. Med. Ass'n v. United States, 317 U.S. 519 (1943). *See also* Arizona v. Maricopa Cty. Med. Soc'y, 457 U.S. 332 (1982).

[11] *See, e.g.*, U.S. Dep't of Justice & Fed. Trade Comm'n, Statements of Antitrust Enforcement Policy in Health Care (1996), http://www.justice.gov/atr/statements-antitrust-enforcement-policyin-health-care.

[12] *See, e.g.*, U.S. Dep't of Justice & Fed. Trade Comm'n, Horizontal Merger Guidelines (2010), https://www.ftc.gov/system/files/documents/public_statements/804291/100819hmg.pdf.

[13] *See, e.g.*, U.S. Dep't of Justice & Fed. Trade Comm'n, Antitrust Guidelines for Collaborations Among Competitors (2000), https://www.ftc.gov/system/files/documents/public_statements/300481/000407ftcdojguidelines.pdf.

[14] *See, e.g.*, U.S. Dep't of Justice & Fed. Trade Comm'n, Antitrust Enforcement and Intellectual Property Rights: Promoting Innovation and Competition (2007), https://www.ftc.gov/news-events/press-releases/2007/04/federal-trade-commission-and-department-justice-issue-report.

ii. Per Se Conduct

Some conduct is considered so unlikely to have redeeming qualities that it is condemned as per se illegal, without the need to examine market conditions or consider possible justifications. Examples include "naked" agreements among competitors to fix prices, allocate markets, or engage in certain types of concerted refusals to deal (boycotts). These agreements are not related to and reasonably necessary to achieve other legitimate goals. For example, in April 2016 the DOJ settled a suit against two West Virginia hospitals that had agreed not to advertise in each other's territories.[15] By contrast, competitors who establish a joint venture that creates a new service, and then set a price for that service, would not be viewed as engaging in per se unlawful price-fixing.

iii. Rule of Reason and Merger Analysis

Most conduct is analyzed under a "rule of reason" to determine whether it will have an adverse effect on competition. The starting point for rule-of-reason analysis is to identify the relevant product and geographic markets (e.g., acute care hospital services in the Houston metropolitan area) that might be affected. In a typical case, the relevant markets encompass the alternative sellers to whom buyers could turn in response to a price increase by the sellers. The antitrust analysis proceeds by considering whether the defendant has market power in the relevant market. This can be demonstrated by high market share, or by direct evidence showing that the defendant has been able to increase prices above competitive levels. The defendant may seek to rebut such evidence by showing, for example, that its market share overstates its competitive significance because of changing market conditions, or that significant entry or expansion by new or existing competitors is probable. If the plaintiff has established that the defendant has market power and the challenged conduct is likely to produce adverse competitive effects, the defendant can try to prove that the conduct has offsetting procompetitive benefits. If the defendant proves that procompetitive benefits exist, the plaintiff then has the burden of proving that those benefits could be achieved with less restrictive means or that they are outweighed by the adverse competitive effects.

The extent of the rule-of-reason inquiry depends on the particular conduct alleged, and often is a crucial issue to be determined by the trial court. A full-blown rule of reason analysis is very fact-dependent and often economically complex, and presents a very high bar for plaintiffs to surmount. In recent years, courts have recognized that a "truncated" or "quick-look" analysis may be sufficient where there is a great likelihood of anticompetitive effects. For example, the Supreme Court held that a detailed market analysis was not required to condemn an agreement among competing dentists not to provide x-rays to insurers who requested them in order to determine the appropriateness of dental services.[16]

While the rule of reason approach discussed above is used for joint conduct cases brought under Sherman Act Section 1, it is generally similar to the analysis used for monopolization

[15] *See* Department of Justice press release, Apr. 14, 2016. https://www.justice.gov/opa/pr/justice-department-sues-two-hospital-systems-agreeing-allocate-marketing-territories.

[16] *See* FTC v. Ind. Fed'n of Dentists, 476 U.S. 447 (1986).

cases under Sherman Act Section 2. In the latter cases, the plaintiff must establish that the defendant has engaged in unjustified exclusionary or predatory conduct that enabled it to obtain or maintain monopoly power in a relevant market. The analysis is also similar to that undertaken in Clayton Act Section 7 cases under the *Horizontal Merger Guidelines*. The *Guidelines* provide that where a merger increases concentration by certain threshold amounts in a market that is already highly concentrated, there is a presumption that it will reduce competition. The principal concerns are that a merger could increase the likelihood of "coordinated interaction" by reducing the number of competitors in the relevant market who might then collude, or produce "unilateral effects" on competition by eliminating close rivalry between the merging parties. Unilateral effects were emphasized in the most recent *Horizontal Merger Guidelines*, which also suggested that evidence of reduced competition such as "diversion analysis" might render formal market definition unnecessary.[17] A presumption of anticompetitive effects can be overcome by showing that market entry will make those effects unlikely, that efficiencies specific to the merger are likely to offset competitive concerns, or that one of the merging parties is either failing or flailing such that the merger will not reduce competition.

iv. Defenses

Three defenses to an antitrust challenge are often relevant in healthcare cases. First, in a long series of decisions, the Supreme Court has established that the antitrust laws do not apply to actions of a sovereign state, nor do they apply to private actors where (1) the challenged conduct has been "clearly articulated and affirmatively expressed as state policy," and (2) is "actively supervised" by the state itself.[18] State action immunity also may apply to subordinate government entities, such as municipalities and professional licensing boards, provided certain conditions are met. In an important case, the Supreme Court recently held that an unsupervised state dental board controlled by "active market participants" could be subject to antitrust liability even though it is formally a government entity.[19] Second, antitrust immunity based on First Amendment rights applies to political action under the *Noerr-Pennington* doctrine, allowing joint efforts to influence governmental actions, including those of the legislature, administrative agencies, and the courts. Political action immunity can be lost, however, if the petitioning is a "sham" and the defendant is using the government process as an "anticompetitive weapon."[20] Finally, the McCarran-Ferguson Act exempts insurers from federal antitrust scrutiny where (1) the challenged practice is part of the "business of insurance"; (2) the practice is "regulated by State law"; and (3) the challenged conduct does not consist of acts or agreements involving "boycott, coercion, or intimidation."[21] As a practical matter, however, health insurers remain subject to the antitrust laws for almost all purposes.

[17] U.S. Dep't of Justice & Fed. Trade Comm'n, Horizontal Merger Guidelines (2010), http://www.justice.gov/sites/default/files/atr/legacy/2010/08/19/hmg-2010.pdf.

[18] Cal. Retail Liquor Dealers Ass'n v. Midcal Aluminum, Inc., 445 U.S. 97 (1980).

[19] N.C. State Bd. of Dental Exam'rs v. FTC, 135 S. Ct. 1101 (2015).

[20] City of Columbia v. Omni Outdoor Adver., 499 U.S. 365, 390 (1991).

[21] 15. U.S.C. §§ 1011–1015 (2012).

c. Public Enforcement

Two federal agencies are responsible for antitrust enforcement: the Federal Trade Commission (FTC), an independent agency led by five commissioners; and the Antitrust Division of the U.S. Department of Justice (DOJ). To a very large extent the agencies have overlapping jurisdiction and their analytic approach is essentially the same. Differences include the following: (1) only the DOJ has authority to prosecute price-fixing and other criminal antitrust offenses; (2) the FTC lacks jurisdiction over the conduct of nonprofit entities; (3) the FTC is responsible for consumer protection as well as antitrust enforcement, more often conducts general fact-finding apart from specific enforcement actions, and engages in "competition advocacy" vis-à-vis state government; and (4) when the FTC challenges a merger, it typically seeks a preliminary injunction in federal court that will prohibit consummation of the transaction pending internal review by an FTC administrative law judge and consideration by the full Commission. By contrast, the DOJ lacks internal adjudicatory processes and must seek permanent relief in federal court.

Both the DOJ and FTC have had a strong interest in healthcare since the late 1970s. Historically, the FTC has focused on matters involving healthcare providers and the pharmaceutical and device industries. The DOJ has focused on insurer/health plan conduct and mergers, conduct involving nonprofits, and possible criminal violations.

The DOJ and FTC have acquired substantial knowledge and experience involving healthcare, which is spread among the lawyers and economists who form the agencies' investigative teams. On an informal basis, the DOJ and FTC also will obtain input from other federal agencies, particularly the Food and Drug Administration. In recent years, both agencies have shared their expertise with the Centers for Medicare and Medicaid Services. For example, the DOJ and FTC issued a joint statement regarding the antitrust issues raised by accountable care organizations participating in the Medicare Shared Savings Program.[22]

State attorneys general vary with respect to health antitrust matters, with the larger states such as New York, California, Florida, and Texas having particularly active enforcement efforts. Much state enforcement is focused on local healthcare provider mergers and allegations of anticompetitive conduct, although task forces spanning many states have been convened for mergers or conduct that covers broad geographical areas, such as "reverse payment" cases in the pharmaceutical industry.

The primary forms of relief sought by the government in antitrust cases are structural remedies that may involve blocking a transaction or requiring a divestiture, or conduct remedies requiring that the respondent not engage in certain behavior in the future. Generally, the federal agencies have a strong preference for structural relief as they believe such remedies are more effective and avoid the need for ongoing expert supervision. On criminal matters, the DOJ can obtain substantial criminal fines, and in unusual cases the FTC has sought disgorgement of ill-gotten gains.

[22] *See* U.S. Dep't of Justice & Fed. Trade Comm'n, Statement of Antitrust Enforcement Policy Regarding Accountable Care Organizations Participating in the Medicare Shared Savings Program, 76 Fed. Reg. 67,026–32 (Oct. 28, 2011).

d. Private Enforcement

Private parties are also active as plaintiffs in healthcare antitrust matters, especially in pharmaceutical cases where class action lawsuits have been brought on behalf of direct purchasers alleging conduct that has driven up drug prices. Antitrust plaintiffs must have standing to sue, and must establish that they have suffered "antitrust injury," which means an injury of the type that the antitrust laws were designed to prevent, and which was caused by the antitrust violation. A successful plaintiff can recover three times the actual damages, plus attorney fees.

II Recent Controversies

Competitive considerations implicate nearly all sectors of the $3 trillion U.S. healthcare system. As many commentators have observed, the healthcare system has been highly fragmented—a product of traditional medical professionalism reinforced by law over the course of more than a century. Since the 1980s, however, many healthcare organizations have consolidated by merger or acquisition, while others have affiliated by contract. Previously independent community hospitals have combined into large regional and national systems, though many remain nonprofit enterprises. Physicians who were in solo or near-solo practice now work in large single-specialty or multi-specialty groups, participate in contractual networks that do business with large health insurers, and increasingly are becoming employees of hospitals and managed care organizations. Nonprofit Blue Cross and Blue Shield plans have affiliated contractually, merged, and in many cases converted to for-profit status, while other prominent private insurers have merged into a few very large organizations. Pharmaceutical manufacturers (and many medical device companies) compete in a global marketplace where size confers advantages; even generic drugs are often produced by large companies. Similarly, giant chain drugstores and pharmacy benefit managers have largely eclipsed small, independent pharmacies.

Antitrust law comes into play in each of these areas. Despite the national and global reach of some aspects of healthcare services, many markets for healthcare services remain local, making dominance by one or a few providers of genuine concern for competition as consolidation accelerates in response to the ACA. U.S. antitrust law has limited ability to break up dominant organizations that already exist, but possesses greater capacity to prevent monopolies or oligopolies from forming and to police agreements among competitors that might result in cartelization or other harms to consumers. This applies to otherwise independent physicians who join together contractually, with or without health facilities, to serve privately insured patients, to large organizations that use agreements to shield their existing business models from new competition, and to pharmaceutical manufacturers attempting to prevent generic drug makers from eroding their patent or regulatory exclusivity. The professional nature of healthcare services continues to influence the legal analysis of transactions involving physicians and other trained, licensed individuals, but the general framework of health antitrust law differs minimally from that applied to other industries.

The examples discussed in this section illustrate these dynamics and more. For ease of exposition, they are divided into three analytic categories: structural cases, conduct cases, and cases that arise from the interaction between competition law and healthcare regulation. It is important to note that DOJ or FTC enforcement actions and private antitrust lawsuits typically assert multiple theories of legal violations and associated harm to consumers, which are defended on all available grounds. For purposes of this chapter, however, it is useful to focus readers' attention on particular aspects of the selected disputes.

a. Structure

i. Hospital Mergers and Healthcare Reform

From the late 1980s through the early 2000s, the DOJ, FTC, and state enforcers lost seven consecutive challenges to hospital mergers.[23] The reasons were multiple, though largely unique to the healthcare industry. Antitrust law exists to protect the welfare of consumers, meaning buyers. In the healthcare system of the time, buyers increasingly were newly formed managed care organizations that negotiated with established medical care providers, mainly hospitals and physicians. To judges, the former were ethically suspect interlopers, while the latter were charitable and professional pillars of the community.

This was in part a moral and political judgment, but it also reflected the economics of the times insofar as hospitals supported local employment, provided charity, and instilled civic pride, whereas health insurers—particularly the large, for-profit variety—seemed to act only on behalf of giant employer customers and their own shareholders and executives. Analytically, the enforcement agencies suffered from a temporary "econometrics gap," in which defendants' experts were able to reinforce the narrative of good and evil by casting economic uncertainty on the government's case—expanding the alleged geographic market to include more competitors or conjuring data on nonprofit hospitals' unwillingness to exploit any market power they might acquire.

This changed a decade later. During the 2000s, as the pace of consolidation slowed, agency economists and academic researchers studied both the mergers that had been allowed and the more general relationship between provider consolidation and market outcomes. This research was collected and analyzed by a Robert Wood Johnson Foundation initiative called the Synthesis Project, which published a report in 2006 and an update in 2012.[24] The Synthesis Project concluded that less competitive hospital markets have higher prices and

[23] *See* Tenet Healthcare Corp. v. FTC., 186 F.3d 1045 (8th Cir. 1999) (Poplar Bluff, MO); California v. Sutter Health Sys., 84 F. Supp. 2d 1057 (N.D. Cal. 2000), *aff'd*, 217 F.3d 846 (9th Cir. 2000) (Oakland, CA); United States v. Long Island Jewish Med. Ctr., 983 F. Supp. 121 (E.D.N.Y. 1997) (Nassau County, NY); FTC. v. Butterworth Health Corp., 946 F. Supp. 1285 (W.D. Mich. 1996) (Grand Rapids, MI); United States v. Mercy Health Servs., 902 F. Supp. 968 (N.D. Iowa 1995), *vacated as moot*, 107 F.3D 632 (8th Cir. 1997) (Dubuque, IA); FTC. v. Freeman Hosp., 911 F. Supp. 1213 (W.D. Mo. 1995), *aff'd*, 69 F.3d 260 (8th Cir. 1995) (Joplin, MO); FTC v. Hosp. Bd. of Dirs. of Lee County, No. 94-137-CIV-FTM-25D, 1994 U.S. Dist. LEXIS 19770 (M.D. Fla. May 16, 1994), *aff'd*, 38 F.3d 1184 (11th Cir. 1994) (Lee County, FL).

[24] *See* Martin Gaynor & Robert Town, Robert Wood Johnson Found., The Impact of Hospital Consolidation—Update 2 (2012); William B. Vogt & Robert Town, Robert Wood Johnson Found., How Has Hospital Consolidation Affected the Price and Quality of Hospital Care? (2006).

may have lower quality. Moreover, there was no relationship between hospitals' behavior and their status as charitable or proprietary entities.[25]

Amid mounting concern over continued healthcare cost increases, with particular focus on exorbitant hospital prices and their indulged, overpaid executives—and with managed care no longer considered a public menace—the antitrust agencies applied their new research findings to enforcement, and succeeded first in unwinding and then in halting several hospital mergers.[26] In the first few years following the enactment of the ACA, for example, the FTC succeeded in obtaining a preliminary injunction in federal district court and then blocked a hospital merger in Toledo, Ohio (upheld by the Sixth Circuit), and a preliminary injunction against a proposed merger in Rockford, Illinois.[27] In reaching these outcomes, decision-makers have focused on the superior bargaining power of merged hospitals with respect to the terms of participation in private insurance networks.

In *ProMedica Health Sys., Inc. v. FTC*, the Toledo case, the government successfully prevented a merger between two of the four hospital systems in Lucas County—ProMedica, the county's dominant health provider, and St. Luke's, a small independent community hospital. Before the merger, ProMedica and St. Luke's were competitors in general acute care services with 46.8% and 11.5% shares of care in the county, respectively. Granting a preliminary injunction pending the outcome of an FTC administrative proceeding, the district court observed that St. Luke's hospital was, before the merger, a low-cost and high-quality provider that was "well-positioned to take advantage of the pending healthcare reform."[28] It distinguished the ProMedica transaction from a potentially procompetitive accountable care organization (ACO) because an ACO "agrees to be accountable for quality, cost, and overall care in exchange for a share of the savings achieved." The district court further reasoned that the shared savings of an ACO can be achieved by arrangements other than merger, such as contractual relationships and joint ventures.

The administrative law judge found that the merger would substantially lessen competition in violation of Section 7 of the Clayton Act and ordered ProMedica to divest St. Luke's. The full Commission affirmed, and ProMedica petitioned the Sixth Circuit for review of the Commission's order. The Sixth Circuit upheld the Commission, finding that the merger would enhance ProMedica's market power to "levels rarely tolerated in antitrust law."[29] The court also upheld the FTC's alleged product market, even though it clustered together different types of healthcare services. The court noted that a merger could potentially overcome a presumption of illegality by creating efficiencies that enhance consumer welfare, such as "lower prices, improved quality, enhanced services, or new products," but found

[25] *See* David Dranove & Richard Ludwick, *Competition and Pricing by Nonprofit Hospitals: A Reassessment of Lynk's Analysis*, 18 J. Health Econ. 87, 97 (1999).

[26] *See In re* Evanston Northwestern Healthcare Corp. & ENH Med. Group, Inc., No. 9315, 144 F.T.C. 1, 521–523 (Aug. 2, 2007) (Evanston, IL); *In re* Evanston Northwestern Healthcare Corp., 2005 WL 2845790 20, 343 (F.T.C.) (Oct. 20, 2005). On review, the full Commission agreed the merger was anticompetitive but declined to order divestiture. *In re* Evanston Northwestern Healthcare Corp., 2007 WL 2286195 375, 521–523 (F.T.C.) (Aug. 6, 2007).

[27] *See* FTC v. OSF Healthcare Sys., 852 F. Supp. 2d 1069, 1095 (N.D. Ill. 2012) (Rockford, IL); FTC v. ProMedica Health Sys., No. 3:11 CV 47, 2011 U.S. Dist. LEXIS 33434, at *50 (N.D. Ohio Mar. 29, 2011) (Toledo, OH); *In re* ProMedica Health System Inc., F.T.C. No. 9346 (Dec. 12, 2011).

[28] FTC v. ProMedica Health Sys., No 3:11-CV-47, 2011 WL 1219281 (N. D. Ohio Mar. 29, 2011).

[29] ProMedica Health Sys., Inc. v. FTC, 749 F. 3d 559 (6th Cir. 2014).

that ProMedica did not even attempt to argue that the merger would benefit consumers—an omission that the court considered "remarkable."

As a result of ProMedica and similar recent cases, large hospitals in markets with few existing facilities are on notice that further consolidation will attract scrutiny and that courts are unlikely to find special circumstances that might except healthcare cases from standard economic presumptions. In particular, both the agencies and the courts have rejected claims by the merging entities that "health reform" (sometimes meaning the ACA specifically and sometimes meaning a broader shift to healthcare value) either forced or blessed the transactions. Instead, antitrust enforcers and the courts typically have concluded that the hospitals would remain financially viable as independent facilities and that the claimed efficiencies with respect to cost and quality were either speculative or achievable in ways not requiring merger.

Continuing this trend, in late 2015 the FTC challenged three more hospital mergers: Advocate Health Care Network's proposed merger with NorthShore University Health System in Chicago (also joined by the Illinois attorney general), Penn State Hershey Medical Center's merger with Pinnacle Health System in the Harrisburg, Pennsylvania, area (also joined by the Pennsylvania attorney general), and Cabell Huntington Hospital's acquisition of St. Mary's Medical Center in the Huntington, West Virginia, area (interestingly *not* joined by the West Virginia attorney general, who supported the transaction after the hospitals made certain commitments about cost and quality). In all these cases, the combined entity would control more than 50% of general acute care inpatient hospital services in the markets alleged by the FTC (which are disputed by the defendants). To the surprise of most economists, the district court hearing the Hershey case found in favor of the defendants, rejecting the government's proposed geographic market as not in keeping with how patients in rural Pennsylvania choose hospitals and opining that long-term agreements that had been signed by the hospitals and large payers would prevent price increases.[30] That case is currently on appeal, and the other cases remain in litigation.

Still, the federal enforcement agencies refrain from challenging the great majority of mergers and acquisitions.[31] Across all industries in 2013, the agencies were notified of 1,326 transactions, of which FTC challenged 23 and DOJ challenged 15. Of 59 transactions involving healthcare services and meeting the Hart-Scott-Rodino pre-merger notification thresholds, the government challenged only three.

ii. Physician Practice Mergers and Hospital Acquisitions of Physician Practices

The competitive analysis of physician consolidation is more varied. Physician practice has been highly fragmented for decades, with many sole proprietorships and small groups still in existence. These physicians are often reluctant to relinquish their independence and share

[30] Federal Trade Commission et al. v. Penn State Hershey Medical Center et al., Case No. 1:15-cv-02362-JEJ, May 9, 2016, Memorandum Opinion & Order

[31] *See* FED. TRADE COMM'N & U.S. DEP'T OF JUSTICE, HART-SCOTT-RODINO ANNUAL REPORT: FISCAL YEAR 2013 (2014), http://www.ftc.gov/system/files/documents/reports/36th-report-fy2013/140521hsrreport.pdf.

financial risk as part of a corporate organization. For this reason, antitrust controversies involving physicians often relate to joint conduct short of full merger, raising important questions regarding price-fixing and other forms of cartelization. These cases are discussed below under the heading "Defragmentation and Clinical Integration."

When physicians do form larger practice groups, most are single-specialty entities that are paid on a conventional fee-for-service basis. Full-service multi-specialty groups tend to be associated with selected markets that are amenable to risk contracting and prepayment; many of these are historically significant organizations such as the [Kaiser-]Permanente Medical Group or the Mayo or Marshfield Clinics. Large single-specialty groups are often associated with hospital-based fields such as anesthesiology, emergency medicine, radiology, and various surgical specialties. These organizations can raise significant antitrust concerns as they grow and merge; although barriers to new competitive entry may be lower for physician than for hospital markets, entry may be retarded by existing physician-hospital contracts, by difficulties in obtaining medical staff privileges, or by entrenched referral patterns from primary care physicians. Still, challenges to these transactions are uncommon, in part because the merging organizations typically have revenues below the legal thresholds for mandatory premerger notification.

When physicians join together in larger organizations, moreover, they often trade sole proprietorship or partnership for employment. They can become employees of other physicians who continue to own the larger practice, they can work for practices under the control of national or regional practice management groups (e.g., US Oncology for cancer care), or they can become hospital employees. When smaller physician groups are acquired by larger organizations, the core of the transaction generally is the absorption of the small group's physicians into the larger organization as employees rather than the value of the small group as a going concern. As a result, some transactions attract antitrust scrutiny because they appear to be corporate combinations (including the *St. Luke's* case discussed below), while others with very similar substance escape notice because they seem merely to be employment arrangements.

In 2012, Renown Health settled charges that its acquisitions of two local cardiology groups reduced competition for the provision of adult cardiology services in the Reno, Nevada, area.[32] Renown agreed to release its staff cardiologists from "noncompete" contract clauses they had signed, allowing up to ten of them to join competing cardiology practices. On one hand, this was an indication that the enforcement agencies regard physician practice mergers as potentially anticompetitive. On the other hand, voiding noncompete agreements does not do much to restore competition if the merged entity in fact has market power, because physicians may not be motivated to leave an enterprise that is able to charge supra-competitive prices.

To date, physician-hospital transactions have not been analyzed as generating efficiencies through true joint production of clinical services. Instead, they have been seen as increasing the risk in conventional fee-for-service markets that physician consolidation will result in market power, that captive physicians will restrict referrals and thereby mute competition

[32] *See* Federal Trade Commission, FTC Order Will Restore Competition for Adult Cardiology Services in Reno, Nevada (Aug. 6, 2012), http://www.ftc.gov/news-events/press-releases/2012/08/ftc-order-will-restore-competition-adult-cardiology-services-reno.

among hospitals, or that hospitals will be able to bill outpatient services at higher, hospital-based rates. Indeed, economic studies performed in the current practice environment suggest that physician-hospital integration is associated with short-term provider price increases for outpatient services paid by private insurers.[33] However, discouraging hospital acquisitions of physician groups perpetuates fee-for-service commerce in random inputs and isolated care processes, and makes it harder to assemble complex services at lower cost and offer them on a packaged and warranted basis, which is a goal of the ongoing move toward "Alternative Payment Systems."[34]

The tension between old-market and new-market perspectives was evident in a 2014 case, *FTC v. St. Luke's Health System, Ltd.*,[35] in which the federal government, the state of Idaho, and a rival hospital sued a hospital system that had acquired a forty-one-physician group practice in Nampa, Idaho, outside Boise, where the hospital already had an inpatient facility. After a hearing, a federal judge ordered the hospital to divest itself of the acquired physicians, finding that the transaction had increased the hospital's bargaining leverage with health insurers in the market for "adult primary care physician" services.[36] The judge construed the geographic market narrowly as only the town of Nampa, not broadly to include Boise about twenty minutes away. The judge also concluded that the acquisition would increase prices for certain diagnostic services ordered by the newly affiliated physicians because the hospital would be able to apply more lucrative billing codes associated with hospital-based care.[37] The district court ruling was affirmed by the Ninth Circuit Court of Appeals the following year.[38]

At the same time, however, the judge praised the hospital for preparing to compete in a post-ACA environment in which payment will be based on patient outcomes rather than the volume of services. The court recognized that using primary care physicians to coordinate care might well increase value for patients, but noted that integrated practice could be achieved through means other than acquisition of a large existing medical group. "In a world that was not governed by the Clayton Act," he wrote, "the best result might be to approve the Acquisition and . . . see if the predicted price increases actually occurred. . . . But the Clayton Act . . . does not give the Court discretion to . . . conduct a health care experiment."[39]

Indeed, keeping physicians economically independent of hospitals is not a desirable policy over the long term because integrated care can be produced more efficiently and offered at a bundled price. Similarly, a market for primary care physician services should lose its coherence as other professionals and other modalities become available to provide basic

[33] *See* Hannah T. Neprash, Michael E. Chernew, Andrew L. Hicks, Teresa Gibson, & J. Michael McWilliams, *Association of Financial Integration Between Physicians and Hospitals with Commercial Health Care Prices*, 175 J. AM. MED. ASS'N INTERNAL MED. 1932 (2015).

[34] *See* Medicare Access and CHIP Reauthorization Act of 2015, Pub. L. No. 114-10, 128 Stat. 87 (introducing the new Merit-Based Incentive Payment System).

[35] *See* Findings of Fact & Conclusions of Law, FTC v. St. Luke's Health System, Ltd., 2014 WL 407446 (D. Idaho Jan. 24, 2014) (No. 1:13–CV–00116–BLW), *aff'd sub nom.* Saint Alphonsus Med. Ctr.–Nampa, Inc. v. St. Luke's Health Sys., Ltd., 778 F.3d 775 (9th Cir. 2015).

[36] *See* Memorandum Decision & Order at 3–4, FTC v. St. Luke's Health System, Ltd., No. 1:13–CV–00116–BLW (D. Idaho Jan. 24, 2014).

[37] *See* Findings of Fact & Conclusions of Law ¶¶ 124–125.

[38] Federal Trade Commission and State of Idaho, et al. v. St. Luke's Health System, Ltd, and Saltzer Medical Group, P.A., No. 14-35173, slip op. (9th Cir. February 10, 2015).

[39] *Id.* ¶¶ 76–77.

medical care, including from more distant locations through telehealth.[40] Retail medical clinics, for example, are actual and potential competitors for a variety of outpatient services that can be provided in a standardized way at low prices using cost-effective staffing such as advanced practice nurses.[41] The court also failed to recognize that Medicare would very likely change its rules to reduce the payment differential for hospital-based and non-hospital outpatient services, as in fact it did in late 2015.[42]

iii. Health Insurer Consolidation

The medical profession has sounded the alarm over insurer consolidation since the 1990s, worrying that large insurers would use market power to lower physician reimbursement.[43] In 2015, a series of high-profile mergers were announced among health insurers, including combinations of Aetna with Humana, CIGNA with Anthem, and Health Net with Centene.[44] The last of these was cleared by the DOJ in March 2016 and has been finalized; the other two remain under close political and legal scrutiny. If the CIGNA and Aetna transactions are approved and consummated, the health insurance industry would consist of a few very large organizations (including United Healthcare, Kaiser, and the largest Blue Cross plans) surrounded by many smaller health plans and financing entities serving niche markets. According to analyses performed by the American Medical Association, the proposed insurance mergers would reduce competition in up to ninety-seven metropolitan areas in seventeen states.[45]

There are several possible motives for sudden consolidation among insurers, including economies of scale, better insulation from adverse selection, countervailing bargaining power against large hospital systems, and maintaining dominance in local markets. An important factor appears to be a perceived need for political strength when doing business with the federal government in Medicare managed care (Medicare Advantage) and with both states and federal regulators in the ACA's health insurance exchanges. Arguably, the largest consolidated insurers would be "too big to fail," potentially insulating them from government payment reductions and strengthening their claims for subsidies or bailouts should

[40] *See, e.g.*, Daniel McCarthy, Note, *The Virtual Economy: Telemedicine and the Supply of Primary Care Physicians in Rural America*, 21 Am. J. L. & Med. 111, 112–113 (1995) (examining "telemedicine" as a method of providing basic medical care to rural communities).

[41] *See* John K. Iglehart, *The Expansion of Retail Clinics—Corporate Titans vs. Organized Medicine*, 373 New Eng. J. Med. 301 (2015); William M. Sage, *Out of the Box: The Future of Retail Medical Clinics*, 3 Harv. L. & Pol'y Rev. 1 (2009).

[42] *See* Medicare Program: Hospital Outpatient Prospective Payment and Quality Reporting Programs, 80 Fed. Reg. 39,200 (July 8, 2015) (to be codified at 42 C.F.R. pt. 410) (discussing a change to Medicare payment for non-hospital outpatient services).

[43] Am. Med. Ass'n, Competition in Health Insurance: A Comprehensive Study of U.S. Markets, 2014 Update (2015).

[44] *See* Robert Laszewski, *Health Insurer Merger Mania—Muscle Bound Competitors and a New Cold War in Health Care*, Forbes, July 27, 2015, 2:55 PM, http://www.forbes.com/sites/robertlaszewski2/2015/07/27/health-insurer-merger-mania-muscle-bound-competitors-and-a-new-cold-war-in-health-care/ (discussing possible motives and effects of insurer consolidation).

[45] *See AMA Releases Analyses on Potential Anthem-Cigna and Aetna-Humana Mergers*, AMA News Room, Am. Med. Ass'n (Sept. 8, 2015), http://www.ama-assn.org/ama/pub/news/news/2015/2015-09-08-analysis-anthem-cigna-aetna-humana-mergers.page.

market conditions deteriorate. In these respects, the consolidation of health insurers today is reminiscent of defense contractors following the end of the Cold War.[46]

However, the competitive implications of health insurance mergers are challenging to model, and the economic outcomes of negotiations between consolidated insurers and dominant hospitals—termed "bilateral monopoly"—are even more difficult to predict. In theory, healthcare financing has few barriers to entry by new competitors, and can cross geographic boundaries in ways that would be impractical for most healthcare services. In practice, however, health insurance is tightly regulated by states and relies on complex local negotiations with hospitals and physicians regarding their inclusion in provider networks and the associated fees they receive for serving enrolled beneficiaries. While the overall gains in price and quality for consumers from this stylized and costly process are hard to demonstrate empirically, one or a few large insurers may be able to use network negotiations to lock up providers, deter potential market entrants, and gain market power. In fact, studies that have been done of health insurer consolidation suggest that the merged entity may act both monopsonistically to reduce provider payments and monopolistically to impose higher premiums on employers and beneficiaries.[47]

Because commercial insurers act as purchasing intermediaries, not actual consumers of healthcare, they are at best weak agents for buyers and at worst self-interested middlemen. Under prevailing conditions, many bear little true insurance risk, serving instead as administrators for self-insured employers or as claims clearinghouses for government programs. This trend was bolstered by the ACA, which simultaneously prohibited many underwriting practices and promised government assistance if actual liabilities exceed projections. All in all, health insurers turn a more-than-respectable profit from the trillions of dollars of claims they process annually, and have every reason to maintain their existing market role and business practices, a deterrent to innovation which consolidation could make even stronger.

On the other hand, an argument for insurer consolidation is that annual churn of covered individuals from insurer to insurer, which competition arguably increases, makes it difficult for any single insurer to capture value from long-term health coverage and therefore spend money today to prevent more costly diseases tomorrow. For example, new drug cures for hepatitis C infection are clearly cost-effective in the long term, but because their very high price must be paid by whatever insurer is financially responsible when definitive treatment is sought, they are harder to justify actuarially than less effective medications whose total cost could be spread over years of chronic disease coverage.[48] ACA exchange coverage and Medicaid are especially transitory markets, in which frequent disenrollment (sometimes but not always in pursuit of lower premiums) can undercut incentives for cost-effective coverage.

[46] *See, e.g.*, Lawrence J. Korb, *Merger Mania: Should the Government Pay for Defense Industry Restructuring?*, BROOKINGS INST. (1996), http://www.brookings.edu/research/articles/1996/06/summer-defenseindustry-korb.

[47] *See* Leemore Dafny, Mark Duggan, & Subramaniam Ramanarayanan, *Paying a Premium on Your Premium? Consolidation in the U.S. Health Insurance Industry*, 102 AM. ECON. REV. 1161 (2012).

[48] *See* Karen Van Nuys, Ronald Brookmeyer, Jacquelyn W. Chou, David Dreyfus, Douglas Dieterich, & Dana P. Goldman, *Broad Hepatitis C Treatment Scenarios Return Substantial Health Gains, But Capacity Is a Concern*, 34 HEALTH AFF. 1666 (2015).

In Medicare Advantage, by contrast, beneficiaries gain permanent eligibility at age 65 and tend not to shift carriers once enrolled (probably because they fear having to change providers). Now that total enrollment has grown large enough to discourage cherry-picking of healthier seniors, Medicare Advantage plans constitute a stable marketplace in which insurers can take a longer view. However, Medicare Advantage markets are also very concentrated, with eighty-one of the one hundred largest by Medicare population deemed noncompetitive in a 2015 report.[49]

b. Conduct

i. *Defragmentation and Clinical Integration*

One of the most daunting problems involving competition and health policy is "defragmenting" the provision of healthcare without either facilitating cartelization—which has always been a risk in professional activities—or swinging the pendulum too far toward consolidation given the relatively small geographic markets typically associated with service industries.[50] As repeatedly documented in recent decades, lack of coordinated treatment, redundant and unnecessary services, poor communication and information exchange, inattention to prevention and follow-up, and inadequate measurement of clinical and patient-reported outcomes have revealed a "quality chasm" between traditional medical practice and what is expected of other industrial sectors.[51] Yet individual physician expertise, compassion, and loyalty—fairly compensated by society without excessive commercialism or government oversight—are still prized as ethical norms.

The American medical profession's influence over the regulation of care delivery and payment has perpetuated fragmentation, even as medical science has advanced rapidly in both complexity and expense.[52] Consequently, physicians practicing in small offices with minimal capital investment of their own can earn substantial amounts performing technically complex procedures that require large physical plants, costly technology, and skilled staffing—with those inputs available on demand from corporate enterprises (or loosely coordinated with other physicians) but billed separately to patients, private insurers, or government programs.

When private insurers finally sought greater control over physicians' fees and referrals in the 1980s and 1990s, physicians attempted a collective response to the perceived economic threat. Rejecting arguments about threats to professionalism and the quality of medical care, however, antitrust enforcers and the courts held firmly to the principle that price-fixing among competitors was a per se violation of Section 1 of the Sherman Act.[53] Physicians

[49] *See* Brian Biles, Giselle Casillas, & Stuart Guterman, *Competition Among Medicare's Private Health Plans: Does It Really Exist?*, The Commonwealth Fund, Aug. 25, 2015, http://www.commonwealthfund.org/publications/issue-briefs/2015/aug/competition-medicare-private-plans-does-it-exist.

[50] The Fragmentation of U.S. Health Care (Einer Elhauge ed., 2010).

[51] *See* Inst. of Med, Crossing the Quality Chasm: A New Health System for the 21st Century (2001).

[52] *See* Paul Starr, The Social Transformation of American Medicine: The Rise of a Sovereign Profession and the Making of a Vast Industry (1984). *See* William Sage's chapter on health law and health policy in this volume.

[53] *See* Arizona v. Maricopa Cnty. Med. Soc'y, 457 U.S. 332 (1982).

lobbied actively in state legislatures and Congress to secure antitrust exemptions that would have allowed them to bargain collectively, but with little success.[54] In order to negotiate jointly with health insurers, physicians therefore must share "substantial financial risk" as do joint ventures among competitors in other industries, must not have market power, and must be equally scrupulous in avoiding behavior that would risk spillover collusion outside the scope of the joint venture, such as coordinating prices charged to other customers.

These restrictions proved both cumbersome (e.g., the now-defunct "messenger model") and ineffective. As a result, since the mid-1990s, the antitrust agencies have permitted independent physicians who participate in provider networks and are "clinically integrated" to jointly negotiate fees with insurers without it automatically constituting unlawful price-fixing.[55] Clinical integration was rationalized by the enforcement agencies as akin to offering a new product, which might justify joint pricing as an "ancillary" rather than "naked" restraint even without shared financial risk.[56] However, nothing approximating the delivery of fully assembled products—which would be indisputably new—has been demanded of physicians. Instead, the agencies have accepted a variety of joint investments in quality or efficiency of care as clinical integration, such as shared health information systems, common treatment protocols, and uniform processes for reviewing the quality and cost-effectiveness of care.[57]

ii. Most-Favored-Customer Clauses and Other "Contracts Referencing Rivals"

"Most-favored-customer clauses" (also called "most-favored-nation" clauses, or MFNs), which assure the contracting party of a supplier's best price, demonstrate the difficulties of applying standard market assumptions to the healthcare industry. Traditionally, courts regarded MFNs as "standard devices by which buyers try to bargain for low prices" and therefore procompetitive.[58] As MFNs became common among large medical and dental insurers in their provider agreements with hospitals and health professionals, however, the weight of antitrust opinion turned against them. This is because MFNs are a subset of what economist Fiona Scott Morton calls "contracts referencing rivals," which can be used anticompetitively.[59]

One concern is that a large insurer may be sufficiently dominant in a given geographic area to demand a true monopsony price, which would depress sales volume below the

[54] *See* Fred J. Hellinger & Gary J. Young, *An Analysis of Physician Antitrust Exemption Legislation: Adjusting the Balance of Power*, 281(1) J. AM. MED. ASS'N 83 (2001).

[55] *See* U.S. DEP'T OF JUSTICE & FED. TRADE COMM'N, STATEMENTS OF ANTITRUST ENFORCEMENT POLICY IN HEALTH CARE 90–91 (1996), http://www.justice.gov/atr/public/guidelines/0000.htm [hereinafter STATEMENTS OF ANTITRUST ENFORCEMENT POLICY 1996]; Letter from Fed. Trade Comm'n to John J. Miles, Esquire, Counsel for MedSouth Inc. 1–2 (June 18, 2007), http://www.ftc.gov/sites/default/files/documents/advisory-opinions/medsouth-inc./070618medsouth.pdf.

[56] *See* Broad. Music, Inc. v. Columbia Broad. Sys., Inc., 441 U.S. 1, 23 (1979) (holding the issuance of blanket licenses does not constitute price fixing per se unlawful under the antitrust laws because, in part, blanket licenses are a new product).

[57] *See* STATEMENTS OF ANTITRUST ENFORCEMENT POLICY 1996, *supra* note 52, at 111.

[58] Blue Cross Blue Shield United v. Marshfield Clinic, 65 F.3d 1406, 1415 (7th Cir. 1995) (finding no evidence connecting MFN clauses to anticompetitive conduct).

[59] Fiona Scott Morton, *Contracts that Reference Rivals*, 27 ANTIRUST 72 (2013).

efficient point and produce dead-weight loss equivalent to a seller monopoly. A second concern is that most health insurers are purchasing disaggregated medical services for resale as covered benefits, not as inputs for their own production processes (much less their direct use as would a normal buyer). Absent regulation to assure that low prices paid by the insurer are passed on to insured individuals as low premiums or reduced cost-sharing, the pro-consumer posture of the antitrust laws should not immunize MFNs from scrutiny. Third, MFNs can be used by dominant insurers to raise costs for smaller rivals or potential rivals in fee contracting with hospitals or physicians. A provider will not cut prices to a new insurance entrant for a small increment of care if the provider is obligated to offer the same discount in connection with most of its insured patients. Fourth, many health insurers came into existence years ago as contracting vehicles controlled by hospitals (the original Blue Cross plans) or physicians (the original Blue Shield plans). Where that control remains in place, an MFN may benefit the providers rather than the insurer by stabilizing prices at a higher than competitive level. MFNs therefore can facilitate provider cartels and harm consumers much like any other collective restraint of trade.[60]

Three lawsuits have been brought against Blue Cross Blue Shield of Michigan for its use of MFN clauses in contracts with hospitals, with the first filed by the DOJ and the state of Michigan in 2010.[61] At the time, the defendant's health plans covered 60% of Michigan's commercially insured population, and it had agreements containing MFNs with over 40% of Michigan's general acute care hospitals. The hospitals were seen as having little choice and were not named as defendants; the court's opinions suggest that a hospital that declined to sign would have been paid up to 16% less by Blue Cross. Michigan subsequently enacted laws banning the use of MFNs by the health insurance industry.

Large hospitals may also disadvantage potential rivals by contract. In *Palmyra Park Hospital, Inc. v. Phoebe Putney Memorial Hospital*, a smaller for-profit hospital alleged that a dominant nonprofit forced health insurers to exclude it from their provider networks for all services, in violation of the Clayton Act's prohibition on tying arrangements.[62] In *United States v. United Regional Health Care System of Wichita Falls, Texas*,[63] the DOJ and the Texas attorney general brought suit to enjoin United Regional from inserting terms into contracts with insurers that prevented those insurers from contracting with its competitors. United Regional had a market share of approximately 90% for inpatient hospital services and 65% for outpatient hospital services, and insurers unwilling to contract exclusively with it paid substantially more for services. Similarly, Sutter Health in California has been accused of using its market power in some hospital markets to force health plans to contract with it in all markets where it does business ("all-or-nothing" clauses) and to promise to "actively encourage" members to utilize Sutter hospitals rather than its competitors'.[64]

[60] *See* United States v. Delta Dental, 943 F. Supp. 172 (D.R.I. 1996) ("The net effect is an alleged detrimental impact on the dental market without any *discernible* competitive benefits.").

[61] *See* United States v. Blue Cross Blue Shield, 809 F. Supp. 2d 665 (W.D. Mich. 2011). *See also* Aetna Inc. v. Blue Cross Blue Shield, No. 11-CV-15346, 2013 WL 1831320 (E.D. Mich. June 14, 2012); Shane Grp., Inc. v. Blue Cross Blue Shield, No. 10-14360, 2012 WL 5990219 (E.D. Mich. Nov. 30, 2012).

[62] *See* Palmyra Park Hosp., Inc. v. Phoebe Putney Mem'l Hosp., 604 F.3d 1291, 1303 (11th Cir. 2010).

[63] United States v. United Reg'l Health Care Sys. of Wichita Falls, Tex., No. 7:11CV00030, 2011 WL 846762 (N.D. Tex. Feb. 25, 2011).

[64] Sidibe v. Sutter Health, N.D. Cal., Nov. 7, 2013 (No. C 12-04854) (order granting motion to dismiss).

iii. Mutual Advantage ("Cahoots")

Breaking up cozy relationships that keep out other competitors is a valuable aspect of antitrust enforcement. Large providers and large insurers often have a mutual interest in maintaining the status quo. For example, a well-publicized "standoff" between Partners HealthCare in Boston and Blue Cross Blue Shield of Massachusetts ended in an infamous "handshake in the snow" that used each party's size and reputation to reinforce the other's market position and was almost certainly adverse to consumers.[65]

Another example is in Western Pennsylvania, which has experienced over a decade of contractual maneuvering intended to keep new competitors out of the market. Private healthcare in Pittsburgh and environs has long been dominated by the University of Pittsburgh Medical Center (UPMC), which owns a majority of the hospital beds and employs a very large number of physicians, and by Highmark, a nonprofit health insurer that combines the former Blue Cross and Blue Shield plans of western Pennsylvania. In the early 2000s, Highmark attempted to undermine UPMC's dominant position by supporting a smaller, financially strained hospital system, West Penn Allegheny Health System (WAHS) and UPMC responded by creating its own health plan to compete against Highmark. In 2005, however, Highmark and UPMC began to act more like allies. UPMC refused to discount fees for hospital services to other health plans that were considering entering the Pennsylvania market, and Highmark increased its reimbursement rates to UPMC. UPMC scaled back its own health plan, and Highmark shut down its low-cost insurance option that had not included UPMC. Highmark declined to refinance its loan to WAHS, and UPMC began a systematic effort to hire away WAHS' best physicians. WAHS eventually filed an antitrust suit against UPMC and Highmark that paints a clear picture of Highmark and UPMC "[conspiring] to protect one another from competition."[66]

iv. Blue Cross Class Actions: Market Division or Trademark Protection?

Lack of strong competition among health insurers has also given rise to accusations of cartelization. For their first half-century of existence, Blue Cross plans (for hospital coverage) and Blue Shield plans (for physician coverage) were large but sleepy entities that were chartered as nonprofit organizations, offered coverage on a community-rated basis that often attracted the sickest enrollees, and existed primarily to assure hospitals and physicians in their communities of payment for services. For these reasons, Blue Cross plans almost died out in the 1980s and early 1990s in the face of competition from for-profit health maintenance organizations (HMOs), only to have their fortunes revived later in the decade as tightly managed care faded and broad networks of providers under contract once again became desirable. This financial success brought new scrutiny to their business practices, however, in part because the Blue Cross and Blue Shield trademarks remained controlled by a national association, which began to allow for-profit health plans to use the marks while still limiting their use to one plan in any geographic area.

[65] Scott Allen & Marcella Bombardieri, *A Handshake that Made Healthcare History*, BOSTON SUNDAY GLOBE, Dec. 28, 2008, at A1, A14.

[66] W. Penn. Allegheny Health Sys., Inc. v. UPMC, 627 F.3d 85, 91–92 (3d Cir. 2010).

Two class action antitrust suits were filed in 2012 against thirty-seven independently owned health plans that use the Blue Cross or Blue Shield brand names, as well as against the national Blue Cross and Blue Shield Association. The suits allege that the Blue Cross and Blue Shield plans act as a cartel and agree to divide geographic markets among themselves, which if proved would likely be a per se violation of Section 1 of the Sherman Act. The insurers, by contrast, assert that non-overlapping markets are a reasonable condition of licensing the Blue Cross and Blue Shield trademarks. In 2014, the federal district judge overseeing the litigation ruled against a motion to dismiss the plaintiffs' claims, and the case remains ongoing.[67]

v. Gamete Donation and Professional Ethics

Bioethics met competition law in *Kamakahi v. American Society for Reproductive Medicine*, an unusual class action lawsuit brought against two professional associations by young women who "donate" human ova for infertility treatment. In their complaint, the plaintiffs alleged a conspiracy among professional associations, fertility clinics, and egg agencies to fix maximum prices for egg donor compensation. Ethics guidelines promulgated by the American Society for Reproductive Medicine (ASRM) suggested that the amount a woman be paid for her eggs not exceed $10,000 so as to "not be so excessive as to constitute undue inducement." These maximum price guidelines allegedly were widely adopted by ASRM-affiliated fertility clinics and the egg agencies serving those clinics. Women providing eggs to these organizations claimed that they were paid less for their services than they would have been absent the ASRM pricing rules, which they alleged to be a violation of Section 1 of the Sherman Act.

ASRM and the other named defendants moved to have the case dismissed, but the U.S. District Court for the Northern District of California denied the motion, holding that the complaint alleged sufficient facts defining the relevant market and did not suffer from any "fatal legal defect."[68] The court rejected as premature the defendants' argument that the suit should be dismissed because the maximum price guidelines were designed to protect the health and safety of egg donors. In February 2016, ASRM settled the case, agreeing to remove language relating to donor compensation from its guidelines, and to pay $5,000 to each of the named plaintiffs plus $1.5 million in attorney fees.

Kamikahi poses interesting questions about the proper relationship between professional ethics and competition in a highly profitable subsector of the healthcare system that primarily caters to the wealthy and well insured.[69] Issues raised include the unrestricted market for sperm donation by men, the very large payments made in unregulated markets for eggs from women with desirable physical or intellectual traits, and whether payment should be prohibited by law (as for solid organ donation under the National Organ Transplant Act) because of the potentially significant health consequences of the hormone regimen that precedes egg harvesting, particularly for women making repeated donations. Some commentators

[67] *See In re* Blue Cross Blue Shield Antitrust Litigation, 26 F. Supp. 3d 1172 (2014).

[68] Kamakahi v. Am. Soc'y for Reproductive Med., No. C 11-01781 SBA (N.D. Cal. Mar. 29, 2013).

[69] *See, e.g.*, Tamar Lewin, *Egg Donors Challenge Pay Rates, Saying They Shortchange Women*, N.Y. Times, Oct. 16, 2015, http://www.nytimes.com/2015/10/17/us/egg-donors-challenge-pay-rates-saying-they-shortchange-women.html?_r=0.

have also argued that pricing guidelines are necessary not only to prevent the exploitation of young women but also to keep donated eggs affordable and accessible for families seeking fertility services, an assertion at odds with conventional economic understandings of supply and demand.

c. Antitrust-Regulatory Interactions

i. Accountable Care Organizations

Health maintenance organizations using dedicated physicians and facilities to deliver comprehensive care for a preset annual premium have been part of the U.S. healthcare landscape since the 1940s.[70] These have often been physician-led, nonprofit organizations, which recent health policy tends to treat sympathetically as "good guys" bearing insurance risk.[71]

"Accountable care" is the name currently favored for physician-hospital collaborations that seek the benefits of defragmentation without the risks associated with "managed care" in its pejorative sense. ACOs tend to function as joint ventures rather than unitary corporate entities. In theory, ACOs fulfill the long-standing promise of primary care medicine, emphasizing holistic, community-based, accessible services that reduce the need for acute or specialized care and manage it well when it is required.[72] In practice, ACOs are frequently controlled not by community-based physicians but by hospitals that have both sufficient capital and a developed organizational structure, adding an additional dimension to the competitive analysis.

ACOs may enable physicians and hospitals to work together more efficiently because of greater transparency, stronger accountability metrics, and better-designed incentives. There are now several hundred ACOs across the country serving both Medicare patients and private insurance beneficiaries. Medicare has launched three separate ACO initiatives: the Pioneer Program, the Medicare Shared Savings Program (MSSP), and the NextGen program, which reward physician-hospital partnerships that meet quality benchmarks at lower cost than traditional, fee-for-service Medicare.

To prevent the accumulation of market power in particular physician specialties and to reduce barriers to entry for potential competing ACOs, the enforcement agencies initially proposed requiring Medicare ACOs exceeding certain physician participation thresholds to obtain antitrust preclearance,[73] but retreated from that position in the final rule.[74] The DOJ and FTC continue to prefer nonexclusive to exclusive physician contracts in ACOs participating in the MSSP. However, opinion among health antitrust experts is beginning to swing

[70] *See* Am. Med. Ass'n v. United States, 317 U.S. 519 (1943).

[71] *See* Edward Hirshfeld, *Assuring the Solvency of Provider-Sponsored Organizations*, 15 HEALTH AFF. 28, 29–30 (1996) (discussing solvency risks).

[72] *See* Stephen M. Shortell & Lawrence P. Casalino, *Health Care Reform Requires Accountable Care Systems*, 300 J. AM. MED. ASS'N 95 (2008).

[73] *See* U.S. Dep't of Justice & Fed. Trade Comm'n, Proposed Statement of Antitrust Enforcement Policy Regarding Accountable Care Organizations Participating in the Medicare Shared Savings Program, 76 Fed. Reg. 21894-98 (Apr. 19, 2011).

[74] *See* Statement of Antitrust Enforcement Policy Regarding Accountable Care Organizations Participating in the Medicare Shared Savings Program, 76 Fed. Reg.67,026–32. (Oct. 28, 2011).

back toward allowing exclusive contracting in order to foster more meaningful clinical collaboration that responds to strongly shared, consistent financial incentives.[75]

Creating a workable framework for ACOs challenges competition law to address a host of specific regulatory interactions. In addition to the statement by the DOJ and FTC clarifying when ACOs would and would not risk antitrust liability, the Centers for Medicare and Medicaid Services issued regulations excusing properly structured ACOs from fraud-related prohibitions on kickbacks, physician self-referral, and physician-hospital gain-sharing. Moreover, the Internal Revenue Service issued an opinion that by saving money for Medicare, ACOs were acting in furtherance of a charitable purpose because they were "relieving the burden on government"—and therefore that nonprofit hospitals operating ACOs remained in compliance with tax-exempt organization law even though the physician practices controlling expenditures and sharing in savings are for-profit actors.

ii. Self-regulation and "Active Supervision" of Professional Licensing Boards

In 1962, libertarian economist Milton Friedman concluded a scathing critique of occupational licensing with the following: "I am myself persuaded that licensure has reduced both the quantity and quality of medical practice; that it has reduced the opportunities available to people who would like to be physicians, forcing them to pursue occupations they regard as less attractive; that it has forced the public to pay more for less satisfactory medical service, and that it has retarded technological development both in medicine itself and in the organization of medical practice."[76] Well-intentioned but often insular and unimaginative, many state medical and dental boards continue to favor their own licensees over potential rivals and to prohibit or restrict new forms of practice organization, marketing, and service delivery. Until recently, most parties seeking to counter anticompetitive board rules or disciplinary proceedings in court were limited to legal theories that favored the licensing boards, such as state administrative law challenges or First Amendment claims.

The Supreme Court's 2015 decision in *North Carolina State Board of Dental Examiners v. FTC*, discussed above, will give professional licensing boards throughout the country significant pause before adopting ad hoc policies that disadvantage competing professionals or nonprofessionals, and should lead to a constructive conversation regarding the accountability of self-regulatory bodies to actual state government.[77] The case concerned cease-and-desist letters sent by North Carolina's dental licensing board to nondentist teeth-whitening businesses, warning them that the unlicensed practice of dentistry is a crime. Affirming the Fourth Circuit Court of Appeals, the court held that a state professional regulatory board controlled by active market participants in the occupation the board regulates cannot claim immunity unless it is "actively supervised" by the state itself.

In the aftermath of the *North Carolina State Board* decision, private plaintiffs have begun to bring antitrust claims against state licensing boards. For example, the Texas Medical Board

[75] *See* Thomas L. Greaney, *The Tangled Web: Integration, Exclusivity and Market Power in Provider Contracting*, 14 HOUS. J. HEALTH L. & POL'Y 59, 88–90 (2014).

[76] MILTON FRIEDMAN, CAPITALISM AND FREEDOM 149–159 (1962).

[77] 135 S. Ct. 1101 (2015).

has been sued under the Sherman Act by a Dallas-based telehealth company that contracts with licensed Texas physicians to provide telephonic consultations to patients in the state, a care model that the board had attempted to discourage for several years by an increasingly stringent set of interpretations and amendments to its rules for issuing prescriptions. A federal district judge in Austin issued an injunction against the Medical Board in 2015, and the case is currently on appeal to the Fifth Circuit.[78]

Because self-regulatory bodies cannot function effectively under a constant threat of private litigation against themselves and their members, the most important issue raised by the case is *how* states will actively supervise their professional licensing boards. FTC staff has issued a guidance document regarding "active supervision," but its analysis leaves more uncertainty on state boards than seems advisable. For example, the guidance requires active oversight not only of blanket rules but also of individual disciplinary actions which, absent a pattern of selective enforcement, are much less likely to be anticompetitive.[79] Medical self-regulation faced an analogous problem thirty years ago when the Supreme Court exposed physicians' collective refusal to grant newcomers hospital privileges to potential antitrust liability, which Congress solved by granting legislative immunity conditioned on compliance with standards for good faith peer review.[80] Federal standards for state board conduct are an outside possibility, but it is more likely that states will enact one or more model practice acts that would promote uniformity among boards and assure their accountability to state government.

iii. Pharmaceuticals, Patents, and Generic Competition

Considerable innovation in healthcare lies at the intersection of patent law, antitrust law, food and drug law, and civil procedure. Since the enactment of the Hatch-Waxman Amendments in 1984, a large number of disputes have involved titrating incentives to develop new chemical and biochemical entities by awarding intellectual property rights while making existing drugs cheaper and more accessible by facilitating generic production.[81]

"Reverse payment" settlements (also called "pay for delay") resolve patent infringement litigation by transferring value from a patent holder to an accused infringer (i.e., a generic drug maker) instead of, as would be expected, from infringer to patent holder. To the antitrust enforcement agencies, a reverse payment agreement between the maker of a patented drug and generic drug manufacturers creates a cartel in which potential competitors, rather than becoming actual competitors, share the spoils of patent-generated market power with a current monopolist. After years percolating in the lower federal courts, the Supreme Court ruled on reverse payment settlements in *FTC v. Actavis* (2012), holding that when reverse payments are "large and unjustified," they may constitute unreasonable restraints of trade prohibited by the antitrust laws. However, the Court applied a "rule of reason" analysis to the practice, rather than declaring it presumptively illegal as the FTC had argued.

[78] *See* Teladoc, Inc. v. Tex. Med. Bd., 122 F. Supp. 3d 529 (W.D. Tex. 2015).

[79] FTC Staff Guidance on Active Supervision of State Regulatory Boards Controlled by Market Participants (Oct. 2015), https://www.ftc.gov/system/files/attachments/competition-policy-guidance/active_supervision_of_state_boards.pdf.

[80] *See* Patrick v. Burget, 486 U.S. 94, 105 (1988); Health Care Quality Improvement Act of 1986, 42 U.S.C. §§ 11101–11152 (2012).

[81] Drug Price Competition and Patent Term Restoration Act of 1984, Pub. L. No. 98-417, 98 Stat. 1585.

Since the *Actavis* decision, the federal courts have held that benefits of various types offered by a patent holder to an apparent infringer conditioned on the infringer delaying generic market entry may violate the antitrust laws. In the *K-Dur* litigation, the Third Circuit held that cash payments for delay were presumptively illegal.[82] In 2015, the California Supreme Court issued a similar ruling under state antitrust law.[83] Most recently, the First Circuit held that a brand drug firm's payment to a generic firm to delay entering the market could violate the antitrust laws not only if it takes the form of cash but also if it includes other types of consideration.[84]

In *New York* ex rel. *Schneiderman v. Actavis PLC*,[85] the Second Circuit departed from usual antitrust practices by approving a "conduct remedy" to redress competitive harm from another patent-related practice of the pharmaceutical industry called "product hopping." Pharmaceutical manufacturer Actavis held the patent for a twice-daily drug to treat Alzheimer's disease, Namenda IR. As Namenda IR neared the end of its patent exclusivity period, Actavis introduced a once-daily version—Namenda XR—carrying its own exclusivity period lasting until 2029. Actavis then withdrew Namenda IR from the market to force Alzheimer's patients to switch to Namenda XR before the generic versions of Namenda IR would become available.

In September 2014, the New York attorney general brought a lawsuit alleging that this "force-switch scheme" violated federal and state antitrust laws. The district court agreed, and issued a preliminary injunction requiring Actavis to keep Namenda IR on the market until thirty days after generic entry, as well as to inform healthcare providers of the injunction and the continued availability of Namenda IR. The Second Circuit affirmed the district court's order. The court reasoned that the combination of withdrawing a successful drug from the market and introducing a reformulated version of the drug was both anticompetitive and exclusionary. However, the court also indicated that efforts to persuade patients to shift to the reformulated version (a "soft" switch) would be permissible.

III Deeper Issues and the Path Forward

Healthcare markets are systematically challenged to achieve both competitive processes and competitive outcomes. Care is rarely produced at the lowest possible expense, prices seldom reflect the cost of production, quality is often ill-defined and unmeasurable, and inexpensive alternatives to established treatments are usually not available. Reversing these problems will require more than vigorous antitrust enforcement against private parties. It will require competition policy-makers to engage in a serious and sustained manner with the market imperfections created by roughly a century of accreted healthcare regulation, professional privilege, and public subsidy. These policies originally were adopted to strengthen and protect the therapeutic relationship between patients and their individual physicians, but now

[82] *See In re* K-Dur Antitrust Litigation, 686 F.3d 197 (3d Cir. 2012).

[83] *See In re* Cipro Cases I and II, 348 P.3d 845 (Cal. 2015).

[84] *See In re* Loestrin 24 Fe Antitrust Litigation, No. 14–2071, 2016 WL 698077 (1st Cir. Feb. 22, 2016). *See also* King Drug Co. of Florence, Inc. v. Smithkline Beecham Corp., 791 F.3d 388 (3d Cir. 2015).

[85] *See* New York *ex rel.* Schneiderman v. Actavis PLC, 787 F.3d 638 (2d Cir. 2015).

often serve mainly to shelter powerful interest groups and impede both competition and innovation. Improving competition also will require looking beneath conventional labels and questioning assumptions that antitrust analysis often takes for granted. Competitive landmarks in healthcare markets can be ambiguous, and substance can depart from form in many transactions and relationships.

Using these insights, competition policy-makers will need to develop workable strategies for dislodging the status quo, including recalibrating decades of regulation. Because U.S. antitrust law has few tools with which to dissipate market power after it has been acquired, a particularly challenging task will be to improve healthcare efficiency without simultaneously creating an oligopoly (or worse) of large integrated financing and delivery systems that cannot easily be deconsolidated later.

a. Agency, Information, and Professionalism

Two forms of agency failure permeate the healthcare system. First, physicians control over two-thirds of healthcare spending as patients' expert agents "ordering" hospitalization, specialty consultation, diagnostic testing, prescription therapy, and a variety of other services. These professional judgments, while usually well intentioned, are made under conditions that virtually guarantee their inefficiency: fragmented decision-making, disorganized production models, limited or biased information, fictitious input pricing even when cost is considered, and financial incentives ranging from studied apathy to outright self-enrichment. Second, financing intermediaries such as insurance companies, employers sponsoring benefit plans, and third-party administrators aggregate medical services into packaged coverage and underwrite (with various public subsidies and cushions) the associated financial risk. These agents do not always honor the preferences of the individuals who ultimately pay for coverage and receive care, an environment that not only creates "moral hazard" for both patients and healthcare providers but also tends to stabilize current market practices including anticompetitive norms.

Information failures justify and are intensified by these flawed agency relationships. Medical knowledge is both incomplete and asymmetric between expert professionals and patients. More generally, norms of medical professionalism coupled with generous insurance have detached pricing from cost and value throughout the system, distorting the contextual information that prices typically convey in competitive markets. Proponents of "big data" believe that generating and sharing comprehensive information about disease burden and treatment alternatives can spawn a "learning healthcare system" that achieves efficiency through collaboration more than competition.[86] However, most data elements currently available in electronic health records and the All-Payer Claims Databases (APCDs) that many states are constructing were collected in order for someone in the current healthcare system to get paid, and may prove less enlightening than expected.[87]

[86] *See, e.g.*, Inst. of Med., Best Care at Lower Cost: The Path to Continuously Learning Health Care in America 101–102 (Mark Smith et al. eds., 2012).

[87] *See also* Gobeille v. Liberty Mutual Insurance Company, 136 S. Ct. 936 (2016) (holding that ERISA preempts state laws imposing claims reporting requirements on self-insured employers and their third-party administrators).

Whether or not medical professionalism requires some degree of market power remains an open question in health policy.[88] Urgency and vulnerability still dominate mental images of medical need, the impulse to rescue is strong, and the notion of valuing life unsettling. The public therefore seeks perfection from its physicians, and character matters as well, justifying limits on the supply of professionals to those who meet peer standards of ethical purity in addition to technical competence. Collegiality and consultation are prized even at the risk of collusion. Compassion and charity are expected of both ethical health professionals and mission-driven nonprofit hospitals.

The result of these ethical preferences, which economist Kenneth Arrow once suggested may partially compensate for the information asymmetries referenced above,[89] is to erect substantial regulatory barriers to both competitive entry and consumer self-help. Deference to professional control also attenuates competition in health insurance, especially in a post-ACA world in which competition is channeled away from risk selection and into care management, where it comes face-to-face with professional and charitable norms.

b. The Regulatory Interface

A chicken-and-egg problem like rent control and the supply of affordable housing, healthcare regulation is so long-standing and so pervasive that it is no longer clear whether market failure necessitates regulation or regulation instantiates market failure. Regulation as much as market forces determines the structure of healthcare delivery, the form and amount of payment, and the opportunities for entry and innovation. Reinvigorating competition therefore requires not only compatible regulation at the federal level but also incremental reconsideration of state law and professional self-governance through organizations such as licensing bodies, medical specialty societies, and the Joint Commission.

The ACA generally invites competition and attempts to channel it into productive health system change, but suffers from several tensions and inconsistencies. Following the standard playbook of "managed competition" from the 1990s, the ACA curtails health plan competition based on risk of illness (e.g., cherry-picking healthy enrollees) by prohibiting medical underwriting and enforcing standardized benefits while using transparency, new payment methods, and new forms of healthcare delivery to intensify competition based on effectiveness and efficiency of care. However, its multiple layers of risk-adjustment through cross-subsidies among health plans participating in individual health insurance exchanges encourage speculative pricing and dampen incentives for careful management. The ACA also tries to defragment healthcare delivery and reorient it to prevention and community health by chartering entities such as ACOs and patient-centered medical homes (PCMHs) but, as discussed above, broad provider collaboration and consolidation can result in oligopoly, facilitate spillover collusion outside the scope of the joint venture, and create bottlenecks that erect barriers to entry by new competitors.

More generally, federal healthcare law—which has mainly been enacted in connection with Medicare payment rather than underlying practice—rests on assumptions of

[88] *See* Ronald Gilson, *The Devolution of the Legal Profession: A Demand Side Perspective*, 49 MD. L. REV. 869 (1990).

[89] *See* Kenneth J. Arrow, *Uncertainty and the Welfare Economics of Medical Care*, 53 AM. ECON. REV. 941, 941–943 (1963).

independent physicians recruiting outside resources to serve individual patients that are increasingly at odds with system-wide competitive priorities. As noted above, waivers or facilitative interpretations were needed from several federal administrative agencies to enable physicians and hospitals to collaborate on accountable care in the Medicare program. Other competitive issues are raised by federal drug and medical device regulation (e.g., FDA, Hatch-Waxman), which also focuses on suppliers to physicians rather than integrated medical practice, including the interactions with federal patent law discussed in connection with reverse payment settlements and product-hopping.

State law presents an even more varied and difficult-to-alter landscape, short of major preemptive federal legislation. Although the FTC frequently engages in "competition advocacy" that urges state lawmakers to avoid blatantly anticompetitive approaches, the state action doctrine reflects long-standing congressional intent that federal antitrust law defer to state regulation. As a result, states responding to stakeholder pressure often disadvantage nonphysician health professionals, impose certificate-of-need requirements on new health facilities, and otherwise erect or maintain barriers to competitive entry.

North Carolina State Board therefore is a potentially significant step along the path that the healthcare system must travel from guild monopoly to ethical but competitive industry. National licensure, or at least reciprocity, for physicians and some nonphysician health professionals may eventually follow. However, even a wholesale revision of state licensing laws would leave in place many other laws that discourage competition and innovation, such as medical staff regulations that partition physicians from hospitals, corporate practice prohibitions that limit the organizational forms of professional services, insurance laws that structure coverage by conventional category and mandate particular benefits, and even medical malpractice and product liability laws that apportion responsibility for harm selectively among market participants.

c. Ambiguous Competitive Landmarks

An important implication for competition policy of the agency-related, informational, and regulatory distortions just discussed is that economic landmarks used by the antitrust enforcement agencies and by courts hearing antitrust lawsuits may be misleading. Over the past half-century, legal analysis under the federal antitrust laws has settled into a generally well-accepted, relatively predictable set of criteria and tools predicated on standard microeconomics, albeit with strategic refinements drawn from fields such as game theory and behavioral economics. This is a far cry from the original premises of the Sherman Act, which included favoring small over large businesses for reasons of personal independence and participatory democracy as well as consumer welfare, a conceptual strand that survived in merger analysis into the 1970s.[90] Even for professional services, few recent courts have strayed from mainstream economic analysis, notwithstanding the leeway offered by a footnote in the Supreme Court's seminal *Goldfarb* decision.[91]

[90] *See, e.g.*, United States v. Von's Grocery Co., 384 U.S. 270 (1966).

[91] *See* Goldfarb v. Virginia State B., 421 U.S. 773, 788 n.17 (1978) ("The fact that a restraint operates upon a profession, as distinguished from a business, is, of course, relevant in determining whether that particular restraint violates the Sherman Act").

Healthcare antitrust law therefore uses standard economic terminology to describe market structure and conduct ("buyers and sellers," "vertical and horizontal"), to measure the product and geographic characteristics of each, and thereby to assess their competitive implications. These analytic frames are summarized and explained in a series of guidance documents issued over the years by the DOJ and FTC, which are not industry-specific and are illustrated using examples from much less regulated sectors than the healthcare system. The agencies make occasional joint pronouncements focused on healthcare, but these tend to offer market participants the reassurance of "safety zones" rather than modifying antitrust analysis.

The problem in a post-ACA world that acknowledges the existence of gross inefficiencies even in seemingly vigorous healthcare markets is that many standard descriptors were not outgrowths of a normal competitive dynamic and therefore should be questioned if those inefficiencies are to be reduced. For example, "vertical" transactions in normal industries are those that combine two or more levels in a standard supply chain (suppliers, manufacturers, distributors, retailers, etc.), while in healthcare the term is used to describe transactions between hospitals and physicians who are seldom part of a standard supply chain but rather are legally partitioned co-producers of complex care. In the *St. Luke's* case discussed above, the court ruled only on what seemed to be a straightforward acquisition of market power in physician primary care and did not grapple with ultimately more interesting issues regarding contractual and employment relationships between hospitals and medical groups that could, in the end, result in more coordinated and higher quality services.

Consider as well the "two-stage model" of competition that antitrust enforcers have used to analyze hospital and physician consolidation for the past twenty years.[92] That model posits that hospitals (and, to a lesser extent, physicians) first compete among themselves for inclusion in private insurance "networks" and then compete a second time if so included for the opportunity to care for individual patients. At the first stage of this model, insurers negotiate the lowest possible prices with each hospital for a full complement of services, making it important that there are enough hospitals to bargain against and that no hospital is so special that beneficiaries (or, more typically, their employers) will not buy insurance that omits it. At the second stage, patients who are sheltered by insurance from all or most of the costs seek out particular providers for particular services based on quality and convenience (and, usually, someone's personal or professional recommendation). In cases that seem worrisome to the agencies, such as hospital mergers in smaller communities, the agencies feed historical data into these models to estimate the potential harm to insurer-provider negotiations of changes in market concentration at either level.

However, broad networks of providers discounting the prices that insurers must pay for randomly aggregated individual services represent one historical moment in the recent evolution of private "managed care," nothing more, and have not delivered true value to patients according to most health policy experts. Such products, particularly preferred provider organizations, were normalized following the political backlash against tightly managed care in the late 1990s, which re-empowered Blue Cross plans and large hospitals as economic actors and rendered unavailable most HMO products with low consumer cost-sharing. By contrast, early "managed competition" theory, from which both the ACA's insurance framework

92 *See* Gregory Vistnes, *Hospitals, Mergers, and Two-Stage Competition*, 67 ANTITRUST L.J. 671(2000).

and the ACO movement are derived, contemplated competition on price and quality by fully integrated organizations such as closed-panel HMOs (e.g., Kaiser) and prepaid group practices. Today's return to narrow-network models, albeit with higher cost-sharing than traditional HMOs, calls "two-stage" competition into serious question. Broad networks will be even less necessary if primary care becomes available from a variety of community-based providers, if specialty care can be delivered through telemedicine, and if complex surgery and chronic disease management are offered by dedicated providers at a bundled price with a guarantee of quality and effectiveness.

Looking ahead, it therefore will be important for antitrust law to be more precise about the roles played by professional and corporate entities in particular transactions, and more open to market configurations that differ from historical norms. Today's insurers may end up in direct competition with today's providers, or in direct collaboration with them—and both, either, or none may bear true insurance risk. Finding real "buyers" in this environment also may be challenging. Furthermore, a sustained move to bundled payment should reveal a new dimension of competition, success of treatment (also called "performance" or "warranty" risk). Bundling will also channel many of today's individually purchased care components into provider (business–to-business) rather than patient (business-to-consumer) transactions.

d. Dislodging the Status Quo

In most industries, antitrust enforcement acts only at the margin, deterring collusion and forestalling monopoly. In healthcare, however, modal competition is weak—particularly with respect to reducing costs of production and charging commensurately low prices. Antitrust alone cannot solve this problem, but as coverage expands under the ACA there are compelling reasons for it to play a more central role in dislodging the status quo.

How might this be done? One promising strategy is to focus on barriers to competitive entry, both those that result from outdated regulations such as certificate of need laws and overly restrictive licensing standards and those that are caused by private bottlenecks such as MFNs. A staple principle of "Chicago School" antitrust theory is that innovation will overcome most market power if government gets out of the way. One lesson for healthcare is that facilitating innovation through both regulatory reform and targeted antitrust enforcement can go a long way toward opening dimensions of competition that have up to now been suppressed, including making care delivery much more responsive to normal consumer preferences.[93]

Addressing power in already consolidated geographic markets is more difficult. Many areas of the country have high concentration ratios for hospitals and some specialist physicians, either because of persistent provider shortages in rural areas or because mergers and acquisitions over the course of three decades have reduced the number of independent competitors. As the result of widespread insurance coverage with generous payment, however, few consolidated markets behave economically as "natural" monopolies (i.e., with increasing scale economies over the expected range of production), and coordinated behavior

[93] *See* William M. Sage & Kelly McIlhattan, *Upstream Health Law*, 42 J. L. Med. & Ethics 535 (2014).

facilitated by compliance with complex regulation is common. Rationalizing capacity and "rightsizing" inventory is therefore a challenging task. One possible approach in these markets is to involve state and local government in oversight of specific markets.[94] In some communities, this strategy might promote competition among politically budgeted provider organizations to serve the aggregate needs of an assigned population-more resembling a European model-instead of competition to provide specific services to individuals.

Another possibility is to leverage government administered pricing systems with associated transparency to discourage managerial slack and force the development of more efficient production processes. Especially in consolidated markets, Medicare and Medicaid provide essential funding streams for hospitals, and Medicare remains influential for most physicians, including specialists, who are unwilling to turn away aging patients. With respect to private payers, targeted regulatory changes might facilitate value-based contracting with dominant providers, and potentially open up alternative sources of supply such as telemedicine. These more market-directive strategies are disfavored by traditional competition theory, but are probably necessary given the overhang of decades of regulation and subsidy.

An additional transitional problem to address is the very high price charged for patented medical technologies, particularly prescription drugs with high development costs but low production costs. In a regulatory environment that requires insurance coverage of "medically necessary" products and services within a provider system that is still highly deferential to individual physician preference, even markets with more than one manufacturer can be uncompetitive. Breakthrough hepatitis C medications, for example, remain extremely expensive because manufacturers can tacitly coordinate their pricing strategies.[95] In the case of drugs such as these that really do have the power to cure, payers may be able to negotiate a money-back guarantee of effectiveness that offsets the high price. For patented technologies that have only incremental benefit, however, government may need to expand the very limited authority that the ACA currently confers on comparative effectiveness research to encompass cost-effectiveness and to use the results to guide coverage and payment decisions.[96] It has also been suggested that sharp price increases for existing drugs may warrant antitrust investigation.[97]

Finally, competition policy-makers must manage the post-ACA transition from fragmented, fee-for-input medical care to organized systems that are accountable for outcomes and value. Healthcare is a capital-intensive industry, and it will not be possible to build

[94] Erin C. Fuse Brown & Jaime S. King, The Double-Edged Sword of Health Care Integration: Consolidation and Cost Control (Fed. 2016) (prepublication draft), http://ssrn.com/abstract=2736310 (discussing Certificates of Public Advantage (COPAs) and other oversight methods).

[95] *See* Troyen Brennan & William Shrank, *New Expensive Treatments for Hepatitis C Infection*, 312 J. Am. Med. Ass'n 593 (2014).

[96] *See* 42 U.S.C. § 1320e (2012).

[97] Daraprim (pyrimethamine) was recently sold to Turing Pharmaceuticals, which promptly raised its price from $13.50 to $750, prompting a public outcry and even a congressional hearing. In connection with the sale, the manufacturer switched the drug from conventional distribution channels to a tightly controlled distribution system usually associated with an FDA-mandated Risk Evaluation and Mitigation Strategy (REMS). However, no particular safety issues exist, raising the possibility that the goal of restricted distribution is to make it more difficult for generic competitors to obtain samples. Michael Carrier & Aaron Kesselheim, *The Daraprim Price Hike and Role for Antitrust*, Health Aff. Blog (Oct. 21, 2015), http://healthaffairs.org/blog/2015/10/21/the-daraprim-price-hike-and-a-role-for-antitrust/.

hundreds of Kaiser-like health systems in a short period of time. Nor would hundreds of thousands of physicians, many at advanced stages of their careers, be willing to abandon their independent practices for employment, even if all states permitted it. "Virtual" integration through contract and shared information and management systems is therefore a practical necessity. As is already taking place with respect to ACOs, antitrust authorities will have to judge the relative merits of exclusive and nonexclusive contractual relationships in many markets, as well as the risk that partial integration will facilitate cartelization for services still provided under conventional fee-for-service payment.[98]

IV Conclusion

Consolidation in American industry as a whole is attracting renewed attention. In a 2015 lecture, economists Jason Furman and Peter Orszag suggested that oligopoly power resulting from mergers in a range of economic sectors over the last few decades may have not only significantly harmed consumers but also may have exacerbated the effects of income inequality.[99] These concerns are relevant to the U.S. healthcare system, which according to expert consensus wastes approximately $1 trillion annually of public and private money. Dramatically improving healthcare competition in the United States could restore our healthcare system to a sustainable path in terms of affordability, accessibility, and quality.

Acknowledgment

The author gratefully acknowledges Robert F. Leibenluft, Esq., of Hogan Lovells for his indispensable contributions to this chapter. University of Texas law student Preston Moore provided research assistance.

[98] *See* Thomas Greaney, *Examining Implication of Health Insurance Mergers*, Health Aff. Blog (July 2015), http://healthaffairs.org/blog/2015/07/16/examining-implications-of-health-insurance-mergers.

[99] *See* Jason Furman & Peter Orszag, A Firm-Level Perspective on the Role of Rents in the Rise in Inequality, Presentation at "A Just Society" Centennial Event in Honor of Joseph Stiglitz Columbia University (Oct. 16, 2015), https://www.whitehouse.gov/sites/default/files/page/files/20151016_firm_level_perspective_on_role_of_rents_in_inequality.pdf.

CHAPTER 28

DRUGS, BIOLOGICS, AND DEVICES

FDA Regulation, Intellectual Property, and Medical Products in the American Healthcare System

LEWIS A. GROSSMAN

I Introduction

Treatises and casebooks on American health law typically devote few pages to the role of the U.S. Food and Drug Administration (FDA). The traditional exclusion of food and drug regulation from the core topics of health law is unfortunate, for the FDA is one of the most important actors in this field. The agency has primary regulatory authority over all drugs, biologics, and medical devices, and its influence has grown in recent decades along with the markets for these products. In 2012, retail sales of medical products regulated by the FDA totaled \$358.3 billion—almost 13% of national health expenditures.[1] And this figure does not include the additional tens of billions of dollars spent on drugs and devices outside the retail context—for example, products used and administered by physicians' offices, hospitals, and other healthcare facilities.

The price of these products reflects the massive costs that industry incurs in gaining FDA approval to sell them. But the agency's impact on the healthcare system is not merely economic. The requirement for FDA approval shapes much of the medical research performed in the United States. The agency regulates the manufacture, composition, labeling, and much of the advertising of the drugs, biologics, and medical devices it approves—and it increasingly restricts their distribution and use as well. FDA approval decisions greatly influence medical practice and insurance reimbursement decisions. Furthermore, because the FDA is a gatekeeping agency, its influence is reflected not only in the selection of products on

[1] CMS, National Health Care Expenditure Data, Table 2, *available at* http://www.cms.gov/Research-Statistics-Data-and-Systems/Statistics-Trends-and-Reports/NationalHealthExpendData/Downloads/tables.pdf.

the market, but also in the invisible universe of products *not* on the market for lack of FDA approval.

This article will set out the basic framework of the FDA's product approval schemes for drug, biologics, and medical devices. It will also consider intellectual property protections and statutory exclusivity periods, which pose additional barriers to market entry for follow-on medical products. Finally, it will explore a number of technological, legal, political, and economic developments that are currently reshaping FDA pharmaceutical and device regulation.[2]

The federal Food, Drug, and Cosmetic Act (FD&C Act) and Public Health Service Act (PHSA) create separate but overlapping regulatory schemes for drugs, biologics (large-molecule drugs), and medical devices. The three FDA subdivisions responsible for these products are the Center for Drug Evaluation and Research (CDER), the Center for Biologics Evaluation and Research (CBER), and the Center for Devices and Radiological Health (CDRH). This article will discuss small-molecule drug regulation in the most detail and will then more briefly describe the schemes for biologics and devices. Although the FDA regulates almost every aspect of the testing, manufacture, labeling, sale, and promotion of these products, this article will focus primarily on the agency's gatekeeping role.

II The Law Governing Each Product Category

a. Drugs

i. Product Approval Scheme

The FD&C Act defines "drug" to mean articles "intended for use in the diagnosis, cure, mitigation, treatment, or prevention of disease" or "intended to affect the structure or any function of the body."[3] The definitions of "biological products" and "medical devices" are similar, but, as discussed below,[4] the former term applies only to large-molecule articles derived from living things, and the latter applies only to products that do not operate primarily through chemical action or metabolization.[5]

The FDA's power over America's drug supply hinges primarily on one sentence—Section 505(a) of the FD&C Act: "No person shall introduce or deliver for introduction into interstate commerce any new drug, unless an approval of an application filed pursuant to subsection

[2] The issues surrounding tort suits against manufacturers of drugs and devices are explored in the article of this volume by Peter Grossi and Keri Arnold.

[3] Federal Food, Drug, and Cosmetic Act (FD&C Act) § 201(g). The FD&C Act is codified at 21 U.S.C. §§ 301-399F. This article follows the widespread practice among Food and Drug Law experts of citing to the FD&C Act rather than to the U.S. Code. FDA's authority to regulate biological products derives from Section 351 of the Public Health Service Act (PHSA), 42 U.S.C. § 262, as well as from the FD&C Act. When discussing biologics, this article will similarly cite to the PHSA rather than to the U.S. Code.

[4] *See infra* sections II(b)(i) and (II)(c)(1).

[5] Public Health Service Act (PHSA) § 351(i); FD&C Act § 201(h).

(b) or (j) of this section is effective with respect to such drug."[6] Subsection (b) sets forth the requirements for a New Drug Application (NDA), which the FDA will not approve unless the sponsor provides adequate evidence of the drug's safety and effectiveness. Subsection (j) creates the Abbreviated New Drug Application (ANDA), a much less onerous pathway to market for manufacturers of generic copies of approved new drugs. This pathway becomes available following the expiration of any relevant patent and statutory exclusivity periods. An ANDA relies on the safety and effectiveness data contained in the pioneer product's NDA and is devoted primarily to showing merely that the generic drug is bioequivalent to its brand-name counterpart.

Although the FDA first acquired premarket review power over new drugs in 1938, with the passage of the Federal Food, Drug, and Cosmetic Act, this function took its modern form only with enactment of the Kefauver-Harris Drug Amendments of 1962. Between 1938 and 1962, the FD&C Act required premarket notification rather than premarket approval; a manufacturer could commence selling a drug within one hundred eighty days after submitting an NDA unless the FDA affirmatively objected. Moreover, an NDA sponsor was required to demonstrate the safety but not the efficacy, of its product—although efficacy considerations began to enter the FDA reviewers' calculations informally well before 1962.[7] The 1962 amendments converted the NDA into a true premarket licensing application and mandated proof of both safety and efficacy. To apply this new efficacy requirement to drugs already on the market in 1962, the FDA implemented a complex transition process that is not finished even today.

The FD&C Act requires the FDA to deny an NDA unless it includes, among other information, (1) reports of "adequate tests by all methods reasonably applicable to show whether or not such drug is safe for use under the conditions prescribed, recommended, or suggested in the proposed labeling thereof," and (2) "substantial evidence that the drug will have the effect it purports or is represented to have" under the conditions of use in the labeling."[8] The act does not explicitly instruct the agency to *balance* the risks of a drug against its benefits, but the agency has nonetheless done so since 1962.

Although the FDA's authority to approve or deny an NDA is its most conspicuous and discussed power with respect to drugs, the agency is involved in drug development well before the NDA stage. Preclinical (in vitro and animal) research can be performed without FDA permission, but a company cannot transport an unapproved drug across state lines for clinical (human) trials unless it first submits an Investigational New Drug Exemption (IND) to the agency. The FD&C Act directs the FDA to condition any such exemption on the investigator obtaining the informed consent of the research subjects. The agency enforces this obligation, and protects the subjects' rights and welfare in other respects, by requiring every proposed protocol to be approved by an ethics committee known as an institutional review board (IRB). Although IRBs have traditionally resided within academic institutions and medical facilities conducting human subject research, independent for-profit IRBs also review some drug trials today. Every significant change in an investigation subsequent to the filing of the IND (for example, the progression from Phase I to Phase II or Phase II to Phase

[6] FD&C Act § 505(a).

[7] Daniel Carpenter, Reputation and Power: Organizational Image and Pharmaceutical Regulation at the FDA149–156 (2010).

[8] FD&C Act § 505(d)(1), (5).

III) must be preceded by additional IRB review and the submission of a "protocol amendment" to the FDA. The FDA can issue a "clinical hold" halting an investigation at any time because of concerns about patient safety, ethics compliance, or scientific validity.

Sponsors strive to avoid FDA challenges to the scientific validity of their clinical studies—either during the investigation or after submission of the NDA—by meeting with agency representatives throughout the drug development process. The act requires the FDA to grant a sponsor's request for a "special protocol assessment" meeting regarding the size and design of its pivotal Phase III trials and binds the agency to the parameters agreed on in this meeting except in limited circumstances.[9]

As noted above, the FDA cannot approve an NDA unless it contains "substantial evidence" of efficacy. The FD&C Act defines this term to mean "evidence consisting of adequate and well-controlled investigations, including clinical investigations."[10] Ordinarily, the pivotal trials supporting an NDA are large Phase III studies. The FDA prefers the use of placebo controls, but it allows active treatment controls when the interests of the patient make the use of a placebo unethical.[11] In addition, the agency almost always demands that such investigations be double-blinded and randomized, if possible.[12] The FDA ordinarily will not approve an NDA unless the sponsor has completed at least two successful Phase III trials, but as the statute permits, the agency will occasionally determine that one such trial plus confirmatory evidence are "sufficient to establish effectiveness."[13]

Before reaching a final decision on an NDA, the agency frequently solicits the views of an advisory committee of independent experts, whose recommendation is influential but not binding. Despite the scientific language of the FD&C Act and the scientific rigor demanded of the supporting studies, the FDA's ultimate decision is not purely objective. Rather, its approval or denial of an NDA is a policy judgment about whether the benefits of the product sufficiently outweigh the risks. The FDA's policy considerations extend only so far, however. Except in occasional situations involving treatments for extremely serious conditions, the agency will not expressly deny an application because the new drug, though shown to be effective, is *less* effective than another drug already on the market.[14] Furthermore, the agency is not supposed to take economic factors, such as cost-effectiveness, into account when ruling on an NDA.

When the FDA approves an NDA for a new prescription drug, it is not simply permitting the sale of a molecular entity, but rather of a molecular entity accompanied by particular labeling. The lengthy, carefully negotiated physician labeling, set forth in the NDA itself, contains, among other information, the approved indications, the dosage, any contraindications and warnings, and a summary of the supporting scientific studies. Written and graphic promotional materials are also considered to be "labeling" under the FD&C Act.[15]

9 FD&C Act § 505(b)(5)(B) & (C). 10 FD&C Act § 505(d).

11 21 C.F.R. § 314.126(b)(2). 12 21 C.F.R. § 314.126(b)(4) & (5).

13 FD&C Act § 505(d).

14 The FDA will consider the comparative efficacy of a new product for a life-threatening disease, a disease causing irreversible mortality, or a serious communicable disease in situations when an effective remedy is already available. 60 Fed. Reg. 39,180, 39,181 (Aug. 1, 1995). Moreover, the FDA will sometimes reject a new product application on the grounds of relative *safety*, and it may require the labeling of a less effective product to specify the therapy of choice.

15 FD&C Act § 201(m).

The dissemination of any sort of labeling that is inconsistent with a drug's approved labeling almost always renders the product an illegal, unapproved new drug. A manufacturer that wants to make a change in the labeling ordinarily must first obtain FDA approval of a supplemental NDA (SNDA). If the SNDA is seeking approval of a new indication, it must be supported by "substantial evidence" of efficacy.

Critically, however, the FDA does not limit the uses for which a physician may prescribe a drug, regardless of the content of the labeling. Since the early 1970s, the agency has foresworn any regulation of the practice of medicine through restrictions on off-label prescribing.[16] Indeed, prescribing inconsistent with the approved package insert is extremely widespread in American medicine, especially in certain fields, such as oncology and pediatrics. As discussed below,[17] the FDA today occasionally shapes prescribing practices through mandatory Risk Evaluation and Mitigation Strategies (REMS) that restrict approved drugs' distribution and use (for example, by requiring that prescribing doctors have particular training or experience). Nonetheless, the fact remains that most physicians can prescribe most of the FDA-approved armamentarium for any purpose.

The FDA has long struggled to preserve the integrity of the SNDA process in the face of its nonregulation of the practice of medicine. If a drug becomes widely used for an off-label indication without a labeling change, its manufacturer will have little incentive to invest in the clinical trials necessary to support an SNDA. Accordingly, the agency fights attempts by manufacturers to promote or advertise their drugs for off-label uses. As discussed below,[18] however, courts have recently weakened the FDA's authority to prohibit promotional communications about off-label uses, ruling that some such prohibitions violate manufacturers' commercial free speech rights under the First Amendment of the U.S. Constitution.

Through the 1980s, manufacturers and some patients vociferously—and justifiably—contended that the FDA took too long to review NDAs. Critics were especially vexed by periods during which new molecular entity (NME) drugs were available in foreign markets but not in the United States, a phenomenon known as the "drug lag." The FDA's protracted review times were due both to a dearth of resources and the agency's conservative approach.

Today, NDA review times are dramatically shorter than they were a quarter of a century ago. The median number of months the FDA took to review and approve an NME NDA dropped from 34.1 in 1988 to 9.8 in 2012.[19] This quicker pace is due largely to an increase in agency personnel dedicated to the drug review process. The bulk of these additional employees are funded by drug applicant "user fees," which Congress first authorized in the 1992 Prescription Drug User Fee Act (PDUFA) and has reauthorized in five-year intervals ever since. The shortening of NDA review periods also reflects a generally less risk-averse attitude at the FDA. The agency's modern view of its role—encapsulated in a mission statement contained within the FD&C Act—includes not only protecting the public health by preventing the sale of dangerous products, but also enhancing the public health by ensuring timely access to useful remedies.[20]

[16] Legal Status of Approved Labeling for Prescription Drugs; Prescribing for Uses Unapproved by the FDA: Notice of Proposed Rulemaking, 37 Fed. Reg. 16,503 (Aug. 15, 1972).

[17] *See infra* section III(c).

[18] *See infra* section III(b).

[19] Peter Barton Hutt, Richard A. Merrill, & Lewis A. Grossman, Food and Drug Law: Cases and Materials 749–750 (4th ed. 2014).

[20] FD&C Act § 1003(b).

In addition to speeding up the normal NDA review process, the FDA and Congress have also introduced various special programs to expedite the availability of drugs for serious and life-threatening diseases. Some of these programs—such as "fast track," "accelerated approval," and the "breakthrough therapy" designation—are designed to shorten drug development and approval times by increasing agency consultations with manufacturers, permitting "rolling" review of NDAs before they are complete, and authorizing provisional approvals of drugs based on unvalidated surrogate endpoints. Other programs, epitomized by the "Treatment IND," allow manufacturers to provide investigational drugs to patients for treatment purposes *prior* to approval if those patients suffer from serious conditions and have no satisfactory alternatives. These early access programs are not implemented frequently, largely because drug manufacturers are prohibited from profiting on the sale of investigational drugs for treatment purposes. Manufacturers also worry that use of an investigational drug outside of controlled studies might complicate the NDA approval process.

Although FDA approval of an NDA does not present quite as high a barrier to market entry as it once did, drug development remains a prolonged, risky, and extraordinarily expensive endeavor. Even as agency review periods have shrunk, the time that sponsors devote to clinical research prior to submission of the NDA has continued to expand.[21] Furthermore, much research—both preclinical and clinical—leads to dead ends. For every ten thousand chemicals screened, only about ten will enter clinical testing. Of these, seven will successfully complete Phase I clinical testing, three will successfully complete Phase II, and only two will successfully complete Phase III and be approved for marketing.[22] When failed research efforts and opportunity costs are taken into account, it costs well over $1 billion to bring an NME drug to market.[23]

ii. Intellectual Property and Statutory Exclusivity

In light of these massive costs and risks, the pharmaceutical industry would not invest in the development of new drugs without the promise of a postapproval period free of generic copies in which the NDA holder can charge monopoly rents. Until 1984, the only tools available to pioneer drug manufacturers to resist the entry of generic competitors were standard patent law plus statutory protections for trade secrets and confidential commercial information. The former body of law barred a generic company from marketing a copycat product prior to the expiration of the pioneer's patent term.[24] The latter prevented generic manufacturers from obtaining the nonpublic clinical data that the innovator company used to support its NDA, and it also prohibited the FDA from relying on these data to support the approval of a generic product's application.

The innovator drug industry was dissatisfied with this system, because the time devoted to research and to obtaining FDA approval ate away much of each drug's "effective" patent life. Meanwhile, generic manufacturers (as well as policy-makers concerned about growing healthcare expenditures) were troubled by the requirement that the NDA for a generic

[21] Hutt, Merrill, & Grossman, Food and Drug Law, at 750.

[22] *Id.* at 674.

[23] *Id.* at 748.

[24] Indeed, even the use a patented active ingredient in a generic manufacturer's premarket studies was considered to constitute patent infringement. *See* Roche Products v. Bolar Pharmaceuticals, 733 F.2d 858 (Fed. Cir. 1984).

product be supported by costly and time-consuming duplicative research even after the expiration of the pioneer drug's patent. The Drug Price Competition and Patent Term Restoration Act of 1984,[25] known as "Hatch-Waxman," was a grand bargain intended to address both sectors' concerns.

Under Hatch-Waxman, generic companies may gain market entry through FDA approval of an Abbreviated New Drug Application (ANDA). An ANDA demonstrates bioequivalence to the pioneer product (the "reference listed drug") but piggybacks on the safety and effectiveness data contained in the listed drug's approved NDA. In other words, the statute circumvents the government's obligation to protect the innovator company's confidential commercial information by permitting generic applicants to benefit from the pioneer's data without actually seeing it.[26]

In exchange for these concessions, Hatch-Waxman grants the innovator drug companies the possibility of a patent term extension to restore some of the protected time (up to five years) that they lost while performing clinical research and obtaining FDA approval. The statute also establishes periods of "data exclusivity" for brand-name drugs during which the agency may not approve an ANDA. These exclusivity periods, which are entirely distinct from patent protections and thus apply regardless of the pioneer drug's patent status, run for five years following the approval of an NDA for a new chemical entity (NCE) drug and for three years following other types of approvals supported by new clinical investigations (for example, SNDAs for new indications).[27]

Finally, Hatch-Waxman creates a special mechanism for brand-name and generic drug manufacturers to resolve patent disputes. Innovator companies are permitted to list every patent purportedly protecting each of their NDA'd drugs in an FDA-published volume known as the *Orange Book*. Every ANDA must include a "certification" with respect to each patent listed for the relevant pioneer drug. This certification must assert that the patent has not in fact been filed with Patent and Trademark Office; that it has expired; that it will expire on a stated date; or that it is invalid or will not be infringed by the generic product. A certification of invalidity or noninfringement, known as a "Paragraph IV" certification, triggers an immediate right by the innovator company to file a patent infringement action within forty-five days. The FDA may not approve the ANDA for thirty months following the commencement of such a suit, unless the court decides prior to that time that the brand-name company's patent is invalid or not infringed. To encourage generic companies to challenge patents, Hatch-Waxman grants the first successful filer of a Paragraph IV certification one hundred eighty days of *generic* exclusivity upon approval of its ANDA.

Because of Hatch-Waxman, generic manufacturers bear much lower costs for product development and regulatory approval than do their brand-name counterparts. Consequently, generics are sold at substantially reduced prices. The first generic competitor prices its product, on average, only about 6% lower than the brand-name drug, but the introduction of a second generic version typically causes the price to plummet to about 50%

[25] Pub. L. No. 98-417, 98 Stat. 1585 (1984).

[26] Hatch-Waxman also overrules *Bolar*, thus permitting a generic manufacturer to use a patented product in the tests necessary to prepare an ANDA prior to the expiration of the patent.

[27] Under separate statutory provisions, manufacturers can extend their exclusivity periods by pursuing pediatric studies. Orphan drugs for rare diseases and conditions are also eligible for additional market exclusivity.

of the price of the pioneer product. Each additional ANDA approval drives the price down further, and the presence of nine generic competitors drops the generic price to about 20% of the brand-name price.[28]

Brand-name drug manufacturers are understandably eager to wring every possible day of exclusivity out of this system. They do so, for example, by obtaining multiple patents for the same drug and by performing pediatric studies to qualify for additional statutory exclusivity under a different section of the FD&C Act.[29] Moreover, they enter "reverse payment" settlement agreements with generic manufacturers, under which an NDA holder agrees to drop its infringement lawsuit and pay the generic company a substantial amount of money, and the ANDA filer in exchange agrees not to market the generic product for a designated period of time.[30] In the years immediately following the passage of Hatch-Waxman, brand-name companies used additional tactics to extend their monopoly position that the FDA and Congress later forbade. For example, pioneer drug manufacturers used to string together prolonged series of separate thirty-month stays, until a 2003 FDA regulation and a 2004 statutory amendment provided that only one such stay is available with respect to each ANDA.

Hatch-Waxman also created another important abbreviated pathway called a Section 505(b)(2) application. Follow-on manufacturers typically use a 505(b)(2) NDA when they seek to make a change to another company's already marketed drug whose patent protection and statutory exclusivity have expired—for example, a change in the drug's dosage form, strength, or indication or a switch of the product from prescription to over-the-counter status. A Section 505(b)(2) NDA relies on the reference listed drug's NDA for all required information except the data required to support the follow-on drug's safety and efficacy in light of the changes. A drug approved pursuant to 505(b)(2) is itself potentially eligible for either a three-year or five-year period of market exclusivity.

b. Biologics

i. Product Approval Scheme

Section 351 of the Public Health Service Act (PHSA), also administered by the FDA, establishes a separate approval pathway for biological products known as the Biologics License Application (BLA).[31] The PHSA defines the term "biological product" to embrace any "virus, therapeutic serum, toxin, antitoxin, vaccine, blood, blood component or derivative, allergenic product, protein (except any chemically synthesized polypeptide), or analogous

[28] FDA, Generic Competition and Drug Prices (2006).

[29] FD&C Act § 505A (made permanent by the FDA Safety and Innovation Act, 126 Stat. 993, 1039 (2012)).

[30] In 2013, the U.S. Supreme Court held that such arrangements may, in some instances, violate the antitrust laws, although it declined to deem them presumptively unlawful. FTC v. Actavis, 133 S. Ct. 2223 (2013).

[31] This distinct regime derives from the Biologics Act of 1902, 32 Stat. 728. The federal government thus began to perform premarket review of biologics more than three decades before it assumed this task for nonbiologic drugs in 1938. The National Institutes of Health (NIH) administered the Biologics Act until the FDA acquired this responsibility in 1972.

product... applicable to the prevention, treatment, or cure of a disease or condition."[32] The FDA interprets the term "analogous product" to embrace human cell and tissue products, including the components of advanced cellular technologies such as gene therapy, stem cell therapy, and assisted reproductive technology. Although it is perhaps impossible to identify a single characteristic common to all biologics, they are generally large-molecule products derived from living organisms, including animals, human beings, and bioengineered bacteria.

Because of their molecular complexity and living precursors, biologics present manufacturing and regulatory challenges different from chemically synthesized, small-molecule drugs. For example, the details of the manufacturer's production process are especially important to assuring the identity, consistency, and purity of a biologic. Indeed, the PHSA used to require a biologics manufacturer to obtain approval of both a product license application (PLA) and a separate establishment license application (ELA). Congress consolidated these applications into a single BLA in 1997, but facility and processing control information remain critical components of this application.

Most biological products also fall within the FD&C Act's definition of "drug."[33] Therefore, apart from the distinct NDA and BLA applications, small-molecule drugs and biological drugs are subject to the same requirements.[34] For example, the FDA uses the same IND procedures for investigational biologics that it uses for small-molecule drugs. Moreover, the NDA and BLA processes themselves are not so different. Although the PHSA's criteria for approving a BLA—"safe, pure, and potent"—are couched in slightly different language than the FD&C Act's standard for approving an NDA, the two statutes are functionally almost identical in this respect. The user fee legislation (PDUFA) applies to BLAs as well as NDAs. Furthermore, in 2003, the FDA transferred some important categories of biological products formerly reviewed and regulated by CBER to CDER, including monoclonal antibodies, therapeutic proteins, and immunomodulators.[35] The FDA's regulation of these products in particular is thus virtually identical to its regulation of small-molecule drugs, apart from the distinct, new regime for follow-on biosimilars, discussed below.[36]

Cellular products, gene therapy products, vaccines, allergenic extracts, antitoxins, and blood products remain within CBER's bailiwick. The FDA has promulgated discrete regulations for human blood and blood products and for human cellular and tissue-based products.[37] These regulations, the details of which are beyond the scope of this article, are based in part on Section 361 of the PHSA, pursuant to which the FDA may issue regulations to prevent the spread of communicable diseases.[38]

[32] PHSA § 351(i)(1).

[33] A few biologics qualify as medical devices, rather than drugs.

[34] The similarity between the regulatory regimes was enhanced in 1997, when Congress both explicitly applied the FD&C Act—except for the NDA requirement—to biological products and instructed the FDA to "take measures to minimize differences in the review and approval of products required to have approved [BLAs] and products required to have approved [NDAs]." 111 Stat. 2296, 2324 (1997).

[35] Transfer of Therapeutic Products to the CDER, FDA website (updated Feb. 22, 2010).

[36] *See infra* section (II)(b)(2).

[37] *See* 21 C.F.R. Parts 606, 607, 630, 640, 1271.

[38] 42 U.S.C. § 264.

ii. Intellectual Property and Statutory Exclusivity

Until recently, no abbreviated pathway existed for the approval of a generic biological product. Although Congress did not explicitly exclude biologics from the Hatch-Waxman scheme, biotechnology innovators maintained, and the FDA agreed, that neither an ANDA nor a 505(b)(2) application was a suitable vehicle for a follow-on biologic. Opponents of an abbreviated pathway for generic biologics contended that because of biologics' complexity and production challenges, the FDA could not rely on the safety and effectiveness data from the brand-name manufacturer's BLA when approving a purportedly similar product.

Lawmakers' and regulators' resistance to the notion of generic biologics began to weaken significantly around the turn of the century, in light of technological advances and escalating healthcare costs. In the late 1990s and 2000s, the FDA approved a few 505(b)(2) applications for recombinant biotechnology products whose reference listed counterparts were marketed pursuant to NDAs rather than BLAs. The agency continued to deny, however, that the 505(b)(2) pathway was available to copies of BLA'd biologics.

In 2010, Congress officially launched the era of generic biological products with the passage of the Biosimilars Price Competition and Innovation Act, or Title VII of the Patient Protection and Affordable Care Act ("Obamacare").[39] The Biosimilars Act amends Section 351 of the PHSA to create a new, abbreviated licensure mechanism for "Biological Products as Biosimilar or Interchangeable."[40] The ultimate feasibility of this "Section 351(k)" pathway, and its cost-saving potential for follow-on manufacturers, will depend on the details of the FDA's implementation. The agency will spell out these details—including, for instance, the precise evidentiary burden on biosimilar applicants—in a series of guidance documents explicitly authorized by the Biosimilars Act.[41] In addition to mandating pharmacokinetic and pharmacodynamics studies, the FDA is likely to require many or most biosimilar applicants to conduct clinical studies demonstrating their products' safety, purity, and potency. The future of the biosimilars market hinges on the size, rigor, and expense of the additional studies demanded by the FDA.

Because Congress recognized that large-molecule products raise distinct issues, it did not simply apply Hatch-Waxman to biologics. The most striking contrast between the Biosimilars Act and Hatch-Waxman is the distinction the former draws between "biosimilar" products and "interchangeable" products. The statute defines "biosimilarity" to mean that the follow-on product is "*highly similar* to the reference product notwithstanding minor differences in clinically inactive components" and that "there are no *clinically meaningful* differences... in terms of the safety, purity, and potency of the product."[42] To establish "interchangeability," by contrast, an applicant must further demonstrate that the follow-on biologic "can be expected to produce the *same clinical result* as the reference product in any given patient" and that alternating between the follow-on product and the reference product does not present any greater "risk in terms of safety or diminished efficacy" than continuous administration of the reference product alone.[43] It remains unclear whether, as a practical

[39] Pub. L. No. 111-148, 124 Stat. 119, 804 (2010). [40] PHSA § 351(k).

[41] PHSA § 351(k)(8). The FDA had promulgated six of these biosimilars guidance documents in draft form by the start of 2015. *See, e.g.*, Draft Guidance for Industry: Clinical Pharmacology Data to Support a Demonstration of Biosimilarity to a Reference Product (2014).

[42] PHSA § 351(i)(2) (emphasis added). [43] *Id.* at 351(k)(4).

matter, a demonstration of interchangeability will ever be possible for a complex biologic. And thus far, every enacted state law permitting generic biologic substitution at retail pharmacies applies only to interchangeable products.

Many other significant differences exist between the Biosimilars Act and Hatch-Waxman regimes. For instance, the former provides for twelve years of data exclusivity rather than five. No *Orange Book* listing of patents occurs for BLA products; instead, the biosimilar applicant and pioneer manufacturer engage in a complex exchange of information to determine which patents are subject to litigation prior to initial marketing of the biosimilar product. Moreover, FDA approval of a 351(k) application is not stayed for thirty months following the filing of a patent infringement suit.

Because large-molecule therapies represent a growing proportion of new drug approvals and of the best selling drugs, the details of FDA's implementation of the new biosimilars regime will likely have a major impact on the country's future healthcare costs. On March 6, 2015, prior to issuing any final guidances on biosimilars (or even a draft guidance on the nonproprietary naming of such products), FDA approved the first biosimilar under 351(k)—Zarxio, used for the prevention of infections in chemotherapy patients.

c. Medical Devices

i. Product Approval and Clearance Scheme

According to the FD&C Act, "medical devices," like "drugs," are articles "intended for use in the diagnosis, cure, mitigation, treatment, or prevention of disease" or "intended to affect the structure or any function of the body."[44] The main distinction between these categories is that a device "does not achieve its primary intended purposes through chemical action within or on the body." The device definition embraces an extraordinary range of products, from thermometers, tongue depressors, adhesive bandages, and contact lenses to PET scans, genetic tests, implanted brain stimulators, and artificial hearts. Although some provisions of the FD&C Act apply to both drugs and devices, the act also establishes many distinct requirements for devices, including device-specific pathways to the market.

The FD&C Act's complex device regulatory regime is a product of the 1976 Medical Device Amendments. The act, as amended, divides the universe of medical devices into three classes, based on the rigorousness of the controls necessary to ensure their safety and effectiveness. Class I devices, the simplest and least risky products, are subject only to general controls applicable to all devices, such as adulteration and misbranding prohibitions, establishment registration requirements, and good manufacturing process/quality system regulations. Class II devices must comply not only with these general controls, but also with any "special controls" the FDA imposes on the type of device in question. These special controls may include, for example, performance standards, postmarket surveillance requirements, patient registries, and the dissemination of guidelines. Finally, Class III devices are—like new drugs—subject to a premarket licensing regime. A manufacturer cannot sell a Class III

[44] FD&C Act § 201(g), (h). The definition of device, unlike that of drugs, includes articles intended to diagnose "conditions" as well as "diseases."

device without first gaining FDA approval of a premarket approval (PMA) application demonstrating safety and effectiveness, and an approved PMA imposes detailed labeling, manufacturing, technological, and compositional requirements.

The FDA has published extensive regulations defining hundreds of different types of devices and assigning each type to Class I, Class II, or Class III. A completely novel type of device that did not exist prior to 1976 is presumptively placed in Class III, although the FD&C Act contains little-used procedures for reclassifying or initially classifying such a product into Class I or Class II.

A medical device's regulatory pathway to market depends primarily on its classification. As noted above, Class III devices cannot be sold without FDA approval of a PMA. By contrast, a device of a type that FDA has classified as Class I or Class II is not subject to the PMA requirement if it is "substantially equivalent" to at least one device that is already legally on the market (a "predicate device"). Sellers of most Class II devices must, prior to marketing, demonstrate "substantial equivalence" to a predicate device in a distinct premarket filing known as a premarket notification, or "510(k)." New Class I devices must also be "substantially equivalent" to predicate devices, but because almost all Class I devices are statutorily exempt from the 510(k) requirement, the FDA reviews the market entry of very few of them. In sum, the most common modes of market entry for new medical devices are: (1) FDA approval of a PMA demonstrating safety and effectiveness (Class III devices); (2) FDA "clearance" of a 510(k) notification showing substantial equivalence to a predicate device (Class II devices); and (3) self-determination of substantial equivalence by the manufacturer with no premarket filing (Class I devices).

The PMA process is similar to the NDA process, although the statutory standards for PMA approval seem marginally more flexible than the counterpart provisions for NDAs. Until the early 1990s, the FDA frequently approved PMAs based on evidence that would have been insufficient for approval of a new drug. Following the 1993 publication of an internal agency committee report criticizing the device review process,[45] the FDA appears to have set the bar higher for PMA sponsors, but the device approval process nevertheless remains somewhat less rigorous than the drug approval process.

PMAs are not the most important premarket filings for medical devices, however. To a degree unanticipated by the drafters of the 1976 amendments, Section 510(k) has become the dominant pathway to market. In 2011, for example, the FDA cleared 3,072 Section 510(k) premarket notifications while approving only 37 PMAs.[46] The prevalence of 510(k) filings is due largely to the fact that FDA has classified many more devices in Class II (approximately 60%) than in Class III (approximately 10%). It also reflects the fact that the FD&C Act defines "substantial equivalence" so broadly that even quite novel devices can use the 510(k) route. According to the act, even a new device with "different technological characteristics" than a predicate device should be deemed "substantially equivalent" if the 510(k) demonstrates that the new product "is as safe and effective as [the] legally marketed device" and "does not raise different questions of safety and effectiveness."[47]

[45] FDA COMMITTEE ON CLINICAL REVIEW, FINAL REPORT (1993).

[46] HUTT, MERRILL, & GROSSMAN, FOOD AND DRUG LAW, at 1219.

[47] FD&C Act § 513(i)(1)(A)(ii).

Whether cleared pursuant to a 510(k) or approved pursuant to a PMA, a device can be legally marketed only for the conditions of use set forth in the premarket filing. In other words, a medical device, like a drug, ordinarily cannot be labeled or promoted for uncleared/unapproved uses. As with drugs, however, the FDA does not purport to regulate the off-label prescription or use of devices by physicians.

The FDA polices clinical research on medical devices through regulations specific to devices along with the same human subject protection rules applicable to all medical products. Although the FD&C Act does not mandate that PMAs be supported by evidence from well-controlled clinical investigations,[48] the FDA demands that most PMAs include such data. The agency also requires some 510(k) filers to perform clinical trials (increasingly, well-controlled clinical trials) to support claims of substantial equivalence.[49] To legally perform clinical studies on an uncleared and unapproved device, a sponsor must obtain an "investigational device exemption" (IDE). The IDE process is similar to the IND system for drugs, with the important difference that only sponsors of "significant risk" devices are required to actually apply for an IDE; sponsors of other devices are deemed to have an approved IDE based solely on IRB approval and the satisfaction of several other requirements.[50]

ii. Intellectual Property and Statutory Exclusivity

Congress has not established a special patent litigation scheme for devices as it has for small-molecule drugs and biologics. Two important special protections exist for manufacturers of innovative medical devices, however. First, the Hatch-Waxman patent term restoration provisions apply to medical devices as well as drugs; the manufacturer of a device marketed pursuant to a PMA can apply for an extension of its patent term to partly compensate for time lost while developing the product and awaiting FDA approval. Second, for a six-year period following PMA approval, the FDA may not rely on the data in the PMA to approve another medical device, regardless of the first product's patent status.[51] Importantly, however, only devices marketed pursuant to PMAs are entitled to these benefits; manufacturers of devices sold pursuant to 510(k) notices have only general intellectual property law to rely on when they seek to block the entrance of competitors.

III Twenty-First-Century Developments

At the dawn of the twenty-first century, the regulatory system for medical products described above seemed relatively stable. Congress periodically tweaked the framework, but the main features endured. These features included the following: (1) the FDA generally approved pharmaceuticals and devices for broadly defined diseases and conditions, rather than for disease subtypes; (2) a period of guaranteed exclusivity for brand-name pharmaceuticals was inevitably followed by the facilitated entrance of multiple low-cost generic competitors;

48 *See* FD&C Act § 513(a)(3)(B).

49 FD&C Act § 513(i)(1)(A)(ii)(I).

50 21 C.F.R. § 812.2(b)(1).

51 FD&C Act § 520(h)(4).

(3) the development and regulation of pharmaceuticals were almost wholly distinct from the development and regulation of medical devices; (4) the FDA rarely sought to regulate medical *practice* (as opposed to medical *products*); and (5) the FDA strictly prohibited manufacturers from promoting off-label uses.

Since around the turn of the century, however, a number of scientific and legal developments have been brewing with the potential to revolutionize FDA medical product regulation. These trends, explored in the remainder of this article, include the emergence of clinically effective and commercially viable personalized medicine and other biotechnology; the application of First Amendment commercial free speech doctrine to food and drug regulation; and the FDA's increasing intrusion into the practice of medicine.

a. The Rise of Personalized Medicine and Advanced Biotechnology

i. The Story of Herceptin

In 1998, the FDA approved the BLA for trastuzumab (Herceptin), a monoclonal antibody therapy for an aggressive form of breast cancer characterized by overexpression of HER2 protein by breast cancer genes. For various reasons, this approval represented the dawn of a new era of biotechnology and FDA regulation of it.[52] First of all, the approval was only for a certain form of breast cancer, and it thus reflected the growing understanding that "[b]reast cancer—as well as other cancers—cannot be viewed as a single disease, but rather as a group of several subtypes, each with its own molecular signature."[53] Second, Herceptin is a *gene-targeted* therapy; it works by deactivating a gene present in some breast cancer patients, but not others. Third, on the same day that the FDA approved Herceptin, it also approved a companion medical device, namely HercepTest, an in vitro diagnostic (IVD) test used to detect HER2 overexpression in breast cancer cells and thus to identify those patients for whom Herceptin might be effective.

Finally, Herceptin was part of an early surge of FDA approvals of monoclonal antibody therapies—one of six such biological products licensed within a ten-month period from 1997 to 1998.[54] Sixteen years later, four of these six biologics, including Herceptin, are among the thirty top-selling drugs in the United States. Six subsequently approved advanced biotechnology products, including four other monoclonal antibodies and three therapeutic proteins, are also on this list of bestsellers. Herceptin was thus on the leading edge of a wave of complex biologics, many of them products of recombinant gene technology, that are earning an ever-increasing share of pharmaceutical expenditures.

[52] *See* FDA, PAVING THE WAY FOR PERSONALIZED MEDICINE: FDA'S ROLE IN A NEW ERA OF MEDICAL PRODUCT DEVELOPMENT 15 (2013).

[53] *Id.*

[54] Herceptin was the sixth of these BLA approvals, and the eighth monoclonal antibody therapy that FDA ever approved. The FDA issued the first two licenses for monoclonal antibody therapies in 1986 and 1994.

ii. The Fragmentation of Disease and Treatment

The FDA itself recognizes the licensing of Herceptin to be a signal event in the rise of "personalized medicine," which the agency defines as "the tailoring of medical treatment to the individual characteristics, needs and preferences of a patient during all stages of care, including prevention, diagnosis, treatment, and follow-up."[55] In particular, Herceptin's approval only for breast cancer patients determined to have overexpression of HER2 protein exemplifies the new science of pharmacogenomics, which "seeks to understand how differences in genes and their expression affect the body's response to medications."[56]

In a 2013 report titled *Paving the Way for Personalized Medicine: FDA's Role in a New Era of Medical Product Development*, the agency considers how the rise of personalized medicine will affect its operations and medical product development generally. One major characteristic of personalized medicine emphasized in this report is the fragmentation of current disease categories. Treatments are increasingly being formulated for *subtypes* of diseases—subtypes characterized by shared genes or other biomarkers.

For years, manufacturers have focused primarily on developing products premised on universal notions of diagnosis and therapy.[57] The epitome of successful medical product development has long been the commercialization of a "blockbuster" pharmaceutical or device intended to treat *all* patients suffering from a widespread disease or condition. Congress, recognizing industry's lack of economic incentive to develop products for diseases affecting small populations, has created special "orphan" product inducements, such as tax credits and extended market exclusivity.[58]

Although pharmaceutical and device companies today continue to aspire to create the next blockbuster, this business model rests on increasingly creaky foundations because of the rise of personalized medicine. The conversion of common diseases into less common (and sometimes rare) subtypes presents both opportunities and challenges. On the one hand, the use of biomarker data may reduce the cost, time, and risk of drug development by allowing the use of smaller, targeted clinical trials that are more likely to succeed.[59] On the other hand, the division of disease categories into distinct subtypes shrinks the potential market for new therapies, leading to either higher prices or reluctance on the part of industry to invest in cutting-edge research in the first place. A systematic fragmentation of disease and treatment might require an extremely widespread application of "orphan" incentives, a development that would impose enormous costs both on the government and on private purchasers of medical products.

iii. Joint Development and Regulation of Devices and Pharmaceuticals

Traditionally, the development of medical devices and the development of pharmaceuticals were almost entirely separate scientific and commercial endeavors. Accordingly, the FDA's regulation of devices was almost totally discrete from its regulation of drugs and biologics;

[55] FDA, PAVING THE WAY, at 6. [56] *Id.* at 8.

[57] *See* Richard Tutton, *Personalizing Medicine: Futures Present and Past*, 75 SOC. SCI. & MED. 75 (2012).

[58] *See, e.g.*, Orphan Drug Act, Pub. L. No. 97-414, 96 Stat. 2049 (1983); Orphan Drug Amendments, Pub. L. No. 99-91, 99 Stat. 387 (1985).

[59] FDA, PAVING THE WAY, at 40.

CDRH had little occasion to cooperate closely with CDER or CBER. This division between product areas began to blur in the late twentieth century, as a growing number of "combination products" that included both device and pharmaceutical components appeared on the market.[60] Personalized medicine promises to take the codevelopment and coregulation of devices and pharmaceuticals to a new level.

In personalized medicine, the investigation and ultimate use of a drug or biologic is typically guided by a "companion" in vitro diagnostic (IVD) device, such as a genetic test, that identifies relevant biomarkers. Both the pharmaceutical and the companion diagnostic test require FDA review and approval, as illustrated by the simultaneous approval of Herceptin and HercepTest. The interdependence of such products poses challenges to both industry and the agency—particularly with respect to coordination between companies and between FDA centers. For example, it is difficult to achieve simultaneous approval of a drug by CDER and a companion diagnostic by CDRH.

iv. *Intellectual Property Questions*

The complex regulatory situation for personalized medicine was complicated further by a recent Supreme Court decision regarding patent protection for companion diagnostics. In *Mayo Collaborative Services v. Prometheus Labs*, 132 S. Ct. 1289 (2012), the Court held that a method for determining an optimal drug dosage based on the concentration of a blood metabolite in the recipient added nothing significant to an unpatentable "law of nature" and was thus not patentable subject matter. The impact of this decision on the availability of patent protection for diagnostic method claims remains to be seen, but if interpreted broadly, *Mayo v. Prometheus* may hinder the progress of personalized medicine by reducing the incentives to develop companion IVDs.[61]

Even outside the context of personalized medicine, innovator biotechnology companies face great uncertainty about how much market exclusivity they can expect for their monoclonal antibodies, therapeutic proteins, and other complex biologics. As discussed above, the details of the new biosimilars system remain to be worked out. In light of the inexorable growth of the market for large-molecule products, the FDA's interpretation and administration of the Biosimilars Act will have a significant impact on American healthcare costs.

b. The First Amendment and Off-Label Promotion

As discussed above,[62] although the FDA does not restrict the off-label use and prescription of medical products, it has long prohibited most communications by manufacturers about

[60] Examples of combination products include drug-coated stents and transdermal patches. In 1990, Congress added to the FD&C Act a special provision, Section 503(g), regarding the regulation of such products.

[61] John R. Thomas, Mayo v. Prometheus: Implications for Patents, Biotechnology, and Personalized Medicine, CRS Report for Congress 7-5700 (2012). Another patent decision with uncertain consequences for personalized medicine and the biotechnology industry was *Ass'n of Molecular Pathology v. Myriad Genetics*, 133 S. Ct. 2107 (2013), which held that a naturally occurring DNA segment does not become patentable simply by virtue of being located and isolated.

[62] *See supra* section (II)(a)(1), II(c)(1).

off-label indications. Exceptions to this policy exist; for example, since the early 1980s, the agency has explicitly allowed companies to provide scientific information about extralabel uses of drugs and devices in response to unsolicited requests by physicians.[63] But the agency has never voluntarily endorsed manufacturer-initiated dissemination of such information, except in extremely limited circumstances. Recently, however, courts have forced the FDA's hand.

In the late 1990s, the agency issued a guidance document that effectively banned most industry distribution of medical journal articles and textbook excerpts about off-label uses, and Congress soon embodied this policy in statutory form. The Washington Legal Foundation (WLF) challenged these actions in court, alleging that they violated the manufacturers' First Amendment right to commercial free speech. In a pair of decisions, the U.S. District Court for the District of Columbia ruled for WLF, striking down the guidance and statute.[64] The court enjoined the government from prohibiting the dissemination of bona fide peer reviewed articles and independently published textbook excerpts focusing on unapproved uses, though it permitted the FDA to mandate that the companies distributing such materials provide certain disclosures.[65] The Court of Appeals later vacated these decisions on technical grounds,[66] but the FDA embraced the terms of the injunctions as a matter of policy. [67] The FDA has regulated off-label communications in the shadow of the First Amendment ever since.

The potential of commercial free speech jurisprudence to revolutionize food and drug law became even more evident in 2012, when, in *United States v. Caronia*, the U.S. Court of Appeals for the Second Circuit overturned the conviction of a pharmaceutical sales representative who orally promoted a product's off-label uses to a physician.[68] Strikingly, the court declared the defendant's communications to be protected by the First Amendment even though he presented the information in his own words, without disclaimers, in a starkly promotional context. The implications of this decision remain to be seen, but if courts read *Caronia* broadly, it has the potential to unravel the FDA's entire scheme for restricting off-label communications and, with it, much of the agency's gatekeeping power over medical products. After all, if manufacturers are permitted freely to promote off-label uses to doctors—who themselves may prescribe an approved product for any use they deem

[63] *See, e.g.*, 59 Fed. Reg. 59820, 59823 (Nov. 18, 1994); DRAFT GUIDANCE FOR INDUSTRY: RESPONDING TO UNSOLICITED REQUESTS FOR OFF-LABEL INFORMATION ABOUT PRESCRIPTION DRUGS AND MEDICAL DEVICES (2011).

[64] Washington Legal Foundation v. Friedman, 13 F. Supp. 2d 51 (D.D.C. 1998); Washington Legal Foundation v. Henney, 56 F. Supp. 2d 81 (D.D.C. 1999).

[65] The court allowed the FDA to require the manufacturer distributing the material to disclose its financial interest and the absence of FDA approval.

[66] Washington Legal Foundation v. Henney, 202 F.3d 331, 336 (D.C. Cir. 2000).

[67] The agency has since issued a "Good Reprint Practices" guidance that permits relatively unfettered distribution of unabridged and unannotated scientific literature about unapproved uses, though it sets forth a list of conditions and mandatory disclosures. GUIDANCE FOR INDUSTRY: GOOD REPRINT PRACTICES FOR THE DISTRIBUTION OF MEDICAL JOURNAL ARTICLES AND MEDICAL OR SCIENTIFIC REFERENCE PUBLICATIONS ON UNAPPROVED NEW USES OF APPROVED DRUGS AND APPROVED OR CLEARED MEDICAL DEVICES (2009).

[68] United States v. Caronia, 703 F.3d 149 (2d Cir. 2012).

appropriate—the manufacturers will lose almost all incentive to pursue FDA approval of new indications for pharmaceuticals and devices already on the market.

c. Growing FDA Regulation of the Practice of Medicine

The FDA's policy of not regulating off-label prescribing practices is part of a broader commitment by the agency "not . . . to interfere with medical practice."[69] Of course, an FDA decision not to allow a pharmaceutical or device to be sold at all represents a practical restriction on the practice of medicine. But the agency has traditionally viewed its role as limited to regulating the manufacture, composition, labeling, and market entry of medical *products*, while it has consistently disclaimed authority over physicians' *use* of these products and over medical *procedures*. In recent years, however, the FDA has become ever more involved in these spheres.

Congress first explicitly empowered the FDA to regulate medical practice in the 1976 Medical Device Amendments. These amendments authorize the agency not only to limit a device to prescription sale, but also to "require that a device be restricted to sale, distribution, or use . . . upon . . . other conditions . . . if . . . the [agency] determines that there cannot otherwise be reasonable assurance of its safety and effectiveness."[70] Although the FDA has not frequently used this authority in a manner that can be viewed as interfering in medical practice, it has, for example, prohibited silicone breast manufacturers from making their products available to physicians who have not completed a special training program.[71]

Until recently, the FDA did not have similar power to restrict the distribution of approved drugs.[72] Consequently, most drugs—with the notable exception of controlled substances—could be prescribed by any doctor for any purpose.[73] Nevertheless, starting in the early 1990s, the FDA began occasionally to persuade manufacturers to "voluntarily" embrace distribution and use restrictions—either as an explicit condition of accelerated approval or as an implied condition of regular approval. Some of these voluntary "risk minimization action plans" (RiskMAPs) included elements regulating the practice of medicine. Consider, for example, the RiskMAP for Accutane, a highly teratogenic acne drug. This plan, still in

[69] Legal Status of Approved Labeling for Prescription Drugs; Prescribing for Uses Unapproved by the Food and Drug Administration: Notice of Proposed Rulemaking, 37 Fed. Reg. 16,503, 16, 503 (Aug. 15, 1972).

[70] FD&C Act § 520(e) (emphasis added).

[71] *See, e.g.*, Approval Letter for Mentor Worldwide MemoryShape™ Breast Implants (June 14, 2013).

[72] *See* American Pharmaceutical Association v. Weinberger, 377 F. Supp. 824 (D.D.C. 1974), *aff'd per curiam* 530 F.2d 1054 (D.C. Cir. 1976) (the FDA could not condition approval of methadone on distribution only to hospital pharmacies and heroin maintenance treatment programs).

[73] The 1970 Controlled Substances Act allows only physicians who are registered with the Drug Enforcement Agency (DEA) to prescribe scheduled controlled substances. 21 U.S.C. § 822(a). The DEA may suspend or revoke a physician's prescription privileges if "such registration is inconsistent with the public interest." *Id.* at § 823(b), (e). DEA regulations mandate that a prescription for a controlled substance "must be issued for a legitimate medical purpose." 21 C.F.R. § 1306.04.

effect, requires prescribing physicians, among other things, to certify that they will provide pregnancy prevention counseling and will obtain a negative pregnancy test before commencing treatment. In 2006, a skeptical FDA official opined that the use of RiskMAPs, while sometimes justified, "cuts directly to issues related to the practice of medicine, and sometimes tugs at where the boundary is between our role at FDA and the role of practicing doctors."[74]

In 2007, Congress added a new section to the FD&C Act formally authorizing the FDA to require the implementation of a "risk evaluation and mitigation strategy" (REMS) as a condition of approval or continued marketing of a drug if the REMS is necessary to ensure that the drug's benefits outweigh its risks.[75] The agency has regularly imposed REMS on small-molecule drugs and biologics ever since. Although many REMS mandate only the provision of information to healthcare providers and patients, many others also include more rigorous "elements to assure safe use," some of which directly impact medical practice. For example, a REMS may require that the prescriber of a drug "have particular training or experience," that "the drug be dispensed to patients only in certain health care settings," or that "each patient using the drug be subject to certain monitoring."[76]

The long-term implications of REMS remain unclear. The FDA could, in theory, approve numerous otherwise unapprovable pharmaceuticals by employing REMS to reduce risks to the point where they are outweighed by benefits. So far, the agency has not manifested an inclination to significantly increase its rate of NDA and BLA approvals in this way. If it chooses to do so in the future, however, the surge of new products will be accompanied by ever more restrictions on the practice of medicine.[77]

Recent advances in biotechnology, particularly with regard to human cell and tissue products, have pulled the FDA further into the realm of medical practice. For example, the FDA in 2010 obtained a federal court injunction prohibiting a medical clinic from performing a procedure in which it extracted bone marrow from a patient, isolated stem cells from the marrow, cultured the cells, combined them with an antibiotic, and injected the mixture back into the same patient. In *United States v. Regenerative Sciences*, the D.C. Circuit upheld the injunction, rejecting the clinic's assertion that the FDA was reaching beyond its jurisdiction by intruding in the practice of medicine.[78] *Regenerative Sciences* left some questions unanswered, such as whether the FDA would have authority over an autologous procedure using manipulated cells but no added substances. Nevertheless, the case permits the agency to remain involved in much cutting-edge medicine involving advanced cellular technologies.

[74] Speech by Scott Gottlieb, M.D. FDA Deputy Commissioner for Medical and Scientific Affairs, before the American Medical Association (June 12, 2006).

[75] Food and Drug Administration Amendments Act of 2007, Pub. L. No. 110-85, 121 Stat. 823, 926 (2007) (codified as FD&C Act § 505-1).

[76] FD&C Act § 505-1(f)(3).

[77] The FDA might also choose to increase its use of REMS to ensure the safety of products that, thanks to the advances of personalized medicine, have undergone smaller trials, because smaller trials are less likely to reveal infrequent adverse events. *See* FDA, PAVING THE WAY, at 40.

[78] United States v. Regenerative Sciences, 741 F.3d 1314 (D.C. Cir. 2014).

IV Conclusion: Who Will Guard the Gate?

In conclusion, it is important to consider not only recent changes in the FDA's regulatory approach, but also a broader phenomenon—the potential disintegration of the FDA's role as the chief gatekeeper of medical products in the United States. Increasingly, FDA approval of a pharmaceutical or device does not, in a practical sense, give the sponsor of the application full market access. A medical product's financial success hinges on which insurance plans will cover it. And these coverage determinations are made using criteria entirely different from those used by the agency in its NDA, BLA, and PMA decisions.

When the FDA reviews medical product applications, it performs an isolated analysis of whether the clinical benefits of the particular product outweigh its risks. This approach leaves out some notable considerations. First, the FDA does not take comparative efficacy into account—that is, it rarely declines to approve a drug, biologic, or device merely because a *more* effective product is already available. Second, it does not consider the product's cost-effectiveness. In other words, the FDA will not reject a product application because the same clinical result can be achieved more affordably using another therapy.

The premarket review provisions of the FD&C Act and PHSA are artifacts of eras very different from our own with respect to the financing of healthcare. One important contrast is the sheer amount that our society now spends on FDA-regulated pharmaceuticals and devices. In 2012, retail outlet sales of medical products represented about 2.2% of the country's gross domestic product; the corresponding figure in 1960 (two years before the passage of the Kefauver-Harris Drug Amendments) was less than 1%.[79] And this 2.2% does not capture nearly all of the nation's expenditures on FDA-regulated medical products; it excludes, for example, pharmaceuticals and devices used and administered in physicians' offices, hospitals, and other healthcare facilities.

Another stark contrast between 1962 and today is the source of the funds used to purchase FDA-regulated products. Consider, for example, prescription drugs sold at retail outlets—the type of purchases today covered by Medicare Part D.[80] In 1970, only 16.5% of retail prescription drug expenditures in the United States were covered by *any* sort of insurance, government or private. There was thus relatively little use of restricted formularies to restrain drug costs. Since then, the percent of retail prescription drug purchases covered by insurance has risen dramatically, to 81.3% in 2012. The enactment of Medicare Part D in 2003 explains only part of this increase; an even bigger factor is the dramatic increase of prescription drug coverage by private insurers in the 1980s and 1990s.[81] The expansion of insurance coverage for prescription drugs has been accompanied by the use of closed and tiered formularies by both public and private insurers.[82]

In light of growing concentration in the insurance industry, a formulary exclusion by even a single private third-party payer can have grave financial consequences for a pharmaceutical

[79] Derived from CMS, National Health Care Expenditure Data, Tables 1 & 2.

[80] These figures thus exclude, for example, expenditures on pharmaceuticals administered in physicians' offices and hospitals, nonprescription drugs, and medical devices.

[81] *See* CMS, National Health Care Expenditure Data, Table 16.

[82] State Medicaid plans use restricted formularies, as do the Veterans Health Administration, and—outside six protected classes of drugs—Medicare Part D plan sponsors. 42 C.F.R. 423.120(b)(2).

manufacturer. For example, sales of the respiratory drug Advair plunged by 30% in the first quarter of 2014 merely because Express Scripts, the nation's biggest pharmacy benefit manager (PB), stopped covering it.[83] This episode illustrates how the FDA is no longer the only gatekeeper with the power to determine the fate of a drug; it shares this role with third-party payers' formulary committees.

When it comes to off-label uses of already approved drugs, the FDA sometimes cedes the gatekeeping function to insurers altogether. Third-party payers make independent decisions about which off-label uses to cover. Medicare Part D, for instance, covers off-label uses that satisfy the definition of a "medically accepted indication."[84] Congress defines this term to mean not only FDA-approved indications, but also unapproved indications that are supported by citations in at least one of three designated nongovernmental drug compendia.[85] In some instances, this system renders the FDA virtually irrelevant. Consider, for example, a widely publicized recent episode concerning the biologic Avastin. In 2011, based on new clinical data, the FDA withdrew the approval of this product for use against breast cancer. It remained on the market as an approved therapy for other cancers, however. Even before the FDA issued its final withdrawal announcement, the Center for Medicare and Medicaid Services (CMS) quieted fierce protests by patient groups and others by announcing that Medicare would continue to cover Avastin for breast cancer regardless of the FDA's decision.

What factors do third-party payers use in constructing their formularies? As illustrated by the Avastin controversy, consumer demand and political pressure play some role. But economic considerations are increasingly the primary factor in formulary decisions.[86] Third-party payers compare the cost-effectiveness of different therapies when they determine which ones they will cover. They do so most obviously when they establish generic substitution requirements, but the phenomenon is also reaching into the realm of brand-name drugs. For instance, when Express Scripts excluded Advair from its formulary (while continuing to cover other brand-name drugs for the same indications), it presented the decision as a part of a company-wide "charge toward cost-effectiveness assessments."[87] Americans remain ambivalent about limiting coverage in this way.[88] Nevertheless, advances in comparative-effectiveness research and the increasing burden of healthcare costs will almost certainly continue to elevate the importance of such considerations.

83 Andrew Pollack, *Health Insurers Are Pushing Back on Drug Prices*, N.Y. Times, June 21, 2014, at A1.

84 42 U.S.C. 1396r-8(d)(B)(i), (k)(6).

85 *Id.* (g)(1)(B)(i).

86 Sometimes, inclusion of a drug on a formulary hinges mainly on price concessions that pharmacy benefit managers (PBMs) are able to negotiate with manufacturers.

87 *Steve Miller—Express Scripts: The Most Influential People in Biopharma Today*, FierceBiotech (Feb. 12, 2014), http://www.fiercebiotech.com/special-reports/steve-miller-express-scripts-2014-influentials.

88 Consider, for example, the Patient-Centered Outcomes Research Institute (PCORI), established by the 2010 Patient Protection and Affordable Care Act. Congress established this entity to perform "comparative clinical effectiveness research" on medical services and treatments, including pharmaceuticals and devices. 42 U.S.C. § 1320e. On the one hand, the statute expressly prohibits PCORI's research findings from being construed as coverage or reimbursement mandates, or even as recommendations. *Id.* at 1320e(j), 42 U.S.C. 299b-37(a)(2)(B). On the other hand, the law expressly states that PCORI's findings should be disseminated not only to physicians and patients, but also to "Federal and private health plans." 42 U.S.C. § 299b-37(a)(2)(A). The statute provides that CMS may consider—but not rely exclusively—on comparative clinical effectiveness research in making Medicare coverage determinations. 42 U.S.C. § 1320e-1(a).

How much will the FDA's influence shrink in such a future? Even if the FDA were inclined to use comparative efficacy and cost-effectiveness as factors in its product approval decisions, it likely could not do so (at least explicitly) without amendments to the FD&C Act. Nevertheless, the FDA may already possess the authority it needs to be an important player in the battle for formulary inclusion. The FD&C Act as written empowers the agency to regulate manufacturers' *claims* about comparative efficacy and cost-effectiveness, whether in labeling, advertising, or communications to formulary committees.[89] Although pharmaceutical and device manufacturers have traditionally made few such claims (largely because they have not wanted to fund the research necessary to support them), industry's reticence might begin to disappear in the modern, competitive reimbursement context. If comparative efficacy and pharmacoeconomic claims proliferate—and the FDA energetically regulates them—the agency will remain near the center of action in the age of restricted formularies. Otherwise, the FDA's once-indisputable status as the main gatekeeper for medical products in the American marketplace will probably continue to erode.

[89] *See, e.g.*, 21 C.F.R. § 201.6(a) (false or misleading representations in a drug's labeling with respect to another drug or a device render the drug misbranded); 21 C.F.R. § 202.1(e)(6)(i),(ii) (prohibiting prescription drug advertisements containing comparative effectiveness claims unsupported by "substantial evidence" or "substantial clinical experience); FD&C Act § 502(a) (providing that healthcare economic information provided to a formulary committee may be deemed false or misleading if it is not "based on competent and reliable scientific evidence" and requiring that information relevant to the substantiation of such information be made available to the FDA upon request).

CHAPTER 29

HEALTH LAW'S UNEASY RELATIONSHIP WITH DELIVERY SYSTEM INNOVATION

RICHARD S. SAVER

WHY has innovation in the healthcare delivery system been so slow, difficult, and limited? Cutting-edge medical advances are incorporated into an outmoded delivery system seemingly locked in old patterns and structures. Changes in care delivery lag behind transformation in other economic sectors and even fail to keep pace with development of new drugs and medical devices.[1] Many commentators blame health law.[2] The law-as-barrier perspective laments that inflexible legal rules constrain delivery system innovation. Under this view, legal rules nominally about patient protection instead are used to block value-enhancing opportunities, often in favor of incumbent stakeholder interests.

Although it has considerable descriptive appeal, the law-as-barrier perspective does not fully capture the many nuances and complexities at play in the law's interaction with delivery system innovation. A plausible alternative, the law as catalyst perspective, considers how law evolves to accommodate and even facilitate delivery system transformation.

Barrier or catalyst? The intriguing paradox is that law seems to be both. This chapter explores the counterintuitive and often confounding duality at play in the way law impacts delivery innovation. Law's dual capacity as barrier or catalyst helps to explain why some delivery system reform has been successful and other change opportunities squandered. Recognizing law's duality also is important for understanding the historically significant transition with the rollout of the Patient Protection and Affordable Care Act (Affordable Care Act)[3] and for envisioning the prospects of future healthcare reform.

[1] Steven Garber, Susan M. Gates et al., CHALLENGES TO VALUE-ENHANCING INNOVATION IN HEALTH CARE DELIVERY 17 (Rand Corp. 2011) [hereinafter CHALLENGES TO INNOVATION].

[2] *See, e.g.*, Timothy S. Jost & Ezekiel J. Emmanuel, *Legal Reforms Necessary to Promote Delivery System Innovation*, 299 JAMA 2561 (2008); Lesley H. Curtis & Kevin A. Schulman, *Overregulation of Health Care: Musings on Disruptive Innovation Theory*, 69 LAW & CONTEMP. PROBS. 195 (2006).

[3] Patient Protection and Affordable Care Act, Pub. L. no. 111-148, 124 Stat. 119 (2010).

Section I of this chapter reviews definitional issues and the common problems that many delivery system innovations try to address. Section II examines representative reforms: comparative-effectiveness research, retail clinics, gainsharing, and coordinated care models such as accountable care organizations (ACOs) and medical homes. These examples reveal law's double-edged relationship with innovation, as it both constrains and advances delivery system reform. However, law has not operated randomly or arbitrarily. Section III identifies common themes and recurring patterns in the representative innovation arcs: how health law's patient protection orientation remains in constant tension with innovation; the use of health law to advance incumbent interests; health law's role in furthering path dependence; the way that health law fosters innovation most effectively through fits and starts rather than incrementally, resembling a model of punctuated equilibrium; the regulatory difficulty in measuring the outcomes and value of delivery system reform; and the critical need for incentivizing physicians and the special challenges and legal impediments that result. Section IV concludes.

I Background: What Is Delivery System Innovation?

a. Definitional Issues

"Innovation," an elusive term, has many possible definitions. In theory, any departure from current practices can be characterized as innovative, however misguided. Innovation typically occurs through a considerable change in products, processes, methods, and organizational structure.[4] Most desirable innovations, however, also feature sufficient novelty, deliberate application, early implementation, and creation of benefit or value.[5]

As applied to the healthcare delivery system more specifically, innovation typically alters the bundle of healthcare services offered, how the services are paid for, the process for delivering the services, the medical personnel involved, the site of delivery, the use of products and technology, or the organizational structure under which care is provided.[6] More generally, innovation tries to improve the delivery of care across the three critical dimensions of the healthcare system: cost, quality, and access.

Scholars and commentators have shown considerable interest in "disruptive" innovations that radically disorder old systems. Disruptive innovations tend to be introduced by new stakeholders and feature novel services, structures, products, and markets.[7] Sustaining innovations, in contrast, are more incremental, follow linearly from existing methods and

[4] Prathibha Varkey et al., *Innovation in Health Care: A Primer*, 23 Am. J. Med. Quality 382, 383–384 (2008).

[5] Vincent K. Omachonu & Norman G. Einspruch, *Innovation in Healthcare Delivery Systems: A Conceptual Framework*, 15 The Innovation J. 2, 4 (2010).

[6] *See* Varkey, *Innovation in Health Care*, at 383; James C. Robinson & Mark D. Smith, *Cost-Reducing Innovation in Health Care*, 27 Health Aff. 1353, 1355 (2008).

[7] *See, e.g.*, Clayton M. Christensen et al., The Innovator's Prescription: A Disruptive Solution for Health Care (2009).

models, support current performance trends, and may improve on things that already exist, but find expanded value in their use.[8]

Truly disruptive innovations in healthcare delivery have been rare. An example is the ambulatory surgery center (ASC). ASCs emerged to claim a successful position in-between traditional sites of care, offering same-day surgeries in facilities with greater quality control and resource capabilities than physician offices but with easier access, lower cost, and less risk of iatrogenic injury than hospitals.

Some innovation remains socially undesirable.[9] Thus, the law-as-barrier perspective may too readily critique any legal restriction as problematic. For example, compared to general hospitals, physician-owned specialty niche hospitals that operate exclusively in particular domains of care (cardiac, orthopedic, etc.) are innovative because of enhanced expertise and access. Certificate of need, healthcare fraud and abuse, and related laws have limited this model's growth. These restrictions have been justified because of specialty hospitals' negative impact on the rest of the delivery system, including siphoning away revenues that support care to the uninsured/underinsured and increasing costs.[10]

b. Common Delivery System Problems

Innovation's slow pace and limited impact stem in part from the seemingly intractable delivery problems that reforms must address. First, fragmentation pervades many aspects of healthcare.[11] Patients see disparate providers in inpatient and outpatient settings who often are not linked administratively, clinically, or economically, fail to coordinate treatment, and do not even work off of the same medical record. Fragmentation also occurs at the organizational level. Physicians typically practice as independent contractors and are legally organized into medical groups that operate as distinct silos from their affiliated hospitals. Fragmentation problems further arise in healthcare financing. For example, patients changing health plans may find that they lack coverage for the same services or to continue care with their long-standing providers.

Second, flawed economic incentives negatively impact the delivery of care. The traditional fee-for-service reimbursement system escalates costs while remaining distinctly quality-insensitive, as providers earn more for delivering each reimbursable unit of service, even if it is suboptimal care. While Medicare and many other health plans have moved to a prospective payment system for reimbursing hospitals for most acute inpatient care, the fee-for-service system remains intact for physician services, resulting in considerable misalignment. In addition, patients and payers are hard pressed to act as prudent consumers when hospital pricing remains highly variable, seemingly irrational, and frustratingly opaque (Frankford, this volume).[12] Meanwhile, alternative financing models are sorely lacking for patients with

[8] Omachonu & Einspruch, *Innovation in Healthcare Delivery*, at 4.

[9] Challenges to Innovation, at ix.

[10] *See* Frank Pasquale, *Ending the Specialty Hospital Wars: A Plea for Pilot Programs as Information-Forcing Regulatory Design*, *in* The Fragmentation of U.S. Health Care 239–254 (Einer Elhauge ed., 2010).

[11] *See generally* The Fragmentation of U.S. Health Care (Einer Elhauge ed., 2010).

[12] Barry Meirer et al. *Hospital Billing Varies Wildly, Government Data Shows*, N.Y. Times, May 8, 2013.

chronic conditions, such as payment for multidisciplinary services and basing reimbursement on longer-term health maintenance.

Third, a serious information deficit exists for assessing the cost, quality, and overall value of many interventions. Treatments diffuse into practice without rigorous demonstration of cost-effectiveness or, importantly, whether they are comparatively better than other interventions for the same condition. For example, clinical variation studies have found that the intensity and volume of healthcare services differs by geographical region, and that more expensive and newer-technology-based care does not necessarily correlate with better outcomes.[13]

Fourth, the healthcare delivery system remains overly complex. It "is characterized by more to know, more to do, more to manage, more to watch, and more people involved than ever before."[14] Providers, for example, must navigate multiple health plans for their different patients, with key distinctions in covered services and reimbursement procedures.[15] Even within single institutions, healthcare providers can find themselves entrenched in unwieldy bureaucratic processes that detract from patient care.[16] Similarly, the Medicare program suffers from an overly complex structure by relying extensively on private contractors, such as carriers and intermediaries, with varying capacity and incentives to enforce the rules on the ground.[17]

II Representative Delivery System Innovations and the Role of Law

As innovation tries to tackle these fundamental delivery challenges, what has been the role of law? This section considers the evidence from several delivery system innovations: comparative-effectiveness research, retail clinics, gainsharing, and coordinated care models such as ACOs and medical homes. By no means an exhaustive list, these examples were chosen because they range from targeted innovation to more disruptive. The Affordable Care Act has advanced several of these reforms and they otherwise have attracted the considerable interest of policy-makers and commentators, making it likely that they will endure in some form.

[13] *See, e.g.*, Joseph P. Newhouse & Alan M. Garber, *Geographic Variation in Health Care Spending in the United States: Insights From an Institute of Medicine Report*, 310 JAMA 1227 (2013).

[14] INST. OF MED., CROSSING THE QUALITY CHASM: A NEW HEALTH SYSTEM FOR THE 21ST CENTURY 1 (2001).

[15] Lawrence P. Casalino et al., *What Does It Cost Physician Practices to Interact with Health Insurance Plans?*, 28 HEALTH AFF. w533 (2009).

[16] David M. Cutler, *Where Are the Health Care Entrepreneurs? The Failure of Organizational Innovation in Health Care*, NAT'L BUREAU OF ECON. RES. (2010), http://www.nber.org/papers/w16030.pdf.

[17] Nicholas Bagley, *Bedside Bureaucrats: Why Medicare Reform Hasn't Worked*, 101 GEO. L.J. 519, 526–539, 549–554 (2013).

a. Comparative-Effectiveness Research

At one end of the spectrum is comparative-effectiveness research (CER), a seemingly modest innovation. CER generally compares competing medical interventions against each other to determine which works best. CER studies can vary in how the interventions are compared, looking to differences in therapeutic outcomes, cost-effectiveness, or other metrics for effectiveness. CER differs from conventional medical research in at least three important features: (1) instead of studying general effectiveness of an intervention, it looks at *relative* effectiveness between differing treatments; (2) it includes a broader range of subjects than in typical clinical trials so the data generated is more representative of real-world patients and attentive to different patient subgroup responses; and (3) it includes even long-standing treatments for comparison.

CER might not ordinarily be thought of as a delivery-side innovation because the research alone does not inherently alter care methods or create new models. Nonetheless, to undergo continual learning, the delivery system critically needs information about the relative value of different interventions. Also, CER can directly compare different delivery models. Recognizing the need for more evidence-based evaluation, the Patient Centered Outcomes Research Institute (PCORI), the private nonprofit corporation that the Affordable Care Act established to oversee the new national CER program,[18] has tried to ensure that some of the research analyzes delivery system change. A representative study praised by PCORI, for example, considers whether chronically ill diabetes patients receive any relative advantage from health-educator-led group visit programs compared to the usual methods of diabetes care.[19]

Law has been instrumental in ushering in the nation's first, comprehensive CER program. With the 2009 federal stimulus legislation[20] and the Affordable Care Act, Congress funded CER at historically record levels. The Affordable Care Act also established a new regulatory framework for oversight of the research with the creation of PCORI to direct the national CER program.

At the same time, law has stymied innovation by defanging CER.[21] To appease concerns about rationing and crude cost control, Congress restricted CER's use. The Affordable Care Act prohibits Medicare from making coverage decisions solely on the basis of CER. It also prohibits PCORI from using dollars-per-quality-adjusted life years or similar measures as a threshold to establish what type of healthcare is cost-effective or recommended. The statute further handicaps using CER to guide health policy, as it requires PCORI to ensure that the research findings do not include coverage recommendations, practice guidelines, or other policy recommendations.[22] Most of the legislative restrictions on CER affect public programs such as Medicare. It remains unclear whether CER will materially affect the

[18] 42 U.S.C.A. § 1320e.

[19] PATIENT CENTERED OUTCOMES RES. INST., WINTER 2014 FUNDING CYCLE: IMPROVING HEALTHCARE SYSTEMS 9 (2013).

[20] American Recovery and Reinvestment Act, Pub. L. No. 111-5, 123 Stat. 115 (2009).

[21] *See generally* Richard S. Saver, *Health Care Reform's Wild Card: The Uncertain Effectiveness of Comparative Effectiveness Research*, 159 U. PA. L. REV. 2147 (2011) [hereinafter Saver, *Health Care Reform's Wild Card*].

[22] *See generally* 42 U.S.C.A. § 1320e-1 for all of the CER restrictions.

reimbursement practices of private health plans as, among other reasons, many private payers look to the Medicare program as first mover in payment design. Another shortcoming is the structure of PCORI itself, which, by statute, must have representatives of drug and device companies and insurers among its board members,[23] raising concerns about industry bias.

Other legal rules complicate the national CER program. The detailed regulatory requirements for traditional clinical research, such as institutional review board approval, reasonable risk/benefit prospects, and specialized informed consent, may be ill-fitting and cost-ineffective when applied to CER. A fair number of the investigations do not evaluate investigational therapies but instead compare treatments already approved and widely used in practice,[24] where a more relaxed regulatory approach may offer sufficient protections.

Tort liability concerns also likely dampen physician enthusiasm for adopting CER into clinical practice. Surveys suggest that physicians worry a more robust CER program increases their liability exposure, as they will face claims for not following CER results even if they had valid clinical reasons for doing so.[25] And in a lose-either-way scenario, other physicians fear that they face increased liability for conforming to CER. Physicians may rightly question whether lay juries will view unfavorably treatment decisions based on CER as stinting on care or as unjustified departures from custom.

b. Retail Clinics

Relative to CER, retail clinics more directly alter existing delivery models. Retail clinics, typically located within large stores, provide simple acute and preventive healthcare. The clinics are ordinarily staffed by nurse practitioners and occasionally involve other allied health professionals. Retail clinics treat routine conditions such as flu, colds, sore throats, and ear infections, and also offer vaccinations and other limited preventive services. They offer walk-in care, remain open during weekend and evening hours, and charge fixed prices based on posted charges. The first retail clinic opened in 2000 and now over twelve hundred clinics are in operation.[26] Retail stores or independent investors own the majority of retail clinics, with physician groups and hospitals owning a growing minority.[27]

Retail clinics are considered innovative because of their cost and access advantages. They can charge lower prices by relying almost exclusively on allied health professionals, avoiding the larger expense of physician services. They also have lower overhead costs compared to other ambulatory care settings because of the more limited range of services offered and the ability to share common expenses with their parent stores. As for access, patients regard the clinics' walk-in appointments and evening/weekend availability as a significant convenience. Moreover, retail clinics do more than just help expand access for already aligned

[23] 42 U.S.C.A. § 1320e(f).

[24] Richard Platt et al., *Ethics, Regulation, and Comparative Effectiveness Research: Time for a Change*, 311 JAMA 1497 (2014).

[25] *See* Joan Sokolovsky, Remarks at the Public Meeting of the Medicare Payment Advisory Commission 103 (Sept. 17, 2009), http://www.medpac.gov/transcripts/0909MedPAC.pdf.

[26] Robin M. Weinick, Craig E. Pollack et al., POLICY IMPLICATIONS OF THE USE OF RETAIL CLINICS vii (Rand Corp. 2010) [hereinafter POLICY IMPLICATIONS].

[27] *Id.* at ix.

patients. Their low cost and accommodating hours attract patients who depend solely on emergency room visits or who otherwise have no regular contact with the healthcare system. The majority of patients who use retail clinics do not have a regular relationship with a primary care provider and an estimated 16%–27% of retail clinic patients lack insurance.[28] Retail clinic use is more likely among minority families, younger adults, and families with children.[29] Thus, retail clinics follow a pattern consistent with innovation theory: Successful innovators capture new customers by offering products or services that cost less and may be simpler, even if not of the same quality as what incumbents provide.[30]

Despite this promise, retail clinics face a somewhat unfavorable legal environment. Professional scope of practice licensing laws limit the types of services that can be independently provided by nurse practitioners and other allied health professionals and also constrain their independent prescribing authority. More complex clinical activities are deemed the practice of medicine, requiring that licensed physicians directly provide or supervise the services (Johnson, this volume). These licensure concerns will magnify if retail clinics, as expected, expand care to other domains, such as managing chronic disease patients or offering weight-loss services. An additional complication is the delivery site. State laws vary as to whether retail clinics are treated like physician offices, ordinarily exempt from facility licensure, or more like other licensed outpatient facilities, negatively affecting the costs and flexibility of the retail clinic model.[31]

Under the corporate practice of medicine doctrine, and related fee splitting prohibitions, a fair number of states prohibit lay entities from directly employing licensed physicians, splitting fees with physicians, or otherwise asserting too much clinical control over clinical decision-making. In most retail clinics, the business owning the retail store also directly employs the clinical staff. For clinics desiring to employ physician medical directors, this business model may not be sustainable. Also, concerns have been raised that staff working at pharmacy-owned retail clinics face incentives to overprescribe and otherwise order services that boost in-store pharmaceutical sales.[32] Such practices invite increased regulatory scrutiny for compliance with the healthcare fraud and abuse laws.

However, the law has not been completely one-sided. The Affordable Care Act's expansion of the number of insured patients is expected to increase demand for primary care providers. This, in turn, will likely increase demand for retail clinics, particularly in areas where patients remain sensitive to price because they are enrolled in high cost-sharing plans or where existing primary care medical practices are not accepting new patients.[33] Indeed, retail clinic providers report significant expansion plans due to the Affordable Care Act.[34] Retail clinics may also be beneficiaries, however unintended, of healthcare reform's push to expand the supply of allied health professionals. The Affordable Care Act's initiatives to increase the number of

[28] *Id.* at viii–ix. [29] *Id.* at 8.

[30] *See* Clayton Christensen, The Innovator's Dilemma: When New Technologies Cause Great Firms to Fail xv (1997).

[31] Kaj Rozga, *Retail Health Clinics: How the Next Innovation in Market Driven Health Care Is Testing Federal and State Law*, 35 Amer. J.L. & Med. 205, 222–227 (2009).

[32] Bruce Jaspen, *Doctors, Retailers Square Off*, Chic. Tribune, June 26, 2007.

[33] Policy Implications, at xiii.

[34] Carol Wolf, *CVS to Double Number of In-Store Clinics After Health-Care Law, CFO Says*, Bloomberg, Apr. 13, 2010, *available at* http://www.investorvillage.com/smbd.asp?mb=4532&mn=7313&pt=msg&mid=8850454.

nurses in clinical practice generally and demonstration grants for nurse practitioner training programs favor delivery models like retail clinics that depend heavily on nurse practitioner staffing.[35]

c. Hospital-Physician Gainsharing

Further along the innovation spectrum, hospital-physician gainsharing programs try to integrate providers virtually and overcome misaligned financial incentives. A gainsharing plan is a formal reward and participation program in which a hospital encourages its staff physicians to suggest and implement productivity improvements. The hospital pays the physicians bonus payments, based on a percentage of cost savings achieved for the institution, if their reform efforts reduce hospital operating costs for a targeted group of patients over a typically annual measurement period. Usually, quality-of-care targets, ensuring that care was not compromised, must also be met before the physicians earn the gainsharing bonuses.

Gainsharing intentionally enlists the reform efforts of staff physicians, who are often in a better informational position than the institution to recognize cost-saving and quality-enhancing opportunities. Gainsharing also better aligns hospital and physician financial incentives than the current disconnect resulting from fee-for-service payment for staff physicians and prospective payment for inpatient hospital care. More generally, gainsharing has the potential to address underlying fragmentation problems. In many institutions, administrators and staff physicians operate at cross purposes and have strained relations. Staff physicians enjoy a considerable degree of independence and self-governance, enhanced by legal rules such as the corporate practice of medicine doctrine and hospital accreditation standards and licensure provisions. These rules constrain, for example, an institution's ability to oversee and discipline staff physicians, including terminating staff privileges, and to implement policies that potentially interfere with individual clinical judgment. As a result, staff physicians can remain insulated from larger institutional objectives, however beneficial. By offering shared financial incentives, and a clear platform for collaboration on productivity improvement, gainsharing in theory narrows the organizational and other forms of divide between hospitals and staff physicians.

Despite considerable industry interest, law has significantly restricted gainsharing. The principal obstacles arise from a civil monetary provision (CMP) in the federal Medicare/Medicaid statute. The CMP imposes penalties on hospitals that knowingly make payments to physicians as an inducement to limit services to Medicare and Medicaid patients.[36] The Department of Health and Human Services Office of the Inspector General (OIG) issued an advisory bulletin in 1999 that cautioned most gainsharing programs would run afoul of the CMP.[37] The OIG has subsequently issued several advisory opinions in which it exercised discretion and declined to impose sanctions under the CMP for specific gainsharing programs.[38] But such approvals have been contingent on ameliorating conditions and

35 Policy Implications, at xii.

36 42 U.S.C. § 1320a-7a(b)(1).

37 Special Advisory Bulletin on Gainsharing Arrangements and CMPs for Hospital Payments to Physicians to Reduce or Limit Services to Beneficiaries, 64 Fed. Reg. 37,985 (July 14, 1999).

38 *See, e.g.*, OIG Advisory Op. No. 01-1 (Jan. 11, 2001), https://oig.hhs.gov/fraud/docs/advisoryopinions/2001/a001-01.pdf; OIG Advisory Op. No. 06-22 (Nov. 9, 2006), http://oig.hhs.gov/fraud/docs/advisoryopinions/2006/AdvOpn06-22NewA.pdf.

background factors that are difficult to replicate and very case specific, resulting in a still unfavorable environment for gainsharing.

Gainsharing raises other legal risks. The bonus payments a hospital makes to a staff physician can be challenged under the federal antikickback statute[39] as problematic remuneration to induce referrals or under the federal physician self-referral law (aka the Stark Law)[40] as creating a financial relationship that restricts the ability of the physician to refer within the hospital system (Krause, this volume). Tax-exempt hospitals interested in gainsharing must navigate additional legal obstacles, ensuring that the bonus payments do not share net earnings with insiders or permit private interests to benefit more than incidentally.[41] In general, apart from limited demonstration projects authorized by Congress, [42] gainsharing opportunities remain constrained. The Affordable Care Act opened the door to more gainsharing, but only incrementally, by authorizing gainsharing-like shared saving programs between Medicare and specially recognized ACOs.[43]

d. Coordinated Care Models

The possibility of even more disruptive innovation arises with coordinated care models. Initiatives such as ACOs and medical homes not only change the method of reimbursing providers but introduce novel delivery structures.

ACOs are clinically integrated networks of physicians, hospitals, and other providers, organized together under a common legal entity. ACOs vary in the type of reimbursement incentives employed, marked by differences in degree for controlling costs. In the simplest form, an ACO contracts with a payer to provide a broad spectrum of care to a group of patients, but the payer reimburses individual providers within the ACO network under traditional methods. If treatment costs for the patient group decrease by a targeted amount, the payer additionally reimburses the ACO a share of the savings generated, in essence a form of gainsharing.[44] Other models sharpen the financial incentives by also introducing penalties for the ACO when treatment costs exceed targeted amounts. Further, other models transfer more downside risk for managing costs to the ACO as the ACO contracts to provide the continuum of care to the group of patients in return for a lump-sum payment.

Medical homes, narrower in scope than ACOs, deliver primary care and social support services to chronically ill patients. In a medical home, the patient's personal physician assumes responsibility for providing direct physician services and managing the patient's needs among a team of health coaches, visiting nurses, and other ancillary providers. Medical homes exclude specialists and hospitals from the core of the home, although they help manage referrals for such services.[45] The goal is to offer continuous, coordinated,

[39] *See* 42 U.S.C. § 1320a-7b(b). [40] *See* 42 U.S.C. § 1395nn.

[41] *See generally*, Richard S. Saver, *Squandering the Gain: Gainsharing and the Continuing Dilemma of Physician Financial Incentives*, 98 Nw. U.L. Rev. 145, 171–172 (2003) [hereinafter Saver, *Squandering the Gain*].

[42] Deficit Reduction Act of 2005, Pub. L. No. 109-171, § 5007c(1).

[43] *See* notes 50 to 52 and accompanying text.

[44] Cong. Res. Service, Accountable Care Organizations and the Medicare Shared Savings Program 1–2 (2010).

[45] Deloitte Center for Health Solutions, The Medical Home: Disruptive Innovation for a New Primary Care Model 1–7 (2008), http://www.deloitte.com/assets/Dcom-UnitedStates/Local%20Assets/Documents/us_chs_MedicalHome_w.pdf.

and readily accessible primary care, engage in specialized health education, and connect patients to social services and public health programs. Medical homes typically also feature enhanced access, such as same-day appointments, electronic communications with providers, and monitoring of all other healthcare the patient may receive.[46] As for financing, the primary care physician typically earns a separate case management fee for each patient. Alternatively, the primary care physician may receive higher than usual fee-for-service payments to reward for the enhanced oversight responsibilities. Sometimes the two different payment approaches are blended and other models include additional incentive payments. Medical homes are not incompatible with ACOs; in some instances, a medical home could join a larger ACO as a primary care provider within the ACO's network.

In theory, ACOs and medical homes address fragmentation concerns by clinically integrating providers into a unified delivery platform, facilitating the sharing of information and harmonization of care. Coordinated care models aim to impose greater accountability for costs and quality at the level of actual care delivery by putting primary care physicians at or very close to the organizational core, minimizing the operational involvement of intermediary health plans. Further, compared to traditional reimbursement, payment to coordinated care models more directly rewards providers for care harmonization and preventive care.[47]

However, coordinated care models raise legal complexities. First, antitrust liability can result from aggregating community providers together into a single ACO if, depending on the specific market conditions, this allows dominant providers to increase market power or otherwise facilitates anticompetitive behavior in payer negotiations. Second, the anti-kickback and physician self-referral laws may limit the ability of coordinated care entities to reward physicians for meeting quality and cost-savings targets, especially when the payments earned vary with the volume or value of referrals. Third, the choice of legal model for organizing an ACO, and the associated governance rules, present additional legal challenges. A tax-exempt, nonprofit hospital, for example, may be constrained in the types of transactions to undertake in joining an ACO. Disproportionate profit-sharing with physician partners or ceding too much operational and organizational control to other stakeholders could jeopardize a hospital's tax-exemption and nonprofit status. Fourth, shared savings payments to physicians can run afoul of the CMP gainsharing provision, as discussed above. Fifth, the model where the ACO is paid a fixed lump sum, and incurs significant financial risk for the cost of care, may require in some states that the entity be licensed as a risk-bearing insurer, which can necessitate maintaining large financial reserves.

Reimbursement rules also threaten to impede the growth of coordinated care models. Many payment systems are not designed to reward primary care physicians for medical-home-critical tasks, such as coordinating social support services and engaging in patient outreach and education.[48] Also, inflexible eligibility rules limit the ability of medical homes

[46] Robert A. Berenson et al., *Will the Patient-Centered Medical Home Transform the Delivery of Health Care?*, Urban Inst., Aug. 2011, at 1–2, http://www.urban.org/uploadedpdf/412373-will-patient-centered-medical-home-transform-delivery-health-care.pdf.

[47] Jessica Mantel, *Accountable Care Organizations: Can We Have Our Cake and Eat It Too?*, 42 SETON HALL L. REV. 1393, 1410–1411 (2012).

[48] AGENCY FOR HEALTHCARE RES. AND QUALITY, COORDINATING CARE FOR ADULTS WITH COMPLEX CARE NEEDS IN THE PATIENT-CENTERED MEDICAL HOME: CHALLENGES AND SOLUTIONS 7 (2012).

to take on new patients. For example, a medical home may determine a high-risk patient is best cared for with home nursing services but, if not truly homebound, the patient is likely ineligible for many home health benefits under Medicare and other health plans.[49]

Despite the legal complexities, healthcare reform has shown considerable interest in coordinated care models. The Affordable Care Act's creation of the Medicare Shared Savings Program (MSSP) serves as the principal boost for ACOs. Under the MSSP, Medicare pays a participating ACO to coordinate care for groups of at least five thousand Medicare patients, and the ACO is eligible to share in any cost-savings generated. The MSSP importantly lessens potential barriers to entry by waiving several of the gainsharing and fraud and abuse restrictions for participating ACOs.[50] In addition, the Department of Justice and the Federal Trade Commission—which jointly enforce antitrust laws—issued parallel guidance providing a regulatory safety zone for ACOs participating in the MSSP, minimizing their antitrust liability exposure.[51] The Centers for Medicare and Medicaid Services (CMS) has also used its demonstration authority to promote a slightly different form of Medicare ACO. Under the "Pioneer" ACO program, participating ACOs share more of the savings, and yet also incur possible penalties for cost-overruns, as a possible transition to global payments.[52]

Growth in Medicare ACOs has outpaced that of commercial ACOs,[53] suggesting the Affordable Care Act's targeted support for Medicare ACOs is having a measurable impact. Because Medicare traditionally plays the role of first mover in reimbursement design, it remains possible that the growth of Medicare ACOs will positively influence later ACO developments in the private market. At the same time, the Medicare ACO experiment has encountered many bumps in the road. Among the initial 114 ACOs participating in the MSSP, nearly half achieved some savings but only 29 saved enough money to be eligible to share some of the surplus.[54] A significant concern for ACOs generally is the difficulty harmonizing ACO performance with participation in the rest of the delivery system. Productivity improvements undertaken for ACO patients, such as managing specialty referrals and ancillary tests according to evidence-based protocols, may negatively impact the reimbursement received by ACO network providers for non-ACO patients, with shared savings or other bonus payments insufficient to offset the losses.

The Affordable Care Act has also promoted medical homes. It offers states the option to enhance Medicaid reimbursement of primary care sites designated as "health homes" with a generous federal funding match and provides bonus payments to Medicare primary clinicians for certain home visits, among other supporting provisions.[55] Beyond the Affordable

[49] Steven Landers, *The Future of the Medicare Home Health Program*, 310 JAMA 1443 (2013).

[50] Medicare Program: Final Waivers in Connection With the Shared Savings Program, 76 Fed. Reg. 67992 (Nov. 2, 2011).

[51] Statement of Antitrust Enforcement Policy Regarding Accountable Care Organizations Participating in the Medicare Shared Savings Program; Notice, 76 Fed. Reg. 67026 (Oct. 28, 2011).

[52] Centers for Medicare and Medicaid Services, *Pioneer ACO Model*, http://innovation.cms.gov/initiatives/Pioneer-ACO-Model/.

[53] Matthew Petersen et al., *Growth and Dispersion of Accountable Care Organizations*, Leavitt Partners, at 3 (2013), http://leavittpartners.com/wp-content/uploads/2013/08/Growth-and-Disperson-of-ACOs-August-20131.pdf.

[54] Rob Cunningham, *The Payment Reform Paradox*, 33 HEALTH AFF. 735, 737 (2014).

[55] *See generally* Berenson, *Will the Patient-Centered Medical Home*, at 9–10; AGENCY FOR HEALTHCARE RES. AND QUALITY, COORDINATING CARE FOR ADULTS WITH COMPLEX CARE NEEDS IN THE PATIENT CENTERED MEDICAL HOME: CHALLENGES AND SOLUTIONS 33–34 (2012).

Care Act, executive orders or legislation in several states have required commercial insurers and Medicaid plans to participate in medical home pilot programs.[56]

III Common Themes and Recurring Patterns

As the previous examples demonstrate, law has both advanced and constrained delivery system transformation. However, despite its contrasting influences, law has not operated randomly or arbitrarily. It may be difficult to predict in each instance whether law will act more as barrier or catalyst, and how it will do so. Nonetheless, several common themes and recurring patterns emerge that offer a deeper understanding and appreciation of law's duality and its complex interaction with delivery system innovation.

a. Health Law's Patient Protection Orientation

Protecting patients at informational disadvantage from incurring unreasonable risk serves as a primary justification for numerous legal rules, ranging from informed consent to provider licensure. Frequently, however, this precautionary orientation operates in direct tension with delivery system innovation. Health law tends to view healthcare as a special social good and patients as vulnerable. Thus, business practices common in other settings can receive different legal treatment in healthcare, such as the heightened scrutiny given incentive payments to physicians under the fraud and abuse laws. There is general reluctance to protect departures from custom without strong evidence of risk minimization. However, "[i]nnovation will not occur if each novel way to organize and pay for care needs to be adjudicated case-by-case."[57]

Inherent tension further arises because innovation theory predicts that the most transformative reforms present the more immediate quality concerns. Significant innovation often occurs when late entrants introduce products and services that may be of lower quality but are more affordable, accessible, convenient, and appealing to new customers, allowing new markets to be captured. Over time, the quality may improve and the innovation model expands, sometimes to the point of completely displacing older providers and suppliers.[58] A classic example is the personal computer, which although inferior upon initial introduction, eventually displaced more expensive mainframes.[59] In healthcare delivery, this pattern arises when new care models offer simpler services provided by less credentialed providers in more flexible settings, as has occurred with retail clinics. The change invites intense scrutiny about patient safety, making it difficult for new models to get out of the starting gate.

[56] Mary Takach, *Reinventing Medicaid: State Innovations to Qualify and Pay for Patient-Centered Medical Homes Show Promising Results*, 30 Health Aff. 1325, 1331 (2011).

[57] Jost & Emmanuel, *Legal Reforms*, at 2561.

[58] Jason Hwang & Clayton M. Christensen, *Disruptive Innovation in Health Care Delivery: A Framework for Business-Model Innovation*, 27 Health Aff. 1329, 1330 (2008).

[59] Clayton M. Christensen, *Will Disruptive Innovations Cure Health Care?*, Harv. Bus. Rev. 1, 3 (Sept.–Oct. 2000).

Here, patient protection may end up protecting too much by imposing standards that, while helpful to some and risk minimizing, exceed the needs of the average healthcare consumer.[60]

Law has been especially vigilant as patient protector regarding innovations that make visible reductions in care. In such instances, law has often bluntly equated care-level reductions with increased risk to patients or inappropriate rationing. Consider the CMP provision that blocks many gainsharing programs. Although the provision could plausibly be read to prohibit hospitals from paying physicians as inducement to reduce *medically necessary* care, the OIG has not enforced the statute this way. Instead, it views a gainsharing program as presumptively suspect and illegal if it has the mere potential to lead to a reduction in *any* healthcare service, regardless of necessity. Here, law's restrictive stance conflates and confuses the complex, nonlinear relationship between cost and quality in healthcare, as more care is not always better care. Opposition toward any service-level reductions also jeopardizes gainsharing initiatives that promote quality-enhancing disease management programs, which inevitably reduce some level of care but replace it with alternative, more optimal services.[61] For example, disease-management programs for congestive heart failure patients have tried to increase the use of prophylactic medications to prevent acute care episodes, while hopefully decreasing the number of hospitalizations and intensive care services. Because of this partial service reduction, financial incentives to encourage physician participation in such programs could run afoul of the gainsharing restrictions.[62] Similarly, rationing was salient in the acrimonious political battles about "death panels" and CER surrounding the Affordable Care Act.[63] In reaction, Congress strictly limited using CER in a variety of important reimbursement contexts and left it unclear as to whether CER studies should regularly incorporate cost-effectiveness review.[64]

A related tension flows from how health law's patient protection orientation privileges identifiable patients in existing treatment relationships. Health law urges undivided loyalty by physicians to individual patients. This arises from the common law view of the doctor-patient relationship as a quasi-fiduciary relationship and related licensure, malpractice, and medical ethics standards. This "relational bias" in health law discourages consideration of how treatment decisions for an individual patient impact the overall healthcare system, the physician's obligations to other groups, and larger societal interests.[65] It likewise discourages attention to whether "doing less" or "doing it differently" for an individual patient through innovative models of care and greater emphasis on social determinants of health, might lower costs and improve access overall within the delivery system, benefiting a larger group of potential patients. This relational bias also calls into question, even if not clearly prohibiting, innovations that reward physicians financially for cost control because of concerns of breaching trust with existing patients.

60 *C.f.* Curtis & Schulman, *Overregulation*, at 199.

61 Saver, *Squandering the Gain*, at 198–217.

62 *Id.* at 212–214.

63 *See, e.g.*, George F. Will, Op-Ed., *Stimulus Math for the GOP*, WASH. POST, Jan 29, 2009, at A19; Peter Ferrara, *The Absolutely Worst Bill Ever*, AM. SPECTATOR (Nov. 11, 2009), http://spectator.org/articles/40573/absolutely-worst-bill-ever.

64 *See* notes 21 to 23 and accompanying text; Saver, *Health Care Reform's Wild Card*, at 2164–2170.

65 *See generally* William M. Sage, *Relational Duties, Regulatory Duties, and the Widening Gap Between Individual Health Law and Collective Health Policy*, 96 GEO. L J. 497 (2008).

b. Protection of Incumbent Interests

Innovation theory predicts that powerful incumbents try to impede innovation that threatens their interests.[66] Law remains a very effective tool for such purposes. Licensure, liability, and reimbursement rules nominally about safety and quality can make it costly or even impossible for new entrants to offer novel delivery models that compete with established providers and suppliers. Under such rules, "the patient is 'protected' against the ability to economize—to use a product, provider, or facility that is 'good enough' to get the job done well. . ."[67]

The debates about retail clinics reflect this pattern. Retail clinic proponents urge liberalization of licensure laws to offer nurse practitioners and other allied health professionals clearer authority to provide a wider range of primary care services in a nontraditional delivery site. Meanwhile, opposition from professional associations such as the American Academy of Family Physicians (AAFP) and American Academy of Pediatrics fuels resistance. These physician groups argue that retail clinics are not the right care environment for infants, chronic care patients, and many other medical needs.[68] The AAFP in particular warns that retail clinics' scope of services not be expanded beyond minor illness because most retail clinics must rely on protocol-based decisions and diagnostic models, rather than physician clinical discretion, resulting in missed opportunities to address more complex medical problems.[69]

Legal constraints imposed on the rollout of CER similarly reflect the strong influence of incumbents. Certain medical providers and suppliers understandably view CER as a threat because the research may question the necessity or relative value of their products and services. These stakeholders have relied on law to block wider use of CER. For example, the now-defunct Agency for Health Care Policy and Research (AHCPR) issued CER-type studies in the mid-1990s questioning the comparative efficacy of common back surgeries. Surgeon groups and medical device manufacturers reacted by successfully lobbying for budget reductions for AHCPR and stripping the agency of legal authority to make reimbursement recommendations.[70]

Likewise, incumbent interests have played a key role in shaping the unique and rather puzzling regulatory structure for the new national CER program. As previously noted, the Affordable Care Act created PCORI, the new oversight entity, as a nonprofit corporation and requires it to have a certain number of board members representing drug and device manufacturers and health insurers, among other private constituencies. Concerns have been raised that this oversight structure "seems almost designed to enable [industry] stakeholders to block studies that threaten their interests."[71] Heavy lobbying by drug industry trade groups is credited with changing the initial versions of the legislation that followed a more traditional regulatory approach and put responsibility for CER entirely within a public agency.[72]

[66] Challenges to Innovation, at 23.

[67] Robinson & Smith, *Cost-Reducing*, at 1355.

[68] Policy Implications, at 14.

[69] Amer. Acad. of Family Physicians, *Retail Clinics*, http://www.aafp.org/about/policies/all/retail-clinics.html.

[70] Michael F. Cannon, *A Better Way to Generate and Use Comparative Effectiveness Research*, CATO Inst., Policy Analysis No. 632, at 7–8 (Feb. 6, 2009).

[71] M. Gregg Bloche, The Hippocratic Myth 51 (2011).

[72] *See* Alicia Mundy, *Drug Makers Fight Stimulus Provision*, Wall St. J., Feb. 10, 2009, at A4.

c. Path Dependence

The ability of incumbents to leverage law to block innovation is part of a larger pattern of path dependence underlying the delivery system. Existing institutions and structures, as well as historical contingencies, have channeled the delivery system along established directions, making more radical, innovative change less likely.[73] And law often plays a key role in furthering this path dependence. For example, the linkage of health insurance to a benefit of employment has favored certain delivery models. Loosely integrated preferred provider networks, which perform weakly in coordinating care or providing preventative health maintenance services, nonetheless have persevered by responding to the needs of large employers through offering discounted rates and an ability to handle an ever-changing roster of covered employees' acute, episodic care needs. The connection between employment and health insurance dates back to the 1940s, when tax law and labor market dynamics made employer-provided health insurance more attractive as a benefit (Hall, this volume; Jost, this volume). Linking health insurance to employment has endured ever since, despite many criticisms.

A more recent illustration of path dependence is the Affordable Care Act's push for Medicare ACOs. Rather than urge more radical restructuring of the hospital-physician groupings and require more robust clinical integration to form a qualifying ACO, the MSSP[74] anticipates that ACOs will build upon existing virtual networks of large medical groups and their affiliated hospitals. Rather than introduce more comprehensive reimbursement changes such as global payments, the MSSP retains fee-for-service payment in many respects. Serious questions remain whether the new ACOs are simply managed-care-lite and whether there are enough changes to have successful impact. As Nicholas Bagley observes:

> First, ACO hospitals and ACO physicians will still be paid as they have before, the only caveat being that they will distribute any shared savings. There is no shift to bundled payments—none—meaning that the sharp divide between... [hospital and physician payment], as well as the perverse incentives of the fee-for-service system will remain entrenched... [H]ospitals may have little financial incentive to reduce hospital care, even if doing so would save the ACO money on the whole. The benefits of keeping admission rates high may outweigh potential shared savings.[75]

A further complication is that the new Medicare ACOs lack the ability to "lock-in" patients. Medicare beneficiaries participating in an ACO have, according to the legislation, easy ability to seek care outside the ACO's network.[76] While this continues a strong tradition of freedom of choice for Medicare beneficiaries, it seriously hampers ACOs' ability to coordinate care and direct patients to network providers that follow common protocols for cost control, quality, and preventive services.

[73] David Wilsford, *Path Dependency, or Why History Makes it Difficult But Not Impossible to Reform Health Systems in a Big Way*, 14 J. PUB. POL'Y 251 (1994).

[74] *See* notes 50 to 51 and accompanying text.

[75] Bagley, *Bedside Bureaucrats*, at 575.

[76] Medicare Program; Medicare Shared Savings Program: Accountable Care Organizations, 76 Fed. Reg. 67,802, 67,851 (Nov. 2, 2011); 42 C.F.R. § 425.304c(2).

d. Law-Driven Innovation as Punctuated Equilibrium?

Despite law's customary role in furthering path dependence, it sometimes breaks this pattern quite dramatically. In this respect, the law-delivery system interaction resembles the evolutionary model of punctuated equilibrium. According to punctuated equilibrium theory, evolution and natural selection do not always work gradually and incrementally. Instead, species can remain quite static for long periods of time, until interrupted by rare bursts of dramatic speciation and change. Often the trigger for disturbing the settled order is some significant endogenous event, such as a harsh environmental change. Commentators have analogized and applied the punctuated equilibrium model to dramatic shifts in other fields of law, such as securities law and administrative law.[77]

The punctuated equilibrium model helps explain not only the evolution of particular fields of law but also how law itself can trigger dramatic changes in the underlying economic sectors it regulates. Within the healthcare delivery system, law has rarely, but quite powerfully, acted as an endogenous force for ushering in innovation, sometimes providing needed governmental support to overcome underproduction of public-good-like services and delivery models. Consider the development of CER. Despite long-standing interest in such research, public and private efforts languished for many years, hampered by a failure to use common data infrastructures and consistent research methodologies, limited dissemination of the research results, and concerns by private health plans that the information could be used by competitors acting as free riders.[78] But legislation changed all this in short order with the American Recovery and Reinvestment Act,[79] followed quickly by the Affordable Care Act, funding CER at historically record levels and creating a new regulatory structure through PCORI for setting national research priorities, harmonizing investigational methodologies, and disseminating the research results broadly.

The development of coordinated care models also reflects law's capacity for punctuating established order. An often controversial coordinated care model, one that developed long before the current interest in ACOs and medical homes, is the health maintenance organization (HMOs). HMOs blend the roles of insurer and provider, providing a comprehensive range of services through a restricted network of providers and facilities. The federal HMO Act of 1973[80] is credited with jump-starting managed care and promoting HMOs as a viable alternative in the private market. It did so by preempting obstructive state laws for federally qualified HMOs and requiring certain employers to offer an HMO option as part of the health benefits available to employees in order to obtain favorable tax treatment for employee health expenses.[81]

While too early to tell, it is possible that the Affordable Care Act will have a similar endogenous shock effect on the development of retail clinics and ACOs. As noted previously, while

[77] *See* Joseph A. Grundfest, *Punctuated Equilibria in the Evolution of United Securities Regulation*, 8 STAN. J.L. BUS. FIN. 1 (2002); Mark C. Niles, *Punctuated Equilibrium: A Model for Administrative Evolution*, 44 J. MARSHALL L. REV. 353 (2011).

[78] *See, e.g.*, Elizabeth Docteur & Robert Berenson, *How Will Comparative Effectiveness Research Affect the Quality of Health Care?* 5–6 (2010), http://www.urban.org/uploadedpdf/412040_comparative_effectiveness.pdf.

[79] 123 Stat. 115 (2009).

[80] 42 U.S.C. § 300e-10.

[81] *See* Eleanor D. Kinney, *Procedural Protections for Patients in Capitated Health Plans*, 22 AMER. J.L. & MED. 301, 305 (1996).

the legislation does not address retail clinics in any express detail, it does provide the clinics with a significantly larger pool of potential customers with insurance who nonetheless desire low-cost primary care.

Punctuated equilibrium theory, as applied to legal and policy-making phenomena, further suggests that external shock events, such as public crises, focus dramatic attention on underlying policy problems and enhance the ability of regulators to move beyond the status quo.[82] In such instances, law may not be the original endogenous force, but it provides an effective tool for powerful societal reaction and, in doing so, accelerates innovation. The downside, of course, is that reactionary regulation may overshoot the optimal mark. ACOs are, in part, the result of accelerated reform due to reactionary regulation. Medicare ACOs, while not necessarily groundbreaking for the reasons previously noted, are still an important experiment in healthcare delivery, including as a possible transition to paying for bundled, episodic care. ACOs were an interesting academic idea initially, drawing on the insight that in most instances a physician is affiliated with a local acute care hospital in the community and operates as a extended virtual, if not actual, member of the facility's medical staff, making that virtual hospital-physician network a valuable focal point for reform efforts.[83] But ACOs did not necessarily show initial chances of widespread adoption. However, in the run-up to the 2008 presidential elections and later debates over healthcare reform legislation, long-standing problems of healthcare access and cost became salient. Also, noteworthy commentary, such as physician Atul Gawande's *The Cost Conundrum*,[84] captured the interest of policy-makers, highlighting fragmentation, the problematic incentives of fee-for-service, the difficulties in serving chronic care patients, and the promising success of ACO-like models in the private market such as the Kaiser Permanente health system. All this conspicuous attention helped support, via the Affordable Care Act, more significant experimentation with the ACO alternative.

ACOs reflect the inherent tension between health law's ability to accelerate delivery system innovation and its oppositional tendency to regress. It remains difficult to predict how the ACO experiment will fare in coming years. The Affordable Care Act has given ACOs a dramatic boost, but most ACOs at present use positive reward incentives such as shared savings, not risk-based incentives that penalize overspending, and the degree of integration within the provider networks varies considerably between ACOs. Continuing momentum may lead to further rollout of more aggressive, innovative models, such as reimbursing ACOs entirely though lump-sum payments, tighter organizational integration of providers within the same legal structure, and restricting patients' ability to move in and out of ACO networks for care. At the same time, patient protection concerns, incumbent interests, and path dependence threaten to hamper the degree of change, leading to continued reliance on more modest ACO models and incremental, second-best innovation.

[82] *See* Niles, *Punctuated*, at 358–359; Graeme Boushey, *Punctuated Equilibrium Theory and the Diffusion of Innovations*, 40 POL'Y STUD. J. 127, 128 (2012).

[83] *See* Elliot S. Fisher et al., *Creating Accountable Care Organizations: The Extended Hospital Medical Staff*, 26 HEALTH AFF. w44, w48–9 (2006); Stephen M. Shortell and Lawrence P. Casalino, *Accountable Care Systems for Comprehensive Health Care Reform* (Mar. 2007), http://research.policyarchive.org/21919.pdf.

[84] Atul Gawande, *The Cost Conundrum: What a Texas Town Can Teach Us about Health Care*, THE NEW YORKER, June 1, 2009.

e. Measurement and Valuation Challenges

When not in an isolated period of punctuated equilibrium, law's customary, wary stance toward delivery system innovation arises in part due to regulatory challenges in measuring the impact and overall value of reforms. A typical legal response is to assess innovation against cost, quality, and related benchmarks and use regulatory controls to restrict changes that appear unfavorable. However, designing optimal safeguards frequently becomes contested. Although healthcare can be measured by a wide range of outputs (survival rates, overall wellness, quality adjusted life years, cost-effectiveness, etc.), it is also a credence good that remains difficult for nonproviders to evaluate, often because the delivery system involves so many moving parts. Also, outcomes are often hard to connect causally to delivery system innovation, given the often indirect effects of delivery system change and the large influence of nonmedical factors on overall health. Moreover, it is hard to measure the lost opportunity costs of blocked innovation, which critics say the regulatory framework frequently overlooks.[85]

One major recurring regulatory question is what time period to use for assessment because innovation may only yield significant returns over longer time frames. Other important, but quite thorny, assessment considerations include whether positive results under the innovation model are achieved by negatively impacting other parts of the delivery system, whether the outcomes achieved by early adopting providers and patients will be replicable with later adopters, and whether results are generalizable across different patient and provider subgroups.

More generally, randomized controlled trials, the gold standard for measuring new medical products, are often not performed for delivery system reforms as such studies may be too costly or infeasible. As a result, delivery system innovations may be less persuasive to stakeholders and leave regulators with considerable uncertainty. For example, the new Center for Medicare and Medicaid Innovation has already come under criticism for extensively using demonstration projects that rely on modeling to evaluate reform's impact rather than randomized trial assessment.[86]

These valuation and measurement concerns are evident in debates surrounding retail clinics. Regulators have a number of control options to consider, and more generally whether to use law as barrier or catalyst for this new delivery model. These deliberations are undertaken, however, in the face of limited empirical assessment to date of retail clinics' performance, particularly downstream effects on the overall healthcare system. On the one hand, retail clinics seemingly offer a more efficient, accessible form of primary care. On the other, they may skim away healthier and more profitable patients, increase pharmaceutical expenses because of the alleged pressures staff face to boost in-store pharmacy sales, present quality problems for treatment of chronically ill patients, exacerbate fragmentation in care delivery, and increase overall healthcare costs. Little wonder, then, that law has moved in typical risk-averse fashion as there has been limited progress in reducing significant barriers, such as liberalizing the scope of practice licensure laws.

Similar measurement challenges complicate the development of ACOs. Even the seemingly simple question of which patients should be counted as ACO patients when measuring

[85] *See* Curtis & Schulman, *Overregulation*, at 205.

[86] Gina Kolata, *Method of Study is Criticized in Group's Health Policy Tests*, N.Y. Times, Feb. 2, 2014.

an entity's performance turns out to be not so simple. ACOs are usually evaluated by annual performance data. But patients typically, as within the Medicare ACOs required to preserve patient freedom of choice, retain the authority to leave the network before the annual measurement period ends or seek care from outside providers. Thus, a patient could be "attributed" to an ACO in a variety of ways, including prospectively and retrospectively.[87] Moreover, under some attribution approaches, an ACO network provider may not even know many of the patients cared for were considered ACO patients until much later after care was rendered, presumably blunting some of the intended reimbursement incentives at the time of clinical decision-making.

f. Challenges Posed by Incentivizing Physicians/Clinical Autonomy

A final common theme is that delivery system innovations, to succeed, critically depend upon effective physician participation. Physicians remain the core and key gatekeepers of the healthcare delivery system, controlling or strongly influencing the lion's share of healthcare expenditures. Defragmentation, efficiency, error reduction, and other improvements require, at bottom, physician willingness to change practice patterns.

A significant reason physicians remain so central to what happens with innovation is the role of law, which fiercely protects individual physician discretion within broadly defined custom. For example, the Medicare statute generally authorizes physicians to prescribe any medically necessary treatments, regardless of high cost or novelty. Law has been generally supportive of physician empowerment, even if this reasonably expects too much of physicians as prudent stewards and does not fit well with the many public responsibilities and nonclinical challenges involved in managing the overall delivery system.[88]

Moreover, physicians have proven resilient in ignoring or evading proposed changes that seemingly threaten their discretion. The high value physicians place on clinical autonomy and individualized medicine, a preference reflecting medical custom, means that many reforms have failed because of physician concerns of ceding individual authority to others.[89] Innovation theory suggests that reforms take hold more successfully when consistent with the belief systems, values, and needs of the targeted adopters. In healthcare, this means that even welfare-enhancing innovations will have trouble if not sufficiently convincing to physicians and tailored to account for the strong medical norms favoring clinical autonomy. For example, "[s]urgeons are not interested in finding new ways to arrive in the operating room on time if they do not care when the surgery starts, or if they know that operations do not start on time."[90]

[87] Valerie A. Lewis et al., *Attributing Patients to Accountable Care Organizations: Performance Year Approach Aligns Stakeholders' Interests*, 32 HEALTH AFF. 587 (2013).

[88] *See* William M. Sage, *Our "Patchwork" Health Care System: Melodic Variations, Counterpoint, and the Future Role of Physicians*, 14 HOUSTON J. HEALTH. L. POL'Y 1, 2–3 (2014).

[89] James L. Reinertsen, *Zen and the Art of Physician Autonomy Maintenance*, 138 ANNALS INTERNAL MED. 992, 993–993 (2003); Mark A. Hall, *Institutional Control of Physician Behavior: Legal Barriers to Health Care Cost Containment*, 137 U. PA. L. REV. 431, 450–452 (1988).

[90] Donald M. Berwick, *Disseminating Innovations in Health Care*, 289 JAMA 1969, 1971 (2003).

As a result, innovations need to change physician practice patterns but, in order to have the best prospects for success, must do so, perhaps counterintuitively, in a manner that still sufficiently respects clinical autonomy. One approach is to enlist physician opinion leaders, who can lead by example. Targeted financial incentives are another effective autonomy-preserving strategy as they avoid direct commands and preserve for the clinician some freedom as to which treatments to order and how to make other allocation tradeoffs.[91] But innovations relying on targeting physician opinion leaders and financial incentives inevitably introduce legal complications, such as running afoul of the healthcare fraud and abuse laws. The troubled rollout of gainsharing demonstrates this. It remains all too easy for physicians to support a hospital's productivity improvement in theory and then doggedly revert to traditional practice patterns, especially when they may feel disconnected from the institution's overall mission. Gainsharing's financial bonuses are key to jump-starting and maintaining physician interest. The financial bonuses provide ongoing incentives to examine and adjust practice patterns on a continual basis. But hospitals have been reluctant to gainshare because of the uncertain legal risk.

Similar difficulties in ensuring physician engagement threaten the viability of CER and coordinated care models. As for CER, the research relies on sophisticated analysis of large datasets, rather than looking to isolated clinical experiences. This emphasis, common to much evidence-based medicine, threatens clinical autonomy as it gives greater authority to statisticians, academic researchers, and others while seemingly devaluing individual clinical judgment.[92] It is not surprising, therefore, that some physicians remain wary about the use of CER to dictate treatment or override professional discretion,[93] and may tune out the research, however valuable, without additional encouragement, such as fine-tuned financial or liability protection incentives. As for ACOs, shared savings without any downside risk may simply be too mild an incentive to reward physicians.[94] Likewise, most Medicare ACO specialist physicians continue to receive traditional fee-for-service reimbursement. In the absence of more clear regulatory direction for engaging specialists with accountability for overall cost and quality, Medicare ACOs will likely experience many difficulties controlling the full spectrum of care.[95]

IV Conclusion

Conservative legal rules seemingly squelch welfare-enhancing innovation for the delivery system. But the law-as-barrier critique is incomplete. It overlooks law's important

[91] David Orentlicher, *Paying Physicians More to Do Less: Financial Incentives to Limit Care*, 30 U. Rich. L. Rev. 155, 174–177 (1996).

[92] *See* Marc A. Rodwin, *The Politics of Evidence-Based Medicine*, 26 J. Health Pol. Pol'y &L. 439, 440–441 (2001).

[93] *See* Alvin I. Mushlin & Hassan Ghomrawi, *Health Care Reform and the Need for Comparative Effectiveness Research*, 362 New Eng. J. Med. E6(1) (2010), http://www.nejm.org/doi/full/10.1056/NEJMp0912651.

[94] Bagley, *Bedside Bureaucrats*, at 575.

[95] Xiaoyan Huang & Meredith B. Rosenthal, *Transforming Specialty Practice—The Patient-Centered Medical Neighborhood*, 370 New Eng. J. Med. 1376, 1378 (2014).

prophylactic role, as some innovation is socially undesirable. Also, there is an interesting duality as law has demonstrated capacity to act powerfully as catalyst in addition to barrier.

This suggests that moving forward what health law needs is not widespread deregulation but determined flexibility and willingness to use its catalyst potential more frequently. Health law itself could innovate. Rather than reflexively protect the patient or further path dependence and incumbent interests, health law critically needs experimentation with more nimble regulatory strategies, such as alternative timing and enforcement methods, regulatory sunsets, and provisional rules.[96] This would facilitate testing innovations and using legal stimulus, either by easing regulatory restrictions or through direct spending legislation, to overcome public goods and logjam problems.

Limitations arise, of course, in viewing in isolation law's relationship with delivery system innovation. There is a danger of legal exceptionalism. The highly contested political environment surrounding social welfare programs such as healthcare certainly shapes the direction of delivery system change. Market forces do as well. Additionally significant nonlegal factors are the professional norms of healthcare providers and the culture of healthcare organizations.[97] As noted, the high importance of clinical autonomy and individualized medicine as a professional medical norm complicates delivery system innovations, which inevitably involve attempting to alter practice patterns.

But even if one should be cognizant of legal exceptionalism, attention to law remains important. Law certainly helps create the background conditions for market forces and the political environment. As for professional norms, law can have a reciprocal effect. The content of law and the way its message is understood can change social belief systems of regulated actors.[98] As such, law can shift norms of healthcare providers regarding delivery system change while also reflecting providers' customary professional attitudes.

Thus, law remains a very important component to understanding how innovation arises and fares within the delivery system. Many innovation attempts, including instances of failure and modest success, have revealed similar themes and recurring patterns: the constant tension between innovation and health law's patient protection orientation; the use of law to advance incumbent interests; health law's reinforcement of path dependence; how health law's role as catalyst resembles the model of punctuated equilibrium; the special difficulties for law in measuring the outcomes and value of delivery system reform; and the considerable challenges, legal and nonlegal, that arise in engaging physicians to participate in delivery transformation, an often necessary condition to successful innovation. Recognizing, anticipating, exploiting, and potentially overcoming these patterns is critical for thinking about what lies ahead as the delivery system struggles with implementing current change initiatives and encounters new opportunities for innovation.

[96] *C.f.* Nathan Cortez, *Regulating Disruptive Innovation*, 29 Berkeley Tech. L.J. 173, 225 (2014).

[97] *See, e.g.*, Reinertsen, *Zen*, at 992; David A. Hyman, *Health Care Fraud and Abuse: Market Change, Social Norms, and the Trust "Reposed in the Workmen,"* 30 J. Legal Stud. 531 (2001).

[98] *C.f.* Cass R. Sunstein, *Social Norms and Social Roles*, 96 Colum. L. Rev. 903, 910 (1996).

CHAPTER 30

LEGAL AND POLICY ISSUES IN MEASURING AND IMPROVING QUALITY

KRISTIN MADISON

I Introduction

Healthcare quality, a long-standing concern of physicians and their patients, has become a central concern of policy-makers. The focus on doing good and not doing harm embodied in the Hippocratic Oath now stands alongside a national call to achieve the aim of better care "by making health care more patient-centered, reliable, accessible, and safe."[1] Despite many centuries' worth of attention to quality issues, neither healthcare professionals' commitment to serving their patients nor external forces such as regulation or competition have resulted in the level of quality that patients deserve.

Why? While providers, regulators, and markets each face their own distinct challenges in ensuring high-quality care, there is one particularly formidable obstacle that they all share: an information void. Providers seeking to deliver high-quality care must understand the relationship between their actions and their patients' health. When providers do not know what high-quality care is, they cannot deliver it. Regulators and patients, on the other hand, must be able to assess the quality of care that a particular provider has provided in the past, is proposing to provide in the present, or is likely to provide in the future. When differences in provider quality are not apparent to those involved in choosing or compensating providers, there can be little hope for the robust competition that delivers higher quality and lower costs in other industries. Commentators lamenting the slow pace of innovation in healthcare have attributed industry stagnation to deficiencies in information about quality.[2]

Information deficiencies are by no means a new phenomenon. The information needed to accurately assess quality has long been lacking. It was not until the late 1960s and the 1970s

[1] Agency for Healthcare Research and Quality, *About the National Quality Strategy*, http://www.ahrq.gov/workingforquality/about.htm (last visited July 9, 2015).

[2] *See, e.g.*, David M. Cutler, *Where Are the Health Care Entrepreneurs? The Failure of Organizational Innovation in Health Care*, Nat'l Bureau of Econ. Research, Working Paper No. 16030, 2010.

that systematic research on treatment practices began to accelerate, and not until the 1980s and 1990s that evidence-based medicine and a commitment to quality assessment began to take hold. Research from that era exposed the widely varying levels of quality that characterize modern healthcare. It also made clear the need for further quality improvement.[3]

Given the central importance of quality assessment to quality improvement, it is not surprising that the attention of providers, regulators, and market participants has turned to quality measurement and reporting. The two influential, turn-of-the-millennium Institute of Medicine reports highlighting quality problems in the American healthcare system, *To Err Is Human*[4] and *Crossing the Quality Chasm*,[5] were soon followed by another Institute of Medicine report, *Performance Measurement: Accelerating Improvement*.[6] The Medicare program provided a financial incentive to hospitals to report quality metrics in the early 2000s, and since then the federal government has steadily expanded the scope of its measurement and public reporting initiatives.[7] An Agency for Healthcare Research and Quality (AHRQ) database now contains over two thousand quality measures, and these constitute only a subset of quality metrics in use today.[8]

The proliferation of quality measures has not halted calls for further measure development and refinement. To reach their full potential as mechanisms for quality improvement, healthcare quality measures must be accurate. They must reflect dimensions of quality that people care about. They must be easily understandable to their users. And they must be technically and financially feasible to collect and disseminate. Carefully crafted law and policy can help achieve these goals.

This chapter will examine how law and policy shapes quality measurement and reporting. It begins by describing how quality measures are used today. It then explores the continuing challenges associated with measurement and reporting. The chapter emphasizes the legal and regulatory mechanisms for addressing one of these challenges: ensuring accuracy. It reviews the actions that payers, providers, patients, and regulators have taken or could take in response to problematic quality information. The chapter concludes by suggesting that to address quality measurement deficiencies, policy-makers should prioritize two goals: expanding research on quality, its measurement, and its reporting, and accelerating the adoption of information technology that will facilitate the development of diverse new quality measures.

[3] *See generally* Kristin Madison, *Donabedian's Legacy: The Future of Health Care Quality Law and Policy*, 10 IND. HEALTH L. REV. 325, 327–345 (discussing the evolution of quality oversight as reflected in medical and legal journals of the period).

[4] INST. OF MED., TO ERR IS HUMAN: BUILDING A SAFER HEALTH SYSTEM (Linda T. Kohn, Janet M. Corrigan, & Molla S. Donaldson eds., 1999).

[5] INST. OF MED., CROSSING THE QUALITY CHASM: A NEW HEALTH SYSTEM FOR THE 21ST CENTURY (2001).

[6] INST. OF MED., PERFORMANCE MEASUREMENT: ACCELERATING IMPROVEMENT (2006).

[7] *See* Kristin M. Madison, *From HCQIA to the ACA: The Evolution of Reporting as a Quality Improvement Tool*, 33 J. LEGAL MED. 63, 76–80 (discussing evolution of state and federal reporting from the 1980s through 2010); Madison, *Donabedian's Legacy*, at 347 (describing expansion of federal reporting).

[8] Agency for Healthcare Research and Quality, NATIONAL QUALITY MEASURES CLEARINGHOUSE, http://www.qualitymeasures.ahrq.gov (last visited May 26, 2014).

II Measurement and Reporting as Quality Improvement Tools

The Patient Protection and Affordable Care Act (ACA) illustrates the growing importance of measurement and reporting in the evolving American healthcare system. The ACA's third section is titled "Improving the Quality and Efficiency of Health Care," and at its heart is a requirement to develop a national quality improvement strategy.[9] The architects of this strategy have identified nine "levers" that can be used to achieve the triple aim of "Better Care," "Healthy People/Healthy Communities," and "Affordable Care."[10] While the levers include some traditional quality assurance mechanisms, such as "Certification, Accreditation, and Regulation," the prominence of quality measurement on the list of levers is striking. In addition to being its own lever ("Measurement and Feedback"), it facilitates the use of three others ("Public Reporting," "Payment," and "Consumer Incentives and Benefit Designs"). Even certification and accreditation processes now incorporate quality measurement.[11]

Quality measures' emergence as a centerpiece of quality improvement activities is relatively recent. Scholars discussing the origins of quality measurement often point to a handful of initiatives undertaken between the early 1900s and the 1950s, but the most influential early contribution to the practice of quality assessment was the framework Professor Avedis Donabedian introduced in the 1960s. He proposed evaluating healthcare quality by examining structures, such as the nature of facilities and medical staff qualifications; processes, such as technical competence in the performance of surgery; and outcomes, such as mortality or disability or patient satisfaction.[12] As the medical profession embraced a commitment to evidence-based medicine, and the principles associated with measurement and quality improvement in other industries found their way into healthcare management, this tripartite framework continued to influence thinking about measurement approaches. By the late 1980s and 1990s, many healthcare leaders had joined Professor Donabedian in writing about quality measurement.[13]

During this period, much of the focus was on healthcare providers' use of quality measures to improve their own care. By systematically collecting data about the quality of

[9] Patient Protection and Affordable Care Act, Pub. L. No. 111-148, 124 Stat. 119 (2010), *as amended by* Health Care and Education Reconciliation Act of 2010, Pub. L. No. 11-152, 124 Stat. 1029 (2010), § 3011.

[10] Agency for Healthcare Research and Quality, *About the National Quality Strategy*.

[11] *See, e.g.*, American Board of Internal Medicine, Practice Assessment, https://www.abim.org/maintenance-of-certification/requirements/practice-assessment/default.aspx (last visited May 27, 2014) (describing quality measurement–related maintenance of certification requirements); Mark R. Chassin et al., *Accountability Measures—Using Measurement to Promote Quality Improvement*, 363 New Eng. J. Med. 683, 683 (2010) (describing 2002 initiation of Joint Commission requirement to report performance data).

[12] *See* Avedis Donabedian, *Evaluating the Quality of Medical Care*, 44 Milbank Memorial Fund Q. 166, 167–170 (1966) (describing ways to assess quality).

[13] *See* Madison, *Donabedian's Legacy*, at 338–339 nn.49–52 (listing articles by authors such as Donald Berwick, David Blumenthal, and Mark Chassin). *See also* Timothy Stoltzfus Jost, *Oversight of the Quality of Medical Care: Regulation, Management, or the Market*, 37 Ariz. L. Rev. 825, 827–841 (1995) (discussing quality oversight trends, including quality measurement).

services they provide, physicians, hospitals, and other care providers can identify areas in which they are falling short of their own expectations and then track subsequent improvements. If providers also have access to the data of others, they can use it to identify top performers and attempt to replicate their practices.

Public reporting of quality measures can reinforce this improvement process in several ways. First, government or accreditation organization reporting mandates may force even the most reluctant providers to devote resources to measurement. Second, reporting adds the possibility of reputational sanctions to the motivations of providers to perform well. Third, it makes competition on the basis of quality metrics possible. Without publicly reported quality measures, patients, payers, other providers, and anyone else who wields influence over a patient's choice of providers must ignore clinical quality as a criterion, rely only on quality information they collect themselves, or make do with weaker measures or proxies for quality, such as friends' comments or accreditation status. If report cards are widely available, however, decision-makers can take this information into account, which could improve care for the patient involved while simultaneously creating a financial incentive for further improvement. In addition, payment levels could be adjusted based on measured quality.

As providers' internal focus on measurement increased, policy-makers sought to take advantage of the benefits of reporting. In 1986, the Pennsylvania legislature imposed a statewide cost and quality reporting requirement intended to promote competition and "facilitate the continuing provision of quality, cost-effective services throughout the Commonwealth."[14] Three years later, the Pennsylvania Health Care Cost Containment Council (PHC4) released a report documenting mortality and complication rates in certain Pennsylvania hospitals; in 1992, it released a report card with mortality rates for bypass surgery patients of individual heart surgeons across the state.[15] In the 1990s and 2000s, a number of other states began publicly reporting provider quality measures, mostly for hospitals, and mostly for just a few types of care and care-related deficiencies, such as infections.

The commitment to quality reporting has been even greater at the federal level. After publishing hospital-specific mortality for a few years in the 1980s and early 1990s,[16] federal policy-makers began to focus on quality measurement and reporting in earnest in the 2000s. Congress incorporated into Medicare payment formulas financial incentives for hospitals to report quality-related data to the federal government, and in 2005, the Department of Health and Human Services (HHS) published the first national hospital quality report card on its website.[17]

Public reporting initiatives have largely been driven by public and private payers and independent organizations, not providers. As pressure to develop reporting systems grew in the 2000s, many physicians articulated serious objections to quality reporting and organized physician groups resisted federal reporting initiatives.[18] Results of a 2005 survey suggested

[14] Act No. 1986-89, § 2, 1986 Pa. Laws 409.

[15] Madison, *From HCQIA to the ACA*, at 72–74 (discussing Pennsylvania's legislation).

[16] *Id.* at 71–72. *See also* William T. Gormley & David L. Weimer, Organizational Report Cards 44–45, 48, 52 (1999); Michael L. Millenson, Demanding Medical Excellence 175 (1997) (describing federal mortality reporting).

[17] Madison, *From HCQIA to the ACA*, at 78–79.

[18] *See, e.g.*, David Glendinning, *AMA Leads Project to Develop Quality Measures by Year's End*, Am. Med. News (Mar. 13, 2006) (noting physician group opposition to CMS voluntary quality reporting

that a majority of general internists opposed publication of physician-specific quality measures even if accurate,[19] a phenomenon that might arise in part because of a deep concern about the reputational implications of disclosure.[20] By the mid-2000s, however, recognizing the inevitability of the performance measurement trend, physician groups had begun to take a more active role in measure development.[21]

Quality reporting efforts continue to expand today. For example, twenty years after Pennsylvania established PHC4, Massachusetts established the Massachusetts Health Care Quality and Cost Council as part of a health reform initiative; the Council now publishes hospital and medical group quality ratings based on data from multiple sources.[22] Medicare's reporting initiatives have expanded to include providers such as nursing homes and home health agencies.[23] The ACA called for the development of new quality measures, established reporting programs for additional types of healthcare entities, and mandated the creation of a website that will report physician quality.[24] The ACA also embedded reporting requirements in other reforms, such as the accountable care organization program.[25]

Government websites are not the only source of information about healthcare quality. Hospital quality information is available through the Joint Commission, which accredits hospitals, as well as through health plans. In many states, broad coalitions of stakeholders such as hospitals, physicians, and health plans have come together to jointly publish provider quality ratings. Nonprofit organizations such as the Leapfrog Group and the Commonwealth Fund, as well as for-profit companies such as Health Grades, also publish provider quality ratings.[26] In addition, organizations that provide quality information about other types of products and services, from Consumers Union to Angie's List to Yelp to *U.S. News & World Report*, also provide information about healthcare providers.

The nature of the quality information supplied through these mechanisms varies. The federal Medicare website now provides aggregate ratings based on patient experiences ("Patients who reported that their nurses 'always' communicated well"), care processes ("Heart attack

program); Andis Robeznieks, *Education Called Key to Acceptance of Performance Ratings*, AM. MED. NEWS (Feb. 9, 2004) (describing physician concerns).

[19] Lawrence P. Casalino et al., *General Internists' Views on Pay-for-Performance and Public Reporting of Quality Scores: A National Survey*, 26 HEALTH AFF. 492, 494 (2007).

[20] *See generally* William M. Sage, *Reputation, Malpractice Liability, and Medical Error*, *in* ACCOUNTABILITY: PATIENT SAFETY AND POLICY REFORM 159 (Virginia A. Sharpe ed., 2004).

[21] *See* Robeznieks, *Education Called Key* (noting calls for physicians to take an active role in providing input); Glendinning, *AMA Leads Project to Develop Quality Measures* (describing efforts of Physician Consortium for Performance Improvement).

[22] Commonwealth of Massachusetts Health Care Quality and Cost Council, MYHEALTHCAREOPTIONS, http://hcqcc.hcf.state.ma.us/ (last visited May 28, 2014).

[23] Medicare.gov, FIND & COMPARE DOCTORS, PLANS, HOSPITALS, SUPPLIERS & OTHER PROVIDERS, http://www.medicare.gov/forms-help-and-resources/find-doctors-hospitals-and-facilities/quality-care-finder.html (last visited May 28, 2014).

[24] *See* Madison, *Donabedian's Legacy*, at 347–348 (describing and providing citations to relevant provisions).

[25] Patient Protection and Affordable Care Act § 3022, 42 U.S.C. § 1395jjj (b)(3).

[26] HEALTHGRADES, http://www.healthgrades.com/; THE LEAPFROG GROUP, http://www.leapfroggroup.org/cp; HOSPITAL SAFETY SCORE, http://www.hospitalsafetyscore.org/ (another site sponsored by the Leapfrog Group); WHYNOTTHEBEST?, http://www.whynotthebest.org/ (site sponsored by the Commonwealth Fund).

patients given aspirin at discharge"), and outcomes ("Death rate for heart attack patients," "Rate of unplanned readmission after hip/knee surgery," "Central line-associated bloodstream infections"). Massachusetts reports similar statistics, along with others such as the percentage of staff who received a flu vaccination, the rate of "serious reportable events," and, for weight-loss surgery, an indicator of hospital and surgeon experience. Presentation format for quality data varies by site and measure type, and includes percentages, rates, descriptions ("Better than the US Average Rate"), stars, and numeric scores. Some sites also allow individuals to post comments.

The rapid growth in the prevalence of quality reporting reflects a belief that reporting adds value beyond that generated by mere measurement. For every new website created, every new type of provider included, every new condition covered, and every new measure added, someone was willing to invest the resources necessary to report the additional information. But does public reporting ultimately improve quality? Skeptics might point to the public's relatively infrequent use of quality measures. In a 2014 poll, just under a quarter of respondents reported seeing comparative quality information on doctors[27]; an earlier poll found that only about half of respondents who had seen physician quality information actually used it.[28] Skeptics might also question patients' ability to interpret ratings properly,[29] or argue that report cards lead providers to turn away sicker patients or game measurement algorithms in other ways, undermining quality ratings' otherwise salutary effects.[30]

Evidence supports all of these claims but also indicates that reporting can have a positive impact. Ratings might affect patient demand even though not every patient reads and understands report cards; some patients will respond appropriately to ratings, as will some family members, health plans, and others that influence provider choice. Report cards can be designed to reduce gaming. Furthermore, providers may respond to public ratings even if their patients do not. Evidence from the early 2000s on report cards' impact on provider market share is decidedly mixed, but more recent studies, such as a 2009 study on fertility clinics and a 2011 study of bypass surgery, find an effect.[31] A few studies have shown a link between report cards and healthcare quality improvement in areas such as nursing-home care and physician services.[32] Hospital leaders have indicated that reporting drives quality

[27] The Associated Press–NORC Center for Public Affairs Research, *Finding Quality Doctors: How Americans Evaluate Provider Quality in the United States* (2014), http://www.apnorc.org/projects/Pages/finding-quality-doctors-how-americans-evaluate-provider-quality-in-the-united-states.aspx.

[28] The Henry J. Kaiser Family Found., 2008 Update on Consumers' Views of Patient Safety and Quality Information 6 (2008).

[29] *See* sources cited in Kristin Madison, *The Law & Policy of Health Care Quality Reporting*, 31 Campbell L. Rev. 215 (2009), at 227 n.62.

[30] *See, e.g.*, David Dranove et al., *Is More Information Better? The Effects of "Report Cards" on Health Care Providers*, 111 J. Pol. Econ. 555, 583 (2003).

[31] M. Kate Bundorf et al., *Do Markets Respond to Quality Information? The Case of Fertility Clinics*, 28 J. Health Econ. 718 (2009); Justin Wang et al., *Do Bad Report Cards Have Consequences? Impacts of Publicly Reported Provider Quality Information on the CABG Market in Pennsylvania*, 30 J. Health Econ. 392 (2011).

[32] Rachel Werner et al., *Public Reporting Drove Quality Gains at Nursing Homes*, 29 Health Aff. 1706 (2010); Maureen A. Smith et al., *Public Reporting Helped Drive Quality Improvement in Outpatient Diabetes Care Among Wisconsin Physician Groups*, 31 Health Aff. 570 (2012). *See also* David Dranove, *Health Care Markets, Regulators, and Certifiers*, *in* 2 Handbook of Health Economics 639, 681 (Mark V. Pauly, Thomas G. McGuire, & Pedro Pita Barros eds., 2012) (table summarizing results of empirical

improvement activity and that public quality measures are incorporated into annual goals and reviewed with trustees and physicians.[33]

Healthcare payers have become increasingly interested in tying payment to measured quality. Financial incentives have been tied to structural quality indicators such as the use of electronic health records, process indicators such as smoking cessation interventions, and outcome indicators such as blood sugar levels. Many private insurers have adopted pay-for-performance programs, as have public payers, including both Medicaid and Medicare.[34] Medicare is reducing payments to hospitals for patients with hospital-acquired conditions, such as certain infections or foreign objects retained after surgery, as well as to hospitals with patients who are frequently readmitted. It has instituted a hospital value-based purchasing program that ties payment to factors such as appropriate antibiotic use and heart failure mortality rates. It will soon introduce a value-based modifier for payments to physician groups.

While some studies have shown a positive impact of pay-for-performance programs, results overall are mixed, with many studies showing limited effects.[35] Given the wide variation in incentive program targets and designs, as well as the studies' methodological limitations, it is difficult to provide an overall assessment of the impact of measurement-based payments on quality. As with reporting, it is clear that pay-for-performance can succeed, and equally clear that it can fail. Ultimately, the most important question is what sorts of designs, in what kinds of contexts, are likely to achieve measure designers' objectives.

Healthcare quality measurement has assumed a central role in today's healthcare delivery system. It is an element of providers' internal efforts for quality improvement as well as an essential tool for outsiders seeking to assess, improve, or assure quality. The potential benefits of quality measurement, reporting, and pay-for-performance initiatives are clear. On the other hand, the limitations and drawbacks of these initiatives are equally clear. Measures that do not accurately reflect quality because of inadequacies in either underlying data or measure design can malign providers, misdirect patients, and lead improvement efforts astray. Measures that are ignored will have no impact, and measures that are used improperly may make things worse. Measures that successfully shift providers' attention to an area in need of improvement will have the disadvantage of shifting attention away from other areas. In addition, measurement is costly. Unless it increases quality in ways that reduce costs, it will require the redirection of resources from other potentially beneficial uses. The potential for

studies on health report cards' effects); Madison, *Law & Policy of Health Care Quality Reporting*, at 223–326 (discussing report cards' effects).

[33] Peter K. Lindenauer et al., *Attitudes of Hospital Leaders Toward Publicly Reported Measures of Health Care Quality*, 174 JAMA Internal Med. 1904 (2014).

[34] *See* Julia James, *Pay-for-Performance*, Health Affairs/Robert Wood Johnson Health Policy Brief (2012) (describing pay-for-performance programs); Medicare Program, 78 Fed. Reg. 50,496, 50,649–650,729 (Aug. 19, 2013) (describing readmissions, value-based purchasing, and hospital-acquired conditions programs); Patient Protection and Affordable Care Act § 3007, 42 U.S.C. § 1395w-4 (value-based payment modifier).

[35] *See* Naomi S. Bardach et al., *Effect of Pay-for-Performance Incentives on Quality of Care in Small Practices with Electronic Health Records*, 310 JAMA 1051 (2013) (reporting results of randomized trial); Julia James, *Pay-for-Performance* (discussing studies of pay-for-performance effects); Pieter Van Herck et al., *Systematic Review: Effects, Design Choices, and Context of Pay-for-Performance in Health Care*, 10 BMC Health Services Res. 247 (2010).

both drawbacks and unrealized benefits suggests that there is reason to seek legal and policy tools that could improve measurement practices.

III Building a Foundation for Measuring Quality

In an ideal world, providers would each see hundreds of patients with a particular condition and dutifully record demographic and health-related characteristics, medical and surgical interventions, and health outcomes in an easily analyzable format. The patients' data would then be aggregated and appropriately risk-adjusted quality metrics calculated. In the real world, however, there are significant barriers to both data capture and data aggregation. Establishing a reliable measurement system requires overcoming these barriers.

Historically, providers have stored data on paper or in other forms not easily transmittable to others. Entities interested in systematic analysis of this data, such as payers, therefore must ask providers to prospectively record or manually abstract data from treatment records, a costly process, or rely on administrative records created for other purposes. As a result, the data available for use in measurement is often sharply limited, which in turns limits the measures that can be calculated. Relevant outcome indicators may never be recorded, and there may not be enough demographic or health-related data collected to allow for adequate risk adjustment.

The development of appropriately structured electronic health records could go a long way toward addressing these data shortcomings. In 2009, Congress passed the Health Information Technology for Economic and Clinical Health (HITECH) Act, which offered hospitals and physicians significant financial incentives to adopt and use electronic health records. More than 370,000 hospitals and professionals had received incentives under the program by mid-2014.[36] Importantly, the incentives were awarded not just for having an electronic system, but for actually using a system certified as meeting program requirements. To satisfy the "meaningful use" requirements, professionals seeking incentive payments must report a number of clinical quality measures using their electronic health record systems.[37] Measures on the reporting menu fall into domains such as patient engagement, patient safety, public health, and clinical processes, and include measures related to blood pressure control, tobacco cessation interventions, childhood immunization status, and functional status assessments. Hospitals seeking incentives must report on measures such as aspirin prescribed for heart attacks and elective deliveries before thirty-nine weeks of

[36] Health Information Technology for Economic and Clinical Health (HITECH) Act, Pub. L. No. 111-5, 123 Stat. 226 (2009) (codified as amended in scattered sections of 42 U.S.C.); Press Release, Ctrs. for Medicare & Medicaid Svcs., CMS Rule to Help Providers Make Use of Certified EHR Technology (May 20, 2014), http://www.cms.gov/Newsroom/MediaReleaseDatabase/Press-releases/2014-Press-releases-items/2014-05-20.html.

[37] *See* Ctrs. for Medicare & Medicaid Svcs., Clinical Quality Measure Basics, http://www.cms.gov/Regulations-and-Guidance/Legislation/EHRIncentivePrograms/ClinicalQualityMeasures.html (last visited July 23, 2014).

gestation. The meaningful use requirements have encouraged the adoption of systems that capture relevant data and the use of these systems for quality reporting.

Certified electronic health records do not end the need for manual extraction of data for use in quality metrics. Record systems do not always support reporting in forms that data collectors demand. However, as systems improve, and as providers gain facility with electronic health records and the workflows needed to support appropriate record use, they should increasingly be able to enter the appropriate patient information as structured data, allowing for later construction of many different quality measures.

Data capture does not always lead to data aggregation. Payers, for example, can access claims data for their own enrollees, but not on other patients, hampering their ability to accurately judge quality. Even if an entity obtains access to all of a single provider's data, varied data collection procedures and information systems hinder aggregation across providers, impeding statistical analysis and comparative evaluations.

Policy measures have begun to address these issues. The HITECH Act's support for electronic data exchange will facilitate data sharing across organizations, as will the federal government's decision to alter data formats and data-sharing policies to make claims data more available to third parties.[38] In addition, the ACA mandated the sharing of Medicare claims data with interested entities holding their own data, so as to promote the development of more reliable quality measures.[39] Leading commentators have criticized this program as too restrictive and have proposed policies allowing broader use and reuse of data and permitting data users to charge for the services they provide.[40] As is so often the case, restrictions adopted to protect privacy and prevent misuse, both important aims, can reduce the usefulness of an otherwise highly valuable data program.

Professor Harold Luft has proposed a different approach to data aggregation: the creation of a public-private data repository that brings together de-identified patient data from numerous payers.[41] He argues that efforts should be directed toward curating data that can be used by providers for quality improvement, rather than toward developing standardized measures for use in consumer reporting. He suggests the creation of a data aggregating entity that would be governed by a publicly appointed board and financed by both public and private funds. The entity would ensure that the data was appropriately standardized and de-identified, and available only to authorized users, who would not include the public. One particularly interesting aspect of the proposal is that providers would be individually identified only with the agreement of the provider involved, a choice that reflects and responds to lingering provider opposition to provider-specific quality measures. This approach may be overly cautious, however, given the momentum toward provider-specific reporting apparent in other reporting initiatives.

[38] On federal data aggregation and management, *see generally* Kristin Madison, *Health Regulators as Data Stewards*, 92 N.C. L. Rev. 1605 (2014).

[39] Patient Protection and Affordable Care Act § 10332, 42 U.S.C. § 1395kk(e) (Supp. 2011).

[40] John S. Toussaint & Donald M. Berwick, *The Need for Access to Medicare Fee-for-Service Claims Data*, 310 JAMA 29 (2013).

[41] Harold S. Luft, *Advancing Public Reporting Through a New "Aggregator" to Standardize Data Collection on Providers' Cost and Quality*, 31 Health Aff. 619 (2012).

IV Focusing Quality Measurement Efforts

As policy-makers work to improve the informational foundation for quality measurement, industry stakeholders have begun to refine measurement approaches. One common criticism of quality reporting is that as report cards proliferate, consumers are often confronted with conflicting information about provider quality, potentially leading them to abandon quality ratings as a guide. Another is that rapidly proliferating and often overlapping reporting mandates drain provider resources while generating little incremental information about quality.[42] One study found that Massachusetts providers were subject to more than four hundred quality measures linked to reporting or payment programs, and that only 11% of these measures were shared across all of the programs examined.[43] These criticisms generate frequent calls for increased standardization of measure collection and reporting. Standardization has drawbacks; it may dampen innovation and competition in measure development, and the selection process involved may be shaped by a political process that "inherently protects the status quo."[44] Nevertheless, some commentators have advocated for greater standardization.

Given the diversity of the stakeholders involved, standardization has long been a challenge. CMS has looked to many entities for the quality measures incorporated in its meaningful use program. Measure "stewards" include accreditation organizations such as the Joint Commission and the National Committee for Quality Assurance and provider groups such as the American Medical Association–convened Physician Consortium for Performance Improvement, as well as other groups dedicated to measure development. One institution that has taken on the task of sifting through measures produced by these groups is the National Quality Forum (NQF), a multistakeholder institution established in the late 1990s to develop standards for performance measures. It continues to play a lead role in vetting new quality measures, including many used in federal programs. But state governments and private entities, including developers of proprietary quality indicators, do not always turn to the NQF. In addition, while the NQF engages in systematic review of measures, regularly approving new measures while retiring others, it does not have the capacity to lead efforts to develop new measure sets. Furthermore, when competing measures exist, developers may have a keen interest in preserving their own measures for financial or reputational reasons.

The ACA sought to address some of these concerns.[45] It required the identification of measurement gaps as well as measures in need of improvement or updating. It sought to minimize duplication and increase the use of common measures within HHS, and called for strategies that would align the efforts of public and private payers. It outlined measurement priorities, including assessment of health outcomes and functional status, management and

[42] On the proliferation of quality measures, *see* Robert J. Panzer et al., *Increasing Demands for Quality Measurement*, 310 JAMA 1971 (2013).

[43] Massachusetts Health Policy Commission, 2014 Health Trends Report 59 (2014), http://www.mass.gov/anf/budget-taxes-and-procurement/oversight-agencies/health-policy-commission/2014-cost-trends-report.pdf.

[44] Luft, *Advancing Public Reporting*, at 620.

[45] *See generally* Patient Protection and Affordable Care Act, Pub. L. No. 111-148, 124 Stat. 119 (2010), §§ 3011-3014.

coordination across healthcare providers, health services equity and health disparities, and patient experience and satisfaction. It also mandated that HHS work with multistakeholder organizations in implementing its measurement-based initiatives. Toward that end, HHS contracted with NQF to bring together the Measure Applications Partnership, which includes organizations representing consumers, payers, labor, healthcare professionals, and healthcare providers; one of its functions has been to help prioritize measures.[46] The Office of the National Coordinator for Health Information Technology has also been working to develop information technology–based strategies to achieve better coordination among payers, providers, and others with respect to quality measures as well as other quality-related tools.[47]

While policy-makers have made significant progress in developing and prioritizing quality measures, much work remains to be done. Many commentators have advocated for more frequent use of health outcome-based measures, rather than process-based measures, but this approach would often necessitate risk adjustment that is especially demanding in terms of data requirements.[48] In addition, while it is clear that reliable quality measures are still lacking in many areas, it is less clear where attention should be focused. One recent article suggested prioritizing measures that would generate the most health gains in terms of quality-adjusted life years.[49] The authors found that 93% of the health gains associated with the thirteen AHRQ quality indicators they examined could be attributed to just seven of the thirteen measures.

V Ensuring the Quality of Quality Measures

Even with voluminous data and carefully selected areas of focus, measurement will fail to improve quality if it is inaccurate. Quality measures will be misleading if the underlying data is intentionally or unintentionally miscoded. Measures may be based on healthcare processes that do not actually improve patient outcomes. Outcome measures may not be appropriately adjusted for patients' health risks. Technically accurate measures may mimic the effects of inaccurate measures, if measure users misconstrue them.

Faulty quality metrics might lead some patients to inadvertently choose lower quality providers, which would harm the patients and limit competition's potential to boost quality. Other patients might be falsely reassured about the quality of their current providers. Misclassifying quality levels might result in personal distress and undeserved reputational harm for some providers. Providers might develop an inaccurate sense of their own quality, leading them to do too little, or too much, or the wrong thing, to address deficiencies. Inaccurate measures could also harm payers' attempts to use financial incentives or benefit

[46] *See* U.S. Dep't of Health & Human Servs., 2013 Annual Report to Congress: National Strategy for Quality Improvement in Health Care 7–8 (2013).

[47] *Id.* at 20.

[48] *See* Robert A. Berenson, Peter J. Pronovost, & Harlan M. Krumholz, Urban Inst., Achieving the Potential of Health Care Performance Measures 12–13 (2013), *available at* http://www.rwjf.org/content/dam/farm/reports/reports/2013/rwjf406195.

[49] David O. Meltzer & Jeanette W. Chung, *The Population Value of Quality Indicator Reporting: A Framework for Prioritizing Health Care Performance Measures*, 33 Health Aff. 132 (2014).

structures to drive quality improvement. The question, then, is how best to ensure that quality measures themselves are of high quality.

Some of the same policies that facilitate data capture could address data quality. For example, HITECH's financial incentives for electronic health record use may help. Electronic health records, particularly when combined with re-engineered workflows that systematically capture quality data, may increase the comprehensiveness and accuracy of reporting, while reducing the potential for gaming, relative to reporting systems that require data collection solely for the purpose of reporting.

Research may also help increase measure quality. Research directed toward determining which structures and care processes generate good patient outcomes would be a helpful starting point for the development of new quality measures. Research that focuses on questions such as how to develop reliable measures in the context of small sample sizes and how best to adjust for risk will help numerous measurement projects move forward. Technical work on measurement algorithms will undoubtedly help to increase the quality of future measures.

A third way to address measure deficiencies is to use legal and regulatory tools. The available tools differ in many ways, including in the types of issues they target, their frequency of use, and their likelihood of success. They also differ in the identity of their primary users: payers, providers, patients, and regulators use different tools to respond to shortcomings in quality metrics.

a. Public and Private Payers' Efforts to Ensure Data Quality

Public payers and private health plans that publish quality metrics have considerable influence over measure quality. In creating or selecting quality metrics, they determine measure design. In deciding how to present information, they affect how information is understood. The accuracy of payers' quality metrics, however, hinges on the underlying data supplied by hospitals, physicians, or other providers. If these data are inaccurate, even the best-designed measures will be misleading, undermining public reporting, pay-for-performance initiatives, and any other arrangement that depends on these metrics.

To ensure greater data accuracy, payers could rely on contractual mechanisms. One such mechanism is contract terms that call for accurate reporting. Another is contractual mandates of specific steps to ensure quality, such as audits comparing reported data to medical records. Contractual provisions that facilitate monitoring would allow for earlier detection of problems. If providers do not live up to their contractual obligations, payers could then sue for breach of contract.

As pay-for-performance and value-based purchasing become more common in public programs, fraud and abuse law may also become a tool to ensure measure quality. For example, if payment of a federal claim is contingent on the provision of information about service quality, then reporting inaccurate information would render the claim false. An action could then be brought under the False Claims Act (FCA) against providers who knowingly submit false claims, including those who act "in reckless disregard of the truth or falsity of the information."[50]

[50] 31 U.S.C. § 3729 (2012).

Admittedly, past quality-related FCA suits have not always been successful. A number of these suits have been premised on the theory that submitted claims were "legally false" because providers had falsely certified the services as meeting the requisite standard of care, when in fact the care was substandard. Many courts are willing to accept this theory only when "a party certifies compliance with a statute or regulation as a condition to governmental payment,"[51] and in some cases establishing that certification of compliance is a condition of payment may not be possible. But in an era of value-based payment, a quality-related FCA claim should be more straightforward. When seeking payment, providers will need to submit not just data on the services they provide, but also data on the services' quality, and payment will explicitly be tied to both. If so, the issue will not be compliance with a quality standard, but a factually false report of quality submitted for the purposes of obtaining payment.

There has been at least one legal action based on an allegation of false reporting of quality information: The Kentucky attorney general investigated a health plan for falsely reporting to the Medicaid program a cervical cancer screening score which enabled it to receive more than $677,000 in bonus money. The plan ultimately agreed to pay more than $2 million in damages.[52] Large penalties available under the FCA or other fraud and abuse laws should encourage providers to put in place systems that facilitate accurate reporting.

b. Providers' Responses to Quality Measure Deficiencies

Hospitals and physicians share similar concerns that inaccurate quality measures may unfairly threaten their reputations, but have responded somewhat differently to the proliferation of quality reporting. Hospitals have devoted institutional resources to direct engagement with measure developers. They have taken an active role in trying to shape the federal hospital measures used in Hospital Compare, which underlie many reporting systems, while touting top ratings they receive in proprietary rating systems, many of which are designed to draw attention to the best performers. They have not tended to engage in high-profile legal actions challenging reporting systems.

Individual physicians, who tend to wield less influence than hospitals, face a quite different quality reporting landscape. While physician groups have certainly been involved in shaping governmental quality measures, federal quality ratings have been slow to develop; government-provided quality information has mainly come in the form of state licensure websites, which often pass along information related to professional disciplinary actions or malpractice, but do not provide quality metrics. Outside of these official sources, the most common types of publicly available quality information on physicians include commentary provided by individual patients and information offered by health plans. Physicians have brought legal challenges in response to both types of quality information.

[51] Mikes v. Straus, 274 F.3d 687, 697 (2d Cir. 2001).

[52] *AmeriHealth Mercy to Pay $2 Million for Submitting False Report*, KY. GEN. NEWS, Jan. 2011, http://ag.ky.gov/news/ky_general_news/kygeneralnews0111.pdf.

i. *Physician Responses to Patient Reviews*

Most posted patient reviews of physician services are positive. Occasionally, however, a patient unhappy with his or her treatment experience or outcome posts negative comments online. Physicians often face difficulties in responding to these reviews. Many reviews are posted anonymously, increasing the difficulty of identifying the poster. Even if they can identify the poster, physicians are limited in their ability to respond publicly to reviews they perceive as flawed, given legal restrictions on the disclosure of patient information.

Physicians have sometimes responded with defamation suits. One suit involved a man who complained online about the treatment a neurologist had provided to the man's father[53]; another involved parents who had complained on the website Yelp about the dental treatment their son had received.[54] Several suits have involved cosmetic surgery patients, such as a suit brought against a former patient who had posted complaints about a surgeon's services and claimed that the surgeon lacked board certification.[55] Another surgeon sued a patient who had received a breast augmentation, alleging that she had posted defamatory comments about the surgery's results on RateMDs.com.[56]

While plaintiffs do sometimes prevail in these cases, doing so can be difficult.[57] The case involving the neurologist was ultimately resolved by the Minnesota Supreme Court, which rejected the defamation claims on the grounds that the challenged statements involved "no genuine issue of material fact as to . . . falsity" or were "not capable of conveying a defamatory meaning that would harm respondent's reputation and lower him in the estimation of the community."[58] Cases fail when a court determines that the challenged statements are merely opinion. A federal district court recently accepted such an argument in a case involving a plastic surgery patient's postings. The court noted that the statements made "were posted on opinion websites; therefore, the natural tendency would be to infer that they are opinion."[59]

Some healthcare providers have turned to a contractual strategy to manage their online reputation: They have asked their patients to assign them copyrights for commentary posted on the Internet.[60] The idea behind such contracts is that if the patient does choose to post a review online, the provider could then demand its removal on the grounds that a copyright violation had occurred. This approach appears to have lost favor, however. Some websites have apparently repeatedly denied such requests.[61] Moreover, in 2011, in the aftermath of a class action suit targeting these agreements[62] and the filing of a complaint with the Federal

53 Alicia Gallegos, *Doctors Win Redress in Online Defamation Suits*, AM. MED. NEWS, Feb. 20, 2012, http://www.amednews.com/article/20120220/profession/302209934/6/.

54 *See* Wong v. Jing, 189 Cal. App. 4th 1354 (2010).

55 *See* Gallegos, *Doctors Win Redress.*

56 Walter Pacheco, *Doctor Sues Patient over Web Comments*, ORLANDO SENTINEL, May 21, 2012, http://articles.orlandosentinel.com/2012-05-21/health/os-doctor-online-defamation-lawsuit-20120521_1_patient-comments-defamation-lawsuit.

57 *See* Sean D. Lee, Note, *"I Hate My Doctor": Reputation, Defamation, and Physician-Review Websites*, 23 HEALTH MATRIX 573, 583–592 (2013) (discussing defamation cases involving online physician reviews).

58 McKee v. Laurion, 825 N.W. 2d 725, 728 (Minn. 2013).

59 Loftus v. Nazari, Civil Action No. 10-279(WOB-JGW), 2014 WL 1908812, at *3 (E.D. Ky. May 13, 2014).

60 For a discussion of these contracts, *see* Ann Marie Marciarille, *"How's My Doctoring?" Patient Feedback's Role in Assessing Physician Quality*, 14 DEPAUL J. HEALTH CARE L. 361, 394–402 (2012).

61 *Id.* at 397.

62 *See* Lee v. Makhnevich, Civ. Action No. 11-civ-8665 (U.S.D.N.Y.).

Trade Commission alleging unethical business practices, a company that had developed and promoted the use of such contracts decided to no longer use them.[63] The legal tools available to physicians to respond to negative reviews therefore are limited, regardless of whether the reviews are accurate or flawed.

ii. *Physician Responses to Health Plans' Ratings*

While physician suits against individual patients garner headlines, much more of physicians' collective energy has been directed toward another source of quality-related information: health plans. By the early 2000s, health plans had begun to share provider quality data with their enrollees in a variety of forms.[64] Some developed and published provider ratings based on criteria the plans had established. Others created programs in which a subset of providers were distinguished based on performance; in some cases, employers established benefit structures that encouraged enrollees to use high-performing physicians. These rating programs often elicited objections from physicians, who argued that the programs generated faulty ratings because of poor-quality data and/or flawed methodologies.

In some cases, the objections led to further discussion and modifications. In at least one case, described in more detail in section V.d on regulators' efforts to enhance measure quality, the American Medical Association and a state medical society worked with other stakeholders and a state attorney general to create a framework for rating systems.[65] In other cases, objections led to litigation, with medical associations frequently acting as plaintiffs.[66] As with suits in response to individual patient reviews, one common claim was defamation; the argument was that through their ratings, health plans had published false statements about provider quality, harming providers' professional reputations. A second cause of action was tortious interference with advantageous relationships, a claim based on the theory that the health plans' actions prompted physicians' patients to turn elsewhere for care. A third type of claim that appeared repeatedly was violation of the state consumer protection act, a claim arising out of the allegedly deceptive nature of challenged ratings programs. Plaintiffs also alleged breach of contract, a viable claim if health plans' rating activities were impermissible under the terms of the contracts between health plans and providers.

These lawsuits met with varying degrees of success. The 2006 Washington State Medical Association suit against Regence BlueShield ended in a settlement under which Regence BlueShield agreed to consult with the Medical Association on methodological issues, to disclose its methodology, to permit physician appeals of ratings, and to allow final, binding review by an independent external reviewer.[67] A judge dismissed the 2010 suit of the California Medical Association challenging Blue Shield of California's Blue Ribbon Physician Recognition Program, finding that the plaintiffs had failed to respond to the argument that the First Amendment shielded the ratings. In addition, the plaintiffs failed to show that the

[63] *See* Alicia Gallegos, *Company Withdraws Contracts Controlling Online Comments by Patients*, AM. MED. NEWS, Jan. 2, 2012, http://www.amednews.com/article/20120102/profession/301029947/4/.

[64] *See* Madison, *Law & Policy of Health Care Quality Reporting*, at 236–240.

[65] *See id.* at 240–250 for a fuller discussion of the attorney general's letter and its aftermath.

[66] *See* Madison, *Law & Policy of Health Care Quality Reporting*, at 236–240.

[67] *See id.* at 240.

public was deceived by the ratings, or that the public had relied on them, given the disclaimers presented on the ratings website.[68] The parties later settled, with Blue Shield agreeing to publicly disclose more information about its program. The Massachusetts Medical Society decided to drop its 2008 suit against two health insurers and the Massachusetts Group Insurance Commission (GIC), which had created a ratings program as part of its health insurance offerings to state employees. The decision was made after a judge dismissed GIC from the case on the grounds that the physicians lacked a direct commercial relationship with GIC, rendering the physicians' claims of interference with advantageous relations moot.[69]

Another claim made in cases challenging ratings is violation of due process rights.[70] For example, the Massachusetts Medical Society claimed that the GIC's executive director had violated procedural rights under the Massachusetts and U.S. constitutions because the GIC tiering program lacked a meaningful appeals process, depriving the plaintiffs of a property interest in their practices and a liberty interest in their reputations.[71] The superior court justice rejected these arguments, finding that reputational injury alone does not constitute deprivation of a liberty interest, and that the goodwill that would be damaged by reputational harm is not a protected property interest.

Some courts have recognized common law due process rights for physicians removed from health plan provider panels, but whether such rights would extend to a quality rating case is unclear. In the 2000 case *Potvin v. Metropolitan Life Ins. Co.*, the California Supreme Court held that when an "insurer possesses power so substantial that the removal significantly impairs the ability of an ordinary, competent physician to practice medicine or a medical specialty in a particular geographic area, thereby affecting an important, substantial economic interest," physicians' removal from a preferred provider list must be "substantively rational and procedurally fair."[72] One could argue that quality ratings, like termination, could significantly impair a physician's ability to practice, and so should be subject to due process requirements in states that recognize them. On the other hand, given patients' relatively limited use of such ratings, low ratings may not affect a physician's practice as much as panel termination. In addition, low ratings need not significantly impair a patient's access to his or her physician, one of the concerns that appeared to motivate the *Potvin* decision. These differences between ratings and panel terminations, particularly when combined with the likelihood that minimal procedural protections would be sufficient to satisfy court-imposed due process requirements, mean that due process challenges, although potentially viable, may not go very far in addressing physicians' concerns about quality ratings.

[68] Cal. Med. Ass'n v. Blue Shield of Cal. Life & Health Ins. Co., No. RG10535619 (Cal. Super. Ct. Mar. 23, 2011) (order granting special motion to strike and dismissing action).

[69] *See* Bruce Auerbach, An Update on the MMS Lawsuit Against the Group Insurance Commission (Sept. 22, 2011), http://blog.massmed.org/index.php/category/group-insurance-commission/.

[70] *See* Stacy L. Cook, *Will Pay for Performance Be Worth the Price to Medical Providers? A Look at Pay for Performance and Its Legal Implications for Providers*, 16 ANNALS HEALTH L. 163, 180–185 (2007) (discussing due process claims).

[71] Mass. Med. Soc'y v. Group Ins. Comm'n, No. 08-2124, 2009 Mass. Super. LEXIS 100, at *35–*43 (Mass. Super. Mar. 30, 2009).

[72] Potvin v. Metropolitan Life Ins. Co., 997 P.2d 1153, 1160–1161 (Cal. 2000).

c. Patients' Responses to Quality Measure Deficiencies

While providers may experience reputational harm as a result of poorly constructed quality ratings, patients may experience physical harm. Imagine the following scenario: A patient who needs treatment uses quality ratings to select a highly rated practitioner. As it turns out, however, the rating is misleadingly high, and the treatment she receives is more consistent with the practices of a low-quality provider than those of a high-quality provider. The patient does not end up faring as well as she could have, had better treatment been delivered. If the treatment provided were below the standard of care, the patient might have a cause of action for malpractice, but this action would be available regardless of the existence or use of quality ratings. Does the presence of quality ratings in this scenario make possible additional claims?

Patients might try to bring claims against organizations that produce quality ratings, but such suits would face many challenges. Rating sites often include disclaimers that could help shield them from liability. The sites may state that they do not recommend particular providers and emphasize that the user is entirely responsible for his or her choice of provider, hindering claims that hinge on the ratings' influence on patient decision-making. Rating services might assert that the quality information provided is merely opinion, undermining claims based on misstatements of fact. Indeed, many of the same arguments that undermined physicians' claims against health plans would apply to similar consumer claims. In addition, rating services might make use of express contractual limitations on liability.

Patients might also try to direct suits against providers who supply misleading quality ratings. A patient could argue that had she been properly informed of the provider's quality, she would have chosen another provider, thereby avoiding injury. A decision to sue might find some support in the much-discussed 1997 informed consent case *Johnson v. Kokemoor*, in which the Wisconsin Supreme Court found that evidence on experience-related mortality differentials was properly admitted, as was evidence about the "availability of other centers and physicians better able to perform that procedure."[73] In light of this decision, it would not be much of a stretch to argue that a physician's provision of misleading quality ratings would be relevant to an informed consent claim.

It is more of a stretch, however, to say that to adequately inform a patient, a provider must take the affirmative step of providing accurate quality ratings. While Professors Twerski and Cohen have made a case for recognizing failure to disclose physician-specific risk information as the basis for an informed consent claim,[74] a number of post-*Johnson* claims based on the failure to disclose information related to physician-specific risk have failed. One scholar observed that "disclosure applies to risks that are attributed to the medical procedure but not risks attributable to competent physicians," and that "skills are policed through negligence law and licensure regulations rather than through disclosure requirements."[75]

[73] Johnson v. Kokemoor, 545 N.W. 2d 495 (Wis. 1997).

[74] *See* Aaron D. Twerski & Neil B. Cohen, *The Second Revolution in Informed Consent: Comparing Physicians to Each Other*, 94 Nw. U. L. Rev. 1 (1999).

[75] Mark A. Hall, *Caring, Curing, and Trust: A Response to Gatter*, 39 Wake Forest L. Rev. 447, 450 (2004).

Even if courts are willing to allow quality rating-based informed consent claims, the claims may fail because of the difficulty of establishing causation.[76] Twerski and Cohen emphasize that in at least one respect, causation arguments are more credible in suits focused on physician-specific risk disclosures than in suits involving more traditional risk disclosures: A statement that the patient would have chosen a lower-risk provider to perform a particular procedure is more plausible than a claim that the patient would have chosen a different procedure. But as Twerski and Cohen acknowledge, for informed consent claims to work, the legal system must also grapple with the challenges of addressing scenarios in which the outcome of an alternative choice is uncertain. If the risk of an adverse outcome with a more highly rated physician is 10% lower than the risk associated with the patient's treating physician, how should a claim that the undisclosed risk differential led to an adverse outcome be resolved? A court would need to be willing to impose liability for the patient's "lost chance."

The nature of quality measures may also impede informed consent claims. Physician-specific risk information is a close cousin to the general risk information traditionally shared; by contrast, the relationship between a quality rating based on patient experience and the magnitude of a specific health risk is unclear. To say that a missing star on a rating "materialized" into a missed diagnosis is quite different from saying that a higher risk of missed diagnosis, as reflected in a metric specifically designed to capture such risk, materialized. Thus, many of today's quality ratings would fit awkwardly within the informed consent framework.

What if a faulty physician quality measure was produced and supplied by a health plan? Perhaps enrollees could make claims based on deceptive trade practice or consumer protection statutes, or claims based in contract or tort. A suit against a managed care organization for subpar quality ratings might be modeled after tort claims based on negligent credentialing, which target poorly functioning evaluation processes. However, many of the same roadblocks at work in the previously described scenarios, from contractual liability limitations to causation difficulties, could also arise in this scenario. The Employment Retirement Income Security Act may also be a stumbling block for suits against health plans.

d. Regulators' Efforts to Enhance Measure Quality

This brief overview has so far suggested that numerous legal tools are at least potentially available to patients and physicians seeking to challenge faulty quality ratings, but that they may not always be up to the task. Only a few suits appear to have yielded outcomes addressing the fundamental issue at stake from a public policy point of view: how best to ensure that rating systems accurately reflect provider quality.

While most of the work now underway to improve quality ratings is technical work undertaken by researchers, provider groups, standards organizations, and other measurement experts, there has also been at least one example of a legal action undertaken to promote responsible development and use of quality ratings. In 2007, the New York Office of the Attorney General sent letters to insurers that had developed quality rating programs,

[76] *See* Twerski & Cohen, *The Second Revolution in Informed Consent*, at 11–15.

expressing concerns about the possibility of consumer "confusion" and the possibility that data might be flawed or information provided inaccurate.[77] But instead of seeking to block the use of rating systems, the Office of the Attorney General eventually turned its attention to how best to improve them. It began to work with provider and consumer groups to develop a template for rating programs. It entered into settlements with major insurers that incorporated principles and practices meant to improve quality and efficiency measures. Core principles included accuracy and transparency, oversight, and fairness. The agreements required insurers to use quality measures based on national guidelines and, if available, measures endorsed by the National Quality Forum or similar entities. They required disclosure of the underlying methodology and the creation of an appeals process. They also required insurers to contract with independent ratings examiners that would review the rating programs in accordance with agreement provisions; the National Committee on Quality Assurance has served in this capacity. Many of the insurers that agreed to follow the model code chose to implement reforms nationwide. Around the same time, a number of insurers signed on to the Patient Charter for Physician Performance Measurement, a document developed by employer, labor, and consumer organizations that reflects similar principles.[78]

The provider-driven litigation trend of the early 2000s appears to have slowed, and there have been no regulator- or attorney general–led efforts to reshape private reporting systems that have achieved the prominence or impact of the New York attorney general's actions. Healthcare leaders, however, have given thought to mechanisms that could improve quality measures. Robert Berenson, Peter Pronovost, and Harlan Krumholz propose the creation of an institution that would define measurement and reporting standards "to improve the validity, comparability, and transparency of publicly-reported health care quality data," thus taking on functions similar to those the Securities and Exchange Commission (SEC) fulfills for corporate financial reporting.[79] The proposed institution would set standards for measure development, "analyze progress," and audit measure data. Citing First Amendment concerns, the authors suggest that the institution not have regulatory authority, but instead seek voluntary compliance with its standards.

The SEC analogy has guided conversations about the direction of quality reporting for many years,[80] and this proposal echoes previous proposals, including the Institute of Medicine's 2006 proposal for the creation of a National Quality Coordination Board within HHS that would designate standardized performance measures, ensure the creation of a data repository, and track quality improvement over time, among other tasks.[81] One of the many difficulties in establishing such an entity is pinning down the details of how exactly it would function. While the SEC has the legal authority to establish reporting standards, it relies on the Financial Accounting Standards Board, a private, independent organization, to create

[77] *See* Madison, *Law & Policy of Health Care Quality Reporting*, at 240–250 for a fuller discussion of the attorney general's letter and its aftermath.

[78] *See id.* [79] *See* BERENSON, PRONOVOST, & KRUMHOLZ, URBAN INST., at 18–19.

[80] *See, e.g.*, WILLIAM M. SAGE, ACCOUNTABILITY THROUGH INFORMATION: WHAT THE HEALTH CARE INDUSTRY CAN LEARN FROM SECURITIES REGULATION (2000), http://www.milbank.org/uploads/documents/0012sage.html ("Advocates of regulatory reform in the health sector frequently urge attention to the information-based regulatory policy of the Securities and Exchange Commission (SEC) and the Financial Accounting Standards Board (FASB).").

[81] *See* INST. OF MED., PERFORMANCE MEASUREMENT.

them; while the SEC sets rules that influence the auditing process, it is independent auditors that conduct audits of company financial statements. The Berenson-Pronovost-Krumholz proposal does not specify the governance or operational structure of the proposed quality measurement entity. It expressly leaves to policy-makers the question of whether the proposed entity "should be housed at AHRQ; should be a public-private partnership, such as NQF; or should be a separate, new government entity." Developing a single, authoritative entity with such a wide array of quality measurement–related responsibilities would clearly be a daunting task.

VI The Next Generation of Measurement and Reporting

Given the relatively early stage of development of the science of quality measurement, and the rapidly evolving healthcare delivery system, it may make sense for policy-makers to prioritize efforts to strengthen the analytical and data foundations for measurement and reporting, rather than focusing on creating new institutions devoted to measure standardization.

First, policy-makers could direct more resources toward research that could guide all industry stakeholders seeking to make the most out of measurement as a quality improvement tool. To create effective quality metrics, measure developers need to know which process or intermediate outcomes are actually associated with improved health. Healthcare providers need to know what sorts of changes might yield better performance on quality metrics, including changes in organizational structure and management practices. Measure developers need to know how best to tackle the statistical and practical challenges present when data is limited and costly to collect. It might be helpful to have a better understanding, for example, of which measures could proxy for quality in areas not directly measured. Similarly, it would be helpful to know more about the correlation between ratings of provider organizations and ratings of individual providers, and what sorts of factors affect this correlation. With more funding to support health services research, agencies such as AHRQ or the Patient-Centered Outcomes Research Institute could lead the effort to answer these questions.

More research is needed, too, on the best way to present quality measures to influence patient decision-making. Many ratings used today are attractive more for their administrative feasibility than for their patient appeal. The inclusion of survey-based patient experience ratings is certainly a step toward achieving the patient-centeredness that is one of the key goals of healthcare reform. It is clear, however, that more can be done. For example, it would be nice for a prospective obstetrics patient's online search to return clearly relevant comparison data—say, C-section rates or patient experience or safety issues in labor and delivery units—rather than forcing the patient to wade through a long list of measures with unclear applicability, such as the hospital's performance with respect to heart failure care. If patients are interested in learning about particular physicians, but only physician group ratings are collected, then physician websites should allow for searches for individual physicians and return any available physician-specific information along with ratings for the group to which the physician belongs. Website developers should work closely with researchers to determine what sorts of reporting might both interest patients and improve quality, and then follow up on research findings.

Second, policy-makers could continue to promote the adoption and meaningful use of information technology that supports diverse quality measurement efforts. An important first step, already underway, is for providers to move to record systems that can capture highly detailed information about patient demographics and health history, current illnesses or injuries, medical or surgical treatments, and treatment outcomes. Providers may need to alter workflows to ensure that the relevant data is actually collected and appropriately entered. In addition, systems need to be integrated so that information can be brought together from multiple systems simultaneously.[82] If this infrastructure is in place, then coping with multiple measurement demands will become much more straightforward. A stronger health record infrastructure will support more and more varied quality metrics and reduce reliance on the inherently limited information available through claims data.

VII Conclusion

Quality measurement and reporting systems can help improve healthcare quality, but only if they are well designed and well executed. System stakeholders may turn to legal tools to address measure deficiencies or their associated harms, but using these tools effectively can be challenging. Government actors and multistakeholder institutions are better positioned to assure measure quality through a holistic approach to measure development, assessment, and oversight, and they can take a long-term leadership role in encouraging standardization of selected core quality metrics.

In the near term, however, the promotion of measure-related research and improved electronic health record systems should be the primary policy focus. In addition to accelerating measurement efforts already underway, these activities will help to build a foundation for the creation of diverse quality measures better tailored to the varied concerns and interests of a truly patient-centered healthcare system. Questions about how best to capture healthcare experiences and outcomes that patients care about will need to be considered alongside more technical questions about measure calculation. Ultimately, the policy goal should be to create an efficient platform for quality measurement that is flexible enough to serve the differing needs and objectives of providers, payers, regulators, patients, and policy-makers.

[82] For a discussion of the practical challenges measure developers face, *see* Phyllis Torda & Aldo Tinoco, *Achieving the Promise of Electronic Health Record–Enabled Quality Measurement: A Measure Developer's Perspective* 1 eGEMs (Generating Evidence & Methods to Improve Patient Outcomes) (2013), http://repository.academyhealth.org/egems/vol1/iss2/3.

C. Health Insurance and Finance

CHAPTER 31

EMPLOYMENT-BASED HEALTH COVERAGE

MARK A. HALL

EMPLOYMENT-BASED coverage is the dominant form of health insurance in the United States. The vast majority of privately insured people—over one hundred fifty million—receive coverage through the workplace. Although the extent of employment-based coverage may contract somewhat in future years, as of 2014, only about 10% of privately insured people purchase their insurance individually; the rest have group coverage sponsored by an employer.

In the 1990s, President Clinton failed in his attempt to make employer-sponsorship the centerpiece of comprehensive healthcare reform. His proposal to mandate that most employers offer insurance through government-run "health alliances" failed to even come to a vote before Congress. Under the Patient Protection and Affordable Care Act (ACA), individual responsibility takes center stage, with government-run insurance exchanges selling subsidized coverage to individuals, and an "individual mandate" that imposes a modest tax penalty if people do not sign up for coverage that is affordable. Nevertheless, employers retain a central spot on the health insurance stage, if only because of the ongoing debate over their appropriate role.

Prominent public policy voices, such as former presidential adviser Ezekiel Emanuel, predict the downfall of employer sponsorship as more people shift to the ACA's subsidized exchanges. Most others, however, including leading policy analysts such as RAND Corporation and MIT's Jonathan Gruber, predict only a modest erosion of employer sponsorship. They point to the long history and entrenched institutional support of employers' role in paying for health insurance, coupled with the ACA's requirement that, if larger employers (with more than fifty full-time workers) do not offer affordable coverage, they pay a substantial tax. Implementation of this "employer mandate" was delayed for two years, and substantial debate continues over whether it should be modified or repealed. Thus, it is a very auspicious time indeed to consider major aspects of the history, future, and complexities of employer-sponsored health insurance in the United States.

I Why Employment-Based Coverage Is Dominant

a. Legal Reasons for Employment-Based Coverage

Employers' dominant position in the private health insurance market arises from a variety of economic and legal factors.[1] Wage and price controls imposed to counter inflation caused by postwar labor shortages provided the initial impetus for the growth of employment-based coverage.[2] Some analysts believe that, because fringe benefits such as health insurance were not counted as wages, expanded benefits were a convenient way for employers to compete for workers. Others, such as Tim Jost in chapter "Access to Health Insurance and Health Benefits," believe this account is overstated, but all agree that a longer-lasting legal impetus for employment-based coverage came from the federal tax code. In 1943, the Internal Revenue Service (IRS) ruled that the amounts employers paid for workers' health insurance do not constitute income to employees.[3]

This tax ruling has little effect on employers[4] because they can deduct workers' compensation as business expenses regardless of whether compensation is paid in the form of wages or benefits. But, for employees, not taxing benefits as income creates a strong incentive to prefer richer benefits even at the cost of leaner wages. In effect, this asymmetric tax treatment allows employers to purchase health insurance for their employees using employees' before-tax compensation, rather than leaving employees to purchase insurance themselves from their after-tax wages. The amount of the implicit tax subsidy is a function of each worker's marginal tax rate (federal and state combined), so its size is larger for higher-income taxpayers because of the progressivity of federal taxation.[5] In the aggregate, this subsidy is worth about a quarter of a trillion dollars in forgone tax revenue per year,[6] the second largest tax expenditure after home mortgage interest.[7]

[1] *See generally* David Hyman & Mark Hall, *Two Cheers For Employment-Based Health Insurance*, 2 Yale J. Health Pol'y L. & Ethics 23 (2001).

[2] *See* Institute of Medicine, Employment and Health Benefits: A Connection at Risk 70 (1992).

[3] *See* Robert B. Helms, *The Tax Treatment of Health Insurance: Early History and Evidence, 1940–1970*, *in* Empowering Health Care Consumers Through Tax Reform (Grace-Marie Arnett ed., 1999). Ten years later, the IRS withdrew this ruling, but Congress amended the Internal Revenue Code in 1954 to expressly exclude employment-based coverage from taxable income. I.R.C. § 106 (1986) ("Gross income of an employee does not include employer-provided coverage under an accident or health plan."). *See* Sherry Glied, Revising the Tax Treatment of Employer-Provided Health Insurance 4 (1994).

[4] There is a small effect because I.R.C. § 3121 (1986) excludes the employer's contribution to health insurance from payroll taxes.

[5] *See* Helms, *The Tax Treatment* at 10; John Sheils & Paul Hogan, *Cost of Tax-Exempt Health Benefits in 1998*, 18 Health Aff. 176, 179, 181 (Mar.–Apr. 1999) (modeling tax subsidy, and concluding that it is "heavily skewed toward high-income groups," with 68.7% of the total subsidy going to the 36% of the population with incomes greater than $50,000).

[6] Congressional Budget Office, Options For Reducing the Deficit: 2014 to 2023 (Nov. 2013), http://www.cbo.gov/budget-options/2013/44903.

[7] *See* Sheils & Hogan, *Cost*, at 178.

The result of this substantial financial incentive favoring employment-based health insurance is that labor unions often negotiate as hard or harder over benefits as they do over wages. In industries in which unions are strong (manufacturing, public sector employment), the result for many has been especially generous insurance coverage with few out-of-pocket costs.[8] Some employers with nonunionized workforces also offered rich benefits to discourage their employees from unionizing.

More comprehensive insurance has positive public health benefits, but these tax incentives have also been criticized for making health insurance too generous. Generous insurance gives rise to what economists call "moral hazard," which is the tendency of insurance to increase the odds that the insured risk will occur, because insurance reduces the natural economic incentive to guard against the risk. For health insurance, the primary concern is not necessarily that people will be more likely to get sick, but instead, that, when they are sick, insurance makes them more willing to receive expensive medical care.[9] The degree to which moral hazard increases the cost of care is hotly debated, but there is no real dispute that this occurs to a considerable extent. As a consequence, many policy analysts see tax reform as a key element of healthcare cost control. The ACA takes an initial step down this path by imposing a hefty excise tax (starting in 2018) on so-called Cadillac health plans that cost more than about $10,000 a year (for individual coverage, adjusted for inflation).[10]

A third, accidental legal factor sustaining employment-based coverage is the federal Employee Retirement Income Security Act (ERISA).[11] This statute was enacted in 1974 primarily to regulate private pension plans, but, almost as an afterthought, Congress also included other fringe benefits in its scope.[12] To create room for effective federal regulation, ERISA preempts state laws that "relate to" employee benefits, but federal regulation has focused mainly on pension benefits, neglecting "welfare benefits." This federal preemption coupled with the near-absence of federal regulation for health insurance has created what many describe as a regulatory vacuum.[13] Although nature abhors a vacuum, insurers and employers relish freedom from oversight, and so they have eagerly defend the economic advantages of ERISA preemption.

ERISA creates two basic levels or categories of preemption. All employment-based health insurance is preempted from most state laws governing dispute resolution.[14] In addition,

[8] JOSEPH CALIFANO, AMERICA'S HEALTH CARE REVOLUTION: WHO LIVES? WHO DIES? WHO PAYS? 44–45 (1986).

[9] Mark Pauly, *The Economics of Moral Hazard: Comment*, 58 AM. ECON. REV. 531, 535 (1965).

[10] Health Affairs, Excise Tax on "Cadillac" Plans (2013), http://healthaffairs.org/healthpolicybriefs/brief_pdfs/healthpolicybrief_99.pdf.

[11] Pub. L. 93–406, 88 Stat. 829, codified in part at 29 U.S.C. ch. 18.

[12] James A. Wooten, THE EMPLOYEE RETIREMENT INCOME SECURITY ACT OF 1974: A POLITICAL HISTORY (2004).

[13] For additional background discussion of insurance regulation and ERISA preemption, *See* Jana K. Strain & Eleanor D. Kinney, *The Road Paved with Good Intentions: Problems and Potential for Employer-Sponsored Health Insurance Under ERISA*, 31 LOY. U. CHI. L.J. 29 (1999); Catherine Fisk, *The Last Article about the Language of ERISA Preemption?*, 33 HARV. J. LEG. 35 (1996); Jeselyn Alicia Brown, *ERISA and State Health Care Reform: Roadblock or Scapegoat?*, 13 YALE L. & POL'Y REV. 339 (1995); Mary Anne Bobinski, *Unhealthy Federalism: Barriers to Increasing Health Care Access for the Uninsured*, 24 U.C. DAVIS L. REV. 255 (1990).

[14] The major exception is for state laws requiring insurers to provide independent medical review of coverage denials that are based on medical criteria. The Supreme Court upheld such statutes reasoning

only self-insured employment benefits are also preempted from state insurance regulation. The difference arises because ERISA contains a "savings clause" that preserves states' traditional authority to regulate insurance, but ERISA also declares (in what is called its "deemer clause") that employers themselves may not be deemed to be insurers.[15] This statutory maze has created a thicket of case law and legal confusion, explained more in section IV, but for now, one consequence is clear: States may not regulate the content or terms of health coverage if employers bear their own insurance risk rather than purchase conventional insurance. For instance, state laws that mandate health insurers to cover specific health benefits apply only to purchased insurance and not to self-insured employer coverage—even though both types of insurance are often administered by the same insurance companies and so are indistinguishable to the people who are covered or the providers who are paid (same provider networks, same member I.D. cards, etc.).

This greater freedom to design benefit packages and to avoid other regulatory costs has resulted, over time, in more than half of the employment-based market adopting self-funded plans. Although the largest employers are most likely to self-insure, self-funding is feasible even for smaller employers because they can purchase "stop-loss" reinsurance to limit the extent of their financial exposure. Self-funding of employer benefits has led employers to be more committed to offering health coverage and to be more involved in the costs and quality of this coverage. Thus, despite its legal and public policy anomalies, ERISA preemption has played an important role in fortifying the employment-based structure of private health insurance in the United States.

b. Economic Reasons for Employment-Based Coverage

Historical accident and legal anomalies are not the only reasons that employment became the dominant platform for private health insurance. Employer sponsorship improves the economics of health insurance in several fundamental ways. First, because employers purchase for groups of workers and family members, they achieve economies of scale that are not available in the individual market. In essence, employers purchase insurance wholesale rather than retail, meaning that the sales costs and profit margins are greatly reduced. This advantage is reflected in insurers' "medical loss ratio," which is the portion of the insurance premium devoted to paying medical costs rather than going to corporate overhead (including profits). Overhead for the largest employer groups is typically 5% or less, whereas these costs reach around 20% for individuals and smaller groups.

Employment-based insurance also addresses market failings caused by "adverse selection" and "medical underwriting"—two additional terms of art that require explanation. Adverse selection is the natural tendency of riskier people to seek more coverage than less risky people. All else being equal, people who expect to need health insurance are more willing to buy it, and want to buy more of it, than those who expect to remain healthy.

that they are more akin to requiring a second medical opinion than to mandatory dispute resolution. Rush Prudential HMO, Inc. v. Moran, 536 U.S. 355 (2002).

[15] 29 U.S.C. §1144(b) (2)(A).

Accordingly, in the individual market, competing health insurers cannot survive unless they screen applicants for health risks. If insurers simply took everyone who applied at average community rates, sicker people would flock to the coverage, driving up the price beyond what healthier people are willing or able to pay, thus causing the average price to increase even more, resulting in further cycles of fewer healthier purchasers and even higher prices. Suppose, for instance, that a health insurer approached a market assuming that all people of the same age and sex have the same risk of disease or injury and so the insurer prices its product accordingly—say, at $5,000 for males aged forty to forty-five. Naturally, not all men this age have the same risk of illness. Some are in excellent shape, some have average health, and some are already sick. If the insurer is not able to act on this information (or is prohibited from learning it), and if only some people purchase insurance, a disproportionate number of sicker people will subscribe, because those with greater than average risk will find the average price more attractive than those of lesser risk.

A pool of sicker-than-average subscribers will obviously end up costing more than $5,000 per person, so an insurer that wants to remain solvent will raise its price—say to $6,000. This does not solve the adverse selection problem, since at any price the insurance is by definition more attractive to higher-risk than to lower-risk subscribers, and so the cycle repeats, with prices going higher and the pool of people who are willing to purchase shrinking. At the extreme, this community rating dynamic can cause the market to collapse entirely into an adverse selection "death spiral"; short of that, even if the market stabilizes, it will be at a higher-priced equilibrium than is optimal, leaving a good number of people without any coverage.

The obvious way for private insurers to avoid this outcome is to screen applicants for health risk and either exclude people or conditions that are too expensive or charge less healthy people more. This risk screening is called "medical underwriting." Because health risks vary so extremely—from people who incur virtually no costs to those whose costs can exceed a million dollars a year—insurers have a great deal more to lose or gain in how they do medical underwriting than in how they manage the overall average costs of medical care.[16] This is why competition in the market for individual insurance historically has focused to such a considerable extent on techniques of medical underwriting. Prior to reform by the ACA, insurers varied rates more than fivefold based on age and gender, and they refused to cover any conditions that existed prior to the start of coverage. Also, they flatly refused to cover many applicants with common health problems simply because those problems (such as diabetes or heart conditions) were too systemic to isolate and limit through exclusions. This process of medical underwriting added to the overhead costs of selling individual health insurance. More important, the inherent dynamic of structuring insurance markets to counter adverse selection meant that many people could not qualify for insurance that covers their most important health needs.

Almost by magic, employment-based insurance solves this snake pit of market failings. Medical underwriting is not needed, and therefore is not used, for larger employer groups (those above about fifty workers). Employer groups avoid adverse selection for three key reasons. First, when employers provide health insurance as an ongoing fringe benefit, it

[16] 47 Million And Counting: Why the Health Care Marketplace Is Broken, Testimony before the U.S. Senate Committee on Finance Hearing, June 10, 2008, http://www.finance.senate.gov/hearings/.

is much less likely that they purchase insurance simply because they expect higher-than-normal medical expenses. Second, with larger groups, the statistical "law of large numbers" predicts that health risks for any given group will be similar to population averages, since a greater number of healthier people will counterbalance the expenses of the unfortunate number who incur large expenses. Third, fine-grained individual assessment is not required to determine which groups are likely to exceed population averages; instead, insurers can base the current year's premium for a larger group simply on its demographic characteristics and on the aggregate medical expenses the group incurred in previous years.

Employment-based coverage is also a convenient nexus for cross-subsidization within heterogeneous risk groups. Because employment-based coverage is not risk-adjusted or underwritten within the risk pool, there are, by definition, systematic cross-subsidies flowing within the pool. Although these arrangements fall well below the degree of social solidarity desired by advocates of single-payer systems, they are real and long-standing.[17] The success of employment-based coverage in maintaining these internal cross-subsidies should be contrasted with the difficulty that states and the federal government have encountered in mandating or maintaining such cross-subsidization.[18]

This happy outcome is the main reason that public policy should favor employment-based coverage. Buying insurance through large heterogeneous groups solves a host of market problems, but the market does not easily give rise to purchasing groups that spread different levels of insurance risk. It is not a simple matter to form a group that is willing to pool their health insurance expenses and arrange for (and subsidize) insurance for everyone in the group, such that most people in the group will opt into coverage. Consider, for instance, the possibility of forming a group of freelance artists who purchase insurance together. If members of the group have widely varying risk profiles and can obtain comparable coverage outside the group setting, the healthier ones will opt out and purchase individually at a rate cheaper than the average cost for the entire group. In other words, the savings to healthier members from disaggregating the group could well exceed the savings from group economies. In these circumstances, legal and regulatory policy that favors group purchase subsidized by employers, serves a useful function. The tax subsidy, for instance, makes it significantly more attractive to purchase coverage through one's employer; therefore, it plays the important role of keeping intact the heterogeneous risks pools that are needed to achieve the administrative efficiencies found in employment-based health insurance.

What has been said about employer groups applies primarily to larger employers—those with more than fifty workers. For smaller employers, the natural market dynamics are a hybrid of those in the individual and large group markets.[19] Economies of scale are less than those for large groups but greater than those for individuals. Absent regulation, insurers used many forms of medical underwriting for small groups, but not as extensively as with individuals. Because small employers often lack the critical mass needed to self-insure, they do not usually enjoy ERISA's preemption from state insurance regulation. Accordingly,

[17] William S. Custer et al., *Why We Should Keep the Employment-Based Health Insurance System*, 18 HEALTH AFF. 115 (Dec. 1999).

[18] *See, e.g.*, THEDA SKOCPOL, BOOMERANG: HEALTH CARE REFORM AND THE TURN AGAINST GOVERNMENT (1999).

[19] Mark A. Hall, *The Geography of Health Insurance Regulation: A Guide to Identifying, Exploiting, and Policing Market Boundaries*, 19(2) HEALTH AFF. 173 (2000).

small employers are substantially less likely to offer health insurance than are large employers. Whereas almost all employers with two hundred or more workers offer their employees health insurance, only about half of employers with fewer than ten employees do so.[20]

Various attempts prior to the Affordable Care Act to reform private health insurance markets can be viewed as, in essence, trying to make the individual and small group markets behave more like the large-group employer market.[21] These state and federal reforms restricted the elements of medical underwriting that insurers could use (guaranteed issue), they required insurers to charge similar rates for people of the same age and gender (adjusted community rating), and they reduced the exclusion of preexisting conditions by allowing people to change insurance without having to undergo new waiting periods (portability). These reforms were incomplete, however. Most applied only to the small group market, where market economies could support such restrictions on insurers; in the individual market, adverse selection problems continued to make it infeasible for patchwork market reforms to succeed. This experience set the stage for the Affordable Care Act.

These reasons explaining the prevalence of employer-sponsored coverage create an unduly rosy picture, however. Basing most private coverage in employer groups creates or exacerbates a number of public policy problems. Among these are that sheltering insurance premiums from income tax creates a bias toward "first-dollar" coverage, which tends to drive up medical spending by reducing patients' out-of-pocket exposure to medical costs. Also, when employers select coverage for a group, they tend to choose the benefits package and provider networks that please most workers, resulting in networks that include most providers and exclude few benefits. These measures also tend to increase overall medical costs and fail to meet the full range of workers' preferences for the right mix of wages and benefits in their compensation packages. Thus, there are good reasons to ask whether employer groups are the best vehicle for providing private coverage, or whether employer-based coverage might evolve to address some of these public policy concerns.

II The Future of Employment-Based Coverage

a. The ACA's Core Provisions

The ACA's most significant market reforms are focused on the individual and small group markets. It also contains many provisions affecting larger employer groups, but, for the most part, the large group market is expected to remain essentially the same, for reasons discussed in section I. In the individual and small group markets, however, the ACA completed the process of incremental market reforms described in the previous section. It prohibits all insurers from turning down any applicants, and it requires them to cover all preexisting conditions. Also,

[20] Kaiser Family Foundation, 2013 Employer Health Benefits Survey, http://kff.org/private-insurance/report/2013-employer-health-benefits/.

[21] Mark A. Hall, *The Competitive Impact of Small Group Health Insurance Reform Laws*. 32 U. Mich. J.L. Ref. 685 (1999).

the ACA prohibits individual and small group insurers from basing rates on gender or health status (although tobacco use is a permitted rating factor within limits). Although insurers still may adjust their community rates based on age, they are limited to only a factor of 3-to-1 rather than the 6-to-1 spread that actuaries typically use. In sum, the ACA makes all Americans fully insurable at average community rates. No longer does anyone need to worry about becoming uninsurable if they change jobs or family situations or if they drop insurance for a while.

Without more, prior experience tells us that these restrictions on medical underwriting would lead to serious adverse selection, potentially threatening market stability. In order for these market rules to function well, the ACA has two key elements that reduce adverse selection: it both subsidizes and "mandates" the purchase of private insurance. Sliding-scale subsidies are available through new government-operated insurance exchanges for people above poverty[22] who do not have affordable employment-based insurance. The smallest employers (with twenty-five or fewer workers) can receive moderate tax credits for offering insurance if they have lower-wage workers. Larger employers—those with more than fifty full-time equivalent workers—are subject to what is called an employer "mandate," but more accurately is only a "play-or-pay" provision: These larger employers are not legally *required* to offer affordable health insurance to full-time workers (thirty hours or more), but if they choose not to do so, they pay a significant tax.[23] Individuals, similarly, are subject to a mandate: They pay a moderate tax if they fail to sign up for an affordable insurance option[24]—either through Medicaid, the exchanges, or an employer policy.

Every aspect of the ACA is controversial, and the employer mandate is no exception. Critics charge that defining employer responsibility according to the number of full-time workers will cause employers to reduce full-time jobs. Also, basing individuals' eligibility for exchange subsidies on the affordability of employer coverage places a bookkeeping burden on employers to calculate and report such matters. Accordingly, the federal government initially delayed the ACA's employer responsibility provisions for a year or two. At the time of this writing, employers' ACA responsibilities do not phase in fully until 2016. Also, at this moment, public policy analysts are actively debating whether the employer mandate is actually essential to the ACA's success. Even some ACA supporters are now arguing that the employer mandate may not be worth keeping, considering all the fuss that it produces, including some of these legitimate economic concerns.[25]

One reason that analysts question the necessity of the employer mandate is that most larger employers are expected to continue offering affordable coverage even without these

[22] States may expand Medicaid to cover everyone near or below poverty, but only half have opted to do so.

[23] If the employer offers no insurance, the tax is $2,000 per employee except for the first thirty workers (so an employer with one hundred workers would pay 70 x $2,000, or $140,000). If the employer offers insurance but it is not affordable to one or more workers, the tax is $3,000 for each such worker who decides to purchase subsidized individual insurance through the exchange.

[24] Affordability is defined in terms of the cost of single coverage as a percentage of income. To satisfy the employer mandate, insurance must cost no more than 9.5% of a worker's wages; the individual mandate applies only if insurance costs less than 8% of household income. Also, the insurance that employers offer must cover at least 60% of medical expenses, on average.

[25] *See* Linda Blumberg et al., *Why Not Just Eliminate the Employer Mandate?* (Urban Institute, May 2014), http://www.urban.org/UploadedPDF/413117-Why-Not-Just-Eliminate-the-Employer-Mandate.pdf.

tax penalties.[26] The contrary logic reasons that, because insurance is considerably more expensive than the $2,000 to $3,000 tax assessments for employers, employers will calculate that it is cheaper to pay the tax and let workers buy their own insurance on the subsidized exchange.[27] But doing that sacrifices the tax advantages of employer-sponsored health insurance and may leave workers feeling abandoned in the face of the individual mandate. A more optimistic logic, therefore, would predict that employers become more, not less, likely to offer coverage, both to avoid the new employer tax and to help workers meet their own, individual-mandate responsibility.[28] The latter speculation was borne out in Massachusetts, which in 2007 enacted a similar set of reforms that coupled an individual mandate with an employer play-or-pay tax. There, however, the employer tax was much smaller—$295 a year per worker—yet employer coverage increased, in part because workers who were subject to the individual mandate placed even more importance on having this fringe benefit.[29]

It remains to be seen how these competing incentives and social forces balance out nationally under the ACA. Undoubtedly, a number of smaller employers will drop coverage. They are not subject to the ACA's employer mandate. Prior to the ACA's reforms, many workers may not have been insurable in the individual market, but now that insurability is not a barrier, employers have more reason to consider sending workers—and themselves—to the subsidized exchanges. If so, old instincts about public policy need to be rethought. With affordable, comprehensive coverage now readily available in the individual market, there is good reason to question whether public policy should instinctively favor employment-based coverage. Maintaining employer sponsorship obviously reduces government costs, but employer groups are no longer necessary to correct the basic shortcomings that previously existed in the unregulated individual market.

b. Private Exchanges and Defined Contribution

For employers who retain coverage, the ACA has galvanized attention to the long-standing idea of using private insurance exchanges to implement superior forms of managed competition. The ACA's public exchanges for individuals and small groups have caused larger employers and their insurers to also consider using similarly structured private exchanges. Private exchanges being offered by major health benefits consulting firms such as Towers-Watson, Mercer, and Aon Hewitt allow workers to select employer-subsidized coverage from among competing insurers. These newly emerging private exchanges differ in several important ways from the structures that preceded them.[30] Many earlier exchanges offered

26 Christine Eibner et al., *The Effects of the Affordable Care Act on Workers' Health Insurance Coverage*, 363 New Eng. J. Med. 1393 (2010).

27 *See* Shubham Singhal et al., How US Health Care Reform Will Affect Employee Benefits (McKinsey & Co., 2011).

28 Linda Blumber et al., *Why Employers Will Continue to Provide Health Insurance: The Impact of the Affordable Care Act*, 49 Inquiry 116 (2012).

29 Jon R. Gabel et al., *After the Mandates: Massachusetts Employers Continue to Support Health Reform as More Firms Offer Coverage*, 27(6) Health Aff. w566 (2008).

30 Paul Fronstin, *Private Health Insurance Exchanges and Defined Contribution Health Plans: Is It Deja vu All Over Again?* (Employee Benefit Research Institute, 2012).

multiple products from only (or mainly) a single insurer. Others in the small group market were designed to exploit regulatory loopholes (which, for the most part, no longer exist),[31] or themselves were the victim of uneven market rules for small groups.[32] Up until recently, private multi-insurer exchanges had emerged only for retiree health benefits. But now we are seeing widespread interest in, and availability of, multi-insurer exchanges for active workers of large employers.

This concept was first discussed in the early 2000s,[33] but the idea did not take hold then, for several reasons. First, the idea was usually paired (under the umbrella of "consumer-driven healthcare") with the also-new idea of offering high-deductible health plans coupled with health savings accounts. Employers realized they could easily enough offer these new plan designs through their existing single-insurer or self-insured structures, without also introducing the complications of a multi-insurer exchange structure. Also, employers were not prepared to leave workers to the vagaries of the less-regulated markets of that time. Now, however, the ACA provides greater endorsement of the exchange idea and greater regulatory protections for workers that engage with the market directly. Also, the ACA has caused large employers to take a fresh look at their health benefits strategies and options. Private exchanges could give workers a broader choice of health plans, including lower-cost, narrow-network options that are unpopular when required by employers.

Private exchanges are not feasible unless insurers are willing to participate on favorable terms. Previously, insurers were very reluctant to compete for group business on a retail rather than wholesale basis, side by side with their competitors—in part because they feared adverse selection. Now, however, risk adjustment tools are more developed and better established.[34] Risk adjustment levels the playing field among competition insurers by requiring those with healthier subscribers to compensate those whose members are sicker. If done well, risk adjustment should make insurers more willing to compete based on the inherent consumer value of their products. Also, insurers see potential in private exchanges to convert self-insured groups to more profitable fully insured coverage. Finally, over the past decade, as high-speed Internet has proliferated and computing power exponentially expanded, people have become much more acclimated generally to the idea of computer-based exchange purchases for other types of products and services.

For all of these reasons, currently there is widespread anticipation that private multi-carrier exchanges could quickly become an established component of the health coverage landscape for active workers. According to various credible surveys, one-quarter or more of larger employers are considering using private exchanges. One key reason employers are interested is the prospect that private exchanges offer to move toward a "defined contribution" approach to health benefits—one that gives workers a fixed "voucher" of employer support that does not vary based on the plan selected. Traditionally, employers have committed to a "defined benefit" approach that pays a large percentage of specified health benefits.

[31] Mark Hall, Elliot Wicks, & Janice Lawlor, *HIPCs, MEWAs, and Association Health Plans: A Guide for the Perplexed*, 21(1) HEALTH AFF. 142 (Jan. 2001).

[32] Elliot Wicks & Mark Hall, *Health Insurance Purchasing Cooperatives: Performance and Prospects*, 78 MILBANK Q. 511 (Dec. 2000).

[33] Paul Fronstin, *Defined Contribution Health Benefits* (Employee Benefit Research Institute, 2001).

[34] Mark A. Hall, *Risk Adjustment Under the Affordable Care Act: A Guide for Federal and State Regulators* (Commonw. Fund 2011).

Under that arrangement, employers and workers share the cost of selecting more expensive coverage. A "defined contribution" approach would instead make workers pay the full differential in costs for selecting a plan that is more expensive than the reference plan that the employer designates.

A defined contribution approach to health benefits has been discussed for over a decade, but this approach has not yet taken hold on a wide scale. One reason is the absence, until now, of an exchange structure that facilitates employees shopping for their own insurance. Defined contribution holds out the favorable prospect of educating workers about the true cost of trade-offs in insurance coverage and design. It might, for instance, make workers more accepting of managed care or high-deductible plans that do a better job of controlling costs. Reductions in benefits or provider networks that employers previously were not willing to adopt for an entire workforce might become more feasible if the reduction is selected willingly by individual employees.

Defined contribution, however, might make it easier for employers to ratchet back from year to year what they contribute to health insurance. Employers might target their contribution levels to "skinny plans" that barely meet the ACA's "minimum essential benefits" standard. Another legitimate concern is that giving each employee a voucher to shop for insurance could make employers more conscious of the fact that older workers cost more than younger ones. The traditional employer group structure obscures this actuarial reality because insurers use "composite rating" to price the group based on the average age of the workforce; thus, on paper each employee costs the same. A voucher system might replace this composite rating with what is called "list billing," meaning that each worker's actual costs are specified. Although various laws prohibit employers from discriminating based on age, medical conditions, or health insurance costs, it is possible that list billing could make employers more reluctant to hire or retain older or sicker workers.

III Some Complexities and Controversies of Employment-Based Coverage, Especially Related to the ACA

a. Health Reimbursement and Savings Accounts

Having surveyed the basics of employment-based coverage, we now consider some of its legal complexities and current controversies, starting with its tax treatment. As noted above, tax law creates a boundary between individual versus employment-based insurance. As with any such artificial barrier, various forces will tend to erode or exploit the legal and economic gradient.[35] Some of this landscaping has been done by Congress and some by private ingenuity.

[35] Mark A. Hall, *The Geography of Health Insurance Regulation: A Guide to Identifying, Exploiting, and Policing Market Boundaries*, 19 Health Aff. 173 (Apr. 2000).

As noted in section I, not taxing employer-paid premiums as income to workers creates a strong incentive to make health insurance more generous, by reducing amounts that patients must pay for care out of pocket, in the form of deductibles or copayments. Such out-of-pocket payments are made from after-tax income, whereas there is no income or payroll tax on increased premiums used to reduce out-of-pocket exposure. This asymmetry naturally led to employees (and their labor unions) preferring more generous insurance than individuals were willing to purchase on their own. More generous insurance in turn drives up the cost of care by making patients and their physicians less concerned about the price and quality of medical care.

One way to mitigate this economic distortion is to level down by reducing the tax preference for employer-sponsored premiums, but another way is to level up by increasing tax protection for out-of-pocket expenses. In 2004, Congress took the more generous route; it authorized expanded tax protection to include amounts that individuals pay out of pocket, through "health savings accounts" (HSAs). When these earmarked accounts are coupled with health insurance that has high deductibles (at least $1,250 for individuals or double that for families), contributions to these savings accounts are excluded from income tax. A similar tax vehicle is called a Health Reimbursement Account (HRA). HRAs differ from HSAs in that they are owned and funded by employers rather than individuals. Also, HRAs, and similar "cafeteria plans," can be used to pay for insurance premiums as well as direct medical care.

Enactment of the ACA caused creative employee benefits advisers to consider whether they might combine the tax advantages of HRAs and cafeteria plans with the government subsidies for individual insurance. Rather than employers buying group insurance, could they use these tax vehicles to simply give employees earmarked funds to purchase their own, individual insurance using pretax dollars? On first read, the relevant statutes appeared to allow this, at least for HRAs, but the federal government shut the door. It ruled that HRAs constitute a type of "health plan," and the ACA forbids health plans from having any annual or lifetime limits. Because HRAs do not provide unlimited funds, they fail to qualify—according to the IRS—unless they are coupled with a health insurance plan that the employer purchases.[36] For now at least, the boundaries between the group and the individual markets must remain distinct.[37]

b. ERISA Preemption and Self-Insurance

ERISA presents another regulatory and market boundary. Despite the ACA's comprehensive breadth, it does not change the basic elements of ERISA preemption. As surveyed in section I, ERISA still precludes states from regulating coverage offered by self-funded employers. The ACA partially mitigates the resulting regulatory vacuum by subjecting self-insured benefits to a few new requirements. All health benefits, including self-funded plans, must cover

[36] U.S. Departments of Labor, Treasury, and Health and Human Services, Application of Market Reform and other Provisions of the Affordable Care Act to HRAs, Health FSAs, and Certain other Employer Healthcare Arrangements, Sept. 13, 2013, http://www.irs.gov/pub/irs-drop/n-13-54.pdf.

[37] One possible exception exists for employer arrangements that earmark a portion of workers' wages for the purchase of insurance, but only on an after-tax basis.

certain preventive services without any patient cost-sharing and must avoid annual or lifetime caps on benefits. This reduces some advantages from self-funding, but employers can still avoid some state taxes and coverage mandates by self-insuring.

The ACA actually increases regulatory incentives for self-funding for some employers. Its market reforms that apply to small employers govern only purchased insurance. Because these rules forbid medical underwriting, they make it attractive for employers with healthier workers to opt out of the regulated market and choose self-funding instead. It might appear infeasible for small employers to bear their own insurance risk, since doing so could easily bankrupt them with only one or two expensive cases. However, employers can protect themselves by purchasing "stop-loss" reinsurance that caps their exposure at specified "attachment points." For instance, reinsurance with attachment points of $100,000/$1 million leaves a self-inured employer exposed only to expenses less than $100,000 for any one worker and less than $1 million for the entire workforce.

Because financial exposure of this magnitude is still far too risky for most small employers, some insurers have been willing to sell stop-loss reinsurance with much lower attachment points—on the order of $10,000 per worker. Such reinsurance is expensive, however, and so few employers saw economic advantage in purchasing it, compared to regular health insurance. The ACA, however, changes the equation. It requires regular insurance to be community-rated, but reinsurance remains risk-rated. Therefore, an employer with younger, healthier workers might easily find a better deal by self-insuring. Self-insuring also allows small employers to avoid having to offer all of the "essential health benefits" mandated by the ACA. And in 2016 the ACA expands its definition of small groups from fifty to one hundred workers, which makes self-insurance potentially attractive for a greater swath of the market.

Many analysts believe that it is not feasible to have a risk-rated (self-insured) market operate side by side a regulated community-rated market.[38] If smaller employers could simply opt in and out of the regulated market based on each year's expected medical claims, this would obviously result in adverse selection. How severe and destabilizing this might be is subject to speculation and dispute. Therefore, state and federal lawmakers currently are taking a wait-and-see approach to this potential problem. If problems do emerge, then, lawmakers have two basic options: (1) prohibit smaller employers from self-insuring, or (2) regulate reinsurance for small employers under the same terms as normal health insurance by requiring such reinsurance to be community-rated and to cover all essential health benefits.

c. Managed Care Liability

ERISA preemption affects private law as well as insurance regulation. Preemption of insurance regulation is limited to self-insured employer plans, but ERISA preempts tort and contract law for all employment-based coverage, regardless of whether the coverage is purchased or self-insured.[39] This creates a distinct anomaly in the legal ability of patients to recover personal injury or punitive damages from managed care insurers whose policies and

[38] *See* Timothy Jost & Mark Hall, *Self-Insurance for Small Employers Under the Affordable Care Act*, 68 N.Y.U. Ann. Survey Am. L. 539 (2013).

[39] Aetna Health Inc. v. Davila, 542 U.S. 200 (2004).

practices might harm patients' health. Whether framed as a tort or a contract action, ERISA precludes these noneconomic damages under any form of insurance sponsored by private employers.[40] These state law remedies are available, however, under individual insurance.

This anomaly survives the ACA, but will likely grow more prominent as the individual market expands. Prior to the ACA, individual coverage accounted for only about 5% of the population, but that market segment is expected to quickly double as a consequence of the ACA's subsidies and market reforms. The individual market may grow considerably larger than this in future years if significant numbers of employers start to drop coverage.

It makes no public policy sense that health insurers are virtually immune from personal injury damages because of the accident of ERISA preemption, or that patients with identical types of private insurance have wildly different legal remedies against managed care plans, depending on which market segment they purchase it in. One might attempt to justify this stark disparity by imagining that individually purchased exchange insurance is more likely to have the stronger managed care elements that give rise to potential insurer liability because individuals are more willing than employers to sacrifice ease of access for lower premiums. However, employer group coverage also contains managed care elements, and employers are likely to turn increasingly to private exchanges that encourage individual workers to select more limited provider networks or plans with other tighter cost controls. Because private exchanges are employer-sponsored, their insurers will continue to enjoy ERISA's tort immunity while people who purchase similar or identical coverage through public exchanges will be protected by normal tort remedies.

If Congress' attention turns from insurance reform to reform of healthcare costs and delivery, liability issues will surely be part of the discussion. Then, Congress should devise, or allow states to devise, a liability scheme that sets sensible default rules that allocate responsibility for medical error in a more sensible and consistent fashion throughout the various components of managed healthcare systems.

d. ACA Mandated Benefits

Any scheme that subsidizes and requires the purchase of health insurance must do something to define what the content of that insurance will be. The ACA is no exception. It has a variety of terms and provisions prescribing what health insurance must cover. Naturally, these provisions produce ambiguity and controversy.

Prior to the ACA, the greatest need for standardization of benefits existed in the individual market. Its natural dynamics, driven by adverse selection, had resulted in policies that failed to cover some critical health needs, such as maternity care. People not expecting childbirth bought cheaper policies without maternity care, driving up the cost of maternity care for those who needed it to such a level that this essential element of coverage was not marketable or affordable in many places. To remedy this market failure, the ACA requires that individual and small group insurance must cover ten defined categories of "essential health benefits."[41] But rather than mandating the specifics of these benefits, the federal government

[40] ERISA does not apply, however, to government employers.

[41] Institute of Medicine, Essential Health Benefits: Balancing Coverage and Cost (2011).

looked to the insurance policies that were currently selling well in the small group market. Each state may select a benchmark plan from among its market's leading small group plans (or, if a state fails to choose, the default benchmark plan is the largest small group plan).

Larger employers usually include most of these same "essential health benefits" voluntarily, so the ACA does not require them to do so. Instead, their "play-or-pay" mandate requires only that larger employers cover "minimum essential benefits" and "minimum [actuarial] value"—terms that appear similar to but in fact are legally distinct from each other and from "essential health benefits." "Minimum essential benefits" refers to what benefits larger employers must cover (to avoid a tax penalty), and "minimum [actuarial] value" refers to how much employees pay out of pocket for those benefits when they are patients. To avoid the ACA's $2,000 per worker tax, larger employers must offer minimum essential benefits, and to avoid the $3,000 tax for each worker that purchases through the individual exchange, those benefits must be affordable and must cover a minimum of 60% of the plan's actuarial value.

The ACA and its implementing regulations so far do not define "minimum essential benefits." Therefore, many benefits lawyers and advisers thought that employers were free to offer greatly pared down "skinny plans," as long as these included the ACA's basic preventive care mandates that apply to all insurance. Taken to an extreme, it was thought possible that an employer meets the "minimum essential" standard with a policy that covers *only* preventive services with no cost-sharing or limits for those services. Clearly, this narrowly literal reading of the letter of law misses its spirit. Therefore, the government ruled that, even though "minimum essential benefits" remains largely undefined, it requires more that covering only preventive services. There must be some substantial coverage of both hospital and physician services.

Nevertheless, employers still might be tempted to leave out major categories of care. If so, these "skinny plans" still will not satisfy employers' full responsibility under current regulatory interpretation. To avoid a tax assessment, larger employers must not only provide minimum essential benefits, this insurance must also cover a minimum 60% of the plan's actuarial value. On first reading, it would appear that this minimum value requirement is an even lower standard, because it suggests that not only may employer plans cover fewer services, but those plans can require workers to pay for up to 40% of the limited services that are covered. In other words, the denominator for 60% minimum value might be the actual minimum benefits the employer choses to provide.

That is not, however, how the implementing regulations currently interpret minimum actuarial value. Rather than link this calculation to the minimum essential benefits required of large employers, the regulations link minimum actuarial value to the essential health benefits required of small employers, which are much more comprehensive. This interpretation is not entirely logical, and so it is possible that it will be challenged. But, until it is, employers that fail to offer something similar to[42] the bronze level coverage available on the exchanges

[42] The employer's plan need not be identical to the actual bronze plans on the exchange because the implementing regulations recognize that larger employers do not need to cover all of the ten categories of essential health benefits. Nevertheless, the regulations appear to require that actuaries use standard bronze plans as their starting point for deriving the plan's minimum value. It is unclear how much deviation from standard bronze plans will be permitted.

(60% of essential health benefits) will be subject to a tax of $3,000 per worker for anyone who purchases subsidized individual coverage through the exchange.

To avoid that exposure, some benefits consultants are advising larger employers to offer both a skinny plan, for free or at very favorable rates, alongside bronze or higher level comprehensive coverage that costs employees considerably more. As long as a metal-level plan offered by an employer costs the worker less than 9.5% of his or her income, the worker will not be eligible to seek subsidized exchange coverage (and the employer thus avoids any tax penalty). Naturally, many lower-wage workers will select the skinny plan, which will cost the employer considerably less. Higher-wage employees are much more able to afford the fairly comprehensive metal-level plan. Therefore, skeptics of this arrangement are concerned that it might violate tax law norms against fringe benefits that discriminate in favor of higher-wage workers. The IRS has not issued relevant antidiscrimination rulings, and so this set of issues remains unresolved. Also, it does not become fully relevant until the employer mandate itself takes full effect, which was also delayed. Until that time, several key legal issues remain unresolved.

IV Conclusion

Ten years from now, we will look back and say that what happened with employer sponsorship was obviously bound to happen, but at this juncture, it is not at all obvious what that future will be. Under the radical change scenario, the ACA will have catalyzed a historic tipping point that caused the private health insurance system's ballast to shift its center of gravity from employer groups to a government-sponsored individual market. Without a tax subsidy that favors full coverage, and with an individual-choice market that favors narrower networks and more tightly managed care, we could experience dramatic changes in the structure and economics of healthcare delivery.

Under a contrasting, institutional-inertia scenario, a decade could produce little, or only modest, change in the employer-sponsored group market. Tax and ERISA law continue to favor employer sponsorship, and the ACA's employer mandate only strengthens reasons for the larger firms (which account for most workers) to continue paying for health insurance. Moreover, the individual mandate may cause workers to place even greater value on their employers helping them to meet the personal and civic responsibility of remaining insured.

Under a third, hybrid scenario, employer sponsorship will change, but not as radically as some people predict. If the ACA's employer mandate is modified or repealed, that will lessen the inducement to maintain sponsorship. Regardless, many employers will reevaluate whether and how to sponsor coverage. Some small employers will drop coverage, and others will decide to self-insure, avoiding the ACA's mandates for community rating and essential health benefits. Larger employers who maintain coverage may decide to offer "skinny" plans or to limit their contributions to fixed amounts that workers can use as a voucher to shop on private exchanges. Yet, even with such changes, employer sponsorship could remain dominant.

To some extent, the die that will determine this future has already been cast, but the forces at play are simply too large and complex to know the unavoidable outcome. But to a considerable extent, this future can still be shaped through thoughtful public policy or interest-group advocacy. This article has outlined why employer-sponsorship has strong advantages but also substantial weaknesses. Its principal alternatives also have competing virtues and drawbacks. How these difficult trade-offs are viewed by lawmakers, employers, workers, insurers, and many others with a stake in the outcome will undoubtedly shape how ACA implementation, and responses to it, impact employer sponsorship for decades to come.

CHAPTER 32

RISK AND REGULATION IN PRIVATE INSURANCE

ROBERT H. JERRY, II

LIFE's uncertainties are the essence of risk. The inherent human aversion to harmful events explains why individuals and organizations are attracted to risk management strategies, one of which involves risk transfer through insurance. This chapter examines risk and its regulation in private insurance, focusing on private health insurance. Part I examines the nature of risk and the different ways individuals and organizations react to it. Part II summarizes the range of risk management strategies individuals and organizations deploy when dealing with risk, including contracts of insurance, the risk management strategy of last resort. This part sets the stage for the examination in Part III of the differences between health insurance and other kinds of insurance products, including how modern health insurance resembles in some respects risk management strategies that are not insurance. In explaining these differences, this part also examines how the business of insurance is categorized and how legal definitions of insurance operate. Part IV takes up the question of why health insurance is different and what this means for regulation of health insurance, and Part V finishes the discussion with a concluding thought.

I Uncertainty and Risk

The essence of human existence is that we cannot know with certainty what the future holds.[1] Although life's events are not completely random, and we can shape the probabilities of occurrences and the course of their outcomes in many situations, information about most of life's future possibilities is insufficiently clear to enable us to say that we are certain whether, when, or how future events will unfold. For example, in virtually every kind of activity or enterprise, we know that accidents will happen, but we do not know where or when or to

[1] For more on uncertainty, the nature of risk, the economics of insurance, and risk management strategies, *see* Robert H. Jerry, II, & Douglas R. Richmond, Understanding Insurance Law 7–13 (5th ed. 2012).

whom; if we did, we would be able to prevent them. The death of every living thing is certain, but its timing cannot be predicted with certainty. The same is true for illness and injury; although someone in the world may exist who has never been ill or suffered an injury of any sort, even this lucky person cannot know with certainty that this good fortune will continue tomorrow. Hurricanes, earthquakes, wildfires, floods, tsunamis, volcanoes, and other natural disasters—even asteroid impacts[2]—are certain to occur in the future, and they will be accompanied by loss of life, personal injuries, and loss of and damage to property, but when these catastrophes will happen and their magnitudes are impossible to know in advance.

The inherent uncertainty of future events can be described in terms of chance or probability. For events that have adverse outcomes, this uncertainty is usually described in terms of *risk*.[3] Many different kinds of risks concern the average person, and it is human nature to desire, to the extent possible, security in the face of these risks. *Risk management* refers in its most general sense to the set of techniques and strategies an individual or organization might use to maximize security in the face of and reduce the uncertainties posed by the circumstances that produce or represent insecurity-inducing risk. Generally speaking, the most worrisome risks involve perils that threaten loss of life, loss of health due to injury or illness (which also can result in loss of inability to work), and loss of or damage to property, both tangible and intangible (including money). Individuals and organizations have many different options for how to respond to such risks, and most will identify and pursue a variety of risk management techniques or strategies, with insuring the risk being just one strategy among many. Insurance involves paying someone else to take over the risk, and this strategy ordinarily will not be pursued until and unless more efficient (in the sense of being less expensive, more effective, or both) methods of risk management are considered and tried first. When it becomes clear that other non-insurance risk management techniques are unavailable or unable to provide the desired level of security against loss, most persons and organizations will try to insure against the risk of loss to the extent insurance products are available and affordable.

A person's attitude about risk will be influenced by several things, including the probability that an event will occur, the potential magnitude of the loss, and the person's ability to absorb the loss. As these variables interact, a person will land somewhere on a continuum that ranges from "risk preferring" to "risk neutral" to "risk averse."[4] As the potential size

[2] This is the one disaster on this list that has some possibility of being prevented through human intervention. *See* NASA, NEAR-EARTH OBJECT SURVEY AND DEFLECTION ANALYSIS OF ALTERNATIVES, Mar. 2007, *available at* http://www.nasa.gov/pdf/171331main_NEO_report_march07.pdf; European Space Agency, *AIDA: Asteroid Impact and Deflection Assessment Study*, YOUTUBE (Sept. 22, 2014), https://www.youtube.com/watch?v=OQ8vp-u-9A4. The others cannot be prevented but are subject to some measures of risk management through strategies that reduce the loss and damage when the events occur.

[3] Some risks are beneficial or "positive" in the sense that they generate gain when the risk materializes. An illustration is the chance of winning a contest where a prize is awarded. The risks we worry about are those that are "negative" and involve the possibility of loss, injury, or some other adverse occurrence. Risk can be defined or quantified as the probability of something occurring times its cost (or benefit, in the case of positive risks) if it does. Thus, insurance is concerned exclusively with negative risks, and risk in this setting is a function of the frequency of an event and its severity.

[4] To illustrate the continuum, imagine several people being forced to choose between a 50% chance of losing $1,000 (which arithmetically speaking equals an "expected loss" of $500) and a 100% (or certain) chance of losing $500. Some people when faced with this choice are "risk preferring" in that they would

of loss increases, most people become more risk averse, even when the probability of loss declines.[5]

Thus, with respect to large risks, most people are risk averse, with the important qualification that as an individual's wealth increases, risk aversion declines and ambivalence becomes more likely.[6] The risk aversion default in human nature can be intuited from the law of diminishing marginal utility, the fundamental economics principle which holds that as the consumption of a commodity increases, the utility derived from each additional unit of consumption decreases. Because the slope of the marginal utility curve (with consumption on the x-axis and utility on the y-axis) declines (until it turns negative at the point where each additional unit of consumption produces disutility), at every vantage point on the curve the loss of utility from reducing consumption by one unit is arithmetically greater than the gain in utility acquired from increasing consumption by one unit. Thus, the law of diminishing marginal utility teaches that it is human nature to fear an actuarially equivalent loss of something more than to value an actuarially equivalent gain of it, which explains why we will frequently choose to avoid risks even when they are actuarially neutral and fair. This also helps explain why, as a default principle of behavior, we are interested in investing in risk management strategies, including insurance, in order to obtain the higher degrees of certainty and security that such strategies produce.

Layered on top of these observations is a set of behavioral principles that describe the irrationality of humans' risk assessment in some situations.[7] Preconceptions from past experiences (especially unusual, outlier experiences), emotions, intuitions, fear, and other psychological tendencies come into play, leading to inaccurate calculations about risk. The net effects are that abstract, ordinary risks tend to be undervalued (e.g., the risk of skin cancer from unprotected exposure to the sun or the risk of riding in an automobile), and risks associated with rare but horrific circumstances (e.g., airplane crashes), widespread media attention (e.g., shark attacks), situations outside one's control (e.g., terrorism attacks), or easily personified and imagined events (e.g., home invasions) are overvalued. This can skew the rationality of human response to risk, causing us to do too little to responsibly respond to

choose to forgo the certain loss of $500 in order to have a chance of incurring no loss, even though there is an equal probability of suffering a $1,000 loss. In this same situation, some people are "risk neutral" in that they are ambivalent about the choices and have no preference one way or the other. The remainder of the population is "risk averse" in that they would prefer to lose $500 with certainty instead of facing the 50% probability that they could lose twice as much, even though they have an equal probability of losing nothing.

[5] To illustrate, when given a choice between a one-in-10,000 chance of losing $10,000 (an expected loss of $1) and the prospect of a certain loss of $1, many people previously indifferent or even risk preferring would opt to lose the $1 with certainty to avoid the remote possibility of a substantial loss.

[6] To illustrate, a multimillionaire is less likely to care about a one-in-10,000 chance of losing $10,000, or about any small or moderate loss for that matter. Given sufficient wealth, a person will not worry about loss and is therefore likely to be less interested in purchasing insurance to manage it. In other words, such a person will either ignore risk or choose to assume it (which is tantamount to self-insurance).

[7] *See, e.g.*, Amos Tversky & Daniel Kahneman, *The Framing of Decisions and the Psychology of Choice*, 211 SCIENCE 453–458 (1981); Benedetto De Martino et al., *Frames, Biases, and Rational Decision-Making in the Human Brain*, 313 SCIENCE 684–687 (2006).

some risks (e.g., the young adult with no history of illness and little experience with the consequences of accidental injury is more likely to undervalue health insurance) and to invest too much in responding to other risks (e.g., media attention on and fear of accidents may lead an individual to invest excessively in accident insurance when investing in improved health insurance would be optimal[8]). When lack of information (i.e., uncertainty) is added to these behavioral principles that cause skewed assessments of risk in some situations, the upshot is that risk management choices, including those made in insurance markets, are likely to be different from those that would be made under conditions of rationality and perfect information about past and present conditions and events.

Yet when stripped of these important nuances and complexities, the basic principles are straightforward: Uncertainty is a fact of human existence; with uncertainty comes risk; risk produces insecurity; and individuals and organizations prefer security over conditions of insecurity. Consequently, the inherent human tendency to be risk averse causes economic actors, in order to reduce risk and increase security, to invest in risk management strategies, including insurance.

II Methods of Managing Risk

The word "insurance" has its roots in the Latin word "securus," which means "safe."[9] The classical Latin matches well with the modern colloquial usage of "insure," which describes making something sure, certain, or safe.[10] Thus, we might hope that preparation "will insure" the success of a future act or that taking precautions "will insure" the safety of the premises for those that occupy it. In these contexts, we would not say that "insurance" against the risk of loss has been procured or acquired. Instead, the word "insurance" (and the idea of "insuring against" the risk of something) is typically used to refer to a contract where one party (the "insured") makes a payment (a "premium") to another party (the "insurer") to assume risk by means of a promise under which the insurer agrees to pay the insured for loss in circumstances where various conditions in the contract are satisfied. There are many ways to make something secure or safe, and certainly the idea of "health insurance" fits squarely within this understanding of "insure." How "health insurance" fits within the foregoing understanding of the word "insurance" is a more difficult question. Before taking up this question, it is useful to understand where insurance fits among the different kinds of risk management strategies commonly encountered in the space where risk-averse individuals and organizations seek security.

[8] In 2013, mortality in the United States from accidents constituted 5% of all deaths, whereas 92% of all deaths were due to illness or disease. The remaining 3% consisted predominantly of death by suicide or homicide. Ctrs. for Disease Control & Prevention, Deaths, Percent of Total Deaths, and Death Rates for the 15 Leading Causes of Death: United States and Each State tbl.10 (2013).

[9] *Insurance Definition*, Oxford Advanced Learner's Dictionary, http://www.oxfordlearnersdictionaries.com/us/definition/english/insurance (last visited Feb. 20, 2015).

[10] Merriam-Webster Dictionary, http://www.merriam-webster.com/dictionary/insure (visited Feb. 2, 2015).

a. Risk Management: The Consumer's Perspective

Short of entering into an agreement to transfer risk to another party, many kinds of non-insurance mechanisms exist through which individuals and organizations seek to manage risk. The landscape of risk management ranges from the simple, where people make daily calculations about risk when engaging in life's most common activities, to the complex, where firms and organizations develop and implement elaborate and sophisticated systems of risk avoidance, minimization, and transference. Reduced to the essentials, individuals and organizations manage risk by limiting the probability of loss, limiting the effects of loss, diversification, risk retention (in the sense of "self-insurance"), insurance, or some combination of one or more of these strategies.

Preventing loss-producing events is the primary way to *limit the probability of loss.* Constructing a building with masonry instead of wood so that fire is less likely to break out, placing collision-avoidance technologies on vehicles, putting a fence around a swimming pool to prevent children from getting access, removing ice from a sidewalk where pedestrians walk, placing a guard on the blade of a machine used by workers, and normal habits of defensive driving are all risk management strategies that seek to limit the probability that a loss-producing event will occur. In healthcare parlance, the analogous techniques that limit the probability of loss are usually called "primary prevention" or "wellness" programs. The objective of these programs is to protect a healthy person from developing a disease or experiencing an injury. Specific examples include education programs designed to inform individuals about and promote good health and fitness habits (such as encouraging regular exercise, deterring smoking, encouraging weight loss when needed, etc.), public policy efforts that regulate behaviors connected to health and injury (e.g., prohibitions on smoking in public places, requirements for proper seat belt and helmet use), immunization programs that prevent diseases from moving through populations, exams and screenings that identify risk factors (so that the individual can adjust behaviors to avoid illnesses that correlate with discovered factors), and programs that control potential injury-producing hazards in the home and in the workplace.[11] Generally speaking, although life, property, and casualty insurers often promote loss-avoiding habits and behaviors through advertising, communications with policyholders, and other means, policies issued by these insurers do not pay for the expenses an insured incurs in taking steps to prevent loss from happening. Health insurance operates differently; loss avoidance activities are not only routinely promoted by modern health insurers but also are frequently paid for by health insurers under their policies' coverage.

Even if an occurrence cannot be prevented, another way to manage its associated risk is *to limit the effects of loss.* The installation of a sprinkler system in a building will not prevent a fire from occurring but will limit the damaging effects should one break out; having a car with airbags and other impact-reducing safety features operated by a driver who insists that all occupants wear seat belts will not prevent an accident from occurring but will reduce the injurious effects should one occur. With respect to healthcare, the analogous risk

[11] *See* James F. McKenzie & Denise M. Seabert, *Prevention: Primary, Secondary, Tertiary,* Encyclopedia of Epidemiology 839–840 (Sarah Boslaugh ed., 2008), *available at* http://dx.doi.org/10.4135/9781412953948.n367.

management techniques are usually called "secondary prevention" and "tertiary prevention" programs. Secondary prevention programs seek to halt or slow an illness after early-stage diagnosis, and, with respect to injuries, seek to limit the period of disability, avoid long-term disability if possible, and prevent reoccurrence. Tertiary programs manage long-term, complicated health problems, essentially seeking to prevent further deterioration and to maximize the patient's quality of life. Thus, exams, screenings, and diagnostic tests screenings that discover existing illnesses and conditions do not prevent the illness or condition from occurring, but they increase the likelihood of catching a condition early when it can be more effectively managed and controlled. Likewise, a diabetes management program does not prevent the disease, but it does reduce the probability that the disease's wide range of severe consequences will arise. Similarly, cardiac and stroke rehabilitation programs can reduce the risk of reoccurrence, prevent deterioration, and improve one's future health prospects. Generally speaking, traditional insurance policies do not pay for ex ante loss mitigation, but, again, health insurance is different. Treatments that mitigate loss are routinely covered by health insurance, and those who have health insurance expect coverage for these kinds of expenses.

Diversification is most easily understood in the context of the risk reduction achieved in an investment portfolio when different kinds of investments are assembled to achieve the best results in the face of a variety of potential market conditions. Diversification also occurs, however, when economic actors disaggregate property and other interests in ways that reduce exposure to particular perils. Thus, a farmer might plant different crops in different locations to reduce the risk of total loss of a harvest due to weather or insect invasion, and an individual or firm might back up and store its data in multiple locations, thereby reducing the risk of loss. In healthcare, the analogue is a patient receiving two or three kinds of treatments for a condition simultaneously, if this can be done without undue risk itself, in an effort to maximize the probability of a successful outcome, or seeking second or third opinions from different physicians before making treatment decisions.

Another way to cope with risk is to do nothing—in other words, retain the risk after assessing the alternatives. Although sometimes this involves doing literally nothing to prepare for a potential loss, a more considered approach is called *self-insurance* and involves a strategy of setting aside reserves to pay for an eventual loss. In insurance policies, risk retention also occurs through loss-sharing—deductibles, copayments, and coinsurance—under which insureds bear the risk of the first layers of loss or retain a share of some or all layers of loss. In health insurance, risk retention occurs in each of the foregoing ways. Loss-sharing provisions are common in health insurance, and risk retention also exists in the form of programs through which individuals (through, for example, health savings accounts[12]) or firms (through self-insurance programs for the benefit of employees[13]) set aside resources to pay for their own healthcare or the healthcare of employees of the firm.

At a certain point, the marginal cost of implementing loss prevention, loss reduction, or other non-insurance kinds of risk management strategies will exceed the marginal benefit (in terms of losses prevented or mitigated) of such efforts. If the risk that remains is too large

[12] A health savings account ("HSA") is a tax-exempt trust or custodial account set up by an eligible individual with a qualified HSA trustee to pay or reimburse certain medical expenses incurred by the individual. For more discussion, *see* Hall's chapter in this volume.

[13] *Id.*

to be disregarded, the individual or firm will consider the remaining option—insuring the risk through the purchase of an insurance policy from an insurance company.

b. The Insurance Contract as a Risk Management Tool

All insurance policies are contracts, and all contracts allocate risk, but not all contracts are insurance policies. What gives contracts of insurance their distinctive character? Even the simple contract for the sale of a good allocates risk; the price term protects the seller from the risk of a future decline in market price (as it forecloses the seller's positive risk of a gain from a future market price increase) and simultaneously protects the buyer from the risk of a future market price increase (as it forecloses the buyer from the possibility of gain from a future market price decline). But the fact that risk is *allocated* in an agreement does not mean the contract is one of insurance. What distinguishes insurance contracts from other contracts that also allocate risk in various forms and fashions is that in the insurance contract *risk is itself is the subject of the exchange*. Because risk has "negative value," the transferor pays the transferee to receive it (unlike a good which has positive value and which the transferee will pay the transferor to convey). But the salient feature in the insurance policy is that risk itself is the commodity being bought and sold; once the risk is shed, the transferor has security, which itself has value in and of itself. Other contracts which allocate risk have as their primary purpose the transfer of a good or service, or the creation of a relationship, with risk transference being collateral to the primary purpose of the exchange.

In addition, the risks insured by most insurance policies tend to be events that occur infrequently, but when they do, the consequences are significant and sometimes transformative. Generally speaking, ordinary expenses thought of as the typical costs of doing business or day-to-day living are not insurable. That a loss be accidental or unexpected in some sense and outside the control of the insured is a fundamental assumption of insurance; largely through the case law[14] but occasionally through statute,[15] insurance law has acknowledged this assumption by making *fortuity* a prerequisite for the validity of an insurance contract. The fortuity requirement is sometimes explained by reference to certainty; losses that are certain to occur, or which have already occurred, are not insurable, whereas losses that are uncertain to occur can be insured ex ante. Fortuity is a surprisingly complex doctrine with many nuances and exceptions, but it embraces the idea, usually also addressed by intentional act exclusions in the language of most policies, that someone cannot deliberately cause or voluntarily incur a loss and then be reimbursed under an insurance policy. It also incorporates the idea that a loss already in progress cannot be insured, which precludes, for example,

[14] *See* JERRY & RICHMOND, UNDERSTANDING INSURANCE LAW, at 413–422.

[15] *See, e.g.*, MCKINNEY'S CONS. LAWS N.Y. § 1101 (2015) (insurance contract is any agreement or transaction where insurer is obligated to confer benefit on insured or beneficiary "dependent upon the happening of a fortuitous event"); WYO. STAT. ANN. § 26-1-102 (2015) (insurance is a contract under which one undertakes to indemnify another against loss "arising from determinable hazards or fortuitous occurrences"); ARK. CODE ANN. § 23-60-102 (2015) (insurance is agreement, contract, or transaction in which insurer is obligated to confer benefit upon another "dependent upon the happening of a fortuitous event").

an insured from securing insurance on his home when it is already on fire (or has burned down) or when floodwaters are rising and the home's destruction is imminent.

Thus, insurance has four key features that together distinguish the insurance contract from non-insurance contracts that have risk allocation effects. Insurance is a (1) *contract* between insurer and insured where (2) *risk* is (3) *transferred* and then (4) *distributed* across a pool of similarly situated insureds. The object of the exchange in an insurance contract is *risk* of some kind of negative consequence that is unexpected or accidental in some sense.

c. Risk Management: The Insurer's Perspective

Interestingly, and somewhat ironically, although not always obvious to consumers, insurance companies, whose business is to accept the transfer of risk from risk-averse insureds, are no less risk averse than the insureds with whom they do business. Thus, insurers will engage in their own risk management strategies. The most important of these involves utilization of the law of large numbers, which operates as follows: The insurer who assumes the insured's risk will seek to make the same bargain with a large number of similarly situated insureds. With the premiums collected from all of these insureds, the insurer will create a fund that will be used to pay claims submitted by any insured who suffers a loss within the coverage. The key to the success of this arrangement is the insurer having a pool of insureds sufficiently large and disaggregated to enable the insurer to predict with a high degree of accuracy the number of losses that will be incurred among members of the pool of insureds. With this knowledge, the insurer can charge sufficiently high premiums to fund a reserve that will cover all valid claims plus the insured's administrative costs (and a profit if the insurer calculates well). Because insureds are risk averse, they are each willing to pay the insurer more than the expected loss, which enables the insurer to cover all of its expenses (and make a profit) while paying all of the claims.

Complicating insurers' risk management efforts are two principles devolving from asymmetric information distribution among insurers and insureds. First, the principle of adverse selection teaches that those who need insurance are more likely to purchase it, which will cause any given pool of insureds to contain a disproportionate number of higher-risk insureds. But insurers are not always able to predict who these higher-risk insureds are, because insurance buyers often know more about their own risks than do the insurers, and some of this information is inaccessible to insurers. Lack of information prevents insurers from setting fully accurate prices, which can lead to market distortions (e.g., too many high-risk insureds in a pool if the price is too low, or too many "good-risk" insureds dropping out of a pool if the price is too high). Asymmetric information also causes coverage to sometimes be extended when it would have been withheld under conditions of full information. To combat adverse selection, insurers seek to increase information gathering at the point of sale so that better underwriting decisions can be made. Also, through the application process insurers seek to position themselves to invalidate coverage when material information disclosed in the application is subsequently found to be inaccurate or when circumstances on which the policy's issuance is conditioned change and are not revealed or corrected.

Second, the moral hazard principle holds that the existence of insurance coverage increases the frequency and size of loss due to the tendency of insureds to reduce loss-preventing behaviors (or sometimes engage in loss-producing behaviors) when the consequences of the behaviors are the financial responsibility of another party. Moral hazard distorts insurance pricing because the insured has more information about its behaviors and intentions than the insurer. Insurers combat moral hazard by requiring the insured to bear a greater proportion of loss through deductibles, copayments, or retentions. When the insured must share a portion of the loss, the insured is more likely to take precautions to prevent it and less likely to engage in loss-producing behaviors. That being said, risk retention through deductibles and so forth is sometimes sought by the insured, who may desire to reduce the cost of the premium by choosing to bear a portion of the risk. Although moral hazard is present in all kinds of insurance, it is especially influential in health insurance; this is because health insurance by its terms encourages consumption of benefit-producing services, unlike traditional insurance's role of providing compensation to indemnify the insured from or otherwise offset the adverse consequences of loss-producing events.

Another important risk management strategy used by insurers is reinsurance, which is essentially insurance for insurance companies. Stated more elegantly, reinsurance "is a contract whereby one insurer transfers or cedes to another insurer all or part of the risk it has assumed under a separate or distinct policy or group of policies in exchange for a portion of the premium."[16] Reinsurance has the effect of dispersing the risk assumed by insurers throughout global markets, which further reduces any insecurity the insurer might have in its portfolio of risks it has assumed from the insureds with whom it does business.

III Comparing "Health Insurance" to Traditional Insurance Arrangements

a. How Insurance Is Categorized

The manner in which insurance is categorized today is largely the result of how markets have emerged throughout history to deal with risks that raise the greatest concerns for personal and commercial economic interests. The first interests to be protected through insurance arrangements were property interests, and the earliest of these products was *marine insurance*, which provided protection for the owners of vessels engaged in maritime shipping and the cargoes they carried.[17] Fire was the first great peril for owners of homes and buildings, and the Great Fire of London (1666) prompted the creation of *fire insurance* in the late seventeenth century. Over time, fire insurance expanded into the so-called "*allied lines*" that protect against loss of property by other perils, such as lightning, rain, wind, and so on. *Life insurance* first appeared in the eighteenth century but did not blossom until the next century, when increased prosperity amplified the risk that a person

[16] La. Safety Ass'n of Timbermen-Self Insurers Fund v. La. Ins. Guar. Ass'n, 17 So.3d 350, 359 (La. 2009).

[17] Marine insurance expanded over time to include *inland marine insurance*, which evolved to include not only shipping on inland waterways but also virtually all kinds of transportation liabilities and losses associated with shipping goods through different modalities (e.g., rail, trucking, and the like) and the various instrumentalities of transportation (e.g., bridges, tunnels, and the like).

could die prematurely and impose financial stress on dependents well beyond the expenses of burial. *Annuities*, the flip side of life insurance, became prominent in the early twentieth century to help manage the risk of living too long and having financial needs exceeding one's earning capacity. *Accident insurance* appeared in the mid-nineteenth century as a corollary of new methods of transportation—primarily railways and steamships—which were thought to pose new risks to travelers. *Disability insurance*, which provides reimbursement for income lost due to one's inability to work (typically in the occupation for which one is suited by experience, education, or training) as a result of illness or injury, had its roots in accident insurance. *Liability insurance* emerged out of the rise of the tort liability system, the primary common law tool through which accident victims were compensated and financial responsibility was imposed on those whose unreasonable conduct caused victims to suffer loss. Liability insurance covered not only this financial obligation but also the costs of defending against covered liability claims. Liability insurance came to be known as *casualty insurance*, and the companies providing it also wrote other kinds of coverage on very different kinds of risks and interests (hence the phrase "*multi-line underwriting*").

These other kinds of insurance were treated as falling under the umbrella of casualty insurance; thus, casualty insurance came to be understood as liability insurance and associated lines such as workers' compensation insurance, business interruption insurance (for loss of income due to the destruction of or damage to property upon which the production of income depends), credit insurance, fidelity and surety bonds, disability insurance, and accident insurance, plus such discrete lines as burglary, robbery, theft, collision, boiler, and plate glass insurance.

Health insurance was initially considered to be one category within casualty insurance, but the impetus for the emergence of health insurance products was quite different from that which led to the creation of other kinds of insurance. The first hospital and medical healthcare benefit plans appeared as provider-controlled plans designed to respond to shrinking demand for healthcare services in the Great Depression.[18] These service benefit plans were essentially prepaid service contracts under which the subscriber received all of his or her healthcare services from a particular hospital or group of doctors in exchange for a fixed periodic premium. As such, these plans had more in common with fixed-price, exclusive dealing service contracts than they did with insurance contracts, and one of the first important decisions to consider whether these plans constituted insurance held that they did not.[19]

Soon thereafter, prepaid group practices emerged, where a hospital and an affiliated physician group offered services financed by the prepayment of care. These were structured in various ways, including corporate ownership of the hospital and a physician practice plan, or a joint venture between healthcare providers and a fiscal entity which served as an intermediary between subscribers and the providers. These also resembled fixed-price, exclusive dealing service contracts, but the existence of intermediaries to collect what looked like periodic premiums gave the arrangements the appearance of traditional insurer risk-bearing activities.

[18] For more on this history, *see* PAUL STARR, THE SOCIAL TRANSFORMATION OF AMERICAN MEDICINE 290–330 (1982).

[19] *See* Jordan v. Group Health Association, 107 F.2d 239 (D.C. Cir. 1939).

The advent after World War II of favorable federal income tax treatment for health insurance gave rise to the growth of employer-provided health insurance and the entry of insurance companies, typically life companies, into the healthcare system in larger numbers. A variety of healthcare delivery structures soon followed, generally organized around the moniker of "managed care," which usually was understood to refer to large integrated financing and delivery systems built by a fiscal intermediary and consisting of hospital and physician networks whose services were either sold as health insurance plans to employers or administered as benefit plans for self-insured employers.[20] The ensuing pushback against managed care in the 1990s, the rise of consumer-oriented funding mechanisms (including health savings accounts), and the advent of the Affordable Care Act are discussed elsewhere in this volume.[21] The history is complicated, but all of the healthcare delivery structures that emerged in the private sector throughout this evolution were commonly understood to constitute "health insurance," both in the legal and the lay vernacular. Yet these arrangements have features that distinguish them from the other categories of insurance, an observation which is developed further below.

b. Legal Definitions of Insurance

For historical reasons unique to the insurance industry,[22] the predominant source of regulation of the insurance business in the United States is state law. Thus, disputes over what constitutes "insurance" have typically arisen when a state regulatory authority (typically a department of insurance or an insurance commission) or someone seeking to invoke that authority seeks to assert jurisdiction over an organization's activities on the ground that they constitute the "business of insurance" subject to state insurance regulation. Most states have statutes that define insurance, but these statutes are typically phrased generally with some variation from state to state in the text. The most common phrasing in the state statutory definitions of insurance typically refers to one party's agreement to pay or indemnify another party upon the other party's loss from contingencies or perils. A number of the statutes place some specific categories of risk-spreading outside the definition, such as, for example, self-insurance, home service contracts, some kinds of warranty programs, and road or travel assistance contracts.[23]

Because many different kinds of contracts allocate risk in different ways, the language of most statutes is sufficiently broad that if applied literally it would cause some relationships not normally understood as involving insurance to be subjected to state regulation. Thus, a body of case law has developed where courts have interpreted the statutes, and the consensus in this body of law is that the existence of indemnification in a relationship between two parties, without more, is not sufficient to establish an insurance relationship. Under this logic,

[20] For more discussion, *see* Jonathan Weiner & Gregory de Lissovoy, *Razing a Tower of Babel: A Taxonomy for Managed Care and Health Insurance Plans*, 18 J. Health Pol. Pol'y & L. 75 (1993).

[21] Jost's chapter in this volume; Hall's chapter in this volume; Frankford's chapter in this volume; Monahan's chapter in this volume.

[22] *See* Jerry & Richmond, Understanding Insurance Law, at 64–67.

[23] *E.g.*, Ala. Code 1975 § 27-1-2(1) (2015); Alaska Stat. § 21.97.900(25) (West 2014); Cal. Ins. Code § 22 (West 2014); Del. Code Ann. tit. 18, § 102(2) (West 2015); Me. Rev. Stat. tit. 25-A, § 3 (2014); Mass. Gen. Laws ch. 175, § 2 (2014); N.C. Gen. Stat. § 58-1-10 (2014); S.C. Code Ann. § 38-1-20(25) (2014); Va. Code Ann. § 38.2-100 (West 2014); Wash. Rev. Code § 48.01.040 (2014).

an indemnity clause in a contract between contractor and subcontractor, under which the subcontractor agrees to indemnify the contractor from loss in the event the negligence of the subcontractor causes the contractor to become liable to the owner for damages, is not insurance.[24] This kind of arrangement is a contract which transfers risk from contractor to subcontractor, but there is no appreciable distribution of risk across similar transactions, and thus the transaction is not insurance. In addition, the purposes for which states desire to regulate the insurance business (the principal one being ensuring the solvency of insurers, upon whose financial security the well-being of all insureds depends) are not implicated by a discrete indemnification relationship.

Another kind of contractual relationship that might upon a casual glance be considered "insurance" is a warranty accompanying the sale of a good. The warranty, which can be part of a contract between the seller and buyer or an obligation from the manufacturer to the buyer in the absence of privity of contract, is the functional equivalent of a transfer of risk from the seller (or manufacturer) to the buyer. That is, the seller (or manufacturer) of the good assumes the buyer's risk that the product will not work as promised. In the sale, a small part of the price of the good is presumably allocated to compensating the seller for assuming the risk of the good's imperfections, and this part of the price might be considered an insurance premium. But courts have consistently held and many state statutes defining insurance have affirmed that warranties accompanying sales of goods are not "insurance" subject to regulation by state insurance departments.[25] The doctrine that has emerged in insurance law to separate insurance from non-insurance transactions is the "principal object and purpose" test.[26] In the case of warranties that accompany sale of a good, the principal object and purpose of the transaction is to convey a good, not to transfer risk of imperfection in the product, and thus ordinary warranties do not constitute insurance.

Determining the purpose of the risk-transferring arrangement is challenging in many situations,[27] but the principle to be applied is relatively easily stated: The distinction between insurance and non-insurance risk distribution transactions inheres in the underlying purpose of the arrangement. For a transaction to fit within the boundaries of the business of insurance subject to regulation under state insurance law, risk transfer and distribution must be the *primary and essential goal* of the contract. Instead of a transfer of beans, toasters, or services (which may or may not be accompanied by warranties or other collateral promises), what is being transferred under the contract is the risk of occurrence of a loss-producing

[24] *See, e.g.*, Pearlman v. Reliance Ins. Co., 371 U.S. 132, 140 n. 19 (1962) ("suretyship is not insurance"); U.S. ex rel. Custom Grading, Inc. v. Great American Ins. Co., 952 F. Supp. 2d 1259, 1266 (D.N. Mex. 2013); Superior Precast, Inc. v. Safeco Ins. Co. of Am., 71 F. Supp. 2d 438, 451 (E.D.Pa. 1999); Herrick Corp. v. Canadian Ins. Co. of Cal., 29 Cal. App. 4th 753, 766 (1994).

[25] Del Code Ann. tit. 18, § 2051(5) (West 2015); N.C. Gen. Stat. § 58-1-15(b) (2014); Va. Code Ann. §§ 38.2-100, 38.2-2618 (West 2014); Tokuhisa v. Cutter Mgmt. Co., 223 P.3d 246, 253, 255 (Haw. Ct. App. 2009); Kaplan v. Wholesale Auto. Supply, 2009 WL 1347404 at *9 (N.J. Sup. Ct. 2009); *see also* Steven Plitt et. al., 1 Couch on Ins. § 1:20 (3d ed. 2014), *available at* Westlaw.

[26] *See* Lemy v. Direct Gen. Fin. Co, 885 F. Supp. 2d 1265, 1270 (M.D. Fla. 2012); Guest v. Allstate Ins. Co., 244 P.3d 342, 355 (N.M. 2010) (*citing* Jordan v. Grp. Health Ass'n, 107 F.2d 239, 248–249 (D.C. Cir. 1939)); H&R Block v. Tennessee, 267 S.W.3d 848, 856–857 (Tenn. Ct. App. 2010); Wayne v. Staples, 135 Cal. App. 4th 466, 476 (Cal. Ct. App. 2006). *But see* Allen v. Burnet Realty, 801 N.W.2d 153, 156, 159 (Minn. 2011) (declining to adopt the principle object and purpose test).

[27] *See* Jerry & Richmond, Understanding Insurance Law, at 19–28.

event, and the primary object of the party shedding the risk is to achieve security in place of retaining a risk that a peril, or set of perils, will materialize and cause loss or damage to an interest of the insured.

c. Health Insurance as "Insurance"

Despite the widely held assumption that "health insurance" must be insurance, where health insurance fits in the legal vernacular of insurance presents is a surprisingly complex question, as the prior discussion suggests. On the one hand, consumers have a risk of incurring serious illness or injury with potentially long-term and financially devastating consequences. This kind of health risk is no less serious than the catastrophic loss of a major asset (such as a home or business) or the loss of financial support for dependents when a financial provider suffers premature death or disability. Whether a serious injury or major illness will be encountered in the future is uncertain, and the timing is plainly unknown. That this kind of risk is the legitimate subject of an insurance contract is indisputable. It has the primary and essential goal of risk transfer and distribution, and it involves a risk of major negative consequence that is not expected and is uncertain to occur.

On the other hand, many kinds of healthcare expenses are not associated with unexpected calamities but are instead the kind of routine maintenance visits and treatments that individuals are encouraged to make (e.g., physical examinations; inoculations; blood tests to check for early evidence of disease; etc.) in order to reduce the probability of serious illness or injury in the future. As explained above, in the traditional insurance world, these kinds of routine and expected "losses," the timing of which are under the consumer's control, are not considered insurable risks and are not within the purview of the products sold by the insurance industry. In the same vein, many health expenses are associated with minor ailments that occur occasionally and somewhat predictably, and thus arguably fit outside the normal understanding of an insurable risk—just as the baker would not expect a property insurer to reimburse the loss of the occasional batch of burnt bread, an event which fits with other ordinary costs of doing business as a baker.

The application of insurance law's fortuity principle yields identical observations. Although the occurrence of an unanticipated illness or injury requiring medical assistance easily meets the fortuity requirement, many services that are universally assumed to be covered by health insurance are not fortuitous in the sense of the insurance law principle. For example, preventive screening, physical examinations, and wellness programs are benefits often provided by health insurance plans, but the "coverage" for these voluntarily incurred expenses do not result from accidents or fortuitous events. Healthcare expenses to avoid the onset of disease—for example, a regimen of medications designed to respond to a condition in an effort to prevent a disease or illness-related event from occurring—are no more fortuitous than, by way of comparison, replacement of worn brakes for an insured automobile (or the expense of a vehicle safety check in order to identify a risk-increasing defect) despite their benefit in reducing the chance of a future accident.[28] As noted earlier, although

[28] There is room to argue that the presence or manifestation of the condition, including the timing of its manifestation, is fortuitous and thus the risk of incurring expenses to treat it is insurable. Generally speaking, in insurance law, ordinary wear and tear (or depreciation) is not insurable and a reduction in

insurance companies in some situations help insureds manage risks through loss prevention and mitigation and risk management programs, insurers do not agree to pay for these expenses in the insurance contract itself, and these programs are not part of the coverage of the insurance policies. This has something to do with the fact that traditional insurance grew out of a purpose to distribute the risk of negative loss, whereas health insurance has its roots in the early twentieth-century prepaid group programs designed to facilitate the sale of healthcare services.

Health insurance presents itself in the marketplace in different ways, and some arrangements resemble traditional insurance arrangements more than others. For example, although more common historically but almost totally absent from the marketplace today, some health insurance arrangements involve the insured paying a premium for coverage that entitles the insured to reimbursement of covered healthcare expenses incurred by the insured or for the direct payment by the insurer to the hospital or healthcare professional that rendered covered services. This structure closely resembles the indemnity framework of most property insurance policies; the insured suffers a loss and either receives reimbursement for the expenses of repairs or benefits from the insurer's payment to the entity providing repairs.

Much more common today is the arrangement where the health insurer represents an array of hospitals and healthcare providers who agree to provide services to the insured as needed in accordance with a schedule of fees paid jointly by the insurer and the insured (through deductibles and copayments). In this structure, the transaction resembles the insurer promising to provide all of the insured's healthcare needs (within the limits of the contract) in exchange for the insured making periodic payments and agreeing to pay shares of the medical bills up to specified limits. Outside of healthcare, these exclusive dealing arrangements tend not to be considered insurance. In the healthcare world, however, where healthcare access is most often provided through arrangements which encourage or require the rendering of healthcare services from designated providers, modern courts have consistently held that these plans constitute "health insurance" for the purposes of state law and various statutory requirements.[29]

value that is associated with ordinary, customary, expected deterioration is not a fortuitous loss. By this analysis, many routine medical conditions that arise in the normal process of aging are not fortuitous losses. Yet strict application of this principle would call into doubt the entire areas of life insurance and disability insurance under the reasoning that death and most disabilities are the result of ordinary aging and normal wear and tear. There is enough play in the fortuity doctrine to have confidence that no health insurance policy would ever be declared invalid on this ground, but the fact remains that many of the kinds of costs covered by health insurance are far removed from what is permissible in insurance generally.

[29] Carter v. State Farm Mut. Auto Ins. Co., 808 A.2d 466, 472–474 (D.C. 2002) (*citing* Pegram v. Herdrich, 530 U.S. 211, 218–229, 120 S. Ct. 2143, 2148-49 (2000)); Express Scripts, Inc. v. Wenzel, 262 F.3d 829, 834–835 (8th Cir. 2001); Smith v. PacifiCare Behavioral Health of Cal., Inc., 113 Cal. Rptr. 2d 140, 150, 157–158 (Cal. Ct. App. 2001); *see also* Omni Healthcare, Inc. v. Health First, Inc., 2015 WL 275806 at *2 (M.D. Fla. Jan. 22, 2015) (describing managed care plans as insurance products); Universal Am. Corp. v. Nat. Fire Union Fire Ins. Co. of Pittsburgh, 959 N.Y.S.2d 849, 859 (N.Y. Sup. Ct. 2012) (same); AlohaCare v. Ito, 271 P.3d 621, 646 (Haw. 2012); Roche v. Travelers Prop. Cas. Ins. Co., 2008 WL 2875250 at *1 (S.D. Ill. 2008) (same). *But see* Hymel v. HMO of La., Inc., 951 So.2d 187, 200-01 (La. Ct. App. 2006) (noting that, in Louisiana, an HMO is not considered an insurer if certified by the state); Jordan v. Grp. Health Ass'n, 107 F.2d 239, 248–249 (D.C. Cir. 1939) (finding that a group health insurance plan constituted a contract for services and did not fall within the ambit of insurance regulations).

In sum, health insurance is different; it occupies a special, unique space in the insurance landscape. The next section suggests a set of reasons why this is inevitable.

IV Why Health Insurance Is Different

a. Nature and Importance of the Asset Protected

Although the history of the evolution of healthcare access and finance in the United States is a complicated narrative driven by competing visions of what "health insurance" should be understood to mean, that healthcare access enjoys a lofty status relative to other public values and assets is undeniable. Noting the magnitude of the government's financial investment in providing healthcare access is alone enough to prove the point. For example, in 2015, 55 million elderly were enrolled in Medicare and an estimated 66 million indigent received Medicaid assistance at a cost to the federal budget of $807 billion.[30] In addition, it is estimated that about 11 million nonelderly people will be covered under the ACA by insurance purchased through federal or state health insurance exchanges, and most of these will receive significant tax subsidies from the federal government to help finance the purchase.[31] Furthermore, the $1.3 trillion in direct public (federal and state) spending on healthcare, which accounts for 47% of total national healthcare spending, will be supplemented by approximately $250 billion in federal tax subsidies for employer-provided health insurance.[32] Relative to other insurance products which protect against loss of other kinds of assets (such as one's life, job, home, automobile, or personal property), health insurance has no counterpart; there is nothing remotely comparable to the magnitude of the federal presence in providing, underwriting, and supporting health insurance.[33]

This is starkly apparent when health insurance is compared to the risks protected in the property and casualty lines. The loss of a large uninsured property asset could be financially

[30] Congressional Budget Office, U.S. Congress, *The 2015 Long-Term Budget Outlook* (Pub. 50250), p. 29–30, 33 (June 2015) (https://www.cbo.gov/sites/default/files/114th-congress-2015-2016/reports/50250-LongTermBudgetOutlook-4.pdf (LongTermBudgetOutlook.pdf, visited June 16, 2015). The CBO estimates that the states contributed an additional $195 billion to Medicaid. *Id.* at 33.

[31] *Id.* [32] *Id.* at 30.

[33] Although the extent of the federal role in enabling healthcare access is massive, there are other areas where a consensus exists that private markets have failed to generate adequate coverage and where the federal government has stepped in to provide or subsidize insurance products. When flood insurance disappeared from the marketplace in the 1960s, Congress created the National Flood Insurance Program to enable property owners to purchase insurance protection from the government against losses from flooding. National Flood Insurance Act of 1968 (P.L. 90-448). With agriculture being crucial to the nation's food supply, in 1938 Congress passed, and has amended many times since, the Federal Crop Insurance Act (Title V of the Agricultural Adjustment Act of 1938, P.L. 75-430), which establishes a federal program of crop insurance and provides subsidies to agriculture producers to the end of mitigating the risk of crop failures and market fluctuations. Other federal insurance programs exist in other niche areas, such as deposit insurance, mortgage insurance, excess liability insurance for nuclear accidents, business risk in foreign trade, crime insurance for certain urban residential and business properties, and excess coverage for terrorism losses.

devastating with multigenerational consequences,[34] but there is no public or political support for universal access to property insurance or for a system where property insurance is provided or subsidized as a public benefit for those who cannot afford it. Similarly, liability insurance—although the consequences of incurring an uninsured liability to a third party could be devastating financially, not to mention its importance to the injured victim—is not viewed as something to which everyone is entitled and which government should provide on a free or subsidized basis. Nor does federal tax law provide a subsidy for employer-provided property or liability insurance, unlike life, health, disability, and long-term care insurance, where a public consensus exists that federal tax policy should be used to encourage more widespread availability of the coverages.[35]

Among the four personal lines supported by tax subsidies, there are stronger public norms favoring access to life and disability insurance, but even these are not nearly as strong as those favoring health insurance. The Social Security system provides, in addition to retirement income for those who have the requisite work history and reach the requisite age, two important insurance benefits: disability benefits for those who become unable to work before retirement age and survivors' benefits for the spouse and dependents of otherwise eligible deceased benefit recipients. These two programs reflect a public norm that recognizes the importance of life and disability insurance as social goods and affirms the role of government in making these benefits available. But the market for life insurance is overwhelmingly a private one, and only a relatively modest program of public life insurance is embedded in the Social Security system.[36] The survivors' benefits program provides an annuity in an amount approximately equal to the current poverty line definitions for survivors of a person who participated in the Social Security system. This coverage receives no public subsidy, as it is presently fully funded by employee and matching employer contributions; thus, Social Security's survivors benefit program is tantamount to government-mandated but privately financed life insurance protections for most U.S. workers. Thus, this program stands as evidence of a social consensus that a minimum level of life insurance for everyone is valuable and should be nearly universally available, but the commitment is far short of the current consensus on the size and importance of a federal presence in health insurance.

[34] A home is typically a household's largest property asset (for those who are able and wish to own one). If owned free of a mortgage, the uninsured loss of the asset could have devastating impact on the household's net worth. It is virtually impossible to purchase a house with the aid of a loan and secured by a mortgage without insurance, but it is possible for the owner-mortgagor to suffer loss to the property under conditions where the owner disqualifies himself from the insurance coverage. *See* Jerry & Richmond, Understanding Insurance Law, at 348–349. The mortgage debt will not be discharged in these circumstances, and its existence could have multigenerational impact since it would survive even as an obligation of the insured's estate.

[35] Federal tax law encourages employer-provided life, health, disability, and long-term care insurance by allowing employer deductions for the expense of providing the benefit and by protecting significant portions of the benefit from taxation to the employee. Because property and liability insurance require individualized and more involved claims processing, these products do not lend themselves to being sold and marketed on a group basis, which is a prerequisite to employer-provided insurance. But this would not foreclose public subsidies of the coverage if the coverage were thought to be a sufficiently important public good.

[36] For more discussion, *see* Robert H. Jerry, II, *Life, Health, and Disability Insurance: Understanding the Relationships*, 35 J.L. Med. & Ethics 80, 83–87 (2007).

Likewise, the private market for disability insurance in the United States is very thin relative to life and health insurance; ironically, a large part of the reason for this is the extension of disability insurance to Social Security participants in the late 1950s.[37] This component of the Social Security system stands as a public version of disability insurance for workers who become disabled before they reach retirement age. But the benefit is modest, the eligibility requirements are not insignificant, and there is no public contribution to the program out of general revenues. Although the Social Security disability benefit reflects a social consensus that a minimum level of disability protection should be provided to all workers who participate in the Social Security system, this, too, falls far short of the size and importance of the federal presence in health insurance.

Although the United States stops well short of recognizing a "right" to healthcare, the foregoing makes clear that access to healthcare is an extremely important value standing well above many other strong values and assets (e.g., housing, employment, education, and the like). This is inevitable; good health is a necessary prerequisite to enjoyment of and prosperity in each of these other assets, and without good health, life itself has greatly diminished worth. With healthcare being so important in the hierarchy of values, one should expect that health insurance, the portal through which most healthcare access is procured, would have special stature in the world of insurance.

b. Market Commodity or Social Good?

Professor Spencer Kimball's prescient observation that "insurance is a small world that reflects the purposes of the larger world outside it"[38] is profoundly evident in the "smaller world" of health insurance, which resides within a "larger world" of healthcare delivery, finance, and access. In the United States, over a century of debate and political contest has not yet answered definitively whether healthcare should be understood as a right or entitlement in the nature of a social good, or whether it should be treated more like an ordinary commodity produced in a market, where access depends on economic wherewithal. The social good answer points toward a national healthcare system where all citizens receive a designated minimum level of healthcare benefits funded through tax mechanisms of general applicability, perhaps supplemented with some payments of fee-for-service billings. The market good answer suggests a traditional insurance mechanism where insurers pool insureds into risk classifications, with higher-risk people paying more and lower-risk people paying less. The U.S. healthcare system, even with the greater priority given to access as reflected in the Affordable Care Act, blends together elements of both answers, thereby reflecting the persistent absence of consensus on the fundamental values of the U.S. healthcare system.[39]

Thus, health insurance is inevitably different in that, unlike other insurance products, it exists at the vortex of a political struggle where its essential character is fiercely and intensely debated. From one perspective, it is urged that health insurance in the United States should

[37] *See* C. E. Soule, Disability Income Insurance: The Unique Risk at 11–12(4th ed. 1998).

[38] Spencer Kimball, *The Purpose of Insurance Regulation: A Preliminary Inquiry in the Theory of Insurance Law*, 45 Minn. L. Rev. 471, 524 (1961).

[39] *See* Monahan's chapter in this volume.

look like the social insurance example of Medicare, a clear example of the social good answer in operation. From a closely related perspective, it is urged that health insurance should be understood as a consumer's financial asset to be deployed to purchase healthcare according to the insured's desires and needs, that is, that health insurance is simply a source of funds that enables paying for healthcare.[40] At the other extreme it is urged that health insurance should operate like traditional insurance, adhering to the principles of actuarial fairness and soundness that guide commercial insurance. The insurance policies sold in healthcare exchanges under the Affordable Care Act embrace the key insurance features of contract, risk transference, and risk distribution, but the federal mandates regarding the coverage of these plans and the public subsidies for those who cannot afford them graft social solidarity principles onto traditional insurance products. Indeed, the attacks on the Affordable Care Act by its opponents are often premised on how the act interferes with the operation of private markets.[41]

Thus, although social and political values have impact in other lines of insurance, nothing elsewhere in the insurance world resembles the sharp debate and struggle for "the soul" of health insurance.[42] This tension is starkly evident in the debate over how health insurance should be regulated, which is discussed in the next subsection.

c. Implications for Regulation

With health insurance being the portal through which most access to the healthcare system is obtained, the question preliminary to how health insurance should be structured is "how much access is desired." This has been a controversial question in the U.S. public policy debate, and there is no clear answer presently or on the horizon. But it has been apparent since the mid-twentieth century that if making healthcare accessible to all citizens is a public norm, health insurance marketed and sold in private markets will not achieve it. This is true for at least two reasons.

First, in a private unregulated market, some individuals will choose not to purchase private insurance under the belief they do not need it. This is especially true of younger persons, who are disproportionately healthy, are in the midst of building their economic futures, and therefore tend disproportionately to eschew the purchase of health insurance. This behavior undervalues the risks of injury requiring health services and of incurring a health condition that is expensive to treat. Although this choice may be rational under conditions of extreme

40 *See* Wendy K. Mariner, *Social Solidarity and Personal Responsibility in Health Reform*, 14 CONN. INS. L. J. 199, 210 (2008) (discussing how pre-ACA reform proposals endorsed "insurance plus services" contracts that in operation would pull the healthcare system in inconsistent directions).

41 *See, e.g.*, The Heritage Foundation, *After Repeal of Obamacare: Moving to Patient-Centered, Market-Based Health Care*, Oct. 21, 2013, http://www.heritage.org/research/reports/2013/10/after-repeal-of-obamacare-moving-to-patient-centered-market-based-health-care (visited Apr. 8, 2015); James Pethokoukis, *Yes, There Is a Free-Market Alternative to Obamacare*, Apr. 10, 2014, https://ricochet.com/archives/yes-there-is-a-free-market-alternative-to-obamacare (visited Apr. 8, 2015); Thomas Miller, *When Obamacare Fails: The Playbook for Market-based Reform*, Dec. 10, 2012, http://www.aei.org/publication/when-obamacare-fails-the-playbook-for-market-based-reform (visited Apr. 8, 2015).

42 *See* Deborah Stone, *The Struggle for the Soul of Health Insurance*, 18 J. HEALTH POL. POL'Y & L. 287 (1993).

wealth, few have the resources sufficient to manage expensive medical treatments with long-term adverse financial consequences. In addition, some percentage of the population will be uninsured in voluntary systems simply for reasons of inertia.

The second, and more common, reason for patterns of lack of insurance in an unregulated market devolve from denials of coverage, unavailability of coverage at affordable prices, or coverage gaps resulting from condition- or status-based exclusions. At least three factors contribute to these patterns.

First, private health insurance's underwriting principles are incompatible with the public goals of extending healthcare to those who need it most. Those principles are premised on premiums being set at a level close to the amount of risk assumed by the insurer, with insurers continuing to make distinctions among low-risk and high-risk insureds as long as it is possible to measure the distinctions at a cost lower than the pricing benefits gained from further subdivision of the risk pool. Different subgroups in the general population present vastly different risk levels; when the price of insurance is matched to risk, the result is that coverage for high-risk insureds becomes unaffordable (or unavailable) and access to healthcare services is thereby foreclosed. Because most people incur most of their lifetime's medical expenses near the end of their lives, the elderly are one of the highest risk subgroups; in fact, it was this market failure—the elderly population's chronic lack of access to healthcare—that led to the enactment of Medicare. Lower incomes, not surprisingly, correlate with a higher rate of adverse health outcomes; this leads to a spiral where higher-priced insurance for those with limited financial means causes less healthcare access and worse healthcare outcomes, which equate to increased risk resulting in more expensive insurance prices, and so on. Medicaid, another social insurance program,[43] was enacted to address access issues facing society's indigent. Whenever access is compromised for a portion of the adult population for any reason (whether the parent cannot afford the coverage, works for an employer who does not provide it for employees, or is ineligible as a part-time or temporary worker for an employer who does provide coverage), the children of those individuals suffer a loss of access also.

Second, to the extent higher-risk individuals are able to purchase health insurance, the unregulated market will generate gaps in coverage, which are the functional equivalent of barriers to access for those whose needs fall within the gaps. For example, in an unregulated private market, some health insurance policies will contain condition-based exclusions that place the healthcare services needed to treat active illnesses or conditions resulting from prior injuries outside the coverage. Individuals with conditions requiring high-cost treatment will encounter dollar caps on coverage, and some policies will contain lifetime caps on total expenditures. Other exclusions will apply to conditions not yet manifest but which correlate to family or genetic history revealed through standard medical tests (such as blood work). In other words, in private markets that operate similarly to traditional insurance markets, insurers will seek to gather information about the risks presented by potential insureds and will subdivide insureds into different risk pools where higher risks pay more (or pay the same for less coverage) and lower risks pay less, to the end that coverage will be limited (or unavailable) for those who present higher risks.

[43] Although Medicaid is often described as a social insurance program, it also has strong elements of a welfare program due to the means testing for eligibility which restricts eligibility to the indigent. Means-testing is frequently used as a basis for drawing a distinction between a social insurance program and a welfare program.

Third, private health insurance markets have difficulty generating adequate, affordable coverage for small employers in the group market. As discussed earlier, insurers in the private market rely on the law of large numbers to secure predictability in their own underwriting. In the group insurance market, small groups (i.e., employers with relatively small numbers of employees) are by definition outside the reach of the law of large numbers, and the lack of predictability of healthcare expense incurred by small groups generates additional risk which makes the product much more expensive, and hence less affordable by the employer—which in turn results in less healthcare access for these employees. The suggestion that insurers should combine small groups into large groups where the law of large numbers will operate is not viable in an unregulated private market because insurers will continue to compete with each other by identifying factors that justify taking lower-risk small groups out of the larger group and offering them coverage at a lower price, thereby driving up the price (perhaps to unaffordable levels) for the remaining higher-risk small groups. Thus, small group insurers face hurdles that are destructive of coverage and access that are similar to those faced by high-risk individual insureds.

One response to the limits of the private market is to regulate those aspects of the market that prevent reaching healthcare access goals. This has, in fact, been a major theme in the U.S. healthcare system narrative. A wide range of regulatory techniques, such as limiting or prohibiting preexisting condition exclusions,[44] mandated benefit requirements,[45] mandated offers of the purchase of health insurance upon certain life events,[46] antidiscrimination provisions,[47] and guaranteed renewability and availability rules[48] all modify the terms under which health insurance is provided in private markets, thereby increasing the scope and reach of coverage. Yet as these regulations increase coverage, they also increase the cost of the product, and when the purchase of insurance coverage is voluntary, fewer individuals and employers will buy it, thereby frustrating public access goals.

When private insurance cannot meet access goals, another regulatory option is for government to create and manage a social insurance system. Social insurance systems are very diverse, but they typically share a number of core characteristics: (1) financing from taxes or premiums paid by, or on behalf of, participants or their employers, usually in an amount sufficient to operate the system (but possibly supplemented by general government revenues);

[44] The portability rules of the Health Insurance Portability and Accountability Act of 1996 (HIPAA) made it easier for those who remain continuously covered under employer-sponsored health plans to change jobs without meeting new eligibility requirements. Pub. L. No. 104-191, 110 Stat. 1936 (codified in scattered sections of 18, 26, 29, 42 U.S.C. (2006–2012)). The Affordable Care Act has extended these protections to small groups and individual markets. *See* Monahan's chapter in this volume; Hoffman's chapter in this volume.

[45] Examples at the federal level include prenatal and maternity services, coverage of mental illness and nervous disorders, and minimum coverages for hospital stays for newborns and their mothers. Many state legislatures have enacted mandated benefits statutes on a wide variety of conditions.

[46] The right to purchase continuation coverage in some circumstances (such as termination of employment, death of the employee affecting dependents, discontinuance of dependents' coverage due to marriage or age, and the like) was created by the Consolidated Omnibus Budget Reconciliation Act of 1985 (COBRA).

[47] This was a feature of HIPAA. Pub. L. No. 104-191, 110 Stat. 1936 (codified in scattered sections of 18, 26, 29, 42 U.S.C. (2006–2012)).

[48] *Id.*

(2) eligibility defined by statute, usually based on taxes or fees paid, time worked in covered employment, or economic status; (3) benefits prescribed by statute that are not directly related to taxes or fees paid; (4) benefits intended for the general public or a defined population within the general public; and (5) either compulsory participation or voluntary participation under conditions of subsidy that make nonparticipation unlikely.[49] Medicare is the obvious example of a social insurance program for healthcare benefits: It is financed by taxes and premiums paid by participants and their employers, eligibility is defined by statute, benefits are prescribed by statute and are intended for individuals who meet the age requirements, and participation though not mandatory is automatic for someone who reaches age 65 and is enrolled in the Social Security system.

The social insurance answer is attractive when one uses the social good perspective as a starting point. The premises of this perspective are that healthcare is necessary and valuable, and something to which every person is entitled without regard to status, personal characteristics, prior health history, age, or ability to pay. Social insurance is responsive to these premises, but it does not escape the fundamental reality that whenever and however healthcare services are delivered, someone must pay the costs. Providing free healthcare access funded by general tax revenues will never receive majority support in the U.S. political process. Thus, a more realistic scenario is a pluralistic system where a variety of approaches are assembled and work together to finance the healthcare system, including a social insurance mechanism with taxes, fees, or premiums (or a combination of all three), some direct provision of services by government agencies and government-supported providers, some government reimbursement of private providers, and some individual payments at the point of service. This is, in fact, a fair description of the current U.S. healthcare system, and its history can be fairly described as a process of incremental expansion of multiple approaches in a very complicated mix that has gradually moved the country closer to universal access.

Notwithstanding the massive role of the federal government in the delivery of healthcare services and in supporting the availability of and regulation of healthcare access, the perspective that healthcare and health insurance should be allowed to develop in unregulated markets has remarkable sway. This "market commodity" perspective begins with the observation that healthcare is a good that should be available in a free market, that individuals are entitled (consistent with fundamental libertarian principles) to purchase it or not as they see fit, and that those who wish to have insurance should pay for it according to actuarial principles that price the coverage according to the insured's level of risk. This perspective acknowledges that it is common for insurance mechanisms to organize in a marketplace where a large number of consumers share risk-averse characteristics. The perspective also believes that the unregulated market will develop the best and most efficient structures of healthcare delivery. As with other kinds of insurable risks, the question becomes whether the private insurance mechanism can adequately serve the public interest or whether regulation is needed to address market inefficiencies. All but the most ardent adherents to the market commodity perspective typically acknowledge that there are some areas where private

49 *See* James Kwak, '*Social insurance,*' *risk spreading, and redistribution*, in DANIEL SCHWARCZ & PETER SIEGELMAN, EDS., RESEARCH HANDBOOK ON THE ECONOMICS OF INSURANCE LAW 133–38 (2015) (reviewing various definitions of social insurance); FEDERAL ACCOUNTING STANDARDS ADVISORY BOARD, ACCOUNTING FOR SOCIAL INSURANCE 7 (Aug. 1999) (describing characteristics of federal social insurance programs).

insurance markets need assistance, although they will stress the pitfalls of government regulation and the risks that government intervention will fail (with flood insurance, crop insurance, and financial institution insurance and regulation being offered as prime exhibits) to produce good public policy.

Thus, one way to describe the U.S. healthcare system is as a system where two competing, opposing viewpoints have met in the middle. On the one hand, healthcare access is a public good, and government should ensure access to it through an insurance mechanism built on a social insurance model. The other view is that health insurance is like any other insurance product, and it should be offered by private institutions in private markets and then (perhaps) regulated to the extent necessary to achieve public goals. One can imagine a more colorful description of the "meeting in the middle," something along the lines of a violent collision with pieces of the healthcare delivery apparatus damaged and scattered in a more or less random disarray. Regardless, the interaction of these two views, which in the early twenty-first century appear to enjoy roughly equivalent political support, has produced a highly pluralistic and extraordinarily complex system of healthcare access, delivery, and finance.

V A Concluding Thought

However one describes the U.S. healthcare system and assesses its premises, structure, and outcomes, it is clear that the "insurance" which inheres in this system is very different from the insurance products that developed in an insurance business with roots in the property coverages offered on sailing vessels in the maritime industry centuries ago. Yet a central underlying purpose of "health insurance," whether one conceives it as a product of private markets or a benefit provided by the government, is to deal with the risks that attach to illness and injury—that is, the risk that someone will be ill or injured and lack access to healthcare services that have the potential to improve quality of life, and the risk of financial loss associated with paying for those services. The importance of the opportunity to live a healthy life ensures that health insurance will occupy a place of great importance in the insurance world's hierarchy, and the likelihood that healthcare access will continue to be expensive is certain to make health insurance a subject of enormous public interest and controversy for many years to come.

CHAPTER 33

MEDICARE AT FIFTY

THEODORE R. MARMOR AND JONATHAN OBERLANDER

WHEN President Lyndon Johnson signed Medicare into law on July 30, 1965, he declared that "no longer will older Americans be denied the healing miracle of modern medicine."[1] On that promise, and much more, Medicare has delivered. During the past half century, it has provided tens of millions of seniors a major measure of financial security and improved their access to medical care. A secure retirement would be unimaginable for most Americans without Medicare. Since 1972, the program has also insured Americans with permanent disabilities and end-stage renal disease. Medicare has always accepted eligible beneficiaries regardless of their health status, has never charged persons with preexisting conditions higher premiums, and has never ended coverage for someone because they developed an expensive medical condition. Put simply, Medicare has been a reliable source of health insurance and economic security for many of this nation's most expensive, medically complex, and hardest to insure populations.[2]

As the single largest purchaser of medical services in the United States, Medicare is an important source of income for hospitals, physicians, and other medical providers. Medicare has an enormous financial impact on American medical care and on the federal budget. In 2013, the federal government spent $583 billion on Medicare, amounting to about 20% of total national healthcare expenditures and 14% of the federal budget.[3] That price tag includes not just spending on program enrollees, but Medicare funding for graduate medical education and supplemental payments to hospitals serving a disproportionate share of low-income patients.

Medicare indisputably occupies a crucial position in the American healthcare landscape. Yet as the program marks its fiftieth birthday, Medicare, like the rest of American medical care, is surrounded by uncertainty and faces significant challenges. Concerns persist about

[1] President Lyndon B. Johnson, *Remarks with President Truman at the Signing in Independence of the Medicare Bill* (1965), http://www.lbjlib.utexas.edu/johnson/archives.hom/speeches.hom/650730.asp.

[2] Jonathan Oberlander & Theodore R. Marmor, *The Road Not Taken: What Happened to Medicare for All?*, *in* MEDICARE AND MEDICAID AT 50 (Alan B. Cohen, David C. Colby, Keith A. Wailoo, & Julian E. Zelizer eds., 2015).

[3] Kaiser Family Foundation, *The Facts on Medicare Spending and Financing* (2014), http://kff.org/medicare/fact-sheet/medicare-spending-and-financing-fact-sheet/.

Medicare's financial future. The specter of impending "bankruptcy," fueled by dire warnings about the fiscal consequences of population aging, frightens many. Critics charge that Medicare is unsustainable in its current form and requires major changes such as raising its eligibility age and converting the program into a voucher or "premium support" system.[4] Meanwhile, long-standing gaps in Medicare coverage leave beneficiaries vulnerable to the financial burdens of both acute and chronic illness. The fragmentation of Medicare coverage across different program components fosters confusion among enrollees. And major Medicare policies are embedded within the Affordable Care Act, whose fate remains unsettled, while partisan conflict over healthcare reform produces new (and often false) anxieties over Medicare's treatment of its beneficiaries.

By examining Medicare's origins, its history, and its evolution, this chapter seeks to illuminate how Medicare developed into the program that it is today. We address central issues in Medicare reform such as the evolution of cost containment policies and benefit changes. We also explore shifts in Medicare politics, including the rise of pro-market ideas and partisan conflict. Finally, we discuss what lessons can be learned from Medicare about healthcare policy and politics, and what they tell us about Medicare's potential trajectories in coming years.

I The Origins of Medicare

Medicare has complicated historical origins that are difficult to understand in today's political environment.[5] Perhaps the best way to understand Medicare is to appreciate how unusual the program is from an international perspective. No other industrial democracy started national health insurance with compulsory insurance for its elderly citizens alone. Rather, almost all other rich democracies started with coverage of their workforce, or, as in the case of Canada, went from special programs for the poor to universal programs for one service (hospitals) and then to another (physicians). This means that peculiarly American circumstances, rather than some common feature of modern societies, explain why it is that compulsory government health insurance began in the United States with the recipients of Social Security cash pensions.

The roots of this particular history lie in the United States' distinctive rejection of national health insurance in the twentieth century. First proposed in the years before World War I, national health insurance fell out of favor in the 1920s. When the Great Depression made economic insecurity a pressing concern, the social insurance blueprint of 1935 broached both health and disability insurance as potentially controversial items that should be included in a more complete scheme of income protection. From 1936 to the late 1940s, liberals recurrently called for incorporating universal health insurance within America's nascent welfare state. But the conservative coalition in Congress, a de facto majority of Republicans and Southern Democrats, defeated this expansionist aim.[6] National health insurance also

[4] Joseph Antos, *Medicare Reform and Fiscal Reality*, 30 J. Pol'y Analysis & Mgmt. 934 (2011).

[5] The first half of this chapter draws on Theodore R. Marmor, *Coping with a Creeping Crisis: Medicare at Twenty*, *in* Social Security: Beyond the Rhetoric of Crisis 177–199 (Theodore R. Marmor & Jerry L. Mashaw eds, 1988).

[6] Theodore R. Marmor, The Politics of Medicare (Aldine, 1973).

aroused fierce opposition to "socialized medicine" from the chief lobbying group for physicians, the American Medical Association (AMA), which regarded it as a threat to doctors' professional, clinical, and financial autonomy.

The leaders of Social Security, well aware of these political obstacles, reassessed their strategy of expansion after President Harry Truman failed to secure congressional enactment of national health insurance. By 1951, they had formulated a plan of incremental expansion of government health insurance to elderly beneficiaries of Social Security. Medicare became a proposal to provide retirees with limited hospitalization insurance—a partial plan for the segment of the population whose financial fears of illness were as well-grounded as their difficulty in purchasing health insurance at modest cost.

Beyond this substantive case, the proposal for what came to be termed Medicare had a political rationale. By proposing to cover only sixty days of hospitalization and exclude physician services, Medicare's architects sought to soften the AMA's opposition to federal insurance. And by limiting coverage to elderly beneficiaries of Social Security, reformers hoped to capitalize both on the political appeal of the aged as a sympathetic group deserving of government assistance and on the popularity of Social Security. Truman administration officials presumed that focusing coverage on the elderly and locating such coverage within Social Security would make federal health insurance harder to oppose and dismiss as socialized medicine, thereby improving its chances of passing through Congress.

These origins have much to do with the initial design of the Medicare program and the expectations of how it was to develop over time. The incrementalist strategy assumed that hospitalization coverage was but the first step in benefits and that more would follow under a common pattern of Social Security financing. Likewise, the strategy's proponents assumed that eligibility would be gradually expanded to take in the rest of the population, extending first, perhaps, to children and pregnant woman. All the Medicare architects took for granted that the rhetoric of enactment should emphasize the expansion of insurance coverage, not the regulation and reform of American medicine. The clear aim was to reduce the risks of financial disaster for the elderly and their families, and the clear understanding was that Congress would demand a largely hands-off posture toward the doctors and hospitals providing the care that Medicare would finance. A half century after the program's enactment that vision seems odd; it is now taken for granted that how one pays for medical care affects the care given. But in the build-up to enactment in 1965, no such presumption existed.

The incrementalist strategy of the 1950s and early 1960s assumed not only that public concern about the health insurance problems of the aged was widespread. It also took for granted that social insurance programs—which relied on contributory financing via payroll taxes, conferred a sense of entitlement on their beneficiaries, and were universally available regardless of persons' income—enjoyed vastly greater public acceptance than did means-tested assistance programs.[7] Social insurance in the United States was more acceptable to the extent that it sharply differentiated its programs from the demeaning world of public assistance. "On welfare," in American parlance, is a term of failure, and the leaders within Social Security made sure that Medicare fell firmly within the tradition of benefits that are "earned," not given. The aged could be presumed to be both needy and deserving because, through no

[7] Theodore R. Marmor, Jerry L. Mashaw, & John Pakutka, Social Insurance: America's Neglected Heritage and Contested Future (2014).

fault of their own, they had on average lower earning capacity and higher medical expenses than any other age group. The Medicare proposal avoided a means test by restricting eligibility to persons over age sixty-five (and their spouses)—contributors to the Social Security system during their working life.

Once this incrementalist proposal was outlined, who and what shaped its fate? The Medicare debate itself was cast in terms of class and ideological conflict: "socialized medicine" versus the voluntary "American way," private enterprise and local control versus the octopus of the federal government. Despite the turn to incrementalism, the dispute over Medicare recreated the polarization that had characterized earlier fights over national health insurance. The AMA was not impressed by reformers' efforts at conciliation. In 1957, AMA president David Allman declared the Medicare proposal "at least nine parts evil to one part sincerity" and "the beginning of the end of the private practice of medicine."[8] Ronald Reagan warned in a 1962 AMA recording that if Medicare passed, then "behind it will come other federal programs that will invade every area of freedom as we have known it in this country."[9] Beneath the public rhetoric, though, was much division of interest and opinion, particularly in the healthcare world. Blue Cross and the American Hospital Association, for example, had much to gain financially from Medicare's coverage of the high-risk aged, but their public testimony before Congress gave little hint of the extent to which they differed from the AMA.

Medicare advocates also had to contend with opposition of Arkansas Democrat Wilbur Mills, who chaired the crucial House Ways and Means committee, and other Southern Democrats in Congress. After 1961, the Democratic leadership in the House altered the committee's composition by replacing some of these opponents with pro-Medicare members. By 1964, Medicare appeared on the verge of passage and Mills seemed ready to relent, though a bill still had not made it out of Ways and Means.

The overwhelming Democratic victory in the 1964 elections transformed the politics of Medicare, practically guaranteeing that hospitalization insurance for the aged would pass in 1965. The outcome of that election redistributed congressional power in such a way that Medicare's opponents both inside and outside of Congress were overruled, breaking the hold of the conservative coalition on Medicare's fate. The question was no longer the desirability of federal health insurance for the aged, but what particular form that insurance would take.

The result was far more complex than expected. After the 1964 elections made Medicare's enactment a certainty, Wilbur Mills maneuvered to alter the legislation. Concerned that Medicare's limited benefits would disappoint beneficiaries and generate pressures to expand to cover physician services via payroll tax funding, and aware that Medicare advocates envisioned it as a first step to national health insurance, Mills sought to build a fence around the program. With the tacit and hidden support of President Lyndon Johnson, Mills adapted a Republican alternative plan to Medicare, adding voluntary but subsidized physicians insurance to hospitalization coverage.[10] Medicare insurance for physicians (what became Medicare Part B) would be funded by beneficiary premiums and general revenues, not the

[8] *Organization Section: Highlights of A.M.A. Clinical Session*, 165 JAMA 2090 (1957).

[9] JAMES A. MORONE, THE DEMOCRATIC WISH: POPULAR PARTICIPATION AND THE LIMITS OF DEMOCRATIC GOVERNMENT (Basic Books, 1990).

[10] DAVID BLUMENTHAL & JAMES A. MORONE, THE HEART OF POWER: HEALTH AND POLITICS IN THE OVAL OFFICE (University of California Press, 2009).

social insurance financing of hospital coverage (Part A). This enabled Mills, who worried about the consequences of raising payroll taxes too high, to preempt the addition of such coverage through Social Security financing.

Even with the addition of coverage for physicians' services, Medicare had significant limitations as insurance protection. The structure of the benefits themselves, providing acute hospital care and intermittent physician treatment, was not tightly linked to the special circumstances of the elderly as a group. Left out were provisions that addressed the problems of the chronically sick elderly—medical conditions that would not dramatically improve and the need to maintain independent function rather than triumph over discrete illness and injury. Medicare's architects presumed that its benefits would be improved over time, but these gaps would persist for decades; indeed, there are still significant holes in Medicare coverage today.

Mills feared that Medicare would expand into a broader system of national health insurance. His concern was well founded given the aspirations of Medicare's designers, for whom insuring the elderly was never the end goal. Over time, the program would expand, its advocates presumed, to cover new populations. Medicare for All was what the reform leaders of 1965 assumed would be the ultimate, incremental result of their first step. Medicare's incrementalism was a means to an end, a political strategy designed to secure the passage of a federal health insurance program that would expand substantially in coming years. That presumption was never made public during the Medicare debate, but it was strongly held by program architects. As Robert Ball, a key participant in crafting the Medicare strategy and head of the Social Security administration from 1962 to 1973, later explained: "[W]e all saw insurance for the elderly as a fallback position, which we advocated solely because it seemed to have the best chance politically ... we expected Medicare to be the first step toward universal national health insurance, perhaps with 'Kiddy Care' as the next step."[11] Despite repeated denials during legislative debates in the late 1950s and early 1960s, Medicare's architects expected that after covering the elderly, Medicare would soon expand to insure children, then workers, and eventually all Americans.

In an effort to forestall that prospect, Mills added Medicaid to the final Medicare legislation. Medicaid covered low-income Americans, building on an AMA proposal and the preexisting Kerr-Mills program that gave states payments to finance care for low-income residents. By taking another potential target of federal insurance out of the equation, Mills hoped that including Medicaid would weaken the case for expanding Medicare. Medicaid was enacted with scant congressional or public debate, and little sense of how important it would become. When Lyndon Johnson signed the Medicare bill into law on July 30, 1965, with former President Harry Truman in attendance to underscore its roots in earlier national health insurance proposals, he did not mention Medicaid by name in his remarks. Instead, Johnson obliquely noted that the bill "will improve a wide range of health and medical services for Americans of all ages."[12]

In sum, the Medicare bill that passed Congress in 1965 emerged as broader than its advocates expected. The "three-layer cake" encompassed Medicare coverage for hospitalizations

[11] Robert Ball, *Perspectives on Medicare: What Medicare's Architects Had in Mind*, 14 HEALTH AFF. 62 (1995).

[12] *See* Johnson, *supra* note 1.

funded via payroll taxes (Part A), coverage of physician services funded by general revenues and beneficiary premiums (Part B), and a joint federal-state program to pay for medical services for certain categories of low-income Americans (Medicaid).[13] The 1965 Medicare law thus took a form that in key respects deviated from the social insurance model that Medicare's designers had preferred. Yet even with these unexpected departures from their vision, Medicare advocates still believed that the program would over time evolve into national health insurance. Their attention now turned to implementing Medicare, a formidable task they viewed as essential to demonstrating the viability and desirability of federal health insurance.

II Implementing Medicare

Medicare was slated to be fully operational only one year after its enactment. Assuring a smooth takeoff for Medicare entailed enrolling eligible seniors into the program and securing the broad participation of medical providers. Social Security administrators went to great effort to maximize beneficiary enrollment, organizing a nationwide sign-up campaign that relied on mass mailings of Medicare applications and leveraged the over seven hundred Social Security district offices around the country.[14] The Social Security Administration (SSA) launched an intense promotional campaign in national and local media, even enlisting the postal and forestry services in publicity efforts, and arranged for door-to-door canvassing to reach persons not covered by mailing lists. The social insurance structure of Medicare, which did not rely on a means test for eligibility, facilitated these efforts; enrollment in Medicare Part A (hospitalization coverage) was automatic for Social Security beneficiaries. Nonetheless, the SSA still had to solicit and process applications from about 8 million persons who were age sixty-five and older, and thus eligible for Medicare, but not then receiving Social Security benefits. Moreover, Part B (coverage of physicians' services) was a voluntary program that required seniors to sign up and pay premiums.

At the end of Medicare's first year, the success of the enrollment campaign was evident. By July 1, 1966, 19 million beneficiaries, representing virtually all the U.S. population age sixty-five and over were enrolled in Medicare Part A, and 93% of those persons had signed up for Part B.[15] Those impressive figures, achieved within one year of Medicare becoming law, seem all the more extraordinary now given the problems that the Affordable Care Act had with its initial open enrollment period during 2013, which came over three years after its enactment.

As Medicare's administrators worked to enroll seniors, they simultaneously sought to ensure that hospitals and doctors would take part in Medicare so that beneficiaries had broad access to medical services. Securing provider participation meant, in practice, accommodating providers' interests in financial, clinical, and organizational autonomy. There had been strong provider resistance to Medicare before its enactment. Medicare's administrative

[13] *See* Marmor, *supra* note 6.

[14] Michael G. Gluck & Virginia Reno eds., Reflections on Implementing Medicare (National Academy of Social Insurance, 2001).

[15] *Id.*

structure and initial policies reflected that opposition and the desire of program administrators to assure provider cooperation with federal health insurance.

Faced with intense resistance from the AMA, including threats of a doctors' boycott, and striving to avoid the stigma of socialized medicine and demonstrate that federal health insurance could succeed, program leaders took steps to conciliate the healthcare industry. The Medicare law itself contained an explicit vow that the federal government would not intervene in the practice of medicine. Private insurers were authorized to handle claims processing for Medicare so hospitals and doctors would not have to deal directly with the federal government. And Medicare adopted permissive payment policies for medical care providers that contained no cost controls. Vague definitions of key legislative terms—"reasonable costs" and "customary charges" in particular—proved significant loopholes that allowed energetic gaming strategies on the part of providers. Unusual allowances for depreciation and capital costs (such costs were taken into account in determining hospital reimbursement) contributed a built-in inflationary impetus.[16] The use of private insurance companies as financial intermediaries preserved physician and hospital autonomy and weakened government controls on reimbursement. It was left to these intermediaries, who had closer than arm's-length relationships with many providers, to determine the reasonableness of hospital costs under Part A and physician charges under Part B.

Medicare's impressive takeoff reflected the SSA's administrative excellence, political skills, flexibility, and extraordinary preparation. In case demand from new Medicare enrollees overwhelmed hospital capacity—a major concern in the run-up to the program's start date—there were even plans to use Army and Veterans Administration hospitals as backups to serve Medicare patients (in reality, no such overcrowding occurred). Once underway, though, Medicare proved far more complex to administer than its parent pension programs within the SSA. Medicare expenditures varied with the use its beneficiaries made of the program and with the charges and costs providers submitted. Technological changes in medicine added costs unpredictably, whereas pensions were based on a formula that related present benefits to past social insurance payments. Medicare had to accommodate both providers and beneficiaries; the pension program could focus on recipients and internal administration. These differences in organizational tasks, coupled with the program's two-part insurance hybrid, produced a historically unprecedented level of complexity for Social Security's administrative elite.[17]

The truth is that in the early years of Medicare's implementation, the program's administrators were not organizationally disposed to confront providers to the extent necessary to restrain costs. Instead, SSA administrators prided themselves on their history of successful implementation of social insurance. They needed the cooperation of all parties for Medicare's implementation to proceed smoothly, and vigorous efforts at Medicare cost control threatened disruption.[18] Medicare's designers, early on aware of the need to build cost-control mechanisms into the program, also were reluctant to make strong cost-control efforts for fear of enraging Medicare providers.

[16] JUDITH M. FEDER, MEDICARE: THE POLITICS OF FEDERAL HOSPITAL INSURANCE (Lexington Books, 1977).

[17] Lawrence D. Brown, *Technocratic Corporatism and Administrative Reform in Medicare*, 10 J. HEALTH POL. POL'Y & L. 579 (1985).

[18] *See* Brown *supra* note 17, and FEDER *supra* note 16.

With the benefit of hindsight, it is easy to criticize the accommodationist posture of Medicare's early administrators. At the time of the program's enactment, however, Medicare's legislative mandate was to protect the nation's elderly from the economic burdens of illness without interfering significantly with the traditional organization of American medicine. With this aim in mind the original Medicare administrators sought to accommodate providers and thereby ensure a smooth, speedy start for the program. Not until later did Medicare come to be seen as a powerful means to control the costs and delivery of healthcare.

There was, however, one area where federal officials aggressively challenged the status quo: civil rights. Many U.S. hospitals, predominantly in the South, were segregated in 1965, and either operated separate wards by race or refused to admit any black patients. But as a condition of receiving federal Medicare payments, hospitals had to certify that they were not discriminating on the basis of race in order to comply with Title VI of the 1964 Civil Rights Act. As Medicare's July 1, 1966, launch approached, the Johnson administration had to decide whether to look past segregationist practices in order to assure that Southern hospitals participated in the new program. The Johnson administration, led by the Office of Equal Health Opportunity, instead chose to aggressively enforce the civil rights requirement, sending field inspectors to hospitals to assess their compliance and pressing hospital administrators to comply with Title VI lest they lose federal funds.[19] The results were impressive; discriminatory practices in hospitals dropped substantially during 1966 as "more than 1,000 hospitals quietly and uneventfully integrated their medical staffs, waiting rooms, and hospital floors in less than four months."[20] Medicare thus played a crucial role in helping to desegregate hospitals in the South.

Apart from Civil Rights, though, Medicare's initial implementation was solicitous of the medical care industry in the ways noted above. The late 1960s witnessed efficient administration of an inflationary design, with predictable results. Medicare expenditures swelled, as did the health outlays of the nation as a whole. In the first year of Medicare's operation, the average daily service charge in American hospitals increased by an unprecedented 21.9%.[21] The average compound rate of growth in this figure over the next five years was 13%. Medicare's definition of "reasonable charges" paved the way for steep increases in physician fees. In the eleven months between the time Medicare was enacted and the time it took effect, the rate of increase in physician fees more than doubled, from 3.8% in 1965 to 7.8% in 1966.[22] The average compound rate of growth in physician fees remained a high 6.8% over the next five years. In the first five full years of Medicare's operation, total Medicare reimbursements rose 72%, from $4.6 billion in 1967 to $7.9 billion in 1971.[23] Over the same period, the number of Medicare enrollees rose only 6%, from 19.5 million in 1967 to 20.7 million in 1971.

Medicare's rising costs made it much more difficult to realize the aspirations of its designers who believed the program would expand incrementally into national health insurance. After Medicare's successful launch, Wilbur Cohen, Secretary of Health, Education, and Welfare (HEW), and allies in the Johnson administration proposed, for example, adding coverage for mothers and newborn children to Medicare during 1967–1968. Yet the plan to expand

[19] David Barton Smith, Health Care Divided: Race and Healing a Nation (1999).

[20] David Barton Smith, Eliminating Disparities in Treatment and the Struggle to End Segregation (2005).

[21] *See* Marmor, *supra* note 6. [22] *Id.* [23] *Id.*

Medicare to encompass "Kiddycare" never came to fruition. Opposition from Johnson administration officials over Kiddycare's costs, in the context of concern over the growing costs of the Vietnam War and their implications for domestic fiscal policy, led to its abandonment.[24]

III The 1970s: Grand Ambitions, Incremental Progress

By 1970, there was a bipartisan consensus that the United States faced a cost crisis in medicine, a crisis fueled in large part by Medicare's inflationary payments. The result was a reawakening of the drive for national health insurance, with Medicare reform subordinated to grander designs. The most influential Democratic voice in Congress on health reform, Massachusetts Senator Ted Kennedy, proposed a national health insurance plan, with the federal government providing "identical insurance to all Americans for all essential health care."[25] In terms of both philosophy and policy, Kennedy's plan embraced the aspiration of universalizing Medicare. Yet Kennedy did not explicitly call for Medicare for All, choosing instead to label his plan the Health Security Program. Kennedy believed that the problems of American medical care required enacting a new health insurance program, one that would subsume rather than build on Medicare.

Other Democratic party reformers in Congress offered no shortage of proposals to remake healthcare during the early to mid-1970s, including a widely discussed plan for catastrophic health insurance by Senators Russell Long (D-La.) and Abraham Ribicoff (D-Conn.).[26] Republican president Richard Nixon also offered a comprehensive plan to expand coverage by building on employer-sponsored insurance. None of these plans, though, envisioned achieving universal coverage incrementally by expanding Medicare group by group as program architects had assumed during the 1960s. And, ultimately, none of the proposals for universal coverage passed Congress. The 1970s thus marked a turning point, with Medicare no longer the cornerstone of plans that envisioned universal health insurance.

A second consequence of the cost crisis was the realization in Congress that something had to be done to restrain Medicare spending. Medicare, thanks to its rapidly growing outlays, acquired a reputation among some prominent policy-makers in Congress and in the executive branch as an uncontrollable burden on the federal budget. By 1969, Russell Long, chairman of the Senate Finance Committee, was warning that Medicare had become a "runaway" program, and in 1970 his committee issued a landmark report detailing problems with Medicare's payment policies and offering recommendations for its reform.[27]

[24] *See* Edward D. Berkowitz, Robert Ball and the Politics of Social Security (2005); Lawrence R. Jacobs, *The Medicare Approach: Political Choice and American Institutions*, 32 J. Health Pol. Pol'y & L. 172 (2007).

[25] Edward M. Kennedy, In Critical Condition: The Crisis in America's Health Care (Simon and Schuster, 1972).

[26] Judith Feder, John Holahan, & Theodore R. Marmor eds., National Health Insurance: Conflicting Goals and Policy Choices (1980).

[27] Jonathan Oberlander, The Political Life of Medicare (2003).

The Senate Finance report became a foundation of the 1972 Social Security Amendments, which contained the first significant policies aimed at controlling the rate of growth in Medicare spending. The measures included the establishment of organizations to review hospital care provided to Medicare patients, limits on hospital payments, and the authorization of demonstration projects in alternative payment methods.[28] These reforms were destined to fail at controlling Medicare costs because they left the basic inflationary structure—retrospective payment without budgetary limits—intact. Congress was not yet willing to confront the power of the medical care industry and federal budgetary pressures were not at that time sufficiently strong to compel more decisive action. Indeed, while Congress took incremental steps to slow Medicare expenditures, it simultaneously expanded Medicare eligibility to cover persons with permanent disabilities and end-stage renal disease. In retrospect, these expansions represented not the next step to Medicare for All, but rather both the beginning and end of significant efforts to widen Medicare's base of beneficiaries. By the mid-1970s, reformers had turned away from the original strategy of securing Medicare for All through incremental expansions of the program to new populations.[29]

Still, the 1972 reforms represented a milestone. The focus of Medicare policy was shifting; the question of how to contain program spending would come to dominate Medicare policies in coming years. The establishment in 1977 of a new Health Care Financing Administration (HCFA) within HEW to administer both Medicare and Medicaid removed Medicare from the Social Security Administration and its organizational orientation of accommodation. Medicare became "one element in the broader universe of federal health care financing programs," rather than a freestanding component of the nation's social insurance system.[30] With this change, Medicare administrators, now within HCFA, soon became more concerned with healthcare policy and spending than with broader issues of social insurance.

Other measures passed by Congress to control spending in mid-1970s—including the establishment of Health System Agencies to oversee area-wide healthcare planning—would prove ineffective in ensuing years. Stronger initiatives to control healthcare costs more broadly across American medical care either failed to pass Congress, as with the Carter administration's 1978 hospital cost containment proposal, or were only temporary, such as the Nixon administration's 1971 wage and price controls.[31] As the 1970s ended, with healthcare costs continuing to rise, the prospects for national health insurance and broader cost controls having faded, and federal budget deficits increasing, policy-makers' interest in reforms to moderate Medicare spending growth was reaching a crucial threshold.

IV The 1980s: Medicare in the Reagan Era

Medicare, after nearly fifteen years of relatively quiet controversy in the specialized politics of health finance, acquired a greater salience in the Reagan era. Always of interest to those in the healthcare industry, Medicare was a second-order topic in the mass politics of the late

[28] *See* Brown, *supra* note 17. [29] *See* Oberlander & Marmor, *supra* note 2.

[30] *See* Brown, *supra* note 17.

[31] Karen Davis, Gerald E. Anderson, Diane Rowland, & Earl P. Steinberg, *Health Care Cost Containment* (Johns Hopkins University Press, 1990).

1960s and the 1970s. The oil crisis of 1973–1974 and the consequent stagflation joined with Social Security finance as the other high-priority items on the national agenda. This is not to say that Medicare was uneventful, but simply that it was a program of ordinary interest group politics, specially protected under the mantle of social insurance entitlement theories and the elderly's reputed political influence. That protected status was what the 1980s were to challenge.

Medicare's original if tacit bargain with the medical care industry—permissive regulation and generous payments in exchange for participation in the program—ended in the 1980s. Three major developments led to its demise: rising program spending, rising federal budget deficits, and the ascendance of conservatism in national politics.

Medicare payments for hospital care rose 22% from 1979 to 1980 and 21% from 1980 to 1981. Payments for physician services increased at a similarly staggering rate, rising 22% from 1979 to 1980 and 23% from 1980 to 1981.[32] Medicare, indeed all healthcare, was consuming a larger and larger piece of the economic pie, seeming to crowd out spending on other goods and services. Meanwhile, the federal budget deficit, which had not been an issue at Medicare's enactment, was quickly rising and moving onto the national agenda. In 1965, the federal deficit had been $1.4 billion. By 1980, it stood at $73 billion, or 2.6% of gross domestic product (GDP), and by 1983, driven upward by the recession as well as the Reagan administration's policies of tax cuts and defense spending increases, had soared to $208 billion or 5.9% of GDP.[33] The emergence of the federal deficit as a national political issue, coupled with rising healthcare costs, made Medicare a prominent target for deficit reduction during the 1980s.

The 1980 election of Ronald Reagan as president and the simultaneous election of a GOP Senate majority fundamentally changed Medicare's political environment. Reagan's victory culminated a shift in American politics away from liberalism, one that had begun in the 1970s amidst economic stagflation and rising disenchantment with the government following the Vietnam War and Watergate. The Great Society and expansion of the American welfare state now gave way to an agenda of tax cuts, deregulation, and welfare state retrenchment. National health insurance, or any comprehensive plan to expand access to health insurance for the uninsured or contain medical care spending across all of American medical care, was off the political radar screen.

Instead, the Reagan administration and congressional policy-makers turned their attention to deficit reduction and restraining the costs of Medicare and Medicaid. The administration sought to achieve savings in federal expenditures by shifting costs to beneficiaries in the form of higher premiums, deductibles, and co-insurance, trimming benefits, and reducing payments to hospitals.[34] But the political popularity of Medicare constrained the administration's options, and it was only able to secure modest increases in the costs shifted to beneficiaries. It was politically more attractive to target the medical care industry for savings—hospitals, doctors, and other service providers—than to impose major benefit cuts on elderly Medicare enrollees. That political calculus, which has shaped Medicare policy for the past three decades, left healthcare providers, with hospitals the leading target since their

[32] Ross H. Arnett III, David R. McKussick, Sally T. Sonnefeld, & Carol S. Crowell, *Health Spending Trends in the 1980s: Adjusting to Financial Incentives*, 6 Health Care Financing Rev. 1 (1985).

[33] Office of Management and Budget, *The Budget: Historical Tables* (2015), https://www.whitehouse.gov/omb/budget/Historicals.

[34] Robert Pear, *Reagan Medicare Proposals Are Broadly Criticized*, N.Y. Times, Feb. 3, 1983.

services comprised the single largest component of Medicare expenditures, squarely in the sights of both administration and congressional policy-makers looking for budget savings. The projection of an impending shortfall in Medicare's hospital insurance trust fund further emboldened Washington to act.[35] The stage was thus set for a transformation of Medicare payment policy.

In 1983, Congress, with the support of the Reagan administration, adopted the Medicare prospective payment system for hospitals.[36] Medicare no longer would pay hospitals retrospectively with little limit on the costs; under prospective payment, the federal government would set a fixed payment per diagnosis (based on Diagnosis-Related Groups, or DRGs). Hospitals now faced incentives to restrain costs for Medicare patients. Ironically, the most consequential health initiative of the Reagan period—Medicare's prospective payment method—was an exceedingly sophisticated, highly regulatory form of administered pricing.[37] Searching for ways to contain Medicare spending and produce budgetary savings that would reduce the deficit, the conservative, anti-government, anti-regulatory Reagan administration ended up with a policy that substantially expanded the federal government's power to regulate healthcare spending. For the first time, Washington sought to impose significant limits on Medicare payments to the medical care industry.

The advent of prospective payment for hospitals was just the start. Physicians were the next targets of Medicare's suddenly aggressive payment regime. After a freeze on increases in Medicare fees to physicians during 1984–1986, Congress enacted the resource-based relative value scale (RBRVS) in 1989 during the George H. W. Bush administration. Payments to doctors for each service were to vary based on measurements of their complexity, the time required, and practice expenses.

As with DRGs for hospitals, Medicare's new payment system for physician services, which began in 1993, rested on a highly technical formula. It appealed both to the goal of encouraging medical care providers to become more efficient and reflected the aspiration of formulating healthcare policy on the basis of scientific, objective measures developed by experts, not politicians. Beneath its technical veneer, though, the new method for paying physicians constituted administered pricing, with the federal government establishing a Medicare Fee Schedule that set, in advance, standard, fixed payments for services.[38] As with hospital payments, Congress could control increases in Medicare per service payments to doctors by adjusting an annual update factor during the budget process. In ensuing years, Congress and presidential administrations in search of budget savings would do just that. Medicare policy was now largely budget policy, with the politics of deficit reduction driving recurrent efforts to slow down increases in program spending. Taken together, the advent of the prospective payment system for hospitals and the Medicare Fee Schedule for physicians amounted to a revolution in federal health policy.[39] The era of permissive payment policy in Medicare was over, replaced by prospective payment.

[35] *See* OBERLANDER, *supra* note 27.

[36] DAVID G. SMITH, PAYING FOR MEDICARE: THE POLITICS OF REFORM (1992).

[37] James A. Morone & Andrew B. Dunham, *Slouching Towards National Health Insurance: The Unanticipated Politics of DRGs*, 62 BULL. N.Y. ACAD. MED. 646 (1986).

[38] *See* OBERLANDER, *supra* note 27.

[39] RICK MAYES & ROBERT A. BERENSON, MEDICARE PROSPECTIVE PAYMENT AND THE SHAPING OF U.S. HEALTH CARE POLICY (2006).

The emergence of an administered pricing regime was not the only surprise during the Reagan years. Another was the first major expansion of Medicare benefits since the program's enactment in 1965. Medicare was never designed to cover all of its beneficiaries' medical care expenses. Medicare offered insurance protection against the costs of hospital care, which represented the largest component of medical care spending and potentially the most catastrophic threat to persons' finances. It insured beneficiaries for physician visits and provided partial coverage for post-hospital and other outpatient services.

Yet there were sizable gaps in Medicare's benefit package. Beneficiaries had to pay a significant deductible for each spell of illness before hospitalization coverage kicked in. They could be forced to pay multiple deductibles in one year, and the number of days of Medicare inpatient hospitalization insurance was capped, placing the small percentage of beneficiaries with extraordinarily long stays in major financial jeopardy. Medicare reimbursed 80% of the charges for outpatient physician services, leaving enrollees responsible for the other 20%, as well as for premiums, and mental health and home health benefits were quite limited. There was no coverage of long-term nursing home stays (a responsibility that fell instead to Medicaid), most dental care, or outpatient prescription drugs. And there was no "stop loss" cap that limited Medicare beneficiaries' annual costs, an omission that put at financial risk beneficiaries with expensive, prolonged illness.

As healthcare costs marched upward, compelling higher cost-sharing payments from and exerting a greater financial strain on Medicare beneficiaries, and as employer-sponsored private insurance plans expanded to cover benefits such as prescription drugs, the gaps in Medicare coverage became more glaring. By the 1980s, most Medicare beneficiaries had secondary insurance coverage, either in the form of supplemental policies sponsored by their former employer, or directly purchasing Medigap plans that covered some of the holes in Medicare coverage, or, for low-income beneficiaries, from Medicaid.

Still, the limits in Medicare coverage and rising costs paid by its beneficiaries for medical services spurred efforts to improve Medicare's insurance protection. In 1988, Congress passed the Medicare Catastrophic Coverage Act. It expanded hospitalization coverage to an unlimited number of days, established an annual limit of out-of-pocket expenses for Medicare outpatient services, created an outpatient prescription drug benefit, and loosened restrictions on home health and skilled nursing facility care. The 1988 law passed with overwhelming bipartisan support. The Reagan administration initially had proposed a limited expansion of Medicare to cover catastrophic expenses and Democratic majorities in Congress enlarged that proposal to encompass a broader array of benefits.[40]

But within sixteen months, another strong bipartisan majority had repealed catastrophic insurance. The program's financing arrangements—which departed from established precedent by having Medicare beneficiaries bear all the costs of the new program without subsidy from the rest of the population and requiring higher-income beneficiaries to pay much higher costs for the new benefits—led to its undoing. Widespread confusion about the law's provisions, spread in part by groups opposed to the program, grew among seniors, and the support of Medicare enrollees for the program fell markedly.[41] In 1989, Congress responded

[40] *See* OBERLANDER, *supra* note 27.

[41] RICHARD HIMMELFARB, CATASTROPHIC POLITICS: THE RISE AND FALL OF THE MEDICARE CATASTROPHIC COVERAGE ACT OF 1988 (1995).

to mounting opposition to catastrophic coverage by canceling the program entirely, a remarkable turnabout that would leave long-standing gaps in Medicare coverage intact even as healthcare costs continued to rise.

V The 1990s: Changing Politics, Changing Program

At no time during the 1980s did national health insurance have even a remote chance of becoming law. During the Reagan years, as prospects for universal coverage and system-wide cost containment faded and federal deficits ballooned, policy-makers focused on restraining the spending growth in Medicare. But a deep recession during 1990–1991, surging healthcare costs and rising premiums for employer-sponsored insurance, concern over the impact of rising costs on the competitiveness of American business, and a surprise victory in a Pennsylvania Senate election by Harris Wofford vaulted healthcare reform back onto the national agenda. America's uninsured population had grown substantially during the 1980s, and the confluence of a sharp economic downturn and resurgence of medical inflation fueled a growing sense of medical insecurity.[42]

In 1992 Bill Clinton became the first Democrat since Jimmy Carter in 1976 to win a presidential election. He campaigned on a promise to revitalize the American economy, and healthcare reform figured prominently in his agenda. Medicare itself played only a modest role in the Clinton health reform plan. Projected savings from Medicare spending were used to help pay for the costs expanded coverage (the administration also proposed establishment of a Medicare prescription drug benefit). The Clinton plan's vision of universal insurance built not on Medicare's social insurance roots, but on employer-sponsored insurance and a regulated marketplace of competing plans.[43] That model embodied the rise of neoliberal thinking among many Democrats who believed that the achievement of liberal ends (promoting access to health insurance) depended on the embrace of conservative means (relying on a competitive, regulated market as the source of insurance). This thinking would in turn come to have a profound impact on Medicare policy in later years.

With broad Democratic majorities in Congress, in 1993 the stars seemed aligned for enactment of universal health insurance. But the administration's Health Security Act never came close to passage. In 1994, only a year after its introduction, the Clinton plan lay dead.[44]

The demise of the Clinton reform effort once again redirected American health policy away from comprehensive proposals and towards controlling the budgetary costs of public insurance programs. In the 1994 elections, Republicans won their first congressional

[42] Jacob S. Hacker, The Road to Nowhere: The Genesis of President Clinton's Plan for Health Security (1997).

[43] Paul Starr, The Logic of Health Care Reform: Why and How the President's Plan Will Work (1992).

[44] *See* Theda Skocpol, Boomerang: Clinton's Health Security Effort and the Turn Against Government in US Politics (1996); Haynes Johnson & David S. Broder, The System: The American Way of Politics at the Breaking Point (1996).

majorities in both the House and Senate in forty years. New Speaker of the House Newt Gingrich saw entitlement reform as crucial to the GOP revolution. In 1995, Congress passed sweeping legislation to overhaul Medicare as well as Medicaid. Those reforms included substantial reductions in projected Medicare spending—savings that were crucial to the GOP's plans to balance the federal budget. Republicans also proposed introducing an annual cap on Medicare spending and new options for beneficiaries to leave traditional Medicare for private insurance plans. Their aim was to transform Medicare into a more conservative programmatic model, injecting competition, consumer choice, and market forces into the program while redefining the meaning of its budgetary entitlement status. Speaker Gingrich predicted that the GOP proposal would cause traditional Medicare to "wither on the vine."[45] Democrats fiercely resisted the plan, and President Clinton ultimately seized the mantle of protector of Medicare and Medicaid, vetoing the GOP legislation with the same pen Lyndon Johnson had used to sign Medicare into law. Clinton would recover from the 1994 congressional elections to win the White House again in 1996, a campaign during which he emphasized his support for Medicare.

This conflict presaged the emergence of dynamics in Medicare politics that today are common. After the 1994 elections, for the first time, a Republican-majority Congress governed Medicare. In its first three decades of operation, both Democrats and Republicans had accepted Medicare's core structure. Reforms were adopted to strengthen the federal government's purchasing power and to improve Medicare benefits, but there was no effort to fundamentally remake Medicare. Moreover, in this period Medicare policy-making was often bipartisan, as both parties supported efforts to rationalize Medicare through prospective payment systems and tighter controls on payments to providers that generated budgetary savings. After 1995, though, partisan divisions on Medicare would become commonplace. Debates over the program would more regularly revolve around fundamental issues of program restructuring rather than incrementalism.[46] The character of Medicare politics was shifting.

Bipartisanship re-emerged temporarily in 1997 with enactment of the Balanced Budget Amendments (BBA). Despite the earlier defeat of GOP Medicare plans, both Democrats and Republicans agreed on the need for sizable Medicare savings to help reduce the federal budget deficit and address another projected impending shortfall in Medicare's hospital insurance trust fund. The 1997 BBA contained significant reductions in Medicare's payments to hospitals and doctors, broadened prospective payment to encompass inpatient, rehabilitation, skilled nursing facilities, and home health services, and strengthened provisions aimed at reducing fraud and abuse. The law also promoted new private plan options in Medicare under the label of Medicare + Choice (what came to be known as Medicare Part C).[47]

The adoption of Medicare + Choice signaled both the emergence of growing congressional support for a greater role for private insurers in Medicare and the influence of changes in the broader insurance market on public programs. Medicare had, since 1982, allowed private insurance plans (typically health maintenance organizations) to enroll program beneficiaries and receive fixed, capitated payments from the government. While the program started modestly, beneficiary enrollment in private plans took off in the 1990s as what was

[45] *See* OBERLANDER, *supra* note 27. [46] *Id.*

[47] *Id.*; THEODORE R. MARMOR, THE POLITICS OF MEDICARE (2000).

called managed care spread throughout American medical care. The number of beneficiaries obtaining Medicare coverage from private plans grew from 467,000 in 1986 to 2.5 million in 1993, with enrollment accelerating to 7 million by 1999.[48] Medicare represented a new, relatively untapped market for private insurers who recruited enrollees with the promise of extra benefits, benefits that were funded in part through federal formulas that give these plans excess payments. Although the BBA's efforts to accelerate private insurance's hold in Medicare did not succeed—enrollment in such plans would actually decline during 2000–2004—its enactment represented a new direction in Medicare policy.

Indeed, the 1997 BBA reflected an important new political reality as pro-market ideas of competition and private insurance would increasingly shape Medicare policy and find adherents in both parties. The law established a National Bipartisan Commission on the Future of Medicare, co-chaired by Republican Congressman Bill Thomas and Democratic Senator John Breaux. Reporting in 1999, the commission initially recommended converting Medicare into a premium support or managed competition system, but it failed to reach the required supermajority to officially forward its recommendations to Congress.[49] Nonetheless, the commission's majority conclusions underscored the growing appeal of such ideas within Washington. Medicare's political environment was changing, and so was the assumptive world of many policy-makers, both Republicans and Democrats.

VI The Medicare Modernization Act

In 1998, the federal government ran its first budgetary surplus in three decades, and by 2000 the surplus stood at $236 billion.[50] Budget deficit politics had driven Medicare policy for two decades, and as fiscal pressures to restrain program spending receded, the availability of a surplus transformed the politics of Medicare, creating conditions ripe for benefit expansion. The rising costs of prescription drugs and the absence of program coverage for outpatient prescription costs caught policy-makers' attention. In 1999, the Clinton administration proposed a new Medicare prescription drug benefit and Democrats argued that the surplus should be used, in part, to help Medicare beneficiaries pay for the costs of medications. The issue figured prominently in the 2000 presidential election between Al Gore and George W. Bush, with both candidates offering plans to expand Medicare benefits.

Once in the White House, Bush pushed ahead with plans for a Medicare drug benefit, urging GOP majorities in Congress to pass such a plan, even after the projected surplus disappeared amidst the 2001 recession. The administration saw Medicare reform as having crucial political benefits; if Republicans could enact a Medicare prescription drug program, they would neutralize an issue that favored Democrats and potentially win over more senior

[48] *See* Alma McMillan, *Trends in Medicare Health Maintenance Organization Enrollment, 1986–93*, 15 Health Care Financing Rev. 135 (1993); Kaiser Family Foundation, *Total Medicare Advantage Enrollment 1992–2014*, http://kff.org/medicare/slide/total-medicare-advantage-enrollment-1992-2014/ Advantage Enrollment.

[49] Theodore R. Marmor & Gary J. McKissick, *Medicare's Future: Fact, Fiction, and Folly*, 26 Am. J. L. & Med. 225 (2000).

[50] *See* Office of Management and Budget, *supra* note 33.

voters. Bush adviser Karl Rove believed that passing a new Medicare benefit would not only aid the president's 2004 re-election bid, but could also help to realign American politics by facilitating a "permanent" Republican majority.[51]

There was, then, a strong political impetus for expanding Medicare coverage to encompass prescription drugs. The question was what form that expansion would take. Republicans predictably favored provision of a benefit by private plans with subsidized coverage limited to lower-income beneficiaries. In contrast, Democrats unsurprisingly preferred that traditional Medicare operate a program that would be universally available to beneficiaries regardless of income.[52]

Ultimately, what became Medicare Part D ended up combining Democrats' belief in universal, non-means tested benefits (drug coverage would be available to all Medicare enrollees) with Republicans' faith in private insurance and competition and a limited financial commitment that produced a bizarre programmatic structure. The Part D benefit contained an odd gap or "doughnut hole" where coverage for prescription drug costs stopped after a certain expenditure threshold had been reached by beneficiaries only to restart again when expenses reached a higher level. This byzantine structure was the result of self-imposed budgetary constraints that limited the amount of money that Congress and the Bush administration were willing to spend on the program. Even as Medicare benefits were slated for expansion, the generosity of those benefits remained limited. Additionally, the Medicare Modernization Act required wealthier Medicare beneficiaries to pay higher premiums for Medicare Part B starting in 2007—an important precedent in varying Medicare according to beneficiaries' income that both parties would look to expand in subsequent years.[53]

When Congress enacted the Medicare Modernization Act in 2003, for the first time a major component of the Medicare program would be entirely privatized, with prescription drug benefits provided exclusively by private plans that contracted with the federal government.[54] Medicare would not regulate the price of prescription drugs; instead the scheme relied on competition between plans to contain spending. The MMA additionally reconfigured the private insurance option within the Medicare Part C program into Medicare Advantage, and increased federal payments to these plans. The MMA thus aimed both to expand Medicare benefits and to alter the program's structure and philosophy by increasing the role of private plans, promoting competition, and emphasizing the virtues of individual choice of plan. Medicare was increasingly a hybrid program, with traditional insurance sponsored by the federal government operating alongside a growing private market. By 2009, over 10 million Medicare beneficiaries, comprising 23% of all program enrollees, had

[51] Jonathan Oberlander, *The Bush Administration and the Politics of Medicare Reform*, *in* BUILDING COALITIONS, MAKING POLICY: THE POLITICS OF THE CLINTON, BUSH & OBAMA PRESIDENCIES (Martin A. Levin, et al., eds., 2012).

[52] *See* Thomas R. Oliver, Philip. R. Lee, & Helene L. Lipton, *A Political History of Medicare and Prescription Drug Coverage*, 82 MILBANK Q. 283; Douglas Jaenicke & Alex Waddan, *President Bush and Social Policy: The Strange Case of the Medicare Prescription Drug Benefit*, 121 POL. SCI. Q. 217 (2004); Jonathan Oberlander, *Through the Looking Glass: The Politics of the Medicare Prescription Drug, Improvement, and Modernization Act*, 32 J. HEALTH POL. POL'Y & L. 187 (2007).

[53] Theodore R. Marmor & Jacob S. Hacker, *Medicare Reform and Social Insurance: The Clashes of 2003 and Their Potential Fallout*, 5 YALE J. HEALTH POL'Y L. & ETHICS 475 (2005).

[54] KIMBERLY J. MORGAN & ANDREA LOUISE CAMPBELL, *The Delegated Welfare State: Medicare, Markets and the Governance of Social Policy* (2011).

joined the private insurance plans as part of Medicare Advantage; in 2014, nearly one out of every three Medicare beneficiaries was enrolled in a private plan.[55] The market has come to Medicare.

VII Obamacare

In 2009, universal health insurance returned to the agenda as President Barack Obama pushed for enactment of major reform legislation. Democrats sought to cover the uninsured by establishing new purchasing pools where those without insurance could obtain subsidized private insurance, regulating private insurers to prevent them from discriminating against persons with pre-existing conditions, expanding Medicaid to reach Americans below the federal poverty line, and requiring most persons to obtain coverage or pay a fine. Many reformers also argued for inclusion of a so-called "public option," a Medicare-like insurance program operated by the federal government that would be available to the uninsured in purchasing pools (insurance "exchanges") alongside private plans.[56] The public plan was explicitly modeled on Medicare and its emergence as a reform option meant that Medicare was once again shaping Democratic thinking about health reform. However, while a plan for a public option passed the House it could not muster a majority in the Senate, and subsequent compromise proposals to instead offer Americans aged fifty-five to sixty-four the option of buying into Medicare also failed to win enactment.

The defeat of the public option and Medicare expansion proposals showed just how far American health politics has moved away from the original Medicare strategy. A Democratic administration and congressional majorities succeeded in winning passage of the most important healthcare reform since 1965. Yet not even a modest expansion of Medicare could pass Congress. "Near" universal insurance had finally arrived in the United States, but when it did, Medicare had been marginalized, playing no role in this major expansion of health insurance.[57] Obamacare rested less on the Medicare strategy and social insurance principles than on conservative and neo-liberal conceptions of healthcare reform's appropriate shape.[58] Indeed, Obamacare's partial reliance on private insurance and health plan competition resembled, in key respects, the 2003 Medicare prescription drug program supported by the Bush administration. That resemblance largely reflected a political calculus; many Democrats believed that only a health reform model that relied on private insurance could pass Congress.[59]

[55] *See* Kaiser Family Foundation, *supra* note 48.

[56] Jacob S. Hacker, *Healthy Competition: The Whys and How of Public Plan Choice*, 360 New Eng. J. Med. 2269 (2009).

[57] *See* Oberlander & Marmor, *supra* note 2.

[58] Jonathan Oberlander, *Between Liberal Aspirations and Market Forces: Obamacare's Precarious Balancing Act*, 42 J.L. Med. & Ethics 31 (2014).

[59] *See* Theodore R. Marmor, *Book Review: Critical: What We Can Do About the Health-Care Crisis*, 25 Notre Dame J.L. Ethics & Pub. Pol'y 481 (2011); Jonathan Oberlander & Theodore R. Marmor, *The Health Bill Explained at Last*, N.Y. Rev. Books, Aug. 19, 2010, at 61; Theodore R. Marmor & Jonathan Oberlander, *The Patchwork: Health Reform, American Style*, 72 Soc. Sci. & Med. 125 (2011).

The 2010 Affordable Care Act (ACA) did have significant implications for Medicare.[60] It expanded Medicare limited prescription drug coverage and enhanced other program benefits, including coverage for preventive screenings. Medicare also served as a source of projected savings to help finance the ACA's insurance expansion, primarily through reducing the expected rate of growth in payments to hospitals and private Medicare Advantage plans. Obamacare additionally raised Medicare payroll taxes on higher-income Americans and subjected investment income to a surtax, while expanding the use of income-related premiums among Medicare beneficiaries. The ACA more broadly treated Medicare as a platform to test a range of new initiatives—including accountable care organizations (ACOs) and bundled payment—that aim to reform the delivery of medical services and control its spending. The law also established the Independent Payment Advisory Board (IPAB), a commission charged with developing plans to slow Medicare expenditures if they rose faster than a defined threshold. In that circumstance, if Congress did not pass an alternative plan to produce the required Medicare savings, IPAB's proposals would be implemented by the Secretary of Health and Human Services.

The ACA reignited partisan conflict over Medicare. Republicans charged that Democrats were "raiding" Medicare funds to cover the uninsured.[61] In fact, the slowdown in Medicare spending growth produced by the ACA would strengthen the program's financial condition and help program beneficiaries by restraining increases in the cost-sharing that Medicare requires. The ACA debate gave rise as well to a series of consequential myths about Medicare—that Obamacare would "pull the plug on grandma," create "death panels," and stop chemotherapy for older Americans. None of these allegations, of course, had a shred of truth. But their spread demonstrated how controversial changes in Medicare can be, the high political stakes associated with program reform, and the anxiety that many older Americans feel about their insurance coverage.

VIII Lessons from Medicare's First Fifty Years

What have the past fifty years taught us about Medicare politics? In some respects, Medicare has been a remarkably stable program. Medicare still primarily covers seniors, it remains a social insurance program, much of its original benefit package is intact, its major financing mechanisms still operate, and the separation between Medicare hospital and physician insurance endures. The relative stability of these arrangements underscores the lasting impact of the choices made in 1965, which continue to shape Medicare policy and politics today.

Notwithstanding these elements of stability, another important theme is that the politics of Medicare can shift substantially. At Medicare's enactment in 1965, policy-makers were solicitous of the AMA and healthcare industry. Medicare administrators sought to ensure

[60] Karen Davis et. al., Commonwealth Fund, The Affordable Care Act and Medicare: How the Law Is Changing the Program and the Challenges that Remain (2015).

[61] Robert Pear, *Reshaping Medicare Brings Hard Choices*, N.Y. Times, Apr. 12, 2011.

a smooth beginning for the program, and permissive reimbursement policies that generated generous payments to medical providers prevailed. Over time, though, the medical care industry's hold on the program weakened. As pressures for deficit reduction intensified, federal policy-makers adopted stronger cost containment policies in Medicare. Therein lies another lesson: while Medicare's political world encompasses numerous powerful interest groups that influence federal policy, those groups do not always get what they want.[62]

Another crucial lesson is that Medicare does not live on an island, and consequently its politics are shaped by broader political currents. Changes in American political alignments, governing philosophies, private health insurance, and medical care delivery—all had substantial repercussions for Medicare's development. In 1965, American liberalism was ascendant. Medicare's design—a social insurance program operated by the federal government and open to all Americans regardless of income—reflected the preferences of its liberal architects and the prevailing political order. Medicare was to be the cornerstone of national health insurance. Yet as American politics moved rightward beginning in the 1970s, Medicare's political environment fundamentally changed. Not only would Medicare be governed at times by Republican presidents and GOP congressional majorities, but there was a profound shift in policy-makers' assumptions about the best way to organize health insurance programs. Competition, choice, and reliance on private insurers became influential ideas in U.S. healthcare policy, with Republicans and some Democrats supporting changes in Medicare to promote market forces.

As a result of both policy initiatives and market developments, Medicare's programmatic structure, its identity, and the boundary between public and private within the program have changed substantially.[63] The rise of pro-market ideas and policies in Medicare, and the growing footprint of private insurers within the program, underscores how wider political and economic developments can alter a government program like Medicare. These market advances in Medicare constitute a creeping privatization of federal health insurance. The question of how far that privatization should go has triggered intense debates in Washington over Medicare reform, a subject we return to in the concluding section.

Comparing Medicare's early experience to that of the Affordable Care Act further illustrates how much U.S. politics have shifted in the last half century, with important implications for healthcare programs. Despite a long, heated debate over its enactment, once it was law the Medicare debate receded. Medicare immediately gained legitimacy, and there were no serious political or legal efforts to overturn it. In contrast, five years after its passage, Obamacare was still fighting for its survival, and trying to overcome legal and legislative efforts to derail its implementation. In large part, the contrasting experiences reflect the growing partisan polarization of American politics, a dynamic that affects not just the ACA but Medicare as well.

A final lesson has to do with the character of Medicare politics. Medicare is periodically the subject of intense political debate, marked by exaggerated claims that the sky will fall unless some fundamental change is made in the financing, benefits, or administration of the program.[64] That political attention often has had less to do with legitimate concerns about

[62] *See* Timothy Stoltzfus Jost, *Governing Medicare*, 51 ADMIN. L. REVIEW 39 (1999); Bruce C. Vladeck, *The Political Economy of Medicare* 18 HEALTH AFF. 22 (1999).

[63] *See* MORGAN & CAMPBELL, *supra* note 54.

[64] *See* Marmor & Hacker, *supra* note 53.

Medicare's real (if usually overstated) faults. Instead, it has been principally fueled by alarmist rhetoric from those ideologically opposed to Medicare's social insurance structure.[65]

Unfortunately, claims of crisis cloud what is fundamentally at issue in Medicare reform and distort the program's actual fiscal condition. Episodic warnings that Medicare is "going bankrupt" or facing insolvency are exploited by would-be reformers to promote adoption of their preferred policy ideas.[66] The frightening specter of bankruptcy is used to justify immediate, and at times, radical policy adjustments. But Medicare is in no danger of going bankrupt or becoming insolvent. There is absolutely no chance that the federal government would ever let a program with tens of millions of elderly beneficiaries run out of funds so that it had to stop paying for their medical care.

The dynamics of earmarked financing—the program's hospital insurance trust fund is financed almost exclusively from payroll taxes dedicated to that fund—is the only reason that talk about future insolvency arises in Medicare. Programs that are instead funded out of general tax revenues, such as Medicaid or defense, do not trigger such bankruptcy rhetoric.[67] The basics of Medicare accounting are not well understood by the public or clearly explained by the media, adding to the confusion and the misleading sense of crisis that regularly accompanies debates over program reform.

IX The Future of Medicare

After a half century of operation, Medicare's centrality to American medical care is indisputable. What is in dispute, though, is whether and how Medicare should change in coming years. For the reformers who yearn for Medicare for All, the program remains a model that should be emulated and expanded. For critics, Medicare is instead a symbol of what is wrong with government-run insurance and it should embrace market competition and privatization. Charges that Medicare is unsustainable in its current form and cannot afford to absorb the baby boom generation continue to figure in the Medicare debate. That Medicare has in fact thrived for five decades, despite perennial worries about its fiscal future, has evidently not given critics much pause.[68] Moreover, over several decades costs have risen more slowly in Medicare than in private insurance as Medicare's cost containment measures have generated substantial savings.[69] These results suggest three crucial—and frequently overlooked—policy lessons from Medicare. First, private insurers are not, as is often assumed, inherently better than the government at controlling medical care spending. Both American public and private insurers have struggled to restrain costs, yet Medicare has fared significantly better than the private sector since 1985. Second, price regulation, often derided in the United

[65] Joseph White, False Alarm: Why the Greatest Threat to Social Security and Medicare Is the Campaign to "Save" Them (2005).

[66] *See* Oberlander, *supra* note 27.

[67] *See* Paul Pierson, Dismantling the Welfare State: Reagan, Thatcher and the Politics of Retrenchment (1995); Eric Patashnik, Putting Trust in the US Budget: Federal Trust Funds and the Politics of Commitment (2000); Oberlander, *supra* note 27; Marmor, *supra* note 47.

[68] Jonathan Oberlander, *Voucherizing Medicare*, 39 J. Health Pol. Pol'y & L. 470 (2014).

[69] Marilyn Moon, Medicare: A Policy Primer (2006).

States as a crude form of cost control, has in fact worked. Much of the savings achieved in Medicare spending since the 1980s has been a function of controlling the prices that the program pays for services. And third, the rate of growth in medical care spending is amenable to policy intervention and not simply a function of changes in technology and demography that produce immutable growth in costs. Policy-makers are indeed able to implement changes to Medicare that substantially slow down the rate of increase in program expenditures, changes that can drastically alter long-term projections about Medicare spending.[70] That is one important reason why long-term projections of Medicare spending and program financing shortfalls should be treated with significant caution.

Nonetheless, the conviction that Medicare is financially unsustainable and must be restructured is widely held by policy-makers and analysts. They often cite population aging, the retirement of the baby boomers, and the resulting substantial increase in Medicare enrollment that is expected over the next two decades as "evidence" that Medicare is unsustainable and requires far-reaching changes.[71] Among the conventional options for reform that promise to reduce federal expenditures are two that regularly appear in discussions of Medicare policy: converting Medicare into a full-fledged voucher or premium support program, and raising the eligibility age for Medicare from sixty-five to sixty-seven, both designed to reduce federal spending on the program (not overall healthcare spending either for seniors or for other Americans).[72]

The popularity of these options among many policy-makers and analysts is testament to the confused state of thinking about Medicare.[73] Medicare spending has grown over many decades at a lower rate than that of private insurance.[74] Since 2006, there has been a pronounced slowdown in the annual rate of increase in Medicare expenditures.[75] What's more, the ACA is projected to generate additional Medicare savings in coming years. In short, Medicare is not in any immediate financial crisis and there is no critical need to transform it into a voucher system or anything else.

Neither does the increased number of Americans aging into Medicare during the next two decades require radical program restructuring. Other rich democracies such as those in Northern Europe have populations significantly older than the United States while spending far less on medical care in their national health insurance systems. That reality belies the assumptions that demography is destiny and population aging requires the adoption of market solutions to moderate growth in healthcare spending.[76] Moreover, raising the Medicare eligibility age would save the federal government little money and raise costs for states, private insurers, older Americans, and other parts of the federal government that would have to pay for alternative sources of insurance to replace Medicare for sixty-five- and sixty-six-year olds. This is a strategy of cost-shifting rather than serious cost containment.[77]

[70] *See* Chapin White, *Why Did Medicare Spending Growth Slow Down?*, 27 HEALTH AFF. 793 (2008); WHITE, *supra* note 65.

[71] *See* Antos, *supra* note 4.

[72] Theodore R. Marmor, Jonathan Oberlander, & Joseph White, *Medicare and the Federal Budget: Misdiagnosed Problems, Inadequate Solutions*, 30 J. POL'Y ANALYSIS & MGMT. 928 (2011).

[73] *Id.* [74] *See* Oberlander, *supra* note 68.

[75] CHAPIN WHITE, JULIETTE CUBANSKI, & TRICIA NEUMAN, HOW MUCH OF THE MEDICARE SPENDING SLOWDOWN CAN BE EXPLAINED? INSIGHTS AND ANALYSIS FROM 2014 (Kaiser Family Foundation, 2014).

[76] *See* Marmor, Oberlander, & White, *supra* note 72. [77] *Id.*

Proposals to limit the supplemental insurance that Medicare beneficiaries can buy and increase their deductibles would similarly shift costs to beneficiaries. Such proposals reflect the myth, prevalent in the United States, that patient cost-sharing ("skin in the game") is essential to containing medical care spending. No other rich democracy relies on patient cost-sharing as a primary strategy of cost control—and all of them spend much less on medical care than the United States. These proposals also ignore the reality that Medicare beneficiaries, because of persistent gaps in program coverage, already pay a significant share of their medical care costs. In 2010, enrollees in traditional Medicare "spent $4,745 out-of-pocket for health care," including premiums and the costs of medical and long-term care services, with beneficiaries in poorer self-reported health paying much more than healthier beneficiaries.[78]

Other Medicare reform options are less controversial but unproven. It is unclear, for all the hype, if payment and delivery system reforms like ACOs will produce substantial savings. The current bipartisan enthusiasm for replacing traditional fee-for-service reimbursement with payments based on outcomes and quality is another case of searching for panaceas in health policy. Bipartisan legislation in 2015 replaced Medicare's troubled Sustainable Growth Rate formula for paying physicians with a new methodology that purports to rewards value. But there is scant evidence that value-based payments will save much money, nor clarity on what constitutes value in medical practice. The Independent Payment Advisory Board, which was to provide a check outside of Congress on Medicare spending, has yet to get off the ground in a polarized partisan environment not conducive to independent commissions.[79]

The debate over controlling Medicare spending, then, is dominated both by ideological and aspirational agendas, neither of which provides a reliable foundation for containing medical care expenditures. In the short run, implementing the ACA's reductions in Medicare's payments to medical providers is the surest way to slow spending growth. In the long run, adoption of all-payer cost controls—setting limits not just on Medicare but private insurance spending as well—would, if politically feasible, strengthen the program's capacity to contain costs.

How Medicare should change is, of course, a different matter than how it will change. Some reforms to Medicare—more tightening of payments to medical providers, a greater reliance on charging higher-income beneficiaries more for Medicare coverage, and continued experimentation with new payment methods—are likely to occur no matter which party holds Congress and the White House. The fate and character of major reform of Medicare, though, depends largely on external political and economic circumstances. Fiscal conditions, including pressures from federal budget deficits that would be exacerbated by another recession, could pave the way for bolder reforms to Medicare's benefits and financing arrangements. Ambitious changes to Medicare that push it further to the market are more likely to occur if a Republican president with GOP majorities shapes its agenda. A government controlled by Democrats would likely pursue more incremental reforms. Following a quarter century of intermittent partisan conflict over Medicare, it remains to be seen whether Democrats and Republicans can overcome their polarization and agree on a bipartisan package of changes—and bipartisan agreement is no guarantee that such a reform package would be sensible. Fifty years after its enactment, then, the Medicare debate continues.

[78] Juliette Cubanski & Cristina Bocutti, *Medicare Coverage, Affordability, and Access*, 39 GENERATIONS 26.

[79] Jonathan Oberlander & Marisa Morrison, *Failure to Launch: The Independent Payment Advisory Board's Uncertain Prospects*, 369 NEW ENG. J. MED. 105 (2013).

CHAPTER 34

MEDICAID AT FIFTY

SARA ROSENBAUM

I Executive Summary

Medicaid is arguably the most unique and complex component of U.S. healthcare financing. Unencumbered by the risk principles that govern private health insurance, Medicaid assumes tasks essential to any healthcare system but beyond the limits of private insurance: insuring people who cannot afford even modest out-of-pocket costs; operating as a safety net, under continuous open-enrollment principles that enable access at the point of illness and disability; coverage that extends beyond the limits of private health insurance and that reaches long-term services and supports; financial support for related social programs; and infrastructure support for providers serving impoverished and medically underserved communities. Structured as a federal/state legal power-sharing arrangement, Medicaid and its basic aims were preserved and strengthened by the Affordable Care Act (ACA). Medicaid's multiple aims give the program its astounding parameters and help explain its many challenges: the continuing political battle over its size and scope; federal/state power-sharing in a health reform era; aligning Medicaid with a restructured, subsidized private insurance market; and preserving Medicaid as a privately enforceable guarantee.

II Introduction

This chapter examines Medicaid's role, evolution, and future. It begins with a discussion of Medicaid's aims, parameters, and impact and considers the impact of the Patient Protection and Affordable Care Act (hereinafter the Affordable Care Act (ACA)). It concludes with an assessment of Medicaid's major challenges and reflects on its future.

Medicaid has been termed the "workhorse" of the U.S. healthcare system.[1] Its unique capabilities, coupled with its relatively low cost in relation to private insurance[2] explain why,

[1] Alan Weil, *There's Something About Medicaid*, 22 Health Aff. 13 (2003).

[2] Medicaid per capita costs about two-thirds of comparable plans sold in the private insurance market ($6000 versus $9000 in 2012 dollars) because it deeply discounts provider payments. *See*

as part of the ACA, Congress chose to preserve Medicaid as the pathway to coverage for low-income and medically vulnerable Americans.

Medicaid is foundational to American healthcare financing. But the program is burdened by size and political and operational complexities that stem from the breadth of its aims and the federal/state power-sharing arrangement on which it rests. Medicaid constantly faces a raft of legal, political, and operational challenges and an incessant drumbeat of calls for radical overhaul or repeal.[3] Yet Medicaid survives; indeed, with the enthusiastic backing of the insurance industry, Medicaid became the foundation for the ACA's coverage expansions.[4]

The policy significance of Congress's decision to rest health reform for the poorest Americans on Medicaid was not lost on Chief Justice John Roberts, even if his legal analysis was flawed. In *NFIB v. Sebelius*,[5] the Chief Justice, writing for the Court, concluded that restructuring Medicaid to cover all nonelderly low-income adults amounted to an unconstitutional coercion on the states. Rather than nullifying the expansion altogether, took the lesser step of barring the Secretary of Health and Human Services from enforcing the expansion as a mandatory condition of state participation in traditional Medicaid. The Chief Justice's coercion opinion rested on a legally flawed characterization of the adult Medicaid expansion as a "new" program in which states were forced to participate as a condition of receiving traditional program funding. Justice Ginsburg unmasked this erroneous legal reasoning by closely examining the statute itself,[6] which expresses the ACA Medicaid expansion simply as an amendment grafted onto a fifty-year-old statute. Regardless however, the Chief Justice was quite correct when he observed the transformational impact of the expansion, which, in his words, fundamentally altered Medicaid from "a program to care for the neediest among us [into an] element of a comprehensive national plan to provide universal health insurance coverage."[7]

With the ACA amendments, Medicaid's position as the principal source of health insurance for the poor was reinforced. Medicaid is designed to perform like health insurance in that it pays for a wide range of (overwhelmingly private) healthcare providers for covered care and treatment furnished to eligible people enrolled in the program. But Medicaid is also structured to operate unencumbered by the risk principles that undergird private insurance such as medical underwriting or the use of exclusionary coverage terms that bar payment for long-term patients, treatments, and conditions. Although the ACA takes the monumental step of barring insurers from denying access to coverage based on health status or preexisting condition, the law's coverage reforms preserve the basic design of commercial insurance products. This design restricts enrollment to specified time periods unrelated to the need for healthcare. It also restrains financing to the relatively limited continuum of healthcare needs shared among most working-age adults and their by-and-large healthy children. In other

Congressional Budget Office, Estimates of the Insurance Coverage Provisions of the Affordable Care Act Updated for the Recent Supreme Court Decision (2012).

[3] A Google search of the words "Medicaid is broken" yields more than 4 million entries. (Google search conducted on May 26, 2014).

[4] *See* John E. McDonough, Inside National Health Reform (2011).

[5] NFIB v. Sebelius, 132 S. Ct. 2566, 2607 (2012).

[6] To see the Court's error, compare 42 U.S.C. § 1396a(a)(10)(A)(i), both before and after the ACA's 2010 amendments. Far from establishing a new program, the ACA simply amended a single provision of the statute.

[7] *Sebelius*, 132 S. Ct. at 2606.

words, even after the ACA, private insurance continues to offer limited access and limited protection at best against the cost of caring for children and adults with serious and disabling health problems. Furthermore, even those services that private insurance does cover are subject to considerable patient cost-sharing; standard "silver level" health plans sold in the health insurance Marketplace are capped at a 70% actuarial value[8] for all but the lowest income populations.[9]

Medicaid steps into this breach, with concepts of coverage and protections against heavy cost-sharing that extend beyond the furthest reaches of private insurance. To be sure, certain components of Medicaid function like the private health insurance market. A prime example is Medicaid managed care organizations that, like private insurers, sell health plans to Medicaid agencies and now account for three-quarters of all Medicaid beneficiaries.[10] Furthermore, states are now in the process of moving even heavily health-burdened beneficiaries into managed care arrangements. In reality however, these companies tend to operate differently from normal insurers; they offer higher levels of coverage and gear their services and networks toward heavily impoverished populations facing elevated health risks.[11] In sum, whereas private insurance of necessity operates under the principles of financial risk avoidance, Medicaid has been built to embrace risk, covering populations and services outside commercial insurance norms.

But Medicaid's size and complexity also have led to a cascade of political problems, culminating in the constitutional challenge to the ACA's adult Medicaid expansion, famously characterized by the Chief Justice in *NFIB v. Sebelius* as a "gun to the head."[12] Medicaid remains a poorly understood program, despite the fact that it has consistently emerged as the solution of choice to a host of difficult problems. Some of these problems, such as the need for long-term care, are present in any healthcare system. Others are the direct result of a national choice to rest healthcare financing largely on a private insurance base. To be sure, health insurers now must sell to everyone who can afford coverage, but they remain free to select their geographic and product markets, and by and large, to design their products.[13] This autonomy, even in the wake of the ACA, effectively enables insurers to bypass the nation's poorest communities in favor of wealthier prospects,[14] to shape their products to avoid hard and costly cases,[15] and to

[8] 42 U.S.C. §§ 18022 (c) and (d) (2014). [9] 42 U.S.C. § 18071 (c)(1)(B)(i) (2010).

[10] Centers for Medicare and Medicaid Services, 2011 Medicaid Managed Care Enrollment Report: Summary Statistics as of July 1, 2011 1, *available at* http://www.medicaid.gov/Medicaid-CHIP-Program-Information/By-Topics/Data-and-Systems/Downloads/2011-Medicaid-MC-Enrollment-Report.pdf.

[11] For an overview of Medicaid managed care, *see* Medicaid and CHIP Payment and Access Commission, Report To Congress: The Evolution of Managed Care in Medicaid (June 2011).

[12] NFIB v. Sebelius, 132 S. Ct. 2566, 2609 (2012). *See generally* The Health Care Case: The Supreme Court's Decision and Its Implications (Nathan Persily et al. eds., 2013).

[13] Congress specified ten classes of essential health benefits as a bare minimum for insurers' product. 42 U.S.C. § 18022(b). Implementing federal regulations, 45 C.F.R. § 156 et seq., provide very little amplification.

[14] Julie Appleby & Jay Hancock, *Thousands of Mississippi Consumers May Not Be Offered Insurance Subsidies*, Kaiser Health News (June 29, 2013), http://www.kaiserhealthnews.org/stories/2013/june/30/mississippi-insurance-marketplace-rural-counties.aspx?referrer=search (reporting on the refusal of private insurers to sell in thirty-six of Mississippi's eighty-two counties).

[15] Federal regulations defining essential health benefits do not stop insurers from discriminating against persons with disabilities. Sara Rosenbaum & Joel Teitelbaum, *A Lost Opportunity for Persons with*

select provider networks oriented to more affluent customers.[16] In a time of market restructuring and concerns over whether the market, so restructured, can withstand risk, Medicaid endures as a powerful backstop to the entire system.

III Medicaid's Missions, Parameters, and Impact

a. A Thumbnail Sketch of Medicaid

Within a single legislative authority, Congress has built a program encompassing several distinct missions. Codified at Title XIX of the Social Security Act, Medicaid has grown exponentially in response to critical external influences—a broad legislative mandate, the rise of poverty, the erosion of private health insurance, an aging society, and the underlying cost of healthcare. While Congress has reined in Medicaid at certain points, in fact lawmakers have not only left its basic parameters untouched but repeatedly have broadened its scope as new needs emerged. In 1966 Medicaid covered 4 million people and cost federal and state governments a combined $1 billion; by 20154 the program reached over 70 million people at an overall cost of roughly $450 billion, about 57% of which was federal expenditures; by 2022 the program is projected to reach 80 million people.[17]

Medicaid is administered by the states and funded jointly by the state and federal governments. Enacted pursuant to Congress's "Spending Clause" powers, Medicaid entitles states to federal funding as long as they comply with program requirements. Its structure is as a series of mandates and options for participating states. States must cover certain groups of people, while other groups are optional.[18] Individuals must be given the opportunity to apply whenever they need help, and states must determine eligibility and furnish medical assistance coverage and services with reasonable promptness and must offer retroactive coverage.[19] States must cover certain benefits and have the option to offer many others.[20] In general, cost-sharing must be nominal and premiums are banned for the most part.[21] With

Disabilities? The Final Essential Health Benefits Rule, Health Aff. (Mar. 11, 2013), http://healthaffairs.org/blog/2013/03/11/a-lost-opportunity-for-persons-with-disabilities-the-final-essential-health-benefits-rule/?view=full).

[16] The ACA establishes only limited network and access requirements, and the administration has implemented even these requirements with a light hand. Compare 42 U.S.C. § 18031(c)(1)(C) (requiring health plans sold in exchanges to contract with "those essential community providers, where available") with implementing federal regulations that narrow the obligation. *See* 45 C.F.R. § 156.120; cciio & cms, 2015 Letter to Issuers in the Federally-Facilitated Marketplace (2014), *available at* http://www.healthreformgps.org/wp-content/uploads/2015-final-issuer-letter-3-14-2014.pdf.

[17] Department of Health and Human Services, 2013 Actuarial Report on the Financial Outlook for Medicaid i-iv; Table 3 at 24 (2013).

[18] The ACA's low-income adult expansion remains on the books as a mandate, 42 U.S.C. § 1396a(a)(10)(A)(i)(VIII), but enforcement is prohibited under *Sebelius*.

[19] 42 U.S.C. §§ 1396a(a)(8) and 1396a(a)(34) (2014).

[20] 42 U.S.C. §§ 1396a(a)(10) and 1396(d) (2014).

[21] 42 U.S.C. §§ 1396a(a)(14) and 1396o(a)(3) (2014).

certain exceptions for "safety net" providers, described below, states are given broad latitude over provider payment levels and methods.[22]

Since its enactment, Medicaid also has acted as a purchaser of both public and private insurance. States use Medicaid to buy Medicare for the poorest Medicare beneficiaries, making them dually eligible for both Medicare and Medicaid. In these situations, Medicaid finances services and cost-sharing that Medicare does not cover, such as Part A and B deductibles and copayments, eyeglasses, hearing aids, and long-term care. Most states now use Medicaid to buy coverage through managed care arrangements,[23] as well as employer-sponsored coverage where available and cost-effective. At least two states have received permission to conduct special demonstrations under § 1115 of the Social Security Act, discussed elow, to use Medicaid to purchase private health insurance through the health insurance Marketplace.

States participate in Medicaid voluntarily, the last entrant being Arizona in 1982, which launched its program as a § 1115 demonstration.[24] (Over thirty years later Arizona retains its federal demonstration, a testament to the tendency of § 1115 demonstrations to operate in perpetuity). State Medicaid plans must be approved by the Secretary of Health and Human Services (HHS), and the federal/state Medicaid administration relationship is a constant loop of plan amendments, Secretarial reviews, and disputes over payment and amendment approvals. A vast body of federal/state litigation exists, a reflection of the frequently contentious relationship between the parties.[25] States rail at federal oversight and the federal government criticizes state mismanagement. Yet, each side depends on the other: the states, for vast amounts of funding, and the federal government for program management, budget controls, and the delivery of healthcare.

Federal funding is open-ended. The level of federal funding varies by state in accordance with state wealth and ranges from 50% to 74% of each dollar spent on "medical assistance."[26] Federal funding for program administration ranges from 50% to 90%.[27] Federal payments for adults falling within the ACA's Medicaid eligibility expansion categories are set at 100% during the 2014–2016 time period, declining gradually to 90% in 2020.[28] Payments for beneficiaries covered under Medicaid's traditional eligibility pathways—dependent children and caretakers, persons with disabilities, pregnant women, the elderly, and other specified pre-ACA populations—remain at the normal federal medical assistance percentages (FMAP);

[22] 42 U.S.C. § 1396a(a)(13) (creating a broad provision for determination of payment rates for services). *But see* 42 U.S.C. §§ 1396a(a)(13)(A)(iv) and 1396r-4 (varying rates for disproportionate share hospital payments); 42 U.S.C. § 1396b(2)(A)(i) (updating payment policies to rural health clinics and federally qualified health centers).

[23] Sara Rosenbaum & Benjamin D. Sommers, *Using Medicaid to Buy Private Health Insurance—The Great New Experiment?*, 369 NEW ENG. J. MED. 7, 9 (2013).

[24] 42 U.S.C. § 1315a (2010).

[25] This extensive litigation is reported in CCH Medicare/Medicaid Guide.

[26] 42 U.S.C. § 1396b (2014); CENTERS FOR MEDICARE AND MEDICAID SERVICES, CMS FINANCIAL REPORT FISCAL YEAR 2012 6 (2012). Family planning services and supplies are reimbursed at a 90% rate.

[27] 42 U.S.C. § 1396b (2013).

[28] 42 U.S.C. § 1396d(y) (2013), added by PPACA § 2001(a). Special rules apply to states that, prior to enactment of the ACA, already had extended coverage to some or most low income adults through the Social Security Act's §1115 demonstration process. 42 U.S.C. § 1396d(z) (2013), added by PPACA § 2001(a).

states thus pay a higher percentage of costs for people who were eligible prior to the ACA expansion, even if they enroll after the effective date for the expansion (January 1, 2014).

Because of the simplified enrollment process and the mandate to enroll in affordable insurance,[29] Medicaid enrollment has risen even in states that have opted out of the adult expansion, as permitted under *Sebelius*.[30] This fact has further stoked state resentment over the ACA, since even the most recalcitrant state has felt the effects of the reforms. The very fact of the ACA's existence has brought forth individuals who were entitled to Medicaid previously yet had never enrolled, a phenomenon referred to as the "woodwork effect."[31]

Medicaid's structure as a program that embraces financial risk arises from its inherent structure, which is open-ended and targeted on high-need populations and services.[32] Unlike its small companion Children's Health Insurance Program (CHIP), which is subject to aggregate federal funding caps,[33] Medicaid offers as much financing as states need to support the programs they run, and more than half of all spending is for optional populations and services. Thus, states effectively control Medicaid's size, growing or shrinking their programs (in terms of eligible persons, covered services, provider payment rates, and level of administration complexity) as political, economic, and social circumstances dictate.[34] Indeed, even conservative states maintain Medicaid programs that are large, if not relative to other states, then certainly in relation to their other social welfare spending activities. In all states, Medicaid plays a pivotal role in addressing critical population health challenges from reducing infant mortality to community integration of persons with disabilities, responding to disasters natural and man-made disasters,[35] and building and sustaining a healthcare infrastructure in medically underserved communities.

b. Medicaid's Multiple Missions

Medicaid's missions have been expanded but never reduced.

[29] The personal responsibility requirement extends to the poor, but they are exempt from the tax penalty. 26 U.S.C. § 5000A(e)(1) (2010).

[30] *See, e.g.*, Vikki Wachino et al., Kaiser Family Foundation, How Is the ACA Impacting Medicaid Enrollment? (2014), *available at* http://kff.org/medicaid/issue-brief/how-is-the-aca-impacting-medicaid-enrollment/ (last visited Aug. 16, 2014).

[31] *See* Stan Dorn et al., Medicaid Expansion Under the ACA: How States Analyze the Fiscal and Economic Trade-Offs, Urban Institute (2013), *available at* http://www.urban.org/UploadedPDF/412840-Medicaid-Expansion-Under-the-ACA.pdf.

[32] *See* 42 U.S.C. § 1396(f)(2) (2014) (authorizing sums "necessary to carry out the provisions of this section.")

[33] 42 U.S.C. § 1397dd (2013) (providing for annual capped authorization of funding for CHIP). *See generally Children's Health Insurance Program Financing*, Medicaid.gov, http://www.medicaid.gov/Medicaid-CHIP-Program-Information/By-Topics/Financing-and-Reimbursement/Childrens-Health-Insurance-Program-Financing.html.

[34] Laura Snyder et al., Kaiser Family Foundation, Why Does Medicaid Spending Vary Across States: A Chart Book of Factors Driving State Spending (2012), *available at* http://kaiserfamilyfoundation.files.wordpress.com/2013/01/8378.pdf.

[35] *See* Sara Rosenbaum, *U.S. Health Policy in the Aftermath of Hurricane Katrina*, 295 JAMA 437, 437–440 (2006).

Affordable health insurance for very low income people. From its 1965 enactment, Medicaid has provided health insurance for very poor people, offering comprehensive coverage with virtually no cost-sharing. Cash welfare recipients comprised the original poverty group; this meant that equally impoverished individuals and families who failed to meet welfare eligibility standards (presence of a dependent child and deprivation of parental support) were excluded. Over the years however, poverty-based Medicaid eligibility was expanded to include low-income children and pregnant women.[36] But other than as persons with disabilities, pregnant women, or recipients of Aid to Families with Dependent Children (AFDC) consisting of deeply impoverished parents or other caretaker relatives and their minor children,[37] indigent nonelderly adults could not qualify for coverage (unless they resided in states operating Medicaid under § 1115 demonstration authority, discussed below).[38]

The ACA added mandatory coverage of nonelderly adults with family incomes up to 133% of the federal poverty level,[39] while establishing a "maintenance of effort" requirement that, for a specified time period, prevents rollbacks in Medicaid eligibility for children and adults except under limited circumstances.[40] However, the impact of *Sebelius* has been profound. By barring the HHS Secretary from enforcing the mandatory coverage expansion, the Court set the stage for states to opt out of covering all nonelderly low-income adults. As of Fall 2015, twenty states still had not expanded their programs to cover all low income nonelderly adults.[41] Because premium tax subsidies are not available through the ACA's private health insurance Exchanges until household income reaches 100% of the federal poverty level,[42]

[36] 42 U.S.C. § 1396a(a)(10(A)(i)(IV), (VI), and (VII) (2013) (mandatory coverage); 42 U.S.C. § 1396a(a)(10)(A)(ii) (2013) (optional coverage groups). *See* Ian T. Hill, *The Role of Medicaid and Other Governmental Programs in Providing Medical Care for Children and Pregnant Women*, 2 U.S. HEALTH CARE FOR CHILDREN 115 (1992).

[37] AFDC was replaced in 1996 by the Temporary Assistance to Needy Families (TANF) block grant. Pub. L. 104-193 (104th Cong., 2d sess.). Medicaid eligibility remains mandatory for TANF recipients as well as for individuals satisfying states' July 1996 AFDC eligibility standards. 42 U.S.C. § 1396a(a)(10)(A)(i)(I) (2013) and 42 U.S.C. § 1396u-1 (2013). *See* Kaiser Family Foundation, *State Health Facts on Medicaid and CHIP*, http://kff.org/state-category/medicaid-chip/ (last visited Aug. 16, 2014).

[38] For a description of Medicaid demonstrations involving coverage of low-income adults, *see* KAISER FAMILY FOUNDATION, AN OVERVIEW OF RECENT SECTION 1115 MEDICAID DEMONSTRATION WAIVER ACTIVITY (2012), *available at* http://kaiserfamilyfoundation.files.wordpress.com/2013/01/8318.pdf.

[39] 42 U.S.C. § 1396a(a)(10)(A)(i)(VIII) (2013). The actual eligibility standard is 138% of the federal poverty level under amendments enacted in the Health Care and Education Reconciliation Act, Pub. L. 111-152 (111th Cong., 2d sess.), § 1004(e), simultaneous with ACA passage. The amendment added a five-percentage-point income disregard to the 133% standard for both children and adults.

[40] 42 U.S.C. § 1396a(a)(74) (2014) and 42 U.S.C. § 1396gg (2013). For adults, the Medicaid maintenance of effort requirement lasts until the "Secretary determines that an exchange established by the state . . . is fully operational . . ." For children, the maintenance of effort period lasts through FY 2018. States may reduce adult coverage earlier under certain conditions. *See* KAISER FAMILY FOUNDATION, UNDERSTANDING THE MEDICAID AND CHIP MAINTENANCE OF ELIGIBILITY REQUIREMENTS (2012), *available at* http://kaiserfamilyfoundation.files.wordpress.com/2013/01/8204-02.pdf.

[41] *The Coverage Gap: Uninsured Poor Adults in States that Do Not Expand Medicaid—An Update* KAISER FAMILY FOUNDATION (October 23, 2015) http://kff.org/health-reform/issue-brief/the-coverage-gap-uninsured-poor-adults-in-states-that-do-not-expand-medicaid-an-update/.

[42] *See* 26 U.S.C. § 36B(c) (2013), defining the term "applicable taxpayer" for purposes of subsidy eligibility as taxpayers with household incomes between 100% and 400% of the federal poverty level.

consequently, in states that reject the Medicaid expansion[43] the poorest nonelderly adults who do not fit into Medicaid's traditional eligibility categories are completely excluded from coverage. The twenty states that to date have rejected the eligibility expansion accounted for over 3 million adults with Medicaid-level incomes, who fall into a "coverage gap"[44] created by the Court-sanctioned state rejection of the expansion, a move that effectively has left millions without affordable coverage. Medicaid-eligible adults in nonexpansion states are, of course, excused from the federal tax penalty, since insurance is unaffordable.[45] But this is small comfort indeed.

As of fall 2016 virtually all Deep South states had rejected the expansion, accounting for 90 percent of those in the coverage gap; their residents experience the highest concentrations of poverty and constitute a disproportionate percentage of impoverished African American adults.[46] They also bear the heaviest burden of poor health arising from conditions especially amenable to medical treatment.[47] The economic implications are also enormous, underscoring the fact that ideology—not common sense—has fueled states' decisions. One authoritative study has estimated that the opt-out states will lose $423 billion in federal funding between 2013 and 2022, a figure that grows more startling in light of the fact that in order to qualify for these funds, the states collectively would have had to spend only $31 billion over the ten-year time period.[48]

A source of accessible and comprehensive healthcare financing for uninsured and underinsured people with significant healthcare needs. Three aspects of Medicaid fundamentally distinguish it from private health insurance and give the program its true power as a source of healthcare financing. First, Medicaid is continuously accessible. Unlike private health insurance, which is structured to avoid adverse risk selection, Medicaid has no fixed "open enrollment" periods; benefits—whether primary or secondary to private insurance coverage—are available whenever the need for healthcare arises. Thus, while much was made of the initial open enrollment period under the ACA, which began October 1, 2013, Medicaid remains continuously accessible and is not restricted to special enrollment periods.[49]

43 In states that expand Medicaid, premium subsidies begin at 138% of the federal poverty level. 26 U.S.C. § 36B(b)(3)(A) (2011). Recently arrived legal immigrants, ineligible for Medicaid for five years, can qualify for premium subsidies even if their incomes are below the threshold. 26 U.S.C. § 36B(c)(1)(B) (2011).

44 *The Coverage Gap: Uninsured Poor Adults in States That Do Not Expand Medicaid – An Update*, *supra* note 41. (noting that the median eligibility level is 46% of poverty for states that have rejected the Medicaid expansion).

45 *See Medicaid Expansion & What It Means For You*, HEALTHCARE.GOV, https://www.healthcare.gov/what-if-my-state-is-not-expanding-medicaid/ (last visited Aug. 15, 2014).

46 *The Impact of the Coverage Gap in States Not Expanding Medicaid by Race and Ethnicity*, KAISER FAMILY FOUNDATION (Dec. 17, 2013), http://kff.org/disparities-policy/issue-brief/the-impact-of-the-coverage-gap-in-states-not-expanding-medicaid-by-race-and-ethnicity/.

47 Brief of Jonathan H. Adler and Michael F. Cannon as Amici Curiae Supporting Appellants, Jacqueline Halbig, et al. v. Sebelius, et al., (2014) (No. 13-623), *available at* http://www.cato.org/sites/cato.org/files/documents/halbig_-_adler_cannon_amicus_2.pdf.

48 Stan Dorn et al., *What Is the Result of the States Not Expanding Medicaid?*, URBAN INSTITUTE (Aug. 2014), http://www.rwjf.org/content/dam/farm/reports/issue_briefs/2014/rwjf414946.

49 *See* HEALTHCARE.GOV, *supra* note 45.

Second, many Medicaid eligibility categories expressly turn on various types of medical need, medical vulnerability, and disability: pregnancy; a breast or cervical cancer diagnosis; and severe disability sufficient to prevent substantial gainful employment, as defined in the Social Security Act.[50]

Third, Medicaid coverage is singularly comprehensive, and cost-sharing is nominal. The definition of "medical assistance" spans preventive, acute, and long-term institutional and community-based care.[51] While states have the flexibility to impose cost-sharing, this flexibility is tempered, and many types of beneficiaries (e.g., most pregnant women and children, women with breast or cervical cancer, and certain persons receiving long-term care) are by and large shielded from even nominal cost-sharing.

These features combine to make Medicaid the indispensable mechanism for financing healthcare for the poorest patients, as well as treatments excluded by both private health insurance and Medicare. Some beneficiaries who depend on the program for costly treatment and long-term care rely solely on Medicaid as their only source of health insurance. But for millions, Medicaid acts as a supplemental insurer both to Medicare[52] and private insurance.

Medicaid's role as a primary and supplemental insurer of persons with disabilities has evolved over the decades. In addition to establishing mandatory eligibility groups, the original 1965 legislation also created eligibility options, including an option to cover "medically needy" persons who spend down their income on medical care. This optional coverage group consists of individuals whose characteristics link them to an eligibility category (age, disability, blindness, welfare eligibility status, or status as an impoverished child), but whose incomes and resources exceed state-specified levels before their medical spending. As of 2012, thirty-four states maintained medically needy programs.[53] The utility of the medically needy program in financing community care for persons with disabilities has been severely hampered over the decades by a provision, enacted in 1967 in response to rapidly rising state Medicaid expenditures, that caps the medically needy income level at 133% of a state's AFDC payment standard.[54] AFDC payments, never high to begin with, plummeted over the decades; in 2012, the average cash welfare payment under the successor Temporary Assistance for Needy Families (TANF) program had sunk to as little as 20% of the federal

[50] For a discussion of Medicaid's role for more than 9 million with disabilities, *see* MEDICAID AND CHIP PAYMENT AND ACCESS COMMISSION, REPORT TO THE CONGRESS ON MEDICAID AND CHIP (2012), *available at* http://www.modernhealthcare.com/Assets/pdf/CH78650315.PDF.

[51] *See* 42 U.S.C. § 1396d(a) (2013) (defining the term "medical assistance"); *see also* 42 U.S.C. § 1396a(a)(14) (2014) and 42 U.S.C. § 13960 (2010) (cost-sharing requirements).

[52] For example, in 2012, 9.4 million elderly and disabled Medicare beneficiaries also received Medicaid. This figure includes both "full duals" who receive complete Medicaid coverage as well as those with slightly higher incomes who receive Medicaid coverage for Medicare premiums and cost-sharing. *See generally* KATHERINE YOUNG ET AL., KAISER FAMILY FOUNDATION, MEDICAID'S ROLE FOR DUAL ELIGIBLE BENEFICIARIES (2013), *available at* http://kaiserfamilyfoundation.files.wordpress.com/2013/08/7846-04-medicaids-role-for-dual-eligible-beneficiaries.pdf.

[53] KAISER COMMISSION ON MEDICAID AND THE UNINSURED, *The Medicaid Medically Needy Program: Spending and Enrollment Update* (2012), *available at* http://kaiserfamilyfoundation.files.wordpress.com/2013/01/4096.pdf.

[54] For a history of early Medicaid, *see* ROBERT STEVENS & ROSEMARY STEVENS, WELFARE MEDICINE IN AMERICA: A CASE STUDY OF MEDICAID (2004).

poverty level or less.[55] As a result, the medically needy program has become virtually useless for treatments other than catastrophic institutional care bills.

Congress ultimately stepped into the breach of its own creation, expanding coverage options for children and adults with disabilities that are de-linked from the medically needy spend-down system and available even to families with reasonable incomes (for example, working parents with a child with a disability). In situations such as this, most states make Medicaid available (especially in the case of children with disabilities living at home) to families under special income eligibility rules, without the need to spend down. This eligibility innovation was first championed by President Ronald Reagan in response to Katie Beckett,[56] a little girl facing unnecessary institutionalization because, without incurring enormous spend-down exposure, her middle-class family could not qualify for the Medicaid coverage necessary to keep her at home. (Medicaid ironically would have paid her nursing home bills, since at the point of institutionalization Katie would have been treated as residing apart from her parents and thus without disqualifying income or assets).

In addition to expanding eligibility, the Medicaid reforms aimed at helping children and adults with disabilities remain in their communities also permit states to expand coverage to include services such as personal attendants, home modifications, special equipment, respite care, and other items essential to community-based long-term care. (Room and board costs in nonmedical institutions and supportive housing are excluded however).[57] The sheer reach of Medicaid for persons with disabilities is underscored by who receives help: one-third of Medicaid beneficiaries with disabilities receive Medicaid to supplement private or public insurance coverage.[58]

The ACA preserves Medicaid's disability coverage provisions but with one important proviso: Supplemental Medicaid is unavailable to people who receive subsidized coverage from a private health insurance Exchange, since with certain limited exceptions, Medicaid is considered "minimum essential coverage" (MEC), which disqualifies individuals from premium subsidies.[59] To be sure, Medicaid coverage unquestionably satisfies the ACA's MEC requirement. But the impact of not exempting Medicaid's disability-based eligibility groups from persons otherwise excluded from subsidies because they obtain MEC through Medicaid is potentially enormous. As long as states continue to extend Medicaid to optional disability eligibility groups whose household incomes exceed premium subsidy thresholds, failing to exempt these groups from the MEC exclusion means that states must bear all costs on a first dollar basis. This in turn creates an incentive to states to eliminate optional eligibility categories, causing a significant number of beneficiaries to lose coverage while shifting substantial financial risk into the Exchange. The jury is still out, of course, on whether this will come to pass.

[55] Ife Floyd & Liz Schott, *TANF Benefits Continued to Lose Value in 2013*, Center on Budget and Policy Priorities (Oct. 21, 2013), http://www.cbpp.org/cms/?fa=view&id=4034.

[56] Katie Beckett died at the age of thirty-four in 2012. Dennis Hevesi, *Katie Beckett, 34; Inspired Shift on Care*, N.Y. Times Mag., May 23, 2012.

[57] Eligibility groups and service and benefit options are described in *Report to the Congress on Medicaid and CHIP, supra* note 50, at 17–27.

[58] *Id.* at 36–37.

[59] *Individual Shared Responsibility Provision—Minimum Essential Coverage*, Internal Revenue Service (Apr. 2, 2014), *available at* http://www.irs.gov/uac/ACA-Individual-Shared-Responsibility-Provision-Minimum-Essential-Coverage.

Medicaid's support for the healthcare safety net. Medicaid is the principal financial support for healthcare "safety net" hospitals and clinics, a somewhat elusive term that has been defined to mean hospitals and clinics that by mission, custom, or law, disproportionately treat low-income, uninsured, and publicly insured patients.[60] Using the most rigorous definition, the healthcare safety net would focus on public hospitals, federally funded community health centers, and other types of publicly funded health clinics receiving federal, state, or local funding.[61]

The relevance of healthcare safety net providers in a post-health reform world remains high, given the millions of people who will remain uninsured for one reason or another (e.g., undocumented persons, the poor in states that have rejected the Medicaid expansion, people who cannot afford insurance or who experience periodic breaks in coverage).[62] The safety net also remains vital for millions of low-income insured people who reside in medically underserved communities that experience heightened poverty, health risks, and a shortage of primary healthcare.[63] Furthermore, safety net providers remain the only reliable source of treatment for uncovered services such as adult dental and vision care, neither of which is considered an "essential health benefit" under the ACA, the standard that applies to health plans sold in the individual and small group markets, including plans that qualify for premium subsidies.[64]

Medicaid contains special features designed to lend additional support to safety net providers, including special payment rules for community health centers (known as "federally qualified health centers" (FQHCs)) and rural health clinics, as well as annual supplemental state payments (through a special federal pool) to hospitals that treat a "disproportionate" share of low-income and Medicaid-insured patients (known as disproportionate share hospitals (DSH) hospitals).[65]

The ACA leaves the Medicaid payment formula for health centers and rural health clinics untouched; indeed, in order to shield health centers from cost-shifting by qualified health plans, the ACA even extends Medicaid's FQHC payment rules to all health plans governed by the essential health benefit coverage standard.[66] But on the assumption that millions of low-income people would gain insurance coverage, the ACA slashed federal Medicaid (and Medicare) DSH funding by 50% at the point of what Congress thought would be full

[60] *See* INSTITUTE OF MEDICINE, AMERICA'S HEALTH CARE SAFETY NET: INTACT BUT ENDANGERED (Marion Ein Lewin & Stuart Altman eds., 2000).

[61] *See generally* THE HEALTH CARE SAFETY NET IN A POST-REFORM WORLD (Mark A. Hall & Sara Rosenbaum eds., 2012) (discussing safety net issues post-ACA).

[62] For a discussion of coverage instability and breaks in coverage, *see* Pamela Farley Short et al., *Realizing Health Reform's Potential: Maintaining Coverage, Affordability, and Shared Responsibility When Income and Employment Change*, COMMONWEALTH FUND (May 19, 2011), http://www.commonwealthfund.org/publications/issue-briefs/2011/may/maintaining-coverage.

[63] *See* Peter Shin et al., *A Profile of Community Health Center Patients: Implications for Policy*, KAISER FAMILY FOUNDATION (Dec. 23, 2013), http://kff.org/report-section/a-profile-of-community-health-center-patients-introduction/.

[64] 42 U.S.C. § 18022(b) (2014).

[65] Prior to 1990, states' federal funding for disproportionate share hospitals payments was open-ended; Congress capped payments in the wake of aggressive state efforts to maximize revenues for public hospitals. *See* ALISON MITCHELL, CONG. RESEARCH SERV., MEDICAID DISPROPORTIONATE SHARE HOSPITAL PAYMENTS (2013), *available at* http://fas.org/sgp/crs/misc/R42865.pdf.

[66] 42 U.S.C. § 18022(g) (2013).

implementation of the law, including the adult Medicaid expansion. In the wake of *Sebelius* and the state Medicaid expansion opt-out crisis, the administration sought to soften the blow by modifying the DSH funding reduction formula while delaying the effective date of the reductions.[67] This move was later ratified by Congress in 2013, which codified the delay while leaving it on the books.[68]

Support for public education and social welfare programs. Medicaid's final mission—one that tends to be understood only by those familiar with its inner workings and interactions with the rest of the social welfare fabric—is its relationship to social welfare programs such as special education for children, child welfare, programs for children and adults with developmental disabilities or mental illness; food and nutrition programs; social and health supports for persons with HIV/AIDS and people who are homeless; school health services; and early childhood development and child care. All of these programs intersect with Medicaid because they serve virtually the same populations; Medicaid funds necessary healthcare (often in community settings, a marked departure from commercial insurance), while education and welfare programs pay for necessary social and educational services.[69]

c. Medicaid's Role for Selected Populations and Services

Reflecting its major missions, Medicaid's population and health system reach is enormous. Together, Medicaid and CHIP insured one-third of U.S. children under eighteen in 2010.[70] Medicaid finances nearly half of all U.S. births, a testament to pervasive childhood poverty.[71] Medicaid plays a similarly dominant role in long-term care, financing 40% of total national expenditures[72] and 40% of all public-sector spending on mental healthcare.[73] Medicaid

[67] *See* Medicaid Program; State Disproportionate Share Hospital Allotment Reductions, 78 Fed. Reg. 57, 293–57, 313 (Sept. 18, 2013) (laying out the methodology for final DSH payment reductions covering FY 2014 through FY 2020).

[68] See, e.g., Medicare Access and CHIP Reauthorization Act § 412 Pub. L. 114-110 (2015), 114th Congress, extending the delay in the DSH reduction to 2025 and removing reductions for 2014–2016.

[69] *See, e.g., Medicaid and HIV/AIDS*, Kaiser Family Foundation (Mar. 5, 2013), http://kff.org/hivaids/fact-sheet/medicaid-and-hivaids/ (over 230,000 Medicaid beneficiaries who are HIV-positive); Brooke Lehmann et al., Center for Children and Families, Child Welfare and the Affordable Care Act: Key Provisions for Foster Care Children and Youth (2012) (describing Medicaid's role in the child welfare system); U.S. Gen. Accounting office, Medicaid and Special Education: Coordination of Services for Children with Disabilities is Evolving (1999), *available at* http://www.gao.gov/assets/230/228602.pdf.

[70] The ACA expanded mandatory eligibility for children ages 6–18 from 100% to 133% of poverty. 42 U.S.C. § 1396a(l) (2013). This amendment was left untouched by the Court in *Sebelius*, which concerned itself only with adults, presumably because children were not part of the "new" program. NFIB v. Sebelius, 132 S. Ct. 2566, 2582 (2012).

[71] Anne Rossier Markus et al., *Medicaid Covered Births, 2008 Through 2010, in the Context of the Implementation of Health Reform*, 23 Women's Health Issues 273, 279 (2013).

[72] *Five Key Facts About the Delivery and Financing of Long Term Services and Supports*, Kaiser Family Foundation (Sept. 13, 2013), http://kff.org/medicaid/fact-sheet/five-key-facts-about-the-delivery-and-financing-of-long-term-services-and-supports/.

[73] Peter Cunningham et al., *The Struggle to Provide Community-Based Care to Low-Income People with Serious Mental Illness*, 25 Health Aff. 694, 694 (2006).

supplements Medicare for over 9 million low-income Medicare beneficiaries and insures some 9 million beneficiaries with disabilities (6 million of whom receive Medicaid only).[74]

As the principal means by which the healthcare safety net is financed, Medicaid has fueled the growth of healthcare access points into medically underserved communities characterized by high poverty and elevated health risks. Community health centers best illustrate this growth. In 1986, fewer than seven hundred health centers served about 8 million patients; but despite relatively flat funding under their base discretionary grant funding, Medicaid revenues have propelled their growth. In 2014, twelve hundred health centers operating in approximately 9000 locations served 22.5 million patients. This exponential growth is the result of two basic policies: Medicaid eligibility expansions for both traditional populations and newly eligible populations in expansion states; and special payment rules that bar deep discounting of Medicaid payments to health centers, thereby preserving grant funds to pay for the nearly 30% of all health center patients who are uninsured.[75]

d. Medicaid's Parameters

Its multiple missions give Medicaid astounding parameters. Medicaid is the nation's largest public health insurance program and the third largest program in the domestic federal budget, accounting for 7% of all federal spending in 2013[76] and one-sixth of all U.S. healthcare spending.[77] Approximately two-thirds of total Medicaid spending is invested in primary, preventive, and acute-care services, but a considerable proportion of even these expenditures involve care for beneficiaries with disabilities and thus reflect far greater utilization than one would assume for a healthy population. One-third of program spending is dedicated to institutional and noninstitutional long-term care services.

Medicaid covered 58 million people on a full-year basis in 2013.[78] But if one counts all of the people whom Medicaid actually touches over the course of a year, the number is much higher, reaching 72 million people covered by Medicaid at some point during the year.[79] Children and adults make up about 75% of total enrollment and account for about one-third of total spending. By contrast, beneficiaries who are elderly or persons with disabilities represent about one-quarter of program enrollment and two-thirds of program spending.[80]

States are heavily dependent on Medicaid, which accounts for 44% of all federal grant funding received. When total program expenditures (both federal and state) are counted,

[74] Medicaid and CHIP Payment and Access Commission, *supra* note 50, Table 1-1 at 13.

[75] Peter Shin et al., *Health Center Patient Trends, Enrollment Activities, and Service Capacity: Recent Experience in Medicaid Expansion and Non-Expansion States* Kaiser Family Foundation, December 2, 2015. http://kff.org/medicaid/issue-brief/health-center-patient-trends-enrollment-activities-and-service-capacity-recent-experience-in-medicaid-expansion-and-non-expansion-states/ [forthcoming, August 2014].

[76] Cong. of the U.S. Congressional Budget Office, The 2013 Long-Term Budget Outlook (2013).

[77] Kaiser Family Foundation, Medicaid and Its Role in State/Federal Budgets & Health Reform (2013).

[78] Medicaid and CHIP Payment and Access Commission, MACStats: Medicaid and CHIP Program Statistics (2013).

[79] *The 2013 Long-Term Budget Outlook*, *supra* note 76, at 37–40.

[80] *Id.*

Medicaid represents nearly 25% of state budgets.[81] Medicaid's primacy as a source of federal funds transfer has, of course, grown even more pronounced as healthcare spending has continued to outstrip overall economic growth, and as federal funding for other key social welfare programs has stagnated or declined in real-dollar terms.

Medicaid's growth is driven by a combination of factors that have their root in the program's fundamental design combination of open-ended financing coupled with eligibility and coverage rules that embrace risk and the high cost of healthcare generally. But it is also the case that states manage Medicaid aggressively, precisely because of its size. In order to control Medicaid's growth—driven largely by enrollment rather than factors such as increased utilization or rising prices—states use an array of cost-containment strategies ranging from strict coverage limits for adults to more sophisticated program management tools such as managed pharmacy benefits and managed care plans offering coverage for a fixed per-capita rate. Because of these aggressive management techniques, Medicaid's future per-capita growth is projected to be slightly below the average per capita growth rate for the U.S. economy as a whole.[82]

Managed care represents a prominent approach to coverage. Following a slow start throughout Medicaid's early years, the shift to managed care happened rapidly in the 1990s as a result of Clinton administration initiatives, with a heavy focus on parents with children; increasingly, however, managed care is being designed to serve high-cost populations.[83] As of 2014, over half of all states were in the managed care planning or implementation phases, in order to develop integrated financing and delivery systems for beneficiaries dually eligible for Medicare and Medicaid.[84] In this latest managed care transition, one sees the same types of speed bumps that affected the 1990s transition for private insurance[85]; this shift is more complicated of course, because of the high-need population involved.[86]

e. Medicaid's Impact on Health and Healthcare

An extensive research literature documents Medicaid's impact on health and healthcare. Medicaid has significantly lowered the U.S. infant mortality rate,[87] chiefly in its impact on the growth of advanced newborn care capabilities. But compared to low-income uninsured

[81] *Id.*

[82] John Holahan & Stacey McMorrow, *Medicare and Medicaid Spending Trends and the Deficit Debate*, 367 New Eng. J. Med. 393, 393–394 (2012).

[83] *See* Medicaid and CHIP Payment and Access Commission, Report to the Congress: The Evolution of Managed Care in Medicaid (2011), *available at* http://op.bna.com/hl.nsf/id/bbrk-8huq3m/$File/MACPAC_June2011.pdf.

[84] *State Demonstration Proposals to Integrate Care and Align Financing and/or Administration for Dual Eligible Beneficiaries*, Kaiser Family Foundation (Mar. 2014), http://kff.org/medicaid/fact-sheet/state-demonstration-proposals-to-integrate-care-and-align-financing-for-dual-eligible-beneficiaries/.

[85] Medicaid and CHIP Payment and Access Commission, Report to the Congress: June 2012 73–78 (2012).

[86] Nina Bernstein, *Pitfalls Seen in a State's Turn to Privately Run Long-Term Care*, N.Y. Times Mag., Mar. 7, 2014.

[87] Karen Davis & Cathy Schoen, Health and the War on Poverty: A Ten-Year Appraisal 107–110 (1978).

children, children enrolled in Medicaid also are significantly more likely to have a usual source of care and receive well-child care and significantly less likely to have unmet or delayed needs for medical care, dental care, and prescription drugs.[88] Research shows an association between Medicaid expansion and reductions in mortality among low-income adults,[89] as well as comparable birth outcomes when results are risk-controlled.[90]

One widely cited study, using a natural randomized approach, examined Medicaid's impact on health and healthcare, compared to being uninsured. Researchers found that Medicaid was associated with more consistent primary care, increased use of preventive care such as mammograms and cholesterol checks, and increased use of outpatient and hospital care and prescription drugs.[91] The research also documented Medicaid's success in nearly eliminating catastrophic out-of-pocket medical expenditures (defined as costs exceeding 30% of income) and ability to significantly reduce medical debt (more than 20%).[92] The study found that adults who gained Medicaid had better self-reported physical and mental health than those who remained uninsured. But consistent with other studies attempting to find short-term health outcomes within a small population,[93] the study detected no short-term improvements in diabetes control, high blood pressure, or high cholesterol, results potentially attributable to numerous behavioral, economic, and health system factors.[94] Other studies taking a larger, more epidemiologic approach to the evidence have documented Medicaid's impact on adult mortality over time.[95] Critics have cited research showing Medicaid's lack of impact on patient health outcomes and its association with worse health outcomes,[96] although the degree of selection bias present in the studies (given Medicaid's tendency to enroll people at the time of greatest health need) raises reliability questions.[97]

[88] Genevieve M. Kenney & Christine Coyer, *National Findings on Access to Health Care and Service Use for Children Enrolled in Medicaid or CHIP*, Urban Institute (Aug. 2, 2012), http://www.urban.org/publications/1001629.html; Tom M. Selden & Julie L. Hudson, *Access to Care and Utilization Among Children: Estimating the Effects of Public and Private Coverage*, 44 Medical Care 434, 440–442 (2006); U.S. Dept. of Health and Human Services, Health, United States, 2012 17–21 (2013).

[89] *See, e.g.*, Benjamin D. Sommers, Katherine Baicker, & Arnold M. Epstein, *Mortality and Access to Care Among Adults After State Medicaid Expansions*, 367 New Eng. J. Med. 1025, 1025 (2012); Benjamin D. Sommers, Sharon K. Long, & Katherine Baicker, *Changes in Mortality After Massachusetts Health Reform: A Quasi-experimental Study*, 160 Annals Internal Med. 585, 590 (2014).

[90] Emmanuel A. Anum et al., *Medicaid and Preterm Birth and Low Birth Weight: The Last Two Decades*, 19 J. Women's Health 443, 450 (2010).

[91] Katherine Baicker et al., *The Oregon Experiment—Effects of Medicaid on Clinical Outcomes*, 368 New Eng. J. Med. 1713, 1719 (2013).

[92] *Id.* at 1718.

[93] For a discussion of the complexities of health outcomes research focusing on insurance reforms, *see* Institute of Medicine, Insuring America's Health (2004).

[94] Katherine Baicker & Amy Finkelstein, *The Effects of Medicaid Coverage—Learning from the Oregon Experiment*, 365 New Eng. J. Med. 683, 684 (2011); Amy Finkelstein et al., *The Oregon Health Insurance Experiment: Evidence from the First Year*, NBER Working Paper No. 17190 (2011), *available at* http://www.nber.org/papers/w17190.pdf.

[95] Sommers, Baicker, & Epstein, *supra* note 89, at 1025.

[96] Avik Roy, The Medicaid Mess: How Obamacare Makes it Worse Manhattan Institute for Policy Research (2012), http://www.manhattan-institute.org/html/ir_8.htm (last visited Apr. 1, 2014).

[97] Austin Frakt et al., *Our Flawed But Beneficial Medicaid Program*, 364 New Eng. J. Med. e31(1), 1–2 (2011).

IV Medicaid's Major Challenges

Going forward, Medicaid faces three fundamental challenges, some of which relate to the ACA, others of which have percolated for decades.

a. The Politics of Size, Scope, and Power-sharing

Medicaid's size and scope subject it to endless controversy. Indeed, the *Sebelius* dissent would have sunk the adult expansion—even as an option—on the basis of Medicaid's size alone.[98] This size and financial impact mean that the federal and state governments are in a constant battle for control, reaching an apex of sorts in *Sebelius* and the Court's unprecedented unconstitutional coercion holding despite the extraordinarily favorable financial terms attached to the adult expansion. Because of *Sebelius* (fully half the states joined the suit as plaintiffs), the expansion survived but effectively only as an option. Federal funding was preserved, but at the cost of state autonomy to reject coverage for the poorest Americans.

The federalism debate has raged for years. Put simply, what states naturally want is open-ended financing with minimal obligations, restrictions, and oversight. For its part, the federal government is divided. Liberals want to maintain Medicaid as an open-ended legal entitlement but with strict coverage standards as the *quid pro quo*. Conservatives desire an end to open-ended financing, with the trade-off being elimination of most (but not all) requirements. The result has been an unending political battle pitting these three viewpoints against one another like a bad but enduring piece of theater.

Medicaid block grant proposals "have been the *leitmotif* of Medicaid policy for the last three decades."[99] In recent years, Medicaid spending reduction proposals have moved beyond conventional block grants. A different proposal, which first surfaced during the epic 1995–1996 Medicaid block grant battle between Congress and President Clinton (which the governors settled by pulling the plug on support for capped funding),[100] would substitute per capita spending limits for Medicaid's open-ended financing structure. Medicaid would continue to grow in terms of population size, but per-beneficiary spending would be subject to annual limits, much like a premium. Ultimately the per capita cap proposal faded but like the perennial block grant idea, is expected to re-emerge, especially as part of a more comprehensive effort following a Republican victory the 2016 Presidential elections to deal with the Affordable Care Act more broadly.[101] Critics of per capita caps have focused on many

[98] See the dissent's discussion of Medicaid's size in NFIB v. Sebelius, 132 S. Ct. 2566, 2657–2660 (2012).

[99] *A Medicaid Block Grant Program: Implications for People with Disabilities*, National Council on Disability 27 App. A, http://www.ncd.gov/publications/2013/05222013/05222013_AppendixA (last visited May 26, 2014).

[100] *See* Jeanne M. Lambrew, *Making Medicaid a Block Grant Program: An Analysis of the Implications of Past Proposals*, 83 Milbank Q. 41, 46 (2005); David G. Smith & Judith D. Moore, Medicaid Politics and Policy: 1965–2007, at 227 chap. 6 (2008).

[101] *See* Amanda Cassidy, *Health Policy Brief: Per Capita Caps in Medicaid*, Health Aff. (Apr. 18, 2013), http://healthaffairs.org/healthpolicybriefs/brief_pdfs/healthpolicybrief_90.pdf; Edwin Park & Matthew Broaddus, Center on Budget and Policy Priorities Medicaid Per Capita Caps

issues: Medicaid's already-low annual growth rates, which would necessitate real-dollar spending reductions in order to achieve federal savings; the potential for low-spending states to suffer relatively deeper losses (sinking a Medicaid reduction proposal typically involves triggering interstate warfare about how to allocate reduced federal funds)[102]; impossible administrative problems such as continually having to reconcile actual federal payments to dated information about beneficiary characteristics; and the inability, under even per capita spending caps, to rapidly respond to changes in medical technology, shifting demographics, and sudden surges in medical care need brought on by man-made or natural crises.

While legislative battles over big Medicaid reform tend to fall apart owing to the impact on state budgets of federal limits on funding, § 1115 of the Social Security Act has come to act like a sort of pressure outlet that enables states to depart from federal rules without paying the consequences. Enacted as a special demonstration authority in 1962,[103] § 1115 authorizes the HHS Secretary to undertake demonstrations that "in [her] judgment" are "likely to assist in promoting the objectives" of Medicaid (as well as other state grant-in-aid programs authorized under the Act).[104] Section 1115 demonstrations can be federally solicited or sought by states. Under long-standing policy dating back to the Carter administration, § 1115 demonstrations must be budget neutral, costing the federal government no more than the federal sums projected under a state's standard Medicaid program,[105] although projecting what "normal" spending would look like is difficult given Medicaid's many state options.

Even in the case of § 1115 however, states have protested federal oversight and the structural limits of federal demonstrations. As broad as it is, § 1115 enables the Secretary to waive only certain aspects of the statute. For example, the HHS Secretary cannot alter the federal matching formula in order to give states a more favorable return on their own investments, although she can permit states to modify many program requirements while still receiving the funding to which they are entitled.

The Obama administration has used § 1115 as an enticement to foster adoption of the Medicaid expansion effectively made optional in *Sebelius*.[106] The most notable demonstration perhaps has been that undertaken by Arkansas, which expands Medicaid to the low-income adult population while enrolling the non-"medically frail" [107] expansion population into qualified health plans sold in the health insurance Marketplace.[108] By allowing Arkansas to utilize an

Would Shift Costs to States and Place Low-Income Beneficiaries at Risk (2012), *available at* http://www.cbpp.org/files/10-4-12health.pdf.

[102] *See* Lambrew, *supra* note 100, at 45.

[103] Public Welfare Amendments of 1962, Pub. L. No. 87-543, 76 Stat. 172 (1962). *See* Bruce C. Vladeck, *Medicaid 1115 Demonstrations: Progress through Partnership*, 14 Health Aff. 217, 217 (1995).

[104] 42 U.S.C. § 1315(a) (2010).

[105] Robin Rudowitz et al., *The ACA and Recent Section 1115 Medicaid Demonstration Waivers*, Kaiser Family Foundation (Feb. 5, 2014), http://kff.org/report-section/the-aca-and-recent-section-1115-medicaid-demonstration-waivers-issue-brief/.

[106] *Id.*

[107] An estimated 20% of all newly eligible adults are expected to be medically frail. Andy Allison, Arkansas Medicaid Director, Princeton Annual Conference, Council on Economics and Health Policy (May 13–14, 2014). Conference proceedings available at http://council.brandeis.edu/conferences/princeton2014.html. The remainder, according to Dr. Allison, can be expected to be healthy, thereby enhancing the stability of the Marketplace.

[108] Rosenbaum & Sommers, *supra* note 23.

approach that depends on private health plans rather than the traditional Medicaid managed care market, a Democratic governor was able to convince his conservative legislature to accept the adult Medicaid expansion, making Arkansas one of only two Southern states (the other being Kentucky) to have adopted the adult expansion. But since private insurance is about 50% more expensive than Medicaid, how the demonstration is budget neutral is a mystery, resting in part on inflated estimates of the cost of the expansion without demonstration authority and in part on theories regarding the impact of expanded enrollment on program efficiencies.

In sum, there are literally hundreds of Medicaid § 1115 demonstrations; evaluations of their impact on access, quality, and program efficiency are almost nonexistent. In many cases the demonstrations enable states to expand coverage or try alternative delivery arrangements. In others however, demonstration authority has been used to reduce eligibility or coverage; indeed, several of the ACA expansion demonstrations impose requirements (such as, in the case of Indiana, payment of premiums and a 6-month exclusion for non-payment) far harsher than would be permissible under traditional program rules. In some cases, beneficiaries have successfully challenged § 1115 demonstrations as exceeding the Secretary's authority given the absence of any real research design or credible evaluation methodology.[109] By and large, however, demonstrations flourish either because what is being attempted makes some sense (e.g., managed care reforms[110] or expanded eligibility)[111]—or because § 1115 becomes a convenient political escape hatch for states.

b. The Operational Challenges of Aligning Medicaid with the Broader Aims of Health Reform

The Affordable Care Act was not only about getting people insured; its loftier purpose is to improve the quality and efficiency of healthcare. To this end, stability of enrollment over time represents a central legislative reform, as do investments in underlying health system reform such as health information technology, payment incentives and performance measurement, and greater clinical and financial integration.

Like all payers, Medicaid struggles with how it can use its financial clout to incentivize better care. In Medicaid's case, the challenge is tougher because provider payment levels already are so low that provider participation outside of the safety net typically is inadequate and there is no excess to cut. Indeed improving Medicaid may require greater investment in certain types of health care; the ACA took a modest, temporary step in this direction through a two-year, federally funded payment increase in Medicaid primary care rates,[112] but the enhancement ended in 2014, and as of 2015, only 15 states had elected to continue paying for primary care at enhanced rates, omitting specialty care, which arguably poses more serious

[109] *See, e.g.*, Beno v. Shalala, 30 F.3d 1057, 1072-73 (9th Cir. 1993); Newton-Nations v. Betlach, 660 F.3d 370, 380 (9th Cir. 2011).

[110] John Holahan et al., *Insuring the Poor Through Section 1115 Medicaid Waivers*, 14 Health Aff. 199, 200 (1995).

[111] Massachusetts' health reform law was built on that state's § 1115 Medicaid demonstration program. *See* Jonathan Oberlander, *Health Reform Interrupted: The Unraveling of the Oregon Health Plan*, 26 Health Aff. w96, w96 (2007).

[112] Payments to Primary Care Physicians, Pub. L. No. 111-152, § 1202 (2010).

access problems.[113] The American Recovery and Reinvestment Act separately incentivized Medicaid adoption of health information technology (HIT) by certain provider groups, and progress continues, although slowly.

In sum, Medicaid struggles with system reform, as do other payers, but it has fewer tools given the health, social, and economic characteristics of beneficiaries, already-low payment rates, the concentration of beneficiaries in medically underserved communities. Some states have attempted large-scale § 1115 demonstrations (known as delivery system reform incentive payment programs) that seek to introduce large-scale system change,[114] but transforming care for entire communities and measuring impact are tall orders, indeed.

Medicaid transformation is further complicated by churning, that is, the constant movement of low-income populations between Medicaid and premium subsidies as incomes fluctuate. Estimates put the potential for cross-market churn during a year at 50% of the population with family incomes below 200% of the federal poverty level,[115] and even in states that have rejected the adult expansion, churn is likely.[116] This is an enormous issue for healthcare quality, since unless the same plans with the same networks participate in both programs, people whose coverage churns may lose their regular source of healthcare. The populations most vulnerable to churn turn out to be younger healthier workers and their children, whose stable participation is crucial to the success of the ACA.[117] Various strategies for reducing churn or mitigating its effects have been offered: smoother administration to reduce breaks in coverage[118]; the use of § 1115 demonstration authority to enable twelve-month continuous

[113] *See* Advisory Board Company, At Least 15 states will continue bump in Medicaid pay for primary care: 23 states have indicated they will not extend the pay hike, https://www.advisory.com/daily-briefing/2015/04/23/states-to-continue-medicaid-pay-bump. *See, also,* Medicaid and CHIP Payment and Access Commission, *supra* note 11, at 41–66 chap. C and D, which attempts to articulate more refined access standards and methods for measuring access sufficiency. Proposed rules that would have established a limited forecasting requirement for state programs were never finalized. Medicaid Program; Methods for Assuring Access to Covered Medicaid Services, 76 Fed. Reg. 26342–26364 (May 6, 2011).

[114] *See, e.g., Redesigning the Medicaid Program: DSRIP Program,* N.Y. State Dept. of Health, *available at* http://www.health.ny.gov/health_care/medicaid/redesign/delivery_system_reform_incentive_payment_program.htm (last visited May 29, 2014); *Delivery System Reform Incentive Payment Program,* State of N.J. Dept. of Health, http://dsrip.nj.gov/ (last visited May 29, 2014); Delivery Systems Reform Incentive Payments, Cal. Dept. of Health Care, *available at* http://www.dhcs.ca.gov/provgovpart/Pages/DSRIP1.aspx (last visited May 29, 2014). *See generally Lower Costs, Better Care: Reforming Our Health Care Delivery System,* Centers for Medicare and Medicaid Services (Feb. 28, 2013), *available at* http://www.cms.gov/Newsroom/MediaReleaseDatabase/Fact-Sheets/2013-Fact-Sheets-Items/2013-02-28.html.

[115] Benjamin D. Sommers & Sara Rosenbaum, *Issues in Health Reform: How Changes in Eligibility May Move Millions Back and Forth Between Medicaid and Insurance Exchanges,* 30 Health Aff. 228, 233 (2011).

[116] Benjamin D. Sommers et al., *Medicaid and Marketplace Eligibility Changes Will Occur Often in All States; Policy Options Can Ease Impact,* 33 Health Aff. 700, 705 (2013).

[117] *Id.*

[118] The ACA envisioned a single point of application and enrollment for any form of subsidy, but to appease states, the administration permitted retention of a separate Medicaid enrollment system. The result has been enormous application backlogs and litigation over state Medicaid enrollment failures. *See Sebelius: Feds May Cut Medicaid Pay So States Clear Enrollment Backlog,* Inside Health Policy (Apr. 14, 2014); Rebecca Adams, *The Hidden Failure of Obama's Health Care Overhaul,* Roll Call (June 3,

Medicaid enrollment[119]; the use of premium assistance *à la* Arkansas to maintain constant enrollment in qualified health plans; and multimarket health plans that use a common provider networks and available for sale in both the Medicaid and exchange markets. Experts also suggest use of the ACA's Basic Health Program option,[120] a special option, which the administration was slow to implement, that enables states to substitute what is effectively a broadened Medicaid program for individuals and families with incomes up to 200% of the federal poverty level in lieu of Marketplace premium subsidies (essentially the Arkansas model in reverse).[121]

c. Medicaid and the Courts

The continuing legal drama that surrounds Medicaid goes beyond federal-state relations and touches on the fundamental question of whether private individuals will have access to the courts in the case of states whose program administration allegedly violates federal protections. This question has been simmering in the courts for decades, as an increasingly conservative Supreme Court has sought to narrow the circumstances in which beneficiaries and providers can proceed with private enforcement actions.[122]

The enforcement cases raise two distinct issues: first, whether the Medicaid statute creates enforceable rights; and second, whether, even in the absence of an enforceable right, private individuals can bring actions to halt unlawful state action violating federal Medicaid standards if the federal government has not sufficiently enforced them. One example of a federal operational requirement held by numerous courts not to constitute an individually enforceable right[123] is the Medicaid requirement (known as the equal access guarantee) that states "assure that payments are consistent with efficiency, economy, and quality of care and are sufficient to enlist enough providers so that care and services are available under the plan at least to the extent that such care and services are available to the general population in the geographic area."[124] State adherence to this guarantee is viewed by many as crucial to reasonable access to care, given the critical provider shortage.[125]

2014, 6:00 AM), http://www.rollcall.com/news/the_hidden_failure_of_obamas_health_care_overhaul-233506-1.html (a 2.9 million enrollee backlog); Preliminary Injunction Order, Wilson v. Gordon, No. 3-14-1492 (M.D. Tenn., Sept. 2 2014).

119 Cindy Mann, Dept. of Health & Human Services, Letter Re Facilitating Medicaid and CHIP Enrollment and Renewal in 2014 (2013), http://www.medicaid.gov/federal-policy-guidance/downloads/sho-13-003.pdf. As of June 2014, only New York State had adopted this coverage stabilization option.

120 42 U.S.C. § 18051 (2010).

121 Mathew Buettgens et al., Urban Institute, Churning Under the ACA and State Policy Options for Mitigation (June 2012), *available at* http://www.urban.org/UploadedPDF/412587-Churning-Under-the-ACA-and-State-Policy-Options-for-Mitigation.pdf.

122 42 U.S.C. § 1396a(a)(30)(A) (2014). *See* Sara Rosenbaum et al., Law and the American Health Care System 424–426 (2d ed. 2012) & 71–73, (Supp. 2014).

123 *See, e.g.*, Sanchez v. Johnson, 416 F.3d 1051, 1068 (9th Cir. 2005).

124 42 U.S.C. § 1396a(a)(30)(A) (2014).

125 Medicaid and CHIP Payment and Access Commission, *supra* note 85, at 2.

Both types of cases—those raising rights issues and those raising questions of federal duties—are complex because the Medicaid statute itself contains no express federal right of action, which would expressly enable a private right of action. A liberal Court used to infer a private right of action from the nature of a statute, but these days are over; the Court now insists on an express right of action.[126] In some cases, this right of action can be found in 42 U.S.C. § 1983, an ancient statute dating back to the post-Civil War era that permits individuals to seek judicial intervention in cases involving federal rights secured under the Constitution or by statute.[127] But, as it turns out, very few provisions of Medicaid—other than the core entitlement to coverage—are viewed by courts as creating a "right" within the meaning of § 1983, and the Court sets a very high bar for when it will consider a right to exist.[128]

In cases that involve a Medicaid operating rule rather than a right, litigants have turned to the Constitution's Supremacy Clause, arguing that the Supremacy Clause itself creates a right of action to vindicate injuries arising out of states' failure to follow binding federal laws. In this regard, the "equal access" cases have assumed major prominence. In *Armstrong v Exceptional Child Center, Inc.* the United States Supreme Court rejected this argument and went further, concluding that the Medicaid statute itself evidences Congress's desire to bar the courts from exercising their inherent equitable powers to intercede in cases brought by providers (and presumably beneficiaries as well) to enjoin potentially unlawful state payment arrangements pending full judicial review.[129] With this decision, *Armstrong* effectively narrows the Court's landmark decision in Ex Parte *Young*,[130] which provides for judicial redress in the case of private interests facing imminent harm from unlawful state conduct. Whether *Armstrong* will in fact unleash suits against the federal government under the federal Administrative Procedure Act for approving unreasonably low payment arrangements remains to be seen. To date, federal agency action to ensure adequate payments has been shown to be strikingly absent.[131]

V Concluding Thoughts

Medicaid's ability to survive as the nation's largest means-tested legal entitlement is essential, not only for the tens of millions of people who depend on it but also as the legal and operational foundation of health reform. Medicaid is immense and incredibly complex. Yet as Medicaid begins its second half century it survives, precisely because, by filling enormous holes and absorbing financial risk, it is essential to a market-driven health economy. Indeed, Medicaid makes the healthcare market possible. States overwhelmingly depend on its revenues; the poor and medically vulnerable depend on its coverage; and the healthcare industry depends on Medicaid as a $400-plus billion dollar shock absorber.

[126] *See* Alexander v. Sandoval, 532 U.S. 275 (2001).

[127] *See* Maine v. Thiboutot, 448 U.S. 1, 1 (1980); Wilder v. Virginia Hospital Ass'n, 496 U.S. 498 (1990).

[128] *See* Gonzaga Univ. v. Doe, 536 U.S. 273, 290–291 (2002).

[129] Armstrong v Exceptional Child Center, Inc. 135 S. Ct. 1378 (2015).

[130] *Ex parte* Young, 209 U.S. 123, 166–168 (1908).

[131] WOS v. E.M.A., 133 S. Ct. 1391 (2013).

The policy and political battles over Medicaid endure, and the judicial battles proceed. But as long as the United States continues to rely heavily on market solutions to the allocation of healthcare resources, it needs Medicaid or a program just like it. And so those committed to the ultimate success of the Affordable Care Act also must root for Medicaid. Do we allow Medicaid to falter, or do we invest in its implementation and fuller integration into a reformed health system? For now, the situation might be best characterized as slow-motion forward movement, coupled with a cautious wait-and-see outlook.

CHAPTER 35

THE INTERACTIONS BETWEEN PUBLIC AND PRIVATE HEALTH INSURANCE

AMY B. MONAHAN

I Introduction

In most countries, there is little need to discuss the interaction between public and private health insurance, because public health insurance is the predominant means by which healthcare is financed. Private health insurance, if it exists at all, typically plays only a limited, supplemental role in healthcare finance. The situation is quite different in the United States. The United States has always been hesitant to adopt any type of large-scale public health insurance system. Originating from a desire to differentiate ourselves from both communist and socialist countries,[1] and to reflect our values of individual liberty and a free market, we have historically relied primarily on market-based mechanisms to allocate healthcare resources, including health insurance. Even in America, however, we acknowledge that markets sometimes do not function properly and that safety nets are sometimes needed. As a result, we have ended up with a system that relies primarily on privately financed health insurance, with limited eligibility safety-net public programs to provide coverage to the elderly and certain populations that are poor or near-poor. This mixed system of public and private coverage creates some unique challenges for healthcare finance in the United States. Prior to the passage of the Affordable Care Act (ACA) in 2010, the public and private systems had significant impact on each other. Private plans often followed the lead of Medicare in making coverage decisions, and Medicare led the way for all payers in devising payment and credentialing systems. Beginning in the 1990s public programs increasingly began to borrow various mechanisms from the private market, by providing beneficiaries with choices of plans and adopting payment structures with market-based incentives. But public plans were also thought to be a potential threat to private health insurance. Medicare's low provider

[1] Christopher N. J. Roberts, *Dynamics of Healthcare Reform: Bitter Pills Old and New*, 45 Vand. J. Transnat'l L. 1341, 1349–1352 (2012).

reimbursement rates were thought to lead to provider costs being shifted to private payers. This cost-shifting may have contributed to price increases for private plans, thereby reducing coverage within that market. Medicaid, on the other hand, by providing no-cost coverage to low-income individuals, was thought to crowd out private coverage by encouraging low-income employees to drop their employer coverage in favor of lower-cost and more generous Medicaid coverage.

The Affordable Care Act (ACA) is pushing the interaction between public and private coverage in the United States in new directions. Most important, the ACA makes fundamental changes to the individual insurance market that align it very closely with public coverage. The individual market will be subsidized, sell products that cover a required set of minimum benefits, and broadly pool health risks. There will be meaningful choice within that market, but competition will be managed rather than unregulated. While Medicare and Medicaid adopted private-like features in the 1990s, the private insurance market is now moving toward public-like coverage. Essentially, both types of coverage are borrowing the best features of the other and moving toward the center. While this movement toward the convergence of our systems of public and private coverage is a positive development, we still struggle to overcome the complications that result from having multiple public and private systems coexisting.

II Public and Private Insurance Globally

a. Public Coverage, Generally

Most developed countries offer some form of publicly financed health insurance to their citizens or residents. In these countries, public coverage is generally the primary means through which individuals access and pay for medical care, and the public system provides universal or near-universal coverage. Public health insurance is generally considered a form of social insurance, which is defined in its most basic sense as "[g]overnment interventions in the provision of insurance against adverse events"[2] or as "government-orchestrated protection against specific risks faced by most if not all people."[3] Public health insurance in almost all cases spreads the risk of medical losses across the entire insured population, rather than classifying participants based on risk and charging sick individuals more than healthy individuals. Spreading risk evenly across a population rather than differentiating among individuals based on their personal risks is referred to as a "social solidarity" approach to health insurance and is a key feature of public insurance systems.[4]

Because public health insurance coverage is premised in part on the idea that basic healthcare is a right of citizens irrespective of their ability to pay for such care, public programs

[2] Jonathan Gruber, Public Finance and Public Policy 322 (2013).

[3] James Kwak, *Social Insurance, Risk Spreading, and Redistribution*, *in* Research Handbook in the Law and Economics of Insurance (Daniel Schwarcz & Peter Siegelman eds., forthcoming) (manuscript at 2), *available at* http://papers.ssrn.com/sol3/papers.cfm?abstract_id=2436508.

[4] Deborah A. Stone, *The Struggle for the Soul of Health Insurance*, 18 J. of Health Pol., Pol'y & L. 287, 290–292 (1993).

typically contain provisions specifically designed to help protect the neediest in society—features that often look more like social assistance (i.e., direct government benefits) rather than social insurance. For example, financing of such systems is usually progressive, meaning that low-income individuals pay less into the system than higher-income individuals. And benefit structures within the plans themselves typically provide coverage with lower cost-sharing for low-income or chronically ill individuals.[5]

Another common feature of public health insurance systems is that they are generally not market-based and do not treat healthcare like a consumer good. This is perhaps most evident in those countries with a national health service, where the government is not only the financier of the health system but also the provider. But even in countries, such as Germany, where private insurers provide the benefits within the public system, the system is strictly regulated with little market influence. In the German system, and others that follow its structure, individuals must generally enroll in coverage through one of several private, nonprofit health insurers (referred to as "sickness funds"), but the content of the coverage they offer is standardized and prices paid to providers are fixed.[6] Public systems in most country do not depend in any significant way on market mechanisms to allocate goods and services.

To simplify, then, public systems typically (1) pool health risks broadly, reflecting a social solidarity approach to health insurance; (2) are subsidized for those of limited means; (3) utilize a standard product or set of benefits; (4) rely on government regulation to ensure quality and desired distribution of resources; and (5) provide universal or near-universal coverage.

b. Private Coverage, Generally

Privately financed health insurance coverage is, in most of the world, a complement to, rather than a replacement for, public coverage. In many countries, public coverage provides universal coverage of at least basic services, while private coverage offers enhanced coverage for those willing and able to pay for it. In most of the developed world, it is only in this supplemental private coverage market where ability to pay comes into play.

Private coverage also often differs significantly from public coverage with respect to how risks are pooled and how coverage is priced. While public coverage involves broad risk-sharing and subsidized coverage based on income level, private coverage is typically priced based on an individual's particular risk level and therefore involves less cross-subsidization and risk pooling than public coverage. Insurance that is priced based on an individual's particular medical risks is referred to as an actuarially-based pricing model, or as medically-underwritten coverage.

Again to simplify matters, for our purposes we can state that private health insurance coverage (1) is generally priced based on an individual's specific health history and risks (an "actuarially based" model of coverage); (2) is unsubsidized, with availability based on

[5] THE COMMONWEALTH FUND, INTERNATIONAL PROFILES OF HEALTH CARE SYSTEMS 6 (2012), *available at* http://www.commonwealthfund.org/~/media/Files/Publications/Fund%20Report/2012/Nov/1645_Squires_intl_profiles_hlt_care_systems_2012.pdf.

[6] Miriam Blümel, *The German Health Care System, 2013*, *in* INTERNATIONAL PROFILES OF HEALTH CARE SYSTEMS 57, 57–61 (The Commonwealth Fund, 2013).

an ability to pay; (3) relies on market mechanisms to allocate goods and services, as well as police quality; and (4) is optional.

III United States' Exceptionalism in Public and Private Coverage

The United States does not conform to the international norms described above with respect to public and private coverage. First, prior to the enactment of the ACA, the United States offered relatively limited public coverage that was not designed to be universal or even near-universal. Our two primary systems of public coverage covered only specific groups. Medicare, a program of the federal government, provided (and still provides) near-universal coverage of the elderly, plus coverage for certain disabled individuals. Medicaid, a joint federal and state program, has historically provided fairly robust coverage for low-income parents and children, as well as the low-income medically needy, but in most states relatively little coverage of adults who are "simply" poor. Anyone not eligible for one of these two programs had to rely on the private market to secure health insurance coverage. And, as discussed in section III.b., prior to the ACA the private market differed significantly between employer-provided and individually purchased coverage, with the latter often failing to provide any coverage for individuals with poor health histories or risks.

a. U.S. Public Coverage Prior to the ACA

The United States has several public health insurance programs: Medicare, Medicaid, TRICARE (for active duty military and their families), the veterans health care program, and the Indian Health Service. Eligibility for each of these is limited and covers only specified populations. None of the U.S. public health programs is designed to provide universal coverage. The two dominant programs, Medicare and Medicaid, are reviewed in more detail below.

i. Medicare

The federal Medicare program is financed through payroll taxes and provides nearly universal coverage of inpatient services for the elderly (Marmor and Oberlander, this volume). It also provides coverage for certain disabled individuals. The basic Medicare coverage is referred to as Medicare Part A, which is financed by a flat payroll tax and covers hospital inpatient services. Once an individual has qualified for Medicare (generally by paying payroll taxes for ten or more years), no further premiums are due to receive coverage under Part A. Medicare also has various optional forms of coverage available to beneficiaries. Part B provides coverage for various outpatient services, such as doctor visits, while Part D covers prescription drugs. Beneficiaries also have the option of enrolling in a Medicare Part C plan, which is a plan administered by a private entity that combines Medicare Part A and B benefits. Often, but not always, Medicare Part C plans utilize managed care to provide benefits.

Medicare's benefit structure is quite unusual for a public social insurance program. As noted above, only hospital insurance is provided as part of Medicare's basic benefit. The cost for any optional Medicare coverage is borne at least in part by the beneficiary. Further, even though Part A is available without further premium, the cost-sharing requirements within Part A are very high for a public program. Beneficiaries must satisfy a deductible ($1,260 in 2015) before Medicare begins reimbursing hospitalization expenses.[7] Once the deductible is satisfied, Medicare will pay the full costs of hospitalization for sixty days. Beginning on the sixty-first day, beneficiaries are charged a copay ($315 per day in 2015).[8] For example, if a beneficiary were hospitalized for seventy-five days, she would have to pay $5,985 in out-of-pocket costs (a $1,260 deductible plus fifteen days with a $315 copay). The out-of-pocket costs are so high, particularly in relation to beneficiaries' income levels, that the vast majority of Medicare recipients purchase private supplemental coverage to protect against these out-of-pocket costs.[9]

ii. Medicaid and CHIP

Medicaid looks and operates much more like a traditional social assistance program than does Medicare. Medicaid is a cooperative program between the federal and state government that was originally designed to provide coverage to the "medically needy" and the "deserving poor." The so-called "deserving poor" were those who were both poor and "categorically" eligible: members of families with children and single parents, the elderly, the blind and the disabled.[10] Eligibility was then expanded to include poor families with two parents and to pregnant women and children at increasing income levels.[11] While Medicaid's specifics vary from state to state, prior to the ACA it generally provided consistent coverage to pregnant women, children, and the disabled who had low or moderate incomes. In most states, however, coverage for the "mere" poor was much rarer. As of January 2016, twenty-four states offered no coverage to even the poorest childless adults.[12]

Children's access to public health coverage, however, increased significantly in 1997 when the Children's Health Insurance Program (CHIP) became law. While details vary by state, CHIP provides health insurance coverage to children with family incomes too high to qualify for Medicaid, but too low to afford private coverage.[13] Combined, Medicaid and CHIP

[7] CTRS. FOR MEDICARE & MEDICAID SERVS., 2015 MEDICARE COSTS 1 (2014), *available at* http://www.medicare.gov/Pubs/pdf/11579.pdf.

[8] *Id.*

[9] KAISER FAMILY FOUND., MEDIGAP: SPOTLIGHT ON ENROLLMENT, PREMIUMS, AND RECENT TRENDS 4 (2013) (reporting that as of 2009, 88% of Medicare beneficiaries had some form of supplemental coverage), *available at* http://kaiserfamilyfoundation.files.wordpress.com/2013/04/8412-2.pdf.

[10] John V. Jacobi, *Medicaid Expansion, Crowd Out, and Limits of Incremental Reform*, 45 ST. LOUIS U. L.J. 79, 89 (2001).

[11] *Id.*

[12] THE KAISER COMM'N ON MEDICAID & THE UNINSURED, WHERE ARE STATES TODAY? MEDICAID AND CHIP ELIGIBILITY LEVELS FOR CHILDREN AND NON-DISABLED ADULTS AS OF APRIL 1, 2016, *available at* http://kff.org/medicaid/fact-sheet/where-are-states-today-medicaid-and-chip/.

[13] For more information regarding CHIP, *see* Medicaid.gov's CHIP website, at http://www.medicaid.gov/Medicaid-CHIP-Program-Information/By-Topics/Childrens-Health-Insurance-Program-CHIP/Childrens-Health-Insurance-Program-CHIP.html.

provide coverage to more than one in three children in the United States, with only 7% of children remaining uninsured as of 2012.[14]

Because of the special populations which it serves, Medicaid covers a wide and generous range of services.[15] Within broad statutory guidelines, however, states have significant flexibility to determine the type, amount, duration, and scope of the precise services they offer.[16] Cost-sharing within Medicaid is limited. States are permitted to charge premiums and impose cost-sharing requirements for Medicaid participants, although such costs are capped. In general, states can impose higher charges for certain groups of higher income individuals. Various vulnerable groups, such as children and pregnant women, are exempt from most cost-sharing requirements, and cost-sharing is prohibited on certain types of services.[17]

Medicaid, then, looks closer to a typical social assistance program than to a traditional social insurance program. The costs are paid for by government rather than through a dedicated tax on participants. Benefits and cost-sharing are very much designed to take into account the limited means of participants, and only certain particularly vulnerable populations are included.

But for those who are ineligible for either Medicare or Medicaid, it is important to remember that the only options for coverage are either the private market or charity care (Jost, this volume). There is no acknowledged right to even basic, nonemergency medical care in the United States.[18] Figure 35.1 provides an illustration of the sources of coverage prior to the ACA, showing the clear reliance on privately financed coverage for nonelderly Americans, which leaves a sizeable portion of the nonelderly population uninsured.

b. Private Coverage Prior to the ACA

As noted above, prior to the ACA most nonelderly Americans received health insurance coverage through private markets. These privately financed markets reflected a very different vision of health insurance than our public programs. The primary distinctions were that private coverage was very much dependent on the ability to pay, as there were no targeted subsidies to increase affordability for low-income individuals. Second, with the notable exception of large-employer coverage, coverage in the private market was generally priced based on an individual's (or small group's) health status. Instead of health risks being pooled, individuals and small groups were charged premiums that reflected their own riskiness. Health insurers in most states were free to reject applications from individuals or small

[14] Robin Rudowitz et al., *Children's Health Coverage: Medicaid, CHIP and the ACA*, Kaiser Family Found. Issue Brief, Mar. 2014, *available at* http://kaiserfamilyfoundation.files.wordpress.com/2014/03/8570-children_s-health-coverage-medicaid-chip-and-the-aca1.pdf.

[15] Sara Rosenbaum, *Medicaid's Next Fifty Years: Aligning an Old Program with the New Normal*, 6 St. Louis U. J. Health L. & Pol'y 329, 333 (2013).

[16] *See* 42 U.S.C. §1396d(a) (2012).

[17] *Id.* §§1396o; 1396o-1.

[18] The federal Emergency Medical Treatment and Labor Act does, however, require certain hospitals to provide treatment to stabilize emergency medical conditions or active labor, regardless of a patient's ability to pay.

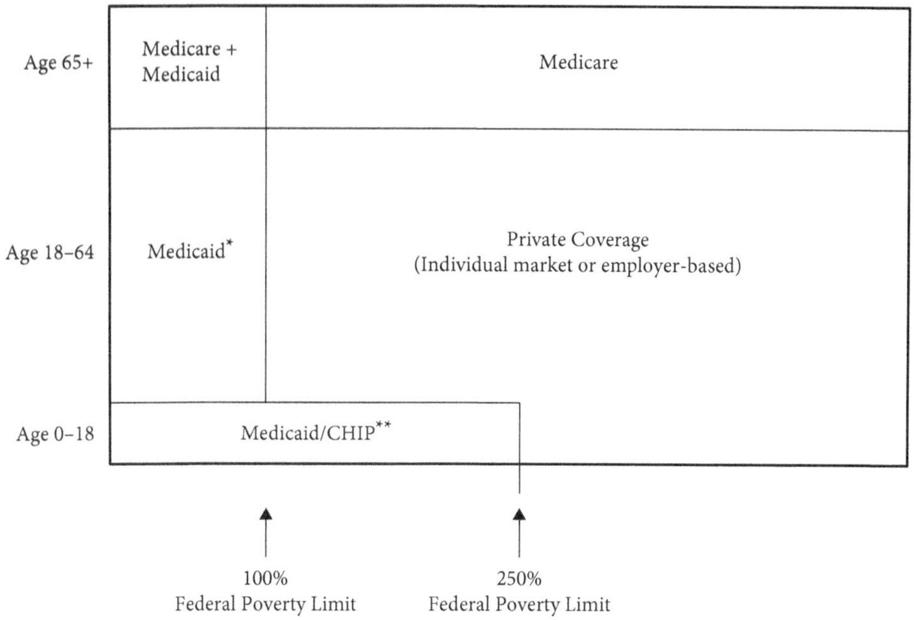

FIGURE 35.1 Pre-ACA Sources of Health Insurance Coverage

*Medicaid income eligibility for adults varies dramatically by state; not all states cover adults with income below the poverty limit.

** Children's Health Insurance Program (CHIP) eligibility also varies significantly by state, with many states covering children in households with income above 250% the federal poverty level.

groups with preexisting conditions or high health risks. Given the different regulatory environments that applied to group versus individual health insurance markets, each is reviewed separately below.

i. Individual Insurance Markets

Privately financed health insurance coverage in the United States has most often been purchased through an employer. If, however, an individual was not employed or was not offered coverage by her employer, the only other option was to purchase an individual policy in a state-regulated market.

Prior to the ACA, markets for individual health insurance were regulated almost exclusively at the state level, and most allowed insurers to deny coverage where an individual was deemed too risky and allowed insurers to vary premiums based on health risk. Despite the ability of insurers to classify individuals based on their risk, these markets were generally thought to suffer from adverse selection, given that the individuals most interested in purchasing health insurance are those with greater-than-average health risks. The general consensus was that high-risk individuals often were either denied coverage altogether, or offered coverage at an unaffordable price, while low-risk individuals often found coverage to be priced higher than they were willing to pay given their low health risks. A handful of states required insurers to offer coverage to all applicants (guaranteed issue), at community-rated prices, where all insured are charged the same rates. While these market rules were designed to protect insurance availability for high-risk individuals, they were often criticized on the grounds that they had the effect of exacerbating adverse selection because they prevented insurers from charging low-risk individuals lower premiums. Ultimately, this made insurance unattractive and unaffordable for low-risk individuals.

In general, financial assistance was unavailable for insurance purchased in the individual market. While self-employed individuals were able to deduct health insurance premiums from their taxable income, employed individuals who were not offered an employer plan or a tax-advantaged health insurance reimbursement arrangement could not. And states generally looked solely to Medicaid to provide assistance for those in need. As a result, many individuals who were not offered employer coverage (or who were offered employer coverage but turned it down because of the cost) remained uninsured.[19]

ii. Employer-Provided Health Insurance

Employer-provided health insurance has been the preferred means for nonelderly Americans to obtain health insurance for two primary reasons. First, purchasing health insurance through a group formed for reasons unrelated to health insurance is more efficient than individual purchasing: overhead costs are lower and health risks can easily be pooled within the group. Second, employer-provided health insurance coverage can be paid for with pretax dollars (whether paid by the employer, the employee, or a combination of both), thereby lowering its effective price.

The ability to pay for employer-provided coverage with pretax dollars operates as a subsidy from the federal government. While this subsidy increases affordability, it is also regressive because it provides the greatest benefit to those with the highest levels of income, not the lowest. Assume Individual A, in the 39% tax bracket, and Individual B, in the 10% tax bracket, both elect employer-provided coverage that costs $5,000 per year. The ability to pay the $5,000 premium on a pretax basis saves Individual A $1,950, while Individual B saves only $500. The tax preference is one of the most expensive tax expenditures in the federal budget.[20]

Federal law regulates how employer coverage can be priced and structured. An employer is not required to offer a health plan, or, if it does offer a plan to make that plan available to all of its employees. However, if it does sponsor a plan for some or all employees, the employer is prohibited from varying eligibility, premiums, or benefits on the basis of an individual's health status. As a result of these nondiscrimination provisions, as well as the tax subsidy, health risks within an employer's group are broadly pooled. Most commentators agree that the large-employer market worked fairly well pre-ACA in providing relatively affordable coverage regardless of health status.

While large employers could rely on the law of large numbers to ensure that their health plans would usually experience roughly average losses, small employers were not so

[19] Kaiser Comm'n on Medicaid and the Uninsured, Key Facts About the Uninsured Population 2 (2013).

[20] Joint Comm. on Taxation, Estimates of Federal Tax Expenditures for Fiscal Years 2012–2017 40 (2013) (estimating a $143 billion tax expenditure for employer-provided health insurance in fiscal year 2014).

fortunate. For small employers, if even one individual in the group had a significant health problem, insurance for the group often became unaffordable because such coverage was priced based on the particular group's risk level. As a result, small employers were much less likely to offer their employees health insurance coverage than large employers, and less likely to be able to do so at community average prices.

But while the large group market was thought to work fairly well pre-ACA, and the small group and individual markets much less well, it is clear that the large group market was not perfect. Even among those lucky enough to be offered attractive coverage from their employer, there remained affordability issues even after employer contributions and tax subsdidies were taken into acocunt. In addition, part-time and other marginalized workers who worked for large employers often were not offered health insurance coverage that was made available to other employees, or were offered it only after significant waiting periods. In addition, even individuals lucky enough to be covered by a large employer plan were at risk of losing such coverage if they lost their employment, making such coverage often insecure over time. The end result was that the mix of public and private coverage prior to the ACA left a significant percentage of the population uninsured. In 2012, 17.7% of the nonelderly population, or 47.3 million individuals, lacked health insurance coverage.[21]

c. Pre-ACA Interactions between Public and Private Coverage

The ends of public and private health insurance coverage prior to the ACA were quite distinct. Public coverage, while not universal, embraced the broad pooling of health risks, along with significant subsidization. Rather than relying on market mechanisms to guide utilization and police quality, the government was generally paternalistic and directly regulated access to services and quality. The private market, at least in most states, was premised on the idea that health insurance was a good just like any other good and should therefore be distributed within a market-based mechanism. Individuals who valued health insurance would find the money to pay for it. If an individual found health insurance to be unaffordable, this simply revealed that she valued other goods more highly. The regulatory framework in most states reflected a belief that it was fair to have individuals pay for health insurance in a manner that at least partially took into account their individual risk level. Quality issues and plan structure were left to traditional market mechanisms, with relatively little regulation.[22] Insurers would respond to consumer demand, design plans accordingly, and ensure their quality in order to attract and retain customers.

Despite these differing ends, there were various forms of interaction between these two distinct mechanisms for health insurance: (1) public and private plans often were required to coordinate coverage for individuals who had dual coverage or who transitioned between public and private coverage; (2) Medicare significantly impacted private payers' administrative and payment systems, as well as coverage determinations; (3) Medicare's reimbursement rates influenced prices charged to private payers in some markets; (4) public programs may

[21] KAISER COMM'N ON MEDICAID AND THE UNINSURED, at 3.

[22] Perhaps the most significant exception to the lack of direct regulation in individual health insurance markets concerns mandated benefit laws, which require all health insurance plans issued in the state to cover specified treatment, services, or providers.

have crowded out private coverage; and (5) public programs borrowed various features of market-oriented private coverage.

i. Coordination between Public and Private Payers

There have always been individuals who transitioned between public and private markets, as well as individuals who had dual coverage in both markets. Low-income workers might cycle between employer coverage and Medicaid, depending on current income levels and employers. Older employees who continued to work were often eligible for both their employer plan and Medicare. These overlaps created the impetus for some coordination of coverage terms between public and private plans. Perhaps even more important, because there were (and are) so many individuals covered under an employer plan who are also eligible for Medicare because they are over sixty-five, rules regarding whether the employer plan or Medicare pay claims first have always had a significant impact on financing and have indirectly influenced plan design.

ii. Medicare's Administrative Influence

In addition to these coordination issues, many other interactions between public and private coverage have resulted from the enormity of the Medicare program. Medicare accounts for such a significant amount of health expenditures that its payment practices, for example, have become the de facto standard for the private health insurance industry as well.[23] Given that nearly all hospitals and many, many providers participate in Medicare, it is understandable why private payers have often followed Medicare's lead in payment practices (such as the use of Medicare's diagnosis-related groups) rather than inventing a separate payment methodology from scratch. And because Medicare is administered by private insurers, those insurers were required to upgrade their administrative services capabilities, such as electronic claims processing systems, with Medicare paying the costs thereof.[24] Private insurers were then able to pass along this increased administrative capability to private payers.[25] Medicare also has had a huge influence on the credentialing infrastructures used by private payers, with many private payers requiring that participating providers be eligible to be participating Medicare (and Medicaid) providers even if they do not actually choose to participate in such programs.[26]

Private plans also often adopted Medicare coverage determinations, particularly with respect to new technology.[27] Again, because of the resources of the Medicare program, its

[23] Stanley B. Jones, *Medicare Influence on Private Insurance: Good or Ill?*, 18 Health Care Financing Rev. 153, 155 (1996).

[24] *Id.* at 153–154. [25] *Id.*

[26] *Id.* at 155. For an example of a private payer's credentialing requirements, see United Healthcare, 2014 Credentialing Plan, at 8, https://www.unitedhealthcareonline.com/ccmcontent/ProviderII/UHC/en-US/Assets/ProviderStaticFiles/ProviderStaticFilesPdf/Tools%20and%20Resources/Protocols/2014_UnitedHealthcare_Credentialing_Plan.pdf ("The Applicant must not be ineligible, excluded or debarred from participation in the Medicare and/or Medicaid and related state and federal programs, or terminated for cause from Medicare or any state's Medicaid or CHIP program").

[27] For a discussion of this phenomenon, *see* John Carroll, *Medicare Coverage Rules Are Not Always Last Word*, Managed Care, Oct. 2007.

evaluation and determinations regarding whether a new treatment, service, or technology would be covered have often simply been adopted by private payers, who perhaps believed it would be inefficient to conduct their own independent evaluation.

iii. Cost-Shifting

Medicare's payment practices are theorized to negatively affect the amounts that private plans are charged by hospitals. This phenomenon, referred to as dynamic cost-shifting, is based on the fact that Medicare reimbursment rates are set by the government, and hospitals, if they wish to participate in Medicare (which, due to demographics, nearly every hospital does), must simply accept those rates. If Medicare reimbursement rates do not adequately compensate hospitals for the care they provide to Medicare beneficiaries (as evidence suggests they generally do not), hospitals will make up this revenue shortfall by increasing the amounts charged to private payers.[28] The extent to which such cost-shifting occurs continues to be debated in the literature,[29] but recent work has suggested that cost-shifting, to the extent it occurs, might result primarily from market power held by consolidated providers, rather than simply Medicare reimbursement rates.[30] Under this theory, the reason hospitals are able to raise prices for private payers is that their consolidated market position allows them to do so. In a truly competitive market, cost-shifting would not occur. Instead, hospitals faced with low Medicare reimbursement rates would seek to cut costs in order to be profitable. Nevertheless, given the reality of provider consolidation in many markets, cost-shifting may in fact result in higher prices for many private payers.

The practical concern associated with this cost-shifting is that, while Medicare has an incentive to set reimbursements rates as low as it can while maintaining an optimal supply of providers, acting on that instinct can raise prices in the private insurance market and end up lowering the number of individuals who elect such coverage, thereby potentially reducing the number of insured individuals. While the extent of cost-shifting continues to be debated, it is possible that Medicare has raised the cost of private health insuance, thereby increasing the likelihood that individuals will be uninsured.

iv. Crowd-Out of Private Coverage

In addition to the possibility that Medicare has raised costs for private plans, Medicaid and CHIP may crowd out employer-provided coverage. The concern is that as public programs expand, rather than reducing the number of uninsured individuals, such expansions may just

[28] Jones, *Medicare Influence*, at 157.

[29] Four well-known articles have found evidence of dynamic cost-shifting: Jeffrey Stensland et al., *Private-Payer Profits Can Induce Negative Medicare Margins*, 29 HEALTH AFF. 1045 (2010); David Dranove, *Pricing by Non-Profit Institutions: The Case of Hospital Cost-Shifting*, 7 J. HEALTH ECON. 47 (1988); J. P. Clement, *Dynamic Cost Shifting in Hospitals: Evidence from the 1980s and 1990s*, 34 INQUIRY 340 (1997–1998); Jack Zwanziger & Anil Bamezai, *Evidence of Cost Shifting in California Hospitals*, 25 HEALTH AFF. 197 (2006). *But see* Chapin White, *Contrary to Cost-Shift Theory, Lower Medicare Hospital Payment Rates for Inpatient Care Lead to Lower Private Payment Rates*, 32 HEALTH AFF. 935 (2013).

[30] James Robinson, *Hospitals Respond to Medicare Payment Shortfalls by Both Shifting Costs and Cutting Them, Based on Market Concentration*, 30 HEALTH AFF. 1265 (2011).

shift individuals insured in the private market over to public coverage. Like the issue of cost-shifting, there is significant debate regarding the extent of crowd-out. Recent estimates, however, have suggested a crowd-out rate as high as 60%—indicating that the number of privately insured individuals fell by about 60% as much as the number of publicly insured individuals rose.[31] The theory is that because Medicaid and CHIP are both less expensive and provide more generous coverage than private insurance, public insurance expansions result in newly eligible individuals dropping their private coverage.[32] Employers of low-income workers can in fact act in their own self-interest and make it even more likely that employees will drop employer coverage in favor of Medicaid. An employer with a low-income work force can set premiums for its group health plan at a rate that is sufficiently high that Medicaid's lack of premiums becomes very attractive. Employers can similarly set cost-sharing requirements for their health plans, such as deductibles and copay amounts, at levels that would encourage low-income workers to opt for Medicaid. Such actions by employers are rational, given that they allow the employer to shift healthcare costs onto the Medicaid program and away from the employer. And workers in such a situation may rationally choose to drop their employer coverage and move to Medicaid.[33] Given both the incentive that employers face to shift employees to Medicaid, along with the empirical evidence of crowd-out, there is a legitimate concern that public coverage expansions may in fact be inefficient, as they substantially shift the source of financing from individuals to the government, without targeting the problem of uninsurance.

v. Incorporation of Market-Based Features in Public Programs

Finally, perhaps the most significant interaction between public and private insurance in the United States prior to the enactment of the ACA was the movement in the 1990s to make public programs operate more like their private counterparts, by adopting various market-based mechanisms to increase efficiency and competition and to lower costs. Within the Medicare program, Part C was added in 1997, which provided for "Medicare+Choice" plans, which were plans provided by private insurers with benefits of both Part A and Part B. In 2003, Medicare+Choice plans were renamed Medicare Advantage (MA) plans, and various minor changes were made to them by the Medicare Prescription Drug, Improvement, and Modernization Act of 2003.[34] The motivating idea behind Part C was to "enable the Medicare program to utilize innovations that have helped the private market contain costs and expand health care delivery options" by allowing a range of private insurers to offer alternatives to traditional Medicare.[35] Medicare Advantage plans are permitted to offer a wide range of

[31] Jonathan Gruber & Kosali Simon, *Crowd-Out 10 Years Later: Have Recent Public Insurance Expansions Crowded Out Private Health Insurance?*, 27 J. HEALTH ECON. 201, 202 (2008).

[32] *Id.* at 203.

[33] Wal-Mart is often cited as an example of this phenomenon, due to a 2006 internal company memorandum that was leaked to the press. In that memo, Wal-Mart disclosed, among other things, that its employees pay on average 8% of their income on healthcare (nearly twice the national average), that only 48% of eligible employees choose to enroll in Wal-Mart's health plan, and that 5% of Wal-Mart employees and 27% of employees' children were enrolled in Medicaid in 2006. A copy of the memo is available at http://www.nytimes.com/packages/pdf/business/26walmart.pdf.

[34] Pub. L. No. 108-173 (codified in scattered sections of 42 U.S.C. and 26 U.S.C.).

[35] H.R. Rep. No. 105-149, at 1251 (1997).

benefits that encompass not only Medicare Parts A and B, but often prescription drugs and additional benefits as well. The cost savings were expected to come from how these private insurers would be reimbursed by Medicare, along with the efficiencies of both private payers and more coordinated care typical of managed care plans. From a beneficiary's perspective, these plans are often attractive because they allow beneficiaries to purchase coverage that provides extra benefits (such as prescription drug coverage) at little or no cost compared to traditional Medicare.[36] The trade-off is that providers are more restricted in MA plans than in traditional Medicare.[37]

In supporting the 2003 legislation creating MA plans, President Bush emphasized the value of individual choice for Medicare beneficiaries. He stated that "seniors who want more choices and better benefits . . . will have the right to select the health plan that fits their needs best—rather than a one-size-fits-all government plan."[38] Medicare Advantage plans have proven to be very popular among Medicare beneficiaries.[39] As of 2013, 29% of Medicare beneficiaries were enrolled in an MA plan.[40] Nearly every Medicare beneficiary has an MA option available to her, with beneficiaries on average able to choose from eighteen different MA plans.[41] While beneficiaries may benefit from greater choice and expanded coverage, the MA program has not been effective in decreasing costs. Medicare Advantage plans have proven to be more expensive than traditional Medicare, although the ACA implements reforms designed to lower MA plan reimbursement rates in order to bring costs in line with traditional Medicare.[42]

Similar changes were made within Medicaid in the late 1990s. In 1997, federal Medicaid law was amended to allow for program administration, at state option, through managed care arrangements.[43] Prior to the law change, states had to obtain a waiver in order to offer coverage through managed care plans. Now, states can make managed care available to beneficiaries on either a voluntary or compulsory basis, although compulsory enrollment has proven by far the most common. The most recent data show that nearly three-quarters of all Medicaid beneficiaries receive coverage through compulsory managed care enrollment.[44] Within Medicaid, however, this movement has not been based on expanding beneficiary choices (as we have seen with Medicare), but rather about helping states control

[36] Timothy D. McBride, *Medicare Advantage: What Are We Trying to Achieve Anyway?*, 1 St. Louis U.J. Health L. & Pol'y 405, 407–409 (2008).

[37] *Id.* at 416.

[38] *Id.* at 411–412 (citing The White House, Fact Sheet: Framework to Modernize and Improve Medicare, at More Choices—Including the Choice to Stay in Traditional Medicare (2003)).

[39] Joseph P. Newhouse et al., *Steps to Reduce Favorable Risk Selection in Medicare Advantage Largely Succeeded, Boding Well for Health Insurance Exchanges*, 31 Health Aff. 2618, 2620 (2012); Marsha Gold, *Medicare's Private Plans: A Report Card on Medicare Advantage*, 24 Health Aff. w41 (Nov. 2008).

[40] Marsha Gold et al., *Medicare Advantage 2014 Spotlight: Plan Availability and Premiums*, Kaiser Family Found. Issue Brief, Dec. 2013, *available at* http://kaiserfamilyfoundation.files.wordpress.com/2013/11/8520-medicare-advantage-2014-spotlight2.pdf.

[41] *Id.*

[42] *See* 42 U.S.C. §1935w-23 (2012) (as amended by the Health Care & Education Reconciliation Act of 2010).

[43] Balanced Budget Act of 1997, Pub. L. No. 105-33.

[44] Ctrs. for Medicare & Medicaid Servs., Medicaid Managed Care Enrollment Report 2 (2011), *available at* http://www.medicaid.gov/Medicaid-CHIP-Program-Information/By-Topics/Data-and-Systems/Downloads/2011-Medicaid-MC-Enrollment-Report.pdf.

their Medicaid costs. By contracting with managed care providers on a capitated basis, states have been able to shift some Medicaid risk onto private payers.[45] While Medicaid beneficiaries generally have a choice among managed care plans, the differences between the plans tends to be only with respect to provider networks and not other plan features such as cost-sharing or coverage provisions.[46] As a result, thus far market-based reform initiatives within Medicaid have been focused on increasing efficiency and cost-containment on the payer side, rather than enhancing choice for beneficiaries.

As one can see, the pre-ACA interactions between public and private coverage were complex. In large part, this complexity was and is a byproduct of the uniquiely American system of health insurance, where three distinct primary sources of health insurance operate alongside each other. In countries with a single system for health insurance, one does not need to worry about complex market effects such as crowd-out or cost-shifting. Additionally, pre-ACA public systems became more market-oriented—another uniquely American feature. Pre-ACA it appeared as though our approach to health insurance was to move toward a market-oriented, if fragmented, approach to health insurance. As the following section will illustrate, however, the ACA significantly changed that trajectory.

IV The ACA's Embrace of a Public Model for Health Insurance

The ACA's primary policy goal was a distinctly public one: to achieve near-universal coverage. To accomplish this goal, the ACA sought to expand both Medicaid and to make changes to the private individual market to address the well-known failures within that market.

a. The Expansion of Medicaid

The most significant attempt to increase public insurace was through an expansion of Medicaid eligibility. As originally drafted, the ACA allowed states to expand Medicaid eligibility to all individuals with income at or below 133% of the federal poverty limit (Rosenbaum, this volume). States that chose to expand Medicaid would receive an enhanced federal contribution for the new population. For the first three years of the expansion, the federal government would cover 100% of the costs of covering the new population. That match gradually would be reduced to 90% by 2020 and beyond. If a state did not choose to expand its Medicaid program, the state would lose all of its federal Medicaid funding. In

45 John K. Iglehart, *Desperately Seeking Savings: States Shift More Medicaid Enrollees to Managed Care*, 30 Health Aff. 1627, 1628 (2011).

46 Utilizing managed care to deliver Medicaid does not relieve the state from the requirement to provide all benefits required by Medicaid. As a result, given some of the nonmedical costs covered by Medicaid, states that utilize managed care must sometimes carve out certain services from the managed care contracts and instead provide those services either directly to Medicaid beneficiaries or contract with a different service provider to do so. John Holahan et al., *Medicaid Managed Care in Thirteen States*, 17 Health Aff. 43 (1998).

National Federation of Independent Business v. Sebelius,[47] the Supreme Court held that the Medicaid expansion was an unconstitutional exercise of the federal spending power and that states that elected not to participate in the Medicaid expansion could not lose their funding for "traditional" Medicaid. As a result of the ruling, states can decline to participate in the Medicaid expansion without forfeiting the federal funding for their existing Medicaid programs. As of the this writing, twenty-four states have either decided not to expand Medicaid or are continuing to debate the issue.[48] Even without all states expanding, Medicaid enrollment has surged. Early reports find that Medicaid and CHIP enrollment has grown by approximately six million as of April 2014, with percentage increases varying significantly among states based on whether such states are participating in the Medicaid expansion.[49]

b. Making the Individual Market More "Public"

Medicaid expansion was not the only method utilized for expanding coverage. The ACA's largest coverage gains were expected to come from the reformed individual market.[50] What is perhaps underappreciated about this design for the expansion of coverage is that the ACA's changes to the individual insurance market make that private coverage look much more like public coverage. Recall the common features of public health insurance identified in section I. Public systems typically pool health risks broadly pursuant to a social solidarity model of health insurance; public systems are typically subsidized; participation is often mandatory; and public system resources are in large measure distributed based on medical need rather than ability to pay. Finally, public systems typically directly regulate the coverage provided, the prices that can be charged, and the quality of care.

The ACA's reforms of the individual market reflect nearly all of these "public" features. First, the ACA dramatically reduces the ability of insurers to vary insurance availability and pricing based on medical risk. Insurers must offer coverage to all applicants and may vary premiums based on only four factors: age, family size, geographic area, and tobacco use.[51] In addition, insurers are prohibited from excluding preexisting conditions from coverage.[52] These reforms result in the individual market embracing a social solidarity approach to

[47] 132 S. Ct. 2566 (2012).

[48] Kaiser Family Found., *Status of State Action on the Medicaid Expansion Decision*, 2014, http://kff.org/health-reform/state-indicator/state-activity-around-expanding-medicaid-under-the-affordable-care-act/. Following the Supreme Court ruling, various parties were discussing the possibility that states might be permitted to adopt a partial Medicaid expansion, at a level below 133% FPL. The Department of Health & Human Services, however, stated that partial expansions were not authorized under the ACA. Ctrs. for Medicare & Medicaid Servs., *Frequently Asked Questions on Exchanges, Market Reforms, and Medicaid*, Dec. 10, 2012, http://www.cms.gov/CCIIO/Resources/Files/Downloads/exchanges-faqs-12-10-2012.pdf.

[49] Ctrs. for Medicare & Medicaid Servs., *Medicaid & CHIP: March and April 2014 Monthly Enrollment* 3 (2014), at http://medicaid.gov/AffordableCareAct/Medicaid-Moving-Forward-2014/Downloads/Updated-April-2014-Enrollment-Report.pdf.

[50] Letter from Congressional Budget Office, to the Honorable Nancy Pelosi 9 (Mar. 20, 2010), *available at* http://www.cbo.gov/sites/default/files/cbofiles/ftpdocs/113xx/doc11379/amendreconprop.pdf.

[51] 42 U.S.C. §300gg. [52] *Id.* §300gg-3.

health insurance. Nearly all health risks will be shared across the insured population; age and tobacco use are now the only health risks that will not be evenly pooled across the insured population.[53] The individual market is also heavily subsidized for low- and moderate-income individuals, with premium tax credits available to individuals with household income up to 400% of the federal poverty level.[54] Not only is the cost of insurance subsidized but the ACA also provides cost-sharing subsidies for those who are low income, thereby reducing the amount of money an individual must spend out of pocket for medical care once insurance has been purchased. Such subsidization is typical of public programs, as it rejects a distribution of medical care based on ability to pay. For the first time, our regulatory system is at least tacitly acknowledging that health insurance is simply unaffordable for many individuals and that, even for individuals with insurance, out-of-pocket expenses charged by plans may lead to an inability to access care or to financial hardship. While participation in the individual market is not mandatory, a financial penalty applies to individuals who have affordable coverage available to them (whether in the individual market or through an employer plan) but choose not to purchase coverage.

The individual insurance market reforms also introduce various restrictions on the market that mimic in various ways the role of government in public systems. Administrators of a state health insurance exchange, which is the insurance marketplace created by the ACA to facilitate the purchase of individual health insurance, have the authority to actively police the quality of plans offered within their state's exchange and may exclude low-quality plans. Further, the substance of the plans is heavily regulated through the requirement that all plans offer "essential health benefits" and comply with cost-sharing limits imposed by the ACA.[55] And while the government is not directly regulating prices as it does within Medicare and Medicaid, the ACA implements medical loss ratio requirements, which limit the amount an insurer can spend on administrative expenses and keep as profit. Under the medical loss ratio rules, insurers are required to spend a certain percentage of premiums (80% in the individual and small group markets; 85% in the large group market) collected on actual medical care or quality improvement activities, leaving only 20% or 15%, respectively, for administrative expenses and profits.[56] Overall, the changes the ACA made to the individual market represent a clear shift toward a "public" approach to health insurance coverage—a notable move given the federal government's historical inclination to take a market-based approach to healthcare and health insurance coverage.

While the ACA enacts a very clear shift toward "public" features, it is important to note that market mechanisms have not been entirely abandoned. Unlike traditional public programs, individual market purchasers will have a choice of health insurance plans offered through the market. While several features of these plans will be highly regulated, they may still vary in terms of plan design, cost-sharing requirements, provider networks, and insurers.[57] The market will still depend on consumers making informed choices that

[53] To be sure, age is correlated with increased risk for many health conditions. As a result, the ACA's allowance of premium variation based on age is likely to limit the degree to which health risks are pooled across the insured population.

[54] I.R.C. §36B. [55] 42 U.S.C. §18022. [56] *Id.* §300gg-18(b).

[57] The extent of this variability depends, of course, on the number of insurers that decide to offer coverage through the state exchange, as well as plan design decisions made by such insurers, and may vary significantly between markets.

satisfy their preferences, a distinctly nonpublic plan feature. In addition, the content of the standardized benefit package (the essential health benefits) are required to reflect the generosity of the average employer plan, thereby indirectly incorporating a benefits standard set by reference to market conditions. Finally, and perhaps most important, products in the individual market will be offered exclusively by private, often for-profit, insurance companies.

c. Small Group Market Reforms: A Mix of Public and Private

The ACA's reforms in the small group market reflect the fact that, while technically group coverage, coverage in this market often operates more like individual insurance given the limited risk pooling that small groups provide. The ACA's small group market reforms are generally identical to its individual market reforms, with the result that the reforms incoporate new public-like features into the small group market. Like the individual market, premiums can vary based only on age, family size, tobacco use, and geographic area of the covered employees; insurers are required to offer coverage to all small group applicants and provide coverage of all essential health benefits. In addition, the ACA creates small business health insurance exchanges whose administrators will have the same authority to oversee plan offerings and quality as in the individual market. As in the individual market, these reforms move the small group market to a social solidarity model, with the vast majority of health risks being pooled throughout the market—a distinct change from the medically underwritten standards that existed in most states pre-ACA. The small group market does not, however, move quite as far toward a public model as does the individual market. Most notably, premium tax credits are not available for low-income individuals who are offered qualifying coverage from their employers. Instead the ACA provides tax credits for small employers that meet various requirements, but the credits are only available through 2016. While the lack of subsidies for small group purchasers make this market look less public in orientation than the individual market, it is still the case that the ACA has incorporated significant public features into the small group market: a social solidarity model with minimum specified benefits and increased direct regulation of product offerings.

d. Leaving Large Employers Alone

The ACA left the large group market largely intact. There were a handful of changes that affected this market, but it is worth examing why the ACA made such dramatic changes to the individual and small group markets but left large group plans to enjoy the status quo.

It seems curious given the movement of public and private coverage closer together that the large group market was left largely unregulated. Yet there is a very practical explanation for this exceptionalism—the large employer market was the one segment of the pre-ACA health insurance system that most people agreed worked fairly well. As a result, it is not surpring that there was no political inclination to rock the boat.

It should also, however, be noted that while the large employer market is very lightly regulated (Hall, this volume), it does in practice have some features that are similar to public coverage. As explained in more detail in section III.b.ii., the large group market broadly pools health risks under a social solidarity model and is subsidized through the tax benefits provided to employer-provided coverage (Hall, this volume). As a result, leaving the large group market alone is not inconsistent with the ACA's embrace of a public model for private health insurance.

e. Existing Public Programs and the ACA

As discussed section III.c.v., the 1990s saw a shift, albeit a modest one, toward incorporating market mechanisms within public programs. The ACA did not fundamentally change the public-with-some-market-pressure approach that has been in place since that time.

The ACA did not directly implement any Medicaid market-based reforms, perhaps other than standardizing benefits between the Medicaid expansion population and the individual and small group markets. All of these market segements are required to cover essential health benefits, and therefore coverage terms within these markets should be nearly identical.[58] One benefit of such consistency is that the individuals who move between them (e.g., between Medicaid and individual market coverage) will have a better chance to enjoy continuity of care, an essential element of quality care.[59] Estimates suggest that there will be significant movement between Medicaid and the individual market once the ACA is fully implemented. For example, one study estimates that 35% of individuals with income below twice the federal poverty level will experience a change in income that will shift them between Medicaid and the individual market within a six-month period.[60]

The ACA did not enact any significant market-based reforms of Medicare. Medicare's premiums were made more progressive, and high-income earners must pay more into the Medicare system, but these reforms actually make Medicare look more like a social assistance program than pure social insurance. The Affordable Care Act added an additional Medicare tax on high-earners effective in 2013, which is equal to 0.9% of wages above $200,000 for individual taxpayers and $250,000 for married individuals filing jointly.[61] This additional tax is imposed only on employees, not employers. The ACA also implements various Medicare payment reforms, such as lowering payment to Medicare Advantage plans and encouraging the formation of accountable care organizations, but these changes are not likely to introduce significant new market forces into the Medicare market. Of course, given the market-oriented reforms of the 1990s to both Medicare and Medicaid, it may make sense that further reforms were not a focus of the ACA.

[58] Specific benefit terms can vary between plans as long as they provide actuarially equivalent coverage to the base or benchmark plan. In addition, "medically frail" individuals in the Medicaid expansion population may be eligible for additional benefits.

[59] Rosenbaum, *Medicaid's Next Fifty Years*, at 333.

[60] Benjamin D. Sommers & Sara Rosenbaum, *Issues in Health Reform: How Changes in Eligibility May Move Millions Back and Forth Between Medicaid and Insurance Exchanges*, 30 HEALTH AFF. 228, 232 (2011).

[61] I.R.C. §3101(b).

f. Prospects for Post-ACA Public-Private Interaction

While the ACA does relatively little to alter public programs' embrace of market features, it does allow for policy entrepreneurs to experiment with new market mechanisms and other reforms. States have in fact always had the ability to experiment by seeking a waiver from the Department of Health and Human Services (HHS) of traditional Medicaid requirements, and that ability continues post-ACA. In addition, the ACA provides a new waiver procedure that can exempt states from many of the state health insurance requirements of the ACA, provided that the state plan provides coverage that is at least as generous as that which would have been provided under the ACA.[62] The waiver provision essentially allows states to utilize the federal funds that would have been paid out in the form of premium tax credits to provide coverage through an alternative mechanism to the individual insurance market as envisioned by the ACA. Two states, Arkansas and Vermont, provide good examples of the types of policy entrepreneurship that can arise from these waiver provisions, as well as a sense of the direction that future interactions between public and private coverage may take.

i. The Arkansas Example—"Privatizing" Medicaid

Arkansas has been granted a waiver from HHS to move to a "premium assistance" model of Medicaid, where beneficiaries are given subsidies to buy insurance available on the individual market, hoping to capitalize on the existing networks and efficiencies within that market.[63] The Department of Health and Human Services has indicated that it is willing to approve a number of such demonstration projects in order to study the effects of moving toward a market-based mechanism for delivering Medicaid.[64]

The Arkansas waiver is an interesting example of the complex relationships that have developed between public and private coverage. The basic idea in Arkansas is that instead of expanding Medicaid through the traditional state program, newly eligible adults will instead select from among silver-level coverage available in the region where they live, through the private individual market, with the state paying the premiums for such coverage. In addition, the state will ensure that the cost-sharing that such individuals face are consistent with Medicaid requirements by subsidizing such payments, if necessary. While most newly eligible adults will be given this so-called private option, individuals who are considered medically frail, or who have exceptional medical needs, will remain in traditional Medicaid. Arkansas applied for the waiver on the grounds that providing Medicaid benefits through private insurance for the expansion population would provide improved continuity of care. Given how often low-income individuals transition in and out of Medicaid eligibility, enrolling such individuals in private plans would allow them to keep the same health

[62] 42 U.S.C. §18052.

[63] Letter from Marilyn Tavenner, Office of the Administrator, Department of Health & Human Services, to Andy Allison, Director, Arkansas Department of Human Services (Sept. 27, 2013), *available at* http://www.medicaid.gov/Medicaid-CHIP-Program-Information/By-Topics/Waivers/1115/downloads/ar/ar-private-option-ca.pdf.

[64] Dept. of Health & Human Servs., *Medicaid and the Affordable Care Act: Premium Assistance*, *at* http://content.govdelivery.com/attachments/USCMS/2013/03/29/file_attachments/200058/Premium%2BAssistance%2BFAQ%2B03-29-13.pdf.

insurance coverage even if they lose Medicaid eligibility. In addition, Arkansas stated that providing Medicaid expansion coverage through the individual market would double the size of that market, thereby helping to drive more competitive premium pricing. Finally, Arkansas explained that providing private coverage for the expansion population would support the equality of provider reimbursment across payers, eliminating the need for cross-subsdiziation (or cost-shifting) among payers. This would have the added benefit of increasing access to providers since the expansion population would be seeking care from doctors participating in private insurance networks, which reimburse at a rate above traditional Medicaid rates.

At first glance, moves like the one in Arkansas appear to run counter to the argument presented at the beginning of this part, that private coverage is becoming more public-like. But moving Medicaid recipients to the private market is in fact a further indication of the public nature of the individual market. Moving Medicaid receipients to an individual market under pre-ACA regulation would have been disastorous in most states, given that insurers could deny coverage and price based on risk. But with the ACA reforming the individual market to contain many public-like features, it makes sense to utilize this market to provide what may be better access to providers and better continuity of care with no increase in cost. And by carving out those with the most significant medical needs from such coverage, traditional Medicaid continues to fulfill its core mission of providing generous coverage to those with the most significant health needs. What Arkansas is effectively doing is simply using Medicaid funds to better subsidize traditional health insurance coverage for those with low-income but no particularly complex health needs. The demonstration project has been approved for three years, and many in the policy community are likely to closely monitor the data in order to determine whether this type of public subsidy for private coverage is a good solution for the low-income population.

ii. The Vermont Example—A Single Payer System

While Arkansas has sought to utilize the newly reformed individual market to provide Medicaid coverage, Vermont has enacted legislation that seeks to move the state toward a universal coverage single-payer system, in part through utilization of federal funds available through the ACA waiver process.[65] Vermont, therefore, is seeking to move its private insurance market even further toward a public model than that contemplated by the ACA's provisions. While many details of Vermont's plan are not yet known, as they are contingent upon both a waiver application and federal government approval, the basic idea is to replace the private health insurance market with a public, single-payer system. Instead of utilizing private insurers, benefits would be provided by a single, public fund. This single payer would then be responsible for setting the reimbursment rates paid to all providers. Medicare and Medicaid funding would remain the same, but such funds would be governed by the same payment and administrative system, thereby creating uniform reimbursment rates. The elimination of private insurers, combined with the de facto price regulation of a single payer

[65] 2011 Vt. Acts & Resolves 48. For more detailed information on the Vermont plan, *see* William C. Hsiao et al., *What Other States Can Learn from Vermont's Bold Experiment: Embracing a Single-Payer Health Care Financing System*, 30 HEALTH AFF. 1232 (2011); Sean McElwee, *Can Vermont's Single-Payer System Fix What Ails American Healthcare?*, THE ATLANTIC, Dec. 27, 2013.

system and universal coverage are the factors that push Vermont's planned system even further into the public model than that created by the ACA.

V Conclusion

Health insurance has long been a puzzle in the United States. In general, American policy reflects the idea that a fully functioning market is the best method to allocate resources. Yet embracing this idea in the context of health insurance has been difficult, as there are well-known market failures that prevent that market from fully functioning. For decades we have made do with a very basic (and incomplete) safety net for the most vulnerable, nearly universal public coverage for the elderly, and an employer-based system for the rest, with large employer groups overcoming some of the market failures that normally plague health insurance markets. There were clear downsides to this system. Individuals who were not eligible for public programs and who did not work for employers that offered them adequate health insurance coverage were often uninsured because the markets for individual health insurance functioned so poorly. And on the public side, there were concerns about the financial sustainability of our public systems, caused largely by the absence of market mechanisms to control cost. Similarly, there were concerns that an absence of competitive pressures within public systems contributed to poor quality care, pricing distortions, and fraud and abuse.

In the 1990s, the federal government responded to some of these concerns by introducing limited market reforms within both Medicare and Medicaid. These reforms had mixed success. While Medicare Advantage plans have proven enormously popular, they have not been effective in lowering costs. Medicaid managed care, on the other hand, has helped states control costs but has not introduced significant participant choice. While these reforms, which introduced some private market features into public programs, have been positively viewed, they were not designed to address the significant problem of uninsurance.

It was not until the passage of the ACA that the federal government meaningfully addressed the issue of uninsurance, and it did so by moving the individual health insurance market toward a public model of health insurance coverage and by significantly expanding the scope of Medicaid. The reforms of the ACA acknowledge a truth often ignored by standard economic theory, which is that health insurance is simply unaffordable for many individuals. The ACA also acknowledges, and addresses, well-known failures in the individual health insurance market by constraining the methods by which insurers can compete in the health insurance market.

This history illustrates that we appear to be moving toward a middle ground: rejecting a fully market-based approach but acknowledging that public systems can benefit from at least limited market forces. I am optimistic that borrowing the best features of public and private markets is a move in the right direction, but we still have a lot of work to do. A system of universal coverage that is made up of several distinct market segments, some public and some private, will always be complicated. We will always have to deal with issues of crowd-out, cost-shifting, and a lack of continuity of coverage and care. Our exceptionalism in healthcare has its costs.

D. Healthcare Costs

CHAPTER 36

MANAGING THE CARE AND COSTS OF A DEFINED INSURED POPULATION

FRANCIS J. CROSSON AND LAURA A. TOLLEN

I Introduction

PERHAPS the greatest fiscal and social challenge of this new century for most countries will be how to afford and provide quality healthcare for their populations. Optimists believe that advances in medical technology, including drugs and vaccines, will lower overall costs by preventing and modifying disease processes. Pessimists believe that population aging and increased rates of chronic illness, combined with other aspects of medical technology development, will bankrupt societies, leading to increased inequities in access to healthcare.

This chapter describes the current state of knowledge about how to manage care and cost for a defined, insured population in the United States.[1] The chapter draws on case studies from Kaiser Permanente, a large, fully integrated healthcare system operating in eight states and the District of Columbia.[2] Kaiser Permanente is often recognized as the leading organization in the United States in managing the cost and quality of care for its insured members. The chapter also describes some of the business, cultural, and legal challenges to replicating important elements of the Kaiser Permanente model. Lastly, the chapter describes policy choices facing the country in the near future, which could have an impact on healthcare systems' ability to manage care and costs.

[1] In this chapter, "population" refers to the universe of individuals enrolled with an insurer, not the population of the United States. In addition, the chapter relies primarily on lessons from commercially insured populations, rather than the approximately 50% of Americans who receive coverage from public programs such as Medicare, Medicaid, and the Veterans Health Administration. This is because public programs, while often able to set unit prices paid to providers, are unable to use broader approaches to manage total population care and costs because of legislative or regulatory restrictions.

[2] A fully integrated healthcare system usually combines insurance coverage, physician services, and hospital services all "under one roof," although specific corporate structures vary.

II Mechanisms of Care and Cost Management in an Insured Population

There are three complementary approaches to managing care and costs in a defined population.[3] Before we address those approaches, we note that care and cost are only two legs of the stool—the third is quality. In this chapter, our focus is on care- and cost-management techniques that preserve and enhance quality. The first approach is to prevent illness in the first place, and to detect and treat illness in its early, less costly stages. The second is to provide only appropriate services, avoiding unnecessary expenditures and potential negative effects of needless or dangerous medical interventions. The third is to avoid overpaying for goods and services used in treatments.

Within each approach, those who pay for care (employers and insurers) and those who provide it (doctors and hospitals) rely on a number of tools. The first tool is the social contract we have, as Americans, that tells us what services are appropriately provided through insurance—the services we believe are legitimately *healthcare* services. The second tool is the design of benefits. The third is design of payment arrangements for healthcare providers. The fourth tool is really a tool-bag of techniques that healthcare providers themselves employ in the clinical setting to manage cost and improve quality.

a. The Social Contract

Any healthcare purchaser operates under a time-specific social consensus about what is "healthcare," and what is not. In aggregate, such distinctions determine what the society wishes to subsidize through health insurance. For example, most purely cosmetic surgery is considered discretionary and is excluded from health insurance coverage. In other areas, there may be a lack of social consensus. For example, there is disagreement in the United States about whether health insurance should cover the cost of habilitation services for children with Autism Spectrum Disorder to improve language, interpersonal, and education functions. Many believe these are healthcare services, while others believe they are educational services. The social contract consensus varies over time and even among developed countries.

b. Benefit Design

Working within the social contract, health insurers develop detailed explications of services covered, in exchange for what monthly premiums, and what "out-of-pocket" payments upon receipt of services. These arrangements are generally referred to as the "benefit plan." In most cases, state and federal regulations moderate the degree to which insurers can limit the actual services covered or the length of coverage, although all benefit plans have some such

[3] Broadly stated, when we discuss "care management" in this chapter, we mean coordination of care, particularly for patients with complex and chronic disease, across providers, care settings, and clinical conditions, and over time.

constraints. Recently, benefit plan designers have sought to limit insurer costs by establishing larger out-of-pocket spending requirements for insured individuals.

There are two components of out-of-pocket spending: deductibles and copayments. Patients must pay an annual deductible directly to their providers before the insurer begins to pay anything. Deductibles are effective at limiting the use of more discretionary, less costly services but have little inhibiting effect on costly services such as hospitalizations, because once the deductible cap is reached, there is no longer a disincentive to use care. Copayments—charges for each visit, hospital day, or diagnostic service—often serve to limit the use of both high- and low-cost services.

Deductibles and copayments reduce use of services but may adversely impact health, as they cause patients to avoid needed services as well as services with marginal benefit.[4] In addition, there is evidence that high levels of copayments may actually increase long-term costs by inhibiting care for chronic conditions, leading to higher use of more expensive services later.[5]

c. Insurer/Payer Actions

Many commercial health plans seek to manage costs and care by contracting with physicians and other providers with a track record of lower costs and better quality. Such providers are referred to as the plan's "network." Recently, plans have begun "narrowing" their networks by eliminating many costly physicians and hospitals. This action has begun to generate legal and regulatory activity in several states.[6]

In the past, payers have used pre-authorization for the provision of expensive or commonly overused services as a means of controlling costs. Under this process, physicians call the contracting health plan to request authorization for the intended services, based upon details of the patient's clinical case. Most health plans believe that the pre-authorization process itself is a barrier to unnecessary service use.

While pre-authorization is still used, it is not as common as it once was. In recent years, insurers are focusing more on "disease management" or "case management," under which health plans work closely with high-using, clinically fragile patients—often through telephone contact—to improve their health and reduce service-use. A large Medicare-directed multiyear effort of this sort produced little value.[7]

One of the most significant payer actions that has influenced cost and care management is the implementation of Diagnosis-Related Groups (DRGs) in Medicare.[8] Since 1983,

[4] Thomas Rice & Karen Y. Matsuoka, *The Impact of Cost-Sharing on Appropriate Utilization and Health Status: A Review of the Literature on Seniors*, 61 MED. CARE RES. REV. 415 (2004).

[5] Amal N. Trivedi et al., *Increased Ambulatory Care Copayments and Hospitalizations Among the Elderly*, 362 NEW ENG. J. MED. 320 (2010).

[6] Elizabeth Johnson, *The Never-Ending Debate over Health Care Narrow Networks*, LAW 360 (Mar. 12, 2014, 5:27 PM), http://www.law360.com/articles/517282/the-never-ending-debate-over-health-care-narrow-networks.

[7] CONGRESSIONAL BUDGET OFFICE, LESSONS FROM MEDICARE'S DEMONSTRATION PROJECTS ON DISEASE MANAGEMENT, CARE COORDINATION, AND VALUE-BASED PAYMENT (2012).

[8] *Acute Inpatient PPS*, CENTERS FOR MEDICARE AND MEDICAID SERVS., http://www.cms.gov/Medicare/Medicare-Fee-for-Service-Payment/AcuteinpatientPPS/index.html (last visited July 8, 2014).

hospitals caring for Medicare patients have been paid a fixed global payment—the DRG—for most stays, irrespective of the length, complexity, or cost of the stay. As a result, hospitals try to manage the cost of Medicare patients by avoiding unnecessary procedures and needless extra days of hospitalization.

More recently, payers have begun experimenting with making direct payments to physicians and hospitals for preferred outcomes, often referred to as "pay-for-performance." Most of these payments are small compared to physician incomes, but material compared to hospital operating margins, and so have had more traction with hospitals than with physicians.

Another technique is the provision of "global" payments or "payment bundles" for the care of patients with specific conditions, such as a heart transplant. Under this approach, the hospital and physicians together receive one shared payment for all related services (including both inpatient and outpatient), regardless of how long the patient is hospitalized, how many tests are ordered, and so forth. Lastly, health plans and other payers are beginning to share insurance risk with providers, or to transfer risk entirely through global prospective population-based payments known as "capitation."

d. Healthcare Provider Actions

Historically the most effective and sustainable attempts to manage care and costs have been led by physicians directly. It is commonly believed that physician decisions affect more than 80% of healthcare costs. Perhaps the longest experience with physician-led population cost management has occurred within medical groups receiving group capitation. But even in the absence of capitation, other physician group practices receiving mostly fee-for-service payments have implemented cost- and quality-management activities. One example is the Geisinger Health System in central Pennsylvania, which developed a cost- and outcome-guarantee program known as "Proven Care," with great success and acclaim.[9] Additional care- and cost-management techniques used by large multispecialty physician group practices include:

- Physician selection and acculturation: attracting and retaining physicians who believe in cost and quality management at the population level as part of their professional responsibility;
- Specialty-specific, evidence-based care guidelines: creating and using such guidelines to assist but never compel physician decision-making;
- Ancillary care providers (nurse practitioners, physician assistants, etc.): substituting for physicians when appropriate, usually at a lower cost;
- Payment and incentive practices: paying physicians a salary rather than fee-for-service payments, and/or providing modest group bonuses for success in reducing unnecessary costs;
- Performance information: providing physicians with detailed information about the cost and quality of their care compared to colleagues' performance, often openly shared within the practice;

[9] *ProvenCare by Geisinger*, GEISINGER HEALTH SYS., http://www.geisinger.org/sites/provencare/ (last visited April 28, 2015).

- Enhancement of prevention and early disease detection: aggressive management of diseases, such as hypertension, which, untreated, lead to preventable and costly conditions such as strokes;
- Shared decision-making: close involvement of patients in decisions about interventions with borderline value, and early consideration of end-of-life choices for appropriate patients;
- Communication technology: substitution of office visits with more efficient telephone and online communication between physicians and their patients, once a therapeutic relationship has been established; and,
- Health literacy and self-care: education of patients about their health and disease processes, empowering them to manage health issues they are capable of handling without professional intervention.

III A Brief History of Kaiser Permanente

Many of the mechanisms used to manage the care and costs of an insured population described above described in sections II.b–d above have evolved within a unique organization, Kaiser Permanente. In its current form, Kaiser Permanente is an evergreen contractual alliance between a not-for-profit insurer, Kaiser Foundation Health Plan, a nonprofit hospital system, Kaiser Foundation Hospitals, and eight physician professional corporations known as Permanente Medical Groups (Figure 36.1).

The Kaiser Permanente model began much by chance. In January 1942, the progressive industrialist Henry Kaiser received a federal commission to build merchant marine vessels, later known as Liberty Ships, to replace ships being sunk by German and Japanese

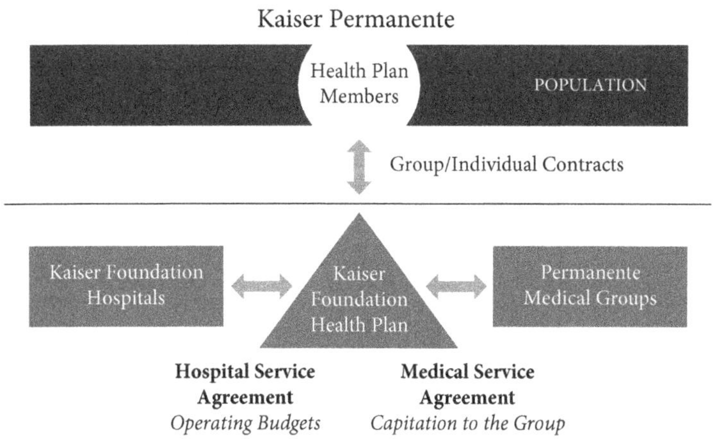

FIGURE 36.1 Kaiser Permanente Structure

submarines. By June of that year, he had built construction facilities in Vancouver, Washington; Oakland and Richmond, California; and Fontana, California, and assembled a workforce of over 90,000 men and women. To provide medical services for these workers he engaged a group of physicians led by Dr. Sidney Garfield, who had provided services to Kaiser at the constructions of the California Aqueduct and the Grand Coulee Dam. This engagement expanded on two innovations used at the two earlier job sites, group practice and delivery system prepayment. Group practice meant that the physicians practiced as one economic unit with mutual accountability to each other and to their patients. The physician group was paid not by fees for each service provided but by a monthly prospective payment from Kaiser that later formed the basis for physicians to be paid a salary.

These innovations reversed the dynamics under which most physicians practiced at the time, creating cooperation among physicians rather than competition and an incentive to prevent illness rather than profit from it. Despite vehement opposition from physician professional associations, the new model grew and thrived in the postwar period, often with the support of labor organizations.

In 1973, Kaiser Permanente's growth began to accelerate following the passage of the "HMO Act." The act required public and private support for the development of "health maintenance organizations" (HMOs), modeled after Kaiser Permanente. The HMO was viewed as a model of insurance and service provision that provided incentives to both improve quality and reduce costs. Unfortunately, by the early 1990s, many newer HMOs—often publicly held, for-profit corporations—seemed to favor aggressive cost reduction over quality improvement, leading to a backlash from physicians, patients, the media, and eventually employers. HMO growth slowed, and the rate of healthcare cost growth began to accelerate, increasing from 8.9% of gross domestic product in 1980, to 17.2% by 2012.[10]

Kaiser Permanente survived the anti-HMO period well intact and continued to grow and expand geographically. Today, Kaiser Permanente provides coverage and services to over 9 million members in eight states and the District of Columbia, with an annual budget of over $60 billion and 18,000 Permanente physicians. In each Kaiser Permanente region, the Kaiser Foundation Health Plan offers health coverage to individuals, called "members," either directly or through employers. The associated Permanente Medical Group provides professional services for a negotiated per-member fee or "capitation." Individual physicians are paid by salary with modest incentive opportunities. Kaiser Foundation Hospitals receive an annual operating budget, also on a prospective basis, and are managed cooperatively by hospital administrators and Permanente physician leaders. Thus, the insurer, the hospitals, and the physicians together have the same incentive—to improve quality through preventive medicine and early detection of disease and to eliminate inappropriate services and costs.

[10] CENTERS FOR MEDICARE AND MEDICAID SERVS., TABLE 1—NATIONAL HEALTH EXPENDITURES; AGGREGATE AND PER CAPITA AMOUNTS, ANNUAL PERCENT CHANGE AND PERCENT DISTRIBUTION: SECOND CALENDAR YEARS 1960–2012, *available at* http://www.cms.gov/Research-Statistics-Data-and-Systems/Statistics-Trends-and-Reports/NationalHealthExpendData/Downloads/tables.pdf.

IV Lessons from Kaiser Permanente: Two Case Studies

As noted, there are three complementary approaches to managing care and costs in a defined population: (1) prevention and early detection of illness; (2) provision of only needed and appropriate services; and (3) avoiding overpayment for goods and services used in the treatment of patients. Kaiser Permanente employs each of these approaches, all of them enabled by the organization's core principles of group medical practice and prospective payment. Here we present two case studies; the first, "Hypertension Detection and Management," is primarily an example of the first approach, and the second, "Pharmaceutical Cost Management," is an example of the latter two approaches.

a. Case Study #1—Hypertension Detection and Management

Blood pressure is the force or pressure of blood against the artery walls. It is usually measured in two parts, the systolic blood pressure, which is the peak pressure exerted by the heart as it pumps blood out to the body, and the diastolic blood pressure, the residual pressure within the arteries between heartbeats. When a person has high blood pressure—or hypertension—the heart has to work harder so that it can send blood throughout the body. There are many biological causes for hypertension, the most common being age-related stiffening of the artery walls, creating resistance to the flow of blood. Hypertension is a major risk factor for stroke, heart attack, and kidney disease, because it gradually and painlessly damages the arterial walls. Hypertension contributed to more than 360,000 deaths in the United States in 2010.[11] It affects 67 million people in the United States, only half of whom have their condition under control.[12]

Hypertension is defined as having blood pressure above specific systolic or diastolic levels, or both. The blood pressure levels considered to be of concern vary depending on the person's age and the presence or absence of diabetes and/or kidney disease. When a hypertensive patient brings his or her blood pressure down below that specific level, generally through life-style changes and medication, the disease is considered to be "in control."

Effective therapies for treating hypertension are well understood and agreed upon, and have been available for nearly fifty years. An estimated 46,000 deaths could be avoided annually if 70% of patients with high blood pressure were treated according to these standards.[13] Further, a 5% reduction in the prevalence of hypertension would save the U.S. healthcare

[11] Alan S. Go et al., *Heart Disease and Stroke Statistics—2014 Update*, 129 Circulation e28 (2014).

[12] Centers for Disease Control and Prevention, *Vital Signs: Awareness and Treatment of Uncontrolled Hypertension Among Adults—United States, 2003–2010*, 61 Morbidity and Mortality Weekly Report 703 (2012).

[13] Thomas A. Farley et al., *Deaths Preventable in the U.S. by Improvements in the Use of Clinical Preventive Services*, 38 Am. J. Preventative Med. 600 (2010); U.S. Dept. of Health and Human Servs., *The Seventh Report of the Joint National Committee on Prevention, Detection, Evaluation, and Treatment of High Blood Pressure*, 289 J. Amer. Med. Ass'n 2560 (2003).

system $25 billion over five years, due to the direct and indirect costs of strokes, heart attacks, and kidney disease avoided.[14]

A major review of clinical trials found that one of the most effective means of improving blood pressure control rates in primary care settings is an organized, comprehensive system of regular population review and intervention—in other words, treating physicians need to know *who* within their population of patients has the disease, and possess an effective and systematic way to *connect* with those patients to initiate and manage treatment.

Because of its unique structure, Kaiser Permanente in Northern California (KPNC) was able to implement a large-scale blood pressure control program for over 3 million patients, resulting in blood pressure control rates increasing from 44% in 2001, to 86% in 2012.[15] The three keys to KPNC's success in managing hypertension were:

- The creation of a registry, or database, that identifies all of the people with hypertension within the covered population;
- An evidence-based intervention that helps these patients reduce their blood pressure; and,
- An ongoing system of measurement to allow the organization to gauge its success and make process improvements in hypertension management when necessary.

i. The Registry

In the mid-1990s, Kaiser Permanente in Northern California began to recognize that hypertension was a growing problem for its members. In 2000, to evaluate the scope of the problem, the organization created a registry—or database—of individuals with hypertension, using outpatient diagnostic codes, pharmacy data, and hospitalization records. Diagnoses were verified through chart audits of random samples of identified members. With the registry established, physicians could begin to proactively reach out to hypertensive members to encourage treatment, a key capability for true population-based care. However, the management of hypertension requires regular blood pressure readings, at least three times a year by trained professionals, and often readings by the patients themselves, then provided to the physicians. In early 2000, the organization was not systematically collecting blood pressure data in an automated way that would provide sufficient information for the highest level of disease management.

At that time, Kaiser Permanente did not have electronic medical records, but it did have a standardized paper form that all physicians used to record basic information, including the patient's diagnosis, for each visit. The hypertension experts within KPNC added a section to the paper form that allowed physicians to mark off each patient's blood pressure from among six ranges that were provided. With this simple step, the elements required to determine

[14] Barbara A. Ormond et al., *Potential National and State Medical Care Savings from Primary Disease Prevention*, 101 AM. J. PUB. HEALTH 157 (2011).

[15] Marc Jaffe et al., *The Kaiser Permanente Northern California Hypertension Project 2001–2012: How an Integrated Care Delivery System Increased and Maintained Blood Pressure Control Rates from 44% to 86% in 11 Years*, 8 J. AMER. SOC'Y OF HYPERTENSION e11 (2014).

hypertension control rates for the registry were available, and it became possible for the physicians to generate regular blood pressure control rate reports.[16]

What was extraordinary about this approach is that it expanded the responsibility for collecting blood pressure readings beyond the primary care physicians, such as internists and family practice doctors. Blood pressure readings were to be taken, when feasible, at every office visit by every primary *and specialty* care physician. So, for example, even if a patient came to see a dermatologist or ophthalmologist for skin or eye care, the intent was to measure and enter blood pressure into the registry for those visits as well. This allowed the organization to populate the registry with multiple blood pressure readings for each patient—a necessity in identifying and managing hypertension.

Within six months, the physicians at KPNC were able to identify three-quarters of all hypertensive patients within the population they served. A medical department or individual physician could then use the registry to identify hypertensive patients with out-of-control blood pressure who had not been in for a visit in a given period of time. This allowed for proactive outreach to these patients to bring them into the office for examination and discussion, intensify their drug therapy, or help them manage any issues they may have had with adherence to their current drug regimen.

It is important to note that KPNC's initial major strides in hypertension control were made using a paper-based form and a simple registry. Kaiser Permanente's full electronic medical record was not uniformly in place until 2007, by which time KPNC had already drastically improved hypertension control rates. Dr. Marc Jaffe, clinical leader of the Kaiser Permanente Northern California Cardiovascular Risk Reduction Program, summed up the process: "You can do everything on note cards."

ii. The Intervention

In concert with the establishment of the hypertension registry, Kaiser Permanente Northern California implemented four innovations that, together, produced dramatic improvement in the hypertension control rate:

- *Development and dissemination of a four-step medication treatment algorithm* to aid physicians in controlling hypertension with medications.[17] Blood pressure control requires frequent adjustment of several medications and intensification to the next level of therapy (either increasing the dose or adding an additional medication) if initial treatment does not result in good control.

  The guideline is based on clinical trials and updated every two years. Physicians are encouraged to use it unless their own judgment, based upon the particular circumstances of the patient, dictates otherwise. KPNC disseminated the guideline to physicians through printed documents, e-mails, videoconferences, lectures, partnering with pharmacy managers, and—later—use of the electronic medical record to electronically facilitate the selection of the appropriate medication.

[16] Marc Jaffe et al., *Improved Blood Pressure Control Associated with a Large-Scale Hypertension Program*, 310 J. AMER. MED. ASS'N 699 (2013).

[17] *Id.*

- *Initial pharmacotherapy with a single-pill combination tablet.* In 2005, the Kaiser Permanente Northern California hypertension guideline was modified to encourage the use of two blood pressure lowering medications combined into a single pill. Most patients with hypertension require two or more medication to control blood pressure; so starting with a single-pill combination reduces the time it takes to achieve control. In addition, initial single-pill combination therapy is more convenient and less expensive for patients, who now have one copayment instead of two, leading to improved adherence. It is also easier for patients to take one pill than several, and patients are therefore more likely to take their full-prescribed regimen.[18] Single-pill prescriptions are also less expensive for the pharmacy to fill.

  Over the period 2001 to 2009, the number of prescriptions for the most frequently prescribed single-pill combination blood pressure medication increased from 13 per month to over 23,000 per month,[19] and by 2012, to 25,700 per month.[20] The single-pill combination accounts for 30% of all prescriptions for these medications in Kaiser Permanente Northern California.
- *Medical assistant blood pressure checks.* Hypertension cannot be controlled if it cannot be measured. With 600,000 hypertensive patients in Kaiser Permanente Northern California, it was neither cost-effective nor necessary to measure blood pressure exclusively at doctor office visits. Therefore, KPNC implemented a program under which medical assistants—trained with standardized guidelines created by physicians and clinic managers—could perform blood pressure checks at follow-up visits, typically two to four weeks after a medication adjustment. Unlike visits with a physician, visits with a medical assistant require no patient copayment. If the patient was found to have poorly controlled hypertension, the medical assistant directed the result to the patient's physician. According to Dr. Joseph Young, Kaiser Permanente's hypertension leader in Northern California, "This system accelerated treatment intensification without significantly increasing the need for repeat clinician visits, while simultaneously improving patient convenience and affordability."[21]
- *Practice alerts in the electronic medical record.* As noted, Kaiser Permanente's electronic medical record was not in place when the wide-scale hypertension control program started. However, the system was fully functional by 2007, and by 2011, included an alert for the medical assistant or physician to repeat the blood pressure test within five minutes if a reading is elevated. This is because many patients are tense when visiting healthcare facilities, in some cases causing temporary "white-coat hypertension." Generally this tension abates over a few minutes, making the second blood pressure reading more indicative of the patient's actual blood pressure. Thus, these alerts helped to improve the accuracy of blood pressure readings.

[18] Alan H. Gradman et al., *Combination Therapy in Hypertension*, 4 J. AMER. SOC'Y HYPERTENSION 90 (2010); Beth Sherrill et al., *Single-Pill vs Free-Equivalent Combination Therapies for Hypertension: A Meta-Analysis of Health Care Costs and Adherence*, 13 J. CLINICAL HYPERTENSION 898 (2011).

[19] Jaffe, *Improved Blood Pressure Control*.

[20] Marc G. Jaffe, personal communication, Oakland, Cal. (July 28, 2014).

[21] Jaffe, *Improved Blood Pressure Control*, at 701.

One of the keys to implementing all of these innovations was a concerted effort to share best practices in hypertension management from across the whole Kaiser Permanente organization. Even before the wide-scale program was implemented, physicians all around Kaiser Permanente were trying various ways to improve medication adherence and blood pressure testing. By examining these varied practices and their results, physicians around the organization could identify what worked best for their own patients, based on local characteristics and needs. Some "homegrown" practices did not work well and were discarded. The best practices identified rose to general awareness among physicians in KPNC and other Kaiser Permanente regions and quickly won over any skeptics in the organization who had concerns about their utility. According to Dr. Joseph Young, "success breeds success." When the evidence was clear, physicians quickly changed their practices, resulting in the impressive doubling of the hypertension control rate from 44% to 86% in eleven years. Today, hypertension control rates in Kaiser Permanente Northern California are much higher than the average rate for national health plans, which hovers around 64%.[22]

iii. Ongoing Measurement

As with any quality improvement project, continuous measurement and sharing of results with stakeholders is critical. At Kaiser Permanente, physicians receive reports every month about the extent to which their hypertensive patients have blood pressure under control. These data are also rolled up to provide feedback at the level of a primary care office/clinic, an entire medical center, or larger geographic regions. Kaiser Permanente has found that this type of feedback is a very strong driver of improvement at the clinic level because clinic managers have the capacity and resources to implement system changes to improve performance, while individual physicians general do not.

b. Case Study #2—Pharmaceutical Cost Management

Prescribed pharmaceuticals account for 9% of healthcare costs in the United States,[23] or about $329 billion per year.[24] This cost is expected to increase at an annual rate of 5.1% per year from 2012 to 2022.[25] Since the development of penicillin during World War II, a steady stream of innovative medications have improved the management of infectious diseases, various forms of cancer, diabetes, mental illnesses, and cardiovascular disease, among others. The absolute economic value of these medications is hard to estimate. At one end of the

[22] NAT'L COMM. FOR QUALITY ASSURANCE, IMPROVING QUALITY AND PATIENT EXPERIENCE: THE STATE OF HEALTH CARE QUALITY 2013 (2013).

[23] CENTERS FOR MEDICARE AND MEDICAID SERVS., THE NATION'S HEALTH DOLLAR ($2.8 TRILLION), CALENDAR YEAR 2012: WHERE IT CAME FROM, *available at* http://www.cms.gov/Research-Statistics-Data-and-Systems/Statistics-Trends-and-Reports/NationalHealthExpendData/Downloads/PieChartSourcesExpenditures2012.pdf.

[24] IMS INST. FOR HEALTHCARE INFORMATICS, MEDICINE USE AND SHIFTING COSTS OF HEALTHCARE (2014).

[25] *NHE Fact Sheet*, CENTERS FOR MEDICARE AND MEDICAID SERVS., http://www.cms.gov/Research-Statistics-Data-and-Systems/Statistics-Trends-and-Reports/NationalHealthExpendData/NHE-Fact-Sheet.html (last visited July 8, 2014).

spectrum, the use of inexpensive generic drugs for the management of hypertension (see case study #1) will prevent or delay death and disability from heart disease and stroke. This appears to be overwhelmingly cost-effective. At the other end of the spectrum, heavily marketed brand-name medications (generally under patent protection) that produce little or no advantage over earlier treatment options represent poor value.

At Kaiser Permanente the challenge has always been to maximize members' health while avoiding unnecessary and wasteful spending. This applies to the use of prescribed pharmaceuticals as well. Because of Kaiser Permanente's prepaid structure, the avoidance of unnecessary expenses on pharmaceuticals provides resources for other patient-care needs. However, this preservation and repurposing of resources for the whole population of patients served by Kaiser Permanente must always be balanced by an allowance for appropriate physician discretion in the choice of treatments for individual patients. In sections i–iii below, we describe key elements of the management approach used in Kaiser Permanente Northern California over the last thirty years to achieve this balance. These approaches have been well described over the last ten years,[26] and are only summarized here.

i. Formulary Development and Management

In 1988, Kaiser Permanente Northern California created a Pharmacy and Therapeutics Committee, comprised of practicing physicians in different specialties, pharmacists, and pharmaceutical scientists. The purpose of the committee was to systematically analyze each drug class, based upon current research, and make recommendations to the Permanente Medical Group physicians about which medications to use in particular clinical situations. The committee still functions today in the same manner. Its recommendations are updated on at least an annual basis. The aggregation of these recommendations is referred to as the "formulary." Formulary recommendations are promulgated to the practicing Permanente physicians and are generally followed. However, in treating individual patients, physicians are allowed to prescribe nonformulary drugs if required by the specific needs of the patient (and the patient pays the same cost-sharing as he or she would for a formulary drug). This same process and the processes described in sections ii–iii are now generally followed in all Kaiser Permanente regions. However the details of this case study most closely reflect the practices in Kaiser Permanente Northern California.

The formulary process in Kaiser Permanente Northern California serves at least two functions: educating physicians about up-to-date, science-based pharmaceutical practice and improving Kaiser Permanente's bargaining power with pharmaceutical companies by producing a larger internal "market share" within drug classes than is the market norm, generally yielding better pricing from pharmaceutical companies. In addition, the formulary process has allowed Kaiser Permanente to achieve very high levels of low-cost generic drug use in clinical settings where appropriate generic drugs are available. Kaiser Permanente

[26] Stanley S. Wallack et al., *Health Plans' Strategies to Control Prescription Drug Spending*, 23 HEALTH AFF. 141 (2004); C. Douglas Monroe et al., *Kaiser Permanente's Evaluation and Management of Biotech Drugs: Assessing, Measuring and Affecting Use*, 25 HEALTH AFF. 1340 (2006); Sharon Levine et al., *Kaiser Permanente's Drug Benefit: A Look at How the HMO Giant Responds to Unregulated Market Pricing of Pharmaceuticals*, 19 HEALTH AFF. 185 (2000).

estimates annual unnecessary cost avoidance from the appropriate use of generics of more than $100 million per year.

ii. *Detailing and Counterdetailing*

One of the mechanisms that pharmaceutical companies employ to encourage physicians to use higher cost brand name drugs is the process known as "detailing." Sales representatives periodically visit physician offices to talk to the physicians and staff about the positive attributes of specific drugs. Traditionally, these representatives have been attractive, able salespersons who provide free samples of their companies' drugs and other enticements such as lunches for the office staff. They argue that they are providing a useful information service to busy physician practices. However, research has demonstrated that detailing increases the average cost of prescribed medications substantially without relationship to the medical evidence supporting such use.[27]

In 1990, Kaiser Permanente implemented a series of policy changes progressively curtailing pharmaceutical detailing to physicians, limiting such activities to the provision of information about formulary drugs, and prohibiting the provision of drug samples and gifts of any kind. The result has been a dramatic reduction in the prescription of nonformulary brand name drugs for both on-label and off-label uses. Others have found similar effects.[28]

In addition to restrictions on pharmaceutical company detailing, Kaiser Permanente in Northern California also began a program of "counterdetailing." Physicians periodically receive visits from Kaiser Permanente clinical pharmacists whose job is to provide, on a one-on-one basis, information about the evidence behind formulary recommendations and to answer questions about appropriate prescribing practices. This process reinforces and personalizes the formulary mechanism.

iii. *Performance Measurement and Peer Pressure*

By 2000, information technology systems were sufficiently developed to allow the regular reporting of pharmaceutical prescribing practices by physicians. The information was first provided only to the prescribing physicians themselves, to allow them to understand their own practice patterns and to compare them with other similar physicians' patterns. Eventually this information was provided to the physician departments on an unblinded basis, so that physicians could see each other's prescribing practices. Since, as described earlier, the cultural bias within Permanente is to avoid unnecessary costs for the members, physicians with significantly aberrant and unscientific prescribing patterns generally modified their practices to fall more in line with formulary recommendations. No financial incentives were ever applied at the individual physician level to direct such modifications. However, formulary adherence by Permanente physicians is among the highest in the nation.

[27] Puneet Manchanda & Elisabeth Honka, *The Effects and Role of Direct-to-Physician Marketing in the Pharmaceutical Industry: An Integrative Review*, 5 YALE J. HEALTH POL'Y, L. & ETHICS 785 (2005).

[28] Ian Larkin et al., *Restrictions on Pharmaceutical Detailing Reduced Off-Label Prescribing of Antidepressants and Antipsychotics in Children*, 33 HEALTH AFF. 1014 (2014).

c. Case Study Implications

These case studies are examples of how a fully integrated healthcare system can improve the value of care by following the principles of prevention and early detection, providing only appropriate and necessary science-based care, and not overpaying for goods and services. Kaiser Permanents is able to do this because of its commitment to the two inextricably-linked core principles of multispecialty group medical practice and prepayment.

In the case of hypertension detection and management, the key to the organization's success was the effort across primary and specialty care providers to collect necessary data. This type of collaboration would have been much more difficult in a more traditional setting in which primary and specialty care physicians are wholly independent of one another and don't share goals, let alone standardized data reporting, feedback, and incentives. Prepayment was also a key to the success of the hypertension program because it allowed Kaiser Permanente to devote resources to the information technology and infrastructure that are necessary to run the program.

In the pharmacy example, prepayment also provides the significant resources necessary to support the rigorous work of the Pharmacy and Therapeutics Committee. The more remarkable aspect of the pharmacy example, however, is the extraordinarily high level of trust and confidence that the Permanente physicians have in the formulary, because it was created by their peers and implemented within a physician culture of individual and collective responsibility for the cost and quality of care. Nevertheless, at least some of the techniques employed by Kaiser Permanente in these case studies, such as the use of registries, counter-detailing, cooperative formulary development, and open performance measurement can be, and are being, applied in other practice settings (see section V).

V Beyond Kaiser Permanente: Challenges to Spreading the Model

Kaiser Permanente leaders and those who study the organization are often asked: If the Kaiser Permanente model makes such eminent sense and works so well to manage care and costs, why isn't it everywhere? Kaiser Permanente is nearly unique in its full integration of healthcare delivery and financing, but nevertheless there are similar organizations that incorporate many of the important characteristics that make Kaiser Permanente what it is. As noted, at the core of the successful initiatives described in the case studies are two linked principles: multispecialty group practice and capitated payments. In 1970, Dr. Ernest Saward, the Medical Director of the Northwest Permanente Medical Group, described the guiding principles at the heart of Kaiser Permanente—its "genetic code"—and included these two principles, in addition to physician–hospital integration.[29]

[29] Ernest W. Saward, *The Relevance of the Kaiser Permanente Experience to the Health Services of the Eastern United States*, 46 Bull. N.Y. Acad. Med. 707 (1970).

That there are other flourishing organizations that adhere to the same principles is evidence that parts of the model are replicable; that they are few and far between is evidence that there are significant challenges to financing and delivering healthcare in this way. This section highlights the barriers—legal and otherwise—that currently constrain the development of more Kaiser Permanentes across the nation.

a. Multispecialty Group Practice

In the early 1900s, Drs. Charles and Will Mayo established in Rochester, Minnesota, the first true multispecialty group practice. The Mayo Clinic was designed primarily as a "destination" medical facility, to which midwestern physicians could send their most complex patients for an expeditious diagnosis and treatment, after which patients would return to their local care. At the Mayo Clinic, all the physicians and diagnostic machines were (and are) housed centrally, and communication among specialists was (and is) rapid and face-to-face. These innovations led to significant efficiencies and genuine coordination of care.

During the twenty years after its founding, the Mayo model was replicated in other parts of the country, either by Mayo-trained physicians (for example, the Guthrie Clinic and the Geisinger Clinic in Pennsylvania), or by other physicians inspired by the Mayo model. By the 1930s, there were two prominent multispecialty group practices thriving in the West: the Ross-Loos Clinic in Los Angeles and the Group Health Cooperative of Puget Sound. In 1933, a federal commission report declared, "Group practice, in one form or another seems essential if the mode in which medical service is rendered is to be consonant with the demands of modern medical science and technology."[30] In the 1940s, multispecialty group practice was chosen as the operating model for Kaiser Permanente. Yet despite these early positive signs, multispecialty group practice did not spread widely or swiftly. Why not?

One reason was early and vocal opposition from organized medical associations, particularly the American Medical Association (AMA). Led by Dr. Morris Fishbein, the longtime editor of the *Journal of the American Medical Association*, the AMA held that group practice was antithetical to the sacred doctor-patient relationship that only solo practice could provide. As a consequence, for many decades, young physicians joining group practices were made to feel like second-class citizens within their profession.

Such opposition gradually became much less strident over the years. For example, in 2010, the AMA House of Delegates voted to allow designated AMA governance representation for group practice physicians, with the establishment of the Integrated Physician Practice Section.[31] However, even as professional norms have changed, and more group practices have formed, the practical difficulties inherent in their establishment have become clear. The first is the need for capital for facilities and equipment. It has been difficult for physicians to generate capital from practice proceeds alone because there is always pressure from the physicians to distribute such proceeds as income. In the case of Kaiser Permanente, facilities

[30] Arthur J. Viseltear, *Medical Care for the American People: The Final Report of the Committee on the Costs of Medical Care. Adopted October 31, 1927*, 64 Am. J. Pub. Health 82 (1974).

[31] *Integrated Physician Practice Section*, American Medical Association, http://www.ama-assn.org/ama/pub/about-ama/our-people/member-groups-sections/integrated-physician-practice-section.page? (last visited Oct. 29, 2014).

and equipment are supplied through a business relationship with Kaiser Foundation Health Plan. Other physicians have formed medical foundations in partnership with one or more hospitals to the same end. Within any such financial arrangement, it is difficult to maintain equity among the partners, leading to many physicians' reluctance to risk their autonomy in such relationships. In addition, the tradition of practice autonomy is often drilled into young physicians in training, making them unwilling to be led as a member of a group, even by fellow physicians. To overcome this inherent resistance, medical group leaders must be skillful managers and, in many cases, charismatic individuals.

Finally, there are particular challenges associated with the creation of multispecialty group practice focused on a local, defined insured population, as opposed to one that serves primarily as a destination healthcare system. Most successful group practices managing defined populations have developed in areas of relative population concentration, generally in large cities such as Los Angeles, San Francisco, Denver, New Orleans, Boston, and Seattle. The population served by the practice must be large enough to support the minimum number of physician specialists required for the model to work—conventionally thought to be about 75 to 100 physicians. In addition, relative geographic concentration of the population allows for acceptable travel time for patients to reach the medical group facilities.

In areas of less population density, medical groups are often forced to contract with non-group specialists in independent practices, either to fill out the group capacity or for geographic access for patients. This disassembly of the group practice can lead to management inefficiencies and lessened care coordination, differences in compensation models, and fragmentation of the group practice culture. In fact, this dynamic played a central role in the ultimate failure of Kaiser Permanente's expansions in North Carolina, Kansas, and New England in the 1990s.

b. Capitation

Dr. Sidney Garfield, the cofounder of Kaiser Permanente, referred to capitation as the "reversal of economics."[32] Under capitation, providers did better economically if patients remained well and used fewer services, in contrast to the fee-for-service dynamic, in which providers made more money for providing more care. Capitation payment creates a strong incentive for preventive medicine, early detection and treatment of chronic diseases, and avoidance of unnecessary hospital use. However, capitation payment to physician groups is only now becoming more widespread, and capitation to hospitals is nearly nonexistent outside of Kaiser Permanente and a few other organizations.[33] If capitation has worked so well, why has it not spread more widely?

Historically, capitation was even more robustly opposed by organized medicine than was group practice. It was viewed by the AMA as a step toward "socialized medicine" and as a risk to patients because of the potential to stint on care services. Many local and state medical

[32] John G. Smillie, Can Physicians Manage the Quality and Costs of Health Care?: The Story of the Permanente Medical Group 15 (1991).

[33] It should be noted again that since 1983 Medicare has paid hospitals a kind of individual "capitation" known as a Diagnosis-Related Groups (DRGs), which creates incentives for shorter hospital stays but not for limiting unnecessary hospitalizations themselves.

associations routinely denied membership to prepaid group practice physicians, a status that was often a prerequisite to obtaining local hospital admitting privileges.[34]

But by the early 1990s, insurers became interested in capitation as a mechanism to help constrain costs under managed care. Some capitation models were successful and persist today, especially among medical groups in Southern California. However, many medical groups that attempted to accept the financial risk inherent in capitation failed, either because of a lack of capital reserves or because the breadth of risk was too great to be managed by inexperienced and under-resourced medical groups.[35]

More recently, interest in capitation has resurfaced, usually under a different name—for example "risk-sharing"—and a more graduated structure. In risk-sharing, the financial responsibility for the cost of care is shared between the payer and the delivery system. Both the degree and breadth of risk assumed by the delivery system vary depending on the desire of the payer and the capacity of the delivery system to manage it. In the simplest form of risk-sharing, the delivery system may agree to a fixed annual reward or penalty based upon performance on quality and cost measures, usually called "shared savings." In more advanced models, such as Kaiser Permanente, physicians may carry full risk for some services, such as physician and referral services, but share risk with another partner for other services, such as pharmaceuticals.

c. Physician–Hospital Integration

One of Kaiser Permanente's early innovations was the co-location of jointly managed physician practices with hospital services, primarily driven by patients' desire for convenience.[36] Patient convenience did and still does convey a strategic marketing advantage to Kaiser Permanente when compared to disjointed, geographically separated individual physician practices, hospitals, laboratories, and pharmacies. This model was, in part, motivated by the early rejection of Permanente physicians from community hospital admitting privileges, as described in section V.a. The model also created a sense of shared responsibility for the performance of the organization among physicians and hospital executives. Furthermore, as medical and information technology advanced, physician–hospital integration fostered the rationalization of care services between the medical office and the hospital, based on cost and quality, without conflicting financial incentives. Such integration and financial alignment was also the basis, eventually, for an integrated patient medical record.

Outside of Kaiser Permanente and other integrated delivery systems, there is seldom such a close working relationship between physicians and hospital executives. Physician committees contribute certain services to hospitals, including overseeing credentialing and privileging the physician staff, but otherwise are not involved in the management of the institution. Over the years, this separation of physician and hospital duties has been enhanced, and

[34] This practice persisted for many years, even after a Supreme Court ruling in 1943 against the AMA and the District of Columbia Medical Association for violation of the Sherman Antitrust Act.

[35] The "breadth" of capitation refers to the number of categories of health care expenditures for which financial risk is assumed, for example, physician services, hospital services, prescription drugs, and so forth.

[36] Saward, *The Relevance of the Kaiser Permanente Experience.*

integration inhibited, by a growing set of laws and regulations. As described in detail by Leibenluft and Sage, these include: antitrust provisions regarding market consolidation; Internal Revenue Service sanctions against "private benefit" relationships between not-for-profit hospitals and physicians or physician groups; and Medicare prohibitions against "kickbacks" from hospitals to physicians for admissions, physician "self-referral" for certain services, false claims, and the provision of inducements to "withhold necessary services" from Medicare beneficiaries.[37] Despite a number of efforts to simplify and modernize these bodies of law, they still serve to inhibit some useful forms of physician–hospital integration.

These legal and regulatory concerns, combined with Medicare payments that often lead to higher reimbursement for the same procedure in the hospital than outside the hospital, have recently led to a rapid increase in direct employment of physicians by hospitals. While this trend is neither good nor bad per se, it has evoked concerns among some physicians about loss of legitimate clinical autonomy, and perplexity among hospital executives about how best to manage this new category of often-cantankerous employees. As a consequence, the American Medical Association and the American Hospital Association embarked in 2013 on a two-year cooperative effort to create a new model for physician–hospital clinical and management integration. The report on this effort is expected in early 2015. It is already clear, however, that some modernization of the legal and regulatory environment will be required if the advantages of physician–hospital integration seen in Kaiser Permanente are to become more widespread.

VI Policy Issues: Delivery System and Payment Reform

Given both the advantages of, and challenges to, designing a delivery system capable of managing care and costs, what public and private policy changes would help move the needle in the right direction? Dr. Paul Batalden of Dartmouth Medical School is known for having said, "Every system is perfectly designed to get the results it gets."[38] Most of the U.S. health system is designed to produce volume and ever-increasing cost, regardless of the impact on health, and that is what it does. The design needs to change.

There is a classic chicken and egg conundrum in healthcare today: to achieve improved management of care and costs, we need integrated healthcare delivery systems at full risk for cost and quality; to get there, we need healthcare purchasers to change the way they pay for care—moving from fee-for-service to paying for value. But healthcare purchasers can't pay delivery systems this way if there aren't many delivery systems that are large and sophisticated enough to manage risk.

[37] Robert F. Liebenluft & William M. Sage, *Overcoming Barriers to Improved Collaboration and Alignment: Legal and Regulatory Issues*, *in* Partners in Health: How Physicians and Hospitals Can Be Accountable Together (Francis J. Crosson & Laura A. Tollen eds., 2010).

[38] Doug McInnis, *What System?*, Dartmouth Med. (2006), *available at* http://dartmed.dartmouth.edu/summer06/html/what_system_03.php.

There may be a way out, however. As noted by Professor Stephen Shortell, a U.C. Berkeley professor and expert in delivery system organization, "We need *co*-evolution of payment and organizational form and capabilities. The chicken *and* the egg, not the chicken *or* the egg."[39] We believe that a step-wise approach to improved care and cost management is possible, with small changes in the way doctors and hospitals are paid, enabling them to adopt more sophisticated models of collaboration and integration over time, enabling them, in turn, to accept even more sophisticated models of risk management.

We see the beginning of this type of step-wise change occurring in certain programs created under the Affordable Care Act. In 2009, the Medicare Payment Advisory Commission (MedPAC), an independent commission chartered by Congress to provide advice on the Medicare program, took up the question of how best to manage care and costs for populations of Medicare beneficiaries. In its June 2009 *Report to Congress*, MedPAC called for the creation of accountable care organizations (ACOs), defined as "organizations of physicians and hospitals that undertook the collective responsibility for the quality and cost of care for a defined population of Medicare beneficiaries."[40] The MedPAC report, in part, led to the incorporation into the Affordable Care Act of two sections designed to promote ACO development. First was the Medicare Shared Savings Program, inviting delivery systems to form ACOs and be paid fee-for-service payments, plus the opportunity to gain (and in later years to lose) payment based upon performance on quality and cost. Second was a new agency, the Center for Medicare and Medicaid Innovation (CMMI), created within the Centers for Medicare and Medicaid Services (CMS), specifically charged with funding and evaluating new models of care delivery. In 2011, CMMI created the Pioneer ACO program, under which Medicare pays Pioneer ACOs on a population basis. There are currently 405 Medicare Shared Savings Program ACOs and 19 Pioneer ACOs operating nationally.[41] In early 2015, CMS announced the creation of a third form of a Medicare ACO, called the Next Generation ACO.[42] One intention in creating this latest form of ACO is to accelerate the movement away from fee-for-service payment toward value-based payments such as global payments and captitaion.

Medicare ACO development has stimulated similar development in the commercial, non-Medicare market. In the commercial ACO model, physicians, or physicians and hospitals, contract with one or more payers to deliver a predetermined set of services to ACO patients, generally accepting some degree of financial risk for the performance of the ACO based on quality and cost of services. By the first quarter of 2015, there were over 300 commercial ACOs (many of which also have Medicare contracts) at various stages of development in 49 states and the District of Columbia.[43]

[39] Stephen Shortell, *The ACA, ACOs, and What It Means for KP*, presentation at internal Kaiser Permanente brown-bag session (2010).

[40] The Medicare Payment Advisory Comm., *Accountable Care Organizations, in* REPORT TO THE CONGRESS: IMPROVING INCENTIVES IN THE MEDICARE PROGRAM 39–56 (2009).

[41] Sean Cavanaugh, *ACOs Moving Ahead,* CMS BLOG, Centers for Medicare and Medicaid Services, December 22, 2014, available at blog.cms.gov2014/12/, accessed April 28, 2015

[42] Patrick Conway, *Building on the Success of the ACO Model, CMS BLOG, Centers for Medicare and Medicaid Services*, March 10, 2015, *available at* blog.cms.gov2015/3/, accessed April 28, 2015

[43] David Muhlestein, *Growth and Dispersion of Accountable Care Organizations in 2015, Health Affairs Blog*, March 31, 2015, http://healthaffairs.org/blog/2015/03/31/growth-and-dispersion-of-accountable-care-organizations-in-2015-2/ (last visited May 3, 2015).

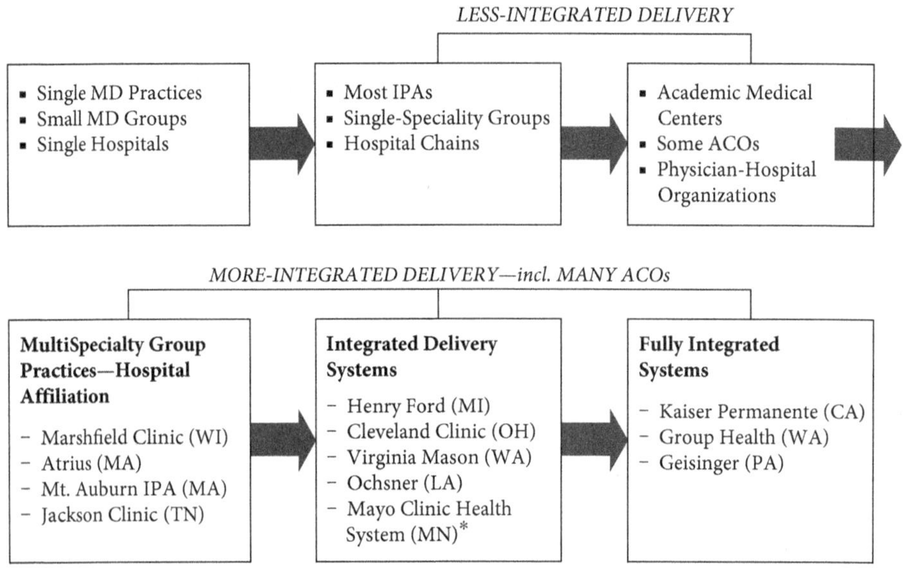

* Mayo Clinic Health System does operate its own, fully integrated health plan, but the plan is open only to Mayo's employees and physicians, not to the general public.

FIGURE 36.2 Integrated Healthcare Delivery Systems in the United States

The ACO "movement" is significant (Saver, this volume). It is a model with the potential to align the incentives of payers and providers to improve quality and reduce costs, much in the way that these incentives are aligned in Kaiser Permanente, but without the formal, organizational structure of Kaiser Permanente. The model may lead to more coordination among physicians, and between physicians and hospitals, leading, in turn, to organizational integration among these providers. Such an integrated system has the scale and resources to succeed financially when paid capitation.

The Kaiser Permanente model, with its integration of physicians and hospitals with prospective payment from an associated health plan, is often referred to as "fully" integrated. However, full integration may not be necessary to improve the health system. There is a continuum of integration in healthcare, from solo physician practice at one end, to full alignment among provider and payer at the other end (see Figure 36.2). Any movement along the continuum represents a step toward improved care and cost management.

More and more, physicians are choosing integrated practice settings.[44] While it is unlikely that the U.S. delivery system as a whole will ever adopt full global capitation and risk-sharing between payers and providers, such complete alignment of incentives may not be necessary to change system outcomes. There are intermediate steps along the way to global capitation that would allow for many of the innovations that Kaiser Permanente and other large multi-specialty group practices have implemented. Medicare's accountable care organizations are

[44] Beth Kutscher, *Making Physicians Pay Off: Hospitals Struggle to Balance Current Costs with Future Benefits of Employing Docs*, Modern Healthcare (Feb. 22, 2014) http://www.modernhealthcare.com/article/20140222/MAGAZINE/302229986

a prominent example. Outside of Medicare, the accountable care movement has given rise to a plethora of new alliances between physicians and hospitals that are capable of accepting various kinds of shared risk from large payers. Examples include bundled payments for specific groups of services and partial capitation for all services across a portion of the care continuum, such as primary care. We believe these experiments will be successful and will eventually lead to a tipping point, in which there are more buyers paying for value in health markets than there are paying fee-for-service.

CHAPTER 37

PAYING FOR HEALTHCARE

DAVID M. FRANKFORD

I Introduction

Healthcare expenditures in the United States, whether measured as a percentage of gross domestic product (GDP) (17.7%) or as dollars spent per capita ($8,508), are nearly 50% higher than the countries with the next highest level of expenditures, the Netherlands (11.9% GDP) or Norway ($5,669 per capita).[1] Recent research has placed blame for our high expenditures squarely on the prices we pay to providers,[2] as well as our high administrative expenses, while ruling out other drivers of expenditures.[3] The population in the United States is no older than that of other advanced, industrialized nations; in fact, the converse is true in many cases. In the United States we don't utilize higher amounts of healthcare goods and services, with the possible exception of very costly technology and some specialty care; and we don't substitute more intensive care for less intensive care any more than in comparable nations. Nor are the higher expenditures in the United States explained by higher quality; again, the converse is often the case. The simple truth is that in the United States we pay providers more money than is paid elsewhere.[4]

[1] Organization for Economic Co-Operation and Development, Health Data 2013—Frequently Requested Data, http://www.oecd.org/health/health-systems/oecdhealthdata2013-frequentlyrequesteddata.htm (accessed June 2, 2014).

[2] Gerard F. Anderson et al., *It's the Prices, Stupid: Why the United States Is So Different from Other Countries*, 22 Health Aff. 89 (2003); Carlos Angrisono et al., *Accounting for the Cost of Health Care in the United States*, McKinsey Global Institute (2007); Alexis Pozen & David M. Cutler, *Medical Spending Differences in the United States and Canada: The Role of Prices, Procedures, and Administrative Expenses*, 47 Inquiry 124 (2010); Paul B. Ginsburg, *Reforming Provider Payment—The Price Side of the Equation*, 365 New Eng. J. Med. 1268 (2011); Miriam J. Laugesen & Sherry A. Glied, *Higher Fees Paid to US Physicians Drive Higher Spending for Physician Services Compared to Other Countries*, 30 Health Aff. 1647 (2011).

[3] *See, e.g.*, Dante Morra et al., *US Physician Practices Versus Canadians: Spending Nearly Four Times as Much Money Interacting with Payers*, 30 Health Aff. 1 (2011); Lawrence P. Casalino et al., *What Does It Cost Physician Practices to Interact with Health Insurance Plans?*, 28 Health Aff. w533 (2009); Stephanie Woolhandler et al., *Costs of Health Care Administration in the United States and Canada*, 349 New Eng. J. Med. 768 (2003).

[4] *See, e.g.*, Uwe Reinhardt, *Divide et Imperia: Protecting the Growth of Health Care Incomes (Costs)*, 21 Health Econ. 41 (2012).

An ineluctable fact of payment is that one person's expenditures are another person's income. As a result, payment is an inherently political and social process.[5] This chapter explores the manner in which this political and social process and the mechanisms of payment are linked and somewhat singular to the United States. In all industrialized nations, providers, particularly physicians, have enormous income-generating capacity, particularly when that power is wielded within and by the organizations of modern, advanced capitalism. The United States has no monopoly on the fact that providers are powerful. However, singular to the United States is an extremely fragmented insurance system in which each payer fends only for itself.[6] Many other nations, like the countries of Western Europe, have multiple payers, but their payment is coordinated through some mixture of private and public power (often referred to as "all-payer" systems).[7] No such coordination exists in the United States. As a result, compared with other nations, the payment equation, "expenditures equal incomes," is tilted heavily toward the income side—physicians, hospitals, nursing homes, device and drug manufacturers, home health agencies, and so forth—as there exists no countervailing power on the payer side.[8] The mechanisms of payment in the United States both reflect and reinforce this imbalance.

As described much more fully below, this structural feature of payment in the United States reinforces and is reinforced by several cultural elements and other structural aspects. Most particularly, in designing and implementing payment, administrators and politicians and much of the policy elite, particularly those influenced by health economics, explicitly try to avoid making the distributional choices that are the hallmark of payment in any nation. They seek to avoid politics by using technical means instead. Absent the use of collective means exercised in a payment system, one can expect growth in expenditures to continue to eclipse that of comparable nations.

The chapter begins by describing how the fragmented structure of insurance and payment became dominant and how it continues. It uses Medicare as the primary example because it is the largest single payer in the United States and because its methods are transparent and often adopted by private payers, while those of private insurers are proprietary and therefore largely unavailable. Using this example, the chapter describes the two most important prospective payment systems used by Medicare, the one for inpatient care and the other for physician services. The chapter makes the point, through examination of the technical apparatus of the payment systems, that the two systems are not nearly as prospective as designed, with the result that expenditures continue to rise. The chapter then connects the technical apparatus of the systems, and the resultant increasing expenditures, to the overall social and

[5] *See, e.g.*, Robert G. Evans, *Coarse Correction—And Way Off Target*, 22 J. HEALTH POL., POL'Y & L. 503, 504 (1997); Uwe E. Reinhardt, *Resource Allocation in Health Care: The Allocation of Lifestyles to Providers*, 65 MILBANK Q. 153 (1987).

[6] *See, e.g.*, Theodore R. Marmor, *American Health Care Policy and Politics: Is Fragmentation a Helpful Category for Understanding Health Reform Experience and Prospects?*, *in* THE FRAGMENTATION OF U.S. HEALTH CARE: CAUSES AND SOLUTIONS 343, 352 (Einer R. Elhauge ed., 2010).

[7] *See, e.g.*, Joseph White, *Implementing Health Care Reform with All-Payer Regulation, Private Insurers, and a Voluntary Public Insurance Plan* 5 (May 3, 2009), http://www.ourfuture.org/files/JWhiteAllPayerCostControl.pdf (accessed June 3, 2014).

[8] *See, e.g.*, Reinhardt, *Divide*; Bruce C. Vladeck & Thomas Rice, *Market Failure and the Failure of Discourse: Facing Up to the Power of Sellers*, 28 HEALTH AFF. 1305 (2009); Jonathan Oberlander & Joseph White, *Public Attitudes Toward Health Care Spending Aren't the Problem; Prices Are*, 28 HEALTH AFF. 1285 (2009).

political context, particularly the eschewal of mechanisms to make explicitly the political distributional decisions at the heart of any payment system. Our systems use some mechanisms common to comparable nations' payment systems, but when these elements are considered as a whole and within larger structure and context, one can see that payment in the United States is exceptional, as are our expenditures.

II History of Fragmented Structure of Payment

The nature of healthcare payment is inexorably linked to the nature of illness and healthcare insurance. Because illness is a probabilistic event, the risk that a particular individual will become ill cannot be predicted with confidence, while, because of the law of large numbers, confidence increases over larger classes of individuals. In the ideal, insurance involves the exchange of a sum certain, the premium, in exchange for certain services, likewise specified in advance, in the event of loss. Health insurance deviates from this ideal in the fact that both the probability and magnitude of loss can be altered after execution of the insurance contract. An insured can affect the probability of loss through behaviors increasing or decreasing the possibility of loss, a "problem" known as "moral hazard." Healthcare providers can affect the existence of loss by defining and locating illness in individuals, and they likewise can affect the magnitude of loss through the services they deem warranted to treat a particular illness, phenomena discussed in economic literature as "supplier-induced demand."[9] Symmetrically, a healthcare insurer can affect the existence and magnitude of loss by denying services altogether or by curtailing their scope, amount, or duration. Neither the probability nor magnitude of loss is easily specified in advance, but, again due to the law of large numbers, the degree of uncertainty can be attenuated by risk pooling.

In industrialized countries other than the United States, this risk pooling is accomplished through either or both of governmentally created systems and social organizations, thereby creating systems grounded in social solidarity and social security. In Western Europe, with its strong tradition of solidarity and mutual aid, the risk of illness is pooled in the sickness funds, which cooperate voluntarily and with varying degrees of state coercion in collecting revenues, spreading risk, and paying providers. In national health system countries, like the United Kingdom and Scandinavia, national governments unite all citizens into a single risk pool. In Canada, Canadian Medicare brings the population together into the risk-pooling systems of the provinces and the territories, with some degree of federal subsidization. All advanced, industrialized countries socialize the risk-pooling function, and they pay with one voice, either as a single payer or as coordinated payers. Payment is "aggregated."

By contrast, the United States is "the odd man out."[10] In the United States, risk pooling was, for present purposes, initially attempted by the creation of the Blue Cross and Blue Shield

[9] *See, e.g.*, Roger Feldman & Michael A. Morrisey, *Health Economics: A Report on the Field*, 15 J. Health Pol., Pol'y & L. 627, 640–641 (1990).

[10] Brian Abel-Smith, *Who Is the Odd Man Out?: The Experience of Western Europe in Containing the Costs of Health Care*, 63 Milbank Q. 1 (1985).

organizations.[11] Unable to collect payment from individuals during the Great Depression, hospitals came together to form Blue Cross, effectively pooling among themselves the risk that a particular one of them would be unable to obtain payment from patients, who became subscribers. Shortly thereafter physicians followed suit with the formation of Blue Shield for payment for outpatient care. The world of provider-dominated, indemnity insurance was born.

Indemnity insurance constituted a method of solving the unpredictability of the occurrence and magnitude of illness in particular patients. In advance, no hospital or physician can identify which subscriber will access its services, and, vice versa, no subscriber can predict whether he or she will need the services of any provider, much less the identity of which one or ones. Because indemnity insurance gave each subscriber the right of access to all providers and, vice versa, granted to all providers the right of access to all subscribers, it provided a mechanism of linking all hospitals and all physicians to all subscribers.

A principal drawback of this approach was that it contained no means to control expenditures. Subscribers were indifferent to price because, aside from relatively insignificant deductibles or copayments, they paid nothing when they used care. Therefore, they had no reason to exercise countervailing power against providers' ability to generate income for themselves, nor did provider-dominated insurers. Providers were "reimbursed" rather than "paid."

To be reimbursed, most hospitals executed participation agreements with the Blue Cross companies, which stipulated that each hospital accepted assignment of subscribers' right to indemnification of loss; to be reimbursed, hospitals merely had to document their "costs." Reimbursement was therefore "cost-based" and "retrospective." Physicians, by contrast, by and large refused to execute such participation agreements. For the most part subscribers paid cash on the barrel, paying for services at the time of delivery, and then sought indemnification from their insurers. Reimbursement was therefore "charge-based" and "retrospective." The whole enterprise was a claims-paying enterprise, effectively operating as a blank check. Predictably, expenditures grew and grew as this form of health insurance became increasingly widespread—the payment, aka reimbursement, side of the payment equals incomes equation—and as healthcare, particularly medicine, increasingly became the technologically driven endeavor it has now become—the income-inducing side of the equation.

Over time, control over the Blue Cross and Blue Shield organizations was wrested from providers. If most people in the United States had been Blue Cross–Blue Shield subscribers, and if the Blues, each created under state law, had remained relatively united in the Blue Cross–Blue Shield national association, then this system of insurance could have exercised countervailing power against providers either to lower the price of care, or to control the volume and intensity of care, or to accomplish both, much as has happened elsewhere in other developed nations. However, in the United States this power failed to materialize for a number of reasons.

For one thing, starting in the 1930s and accelerating in the period after World War II, commercial insurance companies entered the market against the Blues. Unhindered by the obligation imposed on the Blues by state law to accept all comers and to charge a uniform,

[11] For the history of the Blue Cross–Blue Shield organizations, *see* Sylvia A. Law, Blue Cross: What Went Wrong? (1976) *see generally* Paul Starr, The Social Transformation of American Medicine 290–334 (1982).

community-rated premium to all, the commercial insurance companies were able to cherry-pick employer-sponsored groups, which are relatively young and healthy, thereby leaving to the Blues the relatively bad risks. In turn, the Blues needed to increase their premiums, which put them at a competitive disadvantage relative to the commercial insurance companies, which cost them more relatively young, healthy groups, which necessitated increased premiums, and so on in a vicious circle known as the death spiral. The possibility of uniting the entire community within one enterprise fell further away.

For another thing, the entire community was never so united anyway. For a variety of reasons, described in Chapters by Jost and Hall (this volume), in the United States the organization of subscribers into risk pools fell largely to employers. In contrast to the rest of the advanced, industrialized world, other forms of social organization never existed or arose to take on the role of pooling potential patients into risk-bearing groups. Necessarily, given that the health insurance system was primarily employer-based, nonworking portions of the population—particularly the poor, the elderly and the young—were left out.

Nor was there in the United States a Bismarckian moment whereby government brought together increasingly fractured, squabbling groups of risk pools. Instead, government in the United States took on the role of a gap-filler, ameliorating, perhaps, the sharpest edges of a system that left out those not favored by the dominant employer-sponsored model. In 1965 Medicare and Medicaid, in a truly unique, almost revolutionary political moment,[12] insured the elderly and some of the poorest of the poor. Over time other marginalized groups have been incrementally added: the disabled; those needing kidney dialysis; uninsured children in low-income families; and, under the Affordable Care Act (ACA), various categories of persons who have been uninsurable because of prior illness or who lack sufficient income to afford insurance, for example, the "working poor," who fall outside of Medicaid's traditional categories.

III Mechanisms of Fragmented Payment

Given this fragmentation of the social and political function of risk pooling, each particular payer was (and still is) left to its own devices in paying providers. This fragmentation of payment both spawned and reinforced a culture and social structure in which each payer acts only for itself and tries to push risk and cost onto others.

Medicare provides the most prominent example. The Medicare program packs the punch of the largest risk pool by far, and many payers adopt its methods, which are transparent. Medicare is also backed by the sovereign power of the United States; it is not just some private payer acting in the marketplace. However, despite these sources of power, from the very beginning Medicare has operated as only one payer among others, charged by Congress and its administrators to pay only its "fair share," no less and no more. This continuing policy of "Medicare-only" results in structures of payment and administration designed to focus just on Medicare's bottom line, not the wider impacts of its policies.[13]

[12] *See generally* Theodore R. Marmor, The Politics of Medicare (2000).

[13] *See, e.g.*, David M. Frankford, *The Complexity of Medicare's Hospital Reimbursement System: Paradoxes of Averaging*, 78 Iowa L. Rev. 517 (1993).

Because of this narrow view, even Medicare's pioneering move to "prospective" payment has failed to staunch the rise of expenditures in the United States, and prospective payment may have failed to control expenditures even to a great extent within the program itself (although this point is controversial, as indicated in section III.b. below).

In contrast to retrospective reimbursement, prospective payment is designed to impose a constraint on expenditures. To the extent that providers' costs exceed the expected costs embodied in the prospective system, providers lose the difference. To the extent that costs are less than the expected norm, providers retain the surplus. Prospective payment thus is supposed to provide predictability and incentives to control costs.

Yet, a system remains prospective only if the payer or payers hold the line. If, instead, amounts that would be provider losses are forgiven by means of adjustments after the relevant accounting period—that is, "passed through"—then the system, to that degree, becomes retrospective. To a great extent, compared with other nations, that is the history of prospective payment in the United States.

Prospective payment, of course, relies in part on prediction of spending. Some of the difficulty of predicting expenditures is that the delivery of healthcare is relatively variable, subject to standardization to a degree much less than even relatively heterogeneous products such as custom-built houses. The cause of such heterogeneity is debated. One extreme position is that healthcare is so extremely differentiated, because no two patients are alike, that standardization is impossible. In contrast, another extreme position is that providers differentiate their services so as to escape the control imposed by standardization—that is, standardization could be easily accomplished. Most observers fall somewhere in the middle: It is relatively difficult to standardize healthcare.

Standardization, however, is the sine qua non of any payment system for which a goal is controlling expenditures. Take the modern hospital. We could standardize the care provided to all patients across all hospitals by paying for an average day. This "per diem" payment could be cost-based—the cost of the average day in all hospitals, derived by totaling all costs of all days and dividing that sum by the total number of days. However, the per diem need not be cost-based. A payer could decide that it can afford to spend a sum certain, say one million dollars, in an upcoming accounting period, divide that expenditure by the number of patient days expected, and derive its per diem in that manner. The point is that any payment system must use some standardized unit of payment to impose some degree of control on expenditures, as discussed further in section III.a. below.

The particular units chosen for payment in the United States have generally been fairly discrete—they are episode- or activity-based. The two most significant mileposts in the transformation toward prospective payment were the creation of the Inpatient Prospective Payment System (IPPS) and payment to physicians based on the resource-based relative-value scale (RBRVS), a fee structure designed to be divorced from what physicians historically charged and based instead on the "value" of their services.[14] For IPPS, the unit of payment is each inpatient episode of care, differentiated by the diagnosis that led to the stay.

[14] The discussion of Medicare's IPPS and RBRVS-based system draws heavily from SARA ROSENBAUM & DAVID M. FRANKFORD, LAW AND THE AMERICAN HEALTH CARE SYSTEM ch. 12 (2012); Frankford, *Complexity*; David M. Frankford, *Measuring Health Care: Political Fate and Technocratic Reform*, 19 J. HEALTH POL., POL'Y & L. 647 (1994); JONATHAN OBERLANDER, THE POLITICAL LIFE OF MEDICARE ch. 5 (2003); and DAVID G. SMITH, PAYING FOR MEDICARE: THE POLITICS OF REFORM (1992).

This categorization is accomplished though the use of diagnosis-related groups (DRGs), each of which is supposed to represent a homogeneous cluster of patients, the treatment of which does—or should, and the difference, discussed in section III.a. below, is crucial—command an identical use of resources, for example, "concussion," "pneumonia," "myocardial infarction." For the RBRVS-based physician payment system, the unit of payment is the individual service furnished—for example, an initial office visit, a follow-up office visit, an injection, reading a CT scan—differentiated from other services by its "value," as measured primarily by a work relative-value unit (RVU), a practice expense RVU, and a malpractice expense RVU (the cost of malpractice insurance). The two systems are designed to standardize the provision of healthcare to allow comparisons across each provider peer group, hospitals and physicians, and to impose a common payment across each, set in advance and free of provider control—in contrast to the provider-controlled payment methods, discussed previously in this section, with which Medicare started. A blank check no more.

For two principal reasons, things have not quite worked out as intended. The first is internal to the structures of the payment systems, while the second is outside in the systems' interaction with the larger payment environment.

a. Inside

The two systems themselves have remained, to some extent, within the hands of providers, with the result that both IPPS and the RBRVS-based system have, again to some degree, functioned as pass-throughs.

With regard to IPPS, the story begins with the fact that the system was tied to the behavior of hospitals under retrospective, cost-based reimbursement. The DRGs form an ordinal ranking of the value of each hospital stay—more precisely each "discharge" because the "diagnosis" for payment is coded upon discharge—relative to the value of other discharges. The ordinal scale then has to be converted to actual payment dollars. To accomplish this task, each DRG is multiplied by the "base payment rate," also known as the "standardized payment amount" or the "average standardized amount." This "conversion factor" was derived from an actual, historical base period by calculating from that base period the average cost of all discharges in all acute-care hospitals in the United States, and then removing, through a process called "standardization," other known costs that do not vary with diagnosis and over which a hospital has no control. Most important, these recognized costs include certain local variations, particularly local labor costs, as well as factors like teaching status, known to raise costs uniformly because patients at teaching hospitals are sicker than those at nonteaching facilities. This average cost, so standardized, thus represented—again, during an actual, historical base year—the average cost of the average discharge in the average acute-care hospital in the United States. Recognized variations are then added back in for each hospital.

Each year, the base payment rate is updated in a process that mixes expertise with politics. The "update factor" is proposed by the Department of Health and Human Services (HHS), subject to a recommendation from the Medicare Payment Assessment Commission (MedPAC), which is an expert body advising Congress, and then it is codified by Congress in legislation. Leaving aside the lobbying by the hospital sector, the updating process inevitably considers how hospitals are faring under IPPS, perhaps most saliently by considering "Medicare margins."

An analogous point can be made with regard to the DRGs themselves. To begin with, the weights were initially calculated from hospital charges, which can be thought of as a complex set of list prices. To put the matter charitably, charges rarely have any rational relationship to actual resource use and are used simply to obtain greater revenue from payers[15]—so much for cleaving IPPS apart from provider-controlled retrospective reimbursement.

Further, the distinctions among the various DRGs are not airtight and the classification system can be gamed to maximize payment. Hence, twice the system has experienced "DRG creep," in which the value of the weights has risen as providers became more familiar with the coding system and learned how to work it in their favor. This creep first occurred in the early years of implementation. It then occurred again, as actually predicted, after the weights were partially redesigned for fiscal year 2008.

Indeed, this redesign itself was sparked because a MedPAC study showed that the system was highly manipulable by providers. The study concerned the creation of specialty hospitals and allegations by community hospitals that the specialty hospitals were cherry-picking profitable cases. A particularly salient finding of the study was that specialty hospitals were formed in good part to take advantage of particularly lucrative DRGs and, moreover, to cherry-pick the less complex and therefore less expensive cases, with high margins, within those DRGs. This manipulation of the payment system was possible because the DRGs failed to capture so-called "within-DRG severity of illness." Moreover, these differences were highly visible to, and therefore manipulable by, providers.[16] While these issues have been somewhat ameliorated by the rebasing of, and by other changes made to, the weights and the classification system, these reforms were then followed by substantial DRG creep as hospitals became more familiar with the reformed classification system—the newly implemented Medicare severity-adjusted DRGs (MS-DRGs). Although the monetary value of some of this creep has been "taken back" from the hospital sector through a deduction in calculating the base payment update factor, the fact remains that the classification system itself, like the base payment rate, is somewhat controlled by providers. While perhaps on paper Medicare has controlled its inpatient expenditures more successfully than have other payers, it remains the fact that the key components of the system—the conversion factor and the MS-DRGs—render it far less prospective than designed.

The story regarding provider manipulation of the RBRVS-based system is much simpler. The RBRVS was developed by economists and colleagues at Harvard and was tested and refined by HHS and the Physician Payment Review Commission, Congress's expert advisory body for physician payment at that time, the functions of which are now combined with oversight of other prospective payment systems in MedPAC. Two major purposes informed this work. First, the goal was to slow growth of expenditures. Between the enactment of Medicare in 1965 and the mid-1980s, expenditures for physicians' services increased at an average annual rate of more than 13% and averaged 16% a year during the first half of

[15] *See, e.g.*, Uwe E. Reinhardt, *The Many Different Prices Paid to Providers and the Flawed Theory of Cost Shifting: Is It Time for a More Rational All-Payer System?*, 30 HEALTH AFF. 2125 (2011) [hereinafter Reinhardt, *The Many Different Prices Paid to Providers*]; Uwe E. Reinhardt, *The Pricing of U.S. Hospital Services: Chaos Behind a Veil of Secrecy*, 25 HEALTH AFF.57 (2006) [hereinafter Reinhardt, *The Pricing of U.S. Hospital Services*].

[16] *See* MEDPAC, REPORT TO THE CONGRESS: PHYSICIAN-OWNED SPECIALTY HOSPITALS (Mar. 2005).

the 1980s, thereby consistently outpacing growth in both GDP and total healthcare expenditures. Second, the system was explicitly designed to increase payments to generalists relative to specialists as a means to induce more medical graduates to enter primary care. To achieve both goals, the fee structure was designed to be totally independent of actual physician charges and thus provider control.[17]

Unfortunately, it did not stay so independent. Like the MS-DRGs, the RBRVS is an ordinal ranking of the value of different services relative to others, and like the DRG-based system, the RBRVS-based one has to be updated periodically to reflect changes in the relative-value units, particularly the work RVU. In this task, the Centers for Medicare and Medicaid Services (CMS), the agency within HHS that administers Medicare, relies heavily on the American Medical Association's Relative Value Scale Update Committee (RUC). Substantial evidence shows that over time the dominance of RUC in the updating process was skewing the scale toward procedures and imaging, furnished most often by specialists, and thereby actually increasing the differential between payment for specialty and primary care. This adverse impact was (and still is) occurring because (1) RUC is dominated by specialists; (2) most requests for revaluing an RVU come from specialty societies; (3) the great majority of weights reviewed have been ones that were allegedly undervalued, with the result that review has most often led to an increase in value; (4) any increase in one weight diminishes the value of others because adjustments are "budget neutral"; and (5) CMS generally accepts the RUC's recommendations.[18]

To redress the manner in which the updates to the weights have contributed to the increasing tilt toward specialists, particularly procedures and imaging, in 2006 MedPAC issued some fairly strong recommendations, all designed to reduce CMS's reliance, in performing the update, on the medical specialty societies. Most important, MedPAC recommended that CMS form an expert panel of its own to advise it in its review of the RVUs. Under the recommendation, the panel, composed of experts in health economics and physician payment, would not "supplant" RUC but would "augment" it by providing an independent source of expertise. MedPAC also recommended that, separately from the congressionally required five-year reviews, CMS should, based on a number of factors MedPAC specified, identify values that might be ripe for reduction.[19]

CMS has adopted some of the recommendations, some of which were also codified in the ACA.[20] Over the past several years, CMS has begun to identify "misvalued" services along the lines of criteria MedPAC recommended; it has obtained input from nonphysicians; and it has announced that it will conduct annual reviews instead of five-year ones. While CMS has failed to adopt MedPAC's most important recommendation, the establishment of a review panel independent of specialty society control, it has complied with the ACA's mandate to

[17] *See, e.g.*, William C. Hsiao et al., *Results and Policy Implications of the Resource-Based Relative-Value Study*, 319 New Eng. J. Med. 881 (1988); William C. Hsiao et al., *Results, Potential Effects, and Implementation Issues of the Resource-Based Relative Value Scale*, 260 JAMA 2429 (1988); Physician Payment Review Commission, Medicare Physician Payment: An Agenda for Reform 4–5, 20–21, 35 (Mar. 1987).

[18] *See* MedPAC, Report to the Congress: Medicare Payment Policy ch. 3 (Mar. 2006) [hereinafter MedPAC March 2006 Report]; *see also* MedPAC, Report to the Congress: Medicare and the Health Care Delivery System 12–17 (June 2011).

[19] *See* MedPAC March 2006 Report, at 142–148.

[20] ACA § 3134, Pub. L. No. 111-148 (2010).

establish a formal process to review the work RVUs. The broadened process includes input from the medical directors of Medicare contractors, the opportunity for public nomination of codes to be reviewed, and contracts with consultants to validate the work RVUs.[21] Nonetheless, MedPAC continues to express concern with reliance on the RUC,[22] and it is not clear whether these changes will stem the RVUs' drift toward widening the disparity between primary and specialty compensation.

The second aspect of provider manipulation of the RBRVS-based system concerns the substantial power of physicians, particularly specialists, to generate their own income by increasing the volume of care. To account for this "volume effect," the RBRVS-based system employs a mechanism, the Sustainable Growth Rate (SGR) formula, which is an "expenditure target," intended to take back any increase in aggregate expenditures resulting from increased volume. The SGR formula allows the volume of fee schedule services to grow at the same rate as per capita GDP.

In each year from 2002–2012, actual expenditures have exceeded the target. Congress, however, has intervened each year after 2003 to reduce the take-back for that year. The formula then compounds the shortfall in successive years—just like an interest rate compounds each year by adding to the base over which it is taken—and updates in any given year are based on what spending would have been had the full reductions occurred. The effects are now very substantial. For 2013, the take-back would have cut fees by a whopping 24%.[23] Because that level of shock to providers is unreasonable, Congress has again suspended application of the SGR, therefore continuing a payment freeze.

This dynamic further skews the RBRVS away from cognitive services and toward procedures and imaging. Procedures and imaging are churned far more readily than time-intensive cognitive services because the latter, but not the former, are subject to the constraint that face time is needed, and there are only so many hours in the day. Moreover, this dynamic defeats the attempt to wrest expenditures away from a provider-dominated fee system. Nonetheless, because Congress has simply frozen pay, the RBRVS-based system, like IPPS, "on paper" has controlled expenditures for physicians' services to a limited extent and relative to other payers.

All countries face three dimensions of aggregation-disaggregation: (1) whether *payment* is aggregated or disaggregated; (2) whether *units of payment* are aggregated or disaggregated; and (3) whether the *entities paid* are aggregated or disaggregated. Although the United States is distinctive in its disaggregation of payment, its mechanisms to address the other two dimensions bear some similarity to those used in comparative nations, although, importantly, as adapted to its particular structure, history, and culture. In contrast to disaggregation of payment, with regard to the two other dimension we're talking questions of degree, even though as we will see, the sum of each part adds up to a whole that is very distinctive.

[21] *See, e.g.*, Dep't Health & Human Services, Center for Medicare & Medicaid Services, Medicare Program; Revisions to Payment Policies Under the Physician Fee Schedule, Clinical Laboratory Fee Schedule & Other Revisions to Part B for CY 2014, 78 Fed. Reg. 43,282, 43,285, 43,302–304 (July 19, 2013).

[22] *See, e.g.*, Letter from Glenn M. Hackbarth, Chairman, MedPAC to Marilyn Tavenner, Administrator, CMS 6–10 (Aug. 30, 2013), http://www.medpac.gov/documents/083013_MedPAC_PartB_COMMENT.pdf (accessed June 3, 2014).

[23] *See, e.g.*, MEDPAC, REPORT TO THE CONGRESS: MEDICARE PAYMENT POLICY 97, 259 (Mar. 2014).

All payment has to utilize some *unit of payment*, which can be relatively aggregated—"global"—or relatively disaggregated—"activity-based." As discussed in this section previously, hospitals could be paid for discrete services, for a DRG or based on a global budget. The first unit of payment is the most disaggregated, the second method less so while remaining activity-based, and the global budget stands at the extreme side of this aggregation-disaggregation dimension. Payment based on relatively global units are divorced from the quantity and types of services provided—a hospital is paid on a global budget or for a day of care regardless of what is actually done—while episode-based payment is connected much more closely with activity—"discharge-based" payment, as indicated above, is dependent on what is actually done because the coding of the discharge into a DRG is based, in good part, on what services were furnished during the inpatient stay.

The *entity being paid* can likewise be relatively aggregated or disaggregated. A single radiologist, for example, could be paid for the particular services he or she provides, or the radiologist could be paid by an individual salary. Alternatively, radiology could be compensated based on a contract price paid to an entire radiology group servicing an entire hospital. Analogously, a hospital can be paid separately from an after-care facility like a nursing home; or the hospital and the after-care facility could be aggregated into one entity paid through a "bundled payment" among them. Indeed, a major reason for the failure of the IPPS to constrain overall federal expenditures is that as financial pressure has been put on inpatient stays, hospitals have shifted care to more lucrative sites, paid outside IPPS, such as hospital outpatient departments, ambulatory surgery centers, rehabilitation facilities, and so forth.

No level of aggregation or disaggregation is perfect.[24] Smaller units of payment allow payers to monitor and control more of what is performed. For example, if one is concerned that a physician on salary, or a hospital on a global budget, will tend to provide fewer or less intensive services to all patients or to select patients who require fewer or less intensive services, one can instead pay on a fee-for-service, or per diagnosis, basis. However, providers paid on more discrete units of payment have incentives to increase volume of care. Providers also have an incentive to unbundle services because they can make more money by shifting costs to others or increasing volume. Hospitals paid under IPPS have incentives to discharge patients "quicker and sicker" to shift costs of care to whatever provider ends up with the patient next, for example, a nursing home; the hospital's payment for the MS-DRG remains the same regardless of the duration of the inpatient stay. Hospitals likewise have incentives to unbundle services to get paid "twice"—for example, move to an outpatient department, testing that would otherwise occur after inpatient admission, because that way the hospital obtains both inpatient and outpatient payment. Conversely, if one is concerned that a physician paid by fee-for-service, or a hospital per diagnosis, is going to churn volume, thereby increasing expenditures and possibly harming patients, then one can put the physician on salary, or the hospital on a budget (but then it is difficult to monitor activity).

[24] For a comprehensive discussion of the trade-offs among payment methods, *see* R. P. Ellis & M. M. Miller, *Provider Payment Methods and Incentives*, *in* HEALTH SYSTEMS POLICY, FINANCE, AND ORGANIZATION 322 (Gúy Carrin ed., 2009); *see also* Randall P. Ellis & Thomas G. McGuire, *Provider Behavior Under Prospective Reimbursement: Cost Sharing and Supply*, 5 J. HEALTH ECON. 129 (1986).

By and large payment in the United States has tended toward disaggregation on all three dimensions—fragmented *payers* use relatively disaggregated *units of payment* furnished to relatively disaggregated *providers*. While the ACA and other more recent policy initiatives, such as accountable care organizations (ACOs) and a variety of demonstration projects discussed in the chapter by Saver (this volume), represent attempts to bundle payment across the continuum of care, the fact remains that payment in the United States is still disaggregated on all dimensions.

b. Outside

The second major reason that neither IPPS nor the RBRVS-based system is as prospective as designed is due to the fact that Medicare's payment policy is "Medicare-only." As a result Medicare's payment "is assessed relative to the costs of treating Medicare beneficiaries, and [MedPAC]'s recommendations address a sector's Medicare payments, not total payments."[25] In other words, Medicare sets its rates with indifference to the effect on other payers or the healthcare system more generally. As noted, this "Medicare-only" policy has allowed Medicare to control its expenditures relative to other payers.[26]

This fact has led some to charge that Medicare has shifted costs to other payers,[27] while others lay the finger of blame on the failure of private payers to control their expenditures.[28] Regardless of the fact this argument has clear implications for the question whether Medicare is paying "enough," this "push-pull" debate obscures the fact that the continuing escalation of expenditures is a *joint product of all of Medicare and private payers*—they're all in it together because the problem is fragmented payment.[29] IPPS and the RBRVS-based system have allowed Medicare to control its expenditures but *only relative to other payers, not absolutely and not relative to comparable nations*. Whether the failure to control overall system expenditures stems from Medicare's pushing other payers' expenditures up, or whether the continuing escalation of payment is caused by other payers' pulling Medicare's expenditures up, either or both effects push and pull expenditures in the United States to ever higher levels. Without coordinated payment—that is, with the continued fragmentation of payment—the push-pull will simply continue.[30]

[25] MEDPAC, MEDICARE PAYMENT POLICY: REPORT TO THE CONGRESS 30 (Mar. 2011) [hereinafter MEDPAC, MARCH 2011 REPORT].

[26] *See, e.g.*, MEDPAC, MARCH 2011 REPORT, at 51–57.

[27] *See, e.g.*, Allen Dobson, *The Cost-Shift Payment "Hydraulic": Foundation, History, and Implications*, 25 HEALTH AFF. 22 (2006).

[28] *See, e.g.*, Chapin White & Vivian Yaling Wu, *How Do Hospitals Cope with Sustained Low Growth in Medicare Prices?*, 49 HEALTH SERVS. RES. 11 (2014); Austin B. Frakt, *How Much Do Hospitals Cost Shift?*, 89 MILBANK Q. 90 (2011); MEDPAC, MARCH 2011 REPORT, at 51–57; Jeffrey Stensland et al., *Private-Payer Profits Can Induce Negative Medicare Margins*, 29 HEALTH AFF. 1045 (2010).

[29] *See, e.g.*, Reinhardt, *The Many Different Prices Paid to Providers*; Reinhardt, *The Pricing of U.S. Hospital Services*.

[30] This article does not address the more general debate concerning the use of markets to finance healthcare. Switzerland, for example, like the United States, has multiple payers, and they compete on some dimensions of healthcare delivery and finance, while unlike the United States payment is aggregated, or, in other words coordinated.

IV Social and Political Context of Payment: The Denial of Politics

So far we have seen that the singular, extreme degree of disaggregation of payment in the United States prevents the assertion of countervailing power against providers; it also comes at the price of significantly higher administrative costs, perhaps as much as a third or fourth more than other nations, because payment methods are neither standardized, nor (except for Medicare's) are they transparent, both of which cause significant transactions costs.[31]

The reasons that payment in the United States is singularly disaggregated across all dimensions are, obviously, very complicated, but one can say that the relative disaggregation across the board comports with a number of aspects of social and political context in the United States. The most obvious one is that fragmentation of payers and disaggregated units of payment are mutually reinforcing. A hospital, most saliently, cannot be paid on a global budget, as has been traditional in many comparable countries, because payment on a global budget requires coordination among payers. In turn, the fragmented culture and structure tend to support methods of payment that drill down as far as possible to each element of care so as to ensure that no payer pays anything more than the costs of its subscribers[32]—paying anything more would benefit another payer, likewise competing to pay just its costs and nothing more.[33]

To enable each payer to pay just its costs alone, payment must necessarily be cost-based, and "accuracy" is a primary goal of health services research and healthcare policy and administration.[34] Yet, if payment "accurately" reflects costs, then costs just pass through and a prospective system is prospective no more. The search for accuracy thus takes the form of a search for measuring "real" or "true" or "efficient" costs. This search boils down to finding some means to evaluate which costs are eligible for payment. This evaluation, in turn, requires the use of some hypothecation, here: how a hypothetical provider would perform in a hypothetical market free of the "distortions" that characterize the actual markets that exist in healthcare. The hypothecation can define "efficiency" to be the result of competition relative to a chosen "yardstick," which serves as a proxy when markets fail—for example, competing around the average cost of the average hospital—or "efficiency" can be thought

[31] *See, e.g.*, text and notes at note 3; White, *Implementing*.

[32] *Cf.* Elizabeth Kilbreth, *Paying by the Rules: How Eliminating the Cost Shift Could Improve the Chances for Successful Health Care Reform*, 35 J. Health Pol., Pol'y & L. 177 (2010) (cost-shifting is corrosive of social solidarity needed to create consolidated insurance).

[33] For a general discussion of the relationship between adoption of a payment technology like DRGs and social and political context, *see, e.g.*, Thomas D'Aunno et al., *Conclusions: The Global Diffusion of Casemix*, *in* The Globalization of Managerial Innovation in Health Care 346 (John R. Kimberly et al. eds., 2008); John R. Kimberly, *DRGs in Western Europe: Lesson and Comparisons in Managerial Innovation*, *in* The Migration of Managerial Innovation: Diagnosis-Related Groups and Health Care Administration in Western Europe 340 (John R. Kimberly & Gérard de Pouvourville eds., 1993); *see also* Frankford, *Measuring*; David M. Frankford, *The Medicare DRGs: Efficiency and Organizational Rationality*, 10 Yale J. Reg. 273 (1993).

[34] *See* Frankford, *Measuring*; *see also* Joseph White, *Cost Control After the ACA*, Sept./Oct. 2013 Pub. Admin. Rev. S24, S28–S29.

about in standard neoclassical terms as allocative efficiency.[35] Either way, "accuracy" simply means that payers, like those in charge of Medicare, are deciding, through "accurate" determinations of what is "real," the level of resources to inject into the healthcare sector: "The word 'real' thus has an unintended double meaning: (1) 'real' in the sense that a phenomenon occurs independently of measurement; (2) 'real' in the sense that the phenomenon will be recognized as 'happening' by the system and built into rates."[36]

In other nations payment is much less focused on accurately measuring costs and is structured to enable explicit political decisions regarding, first, how much a society can afford to spend on healthcare, as opposed to bridges, highways, schools, defense, and so forth, and, second, the allocation of standards of living to providers.[37] These decisions are made through collective mechanisms, which may mix private and public elements and many of which, from the perspective of the United States, too much resemble collective bargaining.[38] As examples, France applies its DRG weights within overall budget priorities and expenditure targets set for each sector by its Parliament and Ministry of Health, and then by states and regional health authorities, which contract with hospitals, and with rates adjusted for failure to meet expected aggregate expenditures[39]; Germany uses DRGs in combination with volume-adjusted "revenue budgets" negotiated between peak associations, primarily the sickness fund and hospital associations[40]; in decentralized Switzerland, cantons use DRGs within the context of an overall budget negotiated between the hospital and sickness fund associations subject to approval of the relevant canton.[41] These mixed uses can accomplish diverse purposes, like monitoring activity within a budgeting system; allocating funds in internal markets; distributing aggregate federal spending among states or regions in a regionalized system; paying for patients who cross regional or national boundaries.[42] These

[35] *See, e.g.*, Andrew Street et al., *DRG-Based Hospital Payment and Efficiency: Theory, Evidence, and Challenges*, *in* DIAGNOSIS-RELATED GROUPS IN EUROPE: MOVING TOWARDS TRANSPARENCY, EFFICIENCY AND QUALITY IN HOSPITALS 93–94 (Reinhard Busse et al. eds., 2011). For scathing criticism of initial use of average costs in England, as in the United States, as a yardstick to set rates, *see* Andrew Street & Alan Maynard, *Activity Based Financing in England: The Need for Continual Refinement of Payment by Results*, 2 HEALTH ECON., POL'Y & L. 419 (2007).

[36] Frankford, *Complexity*, at 659.

[37] *See, e.g.*, Naoki Ikegami & Gerard F. Anderson, *In Japan, All-Payer Rate Setting under Tight Government Control Has Proved to be an Effective Approach to Controlling Costs*, 31 HEALTH AFF. 1049 (2012).

[38] *See, e.g.*, Wilm Quentin et al., *Hospital Payment Based on Diagnosis-Related Groups Differs in Europe and Holds Lessons for the United States*, 32 HEALTH AFF. 713 (2013).

[39] *See, e.g.*, Zeynep Or & Martine Bellanger, *France: Implementing Homogeneous Patient Groups in a Mixed Market*, *in* DIAGNOSIS-RELATED GROUPS IN EUROPE, at 221; Martine M. Bellanger & Philippe R. Mossé, *The Search for the Holy Grail: Combining Decentralised Planning and Contracting Mechanisms in the French Health Care System*, 14 HEALTH ECON. S119 (2005).

[40] *See, e.g.*, Alexander Geissler et al., *Germany: Understanding G-DRGs*, *in* DIAGNOSIS-RELATED GROUPS IN EUROPE, at 243.

[41] *See, e.g.*, Hervé Guillain, *Casemix in Switzerland*, *in* THE GLOBALIZATION OF MANAGERIAL INNOVATION IN HEALTH CARE, at 176. *See also* INTERNATIONAL PROFILES OF HEALTH CARE SYSTEMS, 2013 (COMMONWEALTH FUND STUDY, Sarah Thomson et al. eds.), at 122.

[42] *See, e.g.*, DIAGNOSIS-RELATED GROUPS IN EUROPE; THE GLOBALIZATION OF MANAGERIAL INNOVATION IN HEALTH CARE; THE MIGRATION OF MANAGERIAL INNOVATION; *see also* Frankford, *Measuring*.

ends all involve distributional decisions, revealing how payment is a political and social process.

Indeed, the mechanics of payment in the United States effectively obstruct the rendering of explicit distributional choice. Clearly, as in all systems using a DRG-like unit of payment, there have been winners and losers under IPPS, but the "rough justice"[43] from the use of averages is much rougher in the United States than elsewhere. IPPS is a remarkably top-down national payment system used across a vast and diverse landscape. Even France, with its Cartesian culture, does not use its version of DRGs—its patient classification system (PCS)—in such a fashion. Its PCS units are applied to expenditures allocated regionally. Further, its PCS is much more highly differentiated than are the MS-DRGs; and certain services like chemotherapy and radiotherapy, which would significantly reduce within-PCS homogeneity if bundled within the PCS, are unbundled and paid separately. The combined result of these features is that the averages generated through these mechanics are much more "granular" and therefore sweep far less broadly than the averages used in the United States, in a trade-off between attaining a much more tailored system at the cost of greater administrative complexity and enhanced ability of hospitals to game the system.[44] By contrast, our use of less differentiated MS-DRGs to allocate an annual national expenditure occurs at such a dizzying height—national flat rates per MS-DRG—that no matter how many adjustments for local variations are allowed one still gets at best a Hubble-like view of the distributional effects being wrought.[45] Therefore, comparatively, the manner in which we use DRGs in the United States serves to preclude the very political distributional choices that are at the center of any payment system.

In the United States, politics is a dirty word and something to be avoided. As a result, we lack collective mechanisms such as exist in other nations to obtain coordination, either voluntary or compulsory, and to resolve disputes; the United States is left with payment policy as its only basic tool. The problems with the SGR and its predecessor, the Volume Performance Standard (VPS) aptly illustrate this point. In their use of the VPS, creators thought they were modeling methods used in British Columbia in the 1980s.[46] However, the designers failed to understand the difference between imposing an aggregate target or

[43] RICK MAYES & ROBERT A. BERENSON, MEDICARE PROSPECTIVE PAYMENT AND THE SHAPING OF U.S. HEALTH CARE (2006).

[44] *See, e.g.*, Or & Bellanger, *France*; *see also* Conrad Kobel et al., *DRG Systems and Similar Patient Classifications Systems in Europe*, *in* DIAGNOSIS-RELATED GROUPS IN EUROPE, at 37. For a fuller comparison of the different construction and usage of DRG-like PCSs, compared with the United States, *see, e.g.*, Quentin et al., *Hospital Payment*.

[45] *See, e.g.*, Bruce C. Vladeck, *Medicare's Prospective Payment System at Age Eight: Mature Success or Midlife Crisis?*, 14 U. PUGET SOUND L. REV. 453, 479–480 (1991). This view was shared by Judith Lave, who was the director of HCFA's Office of Research from 1980 to 1982, the period in which IPPS was developed. *See* Judith R. Lave et al., *A Proposal for Incentive Reimbursement for Hospitals*, 11 MED. CARE 79, 85–89 (1973) (proposing the use of a case-adjusted per-case reimbursement system with cost-sharing between the government and a hospital for deviations from the per-case rate); Judith R. Lave, *Hospital Reimbursement Under Medicare*, 62 MILBANK MEMORIAL FUND Q. 251, 254–256 (1984) (recommending the immediate abandonment of the use of national rates); Judith R. Lave, *The Impact of the Medicare Prospective Payment System and Recommendations for Change*, 7 YALE J. ON REG. 499, 521–527 (1990) (recommending various changes to reduce the reliance upon national rates).

[46] *See* Paul B. Ginsburg & Philip R. Lee, *Defending U.S. Physician Payment Reform*, 8 HEALTH AFF. 67 (1989); *see also* SMITH, PAYING FOR MEDICARE, at 198.

cap and negotiating one, and moreover, they missed the fact that to succeed, a target has to be used in conjunction with the other methods then deployed in British Columbia[47]; most notably, bilateral negotiations among parties who, locked together for the long haul, have to compromise[48]; and control on the supply side, as British Columbia in those years was, in draconian fashion, eliminating *current* physician stock by refusing to grant, or severely restricting geographically, billing numbers for some physicians, and it was actively preventing the diffusion of capital into and within the ambulatory care sector, instead of reimbursing it, as we do, and (worse still) instead of spreading its recovery, as does the RBRVS system, across a relative-value scale.

Because these forms of collective action are too "political" to be used in the United States, our nation denies itself the use of these varying systemwide, "macrolevel" forms of controlling utilization through control of investment in capital, including human capital. As Professor Joseph White quips, "to paraphrase the movie Field of Dreams, if you do not build it they cannot come."[49] Other nations have learned that it is far easier politically to control capacity at the outset than to deny its use after the fact because the latter deprives investors of expected returns and patients of expected benefits. To control expenditures, it is better to nip those expectations in the bud.[50] Such "regulation," however, would be anathema to the avoidance of politics in the United States. Instead, as a weak substitute the attempt to control utilization occurs at the point of service, the "microlevel," through the use of financial incentives and aggressive utilization review at the point of service—when the barn is already on fire.

Given the eschewal of overt politics, the fixation on accuracy of payment at a microlevel comes laden with the technocratic wish to be saved from politics by reliance on technical answers to (non)political questions of what payment should consist of. Both IPPS and the RBRVS-based systems were developed with such goals in the background. Although IPPS's standardized payment amount was based on actual, historical costs, it was expected that the historicity of the base payment rate would fade with time. The aspiration was that it could be updated annually in a scientific manner devoid of politics (or anything else) such that the payment system would reflect only the efficient payment of cases calibrated by their severity. The hope for the RBRVS was similar. It supposedly derived from the scientific analyses of the value of work—the time, mental effort and judgment, technical skill and physical effort, and stress associated with potential risk for a patient—combined with supposedly objective measures of practice expense, including liability insurance. With that foundation in place, scientific and "accurate" updates could preclude extraneous considerations such as politics.[51]

[47] Frankford, *Measuring*, at 660.

[48] As Joe White remarked concerning negotiations and arbitration in Canadian provinces, "Kicking and screaming in many cases, both sides have been dragged into recognizing that they have to live together, that rules are necessary, and neither side should be able to impose its will." JOSEPH WHITE, COMPETING SOLUTIONS: AMERICAN HEALTH CARE PROPOSALS AND INTERNATIONAL EXPERIENCE 69 (1995).

[49] Joseph White, *Targets and Systems of Health Care Cost Control* 24 J. HEALTH POL., POL'Y & L. 653, 659 (1999).

[50] *See, e.g.*, Morris L. Barer et al., *It Ain't Necessarily So: The Cost Implications of Health Care Reform*, 13 HEALTH AFF. 88, 95 (1994).

[51] *See, e.g.*, Frankford, *Measuring*; SMITH, PAYING FOR MEDICARE, at 4, 11, 71–72, 84, 86, 100, 106, 232–233, 246–247. *See generally* James A. Morone, *American Political Culture and the Search for Lessons from Abroad*, 15 J. HEALTH POL., POL'Y & L. 129 (1990); Gary A. Belkin, *The Technocratic Wish: Making Sense

One reads the mountains of technical reports, however, and wonders how anyone can seriously conclude that politics is eliminated. For example, as discussed in section III.a. above, each year MedPAC recommends an annual update to the IPPS base payment rate. At times it has utilized what is called the "discretionary adjustment factor." The elements canvassed have included at various times: beneficiaries' access to care (e.g., number of hospitals and beds, growth of specialized services, volume of services, hospitals' access to capital); quality of care (e.g., safety indicators, satisfaction measures, readmission rates); new technologies; changes in site of care; coding behavior; changes in productivity; provider costs; Medicare margins; total margins; projected costs and margins; costs of "relatively efficient hospitals"; prior underpayments or overpayments; various "one-time factors"; and the general healthcare environment. These considerations are stirred in a pot—a report—and out pops a recommendation, such as the following.

> In considering its update recommendation, the Commission has struck a balance between a number of competing factors. On the one hand, average total Medicare margins are negative (–5 percent in 2009 and projected to reach –7 percent in 2011). On the other hand, our update framework indicators (access to care, including supply and service volume; quality of care; and access to capital) are positive. Furthermore, the negative Medicare margins are due at least in part to the lack of private financial pressure for cost containment, and the set of hospitals identified as efficient have a median Medicare margin of about 3 percent. On the basis of these circumstances, the Commission contemplated an update of 2.5 percent.
>
> However, two additional considerations led the Commission to its recommended update of 1 percent. For inpatient services, the Commission and others have documented past and ongoing overpayments resulting from changes in documentation and coding after implementation of MS-DRGs in 2008. Current law does not allow full recovery of past overpayments and no action has been taken to stop the ongoing overpayments. The Commission believes that all overpayments should be recovered and that the most urgent step is to stop the ongoing overpayments. To accomplish this objective, the Commission would reduce the ongoing overpayment by 1.5 percentage points—that is, the difference between its contemplated update of 2.5 percent and its recommended update of 1 percent. This adjustment would account for 1.5 percentage points of the 3.9 percent adjustment needed to fully prevent accumulation of further overpayments.[52]

Behind technical names like "discretionary update factor" lies a very simple fact: This is simply a very, very global budget. It is a political judgment how much money should be devoted to Medicare hospitals nationwide for acute inpatient care. This extremely macro-level judgment is then drilled down to the individual hospital and to the individual case through the complex mechanisms of IPPS—and not in a well-tailored fashion at all.

Finally, consonant with this focus on microlevel control, as well as the technocratic wish embodied in relatively disaggregated units of payment, is the American penchant to control expenditures through financial incentives as a means of behavioral control.[53] Payment

and Finding Power in the "Managed" Medical Marketplace, 22 J. HEALTH POL., POL'Y & L. 509 (1997). For a discussion of the scientism in such endeavors, *see* David M. Frankford, *Scientism and Economism in the Regulation of Health Care*, 19 J. HEALTH POL., POL'Y & L. 773 (1994).

52 MEDPAC MARCH 2011 REPORT, at 60. *See generally* Frankford, *Complexity*, at 618–635.

53 As Bill Glaser wrote, "policy analysis in health care finance has specialized in technical economics rather than in the construction of politically feasible structures." William A. Glaser, *The Politics of Paying American Physicians*, 8 HEALTH AFF. 129, 131 (1989); *see also* William A. Glaser, *Designing Fee Schedules by Formulae, Politics, and Negotiations*, 80 AM. J. PUB. HEALTH 804 (1990). Quite arguably, Glaser tended

becomes primarily a means to obtain some other end rather than the allocation of income and choice of the amount of expenditures. One can see this concept in the adoption of the DRGs, as just one example among many, as the following illustrates.

> Payment on the basis of a per-case rate for each DRG is intended to create specific financial incentives that encourage hospital management to adopt desirable methods of controlling the cost of care. It was hoped that hospital management, facing a separate payment rate per discharge for each DRG, would have strong incentives to: (1) improve productivity; (2) use less expensive inputs where possible; (3) influence physicians to reduce the length of stay, limit the volume of inpatient services, and use a less expensive mix of services to treat each patient; (4) specialize in treating types of cases the hospital can produce efficiently; and (5) adopt cost-reducing technologies, while avoiding cost-increasing technologies.[54]

One can also see this concept in the latest fad, value-based purchasing—discussed further in the chapter by Saver in this volume that rests on an alleged scientific base that desired outcomes can be scientifically derived and that those ends can be achieved through a scientifically tailored use of financial incentives.[55] IPPS, RBRVS-based payment, and like schemes "promise instrumental control akin to the actions of a skilled watchmaker. When the clock is running too fast, the watchmaker intervenes to slow it down. When the clock runs too slowly, the task is to speed it up. It is all a matter of clockwork."[56] This very strong emphasis on payment as a means of behavioral control is, relatively, another example of American exceptionalism in payment.[57]

In sum, payment in the United States is characterized by disaggregation at all three levels—payer, unit of payment, entity paid—and it uses mechanisms that are failing to control expenditures: methods focused on costs and accuracy that actually obscure distributional effects; the use of payment as the sole lever to control utilization without utilizing collective, macrolevel methods; and the resultant attempt to control price and utilization through use of microlevel, finely tuned, financial incentives—all in the technocratic wish to displace overt political decisions regarding levels and allocation of expenditures and provider incomes. Taken together, these relative, comparative differences combine to render the (non)system of payment in the United States exceptional, singular too in its result, our ever-rising expenditures. We are stuck, as if in mud.[58]

to paint too pretty a picture of consensus rather than the assertion of power. *Compare, e.g.*, William A. Glaser, *Doctors and Public Authorities: The Trend Toward Collaboration*, 19 J. Health Pol., Pol'y & L. 795 (1994), *with, e.g.*, Victor G. Rodwin, *Physician Payment Reform: Lessons from Abroad*, 8 Health Aff. 76 (1989).

[54] Prospective Payment Assessment Commission, Report and Recommendations to the Department of Health and Human Services 16 (Mar. 1, 1990). For criticism of the heroic assumptions behind such behavioral control, *see* Frankford, *The Medicare DRGs*.

[55] *See generally* Sandra J. Tanenbaum, *Pay for Performance in Medicare: Evidentiary Irony and the Politics of Value*, 34 J. Health Pol., Pol'y & L. 717 (2009).

[56] David M. Frankford, *Managing Medical Clinicians' Work Through the Use of Financial Incentives*, 29 Wake Forest L. Rev. 71, 71–72 (1994).

[57] As Joel Cantor wrote to me, this difference "is like European football compared to American football. The rules of the latter are so complex that they require a host of experts, instant replays, and so-forth, to know what is going on. In European football, one simply has to get goals."

[58] *See, e.g.*, David Chinitz & Victor G. Rodwin, *What Passes and Fails as Health Policy and Management*, 39 J. Health Pol., Pol'y & L. 1113 (2014); *see also* Mark Stabile et al., *Health Care Cost*

V Conclusion

Healthcare works best when payers, patients, and providers are joined together for the long haul in integrated pools such that there is continuity of care, incentives to invest in prevention, and stability in revenue generation and payment (two sides of one equation). This chapter has discussed how a very fragmented payment system feeds on itself and becomes entrenched in culture and institutions; and this fragmentation enables cost-shifting, volume generation, shifting of sites of care, risk selection, upcoding, and the like. This behavior is then countered by payers' moves to rebundle services, even to rebundle providers into entities like ACOs (and numerous other examples), in a constant game of move, countermove.[59] However, these efforts are likely to be successful only in a marginal way because they are swimming upstream against so much fragmentation elsewhere—the multitude of private payers (e.g., over one million ERISA plans, over seven thousand exchange plans[60]), which operate with different rules, along with a multitude of public payers (e.g., Medicare, fifty-one state Medicaid plans, Children's Health Insurance Program (CHIP), which likewise operate with different rules. In principle, under highly regulated circumstances the finance side can remain somewhat disaggregated—like in Germany or moreover, in Switzerland and the Netherlands—while the payment side is coordinated.[61] However, in the United States, at least right now, aggregating the payment side is unlikely to occur.

When compensation is short term as part of constantly changing relationships—like the ideal widget of simple neoclasssical models— then no one has any long-term incentives, much less long-term bonds that we describe with terms like "solidarity," "loyalty," and "commitment." In the world of fragmented payers using fragmented units of payment given to fragmented providers, it is very difficult to solve the problem of collective action necessary to "cross-subsidize"—now a pejorative term in the United States—social goods like education and the maintenance of standby capacity like trauma units.

The story of payment in the United States, recounted here, is a bleak one. The expenditure fire in the United States continues to burn out of control. Regardless of rhetoric about "bending the cost curve,"[62] the structure and culture of payment remain the same. Furthermore,

Containment Strategies Used in Four Other High-Income Countries Hold Lessons for the United States, 32 Health Aff. 643 (2012).

[59] *See generally* David M. Frankford, *The Normative Constitution of Professional Power*, 22 J. Health Pol., Pol'y & L. 185 (1997).

[60] Robert Wood Johnson Foundation, Health Insurance Exchange Compare Dataset, http://www.rwjf.org/en/research-publications/find-rwjf-research/2014/03/breakaway-policy-dataset.html (accessed June 4, 2014).

[61] For a truly illuminating discussion of how carefully calibrated such a system must be, *see* Tsung-Mei Cheng, *Understanding the "Swiss Watch" Function of Switzerland's Health System*, 29 Health Aff. 1442 (2010).

[62] For a critique of the alleged cost controls in the ACA, *see* White, *Cost Control*. For contrary arguments that price cuts in the ACA will have spillover effects to reduce expenditures of other payers, *see* Chapin White, *Cutting Medicare Hospital Prices Leads to a Spillover Reduction in Hospital Discharges for the Nonelderly*, 49 Health Servs. Res. 1 (2014); White & Wu, *How Do Hospitals*; Chapin White, *Contrary to Cost-Shift Theory, Lower Medicare Hospital Rates for Inpatient Care Lead to Lower Private Payment Rates*, 32 Health Aff. 935 (2013).

recent evidence exists that growing consolidation in both the insurance and provider sectors, as well as increased vertical integration between them, is correlated with enhanced prices paid to *both* levels.[63] Without some radical change, business will continue as usual, if not get worse.

However, some glimmer of change is illuminating the horizon. Under the ACA's authority to experiment with innovative payment methods, CMS has granted permission to include Medicare spending in an overall per capita expenditure cap to control volume as part of Maryland's all-payer rate-setting system for hospital services—currently the only such system in the United States.[64] Vermont's single-payer system remains on the books,[65] although as of March 2015 the governor has announced that he cannot now put forward the required public financing plan because it would require a substantial increase in taxes.[66] Massachusetts, within its statewide universal health insurance scheme, is experimenting with payment methods that would bring all providers within an overall expenditure target.[67] Finally, given the mounting evidence that price is the main driver of expenditures, and given the fact that nothing else seems to be working, even some members of the policy elite who are generally supportive of markets in healthcare have started to discuss seriously all-payer state rate setting.[68] While it is unclear whether these efforts can spread to other states,[69] we can at least say that a whiff of aggregating payment, at least at the state level, is in the air.

[63] *See, e.g.*, Austin B. Frakt et al., *Plan-Provider Integration, Premiums, and Quality in the Medicare Advantage Market*, 48 HEALTH SERVS. RES. 1996 (2013); *see also* Laurence C. Baker et al., *Vertical Integration: Hospital Ownership of Physician Practices Is Associated with Higher Price and Spending*, 33 HEALTH AFF. 756 (2014); Leemore Dafney et al., *Paying a Premium on Your Premium? Consolidation in the US Health Insurance Industry*, 102 AM. ECON. REV. 1161 (2012); Martin Gaynor & Robert Town, *The Impact of Hospital Consolidation—Update*, Robert Wood Johnson Foundation Synthesis Report (2012), http://www.rwjf.org/content/dam/farm/reports/issue_briefs/2012/rwjf73261 (accessed June 8, 2014); Ann S. O'Malley et al., *Rising Hospital Employment of Physicians: Better Quality, Higher Costs?*, Center for Health System Change, Issue Brief 136 (2011); http://www.hschange.com/CONTENT/1230/1230.pdf (accessed June 10, 2014); William B. Vogt & Robert Town, *How Has Hospital Consolidation Affected the Price and Quality of Hospital Care?*, Robert Wood Johnson Foundation, Research Synthesis Report No. 9 (2006).

[64] *See, e.g.*, Rahul Rajkumar et al., *Maryland's All-Payer Approach to Delivery-System Reform*, 370 NEW ENG. J. MED. 493 (2014).

[65] *See, e.g.*, Ashley M. Fox & Nathan J. Blanchet, *The Little State That Couldn't Could? The Politics of "Single-Payer" Health Coverage in Vermont*, J. HEALTH POL., POL'Y & L, published ahead of print February 19, 2015, doi: 10.1215/03616878-2888381, http://jhppl.dukejournals.org/content/early/2015/02/12/03616878-2888381.abstract (accessed March 16, 2015).

[66] *See, e.g.*, Peter Shumlin, "This Is Discouraging News," RUTLAND HERALD, December 21, 2014, http://www.rutlandherald.com/article/20141221/OPINION06/712219919/1018/OPINION (accessed March 16, 2015).

[67] *See, e.g.*, Robert E. Mechanic et al., *The New Era of Payment Reform, Spending Targets, and Cost Containment in Massachusetts: Early Lessons for the Nation*, 31 HEALTH AFF. 2334 (2012).

[68] *See, e.g.*, Paul B. Ginsburg & L. Gregory Pawlson, *Seeking Lower Prices Where Providers Are Consolidated: An Examination of Market and Policy Strategies*, 33 HEALTH AFF. 1067 (2014). Ginsburg, *Reforming*; Robert Berenson, *Unchecked Provider Clout in California Foreshadows Challenges to Health Reform*, 29 HEALTH AFF. 699 (2010); *see also* Joseph P. Newhouse, *Assessing Health Reform's Impact on Four Key Groups of Americans*, 29 HEALTH AFF. 1714, 1723 (2010).

[69] *Compare, e.g.*, Robert Murray, *The Case for a Coordinated System of Provider Payments in the United States*, 37 J. HEALTH POL., POL'Y & L. 679 (2012), *with, e.g.*, Mark Pauly & Robert Town, *Maryland Exceptionalism? All-Payers Regulation and Health Care System Efficiency*, 37 J. HEALTH POL., POL'Y & L. 697 (2012).

CHAPTER 38

INTEGRATION, FRAGMENTATION, AND HUMAN NATURE

The Role of the Fraud and Abuse Laws in a Changing Healthcare System

JOAN H. KRAUSE

In the years leading up to the passage and implementation of the Patient Protection and Affordable Care Act (ACA), one of the focal points of debate was the fragmented nature of healthcare in the United States. Independent healthcare providers, each reimbursed for their individual contributions to patient care, have little incentive or inclination to coordinate with each other, leading to inefficient, costly, and suboptimal patient care. Moreover, a payment system based primarily on the quantity of services delivered may be rife with both inefficiency and fraud. One solution has been to encourage providers to "integrate" into multilevel entities that can be incentivized and enabled to better coordinate care, thereby improving patient health and reducing costs. Yet such integration may be difficult in light of the healthcare fraud and abuse laws, which restrict financial relationships among providers who generate business for each other. To the extent the current fraud laws inhibit the development of new care models, critics argue that they are antiquated relics posing unnecessary barriers to advances in the healthcare market.[1]

There is some truth to this criticism. The fraud laws were written in a very different context: They assume the existence of a disaggregated healthcare system, with little vertical or horizontal integration and the predominance of fee-for-service (FFS) reimbursement. With virtually every party (including often the patient) benefiting from *more* care, the laws were drafted to prevent the types of financial collusion that might decrease quality and increase costs. By contrast, if payments could be redesigned to reward providers for the quality or

[1] *See generally* U.S. Gov't Accountability Office, GAO-12-355, Medicare: Implementation of Financial Incentive Programs under Federal Fraud and Abuse Laws (2012) (reviewing the challenges posed by federal fraud laws).

value of their services, ideally on a collective rather than an individual basis, the incentives to commit fraud by simply increasing the amount of healthcare services delivered might fade.

Yet experience has demonstrated that fraud can flourish in virtually *any* healthcare system. Fraud may be rampant under FFS reimbursement, but it also exists (albeit in different forms) in capitated systems, in which a set fee is paid for all care during a specified time period regardless of the services actually used. In short, whatever measurement forms the basis for payment—be it volume or value, quantity or quality—there will be incentives for providers to misrepresent that measurement to make more money. The fraud laws may indeed make some forms of integration more difficult, yet they also function as a necessary counterweight to the misguided assumption that integration inevitably reduces fraud. While the underlying premises of the fraud laws remain relevant, however, new healthcare arrangements may require changes in the way the prohibitions are implemented. Future fraud enforcement must respond to the complicated financial incentives providers face in a hybrid system, where new forms of integration coexist with remnants of the fragmented FFS model. This requires not simply more or less fraud enforcement overall, but rather enforcement that is more highly attuned to the realities of an ever-changing healthcare market.

I Fragmentation, Integration, and the Changing Healthcare Market

The dangers of a fragmented healthcare system have been well documented.[2] A decentralized system of independent healthcare providers, each reimbursed for their individual contributions to patient care, offers little incentive or opportunity for collaboration, coordination, quality enhancement, or cost control. The danger is magnified by the prevalence of FFS reimbursement, which Alain Enthoven has characterized as "a centrifugal force that... punishes (with less revenue) coordination that saves resources."[3] Fragmentation characterizes the financing as well as the delivery of care: Insurance is provided through a variety of public and private payers, with patients frequently changing private insurers or transitioning through different public programs. No entity is responsible for, or even capable of, ensuring the provision of cost-efficient, high-quality care across the country's population. Among other ills, this disorganized and inefficient system provides ample opportunity for those so inclined to engage in fraudulent and abusive activities, such as overutilization, overbilling, and abusive referrals.

In contrast, the recent healthcare reform debate invoked the concept of *integration*, a term often used but rarely defined with any precision. Most generally, "to integrate" means

[2] *See generally* The Fragmentation of U.S. Health Care: Causes and Solutions (Einer Elhauge ed., 2010). *See also* Frankford, this volume.

[3] Alain Enthoven, *Curing Fragmentation with Integrated Delivery Systems: What They Do, What Has Blocked Them, Why We Need Them, and How to Get There From Here*, *in* The Fragmentation of U.S. Health Care: Causes and Solutions, at 61, 62.

to "make into a whole by bringing all parts together; unify... [t]o join with something else; unite...."[4] In healthcare, integration refers to the process of discrete healthcare providers coming together in at least a loosely organized form to pursue coordinated, efficient, and high-quality care—attributes sorely lacking in the fragmented healthcare world. While this requires participants to share more than simply cost and quality goals, integration is a broad term that encompasses affiliations falling far short of anything resembling true unity of organization—often consisting of little more than a series of contractual agreements among independent providers.

The ACA contained many provisions designed to encourage and reward providers for higher-quality, more efficient, and better-coordinated services, including adjusting payments to reflect the quality, rather than simply the quantity, of care provided (Saver, this volume).[5] Under a value-based purchasing program that began in 2013, hospitals are eligible for value-based incentive payments if they meet performance standards for the treatment of specified conditions and procedures such as acute myocardial infarction, heart failure, and pneumonia; similar value-based payment modifiers for physician services are scheduled to go into effect in 2015.[6] Other ACA provisions reward improved coordination of care, both episodic and chronic: A national pilot program will examine whether bundling payments "for integrated care during an episode of care," rather than paying providers for their individual services, leads to improvements.[7] Similarly, a new program supports patient-centered medical homes, a model for the delivery of comprehensive primary care that incorporates a wide range of coordinated and interdisciplinary services, including preventive care and management of chronic conditions.[8]

The program with perhaps the greatest chance of transforming the healthcare industry, and the major impetus for provider integration efforts, is the Medicare Shared Savings Program (MSSP). The MSSP encourages multilevel groups of healthcare providers to form accountable care organizations (ACOs), through which they will share accountability for the cost and quality of care for a group of Medicare beneficiaries. Initially, most ACOs will operate on a one-sided risk model in which they will share in any savings achieved if their per capita Medicare expenditures fall below a benchmark; in subsequent years most will move to a two-sided model, sharing both savings and losses.[9] The goals of the MSSP "are to promote accountability for a patient population, coordinate items and services furnished to beneficiaries under Medicare Parts A and B, and encourage investments in infrastructure and redesigned care processes for high quality and efficient service delivery."[10] Yet because healthcare providers who generate referrals (such as physicians) and those who receive referrals (such as hospitals) will work together to coordinate patient care—in return for potential financial gain—ACOs and similar arrangements may implicate the healthcare fraud laws.

[4] American Heritage Dictionary of the English Language 910 (4th ed. 2000).

[5] Patient Protection and Affordable Care Act, Pub. L. No. 111-148, 124 Stat. 119 (2010).

[6] 42 U.S.C. §§ 1395ww(o), 1395w-4(p).

[7] 42 U.S.C. § 1395cc–4(a)(1).

[8] 42 U.S.C. § 256a-1(c)(2).

[9] 42 U.S.C. § 1395jjj; 42 C.F.R. §§ 425.604, 425.606 (2013).

[10] Medicare Programs; Medicare Shared Savings Program: Accountable Care Organizations, 76 Fed. Reg. 67,802, 67,824 (Nov. 2, 2011) (codified at 42 C.F.R. pt. 425) [hereinafter Medicare Shared Savings Program].

II Healthcare Fraud

a. Overview of Healthcare Fraud

It is no wonder that healthcare fraud has captured the attention of policy-makers: The United States spent an estimated $2.8 trillion dollars on healthcare in 2012, with a projected annual growth rate of 5.8% through 2022. Despite both the economic downturn at the beginning of the twenty-first century and the reforms enacted by the ACA, healthcare spending may grow to 20% of gross domestic product (GDP) during this period.[11] With estimates that up to 10% of these funds may be lost to fraud—although no one knows for sure—a strong anti-fraud agenda is both a political and a practical necessity. Fraud concerns drive core aspects of healthcare reform, and the potential savings attributable to stronger antifraud efforts has been offered as a painless method of financing increased healthcare coverage.[12]

These concerns have resulted in new prohibitions and ever-stronger penalties for those who engage in fraudulent activities. Major changes were enacted by the Health Insurance Portability and Accountability Act of 1996 (HIPAA), which defined new federal healthcare fraud crimes and directed more funds to enforcement agencies.[13] HIPAA created the Health Care Fraud and Abuse Control Program (Control Program) to coordinate federal, state, and local enforcement efforts. The core of the Control Program is the Health Care Fraud and Abuse Control Account, which funds fraud inspections, investigations, and prosecutions, in part by using funds recovered through previous enforcement efforts.

The ACA (and the accompanying Health Care and Education Reconciliation Act of 2010) contained no shortage of provisions designed to increase enforcement and strengthen the major fraud laws. Yet recent reforms have also sought to balance deterrence with better detection, adopting a variety of provisions to better control those who submit bills to the federal healthcare programs and to provide more timely assessment of the claims they submit, in contrast to the current "pay and chase" model.[14] In June 2011, the Centers for Medicare and Medicaid Services (CMS) implemented the Fraud Prevention System to run predictive algorithms and other analytic technology against all Medicare FFS claims before payment; as a result, CMS took action against 938 providers and suppliers in fiscal year (FY) 2013, thereby

[11] Gigi A. Cuckler et al., *National Health Expenditure Projections, 2012–22: Slow Growth Until Coverage Expands and Economy Improves*, 32 Health Aff. 1820, 1822 (2013).

[12] *See, e.g.*, Exec. Office of the President, The President's Proposal 1 (Feb. 22, 2010), *available at* http://www.whitehouse.gov/sites/default/files/summary-presidents-proposal.pdf (President Obama's 2010 healthcare reform proposal would put the "budget and economy on a more stable path by reducing the deficit by $100 billion over the next ten years—and about $1 trillion over the second decade—by cutting government overspending and reining in waste, fraud and abuse."); *60 Minutes: The $60 Billion Fraud* (CBS News television broadcast Oct. 25, 2009), *available at* http://www.cbsnews.com/video/watch/?id=5419844n ("President Obama says rising costs are driving huge federal budget deficits that imperil our future, and that there is enough waste and fraud in the system to pay for health care reform if it was eliminated.").

[13] Health Insurance Portability and Accountability Act of 1996, Pub. L. No. 104-191, 110 Stat. 1936 (1996).

[14] Joan H. Krause, *Following the Money in Health Care Fraud: Reflections on a Modern-Day Yellow Brick Road*, 36 Am. J. L. & Med. 343–369 (2010).

saving more than $210 million.[15] Although civil fraud enforcement has been prominent for many years, the Obama administration bolstered criminal prosecutions in 2009 by establishing the Health Care Prevention and Enforcement Action Team (HEAT), a cabinet-level joint Department of Health and Human Services (HHS) and Department of Justice (DOJ) initiative targeting major risk areas by utilizing technology to analyze real-time electronic claims data for patterns that might indicate fraud. These efforts have resulted in a significant number of enforcement actions and recoveries: Between the Control Program's creation in 1997 and the end of FY 2013, more than $25.9 billion was returned to the Medicare Trust Funds.[16]

Healthcare fraud is subject to myriad federal and state laws, which impose a variety of criminal, civil, and administrative sanctions. Some laws, such as the Medicare and Medicaid Anti-Kickback Statute, directly target improper healthcare activities; others, such as the civil False Claims Act (FCA), apply more generally to parties engaged in business with the federal government. Fraud also may be prosecuted under traditional criminal laws, such as mail and wire fraud, as well as state fraud and consumer protection statutes. Potential penalties are severe: criminal convictions under laws such as the Anti-Kickback Statute may subject defendants to imprisonment, and civil statutes such as the FCA may impose remedies in the millions of dollars. Wrongdoers also may be subject to exclusion from all federal healthcare programs, a potentially fatal blow for providers who depend on the revenue stream from such programs. Exclusion is mandatory for those convicted of certain fraud crimes, and the Office of the Inspector General (OIG) has the authority to seek "permissive" exclusion for additional fraud-related activities.[17]

Table 38.1 summarizes the number of new criminal and civil cases, convictions, exclusions, judgments and settlements, and total Control Program recoveries between FY 2004 and 2013. Because settlements and judgments may be collected over several years, recoveries in one fiscal year often include money returned as a result of antifraud efforts in prior years. Despite some fluctuations, nearly every category saw overall growth during this period.

Fraud enforcement targets a wide variety of healthcare providers, and it may be difficult to determine the proportion of fraud attributable to each sector. According to an analysis conducted by the Government Accountability Office (GAO) in 2012, 49% of criminal and 60% of civil healthcare fraud investigations targeted entities rather than individuals.[18] Overall, 40% of criminal investigations involved entities and individuals associated with medical facilities or durable medical equipment (DME) suppliers. Physicians were the individuals most subject to criminal investigation (15.4% of investigations), followed by management employees. On the civil side, hospitals (20%) and medical facilities (18%) were the most frequent targets, with physicians again most likely to be individual targets (12.1%). Although they have

[15] Ctrs. for Medicare & Medicaid Servs, Report to Congress: Fraud Prevention System: Second Implementation Year ii (June 2014), *available at* http://www.stopmedicarefraud.gov/fraud-rtc06242014.pdf.

[16] U.S. Dep't of Health & Human Servs. & U.S. Dep't of Justice, Health Care Fraud and Abuse Control Program Annual Report for Fiscal Year 2013, at 1–2 (Feb. 2014), *available at* http://oig.hhs.gov/publications/docs/hcfac/FY2013-hcfac.pdf.

[17] 42 U.S.C. §1320a-7 (2013).

[18] U.S. Gov't Accountability Office, GAO-12-820, Types of Providers Involved in Medicare, Medicaid, and the Children's Health Insurance Program Cases 14, 27 (Sept. 2012), *available at* http://gao.gov/assets/650/647849.pdf.

Table 38.1 Results of the Healthcare Fraud and Abuse Control Program (FY 2004–2013)

Fiscal Year	Total Judgments/ Settlements	Total Collections	New Criminal Investigations	Defendants Convicted	New Civil Investigations	Exclusions
2004	$ 605 million	$1.76 billion	1,002	459	868	3,293
2005	$ 1.47 billion	$1.71 billion	935	523	778	3,804
2006	$ 2.2 billion	$1.78 billion	836	547	915	3,422
2007	$ 1.8 billion	$1.07 billion	878	560	776	3,308
2008	$ 1.0 billion	$2.14 billion	957	588	843	3,129
2009	$ 1.63 billion	$2.58 billion	1,014	583	886	2,556
2010	$ 2.5 billion	$4.02 billion	1,116	726	942	3,340
2011	$ 2.4 billion	$4.09 billion	1,110	743	977	2,662
2012	$ 3.0 billion	$4.22 billion	1,131	826	885	3,131
2013	$ 2.6 billion	$4.33 billion	1,013	718	1,083	3,214

Source: U.S. Dep't of Health & Human Servs. & U.S. Dep't of Justice, *Health Care Fraud and Abuse Control Program Annual Reports for Fiscal Years 2004–2013*, http://oig.hhs.gov/reports-and-publications/hcfac/ (last visited Oct. 29, 2014).

entered into many of the largest fraud settlements on record, pharmaceutical manufacturers constituted only 0.5% of criminal and 4.6% of civil investigations.

For all the attention, however, there is surprising uncertainty surrounding the actual incidence of healthcare fraud. Critics commonly assert that 10% of healthcare expenditures are fraudulent, yet that estimate has little empirical support. HHS has calculated the rate of improper payments in the Medicare FFS program since 1996; the rate has varied depending on the methodology, but has ranged between 8.5% and 10.8% ($28.8 to $36 billion) since 2009, and is projected to remain close to 10% through 2016.[19] Although the error rate is not a measure of fraud per se—it includes underpayments as well as overpayments, and primarily identifies documentation problems rather than analyzing improper intent—it provides a valuable window into the vulnerabilities of the federal healthcare programs. Press releases and program integrity reports frequently include estimates of the amount of fraud "prevented" by various enforcement and screening initiatives, yet all have one key problem: By definition, they are based only on improprieties that can be *identified*. There is no comparable method to measure activities that manage to evade detection. As Professor Malcom Sparrow has noted: "What you see is not the problem. It's what we don't see that really does the damage."[20]

[19] *Comprehensive Error Rate Testing (CERT)*, Ctrs. for Medicare & Medicaid Servs. http://www.cms.gov/Research-Statistics-Data-and-Systems/Monitoring-Programs/Medicare-FFS-Compliance-Programs/CERT/index.html?redirect=/cert (last visited Oct. 29, 2014); *Medicare Fee-for-Service*, Payment Accuracy, http://www.paymentaccuracy.gov/tracked/medicare-fee-service-2013 (last visited Oct. 29, 2014). For discussion of the problems with such estimates, *see* Krause, *Following the Money*, at 345–347.

[20] Malcolm K. Sparrow, License to Steal: How Fraud Bleeds America's Health Care System 2 (2000).

Success in fighting fraud has been mixed, at best: The $26 billion recouped for the Medicare Trust Funds from 1997 to 2013 roughly equals the improper payments made by the Medicare program *each year*. Billion-dollar settlements are commonplace, especially in the pharmaceutical industry, as few defendants can afford the financial and collateral costs of losing at trial. The high settlement rate, in the words of William Sage, makes "fraud control resemble a rebate program more than a law enforcement exercise."[21] Yet for each case resolved, another two schemes seem to rise, hydra-like, in its place. That conundrum explains much of the seemingly fruitless quest to redesign the law, and the healthcare system overall, to reduce opportunities for healthcare fraud—as well as the hesitation to suspend what little protection exists for the sake of innovation.

b. Key Healthcare Fraud Laws

For proponents of integration, the greatest antifraud impediments are the Anti-Kickback Statute, the "Stark" self-referral prohibitions, and the civil monetary penalty (CMP) provisions that prevent hospitals from paying physicians to reduce or limit services and prohibit the offering of financial inducements to beneficiaries. And no discussion of health fraud would be complete without mention of the role of the FCA in securing settlements, a concern that looms large for providers who contemplate entering into integrated arrangements.

i. Medicare and Medicaid Anti-Kickback Statute

Designed to limit the influence of financial incentives on healthcare referral and purchasing decisions, the Medicare and Medicaid Anti-Kickback Statute prohibits the knowing and willful offer, payment, solicitation, or receipt of any remuneration to induce someone to refer patients or to purchase, lease, or order any item or service for which payment may be made under a federal healthcare program (usually Medicare or Medicaid). Remuneration includes payments made "directly or indirectly, overtly or covertly, [and] in cash or in-kind," extending beyond simple kickbacks and bribes to reach the exchange of virtually anything of monetary value.[22] The statute was enacted in the late 1970s after an investigation by the Senate Committee on Aging concluded that kickbacks and other types of fraud were "rampant" in the federal healthcare programs.[23] To the extent the Anti-Kickback Statute questions the legitimacy of financial incentives designed to affect referral patterns, it poses a direct threat to many integration arrangements.

A wide variety of criminal, civil, and administrative sanctions are available under the statute. Violation is a felony, punishable by five years' imprisonment and a fine of $25,000 as well as exclusion from the federal healthcare programs. OIG has the authority to impose CMPs of $50,000 for each violation, plus three times the remuneration involved in the transaction. The ACA clarified that "a claim that includes items or services resulting from a violation of

[21] William M. Sage, *Fraud and Abuse Law*, 282 JAMA 1179, 1180 (1999); *see also* Joan H. Krause, *"Promises to Keep": Health Care Providers and the Civil False Claims Act*, 23 CARDOZO L. REV. 1363, 1410–1415 (2002) (raising concerns about legitimacy of prosecutions).

[22] 42 U.S.C. § 1320a-7b(b).

[23] S. REP. NO. 95-320, at 2 (1977); *see also* S. REP. NO. 95-453, at 11 (1977).

this section constitutes a false or fraudulent claim" under the FCA, thus permitting a potential private right of action for kickbacks as well.[24]

The Anti-Kickback Statute is extremely broad, encompassing virtually all financial incentives that might influence treatment or referral decisions, including ones that might be neutral or even beneficial in practice. Statutory exceptions insulate certain common transactions, such as discounts and payments to employees, and Congress directed HHS to develop "safe harbor" regulations exempting additional business practices.[25] The narrow criteria of the safe harbors may be difficult for many common business arrangements to satisfy, however, necessitating additional forms of guidance from the OIG to shed light on the risks of these activities. Such guidance includes Advisory Opinions, in which the OIG opines on the permissibility of a proposed transaction, and Special Fraud Alerts, which identify "suspect" activities within the industry. Because a violation of the Anti-Kickback Statute requires proof of prohibited intent, however, few arrangements can be deemed either permissible or illegal per se. As a result, efforts to alter provider referral practices in pursuit of efficiency and quality improvement goals will not automatically be immune from scrutiny. While the majority of arrangements are unlikely to lead to prosecution, the consequences are sufficiently grave that risk-averse actors nevertheless may give the law a wide berth.

ii. Ethics in Patient Referrals Act (Stark Law)

The Ethics in Patient Referrals Act of 1989, informally called the "Stark Law" in honor of its sponsor (Representative Fortney "Pete" Stark), applies to a specific subset of referral arrangements: physician referrals of Medicare and Medicaid patients for "designated health services" (DHS) to entities with which the physician has a financial relationship.[26] Similar to the Anti-Kickback Statute, the Stark Law is designed to limit the effect of financial incentives on healthcare decisions; however, the prohibition is narrower and stricter, responding specifically to concerns regarding overutilization. Financial relationships between physicians and ancillary healthcare providers came under scrutiny in the 1980s, when the introduction of the inpatient Medicare Prospective Payment System (PPS) led to a shift in services from inpatient to outpatient settings, and cost concerns simultaneously created pressure to reduce outlays for traditional physician services.[27] As physicians increasingly sought to capture new streams of revenue by investing in ancillary healthcare services such as laboratories, numerous studies—including two key surveys conducted by the OIG—concluded that physicians who had such financial relationships ordered more services for their patients than did their colleagues.[28] The original (Stark I) legislation applied only to referrals of Medicare patients for clinical laboratory services. In 1993, Congress extended the prohibition to Medicaid patients and expanded it to ten additional categories of DHS, including physical therapy, occupational therapy, and hospital inpatient and outpatient services (Stark II). While some

[24] 42 U.S.C. § 1320a-7b(b), (g).

[25] 42 U.S.C. § 1320a-7b(b)(3)(E); 42 C.F.R. § 1001.952 (2013).

[26] 42 U.S.C. §1395nn.

[27] Office of Inspector Gen., Financial Arrangements Between Physicians and Health Care Businesses: Report to Congress—2 (May 1989).

[28] *See id.* at 14; Physician Financial Relationships with, and Referrals to, Health Care Entities That Furnish Clinical Laboratory Services and Financial Relationship Reporting Requirements, 60 Fed. Reg. 41,914, 41,923 (Aug. 14, 1995) (codified at 42 C.F.R. p. 411).

of these activities might independently violate the Anti-Kickback Statute if prohibited intent could be proven, Stark's primary focus is on financial relationships that might lead to over-utilization instead of those involving bribes or kickbacks.

Rather than requiring case-by-case analysis of intent, as under the Anti-Kickback Statute, Stark imposes a strict liability prohibition on patient referrals subject to narrow exceptions. The law generally prohibits referrals of patients for DHS if the referring physician (or an immediate family member) has an ownership/investment or compensation relationship with the entity providing those services. Stark is not a criminal statute, but the consequences nonetheless are severe: Claims for services will be denied; payments must be refunded; and the knowing submission of a bill for prohibited care is subject to a CMP of up to $15,000 for each service, as well as exclusion from the federal healthcare programs. Because Stark expressly prohibits payment for items and services provided in violation of the statute, courts have held that claims for such services are actionable under the FCA.[29] Indeed, the majority of Stark enforcement thus far has come through FCA suits rather than through government-initiated prosecution.

While Stark contains numerous exceptions, the lack of an intent requirement means that *all* criteria must be satisfied in order to qualify. Exceptions fall into three categories: (1) general exceptions applicable to both ownership and compensation relationships, such as ancillary services provided in a physician's office (a laboratory, for example); (2) exceptions relating only to ownership or investment interests, such as the purchase of publicly traded securities or mutual funds; and (3) exceptions relating solely to compensation arrangements. Stark enforcement has been complicated by the lengthy development of the implementing regulations: although Stark I went into effect in 1992, implementing regulations were not finalized until August 1995, eight months after Stark II became effective. Separate Stark II regulations were not proposed until January 1998, and were finalized in multiple phases in a convoluted process that lasted until September 2007—*fifteen years* after the effective date of Stark I. This delay generated considerable uncertainty for healthcare providers, and may have contributed to the relative infrequency of direct enforcement. To the extent ACOs and other integrated arrangements will include both physicians and entities that provide DHS, such as hospitals, the strict liability Stark prohibition creates legitimate concern for providers.

iii. Civil Monetary Penalties

HHS has the authority to impose civil monetary penalties (CMPs) for a wide range of improper activities involving the federal healthcare programs.[30] CMPs are imposed in administrative proceedings; while the defendant has a right to an attorney, to discovery, and to present evidence, the hearing falls short of a full-fledged trial and the Federal Rules of Evidence do not apply. Conduct that would permit imposition of CMPs also constitutes grounds for permissive exclusion. While many CMPs address claims that are in some way false or fraudulent, two specific provisions are directly relevant to provider integration: the

[29] *See, e.g.*, United States ex rel. Thompson v. Columbia/HCA Healthcare Corp., 20 F. Supp. 2d 1017, 1047 (S.D. Tex. 1998).

[30] 42 U.S.C. § 1320a-7a; 42 C.F.R. § 1003.100.

"gainsharing" CMP preventing hospitals from paying physicians to reduce or limit services, and the prohibition on offering inducements to beneficiaries.

Penalties of up to $2,000 may be imposed on a hospital that "knowingly makes a payment, directly or indirectly, to a physician as an inducement to reduce or limit services" to Medicare or Medicaid beneficiaries under the physician's direct care, as well as on the physicians who accept such payment.[31] As Richard Saver has explained, the prohibition was enacted a few years after the Medicare PPS converted hospital reimbursement to standardized payments based on the patient's primary diagnosis at admission.[32] PPS gives hospitals a strong incentive to control costs, as payments will not increase if additional resources are used. Because physicians control much of the care delivered in hospitals but are paid under a separate fee schedule, they have little financial incentive to help hospitals save money. "Gainsharing" describes hospital efforts to bring physicians into the fold by offering financial bonuses, such as a share of cost reductions, if the physicians assist in achieving cost and quality improvement goals. A 1986 GAO report warned that such arrangements might "compromise the quality of care... because they can result in a close link between a physician's incentive payments and the treatment of individual patients," particularly where payments are based on the performance of a single physician or over a short period of time.[33] The CMP was designed to mitigate the possibility that "payments may create a conflict of interest that may limit the ability of the physician to exercise independent professional judgment in the best interest of his or her patients."[34]

Cost reduction and quality improvement efforts undertaken by the providers in an integrated arrangement might fall within this extremely broad prohibition on indirect as well as direct payments. Such concern may be logical given the extremely restrictive way the OIG has interpreted the provision. In 1999, despite Internal Revenue Service approval of the tax consequences of such arrangements, the OIG issued a Special Advisory Bulletin interpreting the CMP to prohibit "any hospital incentive plan that encourages physicians through payments to reduce or limit clinical services directly or indirectly."[35] Importantly, the agency indicated that the prohibition would apply regardless of whether the incentives were designed to reduce only medically *unnecessary*, rather than necessary, care. To the extent the physicians and hospitals participating in ACOs and other integrated arrangements may reap financial rewards if they work together to control costs, this broad interpretation of the CMP creates a significant risk. Although the Bulletin is not binding on courts, and Advisory Opinions have since approved of individual gainsharing plans, providers understandably remain hesitant to devote resources to arrangements that might be interpreted as falling within the prohibition.

Provider integration also implicates a separate CMP banning financial inducements for federal healthcare program beneficiaries, which authorizes a penalty of up to $10,000 for

[31] 42 U.S.C. § 1320a-7a(b)(1).

[32] Richard S. Saver, *Squandering the Gain: Gainsharing and the Continuing Dilemma of Physician Financial Incentives*, 98 Nw. U. L. Rev. 145, 154–172 (2003).

[33] U.S. Gov't Accountability Office, GAO/ HRD-86-103, Medicare: Physician Incentive Payments by Hospitals Could Lead to Abuse 3–4 (July 1986).

[34] H.R. Rep. No. 99-727, at 444 (1986).

[35] Publication of the OIG Special Advisory Bulletin on Gainsharing Arrangements and CMPs for Hospital Payments to Physicians to Reduce or Limit Services to Beneficiaries, 64 Fed. Reg. 37,985 (July 14, 1999).

offering or paying remuneration that a person knows or should know is likely to influence the choice of provider, practitioner, or supplier.[36] This CMP was added in HIPAA in response to concerns that providers might try to offset the costs of such inducements by delivering unnecessary or lower-quality services, and that smaller providers with fewer financial resources might find themselves at a disadvantage.[37] The prohibition has been interpreted to permit inexpensive gifts and services of no more than $10 (or $50 annually) per patient; several exceptions apply, including for incentives designed to promote preventive care, waivers of coinsurance and deductibles for patients in financial need, and incentives that both promote access to care and pose little threat of harm to patients or the federal healthcare programs. The OIG relied on this latter exception, for example, in an Advisory Opinion declining to impose sanctions on a hospital that sought to provide free lodging and transportation to financially needy patients and family members.[38] Because quality benchmarks will require that ACOs and similar entities develop ways to encourage patients to better manage their own health conditions, there may be a temptation to offer benefits that implicate this penalty. A discounted blood pressure monitor for a patient with high blood pressure might be permissible, for example, while free theater tickets—or the waiver of a copayment for a patient who is not in financial need—would not.[39]

iv. Civil False Claims Act

The FCA was enacted in 1863 to address fraud schemes perpetrated on the Union Army during the Civil War. The statute prohibits a variety of activities, including the submission of false or fraudulent claims to the government, making or using false records or statements, conspiracies, and "reverse false claims" that understate an obligation to pay. The basic FCA prohibition imposes liability when: (1) the defendant presents or causes to be presented a claim for payment or approval; (2) the claim is false or fraudulent; and (3) the acts are undertaken "knowingly," which includes deliberate ignorance and reckless disregard of truth or falsity as well as actual knowledge.[40] Penalties range from $5,500 to $11,000, plus three times the government's damages.[41] Combined with the threat of exclusion, these penalties provide a powerful incentive for healthcare providers to settle fraud allegations.

Although a key component of the modern war against fraud, the FCA is not truly a healthcare fraud law. The law says nothing about the relationships between those who make referrals and those who receive them; it is implicated only when an improper claim for payment is submitted to a federal healthcare program. Yet because Stark bans payment for services rendered in violation of the self-referral prohibitions, and claims for items or services provided in violation of the Anti-Kickback Statute constitute false or fraudulent claims under the FCA, the statute is implicated by many common referral arrangements.

[36] 42 U.S.C. § 1320a-7a(a)(5) (2013).

[37] Publication of OIG Special Advisory Bulletin on Offering Gifts and Other Inducements to Beneficiaries, 67 Fed. Reg. 55,855, 55,856 (Aug. 30, 2002).

[38] Dep't of Health & Human Servs., Office of Inspector Gen., OIG Advisory Op. No. 11-01 (Jan. 3, 2011), *available at* http://www.faegrebd.com/webfiles/OIG%20Advisory%20Opinion11-01.PDF.

[39] *See* Medicare Program; Final Waivers in Connection with the Shared Savings Program, 76 Fed. Reg. 67,992, 68,007 (Nov. 2, 2011).

[40] 31 U.S.C. § 3729(a)(1)(A) & (b).

[41] 31 U.S.C. § 3729(a)(1); 28 C.F.R. § 85.3(a)(9) (2014).

Moreover, the FCA contains a *qui tam* provision that permits a private relator to sue on the government's behalf and to share in any proceeds from a successful suit.[42] Since 1986, when amendments made it more lucrative to pursue *qui tam* actions, the number of healthcare-related FCA suits has grown exponentially: Close to two-thirds of *qui tam* suits now allege federal healthcare program fraud, compared to roughly 10% in 1987.[43] The *qui tam* provision allows this powerful law to be invoked not only by federal prosecutors but also by competitors, employees, and even patients. To the extent the market restructuring necessary to achieve integration will create clear winners and losers, there likely will be no shortage of disgruntled potential relators. While the majority of cases will not result in large recoveries for relators, those that do are notable. For example, when pharmaceutical manufacturer Warner-Lambert agreed in May 2004 to pay $430 million to resolve civil and criminal allegations regarding off-label promotion of the drug Neurontin, the relator—Dr. David Franklin, a former company medical liaison—received $24.64 million as his share of the recovery.[44]

Historically, most healthcare FCA cases involved relatively straightforward misrepresentations, such as the submission of claims for services that had not been provided. By the 1990s, however, both federal prosecutors and *qui tam* relators had begun to file suits in circumstances where items and services had been provided but in violation of underlying legal requirements such as the Anti-Kickback Statute or the Medicare Conditions of Participation.[45] With an influx of federal healthcare funding under the ACA, including through exchange-related insurance subsidies and the federal share of Medicaid expansion, the FCA may be applied to a growing share of referral arrangements.

III Integration and the Potential for Healthcare Fraud

a. The Problem

At the heart of the healthcare fraud provisions is a restriction on financial relationships that may affect referral choices, a broad category that encompasses many efforts to financially incentivize providers to coordinate patient care. While few will face prosecution, many commentators have argued that risk-averse healthcare providers may be disinclined to test the boundaries of these prohibitions and as a result may forgo opportunities to develop innovative, efficient, and patient-centered care arrangements. To the extent the model for medical services has shifted from payment based on volume alone to payment based on value—defined as higher quality plus lower expenditures—the fraud laws may appear to be outdated remnants of an older FFS

[42] 31 U.S.C. § 3730(d).

[43] U.S. Dep't of Justice, Fraud Statistics—Overview 1–2 (Dec. 23, 2013), *available at* http://www.justice.gov/civil/docs_forms/C-FRAUDS_FCA_Statistics.pdf.

[44] Press Release, Dep't of Justice, Warner-Lambert to Pay $430 Million to Resolve Criminal & Civil Health Care Liability Relating to Off-Label Promotion (May 13, 2004), *available at* http://www.justice.gov/archive/opa/pr/2004/May/04_civ_322.htm.

[45] Krause, "*Promises to Keep*", at 1367–1368.

world.[46] These arguments received some support from a 2012 GAO report addressing the fraud and abuse risks of physician financial incentive programs designed to promote high-quality and efficient care, including shared savings strategies.[47] GAO concluded that from the perspective of many providers, the challenges of implementing incentive programs within the current legal framework outweighed any potential benefits. The agency voiced concern that these reservations might limit the broader-scale implementation of incentive strategies and preclude the achievement of quality and efficiency goals.

Perhaps the most commonly cited example concerns the MSSP itself. ACOs, by definition, require a multilevel group of healthcare providers—usually hospitals and physicians, including primary care physicians—to work together to manage the care of a population of Medicare beneficiaries. In return, participants are eligible to receive financial bonuses if they meet quality and savings benchmarks. The essence of a successful ACO, then, is collaborative. Yet arrangements in which primary care physicians work with hospitals and specialists to change patient referral practices, in return for potential financial gain, directly implicate the fraud laws. Responding to stakeholder concerns that these laws would "unduly impede development" of ACOs, HHS developed a process to waive the laws for MSSP ACOs if certain safeguards were present, including authorization by a governing body, a bona fide determination that the arrangement was reasonably related to the purposes of the program, and public disclosure of the arrangement.[48]

Of course, ACOs are by no means the only example of integration efforts that have required the federal government to alter the existing fraud and abuse enforcement model to permit innovation. The growing popularity of managed care organizations (MCOs) in the 1990s, for example, led to concern that these arrangements—in which healthcare providers accepted fee discounts or capitation in return for an increased stream of patient referrals—would violate the Anti-Kickback Statute. In response, Congress enacted a new Anti-Kickback exception for risk-sharing arrangements and mandated a negotiated rule-making process to develop implementing safe harbors.[49] Even without congressional action, HHS has significant flexibility in setting enforcement priorities. Two years after the 1999 Special Advisory Bulletin on gainsharing arrangements, and with little fanfare, the OIG issued an Advisory Opinion approving of a transaction that was in essence a limited gainsharing arrangement; that was followed by more than a dozen additional Opinions, each approving individual gainsharing proposals deemed to present a low risk of abuse.[50] Although the OIG

[46] Medicare Program; Final Waivers in Connection with the Shared Savings Program, 76 Fed. Reg. at 67,993.

[47] U.S. Gov't Accountability Office, GAO-12-355, at 36–37.

[48] *See* 42 U.S.C. § 1395jjj(f) (2013); Final Waivers in Connection with the Shared Savings Program, 76 Fed. Reg. at 68,001. With respect to gainsharing, OIG will permit hospitals to distribute shared savings to physicians as long as payments are not made to induce the physicians to reduce or limit *medically necessary* services. Final Waivers in Connection with the Shared Savings Program, 76 Fed. Reg. at 68,001. With respect to beneficiary inducements, ACOs may provide in-kind items and services if they are for preventive care or advance a "clinical goal" for the patient, as long as there is "a reasonable connection" to medical care. 42 C.F.R. § 425.304(a) (2013). However, innovative arrangements outside the MSSP program remain at risk for fraud and abuse enforcement if federal health care program funds are used.

[49] 42 U.S.C. § 1320a-7b(b)(3)(F); 42 C.F.R. §§ 1001.952(t), 1001.952(u).

[50] U.S. Gov't Accountability Office, Gao-12-355, at 28–31; Joan H. Krause, *A Conceptual Model of Health Care Fraud Enforcement*, 12 J.L. & Pol'y 55, 101–110 (2003) (describing problems with reliance on informal agency advice).

eventually accommodated specific risk-sharing and gainsharing arrangements that otherwise might have been threatened by the fraud laws, those accommodations were made only after the expenditure of a great deal of time and effort by the industry, as well as the intangible costs of operating under prolonged regulatory uncertainty. Piecemeal fraud adaptation, then, has not proven to be the ideal model.

b. Forms of Integration and Their Effects on Fraud

Clearly, there is some truth to the allegation that the fraud laws create barriers to certain provider integration activities. If coordination of care truly became the expectation rather than the exception, however, and payments were redesigned to reward value rather than volume, perhaps it would be inadvisable to continue to rely on laws crafted to respond to the misaligned incentives of the individualized FFS system. Conceptually, integration should be part of the solution: Payment mechanisms could be redesigned to incentivize the provision of higher-quality care, giving providers incentives to organize in more efficient ways in order to maximize payment (and thereby to improve quality, if the payments are calibrated correctly).[51]

Realistically, however, not all integrated arrangements will achieve this full array of benefits; most have far less grandiose visions, implementing discrete rather than fundamental changes. The healthcare system may be evolving, but the process is not complete; the ultimate destination remains unclear, and efforts are disjointed. Significant aspects of the traditional fragmented FFS model coexist with newer payment and organizational structures, resulting in inconsistent systems, oversight, and incentives. In the interstices, both new and old forms of fraud have room to thrive.

Rather than asking whether the fraud laws erect barriers to the concept of integration in the abstract, then, perhaps the focus should be on whether these new arrangements have been adequately designed to prevent fraud. This, in turn, requires an appreciation of the different ways in which providers aggregate, and the differing effects each model may have on the prevalence and form of healthcare fraud. While there is a tendency to use "integration" as shorthand for the changes occurring in healthcare, there is no monolithic model of provider organization. To understand the properties of integration most likely to be most significant from the perspective of fraud prevention, it is helpful to loosely describe integration as primarily *financial*, *structural*, or *operational* in nature. Rather than strict definitions, these terms are meant to function as broad descriptive categories that highlight the fraud-related advantages and disadvantages of different integration arrangements.[52]

i. Financial Integration

One way to categorize provider relationships is to focus on the degree of *financial integration* among the participants. Financial (or economic) integration exists when independent

[51] *See generally* THE FRAGMENTATION OF U.S. HEALTH CARE: CAUSES AND SOLUTIONS.

[52] Note that some of these terms have more specific meanings in the tax and antitrust contexts. *See, e.g.*, Gerald M. Griffith & Brad M. Tomtishen, *IRS Adopts Facts-and-Circumstances Approach for JOAs—Part Two*, 17 EXEMPT ORG. TAX REV. 391, 392 (1997); U.S. DEP'T OF JUSTICE & FED. TRADE COMM'N, STATEMENTS OF ANTITRUST ENFORCEMENT POLICY IN HEALTH CARE 61–179 (1996).

providers tie their own financial success to that of other members of an aggregated group. In the antitrust context, for example, the sharing of substantial financial risk is an indication that a physician joint venture involves the integration necessary to achieve efficiencies.[53] Similarly, an ACO "requires an integration of economic activity by ACO participants," supported by appropriate leadership and management structures.[54] Perhaps the quintessential model of financial integration is capitation, in which a set fee is paid for all care during a specified time period regardless of the services actually used; in the most restrictive form used in the 1980s and 1990s, a capitated payment from a health maintenance organization (HMO) to a primary care physician was expected to cover the costs of referrals for ancillary care as well. By contrast, the shared savings provisions of the MSSP establish much looser financial ties, falling short of fully shared financial risk.

Financial integration is a remarkably broad category, spanning a wide variety of organizational structures. It exists, for example, within fully integrated healthcare systems, such as a staff model HMO with salaried physician employees who may be eligible for bonuses if the organization meets financial targets. Yet financial integration can exist equally in systems where the participants have few nonfinancial links, such as an independent practice association composed of a network of individual physicians who agree to accept capitation. Nor does financial integration require any specific form of payment: While it clearly exists under capitation or salary models, it also encompasses more widespread attempts to modify FFS reimbursement, such as bonuses based on the aggregate performance of a group of physicians. Financial integration may also be attempted on a smaller scale, such as through bundled or global payments that are designed to cover a range of related services (such as pre- and postoperative care).

More important, however, simply knowing that providers are financially integrated tells us very little about their potential for *fraud*. Not to put too fine a point on it, doctors who are engaged in a cross-referral kickback scheme can be described as being "financially integrated": All parties gain when they work together to pursue the shared goal of increasing the number of patients referred. Clearly, this is not the type of financial integration to be encouraged. Moreover, financially integrated entities such as HMOs do, in fact, commit fraud, although of different types than under FFS: Rather than having an incentive to overtreat patients, or at least to overbill for their care, providers may try to benefit from undertreatment or by "cherry-picking" to weed out patients who are likely to need extensive (and expensive) services.[55] Bundled and global payments similarly may be subject to abuse: There may be an incentive to falsify the number of patients for whom such payments should be made, to submit claims for services that fall outside of the bundled rate, or to unbundle services where it will result in greater reimbursement.[56] Thus, there is reason to be skeptical about the fraud-reducing effects of financial integration, at least in the absence of other safeguards.

[53] U.S. Dep't of Justice & Fed. Trade Comm'n, at 67–68.

[54] Medicare Shared Savings Program, at 67,818.

[55] *See* Sharon L. Davies & Timothy Stoltzfus Jost, *Managed Care: Placebo or Wonder Drug for Health Care Fraud and Abuse?*, 31 Ga. L. Rev. 373, 389 (1997).

[56] *See, e.g.*, Ohio Hosp. Ass'n v. Shalala, 201 F.3d 418, 421 (6th Cir. 1999) (citation omitted) (concerning government allegations that hospitals "might have used 'two or more CPT billing codes in

ii. Structural Integration

In contrast to purely financial ties among participating providers, some arrangements rely more formally on *structural integration* to provide incentives and safeguards. Structural integration refers to the use of a legal organizational structure, such as a partnership, corporation, or professional corporation, to form the integrated entity. An underlying assumption is that the requirements of the legal organizational form will function as safeguards against fraudulent behavior. Structural integration encompasses a wide range of arrangements utilizing a variety of payment mechanisms. The MSSP, for example, requires an ACO to have a formal legal structure that enables it to receive and distribute shared savings to providers, and to have a leadership and management structure to oversee clinical and administrative systems; the statute remains agnostic as to what form those structures take, but makes clear that they require shared governance, exercised through a governing body that has the authority to undertake the necessary quality, cost, and patient engagement efforts.[57]

Common assumptions regarding the effect of structural integration on fraud can be illustrated by the leeway given to group practices under the Stark Law. Groups of two or more physicians who legally organize in forms such as partnerships, professional corporations, foundations, or not-for-profit corporations are permitted to make intragroup referrals that otherwise might violate the statute, including referring patients for lucrative in-office ancillary services such as laboratories. Services must be provided through group members, billed under a group number, and treated as group receipts; physicians may not be compensated based on the volume or value of their own referrals; and the methods for dividing income and expenses must be determined in advance.[58] The legislative history of the Stark prohibitions contains no clear explanation for the flexibility given to legally integrated groups. From the perspective of fraud detection, however, it may be easier to track claims billed through a single group number than those billed through individual physician members. Similarly, prohibiting physicians from receiving compensation based on their own referrals, and requiring income distribution rules to be set in advance, limits a physician's ability to profit by overbilling or submitting fraudulent claims. While this may reduce the temptation for participants to commit individual acts of fraud, however, the organization *as a whole* still has an incentive to engage in fraudulent activities. Indeed, Stark explicitly allows group physicians to be paid a share of overall group profits, as long as that share is not directly related to the volume or value of the physician's own referrals—providing an incentive for the overall group to increase utilization (or at least billing).

It is clear that legally organized entities do commit fraud, at times repeatedly. For proof, one need only look to the more than 230 pharmaceutical industry settlements, totaling over $30 billion dollars since 1991.[59] The mere existence of the Organizational Sentencing Guidelines—not to mention the Enron, Tyco, and WorldCom scandals and the passage of the Sarbanes-Oxley Act in 2002—is a testament to the seemingly boundless capacity of

lieu of one inclusive code' when seeking reimbursement for outpatient laboratory services," in violation of the FCA).

[57] 42 U.S.C. § 1395jjj(b)(2) (2013); 42 C.F.R. §§ 425.104, 425.106 (2013).

[58] 42 U.S.C. § 1395nn(b)(1), (b)(2), (h)(4)(A).

[59] *See* Sammy Almashat & Sidney Wolfe, PHARMACEUTICAL INDUSTRY CRIMINAL AND CIVIL PENALTIES: AN UPDATE 4 (Sept. 27, 2012), *available at* http://www.citizen.org/documents/20731.pdf.

organizations to violate the law.[60] Of course, structural integration may have other advantages, such as the potential for achieving efficiency through economies of scale, the ability to provide patients with a broader range of services in a more centralized location, and better coordination of care (although, as learned from the HMO experience, legal structure is no guarantee of patient satisfaction). But this does suggest that fraud prevention, as an independent goal, is not necessarily a hallmark of structural integration. If structural integration is encouraged based on these other attributes, vigilance against the threat of fraud at the organizational level will be necessary.

iii. Operational Integration

From the perspective of healthcare delivery, a more comprehensive set of links among healthcare providers forms the basis for what might be called *operational integration*: All of the operations and functions of the entity are coordinated, not only structurally and financially but also in the delivery of services. Complete operational integration is achieved when the entity operates as an organic whole, rather than a series of independent units. Operational integration can exist within a variety of financial and organizational structures; some fully integrated entities own facilities and employ salaried physicians, while others operate largely on a contractual basis. By analogy, in the antitrust context, joint ventures that do not involve shared financial risk may be permissible if they involve *clinical integration* among the participating providers. As the Department of Justice (DOJ) and Federal Trade Commission (FTC) have explained, "[c]linical integration can be evidenced by. . . an active and ongoing program to evaluate and modify practice patterns by the venture's providers and to create a high degree of interdependence and cooperation among the providers to control costs and ensure quality."[61]

The classic example of operational integration is the Mayo Clinic, founded in Minnesota and later expanded to campuses in Arizona and Florida. As described by a Commonwealth Fund case study identifying "attributes of an ideal health care delivery system," the Mayo Clinic has three interrelated and reinforcing characteristics: a multidisciplinary, salary-based practice that fosters team-oriented care; a strong organizational and technological infrastructure; and a governance structure led by physicians.[62] In essence, Mayo is able to combine financial integration (salary) and structural integration (infrastructure and physician governance) in a holistic, synergistic way to achieve high-quality and efficient care—something that has been difficult to ensure with either financial or structural integration alone. Other operationally integrated systems, such as Kaiser Permanente, include a health

[60] U.S. Sentencing Guidelines Manual ch. 8 (2013); Sarbanes-Oxley Act of 2002, Pub. L. No. 107-204, 116 Stat. 745 (2002).

[61] Statement of Antitrust Enforcement Policy Regarding Accountable Care Organizations Participating in the Medicare Shared Savings Program, 76 Fed. Reg. 67,026, 67,027 (Oct. 28, 2011); Dep't of Justice & Fed. Trade Comm'n, at 72–73.

[62] Douglas McCarthy, Kimberly Mueller, & Jennifer Wrenn, Commonwealth Fund, Pub. No. 1306 vol. 27, Mayo Clinic: Multidisciplinary Teamwork, Physician-Led Governance, and Patient-Centered Culture Drive World-Class Health Care 1 (Aug. 2009), *available at* http://www.commonwealthfund.org/~/media/Files/Publications/Case%20Study/2009/Aug/1306_McCarthy_Mayo_case%20study.pdf.

plan as well as a multidisciplinary range of healthcare providers.[63] Such operational integration comes closest to realizing the full promise of integration. Although each of these systems has served as a model for others around the country, and many of their strategies can be adapted to a variety of organizations, it is important to keep in mind that these entities developed organically in response to the characteristics of specific healthcare markets—such as Dr. Sidney Garfield's innovative industrial healthcare programs for Kaiser construction, shipyard, and steel mill workers in the 1930s and 1940s. This suggests that true operational integration may be difficult to impose from the outside.

Comprehensive operational integration should be particularly meaningful from the patient perspective, as it holds the promise of more seamless delivery of care than can be achieved through financial or legal integration alone. Operational integration was in many ways the piece missing from the most restrictive forms of managed care in the 1990s: In place of true integration, these MCOs relied on centralized administrative utilization controls that, to both patients and physicians, appeared to be designed primarily to deny care. Even when those decisions may have been supported by clinical evidence, "the approach and opaque rules undermined public trust. Physician and patient dissatisfaction fed off each other, leading to a managed care backlash."[64]

The ACA aims to encourage operational integration not only through the financial and structural aspects of the MSSP but also by incorporating both quality of care and patient satisfaction measures into payment calculations. To be eligible for the distribution of shared savings, for example, an ACO must satisfy quality of care measures in addition to financial benchmarks, including the administration of a "patient experience of care survey."[65] Unlike the dominant forms of managed care in the 1990s, it is not enough for an ACO to satisfy basic financial and structural criteria: High-quality, satisfactory care actually must be *delivered*. In this regard, the MSSP criteria and the indicators of clinical integration in the antitrust context are consistent and mutually reinforcing.

Conditioning payment on collective quality criteria will require better coordination of care and should reduce the potential for fraudulent activities that result in poor outcomes or higher costs. In order to succeed, however, these provisions will also put a premium on the ability to select optimal outcomes and process measures. Moreover, as with other forms of integration, the choice of criteria will create additional incentives for fraud—such as cherry-picking those enrollees who are likely to follow care recommendations and demonstrate improvement. Patient satisfaction also remains a concern: Within the first year the insurance exchanges were in operation, concerns arose over the limited choices of physicians and hospitals offered in the most affordable plans. Whether operational integration can deliver on the promise of improving the coordination and quality of care, let alone reduce fraud, remains unclear.

[63] *See* Anthony Shi et al., COMMONWEALTH FUND, ORGANIZING THE U.S. HEALTH CARE DELIVERY SYSTEM FOR HIGH PERFORMANCE 10 (Aug. 2008), *available at* http://www.commonwealthfund.org/~/media/files/publications/fund-report/2008/aug/organizing-the-u-s--health-care-delivery-system-for-high-performance/shih_organizingushltcaredeliverysys_1155-pdf.pdf.

[64] *See, e.g.*, Ezekiel J. Emanuel, *Why Accountable Care Organizations Are Not 1990s Managed Care Redux*, 307 JAMA 2263 (2012) (explaining problems with earlier managed care organizations).

[65] 42 C.F.R. § 425.500(d) (2013).

c. Will Integration Necessarily Reduce Fraud?

Clearly, when it comes to fraud, not all forms of integration are equal: Every type of integration offers opportunities and incentives for improper behaviors. Integration is not synonymous with any particular payment mechanism, and each mechanism creates its own temptations. Experience suggests that rather than reducing overall fraud, integration simply will change the way in which fraud occurs. By way of analogy, PPS may have reduced opportunities for Medicare fraud inside hospitals, but it also shifted the locus of care to home health agencies, nursing homes, and free-standing surgical centers, in turn inviting fraud in those settings. As Pamela Bucy once noted: "In health care, like in everything else, the way we pay people affects the way they cheat."[66] Interestingly, Professor Bucy's comment came not in response to any of the debates surrounding the ACA, but rather in a discussion of the fraud implications of the Clinton administration's healthcare reform proposal in the early 1990s. Her point, borne out by subsequent experience, is that while there may be incentives to commit fraud in *any* healthcare system, that fraud will occur in different ways—and some forms will be much more difficult to detect.

Fraud thrives in a hybrid system in large part because most arrangements achieve only partial integration. Structural organization, for example, is not necessarily accompanied by payment reform. Integration into a multispecialty group practice or ACO does not require providers to be paid on a bundled or even a value-enhanced basis; indeed, MSSP participants continue to be paid under the Medicare FFS program while also being eligible for shared savings.[67] Yet the fraud incentives inherent in volume-based FFS payment are present regardless of whether providers are independent or aggregated into groups. To the extent FFS payment encourages overutilization, inefficiency, and fraud, retaining this form of payment is somewhat at odds with the MSSP's quality-enhancement and cost-reduction goals.

The current enforcement scheme responds to the manifestations of fraud endemic to traditional FFS reimbursement: billing for services not rendered, billing for more expensive types of services than actually provided, mischaracterizing unnecessary services as medically necessary, and paying kickbacks for referrals. Under a global payment system that does not increase payments for additional care, such as capitation, these incentives should no longer exist. But in their place, providers may be tempted to engage in other behaviors to increase payment, such as submitting false cost information in order to qualify for a higher payment rate, enrolling fictitious plan members so as to receive additional per-patient payments, failing to provide medically necessary care, and paying kickbacks for the referral of healthy enrollees.[68] Far from being mere shifts in the locus of fraud, these new activities may pose far greater risks from both the patient and enforcement perspectives. Failing to provide medically necessary care, for example, is physically riskier to patients than an equally lucrative scheme to lie about the complexity of care delivered.[69] Similarly, it may be more difficult

[66] Pamela S. Bucy, *Health Care Reform and Fraud by Health Care Providers*, 38 VILL. L. REV. 1003, 1049 (1993).

[67] 42 U.S.C. § 1395jjj(d)(a)(A) (2013).

[68] Bucy, *Health Care Reform*, at 1009, 1025.

[69] *See* Joan H. Krause, *A Patient-Centered Approach to Health Care Fraud Recovery*, 96 J. CRIM. L. & CRIMINOLOGY 579, 589–593 (2006).

to detect fraud hidden within voluminous cost data than it is to audit FFS claims or to identify systemic fraud in the recruitment of plan enrollees. In short, new forms of fraud will require different expertise and the redeployment of investigatory resources, and the learning curve may be steep.

These experiences should give us pause. Each form of integration—financial, structural, and operational—contains incentives for participating providers to misrepresent *something* in order to increase their payments, whether on an individual or entitywide basis. The lack of any uniformity requirements in terms of payment method and structure, even within a single integration model, suggests that both new and old forms of fraud will continue to coexist, perhaps within the same organization. Under the MSSP, for example, an ACO will prosper if it reports high quality of care and patient satisfaction scores, as well as lower costs. To the extent such information is within the ACO's control, the entity may be tempted to misrepresent the data used to assess achievement; to misrepresent costs; to report a different mix of patient risks; to report better outcomes measures or downgrade initial measurements, making it appear as through greater progress has been made; to direct patient satisfaction surveys to those most likely to report a positive experience; to offer patients overly generous financial incentives to comply with screenings and other care recommendations; or to surreptitiously encourage riskier or noncompliant patients to opt out of the ACO altogether.[70] Moreover, because individual providers will continue to be paid under FFS, all the traditional incentives for improper referrals and overtreatment will remain. The ACA contains specific penalties for many of these activities, and the increasing sophistication of data analysis should make it easier to identify those who stray.[71] Yet these mechanisms are, to a certain extent, already obsolete—those bent on fraud have no doubt already identified these and many other weaknesses in the new systems. In short, experience has demonstrated that these changes are more likely to affect *how*, rather than *whether*, healthcare fraud is able to flourish.

Amid this uncertainty, the optimal antifraud structure remains unclear. HIPAA signaled a government commitment to do *more* to counteract fraud: to define more crimes, to expand and increase CMPs, and to funnel more money to investigators and prosecutors. In contrast, many in the industry argue that new forms of integration could resolve these concerns, if only the fraud laws could be changed to permit them. Perhaps what is needed, however, is not more antifraud prohibitions and not fewer ones, but *smarter* ones: prohibitions that respond to the hybrid incentives providers are most likely to face on the road toward integration. Some long-standing prohibitions—gainsharing, for example—may well be counterproductive in an integrated world that utilizes robust quality and patient satisfaction measures. Others, such as the Stark compensation provisions, have become so complex that they now contribute more to the well-being of healthcare lawyers than that of patients or the public fisc. Less complexity may allow for both more innovation and clearer enforcement. The focus, in short, should be on trying to identify a priori the systemic weaknesses that are likely to be exploited and responding not only with fraud enforcement but also by changing the law to decrease payment complexity and to close unnecessary loopholes.

[70] *See* Jessica L. Mantel, *Accountable Care Organizations: Can We Have Our Cake and Eat It Too?*, 42 SETON HALL L. REV. 1393, 1427, 1435 (describing risks of undertreatment and "upstaging" of patient data).

[71] *See* Kristin Madison, *Rethinking Fraud by Rethinking the Health Care System*, 32 HAMLINE J. PUB. L. & POL'Y 411, 424–426 (2011).

IV Conclusion

At core, the fraud laws may say as much about human nature and self-interest as they do about any particular organizational form or payment model. As one commenter noted during a Senate Special Committee on Aging investigation of Medicaid kickbacks, "there is a little larceny in us all."[72] The authors of the popular book *Freakonomics* put it even more starkly: "For every clever person who goes to the trouble of creating an incentive scheme, there is an army of people, clever and otherwise, who will inevitably spend even more time trying to beat it. . . . Cheating is a primordial economic act: getting more for less."[73]

No one would disagree that the goal should be "a system that encourages as little fraud as possible while making the fraud that is committed easier to detect and prove."[74] However, implementing that goal within a system of hybrid payment methods, ever-changing quality of care expectations, and evolving organizational structures can be difficult. The incorporation of value-based criteria into payment mechanisms is promising, as is the emphasis on operational (rather than solely financial or structural) forms of integration, particularly to the extent that some portion of payment will depend on outcome and satisfaction measures rather than on cost reductions alone. Yet those new metrics will in turn create temptations to game the system in new ways, from the careful choice of patients to the selective usage and reporting of data. In short, ACOs and similar integrated entities undoubtedly will create new opportunities for fraud—opportunities not even contemplated at present. To the extent we cannot legislate human nature, perhaps we should be cautious about heeding calls for the wholesale abolition of the healthcare fraud prohibitions.

[72] S. Rep. No. 95-320, at 28 (1977).

[73] Steven D. Levitt & Stephen J. Dubner, Freakonomics: A Rogue Economist Explores the Hidden Side of Everything 24–25 (2005).

[74] Bucy, *Health Care Reform*, at 1049.

CHAPTER 39

INVISIBLE FORCES AT WORK

Health Legislation and Budget Processes

TIMOTHY WESTMORELAND

I Introduction

After decades of biomedical research and public health advocacy, Congress finally passed comprehensive tobacco control legislation in 2009.[1] Division A of the law deals with "Smoking Prevention and Tobacco Control," including regulation of tobacco by the FDA, required labels and warnings on cigarette packages and advertising, and illicit trade in tobacco products.

Division B deals with "Federal Retirement Reform."

Health experts might genuinely have been confused about what was going on. Did tobacco control affect the morbidity and mortality of federal employees in some heretofore-unrecognized way? Legal archivists of the future will doubtless be scratching their heads. What bizarre backroom deal-making between tobacco-state politicians and labor unions produced this shotgun wedding of a law?

In truth, civil servants and tobacco had no special epidemiological or actuarial relationship. There was no horse-trading involved to get support for the bill; both divisions of the law were adopted by general agreement of essentially the same people. Although they were significant changes, the retirement provisions were barely mentioned in the congressional consideration of the "tobacco bill."

As discussed in detail below, the answer to the riddle is that this combination in law was driven by the mundane workings of the congressional budget process. That process crunched numbers in this instance just as it does on a daily basis with other proposals, largely without regard to the subject matter. A parliamentary form of double-entry bookkeeping had to be completed before this bill could become law. This public health landmark almost didn't happen at all—for reasons having to do only with the deficit and the debt and not with cancer and heart disease.

[1] The Family Smoking Prevention and Tobacco Control Act, Pub. L. No. 111-31 (2009).

Such budget process is not unique to this law. Since the enactment of the Budget Act of 1974,[2] Congress has generally required itself to consider all legislative proposals not just for their respective substance but also for their effects on the federal budget. Whatever political and policy calculations are made about bills, parallel calculations go on about money.

Budget analyses are the dark matter and dark energy of the legislative universe: They are generally invisible, but they exert their own gravity, attractions, and repulsions on lawmaking.[3] If these forces are not taken into account, many proposals just don't add up and they fail. If they are included in the equations, the outcomes may be strange but they work out.[4]

Unfortunately, the congressional budget process is not usually studied or analyzed. When it is, it is usually scrutinized only from the inside out by its experienced practitioners. Lawyers and policy-makers in affected substantive areas such as health or environmental law, who are expert in the intricacies of the Affordable Care Act (ACA) or the Clean Air Act, often have little or no understanding of the budget calculus and its workings. They rarely appreciate the collateral damage that the calculus may have on their principal concerns.

To begin to address this gap, this chapter will lay out the basics for an audience that is assumed not to be made up of budget insiders. Along the way, it will use health-law examples, although similar discussions could include banking, education, and even criminal law—and anything else that might conceivably commit, expend, or raise federal money. Because of the nature of Medicare, Medicaid, and taxes, health law is affected even more than most other areas, but at the federal level budgets are pervasive.

Although far beyond the scope of this chapter and of my own experience, budgeting appears to be fundamental at the level of state government also. However, such basic items as the fiscal year and the horizon for estimation are often quite different from federal practice and, of course, states have diverse limits on spending, revenues, and debt. It is widely reported that most states have "balanced budget requirements," but the meaning of that statement is unclear when states issue bonds, disregard revenues from some sources, and segregate spending and liabilities in some accounts.[5] Readers should recognize that this chapter is only about federal—and mostly congressional—budget practices, and they should apply any information to state actions with great caution.

II How We Got Here

For most of U.S. history, budgeting by the federal government was an ad hoc process. The president was required to submit a comprehensive budget proposal to Congress beginning

[2] The Congressional Budget and Impoundment Control Act of 1974, Pub. L. No. 93-344, 88 Stat. 297 (codified as amended in scattered sections of 2 and 31 U.S.C.) (hereinafter The Budget Act of 1974).

[3] *Cf.*, William Harris & Craig Freudenrich, *How Dark Matter Works*, HowStuffWorks (Sept. 4, 2007), http://science.howstuffworks.com/dictionary/astronomy-terms/dark-matter.htm.

[4] I do not mean to suggest that budget issues make up the same relative proportion of the legislative universe that physicists now theorize dark matter and dark energy make up (i.e., 95% of the physical universe). It's not that bad. *See Dark Energy, Dark Matter*, NASA Sci.—Astrophysics (June 5, 2015), http://science.nasa.gov/astrophysics/focus-areas/what-is-dark-energy/.

[5] *See* Nat'l Conference of State Legislatures, Fiscal Brief: Balanced Budget Provisions (Oct. 2010), http://www.ncsl.org/documents/fiscal/StateBalancedBudgetProvisions2010.pdf.

in 1921,[6] but Congress acted largely through annual laws that each had a relatively narrow subject. Despite Congress alone having the constitutional powers to raise taxes, appropriate funds, and borrow against U.S. credit,[7] there was no formal framework for these activities in the legislative branch.

In the 1970s, however, President Nixon asserted that he had the power to refuse to spend legally appropriated funds (i.e., to "impound" them). Congress disagreed. From this constitutional confrontation came legislation—the Congressional Budget and Impoundment Control Act of 1974 (Budget Act)—that limited executive impoundment authority and, more important in the long run, created the congressional budget process.[8] Much about federal revenues and spending has changed in the past forty years, but most of the basic parts of that statute still govern the process. From the Budget Act emerged the budget schedule, the Congressional Budget Office, and the House and Senate budget committees, as well as definitions and accounting rules.

Many amendments to the Budget Act have come and gone. There have been attempts at capped spending, pledges of "no new taxes," declining deficits, across-the-board cuts, and balanced budgets. Depending on the year, the rules have been observed, waived, disregarded, allowed to expire, renewed, and enforced with a vengeance. Over time, the focus has largely turned away from the amounts of the deficit and the debt and toward the constraints that Congress has placed on itself.

Also over time, the actual size and importance of the budget has changed dramatically, especially in regard to health. In adjusted dollars, annual federal spending (not including tax spending, as discussed below) has tripled, going from about $1 trillion in the mid-70s to about $3 trillion now.[9] Over the same period, the portion of federal spending that is *not* determined on an annual basis in appropriations acts (i.e., that portion that is "mandatory spending," as discussed below) has gone from about 45% of that growing total to about 60%.[10] The subset of that mandatory spending dedicated to Medicare and Medicaid has grown substantially, going from about 5% of spending in the early 70s to about 25% now.[11] Summarized qualitatively, since the time of the first Budget Act, federal spending has grown substantially, it has grown largely through programs based on ongoing promises in statute, and health programs have been the major component of the growth.

III The Basics

To begin to understand federal budgeting, one must appreciate a few basic practices:

- For federal purposes there are three kinds of money.

[6] *See* Budget and Accounting Act of 1921, ch. 18, 42 Stat. 20 (codified as amended in scattered sections of 31 U.S.C.).

[7] U.S. Const. art. I, § 8.

[8] The Budget Act of 1974.

[9] Office of Mgmt. & Budget, Historical Tables (2015), https://www.whitehouse.gov/omb/budget/Historicals.

[10] Mindy Levit, D. Andrew Austin, & Jeffrey Stupak, Cong. Research Serv., Mandatory Spending Since 1962 7 (2015), http://www.senate.gov/CRSReports/crs-publish.cfm?pid=%270E%2C*P%3C[%3C%23P++%0A.

[11] *Id.* at 11.

- To count these different kinds of money, an internal process has evolved to estimate how much will be required by law in the future.
- Each of these kinds of money has its own set of parliamentary and statutory rules limiting what Congress may do with it.
- To make these limits work, an internal process has also evolved to estimate how any proposed legislative changes would affect these limits.

IV Three Kinds of Money

All federal budgets are divided into three parts. These are, respectively, discretionary spending, mandatory spending, and tax spending.[12] They are treated differently in most respects and cannot be easily changed from one type to another.

As the name implies, discretionary spending is money that is spent at the discretion of Congress. In general, it is provided through annual laws containing appropriations (although recent Congresses have been erratic in enacting such laws on any predictable schedule). Most such spending is counted in the year for which it is enacted and must be committed during that year, although it may take years for the projects to expend all the money.[13] Most programs of grants and contracts, as well as the salaries of civil servants and of military personnel, are supported by discretionary spending. Activities of the National Institutes of Health (NIH), the Centers for Disease Control and Prevention (CDC), and the Food and Drug Administration (FDA) are almost entirely funded by discretionary spending, as are those of the Defense Department.

For budget and legal purposes, it is presumed that discretionary spending will not be renewed unless Congress acts to do so. Each year, a new law must be enacted to provide the money. If the money is not provided, the programs supported by this spending will end. In recent years, Congress has provided such funding in dribs and drabs equal to a week or a month of activity, seriously inconveniencing both those who administer the funds and those who rely on them but sending a clear message that the spending is truly at Congress's pleasure.[14] On a few recent occasions, Congress has failed to provide appropriations at all, and large parts of the government have been shut down.[15]

[12] Discretionary spending is often referred to as "appropriated spending" or "appropriations." Mandatory spending is frequently referred to as "direct spending"; a subset of mandatory spending targeted at a defined class of individuals is known as "entitlement spending." Tax spending is frequently referred to as "tax expenditures."

[13] Consider, for example, funding provided to construct a bridge. The money will be provided in full in one law, but it will be expended over years to hire planners and engineers, to buy land, to build the structure, and then to paint and landscape it.

[14] *See* Philip Joyce, IBM Ctr. for the Bus. of Gov't, The Costs of Budget Uncertainty: Analyzing the Impact of Late Appropriations (2012), http://faculty.publicpolicy.umd.edu/sites/default/files/joyce/files/the_costs_of_budget_uncertainty.pdf.

[15] Some discretionary spending programs remain open on an emergency basis during such closures, although most are forbidden to do so by law. *See* Andrew Cohen, *The Odd Story of the Law that Dictates*

By contrast, mandatory spending is money that has been promised in a permanent provision of law (as opposed to a temporary appropriations act). Unless Congress successfully enacts a new law limiting that promise (e.g., by raising the eligibility age of Medicare or reducing the cost-of-living adjustment in Social Security), the funding to make good on the statutory promise will continue to flow. Social Security, Medicare, and Medicaid are the largest mandatory spending programs.

For budget and legal purposes, it is presumed that mandatory spending will be available unless Congress acts to stop it. Consequently, mandatory spending programs have generally been unaffected by government shortfalls and shutdowns.

Statutory language can help the reader distinguish between discretionary and mandatory spending. The phrases "there are authorized to be appropriated" or "subject to the availability of appropriations" make a program discretionary. Likewise, the statement in permanent law that "this constitutes budget authority in advance of appropriations" designates a program as mandatory. Beyond these line-by-line readings of each law, amendments to the Budget Act itself have listed and categorized programs overall, as do the annual congressional budget resolution and the annual president's budget.

In addition to discretionary spending and mandatory spending, there is a somewhat more abstract but increasingly important kind of money: tax spending. Tax spending is revenue that is forgone by the federal government for a specific reason. Such spending may take the form of deductions, credits, exclusions, adjustments, or myriad other baroque ornaments of the tax code. There has long been serious academic debate about whether special tax treatments should be considered "spending" and about whether the lines between revenue-raising and spending can ever be objective. This is sometimes summarized as a disagreement between Boris Bittker and Stanley Surrey about whether there is a coherent concept of what constitutes income and therefore whether exceptions to that concept for tax purposes are part of that definition or simply constitute policy choices for funding.[16] This scholarly tussle acquired practical importance when the proposed budget of President George W. Bush included the comment that "the Administration believes the meaningfulness of tax expenditure estimates is uncertain . . .," a comment that was followed in succeeding years by administration consideration of the theories behind using consumption taxes as an alternative to income taxes, an even farther-reaching and more controversial idea than that of tax expenditures.[17]

The programmatic or distributive effects of doing something through the tax code as opposed to doing it through mandatory spending may be dramatic; for example, most tax spending helps affluent people far more than low-income people. But for purposes of the budget, failing to bring money into the Treasury is functionally the same as bringing money in and then sending it out again. Fortunately for a brief discussion of budgets, this

How Government Shutdowns Work, THE ATLANTIC (Sept. 28, 2013), http://www.theatlantic.com/politics/archive/2013/09/the-odd-story-of-the-law-that-dictates-how-government-shutdowns-work/280047/.

[16] *See* David Weisbach & Jacob Nussim, *The Integration of Tax and Spending Programs*, 113 YALE L.J. 955, 972.

[17] For an erudite discussion of the revival of the debate about tax expenditures, *see* Leonard Burman, *Is the Tax Expenditure Concept Still Relevant*, NAT'L TAX J. (Sept. 2003), http://www.urban.org/research/publication/tax-expenditure-concept-still-relevant/view/full_report.

long-standing and often metaphysical discussion can be sidestepped: The Budget Act created a statutory definition and has then used it.[18]

In recent years, tax spending has grown to be larger than all of discretionary spending and is now more than a trillion dollars a year. Tax spending, however, is rarely listed as part of the federal budget. When it is said that "Medicare makes up X% of the budget" the denominator being divided almost always includes only discretionary and mandatory spending and not the tax revenue forgone for specific purposes. This makes for a distorted view of the scale and dimensions of federal spending. If the denominator included tax spending, the relative size of all types of other spending would be commensurately smaller. As it is, tax spending is regularly out of sight and out of mind, both for policy-makers and for citizens (other than those who enjoy the tax-favored income).

Like mandatory spending, tax spending is generally a permanent promise in statute.[19] Congress can amend the tax code to change the promised tax treatment of income, but until it does so, the existing deduction/credit/exclusion is presumed to continue, producing ongoing decreases in government revenue and ongoing subsidies to the taxpayer. The single largest element of tax spending is a health item: the exclusion of employer-sponsored insurance from income for tax purposes, estimated to cost $250 billion annually in lost revenues.[20]

V Baselines

While both mandatory spending and tax spending are generally based in permanent law, expending the exact same amount of money from one year to the next is unlikely to be adequate to meet statutory obligations. Inflation happens; the same services cost more as time passes. Baby booms happen; more people will qualify for existing programs in the future. New technologies happen; patients will use both x-rays and PET scans, standard surgery and radiosurgery. Each of these changes means that the federal government will have to spend more money (or forgo more revenues) in order to keep its promises in the future. Moreover, these changes interact and multiply: *More* people will use *both* old and new services, and these services will become *more* expensive.

Consequently, for anyone to have an understanding of the required spending (or revenue loss) of the federal government, a model is needed to project what current law requires be done in the future. This model is known as "the baseline." Both the Congressional Budget Office (CBO) and the Office of Management and Budget (OMB) maintain ongoing baselines, using largely similar definitions and assumptions and producing largely similar projections

[18] The Budget Act of 1974: "The term 'tax expenditures' means those revenue losses attributable to provisions of the Federal tax laws which allow a special exclusion, exemption, or deduction from gross income or which provide a special credit, a preferential rate of tax, or a deferral of tax liability." *See generally* JOINT COMM. ON TAXATION, BACKGROUND INFORMATION ON TAX EXPENDITURE ANALYSIS AND HISTORICAL SURVEY OF TAX EXPENDITURES ESTIMATES (Feb. 10, 2015), https://www.jct.gov/publications.html?func=startdown&id=4705.

[19] *Id.* at 16: "[I]n general, once adopted, tax expenditures tend to stay in place."

[20] Matthew Rae, Gary Claxton, Nirmita Panchal, & Larry Levitt, *Tax Subsidies for Private Health Insurance*, THE HENRY J. KAISER FAMILY FOUNDATION (Oct. 2014), http://kff.org/private-insurance/issue-brief/tax-subsidies-for-private-health-insurance/.

(with occasional differences and disputes). Congress relies on the CBO's baseline. The president relies on the OMB baseline.

The baseline represents estimates of the costs of mandatory spending and tax spending if the promises in existing law remain unchanged. It is used to project program costs and revenues, as well as the annual federal deficit and the cumulative federal debt. For most purposes, it includes the coming year and nine years into the future.[21]

The baseline is required to be built on the assumption that current statutory provisions will actually be implemented as written. Thus, the baseline assumes that people who become eligible will enroll in Medicare at a projected rate. It assumes that Medicare and Medicaid will pay for new drugs after they are approved by the FDA. It assumes that the Internal Revenue Service (IRS) will collect income tax in increased amounts when the economy improves—or the converse. If current law actually repeals a program or a tax break, the baseline assumes that the repeal will be implemented.

Future discretionary spending is not guaranteed in law, so a baseline could (and sometimes does) project no spending in the future. In order to provide a more realistic estimate of the overall budget, however, total discretionary spending is usually included in the baseline at a legally specified *maximum* level. There is, however, no requirement that Congress actually provide these funds or preserve the purchasing power of any of its discretionary spending programs (which mandatory spending programs usually do automatically). Moreover, discretionary programs may have static or even increasing appropriations but nonetheless fall further and further behind in their ability to provide more expensive goods or services to an increasing number of people.

Obviously, neither the CBO nor the OMB can foretell the future. Sometimes the baseline will overstate or understate what turn out to be actual costs. A recession or an epidemic may occur. Drugs may be more expensive than projected. Health inflation may slow. To keep the baseline current, the CBO and the OMB adjust their estimates twice a year. This is a complex undertaking that includes interactions among many variables. For example, an observed decline in measles immunizations would likely result in not only a reduction in spending on vaccines but also an increase in Medicaid spending for hospitalizations from the predictable outbreaks. Once these adjustments are made, future projections will be made from this new baseline (until it, too, is updated in the future).

VI Limits

Trying to "stop itself before it spends again," Congress has lashed itself to a budgetary mast and adopted progressively stricter procedural and statutory limits on its own ability to increase spending or cut taxes. These limits differ by kind of money.

For discretionary spending, Congress has created an annual global cap to be the grand total of all discretionary spending in any given year. Total funds for such varied programs as biomedical research, the armed services, and public housing cannot exceed a single specified

[21] This ten-year period is often referred to as "the budget window" or "the snapshot." The nine years beyond the first estimated year are often referred to as "the out-years."

number. Since 1990, various laws have provided that specified number, sometimes only for six months and sometimes for ten years at once.[22] Whatever the period, the existence of the cap itself creates a zero-sum game for all discretionary spending. No new spending for one program can be provided unless other programs are cut from their previous levels.

There are two levels of enforcement of this limit. The first is parliamentary. Legislation that would exceed the cap is not "in order" in either the House or the Senate. This point of order can be waived, but it is an uphill fight to do so in normal political circumstances since it incites opposition both from those opposed to the substantive legislation and from those who might support the underlying bill but are committed to budget restraint.

The second level of enforcement is a statutory doomsday machine—the sequester.[23] If Congress passes appropriations that exceed the cap, the OMB is required to impose across-the-board, pro rata cuts in most appropriated programs to bring total discretionary spending down to the cap. These compulsory percentage cuts are agreed by almost all observers to be "irrational," "stupid," "dangerous," or worse in their effect on programs. But the sequester was purposely devised to be a policy-neutral infliction of political pain so bad that it would drive Congress to meet its preset targets. Inasmuch as the discretionary spending cap has been reset and amended multiple times while sequesters have nonetheless been imposed, it is impossible to say whether this precommitment mechanism has had its intended effect. Health policy-makers should, however, recognize that the overarching cap-and-sequester limits will likely remain in place for the foreseeable future and will complicate and maybe stop any effort to create new or expanded discretionary resources.

For reasons described above in discussing the complexities of baselines, a similar overall cap on mandatory spending and on tax spending would be self-defeating. The inevitable increase in the costs of these programs would erode and ultimately break the promises made in statute. Consequently, mandatory and tax spending are allowed to grow automatically over time, as the internal workings of each statute require. Using existing law to enroll more eligible people in Medicare, thereby increasing spending, does not trigger a sequester. And the sequester does not affect tax spending in any way, another item of structural favoritism given to activities subsidized through tax devices.

Instead of a cap, Congress has adopted a restriction on its own ability to increase mandatory spending or to reduce revenues. This is the "Pay-as-You-go" (PAYGO) requirement. PAYGO creates a parliamentary rule prohibiting the consideration of any mandatory spending or revenue legislation that would make the deficit worse. As with the discretionary spending cap, this point of order can be waived, but it also is an uphill battle to do so even if the legislation otherwise enjoys support.[24]

[22] *See, e.g.*, The Budget Control Act, Pub. L. No. 112-25 (Aug. 2, 2011); The American Taxpayer Relief Act, Pub. L. No. 112-240 (Jan. 2, 2013), The Balanced Budget Act of 2013, Pub. L. No. 113-67 (Dec. 26, 2013); *see generally* D. Andrew Austin, Cong. Research Serv., The Budget Control Act and Trends in Discretionary Spending (Nov. 26, 2014), http://fas.org/sgp/crs/misc/RL34424.pdf.

[23] This sequester is an ongoing statutory requirement, distinguishable from the one created by the Budget Control Act of 2011 (PL 112-25), to respond in an ad hoc manner to the specific failings of the "Supercommittee" to find specified savings. *See* Austin, Cong. Research Serv.

[24] For example, the Affordable Care Act was strongly supported by a number of members of Congress who nonetheless insisted that it conform to difficult PAYGO requirements.

Since 2010, PAYGO has also been enforced by a legal sequester mechanism through the so-called "statutory PAYGO."[25] At the end of each year, the OMB adds up the costs of all new mandatory spending and revenue legislation and subtracts any offsetting savings from other new legislation. If all such legislation in the aggregate is projected to add to the deficit, the OMB is required to impose across-the-board cuts in most mandatory spending programs so that the ultimate impact on the deficit is zero. There are a number of programs exempted from this sequester (notably Social Security, Medicaid, and the Children's Health Insurance Program [CHIP]), and others have limits on the amount that can be cut (notably no more than 4% of Medicare).

Recent Congresses have been extremely reluctant to raise taxes. Consequently, most offsets to meet PAYGO requirements have been derived from cutting existing mandatory spending programs. The rob-Peter-to-finance-Paul nature of these offsets has acted as a substantial brake but not a complete barrier to enacting new programs. CHIP was enacted along with offsets from increased tobacco excise taxes and the auction of licenses to parts of the electromagnetic spectrum. The Affordable Care Act legislation included both slowed growth in Medicare's reimbursement for hospitals and new revenues (e.g., new taxes on medical devices, on generous health insurance plans, and on tanning salons).

VII Scorekeeping

To make the PAYGO limits workable, the costs of new legislative proposals must be estimated. This is known as "scorekeeping." The CBO does such estimation for spending proposals, and the nonpartisan staff of the Joint Committee on Taxation (JCT) does it in tandem with the CBO for revenue proposals. Before any bill is voted on in the House or the Senate, the CBO and/or the JCT must assess whether it affects either the mandatory spending or the revenues contained in the current-law baseline. For example, if a bill would expand Medicare eligibility to a new group of people (e.g., by lowering the minimum age from sixty-five to sixty-two), the CBO would estimate the increased costs to Medicare when compared to the baseline. Conversely, if a bill would limit eligibility of a currently eligible group (e.g., by raising the minimum Medicare age from sixty-five to seventy), the CBO would estimate the decreased costs (or "savings") to Medicare when compared to the baseline.

As with the calculation of the baseline, scorekeeping is a complex activity. Even something as relatively straightforward as an expansion in eligibility would be a major undertaking, involving the estimation of the size of the new group, likely enrollment rates of newly eligible people, prevalence of health needs within that cohort, costs of meeting these needs, and the pricing changes and service responses of providers. More complicated legislation would involve myriad data sets, assumptions, and predictions about individual behavior and market actions. It also would involve many educated guesses and a degree of science fiction, inasmuch as the score is to include ten years of future budget effects.[26]

[25] The Statutory Pay-as-You-Go Act of 2010, Pub. L. No. 111-139 (Feb. 12, 2010).

[26] For example, I was once asked (not by the CBO) to help estimate the cost of AIDS drugs for ten years. I had to ask whether I should assume it was going to be cured or not.

It is important to note that, although the CBO does credible work under intense pressure and within tight timeframes, *no one* (including the CBO) believes that its scores will ultimately be borne out as correct over time. The question of whether the CBO "got it right" misses the real point of scorekeeping. The CBO score is akin to an umpire's call in a sporting event: It is *deemed* to be right and is accepted by participants so that the action can go on. Without such an umpire, the PAYGO process would dissolve into endless bickering among politicians about economics and modeling, topics that politicians are ill-suited to discuss and that have no truly knowable answer. The deemed-correct score of the CBO is a necessary fiction to make the self-imposed limits on the congressional process work.

This defense of the CBO's umpiring is made despite the many quirks and conundrums within the scorekeeping and PAYGO process. There are many—and they can dictate congressional choices more finally than policy analysis, rhetorical flourish, or even moral high ground. Perhaps the most profound of these in recent political history was the CBO's analysis of the Clinton health reform proposal—not so much because of its numbers or its projections but because of its definitional decision. The proposed Clinton plan included payments by *private* employers to *private* insurance alliances; the payments were required, but they were never to enter the Treasury. The CBO, exercising its prerogatives in shaping budget concepts as part of its baseline and scorekeeping roles, concluded that these payments should nonetheless be on the federal books as government receipts (even though they were not to be received). This arcane choice of taxonomy was crucial. No longer a governmental regulatory action such as workplace-safety or minimum-wage requirements, the required payments could be and were opposed as budget-busting government "spending." Additional politics of the Clinton plan weighed it down, but many observers believe that the CBO treatment was decisive.[27]

It has been noted that a similar fate awaits any attempt to create a "single-payer" plan for universal coverage. Official scorekeeping of such a plan would inevitably contain massive new "taxes" many of whose offsetting savings accrue to private employers and would be outside the perimeters of the federal budget. To that extent, the Budget Act structurally favors the continuation of a private health insurance system, even one that is largely financed by tax expenditures.[28]

Not all of the budget process's influence is so visible; much of it goes on far, far below the awareness of the public and even of Congress itself. Nonetheless it is frequently the ultimate source of legislative results. This can be illustrated with a few examples from recent health laws.

VIII Examples

a. Tobacco Control

Take, for instance, that tobacco bill mentioned at the outset. In the annals of tobacco control, there were years of reports from surgeons general, litigation by attorneys general,

[27] *See* Phillip Joyce, The Congressional Budget Process: Honest Numbers, Power, and Policymaking Chapter 6 (2011).

[28] *See* Timothy Westmoreland, *Can We Get There from Here?: Universal Health Insurance and the Congressional Budget Process*, 96 Geo. L.J. 523 (2008).

and proposed and judicially nullified regulations. By 2008, tobacco-farming, tobacco-manufacturing, and tobacco-control advocates were in an uneasy détente about new legislation. Driven by epidemiology, by litigation, and by market share, politicians were prepared to support an era of regulation.

Then the proposal was scored.[29] After considering the legislation, scorekeepers concluded that it would actually accomplish its intended purpose, that fewer people would smoke, and that tobacco use would decline. For the CDC, this might be a cause for celebration. But for the CBO and the JCT it was a problem. This meant that there would be a decline in purchases of tobacco and, therefore, a decline in federal excise-tax revenues from tobacco sales.[30] In this aspect, they concluded, the bill would represent a net loss to the federal budget—a big loss, more than a billion dollars.

This price tag had not been part of the political détente. Budget enforcement limits would stop cold the legislation as written. There would be legislative points of order and potential statutory sequesters.

The intuitive response from health-policy advocates would be that reducing tobacco use would reduce the nation's overall healthcare costs. Those savings could be used to offset the decline in excise tax revenues.

But a return to the basics of congressional scorekeeping and baselines described above shows why that would not be the CBO umpire's call. First, any cost savings that would be produced are not all going to be enjoyed by the federal government. Only those that would be savings attributable to beneficiaries of federal mandatory spending programs (i.e., Medicare and Medicaid) would be counted. Costs and savings to private insurers are not part of the baseline to begin with, and any changes would not have a direct effect on the federal deficit or debt. Even those savings to federal discretionary spending programs (e.g., the Veterans' Health Administration) would not be counted in a score because it is routinely assumed that all discretionary funding under the overall cap would be used for *something* and that any money freed up by lowering health costs from tobacco would be spent on other discretionary programs that are in need of funding.

Even the allowable, on-budget savings within federal programs of mandatory spending (i.e., Medicare and Medicaid), however, would likely be very far off in time. The health effects of smoking do not arise when a person first lights a cigarette; teenage smokers do not immediately incur hospital costs. It takes years of smoking to increase the rates of expensive hospitalization for emphysema, cancer, and heart disease. Consequently, any savings from the reduction of those diseases because of the new law would not arrive soon. For purposes of PAYGO, the CBO score is generally only calculated for the coming ten years; costs and savings beyond that period are not considered.[31] Certainly the scoring period for budget enforcement could be extended (and for some very basic purposes, Social Security is estimated for seventy-five years), but the idea is generally dismissed because such a long-range estimate would require speculation and conjecture that would be almost altogether

[29] *See* CONG. BUDGET OFFICE, COST ESTIMATE OF THE FAMILY SMOKING PREVENTION AND TOBACCO CONTROL ACT (Aug. 25, 2009), http://www.cbo.gov/sites/default/files/hr1256_8.pdf.

[30] These are the same taxes that were increased in order to offset the cost of creating the CHIP program, as mentioned above. What goes around comes around.

[31] Costs and savings outside the ten-year scorekeeping period are frequently referred to as "outside the snapshot" or "not in the window."

untethered from reality. Even more than scores within the ten-year snapshot, longer-range scores would be governed by the scorekeepers' assumptions, not by data.

It might be argued that at least within these narrow boundaries that tobacco control will produce *some* federal savings attributable to beneficiaries of mandatory spending programs within ten years. The most important source would likely be the improvements in pregnancy outcomes for Medicaid beneficiaries. Almost half of all births in the United States are to women on Medicaid, and low-income people are more likely to smoke.

The CBO did, in fact, consider these savings and concluded that there would be babies in the future who—absent the legislation—would be born at a low birthweight and likely in need of expensive neonatal care. Since babies born to women on Medicaid are, by Medicaid's statutory promise, automatically eligible for Medicaid themselves, those neonatal care costs would be covered under Medicaid. Reducing the number of low-birthweight babies would reduce Medicaid spending on neonatal care. Thus the legislation would produce countable savings for this cohort. Those savings might offset some of the lost revenues from excise taxes.

But the CBO also considered another, similar effect: Smoking has been shown to increase the rate of miscarriage. Heartless as it is to consider, miscarriages are usually comparatively less expensive than live births of low-birthweight babies. So, the CBO reasoned, the legislation would also result in fewer miscarriages from smoking and, therefore, there would be a new cohort of living, low-birthweight babies who would not otherwise have survived to become Medicaid beneficiaries. It was estimated that this would create an increased federal cost, one that the CBO projected would altogether offset the savings from the previous effect.

Finally, public health advocates would likely reason that, broadly speaking, reductions in smoking would have a beneficial effect on life expectancy and that this would have some good ripple effects for the tax base. It is a public health truism that without tobacco, Americans would live longer, be more productive, and pay more taxes.

The obvious problem with this reasoning is the same as with Medicare expenses, discussed above: Almost all of these benefits would occur outside the ten-year snapshot for estimation. Over and above that, it must be noted that many of these benefits would accrue to people who are older and not actually working. Extended lives for these people might not actually yield much improved productivity or increased taxes.[32]

Most startling for public health advocates is the final (in all senses of the term) budget conclusion: The improvements in life expectancy might actually increase federal costs overall. Most older Americans are on Medicare and on Social Security. If the tobacco-control legislation were to extend their lives, the result would be Medicare incurring more costs and Social Security paying more benefits.[33] In other modeling, the CBO acknowledges this

[32] In a separate comprehensive and thoughtful review of all tobacco modeling questions published after the enactment of the tobacco-control legislation, the CBO also has raised questions about the many confounding variables about who smokes, why they smoke, what their socioeconomic status and education levels are, and what their employment rates are like. *See* Cong. Budget Office, Raising the Excise Tax on Cigarettes: Effects on Health and the Federal Budget (June 2012), https://www.cbo.gov/sites/default/files/06-13-Smoking_Reduction.pdf.

[33] This effect is sometimes referred to as "survivors' costs." It is the ultimate confirmation of economics as the dismal science. It is not unique to tobacco control. I have written elsewhere about its implications for coverage of vaccines and prescription drugs. *See* Timothy Westmoreland, *Standard Errors: How Budget Rules Distort Lawmaking*, 95 Geo. L.J. 1555 (2007).

outcome, but (fortunately for tobacco control) these increased costs also would be outside the ten-year snapshot and, therefore, would not be scored against the legislation.[34]

These scorekeeping effects are not factual mistakes. They tell some true things about budgeting. They also highlight why budgets alone make truly bad policy. It is perhaps true that it would be cheaper to let people die of preventable illness, to limit insurance coverage for those people who don't add to the gross domestic product, to deny services to terminally ill people, and to end federal reimbursement for neonatal intensive care. It would also be immoral.

Creating parliamentary points of order or triggering across-the-board cuts because the tobacco-control bill might actually reduce smoking would have been wrongheaded health policy. But that was the result that the CBO score seemed about to create. If the bill were enacted, there would be reduced excise-tax revenues. There would be no significant offsetting savings in the legislation to make up this loss. The PAYGO rules did not allow the bill to be considered in either the House or Senate. Waiving the rules was politically impossible. Even if the congressional rules had been waived, the consequent sequester in other programs would have been unthinkable. For a time, it seemed like tobacco legislation had come to a dead end once again, in this instance killed by its own effectiveness.

In this instance, however, there was a deus ex machina. The sponsor of the tobacco-control legislation in the House (Rep. Henry Waxman of Los Angeles, now retired) was the chairman of the House committee that has jurisdiction over health issues. Immediately before assuming that position, however, he had been chairman of the committee that has jurisdiction over government personnel issues. When the tobacco-control bill was in critical budget condition because of PAYGO, he and his staff remembered that in that committee there had been a long-dormant proposal about civil-service retirement issues. Existing law gave federal employees an option to choose to save in a manner parallel to an individual retirement account (IRA), putting untaxed money in an account with the expectation that taxes would be paid on it (and its earnings) when it was withdrawn for retirement, years in the future. Some employees and their unions had proposed that they also have the option to save in a manner parallel to a "Roth" IRA, paying taxes up front at the time of deposit with the expectation that funds (and their earnings) withdrawn in retirement would be tax-free. The proposal had been supported as a matter of fairer employee choice about tax planning and was largely noncontroversial, if not exactly a front-burner political issue.

But this retirement proposal also had a score, a counterintuitive but positive one. Since taxes would be paid in the year in which contributions were deposited in the new Roth IRA, increased federal revenues would be forthcoming immediately, well within the ten-year snapshot. The ultimate loss of revenues from tax-free withdrawals would be far in the future, outside the snapshot. As a result, the proposal was scored as producing significant new tax income—$2.5 billion over ten years.

After some negotiations with the congressman and staff who had taken over the other committee, an agreement was made to add the federal retirement provisions to the tobacco bill.[35] As a result, the combined tobacco/retirement legislation was scored not as losing

[34] Cong. Budget Office, Raising the Excise Tax on Cigarettes.

[35] Other improvements in the federal retirees' program were also included, lowering the net revenue increase by $800 million.

money but as producing a billion dollars in net deficit reduction—an altogether unexpected political bonus for those who voted for it.

This is the clearest form of skewing in policy-making that regularly arises from the budget process. The tobacco bill had political and policy momentum but would be a budget loss and, by itself, seemed stuck. The retirement provisions produced apparent new revenues but would be unlikely to overcome political inertia and be enacted on their own. While unpredictable, the budget process produced two victories and hurt no one (except arguably those taxpayers in the distant future who may someday lament the loss of revenues when Roth funds are eventually withdrawn tax free). But it was mere serendipity that the two bills found each other and were married.

b. Sustainable Growth Rate

Other examples demonstrate less happy outcomes arising in health policy from the budget process. The most notable of these is the long saga of the Sustainable Growth Rate (SGR) in Medicare.[36] Originally adopted in 1997 as part of a large budget-reduction package, the SGR measure was intended to slow the increase in payment of physicians in the Medicare program. By almost everyone's reckoning, it was badly designed to do even that, having created an automatic formula that tied physician fees to the economy's performance in a way that produced unexpected results. But it also became an ongoing problem for Congress because these strange results legally required significant cuts to physician fees without regard to the health needs of patients or to their access to care. As of early 2015, if the SGR had been implemented it would have resulted in 21% cuts in physician fees.

The SGR formula was in permanent statute, so the CBO was required to include projections of the savings that would be produced by its automatic cuts as part of the ongoing baseline for Medicare. In other words, the CBO had to pretend that the law was going to be implemented as written. Any legislation to change that formula or postpone its implementation had to go through scorekeeping, which estimated the increased mandatory spending that would occur within the ten-year budget snapshot.[37] Such legislation either had to comply with the PAYGO rules by including offsetting savings or revenues or face the possibility of triggering a sequester.

Because savings and revenues are hard to find and pass, Congress always just bought time rather than actually fixing the problem. By early 2015, the SGR had been temporarily postponed on seventeen separate occasions for periods of a few months up to a full year. Short-term delays in implementation of the formula were repeatedly enacted because the costs of a permanent change were scored as too expensive and, as time passed, grew ever larger. By 2015, a one-year delay was estimated to add approximately $10 billion to the baseline, and a permanent change was estimated to add $140 billion over the ten years of the snapshot.[38]

[36] *See generally* Keith Fontenot, Caitlin Brandt, & Mark McClellan, *A Primer on Medicare Physician Payment Reform and the SGR*, Brookings (Feb. 2, 2015), http://www.brookings.edu/blogs/health360/posts/2015/02/sgr-medicare-physician-payment-primer-fontenot.

[37] Legislation to postpone or eliminate the automatic SGR cuts was frequently referred to as "the Medicare Doc Fix" or "the SGR Patch."

[38] Cong. Budget Office, Medicare's Payment to Physicians (Feb. 3, 2015), https://www.cbo.gov/sites/default/files/cbofiles/attachments/49923-SGR_Options.pdf. The scores have varied over the years

The specter of dramatic physician-fee cuts was a political nightmare for Congress. Year after year, physicians (and sometimes their patients) described the pain that would result if fees were cut by increasingly large percentages. This in itself was a time-consuming nuisance for all concerned.

More important, patching the SGR under the PAYGO rules over the years catalyzed many other legislative changes just to find offsets for the expense of delaying the automatic formula. To pay for postponing the SGR, cuts were enacted in the payments for durable medical equipment, outpatient prescription drugs, ambulatory surgery, home health care, diagnostic imaging, Medicare Advantage managed care plans, clinical labs, Disproportionate Share Hospitals, dialysis services, diabetic supplies, and inpatient long-term care. Measures were passed to increase electronic prescribing, to coordinate IRS and Department of Health and Human Services data, and to reschedule other Medicare payments. Premiums paid by beneficiaries for Medicare Part B were raised. The ACA's Prevention Trust Fund (for community preventive health projects) was tapped.[39]

Perhaps many of these measures might have been enacted on their own, without the artificially induced demand for offsets that the need for an SGR patch created. Some of them were undoubtedly prudent cost-control or efficient management. But it is equally plausible that some of them might have been defeated had it not been for the need to find savings to pay for the patches. Alternatively, it is also possible that some of them might have been enacted to provide PAYGO offsets for actual enlargements or improvements in other mandatory spending programs such as improved home- and community-based care services that are scored (because of their own counterintuitive budget effects) as costing billions. It is indeed possible that true budget hawks who are agnostic about health policy might have supported these measures solely for the reductions in federal spending that they produce and enacted them simply to reduce the deficit.

Instead, the SGR sat as a black hole in the middle of the mandatory spending galaxy, pulling other programs out of their usual orbits and irresistibly drawing in and absorbing billions that might have gone elsewhere. Dark matter and dark energy indeed.

In May 2015, however, Congress simply fixed it. Since the costs of all U.S. healthcare had slowed (for reasons that are hotly debated but unrelated to the SGR), the CBO's estimated cost of repealing the SGR was at a low ebb, down almost a quarter trillion dollars from its high point. Both political parties in Congress seized this chance to get rid of the black hole that had pulled at them for years. Some offsetting savings were raised to meet PAYGO, including some fundamental changes to how Medicare will pay providers and some increased premiums. But much of the cost of the new law was simply deemed acceptable, with Congress choosing to ignore the estimated $140 billion net increase to the deficit.[40] The last section of that law explains how it was done: "The budgetary effects of this Act shall not be entered on either PAYGO scorecard maintained pursuant to section 4(d) of the Statutory Pay-As-You-Go Act of 2010."[41]

as healthcare cost trends on which CBO estimates are predicated have varied up and down. Years after the snapshot are, of course, not included in the score.

39 *See* Angela Boothe, *Primer: The Sustainable Growth Rate*, American Action Forum App. 1 (Jan. 7, 2015), http://americanactionforum.org/research/primer-the-sustainable-growth-rate#_ednref1.

40 *See* Henry Aaron, *Three Cheers for Logrolling: The Demise of the SGR*, 372 New Eng. J. of Med. 1977 (May 21, 2015).

41 Medicare Access and CHIP Reauthorization Act of 2015, Pub. L. No. 114-10, sec. 525 (Apr. 16, 2015).

c. Universal Coverage

Perhaps the most far-reaching example of the budget process's effects in recent times is the ACA's federal matching rates for its Medicaid expansion.[42] It is not as nuanced or counterintuitive as the stories of tobacco and the SGR, but its reverberating effects are both more basic and more enduring.

During congressional consideration, Democrats who supported both deficit reduction and expanded health insurance ensured that the ACA overall would be required to comply with both parliamentary and statutory PAYGO rules and, thereby, produce a net change in the baseline of at most zero.[43] In addition to these rules, the legislation also had to meet a political promise made by the president that the entire total of the bill would not exceed approximately $900 billion of expenditures, even if these costs were all fully offset to meet PAYGO.[44] Within these parameters, scorekeeping became central and essential.

As any reader of *NFIB v. Sebelius* knows, part of the ACA as enacted would have expanded minimum Medicaid eligibility in all states to cover low-income Americans regardless of their membership in a category.[45] This expansion of Medicaid eligibility to so-called "childless adults" was to complete the patchwork of coverage for poor people that had been gradually stitched together since 1965.

During consideration of the package, it became clear that the CBO-estimated total costs of the ACA's insurance subsidies, the Medicaid expansion, and other provisions were going to run over both the promised price tag of $900 billion and the available offsets for PAYGO. As a first cost-containment effort, a legislative decision was made to increase the income level at which people would be eligible for Medicaid as opposed to the tax-subsidized health-insurance exchanges. This helped with costs because Medicaid was estimated by CBO scorekeeping to be a less expensive package on a per capita basis than would be the subsidies for private insurance. Consequently, the inclusion of more beneficiaries in the Medicaid group and fewer in the exchanges lowered the overall score of the bill. Moreover, when even more cost reductions were needed, a last-minute change was included to increase this Medicaid eligibility level still further by including an additional 5% in the poverty level, creating the near-constant confusion of whether the upper limit

[42] Federal matching rates in Medicaid are referred to as the FMAP (i.e., Federal Medical Assistance Percentages) and, in most instances, vary by state. A state in which the federal government provides one dollar for every one dollar of state spending is referred to as a 50% FMAP state; one in which the federal government provides four dollars for every one dollar of state spending is referred to as an 80% FMAP state. As of this writing, FMAPs in basic Medicaid range from a low of 50% to a high of around 70%. Office of the Assistant Sec'y for Planning & Evaluation, U.S. Dep't of Health & Human Services, Federal Financial Participation in State Assistance Expenditures (Feb. 5, 2014), http://aspe.hhs.gov/health/reports/2014/FMAP2015/fmap15.cfm.

[43] It could, and ultimately did, produce a net positive effect on the budget, saving money over the ten-year snapshot.

[44] President Obama, Remarks to a Joint Session of Congress on Health Care (Sept. 9, 2009), https://www.whitehouse.gov/the_press_office/Remarks-by-the-President-to-a-Joint-Session-of-Congress-on-Health-Care/.

[45] NFIB v. Sebelius, 32 S. Ct. 2566 (2012).

for Medicaid is 133% or 138%.[46] Both of these decisions about eligibility were made largely to achieve a CBO score.[47]

Even more crucially, the ACA design was further changed to achieve the score by reducing the federal matching rate for the Medicaid expansion population over time. Initially, as a policy to assist states in expanding Medicaid, the choice had been made that state health payments associated with these newly eligible people would be matched by the federal government at a higher rate than for the traditional categories of Medicaid beneficiaries—much higher. The federal government was to pay 100% of the costs of this "expansion population," and the states were to pay nothing.

But when scorekeeping revealed a need for further budget reductions, the decision was made to limit that federal payment. As enacted, the Federal Medical Assistance Percentages (FMAP) rate of 100% is to apply only for 2014, 2015, and 2016. But between 2017 and 2020, the federal matching rate will be incrementally reduced, eventually down to 90%. It will then remain at 90% in perpetuity. This decision was made in part to respond to the highly visible political controversy over special "deals" made with individual senators for their home states.[48] But the decision was largely one of budget crunching and scorekeeping as an effort to trim the net and gross cost of the ACA overall to satisfy PAYGO and the president's promised grand total.[49]

The effects of the FMAP decision, however, were not limited to the incremental savings produced for scorekeeping. This future funding reduction provided the fulcrum on which the Supreme Court rested its unprecedented decision that the Medicaid expansion was coercive of the states, beyond the level that the Tenth Amendment would allow. The opinion by Chief Justice Roberts notes, "The Act increases federal funding to cover the States' costs in expanding Medicaid coverage, although States will bear a portion of the costs on their own."[50] The conservative dissenters go further in their focus on the ultimate 90% match in finding coercion of the states, saying:

> [Congress understands] that the ACA offer is not an "exceedingly generous" gift that no State in its right mind would decline. Instead, acceptance of the offer will impose very substantial costs on participating States. It is true that the Federal Government will bear most of the initial costs associated with the Medicaid Expansion, first paying 100% of the costs of covering newly eligible individuals between 2014 and 2016. But that is just part of the picture. Participating States will be forced to shoulder substantial costs as well, because after 2019 the Federal Government will cover only 90% of the costs associated with the Expansion, with state spending projected to increase by at least $20 billion by 2020 as a consequence. [internal citations omitted][51]

[46] The last-minute nature of this change can be deduced by comparing the repeated statutory references to 133% (e.g., Section 2001, "Medicaid Coverage for the Lowest Income Populations") with the 5% increase included by cross-reference in Section 1004(e), "Five Percent Income Disregard for Certain Individuals." The muddle this makes of information and advice is widespread and perhaps most clearly expressed in one blog entry entitled, *ACA Note: When 133 Equals 138—FPL Calculations in the Affordable Care Act*, St. Health Access Data Assistance Ctr. (Jan. 13, 2011), http://www.shadac.org/blog/aca-note-when-133-equals-138-fpl-calculations-in-affordable-care-act.

[47] Personal correspondence with House and Senate staff in 2014.

[48] These were colorfully characterized as "The Cornhusker Kickback" and "The Louisiana Purchase."

[49] Personal correspondence with House and Senate staff in 2014.

[50] NFIB v. Sebelius, at 10.

[51] *Id.*, at 45.

With this argument, the Court struck down the requirement for states to expand Medicaid to all citizens, regardless of categorical eligibility.

The reverberation does not stop there. Once the Court made the Medicaid expansion voluntary, the reduction from 100% to 90% in federal support also provided the central political talking point for governors and legislators to oppose voluntary expansion.[52] Many states refused to expand. The result has been the creation of a "coverage" gap in those states, leaving millions of low-income people ineligible for both Medicaid and insurance-exchange tax subsidies.[53]

It is speculation on my part, but if the reduction in FMAP had not been made, it is hard to see how the Court could have found the provision of 100% federal money to be an unconstitutional coercion of the states: Free is free. If the Court had not done so, then the required Medicaid expansion would have been upheld and would be the law of all fifty states now. Even if the Court had still nullified the enforcement of the ACA's requirement that states expand, it seems likely that many more governors and legislators would have found an expansion that was permanently 100% federal with no state costs to be appealing or at least tolerable.

The platitude is "for want of a nail, a kingdom was lost." In this instance, it might be said that "for want of a PAYGO offset for costs scored against a ten-year baseline, universal coverage of all Americans was lost." It is not poetry, perhaps, but it is a tragedy.

IX Conclusion

In addition to tobacco, the SGR, and the ACA Medicaid expansion, virtually all of the health policy debates of the last twenty years have backstories of budgeting. Proposed expansions of Medicaid to include low-income people with HIV were scrapped because drug costs were immediate and offsetting savings from averted hospitalizations were later, outside the snapshot.[54] The Medicare Part D "donut hole" was enacted without any health-policy rationale and was only to meet a scoring target.[55] The early premium contributions toward the CLASS

[52] *E.g.*, "GOP Govs. Rick Scott of Florida, Bobby Jindal of Louisiana, Nathan Deal of Georgia, Nikki Haley of South Carolina and Rick Perry of Texas have said they, too, will reject a Medicaid expansion, calling it too expensive." *Mississippi Says No Thanks to Federal Medicaid Expansion Dollars*, Modern Healthcare (Oct. 18, 2012), http://www.modernhealthcare.com/article/20121018/INFO/310189979; "Many states with Republican governors and legislatures have rejected the expansion, calling it too expensive." Kelly Kennedy, *Medicaid Expansion Gap Could Leave Poor Shortchanged*, USA Today(Sept. 5, 2013), http://www.usatoday.com/story/news/politics/2013/09/05/100-percent-medicaid/2749143/; "Most of these governors argue the expansion would be too expensive, even though including the poor would only increase these states' Medicaid spending by an average of 3% over the next decade." Sydney Brownstone, *13 Governors Screwing Over the Uninsured*, Mother Jones (Feb. 20, 2013), http://www.motherjones.com/mojo/2013/02/meet-governors-rejecting-expansion-medicaid.

[53] R. Garfield, "The Coverage Gap: Uninsured Poor Adults in States that Do Not Expand Medicaid: An Update" (Kaiser Family Foundation, Nov. 2014), at http://files.kff.org/attachment/the-coverage-gap-uninsured-poor-adults-in-states-that-do-not-expand-medicaid-issue-brief.

[54] Westmoreland, *Standard Errors*, at 1591–1592.

[55] Westmoreland, *Standard Errors*, at 1609.

Act's program of long-term-care insurance appeared inside the snapshot while the expenses of the program were largely outside it, providing apparent offsets for other aspects of the ACA.[56] And there are others.

It is hardly surprising to anyone that money plays a role in lawmaking. Budgeting is a necessary tool for organization, planning, and execution of public policy.

It may, however, surprise many people to find out how central a role it plays, regularly displacing policy judgments that do not fit in the Procrustean bed of PAYGO. In addition to the examples discussed, I can tell similar stories about legislation regarding immunizations, lead poisoning, mental health services, preventive health and screening benefits, and community-based alternatives to nursing homes.[57]

It certainly would surprise almost everyone to know how the very budget process itself deeply skews legislative choices in systemic ways. Current budgeting practices structurally discourage long-term investments, nationwide actions, and transparent government in all areas of government. Most basically, it subordinates all other legal and political values to those that can be monetized.

Nonetheless, all signs are that the primacy of the budget is only going to intensify in the coming years. All parties to legislative action pay some obeisance to limits and scorekeeping. Increasingly, some focus their entire agenda on the deficit and debt. Since 1974, it has been necessary for policy advocates to be able to follow the money by understanding its terms and definitions, its limits and goals, and its precedents and processes. These needs will only intensify over time. It has been the goal of this chapter to provide a useful introduction and a chilling reminder of these invisible forces of dark matter and dark energy at work.

[56] *Health Care Reform: End Game Fiscal Considerations*, THE CONCORD COALITION 11–12 (Dec. 23, 2009), http://www.concordcoalition.org/files/1223FinalHealthCarebrief.pdf.

[57] *See generally* Westmoreland, *Can We Get There from Here?*, and Westmoreland, *Standard Errors*.

CHAPTER 40

THE ETHICS OF RATIONING HEALTHCARE

A. M. CAPRON

I Introduction: Why Talk of "Healthcare Rationing" Is Unavoidable

A specter is haunting medicine—the specter of rationing. Many authorities deny its existence, and fewer sightings are reported now than in the recent past.[1] Moreover, those who observe the apparition describe it in such differing terms that they do not seem to have seen the same ghost. Yet the specter in one form or another is an inevitable presence in clinical medicine and in the debates among experts and the general public about how the United States should respond to the increasing proportion of its gross domestic product spent on healthcare.[2] Although total spending for health may increase more slowly than the Congressional Budget Office was predicting a decade ago, no one doubts that rising healthcare costs will remain a problem and hence that various efforts to restrain total spending, including by rationing healthcare, have to remain options on the policy agenda, however difficult it is in a very partisan atmosphere to talk rationally about the feasibility and ethical acceptability of limiting care.

The inevitability of rationing, both as a topic in policy debates and as a reality in practice, does not make it any less anathema in medicine. Physicians decry it for many reasons.[3] They are depressed by the notion of imposed limitations: What good are their hard-won knowledge and clinical skills and, indeed, all the miracles of modern medicine if they cannot be put to use when needed by a patient? Also, physicians' Hippocratic commitment—always to be guided solely by their patient's well-being—is offended by the prospect of not providing a

[1] Peter A. Ubel, *Why It's Not Time for Health Care Rationing*, 45 Hastings Ctr. Rpt. 15 (Mar.–Apr. 2015).

[2] For recent estimates post–Affordable Care Act, *see* M. Gregg Bloche, *Beyond the "R Word"? Medicine's New Frugality*, 366 New Eng. J. Med. 1951 (2012).

[3] This is true of Americans in general, not just physicians. *See* Philip M. Rosoff, Rationing Is Not a Four-Letter Word: Setting Limits on Healthcare 6 (2014); Alan B. Cohen, *The Debate Over Health Care Rationing: Déjà Vu All Over Again?*, 49 Inquiry 90, 91 (2012).

patient something that might save or improve that patient's life or relieve her suffering. They chafe at the thought that another person—worse, some faceless bureaucracy—will have the power to decide which interventions are sufficiently efficient or effective.

Likewise, patients—or citizens generally—not only experience situations in their own care where coverage for some test or treatment recommended by their physician has been deemed "not authorized" by their insurance carrier, but they also hear that this results from insurance companies trying to avoid paying for beneficial but high-cost treatments and that health policy-makers plan to limit spending on populations, like the elderly, who are disproportionately sick and who can seldom be made fully healthy.

To be sure, physicians themselves sometimes see no benefit in "doing everything," whatever a patient—or the desperate relatives of a patient who is no longer able to speak for himself—may say, if the prospects for truly benefiting the patient are very small and the likelihood of burdening the patient are very large. Indeed, physicians increasingly acknowledge the necessity of initiating difficult discussions with individual patients about whether under some circumstances the patients would prefer to forgo certain life-prolonging interventions.[4]

Physicians also cope with managing scarcity in settings like intensive care units (ICUs) that have a set capacity or when faced with shortage of a particular drug that is critical in treating a lethal disease (such as cancer).[5] Although shortages of this type may be recurrent, they are also usually time-limited, ad hoc, and often invisible to the general public. Rationing arises also from a different sort of physical shortage, one that is persistent and very visible, namely, the scarcity of human organs for transplantation. Moreover, this is a setting where the stakes are very high: Thousands of patients with end-stage disease of the kidney, liver, heart, or other organs die every year while awaiting a transplant. Additional spending would provide no quick fix for this problem, although the related problem of an insufficient number of machines to provide chronic hemodialysis to patients with end-stage renal disease (ESRD) led Congress in 1972 to authorize paying for the care of all ESRD patients whose treatment is not otherwise covered by insurance.

"Rationing" has thus become a trope that reflects the spoken and unspoken concerns and fears of patients and providers—and perhaps even of policy-makers—about a variety of problems with countless causes and multiple manifestations across healthcare. One way or another, the need to ration healthcare seems undeniable.

This chapter examines rationing from an ethical perspective—a companion chapter in the book examines it from an economics perspective—based on defining "rationing" as *a policy or practice of consciously limiting access to medical interventions of known benefit*. Each element could be further elaborated, but it is clear enough as a starting point for the discussion.[6]

[4] This patient-centered approach was quickly swamped by partisan cries of "rationing" as politicians attacked as "death panels" the proposal that Medicare pay physicians to discuss end-of-life care options with patients. Cohen, *supra* note 3, at 90.

[5] Pharmacists and physicians then need to agree on a method for using the limited supply while alternative sources are sought. *See* Rosoff, *supra* note 3, at 48.

[6] It is often said that rationing should not be done "by individual doctors and patients at the bedside." *E.g.*, Daniel Callahan, *Must We Ration Health Care for the Elderly?*, 40 J.L. Med. & Ethics 10, 13 (2012). Rationing is, in the end, manifested in what individual doctors and patients may or may not do, so objections to its occurring "at the bedside" might seem like mere rhetoric. But they are not. Part of the objection to the locale is that given the duties (e.g., loyalty, beneficence) that physicians owe their patients, their relationship is an inappropriate one onto which to place the role of denier

This definition sets the terrain to be explored in the next section and excludes certain phenomena that are sometimes mistakenly equated with, or linked to, rationing.[7]

This chapter proceeds as follows: Part II demonstrates that healthcare is rationed through a wide range of policies and practices and locates them in a three-dimensional topographic space. Part III scrutinizes the principal strategies for making such policies "ethical" and concludes that practical guidance depends on a varied and context-specific combination of "fair process" and multiple principles, including important values that do not on their face relate to rationing. Part IV concludes by arguing that rationing is not one but a number of phenomena, and attention should be on strategies and processes that would bring the more diffused forms closer to the well-elaborated, though imperfect, frameworks developed for handling direct individual trade-offs.

II Separating Different Types of Healthcare Rationing

a. The Topography of Rationing

What factors are germane in sorting out the wide range of policies and practices that involve rationing? Commentators have utilized a number of concepts, though in differing ways. For example, Jeffrey Merrill and Alan Cohen describe "conscious policy decisions to limit access to certain services" as "explicit rationing," which they differentiate from the "implicit rationing" that occurs when "global constraints" are placed on the availability of resources for providing care, such as by requiring certificates-of-need for expensive technologies.[8] In contrast, Daniel Callahan breaks rationing into three types, "direct, indirect, and covert."[9] This chapter's use of these terms differs from both.

The rationing that Merrill and Cohen label "implicit" is still a "conscious decision" that will foreseeably limit some patients' access to certain interventions. The difference between implicit and explicit rationing is not in their effects on access to healthcare but in the candor with which decision-makers own up to the rationing and hence in the ability of others to review such decisions. Not all policies that are "explicit" are formal; indeed, some may be

of beneficial care. *Id. But see* Peter A. Ubel & Robert M. Arnold, *The Unbearable Rightness of Bedside Rationing: Physician Duties in a Climate of Cost Containment*, 155 ARCH. INTERN. MED. 1837 (1995). Part of the objection is that individual acts of rationing that arise entirely from the decisions of doctors and patients, rather than as applications of formal policies, may be idiosyncratic and even biased. And part of the objection is that in order for rationing to be analyzed and improved, in terms of its effectiveness and ethics, it should be reviewable, as a formal policy or discernible practice would be.

[7] In particular, the definition excludes from the province of rationing simple "waste avoidance," the elimination of interventions that produce *no* net benefit to the immediate patient once the burdens they create are taken into account. Further, the definition applies only when access has been limited not when a patient elects to forgo an intervention that he or she concludes is likely to produce insufficient benefits compared to its costs and burdens.

[8] Jeffrey C. Merrill & Alan B. Cohen, *The Emperor's New Clothes: Unraveling the Myths about Rationing*, 24 INQUIRY 105 (1987).

[9] Callahan, *supra* note 6, at 12.

Effects on Access to Interventions		Effects on Individuals: Direct	Effects on Individuals: Indirect
Direct		**1**	**3**
		- Organ from deceased donors - Bed in intensive care unit, when unit is at capacity - Scarce medication for lethal illness - Scarce vaccine for novel, deadly virus	**- Ranking of the condition-treatment pairs that are covered by Oregon Health Plan - Listing drugs on hospital formulary - Coverage terms for "levels" of private insurance**
		- Long waiting lines for certain elective procedures	- Patent protection of pharmaceuticals
		- Not referring certain groups of patients for advanced care, such as dialysis or organ transplantation	*- Building a general hospital without an emergency department*
Indirect		**2**	**4**
		- Eligibility criteria for Medicaid coverage	**- Certificates-of-need for capital projects and expensive technologies**
		- Insurance deductibles & copays	- Reimbursement schedule for healthcare services provided to Medicaid patients set well below market level
			- Selection of physicians for insurance plan's "network" of preferred providers based on level of charges and usage - Incentives to physicians to restrict access to expensive interventions - Physicians' decisions about how to use their own time and skills

KEY: Policy is: A. Explicitly Related toRationing, B. Implicitly Related to Rationing, or C. *Covert* (*Relationship to Rationing Disguised*)

FIGURE 40.1 Rationing as it affects individuals and access to healthcare interventions, categorized by the directness of the effect and the explicitness of the rationing.

practices not yet converted to a written policy and as such may be subject to variation due to particular circumstances. Yet all are overtly about allocating a scarce resource (including insurance coverage) to patients, and this aim would be visible to anyone who applies the policy or examines the activity in question. Callahan takes the matter of rationing's visibility a step further by invoking the category of "covert" policies and practices, which he illustrates with "the unwritten agreement among physicians" in the British National Health Service for many decades to tell patients older than fifty-five "that nothing could be done for their heart disease or kidney failure."[10] On this point, Callahan seems correct, but "covert" is not on the same continuum as the other terms he uses, "direct" and "indirect." Those terms better describe the manner in which a policy or practice produces its effects in providing or not providing particular patients access, or making or not making a particular intervention available, rather than the way in which the policy is expressed.

In Figure 40.1, the columns separate policies[11] according to the way they affect individuals: *Are individuals denied access to interventions as a direct result of a policy or because of an indirect effect?* Since, in the end, one is concerned about healthcare rationing because of the way it affects individuals, these two columns might seem to be the heart of the matter. But the two rows are at least as important because they highlight how policies affect the

[10] *Id.*, citing HENRY AARON & WILLIAM B. SCHWARTZ, THE PAINFUL PRESCRIPTION: RATIONING HOSPITAL CARE (1984). Callahan suggests that a more recent example of "covert" rationing is the use of long waiting lists in the United Kingdom; ironically, that is the example Merrill and Cohen use to illustrate "explicit" rationing.

[11] For the sake of simplicity, from this point forward this chapter uses the terms "policy" or "policies" to encompass both actual policies (such as laws or institutional rules) and practices (the patterns of decision and action that constitute the manner in which a system or organization conducts its activities) that have not yet been translated into policies.

availability of healthcare interventions: *Which interventions are accessible or inaccessible as a direct result of a policy versus indirectly?* This division is especially critical in market-based healthcare because many (perhaps most) policies that ration access do so indirectly through their effects on the whole healthcare system. Policies of this sort may aim to reduce overall spending, lower prices, improve quality, subsidize medical insurance premiums, and so forth; while not intended to affect the supply of particular healthcare goods and services, indirectly they do. Figure 40.1 also displays the third dimension that divides types of rationing: *How apparent is it that a policy rations access to healthcare interventions?* The three categories—explicit, implicit, and covert—are indicated by different typefaces.

This topography shows the range of policies that involve rationing. Much of the literature—particularly the more detailed systems developed by moral philosophers (see Part III below)—focuses on examples drawn from Cell 1, especially policies that explicitly allocate resources between individuals. Yet, while a policy, to constitute rationing, has to eventuate in someone not receiving a medical intervention from which he or she could benefit, many policies are not directly intended to allocate a particular intervention among members of an affected population, much less to separate identifiable "winners" from "losers." Nonetheless, even policies that have other, distinct objectives are properly regarded as instances of "rationing" when a reasonable person formulating or applying them could foresee their effect in limiting some people's access to healthcare interventions of known benefit. Precisely when the connection between the creation or application of a policy and its allocative effects is most attenuated—and, indeed, may not be discerned by those affected—decision-makers who intend to act legitimately in making and applying healthcare-related policies (and those who hold them to account) should attend to the ethical defensibility of their actions.

b. Situating Sample Policies Topographically

The policies in Cell 1 are unquestionably instances of rationing, for they directly affect individual patients and specific interventions; the policies separate patients into those who will receive a particular intervention (an organ, an ICU bed, a vaccine or medication) and those who will not. Such differences can plainly have life-altering consequences. The policies that receive the most attention are explicit about this sorting; the people charged with creating and applying the policy are aware of what they are doing and typically have expressed a wish to act in a way that is ethically (and legally) appropriate.

A second group of policies in Cell 1 also directly limit individuals' access to beneficial medical interventions but do not announce an intention to do so. For example, the persons operating, or making policies for, a particular healthcare institution or system know that if the resources (facilities, surgeons, artificial hips, and so forth) devoted to performing hip replacements are sufficient for 60,000 operations per year but 65,000 new patients are identified each year who could benefit from having a hip replaced, all patients cannot be accommodated as soon as they are diagnosed, so a list must be created of patients who have been cleared for the operation. The existence of a waiting list may demonstrate the unmet need and stimulate those in charge to increase capacity by some combination of increasing efficiency and devoting more resources to hip replacement operations, thus reducing the wait list. But if the increase in capacity, if any, does not eliminate the gap between the number of operations performed and the number of eligible patients, then the waiting list—which is *explicitly* regarded as a means of organizing the provision of care—will *implicitly* function as a means of rationing care, as patients die or remove themselves from the list by seeking treatment outside the health system or deciding to live with their problem rather than continuing to seek hip replacement at that time.

The final policies in Cell 1 are those that ration access to healthcare interventions covertly. The main difference from the prior categories is that covert rationing is not merely implicit but unacknowledged and perhaps even intentionally disguised. For example, the National Health Service practitioners who responded to inadequate resources by restricting older patients' access to treatment for kidney and heart failure simply told the patients that nothing medically suitable was available to respond to their condition.[12] A similar lack of candor—though perhaps for different reasons, including transplant centers' interest in achieving high survival rates—occurs in a local (and largely invisible) fashion in the United States when patients with end-stage organ failure are not listed for a transplant because of advanced age (over 65 years) and/or poor post-transplant life expectancy.[13]

The policies that fall within Cell 2 are those that directly select among individuals but not in terms of their access to a particular intervention (like an organ transplant) but more broadly. The traditional eligibility requirements to enroll in state Medicaid programs provide an example of policies that explicitly ration care by excluding large numbers of people who meet some criteria (such as poverty) but not others (such as youth) and then providing to all those who are eligible insurance coverage for a very wide range of services, including some of little or no value to them. Overcoming the latter problem was the ambition behind the Oregon Health Plan under which the rules that left many poor adults ineligible for Medicaid were removed, while the range of interventions the program would cover for all insured persons was restricted to those that were expected to produce the outcomes most valued by Oregonians. That program therefore appears in Cell 3 because what is unique about it is the manner in which it directly and explicitly limits certain beneficial healthcare interventions.[14]

Similarly, to encourage patients to use their coverage in a prudent fashion and thereby lower overall spending explicit, health insurers have increasingly relied on "cost sharing" in the form of deductibles and copayments, which are supposed to make insured persons behave more like "smart consumers," sensitive to the relative value of various healthcare services. But some of the care that patients forgo or delay seeking could have benefited them and could, indeed, have been vital in protecting or restoring their health.[15] Thus, certain persons do not receive some healthcare interventions of known benefit that they would

[12] *See* Aaron & Schwartz, *supra* note 10.

[13] Mark S. Stein, *The Distribution of Life-Saving Medical Resources: Equality, Life Expectancy, and Choice behind the Veil*, 19 Soc. Phil. & Pol'y 212, 238–240 (2002); OPTN/UNOS Ethics Committee, *Ethical Principles to Be Considered in the Allocation of Human Organs* (June 2, 2015), (http://optn.transplant.hrsa.gov/resources/ethics/ethical-principles-in-the-allocation-of-human-organs/).

[14] *E.g.*, Peter A. Ubel, Pricing Life: Why It's Time for Health Care Rationing 4 (2001).

[15] Dana P. Goldman, Geoffrey F. Joyce, & Y Zheng, *Prescription Drug Cost Sharing: Associations with Medication and Medical Utilization and Spending and Health*, 298 JAMA 61–69 (2007) (higher copayments were associated with lower rates of drug treatment, worse adherence among existing users, and more frequent discontinuation of therapy); Mitchell D. Wong et al., *Effects of Cost Sharing on Care Seeking and Health Status: Results from the Medical Outcomes Study*, 91 Am. J. Pub. Health 1889 (2001) (cost-sharing reduced the use of care for both minor and serious symptoms in a chronically ill population).

receive absent the imposition of cost-sharing.[16] Such policies thus illustrate the category that has a direct effect on individuals but only an indirect effect on interventions (when deductibles and copays do not segregate by the type of treatment). Further, the policies in question are not explicitly about limiting valuable care; quite the contrary, those instituting them profess a belief that having to pay a larger portion of the costs of care will merely orient insured persons toward shopping for value (e.g., accepting a generic rather than a patent-protected drug) rather than skip care because it puts too great a drain on their pocketbooks. Nonetheless, given the empirical evidence, a reasonable policy-maker should recognize that higher deductibles and copays will not only reduce "low-value" treatment but also to some extent ration beneficial care based on insured persons' income or wealth.

Mention has already been made of the Oregon Health Plan as an illustration, in Cell 3, of a policy that indirectly affects individuals but directly rations particular interventions. Another example is the selection of drugs by a hospital formulary committee. The effect is indirect, as the choice is not intended to single out individuals, though it is explicitly intended to limit access, ideally—but often not in practice—by selecting the most cost-effective drugs for the treatment of particular conditions.[17] The coverage terms of private health insurance is a third example of explicit rationing that directly affects access to certain treatments (usually high-cost and often novel) but only indirectly separates individuals (based on their willingness and ability to pay for care that is not covered by their insurance). The choice to purchase a particular insurance policy implicates individual autonomy, a prominent bioethics principle that has played but a small role in discussions of the ethics of rationing,[18] which presupposes that the individual *wants* the rationed intervention. Should the choice of an insurance plan that, by not covering certain interventions, makes them effectively inaccessible be regarded as comparable to an informed refusal of such interventions in a clinical context? Insurance companies do not have the same common law fiduciary obligations of full disclosure toward prospective policyholders that physicians have to their patients, especially as to information about conflicts created by their own interests. But statutory disclosure obligations do exist regarding copays, deductibles, and the like.[19] Yet, to make truly informed decisions, individuals would need to be provided and understand a great deal of statistical and empirical data not only about their likelihood of developing particular medical conditions

[16] "Evidence shows that user charges [e.g., copayments, coinsurance, deductibles] do not stop the escalation of healthcare costs, resulting in rationing in favor of the rich and health." Cam Donaldson et al., *Moving Rationing Forward: An Economic View*, 337 BRIT. MED. J. 905 (2008).

[17] Drug formularies run by American insurance and managed care companies, which are another important source of rationing, rely on special purchasing deals and "closed formularies" to hold down drug costs and only rarely compare the clinical and economic value of new drug to those of existing ones.

[18] A notable exception is a proposal, aimed at avoiding the intransitivity that confounds interpersonal aggregation of utility, to set healthcare priorities based on a population's cumulative choices about healthcare, resulting in the costs not borne by individuals equaling the predetermined total public budget. Alex Friedman & Marion Danis, *Intransitivity and Priority Setting*, 36 J. PHIL. RES. 173 (2011).

[19] Insurance has traditionally been regulated by the states, which retain "significant latitude to impose requirements on health insurance issuers that are more restrictive than the Federal law," so long as they do not modify the required "summary of benefits and coverage." 80 Fed. Reg. 34292, 34303 (2015). These regulations, which the Departments of Treasury, Labor, and Health and Human Services developed collaboratively with the National Association of Insurance Commissioners to implement the Affordable Care Act, aim to ensure that insurance is described in a uniform manner that will facilitate purchasers making informed choices among the available plans. *Id.*

but also about the probable effects of different forms of cost-sharing on their actually accessing particular treatments.[20]

The patent laws are intended to reward innovation but, when applied to medical products for which no good substitute exists, such as novel pharmaceuticals, they can result in prices that individual patients, and even insurance companies, may be unable—or at least very reluctant—to pay. The specificity of the particular drugs or other medical goods, the inaccessibility of which would indirectly affect patients with particular medical needs, make this a good example in Cell 3 of a policy that implicitly rations care by making certain interventions less accessible to large portions of the population.

The final group of policies within Cell 3 consists of those that are covert, such as the decision to build a general hospital without an emergency department, which will limit access to interventions of known benefit by delaying some patients with emergent, life-threatening conditions in obtaining care. The reason for such a decision, however, may not be to "ration" emergency treatment but rather to allow better management of the mix of patients whom the hospital admits or to avoid the uncompensated costs that result from providing uninsured emergency patients with the federally mandated assessment and stabilization.[21]

The policies listed in Cell 4 begin with those that explicitly limit access to healthcare but differ from those just described because they do not target either particular patients or particular interventions for a particular medical need. For example, state certificate-of-need (CON) laws—which were widely adopted in the 1970s as a means of inhibiting the overuse that occurs when the supply of facilities or expensive, high-tech equipment exceeds medically justified demand—require that healthcare organizations receive permission for such capital projects.[22] Although the CON process, which is still in place in more than thirty states, is intended to prevent inappropriate use of healthcare resources, it is a blunt instrument that cannot ensure that access to care will be based on relevant factors.

Many policies that intervene in the market for healthcare services fall into Cell 4. The low fee schedule for healthcare services established by most state Medicaid programs illustrates a policy that rations implicitly. Although intended to hold down public spending, this policy effectively limits access to care across the board (rather than particular interventions) for persons covered by Medicaid by rendering inaccessible many providers who are unwilling to accept payment at the level set by a state's Medicaid program.[23] The effect is indirect because whether a particular person does or does not have access to particular care of known benefit depends on factors extraneous to the policy, such as whether a patient is able to find a provider who can deliver the care for the fee set by the state or who is willing and able to

[20] *See* Mark A. Hall, *Informed Consent to Rationing Decisions*, 71 MILBANK Q. 645, 660 (1993).

[21] Although the Emergency Medical Treatment and Active Labor Act (EMTALA), 42 U.S. Code § 1395dd, which imposes these obligations, does not prevent a facility from billing patients for any emergency care delivered, only a fraction of these bills are ever paid.

[22] Certificate of need programs exist at both the federal (*see* 42 U.S.C. 1320a-1, added in 1972 as Sec. 1122 of the Social Security Act) and state levels (*see* National Conference of State Legislatures, *Certificate of Need: State Health Laws and Programs* (updated Apr. 2015), http://www.ncsl.org/research/health/con-certificate-of-need-state-laws.aspx, including breakdown of regulated facilities and services by state).

[23] *See, e.g.*, Armstrong v. Exceptional Child Center, Inc., 575 U.S. __ (Mar. 31, 2015) (*held*, the Medicaid Act's requirement that State reimbursement levels be "sufficient to enlist enough providers" gives the respondents, providers of "habilitation services," no private right of action against Idaho for setting rates below what providers could reasonably accept).

subsidize the expense of providing care to a Medicaid-insured patient based on income from other, better-insured patients.

The fact that indirect rationing is accomplished covertly does not necessarily make the policy's goals objectionable, as two of the examples at the bottom of Cell 4 show. An insurance company may try to hold down premiums by selecting for its network of "preferred providers" those physicians who charge the least. Such physicians may provide the same care as others in the community but simply be willing to accept a lower fee for providing it, or they may practice in a way that (prudently) utilizes fewer resources. Since the quality of care does not always correlate either with its price or its intensity, patients will not necessarily receive worse care from in-network physicians. But when insurers offer their policyholders substantial financial incentives, by way of lower copayments and deductibles, to use in-network physicians, they encourage physicians to ration care so as to qualify for the network by keeping their costs low.[24]

The last policy in Cell 4, "Physicians' decisions about how to use their own time and skills," illustrates how many decisions in the private, and specifically the professional, sector can have hidden, diffused effects in rationing care for individual patients despite their substantial systemic effects. Consider, for example, decisions about where to practice and in what specialty, which can either prevent or exacerbate the problems certain populations have in accessing medical care. At an extreme, were a large number of physicians to decide to restrict their practice to a small number of patients (i.e., "concierge medicine"), the care available to the remaining persons in the community could be measurably reduced.

c. Refining the Map in Light of the Characteristics of What Is Being Rationed

Many of policies in Cells 2, 3, and 4 aim to hold down healthcare spending by, in effect, rationing the funds from governments, insurers, patients, and other payers that are spent on healthcare rather than on other public and private goods and services. Money is "scarce" only in the sense that people have other things they want to buy with it—it is not scarce in an absolute sense, the way organs for transplantation are. To the extent that the rationing produced by such policies strikes people as unacceptable (on ethical, practical, or other grounds), it can be avoided by shifting money from its present uses to a use that will reduce or eliminate the objectionable rationing of healthcare.

Money is not only fungible but divisible, meaning that funds not spent for one big thing, whether within or outside of healthcare, can be spent on many smaller things instead. In contrast, the "absolutely scarce resources"[25] explicitly rationed by policies within Cell 1 may not be divisible or transferable among patients. A heart removed from a dead organ donor

[24] James C. Robinson, *Theory and Practice in the Design of Physician Payment Incentives*, 79 MILBANK Q. 149 (2001). Physicians "who serve poor and minority patients will not fare well in such an environment" because their costs may be driven up if their community has "a high percentage of sick patients who necessarily demand a more intense and costly provision of services." Note, *The Impact of Managed Care on Doctors Who Serve Poor and Minority Patients*, 108 HARV. L. REV. 1625, 1628 (1995).

[25] Peter A. Ubel & Susan Dorr Goold, *"Rationing" Health Care: Not All Definitions Are Created Equal*, 158 ARCH. INT. MED. 209, 210 (1998).

is nondivisible but is transferable until it is transplanted; once implanted in Patient A, it is cannot then be readily transferred to Patient B. An ICU bed also can only serve one patient at a time (nondivisible) but is transferable, as it can serve Patient A at Time X and then, if that person is removed after the elapse of Y hours, it can serve Patient B at Time X + Y. A scarce vaccine against a novel virus cannot be transferred once given to Patient A but might be divisible if a half-dose would provide some protection for both Patient A and Patient B (and so forth), at least until the manufacturer is able to supply the full amount needed by all patients. But in each case, the policy in question is explicitly about rationing and directly determines which patient gets what.

III Principles and Strategies for Achieving Ethical Healthcare Rationing

The contemporary application of ethical principles to medicine and research is commonly expressed in terms of four principles (beneficence, nonmaleficence, respect for persons, and justice), but discussions of the ethics of rationing, which are often presented in consequentialist, and specifically utilitarian, terms—that action is right which maximizes the net benefit to the population as a whole—are affected by, but not limited to, the iconic four.[26] Instead, in this arena, the concepts in competition are usually utilitarian distribution versus allocation based on theories of justice, as manifested in commitments to egalitarian principles and to fair process. The outcome of applying general principles and particular ethical strategies to various forms of rationing turns on the technically difficult task of specifying assessment measures for the philosophical abstractions and of identifying and gathering the data relevant to performing such assessments; reaching results that seem at once intuitively correct and ethically defensible depends less on having a single grand theory than on accepting mixed strategies, notwithstanding their undeniable imprecision.

a. The Central Principles: The Tension Between Utility and Justice

1. Maximizing Welfare: Achieving the utilitarian goal that the allocation of healthcare will maximize total benefits across the population requires agreement on how to measure benefit. The main options are the number of lives saved, which for example was the aim of the 2006 federal plan to distribute vaccine in the event of pandemic influenza,[27] or the number

[26] The dominant account of the four principles originated with the by now much revised Tom L. Beauchamp & James F. Childress, Principles of Biomedical Ethics (7th ed. 2012). Utility replaces beneficence and nonmaleficence as one of two main principles in organ allocation, along with justice, *in* Robert M. Veatch & Lainie F. Ross, Transplantation Ethics 285–305 (2nd ed. 2015), which also recognizes respect for persons as a "side constraint" on the other two.

[27] Ezekiel J. Emanuel & Alan Wertheimer, *Who Should Get Influenza Vaccine When Not All Can?*, 312 Sci. 854 (2006).

of years of life saved, as illustrated by "the exclusion of people with poor prognoses from organ transplant waiting lists."[28]

The first measure is grounded in a legal and ethical commitment to the equal value of each human life. In addition, it is much easier to administer, since it does not depend on having enough information about people to reliably predict their future with or without the interventions in question. All the same, patients who need the same intervention can have wildly different prognoses after receiving it. Thus, since the desire to maximize one's life expectancy is the primary rationale for most medical interventions, the number of life-years provided by the use of an intervention seems a better measure of its benefit. If, for example, a set of healthcare resources could either prevent the death of six twenty-five year-olds, with a prognosis that each would survive one year, or two twenty-five year-olds each with a life expectancy of forty more years if treated, the view that the latter is the preferable result would not accord with the moral intuitions of many people; moreover, anyone's choice between many short lives or a few long ones may vary in light of many factors, such as the ratio in numbers saved, the length of life extension (e.g., a day versus a year versus a decade), and the patients' ages.

Carrying this reasoning one step further, however, true net benefit can only be calculated if the quality of life as well as its length is considered.[29] Many utilitarians therefore favor using "quality-adjusted life-years" or QALYs (see "The Economics of Healthcare Rationing" chapter elsewhere in this volume). Taking the previous example, if the two survivors were expected to die after spending the next forty years in comas, while treating the six would produce excellent health for almost a year, followed by a very brief period of decline and a painless death, then QALY-maximization would favor saving the six (whose lives would be assigned a utility of 1.0 × 1 year × 6 people = 6.0) rather than the two (with a utility of perhaps .05 or less × 40 years × 2 people = 4.0).

Controversy attends the methods used by consequentialists (especially utilitarians) to determine which allocation of resources will maximize the well-being of a particular population. First, they favor aggregating all consequences to everyone, which is criticized on two grounds. From a Kantian perspective, the person whose great suffering will not be addressed because it is less than the sum of small benefits that the same resources would provide to many people is being treated "as a mere means to the improvement of [the latter's] welfare," and the aggregation of benefits "fails to take seriously the separateness of persons."[30] Further, as Frances Kamm has argued, certain minor improvements should be classified as "irrelevant utilities" that ought not count when comparing the well-being created by different allocations of a set of health resources.[31] Of course, people will differ concerning which benefits are either too trivial when compared to another harm (e.g., thousands of temporary headaches versus one death) or fall outside the realm in question[32] and thus should not count when determining benefits.

Second, a full account of benefit and harm would include indirect consequences. Indeed, policy-makers, such as legislators or heads of agencies, ought to include all consequences of

28 Govind Persad, Alan Wertheimer, & Ezekiel J. Emanuel, *Principles for Allocation of Scarce Medical Interventions*, 373 LANCET 423, 425 (2009).

29 Qualitative factors can also inflect the "lives saved" measure when a survivor's condition (such as permanent unconsciousness) may not constitute an existence that should count as a human life saved.

30 I. Glenn Cohen, *Rationing Legal Services*, 5 J. LEG. ANAL. 221, 269 (2013).

31 FRANCES KAMM, MORALITY, MORTALITY: DEATH AND WHOM TO SAVE FROM IT (1993).

32 Tim Scanlon offers the following hypothetical where one would not aggregate a harm suffered by many as the reason to fail to relieve a much different (and more serious) harm suffered by a single

macro-level allocation decisions that can be measured; this would include not only those that are indirect but also those that are in spheres other than health. But are indirect consequences, such as the better life that the dependents of a man with a mortal injury will have if treating him would restore him to his prior level of functioning, properly part of micro-allocation? Healthcare allocators are understandably "reluctant to take account of benefits and burdens to people other than candidates for treatment," since these calculations are usually impractical and quickly lead to considering "social worth," as illustrated by "the fiasco of the Seattle 'God committee,' which in the 1960s allocated scarce dialysis."[33] This criticism of taking indirect consequences into account seems justified in individual cases, lest "important" people (e.g., an entrepreneurial genius whose company might have to lay off thousands of workers were he to die prematurely) be favored always. When the rules guiding allocation themselves signal social values, however, that consequence should not be dismissed as indirect. For instance, a policy that plainly discriminates against a particular group, such as people with disabilities, could create disutility for group members and those who care about them.

Third, "[p]robably the most troubling implication of the QALY-maximization approach is that we should discriminate against disabled people in the distribution of life-saving treatment, as they have, on average, a lower quality of life."[34] This problem can be avoided if the measure of benefit is the increment (or detriment) in utility between a person's prior state (before he or she developed the need for the intervention in question) and the state the person will be in after the intervention. A disabled person whose prior level of function will be restored would thus not be disadvantaged by the QALY with which he or she began being lower than a nondisabled person's.[35] Moreover, in ordinary cases (unlike the hypothetical of the forty-year coma), differences in length of life swamp differences in quality.[36]

person: Suppose a fifteen-minute interruption of the broadcast of the World Cup's final hour (which would disappoint millions of viewers) is needed in order to extricate one man who has become trapped in the television station's transmitter room, suffering very painful electric shocks. Scanlon's conclusion that we should not delay the rescue seems right because the categories of harm diverge so much in their seriousness. Thomas M. Scanlon, What We Owe to Each Other 238–239 (1998). *See also* the discussion of "separate spheres," *infra* at the text accompanying note 48.

[33] Stein, *supra* note 13, at 213–214. Such third party effects are often included when allocating scarce life-saving treatments and vaccines during an epidemic or disaster to "essential" personnel (e.g., prioritizing the people who manufacture drugs and vaccines, the doctors and nurses who administer them, the undertakers who safely dispose of the dead) The difficulty here is to ensure that people in question are essential to the "function" being supported, rather than simply being well connected to the rule-makers. The instrumental value in enabling *future* usefulness could be extended to priority based on "reciprocity" for *prior* usefulness, to encourage people to make choices that contribute to collective welfare, such as being a living organ donor or serving in the armed forces. Here, too, the question is where to draw the line (e.g., whether to include "healthy lifestyle choices that reduced their need for resources," Persad, Wertheimer, & Emanuel, *supra* note 28, at 426).

[34] Stein, *supra* note 13, at 214.

[35] The proposition that disabilities result in lower QALYs is contested, as people with disabilities report more satisfaction with the quality of their lives than external assessments provide; part of the difference arises because such assessments may be framed in terms of sudden loss (for example, going from being able to walk to paraplegia as result of an accident) rather than as a gradual decline or a condition present throughout life.

[36] *See* Stein, *supra* note 13, at 215. Further, he suggests that, "utilitarian distributive theory should give greater weight to the objective of maximizing the happiness of existing people than to the objective of preserving in existence those people who are happiest."

The deontological counterpart to the utilitarian's focus on collective maximization of benefit is the principle of beneficence, which holds that healthcare professionals' duty is to maximize their patients' welfare (at least to the extent welfare is dependent on health status), without regard to any resultant good for society.[37] In recent years, however, attempts have been made to broaden physicians' obligations to include responsible stewardship of the resources placed under their control "so that as many health care needs as possible can be met, whether in the physician's office, in the hospital or long-term care facility, or at home."[38] Transparency and public involvement that facilitate patients being aware of and accepting—or, better, participating in the making of—the policies that aim to ration care will become increasingly important if this becomes a guiding principle not just for policy-makers but also for individual healthcare practitioners.

2. Justice: The principle of justice relates to rationing in three ways: nondiscrimination, interpersonal equality, and fair process. First, it is basic that neither the state nor the private institutions that provide most healthcare in the United States may lawfully engage in invidious discrimination, which arises when people are denied access to medical goods or services based on an ever-expanding range of characteristics, including their race, ethnicity, or national origin, as well as religion, gender, and sexual orientation.[39] Reliance on personal characteristics that are irrelevant to people's need for and claim on healthcare wrongs them not only by denying them any benefits the care could provide but also by demeaning them as persons unworthy of equal respect and concern.[40] The matter is complicated, however, in light of the role that some policies for allocating scarce resources give to age and disability, two personal characteristics that are protected in some circumstances by antidiscrimination laws but for which principled ethical arguments are made in the context of allocating scarce medical resources. Further, income and wealth have a large impact on access to healthcare but are usually not incorporated into nondiscrimination laws despite the reduced access that "facially neutral" rules for allocating goods and services through marketplace transactions produce for members of racial, ethnic, and other groups that are supposed to be protected from discrimination.[41]

[37] The duty not only places the welfare of patients above benefits to the provider and society but, at its most robust, authorizes providers to treat patients paternalistically so as to produce what in the providers' view would be the best expected outcomes. This pits beneficence against the principle of autonomy, under which the choice of which outcomes to seek lies with patients.

[38] Lois Snyder, *American College of Physicians Ethics Manual, Sixth Edition*, 156 ANN. INTERN. MED. 73, 86 (2012) (discussing "The Ethics of Practice: The Changing Practice Environment").

[39] For example, Title VI of the Civil Rights Act of 1964 prohibits any program or activity receiving federal financial assistance from engaging in intentional discrimination based on a person's race, color, or national origin, and directs federal agencies to adopt regulations that prohibit recipients of funds from using criteria or methods of administering their programs that have the effect of subjecting individuals to discrimination based on these factors even if their actions are not intentionally discriminatory. 42 U.S.C. § 2000d.

[40] Denying equal opportunity "is an existential rejection disproportionate to the value of the good or welfare that the opportunity might have afforded." John Harris, *Justice and Equal Opportunities in Health Care*, 13 BIOETHICS 392, 399 (1999).

[41] Disparate health outcomes for racial and ethnic minorities result not simply from racist policies and attitudes but also from the socioeconomic disadvantages that often align with membership in a minority group. *See generally* W. MICHAEL BYRD & LINDA A. CLAYTON, AN AMERICAN HEALTH DILEMMA: A MEDICAL HISTORY OF AFRICAN AMERICANS AND THE PROBLEM OF RACE: 1900 TO PRESENT (2002).

The second manifestation of justice in the context of rationing is the egalitarian precept that treating people fairly means treating them as having equal moral status.[42] This can translate into making sure that each person receives an equal amount of something valuable or has an equal chance of obtaining it, which is sometimes termed "resource egalitarianism." For certain items, such as being able to cast a vote in an election, simple equality makes sense. But in the medical context, people have wildly unequal needs—a person with end-stage liver failure has a much greater need for a donated liver than a person with temporarily subnormal hepatic function. As a logical matter, then, groups would consist of people that share salient characteristics; as an ethical matter, fairness is manifest when likes are treated alike. This theory of equitable (rather than equal) distribution is sometimes termed "welfare egalitarianism"; it aims for roughly comparable health outcomes as a result of grouping people based on their need for the medical intervention in question or on the benefit they are expected to derive from receiving it.[43]

This turns out, however, to be just the starting point regarding a very contested topic: On what grounds may people be sorted into groups when beneficial interventions will be allocated among the groups? Several reasons have been suggested for treating age, for example, as an easy-to-measure sorting criterion. First, age may be a proxy for prognosis: If a twenty-year-old and a sixty-year-old are both healthy except for having a particular disease, for which only enough medicine is available to treat one (with an equal likelihood of cure), then treating the former would yield more benefit because once cured she has a much longer life expectancy than the latter. Nonetheless, it is often true that many other factors (such as comorbidities) are more important than age when predicting life-expectancy post-treatment, so relying on age may simply reflect a prejudice (older people's assumed shorter life expectancy). Second, even when an intervention would add the same number of years to the life of a twenty-year-old or a sixty-year-old, the marginal utility of life-years may diminish with age. While age does not necessarily determine marginal utility, as a sixty-one-year-old can enjoy life as much as a twenty-one-year-old, the average sixty-one-year-old would probably think that his "life satisfaction would have been reduced substantially more" by the loss of the year between his twentieth and twenty-first birthdays than if he had not made it from sixty to sixty-one, so that "we may think that the years beyond some late age contribute less to our welfare than do earlier years."[44]

Another ground for taking age into account is so-called "fair innings": Older persons have by definition already lived longer than younger ones, so that to give a scarce treatment to an older person and let a younger one die would be "inherently inequitable" since "the younger person would get no more years than the relatively few he has already had, whereas the older person, who has already had more than the younger person, will get several years more."[45]

[42] *See* JOHN HARRIS, THE VALUE OF LIFE (1985). This version of justice coincides with the utilitarian principle of maximizing the number of lives saved, which also rests on the notion of all lives possessing infinite value, which by definition is equivalent for all.

[43] RONALD DWORKIN, SOVEREIGN VIRTUE: THE THEORY AND PRACTICE OF EQUALITY 285–303 (2000) (describing these two types of egalitarianism). Outside of pure dignity, welfare egalitarianism seems the more important concept because access to (enough) *resources* is valued mostly as a means of reaching a beneficial *outcome*.

[44] Stein, *supra* note 13, at 219.

[45] Michael Lockwood, *Quality of Life and Resource Allocation*, *in* PHILOSOPHY AND MEDICAL WELFARE 50 (J. M. Bell & Susan Mendus eds., 1988).

This age-based argument is thus a version of the general proposition that a fair system will aim to make the worst-off group relatively better off. (A young person is worse off in terms of the quantity of something inherently valuable—years of life—which she possesses.) But the principle of favoring the worst off could lead instead to favoring those people who, perhaps burdened by disease, have had the fewest QALYs—not necessarily correlated with their chronological age.

A focus on the worst off (often identified with John Rawls' "maximin" principle[46]) can also translate into the rule of "sickest first," which prioritizes those whose medical conditions are worse (quadriplegia versus paraplegia) or for whom death is most imminent in the absence of the scarce medical intervention (such as a transplanted heart) they need to fix their condition.[47] Like the youngest-first method for allocating resources discussed previously, sickest-first ignores post-treatment prognosis. That is actually more problematic in this case because the very sickest patients are not only in greatest need but often least able to weather a major operation, which is why sickest-first is not used in disaster triage, where the emphasis is on using limited resources to produce the greatest total gains (whether in terms of lives or life-years).

Another objection to using imminence of death to determine which group is worst off is that it does not account for other aspects of people's lives that make them better or worse off than others, although some argue that those are "separate spheres" that should not be considered when allocating healthcare. In that view, prioritizing the sickest is based on the premise that healthcare is an "all-purpose means necessary for the pursuit of nearly all people's aims and ends" such that "its loss may not be able to be compensated for by other goods."[48] Yet the very instrumental nature of healthcare and even of health itself, which is valued because it provides the well-being on which all else depends, supports a more holistic view in which "health care allocations [are] merely one tool" with which to meet the goal of giving "overall better lives to those with overall worse lives."[49] A second objection to using imminence of death is that it focuses solely on a moment in time. If a shortage (say, of a drug) is temporary, then prioritizing patients who will die without immediate treatment, in preference to those who can wait for new supplies to arrive, makes sense. But when scarcity is persistent, as for transplantable organs, focusing solely on urgency would be "myopic,"[50] since assigning a donated heart to Patient A, who will die in the next day without it rather than to Patient B, for whom it is equally well suited, on the ground that that Patient B is expected to survive for a week without a transplant would be arbitrary if the chance of a suitable heart being donated in the next week is very small. Patients A and B are actually equally badly off.

[46] JOHN RAWLS, A THEORY OF JUSTICE 133 (rev. ed. 1999).

[47] The imminence-of-death version of sickest-first is sometimes equated with the "Rule of Rescue," the felt need to save identifiable individuals facing perilous circumstances. *See* Cohen, *supra* note 30, at 259. The usual (and valid) critique of the Rule—that it diverts to efforts to rescue a few people from imminent death resources that could prevent a much larger number of unidentified people ("statistical lives") ever falling into peril—is inapplicable here, however, because sickest-first is typically invoked to determine which of two (or more) otherwise similar *identified* individuals should be prioritized for treatment with a resource that can only treat one.

[48] Dan Brock, *Priority to the Worse Off in Health-Care Resource Prioritization*, *in* MEDICINE AND SOCIAL JUSTICE: ESSAYS ON THE DISTRIBUTION OF HEALTH CARE 362, 368 (Rosamund Rhodes et al. eds., 2002).

[49] Cohen, *supra* note 30, at 250.

[50] Persad, Wertheimer, & Emanuel, *supra* note 28, at 425.

What, then, of adopting justice-based allocation strategies that avoid characteristics that could be regarded as socially or culturally biased? Some have suggested a "first come, first served" allocation as both simple to administer and defensible on egalitarian or prioritarian grounds.[51] Others have critiqued it as "corrupt" in practice, since wealthier and better informed persons queue at multiple centers, which improves their chances, and as insensitive to relevant factors, since one's place in line may have nothing to do with one's need or suitability for the intervention being rationed.[52]

Lotteries, another egalitarian strategy, avoid the problem of corruption but share both first-come's virtues of speed and simplicity and its blindness to significant differences among people's need for, and potential to benefit from, the rationed resource. If such differences are sufficiently critical, separate lotteries could be conducted among groups that have been sorted by the relevant criteria (e.g., prognosis). Or such criteria could be used to assign some people larger numbers of chances in the lottery.[53] Still, to preserve the egalitarian goal, allocators must avoid going overboard in refining the groups, since a main attraction of lotteries is that they "prevent small differences [measured in prioritarian or prognostic terms, such as sickness or age] from drastically affecting outcome."[54]

The arguments discussed thus far concern the substantive content of rules for judging the fairness of rationing, but one could focus instead on fair decision-making processes. Fairness can be based on certain formal procedural criteria, such as the transparency of policy formation or application, the extent to which all affected parties can participate, the appropriateness of the decision-maker (a neutral party to apply rules fairly to individual cases; a broadly representative democratic body to formulate policy), the availability of appeals, the possibility of policy revisions, and the assurance that the procedures will be followed (all of which appear in "accountability for reasonableness," the leading account of procedural fairness in healthcare allocation).[55] Or procedural fairness can be judged by the ethical acceptability or legitimacy of the results. Each version of fair process may work in one circumstance but not another (e.g., selecting the people who will receive a scarce vaccine in an epidemic versus setting eligibility rules for public health insurance), but the former has gained more support because it claims to avoid the substantive approach's weakness, namely that ethical values and strategies are too disputed, both among theorists and among the public and policymakers, to provide solutions to real problems. For example, Norman Daniels urges reliance on fair process because "we have no consensus on principled solutions to a family of morally controversial rationing problems, and general principles of justice for health and healthcare fail to give specific guidance about how to solve them."[56]

[51] American Thoracic Society Bioethics Task Force, *Fair Allocation of Intensive Care Unit Resources*, 156 Am. J. Respir. Crit. Care Med. 1282 (1997); Lockwood, *supra* note 45, at 224.

[52] Persad, Wertheimer, & Emanuel, *supra* note 28, at 424.

[53] Dan Brock, *Justice and the ADA: Does Prioritizing and Rationing Health Care Discriminate Against the Disabled?* 12 Soc. Phil. & Pol'y 159, 168 (1995). This sort of "weighted lottery" might better be described as an egalitarian constraint on a utilitarian (i.e., prognosis-based) allocation because the person who is less likely to benefit still has a small chance of "winning."

[54] Persad, Wertheimer, & Emanuel, *supra* note 28, at 423. "Prioritarian" distribution, which directs benefits to the worst off, can be defended on egalitarian (relativistic) or absolute grounds. Derek Parfit, *Equality and Priority*, 10 Ratio 202, 213–221 (1997).

[55] Norman Daniels & James Sabin, Setting Limits Fairly: Learning to Share Resources for Health (2nd ed. 2008).

[56] Norman Daniels, *Justice, Health, and Healthcare*, 1 Am. J. Bioethics 2, 9 (2001).

Nevertheless, to avoid the countervailing complaint that a purely procedural approach could lead to results that are not well grounded ethically,[57] accountability for reasonableness includes, as one of its four "conditions" (in addition to "publicity," "appeals and revisions," and "enforcement"), the "relevance condition," which is met when the "rationales for limit-setting decisions" provide "a *reasonable* explanation of how the organization seeks to provide 'value for money' in meeting the varied health needs of a defined population under reasonable resource constraints." In turn, a rationale is reasonable "if it appeals to the evidence, reasons, and principles that are accepted as relevant by fair-minded people who are disposed to finding mutually justifiable terms of cooperation."[58] Yet this formulation is at once too vague to exclude anything other than frankly discriminatory processes and too dependent on underlying substantive principles, which "cannot be left aside and replaced entirely with a procedural account that does not specifically address the underlying principles."[59] Even with the addition of further conditions, as others have suggested,[60] Daniels and Sabin's proposal, like any "fair process" for healthcare rationing, ends up as a means of implementing, rather than replacing, principles such as utility and justice.

3. The Interaction of the Principles: Utilitarians and egalitarians often regard their competing theories like Titans in battle, but in the context of articulating strategies for legitimately rationing healthcare interventions they seem more like a married couple whose offspring combine aspects of each. Occasionally, only one is apparent; for example, were the government to establish public insurance for people who cannot afford to purchase insurance, it would be unacceptable—ethically or legally—to exclude on utilitarian grounds (e.g., because saving their lives will provide less benefit to society than the cost of the insurance) some of the people who meet the income-eligibility criteria for the insurance. On the other hand, the principle of utility could be joined with the justice principle in structuring the insurance program, as the particular treatments that will be paid for might be adjusted based on cost-benefit calculations, to get the largest amount of benefit within a set budget, as was attempted by the Oregon Health Plan.

The major proposed strategies for rationing healthcare all involve mixed approaches, though not all acknowledge that reality. Emanuel and colleagues, for example, have developed a "life-cycle" or "complete lives" analysis combining utilitarian and justice principles: They base their system "on the idea that each person should have an opportunity to live through all the stages of life"[61] with "a core commitment to consider entire lives rather than events or episodes,"[62] but also include a modified "youngest first" preference for adolescents

[57] "Kerstein and Bognar [*infra* note 64] stand with us in criticizing the claim that fair procedures, on their own, can ensure just allocation." Govind C. Persad, Alan Wertheimer, & Ezekiel J. Emanuel, *Standing by Our Principles: Meaningful Guidance, Moral Foundations, and Multi-Principle Methodology in Medical Scarcity*, 10 AM. J. BIOETHICS 46, 48 (Apr. 2010).

[58] DANIELS & SABIN, *supra* note 55, at 44.

[59] Lindsay M. Sabik & Reidar K. Lie, *Principles versus Procedures in Making Health Care Coverage Decisions: Addressing Inevitable Conflicts*, 29 THEO. MED. & BIOETHICS 73, 84 (2008).

[60] Ezekiel J. Emanuel, *Book Review: Setting Limits Fairly: Can We Learn to Share Medical Resources*, 347 NEW ENG. J. MED. 953 (2002) (adding "fair consideration" through mechanisms to assess and incorporate every person's preferences, and "empowerment" through means for people to participate in decisions); Annette Rid, *Justice and Procedure: How Does "Accountability for Reasonableness" Result in Fair Limit-setting Decisions?*, 35 J. MED. ETHICS 12 (2009) (adding "consistency" and "impartiality").

[61] Emanuel & Wertheimer, *supra* note 27, at 854–855.

[62] Persad, Wertheimer, & Emanuel, *supra* note 28, at 428. The reference point is the typical life span in a given society, rather than the years needed to afford a fair equality of opportunity to complete one's life plan. NORMAN DANIELS, JUST HEALTH CARE 41 (1985).

and young adults (roughly fifteen to forty years old). As secondary considerations, the system also incorporates "saving the most lives," would rely on people's "instrumental value" in a public health emergency, and uses a lottery to choose between roughly equivalent potential recipients of a scarce intervention. Despite valid criticisms (e.g., can a preference for the lives of fifteen-year-olds over those of ten-year-olds ethically be built based simply on public opinion?), their "framework" is impressive in its aim of simultaneously maximizing benefits, prioritizing the worst off, and treating similar people equally.[63] Yet its inclusion of so many factors, which would impede its practical utility, mostly demonstrates that all are needed, at least in reserve, to adjust counterintuitive results. Thus, notwithstanding some attempts to create a "baseline" algorithm to deal with the conflicts that often arises between principles,[64] Emanuel et al. concede that any achievable multiprinciple framework will be "standard-like," guiding rather than precisely specifying a decision.[65]

Another example, Norman Daniels' "just health care," is a facially egalitarian theory. Access to healthcare for individuals whose "normal species functioning" has been impaired by a disease or disability should be "governed by a principle of fair equality of opportunity."[66] The availability of an intervention to "prevent, cure, or compensate for" their condition should reflect the relative curtailment of individuals' "normal opportunity range."[67] This principle is in line with a Rawlsian requirement that policies should make the situation of the worst off relatively better off. But as formulated, fair equality of opportunity would direct all resources preferentially to the sickest, whose normal opportunity range is the most limited, even though not all these people would experience improvements that they or others would regard as worthwhile.

To avoid this result, Daniels brings in a form of utilitarianism through his account of intergenerational justice, which depends on "prudent deliberators" behind a veil of ignorance designing the institutions that will distribute "fair shares of basic social goods over the lifespan" without knowing the medical conditions they individually will have.[68] Daniels claims that this differs from utilitarianism, which "allows us to take from some people to give to others" when that would maximize total welfare; his prudential deliberation only allows rationing "when it does better for each of us to budget resources over the lifespan in a certain way"[69] (such as by having some personal-care and social-support services available for elderly persons with mild disabilities, rather than only high-tech medical services for acutely ill people of the same age). This is still a form of utilitarianism because "we cannot decide whether one generation would benefit more from resources than another generation unless we know what the best use of those resources is for each generation."[70] That Daniels' recipe

63 Persad, Wertheimer, & Emanuel, *supra* note 28, at 429.

64 *See* Samuel J. Kerstein & Greg Bognar, *Complete Lives in the Balance*, 10 AM. J. BIOETHICS 37, 43 (Apr. 2010).

65 Persad, Wertheimer, & Emanuel, *supra* note 57, at 46.

66 DANIELS, *supra* note 62, at 41 & 57.

67 *Id.* at 35.

68 NORMAN DANIELS, AM I MY PARENTS' KEEPER? AN ESSAY ON JUSTICE BETWEEN THE YOUNG AND THE OLD 40 (1988).

69 *Id.* at 95.

70 Stein, *supra* note 13, at 236. Stein argues that anti-utilitarians like Daniels and Dworkin smuggle in such calculations because considerations of relative benefit predominate in the decision-making of their "hypothetical choosers." *Id.* at 237.

for "just health care" is not purely egalitarian may make it slightly messier to apply, but it also makes it more likely that the results will make sense.

4. An Illustration of the Mixed Methodology: The manner in which the United Network for Organ Sharing (UNOS) allocates organs from deceased donors illustrates how the mix of ethical strategies and methods of decisions depends on the various factors identified in the topography of rationing policies.[71] UNOS strives to produce and rely on scientific evidence regarding the evaluation of donated organs and transplant outcomes, but the allocation systems for various organs diverge both because of differences in end-stage failure with each organ and in the ethical principles on which policy-makers at UNOS have relied in using the evidence.

The framework for liver allocation is both utilitarian (prognosis, based on which group of recipients should do best with an organ) and prioritarian (sickest first). Disturbingly high geographic disparities in transplant candidates' access to livers (and hence how sick they are when they receive a transplant and how likely they are to die while waiting), led UNOS in 2014 to begin rethinking how utility—which produces a preference for recipients being local (or, if not, then within the UNOS region) so as to improve outcomes by minimizing the time between procurement and implantation of the organ—is balanced against fairness. Since the local and regional boundaries are largely artifacts of history, broader and more logically constructed areas might allow donated livers to go to more patients whose need is urgent, thus reducing total deaths.[72]

Given the availability of dialysis, urgency does not play the same role in UNOS' new kidney allocation system, which went into effect on December 4, 2014, after ten years of open (sometimes heated) discussion among a wide range of stakeholders.[73] The mixed system involves egalitarian constrains on a dominant utilitarian strategy, framed in terms of life-years maximized but with the expectation of also benefiting a larger number of kidney patients.[74] Interestingly, some critics of the new policy characterize it as both anti-utilitarian

[71] The United Network for Organ Sharing (UNOS) is the private organization that operates the Organ Procurement and Transplantation Network (OPTN), which was authorized by the National Organ Transplantation Act of 1984, 42 U.S.C. §§273–274, to develop a national system to provide all transplant candidates with equitable access to deceased organs based on objective medical criteria. OPTN Final Rule, 42 C.F.R. §§121 et seq. (2014) (issued on Apr. 2, 1998).

[72] *See* OPTN/UNOS Liver and Intestinal Organ Transplantation Committee, *Redesigning Liver Distribution to Reduce Variation in Access to Liver Transplantation* (2014), http://optn.transplant.hrsa.gov/ContentDocuments/Liver_Concepts_2014.pdf, updated at http://optn.transplant.hrsa.gov/news/liver-forum-and-committee-update-june-2015/ (adding concept of basing allocation on concentric circles around donor location). A survey on the concept paper allowed respondents to indicate the relative importance of factors such as life-years-saved, quality of life, and reduced geographic variations in transplant recipients' illness severity. Although the UNOS committee describes the alternatives mostly in technical terms, http://optn.transplant.hrsa.gov/ContentDocuments/Liver_Survey_Report.pdf, the concept paper explicitly recognizes that the new system should consider how to enhance "utility and efficiency" while looking also to increase "equity or fairness" (p. 8).

[73] Transplant physicians and potential recipients had been dissatisfied with the previous system, which produced a discard rate that was higher than necessary given the quality of the kidneys, variability in access for candidates who are harder to match for biologic reasons, and allocations that resulted in unrealized graft survival years for many transplanted kidneys.

[74] The system will match kidneys likely to function the longest with the 20% of candidates thought to have the longest life expectancy, but utility was bounded by several egalitarian restrictions, such as providing more opportunities to candidates with rarer blood types or immune systems incompatible

(it will not maximize total life-years) and anti-egalitarian (e.g., it disadvantages type 1 diabetics who have typically been in the "worst-off" category for many years).[75]

No absolute, widely agreed formula exists to determine what mixture of which utilitarian strategies and which justice strategies should be used in what process when creating or applying rationing-related policies. Having characterized such policies based on their location in the topography as developed in Part II, decision-makers should apply a framework that can be defended both a priori and a posteriori and, ideally, that is acceptable to, if not wholly embraced by, those affected. As one moves from policies in the upper reaches of Cell 1 to those in the lower reaches of Cell 4, the effects of each policy become more diffuse, and the possibility of providing a refined calculation of relative benefit among those affected becomes lower, so decision-makers should instead employ policies that maximize net utility within the constraints of justice, especially protecting from disparate treatment those who are worse off and members of groups legally protected against overt discrimination.

IV Conclusion

This chapter has made four central points about healthcare rationing. The first and most fundamental is that policies and practices of consciously limiting access to a medical intervention of known benefit are an inescapable reality in contemporary healthcare.

Second, the main mistake in assessing this reality comes from not seeing that it is multiple realities. One involves absolutely scarce resources—paradigmatically, organs donated from deceased persons for transplantation, where the allocation process is broadly accepted, even by those with the most to lose, because it is driven by necessity rather than being imposed by public or private decision-makers for other purposes, such as cost containment, and it adheres to a "fair process" that is transparent and that employs standards which reflect defensible criteria rather than prejudice (age, sex, race, etc.) or privilege, which have been extensively and publicly debated not just by ethicists but also by physicians, patient advocates, and others with a stake in the outcome, and which are periodically revised in light of experience and new analysis. Most important to the legitimacy of this type of rationing is that one person having been deprived of something (e.g., a donated organ) results in its being given to another, more suitable person.

Most rationing (i.e., nearly all of the policies in Cells 2, 3, and 4 in Figure 40.1) is very different because it is not compelled by a scarcity of goods and services but results from public and private decisions. Patients and providers often lack confidence in the rationality and fairness of the outcomes, and some of the policies—for example, incentivizing physicians to employ a diagnostic test that is marginally less effective but substantially less expensive, as a means of containing costs—challenge the ethical basis of the traditional physician-patient relationship. Until the medical profession articulates (as it has begun to), and the public

with most donor kidneys. *The New Kidney Allocation System (KAS) Frequently Asked Questions* (2014), http://optn.transplant.hrsa.gov/converge/ContentDocuments/KAS_FAQs.pdf.

[75] *See, e.g.*, Lainie Ross, *New Kidney Allocation Proposal Is Ethically Unacceptable*, U.S. News & World Report, Nov. 12, 2012, http://www.usnews.com/opinion/articles/2012/11/12/new-kidney-allocation-proposal-is-ethically-unacceptable.

concurs regarding, when and how it is legitimate for physicians to take account of collective interests, rationing based on policies of this sort may be equated with encouraging unethical conduct.[76]

Further, this sort of "structural rationing"—such as requiring certificates of need for capital projects, public and private insurance programs setting low levels in fee schedules for professional and ancillary services—produces very dispersed effects. Many people treat the resulting allocations—who does or does not receive what care in which settings—as simply manifesting "the market" at work, without taking into account how extensively the market for healthcare is a product of policy choices, including the decision to rely on markets to allocate healthcare products and services, and, very significantly, insurance, in the first place. Most important, the lack of transparency means one cannot be sure that any savings such policies generate are being used to benefit other patients or even used for some other socially beneficial end.[77] If U.S. policy-makers want to lower resistance to healthcare rationing, they will need to get our market-based, decentralized "system" to truly operate as one. While the Affordable Care Act includes many provisions that encourage such a development, the debate over that law also underscores that we are very unlikely to see anything like a global health budget anytime soon. Still, the emphasis on organizations taking responsibility for the health of large groups of patients may result in more people recognizing that they will be on the receiving as well as the giving end of healthcare allocations, which has its own ethical payoff: "Making scarcity and priority setting everyone's concern seems, if anything, only fair."[78]

Third, we need to be alert for the rationing inherent in policies developed for other reasons and to ask whether their benefits justify the costs of that rationing. For example, proponents of a policy that would make some patented pharmaceuticals much more scarce and expensive, meaning that it will not be possible to provide them to all patients,[79] ought to have to substantiate rather than merely hypothesize the policy's benefits (such as in underwriting the costs of discovering new treatments), and those should then be compared with the costs not merely of depriving some patients of those drugs but of having to employ mechanisms for rationing, the use of which generates social costs. Relatedly, when rationing is a policy's implicit goal, rather than a side effect, making that explicit should actually improve the acceptance of rationing, as justifications are offered for choices that are now largely opaque.

[76] *See, e.g.*, Mark A. Hall, *The Public's Preference for Bedside Rationing*, 156 ARCH. INTERN. MED. 1353 (1996) (polling data show overwhelming public support for having panels of physicians make rationing choices and some support for physicians doing it "at the bedside," while systems run by insurers, employers, or the government found little support). Individual physicians, who lack both relevant expertise and real authority, are unlikely ever to assume the decision-making responsibilities of officials who aim to be good global welfare-maximizers in setting policies and allocating resources to achieve a wide range of goals; the clinical contexts in which physicians make micro-allocations are not set up to enable them to take into account the full range of benefits and costs generated by those decisions. Cohen, *supra* note 30, at 280, *citing* Dan Brock, *Separate Spheres and Indirect Benefits*, 1 COST EFFECTIVENESS & RESOURCE ALLOCAT. 4, 14 (2003).

[77] *See* Norman Daniels, *The Ideal Advocate and Limited Resources*, 8 THEOR. MED. 69 (1987).

[78] Friedman & Danis, *supra* note 18, at 186.

[79] Amy Kapczynski, *The Trans-Pacific Partnership—Is It Bad for Your Health?*, 373 NEW ENG. J. MED. 201 (2015).

Finally, our attention would be better focused on whether rationing is being done well rather than on whether it should be done at all, as inevitably it must be. Yet no single template exists for evaluating the ethics of all types of healthcare rationing. The major relevant principles, utility and justice, generate competing strategies; when the practitioners of each lay out actual recommendations, they inevitably incorporate aspects of the rival, and neither in its pure form yields wholly defensible results in any but a few cases within the category of absolute scarcity, which is the realm in which they are most frequently invoked. We need more efforts to adjust the existing analyses to structural rationing where policies affect the healthcare system broadly rather than deciding who within a small group of identified patients gets a particular scarce resource.[80] It is particularly within this broader domain that the divide between principle- and procedure-based rationing is illusory: An ethical strategy will be judged legitimate in part based on whether the process that produced it was appropriate for the policy-making setting and embodied transparency, reviewability, consistency, and clarity about the ethical principles being used. Likewise, all attempts to construct a "fair process" for health resource allocation must not only take into account culture and context but also rest on a recognized, sound set of ethical principles. Some such frameworks already exist in state and federal law and in the processes used by private actors. They are not now and may never be perfect, but they can get better as they are revised in light of experience and the public's response. With attention to the multiple ethical approaches and the complex policy terrain described in this chapter, they may be able to function well enough to gain respect for healthcare rationing within a democracy.

[80] This shift in focus to rationales for broader policies would also avoid the dependence of the scarce-resource scenarios on idealized representations of the decisive factors, especially prognosis, which can never be known with such precision in the real world.

CHAPTER 41

THE ECONOMICS OF HEALTHCARE RATIONING

MICHAEL FRAKES, MATTHEW B. FRANK, AND KYLE ROZEMA

ANOTHER chapter in this volume discussed various ethical considerations surrounding the rationing of healthcare. Any study of the rationing of goods and services, however, would be incomplete without the consideration of economic analysis. The need for rationing in the first instance arguably encapsulates the essence of economics itself. Though many definitions abound, economics is often described as the study of how individuals and agents of society allocate scarce resources among competing desires. Clearly, individuals cannot each acquire and consume all of the products and services that they want without limitation. Many, if not all, goods and services must be "rationed" in some manner. In this chapter, we provide a brief overview of healthcare rationing through the lens of economic analysis.

At the outset, it is worth saying a bit about the term "rationing," which is often thrown around rather loosely by the media. In the broadest sense, rationing can be interpreted as *any* means of limiting individuals' consumption of products and services. This perspective implies that prices can ration. After all, those unwilling to pay the price for a particular good or service may be excluded from consuming or receiving it. Moreover, the first fundamental welfare theorem of economics holds that price mechanisms in competitive markets will, under a restrictive set of assumptions, perform this necessary allocation of resources in a Pareto-efficient manner—that is, it would be impossible to reallocate resources so as to make someone better off without making another worse off. Some economists, however, have uneasy feelings about referring to the free market's price mechanism as a means of rationing. Rather, "rationing" is often used as a term of art by many economists to explain any number of ways that policy-makers and industry participants influence who consumes what healthcare services, excluding from this definition the distribution of goods and services via market-clearing forces. For the purposes of this chapter, we largely refer to rationing in this more limited context.

If prices theoretically generate Pareto-efficient outcomes, one may wonder why nonprice means of rationing are even warranted in the first place. One reason lies in the failures of the assumptions of perfect completion inherent in the first fundamental welfare theorem of economics. While it is beyond the scope of this chapter to discuss in depth the various market failures in the healthcare system, it is well known that certain features of this system cause it to deviate from the assumptions necessary to achieve Pareto efficiency. Such sources of failure include, among others, agency costs stemming from informational asymmetries between physicians and patients (sometimes manifesting in "physician induced demand" of excessive services) and moral hazard in healthcare utilization caused by third-party payment relationships. These features of healthcare markets may contribute to supra-optimal levels of healthcare utilization that may be crowding out spending on other nonhealth goods that likewise contribute to social welfare. Total spending aside, such market failures may also lead to inefficient utilization of some types of health services over others. These arguably undesirable outcomes have motivated policy-makers and industry participants to design nonprice means of rationing services, some of which are briefly summarized in this chapter.

A second reason for society's unwillingness to rely solely on price mechanisms to ration healthcare may arise from noneconomic considerations altogether. Even if prices were to generate Pareto-efficient outcomes, it may not necessarily be the case that such outcomes are ultimately desired. Economists evaluate policy issues by attempting to maximize specified social welfare functions. The maximization calculus inherent in this exercise need not collapse to one focused exclusively on economic efficiency, the kind of which price competition is meant to produce. Social welfare optimization criteria can, and often do, incorporate various distributional considerations. Metaphorically speaking, when structuring healthcare rationing programs, we do not just care about the size of the pie (efficiency considerations, generally); we also care about how it is sliced. This analysis necessarily transcends economics. Key inputs into this optimization problem—that is, how exactly do we value different distributions of the pie—derive from ethical and philosophical considerations. Because another chapter in this volume deals exclusively with the ethical side of this coin, we largely abstract away from such matters in the discussion to follow.[1]

[1] Commentators have identified a range of normative frameworks to guide this welfare analysis. Such guiding principles include: (1) "first-come-first-serve" (assigning priority to individuals simply on the basis of time), *see* American Thoracic Society, *Fair Allocation of intensive Care Unit Resources*, 156 AM. J. RESPIR. CRIT. CARE MED. 1282 (1997); *but see* Norman Daniels, *Fair Process in Patient Selection for Antiretroviral Treatment in WHO's Goal of 3 by 5*, 366 LANCET 169 (2005); (2) "instrumental value" (assigning priority to patients who contribute more to society—*e.g.*, giving healthcare professionals priority access to scarce vaccines given that these workers are needed to treat others; or assigning priority based on one's responsibility for their medical need—*e.g.*, providing lower priority to alcoholics), *see* Ezekiel Emanuel & Alan Wertheimer, *Who Should Get Influenza Vaccine When Not All Can?*, 312 SCI. 854 (2006); (3) "best outcomes" (employing a utilitarian principle that aims to maximize social welfare, typically without regard to the distribution of benefits and burdens; this principle generally underlies the economic analyses used for healthcare rationing, *see* Part II); and (4) "equity" (allocating scarce resources based on a fair distribution of benefits and burdens, rather than merely maximizing net benefits), *see* Alan Williams & Richard Cookson, *Equity in Health*, *in* HANDBOOK OF HEALTH ECONOMICS 1863–1910 (Anthony Culyer & Joseph P. Newhouse eds., 2000). Selected equity principles include "prioritarianism" (giving priority to those who are worst off), *see* Derek Parfit, *Equality and Priority*, 10 RATIO 202 (1997), "sufficientarianism" (giving priority to individuals or groups below a predefined threshold level of well-being), *see* Roger Crisp, *Equality, Priority, and Compassion*, 113 ETHICS 745 (2003), and Rawls's "fair equality of opportunity principle" as applied to health (arguing that if there is a social obligation to protect fair equality of opportunity, there is also a derivative obligation to promote health because health has special moral importance given its link with opportunity), *see* NORMAN DANIELS, JUST HEALTH (Cambridge University Press 2007); *see also* JOHN RAWLS, A THEORY OF JUSTICE (Belknap Press 2nd ed. 1999). The above list of guiding principles roughly follows the taxonomy set forth in Govind Persad et al.,

To set the stage for our review of the economics of healthcare rationing, section I of this chapter summarizes the various dimensions across which healthcare rationing operates, or at least has the potential to operate, in the first place. We turn in section II to a brief review the types of economic analyses used in healthcare rationing decision-making, with a focus on cost-effectiveness analysis. In section III, we discuss healthcare rationing in practice. For instance, among other things, we examine how economic analyses inform decisions regarding which services to cover. In section IV, we describe various practical and conceptual challenges that may arise with economic analyses, challenges that span both economics and ethics. Finally, in section V we conclude.

I Overview of Dimensions to Healthcare Rationing

In this section, we attempt to lay the foundation for a basic understanding of healthcare rationing by delineating, in rather broad strokes, the types of healthcare resources that require rationing in the first place and the different levels at which rationing operates (e.g., macro- versus micro-level allocation decisions).

a. Types of Scarcity That May Require Rationing

Healthcare goods and services may be scarce due to financial or physical limitations. While we have separated these two concepts, they are naturally intertwined. Financial scarcity is perhaps self-evident. Individuals, entities, or states only have so much money to devote to the purchase of goods and services, leading to inherent limitations on consumption. To provide an extreme example, robotic surgical systems currently cost upward of $2 million, rendering such devices prohibitively expensive for many healthcare institutions.[2] Physical scarcity arises in various contexts. As a paradigmatic example, organs used in transplantation are often scarce—the need for organs far outweighs the supply.[3] Physician services are also sometimes scarce. With only so many willing and able providers in existence (and only so many hours in the day), demand for labor-intensive procedures is not always fully satisfied. There are concerns, for instance, that the demand for primary care physicians cannot be met given the increasing insurance coverage under the Affordable Care Act.[4]

These sources of scarcity may be absolute or relative in nature. Absolute scarcity refers to shortages that cannot be addressed in the short term by reallocating resources, whereas relative scarcity refers to shortages that may be addressed by shifting resources from one use to

Principles for Allocation of Scarce Medical Interventions, 373 Lancet 423 (2009); *see also* I. Glenn Cohen, *Rationing Legal Services*, 5 J. Legal Analysis 221 (2013).

[2] *See* Emily Singer, *The Slow Rise of the Robot Surgeon*, MIT Tech. Rev. (Mar. 24, 2010).

[3] *See* Judd Kessler & Alvin Roth, *Organ Allocation Policy and the Decision to Donate*, 102 Am. Econ. Rev. 2018 (2012).

[4] *See* Adam Hofer et al., *Expansion of Coverage under the Patient Protection and Affordable Care Act and Primary Care Utilization*, 89 Milbank Quarterly 69 (2011).

another. For example, the shortage of organs for transplantation is a form of absolute scarcity in that the limited supply is presently fixed, although policies could be pursued to increase supply over time.[5] In contrast, a shortage of robotic surgical systems would be a form of relative scarcity to the extent that healthcare institutions may shift funding priorities to purchase the equipment within the short term.[6]

In the balance of this chapter, we are primarily concerned with relative financial scarcity: how should scarce financial resources be allocated in the short term between competing healthcare goods and services?

b. Levels of Rationing

At the outset we would like to distinguish between efficiency considerations between healthcare and other non-healthcare services and efficiency considerations within healthcare.[7] Indeed, the necessity of healthcare rationing manifests itself on both macro and micro levels. With respect to the former, one must determine how many resources should be allocated to healthcare delivery in the first instance as opposed to other services that may likewise contribute to social welfare—for example, education. Analysts often label this question one of allocative efficiency. At the national level, the United States currently spends approximately 18% of its total income on healthcare, up from 7% in 1970.[8] Some believe that social welfare could indeed be better served through a reallocation of these resources to other means. Others believe that much of the healthcare spending growth is justified by associated gains in health. The answer to this macro-level question is undeniably complicated, and an array of policy initiatives (both implemented and theorized) are aimed at curbing overspending in general.[9]

[5] For recent research on various policy levers that can potentially be used to combat the shortage of human organs for transplant, *see* Eric Johnson & Daniel Goldstein, *Do Defaults Save Lives?*, 302 SCI. 1338 (2003); *see also* Judd Kessler & Alvin Roth, *Loopholes Undermine Donation: An Experiment Motivated by an Organ Donation Priority Loophole in Israel*, 114 J. PUB. ECON. 19 (2014).

[6] While it is beyond the scope of this article, we note that dynamic allocation decisions of this nature implicate matters beyond just rationing and cost containment—mainly, innovation policy. There is an inevitable conflict between healthcare rationing policies that aim to constrain spending on the one hand, and healthcare innovation policies that seek to promote research and development on the other. For instance, healthcare utilization of new technologies may sometimes appear to be inefficient and excessive from a static perspective, perhaps arising from moral hazard, physician-induced demand, or related features of healthcare systems. However, from a more dynamic perspective, the promise of such financial returns may stimulate the desire to produce such innovations in the first place. In fact, a leading explanation for growth in U.S. healthcare spending is technological innovation. *See* Amitabh Chandra & Jonathan Skinner, *Technology Growth and Expenditure Growth in Health Care*, 50 J. ECON. LIT. 645 (2012).

[7] *See* ANTHONY BOARDMAN ET AL., COST–BENEFIT ANALYSIS (4th ed. 2011).

[8] *See* Micah Hartman et al., *National Health Spending in 2013: Growth Slows, Remains in Step with the Overall Economy*, 34 HEALTH AFF. 1 (2014).

[9] Determining the optimal amount of resources to healthcare, as any good or service, depends on, among other things, societal preferences, national wealth, and the distribution of that wealth. Contrary to public perception, increases in health spending does not necessarily imply decreases in social welfare or even create a (greater) need for rationing. Naturally, as we become richer, society's willingness to pay for a longer and healthier life increases, which translates into greater healthcare spending overall and perhaps also as a percentage of national income. As a result, some preconceived amount of national

For the sake of tractability, we largely focus in this chapter on the more internal, micro-level counterpart: taking the national amount of healthcare spending as given, how do we allocate scarce healthcare resources among alternative uses—for example, deciding which clinical treatments for which diseases should or should not be covered. For instance, in treating patients suffering from prostate cancer, how many resources should be dedicated to the use of surgery (prostatectomy), proton-beam therapy, or watchful waiting by physicians (expectant management)? Analysts label this inquiry as one bearing on technical efficiency. We now turn in section II to an overview of the various tools employed to guide this technical efficiency analysis.

II Economic Evaluations Used in Rationing Healthcare

Analysts have derived several different approaches to assessing technical efficiency—that is, to determining how competing uses of healthcare resources should be compared with one another—the most well-known of which are called cost-benefit analysis (CBA) and cost-effectiveness analysis (CEA). These two approaches are distinct, though the lines between them are at times blurred, as we suggest in a stylized example below.[10] In this section, we provide an overview of these tools, focusing on the latter.

a. Overview of Cost-Benefit Analysis and Cost-Effectiveness Analysis

Cost-benefit analysis (CBA) is a rather intuitive concept—analysts quantify in monetary terms the costs of a particular healthcare service and compare these costs with a monetary calculation of the benefits. The healthcare service may be deemed appropriate if the calculated benefits exceed the costs. Generally, CBA utilizes a simple alternative decision rule known as the Kaldor-Hicks criterion: "a policy should be adopted if and only if those who will gain could fully compensate those who will lose and still be better off."[11] To be sure, the benefits of CBA actually go beyond a technical efficiency context—that is, beyond the question of how to allocate resources among competing healthcare options. To the extent that it places all benefits—health and nonhealth—on a common monetary framework (assuming

wealth devoted to healthcare, whether it be 18% or even 50%, does not serve as a sufficient condition for which to justify the enactment of policies aimed at rationing healthcare. *See* Robert Hall & Charles Jones, *The Value of Life and the Rise in Health Spending*, 122 Q. J. ECON. 39 (2007).

[10] For a recent literature review on the ways CBA and CEA have been converging, *see* Linda Ryen & Mikael Svensson, *The Willingness to Pay for a Quality Adjusted Life Year: A Review of the Empirical Literature*, HEALTH ECON. (2014).

[11] Nicholas Kaldor, *Welfare Propositions of Economics and Interpersonal Comparisons of Utility*, 49 ECON. J. 549 (1939); John Hicks, *The Valuation of the Social Income*, 7 ECONOMICA 105 (1940).

[12] The necessity of monetizing the benefits of healthcare interventions in CBAs arises because of the need to place a value on opportunity costs used to decide where to employ resources. *See* Alan Garber & Charles Phelps, *Economic Foundations of Cost-Effectiveness Analysis*, 16 J. HEALTH ECON. 1 (1997).

that can be successfully done),[12] it can also be used to assess allocative efficiency—that is, to evaluate whether resources (e.g., land, labor, capital) should be directed toward healthcare or non-healthcare goods and services. A major problem with CBA relates to the difficulty associated with achieving this monetization of benefits.[13] Largely for this reason, CBAs are not commonly utilized in healthcare settings. As such, we will place less emphasis on CBA in this chapter.

Cost-effectiveness analysis (CEA) represents the primary approach to economic analysis of healthcare rationing. One can view CEA as effectively asking: taking as given a particular level of healthcare spending, how do we select among two or more alternative healthcare options to ensure that we receive the most "bang for the buck" from the selected approach? Not immune to the difficulties associated with valuing health benefits, CEA requires the construction of a common set of health outcomes in order to facilitate a comparison across different types of health interventions—for example, the number of life years gained as a result of given treatments. Comparing the ratio of the costs associated with a particular treatment to the value of the outcome metric provides a relative measure of the cost-effectiveness of each treatment. Lower ratios naturally entail greater efficiency. Depending on certain choice parameters (e.g., must only one treatment be selected or may some combination of treatments be selected) and using cost-effectiveness ratios as inputs, CEA then applies certain selection criteria to identify those health interventions that merit priority.

In perhaps the most general terms, CEA involves maximizing population health given a fixed healthcare budget. With perfect information and foresight, the economic framework of CEA collapses to a straightforward constrained optimization problem where policy analysts take as given various treatments i with exogenous health production functions $h_i()$, prices of those treatments p_i, and a healthcare budget W, and maximize aggregate health production by choosing to employ a set j of the various health technologies subject to the production and budgetary constraints:

$$\max_{j \in i} \sum_{j} h_j$$

$$\text{subject to} \begin{cases} W \geq \sum_{j} h_j p_j \\ h_i \leq h_i(p, W) \ \forall i \end{cases}$$

Any discussion of CBAs for health interventions naturally leads to the controversial methods of valuing health and life, which are far from similar. *See* W. Kip Viscusi, *The Value of Individual and Societal Risks to Life and Health, in* HANDBOOK OF THE ECONOMICS OF RISK AND UNCERTAINTY 385 (Mark Machina & Kip Viscusi eds., 2014). The most frequently used terminology for valuing probabilistic decreases to risks to life is called the "value of statistical life" (VSL), which is simply a convenient way of summarizing one's willingness to pay for small reductions in fatal risks. *See* W. Kip Viscusi & Joseph Aldy, *The Value of a Statistical Life: A Critical Review of Market Estimates Throughout the World*, 27 J. RISK & UNCERTAINTY 5 (2003). For clarity, VSL is neither the value of saving the life of a specific identified person nor the value of reducing high probabilities of death, for instance, from 1 to 0. Because many of those health interventions that we associate with healthcare rationing deal with large reductions in risk to life, VSL does not lend itself well to a CBA and should be avoided.

[13] *See* Donald Kenkel, *Using Estimates of the Value of a Statistical Life in Evaluating Consumer Policy Regulations*, 26 J. CONSUMER POL'Y 1 (2003).

CEAs are typically applied in a more simplistic fashion than this general optimization problem entails. For instance, when multiple treatments may be selected among a set of non-competing alternatives, CEA often entails calculating the cost-effectiveness ratio for each treatment relative to the no-treatment option (often known as the average cost-effectiveness ratio for that treatment) and then ranking treatments from the lowest to higher ratios (from most efficient on average to least efficient on average). Society may then select treatments from among this rank ordering, moving down the list until the budget is exhausted. It is important to note that the analysis may take on a form different from this generalized optimization problem and from this stated simplification of that problem when analysts are required to select a *single* treatment among a set of mutually exclusive alternatives, or when analysts are determining whether to adopt a new treatment on the margin to the exclusion of the status quo treatment previously adopted. A "competing" CEA of this latter nature typically follows a particular selection process that we demonstrate in a highly stylized example below.

Before turning to that example, however, we note that much discussion in CEA settings bears on the selection of the necessary common measure of health benefits. Measures employed include the number of illnesses cured, the number of lives saved, and the number of life years gained.[14] In general, this exercise faces real difficulties when comparing the benefits of different treatments. For instance, how should one assess patient A's cataract surgery (to restore sight) against patient B's anterior cruciate ligament surgery (to restore mobility)?[15] Moreover, an obvious limitation with CEA is that the analyst must decide how to define, measure, and combine the quality dimension and the quantity dimension.[16] Economists and other health researchers have attempted to create methods to standardize benefits—that is, methods that seek to make commensurate quantity and quality. CEAs often employ health benefit measures that account for a treatment's impact on length of life (mortality) adjusted for any decrements in quality of life due to functional limitations resulting from the treatment (morbidity), such as the number of quality-adjusted life years (QALYs) or disability-adjusted life years (DALYs).[17] Even the use of measures such as QALYs, however, comes with substantial challenges (discussed further in section IV), not the least of which is the lack of data required to construct QALYs for a particular treatment.

In the stylized example below (and in the Appendix), we demonstrate how CEA and CBA might be applied in practice.

[14] *See* Jeremiah Hurley, *Chapter 2: An Overview of the Normative Economics of the Health Sector*, *in* HANDBOOK OF HEALTH ECONOMICS 55–118 (Anthony Culyer & Joseph Newhouse eds., 2000); Nien-he Hsieh et al., *The Numbers Problem*, 34 PHIL. & PUB. AFF. 352 (2006); Joseph Raz, *Numbers, With and Without Contractualism*, 16 RATIO 346 (2003).

[15] *See* Magnus Johannesson, *Should We Aggregate Relative or Absolute Changes in QALYs?*, 10 HEALTH ECON. 573 (2001).

[16] *See* BOARDMAN ET AL., COST–BENEFIT ANALYSIS, at 464.

[17] Cost-effectiveness analyses that use QALYs or other utility-based measures are sometimes referred to as "cost utility analyses" because the measures serve as a proxy for changes in utility levels. DALYs can be distinguished from QALYs in how "the mortality and morbidity burdens of various diseases" differ in different populations. Christopher Murray & Arnab Acharya, *Understanding DALYs*, 16 J. HEALTH ECON. 703 (1997).

b. Stylized Example

Consider a sixty-year-old patient who suffered from a heart attack and now faces a hospital mortality rate of 10%.[18] Suppose there are three treatment options that differ in effectiveness and cost: (1) streptokinase, which reduces the mortality rate by 5 percentage points to 5% and costs $200 per patient; (2) tissue plasminogen activator (t-PA), which reduces the mortality rate by 7.5 percentage points to 2.5% and costs $2,000 per patient; or (3) do nothing, which does not change the mortality rate and has no cost. For the purposes of the calculations to follow, assume a relevant heart attack patient population of 1,000.

To determine what treatment option should be adopted—*assuming in this case that only one can be adopted*—a policy analyst seeking to ration costs might conduct a simple CEA. CEAs begin by ruling out from consideration strictly dominated treatments, that is, treatments that cost the same or more as another treatment but yielded lower benefits. None of the three treatments in our example are strictly dominated by another. Thereafter, the analysis orders the remaining alternatives starting from the one that generates the lowest benefit but also costs the least to the one that costs the next highest amount and generates the next highest benefit level, and so on and so forth. A CEA in this "competing choice" setting essentially involves incrementally moving up this chain and determining whether the next alternative should be chosen over the preceding alternative in that chain. While the selection framework may be tailored to achieve different sets of objectives, each such determination often rests on whether the incremental cost-effectiveness ratio (ICER) associated with the relevant treatment in comparison with the status quo treatment falls below some specified threshold ratio. To be more precise, the ICER here equals the incremental cost of the treatment in question relative to the next-least effective treatment divided by the incremental benefit of the treatment at question relative to the next-least effective treatment. If the ICER indeed falls below the stated threshold—which often captures our priors regarding the value of a unit of the indicated health outcome—that marginal treatment should be preferred over the prior treatment and we should proceed to evaluating whether the next most effective treatment should be adopted (using the same criteria).

Let us return to our example to demonstrate. Start from the baseline in which we do no intervention. This costs nothing and generates no benefits. Let us then evaluate whether we should adopt the next intervention in this chain—in this case, streptokinase. Is it worth it to adopt this marginal intervention? To assess this, the analyst will calculate the incremental costs and effectiveness of streptokinase versus no treatment. Using the assumed numbers, the incremental cost for the population is $200,000, and the incremental effectiveness is 50 individuals saved.[19] Thus, the so-called ICER becomes $4,000 per life saved ($200,000/50). If $4,000 falls below the specified threshold ICER level—stated differently, if society is willing to accept $4,000 per avoided fatality—then we would determine that providing streptokinase is preferred to no treatment. Assume that we do. Next, we move on to evaluating the

[18] This example was modified from an example presented in BOARDMAN ET AL., COST-BENEFIT ANALYSIS.

[19] The incremental effectiveness is calculated by differencing the expected number of heart attack survivors with the streptokinase treatment [(1−0.05)1000 = 950] with the expected number of heart attack survivors with no treatment [(1−0.1)1000 = 900].

Table 41.1 Cost-Effectiveness Analysis Example

Strategy	Cost	Incremental Cost	Effectiveness	Incremental Effectiveness	Cost/ Effectiveness	ICER
No treatment	$0	$0	900	900	$0	$0
Streptokinase	$200,000	$200,000	950	50	$211	$4,000
t-PA	$2,000,000	$1,800,000	975	25	$2,051	$72,000

marginal adoption of t-PA in place of streptokinase, which we have just established as our new status quo. Using the same analysis we can obtain the ICER of $72,000 per life saved.[20] Whether we adopt t-PA as the sole treatment over streptokinase depends on whether $72,000 falls below the threshold ICER level specified by the analyst (Table 41.1).

To the extent that this competing choice model requires the selection of a threshold ICER level—often meant to capture the value that society places on a unit of the health outcome—the analysis will run into the same problems identified above for CBA—that is, placing a monetary value on health. For this reason, we note that the distinction between CBA and CEA may, in part, be blurred. We note, of course, that the simple, noncompeting model described briefly in section II.a above—in which we exhaust those treatments with the lowest *average* cost-effectiveness ratio before moving on to the next lowest average cost-effectiveness treatment—does not always require a comparison with a value threshold. Thus, as a more general matter, CEA faces at least fewer concerns regarding the need to place a monetary value on healthcare outcomes.

Though our focus in this chapter is largely on CEA, we extend this stylized example in the Appendix in order to demonstrate how a common formulation of CBA would approach the choice as between streptokinase and t-PA.

III Healthcare Rationing in Practice

As suggested in the introduction above, we define healthcare rationing in rather broad terms to capture initiatives aimed at limiting utilization of healthcare services, other than via price mechanisms in competitive marketplaces. To discuss the full array of ways in which rationing takes place is beyond the scope of this modest chapter. Given our decision already to focus on technical (within health) rather than allocative (between health and nonhealth) efficiency, we focus our discussion on forms of rationing that more explicitly incorporate CEA into decisions regarding what healthcare resources society should prioritize. Arguably, it is precisely such types of initiatives that first come to mind when hearing the word "rationing" anyway. We begin this discussion by describing programs in which payers (private or public) use CEA to guide coverage decisions.

[20] The ICER is again calculated by dividing the incremental costs of $1.8 million [(1000)($2000)–(1000)($200)] by the incremental effectiveness of 25 individuals [(1–0.05)1000–(1–0.025)1000].

a. Covered Services

Excluding particular services from insurance coverage is a common supply-side rationing mechanism. While denying insurance coverage does not necessarily prevent patients from receiving desired services, treatments that are not covered—that is, reimbursed—are perhaps substantially less likely to be utilized because patients financially internalize the full cost of care. In some countries, determinations of services to cover are explicitly guided by CEA. In the United Kingdom, for example, the National Institute for Health and Care Excellence (NICE) is responsible for making recommendations to the British National Health Service (NHS) on the coverage of selected medical treatments. These recommendations are based on the cost per quality-adjusted life year (QALY) gained for patients and on the overall impact of the proposed covered treatment on NHS costs. It is believed that NICE employs an implicit cost-effectiveness threshold and recommends coverage of treatments with costs per QALY gained within or below the $30,000 to $50,000 range.[21] For example, if a treatment extends life by 0.5 QALYs, the NHS might pay as much as $25,000 for the treatment, implying a cost-effectiveness of $50,000 per QALY gained.

We briefly digress to note the findings of an empirical literature that estimates the value people place on QALYs. Such valuations can provide a useful benchmark for payers to use in guiding coverage decisions; if the cost per QALY for a particular treatment is lower than the amount by which individuals value a QALY, such services may be deemed worthwhile. A comparison of this nature is evidently helpful for allocative as well as technical efficiency analyses. Depending on the method used,[22] estimated dollar values of a QALY range from $74,000 to $450,000, with practitioners of CEA tending toward the low end of the range.[23]

In the United States, private payers often use CEA to justify coverage decisions. However, CEA is less well incorporated in the publicly financed portion of the U.S. market. While some public insurers use CEA to guide coverage decisions (e.g., the Department of Defense and the Department of Veterans Affairs), the Medicaid and Medicare programs, two of the largest health insurers in the United States, may not, by law, consider the cost of a treatment in determining coverage.[24] Yet some evidence suggests that cost-effectiveness has played an informal role in some Medicare coverage decisions by guiding the level of scrutiny Medicare uses when assessing new treatments.[25] With the rising burden of healthcare expenses as a percent of national income, there is a growing movement toward formally incorporating CEA into more public insurers coverage decisions; the outcome of this debate, however, remains uncertain.

[21] *See* Christopher McCabe et al., *The NICE Cost-Effectiveness Threshold: What It Is and What That Means*, 26 PHARMACOECONOMICS 733 (2008).

[22] For a discussion of the various ways in which QALYs have been valued, *see* Donald Kenkel, *A WTP- and QALY-Based Approaches to Valuing Health for Policy: Common Ground and Disputed Territory*, 34 ENVTL. & RES. ECON. 419 (2006).

[23] *See id.*

[24] *See* Susan Bartlett Foote & Peter Neumann, *The Impact of Medicare Modernization on Coverage Policy: Recommendations for Reform*, 11 AM. J. MANAGED CARE 140 (2005). Medicare has made several attempts to incorporate some form of CEA into its coverage considerations, but it has been unable to do so due to political opposition. *See id.*

[25] *See* Sean Tunis, *Why Medicare Has Not Established Criteria for Coverage Decisions*, 350 NEW ENG. J. MED. 2196 (2004).

b. Demand-Side Initiatives

Health insurers employ an array of cost-sharing requirements—copays, coinsurance, deductibles, and so forth—to discourage utilization of inappropriate care by patients who do not pay the full cost of the care they receive (i.e., to alleviate moral hazard and encourage patients to pursue cost-justified services). Such arrangements have undergone a dramatic growth in recent years with the proliferation of high-deductible health plans (HDHPs) that impose large deductibles on most medical services (averaging over $2,000 for individual plans and $4,000 for family plans).[26] The vast literature on this topic reveals that increases in cost-sharing reduce healthcare utilization.[27] While cost-sharing does not deny coverage of medical services (see section III.a), its intent to discourage utilization of healthcare in some circumstances is arguably in the same spirit. Rather than give a full accounting of such mechanisms, we offer a brief discussion of those cost-sharing arrangements that have incorporated CEA-style components similar to that summarized in section II above, thereby falling within the narrower theme of this chapter.

Cost-sharing mechanisms have historically been somewhat blunt in nature—for example, particular copayment amounts or percentages were—and still often are—applied indiscriminately to all covered services. Over time, insurers developed more tailored structures that attempt to place more cost-sharing pressure on some procedures over others. A particular concern with blunt cost-sharing approaches was that they would discourage utilization of both their intended target—clinically inappropriate care (i.e., where the costs of care surpass its benefits)—and an unintended target—clinically appropriate care (i.e., where the benefits of care surpass its costs). Informational limitations and behavioral irrationalities (e.g., hyperbolic discounting) may cause patients to nonetheless forego valuable and cost-justified care in the face of cost-sharing obligations.[28] Common targets of concern here include chronic-care management (e.g., routine diabetes care), particularly within vulnerable populations.[29]

To address the concern that cost-sharing results in individuals foregoing clinically beneficial care, insurers have begun to modify this blunt, traditional approach to cost-sharing. One increasingly popular idea is called value-based insurance design (VBID). VBID programs promote utilization of clinically cost-effective care by lowering or even eliminating cost-sharing for "high value" medical treatments (such as metformin for diabetes management) and simultaneously discouraging utilization of unnecessary care by raising cost-sharing for "low-value" treatments (e.g., lung volume reduction surgery).[30] VBID programs are more

[26] For concerns with HDHPs, *see* J. Frank Wharam et al., *High-Deductible Insurance: Two-Year Emergency Department and Hospital Use*, 17 AM. J. MANAGED CARE 410 (2011). Regarding growth, 38% of covered workers were in HDHPs in 2013 and enrollment may accelerate under the Affordable Care Act. *See* Amelia Haviland et al., *Growth of Consumer-Directed Health Plans to One-Half of All Employer-Sponsored Insurance Could Save $57 Billion Annually*, 31 HEALTH AFF. 1009 (2012).

[27] *See* Dana Goldman et al., *Pharmacy Benefits and the Use of Drugs by the Chronically Ill*, 291 J. AM. MED. ASS'N 2344 (2004).

[28] *See* Kevin Frick & Michael Chernew, *Beneficial Moral Hazard and the Theory of the Second Best*, 46 INQUIRY: J. HEALTH CARE ORG., PROVISION, & FIN. 229 (2009).

[29] *See* Amelia Haviland et al., *How Do Consumer-Directed Health Plans Affect Vulnerable Populations?*, 14 F. FOR HEALTH ECON. & POL'Y 1 (2011).

[30] *See* Niteesh Choudhry et al., *Assessing the Evidence for Value-Based Insurance Design*, 29 HEALTH AFF. 1988 (2010).

common for prescription drugs where, for instance, generic drugs (e.g., metformin) are covered at higher rates than their more expensive branded equivalent (Glucophage) and more effective drugs (e.g., Flovent for asthma) are covered more generously than their less-effective counterparts (Singulair) within the relevant drug class.[31] Some VBID programs even target patients based on clinical criteria, as the value derived from certain drugs may differ based on patient condition and severity.[32] In addition, VBID has been incorporated into HDHPs, many of which now waive the deductible for selected types of preventive care (e.g., breast and cervical cancer screenings, and well-child visits)[33] and other treatments perceived to be of high value (e.g., medications for chronic conditions).[34]

While VBID programs may consider CEAs only informally when identifying high-value care, they focus on clinical areas with the greatest potential to improve health outcomes and/or constrain costs, including the treatment of chronic illnesses (e.g., diabetes and antihypertensive medications) and secondary disease prevention (e.g., statins that lower cholesterol).[35] Early evidence suggests that such programs have been successful at meeting this potential. For example, Chernew and colleagues evaluated the effect of a VBID program that eliminated copays for generic drugs and reduced copays by 50% for branded drugs in five chronic disease classes.[36] They found that adherence improved in four of the five classes by 2.6 to 4.0 percentage points. Subsequent VBID studies have confirmed this result, reporting statistically significant though quantitatively modest impacts that vary in magnitude across drug classes.[37] The current evidence base regarding the extent to which these improvements will translate into lower costs, however, remains inconclusive.[38]

c. Provider Networks

In addition to denying full coverage or imposing differential cost-sharing amounts for certain services, health insurers have also sought to regulate patient behavior by directing patients to certain providers over others. Insurers often construct provider networks

[31] *See* A. Mark Fendrick et al., *A Benefit-Based Copay for Prescription Drugs: Patient Contribution Based on Total Benefits, Not Drug Acquisition Cost*, 7 AM. J. MANAGED CARE 861 (2001). For example, a VBID plan offered by the University of Michigan lowers copayments for medications to treat diabetes, high blood pressure, high cholesterol, and depression as follows: generics by 100%, tier 2 by 50%, and tier 3 by 25%. *See* Alicen Spaulding et al., *A Controlled Trial of Value-Based Insurance Design—The MHealthy: Focus on Diabetes (FOD) Trial*, 4 IMPLEMENT SCI. 19 (2009).

[32] Inhaled steroids, for example, are effective for treating asthma but not chronic obstructive pulmonary disease. *See* Choudhry et al., *Assessing the Evidence for Value-Based Insurance Design*.

[33] *See* John Rowe et al., *The Effect of Consumer-Directed Health Plans on the Use of Preventive and Chronic Illness Services*, 27 HEALTH AFF. 113 (2008).

[34] *See* Sheila Reiss et al., *Effect of Switching to a High-Deductible Health Plan on Use of Chronic Medications*, 46 HEALTH SERV. RES. 1382 (2011).

[35] *See* Choudhry et al., *Assessing the Evidence for Value-Based Insurance Design*.

[36] *Impact of Decreasing Copayments on Medication Adherence Within a Disease Management environment*, 27 HEALTH AFF. 103 (2008).

[37] *See* Matthew B. Frank et al., *The Effect of a Large Regional Health Plan's Value-Based Insurance Design Program on Statin Use*, 50 MED. CARE 934 (2012).

[38] *See* Teresa Gibson et al., *Value-Based Insurance Plus Disease Management Increased Medication Use and Produced Savings*, 30 HEALTH AFF. 100 (2011).

associated with their plans, extending more favorable coverage to insureds who visit providers within the network (the most common model of this approach is known as a preferred provider organization, or PPO). To see out-of-network providers, patients typically face higher cost-sharing. As a general matter, these plans may achieve cost savings by negotiating favorable prices with participating in-network providers.

Falling more within the spirit of the rationing approaches emphasized in this chapter (aimed at attaining technical efficiency), some provider network programs take matters one step further (i.e., beyond mere price concessions through bargaining power) and try to encourage patients to seek care from providers who offer greater productive efficiency—that is, those who have proven to deliver quality care at low costs. Such alternative approaches are known as "limited network" and "tiered network" plans.

Limited networks typically rank physicians and hospitals based on some cost and quality measures and exclude nonpreferred providers from the network altogether.[39] Tiered networks, in turn, are the network analog to VBID plans (discussed in section III.b above) in that they encourage patients to seek care from preferred providers by structuring cost-sharing differences among tiers.[40] Over the past five years, limited and tiered provider networks have become increasingly popular as the percentage of employers whose largest plan included a limited or tiered network increased from 16% in 2010 to 23% in 2013.[41]

Even if provider networks can effectively steer patients toward preferred providers, provider networks face a number of potential drawbacks. While one of the objectives of networks is to guide patient decision-making with respect to provider selection, such networks may disrupt long-standing existing relationships (and thus the benefits of continuity-of-care associated with such relationships). Another issue is that patients seeking specialty care from in-network providers with long waitlists may have few low-cost immediate alternatives, an issue that is largely mitigated in tiered networks. Finally, questions abound regarding the availability of sound data on provider quality. On this point, physician groups in several states have sued health plans with provider networks on various grounds, including defamation, interference with advantageous relations, and violation of procedural due process, alleging that health plans are misclassifying providers through opaque processes that employ fallible ranking methods and rely on limited (and sometimes inaccurate) data on provider quality.[42] While these lawsuits have failed in the courts, the concerns expressed

[39] *See* Jon Kingsdale, *After the False Start—What Can We Expect from the New Health Insurance Marketplaces?*, 370 NEW ENG. J. MED 393 (2014).

[40] *See* James Robinson, *Hospital Tiers in Health Insurance: Balancing Consumer Choice with Financial Incentives*, 22 HEALTH AFF. 135 (2003). Some insurers have started to experiment with stronger incentives to steer patients toward preferred providers, including larger cost-sharing amounts and greater inter-tier cost sharing differences. *See id.* To the extent that provider networks steer patients toward higher value providers, limited networks have the potential to be more effective than tiered networks because of their more severe incentive structure. On the other hand, relative to limited network plans, tiered network plans preserve patients' ability to choose from a wide range of providers (albeit with higher cost sharing for nonpreferred providers) and thus could be more palatable to patients.

[41] *See* Choudhry et al., *Assessing the Evidence for Value-Based Insurance Design.*

[42] Mass. Med. Soc'y et al. v. Group Ins. Comm'n et al., No. # 2008-cv-2124 (Suffolk Sup. Ct., filed May 21, 2008); Wash. St. Med. Ass'n et al. v. Regence Blue Shield, No. # 06-2-30655-ISEA (King County Sup. Ct. 2006); Fairfield County Med. Soc'y et al. v. CIGNA Corp. et al., No. # CV-075002943 (Conn. Sup. Ct. 2008).

reveal some key challenges with provider tiering. Ultimately, the evidence of the impact of limited and tiered provider networks on utilization and cost containment is mixed though admittedly sparse.[43]

IV Challenges with Economic Evaluations

In this section, we expand our discussion of CEA to highlight several measurement, analytic, and application challenges confronting analyses of this nature. While we discuss these challenges in the context of CEAs that use outcome metrics that incorporate quality of life adjustments—for example, QALYs—most of the issues generalize to other forms of economic analysis as well.

a. Measurement Challenges

By providing a common framework to assess the benefits of competing healthcare resources, measures such as QALYs are useful for cross-treatment comparisons, as noted in section II. However, there are various conceptual issues with how QALYs are constructed. Without setting forth the full details of a QALY calculation, we note a few such issues in this section. One concern is the fact that the quality-of-life adjustment weights used in QALY calculations are derived from elicited utility preferences.[44] Preferences, however, will likely differ across various types of groups due to various social, cultural, or economic differences, and there is a lack of consensus over whose preferences should be used. For example, individuals in manual labor settings may assign greater weight to physical functional limitations than individuals in knowledge-based occupational settings.[45]

Consider also the case of disabled individuals. Interestingly, disabled patients with a given condition often report less limitation on quality of life than community members without the condition. On the one hand, the ex ante preferences of a community member may less accurately capture the effect of a treatment on quality of life than the ex post informed preferences of a disabled person. But on the other hand, the ex post preferences of disabled persons may reflect adaptation to their functional limitations, a lowering of expectations that may provide a less acceptable basis for developing quality-of-life adjustment weights.[46] Relatedly, if community member preferences (assigning greater functional limitation to disabilities) are used in CEAs, then treatments extending the lives of disabled individuals will receive less

43 *See* Matthew Frank et al., *The Impact of a Tiered Network on Hospital Choice*, Health Services Research, in press (2015).

44 These preferences are elicited using a range of valuation techniques, including standard gamble, time tradeoff, rating scale, multi-attribute utility, and person tradeoff techniques. *See* Milton Weinstein et al., *QALYs: The Basics*, 12 Value in Health S5 (2009).

45 *See* Dan Brock, *Ethical Issues in the Use of Cost Effectiveness Analysis for the Prioritization of Health Resources*, *in* Handbook of Bioethics 294 (George Khushf, 2004).

46 *See* Myriam Hunink & Paul Glasziou, Decision Making in Health and Medicine: Integrating Evidence and Values 268–269 (2001).

weight. But if CEAs rely on disabled individual preferences (assigning less functional limitation to disabilities), then less weight will be given to treatments preventing disability.[47]

Another concern relating to QALY construction regards what life expectancy measures should be used.[48] QALYs gained by an intervention effectively capture the amount of time spent in a particular state of health that is made possible by the intervention itself. A calculation of this sort naturally requires some estimate of the general life expectancy facing the patient—after all, an intervention that avoids death and returns a patient to a healthy state will not do so indefinitely. In evaluating a treatment for individuals with a particular condition, it may seem reasonable to use the average life expectancy for individuals with that condition. However, defining QALY gains in this way would result in fewer QALYs gained for individuals with life-shortening disabilities, making treatments targeting these individuals appear less cost-effective. In turn, life expectancies also vary by socioeconomic status, race, ethnicity, and gender. Some of these differences appear largely biological in nature, while others may have been exacerbated by unjust social conditions (e.g., between the poor and wealthy). How should such differences factor into QALY calculations?

A final and related debate frequently invoked bears on whether QALYs should be age-weighted. While CEAs count QALYs the same regardless of the age of the patient, some argue that QALYs should be age-weighted to give priority to the young. One justification, often referred to as the "fair innings" argument,[49] posits that as a matter of fairness, priority should be given to help individuals achieve a normal lifespan; the young, who have enjoyed less of their life share, should therefore receive greater priority.[50] While some forms of preferencing may be deemed discriminatory in certain contexts (e.g., based on race or gender), some argue that preferencing the young is not discriminatory because everyone is young at some point, during which time they would have received priority.[51] Another rationale argues that priority should be given to QALYs gained by adults during their working years, given that they are a primary source of financial, emotional, and physical support for children and the elderly.[52] However, one concern with this argument is that it values the health of adults based on their instrumental value to others.

b. Analytical Challenges

In addition to the measurement challenges described in section IV.a, there are a variety of issues relating to how CEAs are conducted. In this section, we discuss several such issues. The first operational obstacle relates to the perspective from which CEAs are conducted. Often CEAs take the viewpoint of the agent making the decision—for example, the payer—but CEAs may also be conducted from the societal perspective. While CEAs conducted from

47 *See* Paul Menzel et al., *The Role of Adaptation to Disability and Disease in Health State Valuation: A Preliminary Normative Analysis*, 55 Soc. Sci. & Medicine 2149 (2002).

48 *See* Brock, *Ethical Issues in the Use of Cost Effectiveness Analysis.*

49 *See* Alan Williams, *Intergenerational Equity: An Exploration of the "Fair Innings" Argument*, 6 Health Econ. 117 (1997).

50 *See* John Harris, The Value of Life: An Introduction to Medical Ethics 87–102 (1990).

51 *See* Normal Daniels, Am I My Parents' Keeper? An Essay on Justice Between the Young and the Old (1988).

52 *See* Greg Bognar, *Age Weighting*, 24 Econ. & Phil. 167 (2008).

the payer perspective use the prices charged for a treatment as the cost, the societal perspective includes all health benefits and costs regardless of who receives the benefits or bears the costs. The choice of a perspective, therefore, may have a large effect on the results of the analysis.

Consider, for example, a drug and a medical device of equal effectiveness. The drug's cost of production is low, but its price is high (under patent protection, it sells at a substantial markup), whereas the medical device's cost of production is moderate, and its price markup is small. On these facts, the medical device may be more cost-effective than the drug from the payer perspective because it offers equal effectiveness at a lower price to the payer. In turn, the drug may offer greater value from the societal perspective, given that it is less resource intensive to produce and offers equal effectiveness. Although the payer faces a higher price for the drug, from the societal perspective this constitutes a welfare transfer from payer to producer, not a welfare loss.[53]

When CEAs are used to inform coverage decisions, employing the payer perspective may also discourage the offering of preventive care. Given the high rate at which individuals switch health plans ("insurance churn"),[54] payers have less incentive to promote preventative care that provides future health benefits since many of the payer's current members will not be members in the mid/long term, even if the preventive care would be supported from the societal perspective.

A second issue involves which costs and benefits should be taken into account in CEA calculations. Direct health benefits and costs are always included, but should indirect nonhealth benefits and costs be included, as well?[55] An efficient allocation of resources should indeed base its analysis on all costs and benefits stemming from the treatments under investigation, whether indirect versus direct or health versus nonhealth in nature. However, some object on grounds other than efficiency to the inclusion of some items. A prime example here is smoking-cessation treatment. Such programs may extend lives directly, but they may also tend to increase Social Security costs. Including these indirect nonhealth costs in a CEA would result in a lower smoking prevention cost-effectiveness ratio. Some view it unfair to allow a nonhealth benefit of this nature tip the scale in favor of allocation to one patient over another, as this treats patients instrumentally as a means to benefit others.[56] Including nonhealth benefits in other contexts raises fewer eyebrows—for example, the inclusion of enhanced worker productivity and reduced burdens on friends and family resulting from substance abuse treatments.

A final analytical/measurement issue related to QALYs concerns whether health benefits that accrue to individuals in the future should be discounted.[57] While future costs are discounted to reflect the time value of money, which is appropriate, it is not clear that health benefits should be discounted as well. Different interventions will take varying lengths of time to yield benefits, and the discounting of health benefits could result in greater priority

[53] *See* Anupam Jena & Thomas Philipson, *Cost Effectiveness as a Price Control*, 26 HEALTH AFF. 696 (2007).

[54] *See* Bradley Herring, *Suboptimal Provision of Preventive Healthcare Due to Expected Enrollee Turnover Among Private Insurers*, 19 HEALTH ECON. 438 (2010).

[55] *See* Brock, *Ethical Issues in the Use of Cost Effectiveness Analysis.*

[56] *See* FRANCIS KAMM, MORALITY, MORTALITY: DEATH AND WHOM TO SAVE FROM IT 369 (1993).

[57] *See* Brock, *Ethical Issues in the Use of Cost Effectiveness Analysis.*

for interventions that provide small benefits in the short term over interventions that provide larger benefits in the future, including vaccine programs and other preventive interventions. While paradoxes may arise when health benefits are not discounted or discounted at a different rate than costs,[58] an adequate ethical justification for discounting health benefits has not been offered.

c. Application Challenges

Even assuming that the measurement and analytical challenges discussed in sections IV.a and IV.b have been adequately addressed, issues with how the results of CEAs are applied remain. In this section, we review two issues sometimes called the "fair chances/best outcomes problem" and the "aggregation problem."[59]

The fair chances/best outcomes problem concerns rationing decisions between two or more treatments in which allocating resources for one treatment would provide better outcomes for a given group, but those in need of other treatments may nevertheless claim that they should still have a fair chance to receive the resources.[60] Consider the following stylized example: Two treatments yield different levels of value, say treatment A for condition X provides 1.00 QALY per unit of cost and treatment B for condition Y provides 0.99 QALYs at the same cost. A strict utilitarian applying these CEA results would conclude that the resources should be allocated to treatment A. However, most people would conclude that the 0.01 QALY difference between treatments A and B does not, ceteris paribus, sufficiently justify this decision. But what if treatment B provided only 0.90 QALYs (or 0.80, 0.50, 0.20)? In several of these cases, many people may believe that patients with condition Y (who need treatment B) have a reasonable complaint: since the treatments are "close enough" in value, everyone deserves a fair chance to receive the available resources.[61] However, most people believe there is some point at which the value of treatment A so outweighs the value of treatment B that appeals to fair chances should no longer be deemed relevant. In the abstract, one proposal to address the fair chance/best outcomes problem is the use of a weighted lottery.[62] Yet even if this approach could be operationalized, it remains unclear how far intuitions about fair chances extend.

Second, the aggregation problem arises when modest benefits to a large number of individuals are more cost-effective than large benefits to a small number of individuals.[63] Philosophers disagree over the propriety of aggregating benefits across individuals in order to assess how limited resources should be allocated across different groups. An often

[58] *See* Emmett Keeler & Shan Cretin, *Discounting of Life-Saving and Other Nonmonetary Effects*, 29 MGMT. SCI. 300 (1983).

[59] *See* Norman Daniels, *Four Unsolved Rationing Problems A Challenge*, 24 HASTINGS CENTER REP. 27 (1994).

[60] This issue may also arise in other healthcare rationing contexts in determining the allocation of physically scarce resources such as solid organs and units of vaccine.

[61] Some may argue that patients with condition Y already had a fair chance and lost in the "natural lottery," while others (e.g., luck egalitarians) want to compensate for bad brute luck.

[62] *See* John Broome, *Selecting People Randomly*, 95 ETHICS 38 (1984).

[63] *See* Eric Rakowski, *The Aggregation Problem*, 24 HASTINGS CENTER REP. 33 (1994).

cited example of this issue occurred in the state of Oregon Medicaid experiment.[64] In 1989, Oregon decided to expand its Medicaid program, financing the expansion by offering Medicaid beneficiaries a more limited set of healthcare services chosen and ranked based on cost-effectiveness. But when Oregon published its schedule of covered and uncovered services, dental caps for pulp exposure—providing modest benefits to many people—were determined to be cost-effective and therefore covered, while life-saving surgical procedures for ectopic pregnancy and appendicitis—providing substantial benefits to fewer people—were less cost-effective and given less preferential coverage treatment. Comparing the total benefits across these groups proved worrisome for many observers. Controversy over these and other coverage decisions led to the disbanding of the program.

Aside from the aggregation component per se, part of the discomfort in this example comes in comparing treatments with modest health benefits but high cost-effectiveness ratios to those with substantial health benefits but lower cost-effectiveness ratios. One attempt to address the uneasiness appeals to the so-called "rule of rescue," which affords priority to less cost-effective treatments in life-or-death situations, assuming the cost-effectiveness is not unreasonably low.[65] The rule of rescue relates to the notion that the maximand of CEAs should be saving the most lives in a more immediate, "identifiable" sense, as opposed to extending life years in a more predicted and "statistical" sense. Some commentators have been critical of this distinction between identifiable lives and statistical lives, considering that any treatment that extends a patient's life also in a sense "rescues" that patient at some future time.[66] Yet some research suggests that individuals are willing to pay more per QALY for life-saving treatments than for life-extending or life-enhancing treatments,[67] suggesting that perhaps some (though not absolute) weight should be given based on the type of treatment being prioritized.

V Concluding Remarks

A comprehensive discussion of the economics surrounding healthcare utilization and the means by which governments, private insurers, and market dynamics themselves may constrain such utilization (and thus "ration" limited resources) would require far more attention than a single chapter could hope to achieve. Our goals here have indeed been more modest. We have focused on how certain tools of economics, mainly cost-effectiveness analysis, have shaped distinct types of non-price-rationing practices. Indeed, much has been omitted in our discussion regarding the numerous other ways in which governments and private parties may regulate healthcare utilization. For instance, while we have addressed more categorical approaches to regulating which services patients may obtain, we have not addressed

64 *See* David Hadorn, *Setting Health Care Priorities in Oregon: Cost Effectiveness Meets the Rule of Rescue*, 265 J. Am. Med. Ass'n 2218 (1991).

65 *See* Albert Jonsen, *Bentham in a Box: Technology Assessment and Health Care Allocation*, 14 J. L., Med. & Ethics 172 (1986).

66 *See* Cohen, *Rationing Legal Services.*

67 *See* Cam Donaldson et al., *The Social Value of a QALY: Raising the Bar or Barring the Raise?*, 11 BMC Health Servs. Res. 8 (2011).

more case-by-case mechanisms that insurers may employ—for example, utilization review. Nor have we discussed certain modern approaches to rationing care such as global payment systems that retreat from fee-for-service reimbursement models and instead reimburse providers (either individually or in a group) a flat fee for treating specified patients over a given period of time or during particular episodes of care.

Structures of this latter variety—that is, alternative means of reimbursing physicians—are worth emphasizing briefly in these concluding remarks. Our discussion in this chapter largely focused on policies and programs aimed at curbing or shaping patient decision-making. Excessive use of medical care, however, may also arise from another source: physicians. Perhaps one of the most important features of the U.S. healthcare system that may contribute to excessive healthcare utilization is the fee-for-service environment largely characterizing the U.S. healthcare delivery system.[68] Under a fee-for-service approach, physicians are effectively paid more for doing more, creating incentives on the part of physicians to perform an unnecessarily high degree of services, a phenomenon often labeled "physician induced demand." Whether fee-for-service reimbursement structures, in fact, cause physicians to provide an unnecessarily large number of procedures is the subject of an extensive literature.[69] While establishing causation in such studies is empirically challenging, the most convincing evidence put forth to date suggests that at least some physicians may indeed be inducing demand in this manner.[70] With these considerations in mind, more complete discussions regarding healthcare cost containment and healthcare rationing cannot ignore the decision-making role of physicians in this complex interaction between medical providers, insurers, and patients.

Appendix

Return to the heart attack example in section II, in which we evaluated the use of two treatment interventions: streptokinase and t-PA. We now evaluate the choice between these two interventions employing cost-benefit analysis (CBA), as opposed to cost-effectiveness analysis. Assume that the baseline treatment is streptokinase, and a policy-maker is deciding whether to adopt t-PA as a treatment for society, guided by CBA. Effectively, this analysis entails calculating the monetary benefits of t-PA relative to that of streptokinase and asking whether such relative benefits exceed the costs of t-PA relative to streptokinase. If such net benefits are indeed greater than 0, the CBA suggests that efficiency would be enhanced by selecting t-PA over streptokinase.

Assume that the use of t-PA results in a lower risk of death than the use of streptokinase. How should such reduced risk of death be valued? CBAs often approach this inquiry by calculating something known as compensating variation (CV). In this context, CV can be thought of as the amount of money that must be taken away from the individual in order to

[68] *See* David Orentlicher, *Cost Containment and the Patient Protection and Affordable Care Act*, 6 FIU L. Rev. 67 (2010).

[69] For an overview of the empirical literature (up to 2000) exploring this hypothesis, *see id.*

[70] *See* Jonathan Gruber & Maria Owings, *Physician Financial Incentives and Cesarean Section Delivery*, 27 Rand J. Econ. 99 (1996).

leave her just as well off as she was prior to the reduction in risk. Conversely, CV can be interpreted as the maximum amount of money the patient would be willing to pay to obtain the treatment reducing risk of death (t-PA) over the current treatment (streptokinase).

Continuing our example, suppose a representative heart attack patient has lifetime expected utility under treatment t of $E[U(Y \mid t)] = (1 - p_t)u(Y \mid live) + p_t u(Y \mid dead)$, where P_t is the probability of death with treatment t. In words, conditional on obtaining treatment t, the patient lives with probability $(1 - p_t)$ and obtains a utility level $u(Y \mid live)$ and dies with probability P_t and obtains a utility level $u(Y \mid dead)$. Let's denote the probably of death under streptokinase treatment as p and probability of death under the t-PA treatment as q. Assume that $u(Y \mid dead) = 0$, that is, the patient gets no utility if he or she is dead. Further assume that the patient has \$100,000 in income. Solving for CV means that we find the CV that leaves the consumer indifferent between an income of \$100,000 with a probability of death of p and an income of \$100,000−CV with a probability of death of q.

For concreteness, let's solve a simple example by specifying a functional form for the utility function, say, $u = \ln(Y)$, and assuming that $Y = \$100k$, $p = 0.05$, and $q = 0.025$.[71] We can find CV = \$25,562.[72] In words, under the simplified example here, the representative heart attack patient's willingness to pay for the t-PA treatment (as opposed to streptokinase) is \$25,562, which far exceeds the monetary cost of the procedure over streptokinase (\$1,800). If the relative monetary cost of the treatment (\$1,800) equals the social opportunity cost of the treatment, the decision rule from the CBA would be to adopt t-PA as a treatment because it has positive net benefits.

[71] Note that p and q will not likely be the same as the hospital mortality rates in the above example, but for simplicity let's assume they are the same.

[72] Note the expected *monetary* benefits of the procedure in terms of income to the representative individual are: $E[B] = (0.05-0.025) * 100{,}000 = \$2{,}500 < CV = \$25{,}562$. Thus, note that CV is a lot larger than the expected monetary benefit because of risk aversion.

E. Public Health Law

CHAPTER 42

AMERICAN PUBLIC HEALTH LAW

LAWRENCE O. GOSTIN, DANIEL HOUGENDOBLER, AND ANNA E. ROBERTS

> From my perspective, as a White House official watching the budgetary process, and subsequently as head first of a health care financing agency and then of a public health agency, I was continually amazed to watch as billions of dollars were allocated to financing medical care with little discussion, whereas endless arguments ensued over a few millions for community prevention programs. The sums that were the basis for prolonged, and often futile, budget fights in public health were treated as rounding errors in the Medicare budget.
>
> *William Roper (1994)*

POPULATION health and the legal structures that support it are having a renaissance. Once fashionable during the Industrial Revolution and the Progressive Era, the ideals of population health began to wither with the rise of liberalism in the late twentieth century, and with that came hesitancy for governments to use their legal powers to buttress public health. In its place came a heightened focus on personal and economic freedoms with political attention shifting from population health to individual health and from public health to private medicine.

Signs of revitalization in the field of public health law can be seen in diverse national and global contexts—scholarly publications,[1] policy reforms,[2] and empirical research.[3] The resurgence of interest in population-based law deserves vigorous attention in modern

[1] LAWRENCE O. GOSTIN, PUBLIC HEALTH LAW (2nd ed. 2008); WENDY E. PARMET, POPULATIONS, PUBLIC HEALTH, AND THE LAW (2008); JOHN COGGON, WHAT MAKES HEALTH PUBLIC (2012).

[2] Lawrence O. Gostin, Peter D. Jacobson, Katherine L. Record, & Lorian E. Hardcastle, *Restoring Health to Health Reform: Integrating Medicine and Public Health to Advance the Population's Wellbeing*, 159 PENN L. REV. 1777 (2011).

[3] Scott Burris et al., *Making the Case for Laws That Improve Health: A Framework for Public Health Law Research*, 88 MILBANK Q. 169 (2010).

political and social circles. However, it is not easy to sell population health in the contemporary marketplace of ideas.[4]

Why is public health action politically and publicly underappreciated? Here we suggest four key reasons: (1) *the rescue imperative*—society is willing to spend inordinately to save the life of a person with a name, face, and history, but less so to save "statistical lives"; (2) *the technological imperative*—public health services are less appealing and salient than the high-technology solutions of microbiology and genetics; (3) *the invisibility of public health*—when public health is working well (e.g., safe food, water, and consumer products), its importance is taken for granted; and (4) *the culture of individualism*—society often values personal goods (individual responsibility, choice, and satisfaction) over public goods (population health and safety).

To compensate for these perceived disadvantages, the field requires a strong underlying theory and definition (*what* is public health law and what are its doctrinal boundaries?); a well-articulated vision (*why* should health be a salient public value?); and validated legal tools (*how* can law be effective in reducing morbidity and premature mortality?). This chapter begins an exploration of these questions and then goes on to illustrate the field through two lenses: infectious diseases and noncommunicable diseases.

I An Exploration of Public Health Law

a. Public Health Law: A Theory and a Definition

> Liberty does not import an absolute right in each person to be, at all times and in all circumstances, wholly freed from restraint. There are manifold restraints to which every person is necessarily subject for the common good. . . . A fundamental principle of the social compact is that . . . government is instituted for the common good, for the protection, safety, prosperity and happiness of the people.
>
> *Justice John Harlan (1905)*

The literature on the intersection of law and health is pervasive, and the subject is widely taught, practiced, and analyzed. The fields that characterize these branches of study are variously called health law, medical law, and forensic medicine. Notably absent from the literature is a singly accepted theory of public health law and an exploration of its boundaries. We define public health law as follows:

> The study of the legal powers and duties of the state to promote the conditions for people to be healthy (e.g., to identify, prevent, and ameliorate significant risks to health in the population) and the limitations on the power of the state to constrain the autonomy, privacy, liberty, proprietary, or other legally protected interests of individuals for the protection or promotion of the population's health. A fundamental precept of public health law is its aspiration for justice.

[4] Scott Burris, *The Invisibility of Public Health: Population-level Measures in a Politics of Market Individualism*, 87 AM. J. PUB. HEALTH 1607 (1997).

Through this definition, we suggest five essential characteristics of public health law: (1) *Government*—Public health is a special responsibility of government, in collaboration with partners in the community, business, the media, and academia[5]; (2) *Populations*—Public health focuses on the health of populations rather than individual patients; (3) *Relationships*—Public health addresses the relationships between the state and populations (or between the state and individuals or entities who place themselves or the community at risk); (4) *Services*—Public health deals with the provision of population-based services grounded on the scientific methodologies of public health (e.g., biostatistics and epidemiology); and (5) *Power*—Public health authorities possess the power to directly regulate individuals and businesses for the protection of the community, rather than relying on the ethic of voluntarism.

A systematic understanding of public health law requires an examination of the terms "public health" and the "common good." The word "public" in "public health" has two overlapping meanings—one that explains the entity that takes primary responsibility for the public's health, and another that explains who has a legitimate expectation to receive the benefits. The government has primary responsibility for the public's health. The government is a "public" entity that acts on behalf of the people and gains its legitimacy through the political process. A characteristic form of "public" or state action occurs when a democratically elected government exercises powers or duties to protect or promote the population's health.

The population as a whole has a legitimate expectation to benefit from public health services. The population elects the government and holds the state accountable for a meaningful level of health protection. Public health should possess broad appeal to the electorate because it is truly a universal aspiration; however, what best serves the population, of course, may not always be in the interests of all its individual members. It is for this reason that public health is highly political. What constitutes "enough" health? What kinds of services should government provide? What kinds of interventions should governments mandate? How will services be paid for and distributed? These remain controversial questions.

If individual interests are to give way to communal interests in a healthy population, it is important for people to value the common good. How should we understand the common good? Let us first consider "the common." The field of public health would profit from a vibrant conception of "the common" that sees public well-being as more than the aggregation of individual interests. A nonaggregative understanding of the common good recognizes that everyone has a stake in living in a society that regulates the risks shared by all. As members of society, we have common goals that go beyond our narrow interests. Individuals have a stake in healthy and secure communities where they can live in peace and well-being. An unhealthy or insecure community may produce harms common to all, such as increased crime and violence, impaired social relationships, and a less productive workforce. Accordingly, laws designed to promote the common good may sometimes constrain individual actions (smoking in public places, riding a motorcycle without a helmet, etc.) in exchange for the protection and satisfaction gained from sustaining healthier and safer communities.

[5] Bradley C. Karkkainen, *'New Governance' in Legal Thought and in the World: Some Splitting as Antidote to Overzealous Lumping*, 89 MINN L. REV. 471 (2004).

We also need to better understand the concept of "the good." In medicine, the meaning of "the good" is defined purely in terms of the individual's wants and needs. In most cases, it is the patient, not the physician or family, who decides the appropriate course of action. In public health, the meaning of "the good" is far less clear. Who gets to decide in a given case how to balance personal liberties against population health? One strategy for public health decision-making would be to allow each person to decide, but this would thwart many public health initiatives. For example, if individuals could decide whether to acquiesce to a vaccination or permit reporting of personal information to the health department, it would result in a "tragedy of the commons"—in which a group of individuals acting in self-interest (e.g., avoiding the inconvenience and perceived risks of vaccination to an individual) undermine their greater collective interest (e.g., preventing epidemics).[6]

One way forward is to promote greater community involvement in public health decision-making so that policy formation becomes a genuinely civic endeavor.[7] Citizens would strive to safeguard their communities' interest in public health policy through civic participation, open fora, and capacity building to solve local problems. Public involvement should result in stronger support for health policies and should encourage individuals to take a more active role in protecting themselves and their neighbors.

Public health law, therefore, places special responsibility on government to serve the health needs of populations. As a function of government, public health law is highly political and should be highly participatory. Consequently, health advocates should not shy away from energetic, ongoing involvement in the political process and should closely collaborate with affected communities.

b. From Personal Rights to Societal Obligations

> Measures to improve public health, relating as they do to such obvious and mundane matters as housing, smoking, and food, may lack the glamour of high-technology medicine, but what they lack in excitement they gain in their potential impact on health, precisely because they deal with the major causes of common disease and disabilities.
>
> *Geoffrey Rose (1992)*

The twentieth century began with the Progressive Era, characterized by social activism and community consciousness. This was followed by the Great Depression and the New Deal, a time of unprecedented government intervention in society and the economy. The common purpose of World War II and the political activism and social shifts of the 1960s and 1970s also emphasized a more communitarian outlook.

By the late twentieth century, however, this communitarian spirit was challenged by the flourishing philosophy of libertarianism—a worldview that places particular value on

[6] Garrett Hardin, *The Tragedy of the Commons*, 162 Sci. 1243 (1968).

[7] Daniel Callahan & Bruce Jennings, *Ethics and Public Health: Forging a Strong Relationship*, 92 Am. J. Pub. Health 169 (2002).

personal autonomy. This was a time when scholars had great influence in shaping ideas about the salience of the individual. Both ends of the political spectrum celebrated the values of free will and personal choice. The political left espoused the virtues of civil liberties, stressing autonomy, privacy, and empowerment. At the same time, the political right espoused the virtues of economic liberty, stressing freedom of contract, property privileges, and competitive markets. Personal interests in self-determination attained the status of "rights." Citizens were transformed from passive recipients of government largess into rights holders. In this intellectual environment, the individual's own interests often prevailed over the interests of family, community, or country.

Certainly, the power and importance of individual freedom is beyond dispute. However, insufficient attention has been given to the equally strong values of partnership, citizenship, and community. We need to recapture a classic republican tradition that emphasizes communal obligations as well as individual autonomy. As members of a society, our responsibility is not simply to defend our own individual right to be free from economic and personal restraints. We also have an obligation to protect and defend the community against threats to health, safety, and security. Each member of society owes a duty—one to another—to promote the common good. And each member benefits from participating in a well-regulated society that reduces risks that all members share. People may have to sacrifice some small measure of self-interest in order to gain the security enjoyed in a community where public health is recognized as an important value.

c. Why Population Health Should Be a Salient Public Value

> The success or failure of any government in the final analysis must be measured by the well-being of its citizens. Nothing can be more important to a state than its public health; the state's paramount concern should be the health of its people.
>
> *Franklin Delano Roosevelt (1932)*

The public health community takes it as an act of faith that health must be society's overarching value. Yet politicians do not always see it that way, expressing preferences, say, for highways, energy, defense, and tax cuts.

As discussed above, public health offers diffuse benefits, but often impinges on concrete, powerful, and well-organized interests. Its greatest successes are largely invisible, measured by the absence of disease or injury, and even these gains may take years or decades to manifest. For instance, restricting food advertising will likely take years to have an impact on rates of type 2 diabetes. In the meantime, the food industry, with deep pockets and a strong financial interest, will fight hard against any such regulations.

The lack of political commitment to population health can be seen in the relatively low public health expenditures in many national budgets—roughly 5 to 10 percent of total health dollars. Public health professionals often distrust and avoid politicians rather than engaging them in dialogue about the importance of population health. What is needed is a clear vision of, and rationale for, healthy populations as a political priority.

Why should health be a salient public investment, as opposed to other communal goods? Health is foundationally important because of its intrinsic value and its singular contribution to human functioning. Every person understands intuitively why health is vital to well-being. Health is necessary for much of the enjoyment, creativity, and productivity that a person derives from life.[8] If individuals have physical and mental health, they are better able to recreate, socialize, work, and engage in the activities of family and social life that bring meaning and happiness. Certainly, persons with ill health or disability can lead deeply fulfilling lives, but health facilitates many of life's joys and accomplishments. Every person therefore strives for the best physical and mental health achievable, even in the face of existing disease, injury, or disability. Individual health is so instinctively essential that human rights norms embrace state efforts to achieve it as a fundamental entitlement.[9]

Perhaps not as obvious, however, is that health is also essential for the functioning of populations. Without minimum levels of health, people cannot fully engage in social interactions, participate in the political process, exercise rights of citizenship, generate wealth, create art, and provide for the common security. A safe and healthy population builds strong roots for a country—its governmental structures, social organizations, cultural endowment, economic prosperity, and national defense. Population health, then, becomes a transcendent value because a certain level of human functioning is a prerequisite for engaging in activities that are critical to the public welfare—social, political, and economic.

The relationship between public health and societal functioning has been seen throughout the world. The 2014–2015 Ebola epidemic in West Africa destabilized three countries that were on the road to postconflict recovery. That public health disaster had far-reaching effects on Sierra Leone, Liberia, and Guinea, devastating their economies, undermining their governments and institutions, and straining their social fabric, including family life.[10]

Health has an intrinsic and instrumental value for individuals, communities, and entire nations. People aspire to achieve health because of its importance to a satisfying life; communities promote health for the mutual benefits of social interaction; and nations build health-care and public health infrastructures to cultivate a decent and prosperous civilization.

d. Law as a Public Health Tool: Models of Intervention

> [Since the founding of the Republic, p]ublic health regulation . . . [has been] the central component of a reigning theory and practice of governance committed to the pursuit of the people's welfare and happiness in a well-ordered society and polity.
>
> *William J. Novak (1996)*

[8] SRIDHAR VENKATAPURAM, HEALTH JUSTICE: AN ARGUMENT FROM THE CAPABILITY APPROACH (2011).

[9] WENDY E. PARMET, POPULATIONS, PUBLIC HEALTH, AND THE LAW 22 (2009).

[10] Lawrence O. Gostin & Eric A. Friedman, *A Retrospective and Prospective Analysis of the West African Ebola Virus Disease Epidemic: Robust National Health Systems at the Foundation and an Empowered WHO at the Apex*, 385 THE LANCET 1902–1909 (2015).

If government has an obligation to promote the conditions for people to be healthy, what tools are at its disposal? There are at least seven models for legal intervention designed to prevent injury and disease, encourage healthful behaviors, and generally promote the public's health.

Model 1: The Power to Tax and Spend

The constitutional power to tax and spend is ubiquitous. It supports most other types of government intervention and provides government with an important regulatory technique. Besides supporting other interventions, the power to spend directly funds the public health infrastructure, consisting of a well-trained workforce, electronic information and communications systems, rapid disease surveillance, and laboratory and response capabilities. The state can also set health-related conditions for the receipt of public funds. For example, it can grant funds for highway construction or other public works projects on the condition that the recipients meet designated safety requirements.[11] Conditional funding has its limits, however, which Chief Justice John Roberts made clear in striking down the provision of the Affordable Care Act enabling the U.S. Department of Health and Human Services (HHS) to withhold all Medicaid funding to states that refused to expand Medicaid eligibility.[12]

Model 2: The Power to Alter the Informational Environment

The public is bombarded with information and marketing materials that influence life choices and undoubtedly affect health and behavior. The government has several tools at its disposal to alter the informational environment, encouraging people to make more healthful choices about diet, exercise, cigarette smoking, and other health-related behaviors. First, government, as a health educator, can use communication campaigns as a major public health strategy. Second, government can require businesses to label their products to include instructions for safe use, disclosure of contents or ingredients, and health warnings. Finally, government can limit misleading or deceptive information in private advertising. The state can ban or regulate advertising of potentially harmful products such as cigarettes, firearms, and even unhealthy foods. However, such regulation is constrained by corporations' expanding First Amendment protections. The doctrine of commercial speech extends some First Amendment protection even to speech intended to make a profit. The government may only restrict or compel such speech if it meets certain constitutional tests, calibrated according to the purpose of the speech.[13]

Model 3: The Power to Alter the Built Environment

The design of the built or physical environment can hold great potential for addressing the major health threats. Public health has a long history in designing the built environment to reduce injury (e.g., workplace safety, traffic calming, and fire codes), infectious diseases (e.g., sanitation, zoning, and housing codes), and environmentally associated harms (e.g., lead paint and toxic emissions). Improved treatment and control of infectious diseases combined with the twin epidemics of obesity and tobacco have resulted in an epidemiological

[11] South Dakota v. Dole, 483 U.S. 203 (1987).

[12] Nat'l Fed'n of Indep. Bus. v. Sebelius, 567 U.S. ___, 132 S. Ct. 2566 (2012).

[13] *See, e.g.*, Bigelow v. Virginia, 421 U.S. 809 (1975); 44 Liquormart, Inc. v. Rhode Island, 517 U.S. 484 (1996); Cent. Hudson Gas & Elec. Corp. v. Pub. Serv. Comm'n, 447 U.S. 557 (1980).

transition from infectious to chronic diseases such as cardiovascular disease, cancer, diabetes, and asthma.[14] The challenge is to shift urban design to facilitate physical activity (walking, biking, and recreation); improve nutrition (encourage consuming fruits and vegetables, and avoiding added sugar, unhealthy fats, and high-caloric foods); decrease exposure to harmful products (cigarettes and alcoholic beverages); and increase social interactions (helping neighbors and building social capital).[15]

Model 4: The Power to Alter the Socioeconomic Environment

A strong and consistent finding of epidemiological research is that socioeconomic status (SES) is correlated with morbidity, mortality, and functioning.[16] SES is a complex phenomenon based on income, education, and occupation. The relationship between SES and health often is referred to as a "gradient" because of the graded and continuous nature of the association; health differences are observed well into the middle ranges of SES. Some researchers go further, suggesting the overall level of socioeconomic inequality in a society affects health.[17] That is, societies with fewer inequalities between the rich and poor tend to have superior overall health status. This phenomenon is apparent in comparisons of health indicators in Organization for Economic Cooperation and Development (OECD) countries, where life expectancy is higher in countries with well-developed social welfare systems that assure greater equity in resource allocation.

Model 5: Direct Regulation of Persons, Professionals, and Businesses

Government has the power to directly regulate individuals, professionals, and businesses. Public health authorities can set clear, enforceable rules to protect the health and safety of workers, consumers, and the population at large. Regulation of individual behavior (e.g., use of seat belts and motorcycle helmets) reduces injuries and deaths. Licenses and permits enable government to monitor and control the standards and practices of professionals and institutions (e.g., doctors, hospitals, and nursing homes). Finally, inspection and regulation of businesses help to assure safe and healthy working conditions, reductions in toxic emissions, and safer consumer products.

Model 6: Indirect Regulation through the Tort System

Attorneys general, public health authorities, and private citizens possess a powerful means of indirect regulation through the tort system. Civil litigation can redress many different kinds of public health harms: environmental damage (e.g., air pollution or groundwater contamination); exposure to toxic substances (e.g., pesticides, radiation, or chemicals); hazardous products (e.g., tobacco or firearms); and defective consumer products (e.g., children's toys, recreational equipment, or household goods). For example, in the 1990s attorneys general in forty-six states brought lawsuits against four major tobacco companies to recover tobacco-related healthcare costs. In response, these companies negotiated a Master

[14] Lawrence O. Gostin, *Healthy Living Needs Global Governance*, 511 NATURE 147 (2014).

[15] Wendy C. Perdue, L.A. Stone, & L. O. Gostin, *The Built Environment and Its Relationship to the Public's Health: The Legal Framework*, 93 AM. J. PUB. HEALTH 1390 (2003).

[16] MICHAEL G. MARMOT, THE STATUS SYNDROME (2005).

[17] Norman Daniels, Bruce Kennedy, & I. Kawachi, *Justice Is Good for Our Health*, 25 BOS. REV. 6 (2000).

Table 42.1 Pros and Cons of Legal Interventions to Promote Health

Legal Intervention	Pros	Cons
Power to Tax and Spend (e.g., taxes on sugary drinks)	• Uses economic principles to alter individual and industry practices, avoiding direct regulation	• Taxes on harmful behaviors are often regressive, placing financial burdens on those who are already most disadvantaged
Alter the Information Environment (e.g., labeling and health information campaigns)	• Informs the public about risk in ways that enable them to make healthier choices • Does not involve compulsion • Allows individuals to force industry changes through consumer choices	• May require a concerted effort over a significant period of time to change attitudes and behavior • Has the possibility of getting lost among the huge amount of information being presented at any given time
Alter the Built Environment (e.g., zoning laws to encourage safer, more walkable streets and greater access to fruits and vegetables)	• Makes it easier for individuals to make healthier choices without direct regulation • Less likely to come up against protests against government overreaching	• May suffer from the "invisibility of public health" issue • Expensive and time consuming • Often requires private sector buy-in
Alter the Socioeconomic Environment (e.g., education, jobs, and income support)	• Very effective and has widespread benefits beyond simple health	• Difficult to change entrenched social structures • Requires government redistribution, which is often controversial
Direct Regulation (e.g., occupational health and safety, lead removal in gas and housing)	• Effective • Flexible and easy to adjust as needed as controlled by government policy-makers	• Often elicits the tension between individual freedom and societal obligations
Tort Liability (e.g., litigation regarding cigarettes, firearms, food, and alcohol)	• If successful, can dissuade similar behaviors by others, such as related corporations • Can provide effective public health prevention outcomes where successful	• Litigation is expensive, prolonged, and uncertain • May not dissuade companies in other sectors • Set by courts and may not go as far as desired even if successful
Deregulation (e.g., decriminalize distribution of sterile injection equipment)	• Provides opportunities to implement harm reduction interventions • Inexpensive and not resource-intensive	• Public opinion can often be difficult to change • May harm interests that benefited from regulation

Settlement Agreement that required compensation to state governments in perpetuity (among other conditions), with payments totaling $206 billion through the year 2025.

The goals of tort law, although imperfectly achieved, are frequently consistent with public health objectives. The tort system aims to hold individuals and businesses accountable for their dangerous activities, compensate persons who are harmed, deter unreasonably hazardous conduct, and encourage innovation in product design. Civil litigation, therefore, can provide potent incentives for people and manufacturers to engage in safer, more socially conscious behavior.

Model 7: Deregulation: Law as a Barrier to Health

Sometimes laws harm the public's health and stand as obstacles to effective action. In such cases, the best remedy is deregulation. Politicians may urge superficially popular policies that have unintended health consequences. Consider laws that penalize exchanges or pharmacy sales of syringes and needles. Restricting access to sterile drug injection equipment can fuel the transmission of HIV and hepatitis C infections. Similarly, the closure of bathhouses can drive the HIV/AIDS epidemic underground, making it more difficult to reach gay men with condoms and safe sex literature. Further, laws that criminalize sex unless the person discloses his or her HIV status make common sexual behavior unlawful. Such laws provide a disincentive for seeking testing and medical treatment, ultimately harming the public's health.

Each of the legal interventions described above has benefits and drawbacks. Public health advocates must therefore carefully examine the particulars of each issue that they wish to address to determine which intervention is most likely to reach the desired outcome while protecting other important interests. Table 42.1 provides a summary of the seven types of legal intervention, along with a few significant advantages and disadvantages associated with each.

II Public Health Law through the Lens of Two Epidemics

Thus far we have offered a theory and definition of public health law, explained why it should be a key social value, and explored several tools or methods of intervention. Now we want to illustrate these themes and relate them back to the previously outlined principles by examining two salient epidemics: infectious diseases and noncommunicable diseases. In each case law can prevent or ameliorate the hazard, and in each there remain politically charged disputes about the legitimacy of government action.

a. Enduring, Resurgent, and Re-emergent Infectious Diseases

> One can think of the middle of the twentieth century as the end of one of the most important social revolutions in history, the virtual elimination of the infectious diseases as a significant factor in social life.[18]
>
> *Sir Frank MacFarlane Burnet* (1962)

[18] Gerald Pier, *On the Greatly Exaggerated Reports of the Death of Infectious Diseases* (correspondence), 47 Clinical Infectious Diseases 1113 (2008).

Sir Frank MacFarlane Burnet, a winner of the Nobel Prize in Medicine, was one of a large chorus of prominent voices predicting the end of infectious diseases as a public health threat.[19] Their predictions were born of hubris and turned out to be wrong.[20] Pathogens have a way of staying ahead of science, nimbly changing and adapting to changing threats. Endemic diseases such as foodborne and sexually transmitted infections endure, while healthcare-associated infections such as *Staphylococcus aureus* and *Clostridium difficile* affect one in five hospital patients annually. Outbreaks of preventable diseases persist, as localized communities opt out of vaccines (e.g., those for whooping cough and measles) for reasons of religion or conscience. Old threats re-emerge, with pathogens (e.g., tuberculosis and HIV) growing resistant to standard antimicrobial drugs. Society faces new threats from the impact of globalization, such as novel influenza strains (e.g., H5N1, H1N1, H7N9), coronaviruses (e.g., SARS and MERS), and hemorrhagic fevers (e.g., Ebola). Beyond naturally occurring diseases, dangerous pathogens can escape insecure labs, while bioterrorists can create fear and political instability. Can the law respond to these divergent threats? Here, we discuss three examples that are likely to pose significant near- to medium-term threats to public health and outline how different legal modes of intervention have been used or challenged in each example.

i. Healthcare-Associated Infections

Healthcare-associated infections (HAIs) in the United States result in $28 billion to $33 billion in excess medical costs and nearly 100,000 deaths annually—not counting HAIs in non-hospital settings such as long-term care.[21] Perhaps most concerning is that HAIs are major contributors to accelerating highly resistant infections, thus reducing the effectiveness of standard antimicrobials. Most of this morbidity, mortality, and cost is preventable, with large-scale state and regional projects showing substantial decreases in HAIs through systematic adherence to infection control procedures. These projects demonstrate how direct government regulation of industry and appropriate alterations of the built environment can improve health outcomes.

HHS launched a national plan in 2009, which complemented various state-mandated HAI reporting and control requirements. The Centers for Medicare and Medicaid Services offered financial incentives to adhere to the Centers for Disease Control and Prevention's (CDC) infection control guidelines, and all states now have prevention plans in place. Still, these government actions fall short of requiring compliance with good practices and uniformly enforcing those standards. Absent such legal mandates, hospitals continue to have widely variable HAI rates.

HAI illustrates the importance of interventions that take into account both public health and medical approaches. Solving the problem will require a coordinated effort by public health officials, healthcare facilities, and healthcare professionals. Public health can address the population-level impacts of the epidemic, developing surveillance and response

[19] John E. Bennett, M.D. Raphael Dolin, & Martin J. Blaser, Mandell, Douglas, and Bennett's Principles and Practice of Infectious Disease (5th ed. 1999).

[20] Rima F. Khabbaz et al., *Challenges of Infectious Diseases in the USA*, 384 Lancet 53 (2014).

[21] Centers for Disease Control & Prevention, The Direct Medical Costs of Healthcare-Associated Infections in U.S. Hospitals and the Benefits of Prevention (2009).

techniques. However, stemming the spread of HAI will depend on the individual actions and policies of the medical establishment.

ii. Vaccine-Preventable Diseases

Vaccinations are among the most cost-effective and widely used public health interventions, and also exemplify the tension between our culture of individualism and following public health principles that require forgoing some individual choices for the common good. From 1924 to 2012, routine childhood vaccinations prevented more than 100 million cases of serious diseases such as polio, measles, rubella, mumps, hepatitis A, diphtheria, and pertussis.[22] State vaccination laws, moreover, have been a great success, with the rate of complete immunization of school-age children at nearly 95%.[23] But high aggregate vaccination coverage levels mask clustering of unvaccinated children. For example, religious or conscientious opt-outs have fueled major outbreaks of whooping cough and measles from 2012 through 2015.

Once a population reaches a certain threshold of vaccination, community immunity protects the vaccinated and unvaccinated (such as infants and immune-compromised persons) alike, underscoring the invisibility of effective public health interventions. Parents may thus perceive little risk to their child from a failure to vaccinate while failing to perceive how cumulative individual choices may affect the population as a whole. When nonvaccination rises, community immunity may dissipate.

While still a small minority, an increasing number of parents choose not to vaccinate, motivated by fears for their children's safety. Most vaccination fears are rooted in one poorly designed study, since retracted, linking childhood vaccines with autism, and in misinformation about that study spread by celebrities and on the Internet. Efforts by public health officials to dispel these fears through traditional public health messaging have had limited impact. Creative strategies may be needed to reach this population that is often distrustful of government and scientific authorities.

Resistance to vaccines also stems from religious or moral objections. There has been a significant backlash against vaccines such as that for the human papilloma virus (HPV), a sexually transmitted infection linked to cervical cancer. Some parents worry that vaccinating children in their early teens may encourage or condone sexual promiscuity. Others have religious beliefs that prohibit all vaccination.

Vaccination laws fall squarely within states' police powers to legislate to protect health, safety, morals, and general welfare. Requirements that individuals be vaccinated or face a legal penalty have a long history in the United States, and courts have routinely held mandatory vaccination constitutional at the state and federal levels, so long as they are applied without discrimination.[24] In the seminal case, *Jacobson v. Massachusetts*, 197 U.S. 11 (1905),

[22] Willem G. Panhuis et al., *Contagious Diseases in the United States from 1888 to the Present*, 396 New Eng. J. Med. 2152 (2013).

[23] Centers for Disease Control and Prevention, *Vaccination Coverage Among Children in Kindergarten—United States*, 62 Morbidity & Mortality Wkly Rep. 607, http://www.cdc.gov/mmwr/preview/mmwrhtml/mm6230a3.htm.

[24] *See, e.g.*, Jacobson v. Massachusetts, 197 U.S. 11 (1905); Wright v. DeWitt Sch. Dist., 385 S.W.2d 644, 648 (Ark. 1965); Workman v. Mingo Cty. Bd. of Educ., 419 Fed. Appx. 348 (4th Cir. 2011); Check ex rel. M. C. v. N.Y.C. Dep't of Educ., 2013 WL 2181045 (E.D.N.Y. 2013); Maricopa Cty. Health Dep't v. Harmon, 750 P.2d 1364 (Ariz. Ct. App. 1987).

the U.S. Supreme Court upheld Massachusetts' requirement that adult residents be vaccinated or face a fine. Justice Harlan, writing for the majority, stated:

> [I]n every well-ordered society charged with the duty of conserving the safety of its members the rights of the individual in respect of his liberty may at times, under the pressure of great dangers, be subjected to such restraint, to be enforced by reasonable regulations, as the safety of the general public may demand.[25]

Currently, all fifty states mandate that children more than five years old receive a series of vaccinations before enrolling in state-licensed day-care facilities or public schools. However, all states except for West Virginia, Mississippi, and California also grant religious exemptions, while eighteen states grant exemptions for philosophical convictions.[26] Many of these exemptions are easy to qualify for, undermining the efficacy of direct regulation. For example, some states require only a signature on a pre-printed form.

Liberal exemption policies reduce vaccination rates, ultimately increasing the incidence of vaccine-preventable illness.[27] Although states with more restrictive exemption laws face First Amendment challenges under the Establishment and Free Exercise Clauses, courts usually support strict vaccine mandates. Despite the tension between individual freedom and public health, states using their public health powers are therefore able to substantially reduce preventable childhood diseases.

iii. Antimicrobial Resistance

Much drug resistance is man-made, such as the advent of so-called "super bugs" in hospitals fueled by inconsistent infection control in the health system. Antimicrobial resistance is a complex phenomenon with multiple causes: the widespread application of antibiotics to farm animals as a growth-promoting agent; the incorporation of antibacterials such as disinfectants and antiseptics into household products (e.g., soaps, detergents, lotions); physician overprescribing without diagnosing a drug-susceptible infection; and patients who fail to take the full course of prescribed medication.

In each case, legislators and regulators have tools at their disposal such as direct regulation over industry, medical, and individual practices. But, as with vaccines, social and political obstacles to these legal solutions remain. Entrenched interests, such as industrial livestock operations, strongly oppose tighter regulation of antibiotic use. Both physicians and patients resist government intrusion into the doctor-patient relationship. And just as with vaccines, there is a collective action problem—any one individual's overuse of antibiotics is unlikely to cause him or her direct harm, while in aggregate such actions produce great harm to society.

The U.S. Food and Drug Administration (FDA) in 2013 issued voluntary guidelines to phase out antibiotics in food animals for production purposes (e.g., to enhance growth or

[25] Jacobson v. Massachusetts, 197 U.S. 11, 29 (1905).

[26] Johns Hopkins Bloomberg School of Public Health: Institute of Vaccine Safety, Vaccine Exemptions (Sept. 15, 2015), http://www.vaccinesafety.edu/cc-exem.htm.

[27] Saad B. Omer, William K.Y. Pan, & Neal A. Halsey et al., *Nonmedical Exemptions to School Immunization Requirements: Secular Trends and Association of State Policies with Pertussis*

improve feed efficiency) and to bring therapeutic uses (to treat, control, or prevent specific diseases) under veterinarian oversight.[28] Further, in 2014 the White House announced the National Strategy for Combating Antibiotic-Resistant Bacteria, which sets specific national goals and targets to monitor and curb the growth and spread of antibiotic-resistant bacterial strains, including several that directly impact industry.

It remains to be seen whether these approaches will be effective. Little government regulation exists for overuse of antibacterials in household products, although in 2013 the FDA proposed a rule that would require manufacturers of antibacterial hand soaps and body washes to demonstrate that their products are safe for long-term daily use and more effective than ordinary soap in preventing illness and the spread of infection.[29] Physician overprescribing of antimicrobials is well understood, yet government is reluctant to interfere with the physician/patient relationship. Patients continue to expect (even demand) antibiotics, while physicians find that liberal prescribing is often the easier course of action from a financial perspective.

Perhaps the only realm where legislators are willing to regulate is when patients are seen as noncompliant. States empower public health officials to require directly observed therapy, whereby patients are watched while they take medication until the full recommended course of treatment is completed. This approach has proved highly successful, for example, in stemming outbreaks of multidrug-resistant tuberculosis, even though it infringes patient autonomy and privacy.

b. Biosecurity in an Age of Terrorism

> These events revealed totally unacceptable behavior. They should never have happened. I'm upset, I'm angry, I've lost sleep over this, and I'm working on it until the issue is resolved.
>
> *Thomas Frieden upon learning about biosafety breaches in CDC labs* (2014)

Not all infectious disease threats are naturally occurring—some are the product of purposeful genetic adaptation and environmental manipulation. While these dangerous pathogens are generally developed in laboratory settings, they can inadvertently escape from laboratories that are not sufficiently secure, an issue which could be directly addressed through the power of direct regulation.

In June 2014, Centers for Disease Control and Prevention (CDC) scientists were exposed to live anthrax spores after potentially infectious samples were sent to labs that were

Incidence, 296 JAMA 1757 (2006) (explaining that in 2001 to 2004, states that offered personal belief exemptions had higher rates of nonmedical exemptions and, moreover, that easier granting of exemptions and availability of personal belief exemptions were both associated with increased pertussis incidence).

[28] FOOD & DRUG ADMIN., FDA'S STRATEGY ON ANTIMICROBIAL RESISTANCE—QUESTIONS AND ANSWERS (June 11, 2015), http://www.fda.gov/animalveterinary/guidancecomplianceenforcement/guidanceforindustry/ucm216939.htm.

[29] FOOD & DRUG ADMIN., FDA ISSUES PROPOSED RULE TO DETERMINE SAFETY AND EFFECTIVENESS OF ANTIBACTERIAL SOAPS (Dec. 16, 2013), http://www.fda.gov/newsevents/newsroom/pressannouncements/ucm378542.htm.

unequipped to handle them. The investigation also uncovered an even more dangerous lapse, with a CDC lab accidentally contaminating a flu sample with Influenza A (H5N1), a deadly strain that kills around 60% of those infected. And in July of that year, live smallpox samples (supposedly confined to just two locations in the world) were discovered at a National Institutes of Health (NIH) laboratory. These examples demonstrate a lack of sufficient regulation to ensure procedural and structural safeguards to protect public health. If highly secure CDC and NIH labs can make errors, the potential is still greater with less secure laboratories.

Dual use research of concern (DURC) can enhance the function of infectious agents, rendering them more transmissible or pathogenic. For example, in 2012 scientists genetically altered H5N1 to render it more transmissible from human to human. An advisory committee within the National Science Advisory Board for Biosecurity asked the journals *Science* and *Nature* to publish only a redacted version, while similar research was temporarily suspended.[30] Although the committee subsequently reinstated dual use research and permitted unredacted publication, HHS has proposed DURC regulations.

Finally, and importantly, the anthrax attacks following September 11 raised public concerns about dangerous pathogens falling into the hands of bad actors intent on terrorizing the population and causing political instability. State and federal powers to prevent and respond to bioterrorism have been highly controversial. For example, the debate around the Model State Emergency Health Powers Act, drafted in the wake of 9/11 to better define states' powers during public health emergencies, revealed deep fault lines between advocates for public safety and for civil liberties.[31]

Infectious disease powers have been a staple of public health law ever since the founding of the republic. Most state public health legislation focuses intently on infectious disease surveillance and response. Despite the continued relevance of infectious diseases, there has been a modern epidemiologic trend toward noncommunicable diseases. We now turn to the evolving state of public health law in response to chronic diseases caused, in substantial part, by human behavior.

c. Noncommunicable Diseases

> Establishment of community conditions to support healthy behaviours and promote effective management of chronic conditions will deliver healthier students to schools, healthier workers to employers and businesses, and a healthier population to the health-care system.
>
> *Ursula Bauer, et al. (2014)*

Noncommunicable diseases (NCDs) even more sharply implicate the tension between individual liberty and the public good when government proposes using its power to tax, to alter the built environment, to alter the information environment, to subject industry to liability,

30 John D. Kraemer & Lawrence O. Gostin, *The Limits of Government Regulation of Science*, 335 SCI. 1047 (2012).

31 Gostin et al., *The Model State Emergency Health Powers Act: Planning for and Response to Bioterrorism and Naturally Occurring Infectious Diseases*, 288 JAMA 622 (2002).

or to adjust the socioeconomic environment to advance public health. Tobacco, excessive alcohol consumption, poor nutrition, and physical inactivity fuel many NCDs—chiefly, diabetes, cancer, cardiovascular disease, and respiratory disease. Overweight and obesity are emblematic of the epidemiological transition to NCDs, with 35% of American adults currently obese and 69% obese or overweight. Rates of chronic diseases also reflect deep health disparities based on race and socioeconomic status, with 48% of African American adults currently obese.[32] Further, American Indians have the highest smoking rates, African Americans the highest cardiovascular disease death rates, and low socioeconomic status Americans the highest obesity rates.[33]

There is often thought to be a clear demarcation between communicable and noncommunicable diseases, but the lines are, in fact, blurred. For example, more than 20% of all malignancies are causally linked to human pathogens, including hepatitis B and C virus (liver cancer), human papillomavirus (cervical cancer), and *Helicobacter pylori* (stomach cancer). Additionally, the causes of overweight are complex, and in some cases could have an infectious origin.

Although some aspects of infectious disease control remain controversial, it is for the most part well accepted.[34] The same cannot be said of laws regulating human behaviors that are widely viewed as both within the control of autonomous individuals and purely self-regarding. Unlike infectious disease control, where a sick individual can directly expose others to risk of contagion, NCD control measures tend to impact the personal liberties of the same individual the measure is attempting to protect—an aim that is more politically and legally fraught and susceptible to charges of paternalism. Here, we examine the law's diverse roles in NCD prevention and control, while exploring the major reasons for social and political opposition.

i. Prioritize Prevention across Government and Social Sectors

Looking across the spectrum of NCD interventions, it is vital that all society is involved in prevention efforts. Researchers have demonstrated the powerful forces of multiple social determinants in health outcomes—education, housing, gender equality, income, and social support.[35] NCD prevention, therefore, demands engagement from multiple sectors of government, industry, philanthropy, and civil society. An "all-of-government" strategy would coordinate all departments and agencies within the government (e.g., health and human services, economic, education, labor, and urban planning) to encourage consideration of health in all policies. At the same time, industry could develop healthier products, philanthropy could shift funding priorities toward NCDs, and civil society could mobilize for change. The

[32] CENTERS FOR DISEASE CONTROL & PREVENTION, ADULT OBESITY FACTS, http://www.cdc.gov/obesity/data/adult.html.

[33] Ursula Bauer et al., *Prevention of Chronic Disease in the 21st Century: Elimination of the Leading Preventable Causes of Premature Death and Disability in the USA*, 384 LANCET 45 (2014).

[34] *Compare* Richard A. Epstein, *Let the Shoemaker Stick to His Last: A Defense of the "Old" Public Health*, 46 PERSPECTIVES IN BIOLOGY & MED. S138 (2003) *with* Lawrence O. Gostin & M. Gregg Bloche, *The Politics of Public Health: A Reply to Richard Epstein*, 46 PERSPECTIVES IN BIOLOGY & MED. S160 (2003).

[35] *See, e.g.*, MICHAEL MARMOT, THE STATUS SYNDROME (2005).

successful social and political mobilization around both AIDS and tobacco control offers lessons for altering thinking at all levels.

ii. Tobacco Control: The Paradigmatic Case of the Effective Use of Law

The marked reduction in smoking rates could be viewed as proof of concept that law, including indirect regulation through tort, can be an effective public health tool. Cigarette smoking among American adults decreased from 42% in 1965 to 18% in 2011,[36] with similar reductions in most developed countries. No single intervention was responsible for this success, but a suite of policies transformed the culture of smoking—from cigarettes representing an accoutrement of the glamorous life to conveying stigma and social disapproval. Since the groundbreaking report by Surgeon General Luther Terry on *Smoking and Health* in 1964 (demonstrating the scientific link between smoking and disease), national, state, and local policy-makers have increased taxation, passed smoke-free laws, mandated package warnings, and drastically curtailed marketing. Although changing the informational environment has drawn First Amendment opposition, the cumulative effect of these policies has driven smoking rates to historic lows.

Cigarettes are so expensive, their harms so well understood, and the opportunities for indoor smoking so curtailed that they have lost personal and social appeal. None of this would have been possible without massive tort litigation and aggressive regulation of a universally harmful product.

Two discoveries made tobacco control politically palatable: (1) litigation revealed that the industry lied and concealed vital data on the health hazards of smoking, while also targeting children and adolescents in marketing; and (2) research demonstrated the harms caused by secondhand smoke. It was the latter that changed the paradigm from smoking as self-endangering to smoking as causing harm to others.

The next battle in the tobacco forum has begun—over electronic cigarettes. Traditional cigarettes are the archetypal harmful product: They are highly addictive, they are sold using deceptive tactics, and they kill up to half of their users. The fight over e-cigarettes will be more nuanced, possibly dividing the public health community. Proponents argue that e-cigarettes substitute for conventional tobacco products and therefore are effective harm-reduction tools, while critics worry that their glamorization could hook a new generation on smoking. With the FDA having already asserted jurisdiction over electronic cigarettes, this conflict will almost certainly be resolved by public health law.[37]

iii. Regulate the Food Industry

Social perceptions of food and the food industry are very different from perceptions of tobacco. Food is not inherently harmful in the same manner as tobacco and is necessary for health; the industry is not widely seen as deceitful; and consuming food is still thought to be a matter of individual and parental responsibility and an expression of cultural and

[36] NAT'L CTR. FOR HEALTH STATISTICS, HEALTH, UNITED STATES 2012 (2013).

[37] Lawrence O. Gostin & Aliza Y. Glasner, *E-Cigarettes, Vaping, and Youth*, JAMA (June 30, 2014), http://jama.jamanetwork.com/article.aspx?articleid=1886077.

individual identity. In this milieu, the battle to rigorously regulate the food industry will be fraught with complexity and political opposition. But how has law been used—and how could it be used—to facilitate better diet and nutrition?

A package of measures, modeled on tobacco control, would facilitate healthier consumer choices. These include improved food options in schools and other public institutions by altering the information environment via widespread campaigns; direct regulatory measures such as marketing restrictions, particularly on promotions targeting children and adolescents; clear, consistent, and attractive nutritional information (e.g., package labels and menus) designed to help consumers make healthier choices; mandatory reductions in unhealthy ingredients (added sugar, sodium, and highly saturated or trans fats in ultraprocessed foods); portion controls (limiting the size of sugary drinks); and economic tools, such as taxing unhealthy items.

Some public health advocates argue that there is a fundamental conflict of interest between the food industry's profits and public health objectives, leading to significant debate about whether to engage the industry in public-private partnerships and other initiatives, or whether to exclude it entirely, as with the tobacco industry.[38] Some industry-government collaborations have produced healthier products via self-regulation. The National Salt Reduction Initiative, for example, persuaded food companies to voluntarily reduce added sodium.[39] Yet the private sector continues to obfuscate package labels, market junk food, and add sodium, sugar, and trans-fatty acids to processed foods in order to boost sales. Voluntary guidelines also often stave off or stall more effective regulation. The food industry, for example, has adopted weak self-regulatory codes on advertising to children, which has forestalled tougher government regulation.

Although government has introduced innovative policies such as trans-fatty acid bans, package and menu labeling requirements, and improved school nutrition, most of these initiatives have been tamped down by industry opposition and/or criticism of overreach (the "nanny state"). For example, the FDA proposed improvements to the Nutrition Facts Label on processed foods, but its rules do not require clear consistent messages, unlike the United Kingdom's "traffic light" system where products high in calories, sugar, sodium, and fats have four large "red lights" on the package.[40] Even the Affordable Care Act's menu labeling provisions preempt more stringent state or municipal label requirements. Government regulation, moreover, is politically difficult to implement. As countries impose higher taxes or tighter regulations, they risk losing jobs and tax revenues if companies move to more accommodating jurisdictions. In a federal society, cities and states can face a "race to the bottom" as each tries to become more business friendly.

iv. Alter the Built Environment

Healthy activities should be the easy choice where people live, learn, work, and play. Bicycle lanes, bike-share programs, pedestrian walkways, playgrounds, sports pitches, and parks

[38] Kelly D. Brownell, *Thinking Forward: The Quicksand of Appeasing the Food Industry*, 9 PLoS MED e1001254, dx.doi.org/10.1371/journal.pmed.1001254.

[39] NYC DEP'T OF HEALTH & MENTAL HYGIENE, NATIONAL SALT REDUCTION INITIATIVE, http://www.nyc.gov/html/doh/html/diseases/salt.shtml (last accessed Aug. 4, 2014).

[40] David A. Kessler, *Toward More Comprehensive Food Labeling*, 371 NEW ENG. J. MED 371 (2014).

make physical activity safe and attractive. Investing in mass transport reduces driving and air pollution. Schools and employers should dedicate time to recreation, offer healthy menus, and design stairways to be safer and more attractive.

The law could facilitate healthful activity in several ways: incentivizing or requiring the redesign of public spaces, schools, and workplaces; city planning to create safe and attractive walking paths, bike lanes, and parks; funding bike shares and mass transportation; and offering financial support, perhaps through competitive grants, to promote innovative city landscapes or food programs. New York City has introduced multiple policies and programs to expand active transport and other physical activity (such as its "Vision Zero" road safety plan), and has shared the result with other jurisdictions. However, a wide range of barriers, from contentious politics to constrained city budgets to unimaginative city planners, have prevented many municipalities from following New York City's example.

v. *Clinical Prevention Services*

There is perhaps no area where the intersections between public health and healthcare are clearer than in NCDs. Two of CDC's four chronic disease crosscutting strategies entail clinical practice reforms (the other two are surveillance and environmental changes to support healthy behaviors). The first crosscutting strategy is *health system innovations to effectively use clinical prevention tools*, which includes preventive screenings (blood pressure, lipid, and cancer), controlling intermediate risk factors (low-dose aspirin, beta blockers, and statins), and treating chronic conditions (monitoring and lowering blood sugar in diabetics). The second crosscutting strategy is *community resources linked to clinical services*, which is intended to sustain management of chronic disease by supporting good nutrition and physical activity, adherence to treatment, and medical follow-up.

The ACA includes incentives for the healthcare system to prevent and manage chronic disease, while also funding enhanced public health services.[41] For example, it increases the proportion of health insurance coverage costs that employers may link to health-contingent wellness programs, either undertaking a given health-promoting activity (e.g., participating in an exercise program) or achieving a certain health outcome (e.g., not smoking). The CDC's chronic disease strategies dovetail with the ACA's incentives, showing the potentially powerful combined effects of public health and healthcare collaboration.[42]

Of course, with regard to public health programs more is not always better, as illustrated by the recent scale-backs of some prominent screening recommendations. Prostate screening, long urged for all men over forty, was significantly pared back after studies found that the cost of screenings, risk of biopsies, and treatment for prostate cancer outweighed the benefits for many age and risk groups.[43] Breast cancer screenings were curtailed for similar reasons.[44] These examples show that the benefits and costs of screening programs must be

[41] U.S. Department of Labor, Fact Sheet: The Affordable Care Act and Wellness Programs, *available at* http://www.dol.gov/ebsa/newsroom/fswellnessprogram.

[42] Lawrence O. Gostin et al., Law and the Health System (2014).

[43] Andrew Pollack, *Looser Guidelines Issued on Prostate Screenings*, N.Y. Times, May 4, 2013, B4.

[44] Editorial Board, *Shifting Advice on Mammograms*, N.Y. Times, Oct. 26, 2015, A1.

carefully weighed to ensure they are efficacious, provide high value for money, and result in more good than harm for the target population.

vi. Social, Political, and Legal Barriers: A Case Study from New York City

NCD prevention has faced fierce opposition, mostly from those who elevate (or purport to elevate) autonomy and personal responsibility above public health and the common good. Emblematic of these critiques is the reaction to the social action agenda during Michael Bloomberg's term as New York City's mayor (2002–2013), particularly the soda portion limit, which the state's highest court struck down in 2014.

Many of Mayor Bloomberg's policies served as models nationally, such as posting calories in restaurants (adopted in the ACA), the trans-fat ban (currently being phased in by the FDA), and smoke-free public places (now in most major cities). But Bloomberg's policies have also drawn the ire of critics and sometimes the rebuke of judges. Two controversial moves came just as he was leaving office—a portion limit on sugary drinks and a tobacco purchase age of twenty-one years (the highest in the nation). The court of appeals invalidated the portion limit; and the media expressed amazement that a twenty-year-old can drive a car and enlist in the military, but now cannot buy cigarettes in New York City.

Critics often frame their arguments in intellectual terms, claiming that chronic disease policies are unproven scientifically, inconsistently applied, unfair to minorities, and undemocratic. But what really bothers a vocal segment of the public is the steadfast belief that government has no justification for reaching into the lives of adults, who are capable of making choices for themselves. Below we describe these claims in more depth and present a rebuttal to each.

1. *The "Absence of Science" Claim*: Critics claim that NCD policies are not backed by scientific studies and therefore will be ineffective. But corporate actors' real concern is that the policies will drive consumers away from profitable products. As a result, corporate interests have backed media campaigns and aggressively litigated against these policies.[45] In fact, both logic and research guide Bloomberg's policies. Even the soda portion limit is supported by research showing that sugary drinks deliver empty calories; consumption is associated with rising obesity rates; and portion sizes have grown substantially.[46] Because of the complex interactions between different policies and risk factors, policy-makers rarely can demonstrate the effectiveness of any one intervention—a problem also common with respect to economic interventions, which are rarely if ever backed by definitive science. It is also virtually impossible to evaluate a policy unless it is first introduced and then tested. Moreover, the "inconclusive science" critique is faulty because it focuses on a single intervention. Most social change is

[45] *See, e.g.*, Michael Grynbaum, *Fighting Soda Rule, Industry Focuses on Personal Choice*, N.Y. TIMES, July 2, 2012, A10.

[46] *See* Lisa R. Young & Marion Nestle, *The Contribution of Expanding Portion Sizes to the US Obesity Epidemic*, 92 AM. J. PUB. HEALTH 246 (2002); Barbara J. Rolls et al., *Portion Size of Food Affects Energy Intake in Normal-Weight and Overweight Men and Women*, 76 AM. J. CLINICAL NUTRITION 1207 (2002).

not driven by a single intervention but rather on a suite of policies, operating over time, as with changes in the tobacco culture and reductions in the rate of smoking.

2. *The "Inconsistency" Claim*: Related to scientific uncertainty is the demand for consistency. Critics of the soda portion limit pointed out that it applied to McDonald's supersized drinks but not to 7-Eleven's Big Gulps or Starbucks' flavored lattes. The inconsistency critique, however, fails to appreciate the nature of lawmaking. Law is forged through political compromise—shaped by public preferences, lobbying, and trading favors. A tax on sugary drinks would have been a more consistent intervention, but it was outside of Mayor Bloomberg's power. The state's governor was unwilling to impose a tax, despite Bloomberg's requests. The "inconsistency" claim also misunderstands the importance of incremental improvements. Public health agencies tackle problems one at a time, hoping to build a critical mass of policies in the long run. Insistence that policy-makers solve every problem now or not at all is a recipe for doing nothing.
3. *The "Slippery Slope" Claim*: Critics worry that Bloomberg's policies will lead to evermore invasive future policies A host of vested corporate interests can build a common cause around slippery slopes—e.g., the sugar/alcohol/tobacco industries, restaurants, and advertisers. Slippery slope arguments force a speculative analysis without identifying the specifics of policies feared to lie downslope. It should not be necessary to win a debate today about policies that may or may not be proposed in the future.
4. *The "Justice" Claim*: Because NCDs fall especially hard on the poor and minorities, limits on freedom necessarily apply disproportionately to those groups. Tobacco taxes, for example, are regressive because those in lower SES groups have higher rates of smoking—and even if rates of usage were the same, tobacco costs would still take up a larger proportion of those groups' income. A similar concern applies to soda taxes. This is an odd conception of justice, however, as it focuses exclusively on the fair distribution of the downsides of obesity policies (limits on liberty and higher taxes). The justice argument fails miserably in considering the health benefits that accrue from such interventions. The far greater injustice stems from government's *failure* to act to reduce suffering and early death visited mostly upon poor neighborhoods. Health should be seen as a primary freedom, as it underwrites so many of life's options. And the cost of NCDs that the taxes may prevent can far exceed the cost of the taxes.
5. *The "Paternalism" Claim*: Critics' discomfort with Bloomberg's agenda, at its core, is grounded in distrust of government telling autonomous adults how to conduct their lives. Many believe that the state should not interfere with personal decisions that primarily affect only the individual being regulated. Yet, unlike quarantines for infectious diseases, most NCD policies are not significantly intrusive. Many require simply a return to the norms of the recent past—such as smaller food portions and more livable spaces. Other interventions actively create a "new normal" such as reduced trans fat, sodium, and sugar, or limiting advertising to children. Once implemented, many interventions are embraced; few people today are nostalgic for smoke-filled restaurants.

When a corporation offers an unhealthy product to an individual, freedom of choice has already been compromised. The playing field is not level, and it is exceedingly hard for the individual to make a healthy choice. The *corporation* has an economic incentive to sell that product irrespective of the harms that ensue. The *government* helps make that product cheaper by subsidizing the ingredients (e.g., high fructose corn syrup) and more accessible by enacting zoning laws that make fast food retailers virtually ubiquitous. The *courts* grant the corporation free speech rights to market aggressively using inaccurate messages touting fun and vitality—often targeting youth. And the poor, less-educated *consumer* may not have comprehensible information or even affordable access to healthier alternatives. All in all, those burdened with meeting monthly bills and juggling jobs and families find it easier to make the choice that is less expensive, more convenient, and widely marketed. The default choice in today's America is the unhealthy choice, but we can change that default without undermining anyone's fundamental freedoms.

Acknowledgments

This chapter is based largely on previous publications. *See, e.g.*, Public Health Law: Power, Duty, Restraint (2008); Global Health Law (2014); Lawrence O. Gostin, *Bloomberg's Health Legacy: Urban Innovator or Meddling Nanny*, 43(5) Hastings Ctr. Rpt. 19 (2013).

CHAPTER 43

COMMUNICABLE DISEASE LAW AND EMERGING ISSUES

Antibiotic Resistance

ZITA LAZZARINI

I INTRODUCTION

WRITTEN history and the study of prehistory indicate that human populations have confronted and been shaped by repeated encounters with deadly microbes.[1] Although the relative burden of communicable disease to noncommunicable disease has shifted worldwide in recent decades toward noncommunicable diseases in both the industrialized and developing world, the burden of communicable diseases remains substantial.[2] Using "law" to control communicable disease is as old as the Bible and as current as the Ebola outbreak or concerns over a return of pandemic influenza.[3] The United States currently has laws in every state and at the federal level aimed at prevention, detection, and control of communicable diseases. For both historical and constitutional reasons communicable disease control has been primarily addressed by state laws, as part of the police power, but, even under the limited powers granted the federal government by the U.S. Constitution, the federal government plays an important role in law and policy-making related to communicable diseases. This includes not only statutes[4] but also key federal agencies that, through regulation, impact communicable disease prevention, detection, and control (e.g., Department of Agriculture; Food and Drug Administration; Environmental Protection Agency), and others that advance the science underlying our understanding of new and old diseases (e.g., Centers for Disease Control and Prevention; National Institutes of Health).

1 JARED DIAMOND, GUNS, GERMS AND STEEL (1997).

2 GBD 2013 Mortality and Causes of Death Collaborators, *Global, Regional, and National Age-Sex Specific All-Cause and Cause-Specific Mortality for 240 Causes of Death, 1990–2013: A Systematic Analysis for the Global Burden of Disease Study 2013*, 385 LANCET 117, 127–131 (2015).

3 THE BIBLE, Leviticus 14:7; Benjamin Weiser, & J. David Goodman, *The Flu, TB and Now Ebola: A Rare Legal Remedy Returns*, N.Y. TIMES, Oct. 26, 2014.

4 Federal authorities have the power to take measures necessary to prevent introduction and spread of diseases from other countries under section 361 of the Public Health Service Act (42 U.S.C. § 264).

"Law" in the broad sense of state and federal constitutional powers, statutes, regulations, and common law can act at multiple levels in the area of communicable diseases; law can focus on the microbes, it can try to shape human behavior, and it can sometimes change the environment in which we live in ways that alter our vulnerability to disease. Although some laws are specifically designated "infectious disease" or "communicable disease" control provisions in our public health codes, relevant law may appear across a variety of domains including environmental law, licensing and approval of drugs, housing provisions, sanitation, workplace safety, food and agricultural laws, intellectual property, and others.[5] As with other areas of public health, communicable disease control law is potentially very broad in scope.

This chapter will describe the key characteristics of U.S. communicable disease control law. Part II briefly describes the roles of federal and state powers in communicable disease control. Part III begins with a discussion of the relative roles of voluntary and coercive public health programs and continues by describing the police power, the primary source of state authority for communicable disease control, its scope and its limitations. Part IV briefly describes the history of state public health codes and specific types of provisions that are particularly relevant to communicable disease control. Part V considers two emerging issues in communicable disease control, recognition of and attempts to limit antibiotic resistance and expanded use of public health surveillance data.

II Federal vs. State Public Health Powers

In our constitutional system of government, authority is divided between the federal and state governments. The federal government's powers are limited to those specifically allocated it by the U.S. Constitution. States, on the other hand, have far more extensive powers, usually only limited where they contravene the Constitution or federal law. The appropriate scope of federal power and the overall role of federalism in public health are explored in more detail in other chapters in this book.

Public health scholars have vigorously debated the appropriate role for federal and state powers in preparing for and responding to emergencies. A group of scholars who drafted the Modern State Emergency Health Powers Act 2001 and the Model State Public Health Act argue that both federal and state powers need to be strengthened during an emergency, such as extreme natural disasters or a terrorism/bioterrorism event.[6] Others strongly opposed these proposals, arguing that it would be a mistake to sacrifice civil liberties based on fears of bioterrorism.[7]

[5] Lawrence O. Gostin, Public Health Law: Power, Duty, Restraint 155–161 (University of California Press, 2008).

[6] Lawrence O. Gostin, Jason W. Sapsin, Stephen P. Teret, Scott Burris, Julie Samia Mair, James G. Hodge, Jr., & Jon S. Vernick, *The Model State Emergency Health Powers Act Planning for and Response to Bioterrorism and Naturally Occurring Infectious Diseases*, 288 JAMA 622 (2002).

[7] George J. Annas, *Bioterrorism and Public Health Law*, 288 JAMA 2685 (2002) (comment); George J. Annas, *Blinded by Bioterrorism: Public Health and Liberty in the 21st Century*, 13 Health Matrix Cleveland 33 (2003).

Although federal power is limited by what is allocated within the U.S. Constitution, all three branches of the federal government produce policy relevant to communicable disease control. Congress, the executive branch (through federal agencies), and the federal courts each play important roles in public health policy and specifically communicable disease control. Because federal powers are covered elsewhere in the book, this section only provides examples of key powers.

a. Federal Quarantine Power

Since 1796 Congress has adopted and amended legislation establishing quarantine authority. Currently, the Public Health Services Act[8] authorizes the Secretary of Health and Human Services to prevent the spread of communicable diseases from other countries. With authority delegated by the Secretary, the Centers for Disease Control and Prevention (CDC) routinely monitor those entering the country for signs of communicable diseases. The CDC can detain, examine, and either hold or release travelers based on their findings. If necessary, federal officials can use federal isolation or quarantine orders.[9] These are rarely used, however, since most orders for isolation or quarantine are ordered at the state level.[10]

b. Intellectual Property

The Constitution also reserves to Congress specific authority to regulate intellectual property (copyright, trademark, and patent law).[11] In combination with the requirements for drug licensing and approval promulgated by the Food and Drug Administration (FDA), patent law set the terms for the development, testing, licensing, marketing, and sale of pharmaceuticals and devices that are critical to the control of communicable diseases. FDA regulations aim to protect the public from dangerous or ineffective remedies, and intellectual property provisions help reward innovation through granting exclusive rights to manufacture, market, and sell patented drugs and devices. The potential importance of patent law in incentivizing innovation in development of antibiotics and vaccines will be describe in Part V, below.

c. Regulating Interstate Commerce

Congress has adopted a wide range of laws under its power to regulate interstate commerce and commerce between the United States and foreign nations.[12] For example, Congress has adopted measures to protect the food supply and identify and interrupt transmission of food-borne illnesses.

[8] Section 361 of the Public Health Service Act (42 U.S.C. § 264).

[9] 42 Code of Federal Regulations 70–71.

[10] Centers for Disease Control and Prevention, *Legal Authorities for Isolation and Quarantine CDC Reports that Large-scale Federal Orders for Isolation or Quarantine Were Used in the 1918–19 Flu Epidemic*, http://www.cdc.gov/quarantine/aboutlawsregulationsquarantineisolation.html (last visited Jan 14, 2016).

[11] U.S. Const. art. I, § 8. [12] *Id.*

The CDC estimates that up to 48 million people become ill from foodborne disease every year, and up to 3,000 people die.[13] Because our food supply originates not only nationally but also internationally, outbreaks of foodborne disease can affect large numbers of people in multiple communities. In 2011 Congress enacted the FDA Food Safety Modernization Act (FSMA).[14] The FSMA seeks to improve prevention of, detection of, and response to outbreaks caused by domestically produced and processed foods and imported foods. As with most federal laws related to health, it also delegates to the FDA, the CDC, and other agencies authority to implement or enforce its particular provisions.

d. Taxing and Spending Provisions

Congress also impacts communicable disease prevention and control through its power to tax and spend.[15] Congress can tailor federal funding programs to try to shape state or individual behaviors related to health. For example, the Ryan White Care Act of 1990,[16] originally adopted to help states provide costly care for patients with HIV/AIDS, has also been a key tool to shape states' policies related to HIV by conditioning part of annual funding on states having or pursuing specific policy agendas.

Federal programs that condition parts of state funding on states adopting specific policies or programs can be controversial for state policy-makers in that they diminish state autonomy in terms of allocation of resources or policy-making. The federal courts can also invalidate Congress' efforts to link funding to state actions under some conditions. Other chapters in this book discuss limitations on congressional authority.

III Communicable Disease Law in the Public Health System

a. Voluntary and Coercive Measures

Public health provisions, including those devoted to communicable diseases, often reach deeply into individuals' personal lives in the interest of protecting the public's health. Communicable disease laws can infringe on individuals' rights to bodily integrity and individual choices of specific types of foods or services, and may even limit individuals' liberty and freedom of movement in the interest of controlling the spread of communicable disease, through isolation, quarantine, and civil commitment.

13 Centers for Disease Control and Prevention, *Estimates of Foodborne Illness in the United States. January 8, 2014*, http://www.cdc.gov/foodborneburden/index.html (last visited Jan 15, 2016)

14 FDA Food Safety Modernization Act (FSMA), amending the Federal Food, Drug, and Cosmetic Act (21 U.S.C. 301 et seq.).

15 U.S. Const. art. I § 8.

16 Ryan White CARE Act of 1990, Public Law 101-381, 104 Stat. 576.

Ultimately, much of daily public health work involves voluntary programs, cooperation, and compliance, often accomplished through education, outreach, and incentives. For example, prevention of seasonal flu depends predominantly on persuading millions of people to get immunized, wash their hands or use sanitizers frequently, and stay home from work if they develop symptoms of flu.[17] Although legal measures are sometimes contemplated to require some individuals to be immunized against the seasonal flu,[18] these are the exception. Because public health generally has few resources to devote to enforcement, building trust with the public in order to promote voluntary cooperation with public health initiatives becomes particularly important. In the seasonal flu context, the challenge of persuading people to get a shot to prevent a disease they may never experience and frequently underestimate, has been amply demonstrated in recent years.[19]

The power to coerce remains a necessary part of public health and communicable disease law.[20] The state's power is critical to many key elements of communicable disease law. Effective disease surveillance includes mandated reporting for many conditions followed by careful investigation and contact tracing. Some measures preserve individual choice but impose specific consequences for failure to comply, such as immunization provisions, which may include provisions that bar the unimmunized from certain settings during a disease outbreak or require them to wear protective equipment. Others, such as mandatory inspections, seizure of property, physical examinations, counseling, substance abuse treatment, and even confinement, do not.

Using coercive measures remains controversial in many parts of public health law.[21] Use of state power to coerce inevitably results in some abridgement of individual rights (e.g., privacy, autonomy, freedom of movement and association). For public health policy-makers, coercion also fosters worries over possible unintended consequences, including eroding public trust and reducing cooperation with public health programs. From an ethical perspective, coercion also raises the question of the appropriate balance of state power and individual responsibility for preventing disease, or how to resolve the conflict between public health paternalism and respect for individual autonomy.[22]

b. Scope and Limits of the Police Power

States use the "police power," the power to regulate for the purpose of protecting and promoting the common good, to protect the health and safety of their residents.[23] Inherent in the state's authority to act to promote the common good is the power to limit individual

[17] Centers for Disease Control and Prevention, *CDC Says "Take 3 Actions to Fight the Flu,"* Sept. 9, 2014, http://www.cdc.gov/flu/protect/preventing.htm (last visited Jan 15, 2016).

[18] Anemona Hartocollis, *State Requires Flu Vaccination for Caregivers*, N.Y. TIMES, Aug. 18, 2009.

[19] Centers for Disease Control and Prevention, *Flu Vaccination Coverage, United States, 2013–14 Influenza Season,* http://www.cdc.gov/flu/fluvaxview/coverage-1314estimates.htm (last visited Jan 15, 2016).

[20] GOSTIN, *supra* note 5, at 9–12.

[21] Ronald Bayer & Amy L. Fairchild, *The Genesis of Public Health Ethics*, 18 BIOETHICS 1467, 476–485 (2004).

[22] Zita Lazzarini & David Gregorio, *Personal Health in the Public Domain: Reconciling Individual Rights with Collective Responsibilities*, 46 CONN. L. REV. 1839 (2014).

[23] GOSTIN, *supra* note 5, at 91–95.

rights and interests where they threaten or endanger others. The U.S. Constitution supports the broad reach of the police power in that it reserves to the states and the people all power not expressly granted to the federal government.[24]

Public health powers are not unlimited. Constitutional rights can act as functional limits on the scope of some public health powers. In the landmark case of *Jacobson v. Massachusetts* (1905), the plaintiff, Jacobson, challenged a Cambridge, Massachusetts city ordinance that required all persons to be vaccinated for smallpox, on the grounds that it infringed on his individual rights protected by the U.S. Constitution. Jacobson argued that a law that infringes on individual rights must fail.[25] The U.S. Supreme Court noted that the protection of the Constitution did "not import an absolute right in each person to be, at all times and in all circumstances, wholly freed from restraint."[26] Jacobson's rights were, therefore, not absolute but were subject to the "manifold restraints to which every person is necessarily subject for the common good."[27] The Court established theoretical limits on the police power, by articulating the first set of criteria that should be used to justify state actions that limit individual rights. Specifically, the Court set out four criteria courts should consider in weighing the justification for the law or regulation: public health necessity, reasonableness, proportionality, and harm avoidance.[28]

In the century since *Jacobson*, the jurisprudence surrounding how courts describe the specific criteria for judicial review of any regulation under the police power has evolved. Statutes or regulations that limit individual rights for the common good must now meet constitutional standards for both substantive and procedural due process. The provision must be justified in terms of the law's relationship to the underlying government purpose (substantive), and the state must have sufficient procedures in place to ensure that the law is applied fairly to each individual case (procedural).[29]

The next section briefly reviews the history of state public health codes and describes the key types of provisions in those codes that are relevant to communicable disease control. It also considers the constitutionality of such provisions—how constitutional rights including free speech, freedom of movement, equal protection, and due process can all act as functional limits on public health efforts to control communicable diseases.

IV State Public Health Codes and Communicable Diseases

Residents of the United States have used legal measures to protect their communities from communicable diseases since colonial times.[30] State public health codes often developed

[24] U.S. Const. amend. X, ratified 1791. [25] Jacobson v. Massachusetts, 197 U.S. 11 (1905).

[26] *Id.* at 26. [27] *Id.*

[28] *Jacobson, supra* note 25, at 31–39; *but see* Lochner v. New York, 198 U.S. 45 (1905).

[29] Lawrence O. Gostin, *The Future of Communicable Disease Control: Toward a New Concept in Public Health Law*, 83 Milbank Q., 1, 3–9 (2005).

[30] Stephen B. Thacker, *Historical Development*, *in* Principles and Practice of Public Health Surveillance, 3rd ed. 1–17 (Lisa M. Lee, S. M. Teutsch, Stephen B. Thacker, & M. E. St. Louis eds., 2010).

incrementally, with many of their key provisions linked to outbreaks of communicable disease. The resulting code can resemble an onion made up of successive layers of legislation and regulation enacted over many years in response to shifting epidemics. This has resulted in a virtual patchwork of provisions that create sometimes conflicting and confusing rules for different diseases, different healthcare providers, and different locations.[31]

Narrowing the focus to communicable disease law allows us to classify most provisions into one of two categories: (1) traditional medical countermeasures or (2) personal control measures.[32] These categories are not completely separate since some medical control measures also exert some degree of control on individual behavior.[33]

a. Medical Countermeasures

i. Surveillance

One of the most basic tools of public health, surveillance—defined as the ability to identify and count cases, identify sources of disease, and prevent its spread through interruption of new transmissions—requires reliable collection of basic health data. Legally, surveillance begins with *mandatory disease reporting* but also includes *case finding and investigation, contact tracing* or *partner notification* (for some diseases), and *counseling* newly identified cases on recommended treatment and behavioral change. From both legal and ethical perspectives, each of these surveillance-related activities poses a critical question: Can the need for public health action adequately justify the infringements each causes on individuals' rights to privacy, confidentiality, and autonomy?[34] For many communicable diseases, the measures described in this section, while sometimes controversial, form the basis for routine public health practice throughout the United States.

ii. Mandatory Reporting

State reporting requirements require laboratories, physicians, hospitals, or other institutions to disclose what would otherwise be confidential medical information to local or state health departments or both, without the consent or even knowledge of the patient. The information that must be reported usually includes the name, address, date of birth, race/ethnicity, sex, and occupation of the person suspected of having the communicable disease, as well as the diagnosis or relevant lab values.[35] Purposes of mandatory reporting include accurately

[31] Lawrence O. Gostin, Scott C. Burris, & Zita Lazzarini, *The Law and the Public's Health: A Study of Infectious Disease Law in the United States*, 99 COLUM. L. REV. 59, 101–102 (1999).

[32] GOSTIN, *supra* note 5, at 333–420.

[33] All medical countermeasures, when mandated, impose some limits on personal autonomy, whether privacy or bodily integrity, for this reason these categories should not be considered clearly defined.

[34] Lawrence O. Gostin, Ronald Bayer, & Amy L. Fairchild, *Ethical and Legal Challenges Posed by Severe Acute Respiratory Syndrome: Implications for the Control of Severe Infectious Disease Threats*, 290 JAMA 3229, 3229–3230 (2003).

[35] Conn. Dep't Public Health, *Reportable Diseases, Emergency Illnesses and Health Conditions—2015*, 35 CONN. EPIDEMIOLOGIST 2, 2–3 (Jan. 2015).

assessing the burden of disease in a jurisdiction and, where possible, using data on race/ethnicity, sex, and other demographic variables to identify disparities in occurrence or impact of specific diseases. Public health authorities may also use reported data to guide interventions, either at the community or individual level.[36] For example, when a case of tuberculosis (TB) is identified, public health workers are immediately mobilized at the local or state level to interview the patient, try to identify the potential source of his or her infection, list everyone that person might have exposed, and contact each exposed person to offer education, testing, and, if necessary, treatment. Every time a new active case is identified from among those contacts, public health workers repeat the same process.[37] This is called *contact tracing* and will be described in greater detail below.

Connecticut's communicable disease regulations illustrate reporting requirements.[38] In addition to physicians and other direct care providers, the reporting mandate applies to the designated infection control officer of a hospital, the administrator of a public or private school or day care center, the person in charge of a camp, the master of a vessel within the jurisdiction of the state, the owner of aircraft landing within the state's jurisdiction, the owner in charge of any food production, dining, or drinking establishment, and morticians and funeral directors.[39] The list of reportable diseases varies by state, with most states having eighty to one hundred reportable diseases and conditions[40] and nearly as many reportable laboratory findings.

Both legal and ethical issues raised by mandatory reporting provisions center on whether the state has sufficient justification for infringing on individuals' privacy and the potential impact of reporting on the confidentiality of sensitive disease data.[41] While early identification of cases, coupled with prompt investigation and, where possible, treatment or behavioral change, can help prevent epidemics and stop the forward transmission of disease, with each of these interventions public health authorities may be overriding an individual's desire to be left alone and to protect his privacy. Often, once the individual has been treated, the remaining consequences of surveillance are for the benefit of the public, not the individual. The state must have good reasons to justify continued interference with the individual's choices.

Although mandatory reporting provisions have rarely been challenged in court, many have been controversial. Bayer and Fairchild describe substantial resistance to reporting mandates for many conditions, including TB, syphilis, cancer, birth defects, HIV/AIDS,

[36] Amy B. Bernstein & Marie Haring Sweeney, *Public Health Surveillance Data: Legal, Policy, Ethical, Regulatory, and Practical Issues*, 61 Morbidity & Mortality Wkly. Rep. 30, 30–31 (2012), http://www.cdc.gov/mmwr/preview/mmwrhtml/su6103a7.htm (last visited Jan 15, 2016).

[37] Center for Disease Control and Prevention, *Guidelines for the Investigation of Contacts of Persons with Infectious Tuberculosis*, 54(RR15) Morbidity & Mortality Wkly. Rep. 1, 1–5 (2005), http://www.cdc.gov/mmwr/preview/mmwrhtml/rr5415a1.htm (last visited Jan 15, 2016).

[38] Conn. Epidemiologist, *supra* note 35, at 4. [39] *Id.*

[40] Deborah A. Adams et al., *Summary of Notifiable Diseases—United States, 2011*, 60 Morbidity &d Mortality Wkly. Rep. 1, 1–4 (July 5, 2013).

[41] Amy L. Fairchild, Ronald Bayer, & James Colgrove, Searching Eyes: Privacy, the State, and Disease Surveillance in America (2007).

and immunizations, and occupational diseases when they were first enacted.[42] Resistance from healthcare professionals or from persons diagnosed with a specific disease or condition may be based on a variety of different reasons. The final section of this chapter will address expanded surveillance and other emerging issues in communicable disease control law.

iii. Case Finding and Contact Tracing

Case finding and contact tracing refer to public health personnel (or healthcare providers) contacting someone who may have been exposed to a communicable disease by an infected person to inform them of their possible exposure, offer testing, and where possible, treatment. Contact tracing has been used for decades in communicable disease control programs as diverse as TB, sexually transmitted diseases (STDs), Ebola, and investigations of vaccine preventable diseases. Successful contact tracing requires the voluntary cooperation of the index patient (and sometimes his or her family) to identify who might have come in contact with the patient during the time he or she was infectious.[43] Because they rely on the index patient (or the family) to voluntarily identify contacts, these programs should not be described as "mandatory."

Although before the 1960s newspapers often published the names of persons with certain communicable diseases,[44] public health authorities in modern contact tracing programs in the United States do not disclose the identity of the index patient. They inform contacts that they might have been exposed and offer testing and/or treatment.[45] From an ethical perspective, contact tracing does not necessarily represent the same loss of autonomy or breach of confidentiality as other interventions, since names of the infected are not disclosed and disclosure of contacts is usually based on the consent of the patient.

In 1988 the Public Health Service and the Association of State and Territorial Health Officials, followed by the World Health Organization (WHO) in 1989, began using the term *partner notification* to describe "the full scope of outreach efforts that range from an individual informing their own partners, to contact tracing by public health workers, and *even disclosure by physicians without the consent of their patient*."(emphasis added).[46] This led to frequent confusion about the nature of the activity and how it might infringe on individual rights. Federal funding for HIV/AIDS care was linked to recipients moving toward establishing partner notification programs beginning in 1988.[47] Subsequently, the umbrella term "partner notification" was divided into "patient or self referral"—the patient is asked to notify his or her partners and recommend they seek testing—and "provider referral," in which the patient discloses names of contacts and the health department finds them to warn of possible exposure.[48]

[42] Ronald Bayer & Amy Fairchild, *The Limits of Privacy: Surveillance and the Control of Disease*, 10 HEALTH CARE ANALYSIS 19–35 (2002).

[43] Saurabh R. Shrivastava, Prateek S. Shrivastava & Jegadeesh Ramasamy, *Utility of Contact Tracing in Reducing the Magnitude of Ebola Disease*, 4 GERMS 97, 98 (Dec. 2014).

[44] Martin Enserink, *Risk of Exposure: When New or Dangerous Infectious Diseases Strike, Public Health Often Trumps Personal Privacy*, 347 SCI. 498, 498–499 (2015).

[45] Ronald Bayer & Kathleen E. Toomey, *HIV Prevention and the Two Faces of Partner Notification*, 82 AM. J. PUB. HEALTH 1158, 1159–1160 (1992).

[46] *Id.* at 1159. [47] *Id.* at 1160.

[48] CENTERS FOR DISEASE CONTROL AND PREVENTION, PROGRAM OPERATIONS GUIDELINES FOR STD PREVENTION: PARTNER SERVICES, PS-16-PS-18.

Concern that some patients with HIV were failing to inform their partners or disclose the partners' names to health officials to warn the partners led to additional and sometimes problematic policy efforts. The Ryan White Care Act of 1990 (Section 8) conditions certain federal funding on states adopting laws and regulations demonstrating that a "good faith effort be made to notify current and former spouses of known HIV-infected persons of their possible exposure."[49] Notably, Section 8 mentions neither consent of the patient with HIV nor protecting the patient's identity, which diverged from the originally voluntary and confidential model of contact tracing.

The legal theory underlying provisions like Section 8 of Ryan White can be traced to the *Tarasoff* case in which the California Supreme Court established a limited "duty to warn" for a psychotherapist whose patient threatened imminent, foreseeable, and serious harm to an identifiable third party.[50] This obligation conflicted with both existing medical ethics and many local laws, because it required healthcare professionals to breach confidentiality for the benefit of a third party. Technically, the *Tarasoff* decision only applied to psychotherapists in California, but its impact has been much broader. Healthcare providers across many specialties and states questioned whether their actions might incur a duty to warn or to protect third parties whom their patients might put at risk of harm,[51] including those who might be injured as a result of medicines prescribed to a patient, those who might be infected by a patient with HIV or other STDs, and even family members whose risk of future disease was identified through genetic testing of a patient.[52] The *Tarasoff* rule, if applied broadly to all such situations, would represent a significant diminution of individuals' rights to privacy and confidentiality.

Some states responded by adopting statutes that specified under what circumstances a physician or health department could warn partners of persons with HIV about their potential exposure. As with many other aspects of communicable disease law, states' provisions in this area can vary, sometimes substantially.[53]

iv. Immunizations

The CDC identified *immunizations* as one of the ten greatest public health achievements of the twentieth century.[54] The first laws in the United States mandating "vaccination" for smallpox, emerged in late 1800s, most required immunization during an outbreak.[55] The U.S.

[49] Office of the Inspector General, *Implementation of the Spousal Notification Requirement* (Aug. 1999), OEI-05-98-00391, https://oig.hhs.gov/oei/reports/oei-05-98-00391.pdf (last visited Jan 15, 2016).

[50] Tarasoff v. Regents of the University of California, 17 Cal. 3d 425 (Cal. 1976).

[51] Claudia Kachigian & Alan R. Felthous, *Court Responses to Tarasoff Statutes*, 32 J. Am. Acad. Psychiatry L. 263, 273 (2004).

[52] Safer v. Estate of Pack, 677 A2d 1188 (NJ Super. Ct. App. Div. 1996); Pate v. Threlkel, 661 So.2d 278 (Fla. 1995); Kristin E. Schleiter, *A Physician's Duty to Warn Third Parties of Hereditary Risk*, 11 Virtual Mentor: Am. Med. Ass'n J. Ethics 697, 697–700 (2009).

[53] CT Gen Stat §§ 19a-584 (2013); Cal. Health and Safety Code sec. 121015 (2015); *but see* M.G.L. c. 111, § 70F (2012).

[54] Centers for Disease Control and Prevention, *Ten Great Public Health Achievements in the 20th Century*, http://www.cdc.gov/about/history/tengpha.htm (last visited Jan 15, 2016).

[55] *Jacobson, supra* note 25, at footnote 1.

[56] *Id.* at 25.

Supreme Court upheld such laws as a reasonable exercise of state police powers in *Jacobson v. Massachusetts* in 1905.[56] During the twentieth century at least twenty-one new vaccines were developed; eleven of those became part of the regular recommended vaccines for all children.[57] As effective immunizations were developed for more diseases, state legislatures expanded immunization laws to include requiring students to provide evidence of immunization before entering school, preschool, and day care. By the end of the century the proportion of school-age children vaccinated against the most common vaccine preventable diseases was 95% or greater every year between 1980 and 1997 (DTP, polio, and measles, mumps, and rubella vaccines).[58]

All laws in the United States requiring children to be immunized include an exception for those children for whom immunizations are contraindicated for medical reasons—medical exemptions. Forty-eight states allow parents to opt out of immunizing their children if they have a religious objection to immunization. Twenty-one states include a "personal beliefs" or "philosophical" exemption, which allows parents to opt out for other reasons. Children who are unimmunized (due to exemptions or otherwise) are at increased risk of vaccine-preventable diseases. Major outbreaks of vaccine-preventable disease in recent decades have been worse in areas with higher proportions of unimmunized children.[59]

Although remarkably effective and generally low cost, mandated immunizations programs have frequently been controversial. In the wake of *Jacobson*, early cases challenging immunization requirements for school entry appeared in the early 1920s. In *Zucht v. King*, the U.S. Supreme Court upheld the vaccination requirement and permitted the city of San Antonio to bar the student from school even as it recognized that health authorities could exercise discretion in deciding when to enforce the law.[60]

Parents express concern over the number and frequency of immunizations for their infants and young children required by the current immunization schedule recommended by CDC, as well as a range of other fears related to the vaccines themselves.[61] Widespread misconceptions about specific immunizations have fueled parental fears about immunizations. A 1998 article in *The Lancet* purported to find a link between administration of the measles, mumps, rubella vaccine, colitis, and development of autism in young children.[62]

[57] Centers for Disease Control and Prevention, *Achievements in Public Health, 1900–1999 Impact of Vaccines Universally Recommended for Children—United States, 1990–1998*, 48 MORBIDITY & MORTALITY WKLY. REP. 243–248 (1999), http://www.cdc.gov/mmwr/preview/mmwrhtml/00056803.htm (last visited Jan 15, 2016); Centers for Disease Control and Prevention, Advisory Committee on Immunization Practices *Recommended Immunization Schedules for Persons Aged 0 Through 18 Years—United States, 2015, Schedule*, http://www.cdc.gov/vaccines/schedules/downloads/child/0-18yrs-combined-schedule-bw.pdf (last visited Jan 15, 2016).

[58] Centers for Disease Control and Prevention, *Impact of Vaccines, supra* note 57, at 2.

[59] Saad B. Omer, Daniel A. Salmon, Walter A. Orenstein, M. Patricia deHart, & Neal Halsey, *Vaccine Refusal, Mandatory Immunization, and the Risks of Vaccine-Preventable Diseases*, 360 NEW ENG. J. MED. 1981 (2009); Jennifer L. Richards, Bradley H. Wagenaar, Joshua Van Otterloo, Rahul Gondalia, Jessica E. Atwell, David G. Kleinbaum, Daniel A. Salmon, & Saad B. Omer, *Nonmedical Exemptions to Immunization Requirements in California: A 16-year Longitudinal Analysis of Trends and Associated Community Factors*, 31 VACCINE 3009 (2013).

[60] Zucht v. King, 260 U.S. 174 (1922).

[61] Mariam Siddiqui, Daniel A Salmon, & Saad B Omer, *Epidemiology of Vaccine Hesitancy in the United States*, 9 HUM. VACCINES & IMMUNOTHERAPEUTICS 2643, 2643–2644 (2013).

[62] Andrew Wakefield et al., *Ileal-lymphoid-nodular Hyperplasia, Non-specific Colitis, and Pervasive Developmental Disorder in Children*, 351 LANCET 637 (1998), paper retracted,

Although the paper was eventually determined to be fraudulent and was later fully retracted, and the lead author lost his license to practice medicine, the controversy it sparked continues today.[63] The two issues the paper linked—parents' concerns over the small, but real, risk of immunization to children and their fear over the apparent increase in diagnoses of autism spectrum disorders—represent a "narrative" that is difficult to dislodge from many parents' minds. Even parents who cannot cite the specific risk that was supposedly identified may believe there is evidence that immunizations cause disease or contain toxins that are dangerous to children. Public health officials and clinicians struggle to educate parents about the relative risks of immunization as compared to the risks of the diseases themselves.

Another source of controversy has been the introduction of new vaccines, such as the vaccine for human papilloma virus (HPV), which has the potential to greatly reduce the incidence of cervical cancer in women and anal cancer in men.[64] In order to be fully effective, this vaccine requires a series of shots and must be completed before a young person is exposed to HPV—usually before he or she becomes sexually active. The recommended age for these immunizations—between 11 and 12 years old for both boys and girls—was intended to maximize the number fully protected. However, some parents fear that immunization represents endorsement or even encouragement of early sexual activity. Aggressive marketing by companies that manufacture the vaccines may have contributed to this impression and to the overall resistance to the recommendations.[65]

A different type of crisis in childhood immunizations linked to legal issues occurred in the 1980s, when fear of liability suits on the part of vaccine manufacturers led to shortages of some vaccines. In response, Congress enacted the National Vaccine Injury Compensation Program,[66] which largely shields manufacturers from liability while also providing a more rapid and predictable source of compensation for those who can show they were harmed by a vaccine. From a public health perspective, this no-fault system of compensation has had a largely positive impact, tending to stabilize vaccine supplies.

b. Personal Control Measures

Isolation and *quarantine* are the most well-known examples of more coercive public health measures identified with communicable disease control in which the state limits individuals' freedom of movement to prevent disease transmission. Other measures include *mandatory examination and treatment*, including, for some diseases, *directly observed therapy*, in which the state limits individuals' autonomy regarding examination or treatment. During outbreaks of diseases that are easily spread through airborne transmission or casual contact,

Retraction—*Ileal-lymphoid-nodular Hyperplasia, Non-specific Colitis, and Pervasive Developmental Disorder in Children*, 375 LANCET 445 (2010).

63 Editorial, *Silencing Debate over Autism*, 10 NATURE NEUROSCIENCE 531 (2007).

64 Centers for Disease Control and Prevention, *2015 Sexually Transmitted Disease Treatment Guidelines: Human Papilloma Virus (HPV) Infection*, http://www.cdc.gov/std/tg2015/hpv.htm (last visited Jan 15, 2016).

65 Lawrence O. Gostin. *Mandatory HPV Vaccination and Political Debate*, 306 JAMA 1699, 1699–1700 (2011).

66 42 U.S.C.A. sec 300aa(1), National Childhood Vaccine Injury Act of 1986.

health authorities may also use *social distancing measures* to limit large gatherings or order closure of congregate settings that could serve as sites of transmission. Mandatory social distancing measures most directly interfere with freedom of movement and association.

i. Isolation and Quarantine

The terms *isolation* and *quarantine* are often used interchangeably, although they have distinctly different purposes. *Isolation* refers to confinement of a person known to have a communicable disease while he or she is infectious and thus poses a risk of infection to others. *Quarantine* refers to the confinement or separation of a person who has been exposed to a communicable disease in order to determine if he or she has been infected. The period required for quarantine is usually set at the longest known incubation time of a particular disease. Thus, some healthcare workers and family members exposed to persons with Ebola during the 2014–2015 outbreak, were quarantined for twenty-one days, the longest known incubation period for the disease.[67] If, after that time, they had not developed symptoms of the disease, health authorities regarded them as uninfected.

Both states and the federal government have statutes that allow health authorities to limit an individual's freedom of movement if that individual poses a threat to others due to communicable disease.[68] Since the bulk of communicable disease control takes place at the local level, this section predominantly concerns state powers. Federal quarantine power was briefly discussed above.

Isolation and quarantine can be voluntary or mandatory. With diseases such as TB, persons who are acutely ill do not usually resist isolation while being treated, and the state's coercive power to confine them to protect the public health is rarely required. Once patients are not acutely ill, however, they may resist continued interference with their daily activities, and sometimes health authorities must resort to court-ordered treatment or even confinement, where an infected person either does not have a safe and stable residence or continues to expose others.[69] Individuals who are exposed, but symptom free, may also resist the limits (and stigma) created by an isolation or quarantine order. In 2014, U.S. health officials faced a dilemma when considering whether to order the forcible confinement of healthcare workers returning from caring for patients with Ebola in West Africa.[70] Health officials did not want to discourage healthcare workers from volunteering, either through stigma or the prospect of virtual imprisonment, yet they were also responsible for preventing transmission of Ebola from workers who might be infected.

[67] Centers for Disease Control and Prevention, *Interim US Guidance for Monitoring and Movement of Persons with Potential Ebola Virus Exposure, December 24, 2014*, http://www.cdc.gov/vhf/ebola/exposure/monitoring-and-movement-of-persons-with-exposure.html (last visited Jan 15, 2016).

[68] National Council of State Legislatures, *State Quarantine and Isolation Laws* (last updated, 10/29/2014), http://www.ncsl.org/research/health/state-quarantine-and-isolation-statutes.aspx (last visited January 15, 2016); Section 361 of the Public Health Service Act (42 U.S.C. § 264).

[69] Centers for Disease Control and Prevention, *Menu of Suggested Provisions for State Tuberculosis Prevention and Control Laws*, http://www.cdc.gov/tb/programs/laws/menu/treatment.htm (last visited Jan 15, 2016).

[70] Kate Zernike & Emma G. Fitzsimmons, *Threat of Lawsuit Could Test Maine's Quarantine Policy*, N.Y. Times, Oct. 29, 2014; Hartocollis, *supra* note 18.

ii. *Constitutionality of Specific Provisions*

At the state level, the authority to limit an individual's freedom of movement is rooted in the legislature's exercise of the police power.[71] As with other public health measures, the state's power to isolate or quarantine is not absolute. In early cases courts invalidated quarantine orders directed and enforced solely against people of one race where similar restrictions were not imposed on any other group[72] and invalidated an order for isolation for an elderly woman because the conditions of confinement were potentially unhealthy for a woman her age.[73]

Both isolation and quarantine restrict one of the most fundamental liberties, freedom of movement. Consequently, laws that permit either must be based on a compelling public health need, be narrowly targeted so as to impact the fewest number of people, and utilize limitations that represent the "least restrictive alternative" that will reasonably accomplish the health department's goals.[74] Additionally, where an individual's liberty is completely restricted through confinement, the law must afford a wide range of procedural protections to the persons confined to ensure the law is applied fairly and the persons the state seeks to confine have the opportunity to challenge the confinement. Because confinement represents a plenary loss of liberty, procedural due process requires extensive protections for individual rights.[75] In *Greene v. Edwards*, the Supreme Court of West Virginia held that persons being confined for public health purposes are entitled to the same types of procedural protections as those confined for mental health purposes.[76] The state must provide the person they seek to confine with counsel, a fair and impartial decision-maker, an opportunity to present witnesses and to cross-examine witnesses against him or her, clear and convincing evidence that he or she poses a danger to others, a written transcript of the proceedings, and the right to appeal. The person must also have an opportunity for periodic review of the justification for continued confinement.

Many state laws authorizing isolation or quarantine were enacted before the modern era of constitutional review. For example, many states first adopted their TB laws in the early twentieth century. These laws often granted wide discretion to public health authorities to confine individuals, without procedural protections for the infected person. In recent years some state health authorities faced burgeoning U.S. epidemics of TB with only the tools of old laws available. In at least one case where an older law was challenged, the court upheld the old law by recognizing its shortcomings while inferring that modern standards for procedural due process would be applied. The court noted, however, that this should be a temporary fix; ideally, the legislature would act promptly to modernize the TB laws.[77]

Newer laws give health officials more options for helping patients complete TB treatment. Ensuring TB patients complete the full course of treatment is necessary both to achieve a durable cure and to prevent development of multidrug-resistant TB. In these cases public

[71] Gibbons v. Ogden, 22 U.S.1, 25 (1824); Hennington v. Georgia, 163 U.S. 299 (1896).

[72] Jew Ho v. Williamson, 103 F. 10 (C.C.D. Cal. 1900); Wong Wai v. Williamson et al., 103 F. 1, 3 (C.C.D. 1900).

[73] Kirk v. Wyman, 65 S. W. 387 (S. Ct. S. C. 1909).

[74] Conn. Gen. Stat. § 368a-19a-131 (b-d) (2003).

[75] Mathews v. Eldridge, 424 U.S. 319 (1976).

[76] Greene v. Edwards, 263 S.E.2nd 661 (1980).

[77] City of Newark v. J.S., 279 N.J. Super. 178 (1993), 652 A.2d 265.

health personnel may utilize an intervention referred to as directly observed therapy (DOT) to ensure that patients take doses of medication as ordered.[78] Some states have updated their TB provisions to include DOT and other options, while leaving in place older communicable disease quarantine law.[79]

V Emerging Issues in Communicable Disease Law

This section explores two areas where new public health issues or new uses of technology explicitly raise issues of the appropriate use of legal provisions to address public health needs—how the public health and legal community can work together to address antibiotic resistance and how new and improved surveillance programs can offer benefits within public health while respecting individual rights.

a. Antibiotic Resistance

In 2014 the World Health Organization published its first global report on antimicrobial resistance, confirming that scientists have been saying for years—"antibiotic resistance . . . is no longer a prediction for the future. Antibiotic resistance—when bacteria change and antibiotics fail—is happening right now, across the world."[80]

From a public health perspective, the goals of treatment for communicable diseases include not only curing the disease in individuals and reducing or eliminating the spread of disease in the population but also protecting the effectiveness of the medicines used to treat those infections. Medicines lose their effectiveness as treatments for communicable disease as the pathogens develop resistance to the particular drug. Bacteria's ability to develop resistance to antibiotics was recognized almost as soon as the first antibiotics were widely used.[81] For several decades (1950s through the 1960s) drug development moved faster than pathogen resistance. This began to wane, however, in the 1970s. Since 1980, the FDA has approved only sixty-seven antibiotics considered "new molecular entities."[82] Soon there may be no effective treatments for some bacterial infections, much like the pre-antibiotic era of the early twentieth century.[83]

[78] Centers for Disease Control and Prevention, *supra* note 69.

[79] Conn. Gen. Stat. 386g, § 19a-265 (2003); Conn. Gen. Stat. § 368e-19a-221 (2003).

[80] World Health Organization, *Antimicrobial Resistance: Global Report on Surveillance, April 2014*, http://apps.who.int/iris/bitstream/10665/112642/1/9789241564748_eng.pdf (last visited Jan 15, 2016).

[81] Alexander Fleming, *Nobel Lecture on Penicillin*, Stockholm, Sweden, December 11, 1945, 93–94, http://www.nobelprize.org/nobel_prizes/medicine/laureates/1945/fleming-lecture.pdf (last visited Jan 15, 2016).

[82] Kevin Outterson, John H. Powers, Gregory W. Daniel, & Mark B. McClellan, *Repairing the Broken Market for Antibiotic Innovation*, 34 Health Aff. 277, 279 (2015).

[83] World Health Organization, *Antimicrobial Resistance*, *supra* note 80.

International organizations now support concerted action to combat antibiotic resistance.[84] The WHO's 2014 Report identified six common bacterial pathogens responsible for large burdens of disease and collected data on worldwide prevalence of antibiotic resistant strains,[85] as well as reported on the prevalence and spread of drug resistance among three important human pathogens.[86]

In September 2014, the President's Council of Advisors on Science and Technology released a report summarizing its findings and making recommendations to help the United States combat antibiotic resistance.[87] The proliferation of antibiotic resistance among serious human pathogens and the lack of new antibiotics to replace them can be traced to at least three areas of behavior: overuse/improper use of antibiotics in human medicine; use of antibiotics in agriculture for nonhealth purposes; and dwindling investment in drug development. Legal measures have the potential to drive change in each of these domains.

i. Overuse of Antibiotics in Medicine

Because early antibiotics were generally nontoxic to humans and allowed seemingly miraculous cures of potentially deadly diseases, researchers have reported physicians' overprescription at least since the 1950s.[88] Overuse and inappropriate use stem from both expectations of patients for treatment and physicians' failure to adhere to evidence-based practice. Efforts to change antibiotic prescribing practices necessarily must address both patients and physicians, and both outpatient and hospital settings, since the majority of prescriptions are written in outpatient settings. One key intervention that has been implemented in the hospital setting is *antibiotic stewardship*, which means "systematic efforts to optimize the use of antibiotics—not just reduce the total volume used—in order to maximize their benefits to patients while minimizing both the rise of antibiotic resistance as well as adverse effects to patients from unnecessary antibiotic therapy."[89] Stewardship programs devote staff and resources to rapidly identifying the specific pathogen causing an infection, choosing the most narrowly targeted antibiotic that will be effective, identifying the best route of administration, dosing and duration of treatment, and overseeing treatment to ensure it is completed successfully. Research has shown that *antibiotic stewardship* programs in hospitals have been effective in reducing inappropriate use, extending the usefulness of antibiotics of last resort, and reducing the occurrence and spread within institutions of antibiotic-resistant

[84] Carl Nathan & Otto Cars, *Antibiotic Resistance—Problems, Progress, and Prospects*, 371 NEW ENG. J. MED. 1761 (2014).

[85] Common pathogens included: *Escherichia coli; Klebsiella pneumonia; Staphylococcus aureus; Streptococcus pneumonia; Nontyphoidal Salmonella; and Neisseria gonorrhea.*

[86] Other pathogens included: tuberculosis, malaria, and HIV.

[87] President's Council of Advisors on Science and Technology (PCAST), *Report to the President on Combatting Antibiotic Resistance, September 2014*, https://www.whitehouse.gov/sites/default/files/microsites/ostp/PCAST/pcast_carb_report_sept2014.pdf (last visited Jan 15, 2016).

[88] *Abuse of Antibiotics*, 265 LANCET 1059, 1059–1060 (1955).

[89] President's Council of Advisors on Science and Technology, *supra* note 87, at 42.

infections.[90] Unfortunately, these programs have been relatively slow to spread to nonacademic medical centers and community hospitals.[91]

Legal provisions linked to reimbursement could expand active stewardship programs, through Centers for Medicare and Medicaid Services (CMS) regulations.[92] Specifically, CMS could identify adoption of and adherence to antibiotic stewardship practices as a Condition of Participation (CoP), which links reimbursements to good practices and has been shown to be effective in shaping many areas of medical practice. Other incentives related to reimbursement could be used to encourage wiser use of antibiotics in outpatient settings.[93]

Improving surveillance capacity for tracking both antibiotic use and distribution of antibiotic resistant pathogens are also key to effective *antibiotic stewardship*. Current public health infrastructure lacks the capacity to identify and collect comprehensive data on the prevalence of antibiotic resistance or identification of resistant strains. The CDC has a voluntary program for hospitals, the National Healthcare Safety Network (NHSN), which is currently collecting data. Ultimately, a similar program could be made mandatory through the rule-making process of state agencies. Comprehensive collection of data from outpatient settings could rely partially on commercially available data collected by pharmaceutical companies and private insurers.

Developing better and faster diagnostics that will allow antibiotics to be targeted narrowly at the specific pathogen causing a patient's illness is also critical. Typically, culturing a pathogen and testing for resistance takes at least two days, during which time patients may be treated with broad-spectrum antibiotics or even antibiotics completely ineffective against the pathogen. Proposals for encouraging progress in this area include providing prizes for developers of rapid diagnostics for some of the most problematic conditions, streamlining the approval process for such diagnostics, and providing funding for clinical trials.[94]

ii. Use of Antibiotics in Animals Used for Food

Farmers and ranchers use antibiotics both to prevent and treat diseases in animals that produce human food and to promote weight gain, thus reducing the cost of bringing them to market. While the benefits of the former have been generally positive (fewer sick animals, reduced transmission of disease through food to humans, reduction in producers' costs due to fewer animals having to be destroyed), the benefits of the latter are much more mixed. Any use of antibiotics leads to selective pressure on pathogens carried by the animals and development of antibiotic resistance. Increasingly, advocates working to slow the spread of antibiotic resistant strains of human disease have pointed to research that suggests that antibiotic use in animals for non-health-related purposes promotes antibiotic resistance not only in

[90] M. A. Aldeyab et al., *An Evaluation of the Impact of Antibiotic Stewardship on Reducing the Use of High-risk Antibiotics and Its Effect on the Incidence of Clostridium difficile Infection in Hospital Settings*, 67 J. Antimicrobial Chemotherapy 2988, 2993 (2012).

[91] President's Council of Advisors on Science and Technology, *supra* note 87, at 42–43.

[92] *Id.* at 44.

[93] Richard S. Saver, *In Tepid Defense of Population Health: Physicians and Antibiotic Resistance*, 34 Am. J. L. & Med. 431, 482–487 (2008).

[94] President's Council of Advisors on Science and Technology, *supra* note 87, at 48.

the animals themselves but also in people working or living near the animals.[95] Studies also show that disparate species of bacteria can transmit resistance to each other by sharing plasmids (small chains of genetic material that allow bacteria to acquire resistant genes).[96]

For many years use of antibiotics in animal feed was relatively unregulated, and many farmers and ranchers embraced it with enthusiasm.[97] From the producers' perspective, antibiotic use greatly increased productivity at little added cost. However, as societal costs of combating antibiotic-resistant diseases in humans have grown through increased healthcare costs, disability, and even deaths of patients, researchers have characterized non-health-related uses of antibiotics in agriculture as "externalizing the cost," or shifting it from the food producers to the patients and the public who pay for increased insurance premiums, drug costs, and public financing of healthcare.

Although the data on the overall impact of antibiotic use in animals on the burden of human disease from resistant organisms is incomplete, incremental change in the practice is taking place, driven in part by legal mandates.[98] Starting in the 1980s, the FDA began requiring veterinarians to oversee use of new antibiotics in animals. FDA oversight has included establishing a monitoring system,[99] withdrawal of specific classes of antibiotics from use in animals, and introduction of a framework for evaluating the impact of drug resistance into the drug approval process.[100] Since 2008, producers of antibiotics used in animals have been required to report the types and total amounts of antibiotics sold.[101]

The FDA has recently released two guidance documents that aim, ultimately, to discontinue the use of antibiotics in animals to increase production.[102] The FDA Guidance asks producers to voluntarily change the labeling on their drugs to eliminate their use to increase production/promote weight gain, making it illegal to use the drugs for these purposes. It would also require that a veterinarian order and oversee administration of the drugs for disease prevention or treatment. Phasing out antibiotic use to boost production will require education of farmers and ranchers, changes in animal feed manufacturing, and capacity building to ensure sufficient veterinarians are available and educated about appropriate uses of the drugs.

95 *Id.* at 50–52.

96 Tom Vogwill & R. Craig MacLean, *The Genetic Basis of the Fitness Costs of Antimicrobial Resistance: A Meta-analysis Approach*, 8(3) EVOLUTIONARY APPLICATIONS 284 (2015).

97 President's Council of Advisors on Science and Technology, *supra* note 87, at 50–52.

98 *Id.* at 52–54.

99 U.S. Food and Drug Administration, *The National Antimicrobial Resistance Monitoring System*, http://www.fda.gov/AnimalVeterinary/SafetyHealth/AntimicrobialResistance/NationalAntimicrobialResistanceMonitoringSystem/ (last visited Apr 15, 2015).

100 Food and Drug Administration, no. 152, *Guidance for Industry Evaluating the Safety of Antimicrobial New Animal Drugs with Regard to Their Microbiological Effects on Bacteria of Human Health Concern* (2003), http://www.fda.gov/downloads/AnimalVeterinary/GuidanceComplianceEnforcement/GuidanceforIndustry/ucm052519.pdf (last visited Jan 15, 2016).

101 Section 105 of the Animal Drug User Fee Amendments of 2008 (ADUFA) (P.L. 110-316; 122 Stat. 3509) amended section 512 of the Federal Food, Drug, and Cosmetic Act ("the Act") [21 U.S.C. 360b].

102 Food and Drug Administration no. 209, *Guidance for Industry The Judicious Use of Medically Important Antimicrobial Drugs in Food-Producing Animals* (2012), http://www.fda.gov/downloads/AnimalVeterinary/GuidanceComplianceEnforcement/GuidanceforIndustry/UCM216936.pdf (last visited Jan 15, 2016); Food and Drug Administration no. 213, *Guidance for Industry New Animal Drugs and New Animal Drug Combination Products Administered in or on Medicated Feed or Drinking*

Effective implementation of FDA and other regulations aimed at curbing antibiotic use in agriculture will require monitoring sales of antibiotics for animals to ensure sales accurately reflect needs for treatment and prevention of disease rather than a mere shift in the stated justification for the sale.[103] Fully implementing these changes will take time, and their impact on overall antibiotic resistance in humans remains unknown.

iii. Stalled Development of New Antibiotics

Researchers have identified multiple contributing factors for the slow progress in development of promising new classes of antibiotics for drug-resistant infections. From the pharmaceutical companies' perspective, candidates for new antibiotic drug development rarely appear likely to offer as good a return on investment as do candidate drugs aimed at chronic (especially prevalent) diseases. The generally low prices of antibiotics and the limited market uptake for new antibiotics due to lack of proven superiority to existing drugs and potential limitations on use of any drug or class of drugs that could replace last resort antibiotics such as vancomycin means a new antibiotic will generate few profits. Time and financial investment for clinical trials for antibiotics remain high, and, where treatment of drug resistant infections is a goal, recruiting subjects can be complicated. Flat government funding to support innovation means companies have few incentives. As a result, current valuations of the expected return on new antibiotics consistently fall below the $100 million threshold used by many pharmaceutical companies to determine if they should invest in a specific candidate drug.

Governments and other stakeholders have created a range of new initiatives to try to increase innovation, often by directly addressing the failings of the traditional business model to promote growth in this area. A number of scholars have suggested multipronged approaches to encouraging innovation while also preventing resistance.[104] Outterson et al. have described several of these initiatives and their limitations as currently structured.[105] Recent initiatives have included efforts to streamline clinical trials of new antibiotics by bringing drugs to market faster through approval for only limited uses. Although this will result in earlier approval, the safety and efficacy of such drugs would be unknown, and the very limited indications allowed for sale would mean low return and would not significantly improve return on investment.

A range of public-private partnerships in the United States and Europe currently provide new capital for development of "pipeline" antibiotics that are expected to address identified needs. Outterson et al. suggest focusing increased public investment on such projects and further narrowing their focus to candidate drugs that show progress at each step of the development process. Other possible options are incentive programs linked to intellectual property protections, particularly awarding longer periods of market exclusivity to new drugs that are developed to treat "qualifying infections." Current programs, however, do

Water of Food-Producing Animals: Recommendations for Drug Sponsors for Voluntarily Aligning Product Use Conditions with GFI #209, (2013), http://www.fda.gov/downloads/AnimalVeterinary/GuidanceComplianceEnforcement/GuidanceforIndustry/UCM299624.pdf (last visited Jan 15, 2016).

[103] President's Council of Advisors on Science and Technology, *supra* note 87, at 54.

[104] Nathan & Cars, *supra* note 84, at 1762–1763.

[105] Outterson et al., *supra* note 82, at, 280–284.

not grant large enough incentives to make a drug profitable, and the eligibility criteria for drugs to treat "qualifying infections" have been too broad. A better model would use larger incentives and more narrowly tailor qualifying requirements for drugs to address the highest priority needs.

Finally, overall reimbursement reform is necessary to make new drug development profitable. Here policy-makers must balance patients' needs for access to these drugs against the pharmaceutical companies' need for a positive return on investment. One option is de-linking reimbursement from sales volumes. Awarding prizes for antibiotic development, granting "wild-card" patents, exempting new drugs from payment formulas such as the Diagnosis-Related Group system used by Medicare in the United States, and directly rewarding makers of drugs that demonstrate "substantial clinical improvement" are also innovative reimbursement strategies.[106]

Outterson et al. warn that incentives need to be carefully targeted and should focus on actual improvements in drug performance against resistant pathogens. It is not the number of drugs developed but the quality that will make the difference in the long term.[107] They urge a three-part approach to change the business model to enhance antibiotic development: (1) increasing the incentives for antibiotic development across the whole life cycle of the drug; (2) targeting all incentives carefully (quality, not quantity approach); and (3) coordinating efforts globally, specifically through possible adoption of a Framework Convention on Antibiotic Resistance (which could promote improvements in all three areas to combat antibiotic resistance: stewardship in human use; drastically decreased use in agriculture; and innovation among drug companies).[108]

b. Expanded Use of Disease Surveillance Data

Public health surveillance data at the state level contains a wealth of data that can be useful for specific disease tracking, control, and prevention purposes. Traditionally, aggregate data have helped public health officials estimate prevalence in the population and allowed funders to direct resources where needed. Surveillance data that include personal identifiers and location information also allowed public health interventions to investigate cases, provide treatment, identify possible sources of infection, and interrupt or reduce ongoing transmission. These data can also offer broader opportunities for use, some directly relevant to public health, but others less so. This section looks briefly at issues raised by several different types of expanded surveillance.

i. Improving Patient Care

Surveillance data often include more than diagnosed cases. Many states' mandated reporting requires laboratories to report tests that are used primarily for clinical decision-making.

[106] *Id.* at 280–284.

[107] Kevin Outterson, John H. Powers, Enrique Seoane-Vasquez, Rosa Rodriguez-Monguio, & Aaron S. Kesselheim, *Approval and Withdrawal of New Antibiotics and Other Antiinfectives in the U.S. 1980–2009*, 41 J. L., MED., & ETHICS 688, 695 (2013).

[108] Outterson et al., *supra* note 82, at 283–284.

For example, in many states reporting HIV-related data goes beyond mandatory reporting of persons testing positive for HIV antibodies or antigens (signs of infection) to also require reporting of viral loads and CD4 counts.[109] A patient's viral load and CD4 counts are both indicators of disease progression, which can identify persons living with HIV (PLH) who may have fallen out of treatment or for whom treatment is no longer effective. As of January 2013, thirty-six states, plus some territories and cities, require reporting of HIV viral loads and CD4 counts.[110] Required reporting by laboratories may also include clinically relevant tests for noncommunicable diseases, such as testing for hemoglobin A1C, which permits better estimates of long-term blood sugar control for diabetics than other tests. High values for A1C suggest a patient's diabetes is poorly controlled, which may be due to poor diet, inadequate medication, or inconsistent monitoring.

Increasingly, health departments are using these surveillance data to monitor disease progression or to identify persons in need of treatment or other services.[111] In the HIV context this might involve having public health workers contact either the patient or the last clinician of record to try to identify what has caused the rise in viral loads or the decline in CD4 count. Possible problems could include an interruption of care, treatment exhaustion, or lapses due to social or psychological problems, such as homelessness, mental illness, or substance abuse. In the case of diabetes, a patient who cannot afford testing supplies or medications, or whose personal life has become chaotic, may experience poor blood sugar control. Public health initiatives to use surveillance data to reach out to clinicians or patients for the purpose of improving the patients' treatment or their long-term health can cause controversy, primarily because they represent expansions on the traditional justification for surveillance data—identifying cases or preventing transmission.[112]

The U.S. National AIDS Strategy has prioritized improving retention in care numbers as a critical factor in reducing the spread of HIV/AIDS.[113] The immediate beneficiary of outreach that finds PLH who have fallen out of care and provides assistance to reconnect them is the individual patient. Public health officials would argue, however, that such programs will also benefit the public's health, because more PLH with undetectable viral loads will reduce transmission, slow disease progression, and contribute to more healthy years of life for greater numbers of people in the population. Scholars reviewing the expanded use of HIV surveillance data to help retain patients in care and improve clinical outcomes have identified both individual and aggregate benefits.[114]

[109] CONN. EPIDEMIOLOGIST, *supra* note 35, at 3.

[110] Panel on Antiretroviral Guidelines for Adults and Adolescents, 2012, *Guidelines for the Use of Antiretroviral Agents in HIV-1-Infected Adults and Adolescents*, U.S. Department of Health and Human Services, C4–C7, http://www.aidsinfo.nih.gov/contentfiles/lvguidelines/adultandadolescentgl.pdf (last visited Jan 15, 2016).

[111] J. C. Dombrowski, J. B. Kent, S. E. Buskin, J. D. Stekler, & M. R. Golden, *Population-based Metrics for the Timing of HIV Diagnosis, Engagement in HIV Care, and Virologic Suppression*, 26 AIDS 77 (2012).

[112] Janlori Goldman, Sydney Kinnear, Jeannie Chung, & David J. Rothman, *New York City's Initiatives on Diabetes and HIV/AIDS: Implications for Patient Care, Public Health, and Medical Professionalism*, 98 AM. J. PUB. HEALTH 807 (2008).

[113] U.S. National AIDS Strategy, Overview, https://www.aids.gov/federal-resources/national-hiv-aids-strategy/overview/ (last visited Jan 15, 2016).

[114] Patricia Sweeney, Lytt I. Gardner, Kate Buchacz, Pamela Morse Garland, Michael J. Mugavero, Jeffrey T. Bosshart, R. Luke Shouse, & Jeanne Bertolli, *Shifting the Paradigm: Using HIV Surveillance*

ii. Data Matching Across Surveillance Systems

Since the 1990s public health experts have called for greater integration among programs to prevent and control HIV, STDs, viral hepatitis, and TB.[115] In 2009, the CDC's National Center for HIV/AIDS, Viral Hepatitis, STD, and TB Prevention (NCHHSTP) outlined a strategy for promoting program integration and collaboration across programs in these areas.[116] The central goals of this initiative were to promote data sharing across programs and facilitate comprehensive delivery of services to the populations most in need. In 2011, the program released guidelines for confidentiality and data sharing intended to address the disparate data protection and sharing policies in many federal and state programs covering different diseases, which had been identified as a barrier by health departments working on greater collaboration.[117]

Some public health departments have been quietly expanding the impact of their surveillance by combining or matching data sets from previously disparate public health data systems. In combined systems, all data on one individual client will be immediately available in one report, so if a client with HIV is later diagnosed with an STD, the information available to the outreach worker investigating the case will include both diagnoses and a record of the department's previous work with that client. In other states, health departments use computers to periodically (daily, weekly, or monthly) match new diagnoses in one system with existing diagnoses in others. This process can produce similar information that can be used for enhanced outreach to clients with dual diagnoses. In either scenario, having integrated information available to public health specialists who conduct disease investigations can facilitate a more comprehensive assessment of the client to include not only the possible source of the STD infection and efforts to identify subsequent contacts but also a discussion of the risk of ongoing HIV transmission and assessment for needs for HIV-related services. Combining other data systems (viral hepatitis or tuberculosis) could also lead to more comprehensive intervention or service delivery for those diseases. The benefits of efforts aimed at program collaboration and service integration accrue to health departments and the public through more efficient use of resources and effective prevention interventions and also to individual clients through comprehensive service delivery. Integration, whether of data or programs, is not without controversy however.

Data as a Foundation for Improving HIV Care and Preventing HIV Infection, 91 MILBANK Q. 558, 581–583 (2013).

[115] Helen Fox Fields, Association of State and Territorial Health Officials, *The Integration of HIV/AIDS, STD, and TB Prevention and Control Programs* (1998); Beth Meyerson, *Policy and Program Coordination: A Shared Challenge with Miles Yet to Go*, 119 PUB. HEALTH REP. 2, 2–3 (2004).

[116] Centers for Disease Control and Prevention, *Program Collaboration and Service Integration: Enhancing the Prevention and Control of HIV/AIDS, Viral Hepatitis, Sexually Transmitted Diseases, and Tuberculosis in the United States* (2009), http://www.cdc.gov/nchhstp/ProgramIntegration/docs/207181-C_NCHHSTP_PCSI%20WhitePaper-508c.pdf (last visited Jan 15, 2016).

[117] Centers for Disease Control and Prevention, *Data Security and Confidentiality Guidelines for HIV, Viral Hepatitis, Sexually Transmitted Disease, and Tuberculosis Programs: Standards to Facilitate Sharing and Use of Surveillance Data for Public Health Action* (2011), http://www.cdc.gov/nchhstp/ProgramIntegration/docs/PCSIDataSecurityGuidelines.pdf (last visited Jan 15, 2016).

iii. Is Enhanced Surveillance Ethically Justified?

In their comprehensive ethical analysis of surveillance-based outreach to facilitate HIV medical care, Sweeney et al. acknowledge that concerns about the risks to privacy and confidentiality from use of surveillance data have existed since name-based surveillance was first proposed.[118] They argue, however, that the balance of risks and benefits from HIV surveillance has changed dramatically since the late 1980s, driven largely by advances in both HIV treatment and surveillance.[119] Early identification of HIV and consistent retention of PLH in care have been identified as critical elements of the U.S. HIV Control Strategy. In the context of such advances, they argue that the expanded use of surveillance data provides a net benefit for both the individual and society and is justified.[120] In fact, they urge that failing to use these data to improve treatment and care raises serious ethical issues.[121]

Sweeney et al. recognize, however, that concerns about threats to privacy and confidentiality posed by additional uses of these data deserve careful attention and that the perceived intrusiveness of such programs varies, depending on many contextual factors.[122] They recommend that programs seeking to implement expanded surveillance first address a range of ethical, procedural, and strategic considerations,[123] and note that the legal and policy infrastructure must be ready to support surveillance while protecting clients.[124] Other critics have pointed out that in some states, expanded use of HIV surveillance data might increase PLH's risk of being prosecuted under state laws criminalizing exposure. Unless state laws governing health data prevent them from being used to facilitate criminal investigations or prosecutions, or until national prosecutorial guidelines obviate this need, states' efforts to integrate HIV and STD data may have the unintended impact of facilitating prosecutions. Ultimately, as the volume of health data stored electronically grows, there will probably be pressures from others seeking to use these data. Many health insurers already track whether their members have received recommended preventive services and incentivize adherence by offering various discounts. Extending this monitoring to a wide range of laboratory values for those with chronic diseases (such as diabetes) could also be appealing to insurers.

VI Conclusion

Communicable diseases have not been conquered. Even in the early twenty-first-century we struggle to apply some of the oldest known measures for communicable disease control—isolation and quarantine—while still protecting the rights and dignity of the individuals who

[118] Sweeney et al., *supra* note 114, at 560.

[119] Amy L. Fairchild & Ronald Bayer, *HIV Surveillance, Public Health, and Clinical Medicine—Will the Walls Come Tumbling Down?*, 365 New Eng. J. Med. 685, 685–687 (2011).

[120] *See also* Lisa M. Lee, Charles M. Helig, & Angela White, *Ethical Justification for Conducting Public Health Surveillance Without Patient Consent*, 102 Am. J. Pub. Health 38 (2012).

[121] Sweeney et al., *supra* note 114, at 563. [122] *Id.* at 586–587. [123] *Id.* at 578.

[124] *Id.* at 589–590.

are infected or exposed. Although advances in science have brought amazing new insights into the molecular causes of disease, we are still developing the legal and policy tools necessary to effectively incentivize development of novel antibiotics to fight deadly infections. We remain unsure about how to handle the explosion of personal data that advances in medicine, public health, and technology have made available. We must decide, individually or collectively, whether we want to allow broad use of our personal data to improve health and what degree of privacy and autonomy we are willing to sacrifice in order to achieve our goals.

CHAPTER 44

PUBLIC HEALTH
Noncommunicable Disease Prevention

LINDSAY F. WILEY, MANEL KAPPAGODA, AND ANNE PEARSON

ALTHOUGH the infectious disease threats continue to be an important focus of public health law, the primary drivers of premature death in the United States are noncommunicable diseases (NCDs).[1] NCDs also cause two-thirds of all deaths worldwide.[2] Dietary composition and tobacco smoking are the two leading risk factors contributing to disease burden in the United States, with physical inactivity and alcohol use following not far behind.[3] Lung cancer is the leading cause of cancer death in the United

[1] In 2010, the top ten contributors to years of life lost prematurely (YLL) in the United States were: ischemic heart disease, lung cancer, stroke, chronic obstructive pulmonary disease (COPD), road injury, self-harm, diabetes, cirrhosis, Alzheimer disease, and colorectal cancer. Two communicable diseases, HIV/AIDS and lower respiratory tract infections, were ranked among the top ten in 1990, but not in 2010. *See* U.S. Burden of Disease Collaborators, *The State of US Health 1990–2010: Burden of Diseases, Injuries, and Risk Factors*, 310 J. AM. MED. ASSN. 591, fig. 1 (2013).

[2] NCDs cause about two-thirds of all deaths worldwide, but the leading causes of *premature* death (in terms of YLL) worldwide are not dominated by NCDs to the same extent as in the United States. In 2012, the top ten contributors to YLL worldwide were: ischemic heart disease, lower respiratory infections, stroke, pre-term birth complications, diarrheal diseases, HIV/AIDS, birth asphyxia and birth trauma, road injury, COPD, and malaria. *See* World Health Organization, *Regional Estimates for 2000–2011: 20 Leading Causes of YLLs— World (2014)*, at http://www.who.int/healthinfo/global_burden_disease/GHE_YLL_Global_2000_2011.xls.

[3] In 2010, the top ten risk factors contributing to disease burden measured in terms of disability adjusted life years (DALYs) in the United States were: dietary composition, smoking, high body mass index, high blood pressure, high fasting plasma glucose, physical inactivity, alcohol use, high total cholesterol, drug use, and exposure to high ambient particular matter pollution. U.S. Burden of Disease Collaborators, at fig. 3. Worldwide, they were high blood pressure, smoking, household air pollution, diet low in fruit, alcohol use, high body mass index, high fasting plasma glucose, childhood underweight, ambient particulate matter pollution, and physical inactivity. *See* the Institute for Health Metrics and Evaluation, THE GLOBAL BURDEN OF DISEASE: GENERATING EVIDENCE, GUIDING POLICY (2013), 14, fig. 3, at http://www.healthdata.org/sites/default/files/files/policy_report/2013/GBD_GeneratingEvidence/IHME_GBD_GeneratingEvidence_FullReport.pdf.

States, causing more deaths than the next three most common cancers combined.[4] One-third of U.S. adults have high blood pressure, and about 14% have high cholesterol.[5] More than 8% of Americans have been diagnosed with diabetes, with about half as many more estimated to be living with undiagnosed diabetes.[6] Nearly 40% of U.S. adults have abnormal fasting glucose levels designating them as "pre-diabetic."[7] Many of these health problems disproportionately impact people of color and those with low income.[8]

Total healthcare and lost productivity costs are estimated to be more than $315 billion per year for cardiovascular disease and stroke,[9] $245 billion for diabetes,[10] and more than $38 billion per year for lung cancer.[11] In light of these costs, lawmakers at every level of government have made NCD prevention a high priority. State and local governments are employing a wide range of strategies to discourage tobacco use and overconsumption of alcohol and encourage balanced eating and physical activity. At the federal level, the Affordable Care Act emphasizes access to preventive healthcare services, provides funding for community-level prevention initiatives, and organizes federal efforts under the umbrella of the cross-sector National Prevention Council.[12] At the global level, many countries are working with the World Health Organization to implement the Framework Convention on Tobacco Control[13] and the Global Strategy on Diet, Physical Activity and Health.[14]

This chapter focuses on the use of law as a tool for NCD prevention. Until fairly recently, problems like heart disease, cancer, diabetes, and cirrhosis and the risk factors contributing to them were viewed primarily as matters for individual medical care and public health education campaigns. Some continue to argue that medical treatment and education are the only appropriate government responses to NCD epidemics, but

4 American Cancer Society, Cancer Facts & Figures 2014 (2014), http://www.cancer.org/research/cancerfactsstatistics/cancerfactsfigures2014/index.

5 Alan S. Go et al., *Heart Disease and Stroke Statistics—2014 Update*, 128 Circulation 1, 2–3 (2014).

6 *Id.* at 3.

7 *Id.*

8 U.S. Centers for Disease Control and Prevention, *CDC Health Disparities and Inequalities Report—United States, 2013*, 62, no. 3 Morbidity & Mortality Weekly Report 1, 1, 101, 113 (2013).

9 Go, *Heart Disease*, at 3–4.

10 American Diabetes Association, *Economic Costs of Diabetes in the U.S. in 2012*, 37(5) Diabetes Care 1, 1 (2013).

11 U.S. National Institutes of Health, National Cancer Institute, Cancer Trends Progress Report—2011/2012 Update (2012), at http://progressreport.cancer.gov/doc_detail.asp?pid=1&did=2007&chid=75&coid=726&.

12 *See* National Prevention Council, National Prevention Strategy (2011), http://www.surgeongeneral.gov/initiatives/prevention/strategy/report.pdf.

13 World Health Organization, WHO Framework Convention on Tobacco Control, World Health Assembly Resolution 56.1, 1 (2003), http://www.who.int/tobacco/framework/final_text/en/.

14 World Health Organization, Global Strategy on Diet, Physical Activity and Health, World Health Assembly Resolution 57.17 (2004), at http://www.who.int/dietphysicalactivity/strategy/eb11344/strategy_english_web.pdf?ua=1.

a growing body of research indicates that these strategies alone are ineffective. Public health researchers see the physical and social environments in which people make choices about food, tobacco, alcohol, and physical activity as a more promising focus for intervention. This approach is consistent with the "ecological model" that has come to dominate public health science and practice.[15] Law and policy interventions are central to it.[16]

In this chapter, we argue that law and policy interventions can and should be used to prevent NCDs, but some of the most effective strategies for doing so are impeded by political, cultural, and legal barriers. Law and policy interventions—including mandated information disclosures and restrictions on marketing; taxation and pricing strategies; product and retailer regulation; licensing and zoning strategies; spending and procurement strategies; and indirect regulation through tort liability—can change behavior and protect health on a much broader scale than health education. However, the advent of "new public health law"—characterized by an expanded scope that includes NCD and injury prevention with an emphasis on the social determinants of health—has not been without controversy.[17] Opponents of public health intervention invoke charges of government paternalism and attribute ill health to the personal failings of the unhealthy, promoting personal responsibility as an alternative to government action. At the same time, the legal environment is increasingly hostile to the regulation of harmful consumer products, as demonstrated by increasing First Amendment protection for commercial speech and the use of ceiling preemption to limit local regulation. In spite of these challenges, many public health law and policy interventions are being adopted, particularly at the state and local level. Following the ecological model, we discuss legal and policy interventions aimed at influencing the information consumers receive about unhealthy products; the built environment; the marketplace; and the social norms that shape health behaviors, with an emphasis on tobacco control efforts and initiatives that promote healthy eating and physical activity.

[15] Karen Glanz et. al., Health Behavior and Health Education: Theory, Research, and Practice (2008), http://www.sanjeshp.ir/phd_91/Pages/Refrences/health%20education%20and%20promotion/[Karen_Glanz,_Barbara_K._Rimer,_K._Viswanath]_Heal(BookFi.or.pdf at 470 ("Ecological models specify that factors at multiple levels, often including intrapersonal, interpersonal, organizational, community, and public policy, can influence health behaviors. Concepts that cut across these levels include sociocultural factors and physical environments, which may apply to more than one level."); Nancy Adler et al., Inst. of Med., Building the Science for a Population Health Movement (2013), *available at* http://www.iom.edu/~/media/Files/Perspectives-Files/2013/Discussion-Papers/BPH-BuildingTheScience.pdf (accessed Apr. 21, 2014) (experts "view health as the product of multiple determinants at the biologic, genetic, behavioral, social, and environmental levels and their interactions among individuals, communities, time, and place").

[16] Lindsay F. Wiley, *Rethinking the New Public Health*, 69 Wash. & Lee L. Rev. 207, 215–225 (2012) (describing the evolution of public health law in response to changing models of public health science and practice).

[17] *Id.* (describing controversy over "new public health law").

I The Information Environment: Government-Sponsored Speech, Disclosure Mandates, and Advertising Restrictions

Measures that prohibit misleading advertising practices and ensure that consumers have accurate and accessible information about products are necessary adjuncts to government-sponsored messaging campaigns that urge people to adopt healthy habits. However, many of these interventions are facing an uncertain legal environment as the courts have increased First Amendment protection for commercial speech. In this section, we provide an overview of the relevant constitutional framework before discussing government-sponsored speech, compelled disclosures by private parties, and advertising restrictions.

a. First Amendment Protection of Commercial Speech

Until relatively recently, "government had a free hand in regulating advertising."[18] The U.S. Supreme Court consistently held that commercial advertising was entirely unprotected by the First Amendment.[19] In the mid-1970s, however, the Court held that "speech which does no more than propose a commercial transaction [is not] so removed from any exposition of ideas . . . that it lacks all protection."[20] From then on, the Court has recognized a "common-sense distinction between [commercial speech], which occurs in an area traditionally subject to government regulation, and other varieties of speech,"[21] granting less constitutional protection to the former.[22]

Pursuant to *Central Hudson Gas & Electric Co. v. Public Service Commission of New York* (1980),[23] restrictions on commercial speech—for example, prohibitions on tobacco advertisements in certain types of media or restrictions on the use of terms like "low-tar"—are subject to a four-part test: (1) commercial speech is not protected by the First Amendment if it promotes unlawful activity or is false, deceptive, or misleading; additionally, to regulate truthful advertising with regard to lawful activity: (2) the government must have a "substantial" interest in regulating the speech, (3) the regulation must "directly advance[] the governmental interest asserted," and (4) the regulation must be no "more extensive than is necessary to serve" the stated governmental interest. Although this standard has traditionally been

[18] Daniel A. Faber, The First Amendment (2d ed. 2003) at 151.

[19] Valentine v. Chrestensen, 316 U.S. 52, 54 (1942).

[20] Virginia State Bd. of Pharmacy v. Virginia Citizens Consumer Council, Inc., 425 U.S. 748. 762 (1976) (internal quotation marks and citations omitted); *see also* Bigelow v. Virginia, 421 U.S. 809, 826 (1975) (holding that the First Amendment protects commercial speech and invalidating a state statute making it a crime to sell or circulate any publication that encourages or prompts the procuring of an abortion).

[21] Ohralik v. Ohio State Bar Ass'n, 436 U.S. 447, 455–456 (1978).

[22] Bolger v. Youngs Drug Products Corp., 463 U.S. 60, 64–65 (1983).

[23] 447 U.S. 557, 566 (1980).

described as subjecting commercial speech regulations to intermediate scrutiny, in recent cases, the Court has appeared to apply *Central Hudson* in a way that closely approximates strict scrutiny.[24]

The Court's jurisprudence with regard to compelled commercial speech has been somewhat more muddled. Regulations that require industry to communicate health warnings on their products or advertisements (such as graphic warning labels on cigarette packs or text warnings on tobacco print ads) implicate the "right to refrain from speaking,"[25] triggering First Amendment scrutiny. Scrutiny of disclosure requirements has traditionally been weaker than in cases where speech is suppressed. In *Zauderer v. Office of Disciplinary Counsel* (1985),[26] the Court held that laws requiring the disclosure of commercial information are constitutional as long as they are reasonably related to the state's asserted interest. As discussed in section I.c., below, recent decisions signal that the lenient *Zauderer* standard could give way to the more stringent *Central Hudson* standard except in cases where the compelled disclosures are clearly aimed at correcting inherently misleading advertising.

b. Government-Sponsored Speech

Government-sponsored educational campaigns aimed at urging people to eat healthfully, abstain from smoking, and moderate their consumption of alcohol have some influence[27] and are functionally immune from legal challenge.[28] For example, an advertising campaign characterizing the tobacco industry as deceptive and an enemy of public health, which was sponsored by California and financed by a surcharge on cigarette sales, was upheld in the face of a First Amendment challenge.[29] However, funding for educational campaigns is paltry compared to the money spent by industry to advertise harmful products. Governments

[24] Seth E. Mermin & Samantha K. Graff, *The First Amendment and Public Health, At Odds*, 39 AM. J.L. & MED. 298, 299 (2013); Samantha Rauer, Note, *When the First Amendment and Public Health Collide: The Court's Increasingly Strict Constitutional Scrutiny of Health Regulations that Restrict Commercial Speech*, 38 AM. J.L. & MED. 690, 691 (2012).

[25] R.J. Reynolds Tobacco Co. v. FDA, 696 F.3d 1205, 1211 (2012), *citing* Wooley v. Maynard, 430 U.S. 705 (1977).

[26] 471 U.S. 626 (1985).

[27] *See, e.g.*, T. McAfee et al., *Effect of the First Federally Funded US Antismoking National Media Campaign*, 382 THE LANCET 2003 (2013); CDC, *Increases in Quitline Calls and Smoking Cessation Website Visitors During a National Tobacco Education Campaign—March 19–June 10, 2012*, 61 MORBIDITY AND MORTALITY WEEKLY REPORT 667(2012).

[28] Even in cases where a law compels private subsidization of government speech, the Supreme Court has held that First Amendment concerns are not implicated. *See, e.g.*, Johanns v. Livestock Marketing Association, 544 U.S. 550, 553 (2005) (upholding federal assessments to fund government promotional campaigns); Glickman v. Wileman Brothers & Elliott, Inc., 521 U.S. 457 (1997) (upholding federal marketing orders requiring California fruit producers to fund a generic advertising program because it was ancillary to a comprehensive regulatory program); *but see* United States v. United Foods Inc., 533 U.S. 405, 411 (2001) (holding that a federal statute requiring mushroom producers and importers to pay for generic advertising promoting the mushroom industry was coerced speech: "First Amendment values are at serious risk if the government can compel . . . [citizens to subsidize speech] on the side that it favors.").

[29] *See, e.g.*, R.J. Reynolds Tobacco Co. v. Bonta, 423 F.3d 906 (9th Cir. 2005).

attempt to level the playing field by using their regulatory authority to create platforms for government speech, to compel speech by private actors, and to restrict advertising of unhealthy products.

c. Disclosure Mandates

Content labeling requirements mandate the disclosure to consumers (typically on product packaging or at the point of sale) of particular information about product ingredients or nutritional value. Notably, labels on tobacco and alcohol products do not generally disclose ingredients, though a provision of the Family Smoking Prevention and Tobacco Control Act of 2009 requires tobacco manufacturers and importers to disclose ingredient lists to the Food and Drug Administration (FDA).[30]

In 2014, the FDA announced impending updates to the Nutrition Facts Labels required for packaged foods under the Nutrition Labeling and Education Act of 1990 (NLEA).[31] Proposed changes include more prominently displayed calorie counts, serving sizes that more accurately reflect American consumption habits, specific labeling of added sugars, no required labeling of Vitamins A and C (which are not lacking in Americans' diets and are easily added to unhealthy foods to make them appear more beneficial), and revised "calories from fat" labeling (to reflect important distinctions between beneficial and harmful fats).[32] Nutrition labeling requirements not only provide useful information to consumers, they also have the power to prompt manufactures to change their product formulations for the better. The FDA's 2003 decision to require separate disclosure of trans-fat content for packaged foods led many manufacturers to switch to healthier alternatives. In turn, the widespread adoption of alternative ingredients in response to packaged food labeling requirements (as well as local bans for prepared foods, see section II.c below) has made it more feasible for the FDA to propose a de facto ban on artificial trans-fats in all food products nationwide.[33]

Although food labels provide important information about packaged food products, consumers are largely left in the dark when it comes to the calorie content and nutritional value of most alcoholic beverages,[34] produce,[35] and prepared foods.[36] New York City's mandate that food service establishments post calorie counts on menus[37] aimed to fill one of those gaps. The measure met with initial resistance, and there continues to be debate over its

[30] 21 U.S.C. § 387d (2014). [31] 21 U.S.C. § 343(q) (2014).

[32] FDA, Factsheet on New Proposed Nutrition Facts Label (2014), http://www.fda.gov/Food/GuidanceRegulation/GuidanceDocumentsRegulatoryInformation/LabelingNutrition/ucm387533.htm.

[33] The FDA announced a preliminary determination that partially hydrogenated oils (the primary dietary source of artificial trans-fats) would no longer be classified as "generally recognized as safe" for human consumption. 78 Fed. Reg. 67169 (Nov. 8, 2013).

[34] Packaged alcoholic beverages are governed by the Alcohol and Tobacco Tax and Trade Bureau of the Treasury Department. In 2007, the agency published a notice of proposed rule-making regarding nutrition labeling, but has not revisited the issue. 72 Fed. Reg. 41860 (Jul. 31, 2007).

[35] 21 CFR 101.9(j)(10) and 101.45 (exempting fresh produce and seafood from NLEA requirements). Meat, poultry and egg products are governed by the Food Safety Inspection Service of the USDA. As of 2012, Nutrition Facts Labels are required for some meat and poultry products. 9 CFR 317 and 381.

[36] 21 CFR 101.9(j)(2) (exempting food served in restaurants or delivered to homes for immediate consumption); 21 CFR 101.9(j)(3) (exempting bakery and deli foods prepared on the premises).

[37] N.Y., Health Code tit. 24, § 81.50 (2008).

effectiveness,[38] but similar laws were rapidly adopted by other state and local governments. Local disclosure mandate laws such as New York City's must carefully navigate federal preemption, but they can be crafted to withstand challenge.[39] Indeed, local governments have emerged as pioneers of healthy eating interventions, filling gaps left by slow-moving and industry-captured federal legislators and regulators. As of this writing, the FDA was still in the process of implementing a new federal menu labeling requirement under the 2010 Affordable Care Act amid repeated delays attributed to lobbying by grocery stores, convenience stores, and pizza chains for exemptions and weaker penalties.[40]

Warning label mandates go beyond disclosure of neutral facts about the contents or nutritional value of products to convey information about the health risks associated with them. In some cases they openly urge consumers to avoid the product under certain circumstances (e.g., "women should not drink alcoholic beverages during pregnancy") or altogether (e.g., "1-800-QUIT-NOW"). While early warning requirements—such as Surgeon General warnings mandated for cigarettes in 1965[41] and alcoholic beverages in 1988[42]—went unchallenged by industry, recent efforts to update them under the 2009 tobacco control law are running up against increasing First Amendment protection for commercial speech. Warning mandates have only recently emerged as a potentially viable option for particularly unhealthy food and nonalcoholic beverage products.[43] Recent court decisions with regard to tobacco warnings may have a chilling effect on these and many other innovative NCD interventions.

In 2009, long after the original cigarette pack warning messages had lost their impact,[44] Congress mandated that the FDA adopt a rule requiring that warnings include "color graphics depicting the negative health consequences of smoking" that cover 50% of the front and back of cigarette packages and text warnings covering 20% of advertisement space.[45] But in 2013, the FDA withdrew the nine warning labels it had developed[46] after a circuit court split over their constitutionality posed a threat of imminent Supreme Court review.[47] Courts reviewing the graphic warning mandate were divided over the applicability of *Zauderer*'s rational basis test, which courts have traditionally relied upon to uphold legislation requiring the disclosure of information that is intended to positively impact health behaviors, the

[38] James Krieger & Brian Saelens, Impact of Menu Labeling on Consumer Behavior, A 2008–2012 Update (2013), http://www.rwjf.org/content/dam/farm/reports/reports/2013/rwjf406357.

[39] New York State Restaurant Ass'n v. New York City Bd. of Health, 556 F.3d 114 (2d Cir. 2009).

[40] Mary Clair Jalonek, *FDA Head Says Menu Labeling "Thorny" Issue*, Assoc. Press, Mar. 12, 2013; Kira Lerner, *FDA Delays Menu Labeling Until End of Year*, Law 360, Mar. 4, 2014.

[41] 15 U.S.C. § 1335a(a), Pub. L. 89–92. [42] 27 U.S.C. §215, Pub. L. 100–690.

[43] As of this writing, the California legislature was considering legislation that would require warning labels on sugar-sweetened beverages stating that "[d]rinking beverages with added sugar(s) contributes to obesity, diabetes, and tooth decay." If passed, this legislation will be the first of its kind in the United States. http://leginfo.legislature.ca.gov/faces/billNavClient.xhtml?bill_id=201320140SB1000. While this intervention is based on tobacco warning labels, it raises unique considerations, including potential preemption under the NLEA.

[44] Campaign for Tobacco-free Kids, Tobacco Warning Labels: Evidence of Effectiveness, https://www.tobaccofreekids.org/research/factsheets/pdf/0325.pdf ("today's labels are small and easily overwhelmed by the designs on cigarette packages. Moreover, smokers have become habitualized to the style of labels, to the point that the labels go unnoticed altogether").

[45] 15 U.S.C. § 1333(d). [46] 21 CFR 1141.

[47] Nathan Cortez, *Do Graphic Tobacco Warnings Violate the First Amendment*, 64 Hastings L. Rev. 1467, 1470 (2013).

2009 Tobacco Control Act's including calorie postings in chain restaurants.[48] While the Sixth Circuit upheld graphic warning mandate under *Zauderer*,[49] the D.C. Circuit invalidated the FDA's final rule on graphic warning labels, finding that the agency had failed to demonstrate that graphic labels were needed to prevent deception and therefore the *Zauderer* test was inapplicable.[50] In 2014, the D.C. Circuit expressly overruled this holding in an unrelated case,[51] but FDA had already withdrawn its proposed warnings to avoid Supreme Court review.

Furthermore, the D.C. Circuit's decision striking down the graphic warning mandate application of the *Central Hudson* test looked remarkably like strict, rather than intermediate, scrutiny. Diverging sharply from historical deference toward government action to protect public health, the court noted that it was "skeptical that the government can assert a substantial interest in discouraging consumers from purchasing a lawful product, even one that has been conclusively linked to adverse health consequences."[52] The court also insisted that FDA must provide "substantial evidence" that the graphic warnings would "directly" reduce smoking rates by a "material degree," before the intervention, crafted on the basis of the best available science, has even been implemented. The potential implications of this opinion, if taken seriously by the Supreme Court and other lower courts, are staggering. It can take decades to evaluate the impact of an NCD intervention, given the complex web of social norms and habits that determine individual behavior and the long latency period between exposure and the onset of disease. Furthermore, regulators do not necessarily expect warnings by themselves to materially affect behavior. Rather, warnings are designed to work in concert with other interventions to influence health-related behavior.

d. Advertising Restrictions

Several years after mandating warning labels for cigarettes, the United States became the first country to ban cigarette advertising on radio and television.[53] Litigation against tobacco companies by private plaintiffs,[54] the state attorneys general,[55] and the federal government[56] has also played an important role in driving significant changes to the way that tobacco is marketed in this country, with corresponding gains for public health. In particular, the Master Settlement Agreement (MSA) that was negotiated in 1998 between the major tobacco

48 New York State Restaurant Ass'n v. New York City Bd. of Health, 556 F.3d 114 (2d Cir. 2009).

49 Discount Tobacco City & Lottery v. U.S., 674 F.3d 509 (6th Cir. 2012).

50 R.J. Reynolds Tobacco Co. v. FDA, 696 F.3d 1205, 1213-14 (D.C. Cir. 2012) (striking down the graphic warning label requirement based on the *Central Hudson* test).

51 *American Meat Institute*, 760 F.3d at 22-23 (finding that "*Zauderer*'s characterization of the speaker's interest in opposing forced disclosure of [purely factual and uncontroversial] information as "minimal" seems inherently applicable beyond the problem of deception" and expressly overruling previous holdings "limiting *Zauderer* to cases in which the government points to an interest in correcting deception," citing R.J. Reynolds, 696 F.3d at 1214).

52 R.J. Reynolds Tobacco Co., 696 F.3d. at 1218, n. 13.

53 Pub. L. 89–92, 15 U.S.C. §§ 1331–1339 (1969).

54 *See, e.g.*, Henley v. Philip Morris, 114 Cal.App.4th 1429 (2004).

55 *See* Master Settlement Agreement, http://ag.ca.gov/tobacco/pdf/1msa.pdf.

56 *See* United States v. Philip Morris U.S.A., Inc., 449 F.Supp.2d 1 (D.D.C. 2009) (upholding determinations that cigarette manufacturers and trade associations violated the Racketeer Influenced

companies and the attorneys general of forty-six states included bans on outdoor advertising through billboards and transit vehicles and restrictions on sports marketing, event sponsorship, and promotional products. Tobacco advertising restrictions continue to evolve: The 2009 federal tobacco control law restricts marketing for tobacco products represented as having lower risk; bans the use of images and color in most tobacco industry advertising; and bans the use of a variety of other strategies, such as free sampling and brand name sponsorships.[57]

Confined by federal preemption with regard to broadcast and print media, state and local governments have focused on restricting advertising in certain locations, like school zones and at the point of sale. These efforts have been successfully opposed by industry groups on First Amendment grounds, typically faltering on the third and fourth prongs of the *Central Hudson* test. Commentators note that the Court appears to be applying *Central Hudson* in a way that approximates strict, rather than intermediate, scrutiny.[58] For example, in 1996, the Court struck down a Rhode Island law that barred advertisement of the price of alcoholic beverages except inside liquor stores. A plurality of the Court held that the government must demonstrate that the challenged measure would advance its interest "to a material degree" and that "speculation and conjecture" was insufficient.[59] In 2001, the Court struck down Massachusetts prohibitions on indoor, point-of sale advertising lower than five feet from the floor of a retail establishment and on all tobacco advertising within 1,000 feet of schools.[60] Although the court found sufficient evidence that "preventing targeted campaigns and limiting youth exposure to advertising will decrease underage use," thereby satisfying *Central Hudson*'s "substantial interest" prong, it ultimately concluded that the five-foot rule would not directly advance that interest (because children are capable of looking up) and the one-thousand-foot rule would prohibit more lawful speech than necessary.[61]

In addition to raising First Amendment concerns, restrictions on food and beverage advertising have faced unique challenges. Healthy eating interventions have drawn heavily on the tobacco and alcohol control experiences. However, the complexity involved in promoting a balanced diet (as opposed to tobacco abstinence and alcohol moderation), a considerably more conservative political climate, and the lessons the food and beverage industry has learned from the tobacco wars have made healthy eating a tougher fight.

Whereas the FTC played a key role in prompting Congress to institute warning mandates and advertising restrictions for tobacco products,[62] the FTC's efforts to restrict advertising

and Corrupt Organizations Act by conspiring to deceive the public about the health effects of smoking, addictiveness of nicotine, and benefits of "light" and "low tar" products). As of this writing, litigation continued on remand with regard to remedial public disclosures by the defendants admitting their past deceptions.

[57] FDA, Overview of the Family Smoking Prevention and Tobacco Control Act: Consumer Fact Sheet, http://www.fda.gov/tobaccoproducts/guidancecomplianceregulatoryinformation/ucm246129.htm.

[58] Seth E. Mermin & Samantha K. Graff, *The First Amendment and Public Health, At Odds*, 39 Am. J.L. & Med. 298, 299 (2013); Samantha Rauer, Note, *When the First Amendment and Public Health Collide: The Court's Increasingly Strict Constitutional Scrutiny of Health Regulations that Restrict Commercial Speech*, 38 Am. J.L. & Med. 690, 691 (2012).

[59] 44 Liquormart, Inc. v. Rhode Island, 517 U.S. 484 (1996).

[60] 533 U.S. 525 (2001).

[61] Lorillard Tobacco Co. v. Reilly, 533 U.S. 525 (2001).

[62] Unfair or Deceptive Advertising and Liability of Cigarettes in Relation to the Health Hazards of Smoking, 29 Fed. Reg. 8324 (July 2, 1964). (The rule was never implemented, but it formed the basis of

of sugary and fatty foods to children were thwarted early on by a congressional backlash that continues to reverberate today. The ill-fated "kidvid" rule-making launched in 1978 would have imposed significant restrictions on advertising directed at children, with particular emphasis on sugary foods and drinks. [63] The industry-fueled backlash against this failed proposal was "toxic to the Commission as an institution."[64] Echoing the language used by the cigarette industry, and presaging the rhetoric that the soda industry uses so effectively today, critics called the proposed rule "a preposterous intervention that would turn the FTC into a great national nanny."[65]

Although inroads are being made with regard to restrictions on advertising inside public schools,[66] efforts to impose more general restrictions on advertising of unhealthy food and beverage products remain out of reach for public health advocates. As a result, action in this area has been entirely voluntary, with limited effect. The food industry's Children's Food and Beverage Advertising Initiative (CFBAI), the most prominent example, suffers from critical shortcomings. Its nutritional guidelines emphasize the presence of healthy ingredients like Vitamins C and A, rather than excluding foods that are high in calories, sodium, saturated fat, or sugar—allowing manufacturers to fortify their products with nutrients that are not generally lacking in children's diets and thereby convert unhealthy products into "healthy" ones. Furthermore, CFBAI's narrow definition of marketing practices "directed" toward children excludes a great deal of marketing that reaches kids.

In 2009, Congress created an Interagency Working Group (IWG) to develop voluntary principles to guide industry self-regulatory efforts in this area. However, when the IWG released draft guidelines setting forth more stringent nutritional standards and definitions of marketing practices that should be voluntarily restricted, the food and beverage industry fought back with a massive lobbying campaign. Eventually, the draft guidelines were killed by congressional action requiring that they be subjected to prohibitively expensive cost-benefit analysis before being promulgated in final form, an unprecedented requirement for a voluntary program.[67]

Aware of the role that tort and consumer protection litigation has played in driving major changes to tobacco marketing practices, the food and beverage industry has also moved with astonishing speed to quell private lawsuits arising out of harms caused by unhealthy foods and beverages. In the closely watched case of *Pelman v. McDonald's Corp.*,[68] children

the Federal Cigarette Labeling and Advertising Act of 1966); William MacLeod et al., *Three Rules and a Constitution: Consumer Protection Finds its Limits in Competition Policy*, 72 ANTITRUST L.J. 943 (2005).

[63] J. Howard Beales, III, *Advertising to Kids and the FTC: A Regulatory Retrospective that Advises the Present*, 12 GEO. MASON L. REV. 873, 878–879 (2004), quoting Notice of Proposed Rulemaking, 43 Fed. Reg. at 17,969.

[64] *Id.* at 879–880 (noting that Congress allowed the agency's funding to lapse and gutted its law enforcement functions).

[65] *Id.* at 880, quoting Editorial, *The FTC as National Nanny*, WASH POST, Mar. 1, 1978.

[66] *See* 79 Fed. Reg. 10693 (Feb. 26, 2014) (notice of proposed rule-making to restrict advertising in schools of foods that do not meet previously issued nutritional guidelines).

[67] Duff Wilson & Janet Roberts, *Special Report: How Washington Went Soft on Childhood Obesity*, REUTERS, Apr. 27, 2012, http://www.reuters.com/article/2012/04/27/us-usa-foodlobby-idUSBRE83Q0ED20120427.

[68] Pelman v. McDonald's Corp., 237 F. Supp. 2d 512, 519 (S.D.N.Y. 2003) [Pelman I] (dismissed without prejudice to replead); Pelman v. McDonald's Corp., 2003 U.S. Dist. LEXIS 15202 [Pelman II] (dismissing

who experienced obesity and related health problems after regularly eating at McDonald's alleged false advertising and deceptive trade practices in violation of New York's consumer protection law. They pointed to the defendant's advertising campaigns and failure to disclose accurate nutritional information to argue that McDonald's portrayed its products as "nutritionally beneficial and part of a healthy lifestyle if consumed daily."[69] The case was ultimately dismissed. It did have an impact on the food litigation landscape; although probably not in the way the plaintiffs had hoped. In the years that followed, legislatures in twenty-five states adopted Common Sense Consumption Acts, better known as "Cheeseburger Bills." Admonishing those who suffer from obesity and related health harms for their "poor choices," these acts immunize the food, beverage, and restaurant industries from liability (including for false advertising and deceptive trade practices in many states) for health conditions caused by long-term consumption of their products.[70]

Food labeling litigation continues to be an important focus for public health lawyers and industry groups alike. Recent litigation has focused on policing the marketing of foods widely perceived to be healthy, like yogurts, fruit juices, and organics. Public health messaging campaigns have raised awareness about the importance of a healthy diet and a growing number of consumers are willing to pay a premium for products that they perceive to be healthier. When companies manipulate that preference with misleading marketing strategies, consumers are cheated and public health goals are undermined. For example, the FTC has pursued enforcement action against the makers of POM Wonderful pomegranate juice barring the company from making claims that its products are effective against heart disease, prostate cancer, erectile dysfunction, or any other disease.[71] Federal enforcement resources are minimal, however, restricting the Federal Communications Commission (FCC) to high-profile cases. Litigation by state attorneys general and private parties (under state laws that, unlike the NLEA, provide a private cause of action) has filled the enforcement gap to some extent. Plaintiffs assert that food and beverage products are deceptively marketed using terms such as "natural," "fresh," "sugar free," "antioxidant," and "low calorie," or "evaporated cane juice" in place of "sugar."[72]

Litigation strategies have also been used to keep self-regulatory programs honest. For example, in 2009, several state attorneys general announced an investigation of an industry-sponsored voluntary rating system that designated certain food products with a "Smart Choices" logo. The program's nutritional standards were so lax that products like Fruit Loops, Frosted Flakes, and Cracker Jacks qualified for the "Smart Choices" logo. After the attorneys general' announcement, the FDA indicated that it too would investigate. Shortly thereafter, the program was ended.[73]

claims for failure to plead sufficient facts to establish causation), vacated and remanded by Pelman v. McDonald's Corp., 396 F.3d 508 (2d. Cir. 2005).

69 Pelman II, 396 F.3d at 510.

70 Cara L. Wilking & Richard A. Daynard, *Beyond Cheeseburgers: The Impact of Common Sense Consumption Acts on Future Obesity-Related Lawsuits*, 68 FOOD & DRUG L.J. 229 (2013).

71 Opinion of the Commission *In the Matter of POM Wonderful LLC*, Docket No. 9344, *available at* http://www.ftc.gov/opa/2013/01/pom.shtm (reviewed May 9, 2014).

72 *See, e.g.*, Gitson v. Trader Joe's Co., 2013 WL 5513711 (C.D. Cal. Oct. 4, 2013).

73 NATIONAL POLICY & LEGAL ANALYSIS NETWORK TO PREVENT CHILDHOOD OBESITY, PUBLIC HEALTH LAW CENTER, STATE AG ENFORCEMENT OF FOOD MARKETING LAWS: A BRIEF HISTORY 1–2 (2010), http://www.nplanonline.org/childhood-obesity/products/State-AGs.

II The Marketplace: Making the Healthy Choice the Easy Choice

Moving beyond information-focused strategies, some of the most innovative NCD interventions focus on the retail environment in which consumption choices are made. Taxes, subsidies, and regulation affect prices, which in turn influence consumption. Local governments are also pioneering the use of regulation, zoning, and licensing strategies to make retail environments more conducive to healthy choices. The industries whose interests are implicated by these interventions continue to lobby and litigate against them. In this section, we follow the "four Ps" framework used by marketing analysts[74] to discuss interventions in terms of price, place, product, and promotions. Finally, we discuss the preemption issues that play such an important role in this area.

a. Price

The connection between retail price and consumption is well established. When cigarettes cost more, fewer people start smoking, more people quit, fewer former smokers relapse, and those who continue to smoke reduce their consumption.[75] Many states and a few localities have minimum price laws for cigarettes. These laws were enacted to help small retailers, but public health advocates have recommended strengthening them as a public health intervention.[76] Tobacco taxes have been in place for decades in the United States and are widely credited with reducing smoking rates significantly, while also generating revenue for public health programming.

Efforts to extend this approach beyond tobacco control have met with more resistance. Despite scientific evidence indicating that excise taxes on alcohol would reduce consumption and related health conditions, alcohol is not taxed to the same extent as tobacco. This is due to a number of factors, including that many people who drink alcohol do so in moderation and cause no harm to themselves or others.[77] More recently, industry groups and others have lobbied extensively to defeat taxation of sugar sweetened beverages.

Critics of excise taxes argue that they are quite regressive—on average, the poor pay a share of their income that is sixteen times greater than that paid by the wealthiest.[78]

[74] Jerome E. McCarthy, Basic Marketing: A Managerial Approach (1964).

[75] F. Chaloupka, *Tobacco Control Lessons Learned: The Impact of State and Local Policies*, 38 ImpacTeen Research Paper Series, 9 (2010), http://www.impacteen.org/generalarea_PDFs/ITResearch38_Chaloupka.pdf.

[76] McLaughlin et al., *Reducing Tobacco Use and Access through Strengthened Minimum Price Laws*, 104 Am. J. Pub. Health 1844 (2014).

[77] Frank Chaloupka et al., *The Effects of Price on Alcohol Consumption and Alcohol-Related Problems*, 34 Alcohol Research and Health 236.

[78] Institute on Taxation and Economic Policy (ITEP), Who Pays? A Distributional Analysis of the Tax Systems in all 50 States 3 (4th ed. 2013).

Popular support for taxes on sugary beverages declined sharply from 2010 to 2012,[79] largely in response to campaigns by industry groups emphasizing negative impacts on the poor, the middle class, and people of color.[80] Proponents of public health taxes respond that low-income populations and people of color are disproportionately affected by the health conditions caused or exacerbated by the consumption of these products.

Moving beyond taxes and minimum price laws, analysts have also drawn attention to the powerful role of government programs that subsidize unhealthy products, leading public health advocates to call for changes in agricultural subsidies, federal nutrition programs, and government procurement contracts. Deregulation of the agricultural commodity market and agricultural subsidies (adopted and periodically revised through federal "farm bills") have been linked to lower prices for many unhealthy, highly processed foods.[81] "The result is a one foot on the gas, one foot on the brake approach whereby some government programs are aimed at encouraging healthier eating, while others subsidize unhealthy options."[82]

While agricultural subsidies continue to favor grain and oilseed crops over fruits and vegetables, reforms have been implemented in other U.S. Department of Agriculture (USDA) programs. Food and beverages sold in public schools (whether as part of federally subsidized breakfast and lunch programs or in school stores or vending machines) are now subject to more stringent nutritional guidelines.[83] The foods eligible for purchase through the Special Supplemental Nutrition Program for Women, Infants, and Children (WIC) are carefully selected to ensure appropriate levels of salt, sugar, and fat.[84] The defined food packages emphasize reduced-fat milk and whole-grain products, and new mothers are offered incentives to breastfeed.[85] These reforms have increased the availability of healthy foods in WIC-authorized stores, particularly in lower-income areas.[86]

Proposals by state and city authorities to impose similar restrictions on the Supplemental Nutrition Assistance Program (SNAP, better known by its former name, the Food Stamp Program) would require federal administrative approval. These proposals have been criticized by antihunger and antipoverty groups and rejected by both the Bush and Obama

[79] *63% Oppose "Sin Taxes" on Junk Food and Soda*, RASMUSSEN REPORTS, May 6, 2012, http://www.rasmussenreports.com/public_content/lifestyle/general_lifestyle/may_2012/63_oppose_sin_taxes_on_junk_food_and_soda.

[80] Daniel Zingale, *Gulp! The High Cost of Big Soda's Victory*, L.A. TIMES, Dec. 9, 2012, http://articles.latimes.com/2012/dec/09/opinion/la-oe-zingale-soda-tax-campaign-funding-20121209.

[81] LARRY COHEN ET AL., CULTIVATING COMMON GROUND: LINKING HEALTH AND SUSTAINABLE AGRICULTURE, PREVENTION INSTITUTE 2 (2004), http://www.preventioninstitute.org/index.php?option=com_jlibrary&view=article&id=67&Itemid=127; HEATHER SCHOONOVER, A FAIR FARM BILL FOR PUBLIC HEALTH, INST. FOR AGRIC. & TRADE POL'Y (2007), http://www.iatp.org/files/258_2_98598.pdf.

[82] Lindsay F. Wiley, *The U.S. Department of Agriculture as a Public Health Agency? A "Health in All Policies" Case Study*, 9 J. FOOD L. & POL'Y 61 (2013).

[83] The Healthy, Hunger-free Kids Act, Pub. L. No. 111-296, 124 Stat. 3183 (2009).

[84] Nutrition Amendments of 1978, Pub. L. No. 95-627, § 17(f)(11), 92 Stat. 3603 (1978).

[85] VICTOR OLIVEIRA & ELIZABETH FRAZAO, U.S. DEP'T. OF AGRICULTURE, ECONOMIC RESEARCH SERVICE, THE WIC PROGRAM: BACKGROUND, TRENDS, AND ECONOMIC ISSUES 45 (2009), http://www.ers.usda.gov/media/159295/err73.pdf.

[86] Tatiana Andreyeva et al., *Positive Influence of the Revised Special Supplemental Nutrition Program for Women, Infants, and Children Food Packages on Access to Healthy Foods*, 112 J. ACADEMY OF NUTRITION & DIETETICS 850, 855 (2012).

administrations. The USDA has, however, approved several pilot programs to incentivize the purchase of fresh produce, including through local farmers markets.[87]

A few pioneering state and local governments and federal agencies are adopting health-conscious procurement strategies to ensure that food sold in public facilities meets minimal nutritional guidelines.[88] In Washington state, for example, a 2013 executive order directed state agencies to ensure that foods and beverages served to employees, students, persons in custody, and residents of state facilities meet minimal nutritional standards.[89]

b. Place

In addition to influencing the price and content of unhealthy products, local governments can dictate the location, density, and practices of alcohol, tobacco, and food retailers.[90] Not surprisingly, the presence of tobacco, alcohol, and fast food in communities leads to increased consumption of these unhealthy products.[91] Absent preemption, a subject discussed in greater depth in section II.e, localities may regulate the density of retailers in particular areas, prohibit them from locating near places frequented by children such as schools and playgrounds, and limit the total number of retailers in a community.[92] In some cases, these strategies are prompted by aesthetic, rather than health-oriented considerations, but they may have health benefits as well.

Zoning regulations can also facilitate access to healthier food. For example, if a community wants to start a farmers market, it must ensure that the zoning laws permit that use at the market site.[93] In 2011, the city of Philadelphia updated its entire zoning code, incorporating health and sustainability provisions such as density bonuses (which allow developers to build taller buildings or buildings with additional floor area than otherwise would be allowed by right) for including fresh food markets in mixed-use developments.[94]

[87] *See* Wiley, *supra* note 84.

[88] National Policy and Legal Analysis Network to Prevent Childhood Obesity, Understanding Healthy Procurement: Using Government's Purchasing Power to Increase Access to Healthy Food (2011), at http://changelabsolutions.org/sites/default/files/Understanding%20Healthy%20Procurement%202011_20120717.pdf.

[89] Wash. Exec. Order No. 13-06 (Oct. 30, 2013), http://governor.wa.gov/office/execorders/documents/13-06.pdf.

[90] Licensing and Zoning: Tools for Public Health, ChangeLab Solutions, http://changelabsolutions.org/sites/default/files/Licensing%26Zoning_FINAL_20120703.pdf.

[91] D. H. Jernigan, M. Sparks, E. Yang, & R. Schwartz, *Using Public Health and Community Partnerships to Reduce Density of Alcohol Outlets*, 10 Prev. Chronic Dis. (2013).

[92] *Id.*; Larkin v. Grendel's Den, Inc., 459 U.S. 116, 121 (1982) ("there can be little doubt about the power of a state to regulate the environment in the vicinity of schools, churches, hospitals and the like by exercise of reasonable zoning laws"); Arcata, Cal., Land Use Code § 9.42.164 (2008) (limiting the total number of formula restaurants permitted within the community to nine); City of L.A. Planning Dep't, *Westwood Village Specific Plan* § 5B (4), (Oct. 6, 2004), http://cityplanning.lacity.org/complan/specplan/pdf/WWDVIL.PDF (regulating the density of fast-food establishments to every four hundred feet, with one exception).

[93] ChangeLab Solutions, From the Ground Up: Land Use Policies to Protect and Promote Farmers' Markets, http://changelabsolutions.org/publications/land-use-farmers-markets.

[94] Philadelphia, Pennsylvania Municipal Code § 14-603(7).

Licensing is another tool that local governments use to regulate retail outlets.[95] Indeed, because licensing has the potential to regulate not only the location and density of outlets but also the manner in which they operate, licensing is considered a more effective public health tool.[96] A license or permit gives permission to engage in a business, occupation, or transaction that would otherwise be considered illegal. Licensing can impose operational conditions on existing businesses, while zoning and permitting restrictions typically apply only to the opening of new businesses.[97] Long used to regulating alcohol and tobacco outlets, some localities are experimenting with using licensing and permitting to promote access to healthy food. In 2008, Minneapolis became the first city in the nation to use licensing to prescribe nutritional standards for food stores. Its Staple Foods Ordinance requires most small food stores and grocery stores to stock a minimum number of "staple foods" from the following categories: vegetables and fruits; meat, poultry, fish, and/or vegetable proteins; bread and/or cereal; and dairy products and/or substitutes.[98] The same year, Los Angeles sparked controversy by imposing a moratorium on the permitting of any new fast-food restaurants in a thirty-two-square-mile area of the city.[99] The ordinance was expressly intended to "address the over-concentration of [land] uses which are detrimental to the health and welfare of the people of the community."[100]

Some jurisdictions have used licensing to restrict the types of businesses that are eligible to engage in the sale of unhealthy products. For example, in 2008 San Francisco became the first U.S. city to prohibit tobacco sales by pharmacies by banning the practice directly and amending its tobacco retailer licenses to make pharmacies ineligible.[101] This restriction was premised on the notion that the sale of tobacco products by healthcare providers might lead consumers to conclude that tobacco products are safe.[102] Tobacco pharmacy bans have since been enacted in cities throughout Massachusetts.[103]

Unlike with price where it is possible to show, for example, the connection between increased excise taxes and reduced consumption of unhealthy products, the research related to place is less clear. A year after South Los Angeles passed the moratorium on fast-food restaurants, researchers suggested it was unlikely to reduce obesity given that the affected area had fewer, not more, fast-food chain restaurants per capita than wealthier neighborhoods to begin with and that residents of the affected area were more likely than residents of wealthier neighborhoods to purchase food from corner stores and food carts.[104] However, a

95 Heather Wooten et al., *Zoning and Licensing to Regulate the Retail Environment and Achieve Public Health Goals*, 5 Duke Forum for Law & Social Change 65 (2013), http://scholarship.law.duke.edu/cgi/viewcontent.cgi?article=1037&context=dflsc.

96 ChangeLab Solutions, Licensing and Zoning: Tools for Public Health, http://changelabsolutions.org/sites/default/files/Licensing%26Zoning_FINAL_20120703.pdf.

97 *Id.*

98 Minneapolis Code of Ordinances, Title 10, Ch 203.

99 L.A., Cal., Ordinance 180103 (July 29, 2008).

100 *Id.*

101 City and County of S.F., Cal., Health Code art. 19J § 1009.91-98 (92) (2010).

102 M. H. Katz, *Banning Tobacco Sales in Pharmacies: The Right Prescription*, 300 JAMA 1451 (2008).

103 *See, e.g.*, Boston Public Health Commission, Restricting the Sale of Tobacco Products in the City of Boston (2008); Board of Health, Everett, Mass., Regulation of the Everett Board of Health Restricting the Sale of Tobacco Products in the City of Everett (2010); Fall River, Mass., Rev. Ordinances pt. II, ch. 34 § 34-320 (2011).

104 Roland Strum & Deborah A. Cohen, *Zoning for Health? The Year-old Ban on New Fast-Food Restaurants in South Los Angeles*, Health Aff. 28(6w1088–98, (2009).

2013 Health Impact Assessment of the ban found that it did slow the growth of fast-food restaurants in the affected area and may have helped increase the number of grocery stores.[105] Research shows that greater density of alcohol retailers is associated with a variety of public health and safety concerns, including increased alcohol consumption, alcohol-impaired driving, injury, crime, violence, neighborhood disruption, and other harms; however, there is limited research on the health effect of reducing alcohol outlet density.[106] Commentators have argued that density measures raise concerns about disproportionate paternalism toward the poor.[107] In the case of the Los Angeles ordinance, however, the measure appears to have arisen out of a grassroots effort led by the affected community.[108] This kind of democratic engagement—communities coming together to create healthier living conditions—may mitigate concerns about paternalism and equity.

c. Product

Direct regulation of consumer products has long been an important strategy for protecting the public's health and safety. As a general rule, regulation of the way in which a consumable product is produced, distributed, and labeled falls within the exclusive jurisdiction of the federal government, while regulation of the way in which these products are sold and served fall within the bailiwick of states and localities. For example, federal law bans the manufacture and distribution of flavored cigarettes because of their appeal to youth[109] and prohibits the interstate distribution of foods and beverages that have additives that are not considered to be safe,[110] such as alcoholic beverages with added caffeine.[111] States and localities have complemented these efforts by, for example, restricting the retail sale of flavored noncigarette tobacco products[112] and prescribing the maximum alcohol content of particular types of beverages that may be sold in-state.[113]

On occasion, these local efforts "trickle up," prompting the federal government to take broader action to protect the public's health. For example, in 2006, New York City established

[105] Community Health Councils, Inc., South LA Fast Food Health Impact Assessment 2 (2013), http://www.chc-inc.org/downloads/CHC_SLA_Health_Impact_Assessment.pdf.

[106] D. H. Jernigan, M. Sparks, E. Yang, & R. Schwartz, *Using Public Health and Community Partnerships to Reduce Density of Alcohol Outlets*, 10 Prev. Chronic Dis. (2013).

[107] *See, e.g.*, Rebecca L. Goldberg, *No Such Thing as a Free Lunch: Paternalism, Poverty, and Food Justice*, 24 Stan. L. & Pol'y Rev. 35, 40–55 (2013).

[108] *See* LaVonna Blair Lewis et al., *Transforming the Urban Food Desert from the Grassroots Up: A Model for Community Change*, 34 Family & Community Health S92 (2011) (describing the coalition of community groups, informed by research, that led to the adoption of the Interim Control Ordinance in South Los Angeles).

[109] Family Smoking Prevention and Tobacco Control Act, Pub. L. No. 111-31, 123 Stat. 1776 (2009) (amending FDCA, 21 U.S.C. §§ 301–399 (2006).

[110] Food, Drug and Cosmetic Act, 21 U.S.C. § 331.

[111] Alcohol and Tobacco Tax and Trade Bureau, Alcohol Beverages with Added Caffeine, http://www.ttb.gov/main_pages/caffeine-added.shtml.

[112] N.Y.C. Admin. Code §§17-713 et seq.

[113] Many of these limits have been loosened in recent years. For example, Mississippi raised its alcohol by weight limit for beer in 2012, Mississippi S.B. 2878 (2012).

a ban on the sale and service of artificial trans-fats in restaurant foods.[114] Following the enactment of this local law, researchers found that it was associated with a substantial decrease in the trans-fat content of purchases at fast-food chains, without a commensurate increase in saturated fat. Restaurant patrons from high- and low-poverty neighborhoods benefited equally.[115] In 2013, the FDA leveraged the lessons learned from the local law and made a preliminary determination that trans-fats are not "generally recognized as safe," which could amount to a de facto nationwide ban on trans-fats in both packaged and prepared foods.[116]

d. Promotions

Like price, promotions also influence consumption. In response to rising cigarette taxes, tobacco companies have turned to coupons and other kinds of discounts to retain and attract consumers.[117] The 2009 federal tobacco control law leaves state and local governments free to impose restrictions on the sale and distributions of tobacco products. Several have used this authority to restrict the distribution and redemption of coupons.[118] A 2012 Rhode Island law prohibiting the use of coupons and multipack discounts[119] survived a challenge alleging that it violated the First Amendment and was preempted by state and federal law.[120] Federal, state, and local regulations also prohibit the distribution of free samples of cigarettes and smokeless tobacco.[121] Prohibitions on the sale of single cigarettes ("loosies")[122] keep cheap single cigarettes out of the stream of commerce. Similarly, local laws establishing a minimum pack size for cigars address the problem of youth access to cheap cigars.[123]

Some of the most controversial healthy eating interventions also target promotions. In 2010, San Francisco and Santa Clara County imposed minimal nutritional standards on restaurant meals accompanied by toys and other "incentive items" that target children.[124] These ordinances were easily circumvented by retailers, who simply added a nominal charge

[114] Public Health Law Center, Trans Fat, http://publichealthlawcenter.org/topics/healthy-eating/trans-fat.

[115] S. Y. Angell, L. K. Cobb, C. J. Curtis, K. J. Konty, & L. D. Silver, *Change in Trans Fatty Acid Content of Fast-Food Purchases Associated with New York City's Restaurant Regulation: A Pre–Post Study*, 157 Annals of Internal Medicine, 81–86 (2012).

[116] FDA, Tentative Determination Regarding Partially Hydrogenated Oils, 78 Fed. Reg. 67169 (Nov. 8, 2013).

[117] K. Choi, D. Hennrikus, J. Forster et al., *Receipt and Redemption of Cigarette Coupons, Perceptions of Cigarette Companies and Smoking Cessation*, 22 Tobacco Control 418 (2012); X. Xu, M. F. Pesko, M. A. Tynan et al., *Cigarette Price-Minimization Strategies by U.S. Smokers*, 44 American Journal of Preventive Medicine 472 (2013).

[118] Center for Public Health Systems Science, Pricing Policy: A Tobacco Control Guide (2014), at http://publichealthlawcenter.org/sites/default/files/resources/tclc-guide-pricing-policy-WashU-2014.pdf.

[119] Providence, R.I., Code of Ordinances § 14-303.

[120] Nat'l Ass'n of Tobacco Outlets, Inc. v. City of Providence, 731 F.3d 71 (1st Cir., 2013).

[121] FDA, Regulations Restricting the Sale, Distribution, and Marketing of Cigarettes, Cigarette Tobacco, and Smokeless Tobacco: Consumer Fact Sheet, http://www.fda.gov/TobaccoProducts/ProtectingKidsfromTobacco/RegsRestrictingSale/ucm205020.htm.

[122] *See, e.g.*, 21 C.F.R. § 1140.14 (2009).

[123] *See, e.g.*, D.C. CODE § 7-1721.06(c) (2011).

[124] San Francisco Health Code §471; Santa Clara, Cal., Code of Ordinances § A18-352.

to customers' bill for the toy. Nevertheless, they helped prompt voluntary changes by the industry. McDonald's changed the default options for its Happy Meals (to make fry portions smaller, add sliced apples, and promote milk and juice instead of soda) shortly after the ordinances were passed.[125] New York City's 2012 cap on the portion size of sugary drinks sold at food service establishments[126] (effectively banning bonus pricing, which appeals to customers looking for more value while generating big profit margins for retailers[127]), set off a firestorm of controversy and the regulation was ultimately invalidated by the state supreme court.[128] Although public controversy over the measure focused on individual liberty, it is important to be clear that there is no *constitutionally* protected right to sell or purchase particular products or services in particular configurations.[129] Thus, the legal challenge was more narrowly grounded in a particular set of state administrative law issues regarding the authority of the New York City Board of Health in relation to the city council.[130] Nothing in the opinion striking down the portion cap rule suggests that it would have been improper had the city council adopted it, rather than the board of health. Other jurisdictions have expressed interest adopting a version of the sugary drinks portion cap rule, but as of this writing, none had adopted it.

e. Preemption

In many cases, local regulations targeting unhealthy products, marketing, and retailers have prompted industry-backed preemption bills whereby the state legislature prohibits local

[125] Lindsay F. Wiley, *Sugary Drinks, Happy Meals, Social Norms, and the Law: The Normative Impact of Product Configuration Bans*, 46 CONN. L. REV. 1877 (2014).

[126] N.Y. City Health Code § 81.53.

[127] The profit margin on fountain drinks sold at fast-food restaurants is estimated to be around 90%, and bonus pricing is ubiquitous. Paul Ziobro, *McDonald's Bets Pricing Drinks at $1 will Heat Up Summer Sales*, WALL ST. J., Mar. 18, 2010, http://online.wsj.com/article/SB10001424052748704743404575127551110770616.html.

[128] N.Y. Statewide Coal. of Hispanic Chambers of Commerce v. N.Y.C. Dep't of Health & Mental Hygiene, 16 N.E.3d. 538 (N.Y. June 26, 2014).

[129] "[T]he Court declared decades ago its 'abandonment of the use of the 'vague contours' of the Due Process Clause to nullify laws which a majority of the Court believed to be economically unwise.'" In re: Late Fee and Over-limit Fee Litigation, 2014 WL 211729 (9th Cir. 2014), quoting *Ferguson v. Skrupa*, 372 U.S. 726, 731 (1963) and citing *Lochner v. New York*, 198 U.S. 45, 75 (1905) (Holmes, J., dissenting). *See also* Michael J. Phillips, *Another Look at Economic Substantive Due Process*, 1987 WIS. L. REV. 265 (1987) (describing the rejection of constitutionally protected economic rights); Samuel R. Wiseman, *Liberty of Palate*, 65 ME. L.R. 737 (2013) (concluding that there is no constitutionally protected right to consume the foods of one's choosing, based on "the long history of curtailment of food choice, and the lack of any constitutional protection or tradition of broadly protecting food rights"); Abigail Alliance for Better Access to Developmental Drugs v. Eschenbach, 495 F.3d 695 (D.C. Cir. 2007), *cert. denied* 552 U.S. 1159 (2008) (holding that terminally ill adult patients had no fundamental right protected by Due Process Clause to have access to investigational drugs, after surveying the long history of safety and efficacy regulation of drugs for personal use); Lange-Kessler v. Dept. of Ed., 109 F.3d 137 (2d Cir. 1997) (holding that the right to privacy does not encompass a woman's right to choose a direct-entry midwife to assist during childbirth).

[130] N.Y. Statewide Coalition of Hisp. Chambers of Comm. v. N.Y.C. Dep't of Health and Mental Hygiene, *available at* https://www.nycourts.gov/ctapps/Decisions/2014/Jun14/134opn14-Decision.pdf (June 26, 2014).

governments from regulating in particular areas. State-level preemption imposes significant constraints on local authority to regulate alcohol and, in some cases, grocery stores and food markets (this was New York City's explanation for exceptions to the portion cap rule that were challenged as arbitrary).

Recent controversy over healthy eating interventions has fueled sweeping preemption measures. For example, in 2011, Florida and Arizona passed preemption bills prohibiting local governments from regulating the use of toys and other giveaways to promote unhealthy fast-food meals to children.[131] Other states have gone further. Mississippi's 2013 preemption law was dubbed the "Anti-Bloomberg Bill" because it was inspired by New York City's initiatives (no Mississippi jurisdiction had threatened similar action). The state sharply limited local government authority to regulate food service establishments across the board.[132] The same year, the North Carolina legislature tacked a more limited provision barring local governments from regulating the size of soft drinks onto what was otherwise a run-of-the-mill "Cheeseburger Bill" immunity statute for the food and beverage and restaurant industries.[133]

Ohio's broad 2011 preemption law gave the state's agriculture department "sole and exclusive authority . . . to regulate the provision of food nutrition information and consumer incentive items at food service operations" and specifically prohibited local governments from enforcing food content bans and from adopting legal measures to address "food-based health disparities." It was struck down by a state appellate court in 2013 as an "unconstitutional attempt[] to limit municipal home-rule authority."[134]

While the Ohio case was an important victory for public health advocates, the extent of municipal home-rule authority varies from state to state.[135] It is likely that many state preemption bills would be upheld if challenged. But while some states are curtailing the authority of local governments to regulate food and beverage products, others are considering implementing locally pioneered measures statewide. This was certainly the case with calorie labeling for chain restaurant menus and bans on trans-fats, which were rapidly adopted by many states. Adoption has been somewhat slower for other food and beverage interventions, but could ramp up in the near future.

[131] *See* Dale Kunkel & Doug Taren, *Pre-emptive Bill on Fast Food and Kids Reeks of Hollow Politics*, Arizona Daily Star, Mar. 1, 2011.

[132] Mississippi S.B. 2687 (2013).

[133] North Carolina H. 683 (2013).

[134] Cleveland v. Ohio, 989 N.E.2d 1072 (Ohio App. 2013). The court's opinion also describes the preemption bill's origins:

> In response to the city of Cleveland's trans-fats Ordinance, the Ohio Restaurant Association [ORA] . . . sent an email to the Ohio Department of Agriculture with an attached legislative proposal. The email stated that the Ordinance was "exactly what we want to preempt with the attached amendment." The email also stated that the amendment was "a high priority for Wendy's, McDonalds and YUM! [the operator-licensor of Taco Bell, KFC and Pizza Hut]."

Notably, Mississippi's 2013 "Anti-Bloomberg" bill is almost identical to the 2011 Ohio bill.

[135] Some form of home rule has been granted either by constitutional provision or statute in forty-three states, but the precise contours of local authority and its constitutional status with respect to state legislative action vary considerably. Sandra M. Stevenson, Antieau on Local Government Law § 21.01 (2d ed. 2006).

III The Built Environment: A "Health in All Policies" Approach to Promoting Physical Activity

The previous sections focused on using law and policy to regulate and restrict products that cause NCDs. This section considers how legal and policy interventions can promote moderate, daily physical activity, which is known to improve health and reduce the rates of many NCDs. We use one of the key principles to emerge from the ecological model of health, the "Health in All Policies" (HiAP) principle, to frame the discussion. The HiAP principle represents "a reconceptualization of what constitutes health policy" to include "policies in societal domains far removed from traditional health policy."[136] By "highlight[ing] the fact that the risk factors of major diseases, or the determinants of health, are modified by measures that are often managed by other government sectors as well as by other actors in society," the HiAP principle naturally "shift[s] the emphasis . . . from individual lifestyles and single diseases to societal factors and actions that shape our everyday living environments."[137]

As a strategy, HiAP is, by its very nature, broad and somewhat abstract; however, land use and transportation policies that encourage individuals to be physically active throughout the course of their day provide some concrete examples of how the HiAP approach to NCD prevention is implemented. The built environment—which "encompass[es] everything from land use patterns and urban planning, to the design, location, uses and interrelations among buildings, to transportation systems"—has many important impacts on population health, but is a particularly important determinant of physical activity.[138] In this section we review land use planning and zoning strategies, contracting strategies, and spending strategies for encouraging physical activity.

a. Land Use, Zoning, and Design Guidelines

A growing number of communities are incorporating explicit health considerations into their comprehensive land use plans,[139] zoning codes, and design standards that govern what can be built, how it can be built, and what activities are permitted in a given area. The city of Portland, Oregon, has a particularly robust transportation plan that emphasizes walking,

[136] David R. Williams & Pamela Braboy Jackson, *Social Sources of Racial Disparities in Health*, 24 Health Aff. 325 (2005).

[137] Health in All Policies: Prospects and Potentials, Preface, xvi (Timo Ståhl et al. eds., 2006).

[138] Wendy C. Perdue, *Obesity, Poverty, and the Built Environment: Challenges and Opportunities*, 15 Geo. J. Pov. L. & Policy 821, 822 (2008).

[139] Although state law varies with regards to the amount of legal weight these plans are given, they can have tremendous influence over the character of a community. American Planning Association, Comprehensive Planning for Public Health (2011), at 4, http://www.planning.org/research/publichealth/pdf/surveyreport.pdf.

biking, and use of public transportation,[140] all of which have been connected to better population health.[141] Among other key goals, the plan promotes a vision of "a balanced, equitable, and efficient transportation system that provides a range of transportation choices; reinforces the livability of neighborhoods . . . and lessens reliance on the automobile while maintaining accessibility."[142] Louisville, Kentucky's zoning code includes a number of provisions that make the downtown area particularly welcoming to pedestrians.[143] It requires that buildings be easily accessible by pedestrians and parking to be located behind structures rather than on main streets. The code explicitly notes that "parking should be designed to promote comfort and safety for pedestrians on the street and the sidewalk."[144] Jurisdictions across the country are also adopting "complete streets" policies to promote walking, jogging, and biking as modes of transportation and recreation while protecting the safety of pedestrians, cyclists, drivers, and passengers from motor-vehicle related injuries.[145] For example, Columbia, Missouri, enacted an ordinance establishing new street design standards promoting narrower streets, wider sidewalks, and bike lanes or wide shared-use travel lanes.[146]

Design guidelines complement zoning laws by providing a flexible set of approaches to encourage development of a certain form, style, or scale, and can also be used to further a HiAP approach to NCD prevention and the promotion of physical activity. For example, New York City's Active Design Guidelines, developed in 2010, set forth voluntary benchmarks for infrastructure designs that promote physical activity and healthy eating to prevent obesity and related chronic diseases.[147] Building on the success of the Guidelines, a 2013 mayoral executive order required all New York City agencies to use active design strategies in new construction and major renovation projects.[148]

b. Contracting for Shared Use

The government's power to contract is another legal tool that has been embraced by the HiAP movement to promote physical activity, particularly in low-income urban and rural communities where access to safe places to play and exercise are lacking. School facilities like playgrounds, gymnasiums, playing fields, basketball and tennis courts, and running

[140] PORTLAND BUREAU OF TRANSPORTATION, THE TRANSPORTATION ELEMENT OF THE CITY OF PORTLAND COMPREHENSIVE PLAN, *available at* http://www.portlandoregon.gov/transportation/article/370467 (accessed Apr. 18, 2014).

[141] Daniel A. Rodriguez, *Active Transportation: Making the Link from Transportation to Physical Activity and Obesity*, ACTIVE LIVING RESEARCH BRIEF (2009), *available at* http://activelivingresearch.org/sites/default/files/ALR_Brief_ActiveTransportation_0.pdf, (accessed Apr. 18, 2014).

[142] The Transportation Element of the City of Portland Comprehensive Plan, at 3.

[143] Louisville, Ky., Land Dev. Code § 5.5.1(B) (2006).

[144] *Id.*

[145] *See* NATIONAL POLICY AND LEGAL ANALYSIS NETWORK TO PREVENT CHILDHOOD OBESITY, WHAT ARE COMPLETE STREETS? A FACT SHEET FOR ADVOCATES AND COMMUNITY MEMBERS (2010), at http://changelabsolutions.org/sites/default/files/CompleteStreets_FactSheet_FINAL_20100223.pdf.

[146] Columbia, MO Code §105-247.

[147] CENTER FOR ACTIVE DESIGN, THE ACTIVE DESIGN GUIDELINES, http://centerforactivedesign.org/guidelines/ (accessed on May 8, 2014).

[148] New York City Exec. Order No. 359 (June 27, 2013), http://home.nyc.gov/html/om/pdf/eo/eo_359.pdf.

tracks are often kept locked up outside of school hours because officials are concerned about security, maintenance, and liability. "Joint use" or "shared use" agreements among school districts and other local agencies or nonprofit organizations address these concerns while opening up recreational facilities for greater public use.[149] In Charlotte, North Carolina, for example, the city and county governments work together to promote shared use arrangements that include the local school district, the local community college, and the county library system. Similar arrangements are spreading across the country. More generally, alleviating the concerns that school districts, churches, and other property-owners have about tort liability in situations where people are injured while using their facilities—by educating them about existing immunities or creating new ones through legislative action or model contract term—is a priority for public health law organizations.[150]

c. Spending Strategies

Government can also influence the built environment in its role as financier. Direct spending on public transportation, sidewalks, and recreational facilities is crucial, but costly. Many governments are exploring strategies for leveraging public funds to promote health. For example, the Low Income Housing Tax Credit (LIHTC) is a federally authorized program that assists in the production and preservation of affordable rental housing for low-income families and individuals by providing tax incentives for developers to acquire, rehabilitate, and build low- or mixed-income housing.[151] The LIHTC program is administered by states, which are given broad discretion to establish preferences for the types of housing that they finance. These preferences are set out in a state's Qualified Allocation Plan (QAP). Many states have used this financing system to encourage the development of housing that promotes health by including in their QAPs incentives relating to active transportation. Maryland, Georgia, and Massachusetts award points to proposed developments near public transportation stops;[152] Michigan awards points based on a development's walk score;[153] and

149 National Policy and Legal Analysis Network to Prevent Childhood Obesity et al., Playing Smart: Maximizing the Potential of School and Community Property through Joint Use Agreements (2012), *available at* http://changelabsolutions.org/sites/default/files/Playing_Smart-National_Joint_Use_Toolkit_Updated_20120517_0.pdf.

150 *See* Sara Zimmerman &Manel Kappagoda, *The Risk of New Liability Laws to Schools and Students*, ChangeLab Solutions, http://changelabsolutions.org/childhood-obesity/immunity-hazards.

151 *See* 26 U.S.C. § 42); 26 C.F.R. §1.42.

152 Maryland Department of Housing and Community Development, Maryland Qualified Allocation Plan (2013), http://www.dhcd.state.md.us/Website/programs/rhf/Documents/QAP.pdf; Georgia Department of Community Affairs, 2013 Qualified Allocation Plan, (2013) at appendix 2 section 4, http://www.dca.state.ga.us/housing/housingdevelopment/programs/documents/2013QualifiedAllocationPlan_000.pdf; Commonwealth of Massachusetts Department of Housing and Community Development, Low Income Housing Tax Credit Program: 2014 Qualified Allocation Plan (2014), at 38, http://www.mass.gov/hed/docs/dhcd/hd/lihtc/final2014qap.pdf.

153 Michigan State Housing Development Authority, 2013–2014 LIHTC Scoring Criteria, http://www.michigan.gov/documents/mshda/mshda_li_qap_2013_2014_score_sum_final_391278_7.pdf.

Massachusetts uses its QAP to incentivize the development of residential buildings with covered bicycle racks.[154]

IV Law and Social Norms: Promoting a Culture of Health

Health-related behaviors are "encased in a multitude of norms."[155] Public health strategies seek to counter industry-sponsored messages promoting smoking as sexy and liberating or soda consumption as part of a carefree, youthful lifestyle.[156] Social norm change has been a key objective of public health campaigns discouraging alcohol abuse[157] and smoking,[158] among other behaviors. Denormalization strategies are evident in social marketing campaigns—advertisements and educational materials that go beyond straightforward information about health risks to tap into powerful social norms.[159] In this section, we discuss the ways in which *law* also plays an important role in influencing social norms.

Bans on smoking in restaurants, workplaces, public parks, and beaches mean that fewer people—kids in particular—see smoking as a normal, everyday activity going on around them. One of the concerns prompting regulation of electronic cigarettes is that they threaten to renormalize smoking.[160] Regulatory, spending, and procurement strategies that promote the availability of healthy, appealing foods in settings like schools, workplaces, hospitals, and other public facilities (where signals about social norms tend to be particularly salient) have the potential to shape eating habits in ways that persist beyond the time that a person spends at any of those locations. This is similar to how policies that make walking and bicycling easier allow people to incorporate moderate physical activity into their daily lives.

Denormalizing overconsumption of unhealthy food and beverage products has proven more complicated than denormalizing smoking or overconsumption of alcohol. Balanced eating is not a matter of a single meal or a single food or beverage product. It involves complex patterns over the course of days, weeks, and months. Furthermore, denormalization of unhealthy food and beverage products can easily spill over into potentially unhealthy

[154] Commonwealth of Massachusetts Department of Housing and Community Development, Low Income Housing Tax Credit Program: 2014 Qualified Allocation Plan (2014), at 41, http://www.mass.gov/hed/docs/dhcd/hd/lihtc/final2014qap.pdf.

[155] W. A. Bogard, Permit But Discourage: Regulating Excessive Consumption 91 (2011).

[156] *See* Katrina Radic, *"Live for Now"—Pepsi's First Ever Global Campaign*, Branding Magazine, Jan. 5, 2012, at http://www.brandingmagazine.com/2012/05/01/live-for-now-pepsis-first-global-campaign/.

[157] *See* H. Wesley Perkins, *Social Norms and the Prevention of Alcohol Misuse in Collegiate Contexts*, 14 J. Stud. Alcohol (Supp.) 164 (2002), http://www.collegedrinkingprevention.gov/media/journal/164-perkins2.pdf (accessed Apr. 21, 2014).

[158] *See* Xueying Zhang et al., *The Impact of Social Norm Change Strategies on Smokers' Quitting Behaviours*, 19 Tobacco Control i51 (2010), http://tobaccocontrol.bmj.com/content/19/Suppl_1/i51.full (accessed Apr. 21, 2014).

[159] Sonia Greer & Carol A. Bryant, *Social Marketing in Public Health*, 26 Annual Review of Public Health 319 (2005).

[160] *See* Amy L. Fairchild et al., *The Renormalization of Smoking? E-Cigarettes and the Tobacco "Endgame"*, 370 N. Engl. J. Med. 293 (2014).

stigmatization of people based on their size.[161] Law and policy experts are seeking to walk this fine line, particularly with respect to sugary drinks and kids meals.

A sugary drinks portion cap rule has potential to successfully "re-normalize" the smaller portions that were typical just a few decades ago, but which have come to seem tiny compared to the extra-large containers promoted by industry.[162] If such a rule is ever implemented, smaller cups would become far more visible and extra-large cups less so. As many critics have pointed out, the portion rule does nothing to stop a consumer from drinking sixty-four ounces in a sitting. However, by requiring him to purchase four separate cups to do so, the measure sends a strong signal that he is consuming four times the appropriate amount. Ordinances establishing nutritional standards for meals marketed to children have similar potential, signaling that fruit and low-fat milk (rather than fries and soda) are the "normal" accompaniments for a young child's meal.

V Conclusion

Law is a reinforcing expression of social norms. Unhealthy consumption patterns promoted by manufacturers and retailers are burdening the public's health and quality of life. Interventions that require a great deal of individual effort have little population impact compared to those that naturally channel us toward healthier choices.[163] Public health experts and community groups are developing a wide range of strategies that move beyond public education campaigns to encompass advertising restrictions and mandated disclosures, as well as direct regulation of products and retail practices and land use, zoning, and licensing. These strategies demand innovative law and policy tools, pioneering state and local governments willing to pilot their use, and courts willing to protect the gains that legislatures and agencies are making.

The broadening of public health law to encompass a wide range of determinants of non-infectious disease is undeniably controversial. Legislators, regulators, and media pundits debate whether NCD prevention measures are too paternalistic and whether their economic impact on low-income families is justifiable. In the courts, industry groups and others argue that these measures infringe upon the free speech rights of corporations, draw arbitrary distinctions, or exceed the proper authority of particular government actors. The tobacco, agriculture, and food and beverage industries will always be able to outspend public health, consumer protection, and community advocates—promoting "personal responsibility" as an alternative to industry regulation. But the critical response to new public health law also arises out of deep-seated philosophical and cultural views about individual responsibility

[161] *See* Lindsay F. Wiley, *Shame, Blame, and the Emerging Law of Obesity Control*, 47 U.C. Davis L. Rev. 121 (2013) (arguing that obesity stigmatization would be detrimental to public health goals).

[162] The City Record: Official Journal of the City of New York, Sept. 21, 2012, at 2603 (stating that the rule will "reacquaint[] New Yorkers with more appropriate portion sizes").

[163] Thomas Frieden, *A Framework for Public Health Action: The Health Impact Pyramid*, 100 Am. J. of Pub. Health 590 (2010).

and government overreach. The predominant culture of individualism that shapes American politics makes this a tough fight for public health advocates.

In the face of these challenges, should we simply ignore the lessons of social epidemiology and the ecological model, confining our response to measures that we know will have limited effect? Should potentially effective measures be off-limits because they fail to conform to a philosophical ideal of self-sovereignty?[164] Even if these measures are adopted through a democratic process? As public awareness about the burden of chronic diseases on American society has grown, so has concern about the role that industry plays in perpetuating this crisis. But skepticism toward industry does not necessarily translate into support for government initiatives. As for much of public health, the key is to safeguard the public's trust through transparent and participatory engagement aimed at creating healthier communities.

164 Lawrence O. Gostin & Lindsay F. Wiley, Public Health Law: Power, Duty Restraint (3d ed. 2015).

CHAPTER 45

PUBLIC HEALTH EMERGENCY LEGAL AND ETHICAL PREPAREDNESS

JAMES G. HODGE, JR.

I Introduction

In many ways the breadth of emergency legal and ethical preparedness is clear. It concerns how society uses laws, policies, and ethics to plan for, prevent, and respond to catastrophic events that may negatively impact the public's health. These events include natural disasters (e.g., hurricanes, tornados, fires, or earthquakes) that may harm population health, as well as direct threats to health (e.g., epidemic diseases, bioterrorism). Yet, as explained later in this article, public health emergencies may also be invoked by other risks to human health, including food contamination, drug addictions, and seasonal influenza.

Irrespective of the substantive bases for public health emergencies, saving lives or preventing morbidity during or after these events directly relates to adequate preparedness activities at all levels of government and among private sector actors. And the lynchpin to effective preparedness is sufficient legal authority and ethical guidance that support essential activities, or at least do not thwart needed responses when exigent circumstances arise.

Preparedness for these emergencies within and across populations is politically controversial, implicates billions of public and private sector dollars annually, and can be subject to legal and ethical guesswork. Emergency legal and ethical preparedness is constantly mired in interjurisdictional governmental disputes and between various private actors. What is legally permissible or required during emergencies is hardly cut-and-dry. Often at the heart of debates is the juxtaposition of individual and communal interests, often characterized as in direct conflict (even when this is not actually the case). Even when legal options are well set, what is ethically or politically viable may be less clear or even contrary to what the law allows or mandates. Chaos or delays in making critical decisions in emergencies can result, contributing to preventable morbidity or mortality. The fact that people may perish or suffer during public health emergencies because legal or ethical authority or guidance is uncertain, unsound, or unavailable is unacceptable.

Despite pitfalls of planning, prevention, and response, key lessons in emergency legal and ethical preparedness have emerged. This article begins with a brief illustration of historical underpinnings of emergency legal preparedness, notably post-September 11, 2001. It explains legal classifications of varied types of emergencies and associated powers that impact the public's health. Principles of public health emergency ethics, interwoven within legal norms, generate a dynamic "triage" environment for allocation and response efforts in real time. While effective practice of "legal and ethical triage" in real-time events can make a difference, remaining challenges underlie the field. These include: (1) how roles and responsibilities of diverse entities and personnel are coordinated; (2) how to allocate scarce resources legally and ethically; (3) when and how traditional scopes of practice among licensed healthcare workers may be altered; and (4) whether public health and healthcare personnel and entities are liable for negligent acts that may arise during emergency response efforts. Ascertaining effective guidance on these and other topics at the core of emergency legal and ethical triage is the goal, but proving the efficacy of such guidance based on the available empirical data remains elusive.

II Public Health Emergency Legal Preparedness: A Look Back

For decades, public health emergency preparedness was a foreign concept to most Americans. Prior to the terrorist acts on September 11, 2001 and the ensuing anthrax attacks that same fall, preparedness for rapid threats to the public's health was misunderstood, considered nonessential, or ignored altogether by most law- and policy-makers, government officials, healthcare workers, and citizens. Misguided apathy in this context is hard to understand given multiple and diverse public health threats experienced nationally or regionally leading up to September 11. Polio and measles outbreaks were pervasive in the 1940s. Threats of nuclear war and associated mass casualties and injuries were omnipresent throughout the 1950s–1980s. Seasonal flu outbreaks routinely killed tens of thousands in many years. Still, at the beginning of the twenty-first century, these and other public health threats somehow seemed distant and bygone. They were addressed successfully via political maneuvers, tamed by medical science, or merely forgotten despite prominent, advance warnings of potential biothreats through effective surveillance, practice scenarios, and repeated "calls for action."[1]

Even less attention was paid to what role, if any, the law played in preparing for a bioterrorism or mass casualty event. Prior to 2001, only a few, knowledgeable law- and policy-makers argued for legal changes or systemic overhauls. Virtually none foresaw the need for a complete restructuring of government to respond to public health emergencies.[2] Together,

[1] *Dark Winter Exercise*, UPMC Center for Health Security (Oct. 11, 2011), http://www.upmc-biosecurity.org/website/events/2001_darkwinter/.

[2] Cantigny Conference, State Emergency Health Powers & the Bioterrorism Threat (Apr. 26–27, 2001), http://www.heart-intl.net/HEART/Legal/Comp/StateEmergencyPowers.htm (sponsored by the Centers for Disease Control and Prevention, the American Bar Association Standing Committee on Law and National Security, and The National Strategy Forum).

the terroristic acts and unrelated anthrax attacks in September 2001 changed everything. Almost overnight, government could not do enough to combat terrorism in the United States. Facing enormous pressures, federal, state, and local law- and policy-makers viewed existing laws increasingly as potential barriers to effective responses. Critical reforms at all levels of government were demanded.[3] After years of indifference, policy-makers seemed ready for major changes. As a result, law became a central tool of biopreparedness through a series of reforms that:

- rebuilt components of federal, state, and local governments to improve response;
- created the new legal classification known as "public health emergencies";
- rebalanced individual privacy expectations related to government's need to protect populations from national or regional security threats; and
- overhauled existing legal norms that defined roles and responsibilities of public and private actors in emergency response efforts.

A modern legal framework for public health emergency preparedness and response was crafted, but not without sharp criticism among some scholars, civil rights advocates, media, and the public. Characterized by some as "antiquated" or "draconian,"[4] public health emergency laws stemming from traditional and routine governmental public health powers were deemed antithetical to individual freedoms and modern responses.[5] Still, national, state, and local policy-makers systematically used model legal principles and other proposals to reform their emergency laws. Legal changes in response to bioterrorism in 2001, and further public health emergency threats following Hurricane Katrina in 2005 and the H1N1 pandemic in 2009, collectively led to significant alterations in how national public health and emergency preparedness systems respond, as discussed in Parts III, IV, and V.

III Interjurisdictional Coordination and Responsibilities in Public Health Preparedness

At the heart of public health emergency preparedness from the onset was a compelling need for stronger, interjurisdictional coordination among federal, state, and local governments. From the recognition of this need arose a central question: *Which level of government, federal or state, is actually responsible for addressing biothreats that risk national security and community health?* Answering this question required reassessments of the interjurisdictional capacities of American government in emergencies. As President Barack Obama noted in his 2011 Presidential Policy Directive on National Preparedness, integrated coordination

[3] John J. Fialka et al., *Are We Prepared for the Unthinkable?*, Wall St. J., Sept. 18, 2001, at B.

[4] George J. Annas, Worst Case Bioethics: Death, Disaster, and Public Health (2010).

[5] Michael L. Betsch, *Bio-terror Response Plan Would Invade Civil Liberties, Says Critic*, Cybercast News Service (Dec. 11, 2001), http://www.cnsnews.com/ViewNation.asp?Page=\Nation\archive\200112\NAT20011211a.html.

across all levels of government is critical to effective emergency responses.[6] Absent coordination, emergency response efforts would be more happenstance than effective. The need to enhance interjurisdictional coordination was the impetus for significant federal and state legal reforms that moved national policy away from an "all hazards" approach and into a more precise identification of public health emergencies.[7]

For decades, frontline preparedness and response efforts were largely matters for state and local governments tasked with protecting and promoting the public's health within the federalist system. States (and municipalities pursuant to delegated state authority) hold traditional powers to protect the health, safety, and general welfare of populations.[8] Federal agencies like the Department of Health and Human Services (HHS) and its Centers for Disease Control and Prevention (CDC) could provide guidance, expertise, personnel, and resources, but lacked sufficient legal authority or manpower to address specific local public health needs in mass casualty events. While national assistance and resources were generally well received by states, federal attempts to usurp state and local public health preparedness efforts were not, except as related to federal national security interests. Characterizing the 2001 anthrax exposures as a threat to national security implicated and helped expand and cement federal roles in public health emergencies under reformed legal standards, as explained further below.

a. Federal Roles

Multiple federal laws, many of which were passed after September 11, address specific issues arising in a national or regional public health emergency. The Federal Public Health Security and Bioterrorism Preparedness and Response Act of 2002[9] authorizes the implementation of the National Disaster Medical System (NDMS) to coordinate rapid deployment of specialized response teams.[10] The Project BioShield Act of 2004[11] establishes the Strategic National Stockpile (SNS)[12] to expedite distribution of essential medicines and supplies nationally and amended the Food, Drug, and Cosmetic Act[13] to authorize emergency use authorizations (EUAs) of yet-be-approved drugs or devices during declared emergencies.[14] The Homeland

[6] Barack Obama, *Presidential Policy Directive/PPD-8: National Preparedness*, Department of Homeland Security (Mar. 30, 2011), http://www.dhs.gov/xabout/laws/gc_1215444247124.shtm.

[7] Thomas V. Inglesby, *Progress in Disaster Planning and Preparedness Since 2001*, 306 J. Am. Med. Ass'n 1372 (2011), *available at* http://jama.jamanetwork.com/article.aspx?articleid=1104421.

[8] Lawrence O. Gostin, *Public Health Law in an Age of Terrorism: Rethinking Individual Rights and Common Goods*, 21 Health Aff. 79 (2002).

[9] Public Health Security and Bioterrorism Preparedness and Response of 2002, Pub. L. No. 107-188, 116 Stat. 594.

[10] Sarah A. Lister, Cong. Research Serv., RL31719, An Overview of the U.S. Public Health System in the Context of Emergency Preparedness (2007), *available at* http://www.fas.org/sgp/crs/homesec/RL31719.pdf.

[11] Project Bioshield Act of 2004, Pub. L. No. 108-276, 118 Stat. 835.

[12] *Strategic National Stockpile*, Center for Disease Control and Prevention, http://www.bt.cdc.gov/stockpile/ (last visited Oct. 11, 2011) (providing background information on the SNS).

[13] 21 U.S.C.A. §§ 301-399 (West 2008).

[14] 21 U.S.C. § 360bbb-3(a)(1) (2000).

Security Act of 2002[15] and Public Health Threats and Emergencies Act of 2000[16] create and set responsibilities of the Department of Homeland Security (DHS). The Social Security Act was amended to authorize emergency waivers of (1) certain requirements of the Emergency Medical Treatment and Active Labor Act (EMTALA),[17] which typically requires screening and stabilization of all persons seeking emergency care at hospital emergency rooms (and other locations) receiving federal funds, and (2) eligibility requirements for Medicaid and Medicare programs.[18]

Most federal emergency powers are concentrated in the Robert T. Stafford Disaster Relief and Emergency Assistance Act (Stafford Act),[19] the National Emergencies Act,[20] the Public Health Service Act (PHSA),[21] and the Pandemic and All-Hazards Preparedness Act (PAHPA)[22] (which was reauthorized most recently in 2013). Pursuant to these acts, the federal government can declare states of: (1) general emergency, (2) disaster, and (3) public health emergency. The first two declarations may be made by the president via the Stafford Act[23] or the National Emergencies Act. In general, a Stafford Act emergency can be declared only after a state governor requests federal assistance "to save lives and to protect property and public health and safety, or to lessen or avert the threat of a catastrophe."[24] The president may declare a state of disaster on the governor's request typically in response to natural calamities (e.g., tornadoes, earthquakes, snowstorms, or droughts).[25] While these declarations and corresponding federal powers are exceedingly broad and are used to respond to events impacting communal health, they are not tailored to public health emergencies involving mass communication of infectious diseases or other direct and immediate threats to the health of populations.[26]

In contrast, PHSA[27] authorizes the HHS secretary to declare a federal public health emergency[28] whenever "a disease or disorder presents a public health emergency. . ." or in response to "significant outbreaks of infectious diseases or bioterrorist attacks. . . ."[29] Upon such a declaration, HHS can enter grants or contracts, provide awards for expenses, and conduct and support investigations into the cause, treatment, or prevention of a disease or disorder. It can also access emergency funds[30] and waive certain Medicare and Medicaid requirements.[31] HHS has issued multiple public health emergency declarations since the inception of this specific power, including in response to Hurricane Katrina (2005), in response to the H1N1 pandemic (2009–2010), and related to projected shortages of essential medications to allow for use of EUAs.[32]

15 Homeland Security Act of 2002, Pub. L. No. 107-296, 116 Stat. 2135.

16 Public Health Improvement Act, Pub. L. No. 106-505, 114 Stat. 2314 (2000).

17 42 U.S.C.A. § 1320b-5 (West 2008). 18 *Id.* § 1320b-2. 19 *Id.* §§ 5121-205.

20 50 U.S.C.A. §§ 1601, 1621, 1622, 1631, 1641, 1651 (West 2008). 21 42 U.S.C. § 201 (2000).

22 Pandemic and All-Hazards Preparedness Act, Pub. L. No. 109-417, 120 Stat. 2831 (2006).

23 42 U.S.C.A. § 5170 (West 2008). 24 *Id.* § 5122(1). 25 *Id.* § 5122(2).

26 Sarah A. Lister, Cong. Research Serv., RL33579, The Public Health and Medical Response to Disasters: Federal Authority and Funding 4 (2007), *available at* http://fas.org/sgp/crs/misc/RL33579.pdf.

27 42 U.S.C. § 201 (2000). 28 42 U.S.C.A. § 247d (West 2008). 29 *Id.* § 247d(a).

30 *Id.* § 247d(b). 31 *Id.* § 1320b-5.

32 Brooke Courtney, *FDA's Role in Medical Countermeasures: Current Issues and Challenges*, U.S. Food and Drug Administration 27 (Feb. 21, 2012), *available at* http://www.fda.gov/downloads/EmergencyPreparedness/Counterterrorism/UCM296381.pdf.

b. State and Local Roles

As federal authorities addressed the 2001 anthrax threats from its national security perspective, state and local governments attended to answering how to prevent and respond to future bioterrorism incidents that had the potential for systemic, long-term, and widespread disability and death in the population.[33] They sought new routes to address bioterrorism or other public health threats legislatively and via regulation, but recognized a lack of guidance on how best to assess and reform their laws. Together with leading public health authorities, including the American Public Health Association (APHA), Association of State and Territorial Health Officials (ASTHO), and National Association of County and City Health Officials (NACCHO), as well as funding support from CDC, the Centers for Law and the Public's Health at Georgetown and Johns Hopkins Universities drafted what came to be known as the Model State Emergency Health Powers Act (MSEHPA) in December 2001.[34]

MSEHPA introduced a structured and cohesive series of model provisions for state and local governments considering how to respond to bioterrorism or other public health crises.[35] Although sometimes mischaracterized as a federal mandate to state and local governments (due largely to misconceptions about CDC's role and support), the act provides moreso a menu of potential public health powers for consideration and adoption by state and local policy-makers. Its team of drafters sought to balance individual and communal interests underlying modern responses to what it identified and labeled a "public health emergency," defined as:

> . . . an occurrence or imminent threat of an illness or health condition that: (1) is believed to be caused by. . . bioterrorism; the appearance of a novel or previously controlled or eradicated infectious agent or biological toxin [*or other causes*];. . . and (2) poses a high probability of. . . a large number of deaths in the affected population; a large number of serious or long-term disabilities in the affected population; or widespread exposure to an infectious or toxic agent that poses a significant risk of substantial future harm to a large number of people in the affected population.[36]

This definition was initially criticized by some as conceptually overly broad and subject to misuse by state politicians and other actors. In reality, as conceived, this definition of public health emergency is more limiting than existing state-based definitions of "emergency" or "disaster." Historically, state declarations of emergency or disaster, even when applied to public health threats like epidemic diseases, could be made almost completely at the discretion of the governor (or health commissioner in a few jurisdictions). However, a public

[33] Lawrence O. Gostin, Jason W. Sapsin, Stephen P. Teret, Scott Burris, Julie Samia Mair, James G. Hodge, Jr., & Jon S. Vernick, *The Model State Emergency Health Powers Act: Planning and Response to Bioterrorism and Naturally Occurring Infectious Diseases*, 288 J. AM. MED. ASS'N. 622 (2002).

[34] Gostin et al., *The Model*; James G. Hodge, Jr. & Lawrence O. Gostin, *Protecting the Public's Health in an Era of Bioterrorism: The Model State Emergency Health Powers Act*, *in* TERROR IN THE BALANCE: MEDICINE AND MORALITY IN A TIME OF CRISIS (Jonathon D. Moreno et al. eds., 2002); Lawrence O. Gostin & James G. Hodge, Jr. *The Model State Emergency Health Powers Act—A Brief Commentary*, *in* SEATTLE: TURNING POINT STATUTE MODERNIZATION COLLABORATIVE (2002).

[35] Gostin et al., *The Model*.

[36] Model State Emergency Health Powers Act § 104(m) (2001), *available at* http://www.publichealthlaw.net/MSEHPA/MSEHPA.pdf.

health emergency declaration may be issued by the governor (with recommended input from the state health commissioner) only when it can be shown that an act of bioterrorism or other public health threat poses a "high probability" of a large number of deaths, disabilities, or exposures to agents that could cause future harms.[37] These definitional limits are intended to confine a declaration of public health emergency to circumstances where quickly developing factors militate a rapid and effective public health response, such as the H1N1 influenza pandemic or bioterrorism threats like anthrax or smallpox. As discussed in Part VA, below, in reality, what some governments are willing to classify as necessitating a public health emergency diverges from the drafters' original conception.

c. Balancing Public Health Emergency Powers

Upon a declaration of public health emergency, MSEHPA authorizes a series of optional, expedited public health powers among public health officials, including:

- collecting of data and records to facilitate the early detection of a health emergency;
- abating public health nuisances;
- destroying dangerous or contaminated materials;
- taking private property with just compensation as needed to care for patients or to protect the public's health;
- closing roads, implementing curfews, and evacuating populations where justified;
- gathering specimens and using safe handling procedures for the disposal of human remains or infectious wastes;
- testing, screening, vaccinating, and treating exposed or infected persons;
- separating exposed or infected individuals from the population at large to prevent further transmission of communicable conditions;
- garnering assistance of out-of-state healthcare volunteers through licensure reciprocity; and
- informing the population of public health threats through media and language that are accessible and understandable across cultures.[38]

As well, the act authorizes governors to waive existing, specific laws that may impede response efforts for the duration of a public health emergency, coordinate services among public health and emergency actors, allocate state resources, and expend finances as needed to effectuate emergency response efforts.[39]

From this array of public health powers arose perceived infringements of individual rights and other criticism. Some scholars and ethicists criticized MSEHPA as misguided and unbalanced. George J. Annas, writing in the *New England Journal of Medicine* in early 2002, stated: "[t]he model act seems to have been drafted for a different age; it is more appropriate

37 Gostin et al., *The Model.*

38 Model State Emergency Health Powers Act (2001), *available at* http://www.publichealthlaw.net/MSEHPA/MSEHPA.pdf.

39 Daniel G. Orenstein, *When Law Is Not Law: Setting Aside Legal Provisions during Declared Emergencies*, 41(s1) J. L. Med. & Ethics 73 (2013).

for the U.S. of the 19th century than for the U.S. of the 21st century."[40] In their commentary in *Science* in 2002, Ronald Bayer and James Colgrove characterized the act as a "stark expression of the view that a public health emergency might necessitate the abrogation of privacy rights, the imposition of medical interventions, and the deprivation of freedom itself."[41] Though in the minority, these commentators and others suggested that the act presented a skewed prioritization of communal health over and above the interests of individuals during declared events.

Balancing individual and communal interests during public health emergencies can be complex when respective interests conflict. Government cannot, for example, adequately collect surveillance data leading up to and during public health emergencies without potential infringements of individual expectations of health information privacy.[42] What people expect from government to further emergency responses may differ from what they actually receive. As explained in Part VC, below, ethical guidance developed in real time, concerning the distribution of scarce resources, such as vaccines, treatment, or ventilators, during an outbreak of respiratory flu, may not comport with an individual's anticipated needs.

The need to reach appropriate balances in the protection of the public's health and preservation or respect for individual rights escalates during public health emergencies. Answers to thorny law and policy issues do not come easy due in part to the flexibility of public health powers, as well as constitutional norms that vary among autonomous adults and children or other wards of the state (e.g., prisoners, individuals lacking mental competence). Government may be constitutionally required under due process principles to protect the health of wards, for example, but not autonomous adults. American courts typically weigh three factors related to due process claims—the extent of the deprivation of liberty or property, the risk of an erroneous decision, and the burdens that additional procedures will entail.[43]

The design and provisions of MSEHPA reflect an appreciation for these complexities. Although many of the act's provisions heightened significant concerns among commentators and the public, none of its powers present new public health interventions. In fact, powers to report, test, screen, treat, vaccinate, quarantine, and isolate individuals are used constitutionally in routine public health practice. Suggestions that these public health powers exemplified antiquated techniques is contravened by their continued, daily use and strong evidence of their effectiveness in curtailing morbidity and mortality in emergencies.[44] The act also incorporates extensive due process protections related to quarantine or isolation powers that extend well beyond many states' existing statutory requirements. Stopgap protections to limit the duration of a state of public health emergency (to no more than thirty days), absent a re-declaration, help stymie the potential for misuse or overuse.[45]

[40] George J. Annas, *Bioterrorism, Public Health, and Civil Liberties*, 346 NEW ENG. J. MED. 1337 (2002).

[41] Ronald Bayer & James Colgrove, *Public Health vs. Civil Liberties*, SCI., Sept. 13, 2002, at 1811, *available at* http://www.sciencemag.org/content/297/5588/1811.full.

[42] Sheri Fink, *U.S. Mines Personal Health Data to Find the Vulnerable in Emergencies*, N.Y. TIMES, May 15, 2014, at A18.

[43] Parham v. J.R., 442 U.S. 584, 609 (1979) (holding juvenile commitment decision when made by a "neutral factfinder" sufficient to satisfy due process requirements).

[44] Gostin, *Public Health Law*.

[45] Stephen P. Teret, *Health Versus Liberty*, JOHNS HOPKINS PUBLIC HEALTH, Spring 2002, at 5.

Despite some concerns, multiple national public health and policy-making entities openly recognized and supported the premises of the act, including CDC, APHA, ASTHO, NACCHO, as well as the National Conference of State Legislatures (NCSL), National Governors Association (NGA), National Association of Attorneys General (NAAG), and American Medical Association (AMA). Perhaps the most telling support for MSEHPA came from legislatures and regulatory agencies across the United States and internationally. Within months of its completion, state legislatures or agencies in over half of the states and the District of Columbia had introduced legislative bills or regulatory changes based in whole or part on MSEHPA.[46] By 2006, thirty-nine states' legislatures had passed bills related to the act.[47] In 2011, the Network for Public Health Law determined that twenty-six states and the District of Columbia had legislatively crafted "public health emergencies," or like terms, as part of their laws.[48] Prior to 2001, virtually no state (except Colorado[49]) featured this type of emergency classification.

Larger cities and counties with sufficient "home rule" authority explored and used the act's provisions as well.[50] MSEHPA provisions providing licensure reciprocity for healthcare practitioners across states, liability protections for volunteers, and expedited, modern powers to test, screen, vaccinate, isolate, and quarantine individuals and populations were infused in sections of other model public health acts, including the Turning Point Act of 2003[51] and the Uniform Emergency Volunteer Health Practitioners Act of 2007.[52] In 2007, the World Health Organization's overhaul of its International Health Regulations (IHRs) included themes from MSEHPA embedded in IHR's new definition of "public health emergency of international concern."[53] Collectively, the incorporation of MSEHPA principles into international, federal, state, tribal, and local emergency laws and policies over the past decade represents among the most significant public health law reforms in history.

[46] *Emergency System for Advance Registration of Volunteer Health Professionals (ESAR-VHP)—Legal and Regulatory Issues*, U.S. Dep't of Health & Human Servs. (2006), *available at* http://www.publichealthlaw.net/Research/PDF/ESAR%20VHP%20Report.pdf.

[47] Center for Law and the Public's Health, MSEHPA State Legislative Activity Table (2006), *available at* http://www.publichealthlaw.net/MSEHPA/MSEHPA%20Leg%20Activity.pdf.

[48] Public Health Law Network, The Model State Emergency Health Powers Act—Table of State Laws (2011), *available at* http://www.publichealthlawnetwork.org/wp-content/uploads/MSEHPA-States-TableFINAL.pdf.

[49] Colo. Rev. Stat. Ann. § 24-32-2103(1.7) (West 2011).

[50] Evan D. Anderson & James G. Hodge, Jr., *Emergency Legal Preparedness Among Select U.S. Local Governments*, 3 Disaster Med. and Pub. Health Preparedness Supplement S2 (2009).

[51] Turning Point Public Health Statute Modernization National Collaborative, Turning Point Model State Public Health Act (2003), *available at* http://www.publichealthlaw.net/Resources/Modellaws.htm.

[52] Nat'l Conference of Comm'rs on Unif. State Laws, Uniform Emergency Volunteer Health Practitioners Act (2007), *available at* http://www.uevhpa.org/DesktopDefault.aspx?tabindex=1&tabid=69.

[53] World Health Organization, International Health Regulations Art. 2 (2d ed. 2005), *available at* http://whqlibdoc.who.int/publications/2008/9789241580410_eng.pdf.

IV Legal and Ethical Duties to Plan for Public Health Emergencies

One of the central tenets of public health preparedness is the need to effectively plan and train for emergencies. Public health ethics and laws strongly support this objective. Since 9/11, billions dollars at all levels of government have been spent to support or encourage effective planning and training among emergency managers, healthcare workers, and public health personnel, among many others. Recommendations from the federal Institute of Medicine regarding its crisis standards of care guidance may be encapsulated in federal spending conditions underlying receipt of grants or other funds.[54]

Sometimes the mere "power of the purse" stimulates preparedness planning essential to saving lives and preventing disabilities during catastrophic public health events. However, such planning is legally required in many other ways. Federal or state laws like MSEHPA may directly outline and require preparedness planning, or stipulate terms of what it must meet or address. Every state has created a pandemic flu plan due in part to federal funding requirements tied to law. Corresponding regulations among state agencies may similarly require local governments to participate in statewide or regional emergency preparedness planning and training exercises.

Private sector entities may be mandated to prepare for public health emergencies policies. Nearly every hospital in the United States has generated emergency preparedness plans, covering everything from nuclear disasters to "active shooters" on the premises. HHS has allocated hundreds of millions of dollars to hospitals to improve emergency preparedness[55] through comprehensive emergency response plans, and can withhold funds from hospitals that do not meet certain benchmarks.[56] DHS required funded hospitals to adopt its standards within their emergency plans. State laws and licensing provisions call for hospitals to be prepared.[57] The Joint Commission, which sets national standards for hospital accreditation, requires hospitals to demonstrate levels of emergency preparedness through its accreditation processes.[58]

Sometimes the stimulant to plan for public health emergencies is not the availability of major funds or affirmative legal requirements. Instead, it may stem from the potential for liability for abject failures to plan. Such was the lesson of one healthcare entity, Tenet Healthcare, in the aftermath of Hurricane Katrina in New Orleans, Louisiana in 2005. On March 23, 2011, Tenet settled a series of claims for a reported $25 million brought by plaintiffs in *Preston v. Tenet Healthsystem Memorial Medical Center*.[59] They alleged not only that

[54] Institute of Medicine, Crisis Standards of Care: A Systems Framework for Catastrophic Disaster Response (2012), *available at* http://www.iom.edu/~/media/Files/Report%20 Files/2012/Crisis-Standards-of-Care/CSC_rb.pdf.

[55] Public Health Service Act, 42 U.S.C. § 247d-6d (2006).

[56] National All-Hazards Preparedness for Public Health Emergencies, 42 U.S.C. §§ 300hh-2 (2006).

[57] Beth Maldin, Clarence Lam, Crystal Franco, David Press, Richard Waldhorn, Eric Toner, Tara O'Toole, & Thomas V. Inglesby, *Regional Approaches to Hospital Preparedness*, 5 Biosecurity and Bioterrorism: Biodefense Strategy, Practice, and Science 43 (2007).

[58] Joint Commission, Surge Hospitals: Providing Safe Care in Emergencies (2005), *available at* http://www.jointcommission.org/assets/1/18/surge_hospital.pdf.

[59] Preston v. Tenet Healthsystem Mem'l Med. Ctr., Inc., No. 05-11709-B-15 (La. Civ. Dist. Ct. 2008).

that Tenet's emergency responses at its Memorial Medical Center during Hurricane Katrina were insufficient but that Tenet's failure to prepare for a foreseeable emergency caused their harms.[60]

Forty-five patients died at Memorial Medical Center in the aftermath of Katrina and the subsequent citywide flooding.[61] Staff shortages, losses of power, soaring temperatures, delayed evacuations, inadequate supplies, and even involuntary euthanization (via the alleged excess administration of palliative medications without explicit patient consent) all likely contributed to patient injuries and deaths. In *Preston*, the claimants alleged further that Tenet created unreasonable and preventable risks of harm to patients by failing to have a viable patient evacuation plan, an adequate backup power system, or arrangements to care for patients if power was lost for extended periods. Like most hospitals, Memorial Medical Center had a backup power system, but it broke down as floodwaters rose. Tenet may have argued effectively that it was not responsible for patients' damages. Although a healthcare entity may be responsible for faulty designs or dangerous conditions on its premises, it is not usually liable for "acts of God," like flooding, or governmental breaches such as faulty construction of levees that cause patient harms. Liability only exists if Tenet knew its hospital was vulnerable to hurricane-related flooding and still decided not to make recommended changes to elevate backup power switches and pumps from the basement and ground-level to avoid structural damages, as the claimants in *Preston* alleged. Reasonable persons may not expect a hospital to be prepared for every contingency in a catastrophe, but they may conclude it is responsible if hospital administrators foresaw and failed to address potential harms.

While the regulatory consequences for a healthcare entity's preparedness flaws are already dire (e.g., potential loss of licensure, accreditation, or funding), cases like *Preston* up the ante. When patient harms can be tied to an entity's failure to prepare sufficiently for emergencies, defending such claims may be compromised when emergency preparedness is heavily mandated by law, widely endorsed and practiced, and ultimately beneficial to patients. A legal presumption emerges that healthcare entities must avert preventable patient harms through solid emergency planning and training.

Against this presumption are legislative or policy proposals to insulate healthcare entities from liability for their responses, or failures to respond, in public health emergencies. In the absence of comprehensive federal protections from liability, some states' legislatures have enacted liability protections that may apply to healthcare entities in emergencies.[62] Even in Louisiana, where the *Preston* case arose, statutory law in place prior to Katrina immunizes healthcare practitioners and entities from liability for injuries or deaths during declared public health emergencies.[63] This sort of provision may dispel claims of negligence concerning

[60] James G. Hodge, Jr. & Erin Fuse Brown, *Assessing Liability for Health Care Entities That Insufficiently Prepare for Catastrophic Emergencies*, 306 J. AM. MED. ASS'N. 308 (2011).

[61] Sheri Fink, *Trial to Open in Lawsuit Connected to Hospital Deaths After Katrina*, N. Y. TIMES, Mar. 20, 2011, *available at* http://www.nytimes.com/2011/03/21/us/21hospital.html?_r=1&amp.

[62] UNIV. OF N. C., GILLINGS SCHOOL OF GLOBAL PUBLIC HEALTH, GOOD SAMARITAN ENTITY LIABILITY PROTECTION: ISSUE BRIEF, *available at* http://nciph.sph.unc.edu/law/tools/IssueBrief.pdf [hereinafter UNC GILLINGS].

[63] LA. REV. STAT. ANN. § 29:771 (2003).

active emergency responses, but it does not fully address actions asserting entity liability for omissions in emergency planning.

No amount of planning and training activities can eliminate all risks to individuals during public health catastrophes. These events are defined by their unpredictability. Fact-finders may be sympathetic to a healthcare entity's good faith efforts to respond during emergencies, but less so concerning questions of what could have been done *prior* to the emergency to better prepare. Yet, suggesting such entities are liable for all patient harms that could have been prevented through enhanced planning creates an impossible legal standard for entities to meet. Greater clarification of the legal bases in which private sector healthcare or other entities may be liable for failures to plan must account for the (1) foreseeability and magnitude of patient risks, (2) relative costs of adequate planning, and (3) causal connections between preparedness lapses and specific patient harms.[64] Equipping personnel and entities alike with clearer guidance on the potential liability risks may lend to advances in preparedness planning and training that can ultimately save lives.

As in the *Preston* case, some preparedness plans fail to address the needs of a specific group of persons, such as patients, leading to significant harms. In other cases, planning failures may impact entire classes of vulnerable persons. In some jurisdictions, courts have opined that government is legally required to plan for disasters in ways that meet the disparate needs of persons with disabilities. In *Communities Actively Living Independent and Free (CALIF) v. City of Los Angeles*,[65] a federal district court in 2011 reviewed a challenge that the City of Los Angeles' emergency preparedness plan failed to accommodate persons with disabilities under the federal Americans with Disabilities Act (ADA)[66] and other state-based claims. *CALIF* represented over eight hundred thousand individuals with disabilities living within Los Angeles (LA). It alleges that LA's emergency operations plan does not address how the city will meet the unique needs of individuals with disabilities in the event of an emergency. The court noted that LA's plan refers to over two hundred shelter sites, but only a few of these sites were known to be ADA-compliant; most of the sites had never been assessed for their ADA compliance. In 2008, LA's Department on Disability reported that the city was not in compliance with the ADA and made a number of recommendations. Except for conducting limited site assessments, the city had not acted on these recommendations.

At the heart of the case is whether LA violated disability discrimination laws by failing to appropriately provide for individuals with disabilities in its emergency preparedness plan. Granting *CALIF*'s motion for summary judgment, the district court found that individuals with disabilities are disproportionately burdened by the city's failure to consider their unique needs in the administration of its emergency preparedness plans, including provisions on how to notify, evacuate, transport, or shelter individuals with disabilities. These failures allegedly placed the disabled at higher risks than nondisabled persons in the event of an emergency. The city countered that (1) it had not engaged in any affirmatively discriminatory actions, and (2) there was no evidence that anyone with a disability had requested or was

64 Hodge, Jr. & Brown, *Assessing Liability*.

65 Communities Actively Living Indep. and Free v. City of Los Angeles, No. CV 09-0287 CBM (RZx), 2011 WL 4595993 (C. D. Cal. 2011) (California alleges that the city violated: (1) ADA Title II; (2) Section 504 of the federal Rehabilitation Act of 1973; and (3) the California Disabled Persons Act (CDPA), among other claims).

66 Americans with Disabilities Act of 1990, Pub. L. No. 101-336, 104 Stat. 327.

refused reasonable accommodation from the city. The court disagreed. Although the city's actions were facially neutral, the emergency plan placed additional burdens on individuals with disabilities because it did not address their unique needs. Such failures, noted the court, unlawfully discriminated against hundreds of thousands of disabled individuals, requiring a retooling of LA's emergency plans.

In 2013, on the opposite side of the country, a similar result played out in New York City (NYC). After 9/11, NYC prioritized emergency planning and preparedness activities to help assure affirmative and efficacious responses. Its plans were tested during Hurricane Sandy, which slammed the Northeast coast in October 2012. Thousands of persons lacked shelter due to flooding, wind, and fire damage. Hundreds were at risk due to power outages in hospitals and other settings. The public health threats from this massive storm were temporary albeit profound, especially among the thousands of New Yorkers with physical or mental disabilities. In *Brooklyn Center for Independence v. Bloomberg*,[67] a class of disabled persons brought suit in the Southern District Court of New York against NYC for its alleged failure to adequately incorporate accommodations for the disabled into its emergency planning. Approximately 11% of NYC's population is disabled according to the ADA. Members of the class testified that during and after Hurricane Sandy they were trapped suffering inside their residences for hours or days.

As in LA, the New York court found the city liable for its failure to adequately plan to meet the needs of people with disabilities. NYC argued that the disabled were not denied "meaningful access" to key emergency services under its preparedness plans. Yet the court found NYC's plans were deficient in multiple areas, including in its failures to address:

- evacuations, particularly from multistory buildings, and providing transportation;
- physical shelters and related communications;
- power outages;
- recovery operations to check on those who had not evacuated; and
- communications to alert the disabled about what to do in emergencies.

As in *CALIF*, this initial decision (subject to appeal) serves as a strong reminder to communities nationally to take affirmative measures to provide for persons with physical and mental disabilities in all phases of public health emergency planning and response.

V Challenges of Real-Time Practice of Emergency Legal Preparedness

Effective legal and ethical planning and training for public health emergencies are essential, but prevention and response efforts remain key. Good planning may mitigate potential harms and liabilities, curtail incompetent or illusory response efforts, and even obviate the occurrence of select emergency events (e.g., widespread food-borne outbreaks). However, it cannot dispense with the need for viable and efficacious responses during nonpreventable

[67] Brooklyn Ctr. for Independence of the Disabled v. Bloomberg, 290 F.R.D. 409 (S.D.N.Y. 2012).

public health emergencies. Innumerable studies, preparedness exercises, and postemergency reviews consider how public and private sectors respond across jurisdictions in coordinated ways. Nearly all of these assessments reach a similar conclusion: *Public health emergency laws are central to advancing effective response efforts*. In real-time events, laws can either mobilize actors in their efforts to improve health outcomes, or thwart their abilities to the detriment of the community. As a result, significant challenges underlie the application and practice of laws in public health emergencies as described in the sections below.

a. The Dilemmas of Dual (and Dueling) Declarations

One of the unforeseen (and perhaps unhappy) consequences of a decade of systemic legal reform centered on public health emergencies across all levels of government is the potential for overlapping emergency declarations. As noted above, the federal HHS, more than half the states, and countless local governments have crafted explicit authority for political actors to declare states of public health emergency, or like terms, since September 11. As Table 45.1 illustrates, this new type of declaration has been used by a variety of governments at all levels to address various conditions ranging from pandemic flu to local food outbreaks. Many times these declarations present few, if any, conflicts within and between governmental actors. However, when declarations of public health emergency accompany additional declarations of "emergency," "disaster," or like terms, overlap arises leading to detrimental consequences.

In response to Hurricane Katrina, for example, states of emergency and major disaster were declared by the President pursuant to the Stafford Act on August 27, 2005, and August 29, 2005, respectively.[68] On the latter date, the HHS Secretary declared a public health emergency for Louisiana.[69] Responding to multiple declarations, federal agency officials at DHS and HHS were unsure how to deploy their resources best. Major gaps in services and delays resulted. Thousands of victims suffered while stranded by the flooding in New Orleans. Some even died. A lack of strong interagency collaboration and organizational breakdowns[70] led Congress to enact the Pandemic and All-Hazards Preparedness Act (PAHPA)[71] in 2006 to help improve federal coordination.[72] Reauthorized in 2013,[73] PAHPA centralized federal responsibilities and encouraged state-based preparedness capacities for public health emergencies. It clarified that HHS (and not DHS) is the lead agency for federal public health and medical responses to public health emergencies.[74] Still, PAHPA left intact the existing legal architecture that allows for dual declarations of public health emergency and emergency or

[68] Daniel A. Farber & James Chen, Disasters and the Law: Katrina and Beyond 31 (2006).

[69] Lister, Cong. Research Serv., RL33579.

[70] The White House, The Federal Response to Hurricane Katrina: Lessons Learned (2006), *available at* http://library.stmarytx.edu/acadlib/edocs/katrinawh.pdf.

[71] Pandemic and All-Hazards Preparedness Act, Pub. L. No. 109-417, 120 Stat. 2831 (2006).

[72] James G. Hodge, Jr., Lawrence O. Gostin, & Jon S. Vernick, *The Pandemic and All-Hazards Preparedness Act: Improving Public Health Emergency Response*, 297 J. Am. Med. Ass'n. 1708 (2007).

[73] PAPHA Reauthorization Act of 2011, H.R. 2405, S. 1855, 112th Cong. (2011/2012).

[74] Hodge, Jr. et al., *The Pandemic*.

Table 45.1 Select Public Health Emergency Declarations

Date	Jurisdiction	Declared by	Purpose/ Reason	Brief Description
9/2/05	Louisiana	Gov. Kathleen B. Blanco	Suspend licensure of out-of-state medical personnel	Declaration of Public Health Emergency to Suspend Out-of-State Licensure for Medical Professionals and Personnel. Due to statewide shortage of medical professionals and personnel following Hurricane Katrina. La. Exec. Order No. KBB 2005-26 (Sept. 2, 2005).
3/21/08	Alamosa County (CO)	Gov. Bill Ritter	Contamination of public water supply	Declaring a Disaster Emergency Due to the Contamination of the Public Water Supply in Alamosa County. PHE occurred when contamination was identified as the source of community-wide salmonella infection. Colo. Exec. Order No. D 006 08 (Mar. 21, 2008).
5/6/08	Pima County (AZ)	Cnty. Bd. of Supervisors	Measles outbreak	Proclamation of the existence of a public health emergency. County resolution ratifies the local proclamation made on May 1, 2008. Pima Cnty. Bd. of Supervisors Res. No. 2008-107 (May 6, 2008).
1/16/09	U.S.	HHS Sec'y Mike Leavitt	56th Presidential Inauguration	Public Health Emergency Declaration for the 56th Presidential Inaugural. Effective from January 17–21, 2009 in support of emergency actions for the Presidential Inauguration. DHHS Order No. 8 (Jan. 16, 2009).
3/26/09	U.S.	Acting HHS Sec'y Charles E. Johnson	H1N1Outbreak	2009 H1N1 Flu Outbreak: Determination That a Public Health Emergency Exists. Declared via section 319 of the Public Health Service Act, 42 U.S.C. § 247d. DHHS Order (Mar. 26, 2009).
6/17/09	Towns of Libby and Troy (MT)	U.S. EPA Admin. Lisa P. Jackson	Release and threatened release of amphibole asbestos	Determination and Findings of Public Health Emergency for the Libby Asbestos Site in Lincoln County, MT. Declaration made under § 104(a)(4) of the Comprehensive Environmental Response, Compensation, and Liability Act (CERCLA). EPA Region 8, PHE Determination & Findings (June 17, 2009).
8/11/10	Nassau County, Long Island (NY)	Cnty. Exec. Edward P. Mangano	Dramatic increase in reports of domestic violence	Family Violence Public Health Emergency. Declaration made to help victims of domestic abuse. Press Release, Mangano Declares "Family Violence Public Health Emergency" in Nassau County (Aug. 10, 2010) (on file with Nassau Cnty. Press Office).

10/5/10	City of Oakland (CA)	Oakland City Council	Shortage of affordable, safe medical cannabis	Resolution Renewing the City Council's Declaration of a Local Public Health Emergency with Respect to Safe, Affordable Access to Medical Cannabis in the City of Oakland. Oakland City Council. Res. No. 82994 (Oct. 5, 2010).
2/4/11	Marquette County (MI)	Cnty. Health Dep't	Illness due to use of designer drugs sold as "bath salts"	Emergency Order to Prevent Imminent Danger to Health or Lives [concerning sales of "bath salts"]. Marquette Cnty. Health Dep't. Order (Feb. 4, 2011); *see also* CDC, *Emergency Department Visits After Use of a Drug Sold as "Bath Salts,"* 60 MMWR Rep. 19, 624 (2011).
4/8/11	North Dakota	HHS Sec'y Kathleen Sebelius	In anticipation of Red River flooding	Flooding in North Dakota: Determination That a Public Health Emergency Exists. Declared via section 319 of the Public Health Service Act. DHHS Order (Apr. 8, 2011).
7/1/11	Florida	Dep't of Health	Prescription drug abuse related deaths	Declaration of Public Health Emergency. The order was executed by the state surgeon general. Fla. Dep't of Health Order (July 1, 2011).
3/9/12	County of Hawai'i (HI)	Cnty. Council	Food insecurity	An Emergency Ordinance That Finds and Declares That a Public Health Emergency Exists and Makes an Emergency Appropriation of $200,000 to Alleviate Hunger in the County of Hawai'i. Based on 16% of residents lacked food security. Cnty. of Haw. B. No. 199.
8/9/12	Dallas County (TX)	Judge Clay Jenkins	West Nile Virus Outbreak	Public health emergency declared to help control mosquito populations and address the crisis. *West Nile Crisis: Public Health Emergency*, Mosquito Cont. Mag., Summer 2013, at 8.
8/15/13	Pondera County (MT)	Cnty. Disaster/ Emerg. Serv.	Water contamination	Public health emergency declared to address immediate sanitation and drinking water needs of residents in the City of Brady. Water Pol'y Interim Comm. Ex. 11 (Sept. 9, 2013).
3/27/14	Massachusetts	Gov. Deval Patrick	Opioid addiction epidemic	Public Health Emergency Declaration. Declaration made to combat overdose, prevent its escalation, and aid in addict recovery. Press Release, Deval Patrick, Governor Patrick Declares Public Health Emergency, Announces Actions to Address Opioid Addiction Epidemic (Mar. 27, 2014) (on file with Mass. Press Office).

disaster, which arose again in response to the 2009/2010 H1N1 pandemic[75] (fortunately with appreciable better results due to the nonseverity of the flu virus).[76]

The emergency legal environment among many state and local governments is equally overlapping. State and local policy-makers' passage of legislative or regulatory reforms based on public health emergencies are layered on top of the existing emergency legal framework. Every state, for example, featured preexisting classifications of "emergency" or "disaster" prior to their passage of MSEHPA provisions. The capacity for dual declarations led governors in Louisiana (following Hurricane Katrina[77]) and Maryland (during the 2009/2010 H1N1 pandemic[78]), among other examples, to issue competing declarations made possible by commonly shared components of statutory definitions of emergencies, disasters, and public health emergencies.

Duplicate emergency declarations add redundancy, complexity, and confusion to already-strained response efforts by authorizing different state or local agencies to coordinate responses. Typically, emergency management officials coordinate emergency or disaster responses. However, public health officials usually lead public health emergency responses. Simultaneous declarations may vest similar authorities in divergent governmental agents, fail to set lines of demarcation for action among competing governmental entities, or grant powers to act in one instance while restricting them in another. Politically accountable officials seeking to respond to internal and external pressures during a public health crisis may employ their emergency powers even though the potential for duplication, conflict, and controversy may follow.

A simple legal fix for the dual declaration problem in any jurisdiction would be to statutorily limit declarations to no more than one state of emergency at any point in time. However, this may be politically difficult to pull off. Governors may reject efforts to curb their current emergency options. Local officials on the frontlines of response may hold tight to their own emergency powers. Emergency managers exert powerful political voices in many jurisdictions and may disdain restrictions on their present abilities to respond. Public health authorities may also be reticent to pursue legislative changes given the potential that declarations of public health emergency are so limited as to never be invoked. If only one type of emergency can be issued, declarations of emergency or disaster may always come first because they are easier to justify under existing scopes of their definitions. Absent legislative or regulatory reforms, the status quo leading to dual declarations complicates future response efforts.

b. Practicing "Legal Triage" during Crisis Standards of Care

Multiple declarations raise another series of issues, compounded by the need for rapid decisions in altered legal landscapes.[79] Though a critical component of preparedness and

[75] Michael D. Shear & Rob Stein, *Obama Declares H1N1 National Emergency, Easing Rules for Hospitals*, WASH. POST, Oct. 25, 2009, at A1.

[76] James G. Hodge, Jr., *Global Legal Triage in Response to the 2009 H1N1 Outbreak*, 11 MINN. J. L. SCI. & TECH. 599 (2010).

[77] James G. Hodge, Jr. & Evan D. Anderson, *Principles and Practice of Legal Triage during Public Health Emergencies*, 64 N.Y.U. ANN. SURV. AM. L. 249 (2008).

[78] Md. Exec. Order No. 01.01.2009.05 (May 1, 2009), *available at* http://www.gov.state.md.us/executiveorders/01.01.2009.05.pdf.

[79] Hodge, Jr. & Anderson, *Principles and Practice*.

response, the rigors of real-time legal decision-making in declared emergencies are substantial. Yet these skills are nonstandardized,[80] understudied,[81] and, at times, poorly applied. Emergency laws should ideally help direct responses in key areas. In reality, these laws do not provide exact guidance. Framed often in sweeping language and subject to alternative interpretations, emergency laws offer broad powers and options, but no definitive steps on how or when to use them.[82] Still, there are legal limits to what public and private actors can do.[83] Constitutional provisions, statutes, regulations, cases, and contracts may constrain governmental and private actors during declared emergencies.[84]

Through *legal triage*,[85] public and private health practitioners, emergency responders, and their legal counsel must prioritize legal issues and solutions in real time to facilitate legitimate public health responses during declared states of emergencies by:

- identifying legal issues that may facilitate or impede public health efforts;
- assessing and monitoring changing legal norms;
- crafting innovative, legally sound solutions to reported barriers to public health response efforts;
- explaining legal conclusions through tailored communications; and
- revisiting the utility and efficacy of legal guidance to improve public health outcomes.[86]

Practicing legal triage is not easy, but it can be perfected through advance education, training, and exercises. One assessment of legal decision-making in a simulated emergency event conducted by researchers at Arizona State University in 2010 illustrated how varying criteria and substantive skills are used by practitioners to make difficult choices of law and policy.[87] Initial findings showed how multifarious legal, political, and epidemiological bases support key decisions in emergencies, all of which should be incorporated into legal and ethical training to enhance knowledge and skills in real-world environments.

c. Allocating Scarce Resources: An Ethics Approach

Legal triage invariably entails ethical norms, especially when allocating scarce resources. Vaccines, testing, screening, treatment, medical personnel, and other supplies or services

[80] HOMELAND SECURITY PRESIDENTIAL DIRECTIVE-21, LEGAL AND REGULATORY BARRIERS TO PUBLIC HEALTH AND MEDICAL PREPAREDNESS AND RESPONSE 4 (2009).

[81] James G. Hodge, Jr., Timothy Lant, Jalayne Arias, & Megan Jehn, *Building Evidence for Legal Decision-making in Real Time: Legal Triage in Public Health Emergencies*, 5 AM. MED. ASS'N. J. OF DISASTER MED. AND PUB. HEALTH PREPAREDNESS S242 (2011).

[82] James M. Chen, *Modern Disaster Theory: Evaluating Disaster Law as a Portfolio of Legal Rules*, 25 EMORY INT'L L. REV. 1121 (2012).

[83] Rebecca M. Kahan, *Constitutional Stretch, Snap-back, & Sag: Why Blaisdell Was a Harsher Blow to Liberty than Korematsu*, 99 NW. U. L. REV. 1280 (2005).

[84] Anda Botoseneanu, Helen Wu, Jeffrey Wasserman, & Peter D. Jacobson, *Achieving Public Health Legal Preparedness: How Dissonant Views on Public Health Law Threaten Emergency Preparedness and Response*, 33 J. PUB. HEALTH. 361 (2010).

[85] Hodge, Jr. & Anderson, *Principles and Practice*.

[86] James G. Hodge, Jr., *Legal Triage During Public Health Emergencies and Disasters*, 58 ADMIN. L. REV. 627 (2006).

[87] Hodge, Jr. et al., *Building Evidence*.

can quickly become scarce in declared emergencies or during implementation of crisis standards of care. Allocating these resources is hugely controversial. Who should receive life-saving medications first? Who is entitled to vaccines when not all can be served? How should healthcare workers triage an overwhelming surge of patients? These and other questions are pervasive in public health emergencies, but not easily answered. Public health emergency laws and policies may provide allocation options, but not sufficient guidance on exactly who should get what and when. From this legal and political vacuum is a need for ethically sound approaches to assure fairness and justice in the distribution of essential scarce resources.[88]

Yet what ethics principles actually apply? Lack of agreement and specificity of public health ethical norms applicable in emergencies have led to divergent approaches nationally and regionally. At every level of government, public and private actors have engaged in consensus-building efforts to develop principles to guide ethical decision-making in emergencies. From these efforts a series of core ethical norms have been generated with input from actors and entities representing public health, healthcare, emergency management, patients, and other impacted groups.[89] These norms are intended to supplement, not supplant, relevant portions of existing codes of ethics and professionalism, including bioethics, for healthcare workers, public health practitioners, emergency responders, and others. Key differences among public health emergency ethics and other ethics approaches stem primarily from a focus on the health of populations during emergency events, as contrasted with a predominant ethics focus on the health of specific individuals in nonemergency events.

National or regional efforts to recite principles of public health emergency ethics are beneficial, but sometimes deficient in providing real-time guidance. Other models do not comport with, or directly contravene, prevailing legal standards. Correspondingly, some jurisdictions have engaged in consensus building to develop clear guidance on public health emergency ethics applicable in planning, declared events, or implementation of crisis standards of care. While public and private approaches vary, some key norms of public health emergency ethics include, in no specific order of priority:

- ***Stewardship***. Scarce resources must be managed during a public health emergency to prevent and minimize morbidity and mortality among populations to the greatest extent possible while maintaining respect and care for individuals. This may include

[88] *See, e.g.*, I. Glen Cohen, *Rationing Legal Services*, 5(1) J. OF LEGAL ANALYSIS 221 (2013) (discussing how legal service providers may ration their services when they cannot help everyone).

[89] *See, e.g.*, UNIVERSITY OF TORONTO JOINT CENTRE FOR BIOETHICS PANDEMIC INFLUENZA WORKING GROUP, STAND ON GUARD FOR THEE: ETHICAL CONSIDERATIONS IN PREPAREDNESS PLANNING FOR PANDEMIC INFLUENZA 16–17 (2005); Nancy E. Kass, *An Ethics Framework for Public Health and Avian Influenza Pandemic Preparedness*, 78 YALE J. OF BIO. & MED. 235 (2005); Lawrence O. Gostin, *Medical Countermeasures for Pandemic Influenza: Ethics and the Law*, 295 J. AM. MED. ASS'N. 554 (2006); Ezekiel J. Emanuel & Alan Wertheimer, *Who Should get Influenza Vaccine When Not All Can?*, 312 SCI. 854 (2006); Kathy Kinlaw & Robert Levine, *Ethical Guidelines in Pandemic Influenza—Recommendations of the Ethics Subcommittee of the Advisory Committee to the Director*, CENTERS FOR DISEASE CONTROL AND PREVENTION, Feb. 15, 2007; Tia Powell, Kelly C. Christ, & Guthrie S. Birkhead, *Allocation of Ventilators in a Public Health Disaster*, 2 DISASTER MED. & PUB. HEALTH PREPAREDNESS 20 (2008); Douglas B. White, Mitchell H. Katz, John M. Luce, & Bernard Lo, *Who Should Receive Life Support During a Public Health Emergency? Using Ethical Principles to Improve Allocation Decisions*, 150 ANNALS OF INTERNAL MED. 132 (2009).

affirmative duties among qualified personnel to plan for how to allocate scarce resources uniformly and fairly.

- ***Transparency***. Planning and policy decisions (and their justifications) should be open and subject to public consultation and input prior to public health emergencies. Individuals making important decisions should communicate honestly and thoroughly on decisions that affect the public. Plans should be publicly available and disseminated through multiple communication channels. Ideally, the public should be solicited for its input.
- ***Soundness***. Decisions and responses should be consistent with known or empirically supported "best practices," where available. Ad hoc decision-making is to be avoided. Instead, allocation decisions should be based on well-informed situational awareness and known risks, and coordinated with others involved in response efforts.
- ***Duty to Care***. Healthcare practitioners have a duty to provide care during public health emergencies. Despite potential risks to practitioners, they must not abandon patients or others who have a reasonable expectation of care based on prior commitments and available resources. Persons who are ineligible to receive scarce life-saving or life-sustaining resources should be offered appropriate forms of palliative care.
- ***Reciprocity***. Healthcare practitioners who face disproportionate risks or burdens for the benefit of the community in public health emergencies are entitled to receive additional support, including priority for protective measures (e.g., vaccines, protective equipment, curative medications) or services (e.g., childcare services, workers' compensation coverage, job-loss safeguards, or liability protections) where possible.
- ***Fairness***. In a public health emergency, similarly situated individuals and groups should be treated alike. As a result, planning and decision-making criteria concerning the allocation of scarce resources should be applied consistently across healthcare settings, populations, and jurisdictions. Scarce resources may be allocated to individuals or groups with greater needs based on their medical prognoses, likelihood of positive medical responses to available treatment or services, relative risk of harm posed by withdrawing or withholding treatment, and other indications of survivability. Such decisions may not be based on factors unrelated to health status or emergency response needs (e.g., race, gender, ethnicity, religion, social status, education, ability to pay, immigration status, residency, or sexual orientation).
- ***Proportionality***. Less-restrictive public health interventions should be used whenever possible, reserving measures that may impinge individual rights and freedoms only when necessary to effective responses. Decision-makers should balance obligations to protect the public's health with respect for individuals. If more than one equally effective option exists, they must opt for the intervention that less significantly infringes affected individuals' liberty, privacy, or other legally- or ethically-grounded rights. Even when justified, restrictive measures should apply only to those individuals or groups whose interests must be restrained to avoid significant risks to individuals or the public's health.
- ***Accountability***. Decision-makers are responsible for their actions (or failures to act) in a public health emergency. They should monitor the effects and evaluate the efficacy of implemented decisions and responses, providing follow-up services or updated guidance where appropriate. Those making allocation decisions are accountable to the public for failures to abide by applicable plans, standards, or principles.

These principles are neither codified in statutory or regulatory provisions nor is their use during actual emergencies well researched to date. Without doubt, application of these (and other) vetted principles will not always lead to easy choices related to allocations of scarce resources in public health emergencies, but they provide greater support for the ethicality of such decisions while filling the void left by nonspecific laws or noncommittal policies.

d. The Liability Debate: Protecting Practitioners or Patients

Among the most contentious and divisive issues in emergency preparedness are those related to liability. Healthcare and public health practitioners, volunteers, and others are concerned about their personal liability for patients' or others' injuries or deaths in emergencies. Hospitals, clinics, public health agencies, and nonprofits fixate on their potential exposure to liability related to their acts or omissions. Some say these fears are unwarranted because unscrupulous liability claims during and after public health crises are not proliferate. Thus, individuals and entities do not face any real risk of significant liability exposure.[90] Others do not agree. Healthcare workers, for example, point to the significant opportunities for liability claims in attempting to serve or treat patients with limited resources in dire emergency conditions. Cognizant of prominent, national cases[91] following major public health emergencies in which practitioners and entities are hit with catastrophic claims, their perceived threat of liability is real.

Actual costs of liability exposure following emergencies are difficult to measure and assess, but collateral damages related to liability fears are demonstrable. Numerous studies show that health practitioners are unwilling to serve during emergencies due to their potential liability.[92] Countless anecdotal data suggest that the mere possibility of liability drives many healthcare, public health workers, or healthcare entities away from participating during public health emergencies. Correspondingly, in its 2009 Letter Report, *Guidance for Establishing Crisis Standards of Care for Use in Disaster Situations*, the Institute of Medicine suggested that "state and local governments should explicitly tie existing liability protections (e.g., through immunity or indemnification) for healthcare practitioners and entities to crisis standards of care."[93]

[90] George J. Annas, *Standard of Care—In Sickness and in Health and in Emergencies*, 352 NEW ENG. J. MED. 2126 (2010).

[91] Christopher Drew & Shaila Dewan, *Louisiana Doctor Said to Have Faced Chaos*, N.Y. TIMES, July 20, 2006.

[92] Michealle Carpenter, James G. Hodge, Jr., & Raymond P. Pepe, *Deploying and Using Volunteer Health Practitioners in Response to Emergencies: Proposed Uniform State Legislation Provides Liability Protections and Workers' Compensation Coverage*, 3 AM. J. OF DISASTER MED. 17 (2008); Kristine Quereshi, Robyn M. Gershon, & Francisco Conde, *Factors that Influence Medical Reserve Corps Recruitment*, 23 PREHOSPITAL & DISASTER MED. s27 (2008); Jonathan Ives, Sheila Greenfield, Jayne M. Parry, Heather Draper, Christine Gratus, Judith I. Petts, Tom Sorell, & Sue Wilson, *Healthcare Workers' Attitude to Working During Pandemic Influenza: A Qualitative Study*, 9 BMC PUBLIC HEALTH 56 (2009).

[93] INSTITUTE OF MEDICINE COMMITTEE ON GUIDANCE FOR ESTABLISHING STANDARDS OF CARE FOR USE IN DISASTER SITUATIONS, GUIDANCE FOR ESTABLISHING CRISIS STANDARDS OF CARE FOR USE IN DISASTER SITUATIONS: A LETTER REPORT, Sept. 24, 2009; James G. Hodge, Jr., Dan Hanfling, & Tia P.

Still, there are no comprehensive national liability protections for healthcare practitioners, volunteers, or entities in all emergency settings[94] or even during training exercises.[95] Rather, a patchwork of liability protections exists across all levels of government to cover practitioners and entities—particularly volunteers and government entities and officials—who act in good faith and without willful misconduct, gross negligence, or recklessness.[96] These emergency liability protections may immunize or indemnify public health and healthcare actors or entities from specific claims or monetary damages. For example, in the last decade, all states executed the Emergency Management Assistance Compact (EMAC), which provides strong liability protections for state or local agents during declared emergencies.[97] The full extent to which EMAC provisions have been used to insulate government actors from liability claims, however, is not well known. Limited waivers of sanctions or fines for failing to comply with certain federal or state statutes during emergencies offer additional protections.[98]

Concerns over liability risks inherent in distributing or implementing medical countermeasures in emergencies led Congress to enact the Public Readiness and Emergency Preparedness (PREP) Act[99] in 2005. It protects specific entities and individuals implementing certain covered medical countermeasures.[100] Upon a PREP Act declaration by the HHS Secretary, limited immunity from tort liability is extended to "covered persons" (e.g., federal officials, manufacturers, drug distributors, pharmacies, and state and local program planners) involved in the development, distribution, and administration of medical countermeasures. The act expressly establishes a compensation fund for individuals injured from the administration or use of covered countermeasures.[101] PREP Act liability protections are strong, but only apply (1) to persons and covered countermeasures specified by HHS, (2) for a specific period of time, and (3) concerning negligent acts, not intentional or criminal acts.

Powell, *Practical, Ethical, and Legal Challenges Underlying Crisis Standards of Care*, 41(S1) J. of L. Med. & Ethics 50 (2013).

94 Hodge, Jr. & Anderson, *Principles and Practice.*

95 Homeland Security Presidential Directive-21.

96 Sharona Hoffman, Richard A. Goodman, & Daniel D. Stier, *Law, Liability, and Public Health Emergencies*, 3 Disaster Med. and Public Health Preparedness 117 (2009); Sharona Hoffman, *Responders' Responsibility: Liability and Immunity in Public Health Emergencies*, 96 Geo. L.J. 1913 (2008); Sara Rosenbaum, Mary-Beth Harty, & Jennifer Sheer, *State Laws Extending Comprehensive Legal Liability Protections for Professional Health-care Volunteers During Public Health Emergencies*, 123 Pub. Health Rep. 238 (2008); Trust for America's Health (TFAH), TFAH Liability Protections Relevant Statutes (2008), *available at* http://healthyamericans.org/reports/bioterror08/pdf/legal-preparedness-law-review-of-state-statutes-and-codes.pdf.

97 Emergency Management Assistance Compact, Pub. L. No. 104-321, 110 Stat. 3877 (1996); Naim Kapucu, Maria-Elena Augustin, & Vener Garayev, *Interstate Partnerships in Emergency Management: Emergency Management Assistance Compact (EMAC) in Response to Catastrophic Disasters*, Public Administration Review (2007), *available at* http://www.pmranet.org/conferences/AZU2007/ArizonaPapers/Kapucu_Augustin_&_Garayev.pdf.

98 42 U.S.C. § 1320b-5 (2008).

99 42 U.S.C. § 247d-6d (2006).

100 Peggy Binzer, *The PREP Act: Liability Protection for Medical Countermeasure Development, Distribution, and Administration*, 6 Biosecurity and Bioterrororism: Biodefense Strategy, Practice, and Sci. 293 (2008).

101 U.S. Dep't of Health and Human Servs., Countermeasures Injury Compensation Program, *available at* http://www.hrsa.gov/gethealthcare/conditions/countermeasurescomp/.

Though inconsistent, existing federal, state, and local laws collectively provide an umbrella of liability protections, sheltering hundreds of thousands of practitioners, volunteers, and entities who play by the rules. Still, these protections have neither placated healthcare workers (seeking complete immunity) nor dissuaded patient-rights advocates (seeking equal access to courts to adjudicate potential negligence claims). On August 6, 2011, the American Bar Association (ABA) House of Delegates approved Resolution 125 to oppose adoption of laws, particularly immunity provisions, which "would alter the legal duty of reasonable care in the circumstances owed to victims of a natural or manmade disaster by relief organizations or health care practitioners."[102] Though legally lacking enforcement, it reflects the position of at least some ABA members, suggesting that the flexible nature of the legal standard of care adequately protects practitioners from unwarranted liability claims. Others believe that subjecting practitioners and entities to unforeseen claims for negligent acts or omissions for their emergency responses in the chaos and uncertainty in emergencies is contrary to protecting the public's health. This latter position remains the dominant policy choice of existing federal, state, and local governments who have directly addressed liability issues facing healthcare workers and volunteers in public health emergencies.[103]

VI Conclusion

Post-9/11, emergency legal and ethical preparedness has transformed how public and private sector actors prepare for and respond to public health emergencies. Federal, state, and local governments have reorganized and stand mobilized to respond. New classifications and uses of public health emergency have arisen. Emergency public health powers and ethics have been clarified. From these reforms the field has taken root, grown, and matured as a core mission of all levels of government and many entities and actors in the private sector. Preparedness for predictable public health catastrophes or crises is indispensable in an American society that expects public and private sectors to be ready. Virtually no advance in preparedness, however, comes without significant and sometimes controversial implications in law, ethics, and policy. Public and private sector actors continue to debate existing and potential legal reforms and ethics guidance. They question how law and ethics should be used to improve emergency preparedness, derail barriers to response efforts, and prevent morbidity and mortality during major catastrophes that impact the public's health. Finding answers remains a pivotal objective of public and private sectors in an era when unforeseen emergency threats to the public's health assuredly will arise.

[102] ABA Section of Individual Rights and Responsibilities, Report to the House of Delegates Resolution 125 (August 6, 2011).

[103] Institute of Medicine Committee on Guidance for Establishing Standards of Care for Use in Disaster Situations, Guidance for Establishing Crisis Standards of Care for Use in Disaster Situations: A Letter Report, Sept. 24, 2009.

PART IV

THE HEALTH LAW FRONTIER

CHAPTER 46

WHO'S IN?

Immigrants and Healthcare

WENDY E. PARMET

"[W]E have now just enshrined," President Obama stated as he signed the Patient Protection and Affordable Care Act (ACA) on March 23, 2010, "the core principle that *everybody* should have some basic security when it comes to their health care."[1] No doubt the act he signed was designed to reduce the ranks of the uninsured and broaden access to healthcare; but it never aimed at covering *everybody*. Indeed, only six months before he signed the act into law, President Obama pledged to a joint session of Congress that "the reforms I'm proposing would not apply to those who are here illegally."[2] In response, Congressman Joe Wilson, Republican of South Carolina, shattered decorum by shouting, "You lie!"[3] The president, however, did not lie. The law he proposed and signed does not provide coverage for millions of unauthorized immigrants. Nor does it repeal a plethora of other laws that restrict, in varying degrees, the ability of different categories of noncitizens to access healthcare. Even after the ACA, not everyone is a part of "everybody."

Whether and to what degree the tens of millions of noncitizens within our borders are part of the "everybody" entitled to basic healthcare access has long been a contentious question that draws together the heated realms of immigration and health policy. Underlying the issue are complex and often unspoken notions of deservedness and belonging, individual responsibility and communal obligation. Who deserves access to publicly supported healthcare? Who is within the universe when we speak of universal healthcare coverage? How do we allocate and pay for the care that will inevitably be given to the noncitizens who live in the United States?

[1] Press Release, The White House Office of the Press Secretary, Remarks by the President and Vice President at Signing of the Health Insurance Reform Bill (Mar. 23, 2010) (emphasis added), http://www.whitehouse.gov/the-press-office/remarks-president-and-vice-president-signing-health-insurance-reform-bill (emphasis added).

[2] Press Release, The White House Office of the Press Secretary, Remarks by the President to a Joint Session of Congress on Health Care (Sept. 9, 2009), http://www.whitehouse.gov/the_press_office/Remarks-by-the-President-to-a-Joint-Session-of-Congress-on-Health-Care.

[3] Carl Hurse, *In Lawmaker's Outburst, A Rare Breach of Protocol*, N.Y. TIMES, Sept. 9, 2009, http://www.nytimes.com/2009/09/10/us/politics/10wilson.html.

This chapter explores these issues by looking at the nexus between immigration and health policy. Although Americans often think of their country as a nation of immigrants, non-natives have never been considered fully equal and deserving users of the healthcare system. Rather they have long been feared, both for the diseases they are thought to carry and the costs they supposedly place on taxpayers. These fears and the concomitant sense that some or all immigrants simply do not *deserve* health benefits are reflected in laws that deny entry to immigrants who are thought to need healthcare and limit immigrants' access to insurance once they are within the country.

Despite these legal barriers, Americans are not fully comfortable with denying immigrants access to care. For example, federal law requires emergency departments to stabilize patients regardless of immigration status, and numerous other laws provide health insurance to limited classes of noncitizens. Thus while one set of laws limits immigrants' access to care, another set facilitates it. These diverging legal imperatives add complexity to the American healthcare system, increasing costs, and undermining public health. Only by recognizing that immigrants are inevitable participants in the healthcare community, and that when it comes to healthcare, "everybody" means "everybody in need," can we begin to develop a high quality, cost-effective healthcare system.

The chapter explores these tensions by reviewing health law's treatment of immigrants. The chapter begins in section I by exploring how concerns about immigrants' health have influenced laws regulating entry into the United States. Section II surveys the diverse categories of noncitizens within the United States, reviewing their health status and their use of the healthcare system. Section III focuses on immigrants' access to insurance, as well as the pre-ACA laws affecting their eligibility for public insurance benefits. Taken together these laws create a complex and conflicting web of policies that deny noncitizens access to care on the one hand and give it back to them, at least partially, on the other hand, suggesting a deep uneasiness about whether noncitizens are within or without the universe of care. Section IV considers the ACA's treatment of noncitizens, an approach that reinforces the complexity and contradictory messages that predated the act, and complicates the ACA's attempt to rationalize the healthcare system. Section V examines the impact of these laws on healthcare costs, public health, and the lives of noncitizens. Section VI considers the impact of possible immigration reform proposals, explaining why they are unlikely to resolve the conflicts noted above. The chapter concludes by arguing that the laws governing noncitizens' access to care reflect and reinforce the contradictions inherent in our healthcare system; underscoring both its inclusiveness and its exclusivity. The result is a dizzying array of laws and programs that impose needless costs and jeopardize public health. By failing to recognize that immigrants are part of the community served by the healthcare system, our laws have weakened the system for all.

I Immigration Law as Health Law

Populated by succeeding waves of migrants, immigration has been critical to the identity, culture, and economy of the United States. In the nineteenth and early twentieth centuries, immigrants from Europe and Asia worked in factories and built the railroads and urban centers. In the late twentieth and early twenty-first centuries, immigrants from Mexico, Central

America, the Caribbean, and Asia worked in the agricultural and service sectors, providing a younger workforce to an aging country.

Reflecting the importance of immigration to its development, the United States offers noncitizens more rights than do many other nations. Not only are the American-born children of immigrants granted citizenship by virtue of the Fourteenth Amendment, but most state laws that discriminate against immigrants are subject to heightened review under the Equal Protection Clause of the Fourteenth Amendment.[4] Moreover, communities of immigrants and their descendants wield substantial political power, as is evident by influence of the Irish and Italian voters in American cities in the twentieth century, and Latino voters in the twenty-first century.

Despite the country's embrace of immigrants, fears about immigrants' impact on the labor market, as well hostility to the racial and ethnic composition of immigrant populations, has long fueled anti-immigrant sentiment. This nativism frequently centers on the supposed health risks of immigrants, who are often portrayed as dangerous carriers of diseases borne in the less developed (and presumably less socially advanced) world. For example, in 2007 television anchor Lou Dobbs claimed that immigrants were responsible for the spread of leprosy within the United States.[5] In 2014 Congressman Phil Gingrey of Georgia wrote to the Centers for Disease Control and Prevention, "Reports of illegal immigrants carrying deadly diseases such as swine flu, dengue fever, Ebola virus and tuberculosis are particularly concerning."[6] As Arthur Caplan has noted, such comments continue the "long, sad and shameful tradition in the United States [of] using fear of disease, contagion and contamination to stigmatize immigrants and foreigners."[7]

The fear of immigrants as vectors of disease is a long-standing one. Since the late nineteenth century, Congress has used its so-called plenary power over immigration to deny entry to noncitizens who were thought to have a "communicable disease of public health significance."[8] In the late nineteenth and early twentieth centuries, this bar was enforced by the infamous medical examinations on Ellis and Angel Islands. Between 1987 and 2010 this prohibition was applied to immigrants who were HIV positive,[9] resulting in the detention of HIV-positive Haitian refugees in Guantanamo Bay.[10] Although HIV is no longer an excludable condition, immigration law continues to bar those with a variety of communicable diseases or a "mental disorder or behavior" that poses a "threat to the property, safety, or welfare of the alien or others."[11] In order to enforce these bans, immigrants are required to submit to medical screenings.[12]

[4] Graham v. Richardson, 403 U.S. 365, 375 (1971).

[5] David Leondardt, *Truth, Fiction and Lou Dobbs*, N.Y. TIMES, May 30, 2007, http://www.nytimes.com/2007/05/30/business/30leonhardt.html?pagewanted=all.

[6] Maggie Fox, *Vectors or Victims? Docs Slam Rumors that Migrants Carry Disease*, NBC NEWS, http://www.nbcnews.com/storyline/immigration-border-crisis/vectors-or-victims-docs-slam-rumors-migrants-carry-disease-n152216 (last visited Aug. 19, 2014).

[7] *Id.*

[8] 8 U.S.C. § 1182(a)(1)(A)(i)(2014).

[9] Dept. of Health and Human Services, *Medical Examination of Aliens—Removal of HIV Infection From Definition of Communicable Disease of Public Significance*, 74 FR 31798-01 (2009); *USCIS Issues New Guidance on Admitting Aliens with HIV infection*, 86 No. 46 Interpreter Releases 2923 (2009).

[10] Haitian Centers Council, Inc. v. Sale, 823 F. Supp. 1028, 1035 (E.D. N.Y. 1993).

[11] 8 U.S.C §1182(a)(1)(A)(iii)(I-II).

[12] 42 C.F.R. § 34.3 (2010).

Health-based exclusions seek not only to protect public health: They also try to exclude those who are too ill to work and may tap public resources. This concern is reflected in the so-called "public charge" provision, which allows officials to bar immigrants who are thought likely to need or do rely on public support.[13] For many years, authorities enforced this by deporting immigrants who had arrived legally, but later used publicly funded healthcare.[14] Although this policy is no longer in place,[15] federal law continues to proclaim that "[s]elf-sufficiency has been a basic principle of United States immigration law since this country's earliest immigration statutes,"[16] and that aliens should "not depend on public resources to meet their needs. . . ."[17]

II Immigrants among Us

In order to understand immigrants' relationship to the healthcare system, it is important to appreciate the heterogeneity of America's immigrant population. As of 2011, there were nearly forty million foreign-born individuals in the United States, making up approximately 13% of the population.[18] The foreign-born constitute an extremely diverse group, defying the common tendency to divide noncitizens into "legal immigrants," and "illegal" or "undocumented immigrants." They include naturalized citizens, lawful permanent residents (so-called "green card" holders), temporary visa holders (such as international students), refugees and asylees, unauthorized immigrants, and individuals with a variety of other immigration statuses, such as those residing in the United States under a court-ordered stay of deportation.[19]

The vast majority of foreign-born residents are in the United States lawfully. Over 40% are naturalized citizens.[20] Of the noncitizens, in 2012, approximately twenty-eight million were legal immigrants, and approximately 10% of unauthorized immigrants had some other type of quasi-legal status.[21] The Pew Research Center has estimated that the number of unauthorized immigrants declined from a high of 12.2 million in 2007 to 11.7 million in 2012.[22]

[13] 8 U.S.C. § 1182 (a)(4)(A).

[14] Polly J. Price, *Can U.S. Immigration Law be Reconciled with the Protection of Public Health?*, Emory University School of Law, Legal Studies Research Paper Series, Research Paper No. 14-272, 9 (2014), *available at* http://ssrn.com/abstract=2397524.

[15] Brietta Clark, *The Immigrant Health Care Narrative and What It Tells Us about the U.S. Health Care System*, 17 Annals of Health L. 229, 236 (2008).

[16] 8 U.S.C. § 1601(1).

[17] 8 U.S.C § 1601(2)(A).

[18] The Kaiser Commission on Medicaid and the Uninsured, Key Facts on Health Coverage for Low-Income Immigrants Today and Under the Affordable Care Act 2 (2013), http://kaiserfamilyfoundation.files.wordpress.com/2013/03/8279-02.pdf.

[19] It is important to note that many of these categories are fluid; and that data often do not clearly distinguish between the various categories comprising either the foreign-born population or noncitizens.

[20] Elizabeth M. Grieco et al., U.S. Census Bureau, The Foreign-Born Population in the United States: 2010 11 (May 2012), http://www.census.gov/prod/2012pubs/acs-19.pdf.

[21] Jeffrey S. Passel, D'Vera Cohn, & Ana Gonzalez-Barrera, Pew Research Center, Population Decline of Unauthorized Immigrants Stalls, May Have Reversed 3–4 (Sept. 23, 2013), http://www.pewhispanic.org/files/2013/09/Unauthorized-Sept-2013-FINAL.pdf.

[22] *Id.* at 6.

Robust growth in immigration is expected in the years to come. In 2012, the Census Bureau estimated that the United States will experience a net gain of 41.2 million immigrants between 2012 and 2050, and that net annual migration will rise to 1.2 million per year by 2060.[23] Such projections, however, are dependent on a number of assumptions about economic growth, international conditions, and immigration laws. Regardless, immigration has helped, and is expected to continue to help offset, the aging of the overall population.[24]

Foreign-born residents come to the United States from every region of the globe. Most were born in Latin America or the Caribbean, with Mexico being the most common birthplace.[25] Over eleven million people living in the United States in 2010 were born in Asia, and almost five million were born in Europe.[26] Immigration from Africa is also expected to increase significantly.[27] Given the increasing percentages of the non-native population coming from Latin America, the Caribbean, Africa, and Asia, it isn't surprising that immigration policy is influenced by, and often intertwined with, questions of race and ethnicity.[28]

Critics of immigration often claim that immigrants come to the United States for healthcare.[29] The evidence does not support this. Most come to work.[30] Others come for humanitarian reasons or family reunification. As a population, immigrants tend to be younger and healthier than the native-born adult population, a phenomenon known as the healthy immigrant paradox.[31] This may be due, in part, to the fact that it is difficult to immigrate; those who can leave their native country and resettle tend to be young and healthy. It may also

[23] United States Census Bureau, 2012 National Population Projections, http://www.census.gov/population/projections/data/national/2012.html (last visited Aug. 4, 2014).

[24] B. Lindsay Lowell, *Outlook for Labor Mobility*, in The Future of North America 2025: Outlook and Recommendations 122–128 (Armand B. Peschard-Sverdrup ed., 2008), *available at* http://books.google.com/books?id=-NwXSBGJo1wC&printsec=frontcover&dq=the+future+of+north+america&hl=en&sa=X&ei=dwT1U-beEtj_yQS86oHIBQ&ved=oCCcQ6AEwAg#v=onepage&q=the%20future%20of%20north%20america&f=false (The United Nations estimates that about seventy-nine million migrants would be needed to maintain the size of the working population (age 15–64) in the United States); Leah Zallman et al., *Immigrants Contributed an Estimated $115.2 Billion More to the Medicare Trust Fund Than They Took Out in 2002–09*, 32 Health Aff. 1153, 1158 (2013) ("Encouraging a steady flow of young immigrants would help offset the aging of the US population and the health care financing challenges that it presents.").

[25] Passel, Cohn & Gonzales-Barrera, Pew Research Center, at 15.

[26] Grieco et al., U.S. Census Bureau, at 2.

[27] Randy Capps et al., New Streams: Black African Migration to the United States 19 (June 2011), *available at* http://www.migrationpolicy.org/research/new-streams-black-african-migration-united-states.

[28] *See, e.g.*, Kevin R. Johnson, *"Aliens" and the U.S. Immigration Laws: The Social and Legal Construction of Nonpersons*, 28 U. Miami Inter-Am. L. Rev. 263, 281–292 (1997). While the influence of race on the question of immigrants' access to healthcare is undeniable, the present discussion focuses on the contradictory messages of health law, and its ambivalence about the role of government in supporting healthcare access.

[29] Vinita Andrapalliyal, *"Health Care for All"? The Gap between Rhetoric and Reality in the Affordable Care Act*, 61 UCLA L. Rev. Disc. 58, 71–74 (2013), *available at* http://www.uclalawreview.org/pdf/discourse/61-5.pdf.

[30] Kathryn Pitkin Derose, José J. Escarce, & Nicole Lurie, *Immigrants and Health Care: Sources of Vulnerability*, 26 Health Aff. 1258, 1263 (Sept./Oct. 2007), *available at* http://content.healthaffairs.org/content/26/5/1258.full.pdf+html.

[31] Andrapalliyal, *Health Care for All*, at 73 (noting that immigrants are healthier than the native-born); Greico et al., U.S. Census Bureau, at 6 (noting that immigrants are younger than the native born).

result from cultural differences; some immigrants are less likely than those who are born in the United States to view themselves as having health problems.[32] However, despite generally high levels of health, immigrants do have higher rates of some infectious diseases, such as tuberculosis, than the native-born population.[33]

Immigrants utilize health services at significantly lower rates than do citizens.[34] Non-natives are less likely to have a usual source of care, and less likely to receive preventive services, including mammograms, cholesterol screenings, and flu shots.[35] Noncitizens are also less likely than citizens to visit an emergency room.[36] Disparities in utilization are especially large for some specific populations. For example, immigrants from Mexico and Central America are twice as likely as citizens to lack a usual source of care.[37] Undocumented immigrants have especially low utilization rates, visit physicians and emergency rooms less often, and utilize fewer preventive services than other immigrant groups.[38] Given their lower utilization rates, it isn't surprising that noncitizens cost the healthcare system less than do citizens. One 2006 study found that healthcare costs of undocumented immigrants were half of what would be anticipated based on their share of the population.[39]

The striking differences between noncitizens' and citizens' use of healthcare services are likely due to several factors, including a paucity of culturally competent care[40] and fear of immigration authorities. Fears of immigration consequences may even deter legal immigrants living in families with undocumented immigrants from accessing care. A 2014 Kaiser Family poll found that 37% of legal immigrants in California were afraid to sign up for health insurance for which they were eligible because they worried that seeking coverage would bring attention to relatives' immigration status.[41]

[32] Silvia Helena Barcellos, Dana P. Goldman, & James P. Smith, *Undiagnosed Disease, Especially Diabetes, Casts Doubt on Some of Reported Health "Advantage" of Recent Mexican Immigrants*, 31 HEALTH AFF. 2727 (2012).

[33] JACOB S. SIEGEL IN CONSULTATION WITH S. JAY OLSHANSKY, THE DEMOGRAPHY AND EPIDEMIOLOGY OF HUMAN HEALTH AND AGING 572 (2012).

[34] Kathryn Pitkin Derose et al., *Review: Immigrants and Health Care Access, Quality, and Cost*, 66 MED. CARE RES. AND REV. 355, 368 (2009), *available at* http://mcr.sagepub.com/content/66/4/355.full.pdf.

[35] *Id.* at 363; Sarita A. Mohanty et al., *Health Care Expenditures of Immigrants in the United States: A Nationally Representative Analysis*, 95 AM. J. PUB. HEALTH 1431, 1431–1433 (2005).

[36] KAISER COMMISSION (2013), *supra* note 18, at 5.

[37] Derose et al., *Review*, at 363 (*citing* S. Todd Callahan, Gerald B. Hickson, & William O. Cooper, *Health Care Access of Hispanic Young Adults in the United States*, 39 J. OF ADOLESCENT HEALTH 627–633 (Nov. 2006).

[38] Nadereh Pourat et al., *Assessing Health Care Services Used by California's Undocumented Immigrant Population in 2010*, 33 HEALTH AFF. 840, 840–841 (2014).

[39] Dana P. Goldman, James P. Smith, & Neeraj Sood, *Immigrants and the Cost of Medical Care*, 25 HEALTH AFF. 1700 (2006).

[40] Leighton Ku, *Strengthening Immigrants' Health Access: Current Opportunities, Issue Brief*, GEO. WASH. U. SCHOOL OF PUB. HEALTH AND HEALTH SERVS., DEP'T OF HEALTH POLICY, 11 (Dec. 13, 2013), https://sphhs.gwu.edu/pdf/hp/current_opportunities_for_immigrants.pdf; Susan Okie, *Perspective: Immigrants and Health Care—At the Intersection of Two Broken Systems*, 357 NEW ENG. J. MED. 525, 525 (2007).

[41] Drew Altman, *Amid Tensions, Legal Immigrants Fear Signing Up for Obamacare*, WALL ST. J. WASHINGTON WIRE (July 30, 2014, 9:00 AM), http://blogs.wsj.com/washwire/2014/07/30/amid-tensions-legal-immigrants-fear-signing-up-for-obamacare/?utm_campaign=KFF%3A+Drew%27s+Columns&utm_source=hs_email&utm_

As with citizens, utilization rates are lower among uninsured immigrants than among their insured counterparts.[42] Uninsured immigrants are especially dependent on safety-net providers and appear to face significant problems accessing specialty and long-term care services that are not usually available at either federally qualified health centers or emergency departments. There is a striking lack of data on immigrants' use of these services, likely due to the fact that providers usually do not ask patients about their immigration status. However, the practice of medical repatriation (discussed in section V), as well as anecdotal reports by providers,[43] suggest that uninsured immigrants requiring significant levels of chronic care face enormous barriers.

III Immigrants' Access to Insurance

Noncitizens are three times more likely than citizens to be uninsured.[44] Although uncertainty about which immigration statuses fall into each category casts some doubt over the data, a report from the Pew Hispanic Center found that 59% of unauthorized immigrants were uninsured in 2008, as compared to 24% of legal immigrants and only 14% of the native-born population.[45] A 2013 analysis by the Migration Policy Institute using the 2011 American Community Survey estimated that prior to the ACA's implementation, 38% of all adult immigrants (including naturalized citizens) were uninsured as compared to 15% of U.S.-born citizens.[46] Forty percent of permanent resident adults were uninsured, and as much as 71% of unauthorized immigrants (a category that may have included immigrants with varying degrees of legal status) were uninsured.[47] These large disparities in insurance rates will likely continue under the ACA. Indeed, as more citizens become insured, noncitizens are apt to form a larger percentage of the uninsured population than they did prior to the act.[48]

medium=email&utm_content=13631874&_hsenc=p2ANqtz--TdHKE2p6zq5LHc_TYzxkk-WUprTHhm8bY__v3DPVWmH6GWLL32ALSyGaMqKXdvN7IrPhpNYb6lPwR6S_WsJhiCrwh6oyLjxKMNeEM4jnpOoNDrXQ&_hsmi=13631874.

[42] Pourat et al., *Assessing Health Care*, at 845.

[43] Vanessa Grubbs, *Narrative Mattes: Undocumented Immigrants and Kidney Transplants: Costs and Controversy*, 22 Health Aff. 332 (2014).

[44] Grieco et al., U.S. Census Bureau, at 20 (stating that in 2010, the native-born population of the United States was uninsured at a rate of 12.7%, whereas the foreign-born population was uninsured at a rate of 34.3%); Kaiser Commission (2013), *supra* note 18, at 1.

[45] Jeffrey S. Passel & D'Vera Cohn, A Portrait of Unauthorized Immigrants in the United States 18 (Apr. 14, 2009), *available at* http://pewhispanic.org/files/reports/107.pdf.

[46] Randy Capps et al., Migration Policy Institute, A Demographic, Socioeconomic and Health Coverage Profile of Unauthorized Immigrants in the United States 7 (May 2013), *available at* http://www.migrationpolicy.org/research/demographic-socioeconomic-and-health-coverage-profile-unauthorized-immigrants-united-states.

[47] *Id.*

[48] Stephen Zukerman, Timothy A. Waidmann, & Emily Lawton, *Undocumented Immigrants, Left Out of Health Reform & Likely to Continue to Grow as Share of the Uninsured*, 30 Health Aff. 1997, 2002–03 (2011) (focusing specifically on undocumented immigrants, stating that they are likely to form an increasingly large share of the uninsured, up to 25%).

There are many reasons why immigrants are less likely than native-born citizens to have health insurance. Most importantly, foreign-born residents disproportionately work in low wage, agricultural or service jobs that tend not to provide insurance. Although 70% of native-born adults under the age of sixty-five have private health insurance, only 42% of noncitizens immigrants do.[49]

Noncitizens are also less likely to be insured due to the complex and often contradictory tangle of federal and state laws governing their access to health insurance. Taken as a whole, these laws reveal deep, unresolved ambivalences about whether immigrants are deserving members of the healthcare community.

Three broad legal principles help shape the laws governing noncitizens' access to publicly financed healthcare. The first is the lack of an overarching right to healthcare in the United States. Not only is there no constitutional right to healthcare (except for prisoners), but even after the ACA, there is no broad "right" to coverage. Instead, we continue to have a multiplicity of private and public programs, each with their own eligibility criteria.

Coexisting with the absence of any generalized right to care is the widely shared view, enshrined in the ACA, that healthcare is not an ordinary commodity that should be left entirely to the market. At least in some circumstances, our laws recognize that government and providers have obligations to ensure that care is available to those who need it. This understanding is evident in the Emergency Medical Treatment and Active Labor Act (EMTALA), which requires hospitals to treat *all* patients who present with an emergency.[50] For purposes of EMTALA, "everybody" means "everybody," regardless of citizenship or immigration status.

Despite EMTALA, Congress has limited noncitizens' access to many federally funded health programs. For example, most unauthorized immigrants have long been ineligible for Medicare and Medicaid. But until 1996, legal permanent residents and immigrants who were residing under color of law (such as those who have a stay of deportation) were generally able to participate in federally funded health programs for which they were otherwise eligible.

In the 1990s, however, a strong anti-immigrant backlash developed in California and other states facing a large influx of immigrants. Much of the rhetoric focused on the supposed high costs of immigrants' healthcare. In California, voters enacted Proposition 187, which among other things denied publicly funded health services to undocumented immigrants.[51] As harsh as it was, even Proposition 187 evinced some ambivalence, as it continued to permit coverage for emergency care required by federal law.

Although Proposition 187 was only in effect for a very short time—a federal judge struck it down as preempted by federal law[52]—it was quickly followed by two federal acts restricting noncitizens' ability to receive federally funded health benefits. First, the Illegal Immigration Reform and Immigrant Responsibility Act of 1996 (IIRIRA) enables the federal government to seek reimbursement from the sponsors of immigrants who use public benefits, including health benefits.[53] It also requires that the sponsor's assets be used in determining a noncitizen's income eligibility for public benefits.[54]

[49] Ku, *Strengthening*, at 2.

[50] 42 U.S.C. § 1395dd (2011).

[51] Proposition 187, 1994 Cal. Legis. Serv.187 (held to be preempted by federal law in *League of United Latin American Citizens v. Wilson*, 997 F. Supp. 1244, 1253–1254 (C.D. Cal. 1997)).

[52] League of United Latin American Citizens v. Wilson, 908 F. Supp. 755, 763 (C.D. Cal. 1995).

[53] 8 U.S.C. § 1183a(a)(1)(2012).

[54] 8 U.S.C. § 1631 (2012).

More significant was the 1996 Personal Responsibility and Work Opportunity Reconciliation Act (PRWORA).[55] In enacting PRWORA, Congress acted on the belief that many immigrants are not deserving members of the community but are "freeloaders" who come to America to take advantage of taxpayers' largess. PRWORA explains that the "immigration policy of the United States [is] that the availability of public benefits not constitute an incentive for immigration to the United States," and that there is a "compelling government interest to remove the incentive for illegal immigration provided by the availability of public benefits."[56] To achieve those ends, PRWORA divides all noncitizens into those who are "qualified" for federal public benefits, and those who are not.[57] Qualified aliens include legal permanent residents, those granted asylum or refugee status, and a variety of other noncitizens.[58] All other noncitizens, including those who are undocumented and those who have short-term visas, such as international students, are unqualified.

Taken as a whole, PRWORA establishes a complex maze of waiting periods, exceptions, and exceptions to those exceptions. First, most, but not all, qualified aliens remain ineligible for Medicaid and most other federal health benefits for a period of five years following their entry into the United States with a qualified status.[59] According to the Department of Health and Human Services, about four million qualified immigrants have been in the United States for less than five years.[60] Unauthorized immigrants, and other legally present immigrants who are not qualified, are for the most part also ineligible.

But what Congress took away with one hand, it partially returned with the other. Under PRWORA, both qualified aliens who are within the five-year waiting period and unqualified aliens remain eligible for emergency medical treatment and federal public health assistance, including immunizations and programs for communicable diseases.[61] Moreover, the so-called Emergency Medicaid program provides federal support to participating states for the treatment of uninsured noncitizens who need emergency medical care but who are not eligible for Medicaid due to their immigration status.[62] The services covered by this program, however, are quite narrow. For example, some courts have ruled that it does not cover treatment necessary to keep a patient from facing future emergencies or even death, as long as they are not imminent.[63]

In addition, PRWORA gives states discretion to both expand and retract PRWORA's eligibility criteria. States may deny state-funded benefits to most, but not all, qualified noncitizens.[64] States may also choose to cover unqualified (including unauthorized immigrants) in state programs as long as they do so by explicit statutory authorization.[65] Perhaps not surprisingly, there is enormous variation among the states as to what is offered. Some states

[55] Pub. L. No. 104-193, 110 Stat. 2105 (1996). [56] 8 U.S.C. § 1601, §§ (2), (5) (2012).

[57] 8 U.S.C. §1641 (2008). [58] *Id.* [59] 8 U.S.C. § 1613 (2012).

[60] Ku, *Strengthening*, at 4; Nancy Rytina, Population Estimate: Estimates of the Legal Permanent Resident Population in 2012 (July 2013), *available at* http://www.dhs.gov/sites/default/files/publications/ois_lpr_pe_2012.pdf.

[61] 8 U.S.C. §§ 1611, 1612 (2011).

[62] 42 U.S.C. § 1396b(v) (2011). Note that the statute seems to cover only the care of unauthorized immigrants; but in practice it is also used for legal immigrants who are ineligible for Medicaid due to PRWORA.

[63] E.g., Diaz v. Division of Social Services, 360 N.C. 384, 386–391 (2006) (chemotherapy for leukemia is not covered even though the patient will regress into an emergency medical condition without it).

[64] 8 U.S.C. § 1622 (2012). [65] 8. U.S.C. § 1615 (2012).

use their own dollars to provide comprehensive coverage to many categories of noncitizens; other states cover almost no one they need not cover under federal law.[66]

Between 1996 and the ACA's enactment in 2010, federal law gradually liberalized noncitizens' access to federal health programs, even while many states revoked programs that had previously offered state support.[67] For example, in 2002 the Children's Health Insurance Program (CHIP) was amended to give states the option of covering the prenatal care of immigrant women under the so-called unborn child option.[68] As of 2013, fifteen states had taken advantage of this provision.[69] And in 2003 the Medicare Modernization Act allocated $250 million dollars per year to support hospitals providing medical care to uninsured immigrants.[70] This allocation expired in 2008.[71] But in 2009, Congress enacted the Children's Health Insurance Program Reauthorization Act permitting states to use federal funds to enroll lawfully residing (but not necessarily qualified) children and pregnant women in CHIP.[72] As of 2013, twenty-five states had elected under this provision to cover lawfully present children (a category that includes several immigration statuses), and twenty covered lawfully present pregnant women.[73]

In the same period, anti-immigration fervor intensified in many states, resulting in new restrictions on noncitizens' access to state-funded health programs. For example, in 2004 Arizona enacted Proposition 200, which required state and local officials to verity the immigration status of anyone receiving nonfederally mandated benefits, including health benefits.[74] Other states, confronted with budget deficits in the wake of the Great Recession, repealed or limited programs that had previously provided health insurance to PRWORA-ineligible noncitizens.[75]

[66] For example, Wyoming covers only lawfully residing pregnant women, several other states, including Montana, Oregon, and Rhode Island cover lawfully present children. Alaska provides chronic and acute medical care to qualified immigrants and lawfully present ones if they have certain specific medical conditions. Other states such as Massachusetts and New York provide coverage to most categories of lawfully present noncitizens. For a fuller description, see National Immigration Law Center, Table, Medical Assistance Programs for Immigrants in Various States, *available at* http://www.nilc.org/document.html?id=159 (last viewed Apr. 26, 2014).

[67] An exception to this trend is the 2005 Deficit Reduction Act that required states to document the citizenship status of Medicaid applicants, which led to further delays in coverage even for citizens, including newborn citizens. Kaiser Commission on Medicaid and the Uninsured, Focus on Health Reform: Immigrants' Health Coverage and Health Reform: Key Questions and Answers, *3, Dec. 2009, *available at* http://kaiserfamilyfoundation.files.wordpress.com/2013/01/7982 (last accessed Apr. 26, 2014). This requirement was repealed in 2009. Children's Health Insurance Program Reauthorization Act of 2009, Pub. L. 111–113, 123 Stat. 8 (2009).

[68] 67 Fed. Reg. 61956-01 (Oct. 2, 2002) (amending 42 C.F.R. § 457).

[69] Kaiser Commission (2013), at 5.

[70] Medicare Prescription Drug, Improvement and Modernization Act of 2003, Pub. L. No. 108-173, §1101(a), 117 Stat. 2066, 2432 (2003).

[71] *Id.* [72] Pub. L. No. 111-3, §213, 123 Stat. 8, 56 (2009).

[73] Kaiser Commission (2013), at 5.

[74] The Supreme Court struck down provision in the Proposition requiring individuals to produce proof of citizenship to vote. Arizona v. Inter Tribal Council of Arizona, 133 S. Ct. 2247, 2260 (2013).

[75] E.g., Bruns v. Mayhew, 750 F.3d 61 (1st Cir. 2014) (upholding Maine decision to end health coverage for immigrants); Korab v. Fink, 748 F.3d 875 (9th Cir. 2014) (upholding Hawai'i decision to drop certain noncitizens from its general insurance plans and provide more limited coverage instead); Guanam v. Velez, 74 A.3d 931, 943 (N.J. 2013) (upholding New Jersey decision to cease providing state-funded healthcare to immigrants with less than five years residency).

Courts have given mixed signals about the constitutionality of these state restrictions. Under well-settled constitutional doctrine, state laws that discriminate against legal aliens are generally subject to strict scrutiny under the Equal Protection Clause.[76] In contrast, because the federal government has plenary power over immigration, courts apply the less stringent rational basis test to federal laws that discriminate against aliens.[77] State actions that implement uniform federal immigration laws are also subject to rational basis review. As a result, a key question in litigation over state laws affecting immigrants' access to state-funded healthcare has been whether or not PRWORA establishes a uniform federal policy that lowers the standard of review from strict scrutiny to rational basis.

Some courts have found that it does. For example, in rejecting a challenge to a Hawai'i law providing PRWORA-ineligible qualified aliens with less generous health benefits than citizens, the Ninth Circuit found that PRWORA created a uniform national immigration policy limiting state discretion.[78] As a result, Hawai'i's policy was only subject to rational basis review. In contrast, in a case decided under state constitutional law, the Supreme Judicial Court of Massachusetts emphasized the breadth of discretion that PRWORA left to the states and determined that a state law reducing state-funded benefits for legal immigrants was subject to strict scrutiny.[79]

Other courts have argued that because PRWORA prohibits federal funding for health coverage for PRWORA-ineligible noncitizens, state laws that discontinue state support for healthcare for such noncitizens simply do not discriminate, as they do not treat noncitizens differently from citizens. As these courts see it, because only noncitizens are insured through programs that receive no federal dollars, the elimination of programs that only support immigrants does not treat noncitizens differently than citizens who were never eligible for such programs in the first place. Using this logic, the First Circuit found that Maine did not discriminate against PRWORA-ineligible immigrants when it eliminated funding for health coverage comparable in all other respects to the state Medicaid program. According to the court, because citizens never participated in that immigrant-only program, its elimination did not disadvantage them as compared to citizens.[80]

Thus, even before the ACA was fully implemented, noncitizens seeking publicly funded insurance faced a bewildering combination of inclusions and exclusions, constitutional protections and limitations, special programs and specific restrictions. Like everyone else, they were entitled to emergency care in a hospital; and a special program, Emergency Medicaid, existed in some states to reimburse providers for that care. In addition, many noncitizens with legal status were eligible for most federal health insurance programs, but many other noncitizens were excluded altogether from federal coverage. Some noncitizens were eligible for state-funded programs created just for them; and some courts found that laws limiting their access to such programs were unconstitutional. Yet, other courts found that noncitizens had few rights after PRWROA, and large numbers of noncitizens were left without access to any health coverage other than for emergency care. In sum, prior to the ACA, noncitizens existed in the margins and shadows of the American healthcare system, both within

[76] Graham v. Richardson, 403 U.S. 365, 371–372 (1971).

[77] Matthews v. Diaz, 426 U.S. 67, 81–82 (1976).

[78] E.g., *Korab*, 748 F.3d at 884 (citing *Soskin v. Reinertson*, 353 F.3d. 1242, 1256–1257 (10th Cir. 2004)).

[79] Finch v. Commonwealth Connector Insur. Auth., 459 Mass. 655, 678 (2011).

[80] *Bruns*, 750 F.3d at 71.

and without it, as members of the community of care, yet strangers whose exclusion helped to mark the system's boundaries.

IV Noncitizens and the ACA

The ACA aimed at rationalizing the American health insurance system. Recognizing that "[v]irtually every person residing in the United States, sooner or later, will visit a doctor or other health-care professional," and that the "large number of individuals without health insurance . . . burdens the national health-care market" [81] through inefficient cost-shifting, Congress sought to reform the system by requiring everyone to have health insurance, and by ensuring that everyone would have access to some form of insurance. Yet the ACA did not actually establish a broad "right" to healthcare. Rather, it continued the preexisting approach of relying on a plethora of different policies and programs, each with their own criteria. The ACA also followed the established pattern of expanding and restricting coverage for noncitizens, demonstrating anew the deep ambivalence about their inclusion in the healthcare system.

Although President Obama and congressional proponents of the ACA continually stressed that it would reduce the numbers of uninsured and provide access to "all Americans,"[82] they also took pain to insist that "illegal immigrants" were excluded from the act's benefits. As Nathan Cortez explains, this promise was codified by a number of provisions within the ACA that were designed to ensure that unauthorized immigrants were not able to reap the act's benefits.[83] For example, the ACA bars immigrants who are not "lawfully present," a term that is broader than PRWORA's "qualified" classification but still does not cover most unauthorized immigrants, from receiving premium tax credits or cost-sharing subsidies to purchase insurance through the newly created health exchanges, or from purchasing insurance on such exchanges without support.[84] In addition, immigrants who are not lawfully present cannot enroll in healthcare cooperatives or special state plans for low-income individuals ineligible for Medicaid.[85] Interestingly, the Obama administration has ruled that the so-called "DREAMers," the young adults who came to the United States without authorization as children and have received permission to work under an executive order, are not lawfully present for purposes of the ACA.[86] Likewise, the up to five million unauthorized immigrants who will receive authorization to stay and work in the United States if President Obama's 2014 immigration policy goes into effect are also expected to be considered not lawfully present for purposes of the ACA.[87]

[81] NFIB v. Sebelius, 132 S. Ct. 2566, 2609, 2610–2611 (2012) (Ginsburg, J., concurring in part and dissenting in part).

[82] Andrapalliyal, *Health Care for All*, at 67–70.

[83] Nathan Cortez, *Embracing the New Geography of Health Care: A Novel Way to Cover Those Left Out of Health Reform*, 84 S. Cal. L. Rev. 859, 870 (2011).

[84] 111 Pub. L. No. 148, §§ 1312(f)(3); 1401(a), 124 Stat.182, 218 (2010).

[85] *Id.* at §1331(e)(1)(A)-(B).

[86] Benjamin Sommers, *Perspective—Stuck Between Health and Immigration Reform—Care for Undocumented Immigrants*, 7 New Eng. J. Med. 369, 594 (2013).

[87] Tim Henderson, *Immigration Changes Wouldn't Solve Health Issues*, Stateline, Pew Chartiable Trust, Feb. 26, 2015, http://www.pewtrusts.org/en/research-and-analysis/blogs/stateline/2015/2/26/

To enforce its exclusion of those who are not lawfully present, the ACA requires that exchange applicants provide information about their Social Security number, and, in the case of noncitizens, information regarding immigration must be verified by the Department of Homeland Security.[88] Recognizing their inability to attain coverage, the ACA exempts these noncitizens from its requirement that all individuals maintain health insurance.[89] Those who are not lawfully present are thus presumed to be outside the scope of social responsibility and solidarity created by the ACA.

As a result of all of these exclusions, Buettgens and Hall estimated in 2011 that undocumented immigrants were likely to constitute over 24% of the uninsured once the ACA was fully implemented.[90] However, this study, as well as others reaching similar conclusions, was conducted prior to the Supreme Court's 2012 decision giving states the option not to expand their Medicaid programs.[91] As a result of this decision, and depending upon what the states ultimately decide to do, the total number of uninsured is likely to be higher than Buettgens and Hall expected, meaning that the percentage of undocumented immigrants within the group will be smaller. Still, as more citizens become insured, noncitizen immigrants are bound to form a larger percentage of the uninsured.

Importantly, noncitizens who are not lawfully present, and therefore ineligible to participate in the exchanges, may have a more difficult time getting healthcare than they had prior to the ACA's implementation. This is in part because some small businesses are expected to move their group health plans to the exchanges, so that unauthorized noncitizens who receive health insurance via the workplace may lose that benefit. (Estimates of the total number of employees whose insurance may be moved by their employers to the exchanges vary widely from five to thirty-five million).[92] Moreover, in order to finance the benefits it provides, the ACA reduces Disproportionate Share Hospital (DSH) funds for safety-net hospitals, meaning that they will receive less support for providing uncompensated care to noncitizens.[93] Some commentators claim that this will place new pressures on safety-net providers in communities with high numbers of undocumented immigrants.[94] Yet tacking in the other direction, the ACA also increases support for federally qualified health centers, which provide a major source of primary care to noncitizens.[95] And, as noted above, by using the term "lawfully present" the act also permits a broader group of noncitizens to receive federal health benefits than are eligible under PRWORA.

immigration-reforms-dont-solve-health-issues. In February 2015, a federal district court issued a preliminary injunction against the policy in a lawsuit brought by twenty-six states. Texas v. United States, 2015 WL 648579 Civ. No. B-14-254 (S.D. Tex. Feb. 16, 2015).

88 111 Pub. L. No. 148 at §1411(c)(2)(B).

89 *Id.* at § 1501(b).

90 Matthew Buettgens & Mark A. Hall, Who Will Be Uninsured After Health Insurance Reform? 5 (Mar. 2011), http://www.urban.org/UploadedPDF/1001520-Uninsured-After-Health-Insurance-Reform.pdf.

91 *NFIB*, 132 S. Ct. 2604-08 (2012).

92 Timothy Jost, *Employers and the Exchanges under the Small Business Option Program, Examining the Potential and Pitfalls*, 31 Health Aff., 267 (2012).

93 Sommers, *Perspective*, at 594.

94 E.g., Bonnie Jerome-D'Emilia & Patricia D. Suplee, *The ACA and the Undocumented: With Shrinking Charity Care Subsidies, Who Will Care for Those Excluded From Health Care Reform's Benefits?*, 112 Amer. J. Nursing 21 (2012).

95 Sommers, *Perspective*, at 594.

The ACA's ambivalence towards noncitizens is further demonstrated by its treatment of lawfully present noncitizens living below the federal poverty level. Before the Supreme Court ruled that the ACA's Medicaid expansion was optional for the states,[96] Medicaid was expected to cover all citizens with incomes less than 133% of the Federal Poverty Level (FPL). However, the ACA leaves PRWORA in place, so that most legal immigrants who have not been in the country for five years continue to be ineligible for federally supported Medicaid. To compensate for this, the ACA permits lawfully present noncitizens with incomes under 100% of the FPL to receive tax credits and subsidies to purchase insurance on the exchanges, even though citizens with such low incomes were left ineligible for this support on the assumption that they would receive Medicaid.[97] As a result, in states that have decided not to expand Medicaid, lawfully present noncitizens with incomes under 100% of FPL are eligible for federal subsidies unavailable to citizens with equally low incomes, a point noted by Arizona Governor Jan Brewer in arguing for her state to accept the Medicaid expansion.[98] On the other hand, as Leighton Ku explains, the exchanges were not designed for those with very low incomes[99]; and it is unclear whether noncitizens with incomes under 100% FPL will be able to afford coverage, even with support. Moreover, the coverage available on the exchanges is less comprehensive than most Medicaid programs, especially because it does not include long-term care. As a result, both unauthorized and many lawfully present noncitizens will continue to be denied access to the ultimate safety net in the case of serious disease or injury: Medicaid's long-term care provisions.

V Impact of Exclusion

The maze of laws that govern noncitizens' access to healthcare jeopardizes the health of both citizens and noncitizens, while also placing significant financial strains on those who provide noncitizens with healthcare. Although immigrants are generally healthier than citizens, that advantage dissipates the longer they are within the United States. This is likely due in large part to the fact that noncitizens begin to adopt unhealthy aspects of the American lifestyle, such as eating fast food.[100] Lack of access to primary and preventive healthcare may also play a role.[101] As noted in section II, immigrants are less likely to have a usual source of care and less likely to receive many preventive services. Although the full costs of these disparities is not known, perhaps due to the fact that providers generally do not ask patients about their immigration status, making cost studies difficult, it appears likely that these barriers to care leave immigrants vulnerable to a wide range of preventable or controllable conditions.

[96] *NFIB*, 132 S. Ct. at 2606–2607.

[97] Ku, *Strengthening*, at 4, (citing 26 C.F.R. 1.36-2(b)(5)–(b)(7) (2013)).

[98] Fernanda Santos, *Medicaid Expansion Is Delicate Maneuver for Arizona's Republican Governor*, N.Y. Times (Jan. 19, 2013), *available at* http://www.nytimes.com/2013/01/20/us/politics/medicaid-expansion-is-delicate-maneuver-for-arizona-governor.html.

[99] *See* Ku, *Strengthening*, at 4 (noting that the exchanges were designed for individuals with incomes between 100% and 400% FPL).

[100] Yurity Pylpchuk & Julie Hudson, *Immigrants and the Use of Preventive Care in the United States*, 18 Health Econ. 783 (2009).

[101] *Id.*

The impact of the laws governing noncitizens' access to care is most significant for immigrants who suffer from serious accidents and major, chronic illnesses that require long-term, expensive care. Many of these noncitizens have experienced what has become known as medical repatriation, which occurs when hospitals or other care facilities send immigrant patients (often involuntarily) to their country of origin. According to a study by Seton Hall Law School and New York Lawyers for Public Interest, more than eight hundred immigrants were forcibly or coercively transferred by American hospitals to their countries of origin between 2006 and 2012.[102] Although medical repatriations most often involve unauthorized immigrants, legal permanent residents and even the citizen children of immigrants have been affected.[103] In many of these cases, the immigrants were employed prior to a sudden accident. They were rushed to a hospital emergency department and stabilized as EMTALA requires. After they were stabilized, but still in need of need of in-patient care, the hospital chartered a plane to send them to their native country.

The reasons for medical repatriations were explained in 2012 by an Iowa Appeals court in *Cruz v. Central Iowa Hospital.*[104] *Cruz* stemmed from a prototypical fact pattern: Two unauthorized Mexican immigrants, Jacinto Rodriguez-Cruz and Jose Rodriguez-Saldana, suffered traumatic brain injuries when a car they were in was hit by a semi-truck. They were rushed to Iowa Methodist Hospital, where they were stabilized. Although both men had employer-provided health insurance, the hospital was unable to find any rehabilitation facility willing to take them, probably because they were ineligible for Medicaid's long-term care coverage as a result of PRWORA. Unwilling or unable to bear the costs of keeping them as inpatients, Iowa Methodist chartered an airplane to fly them to a hospital in Vera Cruz, Mexico, where they were kept nearly a month before being released to their families, who later sued for false imprisonment.[105]

In its decision affirming the trial court's rejection of plaintiffs' false imprisonment claim, the Appeals Court discussed the "increasingly common use of medical repatriations by hospitals in the United States—a practice that is driven by financial considerations."[106] According to the court, this practice stemmed from the "confluence" of federal laws that require hospitals to treat patients in an emergency and discharge patients only to appropriate facilities, while also denying many noncitizens access to Medicaid.[107] In effect, federal law's conflicting views regarding noncitizens' membership in the healthcare community—recognizing them as within the community for purposes of emergency care, but outside of it for purposes of Medicaid—leaves hospitals with few good alternatives. In response, some hospitals opt to fly their patients back to their native countries, shifting the costs of an accident that occurred in the United States to a less wealthy nation's healthcare system.

Reviewing the trial court's decision, the appeals court in *Cruz* held that the families could not prevail on their false imprisonment claim because they had not specifically objected to the transfer. In addition, the plaintiffs could not show that the patients, who were

[102] New York Lawyers for the Public Interest, Discharge, Deportation, and Dangerous Journeys (2012), http://law.shu.edu/ProgramsCenters/PublicIntGovServ/CSJ/upload/final-med-repat-report-2012.pdf.

[103] *id* at 6. [104] 826 N.W. 2d 516 (Iowa App. 2012). [105] *Id.* [106] *id.*

[107] *Id.* (quoting Phillip Cantwell, *Relevant "Material" Importing the Principles of Informed Consent and Unconscionability to Analyze Consensual Medical Repatriations*, 6 Harv. L. & Pol'y Rev. 249, 252 (2012)).

unconscious during the transfer, had suffered the type of mental anguish protected by the tort of false imprisonment. The court added that the hospital was not liable for any harm the patients suffered once they were in Mexico, as any duty the hospital had ended at the time of stabilization.[108]

Cruz followed an earlier decision by a Florida appeals court holding that an undocumented immigrant could bring a false imprisonment claim for medical repatriation. *Montejo v. Martin Memorial Medical Center* concerned the medical repatriation of Luis Alberto Jimenez, an unauthorized Guatemalan immigrant who suffered severe brain injuries after being injured in a car crash. [109] He was stabilized by Martin Memorial Medical Center and then transferred to a skilled nursing facility that the *New York Times* speculated was willing to take him only in the hope that he might receive a substantial settlement as a result of the car crash.[110] After Jimenez experienced another medical emergency, the nursing facility returned him to Martin Memorial, which was unable to find a suitable long-term care facility after he was stabilized anew. Having been paid for only $80,000 of the $1.5 million it had spent on Jimenez' care, the hospital asked and received permission from a Florida court to transfer Jimenez to a hospital in Guatemala.[111] After the transfer, Jimenez' cousin asked a Florida appeals court to rescind the order. It did so holding that the trial court lacked authority to order what was, in effect, a deportation.[112] The appeals court noted, however, that at trial the plaintiff would have to show that the hospital's actions were unreasonable. An all-white jury found that they were not, exonerating the hospital.[113]

Taken together, *Jimenez* and *Cruz* illustrate both the impact of PRWORA's prohibition on Medicaid's coverage of nonemergency care for ineligible immigrants, as well as the limitations of tort law as a response to the problem of medical repatriations. Tort law, with its focus on the reasonableness of the hospitals' actions, the consent of the individual patients or their families, and the patients' own pain and anguish, utilizes an individualized analysis that is poorly suited to the systemic problems created by health laws' contradictory dictates regarding the treatment of immigrants. Indeed, though many will be appalled by the apparent callousness of hospitals that forcibly deport noncitizen patients, and at least some hospital officials were undoubtedly motivated by their own negative perceptions of immigrants, medical repatriations are a predictable response to the competing commands of American health law. Given that these contradictions remain under the ACA, medical repatriations are apt to continue.

The tort of false imprisonment is also inapplicable when noncitizens "choose" to return to their country of origin due to their inability to attain needed healthcare in the United States. An especially stark example of this occurred in 2009 when Grady Memorial Hospital, the primary safety-net provider in Atlanta, closed its dialysis unit due to a lack of reimbursement

[108] 826 N.W. 2d 516.

[109] 935 So.2d 1266 (Dist. App. Fla. 2006). For further discussion of the *Jimenez* case, *see* Janet L. Dolgin & Katherine R. Dieterich, *When Others Get Too Close: Immigrants, Class, and the Health Care Debate*, 19 CORNELL J. L. & PUB. POL'Y, 283, 286–288 (2010).

[110] Deborah Sontag, *Deported by U.S. Hospitals Immigrants, Spurned on Rehabilitation, Are Forced Out*, N.Y. TIMES, Aug. 3, 2008, at A-1.

[111] Caitlin O'Connell, Note, *Return to Sender: Evaluating the Medical Repatriations of Uninsured Immigrants*, 87 WASH. UNIV. L. REV. 1429, 1429 (2010).

[112] 935 S.2d at 1270–1271. [113] *Id.* at 172.

for the care it offered noncitizens.[114] Although Medicare pays for dialysis and transplants for almost all citizens with end-stage renal disease, this coverage is unavailable to PRWORA-ineligible noncitizens. Except in the few states that support maintenance dialysis for noncitizens, they must rely on charity care or Emergency Medicaid, which pays for dialysis only when the need becomes an emergency. Not surprisingly, the costs for treating patients who rely on emergent dialysis are far higher than those associated with treating patients who receive maintenance care.[115]

When Grady decided to shutter its dialysis unit, all of its patients faced a loss of care, but the noncitizens had a harder time finding alternative providers. Indeed, the situation was so bleak that Grady contracted with Mexcare, an airline that specializes in medical repatriations, to fly its immigrant dialysis patients to their countries of origin. According to the *New York Times*, several dialysis patients took Grady up on the offer.[116] Eventually Grady was able to contract with an outpatient dialysis provider to treat its patients; but in 2011 during a dispute between that provider and Grady, at least one other patient was flown to Honduras.[117]

As these examples demonstrate, conflicting policies regarding noncitizens' access to care imposes significant costs on hospitals and the communities they serve. Laws limiting noncitizens' eligibility for publicly funded insurance programs contributed to Grady's financial problems. When Grady responded to its financial hardships by closing its dialysis unit, all of its patients, including those who were citizens, had to find new providers.

More broadly, the uncompensated costs of treating noncitizens are borne disproportionately by safety-net providers in communities with high concentrations of noncitizens. Although robust, nationwide data is lacking—in 2004 the General Accounting Office abandoned efforts to determine the costs due to problems gathering reliable data about the immigration status of patients—a 2011 paper by Mitchell and colleagues in the *Journal of Trauma* reported that Methodist Dallas Medical Center in Dallas, Texas, experienced a $4.3 million shortfall from 2005 through 2008 due to emergency room costs for indigent undocumented immigrants.[118] This figure took into account DSH funds, as well as money no longer available under the Medicare Modernization Act. When the ACA's reduction of DSH funds and the expiration of Medicare Modernization payments were taken into account, the loss the hospital would have experienced climbed to $7.9 million dollars. This figure likely underestimated the total uncompensated costs associated with treating immigrants, as it looked only at undocumented patients, not those who have legal status but were ineligible for federally funded insurance due to PRWORA.

[114] Kevin Sack, *Immigrants Cling to Fragile Lifeline at Safety-net Hospital*, N.Y. TIMES, Sept. 24, 2009, at A-16.

[115] Rajeev Rhagavan & Ricardo Nuila, *Survivors—Dialysis, Immigration, and U.S. Law*, 364 N. ENGL. J. MED. 2183, 2184 (2011), *available at* http://www.nejm.org/doi/pdf/10.1056/NEJMp1101195 ("Emergency dialysis is good for nobody. It places patients' lives at risk, and it results in more ER visits, more hospitalizations, and more blood transfusions than does scheduled dialysis. In total, these excesses result in costs of more than $200,000 per emergency-dialysis patient annually.").

[116] Kevin Sack, David Agren, & Catrin Einhorn, *Ailing Immigrants Find No Relief Back Home*, N.Y. TIMES, Jan. 1, 2010, at A-1.

[117] Kevin Sack, *Deal Reached on Dialysis for Immigrants*, N.Y. TIMES, Sept. 9, 2011, at A-11.

[118] Christopher D. Mitchell et al., *Who Will Cover the Cost of Undocumented Immigrant Trauma Care?*, 72 J. TRAUMA 609 612 (2012).

Barriers to coverage for noncitizens can also threaten the health of citizens in other ways. As Susan Oakie wrote in the *New England Journal of Medicine*, "laws and barriers that reduce [immigrants'] use of key preventive health services, such as immunizations and screenings for infectious disease make for bad public health policy," and "increase[] health care costs for everyone."[119] The citizen children of noncitizens face a special risk, both due to their parents' untreated illnesses and because their parents are often afraid of placing their children in contact with the healthcare system. More broadly, lack of preventive care for immigrants may help spread communicable diseases such as tuberculosis, which is more prevalent among immigrants than citizens.[120] Such arguments, however, need to be made cautiously so as not to reinforce popular fears about the public health threat posed by noncitizens.[121] As noted in section II, immigrants are for the most part healthier than citizens. The risks that immigrants pose to public health are caused less by their inherent contagiousness than by policies that make it hard for them to access timely and cost-effective care.

VI Conclusion

It is tempting to think that the immigration reform offers a solution to the problem of noncitizens' access to health insurance. It does not for two reasons; one practical, the other theoretical.

As a practical matter, any politically viable immigration reform bill is likely to maintain the status quo regarding healthcare for millions of noncitizens. For example, in 2013, a far-reaching bipartisan immigration reform bill passed the Senate which would have granted so-called "provisional status" to undocumented immigrants who had been within the United States continuously for at least ten years, paid taxes, and met certain other employment or educational criteria. [122] Immigrants with provisional status would have had a legal right to work in the United States and could begin the process of legalization after ten more years if the Secretary of Homeland Security certified the implementation of a southern border strategy. However, during the ten-plus year period in which they had provisional status, these immigrants would have remained ineligible to participate in the ACA health insurance exchanges.[123] Moreover, because the Senate bill reaffirmed PRWORA,[124] immigrants would have had to wait another five years after receiving legal status before becoming eligible for Medicaid or other programs subject to PRWORA. Thus, while providing some new legal protections for unauthorized immigrants presently residing within the United States, the

[119] Susan Oakie, *Perspective: Immigrants and Health Care—At the Intersection of Two Broken Systems*, 357 N. Eng. J. Med. 525, 526 (2007).

[120] Phillip M. Ricks et al., *Estimating the Burden of Tuberculosis among Foreign-Born Persons Acquired Prior to Entering the U.S., 2005–2009*, PLoS One, 6:11:e27405 (2011), http://www.ncbi.nlm.nih.gov/pmc/articles/PMC3226620/ (citing higher incidence of TB among immigrants to the United States than among the native-born population); Price, *Can U.S. Immigration Law*, at 40.

[121] Clark, *The Immigrant Health Care*, at 256–259.

[122] Border Security, Economic Opportunity, and Immigration Modernization Act, S. 744, 113th Cong. (2013), 159 Cong. Rec. S5329-03 (daily ed. Jun. 27, 2013).

[123] S. 744 at §2101(a)(d)(4)(C).

[124] *Id.* at § 2101(a)(d)(3)(A).

bill would have barred them from full membership in the American healthcare system for at least fifteen years.

The Senate bill was never taken up by the Republican-controlled House. And although some form of immigration reform is likely to be enacted in the years to come, it almost certainly will not provide noncitizens with more liberal access to publicly supported health insurance than did the Senate bill. As a result, immigration reform, if and when it comes, is unlikely to reduce the barriers that noncitizens face in accessing health insurance. Indeed, by providing more noncitizens with a quasi-legal status, enhancing their employment prospects and recognizing their right to remain in the country while denying them the right to participate in most publicly supported health insurance programs, immigration reform is likely to exacerbate the tensions at the intersection of health and immigration law.

The more enduring problem is that immigration reform cannot resolve the deep tensions within American health law and policy as to nature and breadth of community, solidarity, and obligation regarding healthcare. Americans both welcome and fear immigrants. We also treat healthcare both as a private good, allocated by the market, and as a public good, deserving of regulation, redistribution, and cross-subsidy. We accept that ability to pay should influence access, yet we also require hospitals to treat everyone facing an emergency regardless of their ability to pay, and we establish a plethora of programs to ensure that those who cannot pay for care on their own receive needed care.

Citizenship and immigration status lie at the crossroads of these conflicting perspectives, serving to demarcate the overlapping boundaries between health law's private and public spheres. In a society that prizes market individualism, citizenship and immigration status fix the borders of social solidarity and shared responsibility. In effect, by functioning as exclusionary criteria, citizenship and immigration status ensure that subsidized healthcare is not available to "all," only to those who "qualify." All others remain subject to the market. For this reason, as the scope of public programs broaden and the sphere of social solidarity enlarges, as they have under the ACA, the exclusion of noncitizens takes on a heightened significance, as it forms the remaining boundary that separates those "deserving" to be within the community of care and those who are relegated to the private market. It should, therefore, come as no surprise that even nations that offer so-called "universal" health insurance deny coverage to many noncitizens. Indeed, some theorists have gone so far as to argue that limitations based on citizenship are essential for the maintenance of social solidarity.[125] For community to exist, these theorists suggest, some groups must be left outside.

Yet regardless of citizenship's role in maintaining social solidarity, the borders of our healthcare system are inevitably as porous as the nation's physical borders. Although we cannot know the exact numbers, as future immigration rates will vary depending on a variety of factors, we do know that immigrants will continue to come in large numbers to the United States. Indeed, economic growth, as well as the financial viability of the Medicare trust fund to which immigrants contribute far more than they cost,[126] requires continued high levels of immigration. And when immigrants come, they will join those who are already here as

[125] *See, e.g.*, Linda S. Bosniak, *Membership, Equality, and the Difference that Alienage Makes*, 69 N.Y.U. L. Rev. 1047, 1053 (1994) (noting the argument that "the exclusion of aliens from access to various rights and benefits in this society properly preserves the benefits of membership for those deemed to belong within the moral boundaries of the nation's community").

[126] Zallman et al., *Immigrants Contributed*, at 1153, 1156.

taxpayers, neighbors, family members, workers, and healthcare providers. Like everyone else, they will contract illnesses and sometimes face catastrophic injuries. They will also experience chronic and preventable illnesses, many of which could be treated for less cost if primary care were more accessible.

Without question, immigrants will continue to need and use healthcare, and their providers will need to be paid. If they are not, the costs of immigrants' care will continue to be shifted to other payers, while straining the budgets of safety-net providers. Although the precise cost of limiting immigrants' access to insurance is difficult to quantify, for reasons suggested above, it will invariably increase as the immigrant population ages and requires more healthcare.

Despite embedded ambivalence, our health laws recognize that immigrants are members of the healthcare community. EMTALA demands that noncitizens receive emergency care, and Emergency Medicaid, the ACA, state programs, and even PRWORA all allow for public support for some healthcare given to noncitizens. Americans are not truly comfortable with leaving noncitizens, even those with less than full legal status, totally outside of our healthcare community.

Indeed, for all of its harshness, medical repatriation is the exception, not the rule. It is a practice that troubles us—it shocks our conscience—even as it illustrates the contradictions, economic costs, and ethical dilemmas that lie at the intersection of health and immigration law. It reminds us that borders are and will be crossed, that costs must be borne, and that while the most vulnerable will inevitably pay the steepest price for our attempts to delineate boundaries that cannot hold, we all end up paying a price.

When it comes to health, borders offer the illusion of security and community, but it is only an illusion, and a costly one at that. Unless we are willing to resolve our ambivalences by allowing noncitizens to die in the streets or be repatriated en masse—options that we rightly seem unwilling to adopt—noncitizens will continue to be a part of our healthcare system. Given that inevitability, the innumerable exclusions and hurdles that health law now imposes on noncitizens' access to insurance cannot in fact keep them out of the healthcare system. Rather, exclusions such as those barring immigrants not lawfully present from the ACA's exchanges and PRWORA's five-year bar simply serve to undermine prevention, overemphasize the use of emergency rooms, and shift costs onto overburdened safety-net providers. In short, by failing to accept that noncitizens are a part of our healthcare community, health law dooms effective health reform.

CHAPTER 47

AGING POPULATION

MARSHALL B. KAPP

I Introduction

THE United States and the international community[1] will be confronted in the coming years with a variety of legal and policy challenges relating to an aging population. Responses to these challenges will affect the regulation of clinical care at the individual level and the structure and financing of healthcare delivery for older persons as a group. This chapter covers an expansive array of issues, ranging from population to community to family to individual concerns, and ventures across financial, clinical, and psychosocial domains.

a. Demographic Background

The population is rapidly aging, both in absolute numbers and as a percentage of the whole. This trend is strongly projected to continue and even escalate for the foreseeable future.[2] In the United States, the proportion of the population aged sixty-five and older is projected to increase from 12.4% in 2000 to 19.6% in 2030; the number of persons sixty-five and older is expected to increase from approximately thirty-five million to an estimated seventy-one million in 2030 and the number of persons aged eighty and higher is expected to increase from 9.3 million in 2000 to 19.5 million in 2030.[3] This demographic phenomenon of delayed mortality is combining with declining national and global fertility rates to change the population makeup.[4]

1 Pew Research Cent, Attitudes About Aging: A Global Perspective (2014), *available at* http://www.pewglobal.org/files/2014/01/Pew-Research-Center-Global-Aging-Report-FINAL-January-30-20141.pdf; Sebastián J. Sánchez Rivera, *Worldwide Ageing: Findings, Norms, and Aspirations*, 79 REV. JURIDICA U.P.R 237 (2010).

2 Admin. on Aging., U.S. Dep't Health and Human Serv., A Profile of Older Americans 2012, *available at* http://www.aoa.gov/AoARoot/(S(2ch3qw55k1qylo45dbihar2u))/Aging_Statistics/Profile/2012/docs/2012profile.pdf.

3 Cent. Disease Control and Prevention, *Public Health and Aging: Trends in Aging—United States and Worldwide*, 52 MMWR 101 (Feb. 14, 2003) [hereinafter CDC].

4 James Hookway, *Baby Bust Spreads to Developing World*, WALL. ST. J. A1 (Mar. 20, 2014).

b. Changing Epidemiology of Aging and Its Disability Consequences

The changing demography is occurring concurrently with an epidemiologic transition in the leading causes of death. We have experienced a trend away from infectious diseases (like tuberculosis) and acute illness as the main sources of mortality to chronic diseases (such as cancer or heart disease) and degenerative illnesses that today can be treated and managed for a long period of time but cannot be cured. The combination of population aging and epidemiologic transition presents public health challenges. In the United States, roughly 80% of the age sixty-five and older population has at least one chronic condition (diabetes is the most common), and half have at least two chronic conditions.[5] Among other things, as Americans live longer, the prevalence of Alzheimer's disease, which doubles every five years after age sixty-five, is expected to increase markedly.[6]

Chronic conditions can lead to severe physical and/or mental disability. For instance, in the United States, arthritis affects almost two-thirds of people age sixty-five and older and is the leading cause of disability.[7] Because of this ailment and a variety of others, as well as the growing prevalence of Alzheimer's disease, other forms of dementia, and other mental conditions (such as depression and organic brain syndrome) adversely affecting cognitive and emotional functioning, many older Americans have substantial impairment in the ability to perform activities of daily living (ADLs).

c. Long-Term Services and Supports

Impaired ADLs are the primary reason that many older individuals require long-term services and supports (formerly termed "long-term care"). Long-term services and supports are "provided to people who need assistance to perform routine daily activities over an extended period due to disability or chronic illness. It includes a broad range of medical and non-medical services and supports provided by professionals as well as unpaid care provided by family and friends. Long-term services and supports may be provided in community-based or institutional settings."[8] Approximately 57% of the twelve million long-term services and supports recipients in the United States is age sixty-five or older.[9]

Largely (although this is beginning to change somewhat), the demarcation between institutional and home and community-based services and supports (HCBSS) depends on the type of physical location where the services are provided. Nursing homes, assisted living facilities, and other residential care communities ordinarily are considered loci of institutional care, while adult day service centers, home care (including home healthcare and

[5] CDC. [6] *Id.*

[7] U.S. Cent. Disease Control and Prevention, Arthritis-Related Statistics, *at* http://www.cdc.gov/arthritis/data_statistics/arthritis_related_stats.htm.

[8] Julie Robison et al., *Long-Term Supports and Services Planning for the Future: Implications from a Statewide Survey of Baby Boomers and Older Adults*, 45 GERONTOLOGIST 297, 298 (2014).

[9] H. Stephen Kaye et al., *Long-Term Care: Who Gets It, Who Provides It, Who Pays, and How Much?*, 29 HEALTH AFF. 11 (2010).

personal and homemaker services), and hospice programs outside of a dedicated hospice "house" have generally been characterized as home and community-based.

d. Financial Concerns and Their Structural Implications

The increased number of older people in American society will lead to increased national healthcare costs. The healthcare cost per capita for individuals sixty-five years old and above in the United States is three to five times greater than the cost for younger persons.[10] The continued growth in the older population, combined with advancing costly medical technology and the prevalence of chronic illness, will create upward pressure on healthcare spending. The primary public means of funding general health services for older Americans are covered in Medicare chapter and Medicaid chapter (this volume); private healthcare financing for older individuals still in the workforce or retired but still covered by an employment-based plan is discussed in chapter by Hall (this volume).

The imperative to contain healthcare expenditures for older people is likely to encourage experimentation with a variety of healthcare delivery structural modifications (Saver, this volume). Among these may be: encouragement of greater consumer reliance on the Medicare Part C (Medicare Advantage) option; development of accountable care organizations (ACOs) under the Affordable Care Act (ACA)'s Medicare Shared Savings program; and testing mechanisms for paying healthcare providers using alternatives to (for instance, prospective payment systems) or modifications of (such as pay-for-performance or value-based purchasing)[11] the traditional fee-for-service (FFS) cost-maximizing model.

The financial consequences associated with providing long-term services and supports to a chronically disabled aging population may be even more substantial. There are a variety of payment sources for long-term services and supports, whether institutional or home and community-based.[12] Private sector payment sources include out-of-pocket payments made by the service receiver or family members or friends on the receiver's behalf. Payments may be made through private long-term care (LTC) insurance policies.[13] However, when paid, formal care is needed, many people cannot afford to cover these expenses out of pocket, and very few people purchase private LTC insurance.[14] Public sector payment sources include, most prominently, Medicare (which pays mainly for postacute care, short-term rehabilitation) and Medicaid (accounting financially for almost half of national LTC expenditures).[15]

Additionally, the Older Americans Act (OAA) funnels federal dollars through a network of State Units on Aging (SUA) and Area Agencies on Aging (AAA) to fund an array of

[10] CDC.

[11] Eleanor D. Kinney, *The Affordable Care Act and the Medicare Program: Linking Medicare Payment to Quality Performance*, 68 N.Y. U. Annual Survey Am. L. 565 (2013).

[12] Institute of Medicine and National Research Council, Financing Long-Term Services and Supports for individuals with Disabilities and Older Adults: Workshop Summary (2014).

[13] Yong Li & Gail A. Jensen, *The Impact of Private Long-Term Care Insurance on the Use of Long-Term Care*, 48 Inquiry 34 (2011).

[14] Leslie A. Curry et al., *Individual Decision Making in the Non-Purchase of Long-Term Care Insurance*, 49 Gerontologist 560 (2009).

[15] Terence Ng et al., *Medicare and Medicaid in Long-Term Care*, 29 Health Aff. 22 (2010).

community-based services, such as home-delivered and congregate meals, transportation, senior centers, legal assistance, health promotion, and adult day programs.[16] Many states and localities authorize programs to serve older community-dwelling residents through separate state or local appropriations or the proceeds of dedicated ballot initiatives. Additionally, the U.S. Department of Veterans Affairs provides funding for community-based services to eligible veterans and their dependents.[17]

Medicaid has relied on nursing homes as the primary locus of care for Medicaid-dependent people with serious ADL impairments.[18] "Whereas most home and community-based long term services and supports are optional for states, nursing facility care is a mandatory Medicaid State Plan service, with the result that states' long-term services and supports spending historically has been skewed in favor of institutional care."[19] States are required to cover nursing facility services, including room and board, for beneficiaries ages twenty-one and over under their state Medicaid plans. The historic reliance on institutional services has been exacerbated by the unintended movement into nursing homes of severely, chronically mentally ill people who in earlier times would have resided in large public psychiatric asylums.[20]

Today, though, a slow but steady process of policy changes and infrastructure development has resulted in increased opportunities for HCBSS rather than nursing home placement, even for Medicaid-dependent people.[21] For the past several decades, the federal government has pushed, at first tentatively and experimentally,[22] in this direction. Some states have been early adopters and vigorous leaders in this effort,[23] while others have lagged behind.[24] Nonetheless,

> states now have a broad range of coverage options to select from when designing their long-term services and supports programs. In general, Medicaid law provides states with two broad authorities, which either cover certain long-term services and supports as a benefit under the Medicaid state plan or cover home and community-based long-term services and supports

[16] 42 U.S.C. §§ 3001-3058ff.

[17] U.S. Dep't of Veterans Aff., Geriatr. and Extended Care, Home and Community Based Services, *available at* http://www.va.gov/geriatrics/guide/longtermcare/Home_and_Community_Based_Services.asp.

[18] Lauren Harris-Kojetin et al., National Center for Health Statistics, Long-Term Care Services in the United States: 2013 Overview 38 (2013).

[19] Kaiser Commission on Medicaid and the Uninsured, Fact Sheet: Medicaid Long-Term Services and Supports: An Overview of Funding Authorities 1 (Sept. 2013).

[20] Gerald N. Grob, From Asylum to Community: Mental Health Policy in Modern America 268–270 (1991).

[21] Rosalie A. Kane, *Thirty Years of Home- and Community-Based Services: Getting Closer and Closer to Home*, 36 Generations 6 (2012).

[22] Robert Applebaum, *Channeling: What We Learned, What We Didn't, and What It All Means Twenty-Five Years Later*, 36 Generations 21 (2012).

[23] Charley Reed, *A Matter of Balance: Washington and Oregon States' Long-Term-Care System Model*, 36 Generations 59 (2012).

[24] Susan C. Reinhard et al., AARP, Commonwealth Fund, & SCAN Foundation, Raising Expectations: A State Scorecard on Long-Term Services and Supports for Older Adults, People with Physical Disabilities, and Family Caregivers (2014), *available at* http://www.longtermscorecard.org/~/media/Microsite/Files/2014/Reinhard_LTSS_Scorecard_web_619v2.pdf.

> through a waiver program which permits states to ignore certain Medicaid requirements in the provision of these services.[25]

The number of American nursing home residents aged sixty-five and older decreased by 20% from 2000 to 2013.[26] Nursing home occupancy rates also are falling.[27]

There are several explanations for the shift among long-term services and supports consumers away from nursing home placement and toward HCBSS. First, most older people prefer to age in place, even with substantial disability, rather than move to an institutional setting. Second, there is widespread support for the position that HCBSS usually are cost-effective in the long run as compared to institutional care,[28] and that support appears to be substantiated by the empirical evidence.[29] A third explanation for the deinstitutionalization of long-term services and supports is the purported robust connection between feelings of independence, fostered by participation in HCBSS, on the one hand, and consumer-experienced quality of life, on the other.[30]

Fourth, the states are under legal,[31] and associated political,[32] pressure to provide long-term services and supports to beneficiaries whose care is subsidized by Medicaid or other state funds in the most integrated (that is, the least institutional) service setting possible, if that is the client's desire. The most integrated service setting model driving many state deinstitutionalization initiatives[33] is based on the Supreme Court's interpretation of Title 2 (Public Services) of the Americans with Disabilities Act[34] in *Olmstead v. L.C.*[35]

e. Family Issues

Healthcare delivery and financing for older individuals are intertwined with family dynamics. Families may be involved in the healthcare of older relatives by supporting the patient's

[25] Kirsten J. Colello, *Medicaid Coverage of Long-Term Services and Supports*, Cong. Resrch Serv. 7-5700, R43328, at Summary page (Dec. 5, 2013).

[26] U.S. Census Bureau, P23-212, 65+ in the United States: 2010, at 134 (2014).

[27] National Investment Center for the Senior Housing and Care Industry, NICMAP Key Metrics 2Q 2014, *available at* http://www.nic.org.

[28] Charlene Harrington et al., *Do Medicaid Home and Community Based Service Waivers Save Money?*, 30 Home Health Serv. Quart. 198 (2011).

[29] Wendy Fox-Grage & Jenna Walls, AARP Pub. Pol'y Inst., *State Studies Find Home and Community-Based Services to Be Cost-Effective*, at 12 (2013). *Contra* Avalere Health, Medicaid-Financed Home and Community-Based Services Research: A Synthesis 12 (2007).

[30] AARP Pub. Pol'y Inst., Beyond 50.3: A Report to the Nation on Independent Living and Disability (2013).

[31] Robert Garner, *Litigation as a Tool for Forcing Accountability in State-Based Long Term Care Settings for the Intellectually and Developmentally Disabled: An Illinois Focus*, 22 Annals Health L. Advance Directives 121 (2013).

[32] Herb Sanderson, *Improving Long-Term-Care Supports Means Advocating Inside and Out*, 36 Generations 74 (Spr. 2012).

[33] Dann Milne, *Olmstead, New Freedom, and Real Choice System Change Grants: Bringing the Disability Movement to Older Adults*, 36 Generations 44 (Spr. 2012).

[34] 42 U.S.C. §§ 12101-12213.

[35] 527 U.S. 581 (1999); Samuel R. Bagenstos, *The Past and Future of Deinstitutionalization Litigation*, 34 Cardozo L. Rev. 1 (2012).

decision-making process (for instance, accompanying the patient to medical appointments and asking questions to and explaining information from the provider). Families also may be involved in sharing or partnering in the decision-making process, serving as a formal or informal substitute decision-maker for a patient who is not decisionally capable, or by supplying or managing the finances needed to pay for care.

In the HCBSS arena, the reliance placed on the role of family caregiving presents serious challenges for the continued success and expansion of this endeavor. Instability of the paid, professional workforce also poses difficult but different questions for the future of HCBSS and for long-term care more broadly.[36]

Demographic trends, changing family structures away from traditional man-woman marriages that produced children and lasted forever, and the increasing involvement of women in the paid workforce portend difficulty in recruiting and maintaining an adequate supply of family members to care at home for needy older baby boomer relatives.[37] Additionally, family caregivers experience, beyond tangible financial and career sacrifices,[38] physical and emotional stresses, often manifesting as adverse changes in caregivers' own health and/or family conflict and dysfunction. The increasing number and complexity of tasks that family caregivers, especially spouses,[39] undertake to keep chronically disabled loved ones at home exacerbate the caregiver stresses. These stresses threaten the continued availability of sufficient numbers of family caregivers.[40]

In light of the clinical, financial, and social forces enumerated above, this chapter selectively overviews some salient challenges likely to arise at the intersection of law, healthcare, and aging during the next part of the twenty-first century. How these challenges are dealt with will impact the clinical care of individual patients and the well-being of the older population collectively.

II Impaired Decisional Capacity

a. Explanation of the Issue

Although not all individuals are affected in the same way, negative age-related cognitive changes, including impaired memory and diminished reasoning ability, do occur at the group level.[41] The prevalence of adverse cognitive changes within the older population will

[36] Edward Alan Miller, *The Affordable Care Act and Long-Term Care: Comprehensive Reform or Just Tinkering Around the Edges?*, 24 J. Aging & Soc. Pol'y 101, 105–106 (2012).

[37] Donald Redfoot et al., AARP Pub. Pol'y Inst., *The Aging of the Baby Boom and the Growing Care Gap: A Look at Future Declines in the Availability of Family Caregivers* (2013).

[38] Susan C. Reinhard et al., AARP Pub. Pol'y Inst., *Employed Family Caregivers Providing Complex Chronic Care* 7 (2013).

[39] Susan Reinhard et al., AARP Publ Pol'y Inst., *Family Caregivers Providing Complex Chronic Care to Their Spouses* (2014).

[40] Debra H. Kroll, *To Care or Not to Care: The Ultimate Decision for Adult Caregivers in a Rapidly Aging Society*, 21 Temp. Pol. & Civ. Rts L. Rev. 403 (2012).

[41] Mary Helen McNeal, *Slow Lawyering: Representing Seniors in Light of Cognitive Changes Accompanying Aging*, 117 Penn. St. L.Rev.1081 (2013).

increase over the coming years, as various forms of dementia and other cognition-altering conditions become more commonplace.[42] This rising prevalence will challenge the United States and other countries economically and socially,[43] as well as ethically.[44] A patient's cognitive impairment does not necessarily rule out the possibility of some level of shared decision-making, or of real patient-centered care more generally.[45] However, age-related cognitive changes interfering with decisional capacity will challenge professionals involved in the medical decision-making context in their endeavors to engage older patients directly in the process of informed consent and shared decision-making.[46] To give perspective to this challenge, according to one large study, at forty-eight hours of hospitalization almost half of older patients required surrogate involvement, including 23% who could not participate in joint decision-making and therefore needed all decisions made by the surrogate.[47]

Difficulties in achieving informed, voluntary decision-making results reflecting the values of decisionally impaired older patients are common when making treatment choices with and for individuals with advanced, irreversible illness who are approaching the end of their lives. Such individuals are not able to make and express autonomous choices at precisely the time when key decisions must be made and implemented. Another particularly challenging and unexamined legal space concerns the burgeoning number of incapacitated "unbefriended" elders who lack willing, available family or friends to advocate or engage in substitute decision-making for them.[48] The "unbefriended" issue arises because of a combination of demographic and family structure changes in American society, namely older individuals today outliving their decisional capacity and either never married or had children or, alternatively, outliving their spouse, children, and other relatives.

b. Relevant Law

This section outlines law relating to medical decision-making for decisionally impaired older persons. Although the relevant law theoretically addresses the problems associated with decisional capacity in elders, including end-of-life decision-making, in reality it often does so incompletely and ineffectively. Consequently, the next section also points out the current law's inadequacies and includes recommendations for legal and other changes aimed

42 Alzheimer's Disease International, World Alzheimer Report 2013: Journey of Caring: An Analysis of Long-Term Care for Dementia (2013), *available at* http://www.alz.co.UK/research/WorldAlzheimerReport2013.

43 *U.S. Senate Comm. on Approp., Hearing, Taking a Toll on Families and the Economy: The rising Cost of Alzheimer's in America* (Feb. 26, 2014), *available at* http://www.appropriations.senate.gov/ht-labor.cfm?method=hearings.view&id=f7a929d6-535d-4264-b9a4-f3c9d2f9947c.

44 Jason Karlawish, *How Are We Going to Live With Alzheimer's Disease?*, 33 Health Aff. 541 (2014).

45 Kenneth Brummel-Smith & Alexander Halperin, *Patient-Centered Care for People with Cognitive Impairment Is Possible in Primary Care*, 37 Generations 87 (Fall 2013).

46 J. Randall Curtis & Mark R. Tonelli, *Shared Decision-Making in the ICU: Value, Challenges, and Limitations*, 183 Am. J. Respir. & Crit. Care Med. 840 (2011).

47 Alexia M. Torke et al., *Scope and Outcomes of Surrogate Decision Making Among Hospitalized Older Adults*, 174 JAMA Intern. Med. 370 (2014).

48 Thaddeus Mason Pope, *Making Medical Decisions for Patients Without Surrogates*, 369 N. Eng. J. Med. 1976 (2013).

at better aligning clinical practice with legal and ethical aspirations regarding autonomy and respect for the older patient.

When an older person with impaired cognitive or emotional capacity lacks adequate decisional capacity, the healthcare provider is not relieved of the duty to obtain informed consent for medical interventions. Rather the provider must work with someone else who is willing and able to act as a surrogate for the patient.

Judicial precedents recognize a federal constitutional right, under the Fourteenth Amendment Due Process protection of liberty, for a decisionally capable adult (with no upper age limit) to make personal medical choices. These precedents also make clear that a person does not forfeit the right to make medical decisions just because he or she has become decisionally incapable; rather the right remains intact but must be exercised for the patient's by a legally authorized surrogate.[49] However, the Supreme Court has held that the extent and conditions of proxy (including family) medical decision-making authority are a matter of state legislative, rather than federal constitutional, policy.[50]

There are several ways in which a surrogate for a decisionally incapacitated patient may become legally authorized to make medical decisions. The older person may, while mentally capable, use an advance planning instrument, such as a durable power of attorney (DPOA) for healthcare, to voluntarily delegate future medical decision-making authority to another. The DPOA consists of a written document in which one individual (the principal) appoints an agent (attorney-in-fact) to make future decisions for the principal. The agent is expected to make specific clinical decisions based on the patient's substituted judgment, choosing what the patient would choose if contemporaneously able to make and express personal decisions.

DPOAs fall into two categories. An immediate power comes into effect as soon as an agent is named. By contrast, in a springing power, the legal authority transfers (springs) from the principal to the agent only when a specified future event occurs, such as declaration of the principal's incapacity by a designated number of examining physicians.

When a patient is decisionally incapable but has not previously appointed a healthcare decision-making agent, in a majority of the states, healthcare providers may rely on legislation empowering family members and specified other persons to make medical decisions for incapacitated patients. In states with family consent statutes, the approved procedure ordinarily consists of documenting unanimous agreement among the attending physician and specified relatives or others, listed in a specified order of preference. Even in almost all the states without family consent statutes, courts nonetheless recognize the family's authority to exercise the incapacitated patient's decisional rights under common law or the state's constitution.

When there is no DPOA, state family consent statute, or judicial precedent empowering the family to act, or in those relatively rare circumstances in which family members strongly and irreconcilably disagree about the best course, a guardianship or conservatorship may transfer decision-making power formally from an incapacitated patient to another. The court may appoint a surrogate (a guardian or conservator) authorized to make certain decisions on behalf of a decisionally incapacitated person (the ward). The process is usually

49 Cruzan v. Director, Missouri Dep't Health, 497 U.S. 261, 275–279 & 287–291 (1990).

50 *Id.* at 280.

initiated by a petition filed by the family or another caregiver. This petition is combined with a review by the court of the sworn affidavit or live testimony of a physician who is familiar with the patient.

Total or plenary guardianship involves extensive deprivation of an individual's decision-making rights. The least restrictive/least intrusive alternative doctrine makes a limited guardianship preferred whenever feasible. Courts possess statutory authority to limit the guardian's power to decide only those particular types of decisions the ward personally is incapable of handling through rational deliberation.

Traditionally, the guardian made decisions consistent with the guardian's view, as a trust agent, of the patient's best interests. Although a few states still expect guardians to act according to the best interests standard, the modern trend is toward a substituted judgment standard under which the guardian is obligated to make those decisions that the patient would make, according to the patient's own values, if the patient were presently able to make and express decisions through a rational process of understanding and analysis.

Despite this legal substructure pertaining to surrogate decision-making, there are problems in harmonizing patient values, on one side, and medical interventions to which patients are subjected, on the other. Only a small percentage of older adults create a surrogate advance directive (AD) while still decisionally capable. When a surrogate has been appointed by the patient, operation of statute, or a court order, the surrogate may not know what treatment the patient would want under the circumstances, may refuse to make any decision because of emotional or other paralysis, may consciously make a choice he or she thinks is best even when it clearly contradicts the patient's previously indicated values, or may act in the surrogate's own financial or other interest rather than consistent with the patient's substituted judgment. Moreover, physicians sometimes purposely nullify through their actions surrogate decisions with which they disagree.[51]

To address some of these problems, particularly regarding end-of-life treatment, a national movement encourages states to use POLST (Physician Orders for Life-Sustaining Treatment) forms for appropriate critically and irreversibly ill patients.[52] POLST is a set of medical orders written by a physician (with the informed concurrence of the patient or surrogate) instructing other healthcare providers, such as emergency medical squads, about the treatment of a patient with advanced, irreversible illness under specific future circumstances. Various states encourage the incorporation of a POLST paradigm into medical practice through a combination of legislative, regulatory, and clinical education and consensus-building strategies. Because the POLST is a medical order written by a medical provider, it is more likely to be honored than a traditional instruction or surrogate AD written by the patient.[53]

However, improving the quality of end-of-life treatment requires educating healthcare providers, the public, and legal and spiritual advisers[54] about the AD and POLST

[51] *E.g.*, Nadia N. Sawicki, *A New Life for Wrongful Living*, 58 N.Y. L. Sch. L. Rev. 279 (2013/2014).

[52] Charles P. Sabatino & Naomi Karp, AARP Pub. Pol'y Inst., *Improving Advanced Illness Care: The Evolution of State POLST Programs* (2011).

[53] Neil S. Wenger et al., *Implementation of Physician Orders for Life Sustaining Treatment in Nursing Homes in California: Evaluation of a Novel Statewide Dissemination Mechanism*, 28 J. Gen. Intern. Med. 51 (2013).

[54] Kathryn Tucker, *Counseling Clients Who Are Terminally Ill*, 37 Wm. Mitchell L. Rev. 117 (2010).

opportunities available under state law.[55] Additional policy efforts could increase the use of POLST and other planning tools. Modifications in Medicare payment policies could incentivize autonomy- and quality-of-care-enhancing behaviors on the part of providers and older patients.[56] States could clarify relevant laws and processes. At the least, states should include explicit authorization, where it does not now exist, for physicians to write POLSTs for consenting patients or surrogates, as well as clear provisions of legal immunity against criminal and civil liability for healthcare professionals honoring a POLST in good faith. States without statutes explicitly conferring default surrogate decision-making authority for incapacitated patients lacking ADs should enact them. Further, legal tools could compel healthcare providers to respect the treatment preferences of patients with advanced, irreversible illness as expressed contemporaneously or through an AD or POLST.[57]

Regarding "unbefriended" elders, a few program models exist as a starting point to develop efficient processes to deal with situations involving treatment decisions for this group.[58] For example, programs experiment with such options as physician consensus, an internal committee structure, emergency guardianship for life-and-death matters, public guardianship offices,[59] professional guardians (when the ward has sufficient assets to pay for this arrangement),[60] and volunteer guardianship projects.[61] Nevertheless, there is potential for the law to continue clarifying theoretical matters and operational details pertaining to decision-making for incapacitated unbefriended persons.

III Long-Term Services and Supports

As explained in the Introduction, a substantial, growing percentage of older individuals require long-term services and supports (LTSS) because of significant impairments in the ability to successfully carry out everyday activities of daily living (ADLs) and/or instrumental activities of daily living (IADLs) independently.[62] LTSS range from skilled nursing care provided within institutions like nursing homes or long-term care hospitals to HCBSS

[55] Harvey M. Tettlebaum, *Quality Measurements, Payment, and the Law: Disincentives to Physician-Patient Discussions of End-of-Life Care*, 6 J. Health & Life Sci. L. 63 (2013).

[56] Muriel R. Gillick, *How Medicare Shapes the Way We Die*, 8 J. Health & Biomed. L. 27 (2012).

[57] Nicole Marie Saitta & Samuel D. Hodge, Jr., *Wrongful Prolongation of Life—A Cause of Action that Has Not Gained Traction Even Though a Physician Has Disregarded a "Do Not Resuscitate" Order*, 30 Temp. J. Sci. Tech. & Envtl. L. 221 (2011).

[58] Rebecca L. Volpe & Deborah Steinman, *Peeking Inside the Black Box: One Institution's Experience Developing Policy for Unrepresented Patients*, 36 Hamline L. Rev. 265 (2013).

[59] Pamela B. Teaster et al., *Wards of the State: A National Study of Public Guardianship*, 37 Stetson L. Rev. 193 (2007).

[60] Alison Barnes, *The Virtues of Corporate and Professional Guardians*, 31 Stetson L. Rev. 941 (2002).

[61] ABA Comm'n on L. & Aging, Court Volunteer Guardianship Monitoring Handbooks, *available at* http://www.americanbar.org/groups/law_aging/resources/guardianship_law_practice/court_volunteer_guardianshipmonitoring.html.

[62] U.S. Census Bur., Amer. Community Survey (2012), *at* http://factfinder2.census.gov/faces/tableservices/jsf/pages/productview.xhtml?pid=ACS_12_1YR_S1810&prodType=table.

provided—on either a compensated or gratuitous basis[63]—by family members or friends,[64] frequently supplemented by paid professionals.[65]

The law and policy around long-term services and supports is in flux. On September 13, 2013, a federal advisory commission on long-term care issued a comprehensive Report with twenty-eight recommendations to Congress, as well as an Alternative Report written by dissenting commission members.[66] The recommendations included: maintaining and strengthening a person- and family-centered LTSS system focused on both the person with cognitive or functional limitations and the family caregiver; revising scope of practice laws to broaden opportunities for professional and direct care workers with demonstrated competency; and adjusting Medicare payment models for postacute care to emphasize the services provided instead of the service location. The main thrust of the Alternative Report was a call for a new public financing program.

Neither the majority Report nor the Alternative Report have been addressed by Congress. The Bipartisan Policy Center, the only Washington, D.C.–based think tank that actively promotes bipartisanship, has signaled its intent to "propose a series of bipartisan policy options to improve the quality and efficiency of publicly and privately financed long-term care."[67] The topics of financing for,[68] and improving quality control over, LTSS will receive substantial regulatory, political, and scholarly attention in coming years.

There are challenges at the intersection of law and geriatric long-term care. One is how to instill a stronger homelike culture into institutional settings, by empowering residents, families, and facility staff to influence institutional policies and details of everyday operations.[69] Another is dealing with changing demographic and family dynamics that threaten to constrict the availability of family members to provide informal, uncompensated care to older relatives. The latter challenge was reflected in a 2014 AARP multistate caregiving advocacy campaign, including endorsement of the proposed Caregiver Advise, Record, Enable (CARE) Act.[70] This act proposed three things: record the name of the family caregiver when a loved one is admitted to a hospital or rehabilitation facility; notify the family caregiver if the loved one is to be discharged to another facility or back home; and require the facility to provide live instruction and explanation of the medical tasks—such as

[63] Marshall B. Kapp, *For Love, Legacy, or Pay: Legal and Pecuniary Aspects of Family Caregiving*, 14 Care Mgt. J. 205 (2013).

[64] Reinhard, *Employed Family Caregivers*.

[65] U.S. Cent. Disease Control, Nat'l Cent. Health Stat., Long-Term Care Serv. in the U.S.: 2013 Overview, *available at* http://www.cdc.gov/nchs/nsltcp/nsltcp_products.htm.

[66] *U.S. Senate, Commission on Long-Term Care, Rep't to Congress* (Sept. 18, 2013), *available at* http://www.medicareadvocacy.org/wp-content/uploads/2014/01/Commission-on-Long-Term-Care-Final-Report-9-18-13-00042470.pdf.

[67] Bipartisan Pol'y Cent., America's Long-Term Care Crisis: Challenges in Financing and Delivery 2 (Apr. 2014), *available at* http://bipartisanpolicy.org/sites/default/files/BPC%20Long-Term%20Care%20Initiative.pdf.

[68] Tracy A. Lustig & Steve Olson, Financing Long-Term Services and Supports for Individuals with Disabilities and Older Adults (2013).

[69] Marshall B. Kapp, *Culture Change in Nursing Homes: Legal Apprehensions and Opportunities*, 53 Gerontologist 718 (2013).

[70] *Available at* http://blog.aarp.org/wp-content/uploads/2014/02/CAREGIVING-CAREAct-OnePager-Design-NATIONAL-2-18-14.pdf.

medication management, injections, wound care, and transfers—that the family caregiver will perform at home.

IV Dangers Posed to, and by, Older People: Societal Reactions and the Healthcare System's Responsibilities

Older persons may be particularly vulnerable to victimization and, conversely, may through their behavior pose special kinds of danger to other persons as well as to themselves. The law attempts to prevent or ameliorate the harmful effects of each of these types of danger.

a. Dangers to the Older Person Posed by Others

i. Explanation of the Problem

Many older individuals, particularly those compromised by cognitive decline,[71] are vulnerable to the risk of physical, psychological, and financial mistreatment at the hands of family members or others. In the healthcare sphere, elder mistreatment often takes the form of a pattern of acts (or omissions) rather than a single instance. In addition to abuse and exploitation, elder mistreatment may be manifested in the form of neglect. These acts or omissions often occur in the older person's home or that of a relative with whom the older victim resides, making it especially difficult for professionals, friends, and other family members to detect in a timely fashion. Only in the last several decades has the social phenomenon of elder mistreatment, both global[72] and domestic, been acknowledged publicly in the same way as child abuse and domestic violence.[73]

This problem is compounded by the reluctance of many older persons to cooperate in reporting and investigating their own arguable mistreatment. For example, a decisionally capable but physically vulnerable older adult may passively accept physical or emotional abuse, financial exploitation, or neglect of basic needs like hygiene or medications at the hands of a family caregiver out of fear that making a report to Adult Protective Services (APS) might result in removal from the home environment to a nursing home.

As discussed in section I.e., families are increasingly involved in caring for older relatives who need some form of long-term care because of deficits in the ability to perform ADLs or IADLs. The family caregiving experience can take a huge physical and emotional toll on the caregivers.[74] Spouses are particularly likely to perform demanding medical/nursing tasks

[71] XinQi Dong et al., *Elder Abuse and Dementia: A Review of the Research and Health Policy*, 33 Health Aff. 642 (2014).

[72] Wendy Lacey, *Neglectful to the Point of Cruelty? Elder Abuse and Rights of Older Persons in Australia*, 36 Sydney L. Rev. 99–130 (2014).

[73] Richard J. Bonnie & Robert B. Wallace (eds.), Elder Mistreatment: Abuse, Neglect, and Exploitation in an Aging America (2003).

[74] Gary Epstein-Lubow, *A Family Disease: Witnessing Firsthand the Toll that Dementia Takes on Caregivers*, 33 Health Aff. 708 (2014).

such as medication management, wound care, and using meters and monitors.[75] Rarely, but sometimes, family care may be deficient, neglectful, or worse, jeopardizing the safety of the vulnerable, dependent older person. Other than tangentially, through general state mandatory or voluntary reporting statutes (noted in section IV.a.ii.), the law has not dealt with how to monitor home care provided by family caregivers.[76] Unresolved issues include whether healthcare professionals should be responsible for directly monitoring the quality of care; what obligation, if any, they have to act in response to knowledge of substandard care; and what legal immunities, if any, they should have if they intervene.

ii. Relevant Law

At the federal level, the Older Americans Act (OAA) includes specific provisions (Titles II, III, IV, and VII) that authorize grant funding to states for programs that combat elder mistreatment.[77] Additionally, an Elder Justice Act (EJA) had been introduced regularly in Congress since 2002 and was enacted (in modified form) as part of the 2010 ACA. The EJA creates a new federal body, the Elder Justice Coordinating Council, to make recommendations to the Department of Health and Human Services about coordinating elder mistreatment enforcement by federal, state, local, and private agencies. Additionally, the EJA authorizes spending federal revenues on: APS (described later in this section); establishment of Elder Abuse, Neglect, and Exploitation Forensic Centers to assist law enforcement agencies in prosecuting elder mistreatment; training programs and support for the Long-Term Care Ombudsman Program (LTCOP) (described in later this section); and training, recruitment, and incentives to attract people to enter or maintain careers in long-term care. However, congressional appropriations to implement these provisions lag substantially behind the authorizing legislation.

The EJA notwithstanding, most of the legal activity targeted at preventing and remedying elder mistreatment has taken place, and likely will continue, at the state and local levels.[78] Every state has in place statutes and regulations dealing with this subject. Some states rely on generic APS laws that set up systems, operating through local government agencies, to make available health and social service interventions to willing older, vulnerable persons to protect them from the risks of abuse and neglect (including self-neglect, discussed in sections IV.b.i. and IV.b.ii.). Some states also deal more specifically with elder mistreatment in state criminal codes, domestic violence laws, and probate statutes.

State laws generally allow local APS agencies to impose beneficial services on unwilling recipients. With small exceptions, under most pertinent statutes, unconsented-to interventions may be instituted for a very short period of time on an emergency basis. However, the intervention must then be discontinued or else continued only under the authority of a

[75] Reinhard et al., *Family Caregivers.*

[76] Will Pridmore, *Expanded Home and Community-Based Services Under the PPACA and LGBT Elders: Problem Solved?*, 22 ANNALS HEALTH L. ADVANCE DIRECTIVE 108, 119 (2013).

[77] Xinqi Dong, *Elder Abuse: Research, Practice, and Health Policy*, 54 GERONTOLOGIST 153, 157–158 (2014).

[78] Marie-Therese Connolly, *Policy Update: How Change Happens*, 21 TEMP. POL. & CIV. RTS. L. REV. 329 (2012).

court order based on a finding that the proposed services recipient lacks an adequate level of capacity to autonomously accept or refuse the offered services.

Relatedly, every state has a statute that either mandates or permits certain named categories of people, such as healthcare professionals, to report cases of suspected elder mistreatment to the local APS agency. There are concerns, however, with mandatory or permissive elder mistreatment reporting statutes as an instrument of health and social policy. It is unclear how many older people really are unable and/or unwilling to speak for themselves. Further, compliance with mandatory reporting statutes is middling. It is not clear that health and human services professionals are uniquely situated to be the earliest detectors of elder mistreatment nor that they possess the necessary knowledge, tools, and inclination to fulfill that responsibility. It may be that at least some professionals require a threat of potential criminal prosecution or explicit assurance of legal immunity to stimulate them to report suspicions to legal authorities. On the other hand, professionals anecdotally claim to often remain silent about suspicions concerning elder mistreatment despite the existence of statutory protections for good faith reporters. Alternatives to the current legal approaches, such as improved professional education and better funding for social services, might be more effective in facilitating early detection, investigation, and appropriate intervention.

One safety and quality oversight model that might be adapted to family caregiving in the home is the long-term care ombudsman program created by the Older Americans Act. Ombudsman programs supply staff and volunteers to investigate and resolve care complaints made by or on behalf of older individuals who are institutional residents. Different programs have different personalities and orientations to their assigned advocacy role, ranging from very adversarial toward facilities to a more consultative and conciliatory approach to problem solving, with many points in between.

b. Self-Imposed Dangers to the Older Person

i. *Explanation of Problems*

The majority of American jurisdictions include self-neglect as a separate category of elder mistreatment in mandatory or permissive reporting and intervention laws. A significant percentage of older adults, mainly living alone, do not regularly attend to their own needs or well-being regarding healthcare, hygiene, nutrition, and other matters.[79] The majority of cases reported to APS agencies by health and social service professionals and family members are triggered by suspected self-neglect. The healthcare system expends considerable efforts trying to intervene in these situations to prevent increased rates of hospitalization, nursing home placement, and even death.[80]

Besides neglecting their own basic human needs, there are other ways in which older individuals, through their conduct, may pose serious risks to themselves. For instance, continuing to drive a motor vehicle after the driver has become temporarily or permanently

[79] Laura Mosqueda & XinQi Dong, *Elder Abuse and Self-Neglect: "I Don't Care Anything About Going to the Doctor, to Be Honest . . ."*, 306 J. AM. MED. ASS'N 532 (2011).

[80] Alexander K. Smith, Bernard Lo, & Louise Aronson, *Elder Self-Neglect—How Can a Physician Help?*, 269 N. ENG. J. MED. 2476 (2013).

seriously impaired physically (such as by sensory diminishment) and/or mentally (such as by confusion) creates the risk of an accident and injury.[81] In a similar vein, maintaining functioning firearms in the home may pose a risk of harm by suicide or accident.[82]

ii. Relevant Law

Most states treat self-neglect by an older person as a category of elder mistreatment justifying, or even requiring, paternalistic government intervention. When an individual refuses offered APS interventions, state statutes generally empower courts to issue orders under the state's parens patriae authority authorizing an APS agency to provide services over the objections of an unwilling beneficiary. The threshold for issuing such an order, at least on a temporary emergency basis, in most states is an individual's need for those services. This means that sometimes the older person's autonomous choice to decline or limit outside interventions may be overruled. For instance, a court operating under a broad interpretation of parens patriae may have difficulty distinguishing between self-neglect justifying APS intervention over the individual's objection, on one hand, and a rational choice made by a cognitively and emotionally capable individual or an authorized surrogate decision-maker to decline or limit some types of medical treatment in specific situations, on the other. Thus, a court may grant an APS motion to admit an older person to a hospital for treatment of an infection even though the person would prefer to stay at home knowing the risk of dying with the infection. Only a few states have enacted statutes clarifying this distinction, expressly protecting the right of an individual to refuse medical treatment even in situations that otherwise might be interpreted as self-neglect.

c. Dangers Posed by Older People to Others

Many of the same behaviors, such as driving a motor vehicle or firearms possession when impaired, that carry foreseeable risks of harm for the older person also entail dangers to others. The obligations, if any, owed by the older individual and perhaps family members to third parties who may be placed at foreseeable risk because of the older person's activities are governed by state tort law.[83] The tort standard of reasonable conduct under the circumstances historically has taken into account the physical and mental infirmities of old age. "At the same time, the conduct of the [infirm older person] must be reasonable in the light of the person's knowledge of his infirmity, which is treated merely as one of the circumstances under which the person acts."[84]

[81] Nazan Aksan et al., *Naturalistic Distraction and Driving Safety in Older Drivers*, 55 HUM. FACTORS 841 (2013).

[82] Brian Mertens & Susan B. Sorenson, *Current Considerations About the Elderly and Firearms*, 102(3) AM. J. PUB. HEALTH 396 (2012).

[83] Vaughn E. James, *No Help for the Helpless: How the Law Has Failed to Serve and Protect Persons Suffering from Alzheimer's Disease*, 7 J. HEALTH & BIOMED. L. 407 (2012).

[84] DAN B. DOBBS, ROBERT E. KEETON, & DAVID G. OWEN, PROSSER AND KEETON ON TORTS 176 (5th ed. 1984).

Similarly, health and human services providers owe reasonable care under the circumstances to innocent third parties who are placed in foreseeable peril because of the behavior of their older patients. Key to the potential imposition of liability in specific cases is the reasonable foreseeability of harm posed by the older person.

For older individuals who pose a risk to others while driving a motor vehicle, statutes in most jurisdictions address the role of the individual's physician by mandating a report to drivers' licensing authorities (ordinarily, the state Department of Motor Vehicles) of any medical condition that might be hazardous to driving. The American Medical Association and National Highway Traffic Safety Administration advise physicians to comply with state mandatory driving hazard reporting statutes, but only after conducting a thorough examination and counseling the risky patient to discontinue or limit driving activities voluntarily.[85]

The physician's legal duties are less clear for firearms in the older person's home. Statutes do not impose an affirmative obligation on the physician to investigate the presence of firearms, but neither do they, or extant case law (with the exception of one Circuit Court of Appeals decision upholding the restrictive Florida Firearm Owners' Privacy Act),[86] prohibit such inquiry. State mandatory reporting statutes pertaining to elder mistreatment, including self-neglect, might be interpreted to include situations in which the physician becomes aware of danger associated with firearms in the home, but there is no case law testing that interpretation. The courts may eventually recognize an affirmative civil tort obligation on the part of at least the primary care provider. This obligation might be drawn from analogy to the two *Tarasoff* decisions imposing, respectively, a duty to warn[87] foreseeable victims about the credible dangers posed by a patient and a duty to go beyond warning to affirmatively protect a foreseeable victim from the credible danger posed by a patient.[88] The duty to protect might also be extended to situations of foreseeable self-harm by the patient.

Another frequent situation in which an older person may place someone else at risk arises when mentally compromised elders act out in an agitated and physically aggressive manner toward their own healthcare workers. In the leading reported case, the California Supreme Court denied recovery to injured healthcare workers in such a situation based on application of the assumption of risk doctrine.[89] This legal doctrine furthers an important policy interest in this context. If families were exposed to liability when their demented loved ones harmed professional caregivers coming into the home, many more families likely would be much quicker to admit the elder to a nursing home rather than keep the person at home (consistent with the person's wishes) where there is exposure to liability for assault. Limiting liability exposure for the acts of agitated, aggressive demented individuals through the assumption of risk doctrine thus encourages families to provide care in the home.

85 Am. Med. Ass'n. & Natl. Highway Traffic Safety Admin., Physicians' Guide to Assessing and Counseling Older Drivers (2010).

86 Wollschlaeger v. State of Florida, U.S. Ct. Appeals (11th Cir.), No. 12-14009 (July 25, 2014).

87 Tarasoff v. Regents of the Univ. of California, 529 P.2d 553 (Cal. 1974).

88 Tarasoff v. Regents of the Univ. of California, 551 P.2d 334, 345 (Cal. 1976); Ann Hubbard *Symposium Introduction, The Future of "The Legal Duty to Protect": Scientific and Legal Perspectives on Tarasoff's Thirtieth Anniversary*, 75 U. Cinn. L. Rev. 429 (2006).

89 Gregory v. Cott, Cal., Supreme Ct., S209125 (Aug.4, 2014).

d. Patient Age, Best Practices, and Standard of Care

For patients of all ages, one of the primary goals of health law is to assure the quality and safety of healthcare. Because older patients often present with complicated medical histories and multiple active comorbidities,[90] and physicians often lack sufficient specialized knowledge and skill pertaining to geriatric patients,[91] the quality of care provided to older patients may be suboptimal.

i. Best Practices

Initiatives have been launched to improve and maximize implementation of best practices in clinical geriatrics. Interventions in the form of screening or diagnostic tests, treatment procedures, or drug prescriptions that are not supported by evidence of sufficient immediate benefit are particularly wasteful and potentially harmful for older patients. In geriatrics, shorter-term quality of life considerations may outweigh the longer-term medical justifications for exposing younger individuals with a longer time perspective to risky, unpleasant, and expensive interventions; in geriatrics, often exercising technological restraint and doing less is the best patient-centered care.

The Centers for Medicare and Medicaid Services (CMS) supports Medicare Quality Improvement Organizations (QIOs). QIOs are private, mostly not-for-profit, organizations staffed by physicians and other healthcare quality experts working directly with healthcare providers such as hospitals, physicians, and nursing homes to ensure that clinically proven practices are put into place to deliver safe, high-quality care to Medicare beneficiaries.[92]

There is a strong movement in organized medicine to reduce the waste and inefficiency that presently characterizes some clinical practice and threatens quality of care. The push, exemplified by the Choosing Wisely program endorsed by the major physician specialty societies, is to encourage physicians to base medical decisions and recommendations more strongly on evidence about the likely value of the intervention than they have done until now.[93] As part of the Choosing Wisely program, for example, the American Geriatrics Society (AGS) in 2013 identified "Five Things Healthcare Providers and Patients Should Question." They include using: percutaneous feeding tubes in patients with advanced dementia; antipsychotics as the first choice to treat behavioral and psychological symptoms of dementia; medications to aggressively control hemoglobin levels in most older people; benzodiazepines or other sedative-hypnotics in older adults as the first choice for insomnia, agitation, or delirium; and antimicrobials to treat bacteriuria in older adults.[94]

[90] Jane S. Saczynski et al., *Patterns of Comorbidity in Older Adults With Heart Failure: The Cardiovascular Research Network PRESERVE Study*, 61 J. AM. GERIATR. SOC'Y 26 (2013).

[91] David C. Thomas et al., *Continuing Medical Education, Continued Professional Development, and Knowledge Translation: Improving Care of Older Patients by Practicing Physicians*, 54 J. AM. GERIATR. SOC'Y 1610 (2006).

[92] American Health Quality Association, Quality Improvement Organizations, *at* http://www.ahqa.org/quality-improvement-organizations.

[93] Nancy E. Morden et al., *Choosing Wisely–The Politics and Economics of Labeling Low-Value Services*, 370 N. ENGL. J. MED. 589 (2014).

[94] American Geriatrics Society Choosing Wisely Workgroup, *American Geriatrics Society Identifies Five Things that Healthcare Providers and Patients Should Question*, 61 J. AM. GERIATR. SOC'Y 622 (2013).

These items were selected because they are very commonly ordered even though the evidence of their ineffectiveness or unfavorable risk/benefit ratio for the older population is compelling.

In 2014, AGS identified five additional common medical interventions of dubious value for older patients.[95] The American Medical Directors Association (AMDA), the professional organization of physicians serving as chief medical officers of nursing homes, also has designated "Five Things Physicians and Patients Should Question." In its position statement, AMDA relies on evidence of lack of efficacy to discourage, for example, routinely prescribing lipid-lowering medications in individuals with a limited life expectancy.[96]

In the effort to rationalize medical practice on the basis of evidence, the age of the particular patient may be relevant in formulating decisions and recommendations to forgo some interventions that might make sense for younger patients. Screening asymptomatic older individuals for low-prevalence conditions may yield fewer true positive results than screening younger individuals would yield. For example:

> No data support mammography for women past 80. . . . [B]reast cancer in older women develops more slowly and is less of a threat especially because many older women suffer from other illnesses that eventually become fatal. According to the U.S. Preventive Services Task Force, the "evidence of benefits of mammography [for women over 75] is lacking." Mammograms for those 75 to 80 only make sense for women in excellent health with no other medical problems—not a large group.[97]

The value of achieving a small number of true positive results for an older patient population must be weighed against the definite costs and the possible risks of the screening procedure itself and from following up on the false positive results. Most important, a true positive screening result may not significantly affect the treatment plan for an older patient whose risk/benefit profile argues against curative medical intervention, even when the same true positive result would suggest such an intervention for a younger patient.

Another example of specialized best practices for evaluating and treating older patients is the 2013 set of joint guidelines published by a consortium of national professional organizations recommending sample policies and procedures for geriatric emergency departments. These guidelines concern the screening of geriatric patients, use of urinary catheters, geriatric medication management, geriatric fall assessment, management of delirium and dementia in the elderly, and provision of palliative care to older patients.[98]

[95] American Geriatrics Society Choosing Wisely Workgroup, *American Geriatrics Society Identifies Another Five Things that Healthcare Providers and Patients Should Question*, 62 J. Am. Geriatr. Soc'y 950 (2014).

[96] American Medical Directors Association, Five Things Physicians and Patients Should Question, *available at* http://www.amda.com/tools/ChoosingWisely_5Things.pdf.

[97] Ezekiel J. Emanuel & Daniel F. Hayes, *Mammograms Aren't Perfect But They Still Save Lives*, Wall St. J. (Feb. 27, 2014), at A15.

[98] American College of Emergency Physicians, American Geriatrics Society, Emergency Nurses Association, and Society for Academic Emergency Medicine, Geriatric Emergency Department Guidelines (2013), *available at* http://www.acep.org/geriEDguidelines/.

ii. Older Patients and the Standard of Care

The push toward more rational care through best practices initiatives is thwarted by physician perceptions of legal standards of care. Physicians often are afraid to reduce screening and treatment for fear of litigation or accusations of unethical rationing.

Physicians' legal anxieties in the geriatrics context are overblown. Older persons have been underrepresented as plaintiffs in medical malpractice lawsuits, for several reasons.[99] First, geriatric practice tends to emphasize conservative management and rehabilitative care. It entails fewer and less severe clinical—and hence legal—risks than practice specialties that rely more on dramatic, curative, technologically-oriented interventions that are calculated to produce immediate, definitive results. Those results may be either clear successes or failures, and unsatisfactory results, especially when they come as a surprise to the patient or family, are the genesis of most malpractice claims. For geriatrics, though, the objectives and expectations of the patient and family ordinarily are more limited and realistic, and therefore the probability of patient dissatisfaction with unexpected bad outcomes is reduced.

Second, older persons are likely to impose more realistic expectations on their physicians than younger patients and to be more satisfied with the quality of medical attention they receive.[100] Older people tend to show greater deference to authority figures generally, and especially in the medical arena, than the population as a whole.[101]

Finally, the legal system deters claims by older citizens in two ways. First, tort doctrine requires that plaintiffs prove by a preponderance of evidence that injury was suffered as a proximate result of the defendant's negligence. Proof of the damages and causation elements frequently presents difficult evidentiary challenges for older individuals who might contemplate medical malpractice claims. Regarding damages, the most significant element of monetary loss figured into a settlement or jury verdict is the amount of future income lost by the plaintiff as a result of the injury. Older persons have fewer income-producing years ahead of them. Thus, the potential recovery in a successful malpractice claim prosecuted by an older plaintiff is likely to be modest (except in those rare cases in which punitive damages are a realistic possibility), deterring pursuit of claims by the patient and family and by attorneys providing legal representation on the basis of a contingency fee.

Additionally, proving causation by a preponderance of evidence is difficult for many older plaintiffs. The allegation that the defendant's negligence was not only the *sine qua non* ("but for") of the patient's injury, but that the error or omission was the proximate or most direct cause, is hard to substantiate when the patient had a preexisting medical condition.

Even though older patients are underrepresented in malpractice cases, the American tort system still may be an impediment to the timely, enthusiastic adoption of evidence-based clinical practices by physicians who perceive that aggressive screening, testing, and treatment is legally required for all patients regardless of age, even when available evidence suggests that specific interventions will likely be wasteful and ineffective for the substantial bulk

[99] Ryan McCarthy, *Aegrescit Menendo: Addressing Barriers to Medical Malpractice Litigation Faced by the Elderly*, 18 ELDER L.J. 391, 391 (2011).

[100] Ann Bowling et al., *Patients' Experiences of Their Healthcare in Relation to Their Expectations and Satisfaction: A Population Survey*, 106 J. ROYAL SOC'Y MED. 143, 146 (2013).

[101] Wendy Levinson et al., *Not All Patients Want to Participate in Decision Making: A National Study of Public Preferences*, 20 J. GEN. INTERN. MED. 531 (2005).

of older patients.[102] For instance, many women over age sixty-five continue to receive annual Pap tests for detection of cervical cancer despite overwhelming evidence that routine screenings are very unlikely to produce information useful in designing a patient care plan.[103]

Key to overcoming physicians' anxieties about potential liability as an impediment to evidence-based medicine is aligning the legal standard of care applied in malpractice actions with the best practices developments described in section IV.d.i. Specifically, evidence-based recommendations promulgated by medical specialty societies and other reputable professional bodies should be formally incorporated into clinical practice guidelines (CPGs) (or clinical practice parameters) that are admissible in litigation as proof of the relevant standard of care in particular clinical situations. In states permitting, for exculpatory purposes, the admission of proof that the physician complied with an applicable CPG (a standard of care announced ex ante), compliance would constitute a legal "safe harbor" protecting against a negligence claim.

This solution has drawbacks. CPGs are controversial within the medical practitioner community. Reasons include objections to the legitimacy of the group developing the particular CPG, concern about the value of data drawn from trials rather than observations and clinical experience, the presence of conflicts of interest tainting recommendations, and claims that recommending less instead of more medical intervention always equates to improper rationing.[104] These objections may be more pointed in the geriatric context because of greater medical complexity and heterogeneity among older patients. This leads physicians to claim that each older patient is a unique outlier demanding customized care for particular needs, rather than an "average" patient as contemplated by the CPG. Additionally, because older adults often are underrepresented in clinical trials, some physicians are resistant to treat them based on CPGs that rely on research results derived from a different population. Certainly, debate must take place within this policy context about what counts as persuasive evidence upon which CPGs promulgated by medical specialty societies and other authoritative bodies should be based and what type of evidentiary value they should hold in court.[105]

Taking a patient's age into consideration at the bedside because it materially affects the relationship between risk or burden, on one hand, and possible benefit, on the other, for the particular person in terms of a specific screening or diagnostic test or treatment option is a desirable element of personalized shared decision-making between healthcare provider and patient.[106] Age-based rationing also may be accomplished as a matter of public policy. Rational, evidence-based medical practice allows providers and patients to take into account the value of a specific intervention for a particular person, where the patient's age-related

[102] Bryan W. Hernandez, *The Crossroad: An Analysis of the Intersection Between Medical Malpractice, Health Care Costs, and Prostate Cancer*, 18 Elder L.J. 361 (2011).

[103] Paula Span, *Pap Smears in Perpetuity*, N.Y. Times (Feb. 24, 2014), *available at* http://newoldage.blogs.nytimes.com/2014/02/24/pap-smears-in-perpetuity/?_php=true&_type=blogs&nl=health&emc=edit_hh_20140225&_r=0.

[104] Eliseo Guallar & Christine Laine, *Controversy Over Clinical Guidelines: Listen to the Evidence, Not the Noise*, 160 Annals Intern. Med. 361 (2014).

[105] Elliott M. Antman & Mariell Jessup, *Clinical Practice Guidelines for Chronic Cardiovascular Disorders: A Roadmap for the Future*, 311 J. Am. Med. Ass'n 1195 (2014).

[106] David A. Gruenewald, *Can Health Care Rationing Ever Be Rational?*, 40 J.L. Med. & Ethics 17 (2012).

problems may make treatment less useful. Such practice is not discrimination because of age bias on the part of healthcare providers, payers, or policy-makers.

By contrast, age-based rationing takes place implicitly at the bedside when healthcare providers deny particular forms of intervention to a patient solely on the basis of that patient's age, without regard for the probable burden or cost/benefit ratio suggested by that person's specific medical picture. Bedside behavior based strictly on the patient's age or a public policy of rationing healthcare solely on the basis of chronological age represent inflexible categorical approaches that present ethical, social, and perhaps legal, challenges precisely because they decide ex ante about certain medical interventions on the grounds of chronological age per se.[107] Such behavior or policy is objectionable because it is predicated on common, but factually inaccurate, presumptions about the value of particular medical interventions for the older population.[108]

The impact of patient age on the setting of legal standards of care for clinical practice will evolve as more evidence accumulates and is interpreted. Serious efforts to enhance the evidence foundation that informs clinical practice are in progress. The chapter by Saver (this volume) discusses the hope that has been placed on comparative effectiveness research being conducted through the Patient Centered Outcomes Research Institute (PCORI) established and funded as a public-private partnership by the American Recovery and Reinvestment Act (ARRA) of 2009[109] and then expanded by the ACA.[110] Given the CMS interest in improving quality of care for older adults and containing the growth of Medicare costs, no doubt a substantial portion of the CER conducted through PCORI will focus on clinical issues in geriatric practice. "Despite objections, the Medicare program has continued to press for the greater use of effectiveness evidence in making coverage policy."[111] Supporting this trend, while safeguarding older persons from unfair discrimination in the form of undue restrictions on beneficial care, will be a continuing, morally and politically delicate, challenge for the health law and policy enterprise as various provisions in the ACA begin to be implemented.[112]

V Conclusion

The aging of the population presents interesting challenges, nationally and globally, for the foreseeable future. The expanding specialty of elder law encompasses a panoply of topics that might affect a particular older person and his or her family members and professional service providers or business associates.[113] Similarly, medical and human services professionals

[107] Michele Mathis, *Health Care and the Aged: Arguing Equality in the Absence of a Right*, 21 Temp. Pol. & Civ. Rts. L. Rev. 337 (2012); Daniel Callahan, *Must We Ration Health Care for the Elderly?*, 40 J. L. Med. & Ethics 10 (2012).

[108] Helmut Gohlke, *Is It Worth Offering Cardiovascular Disease Prevention to the Elderly?*, 20 Eur. J. Prevent. Cardiol. 121 (2011).

[109] Pub. L. No. 111-5, 123 Stat. 115.

[110] Pub. L. No. 111-148, 124 Stat. 727, § 6301.

[111] Kinney, *Affordable Care Act*, at 561.

[112] Michael J. DeBoer, *Medicare Coverage Policy and Decision Making, Preventive Services, and Comparative Effectiveness Research Before and After the Affordable Care Act*, 7 J. Health & Biomed. L. 493 (2012).

[113] Nina A. Kohn & Edward D. Spurgeon, *Elder Law Teaching and Scholarship: An Empirical Analysis of an Evolving Field*, 59 J. Legal Educ. 414 (2010).

are increasingly likely to encounter issues with substantial legal ramifications as they plan, deliver, and evaluate care for older patients/clients and their families. There is an understandable apprehension among some commentators about too readily and reflexively assigning all of the social issues concerning aging and the aged—especially the most morally contentious questions—to the portfolio of law and medicine,[114] but in many instances such a categorization is accurate and helpful, if not imperative. This chapter summarizes salient topics likely to shape the approaching frontier where law, healthcare, and aging population intersect or overlap.

[114] Winsor C. Schmidt, *Medicalization of Aging: The Upside and the Downside*, 13 Marq. Elder's Advisor 55 (2011).

CHAPTER 48

GLOBALIZATION

NATHAN CORTEZ

> Revolutions close with a total victory for one of the two opposing camps. Will that group ever say that the result of its victory has been something less than progress?
>
> —Thomas Kuhn, *The Structure of Scientific Revolutions*[1]

I. Globalization: The Structure of Medical Revolutions?

One of the more striking modern developments in healthcare is globalization. Long thought to be immune to the forces of globalization, nearly all of the inputs and outputs of healthcare have globalized in some meaningful way. Medical workers, medical education, professional credentialing, hospitals, health insurance, clinical research, product manufacturing, and even diagnoses, treatment, and patients themselves are now part of a global trade in healthcare goods and services. Globalization in healthcare no longer is an anomaly.

Transnational healthcare markets derive from broader evolutions in modern travel, communications, technology, science, medicine, and, perhaps above all, intense cost pressures on health systems. "Globalization" is not a steady state but a process—an accretion of cross-border transactions, relationships, and interdependencies by which "capital, traded goods, persons, concepts, images, ideas, and values diffuse across state boundaries."[2] This process of globalization has become so persistent and ubiquitous that it may represent a genuine paradigm shift for the health care sector.[3]

If so, this shift deserves more systematized scholarly attention. Recent scholarship calls attention to the globalization of various healthcare phenomena,[4] but most scholarship of

[1] Thomas S. Kuhn, *The Structure of Scientific Revolutions, in* Int'l Encyclopedia of Unified Science vol. 2 no. 2, 166 (1962).

[2] Derek Yach & Douglas Bettcher, *The Globalization of Public Health I: Threats and Opportunities*, 88 Am. J. Pub. Health 735, 738 (1998).

[3] Kuhn, *Structure*.

[4] *See, e.g.*, The Globalization of Health Care: Legal and Ethical Issues (I. Glenn Cohen ed., 2013).

global scope focuses on public health. The legal literature is thus rich with discourse on infectious diseases, tobacco control, and human rights, for example, with special attention to public international law and public institutions like the World Health Organization (WHO).[5] Although there is also significant scholarship on "private" global health markets and actors (which I discuss extensively herein), it is modest compared to the sprawling literature on global public health.

Yet, healthcare remains one of the fastest growing sectors in the world economy. Health spending continues to rise annually—a persistent frustration for public and private payers. Between 2000 and 2010, worldwide health expenditures rose from 8.2% of the world economy to 9.2%.[6] Per capita spending roughly doubled during that same decade, from $482 per person in 2000 to $941 in 2010.[7] By 2012, total health spending had reached $6.5 trillion.[8]

As globalization in healthcare accelerates, it transitions from anomaly to paradigm. Intense cost pressures have pushed both public and private payers to explore less costly imports of medical products and services from low- and middle-income countries. For example, by 2003, outsourcing to just one country (India) of just two administrative tasks (medical transcription and billing) constituted 2% of the entire U.S. health market.[9] Once a novelty, now outsourcing of medical expertise, education, clinical research, product manufacturing, and other staples of the health sector are well-accepted fact. Even government regulators like the U.S. Food and Drug Administration (FDA) have taken note of "the great rebalancing," in which emerging markets gradually generate a larger share of global economic activity than traditional markets like the European Union and the United States.[10]

This chapter examines globalization as "the great rebalancing" in healthcare. I examine six important health markets that have globalized: medical workers, hospitals, health insurance, drugs and devices, telemedicine, and patient care. This examination reveals two common themes. First, rapid globalization in these markets traces in part to the convergence of practices and standards in these industries, promoted mainly by private, market-driven interests. I call this phenomenon "market-driven convergence."[11] And second, these markets largely operate in a legal and regulatory void, as domestic laws are largely incapable of overseeing these cross-border transactions. These two themes—market-driven convergence, and a transnational legal void—raise important questions about the limits of domestic law, the feasibility of international cooperation, and the ability of various "soft law" levers to correct market failures and inequities in these global markets. As Lawrence Gostin urges, globalization in healthcare means that "law and policy must be transnational, extending beyond sovereign nations. There is no other way to truly ensure the public's health than through cooperation and communal action."[12]

[5] *See, e.g.*, Lawrence O. Gostin, Global Health Law (2014).

[6] WHO, World Health Statistics 2013, at 140, at http://who.int/gho/publications/world_health_statistics/2013/en/ (last accessed Apr. 29, 2014).

[7] *Id.* at 141 (at an average exchange rate, in U.S. dollars).

[8] WHO, *Spending on Health: A Global Overview* (Apr. 2012), at http://www.who.int/mediacentre/factsheets/fs319/en/ (last accessed Apr. 29, 2014).

[9] Thomas R. McLean, *The Future of Telemedicine & Its Faustian Reliance on Regulatory Trade Barriers for Protection*, 16 Health Matrix 443 (2006).

[10] U.S. Food and Drug Administration, *Pathway to Global Product Safety and Quality* 5 (July 7, 2011).

[11] Nathan Cortez, *International Health Care Convergence: The Benefits and Burdens of Market-Driven Standardization*, 26 Wisc. Int'l L.J. 646 (2008).

[12] Gostin, Global, at 32.

II Convergence as a Driver of Globalization

Before considering globalization in various health markets, we should pause to consider a common contributor: convergence. Since the 1970s, scholars have found evidence of "policy convergence" among health systems, noting that policy-makers often emulate earlier policy reforms and innovations from other jurisdictions.[13] In 1994, after a wave of reforms in seventeen countries, the Organization for Economic Cooperation and Development (OECD) found it "remarkable" that later reforms generally borrowed policy tools and ideas from earlier reforms.[14] Although scholars sometimes explained policy convergence as a byproduct of panoramic trends like industrialization, the spread of Western scientific medicine, or evolutions in modern travel, communications, and technology, they largely overlooked convergence driven by the private sector.

"Market-driven convergence" is the idea that market actors, more than policy-makers, are pushing various practices and standards in healthcare to converge, or become more alike across countries.[15] For example, medical education and credentialing standards are converging, which makes medical workers from low- and middle-income countries more portable to high-income countries.[16] Hospital practices are converging in part through voluntary international accreditation, which hospitals use to compete for foreign clientele.[17] In the health insurance industry, more insurers and managed care companies are doing business overseas, creating multinational provider networks with rules that stretch across jurisdictions.[18] The pharmaceutical and medical device industries have helped harmonize regulatory standards for researching and seeking market approval for their products, which can substantially reduce the cost of selling their products in multiple jurisdictions.[19] Related trends have been observed with telemedicine, insurance claims processing, clinical research, and other submarkets in healthcare.[20]

Market interests push convergence because they benefit from it. For example, converging standards and practices can help open new markets for healthcare products and services, facilitating trade. And reducing disparities and inconsistencies between jurisdictions can minimize barriers to trade, which helps sellers operate more efficiently. Market-driven convergence also tends to promote further privatization and commercialization in healthcare, which benefits private industry.

Of course, the line between "public" and "private" is often far from clear in healthcare, which more than most industries relies on a combination of the two to provide services, pay for them, and even regulate their quality.[21] The world's health systems include countless permutations on the division between the public and private sectors.[22] Even the most centralized government-run health systems are marbled with important private sector activities, and vice versa. Still, it is possible to differentiate public-minded activities from

[13] Cortez, *International*, at 647.

[14] Organization for Economic Cooperation and Development, *The Reform of Health Care Systems: A Review of Seventeen OECD Countries*, Health Pol'y Stud. No. 5, 45, 61 (1994).

[15] Cortez, *International*, at 646–647. [16] *Id.* at 664–669. [17] *Id.* at 669–672.

[18] *Id.* at 672–673. [19] *Id.* at 674–676. [20] *Id.* at 677–678. [21] *Id.* at 661.

[22] John Appleby, *Economic Perspectives on Markets and Health Care*, *in* Markets and Health Care: A Comparative Analysis 34, 41 (Wendy Ranade ed., 1998).

market-minded ones. And doing so helps understand the forces pushing globalization in healthcare.

To be sure, market-driven convergence is not inevitable. It is not a theory of technological determinism.[23] But convergence feeds the globalization of healthcare markets. And, perhaps counterintuitively, convergence often serves as a substitute for transnational law and regulation. Section IV examines whether it is a good substitute, and a necessary one.

III GLOBALIZING MARKETS IN HEALTHCARE

Healthcare was long thought to be "peculiarly and tenaciously local,"[24] stubborn against the global pressures that transformed the automobile industry, electronics, manufacturing, and countless other industries. But that is no longer the case. This part considers globalization in six core health markets, evaluating the hydraulics—the "push" and "pull" factors—that stimulate global trade. The irony is that while health products and services are heavily regulated domestically, they largely escape traditional regulation in international commerce. In this legal vacuum, surrogate mechanisms have arisen to fill the gaps, with mixed success.

a. Medical Worker Migration

Of the six global health markets examined here, perhaps the most well established is the global market for physicians, nurses, and other skilled medical workers. A conspicuous number of medical workers migrate to higher income countries.[25] For example, the percentage of foreign-trained physicians exceeds 20% in Australia (25%), Canada (22%), Ireland (27%), New Zealand (36%), the United Kingdom (33%), and the United States (25%).[26] Across all OECD countries, 18% of physicians and 11% of nurses are foreign-born.[27] These ratios have risen steadily over the last twenty-five years, with "radical upward shifts" more recently.[28] Though most studies focus on physician and nurse migration, the trend also extends to paramedics, midwives, pharmacists, technicians, and other health industry workers.[29]

"Destination" countries typically are among the world's wealthiest. Indeed, roughly half of all foreign-born physicians and nurses practicing in OECD countries work in the United States—the only country with a net positive trade balance vis-à-vis all other countries in the world.[30] "Source" countries typically include, in descending order of supply, India, the Philippines, Cuba, Pakistan, Iran, South Korea, Egypt, and China,[31] with more recent

[23] Ted Marmor, Richard Freeman, & Kieke Okma, *Comparative Perspectives and Policy Learning in the World of Health Care*, 7 J. COMP. POL'Y ANALYSIS 331, 337 (2005).

[24] Timothy Stoltzfus Jost, *Comparative and International Health Law*, 14 HEALTH MATRIX 141 (2004).

[25] Jean-Christophe Dumont & Pascal Zurn, OECD, *Immigrant Health Workers in OECD Countries in the Broader Context of Highly Skilled Migration*, *in* INTERNATIONAL MIGRATION OUTLOOK 161, 164–169 (2007).

[26] *Id.* at 169. [27] *Id.* at 163–164. [28] *Id.* at 163.

[29] Rupa Chanda, *Trade in Health Services, reprinted in* TRADE IN HEALTH SERVICES: GLOBAL, REGIONAL, & COUNTRY PERSPECTIVES 35, 37 (Nick Drager & Cesar Vieira eds., 2002).

[30] Dumont & Zurn, *Immigrant Health Workers*, at 163. [31] Cortez, *International*, at 665.

pipelines from Africa and Central and Eastern Europe.[32] Thus, medical workers "are migrating in what is now effectively a global market for talent."[33]

A longstanding concern with this "market" is the severe maldistribution of medical workers, the so-called "brain drain" from low- and middle-income countries.[34] The market logic is simple—global demand for medical workers has long exceeded the supply. In 2006, the WHO estimated a worldwide shortage of 4.3 million health professionals.[35] The greatest burden obviously falls on source countries, particularly in sub-Saharan Africa and southeast Asia. Among 193 members of the WHO, 57 have a "critical shortage" of medical workers.[36] Southeast Asia alone would require 1.1 million more medical workers to meet just 80% of its needs, with acute shortages in Bangladesh, India, and Indonesia. The brain drain also has reached crisis levels in Angola, Antigua and Barbuda, Grenada, Guyana, Haiti, Liberia, Mozambique, Saint Vincent and the Grenadines, Sierra Leone, Tanzania, and Trinidad and Tobago, where over half of all medical workers emigrate to OECD countries.[37]

In addition to the loss of human capital, the economic cost-shifting is significant. One study found that since 1951, Ghana has lost $60 million and the United Kingdom has saved $168 million from Ghanaian-trained workers migrating to the United Kingdom.[38]

The global trade in medical workers is brisk and shows no sign of abating. Demand for foreign workers is being driven by several larger trends, like aging populations that require care for chronic rather than communicable diseases.[39] Moreover, researchers predict that worldwide shortages will be exacerbated by rising demand in emergent economies like Brazil, China, and India.[40] Even the United States will face a shortage of 85,000 physicians by 2020 and 260,000 nurses by 2025.[41]

Medical worker migration is enabled by convergence in medical education and credentialing, as lower income countries adopt Western standards.[42] Groups like the World Federation for Medical Education and the Institute for International Medical Education promote international standards for curricula that are endorsed by the WHO and the World Medical Association.[43] As these standards permeate domestic medical school curricula and regional recognition programs, medical graduates become more portable.[44]

Researchers have examined other "push" and "pull" factors that encourage medical worker migration. Push factors include low domestic wages, heavy workloads, inadequate health facilities, poor access to technology, dim career prospects, and poor overall living

[32] Dumont & Zurn, *Immigrant Health Workers*, at 163.

[33] Nigel Crisp & Lincoln Chen, *Global Supply of Health Professionals*, 370 New Eng. J. Med. 950 (2014).

[34] Allyn L. Taylor et al., *Stemming the Brain Drain—A WHO Global Code of Practice on International Recruitment of Health Personnel*, 365 New Eng. J. Med. 2348 (2011).

[35] WHO, The World Health Report 2006—Working Together for Health 12 (2006).

[36] *Id.* at 11–12.

[37] Allyn Taylor & Ibadat S. Dhillon, *A Global Legal Architecture to Address the Challenges of International Health Worker Migration: A Case Study of the Role of Nonbinding Instruments in Global Health Governance*, *in* The Globalization of Health Care, at 233–234.

[38] Kenechukwu Agwu & Megan Llewelyn, *Compensation for the Brain Drain from Developing Countries*, 373 Lancet 1665 (2009).

[39] Crisp & Chen, *Global Supply*, at 951–952. [40] *Id.* at 951. [41] *Id.*

[42] Cortez, *International*, at 667–668. [43] *Id.* at 667–668. [44] *Id.* at 668.

conditions.[45] Pull factors attracting professionals to wealthier countries essentially include better scores on these same metrics.[46]

Scholars and policy-makers have tried to weigh the most important push and pull factors as targets for intervention. But there is no binding international law that governs medical worker migration. In the absence of such law, source countries try to use unilateral, supply-side interventions that might mitigate push factors, like raising domestic wages or preconditioning medical school scholarships on a minimum period of domestic service.[47] But these have had mixed success, and unilateral policies alone can do little to alleviate global supply-demand imbalances.

Demand-side interventions in jurisdictions like the United States and United Kingdom might have more success. For example, the United Kingdom drastically reduced its intake of foreign physicians by training more of them domestically, by tightening immigration standards, and by entering into bilateral agreements with source countries.[48] As a result, new registrations from South African physicians in the United Kingdom dropped from 3,206 in 2003 to just four in 2004, and new registrations from Indian and Pakistani physicians dropped from 4,626 in 2004 to 1,169 in 2007.[49] Previous efforts to encourage more ethical international recruiting were unsuccessful.[50]

Finally, medical worker migration has been an obvious target of multilateral cooperation.[51] In 2010, the World Health Assembly adopted the WHO Global Code of Practice on the International Recruitment of Health Personnel, which created "voluntary principles and practices."[52] Similar statements have been adopted by groups like the World Medical Association.[53] But these documents are normative, rather than legally binding.[54] Moreover, multilateral institutions sometimes exacerbate the problem—scholars have criticized the World Bank and International Monetary Fund (IMF) for pressuring low-income countries to prioritize repaying debt obligations over investing in domestic medical training, for example.[55]

Still, parts of the Global Code are being incorporated into law in several source countries, including Kenya, Thailand, and Zimbabwe.[56] However, roughly seventy countries, including

45 WHO, World Health Report 2006, at 99 (looking at expatriates from sub-Saharan Africa); Taylor et al., *Stemming*, at 2348.

46 WHO, World Health Report 2006, at 99.

47 *See, e.g.*, Nir Eyal & Till Bärnighausen, *Conditioning Medical Scholarships on Long, Future Service: A Defense*, *in* THE GLOBALIZATION OF HEALTH CARE, at 220; Mary O'Neil et al., *Evaluation of Malawi's Emergency Human Resources Program*, U.K. Department for International Development (2010).

48 Giorgio Cometto et al., *Health Workforce Brain Drain: From Denouncing the Challenge to Solving the Problem*, 10 (9) PLOS MEDICINE 2 (2013).

49 Claire Blacklock et al., *Effect of U.K. Policy on Medical Migration: A Time Series Analysis of Physician Registration Data*, 10 HUMAN RESOURCES FOR HEALTH 35 (2012).

50 *Id.* at 35.

51 Vivian Runnels et al., *Global Policies and Local Practice in the Ethical Recruitment of Internationally Trained Health Human Resources*, *in* THE GLOBALIZATION OF HEALTH CARE, at 203, 206–209.

52 WHO, THE WHO GLOBAL CODE OF PRACTICE ON THE INTERNATIONAL RECRUITMENT OF HEALTH PERSONNEL (2010).

53 Runnels et al., *Global Policies*, at 205.

54 *Id.* at 206–208.

55 *See, e.g.*, Stephanie Taché & Dean Schillinger, *Health Worker Migration: Time for the Global Justice Approach*, 9 AM. J. BIOETHICS 12 (2009).

56 Taylor et al., *Stemming*, at 2349–2350.

most destination countries, continue to examine the Global Code. Only Norway, a country that does not rely heavily on medical worker migration, has begun to implement it, raising doubts about "the effectiveness of this form of international soft law."[57] Indeed, in one survey, 93% of respondents reported that the Global Code had not meaningfully changed domestic policies or practices.[58] The best hope for source countries seems to be bilateral agreements of the type entered into by the United Kingdom.

b. Multinational Hospitals

Like factories, hospitals can be large concrete ziggurats, icons of industry. But unlike factories, hospitals have long resisted the pressures of globalization. As Timothy Jost observed, although "we purchase automobiles from Japan, computers from Korea, toys from China, and clothes from Bangladesh, when we get sick we go to the doctor in our neighborhood or the hospital downtown."[59] Yet, the twin emergence of multinational hospitals and international hospital accreditation points toward rising global competition in the hospital industry.

Multinational hospital chains have become less atypical. United States-based chains include Adventist Health International, which operates 26 hospitals and 70 clinics in 19 countries,[60] and CHRISTUS Health, which operates 54 inpatient facilities and 175 outpatient facilities in the United States and Mexico.[61] European-based chains include Aga Khan Health Services, which operates 9 hospitals and 325 "health facilities" in 4 countries,[62] and Capio, which operates 11 hospitals and 131 other facilities in 5 countries.[63] Columbia Asia Healthcare, based in Malaysia, operates 27 hospitals in 4 countries,[64] and Parkway Paintain Limited, based in Singapore, operates 24 hospitals (including some planned) in 7 countries.[65] India-based Apollo Hospitals operates 51 facilities in 3 countries,[66] and South Africa-based Netcare Limited operates 119 hospitals in 2 countries.[67]

[57] Timothy K. Mackey & Bryan A. Liang, *Rebalancing Brain Drain: Exploring Resource Reallocation to Address Health Worker Migration and Promote Global Health*, 107 Health Pol'y 66, 70 (2012).

[58] Gostin, Global, at 66 (*citing* Jennifer S. Edge & Steven J. Hoffman, "Empirical Impact Evaluation of the WHO Global Code of Practice on the International Recruitment of Health Personnel (2010) on Government, Civil Society, and Private Sectors in Australia, Canada, United Kingdom and United States of America" (paper presented at the Annual Meeting of the American Political Science Association, Seattle, Washington, September 1–4, 2011)).

[59] Jost, *Comparative*, at 141.

[60] Adventist Health International, *About Us*, http://www.adventisthealthinternational.org/article/2/about-us (last visited Mar. 28, 2014).

[61] CHRISTUS Health, *About Us*, http://www.christushealth.org/AboutUs (last visited Mar. 28, 2014).

[62] Aga Khan Health Services, http://www.akdn.org/AKHS (last visited Mar. 28, 2014).

[63] Capio Group, *This is Capio*, at http://capio.com/en/about/capio-in-brief/ (last visited Mar. 31, 2014).

[64] Columbia Asia Healthcare, *About Us*, at http://www.columbiaasia.com/about.html (last visited Mar. 31, 2014).

[65] Parkway Pantai Limited, *Overview*, at http://www.parkwaypantai.com/about_parkway_pantai/overview/ (last visited Mar. 31, 2014).

[66] Apollo Hospitals, International Hospitals, at http://www.apollohospitals.com/international-hospitals.php (last visited Mar. 28, 2014).

[67] Netcare, *Company Profile*, at https://www.netcare.co.za/2390/company-profile (last visited Mar. 31, 2014).

Of course, multinational hospitals are not entirely new. A 1987 study found U.S. companies to be operating ninety-five foreign hospitals at the time.[68] But the trend seems to be accelerating.[69] For a long time, many low- and middle-income countries limited foreign direct investment in their health sectors.[70] But countries like China, India, Indonesia, Maldives, Nepal, Sri Lanka, and Thailand have relaxed these restrictions, creating a surge of investments in new hospitals, clinics, and diagnostic centers.[71]

A parallel development is the emergence of international hospital accreditation. Accrediting bodies from Australia, Canada, France, the United Kingdom, and United States have introduced international accreditation systems inspired by their domestic standards.[72] Some of the more well known include Accreditation Canada International,[73] the Australian Council on Healthcare Standards International (ACHSI),[74] France-based Haute Autorité de Santé (HAS),[75] U.S.-based Joint Commission International (JCI),[76] and U.K.-based QHA Trent Accreditation.[77] There is even an accreditor for the accreditors: the International Society for Quality in Health Care (ISQua).[78]

Perhaps the most well-known international accreditor is JCI, which has recognized over 600 hospitals and medical facilities in 57 countries,[79] many in recent years.[80] JCI accreditation helps hospitals compete for foreign clientele by signaling the hospital's competence and quality.[81] Most accredited hospitals display JCI's golden seal of approval prominently on their websites and marketing materials. JCI accreditation carries the weight of major U.S. trade associations like the American Medical Association and American Hospital Association, which govern JCI's domestic parent, the Joint Commission.[82] Moreover, the

68 Howard S. Berliner & Carol Regan, *Multinational Operations of U.S. For-Profit Hospital Chains: Trends and Implications*, 77 AM. J. PUB. HEALTH 1280 (1987).

69 Jane Lethbridge, *A Global Review of the Expansion of Multinational Healthcare Companies*, Public Services International Research Unit (2007).

70 Nathan Cortez, *Patients Without Borders: The Emerging Global Market for Patients and the Evolution of Modern Health Care*, 83 IND. L.J. 71, 87 (2009).

71 *Id.* at 87; The Advisory Board Company, *U.S. Hospitals Eye Chinese Market for Expansion*, Feb. 7, 2013, at http://www.advisory.com/daily-briefing/2013/02/07/us-hospital-giants-set-their-sights-on-china (last visited Apr. 1, 2014).

72 Cortez, *International*, at 669–670.

73 Accreditation Canada International, *About Us*, at http://www.internationalaccreditation.ca/aboutus/history.aspx (last visited Apr. 1, 2014).

74 Australian Council on Healthcare Standards International, *Accreditation*, at http://www.achs.org.au/achs-international/products-and-services/accreditation/ (last visited Apr. 1, 2014).

75 Haute Autorité de Santé, *International Presence*, at http://www.has-sante.fr/portail/jcms/c_420020/en/international-presence (last visited Apr. 1, 2014).

76 Joint Commission International, *JCI-Accredited Organizations*, at http://www.jointcommissioninternational.org/about-jci/jci-accredited-organizations/ (last visited Apr. 1, 2014).

77 QHA Trent Accreditation, *About*, at http://www.qha-trent.co.uk/#!about2/c4nz (last visited Apr. 1, 2014).

78 ISQua, *Accreditation*, at http://www.isqua.org/accreditation/accreditation (last visited Apr. 1, 2014); Elma G. Heidemann, *Moving to Global Standards for Accreditation Processes: The ExPeRT Project in a Larger Context*, 12 INT'L J. FOR QUALITY IN HEALTH CARE 227, 228–229 (2000).

79 JCI, JCI-Accredited Organizations.

80 Cortez, *Patients*, at 83 (citing "over eighty" accreditations in 2008); Cortez, *International*, at 670 (citing "approximately 140 hospitals and medical facilities" accredited in 2009).

81 Cortez, *Patients*, at 83–84.

82 Cortez, *International*, at 670.

Joint Commission's special status as accreditor for the U.S. Medicare program also imbues JCI's international accreditation with a tint of official government approval.[83]

Both trends—multinational hospital chains and international accreditation—emerged in parallel, driven by competition for patients. Though not as well established as the global trade in medical workers, the global hospital market raises some of the same concerns. For example, similar to the "brain drain" of medical workers, scholars worry that global hospital competition can create a "resource drain" in which private, for-profit hospitals siphon personnel and resources from public facilities.[84] Also, scholars worry that the global hospital market is an outgrowth of efforts by the World Bank, IMF, and World Trade Organization (WTO) to encourage lower income countries to privatize and commercialize their health sectors, thus de-prioritizing public facilities.[85]

In its defense, the global hospital market does offer benefits. For example, the newer private multinational hospitals can entice physicians to repatriate back to lower income countries, stimulating a "reverse brain drain." They can also help improve local health infrastructure. However, there is little evidence that most private, for-profit multinational hospitals produce benefits for domestic patients of ordinary means, particularly the hospitals that cater to foreign clientele. Scholars are just beginning to examine the distributive effects of multinational hospitals, and many doubt that any theoretical "trickle down" benefits or cross-subsidies for the public sector are materializing.[86]

Scholars have also raised important concerns about international accreditation. For example, critics have long worried that accreditors like the Joint Commission grant virtually every application and revoke virtually none, raising questions about the rigors of its review process.[87] Moreover, JCI revenues come from the hospitals it reviews, in the form of applicant fees and from separate "advisory services" sold to prepare applicants for accreditation, raising potential conflicts of interest.[88]

Yet, despite these criticisms, JCI and other international accreditors help fill an important regulatory void in the global hospital market, introducing standards that otherwise might not exist.[89] Although hospital accreditation is a very imperfect proxy for quality regulation, it does measure various structural indicia of quality. Like the WHO's Global Code of Practice on the International Recruitment of Health Personnel, private international accreditation seems to

[83] *Id.* [84] Chanda, *Trade*, at 22–23; Cortez, *Patients*, at 109.

[85] Cortez, *International*, at 681–684.

[86] *See, e.g.*, Y. Y. Brandon Chen & Colleen M. Flood, *Medical Tourism's Impact on Health Care Equity and Access in Low- and Middle-Income Countries: Making the Case for Regulation*, 41 J.L. MED. & ETHICS 286 (2013); I. Glenn Cohen, *Medical Tourism, Access to Health Care, and Global Justice*, 52 VA. J. INT'L L. 1 (2011); Leigh Turner, *Medical Travel and the Global Health Services Marketplace: Identifying Risks to Patients, Public Health, and Health Systems*, *in* RISKS AND CHALLENGES IN MEDICAL TOURISM: UNDERSTANDING THE GLOBAL MARKET FOR HEALTH SERVICES 253, 267–270 (Jill R. Hodges, Leigh Turner, & Ann Marie Kimball eds., 2012).

[87] Cortez, *Patients*, at 86, 110–111.

[88] JCI, *Prepare for Accreditation and Certification*, at http://www.jointcommissioninternational.org/improve/prepare-for-accreditation-and-certification/ (last accessed Apr. 2, 2014).

[89] Nathan Cortez, *Embracing the New Geography of Health Care: A Novel Way to Cover Those Left Out of Health Reform*, 84 S. CAL. L. REV. 859, 908–910 (2011); Nathan Cortez, *Into the Void: The Legal Ambiguities of an Unregulated Medical Tourism Market*, *in* RISKS AND CHALLENGES IN MEDICAL TOURISM, at 187, 197–199.

be a poor substitute for hard law, but preferable to nothing. Moreover, it is doubtful that a multilateral solution, like a WHO Global Code for Multinational Hospitals, would be any more effective. Thus, as with other global health markets, a soft law surrogate helps fill the legal void.

c. Cross-Border Insurance

A third key market inching toward globalization is health insurance, undermining the notion that health insurance is solely a domestic service. Commercial insurers not only do business in multiple jurisdictions, but some also offer cross-border coverage, even beyond unplanned emergency care.

For example, U.S. health insurers have begun experimenting with cross-border plans that encourage beneficiaries to have high-cost treatments overseas. The plans may add foreign providers to their networks or simply outsource specific high-cost surgeries to certain foreign hospitals.[90] A variety of U.S. insurers have explored cross-border plans, including "the four largest commercial insurers in the United States (UnitedHealth, WellPoint, Aetna, and Humana)."[91] Smaller insurers like Blue Cross Blue Shield of South Carolina, Blue Ridge Paper Products, and Hannaford Brothers (a New England grocery store chain) have contracted with foreign hospitals to perform certain high-cost surgeries.[92] In fact, third-party administrators, like BasicPlus Health Insurance, Companion Global Healthcare, and United Group Programs, have collectively contracted with hundreds of U.S. employers to cover foreign providers.[93] More extensive cross-border plans are offered by Blue Shield, Health Net, SIMNSA, and the Western Growers Association, mostly to California residents willing to be treated in Mexico.[94]

Although the actual number of patients sent overseas remains unclear (but seems to be modest), cross-border insurance breaches an important wall between the domestic and the foreign, undermining the notion that health insurance is nonportable. Cross-border plans are inspired by the prospect of using low-cost foreign hospitals and physicians to provide care of roughly equal quality—first-world care for third-world prices. The cross-border plans sold in California can cost 40%–50% less than domestic-only plans.[95]

While cross-border plans remain rare in the United States, they are much less so in the European Union. A simple reason is the close proximity of EU member states. A more complex reason is that layers of EU law (treaties, directives, regulations, and court decisions) help ensure the free movement of goods, services, and capital in a common European market.[96] The common market allows EU citizens to travel more freely to other EU member states for treatment, creating de facto cross-border insurance.[97] The distinction is that

[90] Cortez, *New Geography*, at 882; Cortez, *Into the Void*, at 199.

[91] Cortez, *New Geography*, at 882. [92] *Id.* at 883. [93] *Id.* at 882–883.

[94] *Id.* at 883–884. [95] *Id.*

[96] Directive 2011/23/EU of the European Parliament and of the Council of March 9, 2011 on the Application of Patients' Rights in Cross-Border Healthcare, 2011 O.J. (L 88) 45; Johan W. van de Gronden, *Cross-Border Health Care in the EU and the Organization of the National Health Care Systems of the Member States: The Dynamics Resulting from the European Court of Justice's Decisions on Free Movement and Competition Law*, 26 Wisc. Int'l L.J. 705 (2008).

[97] Nathan Cortez, *The Elusive Ideal of Market Competition in United States Health Care*, *in* Health Care and EU Law 359, 367 (Johan W. van de Gronden, Erika Szyszczak, Ulla Neergaard, & Markus Krajewski eds., 2011); van de Gronden, *Cross-Border*, at 705.

patient mobility in the EU is driven primarily by access to specific treatments, rather than cost considerations.

Like the globalization of medical workers and hospitals, the globalization of health insurance raises important questions. For example, it is unclear how aggressively U.S. health insurers can encourage (or even insist on) foreign care. Domestic law is largely silent on this question,[98] except for a California law that permits certain cross-border plans and a Texas law that largely bans them.[99] Other state laws aimed at traditional domestic-only plans might functionally bar cross-border plans, like state laws that require health maintenance organizations (HMOs) to make providers accessible within certain geographic distances.[100] But for the most part, U.S. domestic laws do not contemplate cross-border plans, which operate in a legal vacuum.

Scholars also raise ethical questions about using financial incentives to encourage patients to leave the country. For example, cross-border plans might use positive incentives (like lowering premiums or waiving deductibles), or negative incentives (like charging higher premiums or deductibles for domestic care).[101] But both forms may be coercive if the financial incentive is great enough.[102] Scholars also worry that the cross-border market will skew towards low-income or marginalized populations, making domestic care a luxury.[103] Finally, scholars note that financial benefits of using low-cost foreign providers will accrue disproportionately to insurers and providers, while the legal and medical risks of having treatment overseas will be borne disproportionately by patients, perhaps the least sophisticated party in these transactions.[104]

To date, there are very few mechanisms that would mute these concerns. Scholars have considered a host of soft law interventions, like using access to the U.S. market as a lever to impose requirements on foreign providers in cross-border plans.[105] There may also be opportunities for public-private cooperation, international networks, and other forms of "new governance" or soft law to help fill the legal void.[106] Again, these can be poor substitutes for traditional regulation, but may play an important standard-setting role given the limits of domestic law.

d. Global Pharmaceutical and Device Industries

Globalization has touched nearly all planes of the pharmaceutical and medical device industries—from clinical research and regulatory approvals to manufacturing and marketing. The result is a brisk trade in both product markets, with impressive annual growth and sharp rises in imports. Global pharmaceutical sales were predicted to double from $605

98 Cortez, *Into the Void*, at 195.

99 California Health & Safety Code §§ 1345, 1351.2; Texas Insurance Code Ann., art. 1216.004.

100 Cortez, *Into the Void*, at 200; I. Glenn Cohen, *Protecting Patients with Passports: Medical Tourism and the Patient-Protective Argument*, 95 IOWA L. REV. 1467, 1557 (2010).

101 Cortez, *Into the Void*, at 199; Cohen, *Protecting Patients*, at 1486.

102 Cohen, *Protecting Patients*, at 1548.

103 *See, e.g.*, Cortez, *New Geography*, at 887.

104 Nathan Cortez, *Recalibrating the Legal Risks of Cross-Border Health Care*, 10 YALE J. HEALTH POL'Y L. & ETHICS 1 (2010).

105 Cortez, *New Geography*.

106 *Id.*

billion in 2005 to $1.2 trillion by 2017.[107] Similarly, the global device market, "one of the fastest growing industries" in the world, was predicted to more than double from $145 billion in 2000 to $302 billion by 2017.[108]

Traditionally, both markets have been concentrated in North America, Europe, and Japan. But that is changing. Pharmaceutical sales growth in these traditional markets looks modest compared to the annual double-digit growth rates in the BRIC markets (Brazil, Russia, India, and China).[109] As a result, the geographic distribution of pharmaceutical sales is flattening.[110] The medical device market is no different. Eighty percent of global device sales occur in just ten countries—all in North America, Western Europe, and Japan. But the geographic distribution of devices is flattening with rising sales in Brazil, China, India, and Mexico.[111]

Import activity is also on the rise. For example, 30% of finished pharmaceutical products (by value) and as much as 80% of active pharmaceutical ingredients used in the U.S. market are imported.[112] Over half of all medical device spending in the United States is on imports.[113]

As with other global health markets, globalization in the drug and device markets derives from several complex factors. One important factor is the globalization of clinical research. The number of principal investigators based outside the United States who were overseeing trials for FDA marketing submissions rose by 15% annually between 2002 and 2006, while the number of U.S.-based principal investigators dropped by 5.5% annually during that same period.[114] The growth of foreign investigators was highest in Asia (29%), Central and Eastern Europe (16%), and Latin America (13%).[115] A 2007 study of Phase III trials by the twenty largest pharmaceutical companies found that roughly one-third were being conducted entirely outside the United States, with over half of study sites located overseas.[116] The contract research industry, which barely existed twenty years ago,[117] is now a multibillion dollar global enterprise.[118] Companies are attracted to low- and middle-income countries, where it is easier to recruit subjects and where the legal obstacles are fewer.

[107] IMS Institute for Healthcare Informatics, The Global Use of Medicines: Outlook through 2015 4 (2011); IMS Institute for Healthcare Informatics, The Global Use of Medicines: Outlook through 2017 5 (2013).

[108] WHO, Medical Device Regulations: Global Overview and Guiding Principles *v* (2003); Lucintel, Global Medical Device Industry 2012–2017: Trends, Profits, and Forecast Analysis (2012).

[109] IMS INSTITUTE (2017), at 34 App. 2.

[110] *id.* at 10–11.

[111] WHO, MEDICAL DEVICES: MANAGING THE MISMATCH: AN OUTCOME OF THE PRIORITY MEDICAL DEVICES PROJECT 15–16 (2010) (citing the World Medical Markets Fact Book 2009); Yair Holtzman, *The U.S. Medical Device Industry in 2012: Challenges at Home and Abroad*, MEDICAL DEVICE AND DIAGNOSTIC INDUSTRY (July 17, 2012), at http://www.mddionline.com/article/medtech-2012-SWOT.

[112] U.S. Food and Drug Administration, *Pathway*, at 12.

[113] *Id.*

[114] Kenneth A. Getz, *Global Clinical Trials Activity in the Details*, APPLIED CLINICAL TRIALS (Sept. 1, 2007), at http://www.appliedclinicaltrialsonline.com/appliedclinicaltrials/article/articleDetail.jsp?id=453243 (accessed Apr. 9, 2014).

[115] *Id.*

[116] Seth W. Glickman et al., *Ethical and Scientific Implications of the Globalization of Clinical Research*, 360 N. ENG. J. MED. 816 (2009).

[117] Richard A. Rettig, *The Industrialization of Clinical Research*, 19 HEALTH AFF. 129, 131 (2000).

[118] ADRIANA PETRYNA, WHEN EXPERIMENTS TRAVEL: CLINICAL TRIALS AND THE GLOBAL SEARCH FOR HUMAN SUBJECTS (2009); Bethany Spielman, *Offshoring Experiments, Outsourcing Public Health: Corporate Accountability and State Responsibility for Violating the International Prohibition on Nonconsensual Human Experimentation*, *in* THE GLOBALIZATION OF HEALTH CARE, at 286, 288.

Globalization of the drug and device industries also traces in part to the harmonization of regulatory approval standards. As early as the 1960s, countries around the world began considering regulatory models based on the U.S. FDA, culminating with the WHO Director-General's 1970 report, *Safety and Efficacy of Drugs: Principles for Drug Control*.[119] Two decades later, in 1990, after countries created their own systems, pharmaceutical regulators and industry representatives created the International Conference on Harmonization (ICH) to harmonize standards for clinical research and marketing approvals.[120] Led by parties from Europe, Japan, and the United States, the purpose of the ICH is "to reduce or obviate the need to duplicate the testing carried out during the research and development of new medicines."[121] The result is a series of international standards and guidelines, many of which have been adopted as domestic law (except in the United States, which generally incorporates ICH standards as nonbinding FDA guidance).[122] Still, the ICH is notable both for the participation of the major trade groups and for its efforts to expand in Africa, Asia, and Latin America.[123]

Similarly, globalization of the medical device industry traces in part to efforts of the Global Harmonization Task Force, formed two years after the ICH and for similar purposes.[124] Like the ICH, the task force once included both regulatory authorities and industry participants, with the stated goal to "encourage convergence in regulatory practices" to promote innovation and stimulate international trade.[125] Although the task force dissolved in 2012, the government participants reformulated to create the new International Medical Device Regulators Forum, excluding industry representatives.[126]

Globalization of the drug and device industries has been subjected to close scrutiny. Most of the literature focuses on the lack of access to essential medicines in low- and middle-income countries. Scholars have studied the tensions created by intellectual property laws, particularly under the WTO's Agreement on Trade-Related Aspects of Intellectual Property Rights (TRIPS).[127] Western legal regimes may also provide data exclusivity periods and patent "linkages" that further inhibit access to medicines.[128]

As with medical workers, there is a maldistribution of drugs. Roughly 80%–90% of patented drugs are sold in OECD countries, while the global "disease burden" falls mainly on low- and middle-income countries, where 84% of the world lives and whose populations

[119] WHO Director-General, *Safety and Efficacy of Drugs: Principles for Drug Control* (EB47/9, Nov. 27, 1970. The first recommendations came via World Health Assembly Resolution WHA15.41 (May 1962). The FDA's regulation of devices is discussed in greater depth in other articles of this volume.

[120] Cortez, *International*, at 674.

[121] ICH, *Vision*, at http://www.ich.org/about/vision.html (last accessed Apr. 9, 2014).

[122] *See, e.g.*, FDA, International Conference on Harmonisation; Guidance on Statistical Principles for Clinical Trials; Availability, 63 Fed. Reg. 49,583 (Sept. 16, 1998).

[123] Cortez, *International*, at 675; Michael J. Malinowski & Grant G. Gautreaux, *All That Is Gold Does Not Glitter in Human Clinical Research: A Law-Policy Proposal to Brighten the Global "Gold Standard" for Drug Research and Development*, 45 CORNELL INT'L L.J. 185, 190 (2012).

[124] Cortez, *International*, at 675–676.

[125] *Id.* at 676 (quoting the now-defunct Task Force website in 2008).

[126] U.S. Food and Drug Administration, *Pathway*, at 2.

[127] *See, e.g.*, Aaron S. Kesselheim, *Think Globally, Prescribe Locally: How Rational Pharmaceutical Policy in the U.S. Can Improve Global Access to Essential Medicines*, 34 AM. J. L. & MED. 125, 132 (2008).

[128] Cynthia M. Ho, *Beyond Patents: Global Challenges to Affordable Medicine*, *in* THE GLOBALIZATION OF HEALTH CARE, at 302.

"are disproportionately sick."[129] Meanwhile, drug companies have financial incentives not to develop drugs to treat "tropical" diseases that occur in less lucrative markets.[130] The United Nations bemoaned that "the lack of life-saving and health-supporting medicines for an estimated 2 billion poor people stands as a direct contradiction to the fundamental principle of health as a human right."[131] Unfortunately, roughly the same criticisms apply to medical devices.[132] Although there is growing multilateral, public-private coordination to improve access to essential medicines in low- and middle-income countries, it must overcome local obstacles like weak public procurement and distribution systems.[133]

There are also long-standing concerns about counterfeits and the quality of imports in the global drug and device markets, particularly in jurisdictions with less-developed regulatory systems.[134] Price discrepancies create arbitrage incentives, giving rise to parallel imports and sales of "grey" market products.[135] The WHO estimated that $431 billion of counterfeit pharmaceuticals were sold in 2012. The FDA's recent effort to open foreign offices is laudable, but is seen as a finger in the dam.

There is also a large scholarly literature on the legal and ethical problems of outsourcing clinical research to low- and middle-income countries. Critics argue that "forum shopping" by large multinational companies for the friendliest legal environments is exploitative.[136] There are serious doubts that study subjects with little to no education can understand informed consent forms or the nature of randomized, placebo-controlled trials.[137] Moreover, study subjects may be unduly swayed to participate because clinical trial compensation may exceed their annual incomes, or the trial may represent their only chance to receive treatment.[138] The infamous Pfizer trial for Trovan in Kano, Nigeria, showcased many of these concerns.[139]

[129] Kevin Outterson, *Patent Buy-Outs for Global Disease Innovations for Low- and Middle-Income Countries*, 32 AM. J. L. & MED. 159, 160 (2006).

[130] *See, e.g.*, David B. Ridley et al., *Developing Drugs for Developing Countries*, 25 HEALTH AFF. 313 (2006).

[131] United Nations Millennium Project, Prescription for Healthy Development: Increasing Access to Medicines 1 (2005), at http://www.unmillenniumproject.org/documents/TF5-medicines-Complete.pdf.

[132] WHO, MEDICAL DEVICES: MANAGING THE MISMATCH.

[133] *See, e.g.*, FREDERICK M. ABBOTT & GRAHAM DUKES, GLOBAL PHARMACEUTICAL POLICY: ENSURING MEDICINES FOR TOMORROW'S WORLD 116–158 (2009).

[134] U.S. Food and Drug Administration, *Pathway*, at 13–17.

[135] Kevin Outterson, *Pharmaceutical Arbitrage: Balancing Access and Innovation in International Prescription Drug Markets*, 5 YALE J. HEALTH POL'Y, L. & ETHICS 193 (2005).

[136] *See, e.g.*, Marcia Angell, *The Ethics of Clinical Research in the Third World*, 337 N. ENG. J. MED. 847 (1997); Marcia Angell, *Ethical Imperialism? Ethics in International Collaborative Clinical Research*, 319 N. ENG. J. MED. 1081 (1988); Fazal Khan, *The Human Factor: Globalizing Ethical Standards in Drug Trials Through Market Exclusion*, 57 DEPAUL L. REV. 877 (2008).

[137] *See, e.g.*, Glickman et al., *Ethical and Scientific*, at 818. *See also* Amulya Mandava, Christine Pace, Benjamin Campbell, Ezekiel Emanuel, & Christine Grady, *The Quality of Informed Consent: Mapping the Landscape. A Review of Empirical Data from Developing and Developed Countries*, 38 J. MED. ETHICS 356 (2012) (finding variable comprehension of informed consent among participants in both developed and developing countries). For an argument that goes beyond informed consent, *see* Ezekiel J. Emanuel, David Wendler, & Christine Grady, *What Makes Clinical Research Ethical?*, 283 J. AM. MED. ASS'N 2701 (2000).

[138] *Id.*

[139] Khan, *The Human Factor*.

Despite a host of ethical rules and guidelines from the FDA,[140] the European Union,[141] the ICH,[142] and the WHO's Council for International Organizations of Medical Sciences (CIOMS)[143]—often inspired by principles from the Nuremburg Code and the Declaration of Helsinki—their enforcement is spotty.[144] In theory, these guidelines encourage compliance by leveraging access to lucrative markets, like FDA rules for foreign trials serving as a gatekeeper to the U.S. market. Indeed, since the 1960s the FDA has been the model for national regulators around the world, one promoted by the WHO itself.[145] But this regulatory model does little to address access to essential medicines or some of the other problems noted above.

e. Telemedicine

Medical expertise is being globalized beyond medical worker migration to include telemedicine—the use of communications technologies to diagnose, monitor, and treat patients remotely.[146] Methods include live video consultations, remote patient monitoring, remote diagnostic and laboratory interpretations, or even remote robotically-assisted surgery. Some of these practices have their own names, like teleradiology, telepathology, or cybersurgery.[147] Although most telemedicine is provided domestically, subspecialties like teleradiology demonstrate how services can quickly globalize.[148]

The global telemedicine market generated $14.2 billion in revenues in 2012 and is expected to grow at an 18.5% compounded annual rate through 2018.[149] It is not clear what proportion is cross-border. Though most services are provided by high-income countries,[150] countries like India are emerging as important suppliers. India has carved out a niche in the

[140] 21 C.F.R. § 312.120(c)(2).

[141] Council of Europe, Convention on Human Rights and Biomedicine and Explanatory Report ch. II, art. 5, Apr. 4, 1997, 36 I.L.M. 817, 821.

[142] ICH Harmonized Tripartite Guideline: Guideline for Good Clinical Practice E6(R1) (June 10, 1996).

[143] CIOMS, International Ethical Guidelines for Biomedical Research Involving Human Subjects (2002).

[144] Kahn, *The Human Factor*, at 887.

[145] *See* Daniel Carpenter, Reputation and Power: Organizational Image and Pharmaceutical Regulation at the FDA 686–726 (2010).

[146] Thomas R. McLean, *The Offshoring of American Medicine: Scope, Economic Issues and Legal Liabilities*, 14 Annals Health L. 205, 233–235 (2005); Joseph Kvedar, Molly Joel Coye, & Wendy Everett, *Connected Health: A Review of Technologies and Strategies to Improve Patient Care with Telemedicine and Telehealth*, 33 Health Aff. 194 (2014). The WHO's definition is broader, but captures the essence of this definition. *See* WHO, Telemedicine: Opportunities and Developments in Member States 8–9 (2010), at http://www.who.int/goe/publications/goe_telemedicine_2010.pdf.

[147] Thomas R. McLean, *The Global Market for Health Care: Economics and Regulation*, 26 Wisc. Int'l L.J. 591, 607 (2008).

[148] Who, Telemedicine, at 37 Tbl. 5; Robert Steinbrook, *The Age of Teleradiology*, 357 New Eng. J. Med. 5 (2007); Thomas R. McLean & Edward P. Richards, *Teleradiology: A Case Study of the Economic and Legal Considerations in International Trade in Telemedicine*, 25 Health Aff. 1378 (2006).

[149] Research and Markets, *Global Telemedicine Market Outlook 2018* (Mar. 2014), at http://www.researchandmarkets.com/reports/2775117/global_telemedicine_market_outlook_2018.

[150] Who, Telemedicine, at 49.

teleradiology market, offering physicians who can interpret X-rays during off-hours in the West, and for one-tenth of the price.[151] Indian teleradiology exports have grown at a 20% annual rate.[152] Other low- and middle-income countries are competing to offer telemedicine services as well. A WHO study found "the highest projected growth" in the "African, Eastern Mediterranean, and South-East Asian Regions."[153]

Telemedicine represents an important innovation in healthcare delivery, with obvious benefits. For example, telemedicine can help alleviate professional shortages in certain geographic areas, with teleradiology as the quintessential example. But other specialists export services via telemedicine too, like dermatologists, who can diagnose patients remotely by accessing high-resolution images and patient histories on secure networks,[154] or even specially trained intensivists, who are utilized in intensive care units (ICUs) in small and rural communities.[155] Demonstration projects have shown positive results in lower income countries,[156] where the populations tend to be more rural.[157]

A second potential benefit of telemedicine is cost savings. For example, a health system in Massachusetts reduced hospital readmission rates for congestive heart failure patients by 44% through remote monitoring and by identifying high-risk patients for early intervention.[158] The program enrolled two hundred and fifty patients, saving $10 million over six years.[159] Hyperspecialization by telemedicine providers might also cut costs through sheer economies of scale.[160]

Telemedicine might also help improve the quality of care and reduce medical errors by allowing providers to continuously monitor patients, make more frequent adjustments, and better coordinate care.[161] Another potential benefit is reducing the variability in diagnosis and treatment, or generating "centers of excellence" that can become hypercompetent at a specific task, like interpreting X-rays.[162]

However, studies recognize that the novelties of telemedicine can also generate novel patient injuries.[163] Any software-based medical system creates a risk of computer errors, user errors, or both.[164] Injuries from robotic surgeries, for example, are estimated to be dramatically underreported. There are also concerns that distance itself generates risk, if a provider cannot physically examine or respond to patients in-person.

[151] McLean, *The Global Market*, at 606. [152] *Id.* at 611 (citing a 2006 study).

[153] WHO, TELEMEDICINE, at 53. [154] Kvedar, Coye, & Everett, *Connected Health*, at 196.

[155] *Id.* at 196–197.

[156] INTERNATIONAL TELECOMMUNICATION UNION, MOBILE EHEALTH SOLUTIONS FOR DEVELOPING COUNTRIES (QUESTION 14-2/2) (2010), at http://www.itu.int/dms_pub/itu-d/opb/stg/D-STG-SG02.14.2-2010-PDF-E.pdf (last accessed Apr. 16, 2014); Gil Siegal, *Enabling Globalization of Health Care in the Information Technology Era: Telemedicine and the Medical World Wide Web*, 17 VA. J.L. & TECH. 1, 8–10 (2012).

[157] Siegal, *Enabling Globalization*, at 9–10.

[158] Ambar Kulshreshtha et al., *Use of Remote Monitoring to Improve Outcomes in Patients with Heart Failure: A Pilot Trial*, INT'L J. TELEMEDICINE AND APPLICATIONS 2010: 870959 (2010).

[159] *Id.* [160] McLean, *The Offshoring of American Medicine*, at 451.

[161] *Id.* at 452; Kvedar, Coye, & Everett, *Connected Health*, at 195.

[162] McLean, *The Future of Telemedicine*, at 452–453.

[163] INSTITUTE OF MEDICINE, TELEMEDICINE: A GUIDE TO ASSESSING TELECOMMUNICATIONS IN HEALTH CARE 96–100 (Marilyn J. Field ed., 1996).

[164] McLean, *The Future of Telemedicine*, at 455; Nathan Cortez, *The Mobile Health Revolution?*, 47 U.C. DAVIS L. REV. 1226–1230 (2014).

As with the other globalizing health markets, there are distributional concerns with telemedicine, such as the potential drain of medical expertise from the public to the private sector. But there is also preliminary evidence, to cite one example, that at least some Indian physicians are repatriating due to opportunities in the Indian telemedicine industry.[165] A systemwide concern is that telemedicine services from higher income countries with well-trained specialists will crowd out opportunities to cultivate home-grown specialists. And on the flip side of that coin, telemedicine providers from lower income countries might threaten their counterparts in higher income countries by undercutting their prices.[166]

Cross-border telemedicine also raises several thorny legal questions. For example, a physician licensed in one country but caring for patients in another may be violating the latter's licensing laws, which can be a criminal offense.[167] Although roughly ten U.S. states grant special limited-use licenses to accommodate telemedicine practitioners,[168] these jurisdictions are exceptional. Second, tribunals hearing disputes over medical malpractice associated with telemedicine must resolve important questions about proper venue, jurisdiction, choice of law, and the standard of care.[169] Moreover, the technologies used for telemedicine raise concerns about patient privacy.[170] Together, these legal ambiguities might deter more widespread use of international telemedicine.[171]

Of course, there is little international law to govern telemedicine.[172] The dispute settlement systems offered under the WTO's General Agreement on Trade in Services (GATS) is not available to private medical malpractice disputes.[173] Domestically, groups like the American Telemedicine Association have introduced standards, best practices, and guidelines for telemedicine providers,[174] though these efforts are largely limited to the United States.[175] There is also private liability insurance for telemedicine providers to reduce the financial risk of medical malpractice, data breaches, and computer errors.[176]

As usual, the European Union's supranational structure enables it to create rules for cross-border transactions between member states, which it has done by writing rules for telemedicine licensing, insurance reimbursement, and patient privacy, among other things.[177]

[165] McLean, *The Global Market*, at 619. [166] *Id.* at 592.

[167] Id. at 632–639; Amar Gupta & Deth Sao, *The Constitutionality of Current Legal Barriers to Telemedicine in the United States: Analysis and Future Directions of Its Relationship to National and International Health Care Reform*, 21 Health Matrix 385, 393–397 (2011); Gil Siegal, *Electronic Medical Tourism and the World Wide Web*, *in* The Globalization of Health Care, at 341, 347–348.

[168] Siegal, *Electronic*, at 348. [169] Gupta & Sao, *The Constitutionality*, at 397–402.

[170] *Id.* at 402–403.

[171] Deth Sao, Amar Gupta, & David A. Gantz, *Legal and Regulatory Barriers to Telemedicine in the United States*, *in* The Globalization of Health Care, at 359.

[172] *Id.* at 375. [173] *Id.*

[174] American Telemedicine Association, *ATA Standards & Guidelines*, at http://www.americantelemed.org/resources/standards/ata-standards-guidelines.

[175] The American Telemedicine Association does partner with counterparts in other countries, but the contours of these partnerships are unclear. American Telemedicine Association, *ATA Global Partnerships*, at http://www.americantelemed.org/about-ata/ata-global-partners.

[176] *See, e.g.*, HUB International, *Telemedicine Overview*, at http://www.hubinternational.com/telemedicine/.

[177] Commission Staff Working Document on the Applicability of Existing EU Legislation to Telemedicine Services, COM (2012) 736 final (Dec. 6, 2012); Communication from the Commission to the European Parliament, the Council, The European Economic and Social Committee and the Committee of the Regions, eHealth Action Plan 2012–2020, COM (2012) 736 final (Dec. 6, 2012).

Similarly, the WHO's Global Observatory for eHealth, created in 2005, serves as an information and standards clearinghouse for telemedicine and related technologies, but lacks a regulatory function.[178] An even earlier agreement by the G8 countries, initiated in 1998, promised to establish global best practices to facilitate telemedicine.[179] But both the WHO and G8 efforts have underwhelmed, according to some.[180] Thus, as with other globalizing markets in healthcare, telemedicine operates largely in a legal void.

f. Global Market for Patients

The last of the six globalizing markets examined here is perhaps the most dramatic—medical tourism. The phenomenon of patients leaving their home countries for medical care is not entirely new.[181] Patients with means have long traveled to seek the best care from the best physicians at the best facilities. Modern patients may travel for a variety of complex reasons, including to access treatments that are unavailable (or even illegal) in their home country, or simply to access more affordable care.[182] This last form of medical tourism has proliferated recently, driven by escalating healthcare prices in high-income jurisdictions like the United States, Canada, and Western Europe.

To meet this demand, a number of low- and middle-income countries like India, Thailand, and Mexico are competing vigorously to attract foreign patients, offering treatments of comparable quality at a discount that often exceeds 50%. Even hospitals in higher income countries, like the United States, Canada, Singapore, and South Korea, try to attract foreign patients to generate revenue. Thus, there is now global competition for patients.

The medical tourism market is perhaps the most opaque of the global health markets. Governments generally do not track how many patients travel, for what procedures, or where. Estimates by foreign hospitals and foreign governments with medical tourism aspirations are often wildly inflated.[183] For what it is worth, one industry expert estimates that roughly eleven million people worldwide leave their countries for medical care each year, spending between $3,500 to $5,000 each; thus generating $38–$55 billion in revenues.[184] The same estimate predicts that in 2014, roughly 1.2 million U.S. residents would leave the country for medical care.[185] A separate survey of the medical tourism industry found the largest growth in cosmetic surgeries, cancer treatments, infertility treatments, and dental care.[186]

178 WHO, *Global Observatory for eHealth (GOe)*, at http://www.who.int/goe/en/ (last accessed Apr. 16, 2014).

179 André Lacroix et al., *International Concerted Action on Collaboration in Telemedicine: Recommendations of the G-8 Global Healthcare Applications Subproject-4*, 8 TELEMED. & E-HEALTH 149 (2002).

180 Siegal, *Enabling Globalization*, at 12.

181 Cortez, *Patients*.

182 Nicolas P. Terry, *Under-Regulated Health Care Phenomena in a Flat World: Medical Tourism and Outsourcing*, 29 WEST. N. ENG. L. REV. 421 (2007); Cortez, *Patients*; Cohen, *Protecting Patients*.

183 Cortez, *New Geography*, at 875–876.

184 Patients Beyond Borders, *Medical Tourism Statistics and Facts*, at http://www.patientsbeyondborders.com/medical-tourism-statistics-facts (last visited Apr. 22, 2014).

185 *Id.*

186 International Medical Travel Journal, *Report Summary: Medical Tourism Climate Survey 2014* (Mar. 2014), at http://www.imtj.com/resources/research-and-statistics/medical-tourism-climate-survey-2014/ (last visited Apr. 22, 2014).

The potential benefits of medical tourism are many. A commonly cited benefit is patient autonomy. Medical tourism also provides an important safety net for patients who cannot afford necessary care domestically.[187] Indeed, many medical tourists are motivated by a combination of desperate medical and financial need—if they could not seek care overseas, they would receive none at all. For domestic providers, competition from abroad might encourage price competition (although it is doubtful that the volume of outbound patients is currently sufficient to induce price reductions by U.S. providers). For host countries, medical tourists can generate new revenues for domestic providers, which in theory could help subsidize care for local patients.[188]

The academic literature has matured beyond considering medical tourism as a novelty to engaging some of the legal, ethical, and policy challenges that it poses.[189] Medical commentators warn that travel is not appropriate for many kinds of treatments and worry about substandard foreign care.[190] Ethical perspectives consider that efforts to attract relatively wealthy foreign patients can drain resources from public facilities.[191] Legal commentators worry that although the benefits of medical tourism are often diffuse—patients and payers save money, while foreign hospitals make it—the legal risks of these transactions fall disproportionately on patients.[192] Indeed, there are troubling practices in the industry to require patients to sign waivers or acknowledge disclaimers that greatly limit their legal recourse in the event of malpractice.[193] From a regulatory perspective, the medical tourism industry largely operates in a transnational legal void.[194]

Scholars have examined countless ways to blunt these risks, ranging from unilateral to multilateral, hard law to soft law, public to private. For example, domestic regulators might try to "channel" patients to high-quality foreign providers or to jurisdictions with sufficient legal protections.[195] Or regulators might oversee the domestic intermediaries that facilitate these trips.[196] Some proposals would simply try to correct information asymmetries or other failures in the medical tourism market.[197] Others would tinker with substantive medical malpractice rules to adjust for the unique circumstances of medical tourism.[198] Restricting patient travel seems to be a nonstarter.[199]

[187] Cortez, *New Geography*, at 876–880.

[188] Cohen, *Medical Tourism* (questioning this frequent assumption).

[189] There are several book-length academic treatments on medical tourism: *see* I. Glenn Cohen, Patients with Passports: Medical Tourism, Law, and Ethics (2015); Milica Z. Bookman & Karla R. Bookman, Medical Tourism in Developing Countries (2007); Risks and Challenges in Medical Tourism: Understanding the Global Market for Health Services (Jill R. Hodges, Leigh Turner, & Anne Marie Kimball eds., 2012); C. Michael Hall, Medical Tourism: The Ethics, Regulation, and Marketing of Health Mobility (2012); The Globalization of Health Care; Medical Tourism and Transnational Health Care (David Botterill, Guido Pennings, & Tomas Mainil eds., 2013); Traveling Well: Essays in Medical Tourism (Ronald Labonté, Vivien Runnels, Corinne Packer, & Raywat Deonandran eds., 2013).

[190] Jessica Wapner, *American Medical Association Provides Guidance on Medical Tourism*, 337 Brit. Med. J. a575 (2008).

[191] Cohen, *Medical Tourism*; Chen & Flood, *Medical Tourism's Impact*.

[192] *See, e.g.*, Cortez, *Recalibrating*, at 1–7. [193] *Id.* [194] Cortez, *Into the Void*.

[195] Cohen, *Protecting Patients*, at 1506–1523.

[196] Cortez, *Patients*, at 118–123; Cohen, *Protecting Patients*, at 1559–1566.

[197] Cortez, *Patients*, at 119; Cohen, *Protecting Patients*, at 1506–1511; Cortez, *Recalibrating*, at 88–89.

[198] Cortez, *Patients*, at 122; Cohen, *Protecting Patients*, at 1563.

[199] Cortez, *Patients*, at 114–118.

Private sector responses have arisen to fill the legal void, like voluntary certification, international hospital accreditation, medical malpractice insurance, industry guidelines, or the use of alternative dispute resolution.[200] Each option underwhelms in some way, either by being too unilateral, too voluntary, or too impractical. Multilateral requirements might be imposed via trade agreements, though this seems unlikely outside of contexts like the European Union, whose Directive on Patients' Rights in Cross-Border Healthcare imposes relatively modest obligations on member states, mostly focused on reimbursement rather than the problems discussed above.[201] Moreover, very few of the twenty-eight EU member states actually implemented the Directive by the 2013 deadline.[202] Thus, like most other globalizing markets in healthcare, the medical tourism trade remains largely underregulated, though surrogate mechanisms have sprouted to partially fill the void.

IV Globalization and Its Discontents

> Globalization today is not working for many of the world's poor.... To some, there is an easy answer: Abandon globalization. That is neither feasible nor desirable.... The problem is not with globalization, but with how it has been managed.
>
> — Joseph Stiglitz, *Globalization and Its Discontents*[203]

The conundrum of globalization in healthcare is that it presents both discrete benefits and burdens. The benefits are often tangible signs of prosperity—a gleaming new hospital, a sophisticated new diagnostic machine, a new foreign-trained physician, or a new revenue stream. Global competition can generate quantifiable gains from trade, shifting resources to their most productive uses.[204] It can also markedly improve the quality of care by accelerating and disseminating scientific advances.[205] Indeed, healthcare in the twentieth century is a story of the broad diffusion of Western scientific medicine. Globalization also creates unique opportunities for market participants from low- and middle-income countries to introduce new sources of revenue and new medical advances to their health systems.[206]

But the burdens of globalization are equally pronounced. Globalization in healthcare inevitably introduces more privatization and commercialization to domestic health sectors, which can undermine public providers.[207] Indeed, countries that lack robust public health sectors often see globalization as worsening domestic inequities.[208] Global market pressures can exacerbate the two-tiered system in many countries in which the private sector caters to healthier, wealthier populations, leaving the public sector to care for poorer, sicker

[200] Cortez, *Recalibrating*, at 78–85. [201] Directive 2011/23/EU.

[202] Denis Horgan, *EU Directive on Patients' Rights to Cross Border Healthcare*, 347 Brit. Med. J. f7694 (2013).

[203] Joseph E. Stiglitz, Globalization and Its Discontents 214 (2002). The title of this book and this section, of course, is a play on the famous book, Sigmund Freud, Civilization and Its Discontents (Dover Publications 1994) (Joan Riviere trans. 1930).

[204] Cortez, *International*, at 688–691. [205] *Id.* at 688. [206] *Id.* at 692–695.

[207] *Id.* at 679–685. [208] *Id.* at 698.

populations. This disequilibrium is often aggravated by multilateral institutions whose policies encourage low- and middle-income countries to further privatize and commercialize their health sectors, corroding the idea that healthcare is a public good.[209]

Moreover, the fruits of globalization often accrue disproportionately to private rather than public interests and to high-income rather than low- or middle-income countries. The latter may be particularly eager to participate in global markets, with participation justified ex post by new revenues, new medical facilities, and new technologies.[210] But domestically, these benefits can accrue mainly to private interests, with little cross-subsidization or positive externalities spilling over to the public sector.[211]

As Stiglitz laments, the problem is not globalization per se, but how it has been managed.[212] Yet there are very few tools for managing globalization in healthcare. Rapid globalization has occurred largely in a legal and regulatory void.[213] There are few supranational legal mechanisms for redressing wrongs, redistributing the benefits and burdens of globalization, or correcting market failures.[214] Domestic efforts to regulate global health markets unilaterally have had mixed success, as demonstrated by efforts to regulate physician emigration, medical tourism, and cross-border insurance.

The most promising interventions, naturally, are multilateral. But even these efforts, like the WHO's Global Code of Practice on the International Recruitment of Health Personnel,[215] are largely normative and voluntary. Public-private cooperation like the ICH have helped harmonize international standards, but do not purport to regulate global transactions in any ordinary sense. The WHO's International Health Regulations sound regulatory in nature but focus on coordinating global responses to public health emergencies, like infectious disease epidemics.[216] Indeed, public international law—as enunciated via treaties and customary international law—focuses on the legal rights and duties of governments, not private enterprises.[217] And public international law governs only by the consent of member states. As Gostin notes, "[t]here is often no supranational authority to monitor, adjudicate, and enforce international law against states."[218] One supranational authority that has been able to impose binding requirements is the European Union, whose Directive on Patients' Rights in Cross-Border Healthcare[219] and telemedicine guidelines[220] do help regulate cross-border transactions. But these only apply within unique supranational regimes.

The lack of hard law has led scholars to push for soft law in global health markets, like leveraging access to domestic markets by imposing private certification or accreditation.[221] Another example is that clinical trials performed overseas must meet certain standards to support marketing applications to the FDA.[222] Gostin, for example, emphasizes the importance of WHO authority to adopt normative standards and soft law, like the Global Code, because they are relatively easy to negotiate and can generate consensus standards.[223]

[209] *Id.* at 681–682, 697. [210] *Id.* at 698. [211] *See, e.g.*, Cohen, *Medical Tourism*.

[212] STIGLITZ, GLOBALIZATION, at 214.

[213] *See, e.g.*, Cortez, *Into the Void* (discussing medical tourism).

[214] Cortez, *International*, at 697. [215] WHO GLOBAL CODE.

[216] World Health Assembly, Revision of the International Health Regulations, WHA58.3 (May 23, 2005); David P. Fidler & Lawrence O. Gostin, *The New International Health Regulations: An Historic Development for International Law and Public Health*, 34 J.L. MED. & ETHICS 85 (2006).

[217] GOSTIN, GLOBAL, at 62. [218] *Id.* at 64. [219] Directive 2011/23/EU.

[220] Commission Staff Working Document. [221] Cortez, *New Geography*, at 905–911.

[222] FDA, International Conference on Harmonisation. [223] GOSTIN, GLOBAL, at 65.

But this kind of soft law often underwhelms and is largely ignored by member states. In one survey, 93% of respondents reported that the WHO's Global Code did not meaningfully affect domestic policies or industry practices.[224] There is no reason to think that a WHO Global Code on cross-border insurance, or telemedicine, or patient mobility would be much different. Other soft law techniques leverage payment on compliance with voluntary international standards—the best example being international hospital accreditation by JCI.[225] But these levers primarily function to ensure access to more lucrative markets in high-income countries. They are not designed to address the vagaries of global markets that harm low- and middle-income countries.

The WHO does have treaty-making authority to generate binding international law through Article 19 of the WHO Constitution[226] but rarely uses it.[227] Gostin makes a detailed case for the WHO to assert this authority more frequently and more ambitiously,[228] though doing so would require the WHO to confront tricky questions about its relationship with member states, its resources, its funding, and its ability to implement a more ambitious agenda.[229] In short, it is not clear that international hard law would be any more effective than international soft law. The emerging scholarship on globalization in healthcare markets must continue to examine optimal strategies for maximizing the benefits of globalization while minimizing its burdens.

V Conclusion

Globalization now touches most of the inputs and outputs of medical care. Although it presents clear opportunities for scientific advancement and economic prosperity, globalization also creates specific burdens, particularly in low- and middle-income countries. The problem is that global trade in health markets largely resides beyond the traditional jurisdiction of domestic regulators, and international law remains largely inattentive to these transactions. Scholars continue to examine the use of soft law in these markets, though soft law has obvious inadequacies. It is particularly good at leveraging access to high-income markets but less good at addressing disparities that primarily affect low- and middle-income countries. The challenge for contemporary scholars is to find mechanisms—legal and otherwise—that will facilitate the tangible benefits of global trade and minimize (or more fairly distribute) its burdens.

224 *Id.* at 66 (*citing* Jennifer S. Edge & Steven J. Hoffman, *Empirical Impact Evaluation of the WHO Global Code of Practice on the International Recruitment of Health Personnel (2010) on Government, Civil Society, and Private Sectors in Australia, Canada, United Kingdom and United States of America* (paper presented at the Annual Meeting of the American Political Science Association, Seattle, Washington, September 1–4, 2011)).

225 Cortez, *New Geography*, at 905–908.

226 WHO, Constitution of the World Health Organization (1948) entered into for April 7, 1948, art. 19.

227 The only treaty negotiated by the WHO under Article 19 is the Framework Convention on Tobacco Control. The WHO used Article 21 to negotiate its International Health Regulations (IHR) and its Nomenclature Regulations (standardizing nomenclature for diseases and diagnostic procedures, etc). Gostin, Global, at 64–65.

228 *Id.* at 103–128.

229 *Id.* at 127–128.

CHAPTER 49

THE SOCIAL DETERMINANTS OF HEALTH

RACHEL REBOUCHÉ AND SCOTT BURRIS

I Introduction

HEALTH is a product of the interaction of genes, people, and places. The "social determinants of health" are the resources we have and the conditions we face in the environments in which we live, work, and learn that influence exposure, vulnerability and immunity to pathogens, toxins, stressors, and other proximate causes of acute or chronic illness.[1] People who are exposed to poor nutrition, preventable disease, unsafe water, poor sanitation, and substandard housing will have poorer health than people who are not. This is no surprise. But even when populations have adequate resources, disparities in income, education, and status still matter. In every country, the relatively rich—those better able to take advantage of a range of resources that support health—live healthier and longer lives than their relatively poorer neighbors.

Quality healthcare is one of the resources that determine health, and healthcare inequities are part of the larger puzzle of the social determinants of health. As the United States demonstrates, however, getting healthcare, even the world's most expensive healthcare, produces neither an optimal level nor fair distribution of health in a population.[2] Healthcare insurance can help an individual pay for needed medical care (and the preventative care that can make future services unnecessary), but a lack of healthcare insurance is not the primary cause of the dismal state of U.S. population health, and expanding access to healthcare services does not guarantee a healthier population.[3]

[1] Scott Burris, Ichiro Kawachi, & Austin Sarat, *Integrating Law and Social Epidemiology*, 30 J. L. MED. & ETHICS 510, 512 (2002).

[2] Scott Burris, *From Health Care Law to the Social Determinants of Health: A Public Health Law Research Perspective*, 159 U. PA. L. REV. 1649, 1651 (2011); David Orentlicher, *The Future of the Affordable Care Act: Protecting Economic Health More Than Physical Health*, 51 HOUSTON L. REV. 1057, 1068 (2014).

[3] Lawrence O. Gostin, Peter D. Jacobson, Katherine L. Record, & Lorian E. Hardcastle, *Restoring Health to Health Reform: Integrating Medicine and Public Health to Advance the Population's Wellbeing*, 159 U. PA. L. REV. 1777, 1781 (2011).

Although we know that education, place, work, and other surroundings exert a powerful influence over health, U.S. health policy still follows the theory—and sends the message—that good health or illness depends solely on individual dispositions and actions—that "people who are healthy deserve praise for their responsible choices and those who are not deserve at least partial blame."[4] Policy (and spending) has tended to focus on strengthening the infrastructure for delivering healthcare services and regulating behaviors, like smoking, that are proximally linked to health outcomes.[5] Thus, when the government acts to regulate health, it often does so through policies targeting individual choices, like buying healthcare insurance, or incentivizing the adoption of healthy lifestyles. Interventions aimed at proximal risk factors like overeating and underexercising, or at specific maladies like hypertension and diabetes, can be effective against their targets and are an important part of healthy public policy. But these interventions do not address the maldistribution of the basic resources for health. Indeed, policies that depend on individuals acquiring additional knowledge about healthy behaviors, or purchasing medical services, can exacerbate existing disparities between the better off and those with less.

Adopting "the broader public health view that all aspects of our lives—in our work, families, and communities—should support active and healthy living"[6] is essential to crafting and implementing policies that afford people the greatest chance to be healthy. Law can and does play a powerful role in perpetuating the social determinants linked to poor health (of individuals or communities) or in ensuring that social environments work toward better health. It shapes, maintains, and mediates the social, economic, and physical structures that determine who gets sick and who thrives.[7]

This chapter discusses the role of law in improving individual and population health and distributing healthcare more or less justly. Part II explains the social determinants of health, noting the racial disparities in health status and healthcare services, and highlights the relationship between low income, inequality, and poor health. Part III considers the Patient Protection and Affordable Care Act (ACA) as an instrument to increase equitable access to high-quality healthcare and to support a better integration of the health and healthcare systems. This part also notes, however, the ways in which the ACA falls short of adopting a social determinants approach. The chapter concludes with a discussion of a "culture of health" and how law can help build one.

II The Social Determinants of Health

One's social position is defined by wealth, education, gender, race, ethnicity, and all the other material and immaterial characteristics that define hierarchy in a community. Social

[4] Emily Parento, *Health Equity, Health People 2020, and Coercive Legal Mechanisms as Necessary for the Achievement of Both*, 58 Loy. L. Rev. 655, 657 (2012).

[5] Paula A. Braveman, Susan Egerter, & Robin E. Mockenhaupt, *Broadening the Focus: The Need to Address the Social Determinants of Health*, 40 Am. J. Preventive Med. S1, S9 (2011).

[6] Alonzo L. Plough, *Building a Culture of Health: Challenges for the Public Health Workforce*, 47 Am. J. Preventive Med. S388, S388 (2014).

[7] Burris, Kawachi, & Sarat, *Integrating Law and Social Epidemiology*, at 512.

position, in turn, largely defines a person's ability to reach resources that support health: a good education, a safe place to live, healthcare, a supportive circle of friends and neighbors. This part of the chapter defines and explains the social determinants of health, including access to healthcare services. We note disparities among racial groups in both health status and in access to healthcare services. This part then explores how a social determinants perspective points to the broad and deep role of inequality in explaining who is healthy and who is not. In short, inequalities in income correlate with disparities in health status and inequalities in access to health resources.[8] Inequality in income, across the U.S. population, drives health (and social) problems and suggests a role for health law reform that takes redistribution of resources—from the haves to the have-nots—seriously.

a. What Are the Social Determinants of Health?

Health depends on the conditions and experiences of daily life: "Health [is not just] something we get at the doctor's office but instead . . . starts in our families, in our schools and workplaces, in our playgrounds and parks, and in the air we breathe and the water we drink."[9] Where people "live, learn, work, and play" shapes individuals' and groups' life expectancies, health, and well-being.[10] Thus, the "social determinants of health" are those factors or resources that define the extent to which people are exposed to health stressors and their capacity to withstand them: education; affordable, dependable housing and safe neighborhoods; good nutrition; clean environments; adequate income; access to healthcare; and safe and manageable employment.[11] The physical environment not only embodies the structural and material conditions of communities but also the patterns of social engagement and sense of security affected by where people live.[12] Where we live is so important that our health can be predicted by our zip codes.[13] Work or employment is a social determinant that includes the risks of one's workplace (handling dangerous materials, for example) as well as the degree of physical workload, the stress produced by and at work, and the level of control one has over his or her position or work life.[14]

Studies on the connection between education level and health provide a good example of social determinants research.[15] Paula Braveman and her colleagues mapped out three interrelated pathways linking education to health. First, education can improve health by increasing health knowledge and behaviors: better-educated people are more likely to make informed

[8] Michael Marmot & Richard Wilkinson, Social Determinants of Health 2 (2005).

[9] Robert Wood Johnson Foundation, Vulnerable Populations Portfolio, A New Way to Talk about the Social Determinants of Health 6 (2010).

[10] Braveman, Egerter, & Mockenhaupt, *Broadening the Focus*, at S5.

[11] Paula Braveman, Susan Egerter, & David R. Williams, *The Social Determinants of Health: Coming of Age*, 32 Ann. Rev. Pub. Health 381, 382 (2011); Bruce G. Link & Jo Phelan, *Social Conditions as Fundamental Causes of Disease*, 35 J. Health & Soc. Behav. (Extra Issue) 80, 81 (1995).

[12] Braveman, Egerter, & Williams, *Social Determinants of Health*, at 385.

[13] Alonzo Plough, *Developing New Systems of Data to Advance a Culture of Health*, 2 eGEMs (Generating Evidence & Methods to Improve Patient Outcomes) 1, 3 (2014). Institute of Medicine, Disparities in Health Care: Methods for Studying the Effects of Race, Ethnicity, and SES on Access, Use and Quality of Health Care (2002).

[14] *Id.*

[15] Braveman, Egerter, & Williams, *Social Determinants of Health*, at 386–387.

decisions about their diets, exercise, and disease management and to adopt health-related recommendations. Second, educational level shapes employment opportunities. Those with higher levels of education have lower rates of unemployment, and are more likely to work in "healthier physical and psychosocial working conditions," receive employer-subsidized health benefits, and make more money than those with little or no formal education. The better off receive all the benefits that attach to having a "good job"—paid sick leave, retirement benefits, enough income to live in a safe neighborhood and in decent housing. Third, education level is associated with higher social status, including a greater sense of control over day-to-day life, higher social standing and prestige, greater social mobility, and better support from family, friends, neighbors, and coworkers. All of these goods and resources correspond to lower levels of chronic illness, such as heart disease or diabetes, and to living a longer life. When people succeed in pursuing an education, they are more likely to experience long-term advantages in physical and mental health.

Thus, a premise of a social determinants approach is that vulnerability and immunity to disease are baked into the human being through exposures that begin early in life and accumulate over a lifetime.[16] For example, studies consistently find that higher birth weights correlate with decreased likelihood of adult disease. Newborns with low birth weights are much more likely to develop diabetes in adulthood by their sixty-fifth birthday.[17] Researchers have focused on early childhood as a particularly important point of intervention.

Studying the social determinants is all the more complicated because resources like education or work do not exist apart from each other. Social determinants are interconnected just as the environments in which people work, learn, and live are interconnected. We often take a social determinant such as safe and efficient transportation for granted. But how we navigate and see our physical space relates to the well-being and safety we experience in our neighborhoods, schools, and workplaces. For example, creating bicycle lanes can help facilitate exercise, which one would expect to improve health status and incentivize healthy behaviors. Thoughtful transportation strategies and road design also support access to jobs and social services. Less cars and more open spaces can help create peaceful communities that reduce accidents, and, in the sense of intangible goods, add to one's sense of wellness.[18]

One's social environment is every bit as important as the physical one. Social norms—on anything from alcohol use to gender roles—can support more or decidedly less healthy behavior. The communities in which we live consist of the material conditions of houses or apartments, as well as the patterns of social engagement and sense of security. Ties of trust and support among neighbors are resources for individual agency and collective efficacy for health. Social determinants of health can make our lives pleasurable and reduce stress through the networks of social support that help define our norms and cultural expectations.

Elevated social status (being closer to the top of any social, economic hierarchy), control over one's life (in terms of profession or mobility), and strong social networks are tied to good health.[19] The World Health Organization has identified the ways in which social exclusion, unemployment, and lack of social support have a documented effect on people's

[16] John Lynch & George Davey Smith, *A Life Course Approach to Chronic Disease Epidemiology*, 26 Ann. Rev. Pub. Health 1, 1 (2005).

[17] World Health Organization, Social Determinants of Health: The Solid Facts 15 (Richard Wilkinson & Michael Marmot eds., 2d ed. 2003).

[18] *Id.*

[19] Michael Marmot et al., *Employment Grade and Coronary Heart Disease in British Civil Servants*, 32 J. Epidemiology & Community Health 244, 244–249 (1978).

physical and mental health and are predictors of poor health.[20] Generally, the longer someone lives in circumstances of disadvantage and stress, the greater the health problems they typically have. That is, studies show that social isolation and poor social support correlates with premature death and higher levels of disability due to chronic disease. Take for example, the social determinant of work. Having little control over one's work day correlates with back pain and cardiovascular disease. And those who receive few rewards from work—in terms of money, status, or self-esteem—have even greater risk of cardiac illness. A policy response that seeks to improve working conditions might consider what the World Health Organization calls a "virtuous cycle": improved work conditions can lead to healthier workers, who are more productive workers.[21]

The fact that health is socially determined to a considerable extent does not mean that we are all exposed to the same health risks. The ability to obtain health services provides a thoroughly researched example of how social position leads to health outcomes. Marginalized populations consistently receive fewer and lower quality healthcare services,[22] and race and ethnicity are well-documented predictors of the type and level of healthcare services individuals receive.[23] People of color suffer disproportionately from preventable diseases, experience worse health on average, and receive less medical care, comparative to the nonminority population.[24] A 2010 National Healthcare Disparities Report, for example, found that Latinos and Latinas received healthcare equivalent to whites in only 17% of tested measures.[25] In part, these disparities are due to a lack of healthcare coverage: People of color make up over half of the uninsured in the United States,[26] and they have less employment-related insurance coverage.[27] Race and ethnicity are powerful markers of people's ability to access to resources.

Even people who get health care are treated differently because of race. Although de jure segregation and, perhaps, conscious discrimination, have receded, race, socioeconomic status, and social position still influence healthcare providers in unconscious ways. People of color, similarly positioned to the white population, consistently receive fewer prescriptions and fewer medical services for the same conditions (bypass surgeries, dialysis treatments, and kidney transplants, for example).[28] The experience of racial discrimination itself can adversely affect an individual's health and correlates with the onset of illness. The stress associated with discrimination can release hormones that increase the wear and tear on the human body and its systems.[29] The disadvantages of race are cumulative and long-term—people of color of varying income levels are statistically less likely to have grown up in households with wealth and are more likely to have experienced discrimination.[30] Moreover, as a direct result of racial segregation, some communities in which populations of color live have significant problems with sanitation, exposure to toxins, access to nutritious foods, and neighborhood safety.

[20] World Health Organization, Social Determinants of Health, at 7–9.

[21] *Id.* at 18–19. [22] Braveman, Egerter, & Mockenhaupt, *Broadening the Focus*, at S9.

[23] Braveman, Egerter, & Williams, *Social Determinants of Health*, at 382; Parento, *Health Equity, Health People 2020*, at 713.

[24] Rene Bowser, *The Affordable Care Act and Beyond: Opportunities for Advancing Health Equity and Social Justice*, 10 Hastings Race & Poverty L.J. 69, 75 (2013).

[25] *Id.* [26] *Id.* at 78.

[27] Lance Gable, *The Patient Protection and Affordable Care Act, Public Health, and the Elusive Target of Human Rights*, 39 J. L. Med. & Ethics 340, 343 (2011).

[28] Bowser, *The Affordable Care Act and Beyond*, at 70. [29] *Id.*

[30] Braveman, Egerter, & Mockenhaupt, *Broadening the Focus*, at S10.

Race, and social position more broadly, carries with it differences in immunities and in vulnerabilities, but it is the *distribution* of health resources within environments that shapes the health of the population.[31] Law plays a key role in that distribution. Discrimination laws, zoning ordinances, and public housing regulations make a difference to individual and group health because governing where and how people live entails managing and distributing valuable social resources. Randomized experiments have shown that low-income public housing residents who move from high-poverty neighborhoods to places with lower poverty rates experience better overall health and well-being.[32] And law is a mechanism that turns social position into health outcomes, because law contributes to the development, stability, and perpetuation of broader social conditions, like racism, that affect health.[33] Evidence indicates, for example, that school discipline policies and drug control laws are sorting a disturbing proportion of African American pupils out of education and into the criminal justice system.[34]

The next section reviews law's relationship with the social determinant of income. Specifically, we engage with research that suggests income inequality is one of the most powerful drivers of health status.

b. Law, Income Inequality, and Reform

This section focuses on how income and class correlate with health outcomes. Income gaps among Americans are disturbingly and increasingly deep, which we argue signals crucial problems in the distribution of health resources. We focus on income inequality because it is a good proxy for the range of social determinants the last section defined, capturing the problems of health disparities noted above and suggesting policy changes that can reverse our present unhealthy course.

The *causal* role of inequality in health is still debated, and possible explanations like hierarchy-induced stress continue to be tested.[35] Still, there is enough evidence and national experience to indicate that lowering inequality will almost certainly help a population improve its health.[36] Studies suggest that when individuals and families have income security, their health improves significantly,[37] and increases in income at the lowest end of the socioeconomic scale produce the greatest improvements in population health.[38]

[31] Link & Phelan, *Social Conditions as Fundamental Causes of Disease*, at 81.

[32] Jens Ludwig et al., *Neighborhood Effects on the Long-term Well-being of Low-income Adults*, 337 SCIENCE 1505 (2012); Jens Ludwig et al., *Neighborhoods, Obesity, and Diabetes—A Randomized Social Experiment*, 365 N. ENGL. J. MED. 1509 (2011).

[33] Burris, *From Health Care Law to the Social Determinants of Health*, at 1652.

[34] *See, e.g.*, Kerrin C. Wolf, *Booking Students: An Analysis of School Arrests and Court Outcomes*, 9 NW. J. L. & SOC. POL'Y 58 (2013) (reporting results from a Delaware study on social position).

[35] John Lynch et al., *Is Income Inequality a Determinant of Population Health? Part 2. U.S. National and Regional Trends in Income Inequality and Age- and Cause-Specific Mortality*, 82 MILBANK Q. 355 (2004) (complicating the relationship between income and inequality).

[36] Braveman, Egerter, & Mockenhaupt, *Broadening the Focus*, at S6.

[37] Orentlicher, *Future of the Affordable Care Act*, at 1070–1071.

[38] Braveman, Egerter, & Mockenhaupt, *Broadening the Focus*, at S7. Kelli A. Komro, Scott Burris, & Alexander C. Wagenaar, *Social Determinants of Child Health: Conceptual and Measurement Directions for Research*, 6 HEALTH BEHAV. & POL'Y REV. 432, 433 (2014).

Social epidemiologists call the relationship between income and health the "social gradient": health outcomes "line up on a steady slope from the have-leasts to the have-mosts."[39] As described by the World Health Organization: "The poorest of the poor, around the world, have the worst health. Within countries, the evidence shows that in general the lower an individual's socioeconomic position the worse their health . . . the social gradient in health [] runs from top to bottom of the socioeconomic spectrum. This is a global phenomenon, seen in low, middle and high-income countries. The social gradient in health means that health inequities affect everyone."[40]

Countries like the United States, with a steep social gradient, tend to have worse problems of obesity, mental illness, violence, and drug use, as well as poorer health outcomes, than countries like Japan and Sweden, where inequality is low.[41] The relationship also holds within U.S. states, so that states like Utah and New Hampshire, which do not have stark gaps in income within their populations, do better across the range of health and social indicators than high-inequality states like Louisiana and Mississippi.[42] When the economic gap narrows, health improves for the poorest; when the economic gap widens, health for the poorest worsens.

If rising economic inequality is a signal of population health distress, the United States has considerable cause for alarm. Since the 1970s, inequality in income in the United States has gone from historical lows to the highest level since the Gilded Age, and wealth inequality is not far behind.[43] In 2014, for the first time, the wealthiest 10% of Americans took home over half of the national income.[44] Yet the United States, with historic levels of income inequality, is doing far less than it should to promote health where we live, learn, work, and play. Our country spends more on healthcare than comparable nations, but the United States continues to be at bottom for key health indicators.[45]

Law plays a crucial role in the distribution and preservation of the income of individuals and of families. Research supports general evidence that inequality in health correlates inversely to the generosity of income-transfer programs. "Negative" income tax experiments of the 1970s demonstrated that providing low-income pregnant women with additional cash correlated with higher birth weights of babies.[46] Moreover, the only time health

[39] Burris, *From Health Care Law to the Social Determinants of Health*, at 1652. Social epidemiology includes the study of "macro-economic factors (such as economic development, poverty, unemployment, and income distribution) and features of social relationships (social cohesion, social exclusion, gender and race relations)." Burris, Kawachi, & Sarat, *Integrating Law and Social Epidemiology*, at 512.

[40] World Health Organization, Social Determinants of Health: Key Concepts 1, http://www.who.int/social_determinants/thecommission/finalreport/key_concepts/en/.

[41] Richard Wilkinson & Kate Pickett, The Spirit Level: Why Greater Equality Makes Societies Stronger 75–77 (2009); Burris, *From Health Care Law to the Social Determinants of Health*, at 1660 n.39.

[42] *See* Gopal K. Singh & Mohammad Siahpush, *Widening Socioeconomic Inequalities in U.S. Life Expectancy, 1980–2000*, 35 Int'l J. Epidemiology 969, 975 (2006).

[43] Thomas Piketty & Emmanuel Saez, *Inequality in the Long Run*, 344 Science 838, 838 (2014). *See also* Thomas Piketty & Emmanuel Saez, *Income Inequality in the United States, 1913–1998*, 118 Q. J. Econ. 1, 1, 32 (2003).

[44] Orentlicher, *Future of the Affordable Care Act*, at 1077.

[45] Braveman, Egerter, & Mockenhaupt, *Broadening the Focus*, at S4.

[46] Hilary W. Hoynes, Douglas L. Miller, & David Simon, Income, the Earned Income Tax Credit, and Infant Health, National Bureau of Economic Research, Working Paper Series 18206 (2012).

outcomes for African Americans improved more quickly than for whites was from the late 1960 through the 1970s, when black-white differences in income narrowed.[47] Measures that strengthen family economic security, through the tax system or welfare and employment benefits, appear to correlate with improved maternal and child health.[48] Research on the effects of tax credits indicates that the expansion of the earned income tax credit (EITC) correlates with better overall health behaviors and lower rates of depression among mothers and children that are EITC beneficiaries.[49]

Yet, there has been very little scientific evaluation of the impact of our core income support interventions—the EITC, the minimum wage, Temporary Assistance for Needy Families, and unemployment compensation—on the health of individuals and families.[50] We know broader investments in education and infrastructure reduce inequalities for lower-income to middle-income groups. Indeed, a major—some argue the primary—driver of inequality in the United States is the skills premium that those with tertiary education have compared to those without.[51] However, we do not necessarily know which policies work better than others, or why they do. Low income and poor health are related, but it is unclear how welfare measures influence health because seldom does rigorous research evaluate how income-support laws directly and specifically impact health outcomes.[52]

We do have models for how law either can help close the income gap or how law permits some to maintain and accumulate wealth, widening the gap between rich and poor. Dean Baker points out numerous ways that law and policy have "increase[d] private sector profits in recent decades"—government-granted corporate tax exemptions or antitrust, patent, and copyright protections, as examples.[53] As a response to the income gap, Thomas Piketty has proposed steeper income tax progressivity and higher inheritance taxes on the wealthy to reduce inequality.[54] Strategies that reduce income inequality may improve individual and population health, even though some of these policies can seem like political impossibilities (and like all current, political "realities," subject to change).

These issues are at the core of political debates, as we see with the Patient Protection and Affordable Care Act (ACA), but politics may be the least of our problems. For decades, almost every element of our health system, from education, to research, to programs, has been organized around disease-specific funding streams and activities. Social determinants may be real, but they feel hard to change and the ethos of evidence in public health law drives the pursuit of measurable objectives. An initiative to reduce inequality will be much slower and harder to assess for health impact than a ten-minute behavioral intervention to increase adherence to high blood pressure medicine.

[47] David R. Williams, Yan Yu, James S. Jackson, & Norman B. Anderson, *Racial Differences in Physical and Mental Health: Socio-economic Status, Stress and Discrimination*, 2 J. HEALTH PSYCHOL. 335, 336 (1997).

[48] Leonard E. Burman, *Taxes and Inequality*, 66 TAX L. REV. 563, 589–590 (2013).

[49] *Id.*

[50] Komro, Burris, & Wagenaar, *Social Determinants of Child Health*, at 436.

[51] David H. Autor, *Skills, Education, and the Rise of Earnings Inequality Among the "Other 99 Percent,"* 344 SCIENCE 843, 845 (2014).

[52] Braveman, Egerter, & Mockenhaupt, *Broadening the Focus*, at S7.

[53] DEAN BAKER, CENTER FOR ECONOMIC POLICY AND RESEARCH, LIVING IN THE SHORT-RUN: COMMENT ON CAPITAL IN THE 21ST CENTURY 1 (2014), *available at* http://www.cepr.net/documents/piketty-comment-2014-04.pdf.

[54] THOMAS PIKETTY, CAPITAL IN THE TWENTY-FIRST CENTURY 1 (2014).

Even though inequality is growing in the United States, so is the appreciation that health is a product of more than healthcare and personal choices. The social determinants model of health, the challenge of inequality, and the need to pursue health in all policies have been recognized as crucial to improving the country's health and healthcare system, but reforms are difficult to implement. The next part of this chapter assesses the role of the ACA in reducing healthcare disparities and addressing the social determinants of health. A social determinants approach calls for policies that respond to the root causes of disparities, which requires attention to resource allocation, poverty, and class status.[55]

III A Social Determinants Perspective on the ACA

Though it plays a smaller role in population health than many people think, healthcare is an important health resource that is not equitably distributed in the United States. And law has played a role in both enabling and preventing disparities in the healthcare system. As the last part explained, law is a tool that can help transform a poorer starting position into a better finish.[56] The Hill-Burton Act and the desegregation efforts of the 1960s, Medicaid waivers, and the Emergency Medical Treatment and Labor Act are all laws that attempt to create more equitable access to health services.[57] Yet there remain socioeconomic disparities in access to healthcare insurance, which in our system is tantamount to access to care, and disparities for groups in the quality and intensity of care. We turn now to the task of using law to reduce health inequities and consider how the country's most important contemporary health reform project—the ACA—addresses health disparities and, perhaps indirectly, the social determinants of health.

The ACA represents an attempt to reduce the gulf between health policy and healthcare policy. Its extended health insurance coverage can reduce disparities in access to health services. Its data-collection requirements can better illuminate the differences in health among populations. Its funding for community health programs can provide direct relief for underserved individuals and neighborhoods. However, each of these provisions or strategies of the ACA face implementation obstacles, funding limitations, or a lack of political will.

The best-known provisions of the ACA concentrate on opening the healthcare insurance market to more Americans through market reforms and protections for insurance buyers. Described in detail elsewhere in this *Handbook*, the ACA's expansion of healthcare coverage will reduce healthcare access disparities by helping middle- and low-income Americans buy health insurance that they could not otherwise afford.[58] For those Americans, the ACA provides means-tested tax credits that subsidize the purchase of private health insurance in new state healthcare insurance exchanges (or markets).[59] A limitation of the ACA's strategy,

[55] Braveman, Egerter, & Mockenhaupt, *Broadening the Focus*, at S7.

[56] Burris, *From Health Care Law to the Social Determinants of Health*, at 1655–1658.

[57] Barry Furrow et al., The Law of Health Care Organization and Finance 227, 509 (7th ed. 2013).

[58] *See also* Bowser, *The Affordable Care Act and Beyond*, at 79.

[59] Furrow et al., Law of Health Care Organization and Finance, at 176.

however, is that low-income Americans who do not have significant medical care expenses may not realize much in the way of cost savings when buying insurance in new state exchanges.[60]

The ACA also expands Medicaid coverage, permitting a greater number of people to take advantage of the "the nation's safety net health insurance program."[61] Twenty-nine states and the District of Columbia, at the time of writing, have expanded Medicaid coverage to all low-income adults under sixty-five years old.[62] As described more in the chapter by Rosenbaum in this volume, the ACA's efforts to increase healthcare insurance coverage have been undercut by a decision of the U.S. Supreme Court. The Court struck down the provision that allowed the federal government to suspend Medicaid funding for states that refused to expand their Medicaid programs.[63] In addition to Medicaid expansion, the ACA promotes broader insurance coverage by including an individual mandate to purchase healthcare insurance (a provision of the ACA that the Supreme Court upheld) and by requiring that employers with fifty or more employees either offer affordable health insurance coverage or pay penalties.[64]

The ACA acknowledges health disparities in the U.S. population by requiring health agencies and programs to gather information about marginalized groups' health, to identify current disparities, and to counteract discriminatory practices in healthcare. First, the ACA continues the work of data collection on "race, ethnicity, sex, primary language, and disability . . . as well as any other demographic data regarding health disparities," by requiring federal health programs—like Medicaid and the Children's Health Insurance Program—to collect information on and to monitor health disparities.[65] Data collection is contingent on funding availability.[66] Second, the ACA addresses health disparities by seeking to remove bias from medical treatment decisions. The ACA supports and funds projects that promote the medical home model of care, outcome-based payments, and evidence-based practices. These measures can encourage evidence-supported treatments for all patients regardless of race or socioeconomic status.[67]

Finally, the ACA has expanded the country's community health centers (CHCs). The ACA's support of CHCs has not received extensive attention as a strategy to reduce health and healthcare disparities among diverse communities. CHCs play a key role in reducing "health disparities for low-income individuals, racial and ethnic minorities, rural communities and other underserved populations."[68] CHCs accomplish this by providing primary and preventative health services to low-income and medically underserved areas throughout the

[60] Parento, *Health Equity, Health People 2020*, at 690–691.

[61] Furrow et al., Law of Health Care Organization and Finance, at 79–80.

[62] Robin Rudowitz, Samantha Artiga, & MaryBeth Musumeci, The Henry J. Kaiser Foundation, *The ACA and Medicaid Expansion Waivers* (Feb. 17, 2015), http://kff.org/medicaid/issue-brief/the-aca-and-medicaid-expansion-waivers/. Of the 32 million expected to receive healthcare coverage under the ACA, half were from the planned Medicaid expansion. Parento, *Health Equity, Health People 2020*, at 691.

[63] National Federation of Independent Business v. Sebelius, 132 S. Ct. 2566 (2012) (striking down the Medicaid penalty).

[64] *Id.* (upholding the individual mandate).

[65] Patient Protection and Affordable Care Act, 124 Stat. 119 §§ 3011, 4302 (2010).

[66] *Id.* § 3011.

[67] Furrow et al., Law of Health Care Organization and Finance, at 32–37.

[68] Juniper Lesnik, *Community Health Centers: Health Care as It Could Be*, 19 J. L. & Health 1, 5 (2004–05).

United States. In addition to primary care and preventive services, CHCs provide patients with a range of ancillary services, including health education, transportation, and mental health services.[69] CHCs also build up communities through educational programs, community outreach, shared decision-making among neighbors, and creation of community jobs and centers.[70] Thus, one way to see CHCs is as service providers that reach the communities hit hardest by the income inequalities described in the last part.

At present, there are approximately 12,000 CHCs that serve more than 21 million patients.[71] To be eligible for federal funding, CHCs must be located in "medically underserved" areas, provide comprehensive health and enabling services delivered in linguistically and culturally appropriate settings, offer services to all residents and bill according to a patient's ability to pay, submit to governance by a community board, and satisfy performance and accountability requirements.[72] The CHCs' "programmatic emphasis on quality improvement" and "community-responsive and culturally appropriate care" have helped establish health services in populations that are typically in poorer health than other non-CHC patients.[73]

Measurements of CHCs' impact suggest that CHCs dramatically reduce hospitalizations and visits to emergency departments—saving, by some estimates, $24 billion in healthcare costs—because CHCs deliver otherwise absent health education or preventative care.[74] The Department of Health and Human Services (HHS) reported in 2015: "the quality of the care that patients receive at health centers often exceeds the health outcomes experienced by patients treated in other settings. Between 2008 and 2012, the percent of low birth weight babies seen in health centers decreased from 7.6 percent in 2008 to 7.1 percent in 2012—lower than the most recent estimated national rate of 8.2 percent."[75]

The ACA dedicated $11 billion over a five-year period (the Community Health Center Fund) for community health workers and the operation, expansion, and construction of health centers.[76] A $9.5 billion portion of the Community Health Center Fund supports the operations of ongoing and new health centers by expanding preventative and primary healthcare services.[77] An allocation of $1.5 billion provides for major construction and renovation projects at existing CHCs.[78] CHC funding was set to expire in October 2015,[79] but in April 2015, the Senate passed a bill that included a two-year extension of funding.[80] The

69 *Id.* The ACA also directs funding toward early childhood home visiting programs (§ 2951), prevention research and health screenings (§4002), school-based health centers (§4101), addressing chronic disease rates and health disparities (§4201), programs for a community health workforce (§5313), and pregnancy assistance programs (§10212).

70 U.S. Department of Health and Human Services, Health Resources and Services Administration, The Affordable Care Act and Health Centers 2, http://bphc.hrsa.gov/about/healthcenterfactsheet.pdf.

71 *Id.* at 1. 72 *Id.* at 6–7. 73 *Id.* at 2. 74 *Id.*

75 Mary Wakefield, U.S. Department of Health & Human Services Blog, *Affordable Care Act Funds to Expand Services at the Nation's Community Health Centers* (June 3, 2014), http://www.hhs.gov/healthcare/facts/blog/2014/06/expand-services-at-community-health-centers.html.

76 U.S. Department of Health and Human Services, Health Resources and Services Administration, at 2.

77 *Id.* 78 *Id.* 79 Wakefield, *Affordable Care Act Funds.*

80 Statement by Sylvia M. Burwell, Secretary of the U.S. Department of Health and Human Services, The President's Fiscal Year 2016 Budget, U.S. House of Representatives Committee on Energy and Commerce Subcommittee on Health, Feb. 26, 2015, http://docs.house.gov/meetings/IF/IF14/20150226/103028/HMTG-114-IF14-Wstate-MathewsBurwellS-20150226.pdf.

additional $4.2 billion in support follows a 2015 report published by the National Association of Community Health Centers, which demonstrated that ACA funding in 2013 helped CHCs expand their patient coverage from 23 million to 28 million.[81] The extended funding will also ensure that 7.4 million patients will maintain access to CHC care and 57,000 Americans will keep their jobs.[82]

These are welcome developments and important examples of how policies that dedicate funding to both health services and community improvement can make real differences in people's lives. CHCs have been traditionally understaffed, oversubscribed, and underfunded. ACA funds have allowed CHCs to expand service hours, build more centers, hire more medical providers, and add oral health, behavioral and mental health, pharmacy, HIV, and vision services.[83] CHCs not only catch people who fall between the cracks—who may not qualify for a government program like Medicaid or Medicare and who do not otherwise have access to affordable healthcare—CHCs also address local needs with resources that reach non-English speakers, assist people of all ages, and provide "enabling services," such as supportive counseling, transportation, and education. In this way, CHCs serve two goals that are foundational to a social determinants approach but are often conflated; CHCs provide healthcare services and, although to a lesser extent, build a health infrastructure for low-income or otherwise marginalized neighborhoods. ACA funding goes a long way in supporting their role in providing for the country's healthcare needs.[84]

The ACA's attention to CHCs, population data, and expansion of healthcare insurance coverage acknowledges the importance of community health and the need to reduce health disparities. However, explicit reference to the social determinants of health does not appear in the ACA's text, and post-ACA policy documents tend to focus on individuals receiving medical care and not on reconfiguring those individuals' work, educational, or residential environments. Two examples—the reports of the Community Preventive Services Task Force and the Healthy People 2020 Report—illustrate the latter point.

First, the ACA charges the Centers for Disease Control and Prevention with supporting the Community Preventive Services Task Force.[85] The Task Force's purpose is to examine institutions, surroundings, and social relationships that typically influence health, such as neighborhood conditions, employment and educational opportunities, civic engagement, and disease and injury prevention.[86] The Task Force's 2011 Report states that health policies need to address "social, economic and physical environments that can have broad effects on health . . . of populations."[87] Although the 2011 Annual Report does not describe or analyze the importance of "where [people] live, learn, work, worship, and play," its recommendations for increasing physical activity demonstrates a social determinants

[81] National Association of Community Health Centers, Community Health Centers Past, Present, and Future: Building on 50 Years of Success, Mar. 2015, http://nachc.com/client/PI_50th.pdf.

[82] For press releases of the HHS on CHCs, *see* http://www.hhs.gov/news/press/2014pres/2014.html (for 2014 press releases on funding).

[83] *Id.*

[84] Bowser, *The Affordable Care Act and Beyond*, at 69.

[85] COMMUNITY PREVENTIVE SERVICES TASK FORCE, FIRST ANNUAL REPORT TO CONGRESS (2011), *available at* http://www.thecommunityguide.org/library/ARC2011/congress-report-full.pdf.

[86] *Id.* (*citing* Patient Protection and Affordable Care Act, 124 Stat. 119 § 4003(b)(1)).

[87] *Id.* at ii, 14.

approach. The Report noted that the lack of sidewalks, crosswalks, and stop signs can keep children from walking to school; the Task Force recommended street scale improvements that address the neighborhood impediments to incorporating more physical activity into a child's day.[88]

However, the Task Force's report's primary focus remains on how policies might shape individual health decisions, which correlate with lower prevalence of heart disease, obesity, and tobacco use.[89] The same is true for the second example—Healthy People 2020 (HP 2020). HP 2020 is published by federal health officials as a decennial guide to the nation's most important health objectives. The current version of this "national blueprint for health" is the first since the series launched in 1979 to refer to the social determinants of health, and it speaks in broad terms of universal healthcare coverage and identifying "ways to create social and physical environments that promote good health."[90] Yet its specific recommendations are much more modest and focused on better school nutrition, helmet requirements, and tobacco control.

Although the Task Force and Healthy People 2020 tend to acknowledge the importance of social determinants, their recommendations tend toward what Paula Braveman and her co-authors describe as "downstream" legal interventions—policies that focus on the immediate decisions or practices that are "temporally close to health effects."[91] "Upstream" interventions, by contrast, are policies that address the root causes of problems that downstream solutions attempt to solve. These root causes are complex, persist over long periods of time, and are often the responsibility of multiple public and private actors. For these reasons, plus issues of funding and research too complicated to describe fully here, the ACA and U.S. health policy generally rely on downstream interventions that attempt to solve systemic health problems with individualistic tools.

As we have argued in this part, the ACA supports better access to health services for more people, and emphasizes healthcare that is prevention-oriented. It also allocates money for programs that target specific diseases afflicting poorer communities and proximal risk factors for those diseases. But even if the ACA worked perfectly, it would not achieve health justice and an optimal level and distribution of health in this country. Doing so requires engaging the difficult question of resource distribution, which social determinants research has shown is the best hope of addressing the deep health inequalities in the United States.[92] A broader effort, with more funding, therefore is still needed.

[88] *Id.* at iv, 14, 11. Aspects of the 2012 Annual Report of the Task Force reflects social-determinants thinking, which gave "addressing disparities in health status (health equity)" the "highest priority status" for review and recommended support for tenant-based rental assistance programs and comprehensive, center-based early childhood programs. Community Preventive Services Task Force, Annual Report to Congress 14 (2012), *available at* http://www.thecommunityguide.org/annualreport/2012-congress-report-full.pdf.

[89] Community Preventive Services Task Force, First Annual Report, at ii.

[90] Office of Disease Prevention and Health Promotion, Healthy People, 2020 Topics & Objectives, Social Determinants of Health, http://www.healthypeople.gov/2020/topicsobjectives2020/overview.aspx?topicid=39.

[91] Braveman, Egerter, & Williams, *Broadening the Focus*, at 383.

[92] Burris, *From Health Care Law to the Social Determinants of Health*, at 1650.

IV Conclusion

Evidence demonstrates that social determinants of health are more important than access to medical care or even one's genetic makeup.[93] A full and active acceptance of a social perspective on health would represent a significant cultural change in the United States. "Culture" encompasses the values we share within the settings we share. It reflects our behaviors and beliefs at all levels of social organization—in neighborhoods, schools, workplaces, towns, and regions, as well as at the national level. A culture of health is one in which being healthy is highly valued, healthy choices are easy choices, and everyone has access to high-quality, affordable healthcare, regardless of background or circumstance.

Law has an important role to play in cultural change. Law sets rules that define minimum standards of behavior, expressing social expectations and disciplining violators. Law also affects culture indirectly, as others observe a change in health-related behavior, perceive it to be both feasible and beneficial, and adopt it as their own. Over time, the legal rule becomes a cultural norm as law influences what people know or believe to be true and shapes what people value. Mere debate on a potential law can bring attention to a problem, change public perceptions, motivate practice innovation, and drive voluntary change.[94]

Work is needed to build and implement normative frameworks that give health, equality, and collective care greater legal weight—in short, that create a culture of health.[95] One reason redistributive policies such as minimum wage laws, compensated family leave, and unemployment benefits are unattractive to segments of the public is that our normative framework for what law should accomplish has moved away from an appreciation of our collective stake in health.[96] One hope is that continued study of the social determinants of health builds a compelling case for policies that redistribute the social, economic, and legal resources that help individuals lead healthy lives. It may not be that inequality causes poor health or death—that draws far too simple a line from poverty to disease. But our laws should acknowledge the persistent correlation between inequality and population health: Fairer societies are healthier societies.[97]

There is no simple way to increase political support for redistribution of health-related and social resources in this country.[98] The social determinants of health are difficult to study and to act on because they represent our country's deepest structural problems—income inequality, lack of educational attainment, substandard housing, and poor living conditions. Any solution must tackle the nuanced and complicated nature of social determinants,

93 Patricia A. Baird, *The Role of Genetics in Population Health*, *in* Why Are Some People Healthy and Others Not?: The Determinants of Health of Populations 133, 158 (Robert G. Evans et al. eds., 1994); Braveman, Egerter, & Mockenhaupt, *Broadening the Focus*, at S14.

94 *See generally* Robin Stryker, *Law and Society Approaches*, *in* Public Health Law Research: Theory and Methods 87 (Alexander Wagenaar & Scott Burris eds., 2013) (describing law's operation as a cultural force).

95 *See* Plough, *Building a Culture of Health*, at S388.

96 *See generally* Wendy Parmet, Populations, Public Health, and the Law (2009).

97 Burris, *From Health Care Law to the Social Determinants of Health*, at 1653.

98 *See, e.g.*, Stacy M. Carter et al., *Writing Social Determinants Into and Out of Cancer Control: An Assessment of Policy Practice*, 68 Soc. Sci. & Med. 1448 (2009).

and move beyond a conception of reform as a one-off fix. What meaningful health reform requires are policies that provide "multi-dimensional interventions" rather than "seeking a magic bullet."[99]

Fairness, equal opportunity, and concern for the welfare of one's community are all generally accepted social goods that do not require justification from public health scholarship. What public health brings to the table is a set of tools for specifying the processes through which we fall short of these ideals, the consequences of falling short, and the ways we can do better.[100] A pragmatic approach to addressing the social determinants of health through law entails specifying discrete initiatives that are consistent with a general theory of promoting the public good but more amenable to action and evaluation.

We can and should draw on a number of established public health tactics. The "healthy public policy" or "health in all policies" approach, for example, recognizes that health flows from many social, economic, and environmental arrangements, and therefore that anything from a gas tax to an economic development statute can have important health effects. Health Impact Assessments are meant to "assess[] a draft policy proposal, based on knowledge of the effects of past decisions and events, to predict the potential health and equity impacts of that policy and influence policy making."[101] This approach promotes cross-sector cooperation, both within and beyond government, and endorses measures that promote health wherever possible and avoid or remedy potentially unintended and unhealthy side effects of policies.[102]

The imperative to address social determinants through structural reform does not require ignoring measures that can prevent immediate harms. Regardless of one's view of the importance of social equality, reasoned investment in effective prevention and treatment of proximal causes of morbidity and mortality can still lead to valuable improvements in population health.[103] We can draw on the success of a wide range of evidence-supported, interventional public health laws, from improved sanitation to road safety.[104] We can look to zoning and tax measures to increase the number of full-service grocery stores and health food stores in underserved communities.[105] Regulation of liquor store density, food safety, the disposal of animal waste, and contamination of water resources are additional policy interventions that seek to promote healthy lifestyles and environments, as well as address specific sites of immediate harm.[106] The same is true for reforming our fragmented healthcare system. Advocating for a social determinants approach does not deny the importance of the ACA

[99] Braveman, Egerter, & Williams, *Social Determinants of Health*, at 391.

[100] Scott Burris & Evan Anderson, *A Framework Convention on Global Health: Social Justice Lite, or a Light on Social Justice?*, 38 J. L. Med. & Ethics 580, 587–588 (2010).

[101] Patrick John Harris et al., *The Essential Elements of Health Impact Assessment and Healthy Public Policy: A Qualitative Study of Practitioner Perspectives*, 2 BMJ Open 1 (2012), *available at* http://bmjopen.bmj.com/content/2/6/e001245.abstract.

[102] *See, e.g.*, Institute of Medicine, The Future of the Public's Health in the 21st Century (2002) (discussing need for cross-sector action to create the necessary conditions for health).

[103] John Lynch et al., *Is Income Inequality a Determinant of Population Health? Part 1. A Systematic Review*, 82 Milbank Q. 5, 7–9 (2004).

[104] Scott Burris & Evan Anderson, *Legal Regulation of Health-Related Behavior: A Half Century of Public Health Law Research*, 9 Ann. Rev. L. & Soc. Sci. 95, 95 (2013).

[105] Bowser, *The Affordable Care Act and Beyond*, at 114.

[106] Burris & Anderson, *Legal Regulation of Health-Related Behavior*, at 95.

and other downstream legislation. Lowering healthcare costs, reducing medical errors, opening access to government programs and the private insurance market, and promoting quality healthcare is still a pressing, if incomplete, agenda.

Law's record in promoting health through safer environments and behaviors is impressive. Law is also a medium through which a nation can imagine better—evoking Robert Cover's image, a bridge to the normative future.[107] Effective day-to-day regulation can be difficult, and depends upon timely evaluation and policy learning. In matters of health, however, the greatest need may well be rebuilding the idea that we share a collective responsibility in providing people in this country with the resources to be healthy and the tools they need to lead full and satisfying lives.

[107] Robert Cover, *The Supreme Court, 1982 Term—Foreword: Nomos and Narrative*, 97 HARV. L. REV. 4, 9 (1983).

CHAPTER 50

GENOMICS AND THE LAW

MAXWELL J. MEHLMAN

Advances in the understanding of the biological instruction book known as the human genome create a number of challenges for the law. Originally the focus of legal inquiry was on "genetics," that is, the impact of the stretches of DNA, called genes, that code for specific proteins. As researchers began to realize the important role played by the regions of DNA between the genes, however, attention has shifted to the legal implications of the entire human genome, or "genomics."

I Scientific Considerations

The modern field of genomics began in the 1860s with Gregor Mendel's observations of hereditary traits in pea plants, which he called "factors." By the end of the nineteenth century, scientists had identified coiled strands of DNA in the nucleus of human cells that they called "chromosomes," although it was not until 1956 that they determined the number of human chromosomes. The term "gene" was coined around 1910 to replace Mendel's "factors." James Watson and Francis Crick identified the basic double-helix structure of the DNA molecule in 1953. In the 1960s, geneticists began to uncover the processes by which the information coded in the human genome, or "genotype," was transformed into the proteins that are responsible for the structures and functions of human body, called the "phenotype." In the 1970s, researchers began to develop the ability to combine functional DNA from different organisms, known as recombinant DNA.

In the early 1990s, Congress authorized funding for the Human Genome Project, a research program aimed at cataloguing all of the roughly three billion units of the chemicals, called "nucleotides," that make up the human genome. A relatively complete map was published in 2003. But geneticists had a rude awakening. Whereas they had previously thought that there were approximately one hundred thousand human genes, corresponding to the number of human proteins, in fact the human genome only comprised about twenty-five thousand genes, roughly the same as thale cress, a member of the cabbage family. It turned out that a single gene could contain the blueprint for producing multiple proteins, depending on the signals that the gene received from the nucleotides between the genes. Geneticists are now endeavoring to understand how the signals system works, including the environmental factors that cause different signals to be activated.

The lesson for lawyers is that human genomics is extremely complex, and major new insights are constantly emerging. Many of the legal problems discussed in this chapter stem from scientific ignorance, misunderstanding, and overconfidence.

II The Legacy of the Past

All of the legal, ethical, and policy challenges raised by the science of human genomics take place against the historical backdrop of the eugenics movement of first half of twentieth century. Led by a diverse group of public health officials and progressive social reformers who thought that they understood how genes produced human traits and how those traits were inherited, the eugenics movement sought to improve the genomic makeup of the population by encouraging people with "good" genes to reproduce, including by awarding prizes to "fitter families" at state fairs, and by using compulsory sterilization to prevent children being born to those with "bad" genes. Indiana enacted the first law authorizing eugenic sterilization in 1907. When some state courts invalidated similar laws on various grounds, a cooked-up case[1] from Virginia called *Buck v. Bell* came to the U.S. Supreme Court and, in an opinion by Oliver Wendell Holmes, the Court upheld the constitutionality of the Virginia version of the law as a permissible exercise of the state's power to protect the public health.[2] A similar law enacted by the Nazis when they came to power in Germany in 1933 laid the foundation for the Holocaust. Eugenic sterilization in the United States nevertheless continued into the 1970s.[3] *Buck v. Bell* has not been reversed, although in *Skinner v. Oklahoma*, the Supreme Court in 1944 struck down an Oklahoma law mandating the sterilization of repeat offenders who committed certain crimes because the exclusion of white collar crimes violated the Equal Protection Clause,[4] and a district court in 1972 held that federal regulations that permitted involuntary sterilization of minors and persons who were mentally incompetent exceeded the government's statutory authority.[5]

Another historical antecedent is the state sickle-cell screening programs targeting African Americans in the 1970s. The test results were delivered without adequate counseling or public education, leading to the mistaken belief that a positive result meant that the person had inherited two copies of the gene for this "recessive" disease and therefore had the disease, when they might only have one copy and therefore not have the disease but be able to pass the mutation to their offspring.[6] Coupled with revelations about the U.S. public health syphilis experiment at the Tuskegee Institute, the adverse effects of the sickle-cell testing program,

[1] *See* Paul Lombardo, *Three Generations, No Imbeciles: New Light on Buck v. Bell*, 60 N.Y.U. L. Rev. 30, 50–62 (1985).

[2] Buck v. Bell, 274 U.S. 200 (1927).

[3] *See* Relf v. Weinberger, 372 F. Supp. 1196 (D.D.C. 1974), vacated as moot, 565 F.2d 722 (D.C. Cir. 1977) (describing Alabama sterilizations).

[4] 316 U.S. 535 (1942).

[5] *Relf*, 372 F. Supp. 1196.

[6] *See* Ira M. Rutkow & Jeffrey M. Lipton, *Some Negative Aspects of State Health Departments' Policies Related to Screening for Sickle Cell Anemia*, 64 Am. J. Pub. Health 217 (1974).

including reports of employment and insurance discrimination, led to distrust of genetic medicine by African Americans and others.[7]

One result of the foregoing history was that, when Congress funded the Human Genome Project, James Watson, who along with Crick had discovered the structure of DNA and who directed the project, insisted that between 3% and 5% of the project budget be devoted to research on the project's ethical, legal, and social implications (ELSI). Many of the insights described in this chapter are the fruits of this ongoing ELSI research program.

III Genomic Research

The basic rules governing human subjects research date back to the Nuremberg Code promulgated in 1947 by the Nuremberg Military Tribunals, which prohibited biomedical research on competent individuals without their consent.[8] Following exposure of the syphilis experiments at Tuskegee, Congress established the National Commission for the Protection of Human Subjects of Biomedical and Behavioral Research. In 1979, the commission issued a set of principles to guide research known as the Belmont Report,[9] which have been embodied in a set of federal regulations called the Common Rule[10] and which govern genomic research using human subjects that is funded by the federal government or submitted to the Food and Drug Administration (FDA).

The following sections discuss the specific legal issues raised by genomic research on human subjects.

a. Informed Consent

The Common Rule, discussed in-depth in the chapter by Mark Barnes and David Peloquin in this volume, contains no provisions specifically related to human genomic research. However, the complexity of genomic science exacerbates the difficulty of fulfilling one of the core requirements, which is to obtain informed consent from competent adults before they may serve as research subjects. Moreover, genomic research poses risks to subjects beyond physical harm, including psychosocial harm from learning genomic information about one's self and one's family, and social stigma and discrimination if the subjects' information is made known to others, which were confirmed by early studies of the effects of genetic testing for Huntington disease.[11] Consequently, researchers must carefully consider the psychosocial

[7] Misunderstanding about the difference between having a recessive genetic disorder and merely being a "carrier" of the genetic mutation is one reason why there have been fears of genetic discrimination in insurance and employment.

[8] Trials of War Criminals before the Nuremburg Military Tribunals 1949, Vol. II, 181–182, (http:// http://www.loc.gov/rr/frd/Military_Law/pdf/NT_war-criminals_Vol-II.pdf).

[9] National Commission for the Protection of Human Subjects of Biomedical and Behavioral Research, Ethical Principles and Guidelines for the Protection of Human Subjects of Research (" Belmont Report") (1979), http://www.hhs.gov/ohrp/humansubjects/guidance/belmont.html.

[10] 45 C.F.R. §§46.01-46.505 ("Common Rule").

[11] *See* Maurice Bloch et al., *Predictive Testing for Huntington Disease in Canada: The Experience of Those Receiving an Increased Risk*, 42 AM. J. MED. GENETICS 499 (1992).

risks of their investigations and preserve the confidentiality and security of identifiable test data,[12] including avoiding publishing results about subjects in an identifiable manner.[13]

Although not addressed in the Common Rule, genomic research also creates the risk of adverse effects on families and ethnic groups to which subjects belong, including stigma, discrimination, and disruption of beliefs about parentage and ancestry. Some have suggested the need to obtain consent from representatives of potentially affected populations.[14] In 2010, the Havasupai Tribe settled a lawsuit complaining that Arizona State University and certain faculty members who had obtained DNA samples from members of the tribe had conducted research on the samples without consent, including research that raised questions about the tribe's beliefs in its historical origins.[15]

The Common Rule also contains specific protections for research on subjects belonging to certain "vulnerable" populations, including prisoners, pregnant women, and children. Genomic research using pregnant women and children as subjects raises special concerns due to the psychosocial risks of learning about the genomic endowment of one's fetus and about genomic diseases that do not manifest themselves until adulthood.

b. Research on Stored DNA

Genomic research can be conducted on DNA obtained specifically for the study or on DNA that has been previously collected, whether for research or other purposes. One legal concern is whether the human sources of DNA collected for nonresearch purposes must give their consent for their samples to be used for research. Litigation has ensued, for example, over plans to conduct research using DNA extracted from stored newborn bloodspots obtained by state newborn screening programs. Texas ended up destroying 5.3 million stored bloodspots in 2011 pursuant to a settlement in one case, and that same year, the Minnesota Supreme Court held that parental consent was required for research using the samples.[16]

Entities that collect and store DNA specifically for research purposes are called "biobanks." One question is whether biobank researchers must obtain consent from the DNA sources for each specific research project. The Department of Health and Human Services (HHS) is considering how to revise the Common Rule to address this issue, but as yet there is no hard legal guidance. Some commentators insist that researchers obtain informed consent for each research project undertaken with stored DNA,[17] while others would be satisfied

[12] However, HIPAA imposes no special privacy or security requirements for entities that possess personal genomic information.

[13] An HHS 1993 guidebook for institutional review boards contains a chapter on human genetic research discussing the special risks it poses. U.S. Dept. of Health and Human Resources, Office of Protection from Research Risks, Institutional Review Guidebook 5-4–5-51 (1993).

[14] *See, e.g.*, Morris W. Foster et al., *A Model Agreement for Genetic Research in Socially Identifiable Populations*, 63 Am. J. Human Genetics 696 (1998).

[15] Amy Harmon, *Tribe Wins Fight to Limit Research of Its DNA*, N.Y. Times, Apr. 22, 2010, at A1.

[16] Bearder v. State, 806 N.W.2d (Minn. 2011). The case was settled in 2014, with the state agreeing to obtain informed consent from parents for research using bloodspots. 23 Health Law Reporter (BNA) 128 (Jan. 23, 2014).

[17] *See* Mary Kay Pelias & Nathan J. Markward, *Newborn Screening, Informed Consent, and Future Use of Archived Tissue Samples*, 5 Genetic Testing 179, 182 (2001).

with "broad" consent, in which the DNA sources agree to allow future research for generally described purposes, is sufficient.[18] Still others maintain that no consent for future research is necessary if the source of the DNA cannot be identified,[19] but there is uncertainty over what makes information unidentifiable, and some types of genomic research, such as efforts to link individuals' genomic variations to their health status, require access to identifiable information, such as medical records. Another issue is whether the sources of DNA retain the right to halt further research with their DNA or to have it destroyed. An alternative is for the repository to have a policy of destroying samples after a certain amount of time.

One of the first, large-scale DNA research projects, a nationwide effort in Iceland called deCode, ran into trouble in part because, although the DNA was obtained from individuals following consent, the researchers planned to obtain access to the individuals' identifiable medical records from a national database unless the donors opted out.[20] Eventually, the company abandoned its plan.[21] The United Kingdom launched a national biobank in 2006 employing "broad" consent and by 2010 had obtained DNA samples from five hundred thousand participants.[22]

c. Return of Results

Another controversy raised by genomic research is whether researchers must inform the DNA sources of the research results. Again there is no clear legal rule. Researchers using biobank specimens object to having to return results for several reasons, including that it may be difficult or impossible to locate the sources and that, since the results presumably would be used for purposes of diagnosis, prevention, treatment or health assessment, laboratories that analyzed the DNA would have to be certified under the Clinical Laboratory Improvement Amendments (CLIA), which would add significant costs to the research.[23] Proponents of returning results argue that subjects have a right to information that would have a substantial impact on their health.

d. Incidental Findings

Researchers conducting genomic tests on large areas of DNA may obtain information of medical value that is not related to the purpose of the study, known as "incidental findings."

[18] HHS endorsed this approach in 2011 advanced notice of proposed rule-making: Human Subjects Research Protections: Enhancing Protections for Research Subjects and Reducing Burden, Delay, and Ambiguity for Investigators, 76 Fed. Reg. 44512 (July 26, 2011).

[19] *See* Office of Human Research Protection, DHHS, Guidance on Research Involving Coded Private Information or Biological Specimens (Aug. 10, 2004), http://archive.hhs.gov/ohrp/humansubjects/guidance/cdebiol04.htm (superseded by http://www.hhs.gov/ohrp/policy/cdebiol.html in 2010).

[20] *See* Lori Andrews & Erin Shaugnessy Zuiker, *Ethical, Legal, and Social issues in Genetic Testing for Complex Genetic Diseases*, 37 VALPARAISO U. L. REV. 793, 797–799 (2003).

[21] *See* David E. Winickoff, *Genome and Nation: Iceland's Health Sector Database and Its Legacy*, 1 INNOVATIONS 80 (2006).

[22] UK Biobank, http://www.ukbiobank.ac.uk/about-biobank-uk/ (accessed June 4, 2014).

[23] 42 U.S.C. § 263a.

A question related to return of results is whether the researchers or clinicians must provide the incidental findings to the sources of the DNA. In the absence of a clear legal rule, some argue that requiring them to do so would distract them from their main objective, add to the cost, and lead subjects to confuse research with clinical care.[24] Others argue that DNA sources have a right to this information.[25] A growing consensus is that researchers should disclose their policy regarding incidental findings in the course of obtaining subjects' informed consent.[26]

e. Ownership of DNA Samples

Collections of DNA can yield information with significant value, raising the question of who owns the DNA and is entitled to benefit commercially. In one case, a prostate surgeon at Washington University in St. Louis named Catalona obtained his patients' permission to conduct research on DNA that he had obtained in the course of their care. When he moved to another university, he contacted the patients for permission to take their DNA samples with him and six thousand agreed, but a court allowed Washington University to retain the samples on the basis that they had become university property.[27]

In another case, parents of children with Canavan disease, who had donated tissue samples and medical information to a hospital research program with the understanding that research results would be made publicly available on an affordable basis, sued the physician-researcher and the program for patenting the disease gene that had been discovered and isolated. A federal district court, following *Moore v. Regents of the University of California*,[28] refused to recognize that the plaintiffs had a property interest in the samples but allowed them to proceed with a claim of unjust enrichment.[29]

[24] Ellen Wright Clayton & Amy L. McGuire, *The Legal Risks of Returning Results of Genomics Research*, 14 GENET. MED. 473–477 (2012).

[25] In a controversial move, the American College of Medical Genetics (ACMG) identified fifty-seven incidental findings that it recommends be reported when DNA is analyzed for health-related or "clinical" purposes, as opposed to in nonclinical genomic research. American College of Medical Genetics and Genomics, *ACMG Recommendations for Reporting of Incidental Findings in Clinical Exome and Genome Sequencing*, 15 GENETICS IN MEDICINE 565–574 (2013).

[26] The same approach is suggested when genomic testing inadvertently reveals misattributed parentage. *See* Jean McEwen, *Genetic Information, Ethics, and Information Relating to Biological Parenthood*, *in* ENCYCLOPEDIA OF ETHICAL, LEGAL, AND POLICY ISSUES IN BIOTECHNOLOGY, vol. 1, 359–362 (Thomas M. Murray, & Maxwell J. Mehlman eds., 2000). In contrast to paternity testing, where the object is to determine whether someone is the biological father of an individual, clinical genomic testing and screening that analyzes DNA from parents along with their offspring can disclose that there is no biological relationship between one or both parents and the offspring. (In the case of misattributed maternity or misattributed maternity and paternity, the cause typically is babies switched in hospitals at birth.)

[27] Washington University vs. Catalona, 490 F.3d 667 (2007), *cert. denied*, 552 U.S. 1166 (2008).

[28] Moore v. Regents of the University of California, 793 P.2d 479 (Cal. 1990).

[29] Greenberg v. Miami Children's Hospital Research Institute, Inc., 264 F. Supp. 2d 1064 (S.D. Fla. 2003).

f. Government Oversight of Genomic Research

In 1974, a group of Nobel laureates and other scientists led by Paul Berg called for a worldwide moratorium on recombinant DNA research due to safety concerns.[30] In response, the National Institutes of Health (NIH) established a Recombinant DNA Advisory Committee (RAC) comprised initially of scientists but eventually including lawyers and bioethicists. Following discussions at a 1975 conference in Asilomar, California, the RAC issued regulatory guidelines that, among other things, required RAC approval for NIH-funded recombinant DNA research.[31] In 1985, the RAC announced that it would begin to consider protocols for recombinant DNA and "gene therapy" research on human subjects that conformed to guidance in a set of "Points to Consider."[32] The RAC approved the first such experiment in 1988.[33]

In 1984, however, the FDA also asserted jurisdiction over "biotechnology products," including modified DNA used for human gene therapy trials, which it deemed "biological products."[34] Since sponsors of privately funded human trials typically obtained RAC approval even though they were not required to do so, virtually all genomic experiments on human subjects were subjected to both FDA and RAC review. The biotechnology industry complained, and in 1997, the director of NIH reduced the size of the RAC and canceled the requirement for the RAC to approve genomic research protocols, thereby ceding regulatory authority to the FDA.[35] Henceforth, the RAC would merely comment on certain "novel" gene transfer experiments that the committee felt merited discussion, propose changes in its Points to Consider guidance document, and convene "gene therapy policy conferences."[36] Although questions have been raised about whether the FDA has access to the RAC's ethical, social, and policy expertise, a 2013 report by the Institute of Medicine endorsed the shift in the RAC's role.[37]

Claiming that they constitute "new drugs" or biological products, the FDA also has asserted regulatory oversight over embryonic stem cell and human cloning research. The

[30] Paul Berg et al., Letter, *Potential Biohazards of Recombinant DNA Molecules*, 185 SCIENCE 303 (1974).

[31] 41 Fed. Reg. 27906 (1976). The guidelines also required institutions conducting recombinant DNA research to create institutional biosafety committees (IBCs) in addition to institutional review boards. The RAC issued less stringent guidelines in 1978 that continued to require RAC approval and IBCs. 42 Fed. Reg. 49596.

[32] DHHS, Points to Consider in the Submission of Human Somatic-Cell Gene Therapy Protocols, 50 Fed. Reg. 33462 (1985). The term "gene therapy research" has been criticized as creating confusion between therapy and research. *See* Larry R. Churchill et al., *Genetic Research as Therapy: Implications of "Gene Therapy" for Informed Consent*, 26 J. L., MED. & ETHICS 38 (1998).

[33] The experiment proceeded after the settlement of a lawsuit to block it brought by Jeremy Rifkin. *See* Joseph M. Rainsbury, *Biotechnology on the RAC: FDA/NIH Regulation of Human Gene Therapy*, 55 FOOD & DRUG L. J. 575, 584 (2000).

[34] Food and Drug Administration, Statement of Policy for Regulating Biotechnology Products, 49 Fed. Reg. 50878 (1984). The policy statement also stated that the agency would impose no new regulatory procedures or requirements for the "products of biotechnology processes," which led to the agency's long-standing refusal, for example, to require special labeling for genetically modified foods.

[35] 62 Fed. Reg. 59032 (1997). [36] *Id.*

[37] Institute of Medicine, Oversight and Review of Clinical Gene Transfer Protocols: Assessing the Role of the Recombinant DNA Advisory Committee (2013).

agency's claim has not been verified by Congress or tested in the courts, and some commentators maintain that stem cell and cloning techniques, as well as gene therapy, are not "products" but the practice of medicine, over which the agency has no authority.[38]

Several states have enacted legislation prohibiting human cloning research and either restricting or endorsing embryonic stem cell research.[39]

g. Germ Line Research

The NIH refuses to fund genomic research that involves altering the human germ line. Germ line alterations occur when changes in DNA are made at a sufficiently early stage of embryonic development that the changes appear in reproductive as well as somatic cell DNA, and therefore can be transmitted to offspring during reproduction. Although researchers have conducted successful experiments in primates and other animals, so far as is known, there have been no attempts to use gene transfer technology to intentionally alter the human germ line.

IV Intellectual Property Issues

Section III(e) discussed ownership of DNA samples. In view of the potentially large commercial value of genomic discoveries, a related legal question is whether the discoveries are entitled to intellectual property protection, in particular, whether they can be patented. Concerns arise about the increase in the costs of clinical genomic testing and treatment caused by patent protection. Critics also point to limitations on research from licensing costs, especially if patents are issued on short segments of DNA and many segments need to be used in a subsequent experiment. Proponents of genomic patents, on the other hand, claim that patent protection is necessary in order to stimulate research and to ensure that discoveries are made public.

Genomic discoveries raise two special intellectual property issues. Naturally occurring living things are not patentable, but what about living organisms created through genomic engineering, such as bacteria altered with recombinant DNA? The landmark case is *Diamond v. Chakrabarty*, in which the Supreme Court upheld a patent on an engineered bacterium.[40] In addition, the U.S. Patent and Trademark Office has granted a patent on the "Harvard oncomouse," a mouse engineered to be especially susceptible to cancer.[41]

[38] *See* Elizabeth C. Price, *Does the FDA Have Authority to Regulate Human Cloning?*, 11 Harv. J. L. & Tech. 619 (1998).

[39] National Conference of State Legislatures, Stem Cell Research (2008), http://www.ncsl.org/research/health/embryonic-and-fetal-research-laws.aspx (accessed Apr. 29, 2014).

[40] 447 U.S. 303 (1980). New plants produced by genomic engineering or more traditional hybridization have long been deemed patentable. *See* J.E.M. Ag Supply, Inc. v. Pioneer Hi-Bred Int'l, Inc., 534 U.S. 124 (2001).

[41] Canada rejected the oncomouse patent, however. Harvard College v. Canada (Commissioner of Patent) 2002 SCC 76.

The second issue is whether genes can be patented. The Supreme Court in the 2013 *Myriad Genetics* case held that naturally occurring segments of DNA—in that case, two genetic mutations that increase the risk of breast cancer—could not be patented, despite the claimant's argument that it had physically isolated the segments and that the isolated segments did not exist in nature.[42] However, the Court held that "complimentary DNA," non-naturally-occurring segments of DNA containing only genes after the "non-coding" sequences have been removed, which are the primary materials now used in genomic research, can be patented.

V Genomic Screening and Testing

Although the distinction is not always kept clear, genomic screening is DNA sequencing of populations while genomic testing is sequencing of an individual's DNA for reasons specific to that individual. Examples of genomic screening include state newborn screening programs and the sickle-cell screening program described in section II. Examples of genomic testing include testing to confirm a suspected genomic disease and "direct-to-consumer" tests sold over the Internet. Currently there are genomic tests for approximately nine hundred diseases and conditions.

a. Regulation of Genomic Testing

Federal regulation of genomic testing, including those tests used in genomic screening programs, is complicated and divided among different federal agencies.[43] DNA is analyzed by laboratories in hospitals and other health facilities using equipment and chemicals called reagents, which may be "home brews" produced in-house or "test kits" purchased from manufacturers. With the exception of some oversight of certain components called "analyte specific reagents," the FDA does not regulate home-brew reagents. The agency has asserted jurisdiction over commercial test kits as "in vitro diagnostic" medical devices but so far has reviewed and approved only a handful of kits for testing human DNA.

A doctor or hospital also may send DNA to an outside laboratory that employs a test that it has developed. The FDA has declared its intention to regulate these so-called laboratory-developed tests[44] but has not yet done so.

In November 2013, the FDA ordered 23andMe to stop selling online genomic testing to consumers except testing related to ancestry.[45] 23andMe is one of a number of companies that sell

[42] Association for Molecular Pathology v. Myriad Genetics, Inc., 569 U.S. ___ (2013).

[43] *See* Amanda K. Sarata & Judith A. Johnson, Regulation of Clinical Tests: In Vitro Diagnostic (IVD) Devices, Laboratory Developed Tests (LDTs), and Genetic Tests, Congressional Research Service (2014); Gail H. Javitt & Kathy Hudson, *Federal Neglect: Regulation of Genetic Testing*, Issues in Sci. and Tech. (2006).

[44] 75 Fed. Reg. 34463 (2010).

[45] FDA Warning Letter to 23andMe, Nov. 22, 2013, http://www.fda.gov/iceci/enforcementactions/warningletters/2013/ucm376296.htm.

genomic testing directly to consumers (DTC). Although proponents of DTC testing argue that it was less costly and more private than testing obtained through physicians, critics complain that many DTC tests have not been validated and that the results, provided online, are confusing, difficult for consumers to interpret without professional assistance, and create health risks such as unnecessary prophylactic surgeries. In its warning letter, the FDA stated that 23andMe could resume the DTC testing only if the FDA approved the tests as medical devices.

Laboratories that conduct clinical genomic testing and transmit the results for health-related reasons to patients or healthcare practitioners are regulated by the Centers for Medicare and Medicaid Services (CMS) within HHS under the Clinical Laboratory Improvement Amendments of 1988 (CLIA). CLIA requires the labs to meet proficiency standards for analytic validity[46] based on the level of complexity of the tests they perform as established by the FDA. The FDA has designated most genomic testing as "high complexity," which would require laboratories to be certified as meeting proficiency standards for that testing specialty, but CMS has not designated genomic testing as a laboratory specialty, and therefore the laboratories are not in fact certified to perform genomic testing. DTC companies maintain, rather dubiously, that they are not covered under CLIA because their website informs consumers that their testing is not for health-related reasons.

New York and Washington State have adopted standards for clinical laboratories that take the place of CLIA requirements.[47]

b. State Newborn Screening Programs

As discussed in section III(b) in connection with research on stored DNA samples, states operate genomic screening programs for newborns. Only Wyoming and the District of Columbia appear to require parents to give consent to the testing, and while a number of other states in theory allow parents to opt out, as a practical matter, parents are not informed of or aware of the option.[48] Some states, such as Texas, only permit parents to opt out for religious reasons. The Nebraska Supreme Court refused to allow parents to opt out for religious reasons, applying a rational basis standard of review and holding that the screening program was a neutral law of general applicability and therefore did not infringe the parents' religious freedom.[49]

c. Prenatal Genomic Testing

Genomic testing prior to birth can be conducted on a fetus in utero or prior to implantation on an embryo fertilized in vitro in a process called preimplantation genomic testing (PGD).

[46] Analytic validity is the ability to accurately sequence the target DNA, in contrast to clinical validity, which is the ability to diagnose or predict a specific health risk or condition.

[47] Amanda K. Sarata & Judith A. Johnson, Regulation of Clinical Tests: In Vitro Diagnostic (IVD) Devices, Laboratory Developed Tests (LDTs), and Genetic Tests, Congressional Research Service (2014).

[48] Rachel L. Schweers, *Newborn Screening Programs: How Do We Best Protect Privacy Rights While Ensuring Optimal Newborn Health?*, 61 DePaul L. Rev. 869, 879–893 (2012).

[49] Douglas County v. Anaya, 694 N.W.2d 601 (Neb. 2005).

In contrast to the United Kingdom and other countries, which limit the conditions that may be tested for using PGD,[50] the United States does not regulate prenatal genomic testing specifically. Nor does the United States prohibit the use of prenatal testing to determine gender, unlike other countries such as Canada.[51]

d. Testing of Children and Adolescents

Genomic testing of minors raises several issues that remain to be addressed by the law, stemming primarily from the concern that testing may reveal information that causes the minor net harm. For example, even when parents request it, practitioners generally refrain from testing minors for late-onset genomic disorders, such as Huntington disease, raising the question of whether the practitioners are inappropriately interfering with parental rights. Genetic testing is not usually performed on minors without parental consent or over parental objection, except if the test is for a serious, treatable disorder or the minor requests testing in connection with their own reproductive decision-making. Similarly, when minors are tested, such as in newborn screening, the consensus is to withhold predictive test results from them until they reach adulthood. It is less clear whether parents and healthcare professionals can test children without their permission or over their objection.

e. Liability Issues in Genomic Testing

The complexity of genomic science and technology creates liability risks for healthcare providers in connection with genomic testing and screening. One area that has generated litigation is sperm donation.[52] In *Johnson v. Superior Court of Los Angeles County*, parents of a child born with autosomal dominant polycystic kidney disease following artificial insemination with donor sperm were allowed to compel the sperm bank to disclose information about what it knew about the donor's genetic risk for the disease.[53] In another case, *Harnicher v. University of Utah Medical Center*, parents were unsuccessful in seeking to hold a sperm bank liable for providing them with the wrong sperm, which allegedly caused the birth of children who were healthy but were not "better looking" and who did not look like the husband, on the basis that the parents had not suffered compensable injury.[54] (Interestingly, the court noted that the plaintiffs had not alleged that the defendants had caused "any racial or ethnic mismatch."[55])

Preconception genetic testing also has generated legal disputes. One type of case concerns the liability of healthcare professionals for failing to warn parents that they were at risk of having children with genetic diseases or conditions. In *Munro v. Regents of the University of California*, an appellate court upheld summary judgment against the parents

[50] Human Fertilisation [*sic*] and Embryology Authority, Embryo Testing, http://www.hfea.gov.uk/5259.html (last visited Apr. 30, 2014).

[51] S.C. 2004, c. 2, § (5)(1)(e)(2012) (Canada).

[52] There are no reported cases involving the liability of egg donors or suppliers.

[53] 95 Cal. Rptr.2d 864 (Cal. App. 2000). [54] 962 P.2d 67 (Utah 1998). [55] *Id.* at 72.

of a child born with Tay-Sachs, a recessive genetic disease primarily found in descendants of European Jews.[56] The court reasoned that, since the parents were not of Jewish heritage, the risk that they were carriers for the disease was too remote to expect their physician to have alerted them to the fact that they might have descended from a small French Canadian community with a higher than normal incidence of the disease. In *Molloy v. Meier*, the Minnesota Supreme Court upheld a denial of summary judgment against the parents of a child born with Fragile X syndrome who claimed that the defendant physicians negligently failed to test a previous child for the disease, thereby depriving the parents of the option of being sterilized to avoid the birth of the second child.[57] The court held that a doctor treating a child has a duty of care toward the child's parents as well as to the patient.[58]

Cases like these alleging that, but for the wrongdoing of the defendants, a child with a genetic disorder would not have been born, are known as "wrongful birth" cases if brought on the parents' behalf, and as "wrongful life" cases if brought on the child's behalf. While a full discussion of these causes of action is beyond the scope of this chapter, it should be noted that they are controversial and not generally favored by the courts, and that a number of states have enacted legislation prohibiting them.[59] In view of the discussion in section II of the history of eugenics, it also should be pointed out that courts in North Carolina and Michigan have rejected wrongful birth actions explicitly because of the eugenic implications of recognizing a parental right to prevent the birth of a child with a disability.[60]

Another context in which liability for preconception genomic testing arises is with preimplantation genetic diagnosis (PGD) following in vitro fertilization. In vitro fertilization typically produces a number of embryos only a few of which are implanted in the mother's uterus. To avoid implanting embryos that have genomic anomalies, a cell from each embryo can be removed harmlessly and tested. In *Doolan v. IVF America, Inc.*, a Massachusetts court refused to allow either a wrongful life claim by a child who was born with cystic fibrosis or a wrongful birth claim by the child's parents following an alleged PGD testing error in which the parents were erroneously informed that the implanted embryo did not have the cystic fibrosis mutation.[61]

Genomic testing takes place in the course of clinical care as well as reproductive decision-making. One concern is that primary care physicians who are not highly knowledgeable about developments in genomic science may not be able to provide appropriate genomic testing to their patients.[62] The Affordable Care Act may heighten the concern because it

[56] 263 Cal. Rptr. 878 (1989). [57] 679 N.W.2d 711 (2004). [58] *Id.* at 719.

[59] *See* Lori B. Andrews, Maxwell J. Mehlman, & Mark A. Rothstein, Genetics: Ethics, Law, and Policy 331, n. 8 (2006).

[60] *See* Taylor v. Kurapati, 600 N.W.2d 670 (Mich. App. 1999); Azzolino v. Dingfelder, 337 S.E.2d 528 (N.C. 1985).

[61] 2000 WL 33170944 (Mass. Super. 2000).

[62] A 2003 survey, for example, reported that only 13% of internists, 21% of ob-gyns, and 40% of oncologists correctly answered questions about the genetic aspects of breast cancer and breast cancer testing. *See* Teresa Doksum, Barbara A. Bernhardt, & Neil Holtzman, *Does Knowledge About the Genetics of Breast Cancer Differ Between Nongeneticist Physicians Who Do or Do Not Discuss or Order BRCA1 Testing?*, 5 Genetics in Med. 99 (2003).

makes genomic testing more accessible by requiring health plans to cover certain tests for women at no out-of-pocket cost.[63]

Another issue is whether physicians owe a duty to notify persons other than their patients about genomic risks. Courts in two cases held that they did, but the opinions differed on the scope of the duty. In *Pate v. Threlkel*, in which a cancer patient alleged that the physician who treated her mother for a heritable form of cancer failed to advise the mother to have her children tested, following which the plaintiff could have taken effective prophylactic measures, the Florida Supreme Court held that the physician could discharge the duty by warning the patient.[64] In another case involving heritable cancer, *Safer v. Pack*, however, a New Jersey court held that the physician must take reasonable steps to ensure that the warning reached the children and that merely notifying the parent-patient about the need for her children to be tested might not be sufficient.[65] *Safer* was particularly interesting in view of the fact that the physician, who was no longer alive at the time of the trial, had treated the plaintiff's father twenty-four years before the plaintiff began to experience symptoms of her father's disease. The case also leaves open the question of whether physicians owe a duty to warn more distant relatives of a risk of heritable diseases, which has yet to be the subject of a reported decision.[66]

VI Genomic Therapy

Genomic therapy began with the use of recombinant DNA-engineered bacteria to produce human drugs, discussed in section III(f). The FDA approved a New Drug Application (NDA) for the first such product, human insulin, in 1982.[67]

In 1985, as also noted in section III(f), the RAC announced that it would entertain protocols for gene transfer experiments on human subjects, but relinquished regulatory oversight to the FDA in 1997. The FDA asserts jurisdiction over gene therapy as a drug or biological product but has not yet approved the marketing of a gene therapy.[68]

The first successful use of gene transfer technology in humans occurred in 1990, in a four-year-old girl suffering from severe combined immune deficiency (SCID); however, the

[63] DHHS, Preventive Services Covered Under the Affordable Care Act, http://www.hhs.gov/healthcare/facts/factsheets/2010/07/preventive-services-list.html (accessed May 1, 2014).

[64] 661 So.2d 278, 282 (Fla. 1995).

[65] Safer v. Pack, 677 A.2d 1188, 1192–1193 (N.J. Super. Ct. App. Div. 1996).

[66] *See* Mark Hallberg & Teresa Fariss McClain, Note, *Recent Developments in Health Care Law: Molloy v. Meier Extends Genetic Counseling Duty of Care to Biological Parents and Establishes That Legal Damages Must Occur Before a Wrongful Conception Action Accrues for Statute of Limitations Purposes*, 31 Wm. Mitchell L. Rev. 939, 954 (2005).

[67] Suzanne White Junod, Celebrating a Milestone: FDA's Approval of First Genetically-Engineered Product, http://www.fda.gov/AboutFDA/WhatWeDo/History/ProductRegulation/SelectionsFromFDLIUpdateSeriesonFDAHistory/ucm081964.htm (accessed May 1, 2014).

[68] FDA, Center for Biologics Evaluation and Research, Cellular and Gene Therapy Products, http://www.fda.gov/BiologicsBloodVaccines/CellularGeneTherapyProducts/default.htm (accessed May 1, 2014).

treatment, involving the reinfusion of white blood cells to which functional genes had been added, was not a complete cure. In 1999, a nineteen-year-old named Jessie Gelsinger died in the course of a Phase I experiment to develop a gene transfer treatment for a genetic liver disease with severe and often fatal effects on newborns. Revelations followed about irregularities in the conduct of the experiment, researchers who had financial conflicts of interest, and the failure of other gene transfer researchers to notify the NIH of serious adverse events suffered by their subjects. The FDA responded by imposing more stringent oversight of gene transfer research, including new tracking systems and greater public disclosure of adverse events.

Another aspect of clinical genomics is a growing understanding of the role that genomic variation plays in how different individuals experience disease and respond to treatment. Clinicians are learning to practice "personalized genomic medicine," including "pharmacogenomics," where prescribing practice varies depending on the patient's genotype. The FDA is grappling with the question of when to permit drug manufacturers to include pharmacogenomic information in the drug labeling, and when to require it.[69] If the drug label describes how different patients respond differently to the drug depending on their genotype, the "learned intermediary doctrine" shifts legal responsibility from the manufacturer to the prescribing physician to take the patient's genotype into account. Physicians therefore may feel compelled to order genomic testing even though the need for it is not certain. Questions have been raised, for example, about labeling required by the FDA for the anticoagulant drug warfarin, which mentions the value of pharmacogenomic testing in determining the proper dosage.[70] One source of concern is that pharmacogenomic testing adds the substantial cost of the testing on top of the cost of the drug itself. Other concerns include that manufacturers will refrain from incurring the cost of developing drugs for patient populations made smaller, and therefore commercially less attractive, by their pharmacogenomic profiles, and that patients with certain genotypes will be stigmatized as being difficult or more expensive to treat.[71]

A controversy related to pharmacogenomics is whether the FDA should approve drugs for use by specific populations such as African Americans. The issue has arisen in connection with BiDil, a drug to treat hypertension. Critics contend that the approval was based on the assumption that African Americans respond differently to the drug than other populations because they differ genomically, when in fact there is more genomic variation within socially defined racial groups than between them.[72]

[69] For a list of FDA-approved drugs with pharmacogenomic information in their labeling, see FDA, Table of Pharmacogenomic Biomarkers in Drug Labeling, http://www.fda.gov/drugs/scienceresearch/researchareas/pharmacogenetics/ucm083378.htm (accessed May 2, 2014).

[70] *See, e.g.*, Stephen E. Kimmel et al., *A Pharmacogenetic versus a Clinical Algorithm for Warfarin Dosing*, 369 N. Eng. J. M. 2283 (2013).

[71] *See* Mark A. Rothstein & Phyllis Griffin Epps, *Ethical and Legal Implications of Pharmacogenomics*, 2 Nature Revs 228 (2001).

[72] *See* Osagie K. Obasogie, Playing the Gene Card? A Report on Race and Human Biotechnology (Center for Genetics and Society 2009), http://www.geneticsandsociety.org/downloads/complete_PTGC.pdf (accessed May 2, 2014).

VII Genomic Enhancement

Increasing knowledge about the relationship between genomics and nondisease characteristics creates challenges for the law. The availability of genomic tests for nondisease characteristics is likely to play a growing role in reproductive decision-making. Parents already select donor gametes based on information about genomically-related donor characteristics, and at least one online dating service matches members on the basis of the results of one genomic nondisease test, topics that are also covered in Judith Daar's chapter in this volume.[73] In the future, parents also may include assays for nondisease traits in preimplantation testing of embryos.

One question is whether parents will be entitled to compensation for negligent nondisease testing; the *Harnicher* case discussed in section V(e), in which the court declined to regard mistakes in relation to nondisease characteristics as compensable harm, suggests that this may be difficult.

A foretaste of the future is gender selection. Parents who desire a child of a specific sex can now employ a number of techniques at various stages of the reproductive process, including genomic testing prior to conception or embryo implantation. Critics of gender selection object that it reinforces sexism and have succeeded in having the practice banned in a number of countries including Canada[74] and the United Kingdom.[75] Similar legislative efforts have been made in the United States, so far without success.

Farther downstream is the prospect of gene transfer for purposes of enhancement rather than to combat disease. One legal issue is how to regulate genomic enhancement research. Since the initial formation of the RAC, the NIH has refused to fund this type of research, but the FDA has approved at least one drug for enhancement use, Botox. Although Botox is not manufactured using genomic technology, its experience suggests that the FDA in the future might be asked to approve the marketing of a gene transfer technique for enhancement purposes rather than to combat disease. The agency therefore would need to determine how to weigh an enhancement benefit against a risk of adverse effects. Since the sponsor would require FDA approval to conduct research crossing state lines to establish the safety and efficacy of the technique, the agency also would need to determine how to balance the risks against the potential benefit in reviewing the research design.[76]

As discussed in section IX below, the Genetic Information Nondiscrimination Act (GINA) currently prohibits employers from requiring genomic testing for job applicants or employees. One question is whether the law should outlaw genomic testing for nondisease characteristics by educational institutions, including for athletic ability. Academic sports programs might be interested in a genetic test developed by the Australian Institute of Sport, for example, which identifies variants of the ACTN3 gene that predict whether the individual has more slow-twitch muscles, associated with activities such as long-distance running

[73] Natasha Singer, *Better Loving Through Chemistry*, N. Y. Times, Feb. 7, 2010, at B3.

[74] *See* S.C. 2004, c. 2, § (5)(1)(e)(2012).

[75] Human Fertilisation [*sic*] and Embryology Authority, Embryo Testing and Sex Selection, http://www.hfea.gov.uk/496.html?fldSearchFor=gender (accessed May 2, 2014).

[76] *See* Maxwell J. Mehlman & Jessica Berg, *Human Subjects Protections in Biomedical Enhancement Research: Assessing Risk and Benefit and Obtaining Informed Consent*, 36 J. L., Med. & Ethics 546 (2008).

that require endurance, or fast-twitch muscles, associated with activities requiring shorter bursts of energy such as sprinting and weightlifting. It also is unclear if the military, which is not covered by GINA, should be permitted to conduct genomic testing on its personnel for nonmedical purposes, such as assignment.

VIII Forensics

The use of DNA testing for forensic purposes, which began in the United Kingdom in 1985, is now widely accepted by the courts. State law enforcement agencies and, to a lesser extent, the FBI, collect and analyze DNA and enter the results into state databases and a comprehensive national database called the Combined DNA Index System (CODIS). The DNA is obtained from persons convicted of an ever-expanding list of crimes, including misdemeanors in some states; persons previously imprisoned; arrestees; crime victims; crime scenes; and rape victims. Although originally the DNA was extracted from blood samples or semen, it can now be obtained from saliva,[77] which facilitates "finding" it on objects such as coffee cups, cigarettes, chewing gum, and stamps. Technological advances such as polymerase chain reaction enable testing on smaller and smaller amounts of DNA.

Questions have arisen concerning whether, like fingerprints, law enforcement officials can require someone who has not been arrested to give them a DNA sample without probable cause. One practice is a "dragnet," in which DNA is sought from persons found near the scene of a crime or who match the suspect's description; the individuals who are asked may not know that they cannot be compelled to surrender their DNA, and it is not clear that this must be disclosed to them.

Only a few states require DNA test results to be expunged following an unsuccessful prosecution or the reversal of a conviction. Many states collect DNA from juvenile offenders, and a 1997 Arizona decision upheld the practice of retaining and continuing to make use of the test results following adulthood.[78]

Currently, forensic tests compare DNA sequences at thirteen different places. Statistical methods generate a probability that a match between two samples could have resulted from chance, rather than from the fact that the samples came from the same person. Although strong statistical inferences can be drawn from a match between two samples of DNA, courts require some additional evidence to support a conviction. For one thing, there is a possibility of laboratory error, such as accidentally mixing DNA from different samples. Furthermore, the reported statistical probability assumes that individuals inherit each of the thirteen tested regions of DNA independently from the other regions, which is less likely the more inbred the population.

Supposedly none of the thirteen currently tested DNA sequences code for proteins, so that the test results do not reveal phenotypic traits such as eye or hair color or body type. The availability of cheaper genomic testing, coupled with greater knowledge of the

[77] Mitochondrial DNA, although not an entire genome, now can be obtained from hair.

[78] Matter of Appeal in Maricopa County Juvenile Action Numbers JV-512600 and JV-512797, 930 P.2d 496 (Ariz. App. 1997).

associations between genotype and phenotype, has led to calls for phenotypic forensic testing.[79] Phenotypic testing might enable law enforcement agencies, for example, to produce a composite sketch of a suspect. Concerns have been raised, however, that phenotypic testing could exacerbate racial profiling and violate privacy rights.

Another controversy involves whether persons convicted of crimes must be given access to postconviction DNA testing in order to try to exonerate themselves. Interest in postconviction testing has been stimulated by the success of the Innocence Project and others in employing DNA evidence to overturn wrongful convictions. In 2009, the Supreme Court declined to hold that inmates had a constitutional right to postconviction DNA testing and left the matter up to the states.[80] State policies vary; most states allow access only for persons in custody, and some states limit access to persons convicted of felonies. States also vary in whether they will provide testing to indigents at government expense. If the results of the postconviction test inculpate rather than exonerate, some states impose penalties on the person who sought the testing.

The influence of genotype on phenotype raises the question of whether a person's genotype predisposes them to commit crimes and, if so, how that should affect their treatment by the law. The eugenicists' belief that genes could predispose a person to engage in criminal behavior led to sterilization programs like the one at issue in *Buck v. Bell*, discussed in section II. As also mentioned in section II, the Supreme Court in 1944 struck down a law mandating the sterilization of repeat offenders because the exclusion of white collar crimes violated the Equal Protection Clause.[81]

In the 1960s, researchers thought that they had discovered an association between criminal tendencies and having an extra Y chromosome, because a large percentage of men institutionalized for violent acts had that chromosomal abnormality. Courts rejected the so-called XYY defense, however,[82] and subsequent research showed that the reason for the apparent correlation was not that the men committed more crimes but that the XYY anomaly lowered intellectual ability, which increases the risk of being caught.

More recently, research has shown an association between antisocial behavior and low levels of an enzyme caused by a mutation in the MAOA gene.[83] One finding is that children with the genetic mutation who are raised in abusive environments are more likely to be antisocial than children with a normal MAOA gene who are raised under similar conditions.[84]

An association between genomic variations and criminal tendencies could affect criminal culpability, punishment, sentencing, and parole. Although it is unlikely that a criminal would be found insane merely on the basis of their genomic makeup, evidence that they were genomically predisposed toward criminal behavior might be considered in mitigation of sentencing, especially if treatments were available that could counteract the genomic effects.

[79] *See, e.g.*, Charles E. Maclean, *Creating A Wanted Poster from a Drop of Blood: Using DNA Phenotyping to Generate an Artist's Rendering of an Offender Based Only on DNA Shed at the Crime Scene*, 36 Hamline L. Rev. 357 (2013).

[80] District Attorney's Office for the Third Judicial District v. Osborne, 55 U.S. 52 (2009).

[81] 316 U.S. 535 (1942).

[82] *See, e.g.*, State v. Roberts, 544 P.2d 754 (Wash. App. 1976).

[83] *See* Sharon Niv & Laura A. Baker, *Genetic Markers for Antisocial Behavior*, *in* The Origins of Antisocial Behavior: A Developmental Perspective 7–14 (Christopher R. Thomas & Kayla Pope eds., 2012).

[84] *See, e.g.*, Avshalom Caspi et al., *Role of Genotype in the Cycle of Violence of Maltreated Children*, 297 Sci. 851 (2002).

In the absence of effective treatment, however, evidence of a genomic tendency could lead to longer or even indefinite incarceration or institutionalization with less chance of parole.

Genomic factors also could impact tort liability. Similar to criminal defendants, for example, defendants in intentional tort cases might assert that they lacked the necessary element of intent, while defendants in negligence actions might seek to be held to the standard of care of someone with their genomic endowment rather than to the standard of a reasonable person.

IX Genomic Discrimination

As the Human Genome Project and its progeny were uncovering associations between genomic variations and disease, concern grew that individuals with unfavorable genomic endowments faced discrimination, especially in access to insurance products and employment. Health insurers were understood to refuse insurance to people with preexisting genomic conditions, to drop insured individuals at risk for genomic diseases if they became ill, and to vary coverage policies so that patients could find themselves without insurance for treatments that they needed. Insurers were also said to be discriminating against healthy persons with genomic risk factors for future illness, which the insurers learned about from genomic test results or family histories. In reality, there was little evidence that this type of discrimination was taking place; evidence came mostly from unverified self-reports from families with members suffering from genomic diseases.[85] For their part, insurers were worried about adverse selection, which would result if people who knew that they were at risk for genomic diseases purchased insurance but those who did not think they were at risk tended not to or bought less; over time, insurers would find themselves in a "death spiral," as insurance became increasingly expensive and only persons at greater and greater risk continued to purchase it.

Initially, the only protection against discrimination for persons who were ill was the Americans with Disabilities Act, enacted in 1990, but it only covered persons who were debilitated enough to be considered "disabled," and it contained an exception for insurance practices supported by sound actuarial data.[86] In 1996 Congress passed the Health Insurance Portability and Accountability Act, which prohibited insurers from considering "genetic information" as a preexisting condition.[87] However, the law only applied to group health plans, such as those offered by employers, it did not prevent employers from declining to offer health benefits altogether or raising the amounts that employees had to contribute so long as all employees paid the same, and it did not require plans to cover treatment for an employee's specific genomic illness. States also began passing genomic antidiscrimination laws, although often they only prohibited insurers from acting on the basis of genomic test results, and they did not apply to self-insured employer health plans qualified under the Employee Retirement Income Security Act.

[85] *See* Mark A. Rothstein & Mary R. Anderlik, *What Is Genetic Discrimination and When and How Can It Be Prevented?*, 3 Genetics in Med. 354, 357 (2001).

[86] 42 U.S.C. §12201(c).

[87] 42 U.S.C. §§300g-300gg-2.

In 2008, Congress passed the Genetic Information Nondiscrimination Act (GINA).[88] GINA prohibits health insurance discrimination against individuals with genomic risk factors, but does not apply to health plans offered by employers with fewer than fifteen employees, and does not cover people who display symptoms of a genomic illness. With the enactment of the Affordable Care Act in 2010, Congress finally completely prohibited health insurance discrimination against persons with genomic conditions. There is still no legal prohibition, however, against genomic discrimination in access to life, disability, or long-term care insurance.

In regard to employment discrimination, GINA prohibits employers from requiring job applicants to undergo genomic testing and from using genomic information in hiring and other personnel decisions. In 2001, the Equal Employment Opportunity Commission (EEOC), which enforces federal laws prohibiting employment discrimination, obtained a settlement in the first lawsuit it had filed alleging genomic discrimination. The defendant, Burlington Northern Railway, agreed to suspend an effort to obtain genetic test results from employees who had filed workers' compensation claims for carpal tunnel syndrome to determine if their condition had a genomic component, which might affect whether or not they were entitled to compensation.[89]

X Future Developments

The expanding understanding of human genomics, including the relationship between genomic factors and the environment, will open up new ways to prevent, treat, and cure greater numbers of genomically-related diseases and conditions. The increasing scope and complexity of the science, however, could expose healthcare professionals to liability if they fail to provide appropriate information and access to their patients. To reduce their risk, providers may rely more on genetic counselors to interact with their patients, which could increase the costs of care and require substantially greater numbers of counselors to be trained and certified.

The increasing ability to identify genomic associations with disease will lead to calls for more thorough government regulation of commercial tests and laboratory practices. It also will facilitate greater use of genomic testing in connection with reproductive decision-making. The law will have to confront the question of whether parents continue to have the right to abort fetuses based on the results of genomic testing for a growing array of conditions and whether to try to restrict the use of genomic testing in choosing reproductive mates, selecting donor gametes, and PGD.

The falling cost of genomic sequencing will facilitate broader types of genomic screening and testing. Together with growing use and sharing of electronic medical records, this will increase concerns about the privacy and confidentiality of individual genomic information.

[88] P.L. 110–233 (2008).

[89] Lori B. Andrews, Maxwell J. Mehlman, & Mark A. Rothstein, Genetics: Ethics, Law, and Policy 922–924 (3d ed. 2006).

It also will heighten calls from researchers to gain access to genomic information collected for other purposes, such as whole genome sequencing data from newborn screening.

If researchers discover clearer associations between genomic variations and antisocial behavior, policy-makers may begin calling for preemptive measures such as screening, monitoring, and treatment. The law will have to determine how significant and how firmly established these associations have to be to warrant government action.

Improvements in gene transfer technology will facilitate its use to combat disease. Eventually the law will have to decide whether or not to permit germ line modification.

Finally, greater knowledge of genomic associations with nondisease traits will confront lawmakers with the question of whether to attempt to restrict the ability of parents to select or modify their children's nondisease characteristics, and in turn whether such restrictions would be upheld as constitutional.

XI Conclusion

As the Human Genome Project passes the quarter-century mark, the broad scientific enterprise that it spearheaded presses on. Interest in using genomic science to combat disease and the resulting commercial prospects combine to fuel a vigorous research effort. Much more will become known about the relationship between genotype and phenotype, and the declining cost of genomic testing will make this knowledge more widely accessible.

Yet there are reasons why genomic research might be slowed or even derailed. Popular visions of the future of human genomics, whether in movies such as GATTACA or novels such as Margaret Atwood's, are universally dystopic.[90] Researchers sometimes make overblown and unsupported claims about the role of genomic factors in human health and behavior, opening them up to criticism from rival fields that focus on the role of environmental factors. Genomics is a battleground in the current culture wars, facing resistance from conservative religious forces that feel threatened by science in general and by genomics in particular. The field also is under pressure from left-wing opponents of genomically-modified plants and animals.

To defend themselves against these challenges, genomic scientists must be judicious in making claims about their discoveries and adhere scrupulously to the scientific, ethical, and legal rules governing their activities. Events like the death of Jessie Gelsinger, which violated all three, are both tragic and avoidable. At the same time, the norms and rules themselves must adjust to developments in ways that protect the public interest without unduly chilling scientific inquiry. For example, the U.S. military is expressing great interest in taking advantage of genomic technologies, such as creating large-scale biobanks with DNA from service personnel, employing genomic testing in connection with recruitment, assignment, and training, and potentially using genetic engineering to improve warfighter performance.[91]

[90] *See* Maxwell J. Mehlman, Transhumanist Dreams or Dystopic Nightmares: The Promise and Peril of Genetic Engineering 11–33 (Baltimore: Johns Hopkins University Press 2012).

[91] *See, e.g.*, JASON, The Mitre Corp., The $100 Genome: Implications for the DoD (Dec. 2010), http://www.fas.org/irp/agency/dod/jason/hundred.pdf (accessed May 2, 2014).

New ethical and legal guidelines are needed for military applications, since the guidelines developed by the ELSI program and others for civilian genomics do not reflect the military's fundamentally different core values.

Finally, genomic researchers must be careful in crossing certain boundaries. One is the boundary between humans and other animals; continued progress in combining DNA from different animal species may spark interest in human experimentation, but researchers must move cautiously. Another boundary divides medical and nonmedical objectives; the same technologies useful in combating disease can be directed at nondisease characteristics, including appearance and mental and physical performance. "Better" humans may produce substantial societal benefit, but genomic science must not become another wedge driving haves and have-nots apart.

Index

Figures and tables are indicated by "f" and "t" following page numbers.